D0657791

So you want to be a lawyer...

Welcome to the 2013 edition of the *Chambers Student Guide* to careers in the law. We've written this book to give you the information, tools and confidence to help you made a sound career decision.

This guide is the only publication to offer these four key ingredients.

- The True Picture: an insight into the training schemes at 120 law firms, based on in-depth interviews with hundreds of trainees. The trainees were selected by us, not by their law firms, and they spoke to us freely and frankly under the protection of anonymity.
- Chambers Reports: a look at life inside 26 barristers' chambers. These reports were written after visits to each of the sets and interviews with pupils, barristers and clerks.
- Law school reviews: compiled after feedback from students who have completed courses at each of the schools, plus interviews with course directors.
- Additional online advice and information in key areas, including: details of the recruitment process at all our featured firms with tips from recruiters and trainees; and in-depth interviews with managing partners and training partners detailing their firms' strategies for the future

Chambers and Partners publishes guides to the legal professions around the world. You will benefit enormously from using our *Chambers UK* guide to refine your search for a law firm or chambers to train with. The best performing firms and sets in over 65 areas of practice are identified by way of league tables in *Chambers UK*, and you can get all this information online, for free, by visiting www.chambersandpartners.com.

All the guides we publish have one thing in common: they are independent. In a market flooded with publications for law students we take great pride in this fact. No one's money influences what we say about them.

This book could be the most useful thing you read this year, so get stuck in, and we wish you great success for your future career.

The *Student Guide* team
October 2012

Published by Chambers and Partners Publishing
(a division of Orbach & Chambers Ltd)
39-41 Parker Street, London, WC2B 5PQ
Tel: (020) 7606 8844 Fax: (020) 7831 5662
email: info@ChambersandPartners.co.uk
www.ChambersandPartners.com

Our thanks to the many students, trainees, pupils, solicitors, barristers and graduate recruitment personnel who assisted us in our research. Also to the researchers of *Chambers UK 2013* from which all firm rankings are drawn.
Copyright © 2012 Michael Chambers and Orbach & Chambers Ltd

ISBN: 978-0-85514-316-9

Publisher: Michael Chambers
Editor: Antony Cooke
Deputy Editor: Richard Simmons
Writers: Elizabeth Sands, Francesca Wright, Haleema Mansoor, Jack Watkins, Natalie Stanton, Paul Rance, Phil Roe, Sam Morris, Sara Veale, Sarah Parkhouse
A-Z Co-ordinator: Saffeya Shebli
Production: Jasper John, John Osborne, Paul Cummings, Pete Polanyk
Business Development Manager: Brad D. Sirott
Business Development Team: Bianca Maio, ...triona Howie, Liz Brennan, Neil Murphy, ...chard Ramsay
...oofreaders: John Bradley, Nicholas Widdows, ...lly McGonigal
...inted by: Butler Tanner & Dennis

Contents

This guide, if used properly, can greatly ease the process of pursuing a career in the law

Use this book in conjunction with www.chambersandpartners.com to find your perfect traineeship or pupillage

Our Editorial Team

Here you can see our editors, deputy editors and researchers. They are all currently (July 2012) working full-time on our range of guides at our head office in central London. (All, that is, except six who are employed in our Hong Kong office.) More biographical information can be found on the 'About Us' page of our website.

Rieta Ghosh
Managing Editor

Catherine McGregor
Managing Editor

Antony Cooke
Student Editor

Andres Jaramillo
Latin America Editor

Dee Sekar
Women in Law Editor

Edward Shum
Global Editor

Georgia Brooks
Editor

James Cowdell
Bar Editor

Jonathan Rubin
Editor

Laura Mills
USA Editor

Rachel Low
In-House Editor

Shi-Ning Koay
Asia Pacific Editor

Stephen Wallace
Confidential Editor

Richard Simmons
Deputy Editor

Alex Marsh
Deputy Editor

Andréa Serva
Deputy Editor

Annie McDermott
Deputy Editor

Cheska Polderman
Deputy Editor

Chris Teevan
Deputy Editor

Crystal Lo
Deputy Editor

Elitsa Yurukova
Deputy Editor

Emma Dougan
Deputy Editor

Giles Thomas
Deputy Editor

Jane Pasquali
Deputy Editor

Jamie Horne
Deputy Editor

Joanna Haber
Deputy Editor

Jon Comlay
Deputy Editor

Liam Whitton
Deputy Editor

Lidija Liegis
Deputy Editor

Luke Kenison
Deputy Editor

Michael Perkin
Deputy Editor

Milena Bellow
Deputy Editor

Peter Whitfield
Deputy Editor

Phil Roe
Deputy Editor

Richard Winter
Deputy Editor

Sarah Kogan
Deputy Editor

Ursula Ben-Hammou
Deputy Editor

Francois Gill
Assistant Editor

Natalia Tejedor
Assistant Editor

Nicolás Obregón
Assistant Editor

Talia Addleman
Assistant Editor

Yvonne Berman
Assistant Editor

Angela Castillo Díaz
Senior Researcher

Daniel Pang
Senior Researcher

Fiona Wong
Senior Researcher

Fran Latham
Senior Researcher

Gareth Hewer
Senior Researcher

Jurgita Meskauskaite
Senior Researcher

Leila Afshar
Senior Researcher

Lucy Craig
Senior Researcher

Michael Bennett
Senior Researcher

Miriam Bishop
Senior Researcher

Miriam Urgelles-Coll
Senior Researcher

Natalie Stanton
Senior Researcher

Oliver Dimsdale
Senior Researcher

Paul Davy
Senior Researcher

Sam Morris
Senior Researcher

Sara Veale
Senior Researcher

Shuma Hoque
Senior Researcher

Stefan Corre
Senior Researcher

Alexis Hercules
Researcher

Andrew Dyer
Researcher

Andrew Freedman
Researcher

Alexander Poots
Researcher

Alice McDonald
Researcher

Beth Warin
Researcher

Bryony Hirsch
Researcher

Calvin Humby
Researcher

Charles Procter
Researcher

Christopher Collins
Researcher

Cillian Logue
Researcher

Claire Oxborrow
Researcher

Claudia Solaro
Researcher

Corey Francis
Researcher

Danielle Vidigal
Researcher

David Watson
Researcher

Deborah Lewis
Researcher

Elizabeth Sands
Researcher

Emma Beatty
Researcher

Francesca Lean
Researcher

Francesca Wright
Researcher

Francis Williams
Researcher

Fredrik Kruse
Researcher

Georgina Simmonds
Researcher

Giverny Tattersfield
Researcher

Haleema Mansoor
Researcher

Hannah Campaigne
Researcher

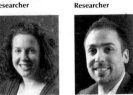
Harriet Carter
Researcher

Houman Barekat
Researcher

Idara Hippolyte
Researcher

Indy Tsang
Researcher

Isabel Story
Researcher

Jack Torbet
Researcher

Jack Watkins
Researcher

Jacob Moffatt
Researcher

James Astin
Researcher

Jamie Yule
Researcher

James Booth
Researcher

James Course-Choi
Researcher

Katherine Hughes
Researcher

Kielan Thompson
Researcher

Keziah Mastin
Researcher

Lindsey Ford
Researcher

Loretta Lok
Researcher

Madalena Andrade
Researcher

Mandeep Sran
Researcher

Marta Krzeminska
Researcher

Matthew Adams
Researcher

Matthew James
Researcher

Mayeni Jones
Researcher

Megan Langham
Researcher

Nick Martin
Researcher

Nicholas Padamsee
Researcher

Nuria Gisbert
Researcher

Paul Rance
Researcher

Rebecca Smith
Researcher

Richard Metcalf
Researcher

Robert Li
Researcher

Rupert Wilson
Researcher

Raquel Holzmann
Researcher

Sara Fantoni
Researcher

Sarah Cosgrove
Researcher

Stella Heng
Researcher

Sue Li-Ciraki
Researcher

Suneel Basson-Bhatoa
Researcher

Summer Hao
Researcher

Timothy Shaw
Researcher

Thomas Carter
Researcher

Tobias Waters
Researcher

Tommy So
Researcher

William Robertson
Researcher

Victoria Sheehan-Dare
Researcher

Zoe Sutherland.
Researcher

Becoming a Lawyer

Calendar of events 2011

Law Fairs

October 2012

11	SOAS
16	University of Cambridge (Solicitors)
17	University of Kent; University of Nottingham
24	City University
29	University of Leeds; Queen Mary
30	University of Leeds; University of York
31	Cardiff University; University of Liverpool

November 2012

1	University of East Anglia; University of Hull
6	LSE
7	Queen's University, Belfast; University of Bristol; University of Reading; University of Sussex
8	LSE; Northumbria University; University of Oxford
10	University of Oxford
12	Newcastle University; UCL
13	UCL; University of Warwick
14	University of Birmingham; University of Leicester
15	University of Essex; University of Southampton
19	Durham University
20	Durham University; University of Manchester
21	University of Bradford; University of Sheffield
22	De Montfort University; University of Exeter
26	King's College, London
27	King's College, London
28	King's College, London; University of Salford

Law fair strategies:

Depending on which approach you take, you'll get very different things out of your law fair experience. What sort of law fair attendee are you?

1. The magpie: You're passive and blend into the crowd. The most you'll get out of the day is a few pens, plastic bags and chocolate bars.

2. The weight-lifter: You pick up all the literature you can. You'll have sore arms and a mountain of material to plough through at a later date... if you ever get round to it.

3. The explorer: You have a rough idea where you want to work and which areas you'd like to specialise in. This is your chance to scout around, have a chat, and hone in on those firms that really take your fancy.

4. The interrogator: You've done your research, and have pinpointed which firms you're interested in. Now's your chance to get the inside scoop on the things that matter to you. What pro bono work can trainees do? Are there any diversity initiatives at the firm? If you're lucky, you might even make some contacts you can mention on the dreaded application form.

Vacation Scheme Deadlines

October 2012

31 Allen & Overy (winter – graduates and finalists)
Berwin Leighton Paisner (winter)
Jones Day (winter, non-law)

November 2012

6 Stephenson Harwood (winter)

15 Cleary Gottlieb (winter)

December 2012

31 Jones Day (spring, non-law)
Latham & Watkins (spring)

January 2013

8 Clifford Chance

12 Freshfields

13 Skadden

15 Allen & Overy (summer – penultimate year undergraduates)
Ashurst

January 2013

18 Hogan Lovells

25 Muckle

28 Cleary Gottlieb (summer)

30 Dundas & Wilson

31

Addleshaw Goddard	Mishcon de Reya
Ashurst	Nabarro
Berwin Leighton Paisner (summer)	Norton Rose
Bircham Dyson Bell	O'Melveny & Myers
Boodle Hatfield	Olswang
Clyde & Co	Osborne Clarke
Cobbetts	Pinsent Masons
Covington & Burling	PwC Legal
Davis Polk & Wardwell	Reynolds Porter Chamberlain
Dechert	SJ Berwin
Dickinson Dees	SNR Denton
DLA Piper	Squire Sanders
Farrer & Co	Stephenson Harwood (summer)
Hill Dickinson	Stevens & Bolton
Ince & Co	Sullivan & Cromwell
Jones Day (summer, law)	Taylor Wessing
Kirkland & Ellis	TLT
Latham & Watkins (summer)	Travers Smith
Lawrence Graham	Walker Morris
Macfarlanes	Watson, Farley & Williams
Maclay Murray & Spens	Wragge & Co
Mayer Brown	
Mills & Reeve	

"Make sure anything you put in your application can be substantiated. It's awful to catch people out."

Trainee

Vacation Scheme Deadlines

February 2013

3	Irwin Mitchell
11	Gateley
14	Holman Fenwick Willan
15	Capsticks Manches
24	Edwards Wildman Palmer SGH Martineau
28	Michelmores Shoosmiths Vinson & Elkins Ward Hadaway Wedlake Bell Withers

March 2013

1	Arnold & Porter Trowers & Hamlins
31	Ashfords Bevan Brittan Bond Pearce BP Collins Lester Aldridge Penningtons Veale Wasbrough Vizards

April 2013

14	Pannone
30	Howes Percival

June 2013

30	Brabners Chaffe Street

"Don't send out hundreds of blanket applications – firms can tell. I knew which firms I wanted to work for and why. I could provide evidence of why each firm was right for me."

Trainee

Training Contract Deadlines

January 2013

15
Herbert Smith Freehills (for finalists/graduates)
Allen & Overy (non-law)

31
Clifford Chance (non-law)
Bristows (Februaruy)

March 2013

29 SNR Denton (non-law)

31 Simmons & Simmons (for all finalists/graduates)

April 2013

30 Hogan Lovells (non-law)

May 2013

1 Freshfields (non-law)

31
B P Collins (for 2014)
Finers Stephens Innocent (for 2014)
Foot Anstey
Kingsley Napley (for 2014)
Morgan Cole

June 2013

14 Bates Wells & Braithwaite

28 Orrick

30
Boodle Hatfield (non-law)
Brabners Chaffe Street
Davenport Lyons
Hill Dickinson (London office)
Lester Aldridge
Veale Wasbrough Vizards

July 2013

1
Gordons
Michelmores

14 Freeth Cartwright

15 Mishcon de Reya

26 Trethowans

31

Allen & Overy (law)	Ince & Co
Addleshaw Goddard	Irwin Mitchell
Ashurst	Jones Day
Berwin Leighton Paisner (for 2015 and 2016)	K&L Gates
	Kennedys (for 2014)
Bevan Brittan	Kirkland & Ellis
Bingham McCutchen	Latham & Watkins
Bircham Dyson Bell	Lawrence Graham
Bird & Bird	Lewis Silkin
Bond Pearce	Macfarlanes
Boodle Hatfield (law)	Manches
Bristows (August interviews)	Mayer Brown (for Sept 2015 and Mar 2016)
Browne Jacobson	McDermott Will & Emery (for 2014 and 2015)
Burges Salmon	
Charles Russell	
Cleary Gottlieb	Memery Crystal
Clifford Chance (law)	Mills & Reeve
Cobbetts	Morgan Lewis
Covington & Burling	Muckle
Cripps Harries Hall	Nabarro
Davis Polk & Wardwell	Norton Rose
Dechert	Olswang
Dickinson Dees	O'Melveny & Myers
DLA Piper	Pannone
Dundas & Wilson	Paul Hastings
DWF	Penningtons
Edwards Wildman Palmer	Pinsent Masons
Eversheds	Pritchard Englefield
Farrer & Co	PwC Legal
Forbes	Reed Smith
Freshfields (law)	RPC
Gateley	SGH Martineau
Government Legal Service	Shearman & Sterling
	Sheridans
Harbottle & Lewis	Shoosmiths
Henmans	Sidley Austin
Herbert Smith Freehills (penultimate year students)	Simmons & Simmons
	SJ Berwin
	Skadden
Hewitsons	SNR Denton (law)
Hill Dickinson (Northern offices)	Speechly Bircham
	Squire Sanders
	Stephenson Harwood
Hogan Lovells (law)	Stevens & Bolton
Holman Fenwick Willan	Sullivan & Cromwell

Training Contract Deadlines

July 2013

31
Taylor Wessing
Thomas Cooper
TLT
Travers Smith
Walker Morris
Ward Hadaway
Watson, Farley &
Williams
Wedlake Bell
Weil, Gotshal &
Manges
White & Case (for Aug
2014 and Feb 2015)
Wiggin
Wilsons
Withers
Wragge & Co

August 2013

1   Trowers & Hamlins

2   Arnold & Porter

11   Capsticks

18   Higgs & Sons

31   Hewitsons
Vinson & Elkins

"Do your application early – the difference between early and late is the difference between five or ten applications that arrive at a firm early in the process and 500 that come in ten minutes before the deadline. Firms do fill up the spaces earlier."

Trainee

What kind of lawyer do you want to be?

Let's start with one of the most basic questions – do you want to be a barrister or a solicitor? Here we give a simple description of each.

Barrister

Ask a solicitor about the key difference between the two sides of the profession and they'll probably tell you it comes down to one thing: ego. At first glance the role of a barrister certainly looks a lot cooler than that of a solicitor. You know the deal – it's all about striding into courtrooms, robes flowing, tense moments waiting for missing witnesses and razor-sharp cross-examinations. Glamorous? It's downright sexy! The truth, of course, is that there's a great deal more to it than looking good in a wig…

Essentially barristers do three things:

* appear in court to represent others
* give specialised legal advice in person or in writing
* draft court documents

The proportion of time spent on each depends on the type of law the barrister practises. Criminal barristers are in court most of the time, often with only an hour or two's notice of the details of their cases. By contrast, commercial barristers spend most of their time on more academic pursuits in chambers, writing tricky opinions and advising in conference on complicated legal points.

Barristers must display the skill and clarity to make complex or arcane legal arguments accessible to lay clients, juries and the judiciary. Their style of argument must be clear and persuasive, both in court and on paper. It has been some time since barristers have had exclusive rights of audience in the courts, though. Solicitors can train to become accredited advocates in even the higher courts. This encroachment hasn't been an utter disaster for the Bar, although solicitor advocates are handling a lot more of the most straightforward cases. When it comes to more complicated and lengthy matters, barristers are usually still briefed to do the advocacy, not least because this is often the most cost-effective way of managing a case. As a point of interest, solicitor advocates do not wear the wig and gown and are referred to as 'my friend' rather than 'my learned friend'.

Solicitors value barristers' detailed knowledge of the litigation process and their ability to assess and advise on the merits and demerits of a case. A solicitor will pay good money for 'counsel's opinion'. Certainly in the area of commercial law, a barrister must understand the client's perspective and use their legal knowledge to develop solutions that make business or common sense as well as legal sense. If you were hoping a career as a barrister would allow you to rise above the rigours and scraping of modern-day capitalism, think again.

Of the UK's 15,500 or so barristers, over 12,600 are self-employed. This is why you hear the expression 'the independent Bar'. The remainder are employed by companies, public bodies or law firms, and they make up 'the employed Bar'. To prevent independence from turning into isolation, barristers, like badgers, work in groups called 'sets', sharing premises and professional managers, etc. Barristers do not work for their sets, just at their premises, and as 'tenants' they contribute to the upkeep of their chambers. A percentage of their earnings also goes to pay their clerks and administrators. Unlike employed barristers and solicitors, those at the independent Bar get no sickness pay, holiday pay, maternity leave or monthly salary. What they do get is a good accountant. To enter practice, LLB grads need to complete the Bar Professional Training Course (BPTC) before starting a much sought-after year of 'pupillage'. Non-law grads need to first complete the Graduate Diploma in Law (GDL) before taking the BPTC. After the pupillage, hopefully, the set you're with will then take you on as a tenant, though you may have to look elsewhere. Once tenancy is established, you're home free (well, except for the gruelling schedule, high pressure, concerns over how much you'll earn, dedicated wig maintenance…).

Being a barrister is a great job, and the fact that this is no secret means competition is truly fierce. If your appetite has been whetted you will find much more information in the final section of this book, where we have detailed the recruitment process and laid bare some of the more obscure practices and terminology. We have also tried to give a fair assessment of some of the difficulties that aspiring barristers may encounter. The main difficulty is that there are many more aspiring barristers than can possibly achieve a career at the Bar. The **Chambers Reports** give invaluable insight into the lives of pupils and junior barristers at some of the best sets. The Bar's professional body is the Bar Council, and it is regulated by the Bar Standards Board.

Solicitor

Most lawyers qualify as solicitors: in fact, there are almost eight times as many solicitors as barristers in the UK. Their role is to provide legal services directly to lay clients, who could be individuals, companies (private or public) or other bodies. In short, clients come to solicitors for guidance on how to deal with their business or personal proposals and problems. These could be anything from drafting a will to defending a murder charge or buying a multibillion-pound business. The solicitor advises on the steps needed to proceed and then manages the case or the deal for the client until its conclusion. They will bring in a barrister if and when a second opinion or specialist advocacy is needed. The solicitor's role is much more like that of a project manager than the barrister's. According to the Law Society, there are over 121,900 solicitors in England and Wales, with practising certificates issued annually by the Solicitors Regulation Authority (SRA). Over 87,900 of them are in 'private practice' in solicitors' firms, and of those, 38,000 are employed in London. Many thousands work in-house for companies, charities or public authorities.

Most readers will be well aware that after an undergraduate degree, law school beckons. Law grads need to take the Legal Practice Course (LPC). Non-law grads must first complete the Graduate Diploma in Law (GDL) before being eligible for the LPC. Next comes the practical training. The most common way of qualifying is by undertaking a two-year training contract with a firm of solicitors, Law Centre, in-house legal team or public body. Much of the rest of this book deals with the nature of training contracts at different firms and how to procure one. The SRA's website gives all the fine detail you could wish for as to the requirements for training.

However, there are changes afoot. Between 2008 and 2010, a SRA pilot examined alternate qualification routes. Candidates clocked relevant work experiences, which were then assessed against skills expected to be acquired in a traditional training contract. Full details of this can be found on the SRA's website at www.sra.org.uk/students/work-based-learning.page. The idea is to dovetail this alternative qualification route with the part-time LPC, possibly blending study and work. From the limited feedback we received, the pilot prompted mixed responses within the profession. The work-based learning model has its fans, but it also has its detractors who question whether it is an appropriate way of introducing new lawyers to the profession. The SRA published an initial evaluation of the pilot in 2011 (available on its website) and will make further recommendations in December 2012. If a work-based learning scheme is rolled out, it is unlikely to provide an easier route to qualification. More on possible changes to legal education later in this guide.

Upon satisfactory completion of their training contract and the mandatory Professional Skills Course (PSC), a person can be admitted to the roll of those eligible to practise as a solicitor and apply for a practising certificate. They are then fully qualified. There are even enrolment ceremonies for anyone who fancies that graduation experience for the umpteenth time!

Where people often trip up is not being fully aware of when they should apply for a training contract. This will depend on the kind of firm you hope to join. If you are studying for a law degree and you want to work in a commercial firm, the crucial time for research and applications is early on during your penultimate year at uni. If you are a non-law student intending to proceed straight to a GDL 'conversion course' before going to a commercial firm, you'll have to juggle exams and career considerations in your final year. Students wanting to enter high-street practice or many of the smaller firms usually don't need to worry about training contract applications quite so early. Unlike commercial firms, which generally offer contracts two years in advance of the start date, smaller firms often recruit closer to the start date, and possibly after a trial period of working as a paralegal.

Larger commercial firms more often than not cover the cost when it comes to their future trainees' law school fees and other basic expenses. Public sector organisations, eg the Government Legal Service, may also come up with some cash. Students hoping to practise in smaller firms soon learn that financial assistance is far from likely and this can make law school a costly and uncertain endeavour.

Needless to say, your choice of firm will shape the path of your career. A firm's clients, its work and its reputation will determine not only the experience you gain but probably also your future marketability as a lawyer. At Chambers and Partners, we've made it our business to know who does what, how well they do it and what it might be like working at a particular firm. Our parent publication *Chambers UK* will also be an incredibly useful resource for you. Its league tables show which firms command greatest respect from clients and other professionals in different areas of practice right across the country. You can search the entire thing for free at www.chambersandpartners.com and use it to help create a shortlist of firms to apply to.

In the **True Picture** section of this guide we've profiled 120 firms in England and Wales. Our goal is to help you understand what kind of firm might suit you and the kind of work you can expect to undertake when you get there. It is the product of many hundreds of interviews with trainees and we think you'll really benefit from making it your regular bedtime reading or favourite bookmark on your smartphone. On the website, we've also interviewed recruiters, training partners and managing partners to give you the low-down on firms' business models, plans for the future and recruitment strategies. You should also read through the **Solicitors' Practice Areas** section of this guide to gain an understanding of what's involved in different fields of practice.

Different types of law firm

There are nearly 10,200 private practice firms in England and Wales. All offer a very different experience. To help you understand the extent and nature of the solicitors' profession, we've grouped them into the following categories.

London: magic circle

The membership of this most exclusive of clubs traditionally extends to Allen & Overy, Clifford Chance, Freshfields Bruckhaus Deringer, Linklaters, and Slaughter and May. To those for whom bigger is better (bigger deals, bigger money, bigger staff numbers), this is the place to be. Corporate and finance work dominates these firms, as do international big-bucks business clients. By organising their training on a massive scale, these firms can offer seemingly unlimited office facilities, great perks, overseas postings and excellent formal training sessions. Although these five giants top many lists, not least for revenue and partner profits, consider carefully whether they'd top yours. Training in a magic circle firm is CV gold but not suited to everyone. One factor to consider is the requirement to work really long hours to keep profits fat and international clients happy. A great camaraderie develops among trainees, but be prepared to not see your other friends too often…

London: large commercial

The top ten City of London firms (including the magic circle) offer roughly 860 traineeships between them each year, representing approximately 16% of all new training contracts registered with the SRA. In terms of day-to-day trainee experiences, there's not such a huge difference between the magic circle and the so-called 'silver circle' firms such as Ashurst, CMS and a few others. Training contracts at these chasing-pack firms are strongly flavoured with corporate and finance deals and, again, international work. The salaries match those paid by the magic circle, which is only fair given that many of the lawyers work equally hard. Many of these firms have recently enlarged further thanks to mergers with large US, Canadian and Australian firms: SNR Denton (formerly Denton Wilde Sapte) and Hogan Lovells (formerly Lovells) are just two examples.

London: American firms

Since the 1970s, there has been a steady stream of US firms crossing the Atlantic to take their place in the UK market. Currently around 40 of them offer training contracts to would-be UK solicitors, with new schemes popping up all the time. We'd suggest staying eagle-eyed if you've a thing for stars and stripes. At the risk of over-generalising, these firms are characterised by international work (usually corporate or finance-led), small offices, more intimate training programmes and very long hours. On the other hand they usually give trainees a good amount of responsibility – famously, many of them pay phenomenally high salaries. Lawyers at the hotshot US firms frequently work opposite magic circle lawyers on deals; indeed many of them were previously magic circle and top-ten firm partners or associates. We've also noticed that since these firms' training contracts are often small, many don't look much further than Oxbridge and London for their trainees: they can afford to be selective.

As we've already mentioned, UK and US firms are increasingly merging with each other, and with Aussie and Canadian firms, further blurring the definition of which are 'American' and which are not. Some firms are quite happy to be labelled as American; others prefer to be described as 'international'. Look at their websites to get an idea of which term to use.

London: mid-sized commercial

Just like their bigger cousins, these firms are mostly dedicated to business law and business clients. Generally, they don't require trainees to spend quite so many hours in the office; however, some of the most successful mid-sizers – eg Macfarlanes and Travers Smith – give the big boys a run for their money in terms of profitability. Generally, the size of deals and cases in these firms means trainees can do much more than just administrative tasks. The atmosphere is a bit more intimate than at the giants of the City, with the greater likelihood of working for partners directly and, arguably, more scope to stand out within the trainee group. You shouldn't expect such an international emphasis to all the work.

London: smaller commercial

For those who don't mind taking home a slightly more modest pay cheque in exchange for better hours, these firms are a great choice. After all, money isn't everything (note: those of you subscribing to Gordon Gekko's 'greed is good' credo see above and read no further). There are dozens of small commercial firms dotted around London: Wedlake Bell and Boodle Hatfield are two examples. Usually these firms will be 'full-service', although some may have developed on the back of one or two particularly strong practice areas or via a reputation in certain industries. Real estate is commonly a big deal at these firms. Along with commercial work, a good number offer private client services to wealthier people. At firms like these you usually get great exposure to partners and there's less risk of losing contact with the outside world.

Niche firms

London is awash with firms specialising in areas as diverse as aviation, media, insurance litigation, shipping, family, intellectual property, sport... you name it, there's a firm for it. Niche firms have also sprouted in areas of the country with high demand for a particular service. How about equine law in Newmarket? If you are absolutely certain that you want to specialise in a particular field – especially if you have already worked in a relevant industry – a niche firm is an excellent choice. You need to be able to back up your passion with hard evidence of your commitment, however. Many of these firms also cover other practice areas, but if any try to woo you by talking at length about their other areas of work, ask some searching questions.

Regional firms

Many of you will agree that there is more to life than the Big Smoke. There are some very fine regional firms acting for top-notch clients on cases and deals the City firms would snap up in a heartbeat. There is also international work going on outside the capital. The race for training contracts in the biggest of these firms is just as competitive as in the City. Some regional firms are even more discerning than their London counterparts in that applicants may have to demonstrate a long-term commitment to living in the area. Understandable, as they hardly want to shell out for training only to see their qualifiers flit off to the capital. Smaller regional firms tend to focus on the needs of regional clients and would therefore suit anyone who wants to become an integral part of their local business community. Salaries are lower outside London, in some cases significantly so, but so is the cost of living. There's a perception that working outside London means a chummier atmosphere and more time for the gym/pub/family, but do bear in mind that the biggest and most ambitious regional players will expect hours that aren't so dissimilar to firms with an EC postcode.

National and multi-site firms

Multi-site firms are necessarily massive operations, some of them with office networks spanning the length and breadth of the country and overseas. To give you just two examples, Eversheds has nine branches in England and Wales plus many overseas; DLA Piper has six in England and many more overseas. These firms attract students who want to do bigger-ticket work outside London – a sometimes unwelcome consequence of which is doing London levels of work for a lower salary. Some of the multi-site firms allow trainees to stay in one office, whereas others expect them to move around. Make sure you know the firm's policy or you could end up having a long-distance relationship with friends, family and your significant other while you move to a new town for a few months or are saddled with a punishing commute. The work on offer is mostly commercial, although some private client experience may be available.

General practice/small firms

If you're put off by the corporate jargon, City-slicking lifestyle and big-business attitude of some of the firms in this guide, then the small firm might be just what you're after. If you want to grow up fast as a lawyer and see how the law actually affects individuals and the community in which you practise, then this is the kind of firm to go for. We go into much more detail over the page.

Larger firms may take up to half a dozen or so trainees a year; the smallest will recruit on an occasional basis. It is in this part of the profession where salaries are the lowest, often the minimum required or recommended for trainees by the SRA. This minimum salary requirement has been scrapped by the SRA after consultations on its regulatory remit. After 1 August 2014, employers will only have to adhere to the national minimum wage rate (currently £6.08 per hour).

Until August 2014:

- Minimum salary Central London = £18,590 pa
- Recommended salary Central London = £19,040 pa
- Minimum salary elsewhere = £16,650 pa
- Recommended salary elsewhere = £16,940 pa

Anyone thinking of entering the Legal Aid sector should be aware that dramatic changes are affecting the public funding of legal services. We discuss this in considerable detail on our website.

High street firms

Choosing a high street firm can lead to a host of rewarding experiences. Among the highlights are daily client contact, a colourful spread of cases and close ties to the local community.

What is a high street firm?

The *Student Guide* is largely devoted to corporate and commercial outfits. We make no apology for this – these firms are the biggest and offer the most training contracts of any group. Still, the firms covered in this guide only account for around 2,400 of the 5,441 training contracts offered in 2010/11. Of the remainder, many are up for grabs on the high street.

There are over 10,000 law firms in England and Wales, many of which are smallish outfits that service private individuals in their local area. High street practices can range from long-established bands of several dozen lawyers in a town centre to sole practitioners setting up shop in the suburbs. They come in all shapes and sizes, but we reckon there are four main characteristics that distinguish the high street firm from its larger corporate/commercial counterparts:

- **Location.** You guessed it – they're based on high streets, whether, that's in a Leeds, London or Birmingham suburb or in a small city or market town. So you might find a firm wedged in between a kebab house and a branch of JD Sports.
- **Practice areas.** High street firms act primarily for private individuals. Their core practices are wills and probate, conveyancing, and private client (tax) on the advisory side, with family, personal injury, employment, immigration, crime and social housing on the contentious side. They might also provide commercial and property advice to small businesses.
- **Legal aid.** State-funded undertakings traditionally make up a large proportion of high street firms' work, though not all of it by any means. In fact, ongoing cuts to legal aid mean these firms are taking on an increasing number of commercial and privately funded clients just to stay afloat.
- **Direct access.** People literally walk in off the street to ask advice from a high street firm, much as they might walk into M&S for a sarnie. This direct access creates roots in the local community, a key hallmark of the high street practice.

Of course, firms vary in endless ways – there are many that fit into some or all of the aforementioned categories yet don't consider themselves high street practices (and rightly so). So be careful with labels as some firms are prouder to assume the 'high street' moniker than others. For all intents and purpose of this guide, however, let's assume a firm that primarily does legal aid work, acts almost exclusively for individuals and has its digs on a shopping street is a high street firm.

Recruitment

Trainee recruitment at high street firms varies wildly, and the ins and outs of the process very much depend on the firm. The biggest might hire as many as half a dozen new starters a year while the smallest take just one every few years. Likewise, some recruit two years in advance, others just a few months before a September start. Many have a formal application process consisting of an application form/cover letter, an interview and skills assessments, but it's not uncommon for selection at smaller units to happen on a more informal nudge-nudge-wink-wink basis. Others still prefer a more indirect approach, taking on paralegals and offering a training contract after six months or so provided they're up to scratch and the budget allows. Interview questions are something that tend to hold true across firms, however – most directly address life on the high street. One of the more colourful examples we heard was: "*What would you do if a client came into the office drunk, demanded their files back and threatened to sue us?*"

High street firms may lack the brouhaha surrounding magic circle behemoths, but that's not to say that getting into one is a walk in the park; in fact, some receive as many as 500 applications for just three or four trainee places. Like with corporate and commercial firms, good academics are essential to getting your foot in the door at a high street fixture. Specific requirements vary from firm to firm – some will happily accept candidates with a 2:2, for example – but the market for training contracts is so competitive that most firms can and do use the 2:1 mark to whittle down applicant numbers. Relevant work or experience is a similarly important factor in landing a spot – experience working in the public sector, volunteering or paralegalling are all seen as big pluses – as is choosing LPC electives that reflect a high street firm's practice. "*Corporate finance doesn't look good when you're looking to practise family law,*" one recruiter told us. Don't underestimate the power of local know-how, either, especially for firms in small cities and provincial towns – familiarity with local folk and their businesses can go a long way in demonstrating a candidate's ability to engage with a town's community.

The work

Like their corporate counterparts, high street trainees spend time across their firm's different departments. The firms we visited offered a mish-mash of stints in crime, immigration, family, private client, personal injury and housing/litigation. Seat options are likely to be somewhat limited given a high street firm's smallish size, but in many ways the system is more flexible than at big firms. Some operate around the classic 4x6 scheme while others offer seats that can last six, eight or nine or even 12 months. "*It's bit of a juggling match as it's not the case that everyone spends the same amount of time in different teams,*" a trainee told us. "*If you're working on a case and a team needs you to stay for an extra month or two, then you'll often do so.*" As such, seat allocation is often arranged one-on-one with the training partner. "*If trainees have a seat they particularly do or don't want to do – or they are not enjoying their seat – they just come and talk to me,*" one high street training partner told us. At smaller firms with only one or two practice areas trainees are occasionally 'seconded' to another firm or organisation to satisfy SRA training requirements.

Wills and probate lawyers draft and provide advice on wills and help executors deal with estates. They also counsel clients on contested probate and disputes over legacies. The job isn't always as office-bound as it sounds. Case in point: "*I went to a car yard in North London to help with a probate valuation of a Lamborghini,*" one trainee told us.

Conveyancing lawyers draft leases and documents related to the sale and purchase of residential property. They also occasionally advise small business or farms on commercial property.

Private client lawyers advise the rich-and-not-so-famous on wealth management and tax issues. (Note that some high street firms also use the term 'private client' to a distinguish individuals paying for services rather than being legally aided.) Tax isn't everyone's cup of tea, but changes to private tax regimes and increasing government scrutiny of tax avoidance and offshore wealth have kick-started many people's interest in the practice.

The bread and butter of **family** law is divorce, be it messy or tidy. While this type of work can prompt some interesting research – "*I had to contemplate whether it was best to organise a divorce in Russia or in the UK*" – some cases are marred by domestic abuse and violence. "*We see the most abject misery coming through the door,*" one trainee lamented, "*including marriage problems, domestic violence, child abuse. Some of our clients are very upset – you see the hardest side of their lives.*" Similarly solemn is childcare law, a niche practice under the family umbrella. Lawyers deal with problems of abused or neglected children, acting either for the child through a guardian or for the parent whose child is being taken into custody by a local authority. "*The issues are very emotional and sometimes we are a shoulder to cry on. That comes with its rewards too: there is nothing better than getting a hug from a client after a successful case.*" You don't get that at Clifford Chance.

Personal injury cases are usually run on a no-win-no-fee basis. (There's been no legal aid for this area of law since the late 1990s.) High street firms act almost exclusively for claimants, with their costs covered by pay-outs from defendants. Cases range from slips and trips to workplace accidents and loss of limb, and their value can be anywhere from a few grand to a million pounds. (An interesting detail: given the large number of Polish workers in this country, many workplace-related personal injury practices offer Polish-language services.)

High street **crime** lawyers defend people accused of misdeeds ranging from common assault and drug offences to rape and attempted murder. Lawyers and trainees often obtain police station accreditation to plump for criminals who've been hauled in by the bill. As one trainee pointed out, "*You're never sure when someone will be arrested. Being called out to a police station at 2am is not everyone's idea of a great job.*" It's the solicitors' job to help the accused give statements and guide them through trial proceedings by instructing counsel and appearing in court. High streets firms were at the forefront of defending those accused of crimes in the wake of the London and UK 2011 riots. One trainee we spoke to had also defended members of the UK Uncut protest against charges of aggravated trespass for 'occupying' Fortnum & Masons in March 2011.

Other contentious areas of the high street practice include **social housing** (landlord-tenant disputes), **immigration** and **employment**.

High-street trainees in contentious practices will almost always get some advocacy experience. "*From day one I've interacted with clients and been involved with simple advocacy,*" one proudly told us. "*I successfully obtained a contact order by consent from of a district judge at the Principal Registry of the Family Division.*"

Trainees are also often tasked with dealing with initial enquiries from potential clients who phone up or walk through the door. *"Our door is always open to the people of Camden,"* one trainee in that London borough told us. *"We get the great and the good dropping by. We'll get a call from reception saying there's someone downstairs, and it's our job to take their details and filter out the nutters."* The reception areas of high street firms are a hive of activity and, much like a doctor's surgery or local council office, can bear witness to some rather surprising enquiries: *"Someone once came in an asked about name changes for transgender individuals."*

Pillars of the community

"Our central position right next to Clapham Junction station is really important to our work and our clients," a trainee at 114-year-old establishment Hanne & Co told us. *"Our client base isn't just local, but it is good to be recognised locally as 'the firm down the road'."* Partners are often pivotal figures in the local business community, sitting on local committees, attending surgeries at local libraries or law centres, giving talks at schools or helping raise money for local charities.

There's a strong personal connection in the job. A client will refer to you as 'their' solicitor, and instruct you on a whole range of fairly simple day-to-day matters from moving house to building an extension on their house. As such, people skills are very important to high street practice, something that was certainly reflected in the working environment at the firms we visited. *"Everyone here has made friends,"* one trainee told us, mentioning that *"some people have lived together as flatmates."* Another told us about their firm's social committee, which organises a Christmas party and two other social dos a year. *"We hold our events at restaurants in the community to support local business."*

Career prospects

We've explained the perks, but what about the downsides to working on the high street? *"Not being paid very much isn't ideal, of course,"* one interviewee admitted bluntly. *"But then again, people work here because they want to, not for the money."* In reality, many high street firms pay the Law Society minimum trainee salary. Fortunately, trainees aren't expected to burn the midnight oil, though it's hardly a nine-to-five job either." *It's not unusual to work until 7pm or 7.30pm,"* one trainee told us. Indeed, thanks to the relatively small size of high street practices it's especially important to show you're committed to the work (seeing as there's much less space to hide).

On average, trainee retention rates are lower on the high street than at corporate/commercial firms, although this varies from firm to firm and year to year. *"My firm's been candid with us – we know they can't promise us anything at the end of the training contract,"* one trainee told us. *"I'm not presuming I'll be offered a job because the firm doesn't have the space to keep on all of its four or five qualifiers."* A partner at the same firm estimated it keeps on around 50% of trainees each year.

The legal aid saga

As a result of government cutbacks, legal aid is being removed from many employment, family, housing, immigration, debt advice and benefits cases. For example, all family and divorce cases in which there are no violence or guardianship issues are now prohibited from receiving legal aid. It is also being removed from all immigration cases except for those related to asylum, human trafficking or other violent activities. *"The impact of these cuts will be significant,"* a high street partner warned, touching on another source's dire prediction that *"the cuts will ultimately cost the government more money in the long term."* Moreover, since legal aid cases often account for a substantial proportion of trainee work, the cuts mean high street firms will likely come under pressure to cut back on their recruitment numbers.

To cope, many high street firms are focusing on bulking up the privately-funded side of the business by garnering more work from local businesses and wealthy individuals. Another strategy is seeking out work in areas that are as yet unaffected by the cuts. Unfortunately, however, it seems inevitable that the cuts will have major consequences. Many small high street firms that rely entirely on legal aid will doubtlessly be forced to close, and the overall number of trainees recruited onto the high street will likely decrease in years to come. You can read more about the consequences of these cuts on our website.

The market is changing in other ways too. An increasing number of corporations are beginning to get involved in high street legal work thanks to the Legal Services Act, which allows businesses like the Co-op supermarket to provide legal advice. Another trend sees multi-site businesses taking on volume legal work traditionally associated with the high street – obvious examples include nationwide personal injury specialists Thompson Solicitors as well as smaller brands like In-Deed, Lawyers4you and QualitySolicitors. Such operations have expanded hugely in the last few years, appearing on more and more high streets, often at the expense of independent local firms.

And finally...

Despite recent changes to the market, working on the high street remains a rewarding experience for many. Trainees get the chance to become closely embedded in their communities, work face-to-face with clients and advocate on their behalf on matters of great personal importance.

What is a training contract?

Basically, a training contract is the step between your academic life and your life as a fully qualified solicitor.

Most training contracts are taken on a full-time basis and last two years. Part-time options are much rarer. The part-time-study training contract lasts between three and four years, allowing you to learn while you earn, balancing the LPC and/or GDL with part-time training at a firm. The part-time training contract is an option for those who have already completed their LPC. It involves working a minimum of two and a half days per week for up to four years.

Training contracts must comply with SRA guidelines. The most important of these are:

- It's a *training* contract not an *employment* contract: this means it is nearly impossible for you to be sacked. For a training contract to be terminated there must be mutual agreement between the firm and trainee, a cancellation clause (like failing the GDL or LPC), or a formal application to the SRA when issues cannot be resolved internally. Instances of trainees being fired are extremely rare.
- Trainees must gain practical experience in at least three areas of English law and develop skills in both contentious and non-contentious areas of law. Some firms send trainees on litigation courses that fulfil the contentious requirement without them having to do a full contentious seat. Firms can also arrange secondments for trainees to gain contentious experience.
- Trainees must complete the Professional Skills Course. The firm has to allow trainees paid study-leave to attend these courses and has to pay the course fees.

The norm is to spend time in four departments over the two years (six months in each). Each stint is called a seat. At some firms you'll find yourself doing six four-month seats or some other more bespoke arrangement. At very small firms it's likely that your training won't be as structured. Repeating a seat is common, more so during six-seat schemes. Typically, repeat seats are in either the firm's largest department or the department in which you hope to qualify.

Besides the SRA's contentious/non-contentious requirement, some firms may require that you do a seat in one or more particular departments over the course of your training. For the other seats, firms usually ask you to identify your preferred departments and try to best accommodate your wishes. However, seat allocation isn't always a simple task and you might not get what you want.

You will be allocated a supervisor in each seat who will be responsible for giving you assignments and (hopefully) helping out with any questions you have. Supervisors are typically mid-level to senior associates/assistants or partners. Usually you will share an office with your supervisor or sit near them in an open-plan setting. You may also have the opportunity to spend a seat (or part of one) seconded to one of your firm's clients or one of its overseas offices. Appraisals are important and most firms will arrange a formal meeting between trainee and supervisor/HR at the end of each seat and probably also midway through. Appraisals typically count when firms are deciding who gets to take up client or overseas secondments and those coveted jobs on qualification.

What the experience entails:

- Long hours are almost a given; however, they are more likely when you work at a large, international or corporate/finance-focused firm. They are less likely at litigation-led firms and smaller domestic advisory or boutique firms.
- There is a hierarchical structure to law firms, and while this is felt more strongly at some firms than others, trainees should be prepared to start at the bottom.
- Luckily, you will have the rest of your trainee intake as back up. Trainees tend to be close-knit and most firms provide some sort of budget for trainee socialising. Larger firms with larger intakes of trainees tend to have more active social scenes.
- You're not guaranteed a job at the end of it. If you've done well, the firm will retain you on qualification, finding you a job in a department that you've come to love… or in a department that needs new junior lawyers. The firm that trained you is not obligated to keep you: your contract with the firm is for the period of your training only. You should regard your training contract as a two-year job interview.

The main thing to remember is that the purpose of training is to learn about several areas of practice and find your spot in the profession. One training partner put it perfectly when he said: "*Trainees should view the training contract as an opportunity to be a sponge and soak up all the right ways to be the lawyer they want to be. Keeping an open mind and soaking up the most idiosyncratic things can really put you ahead.*"

Trends affecting the recruitment market

It's a tough employment market out there for everyone – aspiring lawyers included. In the following feature we'll talk about the various different factors that are combining to make it such a difficult time to break into the profession, and discover if there is any light at the end of the tunnel.

The recession and its effect on the legal profession

The 2008 credit crunch and subsequent recession has, of course, ballsed things up for everybody. How and why we got into this mess is not something that need detain us here, but if you're clueless about this topic, go and do some reading because you'll need to know the basics if you have serious ambitions to be a commercial lawyer.

The legal profession was as hard hit by recession as any other sector. If a property bubble bursts, property and construction lawyers have less work to do. If banks stop lending and companies lose confidence in the economy, corporate and finance lawyers sit idle. Of course, this isn't the whole story. If lots of companies are going bankrupt, insolvency and restructuring lawyers thrive. So do litigators, as creditors battle to retrieve their money. Unfortunately, pre-2008, most large law firms were quite heavily geared towards transactional work. They were cashing in on the boom years, but they'd put an awful lot of eggs in baskets that were subsequently smashed in a big metaphorically eggy catastrophe. Silly them.

So, when the recession hit, law firms were taken by surprise. Most suffered, a few even collapsed. Look up the fates of UK's Halliwells and the US's Dewey & LeBoeuf – two notable law firm failures. The crash exposed mismanagement and flaws at their heart. Even those firms that didn't collapse were forced to take drastic steps. Faced with falling revenue and not enough work, they made a logical decision: remove from the payroll all those lawyers who are sitting around with nothing to do. Hundreds were made redundant in late 2008 and 2009.

The good news is that the worst is – hopefully – over. Law firms have reshaped their practices so they are more balanced and no longer so reliant on certain areas. All those redundancies mean they are leaner organisations, less likely to take heavy damage from any future shocks. And although things are far from rosy with the world economy, and there may yet be more trouble ahead, at the time of writing in summer 2012 transactional lawyers are busier than in the dark days of 2009.

The world of private law has its own problems to face, but major changes are being made to how the UK's Legal Aid system works. You can read about Legal Aid in much more detail on our website.

Law firm mergers

Law firms have always merged with each other, but they're at it like the clappers at the moment. Some of these mergers are genuinely forward-thinking, where two firms come together to increase their international coverage and become global big-hitters. Others are motivated by little more than the need to survive – the recession battered some firms to the extent that they were better off joining forces with another rather than limping on alone. John Quinn, the colourful founding partner of Quinn Emanuel, opined that the merger of US firm Squire Sanders and UK firm Hammonds was a case of *"two rocks that think if they hug each other tight enough they won't sink."* If this is a rather over-the-top analysis, it is true that many firms have decided that there is strength in numbers. It makes sense for two firms with similar practices to merge, thereby reducing overheads and creating a stronger combined firm.

For aspiring trainees, this trend for mergers is one to be aware of. It's perfectly possibly, for example, to be offered a job by a smallish British firm, only to walk up on the first day of your training contract to find it's been taken over by a big American beast. Trainees' contracts are honoured when firms merge, but of course you might end up having quite a different training experience to the one you were expecting.

The Legal Services Act

The Legal Services Act is affecting commercial and private law alike. Introduced in 2007 to much controversy within the profession because of its radical new ideas, the Act permits non-lawyers to invest in and operate law firms. The reforms have been phased in slowly to allow the profession time to adjust, but change is now well and truly upon us. From March 2009 solicitors were permitted to form partnerships with non-solicitors such as barristers, legal executives or other professionals including HR and IT personnel. These Legal or Multi Disciplinary Partnerships (L/MDPs) marked a liberalisation of the partnership model. Nevertheless, a stake in a law firm was still only available via the holy grail of partnership, and under MDPs and LDPs at least 75% of partners still have to be lawyers.

The second wave of reform has been more radical still. Under Alternative Business Structures (ABS) lawyers are now able to team up with other professionals to offer a range of services to clients – accountancy or banking, for instance. Imagine you are a large PLC: your law firm could now handle your annual accounts as well as contract disputes. For individuals, a high-street practice could find a house, secure mortgage arrangements and handle the conveyancing – all under one roof. To give just one example, City firm Mishcon de Reya has already started to explore non-legal revenue schemes, such as private bank relationship management advice, tax advice and even concierge services.

ABSs will also be able to seek external investment. It's early days, but there are indications that several law firms are preparing to dip their toes into this pool of opportunity; national firms Pannone and Irwin Mitchell have confessed themselves keen to take advantage. Those with expansionist instincts should be able to tap into reserves of private capital to fund lateral hires, office renovations or additional branches. ABSs also open the door to the possibility of law firms floating on the stock market. 'Going public' is probably best suited to firms whose legal services are 'commoditised', that is, non-complex services such as personal injury, wills and probate, and conveyancing that can be standardised though investment in technology and processes. Australian PI, family and probate specialist Slater & Gordon was the first to take the plunge when it floated on the Australian Stock Exchange in 2007. Its profits soared and its enhanced war chest enabled it to acquire smaller firms across Oz – and in 2012 it entered the UK market for the first time, taking over Russell Jones & Walker.

While the potential benefits of external investment are clear, the main concerns focus on the influence investors could wield over the management of firms and the potential ethical consequences. After all, investors will want a good return on their money. Furthermore, welcoming outside investment means surrendering some executive decision making. This marks a hugely significant cultural shift in the profession.

Mr Justice Darling commented 90 years ago that "*the law courts of England are open to all men like the doors of the Ritz Hotel.*" Arguably this observation still rings true today. The Act aims to redress this issue by making legal services as accessible as the obligingly open doors of your local supermarket – quite literally – by allowing almost any company to offer legal services. In the not-so-distant future it may be possible to write your will at a bank or buy divorce services alongside your weekly groceries. 'Tesco law,' regarded only a few years ago by some observers as comical or dangerous, is now here. The AA is among the organisations that already offer limited legal services, generally focusing on personal injury. The Co-operative is planning on hiring 3,000 lawyers (and 100 trainees annually) within the next five years in order to offer legal services to the general public. To quote *The Guardian*, the Co-op "*believes its reasonable rates as well as ethical and socially responsible values will attract large numbers of customers who are deterred from approaching more expensive, traditional law firms.*" Meanwhile, in Spring 2011 QualitySolicitors linked up with WHSmith to offer legal services in some of their branches. Although it won't be possible to sell your house while purchasing the Sunday papers, QualitySolicitors' employees can book appointments with lawyers, offer conveyancing quotes and wills services.

All these changes are being introduced in the name of increased efficiency and greater competition, each designed to benefit consumers. And yet surveys in recent years suggest that many members of the public are wary of Tesco Law while large sections of the profession view it as a big threat to profitability. So, while high-street practices may find themselves competing against well-known companies that can take advantage of economies of scale, consumers may decide they still prefer tried-and-tested local firms. The key issues may turn out to be the pricing of services, and familiarity – people may simply become used to getting their legal issues sorted at the supermarket. How this affects the demand for lawyers and the salaries they command remains to be seen.

What about the trainee recruitment market?

The most obvious effect of the recession on the trainee recruitment market was that many smaller law firms stopped hiring trainees altogether, while many larger firms scaled back their recruitment drives and 'deferred' people who were due to start training contracts until such time as there was enough work to go round. The number of registered traineeships fell from 6,303 in 2007/08 to 4,874 in 2009/10.

Once again, the worst appears to be over. Firms have started to hire again. Deferrals have declined as the economy has haltingly recovered (although both Mayer Brown and

Wragge & Co have asked their September 2012 intakes to voluntarily start later than planned).

However, there is still caution in the market, and some question over whether the law will ever need as many junior lawyers as it did pre-bust. With tighter budgets, clients are now demanding greater value for money. They are no longer willing to pay hundreds of pounds for a junior lawyer to sit in a room photocopying when some temp kid could do it for a tenth of the price. Furthermore, new technology may well end the need for firms to employ legions of trainee solicitors. An increasing number of the functions performed by lawyers are now capable of being performed by legal software packages. Of course, there are tasks where human beings are still required, but paying a trainee £50,000 is often not the most economical way of getting them done. Clients will be happy to continue to pay lawyers for their legal expertise but not for processes that can be done by cheaper non-qualified staff. Globalisation means firms can easily outsource low-level tasks, such as document review, to countries like India or South Africa, where they can be completed by equally bright staff for much less. Several top City outfits and national firms are already outsourcing.

With all this in mind, The Law Society has seen fit to publish a 'health warning' telling students that "*you should not view qualifying as a solicitor to be an easy process... competition is fierce and it has been made more so by the recession... the cost of completing the LPC itself is extremely prohibitive.*" It is only fair to say that not everyone shares this bleak view – a 2011 study by the College of Law claimed a recent drop in the number of LPC graduates could lead to a shortfall of rookie solicitors when the economy recovers. Of course, it's in the College's interest to attract more people onto its LPC.

Changes to legal education

A debate is currently taking place about whether 'degree ➤ LPC ➤ training contract' is even the best way of producing new solicitors. A College of Law study even called for the training contract to be scrapped entirely in 2009. The Legal Education and Training Review currently taking place is "*required to ensure that the future system of legal education and training will be effective and efficient in preparing legal service providers to meet the needs of consumers*" and will make recommendations in December 2012. We spoke to a LETR insider, who told us: "*Firstly, it's a much needed and much welcomed review in the world of legal practice,*" and predicted: "*I think a complete overhaul* [of legal training] *would be unlikely; it will most likely be a case of tweaking what we already have. My view is that there is going to be tweaking, but also exponential growth in work-based learning and the validation of work-based degrees. The ILEX course* [see page 35] *will play a far greater role in legal*

training, and people will train via that route instead of an academic one." We'll keep our website updated as things develop.

Conclusions

Law firms have had to re-evaluate what they do, where, for whom, and at what price. They need to be leaner and meaner. Many are cutting back on their recruitment of junior lawyers. And all at a time when law schools are working overtime to churn out more and more GDL, BPTC and LPC students, many of whom have paid for a qualification they will never use.

Our view...

- is that the world will always need lawyers and that good graduates will always have a chance of making it in the profession. Whatever issues the profession faces, that won't change. Even if you are not a top-of-the-class swotty swotface, those of you with decent grades are in with a shout. See our feature **How suitable are you and what do recruiters want?** to assess your chances.

- is that the days when students didn't need to know that much about the firms they were applying to and could rely on being bright individuals with a good degree and potential are over – forever. Even five years ago, training contract applicants weren't expected to show the level of knowledge regarding law firms and the legal marketplace that they are today. Today's applicants have access to more information about the law than ever before – but this also means they are expected to know more. We live in the information age and, that being the case, not having information puts you at a distinct disadvantage. Students who don't prepare sufficiently for application forms or interview will struggle.

- is that likewise, graduates with a 2:2 or below will find fewer doors are open to them. As one training partner told us: "*If you have average or less than average grades, you're really going to struggle. I sometimes feel no one bothers to warn students early enough about that.*" It's a bare fact that a Desmond is less and less likely to get you anywhere in a professional career. Yes, there are always exceptions, but they are just that – exceptions. So work your socks off at university.

- is that you should consider your options very carefully before parting with hard-earned cash to pay for law school. Starting law school with out a training contract or pupillage sorted out will always be a calculated gamble.

How else can I boost my chances?

Firstly, by mastering the art of making applications. Common sense suggests that if you apply to 100 firms, you are more likely to get an interview than if you apply to ten. In this case, common sense is misleading. Recruiters are incredibly adept at spotting copy-and-paste applications. You will almost certainly meet with more success by targeting a dozen or so firms that you really want to work at, researching them properly and spending a great deal of time perfecting your application to them. Quickly dashing off as many application forms as you can and changing the firm name on each identical cover letter is a waste of your time. We bang on about this again in our feature on **Making successful applications**.

Secondly, get as much legal experience as you can as soon as possible to demonstrate your commitment to the profession. By as soon as possible, we mean NOW.

Pay and prospects

Lawyers' pay remains excellent – for now. While some firms made salary freezes or cuts in 2009, most lawyers are pretty well-paid when compared to the rest of the population. Until recently, the Solicitors Regulation Authority set a minimum trainee salary: as of 2012 it was £18,590 in Central London and £16,650 elsewhere.

However, the SRA recently voted to scrap the minimum trainee salary. From 1 August 2014, firms will no longer be obliged to pay trainees more than the national minimum wage (currently £6.08 per hour). Naturally, this has led to intense debate. Supporters of the move say removing the minimum salary will allow more small firms to take trainees, and so more students will be able to get training contracts. Opponents say it will allow firms to exploit legally-trained graduates, employing them as cheap labour for two years, then dumping them at the end of their training contract.

It's impossible to tell if this scenario will actually play out. We'll just have to wait and see. Focusing on the positives, the scrapping of minimum salaries will have no effect at the top end of the market. No top firm is ever going pay its trainees a measly £6.08 an hour. The average starting salary for a trainee in Central London is a very healthy £34,817 according to the last Law Society report in 2011. The lowest average starting salary is in Wales, where it's £17,790.

Finally, those who do manage to get a training contract should be well placed for the future. In a normal year, around 80% of qualifiers stay on at they firm that trained them. There was a noticeable blip in 2009 and 2010, but as the market has readjusted, average retention has returned to pre-recession levels. This year our data shows that 79% of qualifiers were retained by our True Picture firms. You can go to our website for further analysis and retention stats for every firm we've ever covered in the True Picture since 2000.

Pro bono and volunteering

Deriving from the Latin pro bono publico, meaning 'for the public good', the idea of providing free legal advice has been ingrained in the legal profession for centuries.

In 1594 the Lord Chief Justice explained to newly qualified barristers that the "*two tongues*" of linen hanging from counsel's shirt collars in court "*signifies that as you should have one tongue for the rich for your fee... so should you also have another tongue as ready without reward to defend the poor and oppressed.*" Traditionally done in a very British, understated way in the UK, the past decade has seen the rise of structured pro bono programmes at law firms, sets of chambers, law schools and universities. Bringing these all together, ProBonoUK.net was started in 2003 and is the most comprehensive resource on pro bono activities in the UK. 2012's National Pro Bono week will run from the 5th to 9th November.

Why participate?

In 2010 justice secretary Ken Clarke introduced proposals to cut the legal aid bill by £350m a year by 2015, the harshest cut backs the scheme's faced since its inception in 1949. 2011 saw just a few not-for-profit legal advice centres going into administration but Julie Bishop, director of the Law Centres Federation, warns that a third of all centres nationwide are susceptible to closure as legal aid accounts for over 60% of their revenue. Involvement in some form of pro bono or volunteering work is becoming increasingly important, not just because there are people out there who need your help, but now more than ever pro bono experience is a clear winner with recruiters. Experience suggests that those who have been most active have found it much easier to land job interviews. If you have something to put on your CV it will help take you closer to the front of the queue for training contracts and pupillages.

Law schools make a particular effort to introduce students to pro bono. As Jessica Austen, joint director of pro bono at BPP, told us: "*Being involved in pro bono can make a huge difference to student engagement with the courses they are undertaking. They can see the law they are studying come to life in a practical sense and realise the impact their participation can have on the community around them. This is particularly true now, given access to justice is so much more challenging following the legal aid cuts.*"

Many firms now have formal pro bono relationships with organisations such as community legal advice centres. Arguably the increased scope and visibility of pro bono work is in part due to the greater importance placed on pro bono activities by the influx of US law firms into the UK market. Certainly more home-grown law firms now recognise the business case for doing this kind of work, not least because of the PR benefits of telling the world what caring organisations they are.

Real life

Getting involved couldn't be easier when you're at law school as most now offer extensive programmes. Cardiff Law School has the Innocence Project, for example, which deals with long-term prisoners who maintain their innocence and have exhausted the initial appeals process. Kaplan Law School has developed a close relationship with Amicus, and regularly sponsors students to attend training sessions which allows them to assist with defence counsel representations for those facing execution in the US. At the other end of the pro bono spectrum, BPP works in conjunction with the charity Own It to provide free IP advice to the creative industries, while the University of Westminster's LPC course has a clinical law elective, during which students work on a pro bono basis for the CAB and submit a project at the end of the elective. And as if you needed a greater incentive than a warm glow in the pit of your belly, there are various national prizes on offer for students who excel in this field, including the Law Society's annual Junior Lawyers Division Pro Bono Award. At University level, student pro bono opportunities have been more limited, largely because it's too risky for inexperienced undergrads to provide real-life legal advice. This is changing as undergraduates are receiving more support. You can go to www.studentprobono.net for a comprehensive list of opportunities at each institution.

If you hope to go to the Bar or become a solicitor specialising in any contentious area of law then you should seriously consider becoming a ratified member of The Free Representation Unit (FRU), a charity founded in 1972 to provide legal advice, case preparation and advocacy for people who aren't able to claim legal aid.

Vacation schemes

Pack your bags for a holiday placement, if you can... but don't forget to bring your common sense cap.

Still at uni and unsure if you really want to be a lawyer? You wouldn't be the first and you certainly won't be the last. So giving up a week or two of your hard-earned holiday during Christmas, Easter or the summer to sample law firm life ('try before you sign') is a small price to pay. As one training partner told us, vacations schemes are a great opportunity to test the waters, *"a chance to gain an insight into life as a lawyer, get feedback on your work, and grow from the experience."*

But be under no illusions: you will also be on trial, because in this ever-more competitive market most firms (and some more than others) treat the vac scheme almost as a pre-screening exercise when it comes to handing out training contracts. A rare few even insist that you complete a vac scheme with them before they'll consider your training contract application. The prime example of a firm that relies heavily on vac schemes is City firm Nabarro, which now takes almost all of its trainees from people it sees on its three-week placement. Another is US giant Skadden, which informs us: *"We do accept applications from those who haven't done vacation schemes with us; but we really only look at those if something has gone wrong with our placement and it hasn't thrown up enough quality candidates."*

This stance is not (yet) the prevailing recruiting model, and many firms who offer vacation schemes recruit just as many trainees who haven't done one with them as those who have. But the message is clear: whichever vac scheme you end up doing you'll be assessed, no matter how informally, and you should plan and act accordingly. *"It's true we use our vac schemes to assess candidates for prospective training contracts,"* another recruiter admitted.

How do you get on one?

No secret here: our handy-dandy table of vac schemes over the page tells you what places are available with the firms covered by this guide and when to apply. Timing your application is important: certain schemes are targeted at penultimate-year law grads or final-year non-law grads, which can leave other students frustrated. Suffice to say, law undergrads need to start thinking about their application campaign as early as the summer after the

first year at university. The application deadlines for the majority of vac schemes come in January and February, but some firms run schemes in the Christmas and Easter holidays and the deadlines for applying to those can be as early as October. Don't miss out! You'll generally find full details of exactly how to make your application on firms' recruitment websites.

What do firms look for when recruiting for the vac scheme? *"Same as the training contract really,"* one tells us: *"Strong academics and an interest in our practice areas."* As competition for training contracts gets more intense, it's no surprise that competition for vac scheme places is equally so. Obvious conclusion: you'll need to put as much effort into vac scheme applications as you do into training contract applications. For some tips on how to do this refer to our feature on how to make successful applications. On our website we also have detailed advice on the application procedures for each of the firms covered in the **True Picture**. The strongest applicants always manage to secure a clutch of offers, but don't despair if you can't secure a place – it doesn't necessarily mean you'll never get a training contract. Try and build your CV up in other ways – say with voluntary work or other legal or commercial experience – and then have another stab at vac scheme applications.

Even if you navigate the vac scheme obstacle course perfectly, don't get complacent. You'll usually still need to prepare well for a training contract interview.

What will I get to do?

Vac schemes differ as much as the firms themselves. In some cases, your time will be structured down to the minute with talks about the firm and its training contract, followed by tasks and social engagements. At others you might find you have to hunt and gather work. For detailed information on the structure of each firm's vacation scheme, go to our website.

What should I look out for?

When on a vac scheme, become an anthropologist. Observe your environment and its inhabitants; figure out the social structures, the hierarchies, the shared values that bond people (if indeed there are any). Watch how the trainees fit in with all of this. Eavesdrop. You've got to be on your guard though because people will be conscious you're there, and some of our sources did end up concluding: *"It can be an artificial exercise – you see what they want you to see."* Your aim is to peer beyond the mask at the living, breathing, sweating entity behind it.

Try also to get a feel for how different departments work by reading as much as you can. A starting point would be our **Solicitors' Practice Areas**. It'll help you figure out what sort of work might suit you best and will enable you to ask intelligent questions of your supervisors. Intelligent questions pave the road to success, so lay as many down as possible without becoming annoying.

How will I be assessed?

"The vacation scheme is a great way of meeting prospective trainees and giving them a real taster of what life is like here," a recruiter explains. But don't forget that, on the other hand, *"it's a good way of meeting the candidates and seeing them in action working on live files."* Vac schemers are often given research to do as a way of evaluating their abilities; expect to be given some specifics to look into before reporting back to solicitors with your findings. You might be asked to shadow someone, helping them out with their workload. This is an excellent opportunity for you to find more out about the firm while proving yourself at the same time. You might even get to go to client meetings or visit court. Last, but certainly not least, are the mini-assessment tasks designed to test your ability to present, argue and work as a team. *"Don't be over-assertive, but don't fade into the background either. Remember to ask other people what their opinions are – you have to look like a team player."* Some tasks we heard about involved advertising pitches to faux potential clients, mini-transactions and business scenarios.

How should I act?

"Those who are successful have the drive, imagination and confidence to see the scheme for the learning opportunity it really is rather than just an assessment centre in which they are competing with other students," one training partner at a larger outfit advises. *"Students become*

part of the firm when they arrive; many make friendships. And the firm will always make room for excellent candidates it sees on the scheme, whatever the numbers."

While you're busy watching everyone else, don't forget that they're watching you, watching them, watching you. This recruitment lark is a delicate dance, so attune yourself to the characters around you and follow their lead. More than anything else, people will be trying to see if you 'share the firm's core values'. Ultimately, 'professionalism' should be your watchword. This is a job interview, even when you're eating lunch in the canteen. Don't be late for work. Switch off your mobile phone when in the office. Don't bitch or send stupid e-mails. Thinking about browsing Facebook in a slack moment? Why take the risk?

Okay, so don't be an idiot. That much is obvious. But how can you impress? As one recruiter says, it's all about *"marketing yourself well."* Does that sound a little intimidating? It's really not. After all, you marketed yourself well on paper when you sent your application form in, now you are just doing it in person. Asking well-timed questions and showing an interest is an easy way of doing this. Just remember, *"seeking out work and raising your profile without pestering people is a fine line to walk."* A trainee confirmed that you have to strike the right balance, telling us that on the last vac scheme he was involved with, *"there were a couple of people who were too enthusiastic!"*

Coming for a quick drink? Bankers, lawyers, doctors and even priests all know how effective alcohol can be when it comes to greasing the wheels. But the trick is to drink the right amount or none at all. Even when firms take vac schemers out to snazzy clubs, recruiters' mental notepads will still be out. So gauge the situation: is the firm boozy or abstemious?

At the end of the day, a law firm is just like any other office workplace and you'll find all sorts of characters. You'll also find variety within any group of vac schemers. *"You get the quiet ones, the loud ones, the ones who say inappropriate things, the ones who're always smiling."* Obviously, you're being assessed on how good a lawyer you're likely to be, but don't underestimate how far having a normal, attractive personality will get you.

Vacation schemes

Firm name	Vacancies	Duration	Remuneration	Deadline
Addleshaw Goddard	80 – easter & summer	1-2 weeks	Not known	31 January 2013
Allen & Overy	60 – winter – (final year undergraduates & graduates); summer (penultimate year undergraduates)	Not known	Not known	31 October 2012 (winter); 15 January 2013 (summer)
Arnold & Porter	8 – summer	2 weeks	Not known	1 March 2013
Ashfords	Yes	Not known	Not Known	31 March 20
Ashurst	Easter (grads & final year non-law); summer (penult-year law)	Not known	£275 p.w.	15 January 2013
Bates Wells & Braithwaite	24	1 week	£250 p.w.	March 2013
Beachcroft	Summer	Not known	Not known	1 March 2012
Berwin Leighton Paisner	Winter, spring & summer	Not known	Not known	31 October 2012 (winter); 31 January 2013 (summer)
Bevan Brittan	18	Not known	Not known	31 March 2013
Bird & Bird	Summer	Not known	Not known	Not known
Boodle Hatfield	8-10 – summer	2 weeks	Not known	Not known
Brabners Chaffe Street	Summer	Not known	Not known	30 June 2013
Bristows	Winter, spring & summer	Not known	Not known	Not known
Browne Jacobson	Open day in spring	1 day	Not known	17 March 2013
Burges Salmon	40 + 2 open days	2 weeks	£250 p.w.	Not known
Capsticks	Summer	2 weeks	Not known	15 February 2013
Cleary Gottlieb	35 – winter, spring & summer	Not known	Not known	16 November 2012 (winter); 25 January 2013 (summer)
Clyde & Co	Easter & summer	2 weeks	Not known	31 January 2013
Cobbetts	Summer	Not known	Not known	31 January 2013
Covington & Burling	24	3 weeks	£300 p.w.	31 January 2013
Davis, Polk & Wardwell	8-12	3-4 weeks	Not known	31 January 2013
Davenport Lyons	Summer	Not known	£250 p.w.	Not known
Dechert	Easter & summer (aimed at penult-year law)	Not known	Not known	31 January 2013
Dickinson Dees	40 – easter & summer	1 week	£200 p.w.	31 January 2013
DLA Piper	150 - summer	2 weeks	Not known	31 January 2013
Dundas & Wilson	Summer	3 weeks	Not known	30 January 2013
DWF	Summer	1 week	Not known	Not known
Edwards Wildman Palmer	8-10 – summer + open days	2 weeks	Not known	Not known
Eversheds	Summer	2 weeks	Not known	31 January 2013
Farrer & Co	30 – easter & summer	2 weeks	£275 p.w.	31 January 2012

Vacation schemes

Firm name	Vacancies	Duration	Remuneration	Deadline
Freshfields Bruckhaus Deringer	Yes (aimed at penult-year undergrads)	Not known	Not known	13 January 2013
Gateley	Summer	2 weeks	Not known	11 February 2013
Herbert Smith Freehills	Summer & winter, & spring workshops	2 weeks (winter) 3 weeks (summer)	Not known	Not known
Hewitsons	Yes	1 week	Not known	Not known
Hill Dickinson	48	1 week	Not known	31 January 2013
Holman Fenwick Willan	20	2 weeks	Not known	14 February 2013
Ince & Co	15	2 weeks	£250 p.w.	31 January 2013
Irwin Mitchell	Summer	Not known	Not known	1 February 2013
Jones Day	60 – winter (non-law); spring (non-law); summer (law)	2 weeks	£400 p.w.	31 October 2012 (winter); 31 Dec 2012 (spring); 31 Jan 2013 (summer)
Kennedys	Summer	Not known	Not known	31 January 2013
Kirkland & Ellis	Up to 20	2 weeks	£350 p.w.	31 January 2013
Latham & Watkins	Easter & summer	2 weeks	£350 p.w.	31 December 2012 (easter); 31 January 2013 (summer)
Lawrence Graham	24 – summer	2 weeks	£350 p.w.	31 January 2013
Lester Aldridge	Summer	2 weeks	Not known	31 March 2013
Linklaters	Summer (aimed at penult-year undergrads) & workshops	Not known	Not known	Not known
Macfarlanes	55	2 weeks	£300 p.w.	31 January 2013
Maclay, Murray & Spens	Summer	3 weeks	Not known	31 Janurary 2013
Manches	c.20	1 week	£225 p.w.	15 February 2013
Mayer Brown	Easter & summer	2 weeks (easter); 3 weeks (summer)	Not known	Not known
Michelmores	Summer	1 week	Not known	28 February 2013
Mills & Reeve	Summer	2 weeks	Not known	31 January 2013
Mishcon de Reya	20	2 weeks	Not known	31 January 2013
Muckle	Summer	Not known	Not known	25 January 2013
Nabarro	60 – summer	3 weeks	Not known	31 January 2013
Norton Rose	Winter (non-law & grads); summer (penult-year law)	Not known	Not known	Not known
Olswang	20 – spring & summer	2 weeks	£275 p.w.	31 January 2013
O'Melveny & Myers	Summer	Not known	Not known	31 January 2013
Orrick	Open days	Not known	Not known	Not known
Pannone	60	1 week	None	14 April 2013

Vacation schemes

Firm name	Vacancies	Duration	Remuneration	Deadline
Penningtons	Summer + info days	Not known	Not known	31 March 2013
Pinsent Masons	c.120	2 weeks	Not known	31 January 2013
PwC Legal	Summer	3 weeks	Not known	31 January 2013
Reed Smith	Up to 20	2 weeks	Not known	Not known
RPC	Summer	2 weeks	Not known	31 January 2013
SGH Martineau	Yes	2 days	Not known	24 February 2013
Shoosmiths	Yes	Not known	Not known	28 February 2013
Simmons & Simmons	Spring & summer; workshops + open days	3 weeks	Not known	Not known
SJ Berwin	Easter & summer	Not known	Not known	31 January 2013
Skadden	Easter & summer (penult-year law and non-law)	2 weeks	Paid	12 January 2013
Slaughter and May	Summer + workshops & open days	1-2 weeks	Not known	Not known
SNR Denton	Summer (law) + open days (non-law)	1 week	Not known	Not known
Speechly Bircham	Summer	3 weeks	Not known	Not known
Squire Sanders	40 – summer	2 weeks	£230 / £215 p.w.	31 January 2013
Stephenson Harwood	40 – Christmas, Easter & summer winter & open days	1 week (winter); 2 weeks (Easter & summer)	£260 p.w.	4 November 2012 (winter) 31 January 2013 (Easter & summer)
Stevens & Bolton	Summer	1 week	Not known	31 January 2013
Sullivan & Cromwell	Summer	2 weeks	£350 p.w.	31 January 2013
Taylor Wessing	40+	2 weeks	£250 p.w.	31 January 2013
TLT	Yes	1 week	Not known	Not known
Travers Smith	60 – Summer & winter	2 weeks	£275	31 January 2013 (summer)
Trowers & Hamlins	Summer	2 weeks	Not known	1 March 2013
Veale Wasbrough Vizards	Summer	1 week	None	Not known
Vinson & Elkins	Summer	Not known	Not known	28 February 2013
Walker Morris	48	1 week	£175	31 January 2013
Ward Hadaway	Summer	1 week	Not known	28 February 2013
Watson, Farley & Williams	30 – Easter & summer	2 weeks	£250 p.w.	31 January 2013
Wedlake Bell	8 – summer	3 weeks	£250 p.w.	28 February 2013
Weil, Gotshal & Manges	30 – spring & summer	Not known	Not known	Not known
White & Case	12-15 – Easter; 40-50 – summer	2 weeks	£350 p.w.	31 January 2013
Wilsons Solicitors	Summer	1 week	Not known	Not known
Withers	Easter & summer	2 weeks	Not known	31 January 2013
Wragge & Co	Yes	Not known	Not known	31 January 2013

Some other career options

There are a number of different roles and organisations to look at other than becoming a solicitor or barrister in private practice. Here are a few of the main ones.

Working in-house for a company

The commercial sector employs around 15,000 in-house lawyers; for example, there are many in the banking, utilities, telecommunications and entertainment industries. However, the number of training contracts offered in-house is minimal compared to those offered in private practice.

In 2010/11 around 170 individuals began a training contract in house with a company, representing around 3% of the total number of training contracts. Examples of such companies include BT, Vodafone and Standard Life. Check out our website for the full list.

For aspiring in-house solicitors, the Commerce & Industry Group (www.cigroup.org.uk) is a good place to start – it has made promoting in-house legal careers a priority. Aspiring in-house barristers should get in touch with the Bar Council (www.barcouncil.org.uk). It's also worth keeping an eye on the legal press and *The Times* on Thursdays to see who's recruiting, as well as making your interests known in the relevant circles. Indeed, finding out which companies offer training is "*all about networking and making contacts*," according to our sources. "*And the C&I Group has a mentoring system for trainees and dinners, which offer a great way of networking with in-house lawyers.*"

Unless an organisation publicises vacancies, it's likely it recruits trainees from a pool of candidates who already work there in some other capacity – often as a paralegal or equivalent. Even then aspiring trainees are advised to exercise discretion when trying to obtain a contract. A softly-softly approach more in line with the tortoise than the hare usually works best.

We spoke to one junior solicitor who had trained in-house with a major international company. She started working with the company as a legal secretary and then "*when it was discovered I had a law degree, I was encouraged to go to law school.*" The company paid for her LPC and she was asked to help find out how the organisation could become an accredited training contract provider. Four years later our source is a content in-house lawyer: "*I get such a mixed bag of work – I can start the day doing contracts and end on regulatory work.*" Flexibility and good time management are important aspects of the job – "*all day people will turn up at your desk and ask for five minutes of your time*" – as is the ability to take a generalist approach: "*We are the GPs of the legal world as we are not the master of anything but cover a wide area.*" Perhaps the biggest plus of an in-house career path is the perception that it offers good remuneration and better hours than private practice.

If would be remiss of us not to point out that the above tale is somewhat exceptional; most in-house lawyers actually start out working for a law firm and switch to the role some time after qualification. In-house lawyers don't lose touch with private practice: a big part of the job involves selecting and instructing law firms to provide specialist advice. This is another plus as it's likely to keep you knee-deep in invites to parties, lunches and sporting events as different law firms curry favour.

Law Centres

Law Centres are not-for-profit legal practices with local management committees and a remit to 'help people to stay in their homes, keep their families together and get into employment or education.' Advice and representation is provided without charge to the public, with funding coming from local authorities, the Legal Services Commission, and some major charities like the Big Lottery Fund. Community care, all types of discrimination, education, employment, housing, immigration, asylum and public law form the caseload at UK Law Centres. The legal problems handled may vary from one Centre to another, but all who work in the sector are considered social welfare law specialists.

The network of Law Centres in the UK now numbers over 50 and most employ several lawyers. If you're attracted to working with colleagues with shared ideals and a social conscience, it's worth investigating a career in the sector. Routes to a Law Centre position are as varied as the work each handles: newly qualified solicitors with relevant experience in private practice are taken on, as are those who have worked as paralegals for non-profit agencies and gained supervisor-level status. A career may also begin at a Law Centre itself.

Law Centres' horizons tend to be broader than those of Citizens Advice Bureaux, and they tend to take on cases with a wider social impact. A client with a consumer dispute is less likely to be helped than someone who is affected by, say, a local authority's decision on rent arrears. Law Centres identify trends and then use individual cases as a springboard for changing the big picture, perhaps by way of a test case that makes it to the highest courts and the broadsheets. Law Centres are also eager to involve the communities they operate within, providing legal training and education. As a Law Centre employee you might even find yourself at a local comprehensive imparting your legal know-how to teenagers. Recent reforms to the provision of legal aid have required Law Centres to become more target-oriented, but there is still a strong campaigning angle to the sector. Recent highlights include launching a Law Centre for deaf people in conjunction with the Royal Association for the Deaf, using the Equality Act to help a wheelchair-bound MS-patient force Sheffield City Hall to improve disability access to the building, and Avon and Bristol Law Centre winning a discrimination case for a man who was denied work by recruitment agency Adecco because he was not a British citizen.

As a newly qualified solicitor your salary at a Law Centre will roughly match private practice on the high street or local authority salary scales – that's £24,000 to £30,000 (or more in London). However, Law Centres tend to lose their competitive edge when seeking to appoint more experienced lawyers. Let's just say the organisation tends to attract those who feel there is more to being enriched than being rich. In terms of workplace culture, Law Centres operate along different lines from private practices: there's less hierarchy and more of an equal say for staff at all levels – some even operate as collectives with all staff drawing the same salary. Terms and conditions at work emulate those in local government: pensions, holiday provisions and other such benefits are good, and flexible or part-time working options are readily available. Law Centres are keen on the equality and diversity front and actively seek out trainees from their local community. It is an exciting environment, and many lawyers go on to take up influential roles outside of the movement.

Candidates will only be considered if they respond to an advertisement. Look out for these in *The Guardian* (on Wednesdays), in local newspapers, and on Law Centres' websites and the Law Centres Federation website (www.lawcentres.org.uk). Applicants can enhance their prospects by demonstrating their interest in social justice, whether by earning some stripes through committees or community group participation or taking advantage of relevant law school schemes. Work placements at a local authority also offer a taste of the fields Law Centres plough.

Certain Law Centres accept volunteers to assist with administration and (if they're accredited) translation work, though such roles are usually given to those from other non-profit agencies. A voluntary stint with a Citizens Advice Bureau may be easier to get hold of and can prepare you equally well for Law Centre work.

Government Legal Service

The GLS ostensibly has only one client – the Queen. In practice, however, 'clients' include the policymakers and managers within government departments, while lawyers are full-time litigators and solicitors who draft new legislation and advise ministers how best to legally put policy into practice. Despite government budget cuts, the GLS is still currently recruiting. Before you apply, it's important to consider whether you'll be happy working at the interface of law and politics and dealing with matters that directly impact on UK society. If the idea appeals, read our **True Picture** and **Chambers Reports** features on the GLS.

Local government

There are around 3,500 solicitors as well as a host of paralegals, legal executives and barristers employed in the local government sector. Local government lawyers advise elected council members and senior officers on a wide variety of topics including commercial/contracts, conveyancing/property, employment issues, information management, administrative law and governance. Additional work depends on the type of local authority involved and can include litigation/prosecution, social care, children, consumer protection, environmental, highways and planning, education and housing matters, to name but a few. Lawyers tend to maintain broad practices in the smaller authorities, while those in larger ones usually specialise in a single area like housing, planning, highways, education or social services. Duties include keeping councils on the straight and narrow, making sure they don't spend their money unlawfully and advising councillors on the legal implications of their actions. The typical salary for a local authority solicitor is between £29,700 and £39,900, though some senior solicitors can earn more than £40,000.

Local government trainees usually follow the same seat system as those in private practice but have rights of audience in courts and tribunals that outstrip those of their peers. Trainees shadow solicitors and gradually build up their own caseload. Most authorities offer summer placements to give aspiring solicitors a sneak preview of what it's really like, and some are even paid. Contact the head of legal services at a local authority to ask for further information – the more experience you can get the better. Most applicants are graduates, but there is a chance for non-graduates to pursue a career in this direction by starting their training as a legal executive.

Be prepared to wade through the bureaucratic bog and at times be driven to distraction by the slow machinations of local government. Still, the benefits of a government training contract – variety in your day-to-day work, flexible hours and a sense of serving the community – generally outweigh the downsides. A major plus is the ease with which many climb the career ladder – there's the option to hop from authority to authority, and there's a general perception that the glass ceiling is less prevalent in local government as it is in City law firms. In fact, 50% of local authority chief executives have trained as solicitors. Training in local government can also open doors to careers in private practice, the Crown Prosecution Service and the GLS.

The total number of training contracts available each year generally stands at 80-ish, and while government cuts and job freezes are affecting recruitment, we have it on good authority that a solid number of councils are expected to continue recruiting trainees in upcoming years. Because each of the 400-plus authorities in England and Wales acts as a separate employer, there's no central list of vacancies and no single recruitment office. As such, finding out about training contract opportunities is somewhat of a challenge in itself, as is finding out which councils offer sponsorship for the GDL and/or LPC. A good starting point for research is www.lgcareers.com. Most authorities advertise vacancies on their own website and in the *Law Gazette* and *The Lawyer*, so those are worth a look too. Other helpful resources include www.localgovernmentlawyer.co.uk and www.lgjobs.com (both offer useful job-search functions) and www.slgov.org.uk, which provides testimonies from qualified solicitors and trainees. You can also try the law and public service job ads in *The Times*, *The Guardian* and *The Independent*, or even approach local authorities directly.

Crown Prosecution Service

The Crown Prosecution Service is the government department responsible for bringing prosecutions against people who have been charged with a criminal offence in England and Wales. The CPS handles all stages of the process, from advising the police on the possibility of prosecution, right through to the delivery of advocacy in the courtroom.

The CPS employs over 2,700 lawyers to handle more than 1.2 million cases in the magistrates' and Crown Courts. Its prosecutors review and prosecute criminal cases following investigation by the police and also advise the police on matters of criminal law and evidence in order to combat the problem of failed prosecutions. Specifically, lawyers advise the police on appropriate charges for certain crimes and generally split their time between preparing cases in the office and prosecuting in the magistrates' court. A special band of lawyers entitled Crown Advocates prosecute Crown Court cases including murder, rape and robbery.

The CPS's training programme, which we've covered quite comprehensively in the past, was put on hold in 2011 in line with government cutbacks; however, as of spring 2012 it has reopened to those who have completed the LPC or BPTC. According to an official statement, in October 2012 the CPS plans to begin offering places and financial assistance to candidates who haven't yet completed vocational training. For more information visit www.cps.gov.uk/careers/.

The armed forces

Unsurprisingly, the army always needs lawyers, and in good army no-nonsense fashion, it knows how to sell the position: 'No billing, no timesheets, no rat race – a job to be proud of,' declares the website. Fully qualified barristers and solicitors with a good understanding of army activities and preferably some work experience under their belt can join the Army Legal Services (ALS) and expect to see all sorts of work from court-martial to international cases. You should be physically fit and aged between 24 and 32.

Potential applicants should look out for ads in the national press or send their CVs to the service. Recruitment goes as follows: up to nine suitable candidates are called for interview before attending the Army Officer Selection Board at Westbury in Wiltshire. Successful applicants are then offered a Short Service Commission in ALS, which lasts four years, including an 18 month initial probational period. Six months of training will lead on to your first legal appointment, either at home or in Germany or Cyprus. Further international opportunities occasionally arise in Afghanistan, Kenya, the USA and Canada. NATO and the UN are also worth bearing in mind as future job prospects. See www.army.mod.uk/agc/9935.aspx for more details on the ALS.

The Royal Air Force also employs barristers and solicitors to deal with criminal cases and prosecutions, both home and abroad. The Air Force's legal department is small, but the work is juicy – areas of law covered include Air Force law, the law of armed conflict, new legislation plus the host of civil issues that affect RAF personnel. A linear career path can see you rise to the position of Squadron Leader after four years and Wing Commander after a further six. Previous legal officers have found themselves providing advice to people in Iraq, the Falklands, Kosovo and Germany. The starting salary is £37,915 after training, and recruitment is done according to needs rather than annually. Applicants must be aged between 21 and 34. Visit the RAF website to learn more: www.raf.mod.uk/careers/jobs/legalofficer.cfm.

The Navy doesn't have such a clear recruitment path, though we've heard tale of legal opportunities after you've signed on the dotted line and joined the Senior Service.

The police

Only Sherlock Holmes can operate for and outside of the law and get away with it. All other members of the police force are as accountable as everyone else and therefore need good legal representation when their own conduct is called into question. This is where police lawyers step in. They can find themselves working in all sorts of areas, which aside from the aforementioned civil actions, can include: corporate governance; employment law and discrimination; personal injury; and neighbourhood safety matters (for example, issuing ASBOs or Sexual Offences Protection Orders).

We spoke with the Metropolitan Police force to find out more about career opportunities for law grads. Sadly, government cuts in spending have meant that this is one area that has become less active on the recruitment front as of late. However, for those with a passionate interest in police work, our recruiter contacts recommend taking up a voluntary position as special constable, which involves volunteering 16 hours a month and is a common route for lawyers eager to gain experience of the law as it's enacted at street level rather than in the courts. If this sounds like your sort of gig, or if you want any further information about possible vacancies, check online with your local police force. In London, recruitment policies will be reviewed in September 2012 by the Metropolitan Police Force, so make sure that you check www.met.police.uk regularly for updates.

Legal executive

If you haven't found a training contract or are thinking about moving sideways into a legal career, you could consider the Chartered Institute of Legal Executives (CILEx) course. Those who complete it become qualified in what is sometimes known as the 'third branch' of the profession. Day-to-day work is similar to that of a solicitor, although legal executives often deal with lower-value, high-volume cases such as residential conveyancing and personal injury claims. That said, it is possible to progress to more bespoke and complex work with experience.

In the last couple of decades CILEx has helped 92,000 members secure a successful career in law. There are currently over 20,000 Chartered Legal Executive lawyers and trainees across England and Wales, all of whom are independently regulated. No prior legal qualifications are required to enrol on the course, and it is open to those reaching GCSE, A level or university level. This makes it suitable for school leavers, new graduates or those already in a career. It can be taken on a full-time or part-time basis, giving students an opportunity to combine study with practical experience. CILEx members earn while they learn and can be in employment across the full spectrum of legal services, from private practice to government departments, or the in-house legal teams of major companies.

For those with no prior legal training, the CILEx Level 3 Professional Diploma in Law and Practice is the first stage of the academic training. It usually takes about two years of part-time study and costs around £3,500 for tuition and all exam and registration fees, but can cost less depending on where you choose to study. On completion, students become Associate members of CILEx. Associate members are entitled to use the designatory letters A.Inst.L.Ex after their name, but are required to undertake eight hours of Continuing Professional Development (CPD) each year. This qualification also allows firms to charge out their paralegal staff with this qualification as fee-earners, so several people studying for their CILEx have their exam and membership fees funded by their employers.

The second stage is the CILEx Level 6 Professional Higher Diploma in Law and Practice, which is assessed at honours degree level, again typically taking two years to complete at a cost of up to £3,500, but again can cost less depending on where you choose to study. On completion, students become Graduate Members of CILEx. Graduate members are entitled to use the designatory letters G.Inst.L.Ex after their name, and are required to undertake 12 hours of CPD.

For those with a qualifying law degree obtained within the last seven years, CILEx now offers the Graduate Fast-Track Diploma. Students need to choose two subjects from the range of CILEx Level 6 Practice units (one of which must relate to the subjects studied within their university law degree), and take the CILEx Level 6 Client Care Skills unit to complete their academic studies. The qualification takes around a year to complete part-time and costs up around £2,200 (including all CILEx fees), depending on where you choose to study.

With both the full CILEx route or the Fast-Track for law graduates, to become a fully qualified Chartered Legal Executive lawyer (also called a CILEx Fellow), it is necessary to gain five years of qualifying experience in a legal background (at least two after completing the CILEx Level 6 or Fast-Track exams). Timescales for all CILEx courses are flexible, according to personal needs, and study can be fitted around a job. There is no set time to complete the exams, so people can work at their own pace. The qualifications can be studied at a local accredited centre or via distance learning.

Chartered Legal Executive lawyers can continue studying to become Chartered Legal Executive Advocates and represent their clients in open court. They can also be partners in law firms and even apply for judicial appointments.

Whilst being a chartered legal executive can be a rewarding career in its own right. For those who still want to become a solicitor, CILEx can provide a useful route to qualifying as one, even if it is by no means the quickest. Most people can seek exemptions from much of the GDL (having already covered its core subjects). Crucially, they are also usually exempted from the two-year training contract, provided they are already a qualified chartered legal executive before completing the LPC. A full list of institutions offering the ILEX course (including the distance learning option) is available at www.ilexcareers.org.uk.

Paralegal

If you've got time to kill before starting your training contract or have yet to decide whether you're ready to shell out for law school, paralegal work can provide a useful introduction to legal practice. The term 'paralegal' is quite generic, and the job duties that paralegals encounter can vary drastically: some are given their own files to run while others end up with dull doc management tasks for months on end. Experiences do, at the end of the day, depend on the firm. Luckily, legal employers tend to view any time spent paralegalling favourably as it demonstrates a commitment to the profession and enables candidates to gain valuable experience and commercial or sector insight. It's a good idea to take into account factors such as a firm's size and number of trainees when making applications – a smaller trainee intake often means you'll get to see much better quality work. One former paralegal told us: "*A major factor in getting my training contract was the fact that I could talk about my responsibilities as a paralegal: attending court, going to client meetings, drafting documents. I was able to show enthusiasm for the legal process and demonstrate that I would be a committed and enthusiastic future trainee.*" Some firms and companies – though not all – offer traineeships to the most impressive of their own paralegals, though it's important to keep in mind that the job is a valuable position in its own right.

The paralegal market has been massively competitive since the recession, so these days applicants with no legal qualifications or practical experience will find it difficult to secure a position – many large commercial firms require their paralegals to have completed the LPC or BPTC and have at least six months of prior experience. Those lucky enough get a foot in the door might find themselves completing a number of short-term contracts until one firm decides to keep them on a longer-term basis. Some smaller firms insist that prospective trainee solicitors complete a trial period of paralegalling before offering them a contract, a move that occasionally leads to allegations of firms exploiting their paralegals. Be careful to read the small print and keep a lookout for criteria such as whether you get paid for overtime or not. These stipulations can make all the difference, especially if you're handed a BlackBerry and called in on weekends. Should you find yourself in a compromising position, the Junior Lawyers Division or the Law Society are good organisations to contact.

While there are no doubt many upsides to the paralegal experience, an occasional complaint is feeling somewhat left out at the firm. As one source explained: "*Sometimes the paralegals aren't invited to department events. The secretaries go for drinks and the trainees meet for dinner, but a paralegal is neither one nor the other. This might not matter as much in a large firm where there are big groups of paralegals and the partners and associates organise events for their teams; in a smaller firm, however, it can be a bit depressing. The best thing to do is find another paralegal and stick with them.*"

Experienced paralegals with specialist skills can make a decent living. If you're thinking about becoming a career paralegal, the National Association of Licensed Paralegals' website (www.nationalparalegals.co.uk) is a good place to start. Speaking with your law school's careers office, checking the legal press, registering with a specialist recruitment agency and trawling law firms' own websites are all decent ways to get a handle on current vacancies. It's even worth firing off a speculative letter or two as some firms recruit this way.

Legal secretary

"*Being a legal secretary is a good way to get your foot in the door,*" explained one of our lawyer contacts. They would know: it's exactly how they started their career. For anyone unsure of whether they want the full-bore pressure of working as a solicitor, this route could be perfect: "*A major pro is that you're working in law without the more intense responsibility of being a lawyer.*" It's also a smart way to spend a few years if you're struggling to get your finances back on track and can't yet contemplate law school. According to the Institute of Legal Secretaries and PAs (ILSPA), taking a legal secretarial role is suitable for anyone with an interest in law or a background in administrative work. That said, it's important to know that the market is pretty full right now, with firms reducing their support staff to reduce costs and there's a lot of competition for jobs. As such, ILSPA recommends completing a course. For more details visit www.institutelegalsecretaries.com.

People can take on legal secretarial positions at any stage of life, be it instead of university, after a degree or as a complete career change. Whenever you take this step, you'll need to be certain that you have the right qualities and temperament: you need to work well under pressure, have a lot of patience, pay attention to detail and be articulate. You must also get to know your boss quickly, think for them and organise them. One downside is that some people will regard your role as relatively lowly and show precious little respect for your talents. One legal secretary-turned-lawyer confirmed that it can be a challenge working for people who do what you actually want to be doing. For more on the reality of the job see www.legalsecretaryjournal.com.

A legal secretary can be employed as a shared resource for a whole department or just a few lawyers, or they may be more of a personal assistant to just one lawyer. Typical administrative tasks include typing correspondence, filing, arranging meetings and diary management. The salary range is wide and can go up to £40,000 or so a year, though it varies depending on where in the country you work. The most money is to be made in London or other big cities. As in any career, you'll need to start at the bottom of the ladder – especially if it's your first job – although our ILSPA contact reckons that law school grads may be able to start a rung or two up and definitely have scope for climbing higher. Check recruitment sites and agencies for as many options as you can find and apply for any job for which you feel you could be suitable. Look up the law firms in your area, call them and send your CV. Junior positions are often filled via word of mouth or by speculative applicants.

Her Majesty's Courts and Tribunals Service

In 2011, Her Majesty's Courts Service and the Tribunals Service integrated to form HM Courts & Tribunals Service. The Service is an agency of the Ministry of Justice and is responsible for the daily business of the civil, family and criminal courts in England and Wales. Its stated aim is 'to ensure that access [to justice] is provided as quickly as possible and at the lowest cost consistent with open justice, and that citizens have greater confidence in, and respect for, the system of justice.' HMCTS looks after the management of over 1,200 properties and court buildings and deals with the timetabling and management of hearings, as well as lighter matters like making courts available as filming locations. It currently employs around 21,000 staff.

Many HMCTS jobs are administrative in nature; however, the Service also recruits Judicial Assistants (JAs), who are assigned to one of the Court of Appeal's senior judges for a period of up to 12 months. Duties include legal research, advice and providing assistance in drafting judgements. JAs may also help define the shape and nature of appeals in less well-presented cases. There are usually ten positions available at any one time. Applicants need at least a 2:1 and must be lawyers who have completed or are about to complete pupillage or a training contract. Positions are advertised according to need in *The Times* and the *Law Gazette*, as well as on the Justice website: www.justice.gov.uk/about/hmcts/index.htm.

Long-term careers are available for administrative officers, bailiffs and county and Crown Court ushers or clerks. Court clerks do not have a legal advisory role and therefore don't need any legal qualifications. Their responsibilities include maintaining the records of a court and administering oaths to witnesses and jurors. Likewise, magistrates' clerks – who do give legal advice to lay magistrates on issues like self-defence, identification of suspects and inferences from the silence of defendants after arrest as well as points of procedure – don't need a legal background. A commonality among all clerks is the ability to think on their feet and deal confidently with people. Clerks are present at most court sessions (of which there are nine or ten a week) and also issue summonses on behalf of magistrates. One we spoke with described his role to someone from continental Europe as follows: "*In Poland, they would call someone with my level of responsibility a judge!*"

In June 2010, the coalition government announced plans to close 103 magistrates' courts across the country as part of a programme to save over £2bn at the Ministry of Justice. Accordingly, the Service stopped recruiting trainee magistrates' court clerks; however, aspiring court clerks should keep checking the jobs pages of www.justice.gov.uk/about/hmcts/index.htm and www.hmcourts-service.gov.uk for upcoming opportunities as well as other information on HMCTS.

The Law Commission

Many laws are the product of centuries of precedent; others arise from little more than political expediency. Constant reform is needed to ensure that the law is fit for purpose in the modern age, however, the government is not always best placed to see where reforms could be made. The Law Commission, an advisory non-departmental public body sponsored by the Ministry of Justice, was set up by Parliament in 1965 to review the laws of England and Wales and propose reform where necessary. The Commission is engaged in about 20 projects at any one time. Among topics it set out to examine in its most recent reform programme were: shortcomings of the law on contempt committed by publishing information about imminent or active court proceedings; the taxi-cab and private hire regulatory system; the modernisation and simplification of wildlife law; and modernising the Offences Against the Person Act (1861), which uses archaic language, follows a Victorian approach and whose structure provides no clear hierarchy of offences.

It is not just a case of repealing laws that are clearly archaic; it's equally important not to accidentally remove the legal basis for someone's rights. The Commission employs around 12-15 researchers every year to help it fulfil its remit, and as a researcher you would analyse many different areas of law, identifying defects in the current system and examining foreign law models to see how they deal with similar problems. You may also help to draft consultation papers, instructions to Parliamentary Counsel and final reports.

Researchers are normally law graduates and postgraduates, those who have completed the LPC or BPTC, or people who have spent time in legal practice but are looking for a change. The job of research assistant involves some fascinating (and less fascinating) subjects and is intellectually challenging. Candidates should have a First or high 2:1, along with a keen interest in current affairs and the workings of the law. The job suits those with an analytical mind and a hatred of waffle. They must also love research because there's a lot of it, be it devising questionnaires and analysing the responses, studying statistics or examining court files. To read which reforms proposed in 2010 have been implemented and which have been rejected, read the report on the implementation of Law Commission proposals at www.justice.gov.uk/publications/docs/report-implementation-law-commission-proposals.pdf

Keep up to speed with the Law Commission's recruitment needs at at www.lawcom.gov.uk. December tends to be the month when they start looking for people.

Legal Services Commission

The LSC was created by the Access to Justice Act 1999 and replaced the Legal Aid Board in 2000. In addition to its HQ in London, it has operated from 15 offices across England and Wales, helping over two million people a year by managing the distribution of public funds for both civil legal services and criminal defence services. The work of the LSC is essentially divided into the Community Legal Service (CLS) and the Criminal Defence Service (CDS).

The role of the CLS is to ensure people can get information and advice about their legal rights and help with enforcing them: this tends to be in the areas of family breakdown, debt, housing immigration, welfare benefits,

community care, clinical negligence and public law. CLS caseworkers assess the merits of applications for legal funding and means test applicants. The CLS works with legal aid solicitors, Citizens Advice Bureaux, Law Centres, local authority services and other organisations. Recent reforms have seen the CLS working with local authorities to create Community Legal Advice Centres in a bid to provide a more integrated service in relation to social welfare law.

The CDS manages the supply of legal advice to those under police investigation or facing criminal charges using local solicitors accredited by the service. It also performs an audit role in relation to authorised providers of criminal legal advice. Part of the CDS's work is the Public Defender Service (PDS). Its four offices, set up in 2001, advise members of the public 24/7 in what the LSC believes to be a more cost-effective and efficient way. They are located in Cheltenham, Darlington, Pontypridd and Swansea.

The commission is undergoing a great deal of change and will be transforming from a non-departmental public body into an executive agency in the future. As of 1 April 2013, significant changes to the scope and eligibility of legal aid will be introduced – which will affect most areas of the law listed above. These changes will be brought in under the Legal Aid, Sentencing and Punishment of Offenders Act (LASPO), which became law in May 2012. The LSC itself will be succeeded by the Legal Aid Agency, also from 1 April 2013. As a result of the Government's Comprehensive Spending Review, we are unable to comment on possible recruitment opportunities for the future – but keep up to date at www.legalservices.gov.uk.

Patent attorney

Around 1,500 patent attorneys are registered in the UK, usually in private practice firms, large companies and government departments. Their job is to obtain, protect and enforce intellectual property rights for their owners. The website for the Chartered Institute of Patent Attorneys (CIPA), www.cipa.org.uk, has a useful careers section and job vacancy listings. In summary, it takes four or five years to become a UK Chartered Patent Attorney and/or a European Patent Attorney. All candidates must have a scientific or technical background (usually a relevant degree) and the aptitude for learning the relevant law. Attention to detail, good drafting skills and a very logical, analytical mind are crucial.

On completion of a scientific or technical degree, one route for candidates wishing to become a patent attorney is to find a post with a patent attorney firm or in industry. In the UK people take the CIPA foundation exams one year into the profession. After completing the foundation examinations they can go on to take the Advanced level examinations. Candidates are required to have either two years' full time supervision from a patent attorney or to have completed four years of full time patent agency work before they can become a registered patent attorney.

Some people choose to do an intellectual property course prior to looking for a position with a patent attorney firm or in industry. Queen Mary University of London, Manchester University, Bournemouth University and Brunel University all offer courses in intellectual property, which provide exemption to the CIPA foundation papers. Knowledge of other languages are very useful to the profession, but it is no longer a requirement for patent attorneys.

Once qualified, there is the opportunity to obtain a further qualification to become a patent attorney litigator, entitled to conduct litigation in the High Court, although all patent attorneys have the right to conduct litigation and to appear as advocate in the specialist Patents County Court. In order to become a European Patent Attorney, candidates must complete another set of examinations.

Trade mark attorney

A trade mark is a form of intellectual property used to distinguish a manufacturer or trader's particular brand from its competitors. It can be anything from a logo or a picture to a name or even a smell (apparently one Dutch perfume company uses their trade-marked 'freshly cut grass smell' to give tennis balls their distinct aroma). Trade mark attorneys provide advice on the suitability of a word or logo as a trade mark, on the action needed to safeguard a protected trade mark and on how to deal with any infringements by another party.

There are about 630 fully qualified trade mark attorneys in the UK, all registered with the Institute of Trade Mark Attorneys (ITMA). Most work for large companies or at firms of patent and trade mark attorneys. Good communication and drafting skills are required, as is a degree (in any subject). The road to qualification involves completing a law-based course, followed by a practical skills course. It is common for aspiring practioners to study while learning on the job. Candidates with certain degrees, including law, may be exempt from some foundation papers. There is no central admissions procedure, so students need to approach firms or in-house trade mark departments directly. Check out www.itma.org.uk for more information.

Compliance officer or analyst

Banks and other financial services companies recruit law and non-law grads into their compliance units, which take on the vital role of advising senior management on how to comply with the laws, regulations and rules that govern the sector. They also ensure that the banks' own corporate procedures and policies are followed. Other functions relate to the handling of complex regulatory and internal investigations and examinations. In essence, through compliance risk management, banks improve their ability to control the risks of emerging issues, thus helping to protect the organisation's reputation and safeguard its interests. Due to the proliferation of financial regulation, the importance of compliance departments has grown enormously so that in larger banks they are often equivalent in size to in-house legal teams and offer equally solid career prospects.

The role of compliance officer or analyst requires astute advice, clear guidance, reliable professional judgement and the ability to work in a team. Attention to detail and a determination to see the consistent application of compliance policies and practices are essential. Regular exposure to senior management commonly occurs much earlier for trainees in this area than for trainee solicitors at law firms. A minimum 2:1 degree is standard for successful applicants, and salaries are typically comparable with other graduate trainees in the City. With some compliance teams numbering more than 100 staff, there is plenty of scope for career development. Several banks run a two-year compliance analyst training scheme, over the course of which a trainee will gain a broad base of business knowledge and technical experience. It is not usually necessary to have completed the GDL, LPC or even a law degree before undertaking a graduate scheme, although those with a mind to move across to an in-house legal role later in their career would need to find the time to qualify as a lawyer. Being legally qualified opens up the door to general counsel work and it is not uncommon for a bank's head of legal to also lead the compliance team.

Barristers' clerk

Barristers' clerks should not be confused with any other type of clerk, as their role is very different. They help provide all the admin services a barristers' chambers needs: they liaise and organise meetings with solicitors (and the CPS); negotiate and collect fees; allocate cases and plan their duration; administer databases, timetables, finances and diaries; and market their set's members. The most brilliant barristers aren't always the best at selling themselves and so a good team of clerks can be a godsend in this respect.

The traditional image of a barristers' clerk is that of a Cockney barrow boy – think Michael Caine in a suit – with a wide tie-knot, wheeling around a trolley of legal briefs just like his father did before him. As with most professions, these days clerking is now more mixed, with plenty of women and people from other backgrounds, but there are still many burly, earthy types. Certain forward-thinking sets have retitled their clerks as 'practice managers', but it's essentially the same job under a different name.

Clerks are usually school leavers and the minimum academic requirement is four GCSEs at C or above. Some clerks also have A levels and degrees but it's personality along with legal, business or court administration experience that matter most. A senior clerk at a top chambers added: *"Clerks are traditionally school-leavers, but we sometimes take on people with a degree, who have just come out of university and are looking for something to do."* Training is mostly on-the-job, though clerks who want to move up the ladder also complete the BTEC Advanced Award in Chambers Administration.

This is a job where you start at the bottom. Salaries for the most junior clerks are between £12,000 and £14,000, rising to £30,000 to £50,000 for mid-levels. Junior clerks collect and deliver documents (hence the wheelie-trolleys), manage databases, photocopy briefs, deal with court lists and handle day-to-day admin: post, the library, stationary, phone calls. Don't get us wrong: from the off, this is a high-pressure, high-paced career, which requires excellent time-management and people skills. *"As a clerk you have to have a talent for marketing. You are a salesman selling a commodity which has a mind of its own. You need to have an open mind and to be able to see around corners."* No-one is going to hold your hand and the job can be stressful with long hours, tight deadlines and huge workloads. As you make your way up the hierarchy, a clerk's role becomes more managerial. Sets' senior clerks are their CEOs in all but name – they run the place. Senior clerks at top London sets can make as much as £500,000 per year and they're some of the best business managers in the City. *"Someone who makes clerking their profession, like I did, loves the law, but more importantly loves the 'doing business' part of the job."*

For more information, visit the website of the Institute of Barristers' Clerks (www.ibc.org.uk) as well as www.barristers-clerks.com for information on the BTEC qualification.

The road less travelled

So perhaps things haven't gone exactly according to plan, and this year's round of training contract offers has failed to recognise your potential. Or perhaps you didn't graduate in law with the objective of going into legal practice in the first place, as you just wanted the degree as a platform for taking you into other areas. Whatever the case, there are various valuable ways to bide your time until the next round and/or pursue alternative routes that will keep your hand in while beefing up your CV.

The harsh truth is that a cold winter of legal recruitment is fast closing in, especially in the (quasi-)public sector and the policy/regulatory world. That's not to say that all organisations will have frozen recruiting altogether (though many have), but the onus is on you to dig a little deeper.

The policy route was described by one source as a *"magical world,"* and once you've got your foot in the door numerous others should then open for you – as long as you're prepared to be dynamic. But how to make that first step? The feedback we have received suggests that knowing the right people who might champion your cause certainly doesn't hurt (start networking early on, folks) and that luck occasionally has its part to play. Otherwise, it will be a question of researching the various government departments and regulators that might interest you and, if needs be, contacting them directly to see what their current recruitment status is. This is no conveyor belt career path, so you do have to feel your way a little, but the rewards off the beaten track are there to be found. This kind of highly malleable experience can propel you towards your preferred original career of barrister/solicitor or take you into *"other realms,"* as they were so romantically described to us. More prosaically, this means that policy work *"is a profession, but it spans all industries."*

For ideas, try typing 'policy' into the Guardian Jobs website search engine every so often, as well as checking regularly on the websites of organisations such as the Judicial Appointments Commission and Queen's Council Appointments. The Law Society, Solicitors Regulatory Authority, Bar Council and Bar Standards Board websites are all worth looking at for vacancies, as are various industry ombudsmen (check out www.bioa.org.uk). And then there are the heavyweight regulators such as the Financial Services Authority, which runs a graduate training scheme of its own. See www.fsagraduates.com.

Gender and the law

75% of men work within private practice, compared to only 69.1% of women

52% (739) of BPTC students in 2010/11 were women

63% of new trainees in 2010/11 were women

One of the 11 Justices of the Supreme Court is female

89% of Queen's Counsel are men (2010)

50% The number of women making partner in the magic circle jumped 50% in 2012, with 24 made up

1949 Rose Heilbron and Helena Normanton were appointed as the first female silks

17% of High Court Judges are women*

46% of all solicitors are women

Four of the 39 Lords Justices of Appeal are women

All figures from the Law Society and Bar Council in 2011.
*Figures from the Judiciary in 2011.

How suitable are you and what do recruiters want?

The road to training contract or pupillage success is smoother for some than others, but a few nips and tucks to your CV and a healthy dose of self-confidence can improve anyone's prospects.

How impressive is your degree?

So you've not got a law degree. No big. From the top sets at the Bar to the little-known solicitors' firms on the high street, non-law graduates are just as able to secure training positions as their LLB peers. In the few cases where employers prefer law grads they will specify this, so unless you hear differently, conversion route applicants may proceed with confidence. Many recruiters tell us just how highly they regard staff with language skills and scientific or technical degrees, particularly where their clients' businesses will benefit. Humanities degrees require many of the same research and analytical skills needed by lawyers, and believe it or not, being able to discuss literary criticism with your clients could come in handy, since clients – just like lawyers – are people too.

It's a fact of life that many solicitors' firms and barristers' chambers subscribe to the idea of a pecking order of universities; at some the bias is undeniably evident. What is a 'good' university to have attended? This is obviously very subjective, but we've done our best to shed some light on things by tallying the university background of every trainee we interviewed this year. A vast number of institutions were represented (including less 'prestigious' places like Hertfordshire and Bradford) but it's fair to say that about 20 unis are particularly popular among legal recruiters. See our website for more details. If you worry that your university isn't one of the best regarded then you should make sure you get the best degree result possible and work on enriching your CV in other ways.

Your degree result is going to be one of the most important things on your CV. Get a First and you'll impress all and sundry (at least on paper); walk away with a 2:1 and your path to employment will be made smoother; end up with a 2:2 and you're going to have a tough time. In exceptional circumstances the effect of a poor degree result may be softened by a letter from your tutor stipulating the reason why you underachieved, but this is only going to work when the circumstances are actually exceptional. If you were a star student who suffered a serious accident or illness as finals loomed, confirmation of this (perhaps also by way of a doctor's letter) might assist.

Having spoken to a number of trainees and a couple of pupil barristers who left university with a 2:2, we would never presume to discourage anyone from applying for a training position, but these people all had other very impressive qualities and/or CV-enhancing experiences. Some only presented themselves as candidates once they already had other career experience under their belt. If you find yourself at the back of the job queue, think hard about what you can do to overcome that 2:2 – a year or more in a relevant job, a further degree, a commitment to voluntary work perhaps. Of course none of these factors are a guaranteed fix.

Possibly unaware that they could be applying for training contracts and vacation schemes in their second year, many new undergraduates are lulled into a false sense of security concerning their academic performance in the first year. If the only marks you have to show recruiters are thirds or 2:2s, you'll not get far. As obvious as it may sound, working for good results throughout your degree is crucial.

Get involved

Resist the urge to become an expert on daytime telly. Jeremy Kyle, the Loose Women and – much as it pains us to say it – Dick van Dyke in the role of Dr Mark Sloan have nothing to offer you. Instead, take advantage of your freedom and the practically unlimited opportunities on offer. Almost every university has a wide range of societies, meeting groups and sports clubs. Pursuing your interests will give an extra dimension to both your university experience and, crucially, your CV.

Some kind of legal experience, whether it's involvement with the student law magazine or shadowing your aunt's neighbour's lawyer friend, is pretty crucial since you need to convince prospective employers that you're serious about the profession. You can acquire experience later on through open days and vacation schemes, but it's never too early to start, not least because vac schemes and open days are now devilishly hard to get. Non-legal extra-curriculars can be just as useful to show that you play well with others. It also gives you something to write about when an application form asks 'Discuss a time when you worked with a group to achieve a common goal.'

Relevant work experience is vital to almost every successful job application, so search hard for suitable positions and use them to test your own ideas of what you would like to do. Many universities run law-specific career seminars in association with solicitors' firms or barristers' chambers. Be savvy, go along and find out as much as you can by talking to trainee solicitors and recruiters. Networking is a key tactic you should be employing. Our website has further advice on this subject.

Many graduates adopt a scattergun approach, applying to as many firms as possible and hoping for the best. Simply sending the same covering letter to 50 firms will not make you look good. Recruiters can tell very easily which applicants have a genuine interest in their firm and which have put in minimal effort.

It's all about the three Rs: research, research and research. Demonstrating your understanding of what the firm is about, what the work will entail and being able to explain honestly and realistically why you want to do it will be among the most important things to get across. Advice on how to do this can be found in the section of this guide that deals with **making applications** and on our website in the **How to get into** features for every firm, and our feature on **How to research firms properly**.

Be in the know

If you want to become a commercial lawyer you'll need this thing they call commercial awareness. Try and gain a sense of what's going on in the commercial world. At the broadest level, you'll be aware that the recession (yes, still ongoing) has pummelled most of the world economies and the UK's legal sector. Economies in the Eurozone keep needing bailouts and are constantly at risk of being downgraded by credit-rating agencies. Be prepared to talk reasonably knowledgeably about the main themes should you be invited for an interview. If you have zero interest in all this stuff, what on earth makes you think commercial law is a suitable career?

What other topics should you be aware of? How about gaining some understanding of the attraction of the BRIC and MENA economies; the impact of the 'Arab Spring' on the emerging Arab markets; the basic issues involved in UK public spending cuts; the greater emphasis placed on regulation in the financial services sector; and perhaps something from an industry sector to which you are drawn. To give just a few examples, there's a lot going on in relation to energy and natural resources; technology; aviation and travel; and the media. But in any business sector you care to mention there are an infinite number of factors interacting with each other and affecting the commercial

environment. Had you thought about how the health of the UK's construction sector has a direct impact on the financial well-being of archaeologists, for example?

Why not read the *Financial Times* or *The Economist* (it has great podcasts too) now and again, or make friends with the BBC website's business section? BBC Radio 4's *Today* programme also puts out a good daily business podcast. The *Student Guide* has a Facebook page with links to stories that will broaden your knowledge of the business world and major changes affecting private client law. Whichever method suits you best, keep up to date and make sure you're not oblivious to the world around you.

It's also important to understand the role of a lawyer as a service provider. Much like a plumber or an accountant, you will be providing a service to a client and your attitude should reflect this. Lawyers must be able to relate to their clients and know something about their businesses. If the firms you apply to have certain specialisms or target certain industry sectors you'll do yourself a massive favour by finding out about those sectors.

Students looking to go into criminal law should be aware of recent legislation and current issues. Future family lawyers should be able to discuss the major cases that have hit the headlines. Needless to say, anyone interested in administrative and public law issues will have a full-time job keeping up to date with all the various developments. BBC Radio 4's *Law in Action* podcasts are going to be a real help. Hopeful crime, family and human rights lawyers should also be aware of important current issues relating to legal aid. Why not go to our website to get started?

Time out

If you've itchy feet then let them wander – the career can wait. As well as giving you more confidence, navigating your way around a foreign country will develop your organisational and problem-solving skills and it will give you fertile ground for conversation. However, recruiters do appreciate that not everyone has the desire or, more importantly, the money to swan off on a gap year. If travel is the last thing on your agenda, don't stress about it or feel you're going to be marked down for being a stay-at-home. You can stand out in other ways.

Employers being allowed to discriminate against candidates on the grounds of age is officially a thing of the past. Nevertheless, some mature applicants still worry that their years will disadvantage them. Remember (if you still can), with age comes experience and probably an impressive set of transferable skills. You already know how to work, your people/client-handling skills are doubtless better developed, and you may even have relevant industry knowledge. We've chatted with successful barristers and solicitors who've done everything from secretarial work, professional football, journalism, forensic science, physiotherapy and music production to accountancy, policing and soldiering.

But when is old too old? If you're still in your 20s, don't worry your tiny baby face – you're still a kid. If you're in your 30s, ask what it is you can offer a law firm that will make your application stand out. And if you're older still? Never say never. Over the years we have run into a number of 40-something trainees, all of whom were glad to have made the career change. These much older trainees tended to have one thing in common: they brought advantageous industry experience to their firm. Given that each year after qualification a certain percentage of the UK's lawyers move firms or even drop out of the profession for good, the argument that employers expect 30 years of service from new recruits simply doesn't hold water. Of greater relevance is the adage concerning old dogs and new tricks, so if your coat is greying, consider carefully how you'd cope with being asked to revert to puppyhood.

Diversity matters

Long gone are the days of firms and chambers populated exclusively by white men smoking fat cigars. Not only has the smoking ban put paid to the Cubans but women and ethnic minorities are now firmly ensconced in the profession. In the course of our research this year more than 120 firms provided us with lists identifying their trainees. In most, the girls outnumber the boys – something we would expect to see given that more women have gone into the profession than men for well over a decade. The gender balance among new trainees is around 63.5% female (up from 58.8% ten years ago). The names on most of these lists also reflect a healthy spread of ethnic backgrounds. It is worth mentioning, however, that female and non-white trainees still have too few senior role models and there are always a small number of legal sector sex or race discrimination claims going through the employment tribunals.

From 2013 UK law firms will be forced to publish diversity information on their websites. We've jumped the gun and asked our True Picture firms to provide us with diversity data, which we've published on www.chambersstudent.co.uk.

On the subject of sexual orientation, we know scores of gay and lesbian lawyers for whom their sexuality is entirely a non-career matter. Some firms are definitely more gay-friendly than others, but happily we do not tend to hear complaints from our sources about how their employers and colleagues view their sexuality. The Lesbian and Gay Lawyers Association (LAGLA) meets monthly and welcomes student members. You can join up for free online at www.lagla.org.uk and read about other affinity groups on our website.

A number of diversity-related organisations have sprung up and you may see evidence of them at your university. Without doubt anything that encourages genuine diversity in the workplace is to be commended, but before signing on the dotted line with any intermediary – especially if you are asked to hand over any money for their services – make sure you know you are dealing with a respected organisation. Ask if they are affiliated with particular law firms and, if so, how.

The topic of diversity covers more than just gender, sexual orientation, religion and ethnicity. If you think your accent or upbringing could stand in your way then find out if there is anything these organisations can do for you. Addressing the UK's social mobility issues and the dreaded 'glass ceiling' in the legal profession is hot, both in the press and in society generally.

Likewise, if you know your university gets less attention from law firms than, say, Cambridge or Nottingham, then a diversity-related organisation may well be just what you need to get your foot in the door. In 2011, the government launched a business compact aimed at increasing social mobility. Part of this initiative encourages businesses to use name-blank and school-blank applications, wherever possible. Quite a few top firms have signed up, including four of the magic circle. You can read more at www.cabinetoffice.gov.uk/content/business-compact-case-studies. Accessprofessions.com is also a good place to go if you feel you need to be more aware of the right kind of opportunities. It filters relevant work experience and vacation placement opportunities according to the profile you create and make sure they make a timely landing in your inbox.

Despite the legal profession now being more diverse, for students with mental or physical disabilities things are not straightforward. In the experience of the Group for Solicitors with Disabilities (GSD), many applicants with disabilities have great difficulty in securing work placements and training contracts. There are sources of advice and assistance available, and the GSD has been actively involved in approaching law firms to set up designated work placement schemes for disabled students. The group also provides a forum in which students and practitioners can meet in order to share experiences and provide one another with guidance and support. The GSD's website is www.lawsociety.org.uk/productsandservices/specialinterest/disabilities.page. Would-be barristers should refer to the Disability Sub-Group of the Bar Council's Equality and Diversity Committee. You might also be interested in reading an interview with a blind magic circle trainee on our website (seek out the newsletter features at the bottom of the homepage).

Home or away?

London attracts professionals from all over the world, so you can skip this bit if you're a Brit intending to work in the capital. If you hold an EU passport or have a pre-existing right to live and work in the UK and you are following the appropriate path to qualification, you should also proceed with optimism. Applicants who tick none of these boxes may find doors are easier to push open if they apply to firms with business interests in the country or region from which they come. In all cases, excellent written and spoken English is essential, and you will need a convincing reason why you have chosen to commence your career in the UK. Get up to speed on the latest changes in immigration rules: one of the most recent concerns for firms that recruit non-EU candidates is the UK Border Agency's more restrictive approach to issuing visas. Firms have to be able to justify choosing an international student over an able candidate who already has rights to work in the UK.

Regional firms and sets are sometimes more comfortable recruiting candidates with a local connection, be this through family or education. Quite simply, they want to know that whoever they take on will be committed to a long-term career with them. The picture across the UK is a variable one: some firms clearly state their preferences for local lads and lasses; others tell us that most of their applicants do have links with the region but that they are happy to consider anyone.

Use your time wisely

What with studying hard, keeping up with business and professional news, helping out at the CAB, captaining the university rugby and netball teams, debating, acting as student law society president and attending all the careers events that crop up, you'll hardly have time for a pint. Ultimately it's all about finding a good balance. Your years at university are supposed to be fun, but don't waste valuable time that could be spent CV building.

How to make successful applications

Making training applications is an art and a science. In the current ultra-competitive market, the sooner you develop the right techniques the better.

Here's some sage advice from one City training partner on the subject of applications: "*I've seen too many copy-and-paste ones. If you can't be bothered filling in a form properly, then your chances of getting a £30k-plus job are severely limited.*" That is incontrovertible. In all our conversations with recruiters, they never fail to mention this fundamental error. Don't ever be generic in your applications; tailor them to each firm or set of chambers – recruiters can spot a mail merge from a mile away.

We know it's tempting to send off a generic application to as many firms as you can. It's quicker, but you mustn't believe the old adage that if you throw enough mud at the wall some of it will stick. In this more difficult market, we come across fewer and fewer people who have succeeded in getting a training contract this way. The people who are more likely to succeed will target a list of specific firms and take more time perfecting their applications.

Note that we are not saying that it's a bad thing to send off piles of applications. As we have repeatedly mentioned, this is a competitive business and even good candidates may have to turn out dozens, but the more care you take with each, the sooner you will get an offer.

Do your research

Choosing a firm because it's got a cool name and recruitment literature isn't the best policy; neither is random selection. Before you apply, try to work out which firms would best suit you. If you're a 'live to work' type, find an organisation that will give you what you crave. Likewise, if you just have to catch *Hollyoaks* at half six, make sure you seek out firms with shorter hours. If you want to do a certain type of law, apply to the places that specialise in the area. Carefully select your targets – they need to suit your personality and interests, otherwise you'll have a hard time persuading them to hire you, and if you do get hired you might regret it.

- Use the *Student Guide* – it's the best thing we've ever read. **The True Picture**, the **Chambers Reports**, the **Solicitors' Practice Areas** and **Practice Areas at the Bar**, the comparison charts – all are designed to help you work out which employer and area of law is right for you.

- Only marginally less brilliant, our parent publication *Chambers UK* identifies and ranks all the best firms in over 60 areas of practice. It can be read online, for free, at www.chambersandpartners.com.
- Make use of as many other sources as possible. From legal gossip websites through to *The Lawyer*, *Legal Week* and *The Law Gazette*: all can be of value.
- Check the firm's requirements. Check your qualifications and abilities. Do they match? The **Applications and selections** table on page 517 should help with this, as will our detailed online recruitment features for each firm.

Stay organised

- Know the deadlines and diarise the important ones. The calendar at the front of this book should help. Most commercial firms recruit two years in advance, but it might be even earlier.
- Application forms take far, far longer to complete than you'd expect, especially when they're done well. Submitting one two minutes late is too late.
- Some barristers' chambers use the Pupillage Portal, some don't. Make sure you know which is which. Check their websites. The **Bar** section of this guide discusses the Pupillage Portal in more detail.
- If you have to handwrite something, practise with a rough version first (or type it up and then copy it out). If your handwriting is so atrocious that the reader will need a cipher, you'll need to improve it.
- Answer the questions directly – no cutting and pasting or repetition.
- Usually you will be told how much you can write for each question. If you are well under, don't just waffle, keep thinking.
- Keep copies of everything you send out because before an interview or assessment day you will need to remind yourself of what you wrote.
- Increasingly firms are making application forms available only to those who perform well enough in online tests, sometimes verbal reasoning, sometimes numerical. There are books and websites with sample tests and helpful hints on how to perform well. Get in some practice ahead of time.

Good form

Here are a few tips on completing application forms and CVs:

- Avoid chronological gaps in your experience. If you've taken time off, put it down and be prepared to explain why.
- Ignore the fancy stuff and get to the details. Don't waste time with photos or unusual fonts.
- Bullet points and bold text can make things more eye-catching.
- Don't just say what you did at uni – mention sports teams, work experience and volunteering. Show that you've not simply gone through the motions at uni.
- A mistake on a CV can be damning. Technology is there to serve us and make things easier. You have spellcheck: use it. Ask a friend to check your CV as well, because there are some areas in which we feeble humans still come up trumps.
- Don't use glossy terms or jargon. Give concise details, expanding where appropriate – not reams and reams though. Recruiters don't want an essay. A CV should be three pages max, ideally just two.
- Don't just say things; back them up. You can't just claim to be obsessed with debt and equity capital markets; you're going to have to prove your passion with examples. Speak to lawyers whenever you can – it all helps to show that you understand the reality of practice. Likewise, make sure you demonstrate your qualities rather than just stating them.
- You can use any kind of work to prove you have commercial awareness. Even if it was in a pub you can still talk about being aware of costs, budgeting and the marketing the pub did. Think about the simple things you can extrapolate from.
- As well as commercial awareness and a love of the law, applications should demonstrate teamwork and problem-solving skills.

Don't undersell yourself

If you looked at the training contract applications of a handful of different students you'd see that some include more information about their achievements than others. Usually those with less content have omitted to include things because they simply don't appreciate their significance.

- Qualifications, gap-year experiences, 17 A*s at A level, endless vac schemes – these things are obvious essentials.
- Explain to the reader what you learned from your experiences rather than just listing them.
- Write a list of all the jobs you've ever had and consider the list as a whole. You may be able to demonstrate that you're a real grafter who's managed to help pay their way through uni. It won't always be appropriate to list all your part-time employment so you might need to group some jobs into a more general category. Unless the list is extensive, indicate the key aspects of your role in each position but make sure it doesn't appear daunting for the reader, as they plough through many forms or CVs in one sitting.
- If you studied a musical instrument to a high level then say so. It shows you can commit to something and work diligently to achieve it. The same goes for other pastimes or pursuits – eg life-guarding, scuba diving, artistic endeavours, etc.
- Sports are great application fodder. Again, the commitment factor will come through, and if it's a team sport you play then what better confirmation is there of your being a team player?
- Were you ever selected or, better still, elected to a position of responsibility? To be chosen by your peers as a student representative, for example, suggests that people admire you and have confidence in your abilities. It also shows you are naturally the sort of person who likes to take on a challenge. As to how far back in time you reach for such nuggets of gold, well, this depends on your current situation. If you are still at university, or have very recently graduated, then something from your later school days should still be suitable. If it was some time since you left uni then you need to find some more recent examples. Never forget to mention if you were a head boy or girl, the captain of a team or held a position of responsibility in a society.

Unless otherwise stated, always include a covering letter with your CV. It's a golden opportunity to show off your writing skills, explain your motives and show how suited you are to your target firm or set. A good covering letter will highlight the best aspects of your application. If you have any weaknesses (say a poorer than anticipated degree result), it's a place to mention extenuating circumstances.

And finally...

If all this advice seems totally obvious, that's because it is. You wouldn't think anyone makes elementary mistakes any more, but every year recruiters still find themselves reading CVs that look like they've been written by Baldrick. Poor layout, atrocious grammar, banal comments... all this from university graduates. Just think: by the simple act of not making any stupid errors, you're blowing a significant number of your potential competitors out of the water. Conversely, if you accidentally write *it's* when you meant *its* or *there* when you mean *their* – even just the one time – then no matter what your other qualities, in the eyes of recruiters you've just lumped yourself in with all the other Baldricks.

How to succeed at interviews and assessment days

Interviews and assessment days are to be celebrated, not dreaded. You'll send out dozens of application forms and get blanked by many firms. So when you do get an interview, give it your all.

Interviews

The biggest error that can be made while hunting for a training contract is to confuse getting an interview with getting a job. You've worked really hard so far, but it's time to ratchet things up another notch. Turn on the charm, adopt a good posture and be thorough with your homework. It's time for a classic aphorism: 'If you fail to prepare, then you prepare to fail'. As one recruiter acknowledged: "*It's a bit David Brent, but it's true.*"

Before any interview:

Read and think about your application form. Interviewers will pick up on what you wrote and question you on it. A lot of the time, they'll discuss your application form as an icebreaker. It's your chance to speak about things that interest you and to build up rapport. Chat, be expansive, maybe even flash the pearly whites. If you fibbed on your application form, make sure you've got an extensive cover story sketched out to back up your claim or else you'll be found out. Better still: don't lie or over-exaggerate in the first place.

Research the firm. A stock question is 'Why this firm?' Recruiters tell us this is where many people trip up. Make sure you've got something good, innovative and non-generic to say. Read the **True Picture** reports and find out about the firm's strengths, its history and what is being said about it in the legal press. Ideally you will find a topic or two that can be developed into a reason why you and the firm are a perfect match.

Research the people who are interviewing you, if possible. 'Know your enemy', as they say. Practice area, precedent-setting cases they've won, previous firms they've worked at, their favourite sport – all of this is gold and firm websites often contain such details. Don't quote it all back at them though... that's creepy.

Have a finger on the pulse of legal news and current affairs. *The Lawyer*, *Legal Week*, *Solicitors Journal* and *Law Gazette* are all very good, as is Thursday's Law supplement in *The Times*. And have you signed up to the *Student Guide*'s Facebook page? Be ready to see the connections between law and the real world of politics, society and business.

Practise answers, but not too much. It's not hard to guess what sort of questions you're going to get; something along the lines of 'Why do you want to be a lawyer?' is a bona fide cert. It is wise to rehearse a little to collect your thoughts, but as great comedians will tell you, you've got to be ready to deviate from the script. Speaking off the cuff makes you sound more interesting and often a classic question will be slightly altered and you need to be ready to adapt.

Historically, we Brits are modest folk and talking about cash is often deemed vulgar, but at the end of the day it is important. Don't be scared to mention that the excellent financial rewards are a factor in choosing to be a lawyer. You're among friends. Just make sure you give some other, more wholesome, reasons too.

The default setting when going into an interview is to want to be liked, but remember that the interview is a crucial opportunity for you to figure out whether you like the firm back. You can become the questioner; and should have a couple of questions prepared for the end of the interview. There are so many things you might ask and it's best to pick something that isn't already covered in the firm's own literature. You could find out what your interviewers like about the firm or ask them about when they trained. You could ask them what the firm is doing in reaction to [insert your preferred relevant current affair here]. Be confident and use this opportunity to improve the rapport with your interviewers.

The usual interview tips apply:

- Arrive early. Have a contact number ready in case some cruel act of divine vengeance makes you late.
- Dress appropriately. Make 'ordinary' your goal.
- Be polite to EVERYONE.
- A weak handshake is off-putting. Shake hands firmly (not so they lose their balance – that's too much) and make eye contact. Smile non-menacingly.

- Speak to everyone on the panel, ensuring you make eye contact with all present.
- Don't fidget or sit awkwardly. Don't allow your body to tense.
- Do mock interviews beforehand and get feedback from whoever tests you. Even family members and friends can be surprisingly good at this if you explain what sort of questions you want them to ask. They may identify an annoying verbal tic. Do what you can to eradicate any rogue erms and umms.
- Listen carefully to questions so you can establish what it is the interviewer seeks. Don't just shoehorn in pre-packaged answers.
- Finally, be yourself. The interview process is *"about showing your personality, showing yourself as you are normally,"* one graduate recruiter told us. *"There's nothing worse than seeing someone trying to be what they think we want them to be."*

Assessment days

Even though you might have an LPC distinction, a first-class degree, three As at A level, 29 GCSEs and a gold star from Mrs Haslem's nursery class, many firms still want to see you in action and test you with their own assessments. In their arsenal, firms have written and negotiation exercises, personality profiling, research tasks and group tasks. On our website we detail the different hoops you'll need to leap through at each of our profiled firms.

Recruiters are all keen to see whether you can work in a team. Advertising pitches to faux-clients and pretend mini-transactions are two common exercises, but these things are always changing and different firms have different methods. Be careful not to dominate group tasks too much or fade into the background.

There are several types of psychometric test and law firms like to throw a mixture at applicants. Some test verbal or numerical reasoning skills, others test your judgement when confronted by certain scenarios. Although the companies that produce these tests try to keep their secrets safe, the internet is a great place to read up on them. Personality tests aim to find out whether you are a leader or a follower, a planner or impulsive, etc. In theory, there are no right or wrong answers and the standard advice is to be yourself, but before you expose your soul to recruiters, it is worth thinking about why they have set this test and what they are looking for. The general format varies between selecting adjectives that best or least describe you, to choosing a response to a given scenario. Many of the questions on a recent Clifford Chance situational judgement test, for example, began *"your supervisor is extremely busy..."* Obvious attempts to throw the test may be picked up by recruiters; however, profiling yourself as an indecisive, emotional control freak isn't going to help you. Although some people swear that these

tests accurately determine an applicant's personality, others still denounce them.

Numerical and, in particular, verbal reasoning tests are the most important ones and, thankfully, these you can prepare for. Look into the methodologies of the main ones (start on Wikipedia) and ask your careers service for examples. Some firms might post out samples in advance, so take advantage: it is really important to be in the right frame of mind for these. Two common ones are the Watson Glaser and SHL tests. They're usually composed of multiple-choice, reasoning-based questions that look for intellectual rigour and some business awareness. Applicants must typically decide whether a statement is true, false, or impossible to determine given the information available. Accuracy is imperative, as is mental agility, so if your brain cells are as agile as an arthritic grandmother, get practising – they'll need to resemble an Olympic gymnast come test day.

Numerical reasoning tests assess your ability to process data contained in graphs and tables. Questions ask you to find percentage changes and calculate quantities from percentages. Some tests deliberately contain too many questions, as they're designed to assess your speed under pressure. Make sure you know if you're sitting one of these and, whatever the test, try to use your time effectively. Tests may change, of course, but try to quiz people who've taken them already – perhaps your law school classmates – and check out discussion forums on law student websites.

Don't relax too much if there's a social event as these can be just as important when it comes to making a good impression. Some firms have lunches where you sit round with three or four partners and a handful of other applicants and make small talk over the duck à l'orange. Who will your prospective supervisor want to hire? The girl who kept her eyes on the plate for the entire meal and whispered unintelligible answers to every question? The chap who drank too much of the Pinot Noir and spent most of the meal calling him 'buddy'? Or the nice young man who made some pertinent observations on the Greek debt crisis and showed an interest in his taxidermy hobby? Similarly, a drink with the firm's trainees is an opportunity to strike up a rapport with them, not to start making comments about how your vac scheme at Herbert Smith was *soooo* much better.

And finally...

The sad fact is that for many people it could take a while to succeed. Don't let rejection bring you down: treat a failed interview like the end of a relationship; convince yourself you just weren't right for each other. Ask recruiters what led to the rejection and try and learn from it. Chin up, champ: plenty of fish left in the sea. Badmouthing a firm afterwards is optional (and cathartic) but best done privately.

Managing job offers

After all the hard work involved in securing a training contract offer, you'll need to know what to do when you actually land one.

The Solicitors Regulation Authority publishes a 'voluntary code to good practice in the recruitment of trainee solicitors' at www.sra.org.uk/documents/students/training-contract/voluntarycode.pdf.

Read through these guidelines if at any stage you are in doubt as to what you should do. They address the conduct of both recruiters and students. Law firms are not obliged to follow these guidelines, though most will.

On offers, the guidelines say:

- If you're still an undergrad, a training contract offer should not be made before 1 September in your final undergraduate year. If you've impressed a firm during a vacation scheme or period of work experience, it must wait until this date before making you an offer.
- At an interview, you will be told if there is a further stage to the selection process. You should also be told within two weeks of reaching the end of the process whether or not you have been successful.
- Offers should be made in writing. If you receive an offer by phone you don't need to say yes or no: you can ask the firm to send a formal offer in writing for you to consider.

On deadlines, the guidelines say:

- No deadline should expire earlier than four weeks from the date of an offer. If you need more time to mull over an offer, firms are supposed to consider your request 'sympathetically', provided you have a good reason. No definition of 'good reason' is given in the guidelines.
- If a firm is going to pay your law school fees it should set out the terms and conditions of the arrangement in the training contract offer letter. A firm's willingness to provide financial assistance should not affect the time limit for accepting the contract.
- If you feel you need more time, you will have to enter into diplomatic discussions with the law firm, telling them how much longer you need. Ask for written confirmation of any extension to the deadline so both parties are clear what has been decided.

You may want to hang on to an offer from one firm while you pursue applications with others. This is okay, but you must bear in mind the following:

- You should not hold more than two (as yet unaccepted) offers at any one time.
- Students are supposed to respond promptly to a firm that's made an offer, either by accepting or rejecting it. The word 'promptly' is not defined in the code.
- Because offers can and will be made with time limits for acceptance, do guard against allowing a deadline to elapse. The stupidity tax you may otherwise pay doesn't bear thinking about.
- Once you have accepted your preferred offer in writing, you must then confirm to everyone else that you are withdrawing your application. This is only fair to busy recruiters and other applicants who may suffer if you clog up a shortlist.

The guidelines are silent on the issue of what happens if a student changes their mind after accepting an offer. It's a rare firm that will be particularly sympathetic to a post-acceptance withdrawal but, on occasions, these things do happen. We can give no general advice on this subject, as each individual case will have its own merits. What we can say is that the smooth running of the whole trainee recruitment market relies on most parties playing by the above 'rules'. So what if a law firm puts pressure on you to accept an offer earlier than the guidelines say they should? Again, there is no simple answer as the SRA's code of conduct is voluntary. If this situation arises you will have to enter into delicate negotiations with the law firm. You could also discuss the problem with your university or college careers adviser and ask if they can recommend a course of action.

Law School

Solicitors' Timetable

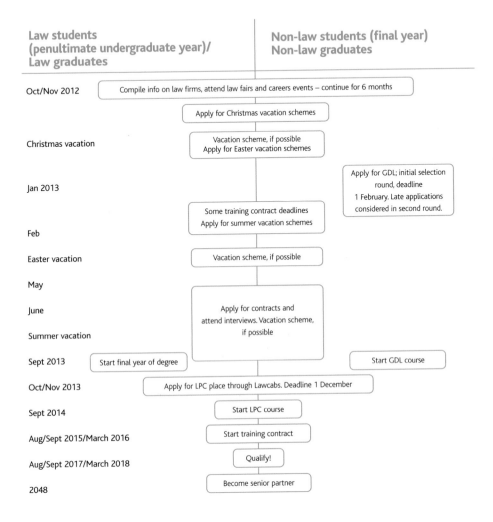

Law students (penultimate undergraduate year)/ Law graduates

Non-law students (final year) Non-law graduates

Oct/Nov 2012 — Compile info on law firms, attend law fairs and careers events – continue for 6 months

Apply for Christmas vacation schemes

Christmas vacation — Vacation scheme, if possible / Apply for Easter vacation schemes

Jan 2013 — Apply for GDL; initial selection round, deadline 1 February. Late applications considered in second round.

Feb — Some training contract deadlines / Apply for summer vacation schemes

Easter vacation — Vacation scheme, if possible

May

June — Apply for contracts and attend interviews. Vacation scheme, if possible

Summer vacation

Sept 2013 — Start final year of degree / Start GDL course

Oct/Nov 2013 — Apply for LPC place through Lawcabs. Deadline 1 December

Sept 2014 — Start LPC course

Aug/Sept 2015/March 2016 — Start training contract

Aug/Sept 2017/March 2018 — Qualify!

2048 — Become senior partner

Notes

1 It is important to check application closing dates for each firm as these will vary.

2 Some firms will only accept applications for vacation schemes from penultimate-year students, whether law or non-law. See A-Z pages for further information.

3 Some firms require very early applications from non-law graduates. See A-Z pages for further information.

4 The timetable refers primarily to those firms that recruit two years in advance. Smaller firms often recruit just one year in advance or for immediate vacancies.

5 This timetable assumes students will progress straight through from university to law school and a training contract. This is not necessarily the most appropriate or achievable course of action for all students.

Barristers' Timetable

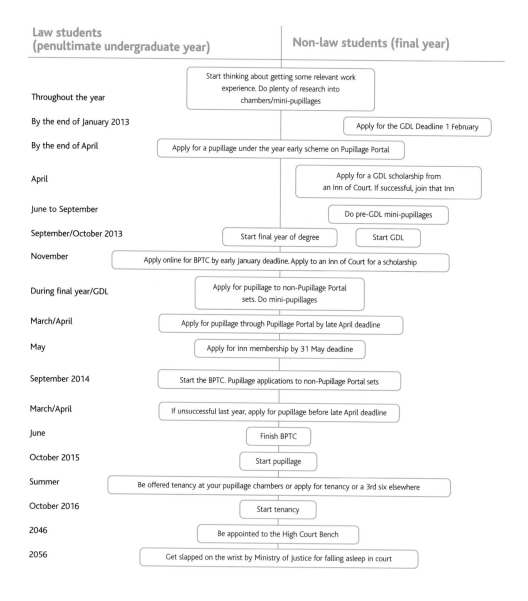

Law students (penultimate undergraduate year)	Non-law students (final year)
Throughout the year	Start thinking about getting some relevant work experience. Do plenty of research into chambers/mini-pupillages
By the end of January 2013	Apply for the GDL Deadline 1 February
By the end of April	Apply for a pupillage under the year early scheme on Pupillage Portal
April	Apply for a GDL scholarship from an Inn of Court. If successful, join that Inn
June to September	Do pre-GDL mini-pupillages
September/October 2013	Start final year of degree / Start GDL
November	Apply online for BPTC by early January deadline. Apply to an Inn of Court for a scholarship
During final year/GDL	Apply for pupillage to non-Pupillage Portal sets. Do mini-pupillages
March/April	Apply for pupillage through Pupillage Portal by late April deadline
May	Apply for Inn membership by 31 May deadline
September 2014	Start the BPTC. Pupillage applications to non-Pupillage Portal sets
March/April	If unsuccessful last year, apply for pupillage before late April deadline
June	Finish BPTC
October 2015	Start pupillage
Summer	Be offered tenancy at your pupillage chambers or apply for tenancy or a 3rd six elsewhere
October 2016	Start tenancy
2046	Be appointed to the High Court Bench
2056	Get slapped on the wrist by Ministry of Justice for falling asleep in court

Note

This timetable assumes students will progress straight through from university to law school and a pupillage. This is not necessarily the most appropriate or achievable course of action for students.

The Graduate Diploma in Law (GDL)

Whether you chose to spend your undergrad years exploring the ritual ceremonies of Amazonians, or grappling with insoluble existential questions, you can still come to the law via a one-year conversion course known as the Graduate Diploma in Law (GDL).

NB: The course is also referred to as the CPE (Common Professional Exam) or PgDL (Postgraduate Diploma in Law).

Because skills like textual analysis, research, logical argument, and written and oral presentation can be acquired in a whole range of disciplines, from English literature to zoology, legal employers tend not to make a distinction between applicants with an LLB and those who take the GDL route.

The GDL is essentially a crash law degree, designed to bring you up to the required standard in seven core legal subjects that would typically be taught in the first two years of an LLB. So that's two years of study crammed into one – not exactly a walk in the park. Taken full-time it lasts a minimum of 36 weeks and can demand up to 45 hours of lectures, tutorials and personal study each week. It is possible to take the course part-time over two years and you will find that course providers offer a surprisingly wide range of flexible study options, from distance learning to weekends or evening-only classes.

The standard requirement for admission is a degree from a university in the UK or Republic of Ireland. It is possible for non-graduates to get onto a course if they've shown the requisite drive and determination, and have exceptional ability in some other field. Such candidates – and those with a degree from an overseas university – must obtain a Certificate of Academic Standing from the Bar Standards Board or Solicitors Regulation Authority before enrolling on the GDL.

Assessments tend to be by written exams taken at the end of the academic year. These will make up the bulk of your final grade, so make sure you are adequately prepared. Most GDL providers offer their students the opportunity to take mock exams throughout the year, and while these are generally optional, it's probably a good idea to get as many as you can under your belt. If nothing else, they will give you an indication of your progress and the chance to receive feedback from tutors. Other assessments and essays completed during the year can count for up to 30% of your final grade so do not underestimate their importance, and coursework does allow for a degree of flexibility, meaning that students can write about areas that aren't necessarily explored in depth on the course, such as immigration or copyright law. Depending on the institution, there will be more or less emphasis on academic essays, written problem questions or practical preparation for classroom debates.

Because the institutions that offer the GDL vary in perceived quality, their approach and the composition of their student bodies, it is well worth doing your research before you apply. City University and Nottingham are renowned for offering more academic courses, thought to be ideally suited to students headed to the Bar. In London, BPP and the College of Law, for example, are packed with plenty of City types and place special emphasis on helping you gain practical legal skills. If you like the idea of a smaller GDL group, then Oxford Brookes could be the place for you.

Be aware that an increasing number of City firms are appointing a particular law school as their preferred provider. If you have your heart set on doing your training contract with a particular law firm, do your research and find out whether they have a preferred provider before you apply to the schools.

There's a huge amount to take in so you need to be disciplined. Try and work out a study timetable early on, and stick to it. Don't count on being able to catch up, as time will fly by. You're there to learn a set curriculum, not to think outside the box. That said, it is important that you gain an overall understanding of how the law works so avoid studying each subject in isolation. Probably the best use of your creativity is to come up with amusing ways of remembering case names. Attend classes! Particularly if you have already secured a training contract before starting the GDL, as some law schools will report on attendance, if asked by your future employer.

Contract

As a practising civil lawyer, you will apply your knowledge of contract law on a daily basis because it underpins nearly every single legal relationship. You'll start by studying the rules that determine when an agreement becomes legally binding and enforceable and which formalities are required to create a contract. You'll then move on to study what terms are permissible and find out what happens when you omit to read the small print. You'll hear about the doctrine of misrepresentation, mistake and duress, and you'll find out what your remedy is when an art dealer has neglected to tell you the Jackson Pollock you've just bought is actually the product of his son's finger painting. Armed with your knowledge of the Sale of Goods Act, you may be tempted to bring any number of small claims against the high-street retailers whose products fall apart the minute you get them home.

Tort

Broadly defined, the law of tort is concerned with remedying wrongs committed by one individual against another via the civil rather than the criminal courts. Beyond this very sensible definition hides one of the most intellectually challenging and stimulating courses on the GDL. The law of negligence is the big subject in tort and you will devote the best part of the year to getting your head around it and applying it to specific situations such as clinical negligence. The course will also cover wrongs ranging from defamation to private nuisance. This is the field which fuels the so-called compensation culture and gives 'ambulance-chasing' lawyers a bad name. While studying tort you will hear about the fate of victims of gruesome work or road traffic accidents and catastrophic events such as the Hillsborough disaster. But you will also come across downright comical stories, including snails in bottles of ginger beer or a case of compensation for scratchy underwear.

Public law

Public law, as it is generically referred to, is a course that includes the study of constitutional law, human rights and administrative law (the order may vary depending on where you study). If you have no interest in politics (shame on you), you may find the whole subject a little obscure, but ten years on since the passing of the Human Rights Act, and with several constitutional reforms in the works, now is arguably the best of times to study this fascinating subject. The course will normally kick off with an analysis of the UK's constitutional arrangements. This part is largely academic and will cover the doctrines of Parliamentary sovereignty, the Rule of Law, the Royal Prerogative and Responsible Government. Those with politics degrees should be able to hit the ground running. You're also likely to enjoy the constitutional bit of the

subject if you're a history or philosophy buff. If you do not fit the description, why not Google 'Dicey' and see where that takes you.

You'll also be taught about the Human Rights Act with particular emphasis being given to the concepts of freedom of speech, the right to privacy, the right to a fair trial and the nitty-gritty of exactly how much force the police can use when they throw you in the back of their van. After the academic bit is over, a large chunk of the rest of the course is devoted to judicial review, the process by which individuals with sufficient standing can challenge the decisions of public authorities. Those who don't enjoy the theoretical feel of constitutional law should appreciate the more practical nature of judicial review.

Crime

Whether it is through reading crime novels, watching *Law and Order* or simply perusing newspaper headlines, you are in contact with criminal activity on a daily basis and you could be forgiven for thinking that the law begins and ends at crime. Studying criminal law will allow you to discover the reality behind the storylines. The syllabus will take you through assault, battery, sexual offences, criminal damage, theft, fraud and homicide. Also covered are the liability of accomplices, attempted offences and the defences available to those accused of committing criminal acts.

Whether your interest is in policy or the gruesome things that people do to one another, the crime course should provide plenty to engage and surprise. Overall, the subject follows a logical pattern and doesn't hide many difficult philosophical concepts. You will find out early on that you always need to identify the actus reus (the guilty act) and the mens rea (the guilty mind) in order to establish an offence. Follow this structure religiously and you can't go wrong. By the end of the course you'll also be in a better position to explain why killing someone is not necessarily unlawful or why you could be guilty of theft without actually making off with somebody else's property.

Equity and trusts

This course will provide you with an introduction to the fundamental principles of equity, an intriguing area of law which calls upon the idea of conscience to remedy injustices brought about by the application of black letter law. Also on the agenda is the concept of trust, which is the legal arrangement whereby one person holds property for the benefit of another.

One preconception about the subject is that it is the preserve of those who have their heart set on Chancery work at the Bar or wish to practise in the private wealth sector. While this is partially true, equity and trusts form a par-

The GDL Providers

Aston University (ft/pt)

University of Birmingham (ft)

Birmingham City University (ft/pt)

Bournemouth University (ft/pt)

BPP Law School, Birmingham (ft/pt)

BPP Law School, Bristol (ft/pt)

BPP Law School, Cambridge (subject to validation)

BPP Law School, Leeds (ft/pt)

BPP Law School, Liverpool (subject to validation)

BPP Law School, London (ft/pt)

BPP Law School Manchester (ft/pt)

Bradford University (ft/pt)

University of Brighton (ft/pt)

Bristol Institute of Legal Practice at UWE (ft/pt)

Brunel University (ft/pt)

Cardiff University (ft/pt available from September 2013)

University of Central Lancashire (ft/pt)

The City Law School (ft)

College of Law, Birmingham (ft/pt)

College of Law, Bristol (ft/pt)

College of Law, Chester (ft/pt)

College of Law, Guildford (ft/pt)

College of Law London (ft/pt)

College of Law, Manchester (ft/pt)

College of Law, York (ft/pt)

De Montfort University (ft)

University of East Anglia (ft)

University of Hertfordshire (ft/pt)

University of Huddersfield (ft/pt)

Kaplan Law School (ft)

Keele University (ft/pt)

Kingston University (ft/pt)

Leeds Metropolitan University (ft/pt)

University of Lincoln (ft)

Liverpool John Moores University (ft/pt)

London Metropolitan University (ft/pt)

London South Bank University (ft/pt)

Manchester Metropolitan University (ft/pt)

Middlesex University (ft/pt)

National College of Legal Training (pt)

Northumbria University (ft)

Nottingham Law School (ft)

Oxford Brookes University (ft/pt)

Plymouth University (ft)

University of Sheffield (ft)

Staffordshire University (ft/pt)

University of Sussex (ft)

Swansea University (ft)

University of Westminster (ft/pt)

University of Winchester (ft/pt)

University of Wolverhampton (ft/pt)

ticularly dynamic area of law, and you'll not only learn about the creation of gifts and trusts in the family context, you'll also see that the concept has many uses in the commercial and financial worlds, particularly where tax evasion or the tracing of misappropriated funds are concerned. The topic is mostly precedent-based, meaning that you'll have to memorise a huge number of cases. On the bright side, these can be amusing and memorable. You'll hear about adulterous husbands trying to set up secret trusts for their mistresses and illegitimate children or wealthy eccentrics attempting to set up a pension for a beloved pet. Be aware that the concept of equity pervades the GDL course, so what you've learned here will also be relevant to your land law and contract modules. Past students report that there's a mathematical side to this module, and that the complex nature of some of the concepts promotes a different way of thinking.

Land law

This module will teach you everything you need to know about the ownership of land, starting with the startling realisation that all of it ultimately belongs to Her Majesty the Queen. Many students may find the subject off-putting to begin with because it uses archaic, mind-numbing jargon and calls on concepts such as overreaching, flying freeholds or overriding interests, which defy any sense of logic. Give it some time and everything will start to fall into place. You'll find the topic has practical implications for your everyday life, including tips on how to handle a dispute with your landlord or how to arrange your first mortgage. The course will also take you through the basics of conveyancing and how to acquire interests in land such as easements or covenants, before going through the detail of how those interests operate.

The subject is formalistic and particularly statute-heavy. In addition to remembering loads of cases, you will be required to memorise countless statutory provisions on the creation and registration of interests in land. Don't wait to familiarise yourself with the most important sections of the Law of Property Act: start creating flowcharts and checklists early on and you will laugh your way through the exam. As with most topics on the GDL, you will need to gain a good overall understanding of land law to be able to deal with specific matters, so don't bet on revising selected subjects for the exam. There can be important overlap between them, particularly with equity and trusts.

EU

Whether the *Daily Mail* likes it or not, EU law now affects our lives in many ways. This course should help dispel a few misconceptions about the British membership of the European Union – it touches on far more than the way in which EU bureaucrats regulate the shape and size of bananas. You'll learn that the European Court of Justice

(ECJ) is effectively the highest court of appeal for all the member states, and that EU law plays a central role in the creation of new rights against discrimination on grounds of age, disability, race, religion or sexual orientation, for example. Students become familiar with the institutional framework, foundations and underlying principles of the European Union before going on to explore certain areas of substantive EU law. Big subjects include the free movement of goods and workers, competition law and the freedom of establishment, as well as the incorporation of the European Convention on Human Rights into our national law. For Europhiles, this course will provide a fascinating mix of politics, history, economics and comparative jurisprudence, but its case law contains some of the longest and most tongue-twisting names you're likely to see.

How to apply

In addition to the seven core subjects, certain GDL providers, particularly those with a City slant, also offer optional classes designed to ease your passage into the corporate world. These may include additional lectures or seminars on company law, intellectual property and international law. Most also organise mooting competitions and pro bono work. These should give you an early opportunity to try your counselling and advocacy skills and find out if a legal career is really for you, particularly if you're headed for the Bar. A number of providers have degree-awarding powers allowing you to upgrade your qualification to an LLB, either upon successful completion of your GDL and LPC or after a summer course following the

GDL. Unlike the GDL, the LLB gives you an internationally recognised accreditation.

All GDL applications are made online through the Central Applications Board (www.lawcabs.ac.uk). Remember there's an application fee and it's worth getting your application in as early as possible if you have your heart set on a particular institution, particularly as Lawcabs need your referee to respond to them before your application is passed on to the schools you're interested in. Many law schools now offer January as well as September starts for their GDL programmes and so the application timetable has been reformed to accommodate this. Replacing the old process involving first and second round offers, law schools will now recruit GDL students on a rolling basis.

The application form for courses beginning in 2013 will be available from early October 2012 and commencing early November these applications will be sent to law schools who may then make offers to students. The later you apply the more flexible you may have to be about where you study. Applications for part-time courses should be made directly to the providers. If you intend to do an LPC or BPTC at a popular institution you might stand a better chance if you choose it for your GDL as many providers guarantee places to their GDL graduates.

The GDL is now offered at around 38 different universities and law schools across England and Wales. Our website has a table detailing course providers' fees and loads of other useful information.

The Legal Practice Course (LPC)

Before starting your glorious career as a solicitor, you'll need to jump through the unavoidable hoop that is the LPC. Just don't let all of those flexible and alluring study options distract from the underlying truth that the LPC is intense, costly, and not a guaranteed pass to a training contract.

Hanging in the balance?

"The legal profession is great at running itself down," said one of our senior law school sources this year. *"Compare the unemployment stats of LPC grads with the unemployment stats of graduates nationally. Compare them with stats for those entering the accountancy profession. The Law Society tries to deter people, and while we don't want to mislead students either, the truth is that it's not easy, but it's not all doom and gloom either."* Optimistic words, but can the *Student Guide* reach the same conclusion? In some ways, yes. According to The Law Society, the number of new training contracts registered between July 2009 and July 2010 totalled a dismal 4,874 (a 16.1% drop on the previous year, and a record decline in numbers). However, the number registered between July 2010 and July 2011 was 5,441, an 11.6% rebound. Does this signal an upward trend and a recovery of the market? Possibly, but let's not be too hasty. The ongoing difficulties of the world economy, and the double-dip recession are hardly a cause for bright-eyed enthusiasm.

Even with the 2011 rebound in the number of training contracts, there are still too many aspiring lawyers for everyone to get one. Around 7,000 students were enrolled on the LPC in 2010, and of course there's a backlog of graduates from previous years who didn't get training contracts at the first time of asking. Note that LPC providers have signalled that enrolments for September 2012 are steady or increasing (*"we actually have record numbers this year,"* one told us), so it doesn't take a rocket scientist to figure out that not everyone who completes the LPC can get a training contract. The SRA puts it as gently as possible: *"If you are planning to apply for a training contract, you need to know that the number of employers able to offer training contracts may be dictated by economic factors and can be significantly lower than the number of LPC graduates."*

The SRA claims that it has no power to cap the number of places that institutions are validated for, so effectively institutions can continue to invite people to the party, even though the dance floor is already full. Course providers have told us that increasingly *"firms* [especially smaller outfits] *are very keen to take on LPC graduates as paralegals and not offer training contracts,"* as trainees are more expensive and smaller firms are not willing to take the risk. *"For a small firm, taking on a trainee is an onerous burden and a risk because if it's the wrong decision, then you're saddled with an ineffective person for a long period of time."* In some cases, paralegalling does lead to a training contract; however the shape of the legal world is changing with increased cost pressures on firms and non-lawyers taking on more responsibility.

Law schools are very proactive when it comes to delivering careers advice to their LPC students, but it is really up to the individual to take a long hard objective look at their prospects of securing a training contract after the course. The Bar Standards Board has introduced a compulsory aptitude test for the BPTC (the vocational course all prospective barristers must pass before being called to the Bar). The aim of the test (called the BCAT) is to assess applicants' chances of securing a pupillage before spending one year and many thousands of pounds on a qualification they may never use. So, is this the way forward for the LPC? No, or not yet anyway. Kaplan Law School attempted to introduce a test for its LPC applicants but was prevented from doing so by the SRA, and most providers aren't exactly enthralled by the idea: *"An aptitude test for what? The market is so broad, and there's quite a bit of difference between someone who wants to be a back-room tax lawyer and someone who wants to be a corporate high-flyer. If you introduce an aptitude test then you can be sure as hell that people will be hot-housed for it. Where would the diversity be?"*

Third time's the charm

The LPC3 was rolled out at law schools in 2009 and 2010 with feedback suggesting that both course providers and students appreciate the increased flexibility of the course and the freedom to 'tailor' the LPC towards a specific area of legal practice. Several providers have re-engineered the compulsory subjects to reflect the interests and future destinations of their students, whether they be more corporate, commercial or high street in nature. LPC programmes are now constantly updated and rejigged, in order to keep up to date with the developments in the legal sector. For example, both the College of Law and BPP are in the process of putting together 'international LPCs', reflecting the increasingly global outlook of many City firms. Add to this the many 'knowledge modules' that have been woven into the LPC to bolster students' business acumen, as well as an ever increasing list of other options, and can see the freedom of the LPC3 in full swing.

Theoretically at least, the option is there to build your very own bespoke LPC. Pretty much anything goes so long as the LPC is completed within five years. The course can be studied full-time, part-time or remotely via online seminars. And it can last anything from seven months to two years or more. Students can even take different parts of the course at different providers. Injecting flexibility into how the course can be studied is intended to widen access to the profession by allowing people to fit the LPC around jobs, families or other commitments.

Another trend in recent years has been law school expansion. The two big course providers – BPP and CoL, who collectively dominate the market – have opened up new centres up and down the country from Bristol to Liverpool. More schools outside the major city centres are to be welcomed, as they allow students the less-expensive option of studying from home and they generally cost less than their City counterparts. However, having BPP or CoL open up in your city can be detrimental, as Anglia Ruskin found out when BPP set up camp in Cambridge: the former was forced to cancel its part-time course due to lack of student interest. Will we see much more expansion from CoL and BPP? A source at CoL said that "*we now have a centre in every region, so I'm comfortable in saying that we wouldn't want to expand any further.*" This doesn't rule out international expansion though, and CoL has its sights set on the Singapore market, while BPP is also looking at potential international opportunities through the US education company Apollo, which it became a part of in 2009.

My money on my mind

Wherever you choose to do it, the LPC is an expensive affair. Unless you've been hooked up by a generous commercial law firm that's sponsoring you, it's time to dig deep. Full-time LPC fees range from £7,150 for the cheapest course, to £13,550 at the top end. Then you must also factor in living expenses. For a comprehensive comparison of course fees look at the **LPC Providers Table** on our website.

Though law firm-funded LPC students may make their peers green with envy, it's important to remember that there's no such thing as a free lunch. With each passing year (especially during the worst of the recession) the conditions imposed upon sponsored students become more and more stringent. Law school/law firm tie-ups are in vogue at the moment. A handful of providers are signing exclusive deals with firms to have their future trainees taught together. Students follow a tailored LPC and in the process become well versed in the firm's style and precedents.

Several grants, discounts and scholarships are available and most providers offer flexible payment of fees. BPP has even introduced a law loan of up to £25k to help its students fund the course – although it's well worth checking out the interest rate on this loan before signing up for it. There are equally useful professional and career development loans available from Barclays and the Co-operative.

There are very few students for whom money isn't an issue. For those chasing elusive training contracts, with scholarships out of reach and loans out of the question, a part-time course may just be the answer. While this option does stall your legal career by another year or so it affords time to continue with a full-time job thereby avoiding the heavy debts carried by the average LPC student. Course providers tell us that part-time enrolments are up and students are migrating back home during their studies.

Law schools are a business: they sell the LPC to prospective solicitors for around £10k and welcome in as many people as they can without compromising on quality. The Law Society and the SRA caution against stumbling into the LPC without considering future job prospects but claim not to have the power to restrict the number of LPC places. A 2:2 degree will pretty much guarantee you a place on a course, but finding a firm that will want to train you afterwards is an entirely different proposition. When faced with a 2:2 candidate, firms usually expect a pretty good reason for the grade (ie valid extenuating circumstances), some outstanding features on your CV or, if you're a more 'mature' candidate, a strong first career under your belt, which show that your degree results are historic and not a true reflection of your abilities. Some law schools, like Kaplan and Nottingham, take an "*ethical approach,*" by asking for a 2:1 in most cases, while others are less prescriptive, earning them some fierce criticism from former students: "*They are taking the piss with how many people they are taking on who are not good enough to get training contracts. It's not fair.*" One such provider does assure us that students with a 2:2 receive "*specialist advice – we always say that they must be alive to the fact that they need to demonstrate something over and above. It's not impossible, but they must also be pre-*

pared to struggle more to get a vac scheme, and seriously consider paralegal work."

So before putting down the deposit it's time to get real: blind optimism won't cut it in the solicitor's world, especially if you're aiming for a top commercial outfit, where only a 2:1 will save your CV from the wastepaper bin. Do make sure you've read all the advice in the previous section of this guide and be realistic about your chances. If you worry that you're not a strong candidate then take steps to improve your market appeal.

The nuts and bolts of the LPC

It's important to remember that the LPC is not an academic course – it's vocational. Treat it like the first year of your professional life. The LPC requires good time management and organisation. *"Do be well prepared for your sessions, otherwise there's not much point in attending,"* advises one LPC survivor. Write up your notes as you go along and pay attention to the outcomes of every class (as these are likely exam questions). Some providers have open-book exams, but beware: sitting at your desk with an exam paper in front of you and a leaning tower of textbooks at your side will not help. Keep on top of things as the course progresses, and perhaps even think about sharing the revision workload with classmates.

Many students complain that the *"learn, apply, regurgitate, pass"* approach of the LPC isn't as stimulating as an undergraduate degree. It's not supposed to be stimulating; it's meant to get you ready to start a training contract. The days of theorising are gone. LLB and GDL essays transform into letters of advice, terms and conditions and points about tax. Forget about that dissertation on Hegelian dialectics or Foucault's contribution to post-structuralism – the LPC strips everyone back to basics. With classes on semicolons and spelling, it can feel like you're back at school, but you'll pick up plenty of tricks and tips along the way, including:

- How to conduct an interview (usually a strong handshake accompanied by the offer of a beverage);
- How to sign off a letter – not 'lots of love' or 'peace', as a rule;
- How to minimise tax exposure – it's about avoidance not evasion;
- How many directors it takes to make a board meeting – this isn't a bad joke;
- When litigation documents must be served on the other side – you will curse the day bank holidays were invented;
- Whether you or your landlord is responsible when the roof leaks; and
- Why it's never a good idea to dabble with clients' money.

Make the right choice

When and how: Timetables can vary wildly between providers, and while some course providers have taken advantage of the freedoms afforded by LPC3 to condense teaching into three or even two days, either mornings or afternoons, others still require attendance four days a week. Term dates and even the length of the whole course can vary substantially. Students can opt to spend anytime between seven months and five years studying for the qualification. Think realistically about what timetable structure will fit most easily into your life. Also think about whether or not you will need a job during the course. While all providers are reluctant to acknowledge that students will be able to fit in a part-time job, they have an increasing understanding of the economic realities and some timetables are more accommodating than others. If working during the course is unavoidable you may want to consider studying part-time.

The use of e-learning resources has become an increasingly popular method of delivering the LPC. CoL, for example, no longer incorporates lectures into its LPC, so instead of sitting in large theatres with 200-odd students being taught in real time by real people, you'll assimilate the lecture information via online i-tutorials. These are backed up and built upon in face-to-face, small-group workshops.

Meanwhile, the use of online learning is becoming even more pervasive at BPP, which is rolling out an entirely distance learning-based LPC, rendering physical attendance entirely unnecessary. Students at Birmingham City University can even access work from virtual law firm 'BCU Solicitors'. Lectures are still available to those that want them, as are face-to-face small-group sessions. Some students thrive on electronic learning methods, and part-time students in particular appreciate being able to fit the work around their already busy lives. However, working from home does require a degree of dedication and self-discipline, so think carefully about what mode of teaching will suit you best before you sign up. Can you actually focus in pyjamas?

Assessments: The vast majority of providers examine their students using open-book exams and written assessments. A notable minority have stuck with the closed-book approach. Think carefully about what method will suit you best. It is easy to feel drawn to the open-book approach, but the timeframes are such that you have very little time to trawl through books in the exams.

Facilities: For every provider at which students must search plaintively for a quiet study corner, there is another where they can spread out in blessed peace in their own 'office'. Take the LPC at a university and you'll belong to a proper law faculty surrounded by chilled-out undergrads and deep-thinking postgrads; elsewhere, leather sofas and acres of plate glass might make you think you've strayed into the offices of a City firm. Given the importance of IT to the LPC, you should consider whether the institution offers endless vistas of the latest flat screens or a few dusty computers in a basement.

Atmosphere and direction: A large institution may appeal to students keen to chug anonymously through the system. Conversely, the intimacy of fewer students and easily accessible tutors may tip the scales in favour of a smaller provider. Some places are known to attract very corporate types destined to be City high-flyers; others cultivate the talents of those headed for regional practice. Still others purport to attract a broad a mix of students, so the commercially minded can mingle with future high-street practitioners. These distinctions are likely to become increasingly pronounced with the variety of courses ushered in by the LPC3, so do consider which flavour you're after.

Money and location: Fees vary and so do the providers' policies on the inclusion of the cost of textbooks and Law Society membership, etc. Even if you have sponsorship, living expenses still need to be taken into account. The cost of living in London can be an especially nasty shock. Plenty of students find that tight finances restrict their choice of provider. Living with parents will save you a packet of course, but if you are striking out on your own (or you haven't lived with The Olds for some time), it's worth considering what you like or don't like about your university or GDL provider and whether you want to prolong your undergraduate experience or escape it. Be aware that certain LPC providers are dominated by graduates of local universities. When weighing up providers in large cities, find out whether the campus is in the city centre or out on a ring road.

Extra qualifications: A current trend among providers is the offer of a top-up LLM, with students using their LPC credits to count towards a Masters in legal practice. Students at CoL can top up their LPC with an LLM in either Professional Legal Practice or International Legal Practice. BPP will pilot a new MA programme ('LPC with business') with Reed Smith-sponsored students from September 2012, while Simmons & Simmons trainees will be able to work towards an MBA through the same provider. A handful of providers also have degree-awarding powers, which means you can turn your GDL and LPC into an LLB.

Social mix and social life: Student-y cities such as Nottingham and Bristol are always a lot of fun, but the bright lights of the capital may be irresistible. Experience tells us that compared to those in other cities many students in London tend to slink off the moment classes end rather than socialise into the evening.

The LPC Providers

Aberystwyth University (ft)

Anglia Ruskin University (ft)

Birmingham City University (ft/pt)

Bournemouth University (ft/pt)

BPP Law School, Birmingham (ft/pt)

BPP Law School, Bristol (ft/pt)

BPP Law School, Cambridge (ft/pt)

BPP Law School, Leeds (ft/pt)

BPP Law School, Liverpool (ft/pt)

BPP Law School, London Holborn (ft/pt)

BPP Law School, London Waterloo (ft/pt)

BPP Law School, Manchester (ft/pt)

Bristol Institute of Legal Practice at UWE (ft/pt)

Cardiff University (ft/pt)

University of Central Lancashire (ft/pt)

The City Law School (ft)

College of Law, Birmingham (ft/pt)

College of Law, Bristol (ft/pt)

College of Law, Chester (ft/pt)

College of Law, Guildford (ft/pt)

College of Law London (ft/pt)

College of Law, Manchester (ft/pt)

College of Law, York (ft/pt)

De Montfort University (ft/pt)

University of Glamorgan (ft/pt)

University of Hertfordshire (ft)

University of Huddersfield (ft/pt)

Kaplan Law School (ft)

Leeds Metropolitan University (ft/pt)

Liverpool John Moores University (ft/pt)

London Metropolitan University (ft/pt)

Manchester Metropolitan University (ft/pt)

National College of Legal Training (ft/pt)

Northumbria University (ft/pt)

Nottingham Law School (ft/pt)

Oxford Institute of Legal Practice (ft/pt)

Plymouth University (ft)

University of Sheffield (ft/pt)

Staffordshire University (ft/pt)

Swansea University (ft)

University of West London (ft/pt)

University of Westminster (ft/pt)

University of Wolverhampton (ft/pt)

Making applications

The Central Applications Board administers all applications for full-time LPCs. The application timetable has been overhauled in response to the fact that several course providers have introduced January and February start dates. LPC admissions will now be processed on a rolling basis with the application form available from early October 2012. Beginning early November 2012 applications will be sent to law schools week by week and the course providers may make offers to students immediately. Obviously the later the applicant the less secure a place, but it should be remembered that there are more validated places than enrolled students on both full-time and part-time courses. Some of the most popular institutions must be placed first on the LawCabs application form – see the **LPC Providers Table** on our website – but students can apply for up to three. Check also whether your university, GDL provider or future law firm has any agreement or relationship with a provider. Applications for part-time courses should be made directly to the individual provider.

Postscript: the future of legal education

The Legal Education and Training Review (LETR) got underway in June 2011, and is a joint project between the SRA, the Bar Standards Board and the Institute of Legal Executives and Professional Standards (IPS). It has been described as "*the big shake-up of the legal profession,*" and is a response to the "*unprecedented degree of change*" currently being experienced in the legal services sector, especially since the Legal Services Act was passed in 2007, and the Alternative Business Structures which have emerged out of it. We go into more detail on our website, but the long and the short of it all is that an in-depth analysis of alternative routes to qualification is definitely on the agenda. In December 2012, recommendations will be delivered in a final report.

At the time of writing, quite a degree of speculation surrounds the LETR and its possible outcomes. A preliminary discussion paper published in August 2012 said: "*Evidence to date... suggests that there are gaps, for some purposes, in core knowledge and commercial skills. More fundamental gaps have been highlighted as regards client relations/communication skills, ethical awareness and organisational skills. If this is correct, it is difficult to see that the* [legal education] *system as a whole is fit for purpose.*" At one end of the scale, the final review may recommend a training system that is broadly similar to what we have now, with tweaks. At the other extreme end it could suggest that we start from a blank sheet, and consider a whole range of alternatives to the training system we have now. We don't think it likely, but it's possible the LPC and/or the training contract could be scrapped altogether. Do keep your eyes on the news for updates.

LPC provider reports

Our website has a table detailing all the providers, allowing a comparison of their fees, student numbers, available option subjects and other helpful information for applicants. Use the following provider reports to make your selection. These reports were compiled after speaking to past students and course leaders.

Aberystwyth University

Number of places: 50 FT
Fees (2012/13): £10,000 with a discount for Aberystwyth and Bangor alumni.

The majority of this provider's LPC students were under-grads in Aberystwyth, which was once voted the UK's favourite university town for its sense of community and facilities. There's guaranteed accommodation at the school thereby liberating students from headache-induc-ing searches for shelter. Some at the school reckon that *"the law library has the best view in the country"* and with its location overlooking Cardigan Bay, it's hard to dis-agree. Students also have access to a well-equipped resource centre, as well as a departmental postgraduate room.

All teaching staff are former solicitors or barristers, and the school believes in face-to-face teaching (there are over 400 hours of it throughout the course). Students are taught through a combination of large and small group sessions: the large group sessions last for one hour, and mix formal lectures with interactive discussions, while the small group sessions focus on practical skills and exercises. Electives include Personal Injury & Medical Negligence and Private Client. LPC students can also add an LLM in legal practice to their name by submitting a 20,000 word dissertation after completing the course. Careers sessions are timetabled into the course, with advice on how to seek training contracts, fill in applica-tions and ace interviews. The school also has an array of local contacts, which allow students to potentially gain experience in nearby firms, local community agencies and county courts. Students can also access a database which regularly posts training contract and work experi-ence opportunities. Placements within the university itself are equally available. Furthermore, there's a Careers and Liaison Officer who will keep students informed of such opportunities directly. Many students at Aberystwyth will go on to high-street practices in Wales and elsewhere.

Anglia Ruskin University

Number of places: 80 FT (Chelmsford), 60 FTE (Cambridge)
Fees (2012/13): £8,500 with a £500 discount for own stu-dents.

Anglia Ruskin runs the LPC full-time across its centres in Cambridge and Chelmsford. The arrival of BPP in Cambridge has had quite an impact (ARU's part-time course has gone the way of the dodo) but after a pro-nounced dip in numbers, student enrolment is *"picking up again for 2012/13."* The Chelmsford branch continues to deliver the full-time LPC four days a week, while the full-time equivalent (FTE) course is taught in Cambridge over two days a week – Tuesday and Thursday – along with six hours of distance learning. The FTE was introduced in response to student feedback, and the flexibility and cer-tainty that comes with having the same days off each week enables students to pursue career development opportunities such as paralegal work with local firms. It is equally valued by students who commute into law school. Around 90% of lectures are web-based, and work-shop numbers are small, engendering an environment where *"students and staff get to know each other really well."*

The law school prides itself on its personal pastoral care. Advocacy skills can be practised in the mock courtrooms which are available in both locations. In addition to the assessed subjects, the school has worked closely with local firms to develop three 'enhanced areas' which run throughout Stage One: Career and Professional Development; Billing, File Management and Commercial Awareness; and Negotiation. These programmes help stu-dents *"position themselves as professionals."* The careers service sends out a monthly legal vacancies bulletin to LPC students and organises careers talks from local prac-titioners. Most LPC students come from East Anglia, and those who gain training tend to go on to regional firms. Students at the Cambridge branch can take advantage of a mentoring scheme with junior lawyers from the

Cambridge Law Society, while those in Chelmsford are invited to join the South Essex Junior Lawyers Division, and establish mentor relationships via that avenue. All students are encouraged to get involved in the National Interviewing Competition, which the school has won six times. Teaching rooms tend to be well equipped, and the Cambridge library recently had a refurbishment to bring it up to date. The social scene among LPC students varies between the two sites. Chelmsford tends to be more vibrant as students are on campus more often than their Cambridge counterparts; however, being in the historic city of Cambridge has its own benefits.

Birmingham City University

Number of places: 60 FT, 40 PT
Fees (2012/13): £8,635

BCU sources tell us that *"we have a small cohort here, which means that we have close relationships with our students – we teach right next door to the main office – and that makes us a bit of a community."* The law school has a fresh new look and houses a range of facilities to enhance the LPC, including a dedicated LPC room and practitioners' library and mock courtrooms. Full-time students attend class three days a week, with Thursday and Friday off to pursue other activities, and electives are timetabled over one or two days. Part-time students are in two evenings a week, Tuesdays and Thursdays. Teaching is delivered through a mixture of small and large group sessions. Skills are integrated into the core practice areas taught to students at Stage One and also through stand-alone skills sessions. On Mondays, the focus is business law and practice, property law and practice on Tuesdays and litigation on Wednesdays. Small group sessions focus on client-related issues and drafting skills, and can be filled by up to 25 students. Audio lectures (which are not meant to be a substitute for face-to-face sessions) are available online alongside other course materials and the law school makes extensive use of the university's virtual town, SHAREVILLE – this is an open resource (for now at least) and we recommend you check it out for yourself! In this virtual world LPC students are part of 'BCU Solicitors'. They access resources from the firm library and receive work from a partner who acts as their 'supervisor'. There's also info about 'life in the office' and talking heads with the office managing partner – *"it's always a work in progress."* Case studies cover the core practice areas and incorporate exercises and quizzes. There are a range of electives aimed at those with an eye for commercial and private client avenues, while advanced criminal litigation and immigration have proved popular this year. Business Transfers will not be running in the year ahead.

A number of BCU graduates stay at the university for the LPC, although they make up less than half the people on the course. BCU grads are also eligible for a loyalty bursary if they do stay and obtain a 2:1 in their degree. Fees include the SRA registration fee, and cover the cost of all books and materials. Students have mixed career aspirations and BCU aims to deliver a broad LPC so that *"students aren't disenfranchised from any potential market."* To help them in their search for a training contract the law school is *"continuing to develop and enhance students' employability through various initiatives."* These include access to the university's careers service and a mentoring scheme which pairs budding lawyers with local solicitors. A guest speaker programme provides careers advice and tips on networking, CVs and interviews. Sources were pleased to report that *"considerable pro bono opportunities"* had been sourced over the past year, and the school has compiled a directory of contacts which are happy to take on students, across a range of areas, including welfare and employment. Students are expected to report back to the school while away on pro bono placements, to *"check that they are getting worth while experiences."* The law school is still considering the possibility of re-introducing a top-up LLM, which, if it happens, will be open to LPC grads no longer at the BCU.

The law school will also be moving into the city centre come 2014: *"We're moving to Millennium Point, where there will be excellent new facilities – it'll be great for local students."*

Bournemouth University

Number of places: 85 FTE
Fees (2012/13): £11,000

LPC students are taught in Bournemouth's shiny executive business centre on its Lansdowne Campus, complete with catering, cafés and multimedia 'technopods'– hi-tech booths with space for eight or so people – for learning and seminar preparation. The school also runs a part-time course, with students attending classes on two or three days each week alongside their full-time colleagues. Students who have successfully completed the LPC can opt to undertake an LLM in legal practice.

The course is delivered via a mix of lectures and more intimate seminars. *"Remote learning might suit some students, but the message we get is that students think the smaller, interactive small group sessions are absolutely essential,"* one lecturer told us. That said, the university acknowledges the value of online learning: specific lectures, such as accounts, are posted online so students can rewind and replay. Students can choose from electives in employment, private client, commercial, family, commercial property, advanced litigation and 'the client in the community', which deals with housing, benefits, children and juvenile crime.

Bournemouth has good links with local firms and law societies, and students have plenty of chances to network with practitioners through events and guest lectures. The all-important commercial awareness is delivered to students in daily doses via news summaries of issues affecting solicitors. Students tend to either have local links or have attended a South Coast university – Bournemouth and Southampton unis are well represented. For those who go on to training contracts, the majority work in the region, often going into high-street practice. Some go to bigger provincial firms with corporate and commercial practices.

BPP Law School

Number of places: See below
Fees (2012/13): £13,550 + £126 (London)

Much has been made of the rivalry between law school giants BPP and CoL. Both insist they are focusing on their own business but where one leads the other seems to follow: with bases in many of England's major cities, a variety of LPCs including 'accelerated' and firm-specific ones, and degree-awarding powers, both seem intent on national domination of legal education. New this year – and mirroring CoL's 'Business of Law' programme – is BPP's 'The Law Firm as a Business' module. This voluntary programme equips students with a certificate of attendance and boosts their commercial awareness: "*They'll learn things about how law firms are governed, the ins and outs of billing, time recording, client care, the market place itself, et cetera...*" The module can be incorporated into the LPC, but also functions as a stand alone programme as well. What else has BPP got up its sleeve to make CoL shiver? An 'international' LPC, run in conjunction with the mightiest of global firms. If all goes to plan, this should be up and running from September 2013.

One of the more expensive providers, BPP does however offer interest-free payment plans; several scholarships for its LPC (there's a total of £300,000 in the pot across all law programmes); and a 'Law Loan' of up to £25,000 in co-operation with Investec Bank. A good idea to help students who have difficulty financing the LPC or just a way of attracting more people into debt?

BPP became a part of the Apollo Group (a US education company) in 2009, which brought all the BPP schools together. It subsequently sped ahead with its expansion plans, opening schools in Bristol and Birmingham in 2010 and more centres in Liverpool and Cambridge in 2011. This pursuit of national dominance hit a bit of a snag when plans to open in Newcastle were shelved due to lack of student interest (and strong competition from the University of Northumbria).

BPP has done well to establish itself as a front runner in the firm-specific LPC market. It has exclusive tie-ups with 24 law firms, including Herbert Smith, Hogan Lovells, Slaughter and May and Norton Rose. Accordingly, the emphasis is very much on commercial and City practice, although there are electives available in family law and private client, as well as a voluntary 'High Street Extra' module, which gives students the chance to focus on typical high-street areas such as conveyancing, partnerships and insolvency. Students now have the chance to complete a non-assessed '4th elective,' in which they can listen to eight online lectures, and also have access to all of the online materials that they will need to complete this additional option. The idea behind it, is, as sources at BPP pointed out, "*based on the fact that there are usually four seats in a training contract, and students come out of law school having only studied three electives on thier LPC. An additional elective will enhance their training contract and make sure that they are fully prepared for it.*" An international trade elective is also on the cards, and should be available from September 2013.

BPP devised a 'fast-track' seven-month LPC for several of its partner law firms (sometimes referred to as the 'city consortium') and now rolls this course out for all students studying in Leeds, London (Holborn), Birmingham and (subject to SRA validation) Manchester. The 'fast-track' option means that students will have two additional hours of face to face teaching, and three extra hours of preparation each week. The remaining full-timers continue to take the course over the usual nine months beginning either in September or, for students at BPP London (Holborn), Leeds and Manchester, in January.

Students at the larger centres – both London sites, Manchester and Leeds – can opt to either attend live lectures or watch them online along with students at BPP's smaller schools, although sources this year hinted at the possibility of launching live lectures in the smaller centres: "*We like to encourage face-to-face learning.*" Students can take classes either in the mornings or afternoons, and over four, three or even two days a week. Further echoing a commitment to flexibility, BPP has introduced 'blended learning', where students from across the UK – and perhaps beyond – can study the course entirely remotely. With a minimum number of face-to-face hours, students join real-time small group sessions led online by a BPP tutor. Those on the part-time course are also given a fair degree of flexibility, and can choose between day, evening and weekend options.

Exams always seem to be a point of contention at BPP, with some students saying that "*I think it's better than CoL because it doesn't have open-book exams,*" while others find the closed-book emphasis to be too "*intense*" and not reflective of a professional situation (in which a solicitor would most likely have access to notes).

As for pastoral care, students have personal tutors; open-door access to their module tutors; and a team of student advisors in every centre. A voluntary mentoring scheme gives students the opportunity to ask for guidance in any area they wish to develop, such as commercial awareness. BPP also offers an LLM programme, which can be taken either full-time over the summer or part-time over a longer period. A new MA (LPC with Business) programme will be available in 2013, and allows students to study the LPC alongside two business focussed modules. Students also complete a 'business intelligence project,' after polishing off their electives in Stage Two. Numerous pro bono projects run at BPP's various sites.

BPP Law School, Birmingham

Number of places: 150 FTE

BPP opened the doors to its Birmingham law school in 2010. It is located within metres of a number of major law firms and no great distance from the city's bars and shops. The building is complete with a student lounge, a TV area and WiFi – or computers if you need them – and the classrooms are all hi-tech. Students are timetabled for small group sessions and lectures can be watched online. Students who commute into the city by car receive special discounts on parking near the law school. Careers advisers are on hand and a range of pro bono activities are on offer.

BPP Law School, Bristol

Number of places: 80 FTE

The Bristol centre was established in 1991 and until 2010 was only authorised to teach professional accountancy courses. As the hub of the legal world in the South West, it made sense to open up a law school here, notwithstanding the competition from UWE and CoL in the city. LPC students access lectures online and can seek careers or course advice from personal tutors. Pro bono opportunities also abound. The law school is situated in the delightful Queen's Square and in addition to taking advantage of Bristol's social scene students can retreat to the lawns outside the law school for study or relaxation.

BPP Law School, Cambridge

Number of places: 80 FTE

The Cambridge centre opened in 2011, providing competition for Anglia Ruskin in the city. Students here are centrally located, and the facilities are all – obviously – shiny and new. Lecture rooms are air conditioned, saving students from the balmy summers often experienced in Cambridgeshire, and there's a state-of-the-art computer suite and WiFi access throughout. Students who drive are advised to use the city's park-and-ride system, while those who opt for a greener mode of transportation can store their bikes in the racks just outside the building. Oh, and apparently there's "*free tea and coffee*" for caffeine enthusiasts.

BPP Law School, Leeds

Number of places: 374 FTE

Students enjoyed the relatively small size of BPP's Leeds law school: "*Everyone gets to know one another, and there's good contact time with the tutors.*" The centre is located just five minutes from the train station, which makes it accessible to those who need to commute from a distance. Facilities include a large library, computer lab, mock courtroom and a good study area plus pool tables. We heard positive comments from former students about the quality of teaching – "*the tutors have all been in practice, and on the whole they're very helpful.*" Careers support was also highly praised, and BPP's Leeds branch runs several pro bono activities.

BPP Law School, Liverpool

Number of places: 80 FTE

BPP's Liverpool branch is also a 2011 newbie, and is conveniently located in Merchants' Court, central Liverpool. It's a bustling part of town, close to James Street station, and not far from the docks. Getting one up on the Cambridge branch, there's "*free fairtrade tea and coffee*" here, as well as a student lounge, computers with free internet access and private study rooms.

BPP Law School, London

Number of Holborn places: 1,850 FTE
Number of Waterloo places: 282 FTE

BPP has two London bases. Most LPC students study in the Holborn headquarters, although late applicants can be placed in the Waterloo branch. The facilities are impressive and easily mistakable for the headquarters of a City law firm rather than a law school. Students rather like studying in BPP's swanky environment, not least because they can see what their money is buying; for example, a rather flashy screen at the Holborn branch informs students where to find available computers in the building. While all BPP's branches are at the expensive end of the scale, the London ones trump them all. The majority of our sources were happy with their experience: "*I thought that it was put together well. They spoon-feed you everything you need to know for your exams. People complain, but I found it relaxing after my Masters!*"

The teaching is roundly praised by students, but complaints have been voiced surrounding *"things that are outside of the teachers' control, like exams. There have been instances of incorrect questions on the paper, and results coming out at the wrong times."* Students admit that the course materials are often a touch uninspiring and, on occasion, rather dry. One commented: *"BPP is generally a hoop which you jump through – it's not the most riveting thing."* To be fair the same could be said of the LPC in general. Many students studying at BPP London are aiming – or destined for – careers in the City and so the atmosphere is quite corporate. A large number are being sponsored by law firms. Few here aspire to serve the high street or toil in the world of Legal Aid. Whatever their career goals, students can get involved with a host of pro bono opportunities, including an environmental law clinic and projects enabling students with foreign language skills to provide legal translation services.

BPP Law School, Manchester

Number of places: 411 FTE

The Manchester law school draws in students from a wide radius encompassing Chester, Bangor, Keele, Liverpool, Lancaster and Salford universities as well as Manchester itself, some of which have guaranteed-place deals with BPP. Students who gain training contracts go on to work everywhere, from the high street to mid-sized firms. Accordingly, a broad selection of electives is offered, the most popular being employment, IP, advanced commercial litigation, advanced property, immigration and media. The school is located in the freshly renovated St James's Building: *"The location is great, and the everything inside is brand new."* Students were equally positive about the teaching and online resources – *"I have no complaints, the teachers were just brilliant, and you could call the tutors whenever and they'd be happy to help."* BPP Manchester has an active careers service. It stresses its links to firms and that its professional advisory panel includes senior HR staff from major local players. Socials have included quizzes, Wii-mbledon tournaments, charity cake bakes and nights out at Dukes 92 and Love Train.

Bristol Institute of Legal Practice at UWE

Number of places: 200 FT, 80 PT
Fees (2012/13): £9,900

"It's been a very exciting year" at UWE, and sources say that *"we're much more tuned in with social media – students are getting savvy and we're keeping up with them,"* meaning that tweets and other technological pilots abound at the moment. The arrival of national providers BPP and the College of Law has done nothing to dent UWE's standing in the South West, so much so that the fees have

been bumped back up by over a thousand pounds, after an initial cut when the competition first arrived a couple of years ago. Students had this to say: *"CoL and BPP have crept in on the Bristol market, but UWE has been providing the LPC in Bristol for years. People told me it was well run and it really was. It was really good. The staff are a lovely bunch of people and we were all on first-name terms. I couldn't praise it highly enough."*

BILP – and UWE's law department – are located on the university's Frenchay campus, outside the town centre but well served by special buses and with ample parking for those travelling in by car. Facilities are fresh and walls are decorated with artwork donated by local firms. Mock courtrooms and a Reuters Financial Trading room allow students to practise their skills. Full-time students are on site for two days (either two full days or one full day and two half days). They can choose when they come in, provided the timetable allows it, and Fridays are always kept free, in time for an *"all-singing and dancing"* email update, which includes general advice as well as job opportunities. The school places an emphasis on small group workshops of two-and-a-half hours. Completing the week's workshops (of which there are four) in two days is popular. Up to 16 students will be placed in four 'office groups' for the team preparatory tasks and these groups are shuffled around every so often to mimic trainee seat changes – it also *"forces them to work with people they might not like so much, so that they work differently."* Lectures are available online a couple of hours after being presented live. At the elective stage 15 options are on offer, allowing those to structure a more corporate and commercial LPC if they choose, however, options range from corporate finance and banking *"all the way down to family law and personal injury."* A charities option is no longer available, but intellectual property, employment and competition remain popular with students.

Bristol offers a multitude of pro bono opportunities and has developed robust careers support with the intention of arming LPC students with a mixed skill set to maximise their chance of obtaining a training contract. On the pro bono side, whether your interest is human rights, criminal law, legal education or housing there are opportunities to devote your time to pro bono projects, including Streetlaw, the Innocence Project, Community Legal Advice and Representation Service (CLARS) and a new project supporting victims of domestic violence. Pro bono is also taking a more business oriented turn at BILP, and student will be helping to *"set up companies and incorporate charities, rather than just doing typical litigation."* Careers advice for the budding solicitor can be sought from supervising principles, a dedicated careers tutor, or indeed any of the law school staff – all practitioners. Ex-students act as mentors and firms come in to pass on interview tips and advice on applications as well as a dose of commercial awareness. An alumni 'LinkedIn' scheme has also been introduced in 2012, and the aim is to have *"80% of our cohort on LinkedIn,"* and to develop it as a handy networking resource. In 2011 the school launched a placement scheme in association with the local law society. It pairs up LPC students with local firms including Bevan Brittan, Ashfords and Veale Wasbrough Vizards for some informal work experience. There are also opportunities at high street criminal practices and in-house at local companies. *"It's really taken off this year – there was demand and we met it. Everyone that wanted a place got one."* In keeping with the technological advances at the school, students can now pretend to be solicitors online for two weeks, and get their work overseen by practitioners in Bristol.

There is a student staff committee that organises events, and students can also participate in clubs and societies run by the wider university. The city of Bristol with all its student distractions is not far away – *"Bristol is hopping in that respect."* Many of the students are *"locally and regionally connected. It would be wrong to pretend that we have a lot of Londoners here who then go onto City firms"* (although the law school is certainly perfectly well-regarded by large commercial outfits). Instead, graduates often remain nearby and commence their careers in either high street or commercial practice. Employability is further boosted by an exclusive *"mini-law fair"* that the school hosts, in which it invites *"over 20 firms from Bristol and the region to see just our students."*

Cardiff Law School

Number of places: 220 FTE
Fees (2012/13): £10,250

Cardiff is a popular university city and is Wales' legal hub as well as its capital. A number of Cardiff Law School's LPC students are Cardiff Uni grads, with the remainder coming from all corners of the UK; usually it's about half and half. Satisfied customers raved about their *"really good hands-on practical experience. The teaching is top-notch and the lecturers were often people who had been in practice themselves."*

A good proportion of students will head to Welsh firms after completing the LPC, with destinations ranging from big commercial operations to smaller family and criminal outfits. Cardiff welcomes full-time and part-time students on to its highly-rated course, which prioritises face-to-face teaching. Students like the small classes and high levels of personal contact at the law school. The vast majority of lectures are delivered live to full-timers, but some have been pre-recorded to *"ease up the timetable"* a little bit. All lectures are uploaded online nonetheless, for part-timers and revision purposes. Teaching continues with small group sessions of around 16 people. Cardiff

attempts to concentrate teaching to mid-week so its LPC students have days free for study or part-time work. Part-time students attend one day a week, on Fridays.

Being part of a university has its advantages, and students can use all campus libraries, study areas and computers, along with the legal practice library area which has practitioners' texts, study space and computers of its own. Online resources are reportedly *"very good,"* and the school is moving more and more towards utilising virtual materials. The law school has nine electives including an optional (non-assessed) course in Welsh advocacy: *"We have a mixture of commercial and high street – we're not based in the City of London, so we can't be painted in that context, but students do go on to commercial firms."* A work placement scheme helps students without training contracts dip their toes in the legal profession and gain some valuable experience, while a host of pro bono opportunities are available. Working with major Welsh firm Hugh James, the civil pro bono unit deals with NHS continuing care cases, challenging decisions by local health boards that refuse financial support. Students can also get involved with the Innocence Project, which supports convicted criminals who maintain their innocence. To celebrate successfully completing the course, a graduation ceremony is held for students, in Cardiff City Hall or elsewhere. From September 2012, Cardiff will be offering a top-up LLM, and from 2013 plans to allow exemptions on parts of the LPC. The school has also signed up for the Law Society's Diversity and Access Scheme, which offers free tuition to the successful candidate.

City Law School, London

Number of places: 420 FTE
Fees (2012/13): £12,500

City Law School (formerly Inns of Court School of Law) aims to imbue its students with a professional ethos towards work and their colleagues from day one: *"We have high expectations, and we provide a one-on-one supportive approach which at the same time does not spoon feed students."* It deliberately recruits less than half of its validated intake and places an emphasis on face-to-face teaching and maintaining small class sizes, with sources highlighting that: *"We have a very distinct course, and we don't want to lose the ethos and personal approach that we've cultivated."* Former students mentioned that *"in class, teachers call on you directly, so you have to make sure that you've done your reading!"*

Students come from *"all over the place,"* from *"Cambridge to Westminster."* The school also receives applications from quite a few international students, *"especially from the Scandinavian countries."* Two scholarships worth £3,000 are available, as well as three financial prizes, which are awarded at the end of the year for the best students. Former City students who have previously completed the LLB or GDL also receive a fee discount.

Split between three buildings at the edge of Gray's Inn, BPTC and LPC students mix together, which bodes well for the social calendar. "*We are a pretty sociable bunch,*" said sources, "*and organise informal events, as well as participate in the many sports and social clubs.*" They can also retire to their own LPC study room for some quiet down time and studious reflection.

The school is committed to making the LPC as reflective of practice as possible, and has an advisory board of firms to keep the course current. Students are in four days a week and can opt for morning or afternoon classes, with the idea being that the entire whole cohort can be assembled at 1pm for large group sessions. Far from following the passive format of traditional lectures, these sessions involve students in research and drafting tasks via networked computers in the lecture theatre. Work produced can then be displayed for all to see. Students attend one large class (containing the entire cohort) for every two workshops (which have up to 16 students), and skills sessions are delivered to sets of six to eight people. Online quizzes and discussion boards supplement learning, and the school may well record some lectures in the future, but having them all available online is unlikely: "*Our approach is very much face-to-face, hands-on and getting the students to do a lot of the work.*" Three clusters of possible electives – litigation, commercial and hybrid – reflect the diverse interests and aspirations of City students; destinations include high street firms, commercial firms, City firms and the public sector. The school is currently in the process of developing a media law elective to add to the mix, which will available from March 2013 subject to validation.

Students can liaise with staff for CV and application advice as soon as they accept a place on the course, while a former law firm recruitment partner runs TCAS – the Training Contract Advisory Service – where students can undergo mock interviews. A new mentoring scheme is also up and running, which sees recently qualified lawyers and City alumni in various firms "*provide advice to students who want it. Work experience opportunities may well come out of that as well.*" As part of City University, students can also attend commercial awareness and practitioner lectures at CASS Business School, and also access all of the careers services that are available through the wider university.

There are plenty of pro bono opportunities, including a community employment clinic, Amnesty International, the London Innocence Project and volunteering as police station advisers (although the latter is subject to availability each year). The school enters various client interviewing and mediation competitions, and students can also top up the LPC with an LLM in Professional Legal Practice.

College of Law of England & Wales
Number of places: 4,750 FT, 2,000 PT
Fees (2012/13): £13,300 (London)

The College of Law has established itself as one of the biggest single providers of professional legal education in the UK, and, after its sale in 2012 to private equity firm Montagu has gained some substantial funding opportunities for future students: "*The buyout effectively created a £200m foundation, and we intend to put that to good use,*" said senior sources. Hopefully this means that a raft of bursaries, scholarships and grants are on the way, although we were assured that there are already 30 scholarships up for grabs. Commenting on the motivation for the buy-out, our sources said that "*being a charity was not consistent with our vision and how we wanted to develop in the future – we needed a different business model, one that would match our appetite for international expansion and future investment.*" Plans to open in Singapore are underway, and, surprise surprise, an 'international LPC' is currently being developed in partnership with CMS Cameron McKenna.

For now, CoL has a network of eight centres across the country, from London to the legal hubs of Bristol, Birmingham and Manchester and the more small-city locations of Guildford, Chester and York. Flexibility and choice are key to the College's ethos. Students can choose between the one year full-time LPC; an 18-month or two-year part-time course with day, evening or weekend study options; and a supervised two-year self study programme ('S' mode), not to mention two special LPC programmes that the College runs for its partner law firms.

At Stage One students can select to pursue a corporate route, a commercial and private route, or a legal aid route. These are complemented by a wide range of electives, from advanced criminal practice to banking and debt finance to personal injury and clinical negligence litigation (with around a dozen more up for grabs as well). Like BPP and Kaplan, CoL has been enormously successful in its bid to sign up exclusive LPC-provision deals with larger law firms. Future trainees of Allen & Overy, Clifford Chance and Linklaters, for example, take 'firm-specific' LPCs at the slick Moorgate branch in the heart of the City. Future starters are fast-tracked on to an accelerated course, which shortens the LPC to a mere seven months. The College has now extended this accelerated option to all its students, but it's worth checking the CoL website for exact details, as the option is mostly applicable to those who have opted for the corporate route (Guildford is the only centre that offers an accelerated commercial and private route) and won't be available at the Chester and Bloomsbury centres. It's also quite a tough ride: "*Five days a week, for seven months, and more workshops.*"

A further 21 partner firms such as Baker & McKenzie and Ashurst have opted for the 'LPC+', where each firm's students are mixed with others for Stage One tuition and then form discrete groups for the electives in Stage Two. All sponsored students are taught using materials tailored to their firms and using scenarios the students will confront as trainees.

Students on the 'S' mode LPC access their work online instead of attending workshops and submit two tasks per fortnight to their supervisor, who then sends back one-on-one feedback. These students also attend a four-day induction and two weekends for oral skills training, and will devote a further 12 days throughout the course to on-site assessments. The 'S' mode is available through the Bloomsbury site, but some of the skills sessions can be attended in Manchester.

Extra qualifications – and the chance to add a handful of letters after your name – are available to LPC students. Those who successfully complete the LPC have the opportunity to top up their qualification with an LLM in Professional Legal Practice or International Legal Practice, or even, for the time being at least, a JD (Juris Doctor, the standard post-grad legal qualification in the USA). This makes students eligible for the New York Bar exam, although only if they possess an LLB (which CoL has been able to award since 2006 to its GDL and LPC graduates) and only if their LPC incorporated enough face-to-face teaching to satisfy requirements for the NY Bar (i.e. not those on the accelerated course). However, CoL has recently announced that it is undertaking a review of this 'US Gateway Programme,' meaning that it won't be running from Spring 2014 onwards – anyone enrolling on the GDL from September 2012 won't be able to pursue the JD. CoL has also introduced a 'business of law' programme which is integrated into the LPC throughout Stage One; it covers professional skills such as commerciality and client relationships. The programme was developed following consultations with CoL's partner firms concerning what they expect trainees to know about how law firms actually work.

One area the College has certainly pioneered is the provision of online teaching. All lecture-format teaching is delivered via 'i-tutorials', which students stream directly from ELITE (an online resource page which carries all the course materials as well as links to online resources such as LexisNexis and Westlaw). I-tutorials contain "*extra learning resources and activities embedded in them*" to enable an interactive experience and are used in conjunction with textbook study and online multiple-choice 'Test & Feedback' exercises as compulsory prepa-

ration for small group workshops: "*The days when things were delivered in lectures are gone. Students like the flexibility and variety of them, and we instruct them how to use them best.*"

Across all of the full-time options, workshops will take up around ten hours a week and are usually spread over four days. On the standard full-time route, students can opt for concentrated timetabling, packing four workshops into two days instead of four. This is popular at the Birmingham, York and Chester centres, where a number of students travel some distance to attend. Underlying CoL's teaching philosophy is the pervasion of skills throughout the course: "*It's very much based on 'learning by doing'; the i-tutorials are created because we want the students to be working actively from the start and not spending learning-time passively taking notes.*"

There is a "*team of 20 careers advisors nationally, and they are specialists, they operate on a different level to most university careers advisors: we are at the top end, and you pay for what you get.*" Students have access to all the same information and opportunities, regardless of which centre they study at: every student is able to log into a database containing a list of up-to-date UK-wide training contract and paralegal vacancies as well as hints and tips for applications. On top of this there are careers workshops, which demonstrate "*how to research and apply for jobs,*" and there's also the Future Lawyers Network, which is an online resource available for anyone to have a gander at. For students hoping to boost their CV, CoL has ample opportunities in the form of mooting, debating and pro bono activities.

College of Law, Birmingham

The location in Birmingham's historic Jewellery Quarter means students can take full advantage of the City's vibrant social scene and many amenities in between or after classes. Students speak favourably of the "*services and teaching environment: we only had 15 people in a class, so it was nice to have that kind of interactive atmosphere.*" The Brum pro bono centre was shortlisted for a Birmingham Law Society Award in 2010, and one of CoL's partner programmes – the Birmingham Legal Advice Clinic – won a LawWorks Award 2010 for Best Partnership. Other extra-curricular activities include BERAL (the Birmingham Employment Rights Advice Line) and the Refugee Council. There is also a legal French exchange with the Ecole d'Avocats in Lyon. On the careers front, CoL has excellent links with the local Law Society and students can take advantage of a mentoring scheme with local firms as well as 'speed networking' events with trainees.

College of Law, Bristol

CoL established a base in Bristol in 2010 alongside rival BPP to compete for a share in the Bristol market, previously dominated by BILP. The city is a fashionable location for students and the business heart of the South West. CoL has made exclusive tie-ups with Bristol-based DAC Beachcroft and Osborne Clarke, and has a non-exclusive relationship with TLT Solicitors. The school is located just ten minutes from Temple Meads station and is a 20-minute walk from the student-heavy Clifton area. Students can get involved in the centre's Legal Advice Clinic and Streetlaw programme, and can benefit from a mentoring scheme with local firms.

College of Law, Chester

The cathedral city of Chester is one of CoL's more rural sites, so if you're looking for urban buzz, this isn't for you. Still, it's a fantastic place to study. Students comment that *"it's a nice, relaxing place, and it's really easy to meet and socialise with people outside of lectures. The building itself is an old building in a Georgian-esque block, with a new modern library to the side."* Many students commute into Chester from the surrounding area and therefore opt to concentrate their face-to-face teaching over two days. Timetable flexibility is highly valued among the students here but they caution *"it's still a one-year course, so it means it's quite intensive on the days you're in."* There's also the chance to get involved in plenty of extra-curricular activities, such as training as a McKenzie Friend to support victims of domestic violence or participation in a witness support scheme. The school has several sports teams and even a choir.

College of Law, Guildford

CoL Guildford is located in a *"really beautiful setting,"* say students. *"It's an old manor house with fountains and deer and rabbits, so a very relaxed setting for quite an intense course."* The location is incredibly popular with those who want to avoid London living but still have relatively easy access to the capital. It is a firm favourite for southern county locals who like the *"campus feel,"* but *"students come from all over."* CoL has numerous sports teams, including rowing and horse riding as well as many student societies. The social scene off-campus also has much to offer. The teaching is *"excellent and the tutors are always on hand to help you."* The location attracts individuals with a range of legal aspirations, both those clinging to their final year out of the fast lane and those preparing for a career in the Home Counties.

College of Law, London (Bloomsbury & Moorgate)

CoL's reputation in London means that many students come here without having really thought too much about their options, or have had the decision made for them by a law firm sponsor. Those that do weigh up their choices are often attracted to CoL's open-book exam policy. Few who end up here are greatly disappointed by their experience, whether they are stationed at the *"more studenty"* Bloomsbury branch or in the *"quite swanky and corporate"* premises in Moorgate.

The Bloomsbury branch operates out of two buildings on Store Street, just off Tottenham Court Road, and is the largest of CoL's centres. The location is popular thanks to its proximity to Covent Garden and Soho, and the cool bars and restaurants of nearby Charlotte Street. Despite the best of London night-life on the school's doorstep, students commonly stray no further than the College Arms next door, which frequently tempts them in with student discounts and other irresistible offers. CoL has an in-house cyber café, in which students can while away the hours between classes. It has to be said that the layout of this branch is far from perfect, but students do at least note that *"the building has character."* Get past niggles regarding the *"less modern"* facilities and the teaching is great, with students mostly praising their tutors. The teachers are also on call to deal with any last-minute panics, thanks to a hotline that operates in the run-up to exams. Bloomsbury students can choose any one of the commercial, private or legal aid routes, resulting in *"probably a wider mix of students, unlike Moorgate where people tend to go to magic circle and City firms."*

College of Law, Manchester

The Manchester centre is making its mark since opening its doors in September 2009. The glass-fronted school building has an extremely open and airy feel to it, but teachers are split between those who are *"inspirational,"* and those *"who weren't helpful at all."* One positive was that *"those initial teething problems that were there when it first opened have been ironed out."* However, one ongoing problem is *"the noise from the gym based on the floor above."* Students have their eyes set on a variety of legal careers, and links with the larger firms in the area, the judiciary, the Coroners Court and the Employment Tribunal all help bring them closer to practice. Pro bono opportunities range from a human rights project to employment law and personal injury advice lines, where students can apply the skills learnt on the LPC while enhancing their CV at the same time. Students can also participate in mooting. Towering above Piccadilly Gardens, the centre has a tempting Kro Bar and Krispy Kreme on its doorstep, while the lure of the trendy Northern Quarter is just a few minutes away.

College of Law, York

York is another of CoL's campus-based locations. Students speak positively of their experiences, one saying: "*I recommend it to anyone who is willing to listen to me!*" Students also like the fact that it's "*in its own little space by the racecourse, and it's a great size for the number of people that attend – there's a very collegiate atmosphere.*" York's rugby pitches and tennis courts mean there's a good range of sporting activities. A social committee organises everything from charity quiz evenings to ski trips. There's an abundance of CV-enhancing activities on offer, including shadowing advocates and advising asylum seekers, plus mooting competitions and an Environmental Law Group.

De Montfort University

Number of places: 80 FT, 80 PT
Fees (2012/13): £7,995

DMU's law school is located in a brand new £35m energy-efficient building, complete with state-of-the-art facilities ranging from a dedicated LPC library and common room to mock courtrooms and interview rooms. After a LPC revamp back in 2010, the Business Law & Practice component took more of a back seat in the compulsories than previously, and face-to-face interactions were condensed to free up time for CV-enhancing activities. Full-timers are timetabled to be on campus on Mondays and Tuesdays during both stages, with optional live lectures on a Wednesday for Stage One. These can also be viewed online. The structure changed for part-time students too: teaching is mostly restricted to the weekends to make it easier for people to maintain full-time jobs. 'Solicitor development' sessions are integrated into Stage One teaching and build on core skills required of future lawyers such as negotiation.

The school aims to have around 15 students in each tutorial. A broad choice of nine electives awaits those who take Stage Two at DMU and the list includes child law, sports and media law, and law and the elderly client. These are "*subject to addition – we're not subtracting.*" When it comes to the student body, "*on the full-time course it's mostly split between local and regional students, but the part-time course is more diverse, and we get students coming from Canada, Hong Kong and the Caribbean – from all over the world.*"

With a potential three days off for full-timers, students can take advantage of the pro bono and careers services available. Students are offered work placements in the not-for-profit sector working with charities including Shelter and Reunite – an international child abduction charity. They can also hone their research and presentation skills with the Streetlaw initiative, where students present relevant legal topics to members of the local community. The school also has links with the Citizens' Advice Bureau. DMU highlights that "*the aim is to give every student an opportunity to engage with law on a practical basis, enabling them to develop their knowledge, skills and experience to enhance their employability.*" A careers tutor organises a programme of events, including talks from in-house and private practice solicitors: "*Students will meet people from all sorts of legal backgrounds, from local recruitment consultants in Nottingham to lawyers at Irwin Mitchell.*" At social events, students can network with practitioners and trainees. Students can also take part in a mentoring scheme with local solicitors, and some have successfully gone on to secure training contracts with their mentors' organisations. Those still wishing to add further shine to their CV can top up their LPC with an LLM, consisting of a short legal research module followed by a 20,000-word dissertation. An alumni scholarship is up for grabs, knocking £500 off of the advertised fees.

University of Glamorgan

Number of places: 90 FT, 40 PT
Fees (2012/13): £7,150

Situated on the university's Treforest campus – a 20 minute train-ride north of Cardiff, the School of Law, Accounting and Finance is located in the Ty Crawshay building. This newly renovated grade II-listed building houses a wide range of facilities, including a mock courtroom where students can build their confidence and hone their advocacy skills in a realistic courtroom setting, dedicated LPC resource rooms, spacious open-plan social learning areas, meeting rooms and study areas.

Full-time students usually work four days a week between 9am to 5pm and are taught in one-hour 'briefing sessions' either with the whole cohort together or in smaller 'practice sessions' taken by classes of up to 15 people. Part-time students are taught in the same way, usually one day per week.

Emphasis is placed firmly on face-to-face interaction and Glamorgan counts among its LPC staff members a Deputy District Judge, Chairs of Asylum & Immigration tribunals as well as Chairs of Employment tribunals. Extra teaching support materials are also available through our online portal called Blackboard, one of the most widely-used virtual learning tools in the UK.

Lecturers encourage students to arrange regular individual face-to-face meetings and the same level of individual student support is applied to pastoral care. Key emphasis is also placed on employability where students can enhance their legal skills in the real world through Glamorgan's work placement scheme.

This scheme allows students to network with local law firms where they can either work on a weekly basis or for a block of time. Past students have secured longer term employment this way and others have joined a variety of commercial firms, high street practices, the CPS; private practice and government. LPC-focused commercial awareness seminars, careers workshops and talks are also organised. Studying at Glamorgan provides a realistic career-orientated experience, with courses and facilities designed in consultation with major companies, private and public sector practitioners. The Glamorgan M Law is an example of a course that has been designed and developed in this way.

This new programme of study is unique in Wales and builds on Glamorgan's reputation for innovative law teaching. Emphasis is placed on a combination of academic learning and providing students with the skills needed to work in an increasingly competitive environment. Furthermore, on completion of the M Law students will graduate with a Masters level qualification, while also achieving a Qualifying Law Degree and exemption from the LPC, therefore enabling students to progress directly to a training contract to become solicitors.

University of Hertfordshire

Number of places: 80 FT
Fees (2012/13): £9,900

After introducing the full-time LPC3 in 2010 (it had previously only run a part-time course), and relocating to a brand new £10m building on the de Havilland campus in 2011, Hertfordshire has "*had a good year: we've got at least the same number of students and the new site is much nicer with plush facilities.*" The full-time LPC blends distance and campus-based learning (around 60% distance and 40% campus based). Classes of 16 to 20 students take place on a Wednesday between 9am and 5pm (9am and 7pm for the electives), with the rest of the work and preparation done via the school's intranet. Online lectures are interactive and downloadable, with links to materials for further study via 'StudyNet.' A notebook (the electronic kind not the paper variety) is given to all students to keep and the library is open 24/7. After Stage One finishes in March, students can choose from any of the 11 electives, or opt for a 'specialism', whereby they select three subjects from either the corporate finance, commercial law, private client or dispute resolution categories. The mediation module has been "enormously popular," and students like "*the mixture of those bigger City electives with the more high street ones.*" There are no plans to extend the choice of electives, and 2012 is "*the third year that they have all been running. There's certainly no prevailing elective.*"

The new building houses a Mediation Centre, which will be the hub for training mediators in the area. The Centre is also used by LPC students opting for the mediation elective, and was used to film an episode of *Silk* in 2011 – those who are curious enough can spot it during episode five... Hertfordshire's new law school also has a state-of-the-art courtroom equipped with a public gallery (replicating a crown court) where advocacy assessments will take place. Students can get involved in various activities, from debating and mooting, to Streetlaw presentations on relevant legal topics, to groups such as the YMCA and women's refuges. A Law Clinic is also run by students under the supervision of practitioners, and clients are met there to be advised on a variety of issues including family, employment and consumer protection disputes. A public lecture series allows students to hear talks and question MPs and Law Lords. Once completed, the LPC can be used as credit towards an LLM, with extra credit being attainable via a work placement: "*it can give you a leg up in terms of finding a job or a training contract.*" Careers advice can be provided by two members of academic staff, who were formerly in the profession, or by the university wide careers and planning service.

A large proportion of the students are Hertfordshire graduates (who are eligible for a fee discount) and the university attracts quite an international crowd, from "*over forty countries.*" Social events are themed around this diverse student intake and include Chinese New Year and Diwali celebrations, as well as Greek and African nights. A Burns Night is great "*for getting international students to read some Scottish poetry.*" Pastoral care is a key concern at Hertfordshire, and each year has its own tutor, and, on a smaller scale, each seminar group has a personal tutor as well.

University of Huddersfield

Number of places: 80 FT, 35 PT
Fees (2012/13): £8,250

Huddersfield is one of a handful of institutions to offer an exempting law degree, and, sources at the school say that this "*is the route which the majority of our practice students take now, rather than the LPC. We've actually had record numbers on our professional practice courses because of this redesign.*" By combining LLB studies with the LPC, students are not required to complete the professional course separately. The university also offers a standalone LPC. Teaching takes place on Mondays and Tuesdays, with the other three weekdays free. LPCers can use the time to find work experience or a part-time job. Part-timers come in one day a week.

The school is proud of its face-to-face and open-door approach, and deliberately limits the number of places on the course to around 40 to allow for better pastoral care:

"We are small enough to know our students and that's important – they are not numbers to us: we give them a lot of feedback." Teaching is delivered through large and small group sessions. The business school is located in a brand spanking new building, with top-notch facilities. LPC students have access to an audio-visual suite, dedicated practitioner library, great computer facilities and a moot courtroom, not forgetting cafés and chill-out areas for socialising.

A dedicated careers liaison counsellor in the law school offers CV and application advice, while a mentoring scheme places students with local practitioners. Many students hail from the region and the surrounding cities of Manchester, Leeds and Sheffield. Huddersfield runs Stage Two electives, and while the main focus of the course is on high street practice, the school also asserts that it caters for those looking to train in a commercial practice. Available electives include commercial, employment, family, and insolvency. All students must complete the 'Wills and Administration of Estates' module in Stage One. There are guest lectures and work placements are on offer with local authorities in the area. In its new premises, the university is developing an enterprise centre for small businesses, and the law school is looking at opportunities to get LPC students involved in that in the future.

Kaplan Law School

Number of places: 300 FT
Fees (2012/13): £12,850

Kaplan is still a relative newcomer to this sector, but it has fast made a name for itself. Nestled in the heart of London, by Borough Market and in between the Thames and Southwark Cathedral (where the school has its glamorous graduation ceremonies), Kaplan Law School enjoys fantastic views from many of its classrooms and there's a good social scene on the doorstep. LPC students have a funded sports and social committee, and the school also organises events – one year it was a boat trip up the Thames – for students as well. Kaplan is affiliated with Nottingham Law School and therefore students have access to Nottingham's facilities and online resources.

Kaplan has been steadily growing and consequently expands its facilities every year, adding new classrooms to accommodate numbers. It remains small enough to guard a *"collegiate feel,"* according to students: *"I wouldn't have moved to a bigger provider as they are so impersonal."* Like rivals BPP and CoL, it has exclusive deals to run the LPC for future trainees of specific law firms – 15 in all, including Bird & Bird, Mills & Reeve and Holman Fenwick Willan. Far from packing students in like the Central line at rush hour, Kaplan maintains small class sizes of around 16-18 people, ensuring that students have ample face-to-face time with tutors. Students said that

"there's a lot more lectures and contact time, which is great. You had direct contact with the teachers, who all properly knew you and if you had a problem, you could go straight to a tutor." It's also much more *"nine to five, which made the transition into working life easier."*

Attendance at all classes is compulsory. Students have traditionally attended Monday to Thursday, with Fridays free to pursue other activities, but this configuration may change in the near future. Although many LPC students are destined for the commercial law firms which are paying for their sojourn at Kaplan, the school also tailors for those with alternative career ambitions, and some do go on to secure positions with high-street firms. At Stage One of the LPC, students can select between a corporate or general study route. Students used to choose between a corporate or general study route in Stage One, but given the overwhelming popularity of the more commercial path, Kaplan now offers a single route for all LPC-ers. Skills such as advocacy are then weaved around the core subjects, and activities are tinged with a distinctly commercial emphasis. Available electives include advanced commercial litigation and advanced commercial property. A new international trade, shipping and arbitration elective has been introduced in 2012, and a relatively new insurance elective has been well received.

The school also runs several pro bono projects for students to put their legal practice skills to the test. Students can assist at a Legal Advice Clinic advising on issues such as employment and housing under the supervision of qualified practitioners. A student who has demonstrated a commitment to pro bono from the start may be eligible for a scholarship. Pro bono scholarships (of which there are three) knock 30% off of tuition fees, while another eight separate awards reduce fees by 15% for recipients. An active careers service supports students without training contracts by polishing up CVs and application forms, interview coaching and organising talks by practitioners. Students are also assigned a personal tutor from whom they can seek advice from the off. Kaplan is very cautious at the outset in enrolling individuals it feels will succeed: it was blocked by the SRA when it attempted to introduce an aptitude test – something that no other provider had made a move towards. Kaplan will nonetheless consider those with a 2:2, but let it be known that most who pass through Kaplan's doors have a 2:1 or above.

University of Central Lancashire

Number of places: 80 FT, 40 PT
Fees (2012/13): £7,400

"Students are not anonymous here – they're part of the department, like an LPC family." UCLan was hit by dwindling student numbers a couple of years ago, but 2012 has been *"a good year, and we've had double the numbers we*

had a couple of years ago." UCLan was validated to offer an exempting law degree to undergraduates from September 2011, and so far there has been a low drop out rate, signalling a positive reception. LPC students study at UCLan's Preston campus. Preston is a "*nice provincial town with a lot happening, and many of the students will meet locally,*" said sources. Part-time students have a full day's study on a Wednesday from 9am to 7pm, while full-timers are at the law school three days of the week, allowing students ample time to focus on pro bono, legal work experience or other part-time work. During Stage Two there are no lectures and the timetable is reduced to two days a week. In class, the students are employees of virtual law firm Preston Harris – "*we do everything within the PH brand, as it makes it more cohesive and professional*" – and every day is different. Monday is litigation day; on Tuesday it's Wills, Probate and Administration of Trusts and Property Law & Practice; and Business Law & Practice runs on Wednesdays. Students are expected to behave as professionals and so, unlike at university, attendance at all sessions is compulsory – "*we're quite stringent on that point.*" Along with lectures, students are taught in small groups of between 12 and 16 people, though in Stage Two there are no lectures and the timetable is reduced to two days per week. A number of tutors have been former partners at firms, adding an additional layer of practical expertise to the classroom. An unusual yet increasingly relevant option for students at the elective stage is 'elderly client law and practice.' Other electives include family; immigration; commercial dispute resolution; and insolvency. A pro bono practice elective is also in the offing from September 2013.

Closed-book short questions and an open-book longer paper examine compulsory subjects, while elective assessments are all open book. There's also a drafting assessment, where students use an online package to draft a legal document. Outside of the classroom students can get involved in a pro bono law clinic, which has "*really blossomed this year – there are plenty of opportunities, from domestic violence matters to consumer complaints. They don't exclude anyone.*" Firms in the North West contact the school to advertise training contracts and paralegal vacancies. The school organises careers talks from training partners and trainees, and there is the opportunity to shadow local practitioners. The school has recently cemented links with local courts, and "*judges are quite happy for our students to go and marshal for them.*" Quite a few of the LPC students are UCLan alumni and "*the cohort tend to have a connection to the region; they have roots here or are returning home after studying at university elsewhere.*" Many head for high-street practice or commercial firms in Manchester and Leeds. UCLan grads also get a discount on fees, as well as a further reduction if they graduate with a 2:1. Part-time students get a 20% discount across the board. End-of-year barbecues are organised to celebrate the completion of an intense year, while football and netball leagues keep LPCers fit and motivated throughout the year.

Leeds Metropolitan University (LMU)

Number of places: 105 FT, 45 PT
Fees (2012/13): £9,000

Students at LMU are based in Cloth Hall Court, which is conveniently located in the city's legal district. The facilities at Leeds Met include a mock courtroom, video suites and laptops for hire, and the building is fully WiFi-enabled. Students get to grips with the course via lectures, seminars and group work. Full-timers are in campus up to four days a week, while part-timers have one day of tuition. Though there is some online preparation by way of podcasts and videos, the school places an emphasis on face-to-face teaching. Optional subjects at Stage Two of the course cater for students with a range of career aspirations, although at Stage One the focus is more on litigation than commercial law.

The school also concentrates on enhancing its students' professional persona. A 'Professional and Career Development' programme aims to help them build a portfolio of competencies to give them a competitive edge in the job market. External speakers come in to present on a number of topics, including CV advice from law firms in the city such as Eversheds, DWF and Pinsent Masons. Other recent speakers have come from the CPS, Leeds Law Society and local recruitment consultants. These talks are combined with networking events. In the past, there have been plenty of law firm-sponsored competitions for students to enter, such as mediation and mooting competitions and essay prizes and others in which winners bagged a summer placement. Students are also assigned a local solicitor as part of the school's professional mentor scheme. For another CV boost, students can use their LPC as credit towards an LLM.

Liverpool John Moores University (JMU)

Number of places: 72 FT 72 PT
Fees (2012/13): £8,585

LPC-ers at LJMU are now taught in the new £38m Redmonds Building. Litigation is the main focus in the compulsory subjects and, those on the full time course can expect to be on-site for between 12 and 15 hours per week. Some part-time students combine the LPC with a part-time training contract. The majority of lectures are now delivered online, and a large portion of the course is taught through small group sessions, with a maximum of 20 students. These are supplemented by larger group sessions, as well as self-study exercises and preparation. All exams are open book, apart from the Solicitors' Accounts component. LJMU worked closely with several Liverpool law firms to enhance aspects of the LPC. With the assistance of Hill Dickinson it devised 'client interview' videos on the basis of which students write letters of advice. DWF works with LPC students on a mediation exercise. Tutors are a mix of research active lecturers, as well as qualified and former practitioners, who maintain links with the profession.

The school has a mix of students – many are local to the North West, with contingents also coming from Ireland and the Isle of Man. The firms they go on to are just as mixed: those who obtain training or paralegal work go everywhere from big commercial firms to high-street ones. A dedicated law adviser within the Graduate Development Centre arranges careers sessions to assist with CVs, applications and mock interviews. A 'Solicitor Mentor Scheme' has around 50 lawyers on its books, and students can spend up to a week work-shadowing. There's also a 'World of Work' programme, which is endorsed by a series of FTSE 100 companies, and gives students the chance to get a certificate which confirms their know-how in the world of business. The law clinic elective will boost the CVs of those looking to improve their advisory skills. All in all, students can receive support from pastoral, careers, and personal tutors. Students can also continue their studies after the LPC to work towards an LLM.

London Metropolitan University

Number of places: 192 FTE
Fees (2012/13): £8,600

Sitting in the shadows of the iconic Gherkin, LMU students find themselves equidistant from the suits and wine bars of Liverpool Street and the gritty markets of Brick Lane. As one of the more affordable LPC providers, sources at LMU were *"cautiously optimistic – we've seen an increase in the number of students we've had enrolling here. We don't have huge budgets for marketing, so people hear about us through word of mouth, from satisfied students."* The introduction of LPC3 in 2010 marked a realignment of compulsory subject concentrations following consultation with students. Litigation now takes up 50%, with Business Law & Practice and Property Law & Practice making up the rest. LMU also took the opportunity to decrease the amount of time students need to be on campus and so full-time students can now expect to be in for two days a week – usually Tuesday and Thursday, providing *"a good opportunity to get work experience."* Part-timers are in either one day a week or two evenings. What's more, students can switch between modes if their circumstances or commitments change. Classes of no more than 16 are taught in three-hour blocks: one hour teacher-led, two hours student-led.

The small staff-to-student ratio means that teachers aren't presenting the same material over and over again, and classes are supplemented with online tests and revision lectures and materials. Students select from 11 varied electives covering everything from Housing to Intellectual Property and Mediation. The law school organises a career development week every year, where students can undertake work placements in law firms, at court or in the charitable sector. It has also started to build careers workshops into the LPC curriculum, and students can get help developing their interviewing and CV writing skills. Students can seek careers advice from dedicated professional mentors, and pro bono opportunities are available to boost CVs as well. From September 2012, LMU is hoping to introduce a 'barrister to solicitor' conversion course, which has emerged from the SRA's decision to allow exemptions on the LPC for those who have already completed the BPTC.

Manchester Metropolitan University

Number of places: 168 FT & 72 PT
Fees (2012/3): £8,800

Manchester Law School is located on Manchester Metropolitan University's main campus in the city. It provides exceptional facilities, with the additional advantage of being adjoined to the new £75m Business School and Student Hub. Set within a purpose built school at the heart of the country's second largest legal hub, students benefit from dedicated LPC facilities and the Law School being a stone's throw away from the student union. Manchester Law School has a strong profile in the legal community and students are provided with many and varied routes to access legal practitioners and begin to build their CVs.

The workshop-based course is taught to groups of 16 to 20 students, with classes spanning two to three hours and supported by online tutorials. For full-timers a two or three-day teaching week can be expected, whereas part-time students attend for face to face contact one day per week, normally Wednesdays. The school is proud that it produces its own materials, which are constantly reviewed and updated. All teaching staff are solicitor practitioners, with some still in practice and coming from all types of firms – from Linklaters and Addleshaws to high-street firms, and in-house teams. As for students, many come from the North West and Northern Ireland, and a number are Manchester Metropolitan University graduates electing to stay and take advantage of the 10% fee discount on offer. Students from across the world complete the LPC and return home to practise very successfully.

UK leavers go on to a range of employers. Students benefit from significant support to gain work experience, legal work and training contracts. This support includes e-mails detailing law firm vacancies; CV clinics; careers talks; the practitioner mentoring scheme; the guest speaker programme providing insightful and highly valuable talks from practitioners; pro bono activities, such as the personal support unit at the Manchester Civil Justice Centre & POPs, a charity that helps the partners of prisoners via an advice centre and a court family support service. A growing number of extremely beneficial work experience opportunities are also available in some of the elective/Stage 2 subjects.

The LLM in Legal Practice gives students an additional option to use their LPC studies towards achieving a Masters degree.

National College of Legal Training

Fees (2012/13): £8,500

NCLT entered the LPC market in 2009 as a partnership between Central Legal Training and the University of the West of England (UWE), with a mission of creating "*geographical and financial accessibility*" to the LPC. Originally conceived as a part-time only course run out of several universities, NCLT's sights are now set on the full-time market. The NCLT now offers the part-time weekend-only option alongside a full-time LPC. Both programmes run in Manchester, London, Coventry, Derby, Southampton and Sunderland, either from NCLT centres or at universities. NCLT's main USP is the price tag: it is one of the cheapest providers. Part-time fees are set at £3,950 p/a at every location (apart from London, where they are £4,250), while the full-time course costs £8,500 in London (£7,900 in the regions). The LPC mirrors that of UWE and students will use the same materials, as UWE is the authorised provider of the course. Full-timers are taught on Fridays and Saturdays over 36 weeks, while their part-time peers come in for one weekend each month for face-to-face lessons. Course materials and self-tests are available online to all students as well as access to UWE's electronic library. At Stage Two of the course students can choose three of 15 electives covering traditional Criminal and Employment Law to Charity and Media Law. From September 2012 a new Immigration Law elective will be available. Each student is assigned a personal tutor as soon as they have enrolled, who is available to discuss progress on the course, and a 'Career Development Unit' provides the usual array of useful information, including advice on CVs, application forms and interview skills. There is also the chance to attend events which are led by visiting practitioners, who dish out tips on what is needed to succeed in the legal world. Students who complete the course can top up their LPC with an LLM for just shy of £2,000.

Northumbria University Law School

Number of places: 150 FT, 100 PT
Fees (2012/13): £9,000

Northumbria University has run a pioneering programme of work-based learning on its LPC for the last few years in the form of its Student Law Office (SLO): "*It's the real deal work – not fake stuff.*" This makes up part of the elective stage of the LPC and is an ever-popular choice among students, who hand in a portfolio of real work experiences – on which they are assessed – at the end of the course. "*You get real mini-office experience,*" say students, "*taking client queries, covering the basics of a case and doing file management.*" Students advising SLO clients find themselves drafting court documents, briefing barristers and generally experiencing all aspects of a case.

Full-time LPC students initially choose between a commercial or general route LPC at Stage One: "*I thought that was fantastic,*" say ex-students, "*as it allows you to focus more on what you want to do long-term.*" Students can opt for teaching over two or four days a week with one lecture, one workshops and one small group session per subject. The school places an emphasis on face-to-face teaching, with workshop and small groups accommodating around 18 students. Students enthused about the teaching, saying: "*Tutors are in part-time practice so they're all on the ball – we got the best quality teaching, and they could give us tips of the trade. They were really supportive as well.*" If students aren't able to turn up for lectures then they are "*uploaded onto the e-learning portal, and also in an iPad-friendly format.*" There's a good selection of 15 general practice and commercial electives, with guest lecturers from local firms holding sessions on a regular basis. "*We do well with 15 options – we don't think that they need any more!*"

Those who don't want to use up an elective on the SLO – "*it's harder and more demanding*" – can get involved in Streetlaw, and occasionally help when organisations come to the campus looking for legal advice. The school runs a top-up LLM for successful LPC students, and the school has careers advice on offer from both a dedicated LPC adviser (who is also a member of the law school faculty) and the university's careers team. It offers students a guaranteed legal placement or professional mentor at law firms in the region, in-house or with local authorities – "*students have really appreciated that and the placement firms have given us some good feedback about our students.*" To increase the chances of students turning these opportunities into real jobs, Northumbria organises an optional 'law as a business' module that runs alongside the electives in Stage Two. It covers issues such as 'the current and future legal landscape', 'profitability and financial management of law firms' and 'looking after clients'.

Northumbria has long been known as a good place to take an exempting degree that incorporates LPC teaching into a five-year undergraduate law course. This gives a very practical emphasis to the study of law, including a compulsory stint in the SLO, and those trainees who've spoken to us about the course have rated it highly. An active social life awaits students here, be it through sport, mooting or pub crawls. An iPad also awaits – it's thrown in with the cost of tuition: "*Some firms are giving fee earners iPads, so we're running a project where we look into using the iPad in teaching sessions.*" What's more, students can knock £1,000 off the price of their tuition, if they apply for a Dean's Award and are successful. "*What we do find,*" said our sources, "*is that we have students continually picking up training contracts throughout the year, but students have to be flexible, and look beyond the region.*"

Nottingham Law School

Number of places: 650 FT, 100 PT
Fees (2012/13): £10,100

Nottingham takes "*an ethical approach*" when it comes to entry requirements: "*It's our USP – we don't want to take on people who won't get a job at the end of it.*" This means that most LPC students will have a 2:1 at degree level, and the odd few that have a 2:2 will have had to have demonstrated "*that they have something more to offer.*" Nottingham grads get a £1,000 progression discount, and new for the 2012/13 academic year are five scholarships worth £2,000 each.

A redevelopment of the law school back in 2011 gave students a new mock courtroom, moot room and high-spec teaching rooms. Additions are always being made at Nottingham, and during the summer of 2012 WiFi access is being set up throughout the school, and student community areas are being tweaked and bolstered.

Underpinning the whole philosophy of Nottingham Law School is flexibility, innovation and dynamism, and this is reflected in the structure of its LPC. In Stage One, students choose either the corporate or general course. For those sure of a corporate career, most often than not with a magic circle firm, the course includes a section on regulatory crime, introduced in 2010, while the general LPC is better suited to those students aiming for the high street, smaller firms, and even the more "*general commercial practices.*" This route seems to be more popular among students as it doesn't narrow down their career options. Another tier of tailoring is introduced via the skills pathways: commercial; public legal services; and a third 'hybrid' option. Core skills exercises on the LPC such as drafting, interviewing and research are thereafter taught within the particular context that the student has chosen. Teaching is delivered in a cocktail of large and small group sessions, and the new 'blended' learning approach, which mixes face-to-face teaching, online group work, video simulations and independent online learning. The online provision has been expanded for the elective stage, where students can take their pick from any of the nine subjects available. From September 2013, two new skills-based electives will be available.

Full-timers tend to be off on a Friday, while part-timers have a large session on Fridays, and small group sessions at the weekend. From 2012/13, full-timers at Stage One, will be able to choose between morning and afternoon teaching, to make it easier to get work experience, or simply to just "*earn and learn*" more effectively. All lecture are live, but also recorded and uploaded online.

Past students have been "*extremely satisfied*" at Nottingham, and claim that "*the vast majority of teachers were ex-City solicitors and the standard of teaching was very high: they'd evidently had valuable and interesting careers. They didn't just take you through the prescribed, black-letter process, but constantly referred to examples.*" The different course concentrations and pathways help students tailor their CVs towards the firms they apply to and, indeed, the school places a huge emphasis on employment. Students go on to a range of firms – from City, American, regional and commercial players to local authorities, the CPS and central government. There are three dedicated careers advisers in the law school and each student is assigned one to help with applications, CVs and interviews (forming a service which is still available a year after students graduate). Events and seminars are organised with practitioners, and there is also a mentoring scheme in place with local law firms, which has expanded over the past year. In 2011 Nottingham commenced a professional practice series of lectures focusing on how law firms operate and to be delivered by practitioners who then network with the students. "*It's been absolutely brilliant – we've had some high calibre speakers, and some students have gone on to get vac schemes out of it as a result.*"

"*Pro bono is the bridge to practice,*" and students can get heavily involved in pro bono. A suite opened in 2010, and the school has an employment tribunal representation unit running in connection with the Free Representation Unit (the first unit to run outside London). There's also an Innocence Project, the opportunity to train at the CAB over the summer, and a mooting team that won the 2010 International Commercial Mediation Competition in Paris. Having completed the LPC, students can again put pen to paper and by submitting a dissertation achieve an LLM. According to the school's stats, 88% of those who completed the full time course in 2010/11 were in legal employment. "*It's all about skills, skills, skills here,*" said our source; "*it's what we're constantly told by our employer board, and we place much emphasis on it.*"

Oxford Institute of Legal Practice

Number of places: 150 FT, 30 PT
Fees (2012/13): £10,250

Former students say that despite having "*less choice elective-wise,*" an LPC at OXILP is "*great – it's a very organised course, the teachers are excellent and they really take their time with you. Plus the intake is small and even the head of the LPC will help you if you need it!*" Located in the dramatic 19th-century Headington Hill Hall (once the residence of media tycoon Robert Maxwell), OXILP is part of Oxford Brookes University. In 2010 its LPC underwent some significant changes. OXILP introduced a part-time course, entered into tie-ups with firms including Manches and Clarke Willmott, and condensed the elective term to allow for greater focus on compulsory subjects. At Stage One, Business Law & Practice was pared down so now all the compulsories have the same weighting, while Wills & Administration of Estates and Taxation were also added to the mix. The move was prompted by feedback from the profession that there is a lacuna in many LPC graduates' knowledge of these subjects. Conscious of the need for students to complete the course with a large dose of commercial awareness if they are to find training contracts, OXILP runs a programme of lectures from the course director and talks from practitioners about marketing and finance in a law firm, and an online business game. The course has, however, been designed to suit both commercial and non-commercial aspirations, and the electives, from commercial law to private client, reflect this.

Full-time teaching can be spread over two to four days. Those who opt for the three to four day a week programme benefit from live lectures, while those who would rather condense teaching down to two days can listen to podcast lectures (which can also be used for revision purposes). Part-timers have two options: to attend 11 weekends per year – either from a Friday to Sunday, or Saturday to Monday – or during the week with the full-timers. The school concentrates on face-to-face teaching, and staff only teach what they've practised. The majority of classes are for groups of 16, and lectures are recorded and put online. Several firms sponsor the electives, with prizes for the best students in each. Students have access to Oxford's old Crown Court for mock trials. Dedicated careers tutors can offer assistance with applications and interviews, and students can make use of the careers service and sports facilities of both Oxford Brookes University and Oxford University. Students have access to an LPC skills suite, common room and study area. For those who feel that their CV is on the light side, a top-up LLM in Legal Practice was introduced in 2010 for an extra fee, and students can also join the OXILP pro bono scheme.

University of Plymouth

Number of places: 80 FT
Fees (2012/13): £8,670

Plymouth University inherited its LPC from the University of Exeter in 2006, when the latter decided to focus on academic courses. The law school has strong links with firms in the South West, and the course remains contemporaneous via "*a small body of practitioners who come in and work with us. There's a mixture of full time academics and practitioners.*" Plymouth runs a full-time LPC and students have working weeks of either two or three days, between 10am and 4pm. "*We have a very structured system,*" which allows students to factor in work experience and other commitments in advance (around 50% of the cohort travel in from surrounding locations). Students mostly attend small group sessions supplemented by podcasts, but lectures are still given for the more technical parts of the LPC, such as accounts. Various additional materials can be accessed remotely using the school's intranet service. Past students recommend the school's materials: "*When I came here I had more practical experience – lots of big law schools churn out the same materials, but smaller providers like Plymouth offer a more tailored selection.*"

"*The focus is on the small*" at Plymouth, and the face-to-face time that students do have is shared among groups of around ten. Eight electives mainly focus on legal issues encountered in regional practice and include private client, private acquisitions and insurance law. Pro bono opportunities are readily available, including work with the South West Employment Rights Centre; the Innocence Project; and the Plymouth City Council.

The school keeps track on its alumni, many of whom practise in regional firms, predominantly in the South West. Former students who have gone on to do well pop in to hand out advice, and visiting lecturers also drop by. All students are afforded the opportunity of a one-week work placement organised by Plymouth with a firm in the region. Such work experience certainly benefits students. In the past around half of them have left Plymouth with a training contract. Fostering relationships with members of the local Junior Lawyers Division has been "*cyclical*" with some years yielding more fruitful connections than others. There are also six LPC tutors dedicated to pastoral support, including advising on CVs and applications. Students can apply for the Saltram scholarship, which knocks £2,000 off the LPC, and former Plymouth and Exeter students are eligible for a 10% discount on fees.

University of Sheffield

Number of places: 180 FT, 35 PT
Fees (2012/13): £9,600

"We're one of the few Russell Group unis to offer the LPC, which gives us some weight," said senior sources at Sheff. Given that the school is based in a research university, there's a *"strong academic side to the law school, but we also recognise the importance of professional legal education."* The LPC at Sheffield takes the form of a part-time course which runs on a Friday and a full-time programme where students have the choice – in semester one – of classes either in the morning (10am until 1pm) or the afternoon (1.30pm until 4.30pm), usually from Monday to Thursday. *"Some LPC providers will ask students to come in for only two days a week, but we think that is too intensive, so we space it out across the week."* The ten electives on offer at Stage Two vary from the general to the commercial, and timetabling may be less accommodating at this point, but the short term means that there are only seven teaching weeks. It is also possible to opt to study the core modules from a commercial or high street point of view, if students want to take their LPC in one direction instead of the other. The majority of teaching is delivered via workshops, each taking in around 18 students, and is supplemented by online lectures, called 'screencasts,' as well as various other online programs, such as 'drag and drop' exercises, multiple-choice questions and short-answer quizzes. Though most lectures have shifted to on-screen streaming, there are still some for students to attend, but these are *"few and far between."* For those who prefer to remain on campus to get their information, a dedicated LPC resource room is *"stuffed with practitioner texts."*

The school has a dedicated careers adviser who offers one-on-one help with CVs and applications. Students can undergo a mock interview with a local solicitor, which is filmed and later picked apart by the student and the careers adviser. Students can add weight to their CVs through pro bono work for the Innocence Project and also through a legal advice clinic – the FreeLaw project – on campus, which provides free legal advice to members of the university and the general public (all advice is overseen by a qualified solicitor). Dedicated students who achieve a commendation or distinction on the LPC can top up to an MA in Legal Practice, which will add a further six months onto the course, but can help students to *"market themselves."* The law school prides itself as being small and friendly, and it takes many of its students from the university's various undergrad courses as Sheffield alumni benefit from a 10% reduction of course fees. Others are drawn from south Yorkshire or north Derbyshire, while some come to Sheffield *"just because they like the sound of us."* Many students do stay in Sheffield, but there's "no set profile, and just as many go further afield, and a lot will go onto large firms." Students say: *"Sheffield is a lot less corporate* [than some other law schools]. *It has a bit more of a friendly feel to it and it's very social."* A postgraduate room helps to cultivate this atmosphere, and given that *"the LPC students form the largest number in the postgrad cohort, they tend to dominate it."*

Staffordshire University

Number of places: 150 FTE
Fees (2012/13): £9,200

Budding solicitors are spoilt for choice at Staffordshire University, which runs a range of LPCs to fit around almost any schedule. Students can opt for full-time study over two intensive days, four short days, or one day and two evenings a week; or a part-time course that runs over one day or two evenings. The law school is reviewing the 'blended learning' mode of study which will be available from September 2013, subject to final validation. This increased flexibility is bound to make the university even more popular with students who need to live at home and study locally for financial reasons or those holding down jobs. Additionally, following the completion of the LPC, students can supersize their qualification to an LLM in Legal Practice with a bit more time, work and cash.

There's a decent mix of eight electives ranging from Corporate and Commercial Practice to Public Child Law, Advanced Criminal and Civil Litigation and Private Client. Staffs has great facilities as well, including mock courtrooms, a simulated solicitors' office, a dedicated law library and lots of IT kit. The law school is conveniently located within walking distance of the mainline Stoke-on-Trent station. The careers department runs a practitioner mentoring programme that connects students with local solicitors and pays for membership of the local Junior Lawyers Division. It also organises a lecture and workshop series to help students understand what recruiters are looking for. Pro bono participation is encouraged in schemes like Streetlaw. Open days are held throughout the year. Staffordshire grads also get a 15% discount on course fees.

Swansea University

Number of places: 100 FT
Fees (2012/13): £9,100

"Numbers are up again this year," say sources at Swansea, after a bit of a dip in previous years. Running since 2009, this LPC is a firm favourite among those who have already tasted life in Swansea, with university alumni making up the majority of the intake each year, as well as those *"who are returning home after studying in England, to save on living costs."* The beautiful Gower

Peninsula with its stunning beaches certainly makes for an attractive learning environment: *"There's nowhere else in the UK like this – there's the sea right next to us and a beautiful ornamental garden as well."* The school places an emphasis on face-to-face teaching and students attend classes four days a week in Stage One (although most manage to cram in everything within three) and three days a week in Stage Two. Workshops take up around four hours each day, often in the afternoons, and materials from large group sessions are placed online on Blackboard for future reference, along with some training modules as well. At Stage Two of the LPC the law school offers three 'high street' and three 'corporate' electives, catering for students with eyes on diverse career paths. The Competition Law & Practice elective no longer runs separately, and has now been incorporated into the Advanced Commercial Law elective. Many use the spare days as an opportunity to gain some work experience at local firms and build up those all-important contacts.

Students have access to the university careers service, and LPC staff collate job vacancies in the area and send out bulletins. Talks from practitioners and the local Junior Lawyers Division on employability are also organised to help students optimise their legal pulling power. Additional CV-boosting activities come in the form of pro bono. Students can participate in the Swansea pro bono law clinic under the supervision of local solicitors, and get involved with the CAB and a StreetLaw programme as well. A number of Swansea grads go on to get paralegal jobs, while a small number will go onto London, and others *"go for jobs in the big maritime law firms, like Ince & Co."* The school has links with the Swansea Law Society, as well as good relationships with local firms in south Wales – *"they tend to advertise through us."*

Being on campus in a real student city means you are never short of welcome distractions from work, with a whole host of student union activities to pursue as well as clubs, bars and pubs. If it all gets too much, students can be sure of support from appointed personal tutors. The school operates an open door policy and students also have five formal meetings with their personal tutor over the course of the year. A part-time version of the course is in the pipeline, and *"we certainly hope that we will have it up and running in the near future."* A new instalment scheme has made paying fees that much easier, and there are also access schemes and a Lord Williams of Mostyn Scholarship prize to pursue as well.

University of West London

Number of places: 60 FTE
Fees (2012/13): £8,970

Formerly known as Thames Valley University, UWL's law school is to be found in the leafy London suburb of

Ealing. Surrounded by several parks, it is a relaxed place to study yet near enough to the buzz of the city centre (about 40 minutes by underground) for students to enjoy it after class. In 2012, numbers dropped slightly, mostly on the part time course, *"which was surprising."* The redesign of the Business Law & Practice module in 2010 led to more of a concentration on Criminal Litigation and Property Law & Practice, better reflecting the destination of UWL's successful students. They join firms and organisations handling everything from social welfare and legal aid to property and high-street practice and occasionally commercial law – especially firms *"that have a number of offices and are expanding to do high street work: commercial hybrids in other words."* Available electives mirror this diversity, and are likely to stay the same in the foreseeable future. A top-up LLM can also be studied for.

A *"significant number"* of LPC students come from the undergraduate course or GDL at the university, taking advantage of a fee discount (a 5% early payment discount is also available), although there are a number of international students too. Students are predominantly taught through workshops in groups of around 20 rather than lectures, with fewer in the elective groups. Preliminary reading is often posted on the school's blackboard, as well as lecture outlines, which are brought up-to-date and repackaged each year. Full-timers can expect to be in for two and a half days a week (Tuesday, Thursday and part of Wednesday), while those on the part-time course attend one day per week, with an additional evening in year two. The elective stage has been reshuffled to benefit those who are working or have other commitments; workshops last longer so that full-time students are only in for three sessions a week, which can, theoretically, be condensed into a day and a half. UWL runs a community advice programme in conjunction with Ealing Equality Council, where students can get involved with fortnightly surgeries. It has gone from *"strength to strength,"* and a new outreach advice clinic on a local estate looks to be heading the same way.

A mini-careers module on the LPC ensures that students' CVs, applications and interview skills are up to scratch. Careers days and firm-matching sessions are organised by the school, making it easier students to know which firms they should be applying for: *"It's all about sensitising them to the quirks and demands of the legal profession."* They can also take advantage of a mentoring and work experience scheme over the summer. A former student who now runs their own firm offers several current students summer work experience. The school has contacts with the Middlesex Law Society, where students can attend lectures, and there are regular talks from practitioners and organisations such as the Land Registry. Sources added that: *"We have a network of professional contacts here – local courts are on board as well, and our students get to go into the magistrates and crown courts to gain experience.*" A new professional development centre has been set up via the school, and students can take advantage of the CPE courses on offer, brushing up on compliance workshops that "*really do keep them up to date.*"

University of Westminster

Number of places: 120 FT, 64 PT
Fees (2012/13): £9,950 FT

Despite "*suffering in recent years due to the financial disaster,*" Westminster's school of law has had a good year and "*pass rates are healthy.*" Conveniently located just off the hustle and bustle of Oxford Street, students commute easily from all across London and are not far from the entertainment that such an area has to offer. Most pay their fees in instalments, but those who can pay the full-whack before the end of September receive a 1.5% discount. Around 5 to 10% of the cohort will come to the school with a sponsorship secured. During Stage One students are in class Mondays, Tuesdays and Thursdays each week between 10.30am and 4.30pm, but the "*intensity relaxes in Stage Two,*" and the timetable can be potentially be reduced down to a day and a half. Full-timers are taught in small groups of 15 to 18 in the morning, and either continue with further tuition in the afternoon or have large group sessions. There's a mixture of live and online lectures – with the more complex subject matter lending itself to an online platform – but the emphasis is nonetheless on live lectures. Sources at the law school tell us that: "*We have a quality assured scheme, and the majority of students say that they prefer live lectures.*" Tutors will regularly upload 'computer assisted learning' exercises to help students, and the school's Blackboard incorporates notes and materials from the small group sessions: "*Everything is duplicated online.*"

There's a bounty of electives – thirteen in total – both private client and commercially oriented: "*The majority want to go to the high street, so the private client electives are generally more popular, but some do go to the City.*" There's also a clinical elective that sees students undertake practical work with the CAB, while those who undertake the popular immigration elective are also given the opportunity to complete Level 1 of the Immigration Accreditation Scheme. For those with other plans for their three electives choices, the pro bono centre sits right next door to the law school, and students can get involved in a host of issues – there are around seven projects going on – from immigration to Land Registry matters. Students have also got involved with mooting competitions and done "*extremely well – two of them had their picture taken with Lord Woolf.*"

All this helps towards building a weighty CV, and the associate director of the LPC routinely sifts through training contract vacancies before advertising them to students via the school's Blackboard site. Careers workshops are also arranged, and law firm representatives visit to offer advice on applications and make presentations. In 2010 a mentoring scheme was set up that links current LPC students with recent Westminster alumni working in law firms. The law school at Westminster is spread over six floors, including an LPC suite that houses a library and computer room that loans out laptops. Students have access to the main law school library and a mock courtroom. The school's Oxford Street location lends itself to a host of social activities, and the school organises drinks events in its foundation week – "*we try to schmooze students and ease them into the course*" – at Christmas and at the end of the course. The student body is quite diverse too, with a mixture of EU candidates and a "*small market of Trinidadian students*" as well. Overall, what Westminster offers is a "*personal touch – students stay with us.*"

University of Wolverhampton

Number of places: 60 FT, 30 PT
Fees (2012/13): £8,750

LPC students at Wolverhampton University were able to make the most of shiny new facilities for the first time in September 2011, when The Professional Legal Studies Centre joined the School of Law on the main campus, in central Wolverhampton: "*We used to be a mile outside and it was a hassle getting the bus, plus all library and careers facilities were based here. Now students like the fact that they have more face-to-face time; we operate from a small number of rooms, and the staff rooms are very close to the teaching areas – it's a lot more integrated.*" Perks of the move include access to the media department's recording studios for interview and advocacy training, a courtroom, easy access to the main library as well as new classrooms and a specialist resources room – "*everything's modern and much better equipped.*"

Wolverhampton views the LPC itself as the first year of professional practice: if students can't come to class, they're expected to ring the centre and explain why. While the majority of students completed undergraduate studies at the university, there's also a Caribbean contingent: as is the case with Manchester Met and Aberystwyth, the school has grown in popularity with students coming from Trinidad especially and the university maintains strong links with law schools on the island. The full-time course is now timetabled over three days – lectures on a Monday; workshops on a Tuesday and Wednesday. Part-timers come in two evenings a week. For each subject there's one one-hour lecture followed by two small group sessions, although the school is considering pre-recording some lectures in the future. Each workshop usually includes 15 students and online materials support studying. These materials are delivered through the intranet system – Wolf – and in the week before Christmas, students group together to work as individual firms, and record their time and receive instructions via Wolf.

The school is active in its careers support. There's a dedicated LPC careers adviser and a mentoring programme involving local firms. The school pins up two lists – one of partners and one of newly qualified solicitors to whom students can send their CVs to apply for work shadowing. Other careers opportunities are uploaded onto Wolf.

Wolverhampton's stated aim is "*to promote access to the profession in the area.*" Several students will have come from the university's foundation degree access courses and many aim to practise in high-street firms. Wolverhampton alumni also get a generous 20% discount of fees, making payment that much easier. Family, employment and insolvency have been the popular elec-

tives over the past year. Commercial options are also offered – a few students have gone on to SGH Martineau – but most tend to go for the more high street choices. The school also arranges the 'LPC Plus', a series of talks throughout the academic year from various practitioners, including the CPS and commercial firms, and is considering hosting introductory talks from practitioners at the beginning of the course from next year. LPC staff have set up a legal advice clinic in the local Mander shopping centre, which students can volunteer in: "*It's a rented shop effectively, and functions as a drop-in advice clinic. It's supported by staff and local practitioners and students will always take down the initial info.*" For those in search of more CV padding, there's also the opportunity to top up the LPC with an LLM. Students enjoy being part of a small intake and all of the social possibilities of being on campus.

Ethnicity and the law

BPTC students 2010/11:
44% (618) – white
42% (600) – ethnic minority
14% (196) – did not disclose

UK domiciled BPTC students 2010/11:
71% (485) – white
20% (140) – ethnic minority
9% (63) – did not disclose

22% of new trainee solicitors in 2010/11 came from ethnic minority backgrounds

11% of all solicitors come from an ethnic minority background (2010/11), just under half of these are based in London

80% of self-employed barristers in 2010 were white

Pupil barristers by ethnicity (2010/11):
White – 349 (79%)
Ethnic minority – 58 (13%)
No data – 37 (8%)

4.9% of QCs identify as coming from an ethnic minority background (2010)

All figures from the Law Society and Bar Council in 2011.

The Bar Professional Training Course (BPTC)

The BPTC is the necessary link between either an LLB or GDL and pupillage for would-be barristers. Nine law schools are authorised by the Bar Standards Board (BSB) to teach the course at locations in London, Bristol, Cardiff, Nottingham, Manchester, Leeds and Newcastle. The full-time course lasts a year; the part-time option is spread over two. Those with the gift of the gab, step up please.

Maybe I'm craaazeey (probably)

"*You would have to be mad to want to be a barrister*," said one course provider we spoke to this year – "*but don't quote me on that.*" While our source shall indeed remain unnamed, the harsh realities to which they allude are very much worth exploring, and echo a 'health warning' put out by the BSB: "*We need to give a signal to those who aren't up to it that they're wasting their money* [or risk] *gaining an army of enemies*," says Lady Deech, Chair of the BSB. Strong words, but at present legions of BPTC graduates are chasing only a fistful of pupillages. Many never make it and all they have to show for their hard work is a £15k hole in their pockets (if not much more). A quick glance at the employment statistics of those recently called to the Bar is enough to give even the most ambitious soul pause for thought. In 2010/11, 1,422 students enrolled onto the BPTC (after 3,099 people applied), but in the same year only 446 first-six pupillages were registered. This figure includes BPTC graduates from previous years who were unsuccessful at their first, second, third or even fourth attempt – remember that the BPTC has a lifespan of five years! So the odds are stacked against aspiring barristers. Most students will veer between "*realism and optimism: they know it's tough, but then again you always think that you will be the one to get a pupillage. The fact is that the number of pupillages being registered is at its lowest point for ten years.*" See page 667 for the exact stats.

Checking out the CVs of those lucky few who do make it paints an even more daunting picture and is a humbling experience for prospective applicants; the academic records of new tenants are quite simply terrifying. Some 35% have First-class degrees, and a similar percentage attended Oxbridge. A further 64% have attended a Russell Group University. Throw into the mix a bountiful array of MAs, PhDs, academic prizes, scholarships, languages and maybe even a few people who have managed to save the world in their sleep once. The point is, winning arguments over the dinner table and fancying yourself as Atticus Finch or Mark Darcy just isn't going to cut it. Bear this in mind before signing up for the BPTC. Back to Lady Deech: "*If you're tone deaf, don't go to music school; if you have two left feet don't go to ballet school*" – said with reference to BPTC students who lack the required command of the English language. Linguistics aside, all prospective applicants need to make a cold, hard assessment of whether they can really cut it in the profession. Think you've got what it takes? Read on…

In 2009 and 2010 the BSB piloted an aptitude test for the BPTC as a more proactive way of protecting wide-eyed students. Maintaining the future strength and quality of the Bar was also on the agenda. As one of the key recommendations from The Wood Report (interesting, do read it), the test involved logic and reasoning questions. After comparing these pilot test results with students' final BPTC scores, approval was finally granted – by the Legal Services Board (LSB) – for the Bar Course Aptitude Test (BCAT) to be installed as a compulsory requirement. From September 2012, all prospective students will have to undertake the BCAT, and they must achieve a minimum required standard in order to take up their place on the BPTC. Oh, and they must also shell out £67 for an application fee to take the test. The move to give the go-ahead for this test has been a controversial one, with the Law Society flagging up various concerns about the viability of the BCAT, especially before the outcomes of the Legal Education and Training Review (LETR) are known. There are further worries about the impact the test will have on diversity, with a homogenisation of the Bar predicted by some. LSB chief executive Chris Kenny has said that the validity of these concerns are "*impossible to verify in absolute terms at this stage by the very fact that the test has not operated in practice, other than in limited pilot circumstances.*" In light of this, the BSB will have to undertake a five-year data gathering and evaluation period, after which a decision will be made about the ongoing use of the BCAT. BPTC providers (apart from Kaplan, which already runs an aptitude test) were on the whole "*unconvinced that aptitude tests tell you much more than a paper application.*" Sources at Nottingham Law School, which runs the exact same course as Kaplan but without a pre-requisite aptitude test, said that "*the profile of the students at both institutions are remarkably similar,*" and that exam results demonstrate an equal level of "*those who are competent and those who aren't.*" One welcome outcome is that the test is likely to protect certain misguided students from the burden of a heavy debt unnecessarily incurred, but we'll have to wait five more years before the true worth of an aptitude test is fully known.

2:2 boohoo

A second contention in enlisting quality candidates onto the BPTC arises from course providers. The BSB's minimum requirement for admission onto the courses is a 2:2 at degree level, and a pass on the GDL (where taken). Several providers have chosen to up the ante. Kaplan Law School, for example, requires all of its shortlisted applicants to attend an assessment day, where they undertake a written advocacy exercise, an oral advocacy exercise and an interview. As sources there say: "*We need students who can fire on all cylinders.*" Bristol Institute of Legal Practice at UWE also runs a system relying on 'admissions points'. Most providers actually require their students to have a 2:1 at degree level. According to the latest data, 12.4% of 2010/11 BPTC students across all providers had a First, while 50.1% had a 2:1 under their belt. A quarter of students had a 2:2. One course leader described it in these terms: "*It's easier to prefer someone with a 2:1, as they form part of that middle group who do have a fighting chance. For those with a 2:2, the numbers are incredibly scary, and official sources from the Bar say that around 3-6% of pupils will have a degree at that level.*" Scary stuff indeed, and it's important to note that the 'Desmonds' who do make it have exceptionally good CVs in other ways and/or a first career under their belts. However, success at the Bar is based on more than impeccable academics. The advice from one BPTC provider on how to improve your prospects? "*Advocacy, advocacy, advocacy.*" Most providers want to assess an applicant's commitment to practice through public speaking experience, such as mooting and debating, plus mini-pupillages and marshalling, etc. and it's no different for the sets offering pupillage.

The mismatch between BPTC graduates and the number of pupillages is tempered to a certain extent by those individuals who have decided that the Bar is simply not for them, and by the significant number of international students (estimated at between 20 and 23% of all BPTC students) who return home rather than seeking pupillage in England and Wales. This contingent may be set to fall as many course providers, prompted by the BSB, are getting tougher on their entry requirements as concerns English language ability. Currently the BSB requires all students whose first language is not English or Welsh to demonstrate that they have a minimum 7.5 IELTS standard, or equivalent. Over the past few years we've heard rumbling criticisms that some students' English just isn't up to scratch, which causes difficulties in the classroom for other students practising key skills that rely on rhetorical ability. It seems that law schools are finally reacting, taking steps to ensure applicants possess the required standard of English: "*We don't have students that cannot cope on the language front – I would say that was more of an issue two or three years ago.*" The BSB did request permission from the LSB to insist that all students sit an IELTS exam as part of the BPTC entry requirements, but this seems to have been forgotten about of late...

Mad skillz

The BPTC has been designed to ensure that wannabe barristers acquire the skills, knowledge, attitudes and competencies needed for practice. Cue: developing students' advocacy, drafting, opinion writing, conferencing, case analysis and legal research skills. As for knowledge, students are schooled in civil litigation and remedies, criminal litigation and sentencing, evidence, and professional ethics. These core areas, especially ethics, are essential because "*barristers are individuals, and they get thrown to wolves more often – when you're a solicitor you have the protection of the firm around you. For barristers it's different, and they have to be equipped with all the knowledge they can get.*" In the final term, students select two option subjects in areas they are targeting for practice. Most teaching is delivered in groups of 12, with the all-important skills taught in groups of six students or fewer. Teaching methods vary slightly between providers, but learning is commonly conducted via case studies which track the litigation process.

Almost wherever you study the emphasis is very much on face-to-face teaching. Still, many use computers in lectures to make learning more stimulating, and writing-skills classes often involve the use of whiteboards. Oral skills classes make increasing use of video-recording equipment in role-plays so students can improve by assessing their own performance as well as that of their peers. It also has the effect of highlighting any nervous tics! The skills acquired are then examined using a variety of assessments in the second and third terms. Written skills are tested through a mix of unseen tests and 'homework', while professional actors are drafted in to take part in oral assessments. One area where the BPTC differs most from its predecessor, the BVC, is its focus on Alternative Dispute Resolution (ADR). A new

'Resolution of Disputes Out of Court' module replaces the old negotiation-skills course, heralding a broader approach to avoiding litigation.

Though skills assessments will continue to be set and marked by the individual providers, the future of testing knowledge has changed. The BSB now sets standardised and centralised exams for civil litigation, criminal litigation and ethics, to ensure confidence in the parity between course providers. The exams consist of a blend of multiple choice questions and short answer questions. The latter are still marked locally by the providers, while the former are centrally marked by a computer. The BSB then samples and moderates the written exam papers.

2012 is the first year in which all this has been done, and the response from both providers and students hasn't been hugely positive. Provider's responses ranged from moderate annoyance to full-on fury: "*I'm upset about it, to the point where I want to run to the BSB with a pitchfork in hand.*" Students were also not impressed, and hundreds signed a petition to the BSB expressing their dissatisfaction. One provider put it thus: "*As long as I can remember exams were set locally: if you did the course at Nottingham, then Nottingham set the exams and marked them. The assessments were aimed at what students could be expected to know based on the teaching at that institution. It's just inevitable when exams are centralised that the questions are going to be one step removed from the providers – the exams may cover things that students haven't come across before.*" Others agreed, saying that "*the BSB have never done this type of thing before – the people putting the papers together are practitioners, not educationalists.*" A BSB syllabus review is potentially on the way to resolve the problems that have arisen this year and to address "*the lack of clarity*" which providers and students have been struggling with. Some students have actually thrived under this new system, while others have done less well, with some providers stating that "*in the end our students actually ended up doing more or less how they expected they would. Our pass rates are not dissimilar this year to what they were last year.*" The problem, then, seems to be with the stress of having to revise a more vast body of material than ever before...

All systems go

Course directors tell us that the BPTC is "*a very demanding, intensive and rigorous course.*" The timetable is described as "*undulating*" – "*intense in parts and boring in others*"– and often the course is "*front loaded.*" But don't use the quieter times to relax. This is your chance to improve your pupillage prospects. As one student advises: "*Organise dining with the Inns, mooting, debating, pro bono, mini-pupillages, marshalling and the like*" to give your CV "*a fighting chance of reaching interview stage.*" It's therefore essential to look carefully at the extra-curric-

The BPTC Providers

BPP Law School, Leeds (ft/pt)

BPP Law School, London (ft/pt)

Bristol Institute of Legal Practice at UWE (ft/pt)

Cardiff Law School (ft)

The City Law School (ft/pt)

College of Law, Birmingham (ft/pt)

College of Law, London (ft/pt)

Kaplan Law School (ft)

Manchester Metropolitan University (ft/pt)

Northumbria University Law School (ft/pt)

Nottingham Law School (ft)

ular opportunities offered at each of the providers and throw yourself into everything you can. Most providers deliberately keep Fridays free of classes to allow students this opportunity.

How to apply through BPTC online

An application for the BPTC costs £40, and the process is all done online. There is no cap on the number of providers you may apply to, although during the first phase of the process only your top-three choices will look at your application. While many providers will say that it's not vital that you put their institution as a top choice, many popular providers fill their places with first and second choice applicants alone. Prioritise your favourites if you want to avoid disappointment.

How to pick a provider

The fight for pupillage is a truly testing one, so choose your course provider carefully. Pick one that's going to arm you well for the challenges ahead in terms of taught skills, support and opportunities. Read through prospectuses and websites, attend open days, try to speak to current or former students. Read our **Provider Reports**. Consider the following criteria:

Cost: Some providers and locations are significantly cheaper than others. London is the priciest but even here there is variation. If you're an international student, look at the differential in price. Part-timers should note whether fees increase in the second year.

Location: Regional providers may be the best option for those looking for pupillage on the regional circuits, not least because of their stronger links and networking opportunities with the local Bar. London students benefit from proximity to the Inns of Court and more easy access to London sets for pupillage interviews; however, compulsory dining and advocacy training courses in the Inns enable regional students to maintain their links with the capital's beating legal heart.

Size: Smaller providers pride themselves on offering a more intimate and collegial environment. Student feedback indicates that this does make a positive difference to the experience, and the friends you make on the BPTC should be a source of support during the search for pupillage and beyond. There's definitely a different feel to those providers that are within universities and those that aren't.

Facilities: Students can tap into a far wider range of support services, sports and social activities by taking the BPTC at a university. Library and IT resources vary from one provider to the next, as does the level of technology used in teaching. Some providers make technology a key feature of the course.

Option subjects: Available option subjects vary. For example, although judicial review and immigration are popular, they are not offered everywhere. The **Table of BPTC Providers** on our website sets out what's on offer at each one. This table also compares fees and offers provider-specific application tips.

Pro Bono: Opportunities range from minimal to superb across the nine providers.

BPTC provider reports

Which of the law schools teaching the BPTC will be right for you? All quotes come from course directors or other official sources at the providers.

BPP Law School, London

Number of places: 264 FT, 96 PT

BPP Holborn's central location – surrounded by the Inns of Court and a sprinkling of barristers' chambers – lends itself well to the extracurricular elements of the BPTC; students can finish classes well in time for dinner at their Inns. With barristers no longer holding the monopoly on higher rights of audience, BPP aims to better arm its students by offering around 30% more advocacy than BSB requirements stipulate. Students also receive written feedback after every class. "*We think that advocacy is advocacy,*" said sources. "*Some providers have the civil and criminal team teach advocacy, but we teach it separately in small groups of four, and dedicate a one and half hour tutorial to it every week.*" The civil and criminal litigation components of the course are then taught in one-and-a-half-hour tutorial groups of 12 students, while professional ethics is "*front-loaded early on, so that students can pick up on ethics points throughout the course.*" The tutors are all qualified practitioners, and some are freelance tutors who are still practising, which is "*valuable to the students and one of the ways in which we maintain links with the profession.*" In the third term, students select two options of interest from a choice of 11, including intellectual property and international trade, which has been "*more popular than ever before.*" The school is also looking into additional public law and advanced commercial options in the coming year.

Part-timers attend school one weekend in four over two years, and although they have the same skills programme as full-time students, more self-study is required for the knowledge elements. With one day a week (usually a Monday or a Friday) free for course preparation, full-timers can commit to pro bono activities. Flexibility increases in the third term, where students "*may have other days in which they do not have classes.*" On the full-time course around "*20 to 25% of students have a first, and the student body is slightly less diverse.*" In comparison, the part-time option has "*greater diversity: we get people who have had the most amazing careers – one once operated on Michael Owen's knee!*"

Students must complete a minimum of five hours of pro bono. The pro bono department has opportunities to suit every interest, from Streetlaw and FRU to the Environmental Law Unit and the Legal Translation Service. Furthermore, if students "*have their own contacts or causes that they would like to devote time to, then we encourage them to be as imaginative and creative as they can be – but helping out a pal won't count!*" Mock pupillage interviews and appointments with careers advisers help the pupillage hungry, and students can continue to use the service for a whole year after leaving. A programme of seminars with chambers, commercial awareness workshops and themed panel discussions with local barristers all bring networking opportunities, which are usually organised by the careers department. A wealth of mooting and mock trial competitions provide ample opportunity to develop advocacy skills, with designated 'mooting officers' available to help orchestrate student involvement.

Current students can call on recent BPP alumni who act as buddies, but are also put into groups of 12, which are each overseen by a designated personal tutor. Those who complete the course can undergo further study to obtain an LLM in Professional Legal Practice.

BPP Law School, Leeds

Number of places: 48 FT, 48 PT

Students can expect the same course as their peers in London, albeit in a more intimate atmosphere. As with other regional providers, students can network with members of the local Bar, and BPP helps facilitate this with meet-and-greet sessions and a speaker programme. Students also have the opportunity to get closer to the profession through pro bono activities such as a legal advice clinic and a human rights unit. Internships are also available at non-profit organisations. Those who complete the BPTC can undergo additional study in the ensuing months to obtain an LLM. Studying the BPTC in Leeds incurs lower fees than in London, and since the course and extracurricular opportunities are more or less uniform between the two cities, the money factor makes the Northern branch an attractive choice. So if you're cost-conscious or have aspirations towards the Northern Circuit consider putting it down as your first-choice provider.

Bristol Institute of Legal Practice at UWE

Number of places: 120 FT, 48 PT

BILP is the only law school to offer the BPTC in the South West, making it a big draw for students interested in pursuing a career on the Western Circuit – or just looking to spend a year in the delightful city of Bristol: "*The nightlife and shopping opportunities are excellent – like London on a more manageable scale.*" Another attraction of UWE's Bar course is the opportunity to qualify as an accredited commercial mediator of the Bristol ADR group. We've heard that this course is hugely popular among students who recognise that "*with an increasing emphasis on mediation in the profession, it's excellent to have that qualification.*" From 2013, ex-students will be able to return to school to specialise in family mediation.

UWE attracts a mix of South West locals, graduates of the various universities in the city and a number of part-timers who fly in from Europe and as far afield as The Bahamas. The majority of offers are made to those who put UWE down as a first choice, and if you have a 2:2, then it's "*essential to have extensive practical experience*" on your CV.

The law school – and indeed UWE's entire law faculty – is situated on the university's Frenchay campus which, though not in Bristol proper, has excellent transport links with the city and plenty of car parking. Commuting is but a minor inconvenience since on-site facilities include two law libraries and dedicated base rooms for BPTC students. These resource rooms are open seven days a week and are equipped with all the technology the modern barrister could possibly need. A Blackboard site enables access to lecture outlines, advocacy demonstrations, power point slides and examples of short answer questions.

BPTC students are usually in class three days a week, with Fridays off for other pursuits, although teaching can sometimes slip into four days. The vast majority of teaching is delivered via small group sessions of six to 12 students (six for skills sessions). Advocacy is practised in mock courtrooms and advocacy 'master classes' are run by local practitioners to properly hone students' technique. There are also three advocacy competitions for students to enter. They are sponsored by two sets of local chambers, and cover family, civil and criminal topics: "*Students get to showcase their talents in front of the local bar, which can in some cases lead to a pupillage.*" UWE even runs several four-hour long mock magistrates' court trials to further enhance the sense of authenticity.

Students can select from a range of options: relatively new offerings like competition law, refugee and asylum law and international trade have gone down a storm, while employment and family remain popular. There is currently a question mark hovering over international environmental law, which may be replaced by a commercial option in the coming year. Pro bono schemes have also "*thrived*" over the past year, and "*students have won various prizes*" working on issues relating to domestic abuse, prisoner rehabilitation and the environment. UWE also has extensive careers advice on offer, whether it's through the main university service; the dedicated BPTC careers tutors who host drop in clinics; or via the local practitioners that come in to give talks. Students in the past have found pupillages in London, Bristol, Cardiff and Exeter, with some "*going up to Manchester or Lincolnshire.*" The focus is, as you'll have guessed, on the South West, though.

Cardiff Law School

Number of places: 84 FT

Cardiff's reputation as an exciting and vibrant city continues to grow, so it's no surprise that a fair number of its undergraduates elect to stay in South Wales to do the law school's popular BPTC: "*We've seen a 60% increase in the amount of applications we've received over the past five years.*" The course receives twice as many first-choice applications as there are places, so classing them as your back-up probably isn't the wisest move.

Cardiff keeps its BPTC intake low to ensure that teaching is limited to small groups, with oral skills taught in groups of six people. A teacher observes oral skills in pairs of students – one pair at a time – and oral and written feedback is also provided to each student. A limited amount of large-group sessions concentrate on knowledge-based content: "*The whole cohort is there, it's our equivalent to lectures.*" Cardiff aims to turn out first-class advocates at the end of each year; the BSB recommends a minimum of 12 advocacy classes on the BPTC course whereas Cardiff runs around 25. Welsh speakers can also practice advocacy in their native tongue through a short optional 'advocacy in Welsh' course – Eiriolaeth yn y Gymraeg. Teaching staff are all practitioners, and the school has course consultants and an advisory board that includes local barristers and judges. Students can also use the school's online "*central learning environment*" to view course materials, previous lectures and other relevant documentation. Podcasts can be downloaded as well.

Classes run from Monday through to Thursday, with Fridays off to catch-up and utilise work experience opportunities. A two-week placement scheme enables students to escape the classroom and spend time marshalling a judge at circuit level or above for a week, followed by a mini-pupillage, further marshalling, or another placement with the employed Bar. The school monitors the number of students attaining pupillage: on average 25% secure one at a UK set. These include students at local pupillages, but sources also wanted to make it clear that "*the BPTC is an English and Welsh qualification – we've had students go on to sets in Manchester, Oxford and Birmingham. I've met people who consider Wales as a separate entity altogether – we're in the UK!*"

Cardiff Law School runs several pro bono projects. It is helping set up a Personal Support Unit to assist litigants in person negotiate court procedure and its Innocence Project has submitted cases to the Criminal Cases Review Commission. An asylum justice scheme is still running after a successful pilot, and there are also appropriate adult and NHS Continuing Healthcare schemes to get involved in. Students can turn to the Cardiff University careers service – which has a dedicated advisor who is attached to the law school – for guidance, but "*what is most helpful is the assistance that course leaders provide.*" A top-up LLM has been approved and is now available for students who successfully complete the BPTC.

City Law School, London

Number of places: 420 FT, 60 PT

City Law School (formerly Inns of Court School of Law) has a long history of educating barristers. Once the monopoly Bar course provider, it has a wealth of famous alumni including Tony Blair and Gandhi, whose portrait graces the student common room. Primarily an "*advocacy school,*" City recognises that its students must be academically strong due to the Bar's increasing role as a referral advisory service. The school accordingly considers applicants' academic abilities and commitment to the Bar – mooting, debating and mini-pupillages – to select those with a realistic chance of completing the course and securing pupillage. Students come from all over the world and in particular the Commonwealth countries, where City enjoys a great reputation, but nonetheless the majority of those enrolled are domestic students. City requires its international students to demonstrate a minimum level of 7.5 on the IELTS scale, to ensure that they can follow classes competently – "*some applicants should consider deferring to improve their language skills.*"

City told us that it deliberately recruits fewer students than it is authorised to teach – about 83% of its maximum full-time intake and approximately 50% for its part-time course. Nevertheless, it is over-subscribed and it's a good idea to put City as a first choice. Full-timers are timetabled for four days a week – "*sometimes it's three*" – while part-time students attend over two evenings, for three hours each.

Members of the teaching staff have written legal texts and the team includes barristers and some solicitors who are able to bring real-life experience to the course. Teaching emulates real-life practice as far as possible, and skills training is integrated with the knowledge requirements. For example, students will learn the procedure of applying for an interim injunction, watch a demonstration, and analyse cases and skeletons before performing the exercise themselves. One-on-one advocacy sessions also boost students' skills. Students follow the same cases through the course, applying each new skill they learn to the scenario, from initial meeting with clients to hearings and even appeals. The rationale behind this is firstly because "*it feels more like the Bar*" and secondly because during pupillage students will be exposed to a higher level of work – under the supervision of their pupilmaster – than they would be doing as a junior tenant and so the BPTC must reflect this. Sources at City explained: "*We don't just want to get students through their exams; we want to train them for the junior Bar, to push them to go as far as they can, so that they don't just reach the standard level.*" The school has also increased its body of online materials, allowing students to access documents such as drafting and cross-examination papers via topic and the week of study.

Students have access to careers advisers at City University as well as a dedicated pupillage advisory team that "*puts students through their paces*" in mock interviews, and also provides application and CV advice. A speaker programme welcomes legal personalities including judges, and a mooting and mock trial competition is useful for boosting CVs. Cross-examining trainee police officers once a year adds a more realistic dimension to mock trials. City runs two criminal elective options and a new(-ish) landlord and tenant module which has gone down "*very well – students go for it if they are entering into a chancery practice. It's complicated, but there's a great deal of work for the Bar in this area.*" Alternative options with FRU and the National Centre for Domestic Violence are still available. For students who don't want to devote a BPTC option to pro bono, a host of other 'free-time' opportunities are available for those wishing to develop their skills and add shine to CVs.

Supplementing the Inns' awards, scholarships are granted based on student performance at the end of the BPTC year. Former City grads get a £1,000 discount, while two new 'Rosie Keene Memorial' scholarships are available for promising female students. A student society has free rein over a budget and organises socials throughout the course, like boat trips up the Thames, and events with an "*international flavour.*"

The College of Law, London

Number of places: 240 FT, 48 PT

The College of Law is validated to offer the BPTC at its London (Bloomsbury) and Birmingham branches. Students can also opt to study for a top-up LLM after the course.

The Bloomsbury branch is less flashy and imposing than its Moorgate sibling, where many LPC students head; it nevertheless houses recently refurbished IT rooms and a revamped cybercafé. Its location near the courts is also desirable. Sources at the branch described its "*buzzy atmosphere – it's bang in centre of the West End, and we now run all of the courses here, so there's lots of inter-program mixing.*" Full-time and part-time weekend study options are offered and teaching is delivered via small-group sessions of no more more than 12 students, each of which last three and a half hours.

Key at CoL is the integration of skills and knowledge, with classes following the litigation process. In criminal litigation, for example, students begin by learning about an offender's rights in the police station and how to make a bail application. Later, they can unleash their inner QC in a mock trial at the Inner London Crown Court or Blackfriars Crown Court. Practitioners play the judges, while trainee police officers make the experience even more realistic. Although the BSB no longer requires compulsory court visits, CoL has retained them and expects its students to report back on their experiences. It has also introduced more multimedia resources such as podcasts and video recordings. These online resources supplement learning and cover niche aspects of procedure such as appearing in youth courts. It is CoL's aim to "*go above and beyond what the BSB require,*" and so students here receive 34 hours of advocacy training, and the ethics component of the course is taught as a discrete module, in order to "*really get those essential qualities which make up a barrister across. It's not like being a solicitor where you can rely on a firm more for guidance – as a barrister you are an individual.*"

Students come from a variety of universities, and the most successful go on to a variety of pupillages. Prospective students should note that CoL expects applicants to demonstrate a commitment to studying at its institutions in addition to looking at academics and relevant work experience. This means it's important to rank it first if it's your top pick. Its careers service – one of the largest in the country – orchestrates an 'employability program,' which offers the usual CV and application advice plus mock interviews, career workshops, a mentoring scheme with practitioners and a speaker programme. Panel discussions with practitioner have, in the past, been streamed as an interactive 'webinar' so absent students can participate.

Students can consult a database of mini-pupillages and also seek help from staff. Tutors are all qualified lawyers – one is a QC – and maintain their links with the profession by returning to practice over the summer months. With one day off a week, full-timers can take advantage of a "*huge number*" of pro bono opportunities include FRU and the National Coalition Against Domestic Violence; this can also be practised as an option on the BPTC (there are nine options in total). There are several mooting and mock trial sessions and competitions, while those on the mediation elective can contend in the 'Plea and Mediation Competition'. If students have any time left, CoL is known for its array of sports and social events.

The College of Law, Birmingham

Number of places: 134 FT, 36 PT

Located in the historic Jewellery Quarter, CoL Birmingham welcomes a small set of students onto its BPTC course. CoL is the only BPTC provider in the West Midlands, and since its opening in 2007, the centre has gone from strength to strength. A new wing was added and the library extended in 2010. In 2011 a part-time course was made available at this centre in addition to the full-time study option, and has "*been going really well*" so far. The course itself is taught in exactly the same way as it is in London, and there are great extracurriculars on offer as well, including assisting with the Birmingham Employment Rights Advice Line, The Refugee Council, the Trades Union Congress and Leasehold Valuation Tribunal service. A representative of CoL added that "*even if students are based in Birmingham, they will still have access to all of our national resources; our employability and careers programmes, our databases etc...*" The law school organises a series of talks from barristers and judges where students can pose questions on their practice and network at drinks events afterwards.

Kaplan Law School

Number of places: 120 FT

The BPTC course at Kaplan was first offered to a group of 60 students in September 2010 and in 2012 this was extended for the second time to account for 120 prospective barristers: "*It's quite a leap, and we need to accommodate that in terms of tutors and resources, but it shows that the word is spreading, and we're not just the new kid on the block any more.*" The school sets the bar high when it comes to entry requirements, with its very own entrance exams for prospective candidates. BPTC applicants need to pass an interview, written exam and advocacy test and demonstrate a commitment to the profession evidenced by previous formal and informal work experience or otherwise. Once in, the professional attitude continues as students are required to wear suits into class and study from practitioners' texts *Archbold* and *The White Book (Civil Procedure)*. Students have to be "*firing on all cylinders*" while at Kaplan, and it's worth mentioning that "*around 40% of the intake are Oxbridge, while another 30 to 40% are from the Russell Group. We rarely offer a place to someone with less than a 2:1.*"

The course itself mirrors that offered at Nottingham Law School: consisting of three civil briefs and four criminal. Class sizes of around 12 for written skills and no more than six students for oral skills are standard. Students can expect to be in class four days a week with one day off, although this is subject to change, as the increase in student numbers may mean that room availability "*won't be quite as flexible.*" BPTC students can select from seven options, subject to demand. The commercial and advanced civil litigation electives are popular, and the "*majority of students will opt for them.*" After a lagging interest, immigration will not be running. Those who can't wait to test out their advocacy skills can enter mooting and mock trial competitions where past students have enjoyed success in the international arena, reaching the final of the International Court mock trial in The Hague. In addition to bragging rights, a 50% scholarship is available for the Master or Mistress of Moots and there are nine other advocacy-based scholarships as well.

The location of the law school building more than makes up for its less than fancy exterior. Surrounded by the history of Southwark Cathedral, the Golden Hinde and Borough Market, it's also a stone's throw away from cool bars and fine restaurants. At the end of the day it's what's on the inside that counts and Kaplan has fresh classrooms, break areas and mock courts. Students searching for a pupillage can seek advice from Kaplan's careers service, which provides mock interviews and application advice. It also invites guest speakers from the Inns of Court and some of the 50 chambers with which it maintains close links to give talks. A bank of interview questions is also being developed, based on the experiences of former students who have applied to specific sets. Students looking to add a bit of shine to their CVs can get involved in one of several pro bono programmes which include representing individuals in council tax issues at Thames Magistrates' Court. Students can also volunteer one or two days a week at the Kaplan Legal Advice Centre and the school is looking to cement links with FRU. According to sources, around 46% of Kaplan students go on to acquire a pupillage: "*That's without this year's figures – we hope that it will go above 60%, which is three times the national average.*" Kaplan has also produced what is quite possibly the legal world's answer to Guns & Roses; a band called 'Barely Legal.'

Manchester Metropolitan University

Number of places: 108 FT

Excellent links with local chambers make Manchester Met an excellent choice for those looking to pursue a career on the Northern Circuit, although prospective applicants should note that the part-time course has been cancelled this year. Students largely come from the region – "*the Manchester, Liverpool, Preston area*"– and are likely to remain local after completing the course. The list of experienced teaching staff numbers Deputy District Judges, mediators, pupil supervisors and Inns' advocacy trainers: "*People have a lot of experience, and the course remains current because of that.*" Students can also take advantage of additional advocacy classes (delivered by practitioners) and the Continuing Professional Development events hosted by the school for members of the Bar. In the past the law school has even brought in voice coaches and trainee police officers to practise cross-examination.

Full-timers are taught across four days. At the beginning of the course students are split up into nine 'chambers' of 12 and further divided into groups of six for practising of oral skills. These 'chambers' are rotated at the elective stage of the course.

Students alternate weekly between civil and criminal litigation. Teaching focuses on knowledge at the beginning of the week, building up to the relevant skill, such as advocacy, at the end. Some lectures are available online and the school has a variety of electronic support, including podcasts. A dedicated careers adviser and a speaker programme enable students to learn about pupillage and the Bar. Students are also assigned a mentor currently practising at the Bar. Pro bono opportunities include the Personal Support Unit at Manchester Civil Justice Centre, the Manchester Mediation Service, visits to Manchester prison and Partners of Prisoners. Some students volunteer with Amicus, which offers legal representation to death row inmates. Mock trial, interview and negotiation competitions are set up – sometimes on a national scale – for students to develop their skills and CVs. There are also scholarship opportunities available for those who list the school as their first or second choice upon applying. Fees do include the cost of course materials.

Northumbria University Law

School Number of places: 100 FT, 24 PT

The law school campus, situated in the centre of Newcastle, houses state-of-the-art facilities including WiFi throughout, several mock courtrooms and a popular student café – all part of a £106m redevelopment in 2007.

In addition to the usual three-year LLB, the law school also offers a four-year exempting law degree that incorporates the academic LLB and professional BPTC course for students who know early that the Bar is for them. As a result, full and part-time BPTC students study alongside undergraduates. BPTC students can also study towards an LLM in Advanced Legal Practice, which they can now do during a two year joint-programme, in which both the BPTC and LLM are taught side by side. The standard LLM 'top-up' option is still available as well. Ten scholarships, each worth £2,000, are available each year.

Full-timers normally attend four days a week, with Friday designated as a research day. Practitioner evenings are also timetabled in, with members of the Bar speaking on recent developments and offering careers advice. Part-time students can attend on a Monday, Tuesday or Thursday. The majority of students studying the BPTC at Northumbria come from the region, and there's more than a handful of international students thrown into the mix as well. Around 90% of staff are barristers, of which a large majority still practise, helping to keep the course current.

The school prides itself on its pastoral care and every student is assigned a guidance tutor with whom they regularly meet. The school's experienced careers service organises networking events with local chambers and practitioners, group marshalling and a mentoring scheme with alumni. Mock pupillage interviews and a CV workshop on the induction programme should also steer students in the right direction. The school runs an *"award winning"* Student Law Office, which is usually a part of the exempting law degree, but BPTC students are also welcomed to get involved in it during the 'option' phase of the course: *"It's actively encouraged that they do, but students tend to shy away from it because it's so hard!"* Here, students take on live cases, researching, preparing and even presenting them in court on behalf of clients. The law school's 'Grey Society' organises a mix of social and serious activities from pub crawls to a law ball and sports to mock trials and mooting competitions.

Nottingham Law School

Number of places: 120 FT

Nottingham Law School remains a highly desirable destination for BPTC students, who flock to the banks of the River Trent from across the country and further afield, as the school attracts a growing international contingent (around 14% of the cohort). Sources said that *"our numbers have gone up exponentially for the year ahead – we've got some very good students applying."* With so much interest the school can afford to be selective and demands high standards from candidates, who must have a *"fighting chance of getting a pupillage"* to even make it through the doors. This generally means a minimum 2:1 at degree, a forte for advocacy and a commitment to the Bar, so ask yourself: have you got mooting or mock trial

experience and a handful of mini-pupillages/other legal work experience under your belt? You also would be doing yourself a favour by putting Nottingham down as a first or second choice on the application form. Five scholarships worth £2,000 each are up for grabs, and there's a loyalty discount for former students.

Teaching is delivered to small groups of 12 students, but the number decreases to six when it comes to advocacy and conferencing. Students take a set of civil and criminal briefs *"from cradle to grave,"* from interim applications right through to trial, mimicking the progress of a case in practice. Wearing suits and dressing smartly when participating in advocacy or conferencing exercises is an *"absolute requirement,"* and adds to the authentic feel of the programme. Online resources include conference demonstrations, as well as a civil and criminal advocacy video library, where students watch excerpts of their peers' adversarial prowess. The law school comes complete with a new mock courtroom and specialist mooting rooms – *"we've recently moved into the building that houses these rooms, so we very much sit on top of the resources."* The daily timetable varies week in, week out, although students will be in class Monday to Thursday with Fridays kept free for class preparation, mooting, pro bono or work experience. Sources added that: *"We're trialling a more patterned timetable, so students will have absolute certainty as to when they will need to attend in advance."* Popular options include advanced criminal litigation and family, but students tend to remain wary of landlord and tenant: *"Most students can't divorce it from their notion of property law."*

Nottingham houses the only Free Representation Unit (FRU) outside the capital and recently set up an Innocence Project, all of which are fiercely popular among students interested in pro bono work. The school is also in the process of expanding its pro bono unit, and there are two set-sponsored mooting competitions – one civil, one criminal – for students to get stuck into. A pupillage interview training day is organised before the course begins, and barristers from local chambers review CVs, undertake mock interviews and provide feedback to students. Subsequently, on hand to provide support throughout the year is the university careers service (including dedicated BPTC advisors), as well as BPTC staff and personal tutors. Nottingham has a high *"pupillage success rate,"* with 42% of students (out of 84% who responded) gaining a pupillage in 2010: *"It's self-perpetuating – if you have students getting pupillages at all four points of the compass, then it has a positive impact on future students who attend the school."* Escaping the serious nature of the course itself, the law school has an active social scene including welcome drinks with local barristers, a formal dinner in February and a guest speaker programme.

How to fund law school

Despite being met with fire extinguisher-throwing hysteria, the Government's plans to raise university tuition fees have come to pass. It's now completely plausible that you'll be saddled with upwards of £30,000 of debt by the time you complete your undergraduate degree. Given that a GDL, LPC or BPTC course is by no means cheap either, how can you ease the increasingly intimidating financial burden of law school?

Secure sponsorship before starting your training contract

If you're interested in commercial law or want to work at one of the larger firms in the UK, there's a chance you might be able to find a firm that will sponsor you through law school. These firms tend to recruit two years in advance of the start of the training contract so you'll need to get your act together well ahead of time. Not only will such firms cover the cost of course fees (LPC and usually GDL too), they may well give you a few thousand pounds towards the cost of living. Details of what solicitors' firms are offering their future trainees are given in our **Salaries and Benefits** table.

The lucky minority of BPTC students will already have a pupillage lined up. At the more affluent sets, the size of the pupillage award is now comparable with City trainee/NQ salaries. Usually a decent chunk of the pupillage award can be drawn down to cover BPTC expenses. At the more modest sets there may be no money available for the BPTC at all. Further information about funding is given in the **Bar** section of this guide.

Local authority grants

LEA grants are hard to get and very limited. It's still worth finding the contact details for your LEA at www.studentfinance.direct.gov.uk and testing the water.

The Inns of Court

If you're training to be a barrister you can apply for a range of GDL and BPTC scholarships from the Inns of Court. Around a quarter of BPTC students get some funding and there's just under £5m up for grabs. Check out page 672 for more details.

Law school scholarships

Individual law schools have scholarship programmes. Go to our website for details.

Where to study

Studying in London could set you back as much as double what it would elsewhere, say in Sheffield, Cardiff or Nottingham, and the quality of training isn't necessarily going to be any better. Go to our website for tables comparing the prices of all the law schools' courses.

Career Development Loans

First of all, if the loan isn't from Barclays or the Co-op then it isn't really a Career Development Loan (CDL), it's just a bank claiming there will be no repayments to make while you study. Though that may be the case, it doesn't mean there is no interest accruing – it could just be piling up, ready to swamp you once your studies finish. A true CDL allows you to borrow up to £10,000, with the interest paid by the Young People's Learning Agency (YPLA) while you study. Because the CDL interest rate may be higher than another loan, some people recommend taking a CDL and when the interest-free honeymoon is over, paying it off using another unsecured personal loan with a lower interest rate. Unfortunately, the GDL is no longer covered by the scheme, just the LPC and BPTC.

Bank loans

There's a good chance that you've already emptied the last pennies out of your student overdraft, but never fear – you may still be eligible for more debt. Despite the credit crunch, there's still money to be had, so check the interest rates of various banks.

Since 2010 most banks have withdrawn the special packages for customers entering the legal profession; however check out graduate accounts because they sometimes offer slightly better overdraft terms. Lloyds TSB provides loans of up to £10,000 with a repayment holiday of up to three months and repayment is made over a maximum period of five years. RBS's FlexiLoan for Graduates goes up to £15,000 comes with an interest rate based on your particular circumstances. Initial payments can be deferred for four or 12 months (if you have travel plans) provided you have a firm offer of employment. The repayment period is up to five or seven years depending on the amount of the loan. To be eligible, applicants must be or become RBS customers. Whatever you do, don't make any decisions lightly: loans involve a big commitment that only continues to grow once the debt starts to accrue.

Get a job!

Law firms are increasingly interested in applicants' commercial awareness and ability to cope in a professional office environment, so what used to be an undesirable option can now be deployed in an interview as proof of your suitability for a career in law. Be sure to set yourself a manageable schedule and think long and hard whether full or part-time study is the most appropriate way forward. You'll also have to decide whether to work full or part-time.

LSC grants

The Legal Services Commission used to award grants to support individuals wanting to go into Legal Aid practice. Sadly, cuts have put paid to this programme.

Benefits, benefactors, begging...

So bunking up with Ma and Pa during your course isn't a dream come true, yet sometimes needs must. Forget ideas of declaring bankruptcy to evade student debt; consider other creative ways to ease the burden.

- A student card will get you low-cost travel, discount haircuts, cinema tickets and even drinks in some places. If nothing else, it'll make you feel young.
- Websites such as www.studentdiscountbook.co.uk and www.studentbeans.com have discounts and deals for meals, entertainment and more.
- Law books are pricey so don't get overzealous before term starts. College libraries will have the core texts and you're sure to find former students hawking books. Check out notice boards and online for second-hand tomes.
- A number of law schools, chambers and solicitors firms run competitions. Do a google search to find them. Winning may bring kudos as well as cash.
- Market research focus groups will pay decent money for an hour or two of your time.

Some Scholarships

- Many law schools offer funding. For instance, the College of Law offers various scholarships to those studying full-time LPC or BPTC courses. It also offers 60 Gold Awards worth £3,000 for students about to start a GDL who have a First Class Honours degree or a distinction at Masters level.
- The Law Society Diversity Access Scheme supports talented people who face obstacles to qualification.
- Inderpal Rahal Memorial Trust supports women from an immigrant or refugee background. Contact irmt@gclaw.co.uk for more details.
- The Kalisher Scholarship works with each of the BPTC providers to ensure that every year one talented but financially disadvantaged student has a free place on the course. For more information: www.thekalishertrust.org/contact.php
- The Leonard Sainer Foundation provides financial assistance in the form of interest-free loans of £10,000 each, to help fund either the LPC of BPTC. For further information go to www.charitiesdirect.com
- The Student Disability Assistance Fund can award up to £500 for people studying on a full-time or nearly full-time basis. See www.bahshe.co.uk/student-disability-fund/student-disability-fund.html
- Universities and publicly funded colleges have discretionary college access funds available to especially hard-up students. The major LPC/BPTC providers usually have a number of scholarships to assist select students with fees, etc.
- The HM Hubbard Law Scholarship is for trainees and solicitors who want to study the law and legal procedures in France, Spain or Canada. Up to £15,000 a year is available.
- The Human Rights Lawyers Association makes up to five awards from a bursary fund of up to £6,000 to those who wish to undertake unpaid/poorly paid human rights work, either during their training or soon after.
- Leeds Legal runs an essay competition with a prize of £1,000 and a summer placement with a top legal firm.
- The Foreign and Commonwealth Office's Chevening Scholarships are available for overseas students wishing to study in the UK. Happily, the scholarship fund amounted to £22m in 2012, a £10m increase on 2011.
- Postgrad Solutions offers a small number of £500 bursaries for LLM students.

"If you have a clear sense that you want to be a tax, corporate, litigation or administrative lawyer, then go to a law firm that will give you a well-rounded experience in that area. If you don't know what area you're interested in, go to the best law firm you can get into and learn how to become a general lawyer, while you figure out what your passion is."

Rudy Giuliani, corporate lawyer and former New York mayor

Read the interview Giuliani gave our US sister publication Chambers Associate on chambersassociate.com

A-Z of Universities
& Law Schools

Cardiff Law School

Centre for Professional Legal Studies, Cardiff University, Museum Avenue,
Cardiff CF10 3AX
Website: www.law.cardiff.ac.uk/cpls

Contact
GDL: Julie Webb
Tel 029 2087 4941
Email law-gdl@cf.ac.uk
LPC: Kerry Lester
Tel 029 2087 4941
Email law-lpc@cf.ac.uk
BPTC: Lucy Burns
Tel 029 2087 4964
Email law-bptc@cf.ac.uk
LLM in Legal Practice: Julie Webb
Tel 029 2087 4964
Email law-cpls-LLM@cf.ac.uk

Other postgraduate law courses:
The Postgraduate Office
Tel 029 2087 6102
Email law-PG@cardiff.ac.uk

University profile

Cardiff Law School is one of the most successful law schools in the UK and enjoys an international reputation for its teaching and research, being ranked 7th in the UK for research. Cardiff offers opportunities for students to pursue postgraduate study by research leading to the degrees of MPhil and PhD and a broadly based Masters (LLM) programme which is offered in full and part-time mode. Cardiff also has a Pro Bono Scheme which gives students an opportunity to experience the law in action, work alongside volunteer legal professionals and develop transferable skills to add to their CVs.

The Law School is the leading provider of legal training in Wales and is validated to offer the GDL, LPC and BPTC. Students are taught by experienced solicitors and barristers who have been specifically recruited for this purpose. The Law School prides itself on its friendly and supportive teaching environment and its strong links with the legal profession. Placements with solicitors' firms or sets of Chambers are available to students pursuing the vocational courses.

Graduate Diploma in Law (full-time or part-time)

The GDL is a one-year (full-time) or two-year (part-time) course for non-law graduates to convert to law. This intensive course covers all of the essential topics of a qualifying law degree. Completion of the GDL allows you to progress to the professional stage of training – the LPC for solicitors and the BPTC for barristers.

Legal Practice Course (full-time or part-time)

Cardiff has delivered its LPC since 1993 and is highly regarded by both students and employers. Cardiff offers the LPC both full-time (3 days a week) and part-time (1 day a week). Through both courses the Law School provides an excellent learning experience which includes a high degree of hands-on teaching. Placements with solicitors' firms are available to students without training contracts or recent work experience.

Bar Professional Training Course

Cardiff delivers a high-quality and highly regarded BPTC. There is a relatively small student cohort and the course provides a highly supportive learning environment with high levels of individual tutor feedback on all live skills performances. The learning mostly takes place in small groups. There is a focus on the development of Advocacy skills, with two hour classes in groups of six or less almost every week across all three terms. Students are offered two weeks of placements giving them the opportunity to marshall with both a Circuit Judge and a District Judge in addition to undertaking a mini-pupillage.

LLM in Legal Practice

From September 2012 Cardiff is offering a one year LLM in Legal Practice which can be taken part-time or by distance learning. The LLM is open to students who have successfully completed the LPC, BPTC or BVC, whether at Cardiff or another recognised institution. Assessment takes the form of a practice-based dissertation.

Facilities

The Law School has dedicated accommodation for the vocational courses which houses a practitioner library, a suite of class rooms with interactive teaching and audio visual equipment and extensive computer facilities. In addition, the main law library contains one of the largest collections of primary and secondary material within the UK. The Law School is housed in its own building at the heart of the campus, itself located in one of the finest civic centres in Britain.

The City Law School

City University London, Northampton Square, London EC1V 0HB
Website: www.city.ac.uk/law

Contact

GDL
(020) 7040 8301
gdl@city.ac.uk

LPC
(020) 7404 5787
lpc@city.ac.uk

BPTC
(020) 7404 5787
bptc@city.ac.uk

Master Degrees (LLMs)
(020) 7404 5787
law@city.ac.uk

College profile

Located in the heart of legal London, The City Law School is one of London's major law schools and offers an impressive range of academic and professional courses. We're the first law school in London to educate students and practitioners at all stages of legal education.

The school's exceptional legal courses are fully accredited by the relevant professional bodies and are developed and delivered by its team of highly respected practitioners and academics. The school takes a personalised approach to your learning experience and aims to develop you into the professional, dynamic, highly motivated, "practice-ready" lawyers of the future.

Graduate Diploma in Law (full-time)

Started in 1976, this internationally renowned course was one of the first Common Professional Examination programmes (Graduate Diploma in Law) for non-law graduates. The course is designed to provide you with the knowledge and skills traditionally gained from an undergraduate law degree in just one year. The school also offers a two-year Graduate Entry LLB (Hons) for non-law graduates wishing to convert to law. Successful completion of these courses qualifies you to progress to the Legal Practice Course for aspiring solicitors and the Bar Professional Training Course for aspiring barristers.

Legal Practice Course (full-time)

The school's Legal Practice Course has been designed to ensure that you're prepared for the evolving demands of the modern legal profession. You are taught the core legal practice areas and a range of specialist elective subjects face-to-face in lectures, workshops and skills sessions that comprise around 16 hours contact time each week. To ensure that you're ready for practice the school provides a Training Contracts Advisory Service and Careers and Skills Development Service. As our course is taught at masters level, you have the unique opportunity to convert this final award into an LLM in Professional Legal Practice by taking an additional dissertation.

Bar Professional Training Course (full or part-time)

The school's well established and world renowned barrister training is designed to meet every demand of the modern Bar. You are taught at Masters level by accredited advocacy trainers with an emphasis on skills-based training and advocacy. To give students the best possible chance of entering the bar the school offers a specialist Pupillage Advisory Service. On successful completion of the course you are awarded a Postgraduate Diploma in Professional Legal Skills, which is required for you to be called to the bar. As the course is taught at masters level you have the unique opportunity to convert this final award into an LLM in Professional Legal Skills by taking an additional dissertation.

Masters Degrees (LLMs) (full or part-time)

The school's LLM courses give you the opportunity to develop your understanding and expertise in a number of distinct areas of law. The firm offers the following masters: LLM in EU Commercial Law; LLM in International Banking and Finance; LLM/M Jur in International Commercial Law; LLM in International Competition Law; LLM in International Energy Litigation; LLM in Maritime Law (UK); LLM in Maritime Law (Greece); LLM in Criminal Litigation and LLM in Civil Litigation and Dispute Resolution. The School's LLMs are offered on a full and part-time basis, allowing you the freedom to fit your study in and around work, family and any other commitments you may have.

The City Law School
CITY UNIVERSITY LONDON

The College of Law

Admissions, Braboeuf Manor, Portsmouth Road, Guildford GU3 1HA
Freephone: 0800 289997 International: 01483 216000
Email: admissions@lawcol.co.uk Website: www.college-of-law.co.uk

College profile

At The College of Law you'll get the best possible start to your legal career. We are the largest professional law school in the world and, with centres in Birmingham, Bristol, Chester, Guildford, London, Manchester and York, we're the first choice for aspiring modern lawyers. Our innovative courses are designed and taught by lawyers, with a clear focus on building the practical skills, commercial awareness and independent thinking you'll need to succeed in the modern world of law.

Graduate Diploma in Law - full-time/part-time/i-GDL (supported online learning programme)

Designed to build knowledge and skills that more than match a law degree – with a clear focus on preparing you for life in practice. Academic training is built around real-life examples and case studies, and you'll be given research assignments that directly reflect the way you'll work as a lawyer. In addition it's unique Preparing for Practice module equips you with the professional skills you'll need as a modern lawyer.

LL.M Legal Practice Course* - full-time/part-time/ i-LL.M LPC (supported online learning programme)

Our new LL.M in Legal Practice LPC*, as well as being your LPC, is also an internationally-recognised Masters qualification with the scope to specialise in international or national legal practice. This exciting development for 2013 is exclusive to The College of Law and already being endorsed by leading law firms.

We are the only globally-recognised professional law school to offer an LL.M LPC with an increased international focus and an unparalleled choice of 18 electives. In addition, our unique Business of Law competencies framework gives you an understanding of the business drivers of your firms and your clients. By taking The College of Law LL.M LPC, you will be better prepared and more employable for modern legal services than graduates from any other law school. Your LL.M will be recognised globally as the leading qualification in legal services.

* Subject to validation

Bar Professional Training Course - full-time/part-time

Our BPTC has been designed to resemble practice as closely as possible. Study follows a logical, realistic process from initial instruction to final appeal and learning is based around the seven core skills and three knowledge areas stipulated by the Bar Standards Board. Most of your learning will be in small groups and you'll have plenty of opportunities to put your learning into action through: practitioner evenings, mock trials, court visits, mooting, negotiating and advocacy competitions, and pro bono.

LL.M Masters Degrees – i-LL.M (supported online learning programme with no attendance required)/ full-time attendance

Our Masters degrees are truly professional qualifications and reflect cutting-edge approaches to legal practice. We offer a wide choice of flexible, specialist modules to suit your area of interest and enhance your expertise. You can study for an LL.M in either Professional Legal Practice or International Legal Practice.

GDL & LL.M LPC full-time
Apply to Central Applications Board www.lawcabs.ac.uk

GDL & LL.M LPC part-time
Apply to The College of Law admissions@lawcol.co.uk

BPTC full & part-time
Apply to Bar Standards Board (BSB) www.barprofessionaltraining.org.uk

LL.M Masters Degrees
Apply to The College of Law LLM@lawcol.co.uk

Find out more
To open up your prospects in the world of law, join the Future Lawyers Network today. Visit our website at college-of-law.co.uk/futurelawyers65

The College of Law
believing in your future

Nottingham Law School

Nottingham Law School, Burton Street, Nottingham NG1 4BU
Tel: +44 (0)115 848 4460
Email: nls.enquiries@ntu.ac.uk
Website: www.ntu.ac.uk/nls

Contact
Nottingham Law School
Burton Street
Nottingham Trent University
Nottingham NG1 5LP
Tel: +44 (0)115 848 4460
Email: nls.enquiries@ntu.ac.uk
Website: www.ntu.ac.uk/nls

College profile

One of the largest and most diverse law schools in the UK, we are committed to retaining strong links to practice. We seek to ensure that all our clients, from students to experienced practitioners, receive the best practical legal education and training. You will be taught by a unique mix of qualified lawyers with a proven track record in practice and legal education.

Nottingham Law School has a proven track record of graduate employability. Our focus on practical skills, award-winning pro bono scheme and dedicated careers and recruitment service has helped to keep our training contract and pupillage rates consistently high. In 2010/11 88% of our full-time LPC graduates were in legal employment and 90% of our GDL students who also completed the LPC were in legal employment six months after graduating.*

*Source: NLS Careers Centre.

Graduate Diploma in Law (full time or distance learning)

This conversion course is designed for any non-law graduate who intends to become a solicitor or barrister in the UK. The intensive course effectively covers the seven core subjects of an undergraduate law degree in one go. It is the stepping stone to the LPC or the BPTC and to a legal career thereafter. It is possible for the Law School to award a Graduate LLB degree to students who have achieved the LPC or BPTC after completing the GDL with us.

Legal Practice Course (full or part time)

Our highly regarded Legal Practice Course has received the highest possible rating in every SRA/Law Society assessment. This course has been designed to be challenging and stimulating for students and responsive to the needs of firms, varying from large commercial to smaller high street practices. Our Legal Practice Course is designed to enable you to select pathways that lead to a specific type of practice, or maintain a broad based professional legal education if you are not sure yet what practice you intend to move to. In addition to our broad-based LPC, we offer corporate, commercial and public funding pathways. Nottingham's Legal Practice Course allows you to select your pathway after starting the course, rather than commit to a particular route in advance.

Bar Professional Training Course (full time)

Nottingham Law School designed its BPTC to develop to a high standard a range of core practical skills, and to equip students to succeed in the fast-changing environment of practice at the Bar. Particular emphasis is placed on the skill of advocacy. The BPTC is taught entirely by qualified practitioners, and utilises the same integrated and interactive teaching methods as all of the school's other professional courses. Essentially, students learn by doing. Students are encouraged to realise, through practice and feedback, their full potential.

Masters in Law (LLM)

Our taught Masters in Law programme offers a flexible approach to postgraduate study. Offered in both full-time and part-time study modes, students are able to build an LLM to suit their individual needs. Subjects can be studied as single, joint or major/minor awards depending on your area of interest. Pathways include: competition law, corporate law, criminal justice, employment law, health law, human rights, insolvency law, intellectual property law, international criminal justice, public international law, international trade law, sports law.

NOTTINGHAM
LAW SCHOOL
Nottingham Trent University

Solicitors' practice areas

Banking and Finance

In a nutshell

Banking and finance lawyers may work in any one of the specialist areas described below, but all deal with the borrowing of money or the management of financial liabilities. Their task is to negotiate and document the contractual relationship between lenders and borrowers and ensure that their clients' best legal and commercial interests are reflected in the terms of loan agreements. It is a hugely technical, ever-evolving and jargon-heavy area of law.

Straightforward bank lending: a bank lends money to a borrower on documented repayment terms. **Acquisition finance**: a loan made to a corporate borrower or private equity sponsor for the purpose of acquiring another company. This includes **leveraged finance**, where the borrower uses a very large amount of borrowed money to meet the cost of a significant acquisition without committing a lot of its own capital (as typically done in leveraged buyouts (LBOs): read our corporate law section). **Real estate finance**: a loan made to enable a borrower to acquire a property or finance the development of land and commonly secured by way of a mortgage on the acquired property/land. **Project finance**: the financing of long-term infrastructure (eg roads) and public services projects (eg hospitals), where the amounts borrowed to complete the project are paid back with the cash flow generated by the project. Asset finance: this enables the purchase and operation of large assets such as ships, aircraft and machinery. The lender normally takes security over the assets in question. **Islamic finance**: Muslim borrowers, lenders and investors must abide by Shari'a law, which prohibits the collection and payment of interest on a loan. Islamic finance specialists ensure that finance deals are structured in a Shari'a-compliant manner. **Debt capital markets**: this generic category covers many types of debt instruments, but generally speaking it deals with a borrower raising capital by selling tradable bonds to investors, who expect the full amount lent to be paid back to them with interest. [We've written a beginners' guide to capital markets – read it online] **Securitisation**: essentially this is where a lender wants to sell its loans to create liquidity. It does so by selling them to a shell company, which then issues bonds to the markets. Bond investors get paid from the interest and principal on the loans owned by the shell company. **Structured finance**: a service offered by many large financial institutions for companies with unique financing needs that traditional loans cannot satisfy. Structured finance generally involves highly complex bespoke financial transactions. **Derivatives**: at its most basic, a derivative is a security used by banks and corporates to hedge risks to which they are exposed from factors outside of their control. They can also be used for speculative purposes by betting on the fluctuation of just about anything from currency exchange rates to the number of sunny days in a particular region. Futures, forwards, options and swaps are the most common types of derivatives. **Financial services regulation**: lawyers in this field ensure that their bank clients operate in compliance with the relevant financial legislation.

What lawyers do

- Meet with clients to establish their specific requirements and the commercial context of a deal.
- Carry out due diligence – an investigation exercise to verify the accuracy of information passed from the borrower to the lender or from the company raising finance to all parties investing in the deal. This can involve on-site meetings with the company's management, so lawyers can verify the company's credit profile. If financial instruments, such as bonds, are being offered to investors, the report will take the form of a prospectus, which must comply with the requirements of the EU prospectus and transparency directives.
- Negotiate with the opposite party to agree the terms of the deal and record them accurately in the facility documentation. Lenders' lawyers usually produce initial documents (often a standard form) and borrowers' lawyers try to negotiate more favourable terms for their clients. Lawyers on both sides must know when to compromise and when to hold out.
- Assist with the structuring of complicated or groundbreaking financing models and ensure innovative solutions comply with all relevant laws.
- Gather all parties to complete the transaction, ensuring all agreed terms are reflected in the loan and that all documents have been properly signed and witnessed. Just as in corporate deals, many decisions need to be made at properly convened board meetings and recorded in written resolutions.
- Finalise all post-completion registrations and procedures.

The realities of the job

- City firms act for investment banks on highly complex and often cross-border financings, whereas the work of regional firms generally involves acting for commercial banks on more mainstream domestic finance deals. If you want to be a hotshot in international finance, then it's the City for you.

- Lawyers need to appreciate the needs and growth ambitions of their clients in order to deliver pertinent advice and warn of the legal risks involved in the transactions. Deals may involve the movement of money across borders and through different currencies and financial products. International deals have an additional layer of difficulty: political changes in transitional economies can render a previously sound investment risky.
- Banking clients are ultra-demanding and the hours can be long. On the plus side, your clients will be smart and dynamic. It is possible to build up long-term relationships with investment bank clients, even as a junior.
- Working on deals can be exciting. The team and the other side are all working to a common goal, often under significant time and other pressures. Deal closings bring adrenaline highs and a sense of satisfaction.
- You need to become absorbed in the finance world. Start reading the *FT* or the City pages in your daily newspaper for a taster.

Current issues

- The market is still feeling the effects of the credit crunch, with the UK slumping into a double-dip recession – the worst in 50 years by some counts. While hopes are high that the recent Olympics will have injected a much-needed kick, economists are predicting a bleak period ahead.
- With fewer deals being done, many law firms have downsized their banking and finance teams. The big City firms were no exception, but they have fared better than initially expected due to their ability to adapt quickly in tough market conditions. They've had to be flexible, advising clients on recapitalisations and restructurings. Particularly noticeable is the trend for borrowers to buy back their own loans at a significant discount.
- The ongoing European debt crisis, which has been paralysing deal markets in Europe, has also had an impact. Law firms are busy helping financial institutions to navigate current conditions – advising banks on how best to deal with their assets across the globe.
- A package of measures intended to strengthen the regulation, supervision and risk of the banking sector was agreed in September 2010. Basel III will be implemented between 2013 and 2019, and banks are already seeking advice from risk and compliance experts on how to stick to the new rules.
- As we went to print, the ongoing Libor lending rate scandal looked likely to result in increased regulation for banks. In fact, the UK appears to be increasingly following in the footsteps of the US, implementing an avalanche of banking regulation to patch up leaks that caused the financial crisis. Money laundering accusations aimed at Standard Chartered and HSBC in 2012, may also lead to the tightening up of screws in the financial sector. This will have a knock-on effect on banks and their lawyers.

Read our True Pictures on...

Addleshaw Goddard	Linklaters
Allen & Overy	Macfarlanes
Ashfords	Mayer Brown
Ashurst	Memery Crystal
Baker & McKenzie	Michelmores
Berwin Leighton Paisner	Mills & Reeve
Bird & Bird	Morgan Cole
Bond Pearce	Muckle
Brabners Chaffe Street	Nabarro
Browne Jacobson	Norton Rose
Burges Salmon	Olswang
Charles Russell	Osborne Clarke
Cleary Gottlieb	Pannone
Clifford Chance	Paul Hastings
Clyde & Co	Pinsent Masons
CMS	Reed Smith
Cobbetts	SGH Martineau
Cripps Harries Hall	Shearman & Sterling
Davenport Lyons	Shoosmiths
Dechert	Sidley Austin
Dickinson Dees	Simmons & Simmons
DLA Piper UK	SJ Berwin
Dundas & Wilson	Skadden
DWF	Slaughter and May
Eversheds	SNR Denton
Farrer & Co	Squire Sanders
Freeth Cartwright	Stephenson Harwood
Freshfields	Stevens & Bolton
Gateley	Taylor Wessing
Gordons	TLT
Herbert Smith Freehills	Travers Smith
Hill Dickinson	Trethowans
Hogan Lovells	Trowers & Hamlins
Ince & Co	Veale Wasbrough Vizards
Irwin Mitchell	Walker Morris
Jones Day	Ward Hadaway
K&L Gates	Watson, Farley & Williams
Kirkland & Ellis	Wedlake Bell
Latham & Watkins	Weil, Gotshal & Manges
Lawrence Graham	White & Case
Lester Aldridge	Wragge & Co

- Commentators have observed a 'flight to quality' by clients, meaning magic circle firms are getting the lion's share of available work. Clients are also putting their faith (and money) into the hands of 'trusted advisers'.
- Secondments to banks are available, even for trainees, and subsequent moves in-house are common. In the past year many banks have laid off large numbers of their own legal personnel, which has increased their demand for law firm secondees at all levels of seniority. Some firms say this has put a strain on their own resources.

Competition/Antitrust

In a nutshell

It is the job of the UK and EU regulatory authorities to ensure that markets function effectively on the basis of fair and open competition. The rules in the UK and EU are substantially similar, but the UK bodies concentrate on those rules that have their greatest effect domestically, while EU authorities deal with matters affecting multiple member states. The UK regulators are the Office of Fair Trade (OFT) and the Competition Commission (CC); on matters also affecting other EU countries, it is the European Commission. Additionally, there are industry-specific regulatory bodies, such as Ofcom for the media and telecoms industry.

Competition authorities have extensive investigative powers – including the ability to carry out dawn raids – and can impose hefty fines. The OFT has become more proactive and litigation-minded in recent years, and you will certainly have heard about Intel's run-in with the European Commission.

What lawyers do

- Negotiate clearance for acquisitions, mergers and joint ventures.
- Advise on the structure of commercial or co-operation agreements to ensure they can withstand a competition challenge.
- Deal with investigations into the way a client conducts business.
- Bring or defend claims in the Competition Appeal Tribunal (CAT).
- Advise on cross-border trade or anti-dumping measures (preventing companies exporting products at a lower price than it normally charges in its home market).
- Regulators investigate companies, bring prosecutions and advise on the application of new laws and regulations.

The realities of the job

- You won't get much independence; even junior lawyers work under the close supervision of experienced partners. In the early days the job involves a great deal of research into particular markets and how the authorities have approached different types of agreements in the past.
- You need to be interested in economics and politics.

- The work demands serious academic brainpower twinned with commercial acumen.
- As a popular area of practice it's hard to break into. Competition-specific studies – say a master's degree – will enhance your prospects.
- Advocacy is a relatively small part of the job, though you could end up appearing in the High Court or the CAT.
- In international law firms you will travel abroad and may even work in an overseas office for a while, perhaps in Brussels, which is the hub for European competition work. Fluency in another language can be useful.

Current issues

- Competition law continues to increase its profile as greater regulatory activity is undertaken by the UK, EU and USA. The European Commission's record-breaking €1.06bn fine slapped on computer chipmaker Intel made headlines around the world, while the OFT recently ordered airlines and other travel companies to abolish hidden fees for paying by debit card.
- The OFT came under criticism after its four-year criminal case against British Airways for price fixing with Virgin Atlantic collapsed in early 2010. It folded after the OFT failed to disclose key documents. The OFT has come under pressure to reform its approach to offering immunity in return for full co-operation in investigations, as it did with Virgin. Critics have said the agency should perform more of its own investigations, rather than relying on the whistle-blowers. Notably, since 2011 it has carried out more of these 'own-initiative' investigations.
- Partly as a respose to these criticisms, The Department for Business Innovation and Skills has announced reforms to competition law in the UK. The Enterprise and Regulatory Reform bill will bring together the CC and the OFT to create a new Competition and Markets Authority (CMA), which is intended to promote enterprise and free markets.
- The recession has caused a dip in merger control work, but there is plenty of cartel and competition litigation work to be had, particularly in damages actions.
- US authorities are particularly active in pursuing cartels. In July 2010, Ian Norris, former CEO of UK company Morgan Crucible, was convicted of conspir-

ing to obstruct justice over price-fixing charges brought against him.

- Competition lawyers are increasingly drawing on the experience of colleagues, such as financial regulation, tax and litigation specialists. They are also bringing in experts to address white-collar crime aspects.

- The remit of the CAT has been widened to allow claims for damages brought by third parties. Private enforcement can be a useful tool for competitor businesses and consumer groups, but thus far has had limited success.

- There are increased opportunities to work for the regulatory authorities; the OFT, for example, employs many more investigators than before. There is also a trend for lawyers to switch between private practice and working for the regulators.

- As the technology sector continues to grow it's coming under increasing scrutiny from regulators. The CC is currently handling 16 complaints against Google, from companies ranging from Microsoft to TripAdvisor.

- Online service providers are also increasingly on the OFT's radar, especially for misleading pricing infringements.

Read our True Pictures on...

Addleshaw Goddard	Kingsley Napley
Allen & Overy	Latham & Watkins
Arnold & Porter (UK)	Linklaters
Ashurst	Macfarlanes
Baker & McKenzie	Mayer Brown
Berwin Leighton Paisner	Nabarro
Browne Jacobson	Norton Rose
Burges Salmon	Osborne Clarke
Cleary Gottlieb	Pannone
Clifford Chance	Pinsent Masons
Clyde & Co	Reed Smith
CMS	Shearman & Sterling
Cobbetts	Shoosmiths
Dickinson Dees	Sidley Austin
DLA Piper UK	Simmons & Simmons
Dundas & Wilson	SJ Berwin
DWF	Slaughter and May
Eversheds	Squire Sanders
Freshfields	Stevens & Bolton
Herbert Smith Freehills	TLT
Hogan Lovells	Travers Smith
K&L Gates	Wragge & Co

Construction

In a nutshell

Construction law can broadly be divided into non-contentious and contentious issues. The first involves lawyers helping clients at the procurement stage, pulling together all the contractual relationships prior to building work; the second sees them resolving disputes when things go wrong. In the past, the relatively high monetary stakes involved, and the industry trend for recovering building costs through the courts, made construction a litigation-happy practice. Since the 1990s most new contracts have contained mandatory procedures to be adopted in case of dispute. Adjudication of disputes has become the industry norm and these tend to follow a swift 28-day timetable. Others are resolved through mediation or arbitration; however, some disputes are so complex that the parties do still choose to slug it out in court.

What lawyers do

Procurement

- Negotiate and draft contracts for programmes of building works. Any such programme involves a multitude of parties including landowners, main contractors, sub-contractors, engineers and architects.
- Work in conjunction with property lawyers if the client has invested in land as well as undertaking a building project. Together, the lawyers seek and obtain all the necessary planning consents as well as local authority certifications.
- Where the developer does not own the land, liaise with the landowner's solicitors over matters such as stage payments, architects' certificates and other measures of performance.
- Make site visits during development.

Construction disputes

- Assess the client's position and gather all related paperwork and evidence.
- Extract the important detail from huge volumes of technical documentation.
- Follow the resolution methods set out in the contracts between the parties.
- Where a settlement is impossible, issue, prepare for and attend proceedings with the client, usually instructing a barrister to advocate.

The realities of the job

- Drafting requires attention to detail and careful thought.
- It's essential to keep up to date with industry standards and know contract law and tort inside out.
- People skills are fundamental. Contractors and subcontractors are generally earthy and direct; structural engineers live in a world of complicated technical reports; corporate types and in-house lawyers require smoother handling. You'll deal with them all.
- The construction world is often perceived as a male-dominated environment, but while some clients might see a visit to a lap-dancing club as par for the business entertainment course, there are many successful female construction lawyers, architects and engineers who avoid such activities.
- Most lawyers prefer either contentious or non-contentious work, and some firms like their construction lawyers to handle both, so pick your firm carefully.
- A background in construction or engineering is a major bonus because you'll already have industry contacts and will be able to combine legal know-how with practical advice.

Current issues

- After a small rise in activity at the start of the year, the construction sector looks set to see another drop in output in 2012. Thanks to a faltering private sector, and government spending cuts, industry insiders predict no recovery until at least 2014. Big contractors are also beginning to struggle as opportunities to work on large scale projects like the Olympics and Crossrail are drying up. The HS2 rail link between London and the Midlands is one project that is still ongoing.
- Construction disputes are increasing in value. In Britain, the average dispute jumped from £4.8m in 2010 up to £6.5m in 2011. (The same was true of the Middle East where they doubled in value up to a whopping £72m.) Party-to-party negotiation has trumped both mediation and arbitration as the most popular method of dispute resolution.

- House building came to a standstill during the recession, and remains at a lull. There is optimism in some quarters, however: the hope is that having battened down the hatches in the downturn, developers will now have money to spare, perhaps for strategic land purchases of both green and brown-field sites in readiness for a revival in the building market.
- Social housing development became a hot area for firms to try and break into, but this sector is fearful for the period ahead because of cuts in government spending.

Read our True Pictures on...

Addleshaw Goddard	Lewis Silkin
Allen & Overy	Macfarlanes
Ashfords	Mayer Brown
Ashurst	Michelmores
Baker & McKenzie	Mills & Reeve
Berwin Leighton Paisner	Morgan Cole
Bevan Brittan	Muckle
Bond Pearce	Nabarro
Brabners Chaffe Street	Norton Rose
Browne Jacobson	Osborne Clarke
Burges Salmon	Olswang
Charles Russell	Pannone
Clifford Chance	Pinsent Masons
Clyde & Co	Reed Smith
CMS	RPC
Cobbetts	SGH Martineau
Cripps Harries Hall	Simmons & Simmons
Dickinson Dees	SJ Berwin
DLA Piper UK	Slaughter and May
DMH Stallard	SNR Denton
Dundas & Wilson	Speechly Bircham
DWF	Squire Sanders
Eversheds	Stephenson Harwood
Freeth Cartwright	Stevens & Bolton
Freshfields	Taylor Wessing
Gateley	TLT
Gordons	Trowers & Hamlins
Herbert Smith Freehills	Veale Wasbrough Vizards
Hill Dickinson	Vinson & Elkins
Hogan Lovells	Walker Morris
Jones Day	Ward Hadaway
K&L Gates	Wedlake Bell
Kennedys	White & Case
Lawrence Graham	Wragge & Co

Corporate

In a nutshell

Corporate lawyers provide advice to companies on significant transactions affecting their activities, including internal operations, the buying and selling of businesses and business assets, and the arrangement of the finance to carry out these activities. Here are some of the terms you'll encounter.

Mergers and acquisitions (M&A): this is where one company acquires another by way of takeover (acquisition), or where two companies fuse to form a single larger entity (merger). The main reasons for a company to execute an M&A transaction are to grow its business (by acquiring or merging with a competitor) or add a new line of business to its existing activities. M&A can either be public (when it involves companies listed on a stock exchange) or private (when it concerns companies privately owned by individuals). **Equity capital markets**: where a private company raises capital by making its shares available to the public by listing itself on a stock exchange and executing an initial public offering (IPO), as a result of which it becomes a public company (or plc). The London Stock Exchange (LSE) and New York Stock Exchange (NYSE) are the most prestigious exchanges, but companies may list in many other exchanges worldwide. Once listed, the shares can be bought and sold by investors at a price determined by the market. **Private equity funds/houses**: manage multiple investment funds comprising investors who commit capital and mandate the private equity house to invest in numerous businesses on their behalf. **Private equity**: covers a range of transactions in which private equity funds are invested in or used to acquire privately held companies which have potential for growth. Private equity houses typically execute leveraged buyouts, using significant bank loans to complete the purchase of these businesses. A private equity fund's aim is to realise its investment by selling on portfolio companies at a profit or by way of an IPO of their shares on a stock exchange. **Venture capitalists**: groups of wealthy investors who provide capital to start-ups and small companies with perceived long-term growth potential. It typically entails high risk for investors but has the potential for above-average returns. **Corporate restructuring**: involves changes to the structure of a company and the disposal of certain assets, either because the company wants to concentrate on more profitable parts of its business; or because it is facing financial difficulties and needs to free up liquidity.

What lawyers do

- Negotiate and draft agreements – this will be done in conjunction with the client, the business that is being bought or sold, other advisers (eg accountants) and any financiers.
- Carry out due diligence – this is an investigation to verify the accuracy of information passed from the seller to the buyer, or from the company raising capital to the investor. It establishes the financial strength of the company; the outright ownership of all assets; whether there are outstanding debts or other claims against the company; any environmental or other liabilities that could reduce the value of the business in the future. If shares or bonds are being offered to the public, the report will take the form of a prospectus and must comply with statutory regulations.
- Arrange financing – this could come from banks or other types of investors; they will wish to have some kind of security for their investment, eg participation in the shareholding, taking out a mortgage over property or other collateral.
- Gather all parties for the completion of the transaction, ensuring all assets have been properly covered by written documents that are properly signed and witnessed. Company law requires that decisions are made at properly convened board meetings and recorded in written resolutions.
- Finalise all post-completion registrations and procedures.

The realities of the job

- The type of clients your firm acts for will determine your experiences. Publicly listed companies, major private equity houses and the investment banks that underwrite deals can be extremely demanding and have a different attitude to risk than, say, rich entrepreneurs, owner-managed businesses (OMBs) and small to medium-sized enterprises (SMEs). To deal with such clients, a robust and confident manner is required and stamina is a must.
- Corporate transactions can be large and complicated, with many different aspects of the company affected in the process. Lawyers need to be conversant in a variety of legal disciplines and know when to refer matters to a specialist in, say, merger control (competition), employment, property or tax.
- Corporate deals involve mountains of paperwork, so you need to be well organised and have good drafting skills. Above all, corporate is a very practical area of law, so commercial acumen and a good understanding of your clients' objectives is a must.
- Corporate work is cyclical and therefore the hours lawyers work can vary depending on the general state

of the market and the particular needs of the clients, whose expectations have risen even further since the widespread use of instant modes of communication.

- The most junior members of a deal team normally get stuck with the most boring or unrewarding tasks. The banes of the corporate trainee's life are data room management (putting together and caretaking all the factual information on which a deal relies) and bibling (the creation of files containing copies of all the agreed documents and deal information). More challenging tasks quickly become available to driven junior lawyers.

- You need to become absorbed in the corporate world. If you can't develop an interest in the business media then choose another area of practice pronto.

Current issues

- The UK is traditionally Europe's biggest market for M&A deals, but in 2011 their volume fell to the lowest levels since records began back in 2001. This was a 8.17% drop on 2010. A slight uptick was recorded in UK deals, but the vast majority – 75.6% of all UK M&A activity, in fact – was thanks to foreign investments.

- Companies have been finding it more difficult and expensive to borrow money from banks, and there has been far less funding available from non-bank lenders such as hedge funds and pension funds. In such a volatile market, buyers and sellers are finding it hard to reach agreement on the value of assets. The result has been a massive reduction in deal volume and value.

- Leveraged buyouts, financed using a significant amount of borrowed money, saw a particularly sharp decline in value and volume after 2008, but made a comeback after 2010. Private equity players have also increased their focus on restructuring portfolio companies.

- Cash-rich investors have their pick of the best assets and often acquire businesses at a significant discount due to lower company valuations. There has been growing interest from emerging markets investors and sovereign wealth funds, particularly from the Middle East, in acquiring assets in the UK and elsewhere. Although the US is still the largest overseas bidder for UK companies, emerging market bidders like China and India are catching up fast.

- Private equity has become a leading source of finance for buyouts. The UK's market is second only in size to that of the US.

- As M&A activity slowed in 2011, private equity grew to account for 45% of the deals by number and almost 75% by volume, according to a study by the Centre for Management Buyout Research.

- Big-ticket energy work – in both oil and gas and renewables – is on the up and up. Joint ventures between companies are increasingly popular on large projects, and government support for investments ensures greater regulatory stability.

Read our True Pictures on...

Addleshaw Godard	Linklaters
Allen & Overy	Macfarlanes
Ashfords	Manches
Ashurst	Mayer Brown
Baker & McKenzie	Memery Crystal
Berwin Leighton Paisner	Michelmores
Bird & Bird	Mills & Reeve
Bond Pearce	Mishcon de Reya
B P Collins	Morgan Cole
Brabners Chaffe Street	Morrison & Foerster
Browne Jacobson	Muckle
Burges Salmon	Nabarro
Charles Russell	Norton Rose
Cleary Gottlieb	Olswang
Clifford Chance	Osborne Clarke
Clyde & Co	Pannone
CMS	Paul Hastings
Cobbetts	Penningtons Solicitors
Covington & Burling	Pinsent Masons
Cripps Harries Hall	Reed Smith
Dechert	RPC
Dickinson Dees	SGH Martineau
DLA Piper UK	Shearman & Sterling
DMH Stallard	Shoosmiths
Dundas & Wilson	Sidley Austin
DWF	Simmons & Simmons
Eversheds	SJ Berwin
Farrer & Co	Skadden
Freeth Cartwright	Slaughter and May
Freshfields	SNR Denton
Gateley	Speechly Bircham
Gordons	Squire Sanders
Harbottle & Lewis	Stephenson Harwood
Henmans	Stevens & Bolton
Herbert Smith Freehills	Taylor Wessing
Higgs & Sons	TLT
Hill Dickinson	Travers Smith
Hogan Lovells	Trowers & Hamlins
Howes Percival	Trethowans
Irwin Mitchell	Veale Wasbrough Vizards
Jones Day	Walker Morris
K&L Gates	Ward Hadaway
Lawrence Graham	Watson, Farley & Williams
Latham & Watkins	Weil, Gotshal & Manges
Lester Aldridge	Wragge & Co
Lewis Silkin	White & Case

- The fastest-growing sector for UK deal-making is technology. The value of these deals trebled in 2011, from £2.7bn up to £9.3bn.

- A sound grounding in corporate finance makes an excellent springboard for working in-house in major companies. Some lawyers move to banks to work as corporate finance execs or analysts. Company secretarial positions suit lawyers with a taste for internal management and compliance issues.

Crime

In a nutshell

Criminal solicitors represent defendants in cases brought before the UK's criminal courts. Lesser offences are commonly dealt with exclusively by solicitors in the Magistrates' Courts; more serious charges go to the Crown Courts, which are essentially still the domain of barristers, not least because most defendants still prefer this. Everyday crime is the staple for most solicitors – theft, assault, drugs and driving offences. Fraud is the preserve of a more limited number of firms, and the cases require a different approach from, say, crimes of violence. Criminal practice is busy, often frantic, with a hectic schedule of visits to police stations, prisons and Magistrates' Courts meaning plenty of face-to-face client contact and advocacy.

What lawyers do

- Attend police stations to interview and advise people in police custody.
- Visit prisons to see clients on remand.
- Prepare the client's defence using medical and social workers' reports, liaising with witnesses, probation officers, the CPS and others.
- Attend conferences with counsel (ie barristers).
- Represent defendants at trial or brief barristers to do so.
- Represent clients at sentencing hearings, explaining any mitigating facts.
- Fraud solicitors need a head for business as they deal with a considerable volume of paperwork and financial analysis.

The realities of the job

- Hours are long and can disrupt your personal life. Lawyers who are accredited to work as Duty Solicitors will be on a rota and can be called to a police station at any time of the day or night.
- Confidence is essential. Without it you're doomed.
- In general crime you'll have a large caseload with a fast turnaround, meaning plenty of advocacy.
- The work is driven by the procedural rules and timetable of the court. Even so, recent figures show that almost a quarter of trials do not proceed on the appointed day.
- Your efforts can mean the difference between a person's liberty or incarceration. You have to be detail-conscious and constantly vigilant.
- You'll encounter horrible situations and difficult or distressed people. Murderers, rapists, drug dealers, con-

men, paedophiles – if you have the ability to look beyond the labels and see these people as clients deserving of your best efforts then you've picked the right job.
- It can be disheartening to see clients repeat the same poor choices, returning to court again and again.
- Public funding of criminal defence means there's a good helping of bureaucracy. It also means you'll never be a millionaire.
- Trainees in fraud find the early years provide minimal advocacy and masses of trawling through warehouses full of documents. Caseloads are smaller but cases can run for years.

Current issues

- Huge changes in legal aid funding are ongoing and many firms that have previously excelled in crime are moving out of the area entirely or no longer accept publicly funded clients. Firms affected by the cuts (or those looking to pre-empt financial difficulties) are either abandoning legal aid altogether, merging, or shifting their focus from the more high-street criminal cases to fraud and the more serious financial crimes.
- The coalition government's Legal Aid (Sentencing and Punishment of Offenders) Act comes into practice on 1st April 2013. This will cut £350m from legal aid's current £2.2bn budget, and remove entire areas – such as employment and immigration – from the scheme. It was reported in 2012 that criminal barristers were considering strike action in protest at the cuts, which will lead to 500,000 fewer instances of legal help to individuals and 45,000 fewer instances of legal representation. Read more about legal aid on our website.
- When the Legal Services Commission (LSC) introduced a compulsory quality mark for firms wishing to undertake legal aid work in 2000, the number of legal aid firms dropped dramatically, and has continued to fall. In 2011 there were around 1,700 criminal legal aid firms, compared to over 2,900 in 2000.
- A change in police station procedures means the police are cautioning more and charging less in an effort to meet government targets. This obviously has a knock-on effect on the number of available cases. The number of police officers in England and Wales had fallen to its lowest level in a decade by September 2011 – 4.3% fewer than the year before. There are fears that it could drop further, as the coalition government tries to plug spending gaps. After the 2011 London riots, how-

ever, support has increased to maintain or increase the current levels of criminal justice spending.

- The nationwide rollout of the Legal Services Commission's Criminal Defence Service Direct is affecting the amount of work available for solicitors. The CDS now provides telephone advice to those detained at police stations for less serious matters – eg drink driving, non-imprisonable offences, breach of bail and warrants.
- More fraud cases are popping up, and with authorities pushing for criminal charges for competition regulation violations, corporations are facing greater criminal liability. This kind of work tends to go to the firms that have traditionally handled white-collar crime. The Bribery Act 2010, which came into force in July 2011,

Read our True Pictures on...

Forbes	Irwin Mitchell
Higgs & Sons	Kingsley Napley

aims to reform the criminal law to provide a comprehensive scheme of bribery offences in the UK or overseas. Companies are now liable for corruption among staff and – for the first time – associated third parties, so white-collar crime lawyers have been busy advising companies on anti-corruption policies and procedures.

- Check out www.clsa.co.uk for other news and discussion on major developments in criminal practice.

The criminal courts of England and Wales

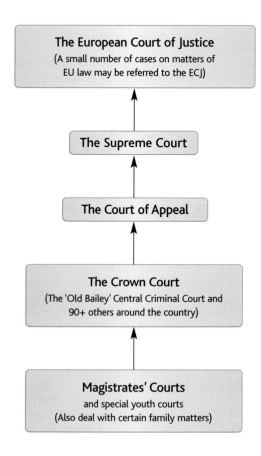

The European Court of Justice
(A small number of cases on matters of EU law may be referred to the ECJ)

The Supreme Court

The Court of Appeal

The Crown Court
(The 'Old Bailey' Central Criminal Court and 90+ others around the country)

Magistrates' Courts
and special youth courts
(Also deal with certain family matters)

Confused by City finance?
A magic circle trainee explains: *"Finance is all about loans. If a business wants to borrow money it can do two things: take out a private contractual loan or raise money publicly through bonds or stocks. Banking is the former. Capital markets is the latter."*

Read more about finance and capital markets on chambersstudent.co.uk

Employment

In a nutshell

Employment lawyers guide their clients through the ever-growing area of workplace-related legislation and are intimately involved in the relationship between employers and employees. The divide between employers' and employees' lawyers is often clear-cut so bear this in mind when you pick your firm. Most will work either largely for employers or largely for employees; a few will straddle both sides of the fence. Usually the job includes both advisory work and litigation.

Disputes are almost always resolved at an Employment Tribunal, or before reaching one, and appeals are heard at the Employment Appeal Tribunal (EAT). The grievances leading to litigation fall into the following broad categories: redundancy; unlawful dismissal; breach of contract; harassment and discrimination. This last type of claim can be brought on the grounds of race, religious or philosophical belief, gender, sexual orientation, disability and age.

What lawyers do

Employees' solicitors...

- Advise clients on whether they have suffered unlawful or unfair treatment and establish the amount to be claimed. This will either be capped or, in the case of discrimination, can include additional elements to cover loss of earnings, injury to feelings and aggravated damages.
- Gather evidence and witnesses to support the claim.
- Try to negotiate a payment from the employer or take the matter to tribunal. If there is a breach-of-contract element to the claim, it might be heard in a court rather than a tribunal.
- If the matter does reach tribunal, the solicitor may conduct the advocacy.

Employers' solicitors...

- Defend or settle the sorts of claims described above.
- Negotiate employment contracts or exit packages for senior staff.
- Negotiate with unions to avoid or resolve industrial disputes.
- Formulate HR policies and provide training on how to avoid workplace problems.

Realities of the job

- You quickly develop an understanding of human foibles. By their very nature employment cases are filled with drama.
- Clients may assume your role is to provide emotional support as well as legal advice, so you need to take care to define your role appropriately.
- Solicitors who want to do their own advocacy thrive here, although barristers are commonly used for high-stakes or complicated hearings and trials.
- The work is driven by the procedural rules and timetable of the tribunals and courts.
- The law is extensive and changes frequently. You'll read more than your fair share of EU directives.

Current issues

- The appetite for redundancy exercises has not tailed off completely, and although it's not as strong as it was in 2008, many clients are still looking to make cost savings by restructuring, outsourcing or simply cutting staff.
- There has been a rise in TUPE work as staff are transferred or outsourced by companies looking to cut costs. In cases where staff have been dismissed or made redundant, or have had changes made to their contracts, there has been more scope for proceedings.
- Employers are more concerned than ever about their staff leaving to set up a competing business, leading to a rise in attempted enforcement of restrictive covenants and confidentiality agreements.
- Some law firms have retained the services of a team of HR specialists or a dedicated hotline to deal with low cost, day-to-day employment queries.
- Many organisations have consolidated their employment legal spend by putting out to tender just one contract and are now looking for a sole legal provider to handle all their needs. This has naturally increased the level of competition between employment practices.
- Employment litigation has risen sharply as a result of a rise in redundancies. Workers have been much more willing to bring whistleblowing and discrimination claims to tribunal proceedings in a bid to force settlement claims from their former employers. Similarly, employers have been more likely to make use of disciplinary and breach of contract charges to avoid making expensive redundancy payoffs. Because of the depressed labour market, many employees have been reluctant to settle at an early stage and made bolder

gambles about extracting higher concessions from their previous employer.

- In response, the coalition government has introduced radical reforms to the tribunal process. More decisions can now be made by legal officers rather than employment judges or a full tribunal. Plus, from April 2012 the amount of time necessary to be employed at a company before being able to take out unfair dismissal charges has jumped from one to two years. Ministers say it will improve what is a *"costly and time-consuming"* employment tribunal system. Employers naturally see these proposals as a good thing; trade unions are angry.

- The default retirement age was abolished in 2011, leading to the number of age discrimination claims exceeding the number of race discrimination claims for the first time ever. It is now third in terms of case volume, behind sex discrimination and disability discrimination. The high average earnings and extravagant bonus schemes of many workers in the financial services sector has led to a spike in employment disputes as the recession continues to bite. The Walker report on corporate governance in the banking industry and changes to the FSA code on remuneration have led to an increased scrutiny of executive bonuses and incentive arrangements.

- Many companies are still leveraging the effects of the recession to make changes at board and senior management level. This has led to an increase in demand for advice on high-value contract termination work from both employees and respondents.

- Businesses are still failing and this has reaped benefits for law firms with a strong insolvency/administration specialism.

Read our True Pictures on...

Addleshaw Goddard	Lawrence Graham
Allen & Overy	Lester Aldridge
Ashfords	Lewis Silkin
Ashurst	Linklaters
Baker & McKenzie	Macfarlanes
Bates Wells & Braithwaite	Manches
Berwin Leighton Paisner	Mayer Brown
Bevan Brittan	McDermott Will & Emery
Bird & Bird	Memery Crystal
Bond Pearce	Michelmores
B P Collins	Mills & Reeve
Brabners Chaffe Street	Mishcon de Reya
Browne Jacobson	Morgan Cole
Burges Salmon	Muckle
Capsticks Solicitors	Nabarro
Charles Russell	Norton Rose
Clifford Chance	Olswang
Clyde & Co	Osborne Clarke
CMS	Pannone
Cobbetts	Penningtons Solicitors
Cripps Harries Hall	Pinsent Masons
Davenport Lyons	Reed Smith
Dechert	RPC
Dickinson Dees	SGH Martineau
DLA Piper UK	Shoosmiths
DMH Stallard	Simmons & Simmons
Dundas & Wilson	SJ Berwin
DWF	Slaughter and May
Eversheds	SNR Denton
Farrer & Co	Speechly Bircham
Freeth Cartwright	Squire Sanders
Freshfields	Stephenson Harwood
Gateley	Stevens & Bolton
Gordons	Taylor Wessing
Harbottle & Lewis	TLT
Henmans	Travers Smith
Herbert Smith Freehills	Trethowans
Higgs & Sons	Trowers & Hamlins
Hill Dickinson	Veale Wasbrough Vizards
Hogan Lovells	Walker Morris
Howes Percival	Ward Hadaway
Irwin Mitchell	Watson, Farley & Williams
Jones Day	Wedlake Bell
K&L Gates	Wilsons
Kennedys	Withers
Kingsley Napley	Wragge & Co
Latham & Watkins	

Environment

In a nutshell

Environment lawyers advise corporate clients on damage limitation and pre-emptive measures, and they defend them from prosecution. In other words, the majority of private practitioners work for, rather than stick it to, big business. Opportunities do exist at organisations like Greenpeace and Friends of the Earth, but these jobs are highly sought after. Another non-commercial option is to work for a local authority, a government department such as the Department for Environment, Food and Rural Affairs (Defra) or a regulatory body like the Environment Agency.

Environment law overlaps with other disciplines such as property, criminal law, corporate or EU law. Environmental issues can be deal breakers, especially in the modern era of corporate social responsibility. However, the small size of most law firms' environment teams means there are relatively few pure environmental specialists around.

What lawyers do

Lawyers in private practice

- Advise on the potential environmental consequences of corporate, property and projects transactions.
- Advise on compliance and regulatory issues to help clients operate within regulatory boundaries and avoid investigation or prosecution.
- Defend clients when they get into trouble over water or air pollution, waste disposal, emission levels or health and safety. Such cases can involve criminal or civil actions, judicial reviews and even statutory appeals. They may also be subject to damaging media coverage.

Lawyers with local authorities

- Handle a massive variety of work covering regulatory and planning issues plus waste management and air pollution prosecutions.
- Advise the authority on its own potential liability.

Lawyers working for Defra

- Are responsible for litigation, drafting of subordinate legislation, advisory work and contract drafting on any of Defra's varied mandates.
- Work in a team of over 80 lawyers, including trainees, on GLS-funded schemes. Defra aims to promote sustainable development without compromising the quality of life of future generations.

Lawyers working for the Environment Agency

- Prosecute environmental crimes – this involves gathering evidence, preparing cases and briefing barristers.
- Co-operate with government lawyers on the drafting and implementation of legislation.
- Work in Bristol and eight regional bases and are responsible for protecting and enhancing the environment. They also regulate corporate activities that have the capacity to pollute.

The realities of the job

- In this competitive and demanding field, all-round skills are best complemented by a genuine interest in a specific area. The way in which environmental law spans disciplines requires commercial nous and a good understanding of corporate structures.
- Excellent academics are essential to help wade through, extrapolate from and present research and complex legislation; so too are sound judgement, pragmatism and the ability to come up with inventive solutions.
- A basic grasp of science helps.
- If you want to change environmental laws or crusade for a better planet, then stick to the public or non-profit sectors. The sometimes uncomfortable realities of private practice won't be for you. Client contact is key and relationships can endure over many years. Environmental risks are difficult to quantify and clients will rely on your gut instincts and powers of lateral thinking.
- With visits to waste dumps or drying reservoirs, and a workload that can span health and safety matters, corporate transactions and regulatory advice all in one day, this is neither a desk-bound nor a quiet discipline.
- Research constantly advances and legislation is always changing in this field, so you'll spend a lot of time keeping up to date.
- A taste for European law is essential as more and more EU directives prescribe the boundaries of environmental law in the UK.

Current issues

- In 2010 the Carbon Reduction Commitment Energy Efficiency Scheme was brought in to put a cap on the amount of carbon produced by organisations. This and other climate change-related legislation coming through is likely to result in an immense amount of regulatory compliance work.

- The EU Environmental Liability Directive was updated in 2009, resulting in more companies taking up environmental insurance. Consequently, firms with an insurance focus have seen an increase in work on this front.
- The Environment Agency has been taking a more stringent approach to clamping down on regulatory offences. Where businesses might previously have dealt with them in-house, lawyers are now being instructed to negotiate with EA. The costs involved can run into the millions.
- An increasingly well-informed public also means an increasingly litigious public. A surge in class actions, usually involving pollution, odour or other forms of nuisance, is being witnessed across the board. Some lawyers speculated that the Environment Agency is slightly more 'trigger happy.'
- The increased focus on renewable energy in the UK has resulted in more work involving alternative forms of power such as biomass, wind farm, nuclear and energy-from-waste projects. With the value of some recent deals reaching hundreds of millions, magic circle firms have been becoming more interested in the sector as well. The energy-from-waste projects are especially topical as they have brought up issues regarding whether waste should be labelled as waste or a fuel.
- ·Climate change isn't just for academics any more. It's a whole legal area in itself. Top-flight international firms are encountering this type of work more often, and international issues are coming to the fore. Initiatives like the Equator Principles and Corporate Social Responsibility are now prominent.
- The carbon trading sector, at least in the UK, seems to be near dead in the water thanks to the recession. Manufacturers have been producing less, which has consequently meant they have needed to buy fewer carbon credits. This is an endemic problem at the moment, and carbon trading specialists are witnessing an all-time low in this type of work. This also means that no new blood/new lawyers have been entering the market, which could result in a dearth of specialists in the

Read our True Pictures on...

Addleshaw Goddard	K&L Gates
Allen & Overy	Linklaters
Ashurst	Macfarlanes
Baker & McKenzie	Manches
Berwin Leighton Paisner	Mayer Brown
Bond Pearce	Mills & Reeve
B P Collins	Nabarro
Brabners Chaffe Street	Norton Rose
Browne Jacobson	Osborne Clarke
Burges Salmon	Pannone
Clifford Chance	Pinsent Masons
Clyde & Co	Shoosmiths
CMS	Simmons & Simmons
Dickinson Dees	SJ Berwin
DLA Piper UK	Slaughter and May
DMH Stallard	SNR Denton
Dundas & Wilson	Squire Sanders
Eversheds	Stephenson Harwood
Freshfields	Stevens & Bolton
Herbert Smith	TLT
Hogan Lovells	Travers Smith
Irwin Mitchell	Walker Morris
Jones Day	Wragge & Co

future. The failure of the Copenhagen Convention also added to the climate change sector's woes in that no real new, substantive legislation or changes were brought in to revitalise or rework the sector and its focus. Speak to a climate change lawyer and they're often quite despondent about the sector's future.

- Keep on top of changes in environmental law courtesy of websites like www.endsreport.com. You should enhance your CV and prime yourself by joining organisations such as the Environmental Law Foundation (ELF) and the UK Environmental Law Association (www.ukela.org). Most environmental lawyers are members of UKELA and students are welcome to attend events across the country. The charity ELF (www.elflaw.org) provides a referral service for members of the public, organises lectures in London and produces regular newsletters for members.

Family

In a nutshell

Lawyers are involved with almost every aspect of family life, from the legal mechanics and complications of marriage and civil partnerships to divorce, disputes between cohabitants, inheritance disputes between family members, prenuptial and cohabitation agreements and all matters relating to children. Whether working in a general high street practice with a large caseload of legally aided work, or for a specialist practice dealing with big-money divorces and complex child or international matters, family solicitors are in court a good deal and fully occupied back in the office.

There is effectively a division between child law and matrimonial law, with many practitioners devoting themselves exclusively to one or other. Some plant a foot in each.

What lawyers do

Matrimonial lawyers

- Interview and advise clients on prenuptial agreements, cohabitation arrangements, divorce and the financial implications of divorce. This can involve issues like inheritance and wills, conveyancing, welfare benefits, company law, tax and trusts, pensions and even judicial review.
- Prepare the client's case for divorce and settlement hearings, including organising witnesses and providing summaries of assets/finances, which will require dealing with accountants and financial and pensions advisers.
- Attend conferences with barristers.
- Represent clients in hearings or brief barristers to do so.
- Negotiate settlements and associated financial terms.

Child law lawyers

- In private cases – interview and advise clients on the implications of divorce with regard to child contact and residence. In some instances this will result in court action. Deal with disputes between parents or other family members over the residence of, and contact with, children.
- In public cases – represent local authorities, parents, children's guardians or children themselves on matters such as children's care proceedings or abuse in care claims. Social workers, probation officers, psychologists and medical professionals will also be involved in cases.

The realities of the job

- When it comes to relationships and families, no two sets of circumstances will ever be the same. Advocacy is plentiful.
- You will encounter a real mix of clients, some at a joyful moment in their lives, others facing deeply traumatic times. A good family law practitioner combines the empathetic, sensitive qualities of a counsellor with the clarity of thought and commercial acumen of a lawyer. You need to retain detachment to achieve the result your clients need.
- Tough negotiating skills and a strong nerve are vital as your work has immediate and practical consequences. The prospect of telling a client that they've lost a custody battle does much to sharpen the mind.
- A pragmatic and real-world outlook is useful, however you'll also need to spend time keeping abreast of legal developments.
- On publicly funded matters you'll face your share of bureaucracy and it certainly won't make you rich.

Current issues

- London is arguably the divorce capital of Europe and the most generous jurisdiction in the world for (usually) women in a divorce situation. International instructions regarding divorce are on the rise as clients with a foot in two or more jurisdictions, not to mention a bundle of cash, seek to get the best outcome.
- There has been an increase in the popularity of prenuptial agreements following the *Radmacher v Granatino* divorce. Prenups aren't automatically recognised by the English courts, but this case saw the Supreme Court rule for the first time that they should have 'decisive weight'.
- In July 2010, the Supreme Court ruled in the Imerman case that claimants in divorce proceedings could not use secretly obtained documents as evidence of their spouse's hidden assets. The court ruled that admission of such evidence breached the spouse's right to confidentiality: many commentators view the decision as a 'cheats' charter'.
- The economic downturn has led to increased demand for advice on wealth protection and some family lawyers report an 'explosion' in the number of cohabiting couples seeking advice on relationship breakdown.
- Taxation is a major theme as, more than ever, clients seek to reach settlements that are structured to mitigate unnecessary tax or other liabilities. As in many other practice areas, it's worth getting close to a tax specialist.

- While it isn't an area traditionally associated with City firms, some have been moving into or developing their family and private client practices during the recession to make up for losses from the corporate sector.
- These are challenging times for the publicly funded lawyer. Many firms are feeling the squeeze and some are choosing to limit, or even cease, legally aided work. This is the case with both matrimonial finance cases and childcare proceedings, although some firms have stuck with the latter on idealistic grounds.
- Social workers are under increased scrutiny and the family courts have been opened up to the press. Many lawyers say that this has made it much harder to do their jobs and has more to do with justice being seen to be done rather than anything else. The family courts have been heavily criticised for the length of time it takes to reach decisions in child law cases.
- In response to an independent review into "*shocking delays*" over family law decision making, the government has implemented a six month limit for the completion of child care cases. Critics say this will have an impact on the quality of decisions, and on childrens' welfare. The government also pledged to pour money into publicly-funded family mediation, in the hope of diverting cases away from the courts. There's little optimism here either – 90% of cases are already resolved before they reach this stage, with only the most serious being heard by a judge.

Read our True Pictures on...

Ashfords	Kingsley Napley
Bircham Dyson Bell	Lester Aldridge
Boodle Hatfield	Manches
Brabners Chaffe Street	Michelemores
B P Collins	Mills & Reeve
Burges Salmon	Mishcon de Reya
Charles Russell	Morgan Cole
Collyer Bristow	Penningtons Solicitors
Cripps Harries Hall	SGH Martineau
DWF	Speechly Bircham
Farrer & Co	Stevens & Bolton
Gateley	TLT
Henmans	Trethowans
Higgs & Sons	Ward Hadaway
Irwin Mitchell	Withers

Insurance

In a nutshell

Insurance is the practice of hedging against financial risk. This practice and its fall-out require a lot of legal work. Insurance and reinsurance (even insurers are vulnerable to financial risk and they transfer part of their risk onto reinsurers) are practised by a significant number of specialist law firms and general commercial outfits across the UK. Insurance can be split into many sub-specialisms (see below). Firms may offer all or some of these services. Personal injury and clinical negligence (including public liability, employers' liability, accident-at-work claims etc.) are also insurance-related practice areas – you can read more about them on page 133. Maritime insurance was the first type of insurance to exist. You can read more about shipping and trade law on page 146.

It's possible to insure pretty much anything against almost any eventuality. Put differently, insurance is taken out to cover risks: human error, accidents, natural disasters etc. The most common types of insurance which lawyers deal with are: insurance against the destruction of tangible assets (eg property), insurance against the loss of intangible assets (eg revenue streams) and insurance against mistakes made by professionals (professional indemnity – the insurance-related bit of professional negligence). So, insurance lawyers work on cases related to property damage, product liability, fraud, insolvency, director's liabilities (D&O), aviation, business interruption, mortgage losses, political events, technology, energy, environment, construction, finance... the list goes on. Disputes arise between the insured policyholder and the insurer; between the insured plus the insurer and another party; or between the insurer and the reinsurer.

Other lawyers specialise in the transactional aspects of the insurance industry, advising on tax, regulations, restructurings, drafting insurance policies, and M&A activity between insurance companies.

What lawyers do

Professional indemnity
- Represent professionals accused of malpractice and their insurers. Professions most often affected include engineers, architects, surveyors, accountants, brokers, financial advisers and solicitors as well as GPs, dentists, surgeons etc.
- Investigate a claim, assess its authenticity and look into the coverage of a given insurance policy to determine an insurer's degree of liability.

- Take advice from experts on professional conduct.
- Draft letters in response to claims.
- Prepare documents for court or out-of-court settlements.
- Attend pre-trial hearings, case management conferences and trials if a case goes to court.
- Attend joint-settlement meetings, arbitrations or mediations in out-of-court cases.

Commercial insurance disputes
- Work on claims related to things as varied as properties damaged by flood or fires; oil rigs destroyed by hurricanes; or mines nationalised by socialist governments.
- Work on disputes between insurers and the insured over insurance pay-outs and what insurance coverage consists of or act for the insurer and the insured together in litigation with a third party.
- Assess coverage and the insurer's liability.
- Interview witnesses to find out how events occurred.
- Value the claim and build up the case for what the client feels is an adequate settlement.
- Attend court or mediations/arbitrations in order to come to a settlement.

Transactions
- Broadly similar to the work of a general transactional lawyer. There are extra rules and regulations governing insurance transactions which lawyers need to take into account.

The realities of the job
- While several legal practice areas fall under the insurance umbrella, the insurance industry itself is a distinct, single block within the City and the UK as a whole. There are a few big well-known insurance companies out there, but over 400 are registered with the famous insurance market Lloyd's of London.
- London is *the* global centre for insurance and reinsurance. It has been ever since Lloyd's of London was founded over 200 years ago. The industry is extremely well-established and has its own rules, traditions and obscure terminology. Businesses based overseas will often be insured with a London firm, and the biggest disputes often have an international angle to them.
- The insurance industry has a reputation for being a bit dull, however the legal side kicks in when calamities occur, making it quite eventful, as any 'wet' shipping lawyer will tell you. It is also home to plenty of colourful characters and big companies organise many events,

lectures and conferences for like-minded insurance-o-philes to rub shoulders.

- Insurance is a complex and technical area. Insurance policies are not the lightest reading material you'll ever come across. Stints in insurance seats are challenging for trainees, even those who have taken an insurance law elective on the LPC.

- Insurance lawyers are known for their precise and fastidious working style. Good organisational skills are crucial, because lawyers are often dealing with a host of claims at various different stages. There are often daily deadlines and clients need to be kept constantly informed.

- In every case lawyers have to pay special attention to potentially fraudulent claims or parts of claims.

- Insurance cases range from huge international disputes to small local squabbles. Trainees might run a small case themselves, but only work on a small component of a large high-value dispute. Lower value work is usually done by small or mid-size regional and national firms, while the largest disputes are the preserve of City firms.

- Many firms regularly act for both insurance companies and insured policyholders. There is a trend towards firms specialising in either policyholder or insurer work.

- The insurance industry is regulated by the Financial Services Authority, which is soon to be abolished. It is not clear what organisation will take over from the FSA as the industry's regulator.

Current issues

- There is an increasing emphasis on using fixed-fee and capped-fee arrangements to save costs both for insurers and the insured.

- You will recall that 2011 was a big year for catastrophic events. From the Arab Spring and the Fukushima earthquake to the aftermath of the Deepwater Horizon oil spill and the UK riots, all had massive insurance implications. In the long-term such disasters will affect the reinsurance market too, causing reinsurance premi-

Read our True Pictures on...

Addleshaw Goddard	Hogan Lovells
Allen & Overy	Holman Fenwick Willan
Ashurst	Ince & Co*
Berwin Leighton Paisner	K&L Gates
Bond Pearce	Kennedys*
Browne Jacobson	Lawrence Graham
Clifford Chance	Linklaters
Clyde & Co*	Mayer Brown
CMS	Mills & Reeve
Covington & Burling	Norton Rose
DLA Piper	Pinsent Masons
DWF	Reed Smith
Edwards Wildman Palmer*	RPC*
Eversheds	Sidley Austin
Freshfields	Simmons & Simmons
Herbert Smith Freehills	Slaughter and May
Hill Dickinson	

*These firms have a particularly strong focus on insurance

ums to rise. The insurance market is called 'soft' when premiums are low and 'hard' when premiums are high because of a recent catastrophe or disaster. (For example, the market 'hardened' after 9/11.)

- The EU's Solvency II directive – aimed at harmonising EU insurance regulations to enhance consumer protection – is due to come into force in 2014. It is already having a major impact on the insurance industry, as companies seek legal advice on compliance.

- Much to the surprise of many observers, the insurance markets have held up well during the recession. Insurance firms are – for the most part – doing well. The recession has led to a slight increase in speculative and fraudulent claims by individuals and businesses looking to make a bob or two, but again not to the degree expected.

- The recession has caused an upsurge in the number of professional negligence claims against mortgage brokers and other financial advisers over their advice on investments and financial products.

Intellectual Property

In a nutshell

Lawyers, patent attorneys and trade mark attorneys work to protect their clients' intellectual property assets. Technical solutions to technical problems are deemed to be inventions, usually protectable via **patents** that provide their proprietor with the exclusive right to stop others working in the claimed area for a period of usually up to 20 years. Preparing a patent specification is a highly specialised task requiring particular scientific/technical expertise and knowledge, combined with experience and knowledge of complex application procedures.

Trade marks used to sell goods or services are protectable by way of a registration procedure and provide a potentially perpetual monopoly right. The aesthetic shape and way a product is designed is also protectable via **registered design** protection for a limited period of time. **Unregistered** rights also exist for a time for various designs of products. Then there is **copyright** which lasts during the lifetime of the creator and for a period after their death, and which arises automatically on the creation of music, artwork, works of literature or reference, databases and web pages, for example.

A single product such as a mobile phone will be protected by several different forms of IP in countries all around the world. For would-be competitors wanting to make or sell something similar, a first costly hurdle is simply finding out what these rights are and who owns them. Worst-case scenario, getting it wrong or overlooking an IP right might result in being on the wrong end of a court injunction or costly damages (fearsomely so in the USA) and ignorance is no defence! The work of an IP lawyer is not only specialist in itself, but increasingly it requires close collaboration with other specialists in areas such as IT, media, competition, telecommunications, life sciences and employment.

What lawyers do

- Search domestic, European and international registers of patents, trade marks and registered designs to establish ownership of existing rights or the potential to register new rights.
- Take all steps to protect clients' interests by securing patents, trade marks and registered designs; appeal unfavourable decisions; attack decisions that benefit others but harm the lawyer's own client.

- Write letters to require that third parties desist from carrying out infringing activities or risk litigation for damages and an injunction.
- Issue court proceedings and prepare cases for trial, including taking witness statements, examining scientific or technical reports and commissioning experiments and tests. Junior lawyers may find themselves conducting consumer surveys and going on covert shopping expeditions.
- Instruct and consult with barristers. Solicitor advocates can appear in the Patents County Court; the advantages of having a specialist IP barrister for higher court hearings are obvious.
- Draft commercial agreements between owners of IP rights and those who want to use the protected invention, design or artistic work. The most common documents will either transfer ownership or grant a licence for use.
- Work as part of a multidisciplinary team on corporate transactions, verifying ownership of IP rights and drafting documents enabling their transfer.

The realities of the job

- Lawyers must be able to handle everyone from company directors to mad inventors. Clients come from manufacturing, the hi-tech sector, engineering, pharmaceuticals, agrochemicals, universities and scientific institutions, media organisations and the arts.
- A degree in a relevant subject is common among patent lawyers. Brand and trade mark lawyers need a curiosity for all things creative and must keep up with consumer trends. Both need a good sense for commercial strategy.
- Attention to detail, precision and accuracy: you must be meticulous, particularly when drafting, as correct wording is imperative.
- In trade mark and design filings and prosecution, everything has a time limit. You will live by deadlines.
- In patent filing, procurement and strategy, you'll need to work seamlessly with a patent attorney. There are hardly any solicitors who are also patent attorneys (and vice versa).
- The volume of information and paperwork involved can be huge on patent matters, though on the plus side you could get the opportunity to visit research labs or factories to learn about production processes, etc.
- The stakes can be big. Commercial research and development in the pharmaceutical sector is motivated by profit not philanthropy. The investment involved will

have been colossal, and even a day's loss of sales can be eye watering. Success or failure in litigation can dramatically affect a company's share price.

- Manufacturing, pharmaceutical and research companies usually employ patent specialists and there tend to be in-house legal teams at all the larger companies. In the media, major publishers and television companies employ in-house IP lawyers.

Current issues

- UK copyright law is becoming increasingly anachronistic, failing to reflect the way that people use digital material. Format shifting, copying tracks from a CD you've bought onto your iPod, for example, is technically illegal.
- The 2011 Hargreaves Report was commissioned to address these problems. The government has approved all of its recommendations, and hopes their implementation will help pull these laws into the 21st century. Just one response is the development of a 'Copyright Hub', which aims to simplify copyright education and licensing.
- The liquidity crisis led to a growing awareness of intellectual property as a valuable asset. Businesses have become more aggressive in protecting their rights and litigation is on the rise. The English courts' reputation for being patent-unfriendly has been challenged by recent judgments.
- International efforts are being made to harmonise aspects of patent procurement. The European, US and Japanese Patent Offices are testing out patent prosecution 'superhighways' to try and streamline the detailed processes of searching and examining patent applications. The European, US, Japanese, Korean and Chinese patent offices are looking at work sharing.
- The EU continues to move closer to getting a pan-European patent set-up, but politics over language has proved a monumental brake on progress for many years.
- Patent litigation costs continue to be a big issue (as highlighted by a £5.2m bill handed to BlackBerry by Allen & Overy in 2008 following a five-day trial) and the judges are most unhappy about it.
- In the trade mark arena many clients are seeking strategic advice on how to tackle the growing problem of counterfeit goods. L'Oréal's case concerning eBay's liability in relation to counterfeit goods sold on its auction site was referred to the ECJ by the French courts. Its decision was heralded as a triumph for luxury brand owners utilising selective distribution channels. The trend for digitalisation is bringing online IP issues to prominence, with the 2011 ECJ referral of *Interflora v Marks & Spencer*, in which the latter bought sponsored links from Google for the words Interflora, Inter-Flora

Read our True Pictures on...

Addleshaw Goddard	Latham & Watkins
Allen & Overy	Lewis Silkin
Arnold & Porter*	Linklaters
Ashfords	Macfarlanes
Ashurst	Manches
Baker & McKenzie	Mayer Brown
Berwin Leighton Paisner	Michelmores
Bird & Bird*	Mishcon de Reya
Bond Pearce	Mills & Reeve
Brabners Chaffe Street	Morgan Cole
Bristows*	Muckle
Browne Jacobson	Nabarro
Burges Salmon	Olswang
Charles Russell	Pannone
Cobbetts	Pinsent Masons
Covington & Burling*	Reed Smith
Cripps Harries Hall	RPC
Davenport Lyons	SGH Martineau
Dechert	Shoosmiths
Dickinson Dees	Simmons & Simmons
Dundas & Wilson	SJ Berwin
DWF	Slaughter and May
Edwards Wildman Palmer	SNR Denton
Eversheds	Speechly Bircham
Farrer & Co	Squire Sanders
Foot Anstey	Stevens & Bolton
Freshfields	Taylor Wessing*
Gateley	TLT
Harbottle & Lewis	Walker Morris
Herbert Smith Freehills	Ward Hadaway
Hill Dickinson	Wedlake Bell
Hogan Lovells	Wiggin
K&L Gates	Wragge & Co

*These firms have a particularly strong focus on IP

and Intraflora. The law in the UK appears unclear on whether buying a keyword that matches another firm's trade mark is lawful. User-generated content is also an issue.

- European patent attorneys and trade mark attorneys now more than ever work as separate professions, but mostly still stick together in private practice partnerships, some of which are LLPs and a very few incorporated.
- While historically some law firms have employed patent attorneys and/or trade mark attorneys, this model has not taken hold widely. Over in the patent attorney profession, there are examples of a more joined-up approach to offering IP legal advice and litigation. Two good examples are HGF and Marks & Clerk. Both have patent and trade mark attorneys now working alongside solicitors' practices. If the new regime of Alternative Business Structures is a hit then the IP advice sector could see some interesting developments.

Litigation/Dispute Resolution

In a nutshell

Litigation solicitors assist clients in resolving civil disputes. Disputes can concern anything from unpaid bills or unfulfilled contract terms to problems between landlords and tenants, infringement of IP rights, construction-related claims, the liabilities of insurers, shipping cases, defective products, media and entertainment industry wrangles… the list is endless. And that's just in the commercial sphere. The most common types of litigation involving private individuals are discussed at length in our personal injury overview.

If disputes are not settled by negotiation, they will be concluded either by court litigation or an alternative form of dispute resolution, hence the interchangeability of the terms 'litigation' and 'dispute resolution'. The most common of these other methods are arbitration and mediation, the former is often stipulated as the preferred method in commercial contracts, the latter is generally achieved through structured negotiations between the parties, overseen by an independent mediator. These methods can still be problematic: mediation is not necessarily adequate for complex matters and some argue that opponents can use it as a means of 'bleeding' money from each other or as covert interrogation.

Confusingly, there are two divisions of the High Court dealing with major cases – the Chancery Division and the Queen's Bench Division (QBD) – and each hears different types of case.

What lawyers do

- Advise clients on whether they have a valid claim, or whether to settle or fight a claim made against them.
- Gather evidence and witnesses to support the client's position; develop case strategies.
- Issue court proceedings or embark on a process of alternative dispute resolution if correspondence with the defendant does not produce a satisfactory result.
- Represent clients at pre-trial hearings and case management conferences.
- Attend conferences with counsel (ie barristers) and brief them to conduct advocacy in hearings, trials and arbitrations.
- Attend trials, arbitrations and mediations with clients; provide assistance to barristers.

The realities of the job

- Work is driven by procedural rules and the timetable of the courts. Good litigators understand how best to manoeuvre within the system, while also developing winning case strategies.
- The phenomenal amount of paperwork generated means that young litigators spend much of their time sifting through documents, scheduling and copying them in order to provide the court and all other parties with an agreed bundle of evidence.
- Litigators need to express themselves succinctly and precisely.
- Unless the claim value is small, the solicitor's job is more about case preparation than court performance. Solicitor-advocates are gaining ground, and once properly qualified they can appear in the higher courts. Nonetheless, barristers still dominate court advocacy and recently the performance of some solicitor-advocates was criticised by the judiciary.
- Trainee workloads largely depend on the type of firm and the type of clients represented. Big City firms won't give trainees free rein on huge international banking disputes – they might not even go to court during their training contract – but they will be able to offer a small contribution to headline-making cases. Firms handling much smaller claims will often expect trainees to deal with all aspects of a case, from drafting correspondence and interim court applications to meetings with clients and settlement negotiations.
- There are a number of litigation-led law firms that handle cases of all sizes and these present the best opportunities for a litigation-heavy training contract.
- The Solicitors Regulation Authority (SRA) requires all trainee solicitors to gain some contentious experience. People tend to learn early on whether they are suited to this kind of work. Increasingly in big City firms, SRA requirements can be fulfilled by a litigation crash course.
- The competition for litigation jobs at NQ level is fierce. Concentrate on litigation-led firms if you are certain of your leanings.
- Despite a few firms like Herbert Smith starting up in-house advocacy units, the courts remain dominated by barristers, who are felt to have the edge when it comes to the skills and expertise needed to advocate. If you are determined to become both a solicitor and an advocate, certain areas of practice have more scope for advocacy – eg family, crime, employment and lower-value civil litigation.

Current issues

- Historically, London has been a popular forum for international litigation and arbitration. Some suggest this could be affected by an ECJ ruling that arbitration anti-suit injunctions are inconsistent with the Brussels regulation, but the sheer volume of cases (and from places as disparate as Russia and South America) does not appear to be slowing. Research in 2010 showed that London was still the most preferred and widely used seat of corporate arbitration.

- Thanks to globalisation, international arbitration is on the up and law firms are bolstering their cross-border capabilities. The recruitment market for hot areas like internal investigations, financial services and international arbitration is at an all-time high.

- Lord Falconer of Thoroton QC predicted a *"tsunami of [post-credit crunch] litigation,"* but the common consensus is that it either hasn't materialised or is taking longer to filter through. Since 2010, though, work has begun to pick up and litigators are generally pretty busy, with the expectation they will become even more so. Insurance litigation in particular has received a boost as more claims are filed and subsequently challenged.

- If there are any litigation tsunamis on the horizon, they're likely to be in response to the Libor scandal. Experts are predicting this will hit the courts hard, with comparisons being drawn to the tobacco litigation which dragged from the 1950s up to 1998 when final settlement was reached.

- Several major cases concern Russian oligarchs and matters from the former CIS, as well as finance-related disputes in the BVI. The bank charges litigation was among the biggest disputes to hit the English courts in recent years, with more or less everyone who's anyone involved. The ruckus over Payment Protection Insurance (PPI) has also been huge for the legal industry, with PPI being the most complained about financial product ever. £1.9bn was paid to victims of the mis-sold product in 2011, and experts estimate there's another £5bn still to be compensated.

- In 2011 the government announced its intention to implement the majority of the Jackson Report's proposals to reduce the costs of civil litigation. This will include reducing the burden of costs on defendants, for example by no longer allowing successful claimants to recover success fees to pay their lawyers from the losing party.

- Third-party litigation funding is emerging. Essentially an organisation that is not involved in a case, say a bank or private equity company, can choose to bank roll the cost of litigation for a share of the winnings.

- The challenges London now faces as an arbitration venue relate to costs and the increasing popularity of other locations, particularly Singapore. Some people worry that emerging economies such as China and India will look east for their preferred venue. Even if Singapore does become more popular, English law will still play a part, meaning UK arbitration lawyers would be likely to spend more time in Singapore.

- Bigger UK firms and US firms in London are handling more arbitration advocacy in-house and not instructing the bar. There is debate as to how successful and effective this is, but it's certainly something these firms are pushing, especially for more run-of-the-mill cases.

Read our True Pictures on...

Addleshaw Goddard	Holman Fenwick Willan
Allen & Overy	Ince & Co
Ashfords	Irwin Mitchell
Ashurst	Jones Day
Baker & McKenzie	K&L Gates
Berwin Leighton Paisner	Latham & Watkins
Bevan Brittan	Lawrence & Graham
Bird & Bird	Linklaters
Bond Pearce	Macfarlanes
Brabners Chaffe Street	Manches
Bristows	Mayer Brown
Burges Salmon	Michelmores
Charles Russell	Mills & Reeve
Cobbetts	Mishcon de Reya
Cleary Gottlieb	Morgan Cole
Clifford Chance	Muckle
Clyde & Co	Nabarro
Covington & Burling	Norton Rose
Cripps Harries Hall	Olswang
Dechert	Pannone
Dickinson Dees	Pinsent Masons
Dundas & Wilson	Reed Smith
DWF	RPC
Edwards Wildman Palmer	SGH Martineau
Eversheds	Shoosmiths
Farrer & Co	Sidley Austin
Freshfields	Simmons & Simmons
Gateley	Skadden
Gordons	Slaughter and May
Herbert Smith	SNR Denton
Hill Dickinson	Squire Sanders
Higgs & Sons	Stephenson Harwood
Hogan Lovells	

The civil courts of England and Wales

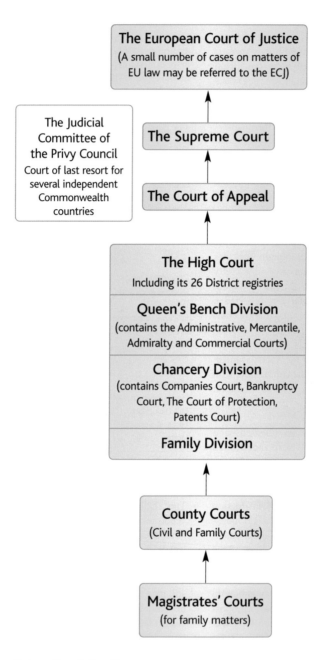

The European Court of Justice
(A small number of cases on matters of EU law may be referred to the ECJ)

The Supreme Court

The Judicial Committee of the Privy Council
Court of last resort for several independent Commonwealth countries

The Court of Appeal

The High Court
Including its 26 District registries

Queen's Bench Division
(contains the Administrative, Mercantile, Admiralty and Commercial Courts)

Chancery Division
(contains Companies Court, Bankruptcy Court, The Court of Protection, Patents Court)

Family Division

County Courts
(Civil and Family Courts)

Magistrates' Courts
(for family matters)

Other Specialist Courts

Employment Tribunals
Lands Tribunals
Leasehold Valuation Tribunals

VAT and Duties Tribunals
General and Special Commissioners (Tax)
Asylum & Immigration Tribunals

Europe

ECJ: Any UK court can refer a point of law for determination if it relates to EU law. The decision will be referred back to the court where the case originated.

European Court of Human Rights: Hears complaints regarding breaches of human rights.

Pensions

In a nutshell

Pensions law revolves around long-term management of large sums of money. Pensions lawyers advise on the creation, structure and funding of pension schemes, their management and resolving any associated disputes. Often created under the form of a trust, pensions are highly regulated and governed by a vast amount of complex and ever-changing legislation. Solicitors typically advise employers, trustees of pension funds, and pension providers.

There are several different types of pension scheme that individuals may buy into; broadly these can be divided into 'occupational pensions' and 'personal' or 'individual' pensions. All employers will soon be required to offer their employees membership of a pension scheme and from 2012 employees will start to be automatically enrolled into a scheme. An overwhelming majority of individuals who contribute to this form of retirement saving will be a member of an employer-sponsored occupational pension, not least because companies contribute to the pension pot.

Most pensions are subject to specialist tax regimes, which makes them very attractive as long-term investments. Members are entitled to tax relief on contributions and a tax free allowance applies to pension income. Solicitors structure pension funds to take maximum advantage of the tax regime, and advise on compliance with the law and regulations in this area.

Pensions teams also work very closely with a law firm's employment and corporate departments. Mergers and acquisitions of businesses may involve the movement of employees from one company to another, alongside the assets, etc, of the target company. This change of ownership will have implications on who has responsibility for funding the pension schemes and questions over which employees (old or new) can become members of a scheme and whether the target company's pension scheme will even continue to exist or if it will be merged into or amended to mirror that of the bidding company.

Pension funds need to be well funded, managed and invested for the money to grow and support the fund's members in their retirement. The difficult economic climate recently has had an impact on pension schemes, with low return on investments contributing to funding deficits in pension funds. Pensioners are living longer than had been predicted or planned for and some compa-nies are struggling to find the resources to keep paying members' pensions for longer periods of retirement alongside funding the scheme for current employees. Such issues affect the public sector just as much as private enterprise – see Royal Mail, for example, which in 2009 had a £10.3bn deficit in its pension fund. Pensions lawyers help companies with restructuring and re-funding their pension schemes where there is such a shortfall and advise on the particular issues arising where companies collapse. Public sector occupational pensions are also subject to the will of the government and lawyers have to be able to anticipate and negotiate amendments to schemes.

Most pension schemes are set up in the form of a trust and therefore strict rules apply to those in charge of administering the money. Trustees often seek legal advice on the discharge of their duties and litigation frequently occurs where they or other parties have failed to administer the funds diligently.

One of the best examples of financial mismanagement is the Equitable Life scandal, which lost its members millions of pounds.

What lawyers do

- Draft documentation relating to the creation, amendment, closure or freezing (closing funds to new members) of pension funds.
- Advise employers on their obligations towards members and pension funds.
- Advise on who can become a member of a pension fund, and when to pay out of a fund.
- Advise on restructuring or securing pension funds which are underfunded or in financial difficulties, including on issues associated with the Pension Protection Fund.
- Advise on regulatory and legislative compliance with tax regimes.
- Handle disputes and litigation related to pension schemes.
- Advise trustees of pension funds on their duties.
- Advise companies, pensions providers and trustees on their interactions with the Pensions Regulator, which regulates UK work-based pension schemes.
- Assist the corporate teams on M&A deals by undertaking due diligence on potential liabilities.
- Negotiating amendments to pension plans with clients.

The realities of the job

- If you're working to corporate deal timetables then the hours can be long.
- Pensions law is technical, highly regulated and often closely intertwined with tax law, which means a lot of time spent reading and interpreting complex statute books. A keen eye and ability to understand very technical information is essential.
- Pensions lawyers need to think long-term and anticipate what policy decisions and legislative proposals the government may make in the area.
- Contentious negotiations (especially in the public sector) with employee representatives/trade union representatives over proposed amendments to employees' pension plans.
- Clients calling every day for advice on small issues such as when to pay funds out of a pension scheme.
- Pensions lawyers need to be personable and able to explain complex law in layman's terms.

Current issues

- Contentious issues surrounding abolishing the compulsory retirement age and raising the age at which individuals can access state pensions. In 2012, it was announced that between 2026 and 2028 the retirement age will be raised to 67.
- As the UK population is living longer, defined benefit (or final salary) pensions are becoming unsustainable for employers to fund. Such schemes are either being closed to new members or wound up completely.
- In order to fund these pension schemes, employers are having to find alternative funding methods such as using the company's assets as security for pension fund.
- The duties owed by the employer funding a pension scheme to its members and how far the employer can

Read our True Pictures on...

Addleshaw Goddard	Linklaters
Allen & Overy	Macfarlanes
Ashurst	Mayer Brown
Baker & McKenzie	Mills & Reeve
Berwin Leighton Paisner	Nabarro
Bond Pearce	Norton Rose
Burges Salmon	Osborne Clarke
Clifford Chance	Pinsent Masons
CMS	Reed Smith
Cobbetts	Shoosmiths
Dickinson Dees	Simmons & Simmons
DLA Piper	Slaughter and May
DWF	SNR Denton
Eversheds	Speechly Bircham
Freshfields	Squire Sanders
Gateley	Stephenson Harwood
Herbert Smith	Taylor Wessing
Hill Dickinson	TLT
Hogan Lovells	Travers Smith
Jones Day	Ward Hadaway
Lawrence Graham	Wragge & Co

consider its own interests when exercising its powers. An example of this is the decision in the 2011 Prudential case, which concerned the employer's discretion over the level of annual pension increases.
- Government changes allowing schemes to change the rate of indexation from the Retail Prices Index to the Consumer Prices Index, which may reduce the pressure on scheme funding.
- How to fund state pensions in the future – almost half of working age adults don't have a pension.
- Automatic Enrolment of employees on to company pension schemes from 2012, making it compulsory for anyone between 22 and state pension age earning more than £8,105 a year to begin to put money away.

Personal Injury and Clinical Negligence

In a nutshell

Personal injury and clinical negligence lawyers resolve claims brought by people who have been injured, either as a result of an accident or through flawed medical treatment. The claimant lawyer usually acts for one individual, but sometimes a claim may be brought by a group of people – this is a class action or multiparty claim. The defendant lawyer represents the party alleged to be responsible for the illness or injury. In most PI cases the claim against the defendant will be taken over by the defendant's insurance company, which will then be the solicitor's client. Local authorities are common defendants in relation to slips and trips, while employers usually end up on the hook for accidents in the workplace. In a majority of clinical negligence cases the defendant will be the NHS, although private medical practitioners and healthcare organisations are also sued.

What lawyers do

Claimant solicitors
- Determine the veracity of their client's claim and establish what they have suffered, including income lost and expenses incurred.
- Examine medical records and piece together all the facts. Commission further medical reports.
- Issue court proceedings if the defendant doesn't make an acceptable offer of compensation.

Defendant solicitors
- Try and avoid liability for their client or resolve a claim for as little as possible.
- Put all aspects of the case to the test. Perhaps the victim of a road traffic accident (RTA) wasn't wearing a seatbelt. Perhaps the claimant has been malingering.

Both
- Manage the progress of the case over a period of months, even years, following an established set of procedural rules.
- Attempt to settle the claim before trial or, if a case goes to trial, brief a barrister and shepherd the client through the proceedings.

The realities of the job
- The work is driven by the procedural rules and timetable of the court.
- There is a mountain of paperwork, including witness statements and bundles of evidence.

- Claimant lawyers have close contact with large numbers of clients and need good people skills.
- Defendant lawyers need to build long-term relationships with insurance companies. Clin neg defendant lawyers need to be able to communicate well with medical professionals and health sector managers.
- PI lawyers have large caseloads, especially when dealing with lower-value claims.
- There is some scope for advocacy, although barristers are used for high-stakes or complicated hearings and trials. Solicitors appear at preliminary hearings and case management conferences.

Current issues
- In 2011 the government announced its intention to implement most of the Jackson Report's proposals aimed at reducing the cost of civil litigation. PI and clin neg are two areas which will likely be most affected by the changes, which include no longer allowing successful claimants to recover success fees from the losing party. Instead, they will have to pay their lawyers' success fees out of the damages they receive, which will likely mean they will be more interested in controlling costs. This will obviously have a profound effect on 'no win, no fee' arrangements. After the event (ATE) insurance will also be abolished, and more of the report's recommendations may be introduced in the near future.
- Claims management companies remain a controversial issue. Some practitioners see their involvement as a way to counter-act the potential challenges from the entry of big high street names into the legal market when the Legal Services Act takes effect. The Jackson Report recommended banning the paying of referral fees to brokers and claims management companies, and there was some surprise that the issue was not addressed along with many of Jackson's suggestions in the 2011 Justice Bill.
- It remains to be seen what the impact of the imminent implementation of the Legal Services Act will be for the personal injury market. The opening up of the legal market to Alternative Business Structures may have a significant impact upon this practice area, as individual clients on the claimant side could be an ideal target group for the kind of service which might be offered by big high-street names entering the legal market. Following the change of government it is possible that certain aspects of the Act may be altered, but currently it seems likely that at least the central ideas will remain.

- There has been a rise in the number of clinical negligence claims being brought. This may be attributed to the recession, with people in need of money more likely to pursue claims that they would otherwise not. Alternatively it may be due to the greater availability of funding through conditional fee arrangements, as well as greater public awareness of the feasibility of making a claim.
- Some concerns have been expressed about the quality of the defence available to clinicians. The NHS Litigation Authority continues to reduce the number of firms on its panel, and increasingly demands that those that remain adhere to very strict rules when responding to claims.

Read our True Pictures on...

Baker & McKenzie	Mills & Reeve
Baker Wells & Braithwaite	Michelmores
Browne Jacobson*	Mayer Brown International
Bevan Brittan	Mills & Reeve
Burges Salmon	Morgan Cole
Clyde & Co	Nabarro
Capsticks Solicitors*	Pinsent Masons
Charles Russell	Penningtons Solicitors
Dundas & Wilson	Pannone*
DWF*	RPC
Eversheds	Shoosmiths*
Freeth Cartwright*	Stevens & Bolton
Herbert Smith	Taylor Wessing
Henmans	TLT
Higgs & Sons	Trethowans
Hill Dickinson	Veale Wasbrough Vizards
Irwin Mitchell*	Ward Hadaway
Kennedys	Wragge & Co
Kingsley Napley	

*These firms have a particularly strong focus on PI and clin neg

Private Client and Charities

In a nutshell

You have money. You need to know how best to control it, preserve it and pass it on: enter the private client lawyer. Solicitors advise individuals, families and trusts on wealth management. Some offer additional matrimonial and small-scale commercial assistance; others focus exclusively on highly specialised tax and trusts issues, or wills and probate.

Charities lawyers advise on all aspects of non-profit organisations' activities. These specialists need exactly the same skills and knowledge as private client lawyers, but must also have the same kind of commercial knowledge as corporate lawyers.

What lawyers do

Private client lawyers
- Draft wills in consultation with clients and expedite their implementation after death. Probate involves the appointment of an executor and the settling of an estate. Organising a house clearance or even a funeral is not beyond the scope of a lawyer's duties.
- Advise clients on the most tax-efficient and appropriate structure for holding money and assets. Lawyers must ensure their clients understand the foreign law implications of trusts held in offshore jurisdictions.
- Advise overseas clients interested in investing in the UK, and banks whose overseas clients have UK interests.
- Assist clients with the very specific licensing, sales arrangements and tax planning issues related to ownership of heritage chattels (individual items or collections of cultural value or significance).
- Bring or defend litigation in relation to disputed legacies.

Charities lawyers
- Advise charities on registration, reorganisation, regulatory compliance and the implications of new legislation.
- Offer specialist trusts and investment advice.
- Advise on quasi-corporate and mainstream commercial matters; negotiate and draft contracts for sponsorship and the development of trading subsidiaries; manage property issues and handle IP concerns.
- Charities law still conjures up images of sleepy local fund-raising efforts or, alternatively, working on a trendy project for wealthy benefactors. The wide middle ground can incorporate working with a local authority, a local library and schools to establish an after-school homework programme, or rewriting the constitution of a 300-year-old church school to admit female pupils. Widespread international trust in British charity law means that you could also establish a study programme in Britain for a US university, or negotiate the formation of a zebra conservation charity in Tanzania.

The realities of the job

- An interest in other people's affairs is going to help. A capacity for empathy coupled with impartiality and absolute discretion are the hallmarks of a good private client lawyer. You'll need to be able to relate to and earn the trust of your many varied clients.
- Despite not being as chaotic as other fields, the technical demands of private client work can be exacting and an academic streak goes a long way.
- The stereotype of the typical 'country gent' client is far from accurate: lottery wins, personal injury payouts, property portfolios, massive City salaries and successful businesses all feed the demand for legal advice.
- If you are wavering between private clients and commercial clients, charities law might offer a good balance.

Current issues

- Private client work has become more popular in the City during the recession, as a way of making up for losses from the decrease in the amount of corporate work available, and taking advantage of the fact that private investors have been filling the void left by diminished corporate funds.
- The private client world is becoming increasingly international. Wealthy people are selecting a wider geographical spread of assets, and London has become a hub for the management of these assets. Many clients come from Russia, the Middle East, the USA, India and France. The Finance Act 2008, which applies strict and complex tax rules to non-UK domiciliaries ('non-doms'), combined with the newly introduced 50% income tax rate, caused some high net worth individuals to consider leaving the UK. Those who've opted to stay have sought advice on restructuring their wealth. The tax rate will drop to 45% in 2013, but either way the UK is still an attractive destination for foreign domiciled individuals to move to, and those wishing to do so have provided a steady flow of work.
- 2009 saw further pressure being applied to offshore financial centres in an attempt to obtain greater transparency as to the ownership and taxation of funds held

there. This resulted in many enquiries about the implications of the rapidly expanding network of international tax information exchange agreements and the consequences for those compliant individuals and families who legitimately wished to maintain their privacy. In addition, 2009 also saw greater efforts by the governments of western economies to facilitate the return of funds to their domestic economies by offering amnesties for the return of undeclared funds.

- More firms have dedicated teams handling legacy disputes. The RSPCA, for example, has been actively involved in these types of claim.
- After a long wait, the Charities Act 2006 was finalised. The Act addresses fundamental questions about what constitutes a charity and what 'public benefit' means. It also provides for greater regulation in some areas, and greater freedom for charities in others.
- Economic uncertainty has brought many challenges for charities, particularly the large ones that rely heavily on public donations and/or government funding. Some charities have seen their budgets cut by up to 40% as a result of a reduction in corporate donations. As a result, many charities are restructuring or becoming more innovative with fund-raising, while others look towards collaborative working with other charities.
- There's been an upswing in charities mergers. The 2002 merger of Cancer Research and Macmillan proved it to be possible, and in 2008 there were almost 500 mergers registered with the Charity Commission. One of the most publicised combinations was that of Age Concern and Help the Aged, to form Age UK.
- Other matters concerning charities are conflicts of interests, 'whistle blowing' and information management. A theme running through these areas is getting governance right – something that tends to come into focus in harder economic times. Economic difficulties aside, the UK is the second-largest charitable donor in the world.
- The government is introducing measures to increase legacy giving, as part of its 'Big Society' agenda. These include a 10% inheritance tax break for those who donate at least 10% of their estate to charity, improving the way donors are thanked, and simplifying donation rules.

Read our True Pictures on...

Addleshaw Goddard	Irwin Mitchell
Ashfords	Lawrence Graham
Baker & McKenzie	Lester Aldridge
Bates Wells & Braithwaite	Macfarlanes*
Berwin Leighton Paisner	Manches
Bircham Dyson Bell*	Michelmores
Boodle Hatfield*	Mills & Reeve
B P Collins	Mischon de Reya*
Brabners Chaffe Street	Morgan Cole
Browne Jacobson	Muckle
Burges Salmon	Pannone
Charles Russell*	Penningtons Solicitors*
Cobbetts	Pinsent Masons
Collyer Bristow*	SGH Martineau
Cripps Harries Hall*	Shoosmiths
Dickinson Dees	Speechly Bircham*
Dundas & Wilson	Stevens & Bolton
DWF	Taylor Wessing
Farrer & Co*	TLT
Freeth Cartwright	Trethowans
Gateley	Trowers & Hamlins
Gordons	Veale Wasbrough Vizards*
Henmans*	Ward Hadaway
Hill Dickinson	Wilsons*
Higgs & Sons	Withers*

*These firms have a particularly strong focus on private client and charities.

- Loss of exempt charity status has affected numerous organisations – schools, religious institutions and museums, among others.
- The introduction of Alternative Business Structures may harm the revenue streams of smaller firms working on will drafting and probate. Some may not survive the increased competition while others may merge, forming a united front against the challenge of 'Tesco Law'.
- In the 2011 budget, the coalition government doubled the lifetime allowance for entrepreneurs' relief to £10m.
- Firms right across the country bemoan a dearth of young lawyers who can claim to be true private client specialists. It looks like a good time to put your hand up and be counted.

Projects and Energy

In a nutshell

Projects

Projects lawyers work hand in hand with finance and corporate lawyers to enable projects to come to fruition. A few City firms and the largest US practices dominate the biggest international projects, but there's work country-wide. Many projects relate to the energy sector (see below) while road, rail and telecoms infrastructure projects are also big business. UK lawyers also work on overseas natural resources and mining projects, while domestically sewage and utilities projects provide work for many regional firms. The Private Finance Initiative (PFI) – an aspect of Public Private Partnerships (PPP) – has also been an important source of work. PFI introduced private funding and management into areas that were previously public sector domains.

Some law firms consistently represent the project companies, usually through a 'special purpose vehicle' (SPV) established to build, own and operate the end result of the project. Often the project company is a joint venture between various 'sponsor' companies. An SPV could also be partially owned by a government body or banks. Other firms consistently represent the organisations that commission projects. Then there are the firms that act purely on the finance side for banks, guarantors, export credit agencies, governments and international funding agencies.

Energy

If a firm has an energy practice most of its work will be based around oil and gas. This breaks down into upstream and downstream work. Upstream refers to the locating and exploiting of oil and gas fields (think 'drill, baby, drill' and you get the picture). Downstream refers to everything related to transport, processing and distribution – pipelines, refineries, petrol stations etc. Many firms that do energy work trumpet their renewable energy and climate change expertise but at any firm this will be a very small practice area. Power and utilities, and environment/regulatory are two other areas which are sometimes considered to fall under the energy umbrella.

What lawyers do

Projects

- The work of an energy or projects lawyer mirrors that of a corporate lawyer – drafting, due diligence, getting parties to sign agreements – with several added layers of complexity.

- There are several components to any project: financing, development and (often) subsequent litigation. Lawyers usually specialise in one of these areas, although they do overlap.
- The field also encompasses specialists in areas like construction, real estate, planning, telecoms, healthcare and the public sector.
- The financing of a project is riskier for lenders than other transactions are, as there is no collateral to act as security for the loan. For this reason risk is often spread across several stakeholders including the SPV, shareholders, the contractor, supplier etc. The agreements which govern the relationship between the parties are the primary domain of lawyers acting for the project company.
- Lawyers who act for lenders check over all project documentation paying attention to the risks the lender is exposed to.
- Site visits and meetings on location are common.

Energy

- Internationally, energy lawyers work on the contracts and licences agreed between international energy companies, governments and local companies. The upstream component of energy work often involves governments, as they have the exclusive rights to certain natural resources.
- Domestically, lawyers often interact with the Department for Energy and Climate Change (DECC). Energy is a highly regulated sector, and there are many government programs and stimuli to encourage certain types of energy projects. EU regulations also frequently come into play.
- Some energy lawyers work on energy infrastructure projects, but usually an energy lawyer is someone who works on contracts and agreements over (oil and gas) resources already being tapped. For example, they might produce so-called Production Sharing Agreements, which detail which proportion of profits go to different parties.
- Because energy companies have very deep pockets, many energy financings happen without the need for a loan (this is called 'off-balance-sheet financing').
- Disputes in the energy sector are often resolved through arbitration, particularly when they have an international element to them (which is often).

The realities of the job

- Projects require lawyers who enjoy the challenge of creating a complex scheme and figuring out all its possibilities and pitfalls. Projects can run for years, involving multidisciplinary legal work spanning finance, regulatory permissions, construction, employment law and much more.
- The value of transactions can vary from a few million pounds for projects to build domestic waste plants to deals worth billions to exploit massive oil fields. You have to get your head around these big numbers and understand what they actually mean: often the sum of money involved is the (potential) value of a joint-venture or natural resource deposit. One of the things projects lawyers like about their job is that the product of their dealmaking is tangible: they can usually watch a mine, bridge or oil refinery being built before their eyes.
- The world's energy resources have helpfully positioned themselves in some of the world's most politically unstable or dubious countries (Venezuela, Russia, Saudi Arabia, Iraq, Iran, Nigeria etc.). This adds an extra layer of interest and intrigue to many transactions. For example, the due diligence on building a diamond mine in West Africa might involve consideration of how many AK-47s and armoured personnel carriers the mine will need to operate.

Current issues

- The difficult market conditions caused by the recession have made it hard for companies to obtain financing for projects. After two years of decline, 2010 saw a 38% rise in the value of global project finance work. But, the number of new deals hitting lawyers' desks reportedly dropped again in 2011/12, with the workload being replaced by restructuring existing projects.
- In July 2012 it was announced that the coalition government would underwrite up to £40bn of funding for infrastructure projects to kick-start the sector.
- Globally, French banks have historically been the biggest projects lenders (and Parisian lawyers handle a large portion of the African projects market). But the financial crisis has meant banks are less willing to lend, so borrowers are seeking funding from different types of lenders like Islamic banks and export credit agencies.
- In Europe, energy security is a key concern for governments as recent political developments have emphasised the problematic nature of relying on a small number of countries (or just one) for domestic energy requirements. An obvious example of the interest in energy security is the development of LNG (liquid natural gas) storage and pipeline projects in Eastern Europe.
- The renewable energy sector is small but booming. Projects have mostly continued unabated despite the economic downturn due to their long-term nature. Renewable energy remains a key area of investment as

Read our True Pictures on...

Addleshaw Goddard	Latham & Watkins
Allen & Overy	Linklaters
Ashurst	Mayer Brown
Baker & McKenzie	Memery Crystal
Berwin Leighton Paisner	Mills & Reeve
Bond Pearce	Nabarro
Burges Salmon	Norton Rose
Clifford Chance	Pinsent Masons
Clyde & Co	Shearman & Sterling
CMS*	Simmons & Simmons
DLA Piper	Skadden
Dundas & Wilson	Slaughter and May
DWF	SNR Denton*
Eversheds	TLT
Freeth Cartwright	Vinson & Elkins*
Freshfields	Watson, Farley & Williams
Herbert Smith Freehills*	White & Case*
Hogan Lovells	Wragge & Co
Ince & Co	

*These firms have a particularly strong focus on projects and energy.

it satisfies both government commitments to energy security and carbon emissions targets. The UK recently overtook Denmark as the world's number one offshore wind energy generator and there are over a dozen offshore wind farms under construction or planned. Biomass also produces a significant proportion of UK renewable energy, while solar remains of negligible importance.

- Nuclear technology is a key focus as being the most potent source of electricity for reducing carbon. The 2011 Fukushima nuclear disaster led Germany to abandon its nuclear power plant program, but it does not seem to have affected UK nuclear policy. Plans are currently being hatched to build five new nuclear power stations, at a total cost of £35bn, financed by the Chinese. This coincides with a reduction of interest and investment in traditional power generation, such as coal-powered stations. There is investment in technology to make these old power stations more carbon efficient where possible.
- City lawyers are working on an increasing number of energy exploration and infrastructure projects overseas, especially in the BRIC countries, but also in Africa. The Middle East, with its oil reserves continues to be a key area for investment. Europe – particularly Western Europe – appears to be more active in renewable energy, although this is driven more by government targets.
- The United States is experiencing a shale gas boom – shale gas is forced out of pockets in layers of rock using a technique called 'fracking'. The UK is known to have significant shale gas deposits and there are plans to exploit these resources. There are several environmental objections to this, but if they are overcome this will become a new growth area.

Property/Real Estate

In a nutshell

Property lawyers, like their corporate law colleagues, are essentially transactional lawyers; the only real difference is that real estate deals require an extra layer of specialist legal and procedural knowledge and there aren't quite so many pesky regulatory authorities. The work centres on buildings and land of all types, and even the most oblique legal concepts have a bricks-and-mortar or human basis to them. It is common for lawyers to develop a specialism within this field, such as residential conveyancing, mortgage lending and property finance, social housing, or the leisure and hotels sector. Most firms have a property department, and the larger the department the more likely the lawyers are to specialise. Note: 'property' and 'real estate' are entirely interchangeable terms.

What lawyers do

- Negotiate sales, purchases and leases of land and buildings, and advise on the structure of deals. Record the terms of an agreement in legal documents.
- Gather and analyse factual information about properties from the owners, surveyors, local authorities and the Land Registry.
- Prepare reports for buyers and anyone lending money.
- Manage the transfer of money and the handover of properties to new owners or occupiers.
- Take the appropriate steps to register new owners and protect the interests of lenders or investors.
- Advise clients on their responsibilities in leasehold relationships, and on how to take action if problems arise.
- Help developers get all the necessary permissions to build, alter or change the permitted use of properties.
- Manage property portfolio investments and advise real estate funds.

The realities of the job

- Property lawyers have to multi-task. A single deal could involve many hundreds of properties and your caseload could contain scores of files, all at different stages in the process. You'll have to keep organised.
- Good drafting skills require attention to detail and careful thought. Plus you need to keep up to date with industry trends and standards.
- Some clients get antsy; you have to be able to explain legal problems in lay terms.

- Despite some site visits, this is mainly a desk job with a lot of time spent on the phone to other solicitors, estate agents, civil servants and consultants.
- Most instances of solicitor negligence occur in this area of practice. There is so much that can go wrong.
- Your days will be busy, but generally the hours are more sociable and predictable.

Current issues

- Arguably the most obviously cyclical legal area around, property practice will always and has always followed the market. In a down economy there's less demand for properties and new developments, values plummet and conventional bank lending becomes increasingly hard to find. Yes, the recession has hit the property sector hard, but this is nothing new. When the economy picks up again, so will this practice area.
- Property markets grew globally in 2011, but 2012 saw UK house prices down 13% on their highest point in 2007. Property in central London, however, goes from strength to strength.
- Generally, banks haven't been lending as much or as often. Lenders are demanding low-risk lending criteria, and borrowers are being forced to raise greater amounts of capital. It's been the cash-rich investors from foreign sovereign wealth funds (particularly Qatar) and big foreign companies (often German) who have been investing into the UK market. However, they've been actively and aggressively pursuing primary investment assets – the big office buildings, shopping centres and tower blocks – meaning that, at that level, there is a high demand and a low supply, keeping prices pretty high. The demand for secondary assets remains lower.
- There has been a shift towards the refinancing of existing deals in the wake of the general downturn in new transactions, with landlords having to be much more flexible than in previous years. Landlords are keen to avoid the dreaded 'empty rates' scenario, where they are forced to pay for buildings without occupiers.
- Apart from big projects like the Olympic Village and Crossrail, the public sector real estate market has slowed. Particularly significant are the cuts to the social housing budget. Firms with existing experience in these sectors largely have the market sewn up; however, there are fears over a drier period ahead.
- The recession caused the real estate transactional market to implode, with some parties who had signed deals, especially buyers, examining/challenging purchase contracts and trying to pull out of deals. This trig-

gered an increase in litigation and firms experienced an upturn in contentious work.

- Generally, property litigation is a booming area at the moment, even though matters are not necessarily going all the way to court due to cost implications. Many cash-strapped landlords and tenants are settling pre-court, or going to mediation.

- The slow economy means more insolvency, with the knock-on result that some former tenants are being pursued when their assignees default. There are also more break clause disputes. The volume of general landlord and tenant dilapidations work is also up – with landlords looking for somebody to blame, they are picking over every last detail.

- There's also an upturn in professional negligence claims against valuers as homeowners are left in negative equity.

- The trends in property finance include: a large number of loans being renegotiated; development finance being thinner on the ground; increased fire sales; and anxiety that UK Real Estate Investment Trusts (REITs) may breach their financial covenants. Banks are beginning to lend again, and the market is now more receptive to new deals, although these are tightly controlled and generally at a much lower level than before. Deals under £100m are no longer considered small.

- German banks are a major presence, while Shari'a finance remains a small but significant area.

Read our True Pictures on...

Allen & Overy	Linklaters
Ashurst	Lester Aldridge
Ashfords	Macfarlanes
Addleshaw Goddard	Manches
Bevan Brittan	Mayer Brown
Burges Salmon	Memery Crystal
Browne Jacobson	Michelmores
B P Collins	Mills & Reeve
Bond Pearce	Mischon de Reya
Berwin Leighton Paisner	Morgan Cole
Bird & Bird	Muckle
Boodle Hatfield	Nabarro
Bircham Dyson Bell	Norton Rose
Burges Salmon	Olswang
Brabners Chaffe Street	Pannone
Charles Russell	Paul Hastings
Clifford Chance	Penningtons Solicitors
Clyde & Co	Pinsent Masons
Cobbetts	Reed Smith
Cripps Harries Hall	SGH Martineau
Davenport Lysons	Shoosmiths
Dundas & Wilson	Sidley Austin
DWF	Simmons & Simmons
Dickinson Dees	SJ Berwin
Eversheds	SNR Denton
Farrer & Co	Speechly Bircham
Freshfields	Squire Sanders
Freeth Cartwright	Stephenson Harwood
Foot Anstey	Stevens & Bolton
Gateley	Taylor Wessing
Gordons	TLT
Hill Dickinson	Travers Smith
Higgs & Sons	Trethowans
Henmans	Veale Wasbrough Vizards
Herbert Smith	Walker Morris
Hogan Lovells	Ward Hadaway
Irwin Mitchell	Wedlake Bell
Jones Day	Wilsons
K&L Gates	Wragge & Co
Lawrence Graham	

Want to work for Chambers and Partners? Our research team is over 100 strong and works on legal guides spanning the globe. If you have good interviewing and writing skills, why not take a look at our website and find out more?

Some of our researchers are with us while looking for a training contract or pupillage. We're especially interested in people who speak foreign languages.

Public Interest

In a nutshell

Human rights lawyers protest injustice and fight for principle at the point of intersection between a state's powers and individuals' rights. Cases usually relate in some way to the UK's ratification of the European Convention on Human Rights (ECHR) through the Human Rights Act and crop up in criminal and civil contexts, often through the medium of judicial review, a key tool in questioning the decisions of public bodies. Civil contexts include claims regarding the right to education or community care under the Mental Health Act, cases of discrimination at work and even family issues. Criminal contexts could relate to complaints against the police, prisoners' issues, public order convictions following demonstrations, or perhaps extradition on terror charges.

Immigration lawyers deal with both business and personal immigration matters – the former has been embraced by the government in its quest to manage economic migration. In this more lucrative area, lawyers assist highly skilled migrants to obtain residency or leave to remain in the UK, and help non-nationals to secure visas for travel abroad. They also work with companies that need to bring in employees from overseas. Personal immigration lawyers represent individuals who have fled persecution in their country of origin. They also take on cases for people whose right to stay in the UK is under threat or indeed entirely absent.

What lawyers do

Human rights lawyers
- Advise clients on how to appeal a decision made or action taken by a public body, such as the police, a local authority, a court, or a branch of government.
- Collect evidence, take witness statements, prepare cases and instruct barristers.
- Pursue cases through the procedural stages necessary to achieve the desired result. The final port of call for some cases is the European Court of Justice (ECJ), so lawyers need to be fully conversant with UK and European laws.

Business immigration lawyers
- Advise and assist businesses or their employees in relation to work permits and visas. They need to be up to speed on all current schemes, such as those for highly skilled migrants and investors.

- Prepare for, attend and advocate at tribunals or court hearings, where necessary instructing a barrister to do so.

Personal immigration lawyers
- Advise clients on their status and rights within the UK.
- Secure evidence of a client's identity, medical reports and witness statements, and prepare cases for court hearings or appeals. Represent clients or instruct a barrister to do so.
- Undertake an immense amount of unremunerated form filling and legal aid paperwork.

The realities of the job

- A commitment to and belief in the values you're fighting for is essential in this relatively low-paid area. Work in the voluntary sector or taking on important cases pro bono can provide the greatest satisfaction.
- Sensitivity and empathy are absolutely essential because you'll often be dealing with highly emotional people, those with mental health issues or those who simply don't appreciate the full extent of their legal predicament.
- Strong analytical skills are required to pick out the legal issues you can change from the socio-economic ones beyond your control.
- In the battle against red tape and institutional indifference, organisational skills and a vast store of patience are valuable assets.
- Opportunities for advocacy are abundant, which means that knowledge of court and tribunal procedures is a fundamental requirement. Often cases must pass through every possible stage of appeal before referral to judicial review or the ECJ.
- The competition for training contracts is huge. Voluntary work at a law centre or specialist voluntary organisation, or membership of Liberty or Justice, is essential.
- Because much of the work is publicly funded, firms do not usually offer attractive trainee salaries or sponsorship through law school.
- If working within a commercial firm, the clients will be businesses and public sector organisations. As such there will be less of a campaigning element to the work and you will not necessarily feel you are 'on the side of the angels'.

Current issues

- Issues of asylum (including detention and deportation) and people seeking permission to stay in the UK on human rights grounds never cease to arouse strong opinions. The government crackdown on all forms of immigration will likely cause an increase in immigration appeals.
- The advent of the Freedom of Information Act, and increased transparency in the public sector in line with Article 6 of the ECHR, mean law firms have seen a greater willingness from the public to challenge the decisions of authorities.
- Many recent human rights and civil liberties cases have related to issues arising out of Guantanamo Bay, Iraq, terrorism, control orders, stop-and-search powers and national security. These cases have taken the form of judicial reviews and public inquiries. The much-publicised Binyam Mohamed judicial review, and the Baha Mousa and Al-Sweady inquiries are examples of such investigations.
- April 2011 saw the Supreme Court rule yet another control order unlawful in *BM v Home Secretary*. It was quashed for being based on 'vague and speculative' evidence. Increasing legal controversy over control orders means they are to be reformed by the current government.
- Other recent big social justice cases have related to equality rights, privacy rights and asylum seeker rights.
- The Points Based System (PBS) of immigration means every employer now needs to obtain an immigration licence under the PBS before being able to issue a Certificate of Sponsorship for each employee it wishes to employ. Some argue that the scheme is now so technical that employers are constantly at risk of unlawful employment.
- Critics believe that restricting highly skilled migrants from working in the UK is farcical.

Read our True Pictures on...

Baker & McKenzie	Lewis Silkin
Bates Wells & Braithwaite	Mishcon de Reya
Bird & Bird	Penningtons Solicitors
Clyde & Co	Speechly Bircham
Irwin Mitchell	Squaire Sanders
Kingsley Napley	

- In early 2011 the government introduced a cap on non-EU immigration of 21,700 – all immigrants must be graduates with job offers or 'exceptional talent' like scientists and academics. All other non-EEA economic immigration has been halted. This is likely to mean more claims by individuals under the Human Rights Act. In April 2012 the government announced the cap would be stabilised until 2014.
- In 2012 Theresa May announced plans to introduce a minimum income requirement for every British 'sponsor' of a foreign spouse. The plans also involved English-speaking tests for those coming to live in the UK on a family visa.
- The past decade has seen an enormous growth in human rights litigation, in UK and European courts – like the General Court (formerly the Court of First Instance), European Court of Justice, European Court of Human Rights – as well as international tribunals. This case-driven development of human rights law is based on fundamental rights standards common to legal systems throughout Europe.
- The July 2010 case of *HJ (Iran) and HT (Cameroon) v Secretary of State for the Home Department* saw the Supreme Court effectively recognise gay asylum seekers' right to have or seek out sexual relationships. Previously, gay asylum seekers could be deported if it were 'reasonably tolerable' for them to conceal their sexuality to avoid persecution in their home country.

Restructuring/Insolvency

In a nutshell

Insolvency law governs the position of businesses and individuals who are in financial difficulties and unable to repay their debts as they become due. Such a situation may lead to insolvency proceedings, in which legal action is taken against the insolvent entity and assets may be liquidated to pay off outstanding debts. Before a company or individual gets involved in insolvency proceedings, they will probably be involved in a restructuring or an out-of-court arrangement with creditors to work out alternative repayment schedules. The work of lawyers in the field can therefore be non-contentious (restructuring) or contentious (insolvency litigation), and their role will vary depending on whether they act for debtors or their creditors. What follows are some of the terms you'll come across.

Debtor: an individual or company that owes money. **Creditor:** a person or institution that extends credit to another entity on condition that it is paid back at a later date. **Bankruptcy:** term used in the USA to describe insolvency procedures that apply to companies, but not in the UK, where the term applies to individuals only. **Restructuring:** a significant modification made to the debt, operations or structure of a company with its creditors' consent. After a restructuring, debt repayments become more manageable, making insolvency proceedings less likely. **Insolvency proceedings:** generic term that covers a variety of statutory proceedings aimed at rescuing or winding up an insolvent company.
Insolvency proceedings include the following actions. **Company voluntary arrangement (CVA):** if it is clear that a business could survive if debt repayments were reduced, it can enter a CVA agreement with its creditors. Under this legally binding agreement, a struggling company is allowed to repay some, or all, of its historic debts out of future profits, over an agreed period of time. **Administration:** when in administration, a company is protected from creditors enforcing their debts while an administrator takes over the management of its affairs. If the company is fundamentally sound, the administrator will implement a recovery plan aimed at streamlining the business and maximising profits. If it is apparent that the company has no future then it can be sold or liquidation can commence.
Receivership: unlike administration, this is initiated by the company's creditors, not the company itself. A receiver is appointed by the court and must look to recover as much money as possible in order to settle the claims made by creditors. Under receivership, the interests of the creditors clearly take precedence over the survival of the company. **Liquidation:** procedure by which the assets of a company are placed under the control of a liquidator. In most cases, a company in liquidation ceases to trade, and the liquidator will sell the company's assets and distribute the proceeds to creditors. There are two forms: voluntary liquidation brought about by the company itself, or compulsory liquidation brought about by court order. **Distressed M&A:** the sale of all or a portion of an insolvent business is an efficient way to preserve going-concern value and avoid the potential for substantial loss of value through a piecemeal liquidation. **Pre-pack sale:** refers to a deal made with an interested buyer to sell the insolvent company's business and assets, negotiated before an administrator is appointed and completed immediately on appointment. Such schemes are becoming increasingly popular and more frequently used in the current economic climate.

What lawyers do

Debtors' lawyers

- Meet with clients to assess the gravity of the situation, highlight the available options and advise on the best course of action to follow.
- In a restructuring, advise the insolvent company on the reorganisation of its balance sheet (such as closing down unprofitable businesses or refinancing its debt) and assist in negotiations with creditors.
- Assist in insolvency filings, and once proceedings have commenced, work closely with the insolvency officeholders (ie those appointed as administrators, receivers or liquidators) and accountants, to achieve the goals set for the insolvent company.
- Provide advice to directors of insolvent companies, explaining their duties to creditors.
- Advise on the sale of assets or mergers and acquisitions of troubled companies.
- Assist clients in insolvency litigation and appeals. Provide preventative advice to debtor clients on liability management and ways to avoid insolvency proceedings.

Creditors' lawyers

- Meet with creditor clients to assess the validity of their security over the insolvent company, the strength of their position in the creditors' pool and the best course of action to ensure full recovery.
- Assist in negotiations with debtors and insolvency officeholders.
- Represent clients in insolvency litigation and appeals.
- Assist in the tracing and valuation of debtors' assets.

- Provide training to their clients on how to deal with insolvent companies.

The realities of the job

- Large City firms deal almost exclusively with large-scale corporate restructurings and insolvencies, and the representation of creditor groups in these matters. Smaller regional firms mostly assist on smaller corporate and personal insolvency cases.
- Corporate insolvency as a practice area is extremely varied, as proceedings affect every aspect of the insolvent company. Lawyers therefore need to be conversant in a variety of legal disciplines or know when to refer matters to specialists in employment, banking, property, litigation, corporate, etc.
- When financial difficulties arise in companies, the rapid deployment of a legal team is necessary to provide immediate assistance. This area of law is extremely fast-paced, and lawyers are often asked to deliver solutions overnight.
- Insolvency and restructuring involves mountains of paperwork, so lawyers need to be organised and able to prioritise their workload, particularly when dealing with multiple assignments. With so much at stake, attention to detail is paramount when drafting asset sale agreements or documents to be filed at court.
- Restructuring and insolvency situations are understandably tense for both debtors and creditors, and lawyers sometimes need to deal with difficult people, so they must be able to hold their ground and show they are not easily intimidated.
- You will need to immerse yourself in both the financial and corporate worlds. Get started by reading the *FT* or City pages of your daily newspaper.

Current issues

- Although the UK economy started to recover from the financial crisis in 2010 and early 2011, the restructuring market remained busy.
- As the financial crisis unfolded, more and more businesses went bust. The predicted massive wave of formal insolvency instructions never came though, with many businesses restructuring without going into administration.
- Sovereign debt defaults form an increasing threat to the world economy. More volatility in this market is having a marked effect on banks and investors. Major restructurings in the private sector now appear inevitable.
- Banks have been sitting on debt rather than litigating it, as assets aren't worth what they once were and litigation is expensive. This has meant less work than expected for insolvency lawyers, so far. If debts continued to build up, this too will probably mean more restructurings.

Read our True Pictures on...

Addleshaw Goddard	Mayer Brown
Allen & Overy	Michelmores
Ashfords	Mills & Reeve
Ashurst	Morgan Cole
Baker & McKenzie	Muckle
Berwin Leighton Paisner	Nabarro
Bingham McCutchen	Norton Rose
Bond Pearce	Olswang
Brabners Chaffe Street	Osborne Clarke
Browne Jacobson	Pannone
Burges Salmon	Paul Hastings
Charles Russell	Pinsent Masons
Clifford Chance	SGH Martineau
Clyde & Co	Shearman & Sterling
CMS	Shoosmiths
Cobbetts	Sidley Austin
Dickinson Dees	Simmons & Simmons
DLA Piper	SJ Berwin
Dundas & Wilson	Skadden
DWF	Slaughter and May
Eversheds	SNR Denton
Freeth Cartwright	Speechly Bircham
Freshfields	Squire Sanders
Gateley	Stevens & Bolton
Herbert Smith Freehills	Taylor Wessing
Hill Dickinson	TLT
Hogan Lovells	Travers Smith
Howes Percival	Veale Wasbrough Vizards
Irwin Mitchell	Walker Morris
Jones Day	Ward Hadaway
Kirkland & Ellis	Weil, Gotshal & Manges
Latham & Watkins	White & Case
Lester Aldridge	Wragge & Co
Linklaters	

- HMRC's Time to Pay (TTP) Scheme means debt-laden small and medium-sized entrepreneurs have been treated leniently in the last few years. As this scheme is cut back – the number of TTP requests refused rose by 50% in the first quarter of 2011 – it is likely to be very harmful to small businesses.
- The sectors hardest hit by the recession – and therefore the busiest in relation to restructuring – were construction and property. Nonetheless, insolvency cases have cropped up everywhere, so lawyers need to be up to speed with a wide range of industry issues. As a result, firms are adapting a more cross-departmental, integrated approach.
- Figures show that individual bankruptcies in the UK have fallen by more than 10% in the second half of 2012 – this may be to do with a rise in fees to declare yourself bankrupt.
- In the same period, retail insolvencies increased by almost exactly the same amount – retail being one of the only sectors to steadily worsen in this area.

Shipping and International Trade

In a nutshell

Shipping lawyers deal with the carriage of goods or people by sea, plus any and every matter related to the financing, construction, use, insurance and decommissioning of the ships that carry them (or are arrested, sunk or salvaged while carrying them). Despite being the preserve of specialist firms, or relatively self-contained practice groups within larger firms, the discipline offers varied challenges. The major division is between 'wet' work relating to accidents or misadventure at sea, and 'dry' work involving the land-based, commercial and contractual side. In extension, disputes or litigation relating to contracts means there is also a contentious side to dry work. While some lawyers in the area may be generalists, it is more common to specialise.

What lawyers do

Wet lawyers
- Act swiftly and decisively at a moment's notice to protect a client's interests and minimise any loss.
- Travel the world to assess the condition of ships, interview crew or witnesses and prepare cases.
- Take witness statements and advise clients on the merits of and strategy for cases.
- Handle court and arbitration appearances, conferences with barristers and client meetings.

Dry lawyers
- Negotiate and draft contracts for ship finance and shipbuilding, crew employment, sale and purchase agreements, affreightment contracts, and the registration and re-flagging of ships.
- May specialise in niche areas such as yachts or fishing, an area in which regulatory issues feature prominently.
- Handle similar tasks to wet lawyers in relation to contractual disputes but are less likely to jet off around the world at the drop of a hat.

The realities of the job

- Wet work offers the excitement of international assignments and clients, so lawyers need to react coolly to sudden emergencies and travel to far-flung places to offer practical and pragmatic analysis and advice.
- Despite the perils and pleasures of dealing with clients and instructions on the other side of the world, the hours are likely to be steady beyond those international-rescue moments.

- Non-contentious work touches on the intricacies of international trade, so it's as important to keep up with sector knowledge as legal developments.
- Dealing with a mixed clientele from all points on the social compass, you'll need to be just as comfortable extracting a comprehensible statement from a Norwegian merchant seaman as conducting negotiations with major financiers.
- Contentious cases are driven by the procedural rules and timetable of the court or arbitration forum to which the matter has been referred. A solid grasp of procedure is as important as a strong foundation in tort and contract law.
- Some shipping lawyers do come from a naval background or are ex-mariners, but you won't be becalmed if the closest comparable experience you've had is steering Tommy Tugboat in the bath, as long as you can show a credible interest in the discipline.
- Though not an all-boys club, parts of the shipping world are still male dominated. Women lawyers and clients are more commonly found on the dry side.
- In the UK, shipping law is centred around London and a few other port cities. Major international centres include Piraeus in Greece, Hong Kong and Singapore. Some trainees even get to work in these locations.

Current issues

- The shipping market was quite severely blown off course in the recession. Some suggested that the top end of the market plummeted between 90% and 100% in a matter of weeks.
- The global shipping market remains volatile. Some areas are slowly recovering, but tanker and dry bulk rates are still dire.
- Decreased demand for raw materials has hit the industry hard. Because shipments and ships are big, slow and expensive, the shipping market is not very versatile. The recent fall in oil prices, however, has enabled shipping companies to operate more profitably.
- The tonnage on order at shipyards has increased over the last year, but shipping finance is still in the doldrums and remains at an all time low. New deals are being done though. For example, Singapore's Neptune Orient Lines recently secured $1.1bn worth of financing for the building of 12 new container ships.
- As this example indicated, the Asian market is doing better than most, with the Chinese government providing financial backing and Chinese commercial banks doing a lot of lending and investing large amounts of

money. 2012 figures showed freight turnover in China had increased 12.4% year-on-year.

- Charter party contracts were put under pressure when value fell out of the shipping industry, leading to a large increase in disputes over shipments.
- The amount of contentious work arising directly out of the economic crisis has tailed off to a degree, as contracts have been renegotiated and remaining businesses have stabilised their positions in the market.
- Shipping is potentially very sensitive to corruption because of its international nature, so the 2010 Bribery Act is having a big impact.
- Piracy remains a significant concern; however legal involvement tends to focus primarily on the status of a ship when seized – ie was it on hire during that period? – to establish who is responsible for the costs incurred. Actual prosecution of pirates remains rare, although in June 2010 a special court to try suspected pirates operating in the Gulf of Aden opened in the Shimo la Tewa prison in Mombasa, Kenya. The future of that court and

how pirates will be prosecuted in future remains uncertain. As yet, pirates have not been brought to trial in the UK, although there have been some civil cases and arbitrations. In 2012, David Cameron signed a Memorandum of Understanding with Mauritius (adding to agreements with Tanzania and the Seychelles) to transfer suspected pirates from Royal Navy ships to land for prosecution.

Read our True Pictures on...

Ashfords	Lester Aldridge
Clyde & Co*	Norton Rose
Eversheds	Pinsent Masons
Gateley	Reed Smith*
Hill Dickinson*	Stephenson Harwood*
Holman Fenwick Willan*	Thomas Cooper*
Ince & Co*	TLT

*These firms have a particularly strong focus on shipping

Sports, Media and Entertainment

In a nutshell

Advertising and marketing lawyers offer advice to ensure a client's products or advertisements are compliant with industry standards, plus general advice on anything from contracts between clients, media and suppliers, to employment law, corporate transactions and litigation. Entertainment lawyers assist clients in the film, broadcasting, music, theatre and publishing industries with commercial legal advice or litigation. Strictly speaking, sports lawyers work in an industry sector rather than a specific legal discipline, and firms draw on the expertise of individuals from several practice groups. Reputation management lawyers advise clients on how best to protect their own 'brand', be this through a defamation suit or an objection to invasion of privacy.

What lawyers do

Advertising and marketing
- Ensure advertising campaigns comply with legislation or regulatory codes controlled by the Advertising Standards Agency (ASA) or Ofcom.
- Advise on comparative advertising, unauthorised references to living persons, potential trade mark or other intellectual property infringements.
- Defend clients against allegations that their work has infringed regulations or the rights of third parties. Bring complaints against competitors' advertising.

TV and film
- Offer production companies advice on every stage of the creation of programmes and films.
- Assist on the complicated banking and secured lending transactions that ensure financing for a film.
- Help engage performers; negotiate a multitude of ancillary contracts; negotiate distribution and worldwide rights; and manage defamation claims.

Music
- Advise major recording companies, independent labels and talent (record producers, songwriters and artists).
- Advise on contracts, such as those between labels and bands, or between labels and third parties.
- Offer contentious and non-contentious copyright and trademark advice relating to music, image rights and merchandising.
- Offer criminal advice when things get old-school rock 'n' roll.
- Assist with immigration issues.

Theatre and publishing
- Advise theatre and opera companies, producers, agents and actors on contracts, funding and sponsorship/merchandising.
- Advise publishing companies and newspapers on contractual, licensing, copyright and libel matters.
- Assist with immigration issues.

Sports
- Assist with contract negotiations, be they between clubs and sportspeople, agents and players, sporting institutions and sponsors, broadcasters and sports governing bodies.
- Handle varied employment law issues.
- Assist with immigration issues.
- Advise on corporate or commercial matters such as takeovers, public offerings, debt restructuring and bankruptcy, or the securing and structuring of credit.
- Enforce IP rights in the lucrative merchandise market and negotiate on matters affecting a sportsperson's image rights.
- Work on regulatory compliance issues within a sport or matters relating to the friction between sports regulations and EU/national law.
- Offer reputation management and criminal advice.

Reputation management (incl. defamation and libel)
- Claimants' lawyers advise individuals – commonly celebrities, politicians or high-profile businessmen – on the nature of any potential libel action or breach of privacy claim, usually against broadcasters or publishers, before it either settles or goes to court.
- Defendants' lawyers advise broadcasters or other publishers on libel claims brought against them. With the burden of proof on the defendant, the lawyers must prove that what was published caused no loss to the claimant or was not libellous.
- Help clients stay out of hot water by giving pre-publication advice to authors, editors or production companies.

The realities of the job
- Advertising lawyers must have a good knowledge of advertising regulations, defamation and IP law.
- The work is real world and fast-paced.
- Clients are creative, lively and demanding.
- The issues thrown up can be fascinating and must be dealt with creatively.

- Many advertising disputes will be settled via regulatory bodies but some, particularly IP infringements, end in litigation.
- Entertainment lawyers need to be completely immersed in their chosen media and have a good grasp of copyright and contract law.
- Clients look to you for the rigour and discipline they may rarely exercise themselves. This is a sector where who you know makes a big difference, so expect to put in serious face time.
- Sports lawyers need to be proactive, passionate and have bags of commercial nous. They must be able to deal with people involved at all levels of all sports.
- Reputation management lawyers need a comprehensive understanding of libel and privacy laws and an ability to think laterally. Individual claimants will be stressed and upset, so people skills, patience and resourcefulness are much needed.
- Solicitors prepare cases but barristers almost always get the glory.

Read our True Pictures on...

Addleshaw Goddard	K&L Gates
Baker & McKenzie	Lewis Silkin*
Bates Wells & Braithwaite	Macfarlanes
Berwin Leighton Paisner	Mishcon de Reya
Bird & Bird	Morgan Cole
Bond Pearce	Olswang
Brabners Chaffe Street	Osborne Clarke
Bristows	Pinsent Masons
Charles Russell	Reed Smith
CMS	RPC
Collyer Bristow*	Sheridans*
Davenport Lyons*	Slaughter and May
DLA Piper	SNR Denton
Dundas & Wilson	Squire Sanders
Eversheds	Taylor Wessing
Farrer & Co	Travers Smith
Harbottle & Lewis*	Wiggin*
Herbert Smith Freehills	Withers
Hogan Lovells	

*These firms have a particularly strong focus on media work

Current issues

- 2012 was the year the Leveson Inquiry dominated headlines. Provoked by the *News of the World* phone-hacking scandal, the inquiry looked into the culture, practices and ethics of the press, politicians and the police. With high-profile arrests and charges (eg Rebekah Brooks), the discontinuation of the *News of the World*, and the Murdoch empire being dragged through the mud, the fall-out from the inquiry will be considerable and will continue to be a major source of legal work.
- In the world of broadcasting, both content providers and platform operators have been keen to introduce high definition services as a means of retaining viewer loyalty and enhancing revenues.
- Changes to the Ofcom Broadcasting Code now permit product placement in TV shows, creating all kinds of new advertising and sponsorship opportunities.
- Online television has grown a great deal and broadcasters are attempting to generate new revenue streams to offset the commensurate decline in advertising revenues.
- Firms are also involved in fighting illegal online content.
- At the heart of many developments is convergence, ie getting multiple services from a single provider.
- The rise of smart phones and tablets has created an explosion in demand for related services like apps, feeding a deluge of opportunities for new players in the market. It's also becoming clear which digital and audiovisual services consumers are and are not willing pay for.
- Web-based interactive, 'smart' advertising is throwing up all kinds of data protection and privacy issues.
- The lines between advertising, news, drama, music, sport, interactive games and user-generated content are blurring as online access becomes increasingly routine.

The attempt to regulate online content in the wake of the Digital Economy Act and the Audiovisual Media Services (AVMS) Directive is increasing demand for legal services.

- The music industry continues to face challenges: illegal downloading and piracy are the biggest concerns. Sales of physical products are declining rapidly, so deals that combine physical sales with merchandising and live appearances are increasingly common.
- Tax credits for film financing have helped boost (foreign) investment in UK film and TV production. Investment in the UK film industry reached an all-time high of £1.26bn in 2011.
- The closure of the UK Film Council in early 2011 was seen as a blow to film financing, but the government is continuing to encourage funding of films in other ways.
- The economic downturn has intensified the public interest in sensitive areas such as gambling, alcohol and products targeting children. Various changes have been made to advertising codes by the Committee of Advertising Practice (CAP), which is the ASA's sister organisation.
- The 2010s have been hailed as a 'golden decade' of sporting events for the UK (glossing quickly over Euro 2012). Following on from the 2012 Olympics, there's the 2013 Champions League Final at Wembley, the 2014 Ryder Cup, the 2014 Commonwealth Games (in Glasgow), the 2015 Rugby World Cup, the 2017 Athletics World Championships and the 2019 Cricket World Cup.
- Football clubs' finances have continued to hit the headlines, and a couple of years back Portsmouth became the first ever Premier League club to go into adminis-

tration. Rangers became the latest top club to fold, when it went into administration in 2012. Other clubs have been sold, bought or invested in by all manner of private investors, many from overseas, providing lucrative work for a whole other set of lawyers and in some cases reversing clubs' fortunes overnight.

- Staying in the world of football: the Premier League is signing increasingly lucrative sponsorship deals – shirt sponsorship deals alone were worth £117m in the 2011/12 season, up almost 20% from the previous year. The Premier League's overseas broadcasting rights for 2010 to 2013 have doubled, from £625m to £1.4bn.

- The new Defamation Bill is likely to be brought onto the statute books soon. It will limit (but not halt) 'libel tourism', and determines that claimants can only sue for defamation if they have suffered serious harm to their reputation. The changes could mean a decrease in the number of cases coming before the courts, but lawyers will continue to be needed for their advice on what does and does not constitute a viable defamation case.

- And finally... as the *Chambers Student Guide* correctly predicted last year, Southampton FC did in fact make it into the Premier League (thanks to being bailed out by 'Saint' Markus Liebherr).

Tax

In a nutshell

Tax lawyers ensure that clients structure their business deals or day-to-day operations such that they take advantage of legal breaks and loopholes in tax legislation. Although predominantly an advisory practice area, on occasion matters can veer into litigation territory.

Tax lawyers in private practice

- Handle tax planning for clients, making sure they understand the tax ramifications of the purchase, ownership and disposal of assets, including advising on structuring corporate portfolios in the most tax-efficient way.
- Offer transactional advice when working with corporate and other lawyers on matters such as an M&A deal, a joint venture or the acquisition of a large property portfolio.
- Deal with investigations or litigation resulting from prosecution by Her Majesty's Revenue & Customs (HMRC). Litigation is always conducted against or brought by the government.

HMRC lawyers

- Investigate companies and bring prosecutions.
- Advise on how new laws apply to different situations.
- Defend cases brought against the government.

The realities of the job

- This is an intellectually rigorous, rather cloistered area of law and is ideally suited to the more academic.
- Corporate tax lawyers are very well paid, treated with reverence by their colleagues and find intellectual stimulation in their work.
- Lawyers must not only have the ability to translate and implement complex tax legislation, but must also be able to advise on how to structure deals in a legitimate and tax-efficient way to avoid conflict with HMRC.
- If you don't already wear specs, expect to after a couple of years of poring over all that black letter law. The UK has more pages of tax legislation than almost any other country, and there are changes every year.
- In time, extra qualifications, such as the Chartered Tax Adviser exams, will be useful.
- It is not uncommon for lawyers to switch between government jobs and private practice. Some tax barristers were once solicitors.

Read our True Pictures on...

Addleshaw Goddard	Macfarlanes
Allen & Overy	Mayer Brown
Ashurst	Mills & Reeve
Baker & McKenzie	Nabarro
Berwin Leighton Paisner	Norton Rose
Bond Pearce	Olswang
Brabners Chaffe Street	Osborne Clarke
Burges Salmon	Penningtons Solicitors
Clifford Chance	Pinsent Masons
CMS	Shoosmiths
Dechert	Sidley Austin
DLA Piper	Simmons & Simmons
Dundas & Wilson	SJ Berwin
DWF	Skadden
Eversheds	Slaughter and May
Freshfields	SNR Denton
Gateley	Squire Sanders
Herbert Smith Freehills	Stephenson Harwood
Hogan Lovells	Stevens & Bolton
Irwin Mitchell	Travers Smith
Jones Day	Walker Morris
Kirkland & Ellis	Weil, Gotshal & Manges
Latham & Watkins	Withers
Linklaters	Wragge & Co

Current issues

- There's been an increased focus on debt restructuring and equity raising.
- Funds work remains active. The restructuring of existing funds, launches of new funds and increases in capital flow all have tax consequences.
- The fall in transactional work during the recession paved the way for other areas such as advisory and litigation to come to the fore. The significant savings achievable mean that tax lawyers' advice is valued more highly than ever.
- Changes to corporate taxes and the introduction of anti-avoidance tax legislation have been keeping tax lawyers on their toes.
- Law firms have come into their own in relation to tax advice. Pre-Enron it seemed accountancy firms were taking over. However, companies now prefer to take advice from sources independent from their auditors.
- The 2011 budget contained several measures aimed at clamping down on tax avoidance. These include the tightening of capital gains rules and an end to disguised

remuneration – a method of paying employees by means of non-repayable tax-free loans.

- Following the row over the tax affairs of celebrities like Jimmy Carr (golden boy Gary Barlow is humiliation-exempt, it seems), the government has hinted that members of tax avoidance schemes may be forcibly disclosed to tax inspectors.
- Osborne's budget aimed to simplify several unclear VAT loopholes – including charging VAT on all hot takeaway food, including that from supermarkets – prompting public outcry on the proposed 50p hike in pasty prices, and David Cameron's assertion that he is a regular eater of pasties.
- HMRC has introduced several 'amnesty' style initiatives, such as the Liechtenstein Disclosure Facility, the Offshore Disclosure Facility and New Disclosure Opportunity – these have resulted in over 50,000 voluntary disclosures of unpaid taxes.
- In recent years resources have been focused mostly on prosecution of indirect fraud – like carousel fraud – over and above direct tax fraud.

Technology, Telecoms and Outsourcing

In a nutshell

Technology lawyers distinguish themselves from general commercial advisers because of their specific industry know-how. They combine a keen understanding of the latest advances in various technologies with a thorough knowledge of the ever-changing law that regulates, protects and licenses them. As forms of media and new technologies converge, clients have come to rely on technology lawyers' innovation and imagination in offering rigorous legal solutions to maximise and protect income and ideas. The majority of the top 50 firms possess dedicated groups of lawyers. There are also specialists within many smaller commercial firms and a number of niche firms.

What lawyers do

- Advise on commercial transactions and draft the requisite documents. There is a heavy emphasis on risk management.
- Assist in the resolution of disputes, commonly by arbitration or other settlement procedures as this is a court-averse sector. Many disputes relate to faulty or unsatisfactory software or hardware.
- Help clients police their IT and web-based reputation and assets. Cyber-squatting, ownership of database information and the Data Protection Act are common topics.
- Give clients mainstream commercial, corporate and finance advice.
- Specialised outsourcing lawyers represent customers and suppliers in the negotiation and drafting of agreements for the provision of IT or other services by a third party.

The realities of the job

- You need to be familiar with the latest regulations and their potential impact on your client's business. Does a website need a disclaimer? What measures should your client take to protect data about individuals gathered from a website?
- You need a good grasp of the jargon of your chosen industry, firstly to write contracts but also so you can understand your clients' instructions. Read trade journals like *Media Lawyer* and *Wired*, or magazines such as *Computer Weekly* or *New Scientist*.
- The ability to think laterally and creatively is a must, especially when the application of a client's technology or content throws up entirely new issues.
- In this frontier world, gut instinct matters. One in-house lawyer made what looked like a risky move from BT to little-known internet auction site, eBay. Six years later he moved to head up Skype's legal team – a perfect example of the convergence of internet and telephone technology.
- High-end private sector outsourcing involves complex, high-value and increasingly multi-jurisdictional work. Mostly, it is the larger law firms that handle such deals. In the public sector, deals involve UK government departments, local authorities and the suppliers of services to those entities.

Current issues

- As tech companies battle for the smartphone and tablet market, we now see an upsurge in patent disputes, notably between the iPhone giant and Samsung.
- Digital convergence throws up many legal problems as the business opportunities created by new technologies move beyond the capacity of existing legal or regulatory structures. Copyrighted content being transferred onto handheld devices; film or TV programme downloads from the internet… the list is practically endless.
- Many firms and their clients now believe that technology, media and telecoms are no longer three distinct markets, and structure their departments accordingly.
- The merger of T-Mobile and Orange's UK operations (a joint venture between Deutsche Telekom and France Télécom) created Everything Everywhere, the largest mobile network in the country.
- The EU cookie law came into effect in May 2011, and the UK was given one year to comply. It requires websites to get consent from visitors to store info on a computer or tablet device. The law was designed to make people aware of their right to privacy – whether it does is another matter.
- The most interesting telecoms work is taking place overseas, particularly in Africa and Asia. India's Bharti Airtel's $9bn takeover of Zain (South African telecoms) is the ultimate example of this. There is plenty of room for manoeuvre in the emerging markets, unlike western Europe.
- There is still plenty to do in the regulatory arena. Telecoms companies in the UK continue to try to chip away the infrastructure that gives BT a massive competitive advantage over its rivals, particularly in terms of how much it charges for its cabling.
- Technology was one of the hardest hit areas during the recession, but the sector has recovered well since then and lots of law firms are building up their work in this

area. Unsurprisingly, growth has been especially strong in emerging markets like India.

- IT outsourcing began in the late 1980s, followed by business process outsourcings (BPOs) that involve handing responsibility to third-party service providers for functions like human resources, finance and accounting. Today, the lines between technology outsourcing (TO) and BPOs are blurred. Smart outsourcing – the concept of outsourcing parts of a company, one part at a time, often using different suppliers – is in vogue at present, as is multisourcing (using many different suppliers on shorter term contracts).

- With the proliferation of so-called 'cloud computing' in business, data protection has become an area of huge expansion for many law firms. One UK source explained that: *"Data protection laws are very strong in the EU but less evolved in the US, so if a head office in New York accesses the HR records in London, you could be contravening the European Data Protection Act."*

- The government recently announced plans to roll out a UK-wide super-fast broadband network by 2015. The government has earmarked £830m for the project, but expects most of it to be paid for by private investors.

Read our True Pictures on...

Addleshaw Goddard	Linklaters
Allen & Overy	Macfarlanes
Arnold & Porter	Manches
Ashfords	Mayer Brown
Ashurst	Michelmores
Baker & McKenzie	Mills & Reeve
Berwin Leighton Paisner	Morgan Cole
Bevan Brittan	Morrison & Foerster
Bird & Bird	Muckle
Bond Pearce	Nabarro
Brabners Chaffe Street	Norton Rose
Bristows	Olswang
Browne Jacobson	Osborne Clarke
Burges Salmon	Pannone
Charles Russell	Pinsent Masons
Clifford Chance	Reed Smith
Clyde & Co	RPC
CMS	Shoosmiths
Dickinson Dees	Simmons & Simmons
DLA Piper UK	SJ Berwin
DMH Stallard	Slaughter and May
Dundas & Wilson	SNR Denton
DWF	Squire Sanders
Eversheds	Stephenson Harwood
Freshfields	Stevens & Bolton
Harbottle & Lewis	Taylor Wessing
Herbert Smith Freehills	TLT
Hogan Lovells	Travers Smith
Irwin Mitchell	Walker Morris
Jones Day	Ward Hadaway
K&L Gates	Wedlake Bell
Latham & Watkins	White & Case
Lawrence Graham	Wragge & Co

The True Picture

The True Picture reports on 120 firms in England and Wales, ranging from the international giants to small regional practices. Most handle commercial law, although many also offer private client experience.

The True Picture

Think all law firms are the same? They're not. Even superficially similar firms can be worlds apart in how they operate internally. Fortunately, one tool exists to sort the wheat from the chaff, the cat's whiskers from the dog's dinners and the Holly Willoughbys from the hopeless wannabes... the True Picture.

Finding the right firm to train with is like finding a relationship: there has to be mutual attraction and you need to be well suited in terms of your interests and style. Between them, the 120 firms covered in the True Picture have thousands of training contract vacancies to fill in 2012. With luck, one of them could be yours. Even if none of these 120 firms wants you, reading the reports will teach you a great deal about the nature of legal training and the experience of working within a law firm.

How we do our research

Every year we spend many months compiling the True Picture reports on law firms in England and Wales, ranging from the international giants to small regional practices. Our purpose is to get to the heart of what you need to know about a prospective employer – what it can offer you in terms of work and working environment. You'll want to know how many hours a day you'll be chained to your desk, the tasks that will keep you occupied and who you'll be working with. Importantly, you'll want to know about a firm's culture and whether colleagues will turn into party animals or party poopers come Friday night.

Most of our chosen firms handle commercial law, although many also offer private client experience. There are a few general practice firms offering publicly funded advice to their local communities. To take part in the True Picture a firm must provide a complete list of its trainees. After checking the list is complete, we randomly select a sample of individuals for telephone interviews. **Our sources are guaranteed anonymity** to give them the confidence to speak frankly. **The True Picture is not shown to the law firms prior to publication**; they see it for the first time when this book is published.

If you'll allow us to blow our own trumpet for a minute, we're the only publication that conducts our research in this way. By chatting to trainees rather than sending them formulaic questionnaires, we can follow up on leads, delve deeper into what makes firms tick and what challenges they face. We think that leads to better, more detailed information for our readers.

Trainees tell us why they chose their firm and why others might want to. We put on our serious faces and talk about seat allocation, the character and work of different departments, the level of supervision and what happens to people on qualification. And we flirt shamelessly to get the gossip on firm politics, office oddities and after-hours fun. We look for the things trainees agree upon, and if they don't agree we present both sides of the argument.

We also speak to senior sources at every firm – managing partners, training partners, recruiters. You'll notice their comments scattered throughout the True Picture features and published in more detail online. We conduct these management interviews to get their insights on what their firm's strategy is for the coming years. We know that by the time you, our readers, hopefully begin your training contracts in 2015 and beyond, market conditions might be very different, so we've tried to make this a forward-looking guide. Each True Picture feature isn't supposed to simply be a review of a training contract, but rather a broader picture of a firm as a whole. After all, it's not much use knowing that 'trainees are Firm X are happy/sad and work reasonable/terrible hours' but not having a clue about the commercial environment in which Firm X operates. Again, we're the only publication to go into this much detail.

What kind of firm do I choose?

Your choice of firm will be based on location, size and the practice areas available... then it's a matter of chemistry. Some firms are stuffier, some are more industrious and some are very brand-aware, involving trainees heavily in marketing activities. Some work in modern open-plan offices; others occupy buildings long past their sell-by date. Some focus on international business; others are at the heart of their local business communities. Some concentrate on contentious work, others transactional. The combinations of these variables are endless.

What we found out this year

The redundancies and falling profits of 2009 and 2010 are now fading into the mists of time, corporate activity has recovered somewhat and, after hearing a lot of talk from firms about 'consolidation' in the last few years, now we're hearing more about growth. This should not imply that the profession is out of the woods yet. The economy is still on shaky ground, government cuts are biting, the Eurozone crisis is lurching to goodness knows what conclusion – the effects on law firms have been and will continue to be profound. Read more about all this in our feature on **Trends affecting the profession** on page 22.

A word on law firm mergers or closures. Mergers are an increasingly regular occurrence in the profession. This is partly due to the recession – strength in numbers, and all that. However, it is also a result of globalisation. The firms with large international networks seem to feel that unless they have offices absolutely everywhere, they will be left out of an emerging global elite. When firms merge, trainees' contracts are honoured, though of course it does mean that new recruits find themselves in a different firm to the one they signed up to. Closures are rarer, but as we've seen with the case of Halliwells and Dewey & LeBoeuf in 2010 and 2012 respectively, they do happen and trainees can find themselves out on their ear.

Since the recession many firms are announcing their qualification job offers extremely late, making it difficult for those who needed to look elsewhere for employment. Pre-recession, usually just over 80% of qualifiers stayed with the law firms that trained them. After a dodgy couple of years, total retention at our True Picture firms recovered in 2011, and stayed strong in 2012, with 79% of trainees staying on at the firm that trained them. It is to be hoped that firms have managed to 'right-size' themselves. If you intend to use retention rates as a determining factor in your choice of firm, do be wary of the statistics being bandied around. Law firms make their own rules on how to calculate retention rates – you may not be getting a full picture from them. We collect our own statistics and include them in each law firm feature. We have collated statistics since 2000 and publish them on our website.

What we hear every year

- Some seats are more popular and there are no guarantees of getting a specific seat.
- Levels of responsibility vary between departments. In property you might have your own small files. In corporate you will generally work in a very junior capacity as part of a team.
- The experience in litigation depends entirely on the type of cases your firm handles; usually a trainee's responsibility is inversely proportionate to the value and complexity of a case.
- In times of plenty, corporate and finance seats mean long hours, commonly climaxing in all-nighters. The size and complexity of a deal will determine your role, but corporate and finance usually require the most teamwork.
- Most firms offer four six-month seats; some offer six four-month seats and others operate their own unique systems. Trainees switch departments and supervisors for each seat. Most share a room and work with a partner or senior assistant; others sit open-plan, either with the rest of the team or with other trainees. Occasionally trainees have their own room.
- All firms conduct appraisals: a minimum of one at the conclusion of each seat, and usually halfway through as well.
- Client secondments help you learn to understand clients' needs. They can be the highlight of a training contract.
- The Solicitors Regulation Authority requires all trainees to gain experience of both contentious and non-contentious work. Additionally most firms have certain seats they require or prefer trainees to try. Some firms are very prescriptive, others flexible. Remember, a training contract is a time to explore legal practice to see what you're best at and most enjoy. You may surprise yourself.

And finally...

Use the True Picture to help you decide which firms to target. No matter how easy or hard securing a training contract is for you, you'll want to end up with the right one.

Jargonbuster

While we're not the biggest fans of legal jargon, the industry is flooded with it, and some of it actually means something. So if there are any terms you don't understand, or you just want to brush up on your legalese for an interview, then look no further.

- **ABS** – Alternative Business Structures: newly permitted arrangements for law firms, which allow non-lawyers to have a financial stake in the business.
- **ADR** –Alternative Dispute Resolution: a way of avoiding the cost or public exposure of litigation. The most common types are arbitration, mediation and negotiation.
- **Agency work** – making a court appearance for another firm that can't get to court.
- **AIM** – Alternative Investment Market: a 'junior' stock market run by the London Stock Exchange, which allows smaller companies and equities to float stock within a more flexible system.
- **Antitrust** – the US term for competition law.
- **Adjudication** – the legal process by which an arbiter or judge reviews evidence to come to a decision.
- **Arbitration** – a type of dispute resolution where the parties agree to abide by the decision of one or more arbitrators.
- **Associate** – a term used to denote solicitors not at partner level but more senior than an assistant solicitor.
- **Bench** – the judge or judges in a courtroom.
- **Best friends relationship** – a situation where two firms have no organisational or financial ties, but use each other as the first port of call when referring work. This is often found across international borders, eg between Slaughter and May (UK) and Hengeler Mueller (Germany).
- **Bibling** – putting together sets of all the relevant documents for a transaction.
- **Billing target/chargeable hours target** – the number of hours lawyers are required to record working for a client; time is usually recorded in six-minute chunks; trainees do not usually have billing targets.
- **Boutique** – a law firm which concentrates on one or a select few areas of law. They do not necessarily have to be small, but often are due to the scope of their work.
- **Brief** – the instructing documents given to a barrister when they are instructed by a solicitor.
- **Bundling** – compiling bundles of documents for a court case.
- **The City** – the commercial and financial centre of London; also known as the Square Mile, but can also include the Canary Wharf financial district.
- **CMC** – case management conference.
- **Coco** – corporate-commercial work.
- **Conditional fee arrangements** – also called 'no win no fee'; an arrangement whereby a solicitor acting in a claim agrees to be paid a fee only if they win the case; such payment is usually made by the losing party.
- **Contentious matters** – legal disputes between parties.
- **Conveyancing** – the transfer of the ownership of property from one person to another.
- **Counsel** – a barrister.
- **CSR** – Corporate Social Responsibility: the practice of companies taking responsibility for the impact of their activities on society; in reality 'CSR committees' at firms will run projects where lawyers paint schools, plant trees and clean playgrounds.
- **Damages** – a sum of money which one person or organisation has to pay to another for not performing a certain duty.
- **Data room duty** – used to involve supervising visitors to rooms full of important documents, helping them find things and making sure they don't steal them. With electronic data rooms the job becomes more of a desktop exercise.
- **Disclosure** – making relevant documentation available to the other parties in a dispute.
- **Dispute resolution** – litigation, mediation, arbitration, etc.
- **Document management** – dealing with the more administrative side of deal documentation.
- **Due diligence** – the thorough investigation of a target company in a deal.
- **Equity partner** – a partner who receives a contractually agreed share of the firm's annual profits. A part

owner of the firm. The other type of partner is a salaried partner.

- **Fee earner** – a lawyer or a paralegal who bills time to a firm's clients. The term doesn't include lawyers who act in a more supportive role.
- **FTSE 100 (pronounced 'footsie')** – an index of the 100 most valuable companies listed on the London Stock Exchange; the value of these companies is used to give an indication of the health of the UK's business world.
- **Grunt work** – administrative (and boring) yet essential tasks including photocopying, bundling, bibling, paginating, scheduling documents, data room duties and proof-reading or checking that documents are intact.
- **High net worth individuals** – rich people.
- **Higher rights of audience** – the qualification necessary to become a solicitor advocate.
- **Highly leveraged** – the practice of having a ratio of few partners to lots of solicitors; leverage is also a term used in finance – the two are not connected.
- **Infant approval** – court authorisation for a settlement involving a minor.
- **In-house lawyer** – a solicitor or barrister who is employed by a company or public body rather than a law firm or barristers' chambers.
- **Injunction** – a court order requiring a party to do, or to refrain from doing, certain acts.
- **IPO** – the Initial Public Offering of shares in a company to the public on a stock market; also known as flotation.
- **Judicial review** – the legal process by which the actions of the government or public bodies can be challenged.
- **Junior Lawyers' Division** – a subgroup within the Law Society set up in 2008 to represent student members of the Law Society, trainees and lawyers up to five years' PQE (see PQE!).
- **Law Society** – the official representative body of solicitors in England and Wales.
- **Legal aid** – a government-funded system which pays for legal representation in criminal and some civil cases for individuals who would otherwise be unable to afford it.
- **Legal Disciplinary Partnership (LDP)** – a business structure whereby a law firm can take on non-lawyers as equity holders. Up to 25% of a partnership can be non-lawyers.
- **Legal Services Act** – the 2007 Act of Parliament encourages the development of one-stop shops that deliver packages of legal services at the convenience of consumers and provides an alternative path for consumer complaints.
- **Limited Liability Partnership (LLP)** – a way of structuring a professional partnership such that no partner is liable to any of the firm's creditors beyond a certain sum.

- **Litigation** – a method of settling disputes through legal proceedings in court.
- **Lockstep** – the practice of increasing solicitors' salaries based purely on seniority.
- **M&A** – mergers and acquisitions; the buying, selling and combining of companies; often the main focus of firms' corporate teams.
- **Magic circle** – the name given to five of the leading London-based law firms; it is generally held to consist of Allen & Overy, Clifford Chance, Freshfields Bruckhaus Deringer, Linklaters and Slaughter and May.
- **Managing partner** – the main boss of a law firm, who leads the partnership and/or management committee in running the business and devising its strategy.
- **Master (in the High Court)** – a judge in the High Court ranking lower than a High Court judge, chiefly responsible for case management. They are called 'Master' regardless of whether they are male or female.
- **Mediation** – a type of dispute resolution where a dispute is resolved with the help of a neutral third party.
- **Moot** – a mock trial used to train or test advocacy skills.
- **Nearshoring** – the outsourcing of work to another organisation, usually in a part of the UK where overheads and salary costs are lower.
- **Notary public** – a qualified lawyer appointed by the Archbishop of Canterbury, who is authorised to authenticate and certify estates, deeds, powers of attorney and other documents, especially for use abroad; the majority of notaries are also solicitors.
- **NQ** – a newly qualified solicitor.
- **Outsourcing** – hiring in an external organisation to perform a part of a company's activities. Frequently this is done overseas to take advantage of lower costs (offshore outsourcing).
- **Panel** – a group of law firms or lawyers chosen for regular consultation by a certain business.
- **Paralegal** – a non-lawyer, often with some legal training, who assists qualified lawyers on legal matters.
- **PFI** – Public Finance Initiative: a way of creating 'public-private partnerships' (PPPs) by funding public infrastructure projects with private capital.
- **Power of attorney** – the legal authority to act on someone else's behalf.
- **PQE** – post-qualification experience.
- **Pro bono** – from the Latin 'pro bono publico', meaning 'for the public good'; legal work done without payment as a public service.
- **Public procurement law** – regulates the purchasing by public sector bodies of products, works or services.
- **Profits per equity partner (PEP)** – the annual profits of a law firm divided by the total number of equity partners in the firm; this statistic is often used to

indicate the financial health of a firm, but it can easily be manipulated by altering the number of equity partners.

- **PSC** – Professional Skills Course: a compulsory course taken during the training contract.
- **Restructuring exercise** (in the context of a law firm) – the reorganisation of the firm to make it more efficient, to react to changes in income or to make the firm more attractive to clients; often a euphemistic way of talking about staff/lawyer redundancies.
- **Rights of audience** – the right of a lawyer (either a solicitor or barrister) to appear and conduct proceedings in court.
- **Salaried partner** – a partner who receives a salary but has no contractual claim on the firm's profits; the other type of partner is an equity partner.
- **Seat** – time spent by a trainee working in a department, usually four or six months.
- **Secondment** – the practice of 'lending' trainees and qualified solicitors to a firm's client to work in their in-house legal department for a certain period; is also used in the context of sending a lawyer to another office in the firm's network.
- **Silo-ing** – encouraging people to work in a specific field rather than being generalists; teams working very independently of others within a firm.
- **Silver circle** – a group of elite English law firms, generally considered as falling just outside the magic circle. This tends to include Herbert Smith, Ashurst, Berwin Leighton Paisner, SJ Berwin, Macfarlanes and Travers Smith.

- **Solicitor advocate** – a solicitor who is qualified to represent clients in the higher courts.
- **SRA** – Solicitors Regulation Authority.
- **Superinjunction** – the informal term for an injunction whose existence and details may not be publicly disclosed.
- **Swiss Verein** – a business consisting of a number of offices, each of which is independently liable for its own obligations.
- **Tesco law** – a nickname for the effect of the Legal Services Act.
- **Tort** – a breach of duty owed to someone else (a 'civil wrong') which leads to injury to a person or damage of their property.
- **Training contract** – a two-year period of working in legal practice in which someone who has completed their LPC is trained by an accredited organisation to become a qualified solicitor.
- **Training partner** – the partner who oversees the training scheme.
- **Trainee partner** – a trainee who acts like a partner. Not an entirely likeable peer.
- **Tribunal** – specialist judicial bodies that decide disputes in a particular area of law.
- **Vacation scheme** – a placement with a law firm designed to familiarise a prospective trainee with a firm and vice versa; sometimes called 'vac schemes' or 'summer placements', they are usually held during the summer or at Easter and can last between one and four weeks.
- **Verification** – the aspect of a deal in which lawyers ensure stated information is accurate.

Firms by size in the UK

	Firm	London	S & Thames Valley	South West	Midlands	East	Yorkshire & NE	North West	Wales	Overseas	Trainees	True picture	A-Z solicitors
1	Government Legal Service	●									50	295	582
2	Eversheds	●			●	●	●	●	●	●	60	275	573
3	Clyde & Co	●	●					●		●	71	234	560
4	Linklaters	●								●	239	351	602
5	Allen & Overy	●								●	210	169	538
6	Addleshaw Goddard	●					●	●		●	70	165	537
7	DLA Piper	●		●			●	●		●	180	259	569
8	Freshfields Bruckhaus Deringer	●								●	186	287	579
9	Clifford Chance	●								●	242	231	559
10	Pinsent Masons	●		●	●		●	●		●	185	404	623
11	Berwin Leighton Paisner	●								●	84	188	544
12	Hogan Lovells	●								●	133	311	589
13	Squire Sanders	●		●			●	●		●	53	450	639
14	DWF	●		●			●	●			44	269	571
15	Norton Rose	●								●	116	385	615
16	Herbert Smith Freehills	●								●	158	302	585
17	Irwin Mitchell	●		●	●		●	●		●	88	325	592
18	Kennedys	●	●	●	●	●	●	●		●	32	333	595
19	Hill Dickinson	●					●	●		●	39	308	588
20	Shoosmiths	●	●		●			●			41	425	631
21	Mills & Reeve	●			●	●	●	●			34	370	609
22	Ashurst	●								●	109	179	541
23	Slaughter & May	●								●	178	439	636
24	Wragge & Co	●			●					●	52	512	660
25	Nabarro	●					●			●	51	382	614
26	Gateley	●			●		●	●		●	29	290	580
27	CMS	●		●						●	125	237	n/a
28	Burges Salmon			●							46	219	555
29	Simmons & Simmons	●		●						●	82	431	633
30=	Dickinson Dees	●					●				30	255	568
30=	Dundas & Wilson	●									25	265	570
32	SNR Denton	●	●							●	50	443	637
33	Baker & McKenzie	●								●	80	183	542
34	Reed Smith	●								●	54	407	626
35	Bond Pearce	●	●	●							20	202	549
36	Taylor Wessing	●				●				●	49	460	643
37	SJ Berwin	●								●	76	434	634
38	TLT	●		●						●	23	467	645
39=	Charles Russell	●	●			●				●	25	224	557
39=	Travers Smith	●								●	41	471	646
39=	White & Case	●								●	57	503	656
42	Trowers & Hamlins	●		●	●		●			●	36	477	648

Note: Firms are listed in order of size as measured by UK partner and solicitor figures provided to Chambers and Partners.

Firms by size in the UK

		London	S & Thames Valley	South West	Midlands	East	Yorkshire & NE	North West	Wales	Overseas	Trainees	True picture	A-Z solicitors
43	RPC	●									31	411	627
44	Olswang	●	●							●	36	388	616
45	Cobbetts	●			●		●	●			36	240	561
46	Macfarlanes	●									59	354	603
47	Stephenson Harwood	●								●	32	455	640
48	Browne Jacobson	●		●	●			●			17	214	554
49	Mayer Brown International	●								●	52	360	606
50	Osborne Clarke	●	●	●							32	393	n/a
51	Farrer & Co	●									20	278	574
52	Mishcon de Reya	●								●	18	373	610
53	Freeth Cartwright	●	●		●			●			18	285	578
54	Pannone	●						●			28	396	619
55	Bird & Bird	●								●	32	199	548
56	Holman Fenwick Willan	●								●	30	314	590
57	Speechly Bircham	●								●	26	447	638
58	Ward Hadaway						●	●			18	488	652
59	Morgan Cole		●	●					●		11	376	611
60	Brabners Chaffe Street							●			11	209	552
61	Lewis Silkin	●	●								13	349	601
62	Skadden	●								●	12	437	635
63	Lawrence Graham	●								●	30	344	599
64	Ashfords	●		●							30	174	540
65	Walker Morris						●				31	485	651
66	Watson Farley & Williams	●								●	28	493	653
67	Penningtons	●	●			●					21	401	621
68	Bevan Brittan	●		●	●						16	191	545
69	Withers	●								●	13	510	659
70	Jones Day	●								●	28	328	593
71	Capsticks	●			●		●				12	222	556
72	Ince & Co	●								●	31	320	591
73	SGH Martineau	●			●					●	20	414	628
74	Latham & Watkins	●								●	34	341	598
75	Wedlake Bell	●									12	496	654
76	Dechert	●								●	23	252	567
77	Veale Wasbrough Vizards	●		●							15	480	649
78	K&L Gates	●								●	15	331	594
79=	Kirkland & Ellis	●								●	10	338	597
79=	Weil, Gotshal & Manges	●								●	20	498	655
81	Michelmores	●		●							9	368	608
82	Manches	●	●								20	357	605
83	Kingsley Napley	●									10	336	596
84	Gordons						●				11	293	581

Note: Firms are listed in order of size as measured by UK partner and solicitor figures provided to Chambers and Partners.

Firms by size in the UK

		London	S & Thames Valley	South West	Midlands	East	Yorkshire & NE	North West	Wales	Overseas	Trainees	True picture	A-Z solicitors
												Pages	
85	Bristows	●									19	211	553
86=	Bircham Dyson Bell	●									14	197	547
86=	Forbes						●	●			8	283	577
88	Stevens & Bolton		●								8	458	641
89	Cripps Harries Hall	●	●								16	247	564
90	Shearman & Sterling	●								●	25	419	629
91=	Howes Percival	●	●		●	●		●			15	317	n/a
91=	Sidley Austin	●								●	19	428	632
93	Davenport Lyons	●									17	249	565
94	DMH Stallard	●	●								14	262	n/a
95	Cleary Gottlieb	●								●	19	227	558
96	Bates Wells & Braithwaite	●									8	186	543
97	Lester Aldridge	●	●								12	347	600
98	Harbottle & Lewis	●									10	298	583
99=	Boodle Hatfield	●	●								10	205	550
99=	Higgs & Sons				●						10	305	587
101	Muckle						●				8	380	613
102	Edwards Wildman Palmer	●								●	15	273	572
103	Wilsons	●		●							8	508	658
104	Henmans		●								5	300	584
105	Paul Hastings	●								●	5	399	620
106=	Covington & Burling	●								●	14	245	563
106=	Memery Crystal	●									8	365	607
108	Fisher Meredith	●									11	281	n/a
109	Collyer Bristow	●								●	8	243	562
110	Trethowans		●	●							7	474	647
111	Orrick Herrington & Sutcliffe	●								●	13	391	618
112	McDermott Will & Emery	●								●	10	363	n/a
113	Sheridans	●									2	422	630
114=	BP Collins		●								7	207	551
114=	Bingham McCutchen	●								●	5	194	546
116	Wiggin	●		●							6	506	657
117=	Arnold & Porter	●								●	2	172	539
117=	Vinson & Elkins	●								●	8	483	650
119	Thomas Cooper	●								●	8	463	644
120	Morrison & Foerster	●								●	6	378	n/a

Note: Firms are listed in order of size as measured by UK partner and solicitor figures provided to Chambers and Partners.

Addleshaw Goddard LLP

The facts

Location: London, Manchester, Leeds

Number of UK partners/solicitors: 160/650

Partners who trained at firm: 28%

Total number of trainees: 70

Seats: 4x6 months

Alternative seats: Secondments

On chambersstudent.co.uk...

- How to get into Addleshaws
- Team building in Romania

Expect all things bold and big from this Northern colossus, which "*continues to innovate*" in its quest to dominate in the City.

Journey south

Addleshaw Goddard reported a 5% hike in turnover and a 37% rise in partner profits in 2012 – a welcome improvement from the previous year, which saw each dip considerably. This financial amelioration did not come without a price, namely a round of redundancies in which 24 senior associates were let go due to, as managing partner Paul Devitt told the legal press, "*natural attrition falling in recent years.*" After a few years of depressed profits, however, it looks like AG's recession-busting measures are finally coming good. For trainees, the firm's next moves are clear: "*Increase our profile in London, and maintain it in Yorkshire.*" According to training principal Andrew Blower, Addleshaws maintains a strident TOOT ('Three Offices, One Team') stance that ensures "*the overarching strategy across the three offices doesn't differ although each also has its own local markets focus too. Overall, we're heavily focused on FTSE 100 clients and equivalents. We align ourselves across four market sectors, which are: financial services; real estate; government, energy and infrastructure; and retail and consumer.*"

They may act as one team, but each Addleshaws hub has its own distinct identity. The London office reigns in the corporate mid-market, whereas Manchester's transactional team excels in banking and finance and Leeds gets a lot of its corporate work from jumbo building society takeovers. The Northern offices are top of the pops when it comes to real estate, while London's niche lies in construction and social housing finance. For trainees, deals often have their roots in other offices, with many supervised by seniors based in another city. "*The market sector focus is cross-practice and cross-office. Trainees are encouraged to involve themselves in that from the start,*" Blower confirms. Add to this an ever-increasing amount of international work – indeed, long-awaited arbitration-focused outposts in Singapore and Dubai are finally due to open in 2012 – and this sounds like a training contract that's going places. "*We're still more of a national than international firm for sure, but the changes are appealing,*" trainees thought.

Trainees visit each of Addleshaws' key areas: corporate, litigation, commercial services, finance and projects, and real estate. A brand-new HR team recently joined the firm and brought with it a fresh approach to seat allocation. "*There's the sense that they're trying to make the system more transparent than before,*" sources told us, explaining that they're now given the chance to "*map out our ideal training contract from start to finish*" and have "*occasional progress chats with HR to establish how things are going.*" If there are any grumbles, it's because the process "*can seem inflexible at times.*" That said, trainees emphasised the firm's endeavours to "*do their best for third and fourth-seaters*" – some are even allowed to switch offices in order to spend time in an oversubscribed department. Client secondments are also available.

Fancy FTSE work

Addleshaws' corporate group has plenty of FTSE 100 clients "*the firm's always keen to mention*" such as Diageo, Barclays, Capita and Aviva. London's team tends to gravitate towards mid-market M&A work, for which it is top-ranked in *Chambers UK*; Manchester and Leeds,

Chambers UK rankings

Banking & Finance	Information Technology
Banking Litigation	Insurance
Capital Markets	Intellectual Property
Charities	Life Sciences
Competition/European Law	Local Government
Construction	Outsourcing
Consumer Finance	Partnership
Corporate Crime & Investigations	Pensions
Corporate/M&A	Planning
Defamation/Reputation Management	Private Client
	Private Equity
Dispute Resolution	Product Liability
Education	Professional Negligence
Employee Share Schemes & Incentives	Projects
	Public Procurement
Employment	Real Estate
Energy & Natural Resources	Restructuring/Insolvency
Environment	Retail
Financial Services	Social Housing
Fraud	Tax
Health & Safety	Transport
Healthcare	

meanwhile, square up to the likes of DLA Piper and Eversheds in the tables and frequently work on transactions to rival the magic circle, on behalf of some big national players like Costcutter, Travelodge and Lloyds TSB. Up north, corporate seats have a specific concentration like "*private equity or straight M&A*," while new starters in Leeds can choose a transactional seat "*with a focus on building society and projects work*," which offers the chance to get involved with deals like the Norwich & Peterborough Building Society's recent merger with Yorkshire Building Society – a matter that involved the transfer of assets worth £3.7bn. On the private equity side, there's a lot of work with 3i and, across the Pennines, the Mancunian team looks after the portfolios of companies like communications providers Daisy and plumbing supplier (not to be confused with swanky Piccadilly café) Wolseley. Work-wise, trainees can and do "*get a mixture of everything*," although "*the deals are pretty vast, so tasks like drafting can be limited.*" Indeed, because "*some of the deals are so huge*," it's not uncommon to "*find yourself mainly project-managing and co-ordinating due diligence – if there are a lot of completions, you're the person making sure that all the documents are on the table for parties to sign.*" Trainees assured us their role is far from that of a lowly paper-pusher, though – several spoke of trying their hand at "*more complicated*" tasks such as legal research and drafting.

Corporate clients often spill over into contentious and commercial groups and occasionally permeate office boundaries. "*Sharing the workload is viewed as really positive – there's no sense that because a client is based in London the work can only be done there*," agreed trainees. On the commercial side of things there's "*competition, advertising, public procurement and contentious and non-contentious IP work*" for big-ticket clients like HarperCollins, ITV and Primark as well as a handful of TV and film production companies including Tiger Aspect (*The Vicar of Dibley*) and Celador (*Slumdog Millionaire*). Trainees informed us that day-to-day tasks can vary wildly: "*One day you're working out the mechanics of a shared trade mark between a UK and a Belgian company and the next you're drafting the heads of terms for an endorsement contract between a celeb and a toiletries maker.*"

Litigation in particular is an area earmarked for expansion, especially within the recently boosted London base. Much of Addleshaws' contentious work is commercial or construction-related. There's much more beyond these areas for trainees to get their teeth into, however: between its contentious practices, AG lawyers handle everything from fraud cases to insurance litigation to support work stemming from vast corporate takeovers. Trainees often sit with specialist teams, but "*you actually end up with a lot of general work. It would be difficult to be pigeon-holed here*," they told us. Manchester and Leeds represent many of the firm's financial clients – "*often on the claimant side*" – as well as commercial enterprises like Lloyds Pharmacy, Sainsbury's and William Hill, while a chunk of London's current workload stems from claims brought by renowned oligarch Boris Berezovsky against legendary business tycoon and Chelsea FC owner Roman Abramovich. It would take more time than we've got to delve into the strange world of Russian billionaires, but let's just say the drama kicked off when AG's client spotted his nemesis during a shopping outing on Sloane Street and decided to take it upon himself to hand-deliver his writ. Even with disputes approaching the billion-pound mark there is "*the chance to get quite involved*," doing "*a bit of everything – research, attending trial and drafting witness statements and instructions to counsel.*"

Shifting gears

Real estate's another field in which Addleshaws excels: both Leeds and Manchester are top-ranked in *Chambers UK* for their efforts on the transactional and contentious real estate and construction fronts. The Leeds team acts as the sole adviser to Travelodge, completing over 50 matters for the hotel chain in 2011 alone. Yorkshire lawyers also handle a number of agricultural clients – namely, landowners who are buying or selling land. In London, it's all about social housing and real estate finance work. Trainees in the latter group often work closely with the banking team, "*doing lease reports for banks and producing the certificate for the title report if we're acting for the buyer.*" On the whole, mainstream property clients tend to be "*large retail tenants and financial service providers*" like The Co-operative Group, Threadneedle, Scottish Widows and Standard Life. Massive clients don't always equate to minuscule responsibility, though. "*The size of the actual matters can be quite small, so you don't always have that much supervision,*" testified one trainee. "*From day one you get your hands on the same files as a junior associate. Rather than working on independent tasks, you get to deal with the other side, handle negotiations and close the file. It's rewarding to see a matter take shape like that up close.*"

Though certain groups – real estate included – tend to be rooted in local clients, there's a lot of national work, particularly in corporate, litigation and projects – all areas in which "*it's not uncommon to be supervised on a matter by an associate from another office.*" That said, trainees admitted that despite the firm's adamant TOOT ethos, "*there's not always as much overlap as they'd like you to believe*" in terms of workload or working style. The degree of supervision appears to differ from office to office, for example: a source up North reported supervisors "*running through my workload every week and checking up on my hours,*" while a London interviewee found that partners there "*sometimes treat trainees like somewhat of an afterthought as their primary focus is winning business.*" Moreover, some sources pointed to evident "*shifts in culture*" in AG London – "*they're starting to focus on operating more as a business than a training centre*" – but most chalked up such differences on that end of the M1 to AG's ardent desire to prove itself in the capital's legal scene. Thought one: "*The Northern offices know where they are in the market and are more assured. London is still pushing to get better work, and there's a keen awareness that there's competition in the City.*"

Making a CityPoint

Trainees get to know each other before they even begin training, as the entire cohort are sent to Romania for a week to help build housing for the charity Habitat for Humanity. Although trainees admitted to "*sticking with people from our office at the beginning,*" they found the trip "*a great way to bond with future colleagues, which makes starting out so much easier.*" Back at the firm, there's no doubt that Manchester trainees have the fullest social calendars. "*We all live centrally, so we can always spare a bit longer after work to let our hair down. We'll go for a drink three or four times a week, have lunch together, maybe go to the races.*" In Leeds, it's all about the free monthly drinks, while Londoners enjoy a spread of sports teams and sporadic events like a summer barbecue/sports day – "*an egg-and-spoon and sack race kind of affair.*" Still, outside of Manchester most agreed the firm could stand to be "*a little bit more creative about offering chances to socialise – it's important to have those opportunities to raise your profile as a trainee.*"

For many in the capital, the recent move from Aldersgate Street to swish new premises at CityPoint Tower is "*indicative of where the firm sees itself going. We're opposite Slaughters and around the corner from Linklaters – it's clear the firm wants to compete for magic circle-quality work.*" By the sound of it, the hub's interior is as impressive as its location. Along with a "*funky*" new subsidised canteen, there's a "*fresh, minimalist*" open-plan design that renders "*the hierarchy less obvious*" and makes it "*far easier to approach people,*" interviewees found. The Mancunians over in Barbirolli Square have an equally popular and rather wholesome-sounding canteen "*with lots of healthy choices. It's nice to have an area where you know you'll be able to catch up at lunch, even if you haven't got much time.*" In Leeds, there's a similarly enthusiastic focus on lunching as "*most people live out of the city, so it's not always feasible to stay late after work.*" An atrium replete with greenery and a fountain and a patio backing onto a canal are also lunchtime hotspots.

And finally...

Trainees emphasised that *"being enthusiastic goes a long way"* at Addleshaws. *"Working hard and making the effort to get to know people – that's the best way to get noticed."* In 2012, 34 out of the 41 qualifying trainees were lucky enough to stay on at the firm.

ALLEN & OVERY

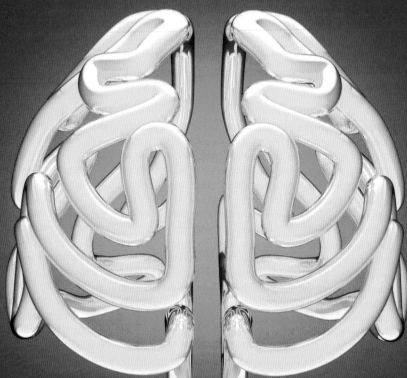

Setting precedents, not following them.

At Allen & Overy you will have to be able to think beyond what has been done before. You'll be supporting ambitious businesses that are themselves breaking new ground and your ideas can make the difference. So, from your first day as a trainee – and even as a student on a vacation scheme – what you do and say will matter, both to your team and to your clients.

Visit **www.allenovery.com/careeruk** to see more.

Join Allen & Overy to do more.

www.facebook.com/AllenOveryGrads

Allen & Overy LLP

The facts

Location: London
Number of UK partners/solicitors: 186/662
Total number of trainees: 210
Seats: 3 or 6 months long
Alternative seats: Overseas seats, secondments
Extras: Pro bono – Battersea Legal Advice Centre; language classes

On chambersstudent.co.uk...
- How to get into A&O
- A history of the firm

Everything about Allen & Overy is big: its size, its reputation and its strategy. Just make sure you don't call it "*cuddly.*"

A right royal affair

The creation of the man who advised Edward VIII on the abdication crisis and his pug-ugly mate who had a habit of urinating in sinks (see our website), Allen & Overy has grown to become one of the world's most famous law firms. Its financial practices shine brightest, earning top-tier ratings from *Chambers UK* in everything from asset finance to Islamic finance to structured finance and derivatives. However, A&O can turn its hand to more or less anything and groups as diverse as insurance, international arbitration, environment and restructuring are also at the very top of their game.

In 2011, almost 60% of A&O's £1.12bn turnover was generated by offices outside of the UK and in the last three years alone it has opened 12 new offices, most recently in Casablanca, Jakarta and Istanbul. "*We took a calculated bet on globalisation,*" explained graduate recruitment partner Richard Hough, "*and it's reaping dividends.*" And don't expect the pace to slow down any time soon. According to Hough: "*We won't spread ourselves too thinly, but Africa is an exciting economy. We hope to use our presence in Morocco as a stepping stone for further development in Africa in due course.*"

All this tinkering at the macro level is having a direct impact on those in A&O's Spitalfields HQ. Work has become increasingly collaborative, and in 2011 half of all cases involved three or more offices. For trainees, "*it used to be the case that people came to A&O for opportunities to travel. Now, there will be more of an obligation to travel.*"

Big money

Seats are either six or three months long, depending on demand, and trainees must spend at least twelve months in the firm's core practice areas – banking, corporate and international capital markets (ICM). Big-ticket corporate and financial work is unavoidable at A&O, but "*each of those departments breaks down into subteams which cover very different things, so it's not difficult to find areas you're interested in.*"

For their first seat, newbies are guaranteed the broad practice group of their choice, but are dropped into one of its subgroups at random. Three months in, there's a seat planning evening: "*It's like a careers fair where all the departments sell their wares to you.*" Trainees pick a 'priority seat' which the firm will "*bend over backwards*" to squeeze them into, and another 'request seat'. Pretty much every trainee will spend their final six months on secondment to either a client or an overseas office that complements the department they hope to qualify into. In general, "*the only people who have had issues are those who tried to put down three very tiny departments,*" explained one source. "*It'll be difficult for you to sit in more than one of those.*"

The firm's enormous banking practice is the biggest department by turnover and is split into subgroups including leveraged finance, regulatory and funds, structured, asset and project finance. Two things common to each subgroup are "*heavy-duty*" clients – the likes of Citi, HSBC, RBS and Goldman Sachs – and the high level of client contact afforded to trainees: "*They're generally happy for you to liaise with clients, even as a first-seater.*" There are so many seats on offer that we can't touch on them all, but we'll try to give a broad overview. Asset finance involves

Chambers UK rankings

Administrative & Public Law	Information Technology
Asset Finance	Insurance
Banking & Finance	Intellectual Property
Banking Litigation	Investment Funds
Capital Markets	Life Sciences
Commodities	Outsourcing
Competition/European Law	Partnership
Construction	Pensions
Corporate Crime & Investigations	Pensions Litigation
	Private Client
Corporate/M&A	Projects
Data Protection	Public International Law
Dispute Resolution	Public Procurement
Employee Share Schemes & Incentives	Real Estate
	Real Estate Finance
Employment	Real Estate Litigation
Energy & Natural Resources	Restructuring/Insolvency
Environment	Tax
Financial Services	Telecommunications
Fraud	Transport

funding seriously big purchases like planes, yachts, ships and oil tankers. "*About a third of time is spent doing pretty administrative tasks – bibling, and drafting cover letters for documents – but the rest of the time they really encourage you to take an active approach on deals. Because of the high volume of work, trainees can step up and take ownership. One guy got sent to deliver 60 jumbo jets.*"

Renowned for its technical nature, the regulatory and funds group is heavy on "*black letter law,*" and trainees can expect plenty of drafting experience. The busy leveraged finance seat involves work for private equity houses – "*they're quite aggressive, as they come in and buy out companies, so it's pretty full on.*" Trainees reported drafting fee letters and legal opinions, and even being sent overseas on signings. "*On those transactions where timing is tight, they have to trust you. If you show yourself to be organised without making too many mistakes, there's quite a lot of scope.*" The project finance department is in high demand and covers energy, utilities and infrastructure law. It's the trainees' job to put together the first draft of documents, and ensure closings run smoothly.

"*In most City firms, capital markets is part of the general banking and finance practice, but here it's so big it's standalone, and a core department.*" Securitisation "*is probably the most legal area of the capital markets group.*" Trainees are forced to pick up complex ideas quickly, running due diligence efforts and drafting documents. The same is true of general securities where, "*once they trust you, you're very much left to your own devices,*" and can occasionally even run smaller transactions with

partner supervision. A&O is particularly big on derivatives and structured finance – "*we're one of the most pre-eminent firms in that,*" noted one interviewee. "*It's a little scary at first,*" but "*trainers assess how comfortable you are, and the work you're given matches that. If you're raring to go, you get interesting work. If you're apprehensive, work is tailored to that.*"

The corporate department is also divided into subgroups, but "*the workflow between them is very flexible.*" Like banking, trainees tend to be involved in drafting documents and closing deals, although "*it's widely known that training tasks are research and admin,*" often for gargantuan transactions such as Virgin Money's £747m acquisition of Northern Rock. In smaller teams, our sources found work to be "*a lot more substantive.*"

Great power, great responsibility

Over on the contentious side of the business, "*the arbitration group has a very aggressive growth plan.*" A source in the group reported having "*quite large levels of responsibility thrust on my shoulders from day one,*" mainly involving "*drafting arguments, and research, research, research.*" If a trainee gets lucky with timing, there are also opportunities to attend hearings, "*working with senior associates and partners to prepare opening and closing submissions.*" Every trainee in the litigation department needs to undergo a time-consuming, but ultimately very helpful, research task described as "*the LPC on steroids.*"

Picking final seat secondments is very much a "*game of strategy,*" as trainees bid for their destination of choice. Options vary from year to year, but opportunities have recently cropped up in Paris, Amsterdam, Milan, Bucharest, Moscow, Hong Kong, Dubai, Abu Dhabi, Sydney and New York to name a few. Check out our website for more details.

"*People say if you go to a big firm like A&O you'll be a small cog in a big machine and not get much work,*" said one source. "*I haven't found that to be the case, to be honest. You get as much responsibility as you can handle, but if you're completely swamped there's a big enough infrastructure to get some help.*" Trainees find their experience in each seat ultimately comes down to their supervisor – or "*trainer*" in A&O-speak – with whom they share an office. Partner trainers have a tendency to funnel a vast amount of work down to trainees. If it's a senior associate, sources reported being "*passed around different associates in the group, getting involved in various things and managing different work streams.*" While there is inevitably the odd personality clash, most trainees find their trainers "*take a genuine interest in developing you as a lawyer.*"

Anger management

"There's no escaping the fact" that there are going to be some long nights in the office. It does all depend on what department you're in, and when. During quieter phases, trainers tend to shoo their wards out of the office at the earliest opportunity – *"I was out before 6pm every day last week,"* one source told us. At busier times, it's pedal to the metal. *"100% capacity means that 100% of your time is filled with work. When I finished my last seat, I was at over 200%,"* a trainee lamented. Another continued: *"It's slightly soul-destroying sometimes, especially when you start out. There have been moments when I'm sat at 2am reading a 200-page document thinking, 'Is this what life's all about?' But that passes: you realise you're being melodramatic."* Ultimately, A&O trainees know better than anyone that you *"do work first, and sleep around it."*

Fortunately, these long hours are made bearable by the fact that A&O quashes so many other negative magic circle firm stereotypes. For starters, many interviewees expressed surprise at the mish-mash of characters at the firm. *"In other places there was a core of white, male, Oxbridge people. There's not really an old boys' network here, so to speak."* The firm has done a decent job of refreshing itself, keeping its more dinosaurish partners at bay. One articulate source explained: *"Honestly, the old stuffy ones don't tend to last. There's a real emphasis on technology and innovation. The atmosphere doesn't foster those old-school, red braces kind of people."* Of course, working in a high-pressure environment, tempers can get frayed, but on the rare occasions that people shout, it's *"out of frustration, not at each other."*

These factors combine to give A&O its reputation as *"the friendly face of the magic circle."* Richard Hough receives the compliment diplomatically: *"We are collegiate and friendly, but that's not what drives us."* He continues: *"If you take friendly to mean cuddly and easy, that misrepresents the firm and we may attract the wrong sort of candidate. We might also put off those focused, hungry, ambitious young lawyers who think, 'I don't want friendly, I want deals'."* The culture, of course, varies between teams, but according to trainees, the one thing common to them all is *"an absolute commitment to excellence. You really get the impression you're learning with people absolutely at the top of their field."*

Para bailar a Levanda

"The offices help promote work/life balance," one trainee joked: *"Your life is in work!"* In fact, trainees could quite happily remain within the confines of A&O's flashy Spitalfields office for the entirety of their training contract. Its *"unbelievable"* facilities include a shop, GP, physio, dentist, beautician, music rooms, beds and even a full-on Nuffield gym complete with mini football pitch. There's two canteens jam-packed with food options, including *"a chef who cooks your choice of food fresh for you in a wok."* Levanda on the sixth floor is a posh café by day and a bar by night, with barbecues on the landscaped terrace every Friday during the summer months. In fact, it's a minor miracle that, as one interviewee pointed out, *"the one thing common to all trainees, is that none of them are fat."*

More concrete trends among Allen & Overy trainees include that *"everyone here is a massive overachiever."* Most have top grades from a first-class uni and a raft of extra-curricular interests. We're informed *"their effort to recruit people from diverse universities is genuine."* Recruitment, trainees explain, is more about personality and 'fit'. *"It's about satisfying the 3am test,"* claims one. *"If you're working until beyond 3am, you want someone you can take a break and have a laugh with."*

Having completed their LPC together in Moorgate, new arrivals at the firm have a ready-made group of close friends to get *"Levanda'd"* with on a Friday night. When work allows, the whole firm heads up to the bar at 6-ish for a mass mingling and mojito session. There are also office-wide, departmental and trainee-only events on a regular basis – more often than not these have a generous budget, and *"are held in really interesting places."* The banking team had its Christmas bash in Tower Bridge – *"the bits that go across between the two towers."* If trainees can squeeze anything else around their work, sports clubs include football, rugby, netball, squash and sailing. *"They're all quite sociable in terms of heading to the pub after a game."*

Trainees who conclude that the fast-paced A&O lifestyle is for them are desperate to stay on at the firm. They are, however, realistic about their chances. *"It's not unfair to say if it's a small team, and very popular, it will always be difficult to qualify into."* That said, in 2012 the firm managed to keep on 97 out of 115 qualifiers.

And finally...

A&O may be friendly but it certainly isn't an easy ride. Those willing to knuckle down to some serious hard graft will be rewarded with first-rate training, excellent prospects and a sparkling name on their CV.

Arnold & Porter (UK) LLP

The facts

Location: London

Number of UK partners/solicitors: 18/22 (+3 non-UK-qualified)

Total number of trainees: 2

Seats: 4x6 months

Alternative seats: Ad hoc overseas seats and secondments

Extras: Pro bono – TrustLaw, i-Probono and others

On chambersstudent.co.uk...
- How to get into Arnold & Porter
- Interview with training partner Richard Dickinson

Take your notion of a US firm and turn it on its head. Welcome to the world of Arnold & Porter.

Hey Arnold!

Arnold & Porter has never been afraid to do things a little differently, having been the only major law firm in the USA willing to represent the victims of McCarthyism back in the 1950s. In 2012, it still refuses to tick all the expected boxes. It's a huge global operation with only a couple of trainees in London; a US firm with small firm hours; a corporate leviathan with a boutique-like expertise in IP and life sciences. Trainees at A&P are privy to a pretty unique training experience.

While the US part of the firm excels in everything from antitrust to government contracts work, the small UK office is much more specialised. *"Our main focus in London to date has been on life sciences, healthcare, competition and IP,"* explains training partner Richard Dickinson. *"We are, however, continuing to bolster other areas to grow the London side of the firm. We're currently growing our corporate, international arbitration and white-collar crime capabilities."*

In fact, since we last True Pictured Arnold & Porter, it has done an awful lot of growing. It has jumped from 14 UK-based partners up to 20 – largely a result of a lateral hiring spree. It's also become embroiled in some headline-hitting cases, such as defending the Management and Standards Committee of News International on the criminal side of its recent phone-hacking misadventures. Trainees say: *"The office is always looking to grow and take on new areas of work, but we're not all of a sudden going to change our spots."*

Heal the world

Seats are available in life sciences, corporate, IP, and competition, with international arbitration and white-collar crime new additions as of 2012. Perhaps the most important thing to note about the training contract at Arnold and Porter is that, at the moment, it only takes on two trainees every other year. This comes with serious perks. *"There's an open dialogue about when you do a particular seat. You can have a chat about at what stage it'd be beneficial for you, and the department's needs at the time."* What's more, the twosome are encouraged to integrate themselves into all aspects of the firm – digging out the work that they want, from the partners that they want – even if they're not necessarily sitting in that seat at the time. *"If an employment partner needs a hand, he'll ask them if they're free,"* Dickinson says. *"It's up to them to manage their own work-flow. It encourages them to grow as lawyers."*

The pharmaceuticals department is arguably the crowning glory of Arnold & Porter London. With big hitters like GSK and Sanofi on its books, it's ranked among the top in the nation by *Chambers UK* for both its regulatory and product liability work. *"It's quite nice as you get a real mix of them both,"* said one source. Trainee tasks in the department tend to filter down to trainees via associates, and include bits and bobs of drafting guidance notes, writing letters to other parties, *"research on certain drugs or requirements from medical standards agencies across Europe,"* and *"pulling out data from expert reports."* There are quite a few doctors and science boffins in the department and while an interest in pharmaceuticals *"might help in terms of motivation, you can always look up terms on the internet or ask a partner,"* if you're really stuck.

Chambers UK rankings

Competition/European Law	Product Liability
Intellectual Property	Retail
Life Sciences	Telecommunications

One-third of all A&P's London lawyers work in the IP group. Heading an impressive portfolio of patent work for pharma clients, the team has advised clients as diverse as dating website Plenty of Fish and the estate of Michael Jackson on protecting their trademarks. Trainees *"absolutely love"* their time in the seat. *"It was about 50/50 transactional and litigious work,"* said one. *"On the one hand helping out with patent work, soft IP and copyright advice, and on the other drafting witness statements and sitting with counsel in court."*

A&P's corporate group in London is tiny – it has only three partners, and quite a few of its matters originate in the USA. It dips its toes into sovereign debt work, helps out the firm's pharmaceutical clients with their corporate requirements, and works for some big-name retail brands, including trendy Urban Outfitters and Anthropologie. The even-smaller competition seat quite often sends trainees out to the Brussels office, where they're able to get involved in work for clients like Kraft, AT&T and Monsanto. *"I had some quite substantive work – things like reviewing contracts for dominant clients – but it wasn't regular,"* claimed one trainee. Trainees in these groups regularly find themselves getting *"dragged into a whole mish-mash of things"* by other rogue partners – particularly *"bits and bobs"* for real estate and *"research on foreign jurisdictions"* for telecoms.

There are few trainee-specific training sessions at A&P *"but the quality of work you get given trains you in a less formal way."* Of course, there's the odd *"doc review from hell,"* but on the whole sources agreed that: *"All my work is really worthwhile, and I'm spending time fruitfully rather than photocopying."* They're particularly encouraged to strut their legal stuff by taking on pro bono work. The office has its own pro bono co-ordinator who alerts everyone to incoming cases. *"We're encouraged to get involved in those matters from the beginning – we do everything from LGBT matters to the use of CCTV. You get work you wouldn't necessarily be doing in your practice group."*

There's plenty of UK-based work floating around but *"a pretty substantial chunk has an international connection."* All new qualifiers get to visit *"the mother-*

ship" in Washington, DC for a firm-wide New Associates' Retreat – a week of seminars and socialising. This regular contact aside, trainees *"do quite often feel like we're just a good London City law firm, rather than part of the bigger American side. It's nice to be a bit independent."* It's also nice to have more easygoing hours. Trainees do sometimes graft into the early hours but in general, *"most people are out of the office by 7.30pm."*

Garden room with a view

It might be growing apace, but there's no denying that A&P is very cosy for a City firm. *"By the end of my training contract I knew everyone in the firm and had worked with all the partners, and most of the associates,"* noted one NQ. It's a pretty tight-knit place – the type of firm where partners will chat with trainees over the water cooler. The two current trainees and a group including London managing partner Tim Frazer even decided to embark on a charity cycling trip together. It's not all bike rides and hand-holding, however, and newbies are expected to bring a healthy dose of oomph to their training experience. *"If you're interested in a certain type of work, you can't wait for someone to offer it to you. You need to be proactive about making your wishes known."*

Based up in the clouds in the City's Tower 42, A&P's office is all about the *"breathtaking"* views. *"I don't know how I get any work done up here"* mused one distracted source, looking out over St Paul's. Every Thursday everyone from admin staff up to partners takes in the vista at the 'Garden Room' – the weekly drinks and nibbles event fondly named after the conservatory in the firm's original DC office. *"There's generally a pretty good turnout."* Our sources do occasionally miss the buzzing social scene of some bigger firms, but assured us that *"for a small firm, they do try more than most,"* and always put on events for birthdays and special occasions.

Competition to train at A&P is hot, with about 700 applications for the two prized training contracts. Those candidates who get lucky don't always have a background in pharmaceuticals – it's worked out as a 50/50 split in the last few years – but do have a good reason for choosing A&P. *"We want well-rounded, academically good people,"* says Richard Dickinson; *"people with a spark, who want us for the right reasons. We want it to be an almost symbiotic relationship."* If this sounds appealing, we have good news – increasing the size of the trainee intake is *"actively under consideration."*

And finally...
Since the firm started its training contract in 2002, it has kept 100% of its qualifiers. Even more impressively, only one of those has left the firm since then.

Ashfords LLP

The facts

Location: Bristol, Exeter, London, Plymouth, Taunton, Tiverton

Number of UK partners/solicitors: 73/96

Partners who trained at firm: 21%

Total number of trainees: 30

Seats: 4x6 months

Alternative seats: Secondments

On chambersstudent.co.uk...
- How to get into Ashfords
- Doing business in the South West

Already the largest law firm based in Exeter, this top South West outfit is making a push into Bristol and London.

South by South West

Ashford's history dates back to the 19th century, but it has existed in its present form since a 2004 demerger with the firm that is now Bevan Brittan. It has five offices in the South West and one in London. Exeter is by far the largest and home to around 290 of the firm's total 500 employees. On 1 March 2012 Ashfords merged with 35-lawyer London firm Rochman Landau, expanding its fledgling London office and creating a firm with total revenue of around £30m. *"It is easy to think of us as not-a-London-firm that doesn't do good commercial work – but we do, and now we have a London office we will be able to bring in more work like that,"* one trainee enthused. *"The firm has remained steady in the past few years, but now our business plan is to expand."* During 2010 and 2011 Ashfords did welcome an array of lateral hires from City and national firms like Beachcroft, BLP, Herbert Smith and DLA Piper.

Ashfords has a strong range of commercial practices and sweeps over a dozen South West rankings in *Chambers UK*. Its practice is centred around corporate/commercial, litigation and property, but it has a host of other groups too, ranging from private client and personal injury to projects and construction, while the Plymouth office has a notable shipping specialism. On the firm's client list you'll find South West companies like insurer Cornish Mutual, the University of Exeter and Viridor Waste, as well as London-based, national and some international businesses. The firm also handles work for several local authorities, including a few London boroughs. The sizeable trusts and estates team, meanwhile, advises wealthy individuals from the immediate region and beyond. One of the testimonials on the firm's website is from the Earl of Iddesleigh (it's in Devon) – demonstrating Ashfords' high-profile connections in the region.

Trainees spend time in at least three of the firm's four core areas: corporate/commercial, property, private client and litigation. Within those areas trainees can complete seats in insolvency, corporate/banking, projects, planning, commercial property, construction, trusts and estates, family, marine, employment, personal injury, commercial litigation and property litigation. *"The range of seats is very broad, which is a really good thing"* – our interviewees had experienced an interesting mix of seats, often blending property, corporate and private client options. Not all our interviewees had got their preferred seat options and some felt allocation *"is not as transparent as it could be. There can be a bit of wheeling and dealing about who goes where."* Our first-year sources were notably more positive than second-years, reflecting recent improvements to the system. The HR team now organises seat swaps several months in advance.

At the time of our calls in summer 2012, half the cohort of 30 was based in Exeter, there were seven in Bristol, four each in Taunton and London. Exeter offers all the seats mentioned above, while the other offices have fewer options: Bristol offers an increasing number of mostly commercial seats, while Taunton has private client and commercial. Trainees can and do switch offices. *"Ashfords does like people to move offices to see more of the firm,"* and trainees will be increasingly encouraged to do so in the future. Trainees outside Exeter are currently more likely to move than those in the head office. At the

Chambers UK rankings

Agriculture & Rural Affairs	Intellectual Property
Banking & Finance	Local Government
Construction	Planning
Corporate/M&A	Private Client
Dispute Resolution	Real Estate
Employment	Real Estate Litigation
Family/Matrimonial	Restructuring/Insolvency
Information Technology	Shipping
	Sports Law

time of our calls the legacy Rochman Landau office in London was still operating as a separate training entity with four trainees in total, but South West trainees could apply for London seats from September 2012, and in future all trainees will be expected to spend at least one seat in Exeter.

On the run

Development work is big business for the real estate department, whose clients include regional developers, house builders like Persimmon Homes and Landmark, and the Homes & Communities Agencies. The firm has also advised Devon Primary Care Trust on the £3m sale of Newton Abbot Hospital and acted for Gwent College on the £38m lease and redevelopment of an old steel works owned by Blaenau Gwent Council. Trainees assist on big projects like this but also *"run our own smaller files: some are developments, some are leases, but they are predominantly plot sales for large developers."* Another source added: *"Generally I didn't take the initial instruction, but I did everything from then on: drafting, negotiating and doing the completion. They let you run with it to the point where you feel the ground disappearing under your feet."*

Both the corporate and commercial litigation departments have quite a few energy, waste and water clients, as well as acting for regular widget-producing businesses. The corporate team acted for Devon-based gas turbine producer Centrax on a £100m joint venture with Bahraini shipbuilder ASRY to build power barges (those are boat-based power stations if you were wondering). It also advised R&R Ice Cream on a £2.5m investment in frozen yoghurt people YooMoo. *"You work on a deal very intensely while they are active,"* recalled one trainee. *"I was helping to draft clauses, ancillary documents and board minutes as well as dealing with bundles and closing documents."* Lawyers also work on banking deals and their clients include Clydesdale, HSBC and Lloyds. Another blue-chip client is EDF, which Ashfords recently advised on the construction aspects of the building of two new nuclear power plants in Somerset and Suffolk. The

projects and PFI practice makes up a sizeable chunk of Ashfords' transactional practice. *"Projects probably has the biggest files,"* said one trainee. *"The partners run them and the trainee's job is more behind the scenes: proof-reading and drafting – although certainly not just the dogsbody work."*

"People are always keen to do a commercial litigation seat." The department has regional, national and some international clients such as Amsterdam-headquartered digital security firm Gemalto and energy firm EGL Italia. Trainees can also fulfil their contentious requirement in employment, construction, marine, personal injury and property litigation (among others). One trainee told us of their employment seat: *"I got to progress files myself rather than just working in the background. I took the initial instruction, liaised with the insurer about the prospects of the claim, then drafted claim forms and witness statements and made applications to court."* The experience in an insolvency seat is similar: *"I was impressed by the amount of stuff I got to do,"* said one source. *"I was drafting High Court papers, spoke during meetings in chambers and went to the Court of Appeal."* The department represents trustees in bankruptcy as well as administrators like KPMG, Bishop Fleming and Grant Thornton.

Cider inside, hog in a bog

Several sources said they were attracted to Ashfords for the *"healthy work/life balance."* A standard working day for trainees is from around 8.30am to 6pm. *"My latest night was when I stayed until 9pm,"* said one. *"No department is here until 10pm every evening, but some have more late nights than others. Projects is known for its long hours. The partners got in pizzas when we had to stay late and have taken us out to lunch and drinks to thank us."*

Plenty of time is certainly left for lawyers to have private lives and socialise with their colleagues. In Bristol and Exeter *"there's wine and cider in the office one Friday a month."* The Exeter office is located on a business park by the M5, but *"trainees get a group together and go into town for drinks quite often."* Socialising also occurs at networking events and during sports matches against other local businesses. Firm-wide, there are Christmas and summer parties. *"There was a band and a hog roast,"* one trainee recalled of the most recent one. *"It was in Bridgwater, in Somerset, in the middle of a field."* How bucolic.

Although the trainee intake offers *"an instant friend group if you are new to the area,"* most of our interviewees came to Ashfords with strong links to the South West already. Several attended university in Exeter or studied elsewhere in the South West; others had grown up in the region. "*When I was interviewed I was asked why I wanted to work at Ashfords and it was important to show I had roots in the area,*" said one interviewee; however, local links are not vital. "*People certainly need to be committed to working and having a career in the South West,*" says trainee recruitment partner Ruth Murray, "*but I am not that concerned about whether they have pre-existing links.*" We also noticed that many trainees had had substantive work experience (or previous careers) before joining Ashfords. A few had paralegalled with the firm or elsewhere. "*An overwhelming number of us have done something else before coming here. Very few trainees came straight through from school and university.*"

Tap dancing

Perhaps it's because our interviewees were a little older, but we detected a mature feel to this firm. "*It is very business-oriented,*" said one trainee. "*There is a very commercial feel.*" Trainees are expected to look after themselves quite a lot. "*You have to have your own agenda as a trainee and know what what you want to get out of each seat. If I had expected my supervisor to chart out my work for me I would have been disappointed.*" Happily, supervisors and most other solicitors and partners are "*approachable*" and "*welcoming.*" The open-plan office layout contributes to this. "*We are all mixed together. I sit next to partners, secretaries, support staff and solicitors, so there is a very friendly team spirit. If I have a problem I can just lean across the desk and talk about it.*" The smaller offices – especially Bristol – have an intimate feel to them. "*Bristol does a lot of things together. It's all very informal. We go out for team meals and things like that.*" In Exeter, "*it is more the atmosphere in your department that determines your experience. Some floors are quite noisy with people chatting freely. Other departments – like property – are a lot quieter as people are working on their own files, not on a group project.*"

The style of supervision is also "*department-specific – a lot about your experience at this firm depends on the personality of your supervisors.*" Most interviewees spoke highly of their supervisors: "*They are aware we are here to learn and develop our skills as much as possible. All the partners I have worked with have tried to give me good-quality work and get me involved.*" The firm also has "*a career support trainer, Nina Carroll, who organises training sessions and webinars.*"

Trainees felt the HR department takes a light-touch approach to retention and that it's mostly left to departments to offer individuals NQ jobs. "*Across the board, there is no clear system in place. There are no interviews and there is no jobs list. If a department wants you, you just get a tap on the shoulder and are asked if you want the job. If you don't get a tap on the shoulder you don't know if you have a job.*" Second-years agreed the qualification process could definitely be improved. "*It needs to be more structured, open and fair,*" they said. HR sources told us they are engaging with trainees to improve the system. 11 of 15 qualifiers were kept on in 2012.

And finally...
Despite some grumbles about the qualification process, trainees agreed this firm offers *"a hands-on training contract which gives you a lot of of responsibility."*

"It sounds really cheesy, but I think it's important to do your work with a smile and a cheerful attitude. When people give you work, it won't always be exciting. When you have to walk to court in the rain, say 'Yeah, no problem'. You think people don't notice but at your appraisal you'll see they do."

Trainee

make your presence felt

We're looking for natural leaders, agile thinkers and real entrepreneurs with the strength of character to quickly become respected figures in their field.

If you want to inspire colleagues and clients alike, find out more about us:

 020 7638 1111

 gradrec@ashurst.com

 www.ashurst.com/trainees

 www.facebook.com/AshurstTrainees

 www.youtube.com/AshurstTrainees

Australia Belgium China France Germany
Hong Kong SAR Indonesia (Associated Office)
Italy Japan Papua New Guinea Singapore
Spain Sweden United Arab Emirates
United Kingdom United States of America

Ashurst LLP

The facts

Location: London

Number of UK partners/solicitors: 120/300

Partners who trained at firm: 35%

Total number of trainees: 109

Seats: 4x6 months

Alternative seats: Overseas seats, secondments

Extras: Pro bono – Toynbee Hall Legal Advice Centre; language bursary

On chambersstudent.co.uk...
- How to get into Ashurst
- Ashurst's beginnings
- Overseas seats

Ashurst has transformed itself from an old-line City firm into a significant international player without losing its sense of community.

Say g'day to Blake

Ashurst *"isn't the first name that pops into your head when you start looking,"* say its trainees, *"but after a little research you realise the firm is top of the league in many of its practices."* A well-established member of the UK's top 20 firms, Ashurst has an especially strong offering in most areas of financial practice, and does indeed come top of the league (or the *Chambers UK* rankings, anyway) for big-ticket real estate work and PFI/PPP projects, to name but two areas.

2012 has been a busy year for the firm. In the UK, it acted for the non-executive directors of RBS in relation to the FSA report into the near-collapse of the bank, and advised The College of Law's management team on its £200m sale to Montagu Private Equity. Internationally, the big news was the firm's combination with one of Australia's 'Big Six', Blake Dawson, which was *"our first step to becoming a premier global firm,"* training principal David Carter told us. *"Our intention is to continue to grow as a firm and client demand is at the core of Ashurst's targeted growth strategy. We intend to be practising law in all major financial areas."*

Trainees repeatedly remarked upon *"how international the firm feels. There's a concerted effort from management to push the global reputation. That's how we want to be seen and represented. We want to be at the top of our game on a worldwide scale. The various mergers and expansions are a sign of that. It is a very exciting time to be at the firm."*

Virgin' on super-friendly

Most of our sources had received their first choice of seat every time and were naturally happy with the allocation process. *"People know what they're getting into when coming to Ashurst. You know you have to do a finance seat and a corporate seat, so you just accept it when you're placed in those departments. It alleviates at least two allocation rounds of stress."* Trainees must usually also complete a seat in a contentious area of practice as well, although they can opt to take a two-week litigation course instead. The corporate and finance departments are both broken down into various subdivisions. Additionally, dispute resolution; energy, transport and infrastructure (ETI); employment, incentives and pensions (EIP); real estate; tax; and competition all take trainees.

Many trainees choose Ashurst for its *"excellent corporate and finance reputation,"* and an interest in these areas is certainly important for anyone considering applying to the firm, but actually *"the HR team wants you to get sufficient exposure to different areas of law"* and so taking multiple seats in corporate and finance isn't the norm. *"Saying that, most of the international secondments are finance-based, so you might end up doing one in London and one abroad. The corporate seats can be particularly popular, so it's not fair to give one person two whacks."*

The corporate group handles transactions that are about as big as they come; however, trainees also added: *"Given the financial market, Ashurst is also looking to broaden its client range and take on more mid-tier, growing clients."* The firm recently acted for HSBC and RBC Capital Markets when they were joint financial advisers

179

Chambers UK rankings

Banking & Finance	Intellectual Property
Banking Litigation	Investment Funds
Capital Markets	Life Sciences
Competition/European Law	Local Government
Construction	Outsourcing
Corporate Crime & Investigations	Pensions
	Pensions Litigation
Corporate/M&A	Planning
Dispute Resolution	Private Equity
Employee Share Schemes & Incentives	Product Liability
	Projects
Employment	Real Estate
Energy & Natural Resources	Real Estate Finance
Environment	Real Estate Litigation
Financial Services	Restructuring/Insolvency
Fraud	Tax
Information Technology	Telecommunications
Insurance	Transport

heavy mathematics and at the beginning the lingo makes you feel totally lost;" however, the *"super-friendly"* team are a great help *"and there's a very thorough training program."* Life in the finance department often involves all-nighters and occasional weekend work, *"but your supervisors always acknowledge how committed you've been."*

RUSAL brand

"No one's tied down to a certain type of litigation" in the dispute resolution group. *"If you hit a massive case, then you'll be focused on that, but otherwise there's the potential to do all types of work."* Clients are generally *"major banks or big corporate heavyweights"* and *"cases have good meaty stuff to them."* Ashurst acted for Imperial Tobacco in Court of Appeal and High Court hearings regarding the bans on tobacco vending machines and displays. It also acting for aluminium producer RUSAL in its shareholder dispute with Norilsk Nickel. There's *"no avoiding the standard bundling and doc review, but the department as a whole is keen to get you doing research and give you regular court attendance."* The arbitration department offers the chance to eventually gain higher rights of audience qualifications and there are *"plenty of advocacy opportunities"* for trainees.

Seats in ETI are *"always oversubscribed."* The department is nominally split between energy and projects work, *"but capacity e-mails go out to the department as a whole."* Ashurst is a leader in the energy from waste (EfW) sector – creating power by incinerating waste – and works on projects related to this across the UK. Google 'Riverside EfW' for a typical example. Trainees had experienced plenty of this type of work as well as *"construction-related projects, matters relating to wind farm regulation, and international development work in countries such as the Philippines and Senegal."*

"Extremely exciting" overseas seats include: competition in Brussels; corporate/finance/ETI in Dubai, Madrid, Milan, Paris, Tokyo and Singapore; finance in Frankfurt; and varied options in Hong Kong. Secondments are also available at clients including Tesco, Westfield, Goldman Sachs, Honda and BNP Paribas. For certain European placements, such as Milan or Paris, *"they prefer you to have a grasp of the language,"* although complete fluency isn't required. Looking ahead, trainees theorised: *"We're opening new offices all the time, so there can only be more opportunities in the future."* Ashurst says it hopes to launch a reciprocal secondment with the Sydney office in 2013.

Brew-ski

"From secretaries to partners, everyone is respectful of each other and works really well together. You're happy to stay and work late with all teams." Ah, there's the kicker.

to the Hong Kong consortium UK Water during its £2.4bn bid for Northumbrian Water. It also worked for supermarket chain Morrisons on its £70m acquisition of online baby products retailer Kiddicare, and for Real Estate Opportunities on the demerger of Battersea Power Station's assets. At the time of our calls there were 27 trainees in corporate seats, which gives you an indication of the department's size. It is split up into M&A, funds, financial institutions, private equity, restructuring, equity capital markets and 'technology and commercial', *"which is essentially IP. You can apply for a specific seat or simply ask for corporate and get a pot-luck choice. Realistically, funds is probably the easiest to get into, but that team does prefer third or fourth-seaters,"* trainees explained. When it comes down to it, though, *"you'll probably end up doing a range of work. You'll focus more on what your supervisor does, but you're never simply shoehorned into one area. If you have a particular corporate interest, you're encouraged to put yourself out there."* Supervisors *"are very good at getting you involved and giving you work that you're interested in."* Typical tasks include drafting board minutes, research, verification and attending client meetings. Interestingly, trainees qualifying into corporate continue to rotate round its sub-groups for their NQ year before settling down into a specific one.

The international finance department is advising RBS on the financing of Virgin Money's £747m acquisition of Northern Rock. It is *"officially broken down into three subgroups for trainees: banking; a securities and derivatives group (SDG); and a real estate finance team."* Securities and derivatives are *"a very technical and specialist area of the law. There's a lot of terminology and*

"*By the very nature of our size and the work that we're doing, there are going to be periods where you're working all night and on weekends. People trust us to get the work done and the hours aren't always conducive to having a social life.*" However, "*there are times when you can head off at 6.30pm. Trainees don't get completely shafted, and our efforts are definitely appreciated.*"

This firm has been nicknamed 'Lashurst' due to its "*work hard, play hard*" reputation. When we asked what they thought about that, trainees said: "*Actually, the Lashurst thing reflects that we really don't take ourselves too seriously,*" but didn't try too hard to deny that this is a fun-loving place. If you're looking for extra-curricular, "*we have it,*" they said. There are all the usual sports teams, plus wine-tasting evenings, the annual carol service and feasting at "*charity picnics on the roof terrace.*" Several departments run regular ski trips, alongside their own "*amusing evenings out.*" On Friday afternoons, "*everywhere you look there'll be cake and ping-pong tables. People just bring in cake and share.*" Trainees are also treated to an annual ball. "*Every year has a theme and this year was a 40s jitterbug, black-tie do. It was held at the Imperial War Museum, which was really good fun, and almost everyone went. People love getting into themes.*

Another year it was at a zoo and someone came dressed like a tiger. People go all-out." One source did add: "*Please don't think that means the social stuff is somehow enforced. No one is obliged to attend anything or pushed to drink, and there are plenty of people that don't.*" We think the Ashurst attitude was summed up perfectly by the trainee who said: "*Of course you're not forced to join in, but people want to be included – I mean, you wouldn't want to miss out!*"

Alongside the 'play hard' reputation, Ashurst also used to be known as being a bit rah, but to be fair the firm has done a decent job of ridding itself of this image. The firm is a lot more international than it was and one source noted: "*It is becoming more obvious that an international outlook is very important to those hiring. There's a real mix of ethnicities and backgrounds.*" True enough, many of our interviewees came from overseas – while the Brits we spoke to had attended a range of universities, not just Oxbridge.

Retention has been continuously good at Ashurst and trainees felt "*the graduate recruitment team do their absolute best to keep people on.*" In 2012, 45 out of 57 second-years were retained on qualification.

And finally...

Ashurst isn't a member of the magic circle but in terms of the work and lifestyle it offers a pretty similar experience. Take that comment as it is intended – high praise.

Baker & McKenzie. Born global.

Join Baker & McKenzie and you'll have the best of all worlds.

Global is the first word people associate with Baker & McKenzie. We were established to offer a genuinely global perspective and operate without boundaries around the world.

Other law firms can open offices worldwide to try to match what we have. But they can't readily match how we think, work and behave.

Our global reach means we have well-known clients; we have fantastic relationships because we are business people who are great lawyers (not the other way around).

Our approach is friendly and inclusive; we are nice people and good citizens.

You'll find this a challenging and stimulating place to work, but one where you will also be inspired to always be your best.

Visit **www.bakermckenzie.com/londongraduates** to find out more.

Baker & McKenzie

The facts

Location: London

Number of UK partners/solicitors: 86/213

Total number of trainees: 80

Seats: 4x6 months

Alternative seats: Overseas seats, secondments

Extras: Pro bono – Save the Children, United Nations High Commissioner for Refugees, Bethnal Green Legal Advice Centre, A4ID and others

On chambersstudent.co.uk...

- How to get into Baker Mac
- Interview with training partner Simon Porter
- From small beginnings to global giant

If ever there was a definition of a global law firm, then B&M is it.

Taxi natter

Not many people know that the origins of one of the world's largest firms can be traced back to a chat in a taxi, but that's where B&M's founders first met. It now has over 3,800 locally qualified lawyers staffing 71 offices in 44 countries. This extensive international reach means that despite originating in the US, it is difficult to regard B&M as simply an American outfit with a string of foreign offices, and the firm's Swiss Verein structure has a lot to do with this: each office is semi-autonomous, focusing on the immediate domestic market while simultaneously acting for clients on an international scale. Trainees *"can feel the big global network around us, but at the same time we stand on our own here. It's our own gaff."*

The London office is a prime example of B&M's pioneering spirit: opened in 1961, it was the first US-founded firm to establish a presence in the UK capital. The office – now the largest in the B&M network – is mostly populated by UK-qualified lawyers, and the client base primarily consists of multinational corporates and financial institutions. Although the emphasis is on cross-border corporate and finance work, B&M London is not quite up there with the magic circle firms, with *Chambers UK* ranking its M&A work a few tiers below the top band in which the likes of Slaughter and May and Allen & Overy compete. One source opined that *"those magic circle firms have an entrenched reputation as the go-to firms in those areas, and it's hard to break into that, but I think we're getting there slowly but surely."* Time will tell, but for now, B&M London has a sturdy all-round reputation, and is especially well regarded in the areas of administrative and public law, employment, IT, outsourcing, private client and telecommunications (all of which are top-ranked by *Chambers UK*).

There are many things that bring trainees to B&M. The size: *"I was looking for a firm that wasn't as gigantic as the magic circle firms, but still big enough so that you can get interesting and international work for big clients."* The variety of the work itself: *"I was quite impressed by the combination of more mainstream practices like corporate with more independent and niche areas like IP, IT and pensions, which have good reputations of their own and aren't just corporate support practices."* The atmosphere: *"The people here had a lot of character but were not pretentious. I found other global firms to be much more intimidating."*

Transparency International

All trainees must spend at least one seat in the corporate department, and many fulfil this requirement during their first year. Trainees also state a 'preference seat' which they are guaranteed at some point, and can list three preferences before each seat rotation as well. *"A lot of people request their guaranteed preference during their third seat – if possible – as generally they feel more ready for it then."* After a few grumbles last year about the transparency of allocation, our sources this time round were on the whole content with the process: *"HR does as good a job as possible under difficult circumstances. We are a lot more transparent than other places. I know that some firms have more of an application procedure for oversubscribed seats, but we don't have a large bureaucracy here, and I like that."*

Chambers UK rankings

Administrative & Public Law	Information Technology
Banking & Finance	Intellectual Property
Banking Litigation	Investment Funds
Capital Markets	Media & Entertainment
Competition/European Law	Outsourcing
Construction	Pensions
Corporate/M&A	Pensions Litigation
Data Protection	Private Client
Dispute Resolution	Private Equity
Employee Share Schemes & Incentives	Product Liability
	Professional Discipline
Employment	Public International Law
Energy & Natural Resources	Public Procurement
Environment	Real Estate
Financial Services	Restructuring/Insolvency
Franchising	Sports Law
Fraud	Tax
Immigration	Telecommunications

B&M's corporate department is divided into four teams: North, South, West and East. West deals with general M&A and restructuring/insolvency. The group represented Prestige on its acquisition of 17 healthcare brands – including heartburn saviour Gaviscon – from GlaxoSmithKline. Trainee tasks include the typical *"due diligence and a lot of drafting documents,"* but interviewees enjoyed being in a department *"where you're very much the hub of the deal: often these transactions have an IP element, or an employment element, and you have to constantly liaise with the other departments and be very organised."* Corporate North is focused on project finance and infrastructure work, with an emphasis on oil and gas deals. Sources found the work interesting, stating that *"the energy work we do can have huge political implications – I'm fascinated by that real-world application."* It's a fast-paced seat and trainees do *"everything they throw at us!"* For more detail on Corporate South (private equity and telecoms matters) and East (securitisation, financial services), plus other seats such as IP, head to the bonus feature on our website.

B&M's banking department has been especially busy with acquisition finance work, handling primary and secondary buyouts among private equity firms in the Nordic countries. In the past year the firm advised EQT on the financing of its acquisition of Atos Medical from Scandinavian rival Nordic Capital Fund V. One source estimated that *"75% of my work has been acquisition finance,"* which means *"assisting with the drafting of ancillary documents, shareholder approvals and company guarantees."* Project finance is another source of work, despite the worsening Eurozone crisis affecting the ability of banks to commit to long-term funding. Regardless, B&M has still received instructions, and advised the Gulf JP Company on a £760m project to develop a natural gas-fired power plant in Thailand. Trainees described the seat as *"quasi-corporate"* due to the transactional nature of much of the work, and found that they *"got to work with almost everyone in the department,"* picking up some restructuring matters and advising on anti-bribery issues as well.

Right up your Baker street

Employment is a particular area of strength for B&M, in London and firm-wide. *"We really do have some stellar clients,"* commented one source, and the Camelot Group, Prudential and Hewlett-Packard have all chosen the firm to handle their employment-related issues. British Airways utilised B&M's expertise after 100 claimants took industrial action against the airline over contested pilot salaries. *"Transactional work is quite a small part of what trainees do: most of the time you'll be working on litigious matters, cracking away at the disclosure, drafting letters to the other side, attending witness interviews and writing statements."* Sources felt that they *"knew cases inside out, as you're the person people come to for information."* This means quite a bit of *"document handling and bundling,"* but for the most part sources were happy to be a part of the *"hot topic cases that you see in the press."*

Dispute resolution can be *"glamorous,"* with *"big banking litigation matters and quite a lot of crossover with the banking teams."* The team has defended Bank St Petersburg against allegations of fraud and conspiracy, while other departmental highlights include representing Globe Motors – an automotive manufacturer – in a damages claim worth €30m, after an exclusive supply agreement was breached. The commercial nature of work in this department is supplemented by a number of smaller teams which specialise in areas such as product liability and recall, competition and fraud. Product liability disputes in particular come with *"lots of research, searching for data that may be of interest, putting in some analysis and drawing out your own conclusions – they like you to have your own mind."* Trainees enjoyed the fact that they weren't *"pigeon-holed"* and could work with a variety of teams, and also get exposure to international arbitration cases (the Bank St Petersburg matter being a prime example).

Overseas secondments to B&M offices have resurfaced after a reduction in offerings last year. Sources mentioned that the pause *"did aggrieve people, especially because the firm markets itself as – and is – an international firm. This dissatisfaction was fed back quite strongly to the powers that be, and now the chance to go away seems a lot more available."* Trainees went on to explain that *"the main rule is that they will only let you go overseas if by your third seat it looks like you have two decent qualifi-*

cation options. *If you've not been keen on the seats you've completed so far, then you're told that it's not a good idea to go.*" Most overseas placements have a corporate focus, as deals are predominantly multi-jurisdictional and it's easier to slot trainees in. This year, trainees had been posted to destinations including Singapore, Sydney, Moscow, Tokyo, Amsterdam, Brussels and Washington, DC. Sources who wanted to stay closer to home had opted for client secondments, which are numerous, and said that "*people often have this idea that you take it easy on secondment, but it's really not the case – you learn to juggle a lot of different matters, and when someone asks you a question they expect an answer straight away. You have to take a deep breath and get them to tell you – honestly – how urgent what they are asking is!*"

Chocs, Turkey and LeBoeuf

"*I wouldn't think twice about talking to a partner,*" said one interviewee, who joined the chorus of praise bestowed upon B&M's pleasant atmosphere. "*It's not dog-eat-dog,*" added another. "*The general mentality is based on an 'all in it together' approach – that is the B&M culture.*" We asked for specific examples: "*Say if you had a massive project, and you sent an e-mail around to the rest of the trainee intake because you knew that you were going to be swamped – they would come and pitch in, and they would volunteer because they know you need the help.*" We also heard about a partner who sent around "*a little box of chocolates to everyone who had worked on this horrifically busy deal – he didn't have to do that, but it made the whole process a little easier.*" Others put it into more of a global context: "*It's so easy to be a person on the other end of an e-mail, but whenever we are communicating with foreign offices we are encouraged to pick up the phone – depending on the time zone – so that there's a more personal interaction.*" B&M is also "*big on diversity*" and devotes much of its CSR work to increasing social mobility: "*The firm just tries to have a social conscience: we go to certain schools to encourage students to undertake work experience with us. It's something that a lot of firms talk about in marketing brochures, but B&M actually does it.*"

Despite all of this "*warmth,*" it would be a mistake to think that life at B&M is always fluffy and easy-going, as one trainee put it: "*We are obviously a global firm, and aim to be the biggest and the best. We always think with our global hat on!*" This is still a deeply ambitious place, and work hours can be tough, especially within corporate and banking. "*It does depend on the client – I remember one that certainly didn't believe in weekends! There can be a lot of unpredictability, but at the same time they're serious about enforcing days off in lieu.*"

Based on New Bridge Street, close to St Paul's, the office doesn't have "*that Canary Wharf feel – we're just before Fleet Street so we're not quite in the pressurised environment.*" The office itself has a "*90s-esque façade, and we're just above Pret,*" but inside some renovation work has begun to transform the space: "*They've spent some time doing up the conference rooms and reception, laying down new carpet, painting the walls white and putting in some more espresso machines – and the restaurant's got a lot better.*" Trainees share offices with their supervisors or associates.

Trainees study the LPC together at the College of Law. They remain close, even if "*as you get older and busier there isn't so much time to socialise as a group.*" This is also quite a sporty firm: "*There's hockey and football teams, and cricket in the summer, and rugby sevens in September.*" Christmas parties are usually held in a posh hotel and incorporate a special awards ceremony, "*for people who have contributed to the firm – they have awards like the 'nicest person' award and the 'fluency' award*" ('fluency' is a key word at B&M, denoting a desire to be the most cohesive of all global firms). Team drinks and dinners are also scheduled, and successes are often celebrated in style: "*When we opened in Turkey we had a client reception in the British Museum.*"

B&M generally has good qualification rates. "*We have a meeting well in advance and discuss our options with the graduate recruitment representative and the training partner. They take us through the whole process – they're open with you and let you know if you're going for an oversubscribed seat.*" In 2012, 32 out of 38 qualifiers were retained.

Trainees commented on the latest office openings in Casablanca, Johannesburg (involving the rescue of lawyers from the collapsing Dewey & LeBoeuf), Istanbul and Doha as a clear indication that B&M isn't slowing down, but instead "*focusing on making the network as efficient and co-operative as it can be.*" Our interviewees were sure about one thing though: no matter how much B&M London strives to bolster its corporate and finance capabilities, it will never have "*that cold corporatey shiver that you find in other firms.*" Let's hope not.

And finally...
Baker & McKenzie is ideal for those seeking a global firm that incorporates a blend of mainstream and niche practices in a mid-sized setting.

Bates Wells & Braithwaite London LLP

The facts

Location: London
Number of UK partners/solicitors: 28/56
Partners who trained at firm: 28%
Total number of trainees: 8
Seats: 2x6 + 3x4 months
Alternative Seats: None
Extras: Pro bono – LawWorks, A4ID

On chambersstudent.co.uk...
• How to get into BWB
• The Third Sector
• More cases and deals

A fast-expanding corporate department has given charity-centric Bates Wells & Braithwaite a new dimension.

Feisty one you are

Bates Wells & Braithwaite is a real big-shot when it comes to charity and social enterprise. For over 40 years this little London firm has been a market leader in the field and represents over 1,000 charities, including start-ups as well as household names such as Barnardo's, the RSPCA and the Samaritans. BWB's work in this sector accounts for roughly 60% of the firm's turnover and you'll find there's a sprinkling of it throughout all departments.

The firm is not exclusively charity-focused, though, and the corporate and commercial practice has seen sustained expansion recently. *"We have significantly increased our corporate department since Mark Tasker arrived as head of department 18 months ago. That will continue full steam ahead for the next few years,"* commented training principal Paul Seath. A trainee joked: *"We're definitely trying to become a bit more corporate without completely going over to the dark side."* With an eclectic client base including multinational corporations, financial institutions, private companies and high net worth individuals, the corporate team focuses predominantly on the small to mid-cap M&A market. There has been a dramatic increase in M&A work for the firm over the past twelve months, with both work volumes and turnover increasing by approximately 150%. Despite this, one first-year concluded: *"Charity will always be the lifeblood of Bates Wells. It may be evolving in other areas, but it will always have the hallmark of a charity law firm."* BWB is also highly ranked by *Chambers UK* for its immigration, media and public law work.

Come fly with me

Trainees choose from four 'flight path' seating plans before they start. Each is a five-seat training contract mapped out by the firm in advance. Trainees select their preferred flight option, with reviews from previous trainees included to help them decide. Each flight path includes stopovers in charity, dispute resolution and either employment or property. Other seats include immigration; public and regulatory; and corporate/commercial. All of our interviewees praised the format: *"Although there is little flexibility, there is also no in-fighting or insecurity about getting certain seats. There isn't that competition you may feel elsewhere,"* said one.

Charity is the biggest department at BWB and the team plays an active role in policy and legislative change in the public benefit sector. Senior partner Stephen Lloyd was even appointed by the Cabinet Office as the expert lawyer advising Lord Hodgson of Astley Abbotts on the government-led review of the Charities Act 2006. Although David Cameron's 'Big Society' has led to significant cuts in the Third Sector, this has actually created a substantial stream of work for the department. Trainees were thrilled to be working with *"people at the cutting edge of the sector."* Sources told us that *"the standard trainee task is drafting,"* and all our interviewees were immersed in some really high-level work. *"I was running my own files, seeing them through from the initial client meeting right to the end,"* said one. Another mentioned *"sitting in on round-table discussions when amendments to legislation were being proposed."* There is also a wealth of client contact for trainees, especially in the numerous pro bono cases the firm gets its teeth into. Despite the supervisors

Chambers UK rankings

Administrative & Public Law	Healthcare
Charities	Immigration
Data Protection	Media & Entertainment
Defamation/Reputation Management	Partnership
Education	Professional Discipline
Employment	Real Estate
	Real Estate Litigation

being some of the biggest names in charity law, trainees said: "*Your views are taken into consideration. There's no right way of doing things a lot of the time so if you've got a suggestion they do listen.*"

Top Dogg

The immigration department is top-ranked by *Chambers UK* and team head Philip Trott is named as a star individual by our parent publication. "*It was amazing to be working with the market leader,*" said one trainee lucky enough to work under Trott's tutelage. The department has a 50/50 business and personal immigration split. Business clients include Nike, Endemol and numerous US law firms such as Morgan Lewis and Debevoise. The personal immigration branch has many interesting clients to doggument, but there's one who really stands out as the doggfather. You may have guessed from the dodgy puns that the firm represents Snoop Dogg, with Trott directly helping out when he was barred from entering the UK, reportedly even going so far as to accompany him on his private plane to ensure smooth passage through immigration control. A big player in the rap game, Trott has also worked with the likes of P Diddy, 50 Cent and Busta Rhymes on issues involving their entry to the UK. "*Work ranges from commercial immigration to family-based work,*" said one source. "*You get a lot of hands-on experience with a number of quirky clients who have complicated immigration histories.*" Although the department is "*quite small,*" all our sources said they were "*in one client meeting, minimum, every day.*"

As a result of the firm's recent success in the corporate field, Paul Seath says: "*We are thinking of developing and amending some of the flight paths so they will include more time in corporate.*" Trainees said the seat involves

working on reductions of capital, restructuring, commercial contracts and, of course, M&A. The department was labelled as "*the most demanding,*" with partners "*relying on you to complete a lot of research and drafting.*" Overall, trainees felt time here was a "*great learning curve*" and had been involved in a lot of "*juicy stuff.*"

The dispute resolution seat is very diverse, both in terms of the clientele – "*you could be working with big organisations or the man on the street*" – and the cases that came in. "*I worked on defamation cases, but also issues involving parking fines,*" said one. It was also said to be the most research-heavy seat at BWB. "*You cannot underestimate how much research you need to do,*" one trainee told us. However, it also gives you a "*good experience of all court procedures.*"

No quarrels over morals

With the majority of our interviewees involved with good causes before starting at BWB, we asked Paul Seath whether the firm actively recruits people with that experience. "*Of the applicants we get, a very good proportion do have a background in charity or volunteer work,*" he said. "*But for a firm as broad as we are, we also want trainees who'll focus on other areas. We don't just want people who want to go into charity.*" What sort of characters do end up at BWB then? "*People who have the same moral belief system as the firm,*" offered one trainee. "*None of us have come into law for the money and we all generally wanted to do some good – we're all pretty liberal.*" Indeed, founding partner and Lib Dem peer Andrew Phillips still pops by the office now and then "*just to have a chat with everyone.*"

The offices are located opposite St Paul's Cathedral and have a gym in the basement which offers lunchtime keep-fit classes. An active social committee organises monthly events including trips to the Harry Potter studios and spots on the Jack the Ripper tour. There's an annual 'away day' where the whole firm ventures out together. This year's included an open-top bus tour round London, followed by lunch and a treasure hunt in Regent's Park, before rounding off with dinner in The Grange Hotel. There are also a number of "*small, quirky*" touches, such as a day off to go Christmas shopping, which trainees really appreciate. The Wine Tun is a popular watering hole – and conveniently located under the office.

And finally...

BWB has a pretty strong record when it comes to retention. In 2012, three of four qualifiers took up NQ position at the firm.

Berwin Leighton Paisner LLP

The facts

Location: London

Number of UK partners/solicitors: 186/381

Total number of trainees: 84

Seats: 4x6 months

Alternative seats: Overseas seats, secondments

Extras: Language classes

On chambersstudent.co.uk...
- How to get into BLP
- Interview with managing partner Neville Eisenberg

You can smell the ambition at Berwin Leighton Paisner, a 21st-century success story.

Silver service

Just over a decade on from the merger that created it, Berwin Leighton Paisner has forced its way into the 'silver circle' – that ill-defined group of firms deemed to be the magic circle's closest competitors – and retains the *"ambition and drive"* that got it there in the first place. With revenue up 8% to £246m in 2012 and clients such as Tesco, UBS, Barclays, the *Financial Times* and the Football Association, to name a few, there's no wonder trainees maintain: *"This is a very exciting place to be. You can feel it in the levels of work coming in, the e-mail updates and the general buzz. People tend to be young and energetic and the firm is constantly trying to improve and be more efficient."*

BLP has its roots in commercial and real estate work; and in the four-seat training contract, *"officially the firm wants you to do a core corporate, a core real estate and a contentious seat,"* interviewees explained. *"They strongly encourage the corporate and real estate departments from a common-sense point of view. They are still BLP's strongest departments and have the most NQ positions available."* One source added: *"The two departments still bring in about 50% of revenue."* The firm has what it calls a 'five-pillar strategy' – five key areas on which it concentrates – and is accordingly split into corporate, real estate, finance, tax and dispute resolution departments, *"with about 25 subgroups within them."*

"A real highlight of 2011/12 was opening offices in Hong Kong, Frankfurt and Berlin," managing partner Neville Eisenberg told us. *"Our international expansion tends to be focused on emerging markets and centres of capital.*

Having opened in Moscow, Abu Dhabi and Singapore, Hong Kong was a natural step for us. Germany has an internationally active real estate market, so it was also important for us to create a presence there." Our trainee sources also thought there would be increasing opportunities in the banking and finance departments, and Eisenberg said: *"We continue to expand our finance department, particularly in regards to banking, capital markets, asset finance, structured finance and project finance. As it develops, there will definitely be more scope for trainees to be involved. The finance area at BLP is going to be a very exciting place for young lawyers."*

Give the people what they want

The seat choices themselves are divided into four categories: real estate, corporate/finance, contentious and 'other', which includes IP, competition, employment, construction and contentious planning, among others. Core corporate is divided into M&A; public markets, which is mostly AIM work; funds and financial services; and private equity. Real estate consists of three groups, devoted to different types of client, while the contentious requirement can be fulfilled by completing a stint in core litigation, contentious tax, IP, employment, restructuring or planning.

The HR department *"makes a very conscious effort to give people what they want. They are accommodating and listen to presentations of what you think you've already achieved, and what you hope for the future."* Of course, *"there are 80 trainees to satisfy,"* and so a bit of give and take in the allocation process is required. The basic policy is *"over the four seats, everyone will get their first*

Chambers UK rankings

Asset Finance	Investment Funds
Banking & Finance	Licensing
Banking Litigation	Local Government
Capital Markets	Media & Entertainment
Charities	Outsourcing
Competition/European Law	Parliamentary & Public Affairs
Construction	
Corporate Crime & Investigations	Pensions
	Planning
Corporate/M&A	Private Client
Defamation/Reputation Management	Projects
	Public Procurement
Dispute Resolution	Real Estate
Employment	Real Estate Finance
Energy & Natural Resources	Real Estate Litigation
Environment	Restructuring/Insolvency
Financial Services	Retail
Fraud	Social Housing
Healthcare	Sports Law
Information Technology	Tax
Insurance	Telecommunications
Intellectual Property	Transport

choice at least once. You often won't get more than one seat from the 'other' category – unless you're in one to fulfil your contentious SRA requirement – and second-years' wishes are given higher priority."

Young man, there's no need to feel down

The various corporate subgroups *"are all pretty large and have between 30 to 40 fee earners each."* Trainees go into a specific team but *"can end up helping out other divisions."* Wherever they go, *"the firm also provides general corporate training."*

There's no lack of interesting work in the equity capital markets team. BLP advised Playtech on a placing of new shares on AIM to raise £100m, and acted for J.P. Morgan Cazenove and South Africa-based coal producer Coal of Africa on the $106m placing of shares on both AIM and the Johannesburg Stock Exchange. Trainees *"liaise with lawyers across the globe, draft ancillary documents and get really involved in deals."* The public matters team *"deals with public companies and those wanting to go public. There are several international clients, particularly in Asia and the Middle East. Trainees get very involved and get great support from the partners."* The department's M&A work, meanwhile, is *"very varied. We work with extremely large international clients and small start-ups."* In 2011, BLP advised Balfour Beatty on a joint ven-

ture agreement with Royal Mail; and acted on the £637m sale of Kwik-Fit to Japanese conglomerate ITOCHU.

"If you're interested in real estate, this really is the place to be," trainees claimed. *"BLP will always be known for its real estate work. It is brilliant at it."* Consistently highly ranked by *Chambers UK*, the department is separated into three groups. *"Group two is informally known as the 'Tesco team', as they're more or less devoted to Tesco."* The supermarket chain is a key client and has a relationship with BLP which dates back more than 30 years, to the days of the firm's predecessor, Leighton & Co. *"Groups one and three focus more on large corporate developments, including acquisitions and deals for banks, hedge funds, investment companies and hotels. It's a broad mix of institutional clients."* One source revealed: *"It's well known that group two has the better hours,"* but opined that *"you get broader real estate and corporate experience in the others."* Clients include the English National Opera, the Royal College of Nursing and Goldsmiths College. BLP also advised the YMCA on a £30m redevelopment in Wimbledon. Trainees say they are *"never short of work"* in this department. *"At one point I had about 40 files to deal with and it can be super-hectic. It's such good work and experience."* Interviewees reported *"overseeing property management, doing research, negotiating and drafting all sorts of letters and Land Registry documents."*

Bricks and banks

Several teams have strong connections with real estate, including construction, real estate finance, PFI projects and the highly regarded real estates dispute team. Trainees said: *"Some of the work we do as trainees is almost of NQ standard. It's a small team, so you get to work with everyone. You have several of your own smaller files and then assist on the larger litigation."* Cases the team has worked on include property developer Almacantar's dispute with the MCC over the aborted redevelopment of Lords cricket ground.

Although BLP's banking team has had some departures this year, managing partner Neville Eisenberg assures us: *"We actually had more partners joining the firm than leaving this year. In keeping with our hopes to broaden our finance practice, our banking team is stronger than ever."* Trainees thought: *"The market in general is very difficult, and we're all interested in the future of this department. The team is definitely still strong and our structured finance team is particularly busy. We also regularly receive work that's comparable to any magic circle firm, so you can gauge the level we're working at."* Clients include Deutsche Bank, the Olympic Delivery Authority, ABC Islamic Bank, Lloyds TSB and the Gulf International Bank.

The commercial dispute resolution (CDR) pillar includes commercial litigation, IP, real estate disputes, contentious construction and insurance/reinsurance. Recognisable names are aplenty, such as the Central Bank of Trinidad & Tobago and Kellogg Brown & Root. Core litigation offers trainees *"really good work and you get very involved in big trials."*

Over the hills and far away

Other departments include the IP group, which *"has close links to the corporate department."* BLP successfully represented the Newspaper Licensing Agency (NLA) and six of the eight national newspapers in deciding that newspaper headlines were capable of being protected by copyright as literary works. The trusts and personal tax team, which achieved its highest ever Chambers ranking in 2012, has *"an increasing amount of international clients"* alongside a host of traditionally wealthy individuals. The commercial department has clients ranging from *"large international banks to asset-holding, media and betting companies."* Another and growing department is competition, EU and trade. This team advised National Grid on a cartel damages claim, and the Association for Financial Markets in Europe on the European Commission's investigation into the proposed merger between Deutsche Boerse and NYSE Euronext.

BLP has secondments to clients in the UK and overseas, and all secondments are *"linked to departments."* So, for example, a trainee in the commercial team can be sent to Tesco, Schroders or Barclays for three months. The competition group sends trainees to a Brussels seat for six months, the corporate department can get you to Moscow, while contentious construction offers six months in Abu Dhabi. A three-month secondment to Thames Water can make up half a CDR seat. Trainees said: *"The general sense is they are trying to expand overseas placements, particularly in Singapore."* Three-month client placements give *"the chance to properly meet both the team in the office and the team you go to on secondment, and never lose touch with the firm in case it's a department you want to qualify into."*

Magic mirror?

"I would definitely say that this is NOT just another quite boring London firm," one trainee declared, pointing to the *"youthful"* feel of BLP, and growth in the form of new overseas offices and expanding practice groups – *"there are lots of new hires, and some of them are real heavy-hitter partners."* This is definitely an exciting place to be at the moment, but though growth and ambition are exhilarating, *"the vibe of the office has hardened as a result,"* trainees said. More than one second-year source declared that *"it's not as warm as before,"* and felt *"the atmosphere is more focused and heads-down than it used to be."* One added: *"We are aiming to climb up the rankings, but it means there's more of a corporate feel."* The *"main fear that trainees have is, where is it going? With all these lateral hires, is BLP going to become a magic circle alumni club? I don't think we can cope with that."* Our feeling is that these fears are probably unfounded – trainees may work harder, but all agreed that *"there is still quite a chatty atmosphere, on the whole,"* and that *"partners are very open and approachable, and if you ever have an emergency or personal problems, the firm is extremely understanding."*

BLP has never exactly been what you'd call a lifestyle firm, but at the same time it's historically tended to attract bright trainees who didn't fancy the fearsome reputation of the magic circle. This remains broadly true; however, anyone hoping for a gentle ride will be disappointed. Trainees said that the length of working hours *"depends on the department"* and there's *"absolutely no face time,"* but did comment that *"as we get larger and larger, the hours are getting longer."* All-nighters and weekend work are definitely called for, if not yet the norm. *"I have regularly stayed until 10 or 11pm,"* said one source, and *"in real estate, the office is definitely still full at 8pm,"* added another.

The Fine Line and The Monument remain the pubs of choice for Friday night drinks, and trainees try to meet up for *"a Friday morning fry-up in the canteen every so often, just to see everyone."* Sporty types won't be disappointed: *"We have hockey, netball, eleven and five-a-side football, and cricket in the summer. The football team went to Amsterdam this year and the annual cricket match is actually at Lords. It's great and there's normally a barbecue involved. We also have tennis in the summer, run by a professional coach, and the charity committee organises a firm bike ride. We're cycling in the Loire Valley this year."*

BLP is *"quite upfront about the whole NQ job process. Because they only take 40 trainees each year, they want to try and keep everyone. They will try and fit people into departments if they can."* In 2012, BLP retained 31 out of 37 qualifiers, following on from 97% retention in 2011.

And finally...

Graduates used to come to BLP because it was a more easy-going alternative to the magic circle. Maybe that's still true, but we'd suggest it's not the best reason to choose the firm any more.

Bevan Brittan LLP

The facts

Location: Bristol, Birmingham, London

Number of UK partners/solicitors: 44/113

Partners who trained at firm: 20%

Total number of trainees: 16

Seats: 4x6 months

Alternative seats: None

Extras: Pro bono – ProHelp

On chambersstudent.co.uk...

- How to get into Bevan Brittan
- Interview with training partner Steve Eccles

With a renewed public sector focus, a fresh face at the top and "*a real buzz around the firm*," the future looks bright for ballsy Bevan Brittan.

Weir making some changes

The credit crunch has had all sorts of weird and wonderful effects on law firms. Bevan Brittan is a prime example. The firm hit a low in 2008 – it was an oversized organisation with corporate ambitions and a gaping hole in its wallet – but thanks to a blast of managerial wizardry it has emerged in 2012 as a lean, public services-focused firm with sustainable profit levels and no real debt. So, what happened?

Well, non-lawyer chief executive Andrew Manning took up the reins in 2008, and set about patching up the firm's leaks. There was little room for sentimentality, with management opting to cut BB's least profitable practice areas (licensing and tax among others) and rebranding as the UK's go-to "*public services law firm*." The percentage of revenue bought in by public services work snowballed from 65% in 2009 to a whopping 90% in 2011 – a big chunk of this being manifested by "*private sector clients working with the public sector*," such as waste management company Viridor. With everything back in good working order, Manning departed in April 2012, leaving the firm with a more traditional management structure and his close ally and fellow board member Duncan Weir as managing partner. Trainees predict: "*He'll bring a fresh approach, but no drastic changes. The focus will always be on the public sector, but we're trying to get our name out there more*."

Chambers UK recognises Bevan Brittan's public sector talent across all of its Bristol, Brum and London offices. Hardly surprising, given that the firm represents over 30% of all local authorities and more than 40% of all health trusts. It's also tipped nationally for its construction and healthcare departments, and in Bristol for employment and social housing work.

Building works

Bristol is home to most Bevan Brittan trainees – eight at the time of our calls in June 2012, as opposed to five in London and four in Birmingham. Bristolians get to pick four seats from a selection including corporate and commercial; property; commercial dispute resolution (CDR); employment; construction and engineering; commercial health; clinical negligence; projects; and project finance. There are slightly fewer options in the smaller offices. Our sources were content that "*they do take your preferences into account as much as possible*."

The firm's recently created commercial infrastructure umbrella covers five main subgroups: commercial (local government and health); procurement; major projects (PPP/PFI/waste/energy); corporate/IP/IT; and construction/engineering. Trainees are likely to spend at least one seat here, more often than not getting involved with projects work, which will have a specific slant depending on their supervisor's interests. The bulk of the project group's work involves major PPP and PFI initiatives: the last dregs of the scrapped Building Schools for the Future programme, Primary Care Trust and local authority restructuring for NHS LIFT, plus a wealth of other health, education, leisure, housing and energy matters. "*It tends to be multimillion-pound projects*," explained one source. "*I often read something in the paper and think 'we're working on that'*."

Chambers UK rankings

Administrative & Public Law	Information Technology
Clinical Negligence	Local Government
Construction	Professional Discipline
Dispute Resolution	Projects
Education	Public Procurement
Employment	Real Estate
Healthcare	Social Housing

Renowned as "*a slightly daunting*" seat, trainees find that "*actually, it's fantastic. You get really good experience and just a huge amount of responsibility.*" Our sources had been able to get their teeth into huge projects, not only gaining "*exposure to commercial work, but to local government work too.*" Responsibility is indeed pitched high – "*there's lots of drafting, and quite a lot of market research. It's less about case law and more finding out about possible or existing projects happening all over the country.*" If there's a deal closing, trainees are the first to be drafted in. On those, "*there's obviously loads of document work – numerous nights in the office checking and cross-checking – but there's champagne at the end to celebrate.*" All trainees leave the seat with a smile on their faces and bulked-up commercial awareness. "*It's the most commercial seat you can do,*" claimed one.

Commercial health work is "*similar to projects,*" explained one trainee, "*but it's different because of the scale. One case doesn't take up three months of your life. Sometimes clients need advice immediately, or they're trying to procure new services which will be an ongoing contract.*" Another source appreciated the variety of work in the healthcare seat: "*A lot of it is ad hoc queries and bits and pieces that don't fit into other teams' work. I had loads of proof-reading, researching whether certain bodies could enter particular contracts, and helped set up the governance of new foundation trusts.*"

Pneumonoultramicroscopicsilicovolc anoconiosis

BB is well known for its clinical negligence work, often representing the "*really interesting*" NHS Litigation Authority (NHSLA). It's been involved in some big cases for the medical profession within the last year or so – not least its effective mediation between the Cornwall Partnership NHS Trust and 286 learning disabled adults with abuse accusations. Terms like 'angiography' and 'nectosectomy' might not be in your standard legal trainees' vocabulary but our BB sources assured us: "*You do pick up things quite quickly – and Wikipedia always helps!*" What's more, they're afforded heaps of responsibility, particularly when it comes to corresponding with experts and getting out and about. "*You get to go to court,*

issue applications before masters and go to all the summer parties at chambers,*" said one content trainee. "*You do miss that once you move seats.*"

For more diverse clients, head to employment. While NHS trusts and local authorities are on the books, the firm also represents a number of private sector clients. The odd bit of bundling in the seat is inevitable, but trainees reported: "*If I want to do something, I just ask and I have the freedom to do it.*" Daily duties tend to include drafting witness statements and court applications, interviewing witnesses, and meeting with counsel and clients.

While the private sector real estate market has taken a bashing in recent years, BB's team has been beavering away restructuring NHS estates, redeveloping schools, bidding on multimillion-pound energy and waste site deals, and extending community leisure centres for local councils. The department "*lends itself to doing more small-value matters,*" which means that trainees are able to run their own files. Long-running deals tend to get passed from trainee to trainee, which "*means we're able to lead our own little things, as well as getting involved in the bigger stuff,*" explained one. Teams are leanly staffed, and supervisors always on hand for feedback and advice.

The commercial dispute resolution group has a high contingent of private sector clients – think Lloyds Banking Group, Johnson & Johnson and Action for Children – as well as the public sector staples. It continues to be heavily involved in judicial reviews resulting from the government's recent cuts, particularly in the healthcare and education sectors. There's the odd bit of bundling to be done in the seat, but an excellent admin team "*means trainees get involved in the real, interesting work, and on the drafting side of things.*" In fact, we hardly heard any grumbles about work from trainees across the whole of Bevan Brittan. "*From the very first seat, you get a lot of responsibility but never feel like you're thrown in at the deep end,*" they concurred. "*There's always someone you can go to or a support network of some sort.*"

Bevan Brittan makes a big deal about perfectionism, and trainees' work is no exception. "*Every word counts,*" they told us. "*At BB they want to see very polished work every time.*" Fortunately, there's plenty of training on hand to ensure juniors' work is up to scratch. After an initial induction in Bristol, training sessions tend to be department-wide – "*lunchtime updates with counsel or colleagues*" take place every few weeks. There are also plenty of precedents on the firm intranet, support lawyers in each department and a library information team. "*If I ever need clarification on something, there are people I can go to who will direct me to a precedent or publication,*" said one trainee.

Feeling (not so) gloomy

Any gloomy vibes still lingering in the corridors of Bevan Brittan seem to have been ousted by the firm's recent changes. *"There was a lot of negative energy in the air, but we've recently won quite a few awards within the public sector – people are now looking forward to us doing well, and there's a real buzz around the firm generally."* This optimism is largely down to improved internal communications, after management took great pains to make things more transparent. *"They've made a deliberate decision to be clearer internally and externally about the work we do, and want to do."* Trainees have access to exactly the same information as their seniors, via online memos, workshops and 'Meet the Partners' lunches.

"No one gets put on a pedestal or segregated." In fact, every single one of our interviewees made a point of telling us about just how *"approachable"* the firm is. It's a bit of a cliché, but we get the impression that BB really is an inclusive sort of place. *"It's quite a good, friendly atmosphere,"* said one source. *"Everyone is willing to chat and get involved, and it's very welcoming. Everyone makes an effort – even with the work experience boy."* The fact that even the most senior partners at the firm share a pod with trainees probably helps this community feel. *"There's no restriction about kidding around with partners – everyone can take a joke."*

Bevan Brittan is no corporate jungle, and the hours reflect this. Most trainees desert their desks by 6.30 or 7pm on average, and late nights are extremely rare. *"If you're coming up to a big trial, people will stay really late, but there's not really a long-hours culture."* The consensus among trainees is that *"we're fortunate to be somewhere that's not obsessed with time recording. When you've done your work, you've done your work. There's no faffing about."*

The Britt-ish Empire

Located centrally in their respective cities, each of BB's open-plan offices has its own distinct quirks. The Bristol office – very pleasantly situated next to Castle Park – is a big hit with trainees, who make full use of the in-house gym and canteen. There's a healthy Friday night drinks culture, and *"you could probably walk down to The Bridge pub on your own and find people you know,"* but *"everyone has their own lives as well."* Each year, our first-year Bristolian sources are slightly traumatised from their annual initiation ceremony: *"Putting on a sketch and taking the mick out of the biggest partners"* at the office Christmas party. It's a tough job, but *"everyone else always loves it!"*

"I think we're known to be the friendliest office," claimed a Birmingham trainee. *"We're pretty small and there are an awful lot of social events."* In fact, BB's Brummies tend to put on a do in the *"smart, modern and comfortable"* building every few weeks, recently holding a *"Jubilee party in the client suite."*

The Londoners have spent a busy 2012 relocating one floor of its office building near the Old Bailey – *"it's much brighter and nicer, and we're all closer together,"* explained one source. They're only one extra flight of stairs away from ground-floor haunt Jamie's Wine Bar, which is always well frequented at the end of the week.

All three offices share expertise and trainees find *"it's actually very fluid: there's no segregation"* between them at all. Everyone tends to travel around quite a bit, which trainees outside Bristol definitely appreciate: *"Even though we work in a smaller office, we still meet people and get our names known."* They also get to mingle at the annual summer party, last year held at the swanky Bath Racecourse, the only grumble being that *"it'd be nice if we could meet up more."*

Bevan Brittan trainees come from a wide range of universities and walks of life – some straight out of law school, and others with years of public sector experience under their belts. Either way, *"they like to employ people who get involved in social events, and people who they feel can take responsibility and hit the ground running."*

If this sounds up your street, paralegalling at the firm is one way to get a foot in the door, but we'll leave the final word to the trainee who told us: *"If you're interested, do a vac scheme."* In 2012, the firm was able to keep on seven of its nine qualifiers.

And finally...

"If you want to do public sector work, this is the firm to be at. But keep in mind that what we do is different to corporate-heavy firms, who work for massive companies. The public sector is changing, and I came to Bevan Brittan because I wanted to do something which doesn't become routine, where you learn something new every day."

Bingham McCutchen (London) LLP

The facts

Location: London

Number of UK partners/solicitors: 18/20 (+8 non-UK-qualified)

Total number of trainees: 5

Seats: 4x6 months

Alternative seats: Overseas seats

Extras: Pro bono – LawWorks

On chambersstudent.co.uk...

- How to get into Bingham
- We talk to grad recruitment partner Vance Chapman
- Bingham's history

For a cosy yet challenging work environment, look no further than Bingham's 50-lawyer City branch, which charms a handful of trainees each year with its high-quality deals and dazzling NQ salary.

Doing the dip

This is normally the part of our feature we dedicate to updating our audience on the progress of the firm at hand's recession recuperation. We've no tales of recovery to report in this one, however; Bingham McCutchen's City branch sidestepped the market trend of plummeting turnovers altogether, continuously upping its revenue throughout the downturn. Its 2011 performance – which saw a healthy 14% jump in revenue – is the latest evidence of ongoing prosperity at the American firm's London leg. Trainees credited the office's focus on financial restructuring – "*it's the kind of work that does well in good times and bad*" – but graduate recruitment partner Vance Chapman explains there's more to it than that: "*The main reason we've had a steady upward curve in revenue is because our financials are linked to what our clients are doing. Our client base of investment funds, hedge funds and investment banks is what sets us apart. These clients are always active because they are always looking to invest – we therefore remain busy throughout the economic cycle.*"

Bingham's London practice is relatively boutique compared to some of its full-service offices elsewhere. It's best known for financial restructuring and banking litigation. However, our sources were quick to label those who view the City digs as a distant uncle within the Bingham family as sorely mistaken. "*We don't do cast-off US work: we have our own work that comes through our partners here, which is indicative of the firm's global rather than American approach. The firm recognises our growing* involvement in high-profile deals and very much sees us as an important office – so much so that people from other offices are clamouring to come to London!*"

Growth spurts

Bingham historically takes on two new trainees a year, but insiders say expansion efforts to the training scheme will see three new starters join in 2012. The number of seat choices is set to increase in the near future: to supplement traditional spots in financial restructuring (FRG), finance, litigation and corporate, management is looking to add full-fledged seats in competition, tax and regulatory – areas which trainees until this point have only experienced through crossover work. "*Your corporate seat might touch on work with the competition department, for example, but now they're moving towards making those seats in their own right,*" one explained. Under the current four-trainee/four-seat system, seat allocation is done on a rota: "*Second-years are asked for their preferences and first-years are placed in the remaining two seats. The order of your training contract might be different, but everybody visits all the areas of the firm at some point.*"

FRG is London's largest department and its biggest money-maker. According to trainees, the group is known for its "*innovative approach*" in the field, which has earned it a top-tier ranking in *Chambers UK*. If numbers are anything to go by, top-tier is a pretty good descriptor on the size front, too: Bingham lawyers have had a hand in many of the market's largest matters, including the respective €1.8bn, €1.6bn and $1.9bn financial restruc-

Chambers UK rankings

Banking Litigation	Restructuring/Insolvency
Financial Services	

turings of Wind Hellas, Vivacom and Preem. Along with strengths in the marine and offshore sectors, the firm has "*a speciality in Norwegian bond deals*," trainees told us, mentioning Bingham's key role in the 2011 restructuring of offshore installation manufacturer Sevan Marine – a move that prevented one of Norway's largest bond defaults. Considering the scale of clients and money at stake, it's hardly surprising that "*matters tend to get quite complicated.*" As such, trainees chiefly act as adjuncts in the department, "*helping out the partners and associates by performing research tasks and handling admin for bondholders.*" Still, "*there's a huge amount of client contact*" to balance out such lower-level labours. "*You're constantly liaising back and forth with them in order to deal with queries and obtain documents.*"

The corporate department's scope "*isn't as large as that of other firms,*" sources informed us, explaining that "*it's often used to play a supporting role within larger restructuring matters.*" As such, spin-off issues like distressed M&A transactions constitute a significant chunk of the corporate group's undertakings. That said, the practice still holds its own on the funds front, advising on high-profile standalone matters like claims made by creditors and investors following the Lehman Brothers bankruptcy. Bingham's corporate team is also "*gaining momentum*" in the M&A scene – lawyers recently handled US technology outfit Kopin's $11m acquisition of British optoelectronics company Forth Dimension Displays. As a trainee there's due diligence to be completed during the closing of large-scale deals – "*drafting minutes and so forth*" – though "*the real responsibility comes into play during smallish matters like incorporating UK companies for US clients – that's the kind of deal you complete almost on your own.*" Client contact is a given: "*You're often the intermediary, answering client questions about filing and renewing subscriptions on a daily basis.*"

The finance team "*often works closely with FRG,*" particularly when distressed debt matters are involved. "*We work on drafting the loan agreements and security packages from the finance side while the other team handles logistics,*" explained an insider. There's also a substantial amount of work done on credit arrangements and debt securities, acting for investors like insurance companies, often in a cross-border context. "*The noteholders we act for are looking to invest so you get to see the negotiation side of things from the outset,*" one source said. An emblematic undertaking from 2011 saw the firm act for investors in a private placement of $530m worth of notes

by a subsidiary of Yorkshire Water Services. "*I spent a lot of my seat looking through securities and facility agreements and even got to do the initial draft a few times,*" said an interviewee. "*As the only trainee, you're also in charge of normal transactional duties like collecting signature pages.*"

Bingham's litigation department is one of the few in the UK that focuses solely on financial disputes, including those arising from investment banking, structured products, pensions, regulatory and distressed debt issues. High-value, complex cases are a forte: last year lawyers acted for Credit Suisse in a $1.2bn credit default swap claim against Abu Dhabi Commercial Bank and represented a group of nearly 70 prominent financial institutions holding more than $20bn of bonds issued by three insolvent Icelandic banks. "*During my seat I got to see two sides of litigation,*" one trainee said. "*On one matter I was exposed to the advisory facet of what we do, analysing the law and giving advice on possible future courses of action; on another I was able to experience the practical aspects of the court process, preparing for hearings and instructing counsel.*"

Catch you on the flip side

Our interviewees unanimously declared Bingham's small environment "*the best part of being a trainee here, hands down.*" "*There's a degree of flexibility here that you don't find at larger firms,*" one elaborated. "*Procedures aren't totally rigid – for example, you can ask to gain experience in a certain area of work and HR will try its best to make it happen for you. Plus, there's a lot of focus on you as an individual as you're not just one of a hundred trainees.*" Of course, the flip side to being part of a small intake is that "*there's nowhere to hide – you have to be prepared to work hard and accept responsibilities as they're given. If that's the kind of thing that scares you, Bingham's not really the place for you.*" For those who relish a steep learning curve, however, it's just the ticket. "*We're staffed so leanly across the firm that it's inevitable you'll end up with a high degree of responsibility,*" one trainee said, citing a time when "*I was sent to a meeting alone regarding a topic I had no clue about! That's the kind of exposure that forces you to learn quickly.*" Others agreed: "*Trainees are relied on heavily and thus tend to be treated on a par with junior associates.*"

Bingham offers the City's highest NQ salary – a whopping £100k. "*It's mainly to do with the fact that that's what our counterparts in New York make,*" trainees said. Is there a catch to this figure when it comes to working hours? Not so much, trainees responded. "*There's a misconception that you'll be worked to the bone in exchange for our high salary, but that's not been the case so far. We work long hours for sure – everyone is expected to put in long shifts – but it's nothing ridiculous.*" As far as office politics go, our sources described a "*supportive and friendly atmosphere*" in which "*people take the time to help each other out.*" Despite the firm's US heritage and Boston headquarters, there's little in the way of day-to-day American influence. "*It seems like London is very much its own operation: our lawyers are mainly English-qualified and most of our deals come through the UK. It's only really apparent when American partners visit the office and you hear their accents. Oh, and on Thanksgiving – we always celebrate that.*"

While interviewees had nothing but nice things to say of their colleagues, they did mention that "*applicants after a firm with a big social scene might want to look elsewhere. We're not the kind of place with societies and regular events – we don't spend much time together outside of work, and when we do it's usually through a low-key affair like drinks or dinner.*" Still, we heard tell of "*a great Christmas party where everybody lets their hair down*" and the odd holiday-related get-together. "*We had afternoon tea for the Jubilee and a turkey luncheon for Thanksgiving, though nothing for the Fourth of July – I was hoping for free hotdogs!*" one interviewee added with perhaps a touch more audible disappointment than a frankfurter-less Fourth warrants.

While camaraderie and chumminess are all well and good, "*you're expected to have a high degree of independence*" in order to get on, as well as the willingness to "*throw yourself into things and get your hands dirty. Because of the high quality of work, you're guaranteed to run into things you're not totally comfortable with, so you have to be the kind of person who can tackle that and complete it to the best of your ability.*" Grad recruitment partner Vance Chapman adds: "*Showing a real passion for what we do*" is an asset. "*We do a limited range of relatively niche practice areas, so an interest in that is a good start,*" other sources chimed in. "*A strong knowledge of bond markets in particular should serve you well at interview, as well as an understanding that we act for lenders instead of borrowers – knowing these things will alter the way you answer questions about the firm's day-to-day work and position in the market.*"

And finally...

In 2012, the firm retained both of its second-years. *"That we're not a full-service firm means a training contract here won't suit everybody, but if you're interested in the stuff Bingham does, it's a brilliant place to get experience."*

Bircham Dyson Bell

The facts

Location: London, Edinburgh
Number of UK partners/solicitors: 43/61
Partners who trained at firm: 30%
Total number of trainees: 14
Seats: 4x6 months
Alternative seats: Secondments
Extras: Pro bono – Migrants Resource Centre, Paddington Legal Advice Centre

On chambersstudent.co.uk...
• How to get into BDB
• Parliamentary and public law

With the paint still drying on an online rebrand, and an almost-but-didn't-quite-happen merger with Dundas & Wilson fresh in the memory, Bircham Dyson Bell is "*in that transitory stage.*"

Bellissimo!

Best known for its parliamentary and private client work, Westminster-based Bircham Dyson Bell is looking to the future. "*We are trying to portray ourselves more as consultants rather than just straightforward lawyers,*" one trainee reflected. "*There's a push to improve all the time and an ambition to become more of a City-type firm. It's ambition, but without the aggression.*" However, "*there seems to be some tension as to how far we should go. BDB has a very strong brand image and clients who are accustomed to our current reputation and approach.*" Training principal Nick Evans told us: "*Our aim has always been to push forward and offer a truly full service, but we recognise our particular strengths and are proud of our current reputation in the areas where that strength is recognised by others. If the opportunity to grow through merger arises, we will consider it, but we remain focused on organic growth. We have aspirations to grow in every part of the firm, but does becoming substantially bigger automatically make us a 'City-type firm'? I don't know. The rebranding of the firm has been done with real thought and we have a defined and appropriate strategy moving forward.*" The new website certainly looks mighty snazzy to us, even if the online 'fortune cookie' (sample message: 'Reflect now. Your future could lie with us') is a bit naff.

In a four-seat system, "*beyond the contentious requirement, there isn't any seat you actively have to complete,*" trainees said. "*We aren't driven by any one department, as other firms are.*" The seat choices are government and infrastructure (G&I); litigation; private wealth; real estate;

charities; corporate/commercial; and employment. "*There's also always a trainee on secondment.*" It's "*quite common for people to get more or less what they want. The firm does do its best to accommodate everyone, although not everyone can get their first choice every time.*"

Cable cars and fancy stars

The firm's biggest revenue generator, G&I is "*extremely diverse. You could ask ten different trainees what they did in this seat and you'd get ten different answers.*" It covers planning, environment, public law, public procurement, public affairs and related property agreements. Trainees said: "*There's a lot of research involved in this seat and planning work tends to be a focus for juniors.*" One added: "*Even the planning work is varied, though. There was a project on the disturbance of ancient burial grounds, for instance.*" Projects BDB has worked on include the new cable car crossing the River Thames and the proposed HS2 high-speed railway to link London to the West Midlands.

The private wealth department is "*still very prominent.*" The firm works with high net worth individuals and is "*involved in a lot of trust work. There's also a specialist tax team.*" One trainee said: "*There is so much cross-selling within BDB and the private wealth clients are a hugely important part of that.*" The charities department was "*born out of the private wealth group, so we act for a number of rich philanthropists.*" BDB also advises hospital trusts, schools, religious organisations and arts groups. Recently, for instance, it acted for the British Film Institute on changes to its Royal Charter following its

Chambers UK rankings

Administrative & Public Law	Planning
Agriculture & Rural Affairs	Private Client
Charities	Public Procurement
Family/Matrimonial	Real Estate
Local Government	Real Estate Litigation
Parliamentary & Public Affairs	Transport

takeover of the responsibilities of the now-abolished UK Film Council. It also helped establish and register the World Book Night charity, and other clients include St John Ambulance and the BBC Children in Need Appeal. Trainees told us: "*The team are small enough that you can get involved with really interesting work.*" There is, for example, "*a lot of work on behalf of charities that are going through structural reorganisations or director disputes.*" Said one source: "*I drafted parts of charity constitutions and participation agreements. I also went to meetings with trustees and executors.*"

The business services department includes coco, charities and employment. In coco, the firm has "*a number of very fast-growing and valuable private companies and entrepreneurs who are very interesting to advise,*" trainees said. They include film rights management and distribution company Metrodome Group and mining company Woodburne Square. "*Everyone sits together, so you can get involved with a variety of work.*" Trainees are "*thrown straight into the thick of things, and even in the first week you're meeting clients. You're considered a valuable resource.*"

"*Every trainee's experience in litigation is quite different, and you can be involved in everything from property litigation, IP, healthcare litigation, construction litigation, family, commercial litigation and judicial review,*" sources explained. "*Although you tend to focus on work your supervisor does, you are encouraged to approach other fee earners to ask for experience that you're interested in. The supervisors themselves all have quite diverse practices, and they'll constantly throw different types of work your way.*" BDB also "*encourages advocacy*" for trainees. "*I think it's almost expected in the department and is one of its real advantages. Advocacy is such a fundamental skill and if you demonstrate an interest they are happy to get you involved.*"

A secondment to Esso "*gives you a huge amount of responsibility,*" trainees said. "*Although it's classified as a real estate seat, it's actually more of a commercial, procurement and employment experience. You are seen as a safe pair of hands if you're sent to the client. It's taken very seriously.*"

The work/life balance at BDB is generally good. Though "*there are evenings when you'll be working late,*" on average "*the office empties by about 7pm, with a definite 6pm finish on Fridays.*"

Practice just ruins the fun

BDB profiles all its trainees on its website and from this we can tell you that the 14 working at the firm in summer 2012 graduated from 11 different universities. Only two had studied law as undergraduates, and women outnumbered men by ten to four. Knowing the firm's practices, it shouldn't come as a surprise that one had worked for an MP, another as a policy analyst for HM Treasury and another for a charity. In fact, most had gained two or three years of experience in the world of work before coming to law.

There are three big formal social events each year. First is the carol service, "*at a little church next to Westminster Abbey. We hold it in conjunction with another firm and have a joint choir.*" Then there's the Christmas party, where "*we get the full banqueting experience. There's usually a strong karaoke contingent towards the end of the evening: the partners are particularly enthusiastic.*" Finally comes a summer regatta. "*It's a rowing race held in Putney and each department has to enter at least one boat, with at least one novice. The rest of the firm comes down to the banks to cheer and enjoy the nibbles and drinks.* The charities department were the champions, helped in no small measure by a somewhat enthusiastic partner who kindly funded some "*extra training sessions.*" That's practically cheating, in our view, so we were glad to hear G&I took the crown in 2012. There's also a trainees v partners race, "*which, funnily enough, trainees have never won.*"

Trainee retention at BDB has had its ups and downs. "*An issue faced by trainees at a firm with such distinct practice areas is that if you're only interested in one of them, you probably won't find anything terribly similar if that department doesn't have space. It's not just a choice of this finance seat or that finance seat.*" However, trainees maintained that "*the firm is very open about timetables and what's basically going on,*" and in 2012, BDB kept on five out of its seven qualifiers.

And finally...
It may be ramping up its corporate/commercial offering, but the things that make BDB unique won't be vanishing any time soon.

Bird & Bird

The facts

Location: London

Number of UK partners/solicitors: 75/120

Total number of trainees: 32

Seats: 4x6 months

Alternative seats: Overseas seats, secondments

Extras: Pro bono – LawWorks, Own-it, South Westminster Legal Advice Centre, language classes

On chambersstudent.co.uk...
- How to get into Twobirds
- Interview with training principal Christian Bartsch

Famous for its IP and commercial divisions, Bird & Bird's corporate and dispute resolution wings continue to soar.

The sector factor

"On the website you see fashion houses, computer game manufacturers and sports groups and frankly it makes you want to come here." Bird & Bird's client list is certainly something to tweet about: with Amazon, Yahoo!, Everything Everywhere (formed from a JV between T-Mobile and Orange), Virgin Atlantic, BT, PayPal and last-minute.com, the firm's *"trendy, techy flavour"* is evident. The firm's larger wings of IP and commercial attract the top-line clients, but less well known are its extremely respectable *Chambers UK* rankings in areas as diverse as corporate, aviation and data protection. Key to the firm's growth plan is cross-selling. *"We're taking a much more holistic view of client relationships across the globe, and we're finding as we do so that we're getting more opportunities to win work on a cross-border basis,"* training principal Christian Bartsch told us. *"We are constantly looking for areas where our knowledge can be applied to specific sectors – our energy and utilities and financial services sector groups are two areas where we have seen strong growth due to our mix of regulatory and technology expertise."*

Twobirds' key sectors range from food to healthcare to life sciences, and trainees agree that it pays to *"experience the breadth and find out what you like,"* at first, though eventually the firm wants you to take a deep interest in something. *"You should eventually focus in on something that you can be expert in,"* thought one. *"The partners who are going far are the ones who take a personal interest and make it their own."* Bartsch sees the benefits for trainees of the firm's sector strategy primarily being *"getting the opportunity to work with clients they know are*

best of breed in those sectors," but also *"work not being limited by territory. There's the opportunity to assist with international pitches, and help with marketing activities – great in developing soft skills in an international context."* And there are a lot of offices – for a firm still regarded as mid-size in the City, TwoBirds' global reach is significant, with 23 offices across 16 different countries, mostly in Europe. A social media-focused Hamburg office brings TwoBirds' Deutsch count to four, while a recently opened base in Abu Dhabi has been bolstered by the head of the firm's corporate group, Mark Pinder.

"Like most organisations, dispute resolution has had a stellar few years," says Bartsch. Additionally, *"smaller areas like automotive, food and beverages and the aerospace, defence and security sectors have seen growth."*

Bird vs birdwatchers

No seats are compulsory, and *"the statistic they give us is that you'll get three out of four choices,"* said one source. Seats are currently up for grabs in commercial, dispute resolution, IP, corporate, banking, real estate, employment, aviation and sport. A tip from trainees: *"Make it very clear where you want to go. We get catch-ups with grad recruitment every couple of months, and you're asked what you think you'd like. You learn to be upfront and a bit politically minded."* Many flock to Bird & Bird because of its IP prestige but eventually discover they want to qualify elsewhere.

Though most agree *"you're at an advantage if you have a science background,"* IP remains a seat where *"there's*

Chambers UK rankings

Asset Finance	Intellectual Property
Aviation	Life Sciences
Banking & Finance	Media & Entertainment
Capital Markets	Outsourcing
Corporate/M&A	Private Equity
Data Protection	Product Liability
Dispute Resolution	Public Procurement
Employment	Real Estate
Fraud	Real Estate Finance
Healthcare	Sports Law
Immigration	Telecommunications
Information Technology	Travel

scope to get a wide range of work if you ask for it. I let HR know I wanted a variety," said one non-scientific source. 'Hard' IP is where the department picks up top rankings in *Chambers UK* – its life sciences and patent practice is seen as a nationwide leader. The firm is acting for Nokia on a large number of patent infringements stemming from IPCom's issue with patents the phone supplier bought from Bosch. There's also a lot of drugs work, with the group acting for major pharmaceuticals companies Teva, Regeneron and Novozymes. *"You do so many varied things,"* said one trainee. *"I worked on a patent dispute on a drug, which involved learning a lot of biology and chemistry. The trial involved reviewing disclosure documents from the past, like lab reports and drug development summaries. There's also research – as when we call a witness, it's good to have some background on who the expert is and specifically why we want their opinion."*

The dispute resolution group isn't as famed as IP, but trainees enjoy the quantity and quality of work they get. There's opportunity to seek out work from partners who specialise in aviation, banking, commercial contracts, finance litigation, media, arbitration and telecoms, and for trainees there's a lot of back-and-forth party correspondence and drafting witness statements. *"It's enjoyable when you see what you've drafted hasn't been changed."* Trainees will generally work on multiple matters at once – *"saying 'no' to people can be an issue at the start,"* – but are often able to *"get under the skin of litigations for several weeks at a time."* Clients here don't tend to be household names, but plans are to grow the group through the communications, life sciences and technology sectors.

Real estate's an area still more litigation-focused since the start of the recession, and trainees will encounter lots of insolvency and bankruptcy work, as well as property finance. The team handling the latter counts RBS, Santander and Clydesdale Bank as clients, while major players in transactional property include Philips, BT and

The Arts Council. Like most property departments, there's scope for trainees to run their own small files, *"sending e-mails out and talking to the client directly."*

Keepy uppy

Bird & Bird's commercial wing includes IT, telecoms, technology, data protection, outsourcing and sports. The latter acts for associations like the International Cricket Council, The FA, the Premier League and the International Basketball Association, events like the Six Nations, and in addition Sky Sports, Twickenham and Wembley. Much sports work has moved in-house post-credit crunch, so TwoBirds' forte is large, complex legal matters. Trainees, therefore, *"get quite standard tasks. There's not much drafting, as partners are quite busy and it's hard to get involved with what they're doing all the time."* Cases are *"massive,"* like advising The FA on the implications of the Murphy case (landlady Karen Murphy used a Greek decoder instead of the £700 a month Sky licence to screen games at her pub in Portsmouth, and when charged successfully took her plea to the ECJ). There's also disciplinary work, which has inherently tight deadlines. *"A player can get a red card in a game on Sunday, and by Wednesday there's a tribunal. In the time it might take a partner to instruct a trainee, he can have the relevant calls with the FA."*

Workload in corporate fluctuates to the extent that *"different trainees will have very divergent experiences."* When busy, there's a lot of good work – the department is active in the lower mid-market and acts for many AIM-listed clients. Trainees working on M&A may be *"placed in charge of disclosure letters, go through verification documents and, on smaller deals, take client calls."* The team advised financial services group Evolution on its takeover by South African bank Investec for £233m, and Evolution's subsidiary, Williams de Broe, on its takeover of BNP Paribas Private Investment Management.

Many trainees get to spend three months in-house as part of seats like sport, commercial, IP or dispute resolution. There are also international seats on offer in Helsinki, Brussels, Madrid, Stockholm, Milan and Warsaw. *"It would be great to do a client secondment and go abroad,"* said one first-year, wistfully. *"It's almost as if four seats aren't enough."*

Trainees praised the grad recruitment team, who are *"brilliant at staying in touch"* during secondments, seat moves, appraisals – which are *"frank, honest, but always nice"* – and as qualification approaches. With no jobs list published, trainees agree the process *"could seem opaque,"* but that it merely relies on good communication. *"You have to let partners know as soon as you do that you want to qualify in a department. You also have to ask them to tell you that there definitely won't be a job going in a certain department.*" Prospects are promising, with 11 out of 12 qualifiers staying with TwoBirds in 2012.

A bird in the hand...

Each year, the firm receives around 2,600 applications for 16 training contracts. What makes candidates stand out among the throng? Bartsch details: "*Candidates with industry knowledge or with a rich extracurricular experience. Someone who's been in commerce would be interesting to us, and we always like people to have language skills.*" Phew. Not too much, then. Bartsch mentions the firm "*recruits very heavily from the summer scheme. We consider the scheme to be a vital part of the assessment process, as it provides an in-depth insight for both the firm and candidates.*" Trainees attest to this, believing that "*the firm needs different kinds of personalities, but everyone has something that's a bit quirky or unusual about them. They like you to have a real character of your own.*" The background of Bird & Bird's lawyers means the firm retains a reputation for "*quirkiness.*"

Trainees believe that, generally speaking, the vibe is "*collaborative, team-focused and open – there's still obviously a hierarchy, but you feel able to talk to anyone.*" The firm remains split between three offices on Fetter Lane. The client-facing number 15, which houses commercial, real estate, banking and aviation, recently had a swanky revamp. These offices are "*clean, very white and none of the offices have doors.*" It's also the place to come if you want to take a shower or play a spot of table football. Up at number 90, you'll find dispute resolution and corporate, while IP has its own building and a slightly different atmosphere. "*You often feel like you're at a different firm, as the people are so different and the way they interact is so informal,*" thought one source. "*People are very good at what they do, but don't take themselves too seriously – there are lots of practical jokes to make the long days pass.*"

As a result, there's lots of department socialising, with IP having its own summer party, "*which last year involved a pub quiz and then playing on a Wii.*" Techies, eh? Come Friday, there is always a group at The Castle and The White Swan, which is "*the real test – when people go out of their own accord, you know they enjoy each other's company.*" There are football, cricket, netball, softball and touch rugby teams "*all captained by trainees.*" The current group like each other so much that they go on holiday of their own accord – "*last year to Amsterdam and this year to Suffolk.*"

And finally...

TwoBirds will always provide a good commercial training but to get the very best experience possible here, you do have to be prepared to speak up for yourself.

Bond Pearce LLP

The facts

Location: Plymouth, Bristol, Southampton, London, Aberdeen
Number of UK partners/solicitors: 76/200
Total number of trainees: 20
Seats: 4x6 months
Alternative seats: Secondments

On chambersstudent.co.uk...
- How to get into Bond Pearce
- Interview with training principal Simon Hughes and recruitment manager Sam Lee

Commercial firm Bond Pearce offers the full package: big clients, secondments, a social scene and that all important work/life balance.

Sou'wester?

"Bond Pearce is not a South West firm, it's a national firm," training principal Simon Hughes told us. Certainly, though its traditional stomping ground is around Bristol, Plymouth and Southampton, the firm has offices in London and Aberdeen, and *Chambers UK* gives it national recognition for its expertise in areas including education, energy, health and safety, product liability, local government and retail. A trainee elaborated: *"As much as you read on our website and in the news, you don't appreciate the large clients until you start working here."* They include the BBC, Virgin, Carlsberg, B&Q and Royal Mail.

Life is good at Bond Pearce at the moment. It was a finalist at *The Lawyer* magazine's awards in 2011, up for nothing less than the title of Law Firm of the Year. Its six competitors were all major City firms with international offices, making the South West-headquartered, UK-only Bond Pearce stand out like a beacon. Trainees told us this is *"certainly not a stuffy old law firm."* Its website is packed with images of colourful body parts and Lego bricks which our younger selves might have scribbled back when we could buy a 64-pack of Crayola from the local Woolworths. But this is no legal novice – it was actually founded in the late 19th century.

Trainees are recruited into the Bristol, Southampton and Plymouth offices, while there are opportunities for secondments to a client or to the firm's smaller outposts in London and Aberdeen. Bristol is the largest office and Bond Pearce is one of half a dozen sizeable commercial firms in that city. In Plymouth meanwhile, trainees claim

it's *"the best in this part of the world. There are some decent firms in Devon, but Bond Pearce has the draw of sexier clients."*

The available seats vary with each rotation. *"We're given a list with the available seats and list up to five in order of preference, giving our reasons. The NQ process takes place quite early in our fourth seat, so the second and third ones are the most important ones to work out."* Some of the options include banking, commercial litigation, commercial property, corporate finance, insurance, IP/IT, oil and gas, planning, property litigation and regulatory. Be aware, though, that while *"Bristol has a great choice of seats, Plymouth and Southampton don't have so many – but they recruit less trainees."* We've already mentioned the secondments to London and Aberdeen, but it isn't usual for trainees to hop around between the South West offices during the course of their training contract.

Litigation around the nation

In 2011, contentious work accounted for nearly half of Bond Pearce's turnover, and around 60% of that came from the commercial litigation group. This is a *"really popular"* seat among trainees across all offices. The team acts for a variety of large corporates and wealthy private clients and has recently featured in the legal press, when advising two financial services businesses in a professional negligence claim against some surveyors. It's the smaller cases, however, that make the seat *"great for trainees."* Said one: *"I was running my own debt recovery on commercial contracts. It was a case of either trying to settle or issuing the claim and seeing it through to medi-*

Chambers UK rankings

Administrative & Public Law	Intellectual Property
Banking & Finance	Licensing
Banking Litigation	Media & Entertainment
Construction	Pensions
Corporate/M&A	Planning
Dispute Resolution	Product Liability
Education	Professional Negligence
Employment	Real Estate
Energy & Natural Resources	Real Estate Litigation
Environment	Restructuring/Insolvency
Health & Safety	Retail
Information Technology	Tax

ation or trial." From another: *"I was liaising with clients every day. Bond Pearce puts a lot of trust in you."* The Southampton office has *"a retail slant to a lot of its litigation work, and has also started taking on oil and gas clients."*

Commercial litigation is *"closely linked"* with commercial property. *Chambers UK* ranks the firm's real estate team in the top two in the Hampshire and Dorset area and among the top seven in the South West. Another popular choice among trainees, a Southampton source told us: *"It's solely commercial property. We don't do any residential work in this office."* Trainees are handed *"a lot of responsibility. I had a caseload of my own to run. It was quite pressurised at times but you gain confidence."*

Insurance is one of the firm's key practices, and there are two seats offered in this area: liability risks and professional risks. *"Professional risks is acting for insurers, defending claims made against professionals – such as surveyors and solicitors – often where they have been negligent. Liability risks is again defending insurers, this time defending claims against individuals such as people involved in workplace accidents or car crashes,"* one helpful trainee explained. QBE, Travelers and Chartis are among the insurers represented. These seats aren't available in Plymouth, but insurance-hungry Janners can head up to Bristol and London for a seat. We even heard of opportunities to do advocacy in the Royal Courts of Justice.

Professional risks *"is really good fun,"* one source said, while another simply summed it up as: *"Fantastic. Brilliant."* In Bristol, this is a *"massive"* department. Trainees there see *"a bit of photocopying, but it tends to be if you're working on something bigger, rather than as a standalone task. I've had lots of drafting and attended a few mediations. I've gone to court hearings and was encouraged to do a telephone hearing as well."* Over in

liability risks, meanwhile, trainees *"get a broad overview of the litigation process,"* but *"it's the sort of work that has a lot of claims, so you're constantly pumping documents. They expect a high level of return very quickly. You become very good at drafting the same letter."*

Ports of call

Energy is another specialism of the firm and there are a number of teams in which trainees will see a lot of work coming from this sector. Corporate finance is one such department. For example, it worked on the sale of the AIM-listed company Aurelian Oil & Gas (Romania) to Raffles Group, and advised the shareholders of oil and gas exploration company Volantis on its sale to Atlantic Petroleum. Non-energy clients include bookmakers Coral Group and bed makers Airsprung Group. The value of deals this group is handling ranges from about £2m to in excess of £30m. Plenty of energy clients (Eneco, ScottishPower Renewables) can also be found in the planning team, and there is also the opportunity for trainees to complete an oil and gas seat, either in the Bristol office or up in Aberdeen.

A Southampton trainee told us that *"the banking seat comes up each and every time. It's renowned as the hardest, most challenging seat to do."* The team advises on multimillion-pound matters and clients include Lloyds, Barclays, Santander and HSBC, as well as borrowers. *"Off the top of my head, I'd say we act for the banks 70% of the time,"* said one source. *"As a trainee, I got asked to prepare and draft loads of documents. I was liaising with the other side continually. I'm trusted and given the opportunity to run with files and contracts. It's hugely satisfying."* Days in the office can last until 1am, but on average trainees are more likely to exit at around 7pm.

"One of the best things about Bond Pearce is the secondments." They are really encouraged: *"All the Southampton second-years have been out on one."* Clients that have taken trainees in the past have included New Look, B&Q and Sainsbury's.

With age comes wisdom

"I like that not everyone here has followed the traditional route of school to university to training contract," one of our sources said. There's a real mix of second-careerers, fresh-out-of-schoolers and a few in-the-middlers. *"I think the firm values some form of commercial work experience outside the law,"* one said. *"Most of us in the Bristol office are in our mid to late twenties."* Recruitment manager Sam Lee tells us that only two of the 11-strong recent intake were *"straight from education."*

In fact, one trainee thought the only people who wouldn't fit in at Bond Pearce are *"those who don't like socialis-*

ing." Every office has a social committee. In Bristol it's made up of "*partners, senior associates, trainees, paralegals and secretaries,*" and "*organises an event a month. There are lots of sports to get involved in, an annual trip to Bath races, live music events, 10 km runs, wine tasting and massages in the office that the firm subsidises. There are also partner drinks every three months, which are paid for by the partners and they serve us the wine.*" In Southampton, "*most Fridays we go to the pub. The social committee organises sports, bowling, curry nights and they're planning a bike ride in the New Forest soon.*" In Plymouth, "*individual teams arrange social activities.*"

The "*modern*" Bristol and Southampton offices are open-plan. Plymouth trainees, however, share a room with a supervisor in their "*ugly former BT call centre.*" Trainees didn't take too kindly to the layout: "*It feels like there's someone watching over you all the time.*" On the up-side though, there are excellent views of the sea. Across all offices, "*every Friday there is a dress-down day.*"

The consensus was that a 6pm home time was average. To get trainees to stay a bit longer, there's a billable-hours bonus incentive but "*it's really informal: there's no pressure for us to meet it. It's simply preparing us for when we qualify.*" They get a Christmas bonus regardless.

And finally...
There were some nerves about NQ jobs this year, since the recession's trainee deferrals meant there was a larger qualifying class in 2012. In the end, 12 out of 17 stayed on.

Boodle Hatfield LLP

The facts

Location: London, Oxford

Number of UK partners/solicitors: 30/44

Partners who trained at firm: 13.3%

Total number of trainees: 10

Seats: 4x6 months

Alternative Seats: None

On chambersstudent.co.uk...
- How to get into Boodle Hatfield
- Digested Dukes of Westminster
- Past Boodles

Mayfair's Boodle Hatfield has been advising the wealthy for almost 300 years.

Hats off to you

Founded by the estate manager of the Grosvenor family in 1767, Boodle Hatfield is predominantly known for private client and niche property work and has been providing a bespoke service to that end for generations. "*2012 has been a successful year for us,*" HR director Katie Kirkhope said. "*We continue to focus on private wealth, property and smaller business market sectors and have seen positive results in all. We continue to grow organically, but have no plans to change dramatically.*" However, Boodle did take on LLP status in 2012 and spruced up its brand a bit as well.

Trainees complete their four seats from options of property, private client, litigation, construction and corporate. "*You'll almost definitely do a property seat,*" sources advised. "*Almost half the firm is property-based, so it makes total sense. There's so much work to do in that department, you'd be mad to come here and not have a slight interest.*" One added: "*If you wanted to do two property seats, the firm would probably be absolutely thrilled.*" Almost everyone "*also does a private client seat.*" At the time of our calls, "*the firm no longer advertises a family seat, but you might end up doing some family work in litigation.*" HR director Katie Kirkhope commented: "*Although for the last year or so there was no business need for trainees in the family team, we have recently reviewed the situation and there will be a family seat from September 2012.*"

Although most of our interviewees were happy with their seats, it was understood that "*Boodle Hatfield is a smaller firm and trainees have to adhere to business need. Although the HR team really tries to accommodate your preferences, you aren't always going to get your first or second choice. You have to be realistic.*"

Monopoly board-tastic

The property department, consistently highly ranked by *Chambers UK*, is a strong presence in the London mid-market. Split between estates and commercial teams, trainees "*pretty much get allocated at random,*" although they can express a preference for one or the other. Boodle also maintains strong property litigation and construction teams.

"*Obviously, the clients in the estates team are those with large landed estates,*" trainees said. "*There tends to be a UK focus and we also do some high net worth residential transactions. You're involved from day one and get several of your own small licence and leasing files to manage.*" The firm's first client, the Grosvenor Estate, is still on the books. In case you haven't a *Debrett's* to hand, the Grosvenors are the Dukes of Westminster – the current Duke owns £2–3bn worth of real estate around London, making him the city's biggest, wealthiest landlord. Boodle is advising the Estate on its £10m investment with Westminster City Council to make Mayfair's Mount Street and Carlos Place an exclusive shopping district.

Commercial property "*is generally development-related.*" Although one partner has a line in offshore commercial property work, most is "*London and South-focused*" and includes several large West End property management clients. The team advised on the £60m acquisition and subsequent redevelopment of Berners Hotel by the Marriott Hotel group and is acting for healthy fast-food retailer POD on its expansion programme in central

Chambers UK rankings

Agriculture & Rural Affairs	Private Client
Charities	Real Estate
Family/Matrimonial	Real Estate Litigation

London. Trainees "*draft leases and licences, speak to agents and get as involved as possible.*" One said: "*I made sure my supervisor knew what I was interested in doing and the team made every effort to give me good work.*"

The highly regarded private client department is still one of Boodle's big guns. It is split into three teams: private wealth, contentious trusts and corporate tax. "*As a trainee you end up working in all three areas at some point.*" A proportion of the department is based in Boodle's satellite office out in Oxford and "*it's really just considered one team. There is so much interaction between the two offices and people travel back and forth the entire time.*" Trainees can also complete a seat in the Oxford office, where they are "*fully supported, both in terms of training and housing arrangements,*" according to HR director Katie Kirkhope. Clients are all wealthy, "*with a fair amount of international individuals*" among them. Trainees said: "*A lot of the time you're the first point of call for clients and the work is so interesting. You also get a lot of drafting experience in the probate work.*"

Corporate "*is definitely very active and certainly has the feel of an ambitious department.*" Clients used to be largely domestic companies, "*but as we've taken on more partners, the work has become more varied and international. We mainly work for mid-size offshore companies and the corporate ventures of our wealthy private clients. There are also several multinational corporations and smaller start-ups.*" Boodle has advised Australian-listed mining conglomerate Straits Resources on the sale of the multinational Magontec metals group to Advanced Magnesium, and acted for the executive directors of Group NBT, a domain name registrar, on a £153m recommended cash offer by HgCapital. "*The team are so good at including you and keeping you aware of everything that's going on,*" trainees agreed. "*With the nature of the work, it isn't appropriate for trainees to lead deals. But you get a lot of drafting and you're taken to all sorts of meetings and closings.*"

Sources said: "*Although we're very busy, the corporate hours at Boodle really aren't that bad.*" In fact the work/life balance is good across the firm. "*It depends on what's on, but the average leaving time is about 7pm. Litigation is the latest in terms of hours, but even in that department a very late night is rare. If there's work to be done, you'll stay, but we can almost always make our social arrangements.*"

Finally, the "*growing*" litigation department "*is enormously busy,*" confirmed trainees. "*There are basically two litigation seats. One is property-based, while the other is more general commercial work.*" Trainees said they "*did pretty much everything, from drafting and being involved in instructions to counsel, to attending hearings and helping with witnesses.*"

Spice up your life

Boodle "*certainly doesn't ignore its heritage,*" trainees said, "*but we have a modern and fresh approach to the law. Applicants are partly attracted to the firm because of the history and tradition, but that doesn't mean we're old-fashioned and fuddy-duddy.*" Trainees praised "*several young and dynamic partners,*" including the "*very impressive female partners. Although the older partners are also wonderful at what they do, the younger generation are keen to keep the firm moving forwards.*" It was admitted that "*there are the Eton and Oxbridge types, but it's not an old boys' club. You never feel like you have to come from a certain background. People across the board are approachable and kind.*"

2012 saw the first ever 'Boodle's Got Talent' event. "*It was a talent show and people sang and danced and did tricks. The whole evening was brilliant and so funny,*" trainees reflected. "*Everyone got involved from partners to staff. The first-year trainees did a Spice Girls tribute mash-up, and that includes the boys. It was utterly ridiculous, but hilarious.*" The corporate team ended up taking the prize, with "*a perfectly choreographed Bollywood dance.*" Otherwise the firm has all kinds of sports groups, from football and netball to yoga and "*a table tennis tournament for Wimbledon.*" Informally, "*people often go for drinks after work and at the end of every month there's a dress-down Friday and drinks for charity.*" Plenty of lawyers "*end up at the Duke of York or in Bonds, but really, in our location, there are a multitude of places to go.*" Boodles is based on Bond Street – shopaholics beware...

In 2012 the firm retained three out of six qualifiers. The firm says this was due to trainees all wanting to qualify into particular departments rather than a spread across the firm.

And finally...

All our sources wanted to work in "*a smaller, slightly more relaxed firm.*" Many also wanted exposure to top-end private client work. If you do too, then Boodle's for you.

B P Collins LLP

The facts

Location: Gerrards Cross

Number of UK partners/solicitors: 16/30

Partners who trained at firm: 25%

Total number of trainees: 7

Seats: 4x5 months + 1x4 months

Alternative seats: Occasional secondments

On chambersstudent.co.uk...

- How to get into BPC
- What goes on in Gerrards Cross?
- Interview with HR manager Jacqui Symons

In a galaxy far, far away lies a little full-service firm offering its expertise to individuals and businesses alike...

4 + 1 = 5 (seats)

Actually, when we say 'a galaxy far, far away' we mean 20 minutes down the line from Marylebone in the small town of Gerrards Cross. Strategically located between the M25 and the M40, the firm attracts clients from London, the northern Home Counties and beyond. It's certainly not that little either: BPC has over 100 staff and takes on three or four trainees a year.

One thing our standfirst didn't lie about is that BPC is a full-service firm. It has six practice groups: property, dispute resolution, corporate/commercial, private client, employment and family. *Chambers UK* ranks all six in the Thames Valley region. Trainees can work in any of the departments and our interviewees praised the *"range and good clients that you'd generally find in London."*

The location *"plays a large role in defining the firm."* Sandwiched between the local library and a kids' clothes shop, BPC looks every inch the bog-standard high-street operation, but this is no ordinary high street; Gerrards Cross is *"predominantly a commuter town for very affluent people."* Many a pinstriped businessman and cigar-smoking captain of industry has retired here from life in the City, and numerous celebrities own houses nearby, including Cilla Black, the Osbornes and Angelina Jolie. So the logic behind BPC's location is obvious. It handles the business and personal needs of the extremely wealthy, and *"these people don't want to feel like they're in and out of London all the time. We give clients the attention they need."*

As a general rule, trainees complete four seats of five months each. *"Then four months at the end of the contract are left where we go back to the department we want to*

qualify in." That's the system in simple terms – it's actually very flexible and seats can last up to seven or eight months. *"Trainees don't get to choose how long they spend in a seat though, that's up to the firm."* Trainees *"tell the HR team one seat we definitely want and one we don't, then rank the others in order of preference."* Not all manage to bypass their chosen Seat of Woe (our term, not theirs), and family and litigation *"always need multiple trainees, so it's harder to avoid these departments."* However, *"95% of the time people get the seat they want and avoid the one they don't."*

Roughly 20% of the firm's work is property-related. Although the department handles some residential property work for wealthy locals, it works mainly on commercial property matters and has been known to line up alongside the likes of Slaughter and May. Clients include several waste management companies such as Biffa, tyre manufacturer Continental, and AMF Bowling, the world's largest operator of bowling alleys. *"The property seat allows you to get really involved,"* one trainee told us. *"It's quite transactional, so there are a lot of papers you can write and get checked before it goes anywhere. So you can have your own little files."* Another elaborated: *"I've also been to client meetings on my own. In some of the other seats it's more difficult to handle your own matters."*

Not in dispute resolution, though. *"For some of the cases, I was effectively running on my own with partner supervision,"* one source said. *"Everyone speaks to clients on the phone all the time and you get a chance to go along to meetings, too."* The dispute resolution department accounts for about a fifth of the firm's work and is split into work-related 'pods'. They cover things like commer-

Chambers UK rankings

Charities	Family/Matrimonial
Corporate/M&A	Private Client
Dispute Resolution	Real Estate
Employment	Real Estate Litigation
Environment	

cial litigation and property litigation. The hours can sometimes be long and the cases large. Clients include HMV and the National House-Building Council. Corporate/commercial (aka coco) "*does quite a lot of work for charities and companies in the waste sector.*" Charity clients include the Federation of European Microbiological Societies. The team also handles M&A, company secretarial work, partnership agreements, IP, refinancing, and the setting up of companies. "*Company secretarial work tends to be a trainee job, but we get quite a mixture. I drafted a partnership agreement and did the terms and conditions for a loyalty scheme award. They give you as much responsibility as you want as long as you show willingness to learn.*"

"*Employment is a popular seat.*" It's even got its own claim to fame: head of department Jo Davis is a returning guest on BBC Radio 4's *Women's Hour.* "*There's a mix of clients. At the moment, we have more employers than employees. We sometimes have quite big clients with an American parent company, but they wouldn't necessarily be ones that everyone has heard of.*" A name you will know is BIC (of pen and razor fame), while one you may not is pharma company Daiicho Sankyo. Trainees "*see a lot of contentious work, for example preparing bundles, listing documents, research and instructing counsel and expert witnesses.*"

The family practice deals with "*the type of clients who would generally go to London firms.*" Although "*most are local,*" there is a significant amount of work involving overseas assets. Though we obviously can't bandy names about, a fair few celebs seek out the family department's expertise. "*I'd say 90% of my work was divorce,*" one trainee estimated. "*I can't fault my time in family. It was very stressful, but I learnt so much and it's incredibly hands-on. I even attended court and went to client meetings on my own. I made a lot of applications and drafted statements. And although I had lots of responsibility, I was always shadowed.*"

The pen is mightier than the Word.doc

B P Collins has two premises on the same street. Collins House is the aforementioned, library-adjacent one, and is the smaller of the two. It houses the family and property teams, while Sterling House is a more typical office building and is home to the litigation, private client, employment and coco departments. The litigation and private client teams sit in open-plan areas, whereas the other departments are office-based. Trainees in the latter share an office with their supervisor. Litigation "*has a nice breakout area with a kitchen and sofas, and even a TV.*"

While BPC attracts plenty of ex-City lawyers, "*a lot of people train here and move up the ranks,*" interviewees told us. "*The HR team often points to partners who trained at BPC.*" "*We have a low turnover: people even leave and come back, which is a good sign,*" HR manager Jacqui Symons says. In the firm's search for committed trainees who won't vanish to London after two years, Symons has a rather unusual hiring requirement: "*I ask for a handwritten covering letter. It assists with the selection process, because a lot of people can't be bothered. It's difficult to compose a hand-written letter, so we look at the content and structure, rather than conducting handwriting analysis as many think.*"

Spending an afternoon manually spell-checking your covering letter is worth the effort if you bag yourself a training contract. Life at the firm means "*good hours, a good salary and a good pension scheme,*" trainees said. "*Family and litigation work longer hours than the other departments, but by late I mean 7pm, not midnight. We do not have a long-hours culture here,*" Jacqui Symons says. "*However, on occasion trainees will be expected to work weekends.*" Our interviewees confirmed this account, and one commented: "*One of the best things about working here is that you get evenings to yourself.*"

Trainees either commute from London or live in Buckinghamshire, which makes socialising tough. "*There's not loads to do in Gerrards Cross.*" The Londoners go out together in the capital; however, it's a bit more difficult for Bucks-based trainees to get involved in socialising. We did hear of "*ice skating at Somerset House, trips to a local racecourse, and bowling,*" though, and "*all departments get a day out in the summer. We went for a treasure hunt in Hyde Park. It's just an excuse to get drunk in the park.*" Also, "*every quarter the firm gives trainees £25 a head to do something, and last time we went to Marylebone for dinner and drinks.*"

And finally...
For a really good commercial/private client training and a slightly quieter pace of life than you'd get in London, B P Collins is your firm. All three qualifiers were retained in 2012.

Brabners Chaffe Street

The facts

Location: Liverpool, Manchester, Preston
Number of UK partners/solicitors: 77/100
Total number of trainees: 11
Seats: 4x6 months
Alternative seats: Secondments

On chambersstudent.co.uk...
- How to get into Brabners
- Recent cases and deals

North West firm Brabners Chaffe Street offers an all-round commercial training and is known for its strong sports practice.

BCS we want to

Brabners married Chaffe Street back in 2001 and the past decade has seen major expansion. Major doesn't mean rapid though, as BCS carefully cherry-picks its additions, which have propelled it to its current position as one of the leading law firms in the North West. Of particular note are charities, private client and social housing practices, which all come highly recommended by *Chambers UK*. The corporate/commercial side of the firm is also strong and we mustn't forget to mention the nationally recognised sports law practice.

Of late, Brabners has been taking on fewer trainees than in previous years. In 2011, just six joined: three in the firm's Liverpool office, three in Manchester but none in Preston (though it has takes trainees occasionally). Trainees told us that the firm doesn't just recruit for the sake of it: "*If they are looking for three trainees and have 100 applicants, they won't recruit three from those if they don't find the right people.*" So what is this picky firm looking for? Brabners attracts "*people with personality and a sense of humour*" and we hear "*they're not afraid of an accent either.*" Nearly all of the current trainees were born and bred in the region. With its excellent reputation for sports law, Brabners does have some ex-pro and talented athletes in its ranks, but "*you don't need to be a high-level athlete to get a training contract here,*" one source assured us.

There are a wide range of seat options, including corporate, commercial, commercial property, employment, family, litigation, private client, social housing and sport. Client secondments are also an option. Every 18 months a commercial seat at Manchester United is offered: not surprisingly "*it's fantastic*" and "*everybody wants it.*"

There's also been a placement at adidas in the past. "*Litigation and employment are the most sought after,*" and commercial and sports are popular choices too.

We heard unanimous praise from our interviewees for the firm's efforts to accommodate their preferences. Trainees tend to return to their favoured qualification destination for their fourth seat, and as the level of responsibility vastly increases over time, double seats are "*definitely worth doing.*"

A lot of wind

Property is an important area for the firm. Last year we reported that it's a mandatory seat but this year we heard: "*The firm said we'd all have to go to property to start with, but that doesn't seem to have been the case.*" The firm says it still encourages trainees to visit property, and the majority do still complete it. A good thing too, thought one source, as "*the property department is well known here and it helps your CV to have done it.*" The team deals with "*really varied*" cases, "*from multinational multimillion-pound projects to work for small businesses.*" A recent biggie was advising on building the world's largest offshore wind turbine (it's going to be taller than the Gherkin). The team is working alongside the giant US firm Reed Smith. The big cases are "*great experience*" for trainees, who can get "*heavily involved,*" but it's the smaller ones (which tend to be leasehold work) that they can run from start to finish. The team has long-standing clients "*who are much friendlier and the partners are happier for trainees to speak with them.*" The partners themselves are "*very helpful*" and we even heard of one who worked his way up from the post room.

Chambers UK rankings

Agriculture & Rural Affairs	Intellectual Property
Banking & Finance	Media & Entertainment
Charities	Private Client
Construction	Real Estate
Corporate/M&A	Real Estate Litigation
Dispute Resolution	Restructuring/Insolvency
Employment	Retail
Environment	Social Housing
Family/Matrimonial	Sports Law
Information Technology	Tax

Corporate is "*always really busy.*" One of our sources recommended it as a good first-year option, as "*it encompasses a lot of different issues and areas.*" The work overlaps with the banking department but it's "*not always million-pound transactions,*" which means trainees can bag greater levels of responsibility. "*I managed to see two deals from start to finish in three months,*" one told us, adding that they were "*heavily involved*" in both. "*I was collating responses to go into the disclosure letter and going through warranties on the phone with clients.*" The highest-value individual deals the corporate team has worked on recently have topped out at about £25m, but it has handled a number of matters for the AIM-quoted company Restore with a combined value of £70m.

Premier League

Seats in the Manchester-based sports team are always sought after – unsurprising when the client base includes Manchester United, Everton and Arsenal FCs and The Professional Footballers' Association itself. "*Trainees in Liverpool always ask whether they can do it,*" but this is unfortunately unlikely. In Manchester though, four current trainees wanted to complete the seat – and all four did. "*The big department means you get a lot of experience and a wide range of work. You are busy but it's not an unreasonable workload. There's a lot of liaising with the other side or dispute resolution bodies, drafting, and client contact on the phone and in meetings.*"

The sports and commercial departments are one team. They "*overlap in terms of clients but they have different heads. The sports team does more of the regulatory work; the commercial team does the contractual drafting side, like image rights agreements, sponsorship agreements and promotional agreements.*" A couple of sources named commercial contracts as their favourite seat due to "*most of the work being drafting, and an exciting subject matter. The work has wider considerations rather than being just a point of law with an answer. We try and get the best for the client in a wider context. There's not a definitive answer all the time.*"

Cheeky beers and big ideas

At Brabners, "*nobody is sitting in their ivory tower.*" That's not to say trainees can't identify the paralegals from the partners, but rather: "*People are sensitive to the fact that you are a trainee and won't know everything. We get great advice and tips from people who have been practising for decades.*" The working hours are generally 8.30am to 6pm "*but when we stay late so do the seniors.*"

The offices themselves are "*self-contained, with their own departments and clients.*" Although they have the same recruitment process, we found out that the trainees in each are really quite different... or maybe that's just the social life. Brabners' Mancs are right in the city centre; however the social scene is "*a bit crap actually. We have good sports teams but we don't go out much,*" one trainee told us. There are staff drinks every six weeks but "*the trainees are quite settled in terms of home life.*" In Liverpool, on the other hand, trainees are party animals – according to themselves, anyway. "*Thinking back to my interview, I don't think they asked us, 'How many times a week do you go out drinking?' but somehow they knew we were all very social. I'd say we have an over-the-top social life,*" one revealed. Not only are there payday staff parties at nearby bar Noble House, where trainees can get to know everyone in the office ("*the partners butt into our conversations and vice versa*") but there are booze cruises down the Mersey, Friday lunches and half-day holidays to Aintree Races. Then they all meet up again on Saturday to go out on the town. In true Liverpudlian fashion, trainees enjoy "*Brabners discounted in-house beauty treatments.*"

When they aren't glamming themselves up to hit the town trainees can be found doing charity work. "*We have Brabners' Big Idea – the offices compete against each other in an Apprentice-style competition.*" Manchester trainees have been known to spend half a day running a nearby charity shop, while in Liverpool, The Prince's Trust Fairbridge provides £500 for local businesses to compete to make as much money as they can by putting on an event. Trainees are in charge of organising the firm's event, "*but the partners muck in and get sponsorship money from clients.*

And finally...

When it comes to qualification, trainees can apply for any position across the three offices. In 2012, four of the eight qualifiers stayed on.

Bristows

The facts

Location: London

Number of UK partners/solicitors: 32/73

Partners who trained at firm: 26%

Total number of trainees: 19

Seats: Seats of 3 to 6 months

Alternative seats: Secondments

Extras: Pro bono – Islington and Tower Hamlets Legal Advice Centres, A4ID; language classes

On chambersstudent.co.uk...
- How to get into Bristows
- Unilever House

IP heavy hitter Bristows is far more than just a haven for techies. Trainees can expect a well-rounded experience across the firm's emerging full-service line-up.

Partying like it's 2012

Amid all the hullabaloo from the Olympics and the Queen's Diamond Jubilee, one recent celebration may have slipped under your radar: the birthday of Bristows. This was no ordinary anniversary, though. In 2012, Bristows reached the grand old age of 175.

Yet despite its age, nothing about this small London firm seems old-school, from its refreshing working ethos – the firm has rejected billable hours targets in favour of nurturing teamwork and quality – to its down-with-the-kids line-up of entertainment and TMT clients. MTV, Google, Nintendo, Sony, Sega and SAMSUNG are just some of the names that Bristows represents. Alongside this enticing array of consumer brands and big technology companies, the firm also has a following in the life sciences industry, advising pharmaceutical juggernauts such as AstraZeneca, Bayer and Novartis. Back in 1837, founding lawyer Robert Wilson set the tone for the firm when he was instructed to draft the patent agreement for the first electrical telegraph. To this day the firm flies high in IP, and is consistently ranked in *Chambers UK* among the elite for intellectual property work. However, training principal Mark Hawes says this firm is "*most emphatically full-service and always has been. We have strong practices in all the mainstream areas and some specialised areas that many firms don't cover, such as data protection and charities. However, our IP department is the largest in the firm – and Europe – which naturally influences perceptions of the firm.*" Roughly half of Bristows' output is IP-related, and the firm divides its workload into seven areas: life sciences; consumer products; industrial mar-

kets; TMT; charities; financial services; and real estate. It is fair to say, however, that the firm's *Chambers UK* rankings are generally related in one way or another to IP, technology or life sciences. "*I think it's trying to become full-service, but it's still on the path there at the moment,*" averred one interviewee, with another adding: "*IP litigation is and always will be the powerhouse of the firm.*"

They're lovin' it

Trainees at Bristows can expect to sit in the core areas of corporate, real estate, IP litigation and commercial disputes, with other seats on offer including EU/competition, commercial IP/IT and regulatory. The firm maps out trainees' full seat plan before they start. "*You have no choice at all, which really surprised me,*" claimed one first-year. "*You can't even give preferences at the start.*" However, the system is actually not as rigid as it sounds, and seats are likely to be shuffled on request. Mark Hawes says: "*If a trainee is worried where a particular department is placed in his or her training plan, or if it hasn't been placed at all, in most instances we can do something about it.*" Trainees agreed: "*If you do want to change seats they are very accommodating.*" One guarantee, however, is that all trainees will complete the compulsory seat in IP litigation.

Bristows views secondments as an essential part of the training contract. Most trainees can expect to spend three months working for the in-house legal teams at big names like McDonald's Europe, Google or advertising heavyweight WPP. The time spent away from Bristows was consistently described by our interviewees as "*the highlight*

Chambers UK rankings

Data Protection	Media & Entertainment
Dispute Resolution	Outsourcing
Information Technology	Partnership
Intellectual Property	Real Estate
Life Sciences	Telecommunications

of the training contract." Don't think this means Bristows will be glad to be rid of you though. One trainee told us: *"The firm offers you a lot of support while you're away. If there is any issue, you do feel you can pick up the phone to them."*

Apple rumble

In IP litigation, trainees should expect exposure to some high-profile cases. Lately the team has been in demand with SAMSUNG in the so-called *"smartphone wars"* against Apple. In one of the most important IP disputes worldwide, Bristows is asserting SAMSUNG patents while also defending the electronics giant against Apple's counter-attack. With parallel proceedings in ten jurisdictions, the case is potentially worth billions. Bristows has also claimed a win on behalf of L'Oréal against eBay, which was advertising products that *"weren't strictly kosher L'Oréal goods."* The team also acted for Kraft Foods' Cadbury arm to defend claims made by Nestlé that its new range of chocolates – Chocos – infringed the Rolo 3D shape trade mark. Trainees who spent time in this department either get involved in hard IP – usually involving the patents of large pharmaceutical or telecoms companies – or soft IP, which is all about the protection of trade marks and copyright. Sources reported getting really involved in some high-value disputes, with many *"spending whole weeks at court for cases."* More commonly, there's plenty of research, drafting and preparation of court documents to get involved with. Although trainees praised the amount of responsibility they were given in IP litigation, *"everyone does have to go through a bit of bundling."*

The commercial IP department brings under its wing subsets such as data protection, licensing and IT. The main focus here is the transactional side of intellectual property, and trainees reported greater client contact here than in IP litigation. *"I was directly involved in advising small start-ups on IP or some meaty contract law, either in person or by drafting documents,"* said one second-year. The department was described as *"very fast-moving and busy"* but trainees enjoyed the amount of variety this brought. *"You could be doing one thing in the morning and something completely different in the afternoon. You never really know what might come in."* The tip-top data protection team at Bristows advises Google – most recently on the Street View case, managing the global response to

claims that Street View cars had illegally collected personal data from insecure home internet networks. Other high points include representing the internet giant on numerous aspects of the launch of Google+, including the introduction of the controversial Find My Face facial recognition feature.

War of the Oranges

The corporate department at Bristows is growing, with a third of 2012's retained trainees qualifying here. The trainee experience varies in this seat depending on the volume of cases on the boil: *"You don't really want to be around if there are no deals."* Trainees in this situation bemoaned having to *"get stuck into due diligence,"* or *"undertake company secretarial work and deal with registration issues."* That said, most of our interviewees were thrilled with the levels of responsibility they were given in the seat: some reported directly liaising with clients; others reviewed contracts or *"saw cases through from start to finish."* Trainees like how the department is run, citing the *"infectious"* supervisors and a focus on career development. One second-year told us: *"If there's something particular you want to get experience in, they try to help you with that."* Corporate work varies from M&A, often with an international leaning, to advising on financial regulations or tax. The team is frequently found lending corporate advice to its sizeable IP client-base. One recent example was acting on the $40m private equity funding of AstraZeneca's biotech spin-out company Albireo.

The commercial disputes team's string of A-list clients includes Chrysler and Everything Everywhere, the product of the Orange and T-Mobile JV. Our interviewees worked on matters including defamation, preliminary injunctions and breaches of confidential information. Time spent here was described as *"challenging"* but not unbearable. *"There was an appropriate amount of pressure. I was fully engaged but not stressing or doing tasks which were beyond me,"* one second-year told us.

Those who sat in real estate enjoyed a great deal of responsibility. *"I was in charge of files from day one,"* said a source. *"It's very rare in other departments that you get to be the first port of call for clients. They know who you are – you're not just a trainee to them."*

Whizz-kids or biz-kids?

Only one of 2012's qualifying class had an undergraduate degree in law, with most having backgrounds in the arts and humanities. This in itself is rare for the firm, which is known for the high proportion of science and engineering grads among its lawyers. Indeed, the wealth of science PhDs in Bristows' ranks prompted one trainee to call the firm *"a bit geeky,"* before quickly qualifying: *"But nice geeky. Maybe I'm just stereotyping the techies."* Training principal Mark Hawes commented: "*Science and engineering students interested in law generally have an interest in IP, so they're naturally attracted to Bristows. But we seek people from a mixture of backgrounds including the law and the arts. We are training lawyers, not scientists.*" Hawes says Bristows nurtures a "*collegial environment rather than one that is profit-driven. The basis for this is mutual respect. It's not aggressively competitive here.*" Our interviewees echoed this: "*I never imagined working somewhere that's so friendly and centred on your own development, rather than just making money and promoting business.*"

Perhaps unsurprisingly, this "*ridiculously friendly*" firm does not expect its trainees to stay glued to their desk. "*If it's quiet, you're not expected to sit around and pick up brownie points for staying,*" said one. The average day is 9am until 6.30pm, and those who work later are in the minority. "*When I did work late people noticed,*" one trainee said. "*A partner e-mailed me telling me to go home.*"

The Grade II listed Unilever House next to Blackfriars Bridge is home to Bristows. Its neoclassical art deco design is "*stunning,*" and was a pull factor for our interviewees when they were applying. "*It certainly struck me during my interview. I thought I'd be really proud to work there.*" Bristows actively promotes a cycle-to-work scheme and provides bike lockers and showers. The firm also offers in-house language classes and numerous seminars to encourage personal development. One second-year surmised: "*Bristows invests as much in you as they do in the company.*"

Party time

The social life is there for the taking. There's the usual array of sports teams to get stuck into, and last Friday drinks rituals in what is affectionately known as the 'Hub' – which we're told is best described as a glorified staff room. Bristows puts on formal parties throughout the year and there are Christmas drinks dos organised by each department and sports team, so expect the season of excess to be, well, excessive. One trainee reported going to seven (!) festive knees-ups. The 175th anniversary party was a glitzy affair held at the Science Museum, while the entire seventh-floor restaurant at the Tate Modern played host to this year's client shindig.

What is the firm looking for in its trainees? "*It's not only about having brains,*" Mark Hawes told us. "*So often people look great on paper and would undoubtedly make great technical lawyers, but we want more than that. At a human level, we're looking for interpersonal skills and a genuine passion for working for clients in the science, technology, media and brand-based industries. Anyone aggressively competitive, however able, wouldn't be the right person for us.*" In its quest to form a dream team of trainees, Bristows has been experimenting with some novel recruitment ideas, more information on which can be found on our website.

And finally...

Fancy carving out a career at this chummy yet geeky establishment? Prospective applicants will be pleased to know that in 2012, Bristows kept on six of its eight qualifying trainees.

Browne Jacobson LLP

The facts

Location: Nottingham, Birmingham, Manchester, London

Number of UK partners/solicitors: 79/147

Partners who trained at firm: 19%

Total number of trainees: 17

Seats: 4x6 months

Alternative seats: Occasional secondments

Extras: Pro bono – CAB, ProHelp, The Prince's Trust, Criminal Injuries Compensation Scheme, Birmingham Employment Rights Advice Line

On chambersstudent.co.uk...

- How to get into Browne Jacobson
- Words from training partner Brian Smith

Further merger-based expansion is a real possibility as this growing Midlands-based firm shifts into a new gear.

Location, location, location

Although it was founded as far back as 1832, it has been in the last ten years that Browne Jacobson's development really accelerated, as the firm quadrupled in size. "*The firm's been progressing and it has done so well*," said trainees, predicting that in a few years BJ will have "*a much stronger national presence.*" This could well happen. In 2011/12 turnover rose by 17.3% to £41.3m, the firm added 79 new staff and it opened a Manchester office. This new outpost – established in January 2012 – is part of BJ's ambitious aim to "*break the North of the country.*" Managing partner Iain Blatherwick said of the revenue growth: "*It is a phenomenal achievement by all involved, well above the average growth anticipated across the UK's top 100 law firms.*"

BJ's largest presence is still in its home town of Nottingham, but there's also a sizeable office in Birmingham and a smaller base in London. The firm concentrates on four sectors: healthcare, insurance, public sector and corporate. Its strong suits have traditionally been insurance and personal injury, but much revenue now comes from its commercial and healthcare work. Blatherwick says: "*All areas of the business have performed well, exceeding our expectations. It is particularly pleasing considering this growth is purely organic and has been achieved without merger or acquisition, although we do not rule out acquisition being part of our strategy going forward.*" London has been the focus of a recent recruitment drive, with lawyers added to the insurance and construction, and property risk teams.

Changing Places

Most trainees are based in Nottingham, though a fair sprinkling from each intake go to Birmingham. There are fewer seats on offer in the latter than the former: "*It's a lot more limited. Brum is good for insurance, health and professional indemnity, while Nottingham also has property and private client work.*" Trainees can move between the two offices, with Brummies more likely to spend time in Nottingham than vice versa, since taking at least one seat in the head office is expected. At the moment, Manchester doesn't have any trainees, and a stint in London is a rarity.

For the first seat, "*HR slots you in as and where they need you.*" However, most sources didn't mind this, and found they still managed to get one of their three preferences at each subsequent seat rotation. Trainees can select from quite a wide selection of teams, which fall under one of the firm's four umbrella departments: business and professional risk (BPR); business services; insurance and public risk (IPR); and property. Potential seat destinations include: healthcare, social care, environment and advocacy, clinical negligence, and personal injury in IPR; commercial litigation, IP, professional negligence, employment, and construction and property risk in BPR; corporate, education, private client and commercial in business services; and public authority, development and retail in property.

Chambers UK rankings

Administrative & Public Law	Healthcare
Banking & Finance	Information Technology
Clinical Negligence	Intellectual Property
Competition/European Law	Local Government
Construction	Personal Injury
Corporate/M&A	Private Client
Court of Protection	Professional Negligence
Dispute Resolution	Projects
Education	Real Estate
Employment	Real Estate Litigation
Environment	Restructuring/Insolvency
Health & Safety	Social Housing

Before the guillotine comes down

Almost all of our sources had spent time in IPR. The clinical negligence team wins national recognition in *Chambers UK* and the firm sits on many legal panels including those of the NHSLA, the Medical Protection Society, the Care Quality Commission and the Treasury Solicitor's Department. It's a busy team, with the volume of claims peaking in light of the forthcoming 'Jackson Guillotine' – an outcome of the Jackson Review which will affect the way civil claims are funded. BJ's lawyers take on mainly defendant work, and regularly advise clients in situations where multimillion-pound settlements are expected. Trainees said: "*The team is really good at getting you involved: you interview the witness and take a statement, draft reports to insurers, and attend a lot of inquests.*" It can also be a challenging seat, with "*saddening cases*" surrounding severe injuries and birth defects leaving trainees unable to not "*read them from a human perspective.*" Sources were also able to get stuck into some Court of Protection work, which involves circumstances when "*someone with mental health problems is unable to make decisions about their healthcare, so a course of action that would be in line with their best interests has to be decided on.*"

Personal injury can be equally intense, with similar issues cropping up. Interviewees said they "*mainly act for the NHSLA, but there are also big insurer claims, so you often liaise with the insurer and their client, chase the records and organise things.*" Trainees were also happy to have been given their own cases on which "*we're allowed to decide where we want to take things.*" Cases can be varied and comprise employer liability issues, catastrophic incidents and multi-action claims, "*for instance, when there's been a pile-up on the motorway.*" The group also has a growing fraud team, who have seen a marked increase in counter-fraud work: "*They are really quite busy, which is*

connected to the economic climate and the fact that people are taking risks to make money where they can.*"

Conversion immersion

Within the BPR department, professional negligence lawyers have been kept on their toes by lenders' claims which have arisen out of the collapse of the property market in 2007/08. Clients include familiar names in the insurance sector – Hiscox, Aviva, Chaucer – and a particular highlight for the team was a £3m claim related to the misselling of payment protection insurance. Trainees commented that their time here was "*really enjoyable as the matters are often highly complex and involve a number of parties. You really have to think about what issues are at stake.*"

BPR is also home to the popular employment and IP teams. Employment was praised for allowing trainees to "*go to tribunals an awful lot – most weeks there will be one day when you're out attending a hearing.*" Another source noted that "*in comparison to other civil litigation cases, employment matters move quite quickly, so you often get to see matters from start to finish. You are forever trying to keep up!*" The "*usual suspects*" are in evidence in this seat, including unfair dismissal, sex and race discrimination, and equal pay claims. Clients include TK Maxx, Peugeot and Wolverhampton City Council. The IP group has expanded over the past couple of years – this is in contrast to the situation at many bigger firms where the practice's strategic significance is being questioned. The team is currently advising the construction company Mace – which has worked on developing the Olympic Village – on its global brand registration and infringement programme.

The business services department contains the corporate team, which *Chambers UK* ranks as one of the top three in the East Midlands. The team regularly advises owner-managed businesses. For example, it acted for Oakwood Fuels – a Nottinghamshire-based fuel manufacturer and hazardous waste collector – during its £30m sale to DDC Environmental. There have been a couple of international deals as well, with BJ's lawyers representing Holland's Macintosh Retail Group in its acquisition of UK shoe retailer Jones Bootmaker. Within business services, trainees can also opt for commercial and private client seats. In private client, the partners are "*keen to let you keep files, begin tax planning for high net worth individuals, work on various trust funds for children and conduct client meetings.*" Clients range from those with a more entrepreneurial and commercial bent to trustees of landed estates.

BJ's property department comprises retail, education, health, development and public authority teams. On the retail side, the group has acted for the buyers of four properties on New Bond Street, including the Louis Vuitton 'Maison' and the Dior flagship store. The education team is, according to the firm, currently instructed on 17% of ongoing academy conversions nationwide. Sources said: "*Property is a great seat for getting your own files, especially if you work on the academy conversions: they're formulaic because we do so many, so there's a step-by-step guide on the process in place.*"

Fare thee well, Hogwarts

"*There's no Browne Jacobson mould,*" according to trainees, who commented on the various personalities at the firm. One source added: "*I got the impression at law school that there's a certain Linklaters personality and a Clifford Chance personality – but here there is more of a range, people with completely different interests and backgrounds.*" In the end, trainees felt that the offices didn't have a typical "*corporate feel,*" and instead described BJ as "*quite a large firm with high-profile clients but a small community feel: people have photos of their children and grandchildren on their desks, and you'll have chats with the post team when they come round. Everybody knows everybody's name.*"

The old Nottingham office resembled something akin to "*Hogwarts – all of a sudden you'd find yourself on a different floor,*" but in June 2012 the Nottingham office moved to swish new premises in the Castle Meadow complex. Read a bit more about it on our website. Sources felt that this new space will "*reflect the firm we've grown into.*" The future open-plan layout was a slight cause for concern: "*The desks will be smaller, storage is minimal, and I'm not sure how people will adapt to a different level of noise.*" These concerns aside, most were excited about the imminent move. The Birmingham office – based on Victoria Square – is "*open plan and really high-spec,*" with The Chameleon Bar, "*a firm favourite,*" conveniently located next door. However, trainees mentioned that "*we're not far from saturating the office,*" and predicted

expansion either within the building or elsewhere in the near future.

What about the London office? We heard that "*there haven't been any trainees down there for years!*" Despite this, "*it does feel attached to the rest of the firm,*" according to one source: "*I deal with the London office quite a lot, and if you're on a trip to the RCJ or in town for a conference, then you're always welcome to pay them a visit.*" Trainees can and have qualified into the London office.

School of rockaoke

"*In general we are a social firm,*" trainees said. There's a central trainee social budget allocated proportionally between Birmingham and Nottingham. Each office will generally do its own thing, but events are also organised for both trainee groups together. Recently the Birmingham trainees went to Nottingham for a curry night, while back in December the Nottingham folks came to Birmingham to tour the Christmas market – "*we manage to see each other quite a lot.*" Sports and social committees in each office also schedule events, which in the past have included comedy club nights, cocktail-making evenings and ghost tours. Nottingham is "*the hub*" when it comes to firm-wide events, and buses are laid on to get staff from Birmingham on site. The summer party in particular is a hit: "*It's quite a big do, and the firm is keen for staff to bring their families. There are clowns for the kids as well as 'rockaoke' for the grown-ups – but trust me, you don't want to hear the partners sing.*"

As for the future, trainees were optimistic about the year ahead. "*The feeling right now is that there will still be year-on-year growth despite the continuing tough economic times. Further expansion is on the cards, but it will be cautious not unreasonable.*" As if to prove the business's success, the firm has had good retention rates since 2010, offering a large number of NQ jobs. In 2012 it retained all eight of its qualifiers.

And finally...
BJ's burgeoning capabilities haven't come at the cost of its *"small community feel."* Let's hope it stays that way now the firm's shed its Hogwarts-style digs.

"Don't forget a job isn't guaranteed at the end of your training contract. Market conditions will dictate whether a firm can take you on, no matter how much you impress. Be loyal, but not so loyal that you don't think you can look elsewhere if you have to."

Trainee

IT'S THE WAY WE WORK THAT MAKES US DIFFERENT

We work with **high profile clients** on well publicised deals

We give our trainees **early responsibility** to run their own smaller matters

We offer a **six seat training system** to allow trainees to make an informed decision

We have a **broad range of practice areas** so we can fit our expertise to our clients' needs

We think about the future – **we recruit future partners**, not just future trainees

We are based in the UK but that doesn't stop us having a **global reach**

We work together in a **collegiate environment**

For more information about trainee solicitor recruitment, please go to
www.burges-salmon.com/careers or call the team on **0117 307 6982.**

f **www.facebook.com/burgessalmontrainee**

@burgessalmon

Burges Salmon LLP is an equal opportunities employer

BURGES SALMON

Burges Salmon LLP

The facts

Location: Bristol

Number of UK partners/solicitors: 77/258

Partners who trained at firm: 24%

Total number of trainees: 46

Seats: 6x4 months

Alternative seats: Secondments

Extras: Pro bono – Bristol University Law Clinic

On chambersstudent.co.uk...
- How to get into Burges Salmon
- The new office
- Interview with trainee recruitment partner Keith Beattie

Burges Salmon has "*come a long way from its West Country beginnings*," but still remains a one-office operation firmly rooted in the heart of Bristol.

Avon is a place on Earth

Those who have difficulty seeing beyond London for the training contract experience should listen to Burges Salmon trainees: "*We couldn't have got it any better in London,*" trainees told us. Certainly, BS has a client list that any London firm would be proud of. International corporates instruct the firm, and many other clients come from outside the South West. Numerous top-tier *Chambers UK* rankings for that region come alongside national recognition for the firm's work in areas as diverse as construction, environment, capital markets, rail transport and pensions litigation. All of which should tell you that this is no country bumpkin. In fact, we'd say that if there was a 'best independent firm outside of London' award, BS would certainly be one of the firms in the running.

"*Corporate, real estate and finance are the core of the firm,*" recruitment partner Keith Beattie tells us. "*However, a lot of the firm's work relates to industry sectors.*" Building up real sector expertise in order to attract clients from that area is a common trend among law firms at the moment, and Beattie cited energy; transport; food and farming; and aerospace and defence as some of Burges Salmon's main target industries. You can see the full list on the firm's website. "*We watch the market closely and stay slightly ahead of it,*" says Beattie. "*For example, the energy team was focusing on wind farms, but now it's working on major tidal projects.*" Trainees say: "*Projects often cross practices, so you can see aspects of them from different departments.*"

Trainees complete six seats of four months each. Real estate is compulsory. The contentious seat can be completed in construction and engineering, commercial disputes (including agricultural disputes) and environment. Two more seats must come from the following list: corporate; banking; commercial; tax/trusts; employment; private client; planning; and pensions and incentives. The fifth seat is a free choice, and then trainees return to their preferred area of qualification for the last four months of their training contract. For that all-important sixth seat, there is "*no formal application process. You have a meeting with HR just before the fifth seat starts and give your first and second choice. You don't know what your last seat will be until you know if you've got a job offer.*" We thought that by this time the atmosphere might be pretty tense, but apparently, "*by the sixth seat the atmosphere is good. The majority of people are happy.*" This is borne out by excellent retention rates: all 22 qualifiers stayed on with the firm in 2012.

Beefy deals

The real estate group always has "*a team of trainees,*" who help out on million-pound transactions while running smaller files themselves. "*I was running a file for a major client. It was challenging but I was well supported,*" one source told us. Another praised the seat for the "*client management experience that trainees get.*" The team acted for The Crown Estate on its acquisition of five retail parks with a total value of around £400m.

The banking and tax departments recently advised bottling company Coca-Cola Hellenic on a five-year €500m

Chambers UK rankings

Agriculture & Rural Affairs	Outsourcing
Banking & Finance	Partnership
Capital Markets	Pensions
Charities	Pensions Litigation
Competition/European Law	Planning
Construction	Private Client
Corporate/M&A	Private Equity
Dispute Resolution	Professional Negligence
Employment	Projects
Energy & Natural Resources	Public Procurement
Environment	Real Estate
Family/Matrimonial	Real Estate Litigation
Health & Safety	Restructuring/Insolvency
Information Technology	Tax
Intellectual Property	Transport
Investment Funds	

revolving credit facility with a syndicate of ten banks. Magic circle firm Clifford Chance was acting for the lenders. One source who had completed the banking seat "*didn't work for any clients based in the South West. Banks tend to have a lot of involvement in the work we do. Often, part of the job is trying to impose the bank's will on the transaction. On a day-to-day basis, there's lots of stuff to be checked and processed, and conditions to be fulfilled. Trainees manage the flow of what's going on and we're often the internal point of contact.*"

One trainee told us: "*On day one of my corporate seat I went to a client meeting. After that, I was always involved in three or four deals at any one time, and I did all the drafting on a smaller deal.*" The larger corporate matters are often a "*long process*" and it's unusual for a trainee to work on a deal from beginning to end. "*Trainees don't draft the big documents, so we do a lot of research.*" The corporate team recently advised the shareholders of RWM on its sale to the ABP Food Group. RWM is a beef and lamb processing company. Meanwhile, the commercial seat covers a variety of areas, including IP, IT and competition. "*The best thing about commercial is that it's great at honing drafting skills. It's not task-based work, it's not admin work – it's genuine legal work.*"

Trainees in commercial disputes "*research cases and write letters of advice to clients. To start with, drafts are reviewed by superiors, but once you're good enough they can go out unamended.*" There is the opportunity to experience a range of different areas: "*I did a bit of property litigation and commercial litigation at the same time,*" one source told us. Star sports litigator Mark Gay recently joined from DLA Piper and trainees who show an inter-

est can get involved in this area too. Work is passed down from supervisors, but trainees are encouraged to seek out projects that appeal to them. "*They like initiative. I asked to go to a mediation that was related to my extracurricular interests,*" a trainee explained.

Handling both contentious and transactional work, construction "*is a scary but incredible seat,*" one trainee revealed. "*I was constantly on conference calls with clients and attending long client meetings in Bristol and London.*" BS has an unmanned office in the capital which trainees often visit for meetings. Sources had encountered "*quite a bit of renewable energy work, including wind turbine projects.*" "*We work closely with the environment and real estate teams. There is an adjudication side to the group as well: people come to us when they have disputes with contractors.*" Clients come from both the public and the private sector and include the Nuclear Decommissioning Authority, Kew Gardens, Tata Steel and HSBC. The group recently advised Exeter University on a £40m development project, and Bristol Airport on its plans for terminal expansion.

Secondments opportunities are "*based on client needs.*" A few trainees have been keen on going recently. "*One went to the European Court and another went to a bank. The six-seat system allows trainees to complete secondments without sacrificing a quarter of the training contract.*"

Which fish are you?

Until very recently, BS pitched adverts with a 'SARDINES / SALMON' theme at students, with the implication that strolling to work in the fresh air of Bristol is infinitely preferable to squeezing onto a Central Line tube carriage every morning. That should tell you that the firm is targeting graduates good enough to work at the best London outfits. However, although some trainees have a connection to the South West, simply 'wanting to work in Bristol' is not enough motivation to apply here. "*It was more about the firm itself,*" said one source. "*Location is important but so is reputation,*" added another. "*You don't want to give up top-quality work, so you must look at both factors, along with the atmosphere and working environment that you are going to be in.*"

So is this what you'd call a 'lifestyle' firm? Trainees told us their "*hours are generally very good.*" It varies between departments, but the majority work from "*around 8.45am to 6.30pm.*" However, said one source: "*Leaving at 6pm would be a good day. I leave after 8pm at least once a week. The aim of the game is to impress. You want a job so you volunteer to stay late.*" Another told us he'd "*worked an 80-hour week*" and all of our interviewees agreed they would be "*expected to stay later if needed.*" Fortunately, "*Burges Salmon doesn't really enforce billable targets for trainees, so we get the opportunity to learn for the sake of learning. I went to a tribunal just to watch. I doubt the client was paying for me to be there.*" How many hours do they bill? "*Something like three or four a day. It's never discussed.*"

As for the commute, "*a couple of trainees live out Cheltenham way, some of us are in Clifton and a few in south Bristol.*" Burges Salmon itself is conveniently located in the city's Temple Quay – arriving at Bristol Temple Meads station, you can't miss the firm's brand-new office building, which it moved into in 2010. Resplendent in salmon-pink cladding, and with the firm's name emblazoned in MASSIVE LETTERS on the side, it really is very impressive. It's a "*phenomenal facility,*" said trainees, "*with a really good, subsidised canteen.*" Our sources liked "*having the whole firm in one building,*" thinking it added a lot to the ethos of BS: "*Everyone knows everyone, and it's effortless to go and see someone from any department. The cross-team work wouldn't happen so easily if we were in different offices.*" Trainees share a room with their supervisor.

Eat your heart out, Ant & Dec

"*I've seen four trainee intakes,*" said one seasoned finalseater, "*and their commercial awareness always stands out. You can't just be a legal genius: you need to have more about you. You have to be able to look at facts from a client's perspective and understand the end result that the client wants.*" BS trainees range in age from early 20s to early 30s and a fair few have a previous career behind them. There are a fair few Oxbridge and Bristol graduates, and the rest tend to come from similarly well-regarded institutions. All of our sources said that the trainee group "*gets on really well,*" and one claimed that the bunch "*is the best thing about the firm.*" They admitted to frequenting the local Wetherspoons, which one described as "*horrible. It's just very near. As soon as everyone's there we head into town,*" often to the Apple, a lovely little cider bar(ge) moored on the waterfront. Second-years organise weekends away for the whole trainee group: "*Last year we went to Devon.*" The firm-wide parties sound pretty good too: "*Our summer party was a sit-down meal in a hotel. There was a photo booth and a chocolate fountain. This summer we are voting whether we go back to that hotel or have it at Bristol Zoo.*"

Burges Salmon is quite a sporty firm and trainees can participate in football and netball teams, pilates and charity fund-raisers such as Bristol's annual dragon-boat race. Law firms often produce their own rip-offs of TV game shows – variations on *The X Factor* are a perennial favourite – but we must admit that BS has upped the standard with an event called I'm a Trainee Get Me Out of Here. "*The aim was to get as far from Bristol without paying,*" a source explained. And the results? "*Some trainees made it to Barcelona in a weekend. Others were still paddling across the Avon to Wales.*" The less free-spirited can join the social committee, "*which organises theatre trips and cupcake-making classes.*"

And finally...

With good training, good qualification prospects and an upbeat working environment, Burges Salmon isn't just an excellent option in Bristol, it's an excellent option, full stop.

Capsticks Solicitors LLP

The facts

Location: London, Birmingham, Leeds

Number of UK partners/solicitors: 41/110

Partners who trained at firm: 22%

Total number of trainees: 12

Seats: 6x4 months

Alternative seats: None

Extras: Pro bono – Putney Law Centre

On chambersstudent.co.uk...

- How to get into Capsticks
- The latest on healthcare reforms
- Interview with training principal Annie Sorbie

The future looks bright for Capsticks, the Wimbledon firm working at the very heart of David Cameron's latest healthcare reforms.

A healthy prognosis

Formed over 25 years ago from the ashes of an in-house NHS legal department, Capsticks has blossomed to become one of the leading firms specialising in healthcare law. South West London is its base and home to all its current trainees, but the firm has expanded from its office close to Wimbledon station in recent years, opening in Birmingham and Leeds in 2008 and 2011 respectively. The first Leeds trainee will arrive in 2013.

If healthcare is your thing, it doesn't get much better than this. At last count, 76% of the firm's business was on behalf of the NHS, and it represents everyone from the Department of Health, to NHS trusts, to regulators like the General Dental Council. It regularly takes on headline-grabbing cases, most recently advising the London Ambulance Service in the inquest into the 7/7 London Bombings – one of the largest ever held in the UK.

The Health and Social Care Act of March 2012 is one of the most radical plans in the history of the Health Service. The main aims of the £1.4bn programme are to increase competition and the role of the private sector, to downsize the Department of Health, and to pass the many responsibilities of primary care trusts (PCTs) and strategic health authorities over to clinical commissioning groups (CCGs) led by GPs, hospital doctors and nurses. Training principal Annie Sorbie says: *"Obviously, it's a massive change in the area of healthcare, but we see it as an opportunity rather than a threat."* Indeed, the firm has become quite adept at navigating the choppy seas of healthcare policy – *"change is nothing new for us: it happens constantly."* Trainees reported seeing an uptick in work as a result of the latest reforms, which shows no signs of slowing. According to one: *"Our strategic direction is to combine our excellent reputation with public sector health bodies with our growing body of private sector health clients. Following NHS reforms, the healthcare market will become much more varied, and we're best placed to provide legal services to those bodies."* The consensus is, and Sorbie agrees, that *"it's exciting and innovative, and a great time to be a lawyer in this area."*

A very different body of law

There are six seat options within Capsticks' five departments: clinical negligence, clinical advisory (both within clinical law), dispute resolution, real estate, commercial and employment. The majority of trainees move through five of these, and spend the final four-month stint of their training contract revisiting the seat they hope to qualify into. Everyone will visit their first choice at some stage. Due to Capsticks' small size, there are no holds barred when it comes to responsibility. *"They treat you like a qualified lawyer from the off. You can't get away with hiding in the background and doing the boring work. They'll have you drafting advice from scratch in your first or second seat."*

Clinical negligence work is widely regarded as *"the bread and butter of Capsticks."* The department represents more than 300 NHS and private sector health clients, and saw the number of cases it handled increase by a hearty 38% in 2012. It's something of a trainee magnet, largely because *"it's for those interested in medicine and how the law applies to medicine at the front line."* The law is a

Chambers UK rankings

Administrative & Public Law	Employment
Clinical Negligence	Healthcare
Court of Protection	Professional Discipline

combination of NHS and insurance work – "*basically defending the NHS from negligence claims*" – and the subject matter ranges from tattoo removal to brain-damaged babies. As you can imagine, these more serious negligence cases aren't for the faint-hearted. According to trainees, it's best to look at them as "*harrowing factually, but interesting medically.*" They continued: "*Everyone takes a professional stance, and you can't let the subject matter affect things.*" Responsibility in the group is pitched high, and trainees will be on their toes "*instructing experts, attending round table meetings and lodging papers at the RCJ.*"

The firm's clinical advisory seat is one of a kind. "*It's fundamentally about the relationship between people and the healthcare system.*" Lawyers in the department are primarily involved in big mental health issues, information law and huge judicial review cases. Those more senior are used to receiving urgent calls from doctors in the middle of the night with queries about "*Jehovah's Witnesses who are refusing blood transfusions, or parents refusing treatment for their kids.*" At trainee level, advice tends to be more low key – how to implement particular programmes, and basic judicial review work. The group is packed with "*very clever and slightly eccentric specialists,*" and there's more chance of getting bogged down in grunt work than in some other departments. According to trainees, however, "*it's quite gratifying, as the work you're doing will have a profound effect on someone else's life. Is it stressful? It can be. But the partners keeping an eye on you are the go-to people in the country for this kind of work. You're learning from the best, and being supported by the best too.*"

Despite the prominence of the clinical teams, dispute resolution is at least equal in terms of headcount. Split into three subgroups – property litigation, regulatory law and commercial litigation – it's a favourite among trainees, partially because it's "*not as high-stress as some other departments.*" Work tends to consist of standard dispute resolution with a medical twist. "*One thing I enjoy, as well as the black-letter law, is that there's a second layer of law on top of that imposed by the Department of Health,*" a trainee explained. "*You have to be sensitive to small political concerns between organisations. Plus, it's an issue that a lot of people in the UK care about. You need to factor that into your legal answers.*"

The non-contentious commercial seat "*isn't what people tend to come here for, but it's essential for trainees as you learn so much about the NHS that you'd never know otherwise.*" It's currently at the heart of the health service reforms, and trainees should expect to "*hit the ground running*" helping construct NHS and PPP contracts, and setting up private healthcare bodies and clinical commission groups. The real estate group is also at the sharp edge of the changes, "*future-proofing the NHS estate.*"

White coats and golden tickets

"*Everyone is pretty close,*" claimed one source; "*we feel like a little family,*" and "*everyone's mates as well as colleagues.*" People "*tend to work really hard in the day so they can have fun afterwards,*" and trainees and partners alike are regular faces at The Alexandra or All Bar One across the road from the firm's office. There are more social and sports events than you can shake a stethoscope at – our sources were still recovering from last year's karaoke event ("*there were things we should never have heard or seen*") and looking forward to this year's summer party on one of the office's two "*sun trap*" balconies.

If Capsticks sounds up your street, make sure you apply for the firm's vacation scheme as it is "*still the golden route in,*" although some current trainees had initially impressed while paralegalling at the firm. A handful have some sort of science degree under their belt, while others have more of a passing interest in the health sector. Either way, hiring partner Annie Sorbie reckons she recognises a healthcare keenie when she sees one: "*You can tell when candidates come to interview – seeing that spark is really important.*" According to trainees, making the grade comes down to personality: "*All the trainees and NQs are really quite confident people – there are no shrinking violets. At interview, make sure you show your personality and be chatty.*"

And finally...

You don't have to be House MD to work at Capsticks, but an interest in healthcare certainly helps. *"It's weird how you find yourself being able to understand ECGs and ultrasound scans!"* In 2012, the firm kept on all five of its new qualifiers.

Charles Russell LLP

The facts

Location: London, Guildford, Cheltenham, Oxford, Cambridge

Number of UK partners/solicitors: 96/160

Partners who trained at firm: 16%

Total number of trainees: 25

Seats: 4x6 months

Alternative seats: Overseas seats, secondments

Extras: Pro bono – LawWorks, A4ID, RCJ CAB, Bethnal Green Law Centre

On chambersstudent.co.uk...
• How to get into Charles Russell
• Give it up for Guildford

Trainees say the combo of traditional private client and trendy commercial work means Charles Russell "*should be on everyone's list.*"

A family affair

Established by the son of a Lord Chief Justice, Charles Russell has been advising the wealthy since 1891. Star family and private client groups are a legacy of its impressive history, but it's actually dispute resolution and corporate/commercial work that now make up the bulk of its business. As senior partner (and great-great-nephew of the founder) Patrick Russell told us: "*The roots of the firm are in private client and litigation; however our work is now much broader and commercial advice is at least 50% of our business and also much more international in outlook. What is most important though is that while the work has grown, we still maintain the traditional qualities that have made the firm what it is.*" In 2011 CR adapted its business model to focus on nine sectors: charities; energy; family; healthcare; private wealth; property; retail, design and leisure; sports and media; and technology and communications.

Charles Russell has other offices in Cheltenham and Guildford and overseas outposts in Bahrain and Geneva, the last of which has two trainees resident for each rotation. The idea is to win corporate instructions from the many private wealth clients CR already has. "*There's a gap in the market,*" explained one trainee. "*There are a huge number of corporations with headquarters in Geneva: the idea is to tap into that.*" The Bahrain outpost also takes one trainee every seat.

"*I wasn't sure what area of law to go into, and Charles Russell has a wide spread of practices,*" was the feeling of most of our sources. The firm's London HQ offers the most variety, with seats in litigation, coco, real estate,

employment and pensions, family and private client. The smaller group of Guildford trainees can choose from family, employment, litigation, property litigation, insolvency, private client, real estate and construction, while in Cheltenham they rotate between coco, litigation, private client and real estate. Guildford trainees rank preferences in order before they begin – after this "*it's simply a case of speaking to HR and stating what we want.*" London is "*a little more formal,*" with trainees completing a form two months before each seat change. Family and employment are always "*very popular,*" and because coco "*takes five or six trainees, it's highly likely that you'll go there.*" Consequently some "*opt for it first to get it out of the way.*"

Mid-market matters

Coco covers capital markets, M&A, banking, tax, competition, IP, funds, media and sports law on top of general commercial work. In London, Charles Russell mines the corporate mid-market, and receives *Chambers* rankings for its capital markets work for AIM clients. Many clients come from the worlds of energy (mining company Centamin), healthcare (pharma company Shire) and media and telecoms (ITV, US publishing empire Meredith Corporation). The group has acted for IT and communications consultancy Bluefish in its disposal of Vodafone's multinational communications business, Vodafone Global Enterprise. It also represented the government of the Bahamas in the process of privatising the Bahamas Telecommunications Company. On large deals trainees can find themselves working on quite menial tasks, such as "*uploading and reviewing documents, printing,*"

Chambers UK rankings

Agriculture & Rural Affairs	Intellectual Property
Banking & Finance	Media & Entertainment
Capital Markets	Planning
Charities	Private Client
Construction	Professional Discipline
Corporate/M&A	Real Estate
Defamation/Reputation Management	Real Estate Litigation
Dispute Resolution	Restructuring/Insolvency
Employment	Retail
Family/Matrimonial	Sports Law
Fraud	Telecommunications
Healthcare	

bundling and checking the bundles against the originals," although this is balanced with *"drafting board minutes and shareholder resolutions and giving advice on the issuing of new shares."*

In the commercial half of the seat, trainees may get the opportunity to take on sports, IP and media-related work: *"If you're interested, you only have to speak to the relevant people to get involved."* The firm picks up *Chambers UK* accolades for its sports practice, and has clients like The FA, Paddy Power and Man U's merchandising arm. When Wayne Rooney received a three-match ban after his red card representing England against Montenegro, CR successfully got it reduced to two, not that it did him much good in Euro 2012. It also advised Thierry Henry on his return to Arsenal on loan and the British Horseracing Authority on the introduction of the controversial whip rule.

The firm has a strong reputation for privacy and libel work, but has made some lateral hires to increase its visibility in the advertising and digital marketing spheres. It has advised Westfield, both on the shopping centre chain's brand partnerships with AmEx and adidas, and on social media-related issues like data protection and prize draws. ITV, Barclays and YouView are other key clients, as is Noel Gallagher, whom CR represented when brother Liam sued him, claiming Noel had pulled out of a festival performance because he was *"hungover."* Boys, boys.

The colour purple (Pantone 2685C)

The firm's IP expertise is clustered around patent, trade mark and brand protection in the arenas of retail, media, technology, sports and life sciences. Clients include Wagamama and Arcadia (which owns much of the high street, including Topshop and Bhs). The firm recently defended Cadbury against opposition from arch-competitor Nestlé in the extension of the trade mark for its shade

of classic purple. Trainees report a mixture of *"bundling and disclosure exercises"* with perks like *"getting to sit in on conferences with counsel and attending client meetings."*

The vast litigation and dispute resolution (LDR) department encompasses teams in insolvency, pharmaceutical litigation and property litigation. Trainees raved about the consequent *"variety of chunky, high-profile work for household-name clients."* LDR newbies get their own small debt claim files to run with. *"You report back every so often to the fee earner, but you're essentially given autonomy to process the case as you see fit. As the litigation process can be quite lengthy, you may only get to dip in and out of a high-value claim in your six months – the small fast-track work allows you to get the investigations done, issue the claim and see it through to the end."* Some of the larger matters have included acting as administrator to the defunct Awal Bank of Bahrain, a multibillion-dollar issue with multi-jurisdictional fraud allegations. On matters like this, *"you spend a lot of time making sense of what's going on,"* but as a trainee, *"you're encouraged to get stuck in. There's admin, but you feel an important part of the team."* Trainees may work on contentious trust and probate as part of their litigation seat, where there's plenty of client contact and the opportunity to attend hearings and draw up first drafts of witness statements.

"If you want private client work, I can't think of a better firm to train with," one source declared. A recent step-up in international work using the Geneva hub hasn't put paid to the firm's staple private client business of *"wills and probate, powers of attorney, trust administration and tax."* There's also a niche practice in mental capacity work. Despite the natural *"hand-holding"* that takes place between partners and their established clients, trainees report good responsibility – *"drafting wills, appointing and resigning trustees, helping out with probates and researching discrete tax issues."* Trainees keen on private work tend to be *"interested in people not companies,"* but there's a growing demand for research on Shari'a law and giving resultant corporate advice. Further, there are *"so many cross-referrals between departments you'll get to see business disputes."* One trainee each rotation sits in Geneva's private client department. A secondee there became intimately acquainted with the Liechtenstein Disclosure Facility (a service identifying individuals with registered companies in the principality who may be UK tax-liable).

The family seat is renowned for providing contact with high-profile and wealthy people. *"From the off, you'll get to hear at first hand the advice the firm is giving to clients."* Work revolves around divorce petitions and financial settlements, and there's a small but strong children practice, although "*we try to get people to settle matters for themselves, as it's nicer for everyone concerned.*"

In addition to secondments to The FA, Actis Capital and Cable & Wireless, trainees have the opportunity to spend time in Bahrain or Geneva. The overseas seats "*aren't that popular, as people aren't that keen on upping their lives,*" so "*if you want to go, it's almost guaranteed.*" Geneva's corporate practice has only been around for a year and a half, so "*things are very focused on business development – when you're there, you're often representing the firm at networking events.*" Across the board, trainees reported increased levels of responsibility away from home, and appreciated the firm's pastoral care: "*They're aware that moving to another country is difficult, so they'll do things like pick you up from the airport.*"

Appraisals come every three months. The mid-seat one is "*helpful in order to be put on the right track,*" and the end one "*great, as you can focus on improving skills for your next department.*"

Desert island discussions

"*I've never met anyone here I wouldn't be delighted to go for a beer with,*" said one trainee. People are "*very friendly – if you have a day off, they'll ask what you're doing, and if you're upset, they want to know what they can do to help. There aren't many boundaries, but it's really nice being friends with your boss.*" London trainees go for drinks "*most Fridays*" and recently ventured into All Star Bowling. The last Christmas party was James Bond-themed, although a few sources complained: "*They started clearing everything away at 8.30pm so we moved onto a bar, although none of the partners followed with credit cards.*" In Guildford and Cheltenham, "*it's not every Friday in the pub, but we go for drinks and dinner every couple of months.*" There is "*netball for girls and football for boys,*" as well as a book group and frequent fund-raising events for the firm's charity of the year – currently child bereavement foundation Winston's Wish.

The firm's HQ just off Fleet Street is "*brand new and very plush.*" The Guildford office is conveniently placed by the River Wey, so lunch is often al fresco come summer. The Cheltenham office used to be a Georgian town house and sits just off the A40, in "*boutiquey*" Montpellier – great for both shopaholics and the office's many commuters. There's a one-firm policy – although those in the regional offices sometimes feel forgotten: "*We get constant firm-wide e-mails about cakes in the London kitchen – it can feel like they forget we're here.*"

Charles Russell's application form is known for including a couple of "*quirky*" questions. Recent ones include 'What two items would you take on a desert island?' and 'If you could have a superhero power, what would it be?' These are often tempered with a less left-field, but still non-legal question, such as 'What one measure would you take to improve the green issues at your current place of work?' Advice: "*All they want is for you to interest them and show you've got a personality. If your answer raises a smile it indicates there's something going on behind your ears that isn't purely academic.*" Trainees who made the cut see it as an efficient filter: "*It's easy to send off blanket applications when you're applying to similar firms. Unusual questions put a lot of people off – if you like it, you'll complete it.*" Despite off-putting questions, Charles Russell still receives around 1,400 applications for just a dozen or so training contracts.

And finally...

Charles Russell provides an excellent all-round training but come qualification *"it's worth bearing in mind that the two biggest departments are coco and litigation."* In 2012, 18 out of 19 qualifiers accepted NQ jobs with the firm.

Cleary Gottlieb Steen & Hamilton LLP

The facts

Location: London

Number of UK partners/solicitors: 11/50 (+24 US-qualified)

UK partners who trained at firm: 28%

Total number of trainees: 19

Seats: 4x6 months

Alternative seats: Overseas seats, secondments

On chambersstudent.co.uk...

- How to get into Cleary
- Interview with grad recruitment partner Richard Sultman
- Internationalists

"*If you are a self-starter,*" internationally minded Cleary "*is an ideal place for you.*"

Something Gottlieb started

Cleary made its ambitions clear when it leapt across the Atlantic and landed in Paris a mere three years after it was founded in the US in 1946. Cleary has long been more than just an American outfit with foreign ambitions. Its London office emerged in 1971, focusing on US elements of global transactions and eventually building a practice that is now widely recognised for a capital markets, M&A and finance practice which touches practically all continents. When recession put a dampener on corporate transactions, Cleary paid the bills by working on restructuring matters, for both corporate and sovereign entities. The firm has been providing counsel on debt restructuring to both private and government sector officials in Greece, so far resulting in a historic €100bn debt write-down and a bail-out agreement for €130bn.

This is not to downplay Cleary's traditional strengths, which are as strong as ever. The firm recently advised on the second largest IPO in 2012 after Facebook – working on Malaysian state-owned palm oil company Felda Global Ventures' £2.1bn listing. *Chambers UK* ranks the firm's capital markets practice as one of the best in the country, also recognising its banking, corporate, dispute resolution and competition capabilities. "*The big interesting story will be the growth of the competition and litigation practices,*" commented trainees. "*Watch those spaces.*"

Expand your horizons

Cleary trainees talk about lockstep remuneration and "*generalist*" training, often and with pride. They couldn't stress enough on how much they like the "*non-hierarchical*" lockstep system (where everyone in a class year earns the same regardless of how much they bill, which is different from some US firms), and how it contributes towards a "*positive working environment... teams of people achieving things without competing with each other.*" They were also happy that Cleary doesn't silo lawyers into discrete categories: "*Not being pigeon-holed is good, you expand your horizons. When one market quietens down, you can reallocate resources.*" The benefits of training as a generalist wasn't lost on trainees, who felt the firm could stay leaner in meaner markets without heads rolling.

Seats are allocated after a couple of chats with HR before each rotation. "*Part of the discussion is about what kind of training you want: you're not dumped with a partner who is hands-off if you don't want that.*" Before assigning a trainee to a seat, the firm "*actually thinks about what this person can contribute, rather than simply stashing them in a seat because there is capacity there – it's a bit more tailored.*"

Work doesn't change abruptly with each seat move: "*You can follow work through from one seat to the other.*" Trainees are allowed to do this "*if* [they are] *interested in something – it's not forced upon you.*" It's also handy for keeping "*a foot in the door*" in areas they want to qualify into. The "*many late nights*" and "*issues in juggling your time*" are worth it if it means "*you see your work gradually appearing in the Financial Times.*" Most supervisors understand "*you have unique knowledge of working on a deal and it would be counterproductive to the firm and the*

Chambers UK rankings

Banking & Finance	Corporate/M&A
Banking Litigation	Dispute Resolution
Capital Markets	Private Equity
Competition/European Law	

client" if a new trainee replaces the old one. Our "*driven*" sources emphasised "*it cuts both ways,*" as some started seats with an empty docket.

It's a whopper!

A few lawyers, a few billion-dollar deals – that's how the London M&A practice rolls. It recently advised Barclays Capital on Justice Holdings' acquisition of a 29% stake in Burger King Worldwide worth $1.4bn – resulting in the 'Home of the Whopper' returning to the NYSE after going private in 2010. A London-led team advised private equity group TPG in the sale of its £1.3bn majority stake in Mey Ici, a Turkish spirits manufacturer, to Diageo. Cleary is also advising Agilent in its $2.2bn purchase of Dako, a Danish manufacturer of cancer diagnostic equipment. "*The first deal I was on was a cross-border merger involving two Finnish companies and an English law agreement. I spent a few weeks reviewing documents thinking I was doing trainee tasks, but a couple of months into the seat my supervisor asked me to draft one because I had seen what they looked like. That was quick progression!*" said one source. Another trainee "*redrafted articles of association and shareholders' agreements and drafted new ones for new ventures. I really liked having the opportunity to do that, as it's not often trainees are able to draft whole agreements – that's more junior-associate level work.*" Because partners don't belong to discrete practice areas, trainees sitting in M&A might be working on "*emerging markets, because the partner I was sitting with also had a focus on the Middle East and North Africa,*" or "*on a minority investment in a South American asset management company. We don't have lawyers who solely do one continent: if you work with a lot of Russian clients you might know more about that country but no one will pigeon-hole you.*"

"*You know when you've been used to working all night as a student? You think: how hard can it be? I'm young, I can handle it,*" mused one trainee. "*The reality is that, by the end of your training contract, this is true – but it does take time to get used to it.*" Wise words, especially for those in Cleary's capital markets team. "*On one particular deal, the other side was in the US and as a result we had conference calls that started at midnight. That wasn't so pleasant but it only went on for a week or ten days.*" The hours "*can get really bad, capital markets is notorious for that,*" a contrast to corporate, where our sources had usu-

ally been able to get out by 8pm. Carrying over other work to this seat would be a bad idea, cautioned our sources: "*You would have too much on your plate.*" Some trainees had worked on debt listings , being responsible for "*filing the prospectus with the UKLA* [UK Listing Authority]*, liaising with them regarding the timetable, getting people's comments on comment sheets.*" Those working on debt take-downs found themselves in a fast-paced environment where there's real pressure to trainee tasks like "*updating prospectuses, annotating them and making sure you have all details on hand, and liaising with clients.*"

Sunil days are here again

"*When I joined, the litigation team was a basically a US arbitration practice in London,*" commented a second-year trainee, "*but at the beginning of 2010 we started an English-law litigation practice. Now we have two UK qualified partners and ten associates and we are all kept busy.*" While new arrival Jonathan Kelly "*specialises in finance, banking and regulatory litigation,*" trainees anticipate the addition of former Stephenson Harwood CEO Sunil Gadhia, who is widely credited with reviving that firm's fortunes, will bring professional negligence and fraud work to the mix. Gadhia "*is a lovely man, very respectful, very engaged – you don't feel like you're working with a partner, you don't have to make sure everything you say is very well thought out!*" gushed one source. Though "*a fair amount of standard tasks like bundling*" can be expected, "*the grunt work is never too bad.*" Trainees also see "*a lot of legal research,*" prepare first drafts of witness statements, help with correspondence and "*draft things like mediation position papers.*" Cleary provides counsel to the Republic of Congo, Sierra Leone, Argentina and Iraq, as well as companies like UBS and Rosneft Oil.

Trainees in finance dabbled in leveraged buyouts, project finance, bond work and restructuring. "*I had a huge amount of independence: if you're inclined to take things on yourself, the sky is the limit.*" They take long hours in their stride without any moaning, reflecting the kind of person who really thrives at Cleary. "*Theoretically, until you've filled 24 hours in a day, you have more capacity. At the moment I am in a deal that's taking up 90% of my time and a partner rang me up to do something fun, so now I'm working 120% of my time. It is fun. But people are understanding and you can say no.*" This enthusiasm came with the caveat: "*It can be stressful, it's worth acknowledging.*"

Brussels, Paris, New York, Moscow and Hong Kong secondments are usually on offer. Others crop up now and then, but "*if you really are interested in, for example, antitrust and want to go to DC, it's always a possibility.*" Our sources gave glowing reports of their time abroad: "*I was basically an associate there.*" Trainees don't need to leave the office to work with their Cleary counterparts overseas. "*You'll just get a call from someone in Brussels, saying, 'Hi, you've worked on this matter, are you the right person to talk to?' Or I might call a librarian in Paris asking for help.*"

In addition to a generally supportive office culture, where most seniors are prepared to offer guidance, each trainee is assigned a mentor trio: a trainee, associate and partner. The latter is "*the most important relationship, it's someone who hasn't supervised you but can give you an overall, impartial review of your performance.*" Official training sessions run "*on most Thursdays*" throughout the year and the firm also started an online "*mini-MBA programme.*"

Where did all the women go?

We do note that for the last two years, male trainees have noticeably outnumbered female trainees – unusual these days – and female trainees "*wondered why there aren't any female partners in London,*" though they hadn't experienced "*an old boys' club mentality*" either. "*I think the firm is trying to improve things,*" suggested one. "*There is a Women's Working Group: female partners from New York come over and we discuss issues over coffee and cake.*" Female senior associates with young families have flexible working arrangements. "*We are conscious that currently we don't have any female partners in London but that is not likely to remain the case in the short term given the talented female associates that we have among the ranks. Having female partners is very much part of our strategy, as evidenced by our situation in other firm offices, but until recently circumstances have played against us in this respect in London. We feel this will change shortly,*" says graduate recruitment partner Richard Sultman.

We've also noticed a particularly heavy Oxbridge bias among our interviewees. In fact, looking back through our talks with randomly selected Cleary trainees over the last six years, nearly three-quarters of them attended either Oxford or Cambridge. "*It doesn't surprise me to hear that,*" said Richard Sultman when we quizzed him, "*but we don't make our recruitment decisions based on which university candidates attended.*" The current trainee group does also include UCL, Edinburgh and LSE grads, and the firm additionally attends law fairs at Queen Mary, Durham and King's.

"*It's a tough place, with great opportunities to thrive,*" reflected one trainee. Others were more blunt: "*If you just want to come in, do a decent job and go home, then this isn't the place for you.*" Most of our sources had come in expecting hard graft, and found the firm fair and "*open to you regulating your own hours*" depending on how busy things are. Cleary trainees work for the "*rush*" and have the confidence to ask for help or reserve 'me time' when they need it. Basically, Cleary's a firm that expects "*you to work hard but is human, not imposing or stuffy.*"

Cleary is housed in a modern-looking glass, concrete and steel structure between Moorgate and Mansion House. Equipped with a canteen that has "*fresh, subsidised food*" and shower facilities, there is one dreaded perk trainees are thankful to not have at work: "*sleeping pods.*" Our sources agreed the offices are "*a bit tired*" but were happy to get their own room on qualification.

"*The social life is there, but you aren't pressured to partake in it. If you want to go for drinks on a Friday, there will always be a bunch of Cleary people somewhere near.*" Trainees found things are more social "*in the first six months. Then you splinter off more into your friendship groups.*" This is by no means a "*bid to exclude anyone, it's just because we are all different.*" The firm is trying to improve the social scene and a social committee has recently organised quiz nights and bowling events, while summer barbecues are in the offing. An annual trip to an EU office to meet people from around the network is open to anyone who started at Cleary in the previous twelve months.

And finally...
Unless trainees qualify into litigation or competition, they remain generalists as NQs. 12 out of 14 second-years were retained in 2012.

DIVERSE, INTERNATIONAL AND COMMERCIALLY AWARE, WE WORK TOGETHER.
TOGETHER WE ARE CLIFFORD CHANCE.

Joining us as a trainee means sharing our ambition and drive to set the pace among the global elite law firms. You will develop your potential as part of an exceptionally talented legal team, and tackle the issues and decisions that shape our clients' success – helping them to achieve competitive advantage in challenging business circumstances.

Find out about opportunities at Clifford Chance – a law firm built on collaboration, innovation and a relentless commitment to quality, and with more leading cross-border practices than any other firm *(Chambers Global 2012)*.

Together we are Clifford Chance.
www.cliffordchance.com/gradsuk

CLIFFORD CHANCE

Clifford Chance LLP

The facts

Location: London

Number of UK partners/solicitors: 177/480

Total number of trainees: 242

Seats: 4x6 months

Alternative seats: Overseas seats, secondments

Extras: Pro bono – Various legal advice centres; language classes

On chambersstudent.co.uk...

- How to get into Clifford Chance
- More about seats and secondments
- A history of the firm

Everything's bigger at Clifford Chance – offices, deals, prestige and opportunities – and it continues to impress as a permanent fixture of the so-called "*global elite.*"

Take a Chance

As it blows out its 25th anniversary candles, Clifford Chance can celebrate its position as one of the world's top ten highest-grossing law firms. It has 3,400 lawyers spread across 34 offices in 24 countries, and stacks up more first-class rankings in both *Chambers UK* and *Chambers Global* than any of its rivals. "*It demonstrates the strength and the depth of the firm,*" says recruitment committee member Emma Matebalavu. "*It shows we're not just good at one thing, but we're very consistent.*" While it shines in diverse areas, from construction to Islamic finance, CC is probably best known for banking and finance. As the long-standing go-to firm for massive financial institutions, it can list Credit Suisse, Barclays, JPMorgan, ING and Santander among its clients. The firm's rep is certainly not lost on its trainees. "*I think it's one of the only firms whose reputation extends outside of the law,*" mused one. There's no denying that "*a training contract at Clifford Chance will score you good CV points in the future, regardless of where you go.*"

While CC's turnover increased by 1% in the UK in 2011, it is telling that it soared by 16% in the Asia-Pacific region and 17% in the Middle East. This shouldn't really come as a surprise, given the firm's expansionism in recent years – 2011 alone saw shiny new CC offices pop up in Sydney, Perth, Casablanca, Istanbul and Qatar. It will also soon be the first international firm to obtain a licence to open in Seoul. "*We have no strategy to radically change what we're doing,*" Matebalavu says. "*We plan to be one of a small number of global firms, doing elite work for high-*

end clients." This international aspect is a big draw for the firm's new recruits. "*A lot of firms don't send trainees to the offices they boast about, but at CC you're almost expected to spend time abroad.*" About 80% of trainees opt to spend six months overseas or with a client.

Dipping into deals

Clifford Chance's multitude of departments fit neatly into six core groups: corporate; finance; capital markets; real estate; dispute resolution; and tax, pensions and employment. For each seat, trainees are able to select preferences – HR does its best to allocate these fairly. It's crucial to note that every single trainee at the firm must spend at least two of their seats within the firm's core corporate, finance and capital markets groups. One source urged: "*The readers of Chambers need to be aware that smaller seats – like real estate, construction, employment, pensions, antitrust and funds – are always oversubscribed.*" If big-ticket finance is your thing, you'll be in your element at CC, but bagging niche areas, said some sources, is "*pot luck.*" The firm says (and we're paraphrasing here) it's down to appraisals and trainees' persistence in applying for niche seats.

The prestigious finance group is divided into numerous areas including general banking; asset and project finance; financial markets and structured products; derivatives; real estate finance; and insolvency, restructuring and liability management. Document management provides the staple diet in all, but trainee experiences vary enormously by seat. In asset management, for example,

Chambers UK rankings

Administrative & Public Law	Insurance
Asset Finance	Investment Funds
Banking & Finance	Outsourcing
Banking Litigation	Parliamentary & Public Affairs
Capital Markets	
Commodities	Partnership
Competition/European Law	Pensions
Construction	Planning
Consumer Finance	Private Client
Corporate Crime & Investigations	Private Equity
	Product Liability
Corporate/M&A	Professional Negligence
Data Protection	Projects
Defamation/Reputation Management	Public International Law
	Real Estate
Dispute Resolution	Real Estate Finance
Employee Share Schemes & Incentives	Real Estate Litigation
	Restructuring/Insolvency
Employment	Retail
Energy & Natural Resources	Social Housing
Environment	Tax
Financial Services	Telecommunications
Fraud	Transport
Information Technology	

"*deals tend to be small so you can get quite a lot of exposure to running day-to-day transactions.*" Many trainees, however, find the projects side "*more interesting,*" and report that "*your e-mails and documents do get read and used.*" The intriguingly named "*finance X*" is a large general banking group. Trainees do have a tendency to disappear into a black hole of admin work – "*there can be up to 500 documents to keep track of on a daily basis*" – but this is bulked up by "*plenty of drafting, and general dogsbody tasks, especially if someone needs help with research.*" Advisory, rather than transactional, work can be found in financial regulation. Trainees in this seat revel in substantial research and drafting, "*basically managing the aspects of small cases with minimal advice from supervisors.*" A quick taster of CC's high-profile finance work: in 2011, it advised JPMorgan, BNP Paribas and other big-name banks on the senior financing of the £1bn acquisition of the RAC by The Carlyle Group.

The corporate side of the firm is split into the likes of M&A; private equity; private fund formation; communications, media and technology; financial institutions; and European competition and regulation. In 2011 it advised Citi on its mind-bogglingly complicated purchase, restructuring and onward sale of the EMI Group, and Mitsubishi on its $5.3bn acquisition of a stake in Chilean copper min-

ing business Anglo American Sur. Most trainees sit within the general corporate division. Work tends to have a seriously international twist: "*At the moment I'm on a deal involving almost 30 jurisdictions, and pretty much all the documents get sent out through me.*" Smaller subgroups allow trainees to get immersed in the nitty-gritty of deals. Private fund formation is a hit for its "*juicy drafting*" work – "*every fund is different so you get to draft from scratch.*" Financial institutions is "*the corporate department's regulatory side,*" allowing trainees to get involved in drafting, research and trips to court.

The capital markets department recently advised Northern Rock on a £1.2bn securitisation transaction, HSBC on the restructuring of its €25bn bond programme, and states including Croatia, the Czech Republic, Denmark, Israel and Romania on their sovereign debt. On the debt and equity markets side of the group, "*I assisted with updating prospectuses with legal changes,*" explained one. "*They'd let me have a go at doing it on my own, then check over it.*" For another: "*I was in charge of liaising with solicitors in other jurisdictions and making sure we were happy with their opinions.*" At the time of our interviews, the securitisation group had "*the worst hours by a country mile,*" although reports that "*it's changing due to the financial markets, and slanting more towards advisory work,*" bode well for trainees' sleeping habits. Our sources reported drafting memos and checking mark-ups on documents.

From Lehman to Leveson

According to Matebalavu, "*litigation is going all-guns at the moment.*" Trainees in this group reported being involved in some of the firm's biggest cases, from Lehman-related litigation, to representing James Murdoch in relation to the Leveson Inquiry and an unnamed investment bank in the Libor investigations by the European Commission. For details about other seats, including secondments, see our website.

While a healthy dose of bundling and bibling is inevitable at CC, it tends to be backed up by some pretty substantial responsibility. "*People use the analogy of being a small cog in a big machine, but being at a large firm gives you more opportunity to be involved in really large transactions,*" explained one trainee. "*You'll be given more mundane tasks, but if you want to take on more than that, supervisors always try to accommodate your requests.*" We get the impression that most supervisors really do care about trainees getting a broad, well-rounded experience, and "*they'll always stop and examine an issue if you have a question.*" One trainee recounted "*spending a good 45 minutes really debating what a law means with a supervisor.*" This world-class training is one of the things that attracts people to CC, and they're not disappointed. With front-loaded training in every new seat, regular lectures and seminars throughout, and online training to top it off, trainees agree: "*It's really excellent.*"

Smart but sleepy

Are horror stories about astronomical hours at global mega-firms just urban legends? Comments like: "*The working hours are completely inhumane,*" "*the hours in my first seat nearly killed me,*" and "*I was so exhausted for such a consistent amount of time, I'd regularly fall asleep on the toilet,*" suggest otherwise. The crux of the problem is the disparity in hours between different groups at CC. It's accepted that the firm's more general finance, corporate and capital markets seats have "*the most punishing hours,*" occasionally running on until 2am or 3am for weeks on end. This is compounded by the fact that trainees just don't feel able to address the problem. "*I didn't think there'd be any point,*" mused one. "*They would've said, 'You signed up for it, so get on with it.'*" Another lamented: "*Nobody wants to be seen as the one person who is less committed. At the moment it's a great unspoken thing, which causes people a great deal of difficulty.*" Of course, it isn't all doom and gloom – some trainees relish the challenge and excitement of unpredictable hours. These are the type of people the firm hopes to attract, as Matebalavu notes, "*if you'll be working for the best clients on leading transactions, there may be long hours involved. We want trainees who will thrive and enjoy that sort of atmosphere.*" The final word should go to the weary source who urged: "*My message is to be very careful, and think about how happy you are to put your life on hold.*"

This sort of work ethic fills the corridors at CC. "*It's a healthy environment,*" says one trainee. "*People appreciate they have a good job, and there's a high level of motivation. People don't just sit on their hands, they go out and get stuff done.*" There's acknowledgement that the place is bursting with talent. "*If you ask a question on an issue, the partners responding are some of the best lawyers in their chosen field. It's very fulfilling.*" 'Prestige' is everywhere, but this doesn't translate into stuffiness. "*No one wears a tie, everyone is on a first-name basis and if I have to talk to a partner I'm treated like an adult.*" Fortunately, partners have a seemingly infinite tolerance for working in a pressure cooker. "*You'd be amazed how calm and collected people can be. I've heard one or two instances of people losing their rag, but it's definitely not common.*"

Perhaps it's easiest to view CC as "*a broad church with no particular ethos,*" and every trainee we spoke to was struck by its diversity. "*The trainee intake is made up from people from all over the world,*" and "*ethnic differences are so natural here that you don't notice them.*" It's clear to us, however, that there's an obvious "*CC type*" – sharp, articulate high achievers. As Matebalavu stresses, "*intellectual ability is taken for granted here. We're also looking for people with strong communication skills, a lot of get up and go, initiative, drive and commercial awareness.*" A hefty contingent of trainees attended Oxbridge (Oxford in particular), but CC is also home to plenty of graduates from Russell Group unis. Trainees are satisfied that "*recruitment is expanding its reach a little bit.*"

Beware the pool fairies

Clifford Chance is almost the only City law firm headquartered in Canary Wharf, and it's testament to trainees' willpower that they're able to get any work done with a hairdresser, prayer room, games room, sleeping pods, bar and Starbucks-stocked canteen on the premises. The office even has "*spectacular views*" from the gym, where trainees have access to squash courts, fitness classes and a swimming pool, though CC legend has it that "*the moment you touch the water, paper magically appears on your desk.*"

Like use of the amenities, the firm's social life is ultimately dependent on hours, but there's plenty on offer if you're at a loose end. Much of this takes place at department level, but trusty basement bar The Budgie is the perfect setting for a couple of drinks and a catch-up. "*On Thursdays and Fridays they have a licence to sell alcohol. At first, I thought that sounded really lame but it's a place you see people from all levels. You can speak to partners and have a laugh.*" Regular trainee-oriented gatherings include biannual alcohol-free events, and there are a multitude of sports teams. By the time trainees have completed their LPC together, however, they have a ready-made group of mates to hang out with informally. "*That's something I really value,*" said one trainee. "*The best part of my day is getting to see and work with those people.*"

Trainees state two seats they'd like to qualify into. "*It's a gamble to choose two niche ones.*" The HR team are "*pretty good at telling us who's recruiting, and if you speak directly to partners you usually get a good idea of your chances.*" In 2012, the firm kept on 87 of its 113 qualifiers.

And finally...

It takes a certain type of person to succeed at CC: the type who says: "*I felt if I was going to do law, I wanted to do it at the top level.*" If you fit the bill, you'll reap serious rewards.

Clyde & Co LLP

The facts

Location: London, Guildford, Oxford, Manchester

Number of UK partners/solicitors: 172/712

Total number of trainees: 71

Seats: 4x6 months

Alternative seats: Overseas seats, secondments

Extras: Pro bono – Lambeth and Surrey law centres, Brent and RCJ CABs

On chambersstudent.co.uk...
- How to get into Clyde & Co
- Barlow (C)Lyde & Gilbert
- Clydes' international strategy

Clyde & Co's no longer just an insurance and shipping juggernaut, and its recent expansion plans have bred a mixture of excitement and trepidation in trainees...

Won't stop till it's silver

"I came to Clyde & Co first and foremost because I saw myself as a litigation lawyer," said one of our sources, and that's probably not a bad place to start, given that the firm is so well known for its contentious work. Litigation teams abound here. Traditionally regarded as one of the go-to practices for insurance and shipping-related matters, Clydes in fact casts its net much further, and trainees love that *"the firm has more specialist areas like aviation, marine litigation and insurance work, but also contains typical City practices like corporate, employment and real estate."*

Clydes has undergone a process of significant expansion in recent years: first came a merger with Beaumont & Son, which boosted its aviation capabilities; then Shadbolt, a *"small, niche construction firm,"* hopped on board; and most recently, in November 2011, a much larger merger with Barlow Lyde & Gilbert strengthened the firm's insurance, reinsurance and employment practices (among quite a few others). The merger also added bases domestically – in Manchester and Oxford – and strengthened the firm internationally. Clydes now has 27 offices worldwide. Add to the mix bases in Sydney and Perth from October 2012, and more offices apparently on the cards, and you have a firm that won't be hitting the brakes any time soon.

London is *"the hub of Clyde & Co's global network,"* according its own website. *"We're trying to branch out internationally as much as we can,"* said one source:

"We've moved on from being just an insurance and shipping firm, and we've delved into all sorts of areas, which makes it viable for us to keep growing – we're not just relying on one type of work. Clydes desperately wants to be silver circle, and it won't stop until it gets there." Other trainees were slightly more hesitant when talking about the firm's future: *"You hear people say that it's unsustainable growth. I just don't know. When I applied to Clydes it felt like it was half the size that it is now."* The firm says that its expansion is consistent with its strategy of *"providing a full service to clients in* [its] *core sectors in key strategic locations"* and adds that it has *"the willingness to invest, and operate profitably, in markets where other law firms fear to tread or have a record of losing value."* Bold words, and the financials are certainly strong.

Surrey sojourns and professional concerns

Trainees discuss their seat preferences with the HR team before each rotation, and the process *"seems to work out well: most are quite content with what they get."* There's a good amount of flexibility to choose from the vast selection of teams on offer. Sources say that *"there's scope to talk to partners about seat allocation as well. HR discourages it, but it's perfectly natural to engage with the partners on this point."* There's still – ostensibly – an obligation to spend one seat in Guildford, which does a range of work including marine, employment, coco, litigation and real estate. However, due to the increase in trainee numbers post-merger, the likelihood of going had been reduced: *"They just say that it's compulsory so that peo-*

Chambers UK rankings

Asset Finance	Personal Injury
Aviation	Planning
Banking Litigation	Police Law
Clinical Negligence	Product Liability
Commodities	Professional Discipline
Construction	Professional Negligence
Corporate/M&A	Projects
Dispute Resolution	Public International Law
Employment	Real Estate
Energy & Natural Resources	Real Estate Finance
Environment	Real Estate Litigation
Fraud	Restructuring/Insolvency
Health & Safety	Retail
Healthcare	Shipping
Immigration	Transport
Insurance	Travel

ple expect to go." The firm says 15 will go every rotation. Although most dread being given the order to journey into darkest Surrey, those that had been enjoyed it. *"The teams based there are mainly smaller versions of the London ones, with the added bonus that there are areas of work that we don't have in London. The exposure to the work is no different; in fact, you possibly get more than you would in London."*

The firm's professional and commercial disputes practice (PCD) is a popular team and a legacy of Barlow Lyde & Gilbert. Around half of our sources had completed a seat here. *"It's high-value litigation, and mostly professional negligence work for lawyers, accountants, brokers and accountants. It's defence work and we act for the insurers. There's also a more general commercial wing, which deals with issues like trade mark infringements."* Clients include familiar names in the insurance sector (Aviva, Chartis) and claims have revolved around mis-selling investment in property funds and the exploitation of mining assets. Cases are *"often complicated and large, and don't move quickly, which means that you don't get exposure to many, but the exposure you do get is on a deeper level."* Tasks include drafting research notes, settlement agreements and other court documents, as well as doc review duties: *"On one case I had to review 750 mortgage files."*

Seats in insurance litigation and reinsurance litigation offer a further chance to explore the insurance world in a contentious context. Lawyers in this field have been representing major insurers after a $1bn claim arose out of the significant damage caused to a workers' encampment in the Amazon (around 22,000 people were affected). On a smaller scale, Clydes has also been acting for an insurer in a claim which features a high-profile 'toxic sofa' (think twice before sitting down...). Insurance litigation includes *"huge multimillion-pound Commercial Court cases,"* in addition to *"smaller cases in which you can get more involved in, drafting witness statements and instructions to counsel."* With reinsurance, cases often revolve around coverage disputes, and *"there are many opportunities to read policies and really get to grips with how the insurance market works."* For those with a taste for this kind of work, further seat options are available in political risk insurance (*"it's big stuff which has the potential to change markets"*), and corporate insurance, which offers a more transactional experience.

Snakes on a plane?

Trainees in shipping finance get stuck into transactions involving *"the buying and selling of vessels,"* and *"dealing with shipping registries all around the world,"* as well as helping *"new companies to get set up so they can own the vessel."* In contrast, those with a contentious preference can undertake a seat in marine litigation, and get *"more responsibility than you get elsewhere – you can run your own cases and plan your day accordingly."* We were told that many of the smaller 'trainee' cases settle out of court, but larger cases can be worth millions, perhaps involving claims brought against builders whose vessels have buckled and ruptured mid-voyage.

Similarly, both aviation finance and aviation litigation seats are available. Finance is *"quite a big team to work for, with some big clients too."* Luckily for trainees, they're *"not just observing – you actually get involved, doing the first draft of documents and managing smaller segments of deals."* Trainees even had the chance to go abroad to attend a special conference on air and space law: *"There were some important people talking and I realised that the work we are doing is really paving the way for the future of the industry."* Aviation litigation cases can range from *"small scale personal-injury-on-an-aircraft claims to full-on plane crashes."* Trainees help out when it comes to assessing how much airlines should pay in damages to victims or families of the deceased. *"One afternoon you'll be reading through bank statements and during another you'll be watching videos of plane crashes."* In one case, a plane overshot the runway, fell over a cliff and caught fire. Luckily, *"no one in the department is scared of flying."*

Additional seat options include: corporate; employment; banking litigation; commercial litigation; casualty (another legacy Barlows team); real estate; international trade and energy; and construction and projects. Read more about some on our website. Overseas seats are available, but this proved to be a bit of a sore point: *"Clydes says, 'Look how many international seats you can do,' and it's* something that the firm prides itself on, but in reality there are only one or two options. People go to Dubai and have a great time, and sometimes they go to Abu Dhabi, but there are always question marks over Hong Kong and Singapore." Other interviewees emphasised that 'overseas' essentially means 'the Middle East', unsurprising given the firm's long track record in the region. Clydes says: "Going forward we will be looking at potentially offering seats in the US and Hong Kong but this must take into account the business needs of the office at the time of each secondment."

Ticket to ride

Trainees didn't know whether to use "aggressive" or "ambitious" to describe Clydes' recent expansion. "I mean, it's hard not to use 'aggressive' when there have been three mergers in such a short space of time." They were also ambivalent about what this could mean for the future of the firm: "In a way I'm very pleased to hitch my wagon to this firm, as it's clearly going places, but I think there's an element of moving away from the family firm that I thought it was. I got the impression that five years ago every partner knew every partner – now it's becoming a huge corporate entity."

All in all, we heard conflicting thoughts about firm 'culture', especially in relation to the recent mergers. "What has happened," said one trainee, "is that each department is like a separate firm in its own right, instead of operating inside a larger one – it's much harder to have a coherent thing now." On top of that, there's the added complexity that some teams are "a mish-mash of three different firms." Cultural confusion is no doubt exacerbated by the fact that, in London, the firm operates from two separate buildings, facing each other on Aldgate. One, affectionately labelled the "big blue box," is the swanky St Botolph Building: modern, slick and very blue. The other is Beaufort House, or the "Barlows building," which is "not quite as nice" and "a bit too brown." Despite some crisscrossing of teams, the situation still remains that most of the legacy Barlows teams reside in the brown building, while most of the legacy Clydes teams are in the blue box.

Let's make this clear, though: trainees are not unhappy. Yes, there's more work to be done on the integration front, but as one source pointed out, "these are issues that most large firms are grappling with at the moment." Former Shadbolt and BLG trainees were especially chuffed at finding themselves under the Clydes name. "I would describe the advantages in three ways," said one. "Firstly, there are more opportunities because of the broader practices available; secondly, it's reassuring to be part of a larger firm, as there are greater resources and hopefully more stability; and thirdly, Clydes has a good approach to business development – the partners are far more likely to get you involved in that, and you have more direct contact with them."

Hitting the Botolph

Socially, unity is encouraged every Thursday night with drinks in St Botolph's 13th-floor restaurant. Sources weren't too hard on the old brown building, as apparently it boasts a "really nice terrace with little gardens." Much effort is put into the "elegant" firm-wide Christmas parties, the most recent of which was held in the grounds of Armoury House. A social committee organises this and "another two random things throughout the year," but there's also a trainee social committee and budget, and trainees have got together for events. "The karaoke was really popular – around 40 people showed up out of an intake of 70." Inevitably, smaller clusters of trainee friendship groups form, and they'll often meet at The Alchemist before "moving somewhere more interesting."

Trainees love the facilities that St Botolph's has to offer (the showers were identified as great for breaking down any pretence of hierarchy, as "suddenly that partner you've been working for becomes that half-naked guy in cycling shorts"). They also appreciated touches like an international weekly newsletter and specific sector updates which fly into their inbox on a daily basis. They were even satisfied with the qualification process, which, despite "taking longer this year because of the increase in numbers," still came off well: "They made a concerted effort to take on as many trainees as possible post-merger." In 2012, 42 out of 48 qualifiers stayed with the firm.

And finally...

Clydes is certainly at an interesting juncture in its development, and while there may be an air of cultural uncertainty, trainees seem on the whole pleased to be part of a firm where they have prospects and a nice mix of strong mainstream and niche practices.

CMS

The facts

Location: London, Bristol, Scotland

Number of UK partners/solicitors: 119/232

Partners who trained at firm: 14%

Total number of trainees: 125

Seats: 4x6 months

Alternative seats: Overseas seats, secondments

Extras: Pro bono – LawWorks, A4ID, TrustLaw Connect and others; language classes

On chambersstudent.co.uk...

- How to get into CMS
- Secondments
- Environmental expertise

This City firm with a strong European network has now made a US merger a priority.

What's in a name?

Go to this firm's homepage and you may be confronted with a photo of the onion-domed cupolas of the Kremlin. It's a good clue to one of this firm's biggest strengths: it was one of the first to expand into Eastern Europe after the fall of the Iron Curtain. Today, CMS Cameron McKenna has offices in London, Bristol, Aberdeen and Edinburgh, as well as six locations in the former Warsaw Pact countries, plus Beijing and Rio de Janeiro. What's more, there are firms in a further 34 locations across Europe, North Africa and Asia which are part of the 'CMS network'.

"We want to be known as a European firm, but on an international stage," a trainee told us. *"Management have said they want to focus on the BRIC countries."* The CMS network is already present in three of those four countries, and has been building a relationship with Indian firm Khaitan & Co. Now there are plans to expand further still, with the firm announcing in mid-2012 it was 'prioritising' a US merger. *"We're looking at possibilities for tying up with the right US firm, but nothing has developed yet beyond conversations,"* training partner Simon Pilcher told us. *"We may also not choose to merge, but to seek a US firm that can become a partner in the CMS network."*

Now, the make-up of the firm's international CMS network has led to some confusion about... what exactly this firm is called. Recently management has been pushing the use of the name CMS – dropping the Cameron McKenna bit entirely. *"The official line is that everyone should call the firm CMS rather than Camerons, whether you're in a meeting or just down the pub. But once you work here, some people call us CMS, some call us CMS London or even McKenna's, but almost everyone still just says Camerons."* We have the luxury of being able to ignore the official line and use the frankly nicer-sounding Camerons in this feature, but suggest you stick to CMS if applying to the firm. Anyway, we wouldn't be surprised to see another name change in future, especially if the firm pulls off that US merger...

In London, Camerons is especially known for its energy, insurance, construction and projects work, and picks up top-tier *Chambers UK* rankings for all these areas. The firm combines these more specialised practices with strong mainstream corporate, litigation and real estate departments, which *Chambers* ranks at the top of the mid-market. And don't get us started on the scores of rankings that the CMS network clocks up in *Chambers Europe*. As one typical trainee put it, *"Camerons stood out because of its European focus. Given my language skills I knew it would offer great opportunities to do cross-border work."* At present, future Camerons trainees complete their LPC at BPP, but from September 2013 onward will do a bespoke 'international' LPC at the College of Law.

Euro-vision

Seat options in London include corporate, banking, energy, energy disputes, projects, construction, competition, commercial/technology, insurance, commercial litigation, real estate, financial services and employment/pensions. For Bristol's four trainees, the options are insurance litigation (prof neg), banking litigation, property, property disputes and IP. Judging from the experience of our inter-

Chambers UK rankings

Banking & Finance	Life Sciences
Banking Litigation	Media & Entertainment
Competition/European Law	Outsourcing
Construction	Pensions
Corporate/M&A	Planning
Data Protection	Private Equity
Dispute Resolution	Product Liability
Employee Share Schemes & Incentives	Professional Negligence
	Projects
Employment	Public Procurement
Energy & Natural Resources	Real Estate
Environment	Real Estate Finance
Financial Services	Real Estate Litigation
Information Technology	Restructuring/Insolvency
Insurance	Tax
Intellectual Property	Telecommunications
	Transport

"As a first-seater there is not a lot of high-level work you can do," one source admitted, *"but that's understandable. We work on very complex transactions, so trainees handle the admin. You draft board minutes and resolutions, manage data rooms, ferry documents around and do the bibling."* One recent complex transaction was the £422m sale of RBS's pub group Galaxy – consisting of almost 1,000 pubs across the UK – to Heineken. Other deals reflect the firm's strong reputation in Central and Eastern Europe: Camerons recently advised Belgian supermarket chain Delhaize on its €932.5m acquisition of Serbian multinational food chain Delta Maxi. Second-years *"don't do as much of the admin-y work."* One told us: *"My supervisor gave me more technical and legalistic tasks. For example, I got to review and analyse hedge fund agreements."* Whenever they visit the seat, trainees will experience *"the urgency and buzz of your inbox going crazy with all the emails you're getting."* The department can get *"very hectic"* with some *"loud personalities."* It has a reputation for being more *"boisterous"* than the rest of the firm and for the fact that *"on Thursday and Friday night the Hand and Shears pub is the big corporate hangout."*

viewees, you can tailor your training contract considerably, focusing on corporate seats, or energy ones, or on insurance (especially in Bristol), or spending time in a mix of departments.

A seat in either banking or corporate is compulsory, but these headers are open to broad interpretation (so a project finance seat counts as banking, and energy counts as corporate). Seat allocation *"works well on the whole. They try to do it as fairly as possible."* Trainees almost invariably spend their second seat (or, in Bristol, third) away from the office on a client secondment, overseas or in Bristol, Edinburgh or Aberdeen. See p.532 for the overseas options the firm offers, while secondments include postings at Amazon, IBM and MetLife.

The secondments and overseas seats came in for universal praise from our interviewees. *"It was a bit scary at first,"* one trainee said, describing their experience in Eastern Europe, *"but everything is done for you: accommodation, travel. And my supervisor really looked after me."* And don't think these European outposts are at the periphery of the CMS network. *"I worked on a big cross-border transaction which was led out of our office. There were 12 jurisdictions involved."*

Eastern Bloc around the clock

The corporate department counts well-known names among its clients – Coca-Cola, RBS, Royal Mail – and advises private equity investors like GE Capital and Lloyds Development Capital. The trainee experience differs depending on whether you're a first or second-year.

Lloyds, HSBC, Santander and Barclays are frequent clients of the banking department, which recently advised six banks on a £230m loan to Chemring – a company which produces explosive decoys and pyrotechnics for military use. The project finance team works on energy, waste, transport and hospital projects both in the UK and overseas. *"Some of the projects have rumbled on for years and are massive. You play a small part in those as a trainee. But we have lots of smaller projects too, where as a trainee you can be managing the closing documents. You get quite a lot of responsibility. I have direct client contact and go to lots of meetings."*

"Banking is just as busy as corporate," with both teams known for their *"long hours."* That means trainees may once or twice have to stay until 2 or 3am or work on the weekend, and *"when it's busy you are leaving at 9 or 10pm."* Elsewhere *"the standard core hours are 9.30am to 7pm,"* but staying until 8 or 9pm didn't sound too rare to us. Here is an attitude most of our interviewees took to their hours: *"I do take my career quite seriously and I don't mind sacrificing my personal time for a short period, say a week, to get work done. But in the long-term I care about my work/life balance and I see it as my own choice when I work late."*

Black gold

Camerons' energy department is equal in size to both corporate and banking. *"It really lives up to expectations,"* said one energy aficionado. Clients include some of the *"big names"* – National Grid, ConocoPhillips, BP – and the department offers the chance to work with a *"hugely interesting and international"* industry. Recently

Camerons has worked on a solar energy project in Gujarat in India, advised the government of Kosovo on the privatisation of its electricity industry, and counselled BP on its interests in Iraq's giant Rumaila oilfield (which produces almost a million barrels of oil a day). *"I helped a senior associate with a large oil drilling contract in Kenya and Tanzania,"* one trainee told us. *"I helped research the clauses and drafted a few of the boilerplate documents."* The department is split into oil and gas, power and utilities, renewables and environment teams. There is also a separate energy disputes department, which works on quite a few arbitrations. *"For one case I had to go back through years of correspondence to find out where a dispute had first arisen,"* one trainee told us. *"Then I had to write up a huge memo about what I had found to help us advise the client on their strategy."*

We'd be very interested to hear the strategic advice given to the client in this case: the commercial litigation department recently represented Nestlé in a High Court case against Cadbury over alleged IP infringement related to the shape of Rolo chocolates. The litigation department is better known for its insurance work. For example, it has been defending ship broker Clarksons in the much-publicised 'Fiona Trust' shipping and insurance case. Bristol has a distinct insurance litigation department, which deals with professional negligence cases. *"I always think we get a lot more responsibility than the London trainees,"* boasted one source there. *"There are lots of smaller matters and we get to run some files ourselves."* The team was recently hit by the departure of 18 lawyers to RPC's Bristol office. Far from depressing matters, trainees said management had *"gone mental on"* the attention paid to Bristol and insurance since the defection. London insurance partners have been redeployed to Bristol and there are still three seats in the department.

The United States of CMS

"We sometimes say the different departments here are like the different states of the US," one trainee mused. *"They're united but each has its own culture and character."* We described the character of the corporate department above – trainees said the atmosphere elsewhere is *"more relaxed."* Banking and project finance *"go out for drinks a lot,"* teams like energy and property are *"also sociable and have a flatter structure than corporate or banking, with people chatting together,"* while elsewhere *"it is more hierarchical and you can really tell who the partners are."* Energy was singled out as a *"really nice"* team. It apparently has a table tennis table and *"everyone gets involved when they have a free moment and we have a leadership board to keep track of the scores."* In general trainees agreed on this point: *"Friendliness was a real buzzword when I applied to this firm and it really lives up to that reputation."*

The firm's reputation seems to have attracted a certain type of trainee: *"Everyone is similarly hard-working and bright, but also fun and sociable. There are no big personalities."* The bunch we spoke to certainly struck us as a sociable and cheerful lot. *"Our intake is really close,"* sources agreed. *"There are lots of activities that we organise together. Because we almost all did the LPC together we carried over personal relationships from that which are sociable and not very business-y."* Recent socials have include bowling, pub quizzes, paint-balling, payday dinners and a trainee ball. And as we mentioned above, on Friday nights departments gather in one of several pubs near Camerons' Smithfield office. There are also rugby, football, cricket and hockey teams which *"anyone can sign up for."* And we mustn't forget the CMS World Cup – held in Madrid in 2012, it pits different offices from the network against one another.

Camerons has always posted decent retention rates and 2012 was no different with 51 of 62 qualifiers staying on. Sources agreed *"graduate recruitment does a good job in terms of the timing and transparency of the NQ process."* That process does involve *"a bit of networking. You need to make sure you have a conversation with the right partners in the right team. I went to the head of the department I wanted to work in to express my interest. It was pretty straightforward and only took ten minutes."* There is still *"a formal process where the job list is released. You apply for up to two jobs and for some positions there is an interview. But by that stage most of us know which departments are taking on which trainees."*

And finally...
This solid City firm should be of particular interest to anyone interested in energy or looking for a firm with a *"fun"* and *"sociable"* corporate culture.

Cobbetts LLP

The facts

Location: Manchester, Birmingham, Leeds, London

Number of UK partners/solicitors: 74/156

Partners who trained at firm: 12%

Total number of trainees: 36

Seats: 5x5 months

Alternative seats: Occasional secondments

On chambersstudent.co.uk...
- How to get into Cobbetts
- Words from managing partner Nick Carr

Cobbetts could have been the blushing bride in a Corrie romance, but after the planned marriage with fellow Mancunian DWF fell through, this plucky firm is continuing to go it alone with a *"sense of energy and a desire to go out and win new work."*

A Nick Carr with desire

Traditionally seen as the Manchester firm, Cobbetts also has large offices in Leeds and Birmingham and a small outpost in London. *"This firm is national but proud of its regional focus,"* trainees said. Its full-service offering includes a smorgasbord of commercial practices. Dispute resolution, corporate M&A and real estate bring in around 60% of the dough and *Chambers UK* ranks the Manchester, Leeds and Birmingham offices for all three of those practices. Trainees share the firm's outside-London focus: *"Primarily, trainees tend to be from the region where they work, although there are some people from other parts of the country too."* Despite the firm's Manchester origins, the three big offices all have a similar standing in their markets – not bad given the Leeds and Birmingham offices were only set up in the early 2000s.

Since the mid-2000s the firm has rebalanced itself. *"Before 2008 we used to be largely driven by real estate,"* observed one trainee. *"But that department is smaller now, while corporate, disputes and banking litigation have grown."* Since the start of the recession, the firm has charted a course of steady, slow recovery. Revenue nudged up to £45.2m in 2011/12 (still below 2007/08's £58m) and trainees were upbeat about the firm's future: *"I have been busy throughout my training contract and it's clear we are headed in the right direction."*

2012 has been a year of transitions for Cobbetts. A merger with DWF was mooted but shelved early in the year. As DWF is known as a rapidly growing firm, while Cobbetts has had a relatively flat few years, some market commentators saw the merger as a bailout for the latter. We think this may be going a bit far, but other changes show Cobbetts is having a rethink about its business plan. Long-serving firm head Michael Shaw stepped down in mid-2012 and was replaced by Nick Carr. At the start of his tenure, the firm has realigned management around three core practice groups: business services, dispute resolution and real estate. Business development is also being pushed.

Nick Carr told us having an *"international outlook"* is one way the firm is trying to grow. Trainees felt the same way. Quite a few of our interviewees had worked on matters with an international component, and revenue from global clients grew from £2.5m in 2010 to £3m in 2011. A few years back the firm launched Cobbetts International: a Swiss Verein aimed at building up an international network. At the moment the only members are the UK LLP and the four-partner Cobbetts International Cairo.

High five

When we spoke to trainees in June 2012, exactly half of the 32 were based in Manchester, with eight in Leeds, seven in Birmingham and one in London. *"London is*

Chambers UK rankings

Banking & Finance	Employment
Banking Litigation	Intellectual Property
Capital Markets	Licensing
Charities	Pensions
Competition/European Law	Private Client
Construction	Real Estate
Corporate/M&A	Real Estate Litigation
Dispute Resolution	Social Housing

used to supporting the regional offices" and there are no plans to increase the number of seats on offer there. Unusually, trainees complete five five-month seats. The system was introduced in 2009 and trainees like it. *"You get a good breadth and depth of experience which you don't get from either a four-seat or six-seat system."*

Trainees usually complete their training contract in one office (though on rare occasions office moves are possible). Seats in dispute resolution, corporate, employment, real estate and commercial/IP are available in all three main offices. Trainees can also do banking and banking litigation in Manchester and Leeds, restructuring in Manchester and Birmingham, as well as planning, construction and property litigation in Manchester. Trainees rank three seat preferences prior to each rotation and *"not many people are disappointed in the seats they get"* as *"the firm goes out of its way to make the seats people want available."* Employment and commercial litigation are perennial favourites.

Getting real

It would be *"surprising not to do a seat in real estate."* The department is *"busy and getting busier – the fact the team has shrunk in the last few years means that people have a good workload."* This seat is said to have the longest hours, with trainees regularly working until 7pm or 7.30pm. Most of the work is commercial: sales, leases, sublettings and some development. The firm recently acted for the De Vere Group in the £8m sale of a former gin distillery in Warrington to be redeveloped as care homes, and advised Burnley Borough Council on the £100m redevelopment of the Weavers' Triangle area. Clients come from both the public and private sector, and include national and local outfits, ranging from KFC and Premier Inn to Salford City Council and the Homes & Communities Agency. Trainees start out assisting on big deals with *"standard trainee tasks like SDLT, Land Registry and drafting leases."* They often also get to run small lease and subletting files. *"I set up the file on the system and prepared the engagement letter,"* one told us, *"then did the searches, enquiries and registration. I*

liaised with the client from start to finish and created a real rapport with them."*

In corporate *"the work is really interesting"* and includes regular M&A, management buyouts and (especially in Manchester) private equity. For example, the firm advised on the MBO of Wells Plastics backed by private equity house Key Capital. There is also AIM work in Leeds, although *"as a trainee you don't necessarily get a lot of exposure to it."* Sometimes work has an international flavour: Cobbetts recently advised Hummingbird Resources – a UK mining company engaged in gold exploration in Liberia – on its £89m AIM float. *"There is a perception you are the document jockey in corporate,"* admitted one trainee, *"and of course bibling is a trainee task at first. But doing the bible at the start of your seat helps you understand the documents. Later on in the seat, when you are asked to draft those documents and work with the client you understand what you need to do."*

The banking team advises major banks – Santander, HSBC, Co-op, Barclays – on multimillion-pound loan agreements. A similar array of banks and lenders instruct the bigger *"busy and hectic"* banking litigation team, which recently acted for Lloyds in litigation to recover £980,000 from various parties after fraud committed by a mortgage broker. Besides fraud, it is professional indemnity and (in Manchester) debt recovery that are the department's main stock-in-trade. *"I probably ran about 20 debt recovery files myself,"* said one trainee, *"and I worked on two fraud cases and a negligence case with my supervisor."* Trainees occasionally get advocacy experience or at the very least *"witness your supervisor attending court with counsel."*

Commercial litigators work on a range of high-value cases, including copyright, property, contracts, professional negligence and insolvency claims. The team recently defended Salford City Council in a judicial review brought by the owners of a shopping centre over the sale of adjacent land to Tesco. *"I got work from everyone within the team,"* one source said. *"A high point was when I worked closely with a senior partner on a swaps and derivatives dispute. I filed the statements of case, got together documents for the witness statements, liaised with counsel, compiled trial bundles, attended hearings and drafted letters of advice to clients."*

Commercial and IP lawyers work on things like procurement, confidentiality agreements and terms and conditions for websites. The group also advises clients on digitisation, technology and media projects. It acted for the organisers of the Manchester International Festival on a range of issues for the 2011 festival, including the performance contracts for Björk, Damon Albarn and Victoria Wood.

Breakfast Club

Trainees enthusiastically told us that in all departments *"you get the opportunity for, and are encouraged to be involved in, business development."* One added: *"I have recently attended breakfast seminars and other meetings, liaising with potential clients. We managed to bring in work which we wouldn't have had otherwise."* Networking is also pushed and *"everyone is involved."* Cobbetts Young Professionals is a networking group run by Cobbetts lawyers, which organises events to gets young lawyers together with peers from other professions and industries.

Trainees said business development work had been *"increasingly prevalent over the past two years."* It's all part of the firm's new 'Future Proof' strategy. Given the attempted merger with DWF, we wondered whether a future merger is part of that strategy too. *"Merger is not our strategy,"* Nick Carr told us in mid-2012. *"The aim over the next three years is to consolidate and grow without the need to merge, but if the right business opportunity arose we would consider it. We are currently looking to invest significantly in lateral hires and bolt-ons."* A trainee added: *"We have seen a few people leave the firm since the suggested merger – when things were briefly a bit unsettled – but we are bringing in new people too."* Another said: *"The foundations to build the firm up have now been laid. With Nick at the helm I think we will go from strength to strength. His election has reinvigorated everyone and I think things are going to be changing going forward."* We will have to wait and see where the firm goes from here.

As part of Cobbetts' revised strategy it has slowly decreased its trainee intake from 25 in 2007 and 16 in 2010 to 13 in 2012. The decrease is probably good news as Cobbetts hasn't posted particularly good retention rates over the past few years. 2012 was a better year with 12 of 15 qualifiers kept on (three of four in Birmingham, all four in Leeds, and five of seven in Manchester). The firm did boost its 2013 intake with an extra recruitment round in 2012, showing the business is doing better than expect-ed. Several sources said they hoped that as fee income increases *"the firm will be able to address the issue of pay – salary levels were dropped a few years ago and haven't recovered."* The NQ salary was cut from £37,000 to £30,000 in 2008 and increased marginally to £31,000 in 2011.

Pints and pigs

All this shouldn't detract from the main message we heard from interviewees: *"Trainees are very well looked after here."* As in previous years, we were impressed by the level of support, supervision, mentoring and work trainees are offered. *"Supervision has been excellent throughout the seats and my supervisors have all been of a high standard,"* trainees agreed. In part, they put this down to Cobbetts' *"key values,"* at the core of which is *"an open culture in which people want to help you build your knowledge."* Said one trainee: *"I have never been frightened of approaching any of the more senior people. Because the offices are open-plan there is less of a feeling of hierarchy. It sounds cheesy but the best way of describing the firm is that it feels like a family. Everyone here has time for a conversation and likes to spend time having a bit of laugh."*

This positive vibe spills out of the office doors too. *"Because the trainees did the LPC+ together we are quite close-knit. We're all very good mates and do a lot together."* For example, just before we spoke with trainees they had completed the Otley Run: *"It's a famous pub crawl in Leeds with visits to 18 pubs,"* one surprisingly sprightly interviewee explained. *"We left Manchester at 11.30am and didn't get back until 4.30... am!"* Besides this, *"each office has its own special events,"* which anyone can attend, organised by a 'social club'. Manchester, for example, has *"end of the month drinks in the canteen and on a Friday there are a few bars down the road where we congregate."* Firm-wide events include a Christmas party and a *"hog roast and barn dance summer barbecue."*

And finally...
With a new managing partner and revised strategy, change is in the air at Cobbetts, but it remains home to some very fine lawyers and offers *"high-quality training."*

Collyer Bristow LLP

The facts

Location: London

Number of UK partners/solicitors: 28/28

Partners who trained at firm: 14%

Total number of trainees: 8

Seats: 4x6 months

Alternative seats: None

On chambersstudent.co.uk...
- How to get into Collyer Bristow
- Details about some of CB's commercial practices

This little commercial and private client firm on Bedford Row has been right in the middle of one of the major stories of the day – the Leveson Inquiry.

From Bob Crow... to courtroom show

Scrolling across the top of Collyer Bristow's homepage are the following words: 'From salaries... to galleries / From planning appeals... to recording deals / From prenups... to winner's cups / From corporation... to defamation.' We don't need rhyming couplets to realise that Collyer Bristow is full-service, but we love them anyway. We only wish there was a song to go with it.

Despite its mix of commercial and private client work, these days CB is most often in the news for defamation and reputation management work. At the Leveson Inquiry the firm has represented no fewer than 50 victims of phone hacking and if you'd watched any of it you may have seen CB litigator Dominic Crossley sat at the back. The firm's also been making headlines working on the first ever Twitter libel case and backing an international sportsman all the way to the ECHR. But don't forget that the family, IP, private client and property litigation departments here are all also ranked by *Chambers UK*, even if they don't make it into the headlines on a daily basis.

Trainee seat choices include tax and estate planning, dispute resolution, family, property and corporate/commercial. Due to the small class sizes, second-years pretty much always get the seats they want and first-years are then slotted in to fit.

Dispute resolution brings in some 30% of CB's turnover. As the firm's largest practice, it usually takes two or three trainees, and in a class of three or four it's "*pretty unavoidable.*" Although we can safely assume the Leveson earned the group a bob or two, they've taken on

other matters too – for example, defending Boris Johnson after Bob Crow took offence to the Mayor's 'Not Ken Again' campaign. Leaflets and posters suggested that a return of Livingstone to the mayoralty would mean a return to "*council tax rises, broken promises, cronies, scandals, waste, Bob Crow...*" Shockingly, Crow took offence at this and sued for defamation. The dispute resolution seat handles employment, property litigation, IP, financial services and commercial litigation as well as defamation and privacy cases. By no means is all the work related to the world of media, and clients include Air France, Bangkok Bank and KPMG.

Obviously, in the most high-profile cases trainees aren't going to be arguing their case in front of a judge. Instead, they "*deal with the document management side of things.*" However, there are plenty of smaller cases that trainees can run with minimal supervision. "*For a number of matters I was the main point of contact with the client. We are encouraged to take on initial drafts of advice or letters,*" one trainee told us. Some even get to do their own advocacy: "*I went before a Master on a number of occasions,*" said one.

From checking facts... to offshore tax

What most firms call private client, CB calls trusts and estate planning. Why? "*Most of the work we do is for private clients,*" a source explained, but "*the firm acts for two wealthy individuals who have varied private client needs and so they also instruct the firm on property matters and business advice.*"

Chambers UK rankings

Defamation/Reputation Management	Private Client
Family/Matrimonial	Real Estate Litigation

The trusts and estate planning seat brings a *"mix of contentious and non-contentious work."* Cases can go to the High Court and the Court of Appeal. If the work is basic, *"it's left to me to write the first drafts of advice, wills and trusts. It's all checked and maybe most of it will be changed, but maybe not. In this department no one thinks you are just a useless trainee, you're seen as an asset to the firm,"* said one interviewee. However, the more complex work is left to the partners. Read more about the commercial side of the firm on our website.

In 2004, CB became the first UK firm to open a Geneva office, which now *"focuses on private clients. It's getting a lot of interest at the moment."* The firm also has three international desks – Brazilian, Italian and American – and a lot of work is carried out in Portuguese and Italian. *"There's a database stating everyone's language capabilities and I hear a lot of people speaking different languages around the office,"* one trainee said. These desks cross all of the firm's departments. The Italian one won a libel case for footballer Marco Materazzi against the *Sun*, *Daily Mail* and *Daily Star* in light of his famous argument with Zinedine Zidane in the 2006 World Cup final. The Brazilian desk is a little less tabloid-worthy and clients include Banco do Brasil, TAM Brazilian Airlines and the cachaca producers Sagatiba Spirits. If you don't know what cachaca is we suggest you get yourself down to Waitrose and try some of the delicious sugarcane liquor.

From art galleries... to decent salaries

Based on historic Bedford Row, CB isn't a place to come if the glass towers of Moorgate are more your idea of what law should look like. *"Collyer Bristow has been around for over 250 years and I think people are keen to preserve the tradition,"* one trainee told us. However, another stated: *"The outside of the building is traditional – but the inside has a contemporary art gallery. It reflects the culture: both informal and hard-working. You only wear a tie if you see a client."*

Ah yes, the art gallery. It's a nice little feature that testifies to this firm's slightly quirky nature, hosting exhibitions that rotate every three months. The space allows for numerous networking opportunities and CB isn't shy of putting trainees right in the middle of these. Informally, the firm holds a monthly social event for everyone – maybe drinks, bowling or karaoke – and has big Christmas and summer dos as well. Due to the small size of the firm and the cross-departmental work, *"everyone knows everyone's names"* and *"trainees get a lot of interaction with partners from the off."*

Trainees at CB are *"happy"* with their salary and the *"good hours."* A few sources mentioned that trial work had kept them in the office until 2am on occasion, but *"the building actually shuts at 9pm. It's very rare for a trainee to be here past that time and the usual hours are 8am to 6pm."*

From being a slob... to getting a job

"When I came in the first time I was met by our graduate recruiter and the first thing she said to me was that she liked my handbag, which put me at ease straight away," said one source. See the bonus feature on our website for more details about the recruitment process. Collyer Bristow apparently *"doesn't have a 'type' of person it hires, but people do tend to have outside interests and you see that with the partners too. For example, some are into writing, others into art... and they are active in those interests. You often see people heading off to the choir or to play sport – generally people are able to manage their workload around their interests."* A fair few of the current trainees are second-careerers – among the mix were a journalist, a foreign tour guide and a translator. Possessing language skills doesn't hurt either: we heard three of the four second-years were at least bilingual.

And finally...

Three of four second-year trainees were retained by the firm in 2012. *"We all got our first choices,"* they said and praised the firm for *"keeping us informed as the decisions were being made."*

Covington & Burling LLP

The facts

Location: London

Number of UK partners/solicitors: 18/30 (+10 non-UK-qualified)

Total number of trainees: 14

Seats: 4x6 months

Alternative seats: Secondments

Extras: Pro bono LawWorks, TrustLaw, A4ID, FRU, PILPG

On chambersstudent.co.uk...
- How to get into Covington
- Pro bono at Covington

Covington & Burling is a full-service US firm with a sizeable corporate capacity and a leading life sciences practice.

Eastern promise

Covington has growth on its mind. New offices are expected to open in Seoul and Shanghai once regulatory approval has been granted. This expansion eastwards reflects what training partner Grant Castle refers to as "*an increased focus on international work. The world is changing: firms can no longer focus primarily on the USA and the UK.*" This realisation has led the US-headquartered firm to continue on the path of highly selective growth in emerging markets: Shanghai, a rising financial centre, will complement much of the corporate transactional work the firm already does, while Seoul is home to Covington's biggest client, SAMSUNG. Castle says that Covington will "*never just suddenly open in 40 places. Our focus is on quality, and that can be difficult to achieve if you're running a franchise system.*"

The London office has been operational since 1988. Five partner hires from Morrison & Foerster in 2011 have given the office a larger life sciences corporate team, as well as a number of public and growing companies as clients. The London base is strong in Covington's chief areas of life sciences, technology and media, but the corporate department is the largest.

After hitting a target to have 80 lawyers in the office a year earlier than planned, Castle adds that "*in theory we have the whole of this building to expand within, and there's space for around 400 lawyers. It's not like we're going to stop once we get to 100.*"

Balm in Gilead?

Trainees set out their seat preferences a few months before joining the firm, knowing that they must spend time in both corporate and dispute resolution. Other options include life sciences; tax; employment; and IP, technology and media. "*There are times when business need has to be met, but if you have a preference you just have to make it known.*" Client secondments are increasingly likely, with most trainees now completing a stint away: "*It's brilliant to experience the in-house culture. You have to be a jack-of-all-trades, and do everything, from supply contracts to distribution agreements – anything with a legal spin.*" The likes of GSK, Gilead and Vifor have been past destinations.

Trainees in corporate "*work for everyone – you go to associates as they need you.*" A call from the funds team "*means working hard with a lot of responsibility,*" and our sources said that "*it's quite an infamous seat*" for its "*steep learning curve.*" Trainees often help out with commercial negotiations: "*You have to read through all of the documents within a day or so, digest a lot of information, add your comments, forward to the client and establish how strong their position is.*" In less specialised parts of the department, trainees assist "*merging entities in a large number of different countries.*" Matters also include the restructuring of global pharma companies, and trainees draft termination deeds, shareholder resolutions and share purchase agreements. The firm recently advised ReNeuron Group on a fund-raising attempt to finance further research into stem cell therapy for stroke victims.

Chambers UK rankings

Capital Markets	Investment Funds
Corporate Crime & Investigations	Life Sciences
Data Protection	Parliamentary & Public Affairs
Dispute Resolution	Private Equity
Insurance	Product Liability

Life sciences seats are divided into two strands: transactional and regulatory. A stint in transactional offers a similar experience to corporate *"with more of a life sciences edge."* Sources agreed that *"it's mostly contractual drafting work"* they take on and had spent quite a bit of time working on distribution, supply and template licensing agreements. On the regulatory side, trainees encounter advisory work: *"You get given a problem from a client, and you go away and research the problem and write up the memo."* Sources reported working *"for most of the big pharma companies,"* and gave advice in relation to medical devices, clinical trials, product labelling claims and stem cell supply agreements. Despite the seat involving some *"very esoteric stuff,"* there's a *"solid amount of guidance,"* and *"if you don't have a science background it's easy to get well acquainted with what goes on. The team is very supportive."* It has provided advice to Microsoft on its health software and compliance with EU medical device regulations, and assisted RAFT – a charity which focuses on improving treatments for skin traumas – on a range of regulatory issues.

Fighter jets

Of late the dispute resolution team has been particularly busy representing everyone's favourite budget airline, Ryanair, in a competition case against the Office of Fair Trading. In this group, there's *"a pool of trainees, who are accessible to everyone,"* but some will steer towards a specific area, like arbitration or white-collar work, depending on their interests. Matters here can be *"quite juicy,"* especially when they involve cross-jurisdictional investigations and *"you get to play detective."* Such cases have involved representing large oil and petrol companies against Latin American governments: *"Basically the company alleges that the state has breached the international treaty with the UK. A lot of it relies on the interpretation of black-letter law."* A high point of the seat is being able to attend and take notes during *"follow-up interviews with key personnel within the companies that are undergoing investigation."* Product liability cases allow trainees to draft and file defences, attend client meetings and take calls with experts.

The IP, tech and media department is currently wrangling with issues such as the difficulty of upholding intellectual property rights in emerging markets such as China and the level of aggression to take against IP theft online. Recently, the firm's been working for big sports clients against websites that were unlawfully streaming Olympic Games coverage. The seat comes with a good amount of pro bono work, according to our sources, who were able to assist charities on copyright issues and help artists remove work published on websites without permission. *"It's a great way for you to gain responsibility for your own clients."*

Trainees receive mid and end-of-seat appraisals, although *"sometimes the mid-seat will turn into a two-thirds-of-the-way-through-seat review."* Despite the occasional timetabling lapse, sources said that they *"benefit from them – at the end of the seat it's nice to combine a lunch and review with your supervisor, as you can talk frankly outside the office."*

Washington post

"You come to a place like this and you can't hide – you're thrown in at the deep end, which can be intimidating, but once you get used to it, it is incredible." This feeling was echoed several times throughout our interviews, with others adding that a Covington trainee *"has to stand on their own two feet."* Don't expect to be spoon-fed at this firm. Trainees must be confident and independent, and need to be in order to meet the challenges thrown at them by the intellectually rigorous nature of the work. *"This is an academic firm,"* says Grant Castle. *"Covington has a history of dealing with difficult legal and regulatory questions, as well as high-end litigation. There are practice areas that have a lot in common with the work you would do in some public law barristers' chambers."*

Trainees enjoy the chance to go to DC for a firm-wide retreat at the beginning of their second year. *"It's great, as you get more of an idea of what's behind the London office."* Monthly management committee notes from DC also keep trainees in the know, while closer to home the 'London Notes' provide an insight into what's going on in various departments.

There's no shortage of social activities throughout the year, and we heard of boat trips up the Thames for vac schemers, a Christmas party held at the London Aquarium, a ski trip to Italy, ludicrously-named netball team the Covington Cupcakes, summer softball leagues and fortnightly drinks trolleys. Of late, a special 'payday lunch' has been very popular, which is prepared by in-house caterers and *"delicious – last time it was Greek-themed, and the five or six pounds that you pay goes towards one of the charities we support."*

And finally...
Covington retained six out of its seven qualifiers in 2012.

Cripps Harries Hall LLP

The facts

Location: Tunbridge Wells, London

Number of UK partners/solicitors: 38/62

Partners who trained at firm: 21%

Total number of trainees: 16

Seats: 6x4 months

Alternative seats: None

On chambersstudent.co.uk...

- How to get into Cripps
- Cripps' history
- About Tunbridge Wells

One of Kent's brightest stars, Cripps Harries Hall is strong in commercial, real estate and private client work.

In England's Garden

Cripps Harries Hall is a proud resident of Tunbridge Wells. With roots as a private client practice catering to the region's wealthy, the firm has since developed a full commercial offering, with particular strength in property. Director of HR and development Alan Geaney told us: *"Our greatest satisfaction over the past twelve months has been to maintain our profitability and staff numbers during very difficult economic circumstances. We are confident that we have a solid platform that will enable us to perform well as the economy improves."*

The still-recent rebrand of the firm has definitely proved to be a positive move by the firm. *"Despite originating from an old-school private client background, you can really feel the vibrancy at Cripps,"* trainees said. *"The whole point of the rebrand was to look forward and broaden our thinking and capabilities, and although it's a slow and steady transition, you can definitely sense a buzz."* One source added: *"It's particularly evident in the people the firm has hired recently. All seem to be very open, interesting and energetic,"* while yet another said: *"Cripps wants to retain its expertise in private client and property, but also expand further in the corporate/commercial London market. This ethos is reflected in our office space. We're still in a beautiful old period building, but the layout is predominantly open-plan and lively."*

"I wasn't specifically looking in Tunbridge Wells," said one interviewee, *"but knew I didn't want to be in a hectic London legal environment. Cripps had the best of both worlds – located in a calmer place, while doing comparable work to the capital's mid-sizers."* Trainees stressed the importance of *"showing a genuine interest in the firm."*

One said: *"Cripps wants people who are looking to make a long-term commitment to the firm and possibly become its future partners."*

Seats include commercial, dispute resolution, employment, specialist dispute resolution (private client disputes), family, corporate, the wealth preservation group (WPG) and a whole host of property teams. Trainees complete six seats, and *"before you join, you submit preferences for all six. You're then given your full two-year timetable. Realistically, people get at least their top three choices, if not four."* Interviewees commended the system, saying: *"It's such a relief knowing in advance. You're never in a state of worry and can prepare for the future."* One added: *"It's also never set in stone. If once you begin, you decide you'd like to try a different path, the HR team are very accommodating."* You do need to be *"reasonable,"* however, as switches aren't guaranteed. *"It's fair to say that most people will do at least one, if not two property seats,"* trainees said. *"The firm is heavily property-based and there are more qualification options there."*

Full Speed Ahead

Cripps' property group is top-ranked by *Chambers UK* for real estate in Kent, and property-related teams include: portfolio property (commercial), the residential investment department (RID), plot sales, planning, property dispute resolution and development. The portfolio property team has Cripps' biggest clients, including government departments, retailers and investor companies. The firm acted for Argent Group in its £40m development of a 67-acre site at King's Cross in London, and represented London and Continental Railways in the acquisition of

Chambers UK rankings

Agriculture & Rural Affairs	Intellectual Property
Banking & Finance	Partnership
Charities	Planning
Construction	Private Client
Corporate/M&A	Professional Negligence
Dispute Resolution	Real Estate
Employment	Real Estate Litigation
Family/Matrimonial	Social Housing

land for the High Speed 1 rail link. *"Starting this seat can be a bit overwhelming. There are so many files and seemingly so much to do, but once you get into the swing of things the work is great."* One source said: *"Due to the nature of the work, you're not going to be given your own files, but you're very much a part of the team and heavily relied upon. I was drafting contracts and leases, doing all sorts of research and frequently travelling to London for meetings."* The RID team does conveyancing work for overseas clients, mostly from South-East Asia. *"As a trainee, this seat is quite admin-based, but it's an excellent learning platform for emerging economies. We have a partner who lives in Thailand, so there is a regular flow of cross-border work."*

The Wealth Preservation Group is split into teams including family, trusts, tax, administration of estates, residential conveyancing and general wills and probate. Trainees *"really help out everyone"* in this department. One said: *"I was drafting wills and powers of attorney, monitoring the accounts of estates and every going to client meetings on my own. You learn such a lot in terms of legal and organisational skills."* Interviewees did add: *"I think your experience in this seat can depend on whether you've completed the private client elective on the LPC. Your background knowledge acquired from there is incredibly useful."* The residential conveyancing seat deals exclusively with private clients of high net worth. *"It's focused on properties in London or expensive estates around the South and most are connected to our private client department,"* trainees said. All reported having *"a huge amount of client contact"* in this seat. *"The responsibility builds up throughout,"* one said. *"By the end you're negotiating, drafting and even potentially running your own files all the way to completion."*

The corporate division is split between employment, corporate, commercial and commercial dispute resolution work. Core corporate is mainly occupied with M&A. Clients vary from small local businesses to AIM-listed national companies and *"as a trainee you really see the full range of work."* Cripps represented Clydesdale Bank in its £25m refinancing of The Holidays Extra Group. Other clients include AmBank, European marketing company Altavia and retailer Eden Park. *"The team is very good at getting trainees involved in deals. I was doing the first drafts of purchase agreements and a large amount of company secretary work, and going to meetings regularly."*

Finally, commercial dispute resolution *"is actually quite a small department at Cripps."* The work varies from commercial disputes to private client and professional negligence matters. *"It's definitely not bundling all the time. From drafting particulars of claim to issuing court proceedings, you're constantly asked your opinion on cases. As it's not a very big team, they need the trainee to be an integral part of what's going on."*

I want it that way

The office has *"an almost informal attitude,"* trainees said. *"People definitely don't have their ties on the whole time."* Hours vary between departments, but *"on average most people leave about 6 or 6.30pm,"* trainees said. There are longer evenings at busy times, *"but it's rare to stay past 9.30pm even on a bad night. Compared to City firms, Cripps' hours are very reasonable."* Interviewees praised the *"particularly good relationships between trainees. We're actually friends. Beyond going for lunch, we also meet up at weekends and go to each other's parties."*

Beyond football, netball, cricket, squash and polo (you don't need to have played before, but do need to know how to ride), there are bake-sales, quizzes and charity summer fêtes. *"There's also a Cripps band, Corporate Jam, who are genuinely really good."* The highlight of the social calendar is the summer ball. *"The second-year trainees organise the evening and it always has a theme. Last year's was 'Hollywood Glamour' and this year we did a 1920s murder mystery in this beautiful old country house. There was a live jazz band and the second-years actually learnt the Charleston to perform for everyone. Then between meals we had actors come in and got some of the partners secretly involved. It turned out really well."* In a charity Cripps' Got Talent evening, *"the trainees, as expected, made complete fools of themselves. The girls all dressed up like Dolly Parton and performed as The Dollys, while the boys did a brilliant rendition of a Backstreet Boys medley. The whole evening was brilliant."* There are end-of-quarter drinks in the office or Friday night bevs at wine bar Sankeys down the road. *"On a Friday night you'll definitely find people out and about. We're in the centre of town, so there a lots of options."*

And finally...
In 2012 the firm kept four out of its seven qualifiers.

Davenport Lyons

The facts

Location: London

Number of UK partners/solicitors: 47/43

Partners who trained at firm: 4.5%

Total number of trainees: 17

Seats: 4x6 months

Alternative seats: None

Extras: Pro bono – LawWorks

On chambersstudent.co.uk...

- How to get into Davenport Lyons
- Interview with training partner Michael Hatchwell

This lively West End firm is perfect for those interested in commercial work.

Top Gear

Tucked away in its Mayfair office, Davenport Lyons feels a million miles away from the bustle of the City. Featuring in the True Picture for the first time this year, Michael (pronounced 'Mikhail') Hatchwell – training partner, management board figurehead, head of corporate, and general bigwig – summed up DL as a small-to-medium-size, full-service, law firm delivering conventional legal services plus real specialisms in certain areas: *"We've always been one of the leaders in film and TV financing, production, music and rights... but the firm has grown significantly in more conventional areas like corporate."* This is evidenced by HSBC becoming one of the firm's biggest clients in recent years. Regarding media, Hatchwell assures us: *"We're not planning to move away from those areas at all, but relative to the whole they've become a smaller part of it."* Corporate work today accounts for a sizeable slice of the DL pie – 36% in fact, as opposed to media's 13%. It's also recognised by *Chambers UK* for its employment, IP, real estate litigation and travel regulatory work.

Available seats include banking, company commercial, dispute resolution, employment, property, matrimonial, private client, media/entertainment, music and occasionally IP. Newbies are strongly encouraged to pass through two of the firm's three core practice areas – company commercial, dispute resolution and property – but can fill the remaining 12 months with their 'wish list' from the above selection. In general, *"seat allocation is pretty effective. They try hard to combine what you want with how your seats might best tie together."*

Three Lyons

We're told *"in every new intake there are more and more trainees who are attracted to our corporate work."* In fact, the group has ballooned by almost a third in the past year. *"I have friends in City firms who did corporate seats, and it seemed quite different,"* one trainee mused. *"It's not really your traditional big M&A stuff, which can be quite dry. It's a mix of commercial work, with interesting clients like media labels or new companies and start-ups."* The likes of investment banking and private equity group Evans Randall and international conglomerate Noble Group instruct the group. In the past, the department has also dealt with a fair few AIM floatations. *"They're not as big as FTSE ones, so easier to get your head around."* Responsibility is pitched high and, while the odd admin job is on the cards, *"what's really good in corporate is that you're asked your opinion on things. You often have an open discussion with the partner, and get heavily involved in each matter."*

The dispute resolution department is another central column of the firm, and one of the larger departments, housing up to three or four trainees at a time. The group has some brilliant clients on its books, including *The Mirror*. Some trainees were involved in *"reviewing all of a comedian's material"* to see if accusations of racism were founded, or trying to settle a dispute over *"a new theme park-type thing based around the horse riding community."* No, we have no idea either. Its not all puns and ponies, however. These projects are also topped up with a healthy dose of *"more general commercial work"* for the likes of Interdean and the Covent Garden Market Authority.

At this juncture, DL's prized defamation group is also worth a mention. According to trainees, *"quite a lot of*

Chambers UK rankings

Defamation/Reputation Management	Partnership
Employment	Real Estate Finance
Intellectual Property	Travel
Media & Entertainment	

people come here for that, and most end up doing it at some point." The team is highly ranked by *Chambers UK*. It has has stepped in to help out many a celeb in bother or potentially libellous publication. In the past couple of years alone, it helped to unveil the identity of The Stig, represented Ian Hislop in the Leveson Inquiry, and partially lifted a super-injunction keeping Gordon Ramsay's father-in-law's 'secret family' under wraps. A niche area within litigation, it also works for clients like Harper Collins, and even casts an eye over each new issue of *Private Eye* before publication. Much like the rest of the litigation department, trainees have their fair share of bundling, but *"you get to do interesting, different things. It's not just boring paperwork."*

Property, the last of the big three, exposes trainees to a wide range of both transactional and contentious work. *"The property department here is quite big so we have lots of different work. There's residential conveyancing, construction and development, property litigation and property funding. Depending on what you're interested in, you get into different bits."* The *"very nice, chilled out department"* offers trainees loads of client contact, with the likes of Ryman the stationers in recent years. *"We work on some exciting developments. If you're into property, this is a great firm to be in."*

Legal maestros

The firm's private client team is small, with *"only two partners and one or two assistants."* There are plenty of juicy cases to go around. *"I've worked on a couple of estates of famous people, and the firm has some international clients, so you meet interesting folks from all over the place,"* a trainee beamed. Probate and tax work is on the menu in this seat, where *"you get to know people rather than dealing with corporate affairs, and get an insight into how people think about their money."* Trainees regularly get to take care of their own smaller cases, and have masses of client contact. *"The work can be quite pedantic,"* but when cases have a direct impact on individuals' lives, *"the difference between getting it right and wrong is huge."*

In the past year, the music team has helped hash out tour agreements involving the likes of Elton John and Beardyman, and advised BMG on its bid for EMI's music publishing division. While partners take care of the more

substantial work, trainees get a look in drafting and proof-reading recording agreements and contracts. On contentious matters such as disputes over royalties, they can expect to *"draft long, detailed letters to the other side."* Music law sounds exciting, but keep in mind: *"At the end of the day, document drafting is document drafting. The subject matter is either an interesting thing for you, or a bit dry. If you have an interest in music it's very interesting to see the machinations behind it, but I'm yet to attend any glitzy, glamorous parties."* Basically, *"the area is quite technical and specific. You'll need to have an interest in the nitty-gritty of the law."*

"I was expecting far more direct contact with my supervisor," one source said. *"Supervisors here are more someone in the background to go to if you need help, than a conduit for work. That very much comes from whoever needs a trainee at the time."* Most trainees sit among paralegals and secretaries in the open-plan part of the office, rather than in private rooms with partners, which they considered a massive plus. *"In terms of being versatile, it's great to be in the middle and accessible to everyone."* DL trainees are no shrinking violets, and embrace a proactive approach to sourcing work. *"Express what you're interested in, as people are happy to accommodate,"* they urge. *"There's no point in keeping your head down. Talk to as many partners as you can."* Hours *"vary wildly from seat to seat and case to case."* If work's all done, trainees can be out by 6pm, but during the rare 2am finish *"the trenches humour comes out. You're very well looked after and hardly ever stuck in the office on your own."*

Departmental training sessions *"are good, as trainees are usually encouraged to chip in and join discussions."* The only gripe is at the lack of trainee-specific sessions to kick off each seat. *"Maybe just a day or two would refresh your memory and get your mind focused."* Fortunately, trainees feel perfectly happy to pipe up with questions – whether to their fellow trainees or partners. Plus, if you're stuck, *"always remember that the secretaries and support staff run the firm. Secretaries are the font of all knowledge – the first port of call!"*

Wherever the music takes you

"This is definitely a quirky place," trainees agreed. Given the number of times they told us this, it should probably be on the firm's banner. The good vibes are largely down to its people, who trainees joked *"tend to get more normal as you go down the firm."* Given the charismatic sources we spoke to, however, we don't dare guess at the partners' antics. *"They're very serious but in their own eccentric sort of way."* Almost all of them are extremely friendly and approachable. They're pally with trainees, who report *"still going back to old departments to chat with partners about football and stuff."* We genuinely get the impression

"there's a good atmosphere, and a lot of banter going around."

There were concerns among our sources, however, that the culture might be shifting. *"There are definitely two schools of thought: the people who want to become slicker and more like a City firm, and those who want it to be like it was five years ago – very, very woolly but a fun place to work. It's pulling in those two directions and striking the correct balance is the key."* Right now, the firm appears to be at a crucial crossroads. *"It needs to make up its mind as to exactly what sort of firm it wants to be,"* another trainee echoed. *"It's in an unsettled period and it needs to re-define itself, but I think it's getting there."*

Recent efforts to increase transparency in the qualification process appear to be paying off, and *"they're very upfront about job opportunities and wanting to keep trainees on."* In 2012, the firm retained four of its eight qualifiers, in the banking, employment and litigation groups. Bear in mind that there are no guaranteed jobs in the sexier defamation, music and IP groups. *"It's nice to get involved with that work, but don't come here expecting to definitely get a job in music."*

Advance to Mayfair

Split across two neighbouring buildings, DL's offices aren't *"state of the art by any stretch of the imagination,"* but trainees enjoy their social set up. Sitting together in most departments, trainees say: *"When you're sitting in a* pod with three or four trainees it's a good laugh."* We're informed that the cosy office might be in for a shake-up. *"Our lease comes to an end in June 2013,"* said Hatchwell. *"Rents are crazy in Mayfair, but we'll stay as close to here as we can."*

Thanks to the turbulent economy, *"sandwich lunches aren't always as forthcoming as they used to be,"* but a good effort goes into the annual Christmas party and there are plenty of informal social events to keep trainees busy. A strong contingent can be found in local watering holes The Burlington Arms or The King's Head on Fridays. Trainees form close ties with the secretaries, and *"at firm-wide events there are always a few partners there 'til the bitter end."*

"We need people's people," demands Hatchwell, who was described by trainees as *"a mini Richard Branson... he's quite a charismatic guy – an entrepreneur."* Funnily enough, we get the impression that he seeks out the very same qualities in his employees. *"We want someone enthusiastic, who will make good connections with clients,"* he says. *"Someone who is practical, commercial and will deal with problems in an efficient and sensible manner. You don't always find those things in the most obvious places. Sometimes people with amazing academics won't necessarily have those qualities."* Hence, DL trainees comes in all shapes and sizes – many with interesting life experiences under their belt. Bear in mind that the firm doesn't cover the cost of the LPC, so be prepared to pay your way.

And finally...

The direction of DL might be shifting, but it'll be difficult to knock the personality out of this bouncy firm. If you're interested, we recommend checking out the vac scheme. *"About half of us did one,"* claim trainees.

Dechert LLP

The facts

Location: London

Number of UK partners/solicitors: 41/87

Total number of trainees: 23

Seats: 6x4 months

Alternative seats: Overseas seats, secondments

Extras: Pro bono – Islington Law Centre, Prince's Trust

On chambersstudent.co.uk...

- How to get into Dechert
- Interview with grad recruitment partner Jonathan Angell
- Trainee life in Brussels

"At the moment, you wouldn't know there was a recession on" at Dechert, which is hiring as if its life depended on it.

Passing the Titmuss test

This Philly firm's first foray into the London market in 1972 wasn't its defining one. That came in 2000, through a tie-up with mid-sized City outfit Titmuss Sainer. Today, the London office is the third-largest in Dechert's network of 26 – a network that has seen some significant expansion of late. The firm opened offices in Frankfurt, Almaty, Dubai, Tblisi and Chicago, all in the first six months of 2012. The London office is known for its top-notch investment funds practice and is well ranked by *Chambers UK* in the corporate mid-market. Corporate and finance are the key drivers of this office, though it provides a pretty broad service, and practices such as dispute resolution, real estate, IP, employment and tax are also Chambers-ranked.

"Within the corporate department, we've taken a team from Dewey & LeBouef London, which focuses on emerging markets, and that has partly driven the opening of offices in Dubai and Tblisi as, along with the team in London, we took a team in both of those locations," says joint graduate recruitment and development partner Jonathan Angell. *"The emerging markets group is led by Camille Abousleiman and is really the premier emerging markets group operating out of London."* In case you haven't been keeping up to speed with the legal news (and if not, why not?), Dewey was a law firm that collapsed in 2012 – it was the largest law firm bankruptcy in history.

Dechert was one of the beneficiaries of its demise. *"Dechert prides itself on being very good at everything it does, but it doesn't strive to be all things to all people,"* says Angell of the firm's recent growth spurt. Identifying

life sciences, regulatory and energy as some of the areas the firm is now seeking to develop, he says *"there will be measured growth in London, recognising that in London, Dechert is still a work in progress."* Trainees were *"under the impression that Dechert sees this period as a bit of an opportunity. Unlike the late lamented Dewey & LeBoeuf, we aren't burdened with large quantities of debt and Dechert is starting to explore the possibilities of taking advantage of low morale at other firms."* Talking to trainees, we get the impression that the appointment of a new, more *"vocal"* London managing partner, replacing one who had been in charge since before the 2000 merger, has given the office a bit of a boost too.

Fun, fun, funds!

"I like the fact that Dechert has a six-seat rotation rather than a four-seat one. It's really showed how many different areas of law there are to sample and four seats wouldn't have made me happy." If four-month-long seats prove a bit short, trainees have remained in them for longer, or honed their interest by opting for a subgroup. Whichever way trainees spin it, time in corporate or financial services (FS) is expected: *"If you're not interested in those areas, there is no point in applying to Dechert. You can qualify wherever, but those seats are expected."* Trainees are asked for their preferences for the first three seats but *"priority is given to the second-years for obvious reasons."*

Within the FS department *"a majority of the work is launching, helping to maintain and on occasion winding down funds – our clients are almost always the funds themselves."* Trainees say: *"When you first start there are*

Chambers UK rankings

Banking & Finance	Financial Services
Capital Markets	Intellectual Property
Corporate Crime & Investigations	Investment Funds
Dispute Resolution	Tax
Employment	

an awful lot of acronyms and jargon to get used to," but the "very well-oiled department" offers training to help "overcome the language barrier." Supervisors "talk you through why a fund is structured a certain way, and how some are different from others." Working in this technical area means "you are never in your comfort zone, constantly learning." Trainees draft skeleton prospectuses, assist with setting funds up and dabble in cross-jurisdictional work. "For a cross-border registration for an Irish UCITS, I ran the file management on my own, running everything past the associate but staying in constant contact with the client and foreign counsel." The time-pressured environment is "exciting enough to keep you going" through late nights.

Linked with the FS department is a client secondment with a global asset and fund management company. The secondee provides support to the in-house head of legal and as a result takes on a lot more responsibility than they'd get during the rest of their training contract. Other secondments are on offer with the Royal Courts of Justice, a financial regulatory body and a US banking giant. There's also a regular Brussels seat, which serves up slices of EU law, corporate and FS, and a Dublin seat entirely focusing on FS. Paris seats are occasionally open to French speakers, while a stint in Dubai is currently under consideration: "We're keen for a trainee to go there regularly," says Angell.

Corporate and securities is another core area for the firm and the London practice is recognised for its work in the City's mid-market. It represented Kerry Group, which manufactures food ingredients and products, in its $230m acquisition of Cargill Flavor Systems. The newly arrived team from Dewey handles "interesting international matters for clients based in places like Africa, Lebanon and Georgia, such as bond issues for companies based there." Since arriving at Dechert, the team has already represented Congolese company High Grade Minerals in its £306m sale to Glencore, and advised Lebanon's Bank Audi on selling a majority stake in LIA Insurance to Moroccan company Saham Finances. Trainees found corporate a "great seat" which had allowed them to work on a "variety" of tasks. Said one: "There was an evening when the associate and the partner on a deal were out of the office and there were some very minor amendments to be made to a deed, and I was entrusted to negotiate with

the associate on the other side. For a trainee to be on the phone to the other side is quite an exciting experience." As with corporate departments across the City, the hours are "unpredictable. You could be sitting there at 3.30pm with essentially nothing to do; other weeks you'll be in at midnight every night."

The litigation department is divided into a number of subgroups: white-collar crime, international arbitration, EU trade and government affairs, employment and commercial litigation. While trainees are assigned to one subgroup, the firm "lets you act as a floating trainee," so trainees can seek out all types of interesting matters. Our sources had been busy on one of the more prominent cases of the year, Cherney v Deripaska. Oleg Deripaska, chief executive of Rusal, the world's biggest aluminium producer, has been accused of breaching contract by Michael Cherney, who claims he has a rightful stake in the company. It's an "enormous, all-consuming," matter and trainees had been tasked with lots of document management and bundling, "which is to be expected on really large cases." The white-collar crime subgroup recently arrived from DLA Piper and does a lot of work with HMRC, "guiding clients through investigations as, rather than doing dawn raids, the FSO is encouraging clients to self-report." The group's very busy and "needs more people." Trainees are kept on their feet assisting with the self-reporting process, attending client meetings, and taking on "a bit of document management."

Dechert trainees work hard and in complex areas, but are supported on all sides. There's department-tailored learning, "panel partners who attend your appraisals as a neutral party and monitor your progress through the training contract" and "a seamless network of international offices that you can rely on." Other seats include tax, employment, finance and real estate (FRE), and IP.

Born in the USA

Despite being American by birth, Dechert retains the feel of a City firm in London (though the majority of partners from the Titmuss Sainer days have now gone elsewhere). It does "take the best bits" of US culture, though, in the form of things like "staff appreciation days." The only question trainees had was one of autonomy. "There is some confusion. It's promoted that we're autonomous, but sometimes it's not clear where the buck stops with trainee decisions." Senior sources told us that the large departments are very autonomous while smaller ones go through the US for certain budget decisions. Overall, trainees feel "the Americans are good at deferring to our Englishness."

Dechert's digs are opposite Blackfriars station, "on the doorstep of the City but only a short walk away from the West End." Housed in a "glassy new building," it has *"breakout areas on every floor,"* showers (*"but no sleeping pods!"*) and a good range of food in the canteen – trainees *"can't imagine it gets better than this."* What's more, there are *"pubs everywhere,"* so Friday evening drinks trip are easy. A favoured destination is the unusually-named pub Shaws Booksellers. The annual Dechert Punch Tavern Quiz is *"something everyone makes an effort to go to,"* while summer brings out the firm's sporty side: softball on Mondays, football on Tuesdays and an annual cricket match with the partners.

And finally...

It might be one of the lesser-known US firms in the City among law students, but Dechert can provide as good a corporate and finance experience as any. It retained five out of seven qualifiers in 2012.

Dickinson Dees LLP

The facts

Location: Newcastle, Stockton-on-Tees, Leeds, London

Number of UK partners/solicitors: 60/270

Partners who trained at firm: 37.5%

Seats: 4x6 months

Total number of trainees: 30

Alternative seats: Brussels, secondments

On chambersstudent.co.uk...
- How to get into Dickie Dees
- More seat information
- Newcastle's legal market

Long recognised as Newcastle's "*biggest and best,*" Dickinson Dees hopes a new business strategy will allow it to reinvent itself as "*more of a national firm rather than a regional firm that does national work.*"

Vision and perspective

With over 200 years of history on the banks of the Tyne, Dickinson Dees stands firmly at the top of the Newcastle legal market. Every single practice in its full-service offering is recognized by *Chambers UK* as a leader in the North East. "*I wanted to be in the North and I wanted to be at a bigger firm,*" one trainee told us. "*And Dickinson Dees is the obvious choice in Newcastle.*"

Besides Newcastle, Dickie Dees has offices in Stockton-on-Tees and Leeds, as well as a small outpost in London. Its work spans the country, though, and while it represents a host of North East clients – Grainger, Teesport and Durham County Council spring to mind – it also acts for major UK and international outfits, such as Age UK, HSBC and Gap.

In mid-2011, the firm's management announced a new business strategy, dubbed '2020 Vision'. It denotes a change in mindset at the top of the firm. "*In common with a lot of regional firms, we took the view a few years back that we could be successful winning work from other regions without needing a presence there,*" senior partner John Marshall told us. "*Back then that worked, but changes in the legal and economic landscape mean it won't work in the future.*" We think a new business plan is just the ticket for Dickie Dees. Despite its rep as top dog in the North East, in the past few years it has at times seemed a little stuck in the mud. Three straight years of revenue decline between 2007 and 2011 haven't helped either.

So, 2020 Vision includes the aim to be a top firm – some trainees guessed a UK top 20 firm – by the year 2020. Given Marshall's comments, that clearly entails the firm building up a greater national presence. Moves are already afoot. The entire 30-lawyer York office has upped sticks and moved to the more developed legal market of Leeds.

Meanwhile, there are now seven employees working in what was a previously unmanned London office. Partner pay is also to be reviewed and made merit-based, and there is to be a focus on eight core "*£1m clients.*" There is even talk of a merger with a mid-size London or Leeds firm. "*We have charted ourselves on a path which has goals that will not be achieved just by organic growth,*" John Marshall said. "*As part of our journey we will be looking at mergers with or acquisitions of other firms, and not just lateral or team hires, important though those are.*" Nothing, it seems, will ever be the same again for Dickie Dees. "*We are trying to change the nature of the firm,*" one trainee emphasised.

Geordie, sure

This strategy stuff is all well and good, but Dickie Dees' down-to-earth and talkative trainees were far more focused on their quality training. "*I couldn't really fault it,*" one source said laconically. The broad practice remit means there are around 35 seat options to choose from in Newcastle. This means that almost all trainees sit in a department on their own. Only corporate and property take two (and very rarely three) trainees at a time. All

Chambers UK rankings

Agriculture & Rural Affairs	Intellectual Property
	Local Government
Banking & Finance	Pensions
Charities	Pensions Litigation
Competition/European Law	Planning
Construction	Private Client
Corporate/M&A	Projects
Dispute Resolution	Public Procurement
Education	Real Estate
Employment	Real Estate Litigation
Environment	Restructuring/Insolvency
Health & Safety	Social Housing
Information Technology	Transport

lawyers work in two-person offices and trainees usually share an office with their supervisor.

Seat options include: corporate; corporate rail; corporate recovery (insolvency); corporate finance; banking and finance; commercial/IP; energy; environment; commercial litigation; employment; insurance litigation; property litigation; property planning; commercial property; property finance; agriculture; construction; education; and private client. Now, in theory seats in corporate/commercial, property and litigation are compulsory. But the options within each of these areas are so varied that trainees can craft a very distinctive training contract. So, for corporate you could do an insolvency seat; employment or property litigation could count towards your contentious requirement; while planning and agriculture both count as property seats.

The Leeds and Tees Valley offices take one or two trainees in each intake and offer seats in property, corporate and litigation/employment. Trainees in these two offices occasionally complete a seat in Newcastle too, though it's rare for Geordies to head south. London doesn't currently take trainees, though an NQ position was on offer in the most recent jobs round, and was taken up by a Newcastle trainee. There's also a short secondment to DD's affiliate firm in Brussels and a client secondment to Virgin Money (formerly Northern Rock).

Although Dickie Dees attracts people who grew up in the North East, we spoke to plenty of non-Geordies. Ties to the region are important, though. "*During the interview they did grill me quite extensively on why I wanted to be in Newcastle,*" one source said. Most of our interviewees had also applied to firms in other Northern cities.

The waste land

Straight corporate M&A is probably the most common seat. This team recently advised Newcastle's Attends Healthcare during its €180m sale to Canadian paper manufacturer Domtar and helped York University develop a new £9m 'Sports Village' with York City Council and Sport England. Other clients include energy, utility, engineering and chemical firms. Corporate recovery has recently been very busy. "*Tight deadlines meant we sometimes had to cram a day's work into two or three hours!*" one trainee exclaimed.

Property is Dickie Dees' largest single department and we're told it's really picking up speed post-recession. "*Property owners are looking at expanding or maintaining their portfolios, rather than just trying to sell with no one there to buy, which was happening a few years ago.*" The firm recently helped Gap with leases for eight new stores and has been advising Partnerships for Schools on the government's new education hobby-horse, Free Schools. It also advised property developer Terrace Hill on the £75.3m sale of a host of flats in and around London to Akelius, Sweden's largest private housing company. On big transactions like this trainees "*get involved with negotiating leases, drafting licences to occupy, but also do some admin work like dealing with stamp duty applications and land tax returns.*" Trainees also run a few of their own "*low-end transactions.*"

Dickie Dees' litigators recently acted for Durham's Premier Waste during a Court of Appeal case against a former director who used equipment belonging to one of Premier's clients to renovate his own house. It also worked for the operator of Teesport in litigation against the Pilots' National Pension Fund over who was responsible for a £300m deficit in the pension fund. "*There is a lot of problem-solving in litigation, rather than actually making something happen,*" one trainee reflected. "*For example, I drafted a couple of letters of claim to try to resolve a contested debt, as well as doing legal research into case law.*"

Trainees in contentious seats usually don't have long hours – leaving at 5.30 or 6pm isn't uncommon. The hours are similar in private client and in property where, as one source told us, "*it was nine-to-six, except at certain crunch points where I stayed until 8pm.*" Trainees told us corporate and corporate recovery had the most demanding hours. "*When it was quiet I would work 9am to 5.30pm, but there were days when I was in until 8 or 9pm and on one occasion I stayed late at night and worked on the weekend.*" Trainees felt the job allowed for life outside work: "*If something really urgent comes up you might have to cancel evening plans, but generally I don't have to and I don't have to work weekends.*"

All the strategy talk earlier leaves us a little short of space to talk about the numerous other teams, but never fear – you can head over to our website for more on seats including agriculture, employment, commercial and corporate rail.

Marrvelous

In past years we've reported on trainee gripes related to communication and the qualification process. There's been a marked improvement on this front. "*If you had asked me how communication was just three months ago I would have said 'not at all good',*" one trainee told us in March 2012. "*Making things more transparent and consulting with us was something that needed to happen. They have really gone all-out to improve communication: there have been presentations by the senior and managing partner about the '2020' strategy and the NQ process.*" To trainees' joy the September 2012 jobs list was announced in early March, with 17 positions on offer for the 15 qualifiers. In the end 13 of them stayed with the firm (nine in Newcastle, three in Leeds and one in London).

Trainees said the late-2011 hire of former lawyer Helen Marr as graduate recruitment supervisor was an excellent development. "*You can call her and ask things on a one-to-one basis.*" She has helped improve appraisals too. "*Often appraisals used to be delayed or you felt the firm wasn't giving you its full attention. Things have got much better since Helen's arrival.*"

So, communication is improving. We also think that having a clear and ambitious strategy will help the firm breed upbeat and optimistic trainees. "*The way the firm is going about things at the moment, I think they probably have the right idea. Dickie Dees has ambitious plans to expand, but wants to take small steps and build things up steadily in London.*" York trainees were positive about the move to Leeds. "*The firm felt it had used York to its full potential and that it was a good springboard into Leeds. Leeds is a big legal market and the extra work there should make it a good move. They have taken a brave step – we will have to wait and see if it pays off.*" It's a half-hour commute from York to Leeds, but all staff are to receive travel reimbursement for a whole year after the move.

Fight for this love

Two points where trainees "*definitely still see room for improvement*" are salary and seat rotation. "*Last time round we only heard a couple of days in advance where we going to, and previously it was maybe a week. It would be nice to hear a few weeks in advance.*" When we checked back with the firm, it told us at the most recent rotation, trainees were informed several weeks in advance. Trainees also admitted that "*pay is not wonderful*" – the first-year salary is just £20,000, which is not the highest in the Newcastle market. Trainees do "*set the salary off against the quality of training and having a good work/life balance.*"

However, all things considered, Dickie Dees trainees have consistently remained positive about training and their work environment. "*The supervisors are generally keen to teach you. Everyone from partners to NQs is really approachable,*" one said. Another added: "*Everyone seems to get on quite well. As anywhere, there are some exceptions: there are some real characters – what you would think of as old-school lawyers.*" A third trainee had this to say: "*There is a very professional atmosphere. We are not sat around in open-plan offices joking all day. Property and private client are more relaxed departments – corporate feels more formal and everyone is always in a suit.*" Trainees in the smaller offices appreciate that you "*get to know everyone. You will be sat in a staff room at lunch and talk to everyone from partners to secretaries.*"

Dickie Dees lawyers also find time to rub shoulders outside the office. Social events are often organised on a departmental basis. "*All the Newcastle departments have Christmas parties – all the trainees are invited to the commercial department's party and there is also a trainee Christmas social.*" Other social events include dinners for birthdays, days at the races and curry nights. There was recently a charity ball for The Prince's Trust, which apparently involved a bunch of lawyers "*dressed up in Cheryl Cole outfits.*" The local Pitcher & Piano next to Dickie Dees' two Quayside offices is a popular hang-out. "*The trainees do socialise together, but not every week. After hours some people want to go home and some want to go for a drink. On a Friday you might find four or five of us down the pub.*"

And finally...
We think that if it adheres to its new strategy Dickinson Dees has a lot of potential for the future, either independently or with a merger partner.

SQUEEZE MORE INTO TWO YEARS
WE OFFER YOU ONE OF THE SHARPEST TRAINING CONTRACTS AROUND

Everything matters and every day counts when you're a trainee at DLA Piper. We squeeze huge amounts of experience, responsibility and personal development into your 24 months with us. That means you get to know more about the law, our firm and about yourself.

Working with one of the world's leading practices also means more opportunities: the chance to try the things you want to try, work on secondments abroad or with clients, and get involved with headline making matters.

Enjoy every last bit of your training contract and develop the all round skills that all top lawyers need.

Visit our website for more details: www.dlapipergraduates.co.uk or follow us on Facebook.

www.dlapiper.com | DLA Piper UK LLP

EVERYTHING MATTERS

DLA Piper is a global law firm operating through various separate and distinct legal entities.
Further details of these entities can be found at www.dlapiper.com

JUL12 | 2373071

DLA Piper LLP

The facts

Location: Birmingham, Leeds, Liverpool, London, Manchester, Sheffield, Scotland

Number of UK partners/solicitors: 274/515

Total number of trainees: 180

Seats: 4x6 months

Alternative seats: Overseas seats, secondments

Extras: Pro bono – LawWorks, A4ID, Bar Pro Bono Unit, FRU, London Legal Support Trust, i-Probono, several legal advice centres and more

On chambersstudent.co.uk...
- How to get into DLA Piper
- Interview with training principal Siân Croxon

With a management hell-bent on global domination and a client base that ranges from Disney to the local Boots optician, DLA Piper's training contract is not unlike a box of chocolates: trainees never know what they're gonna get next...

All things to all people?

You'd be hard-pressed to find someone who can neatly sum up DLA Piper's place in the legal market. It is clearly in a class of its own, as evidenced by its idiosyncratic combo of *"intensely high-profile"* and *"fairly run-of-the-mill"* work for both huge international and tiny local businesses. *"We've always tried to be different in the way we go about things,"* training principal Siân Croxon tells us. *"We've been brave and innovative, and have taken the lead on things rather than followed other people – and look where we are now."* Indeed, with over 4,200 lawyers sprawled across 77 global offices, this juggernaut is practically omnipresent. *"Go to any major city and we'll probably be just around the corner!"* quipped one source.

In May 2011, following a merger with a partner firm in Australia, DLA Piper officially nabbed the title of world's largest law firm by head count – not too shabby for an enterprise only formed in the mid-noughties. *"The firm's history of rapid expansion lends it a real up-and-coming energy,"* one trainee commented. *"You can tell there's strong leadership here."* The firm took up its latest digs in Mexico City in 2012, while Croxon singles out Asia as a definite growth area: *"There's a real need for more lawyers there."*

The end-goal of all this expansion is clear: *"To be the global leading business law firm"* was the catchphrase trainees repeated on more than one occasion. *"There's a visible sense of pushing forward and wanting to offer the best service possible,"* one source elaborated, mentioning

that each department has developed its own vision of how it can improve to service the firm as a whole. Financial figures for 2011 showed an 8% rise in equity partner profits, while the firm increased its turnover by a satisfying 15% for a record gross revenue of £1.4bn.

The brand's grand across the land

The firm's global reputation is a big draw for trainees – the majority of our interviewees cited it as a primary reason for joining – as is the chance to work on a diverse mix of local, national and international work. There's an office in London, of course, plus outposts in Birmingham, Manchester, Liverpool, Leeds, Sheffield (the UK part of the firm's spiritual home) and Scotland. While DLA Piper's British presence represents just a sliver of its entire practice, the UK offices are considered big players in their respective regions – meaning this is an enticing prospect for those keen on a big name outside of the City. *"I didn't want to move to London, nor did I want to settle for a regional firm where I lost out in terms of quality of work,"* one trainee testified, echoing a sentiment we heard many times from DLA trainees outside of the capital. *"Here in Birmingham I still get all of the benefits of the DLA Piper brand – international work, high-quality training, opportunities to travel – without sacrificing my desire to stay local."*

The firm handles a full range of work, but operates on three main tiers: local/regional; national; and international. While

Chambers UK rankings

Asset Finance	Investment Funds
Aviation	Licensing
Banking & Finance	Local Government
Banking Litigation	Media & Entertainment
Capital Markets	Outsourcing
Commodities	Parliamentary & Public
Competition/European Law	Affairs
Construction	Pensions
Consumer Finance	Personal Injury
Corporate Crime & Investigations	Planning
	Private Equity
Corporate/M&A	Product Liability
Data Protection	Professional Negligence
Dispute Resolution	Projects
Employment	Public International Law
Energy & Natural Resources	Public Procurement
	Public Procurement
Environment	Real Estate
Financial Services	Real Estate Finance
Fraud	Real Estate Litigation
Health & Safety	Restructuring/Insolvency
Healthcare	Retail
Information Technology	Sports Law
Insurance	Tax
Intellectual Property	Telecommunications
	Transport

each office provides a mix of all three tiers, the ratio varies by location. To generalise massively, London and Leeds have the greatest international slant, Liverpool and Manchester tend slightly more towards local work, while Birmingham and Sheffield's scope lies somewhere in between. That said, if you're after international assignments, DLA is certainly a good place to come: "*It's an aspect they push in the recruitment literature because it really is a big offering of the firm. You might have to wait your turn to get involved with a global deal that makes the front page of the paper, but the possibility is certainly there.*"

There are a host of seats on offer, and trainees aren't beholden to any mandatory ones. In addition to pretty standard offerings like employment, real estate and corporate, there's the option to pursue more specialised seats such as energy, infrastructure finance and commodities (EIFC) in London, a subset of the finance and projects group. Before each rotation, trainees submit three preferences in no particular order and are "*usually*" given one of their picks. "*Graduate recruitment tries to make it happen for everyone,*" most agreed. "*They make us explain why we want each particular seat so they can suggest other ones if they don't think we want it for the right reasons.*"

Busy, busy

DLA has one of the largest litigation practices in the UK. The department is divided into specialist subgroups including real estate, aviation, sports, media, insurance and construction. An increase in contentious undertakings in recent years has seen the team's client list grow tremendously: teams in London are representing Silvio Berlusconi and former News of the World editor Andy Coulson in addition to a host of international financial players – among them Barclays, RBS and Deutsche Bank – while recent years have seen regional teams act for Vodafone, EAT and Polo Ralph Lauren (the Sheffield office); Kodak, Kraft and West Midland Police (Birmingham); and Liverpool and Wigan Athletic FCs (Liverpool and Manchester). "*I was able to work on some low-value, high-volume commercial recovery work and a few large cross-border cases,*" reported a Sheffield source, while others mentioned involvement with mortgage fraud cases and "*bog-standard*" financial and commercial matters. Trainees regularly bundle, proof-read and draft documents, and many enjoy a front-row view of the action: "*I've spent the past two weeks of my seat in the Crown Court, assisting and taking notes for counsel, and I have another hearing to attend next week,*" said a Liverpool interviewee.

The corporate group is primarily M&A-focused and business has been booming: DLA retained its title of busiest M&A adviser in the UK for the fifth time in six years in 2011. London and Leeds tend to shoulder the bulk of international transactions, with the former recently advising on Santander's €4.3bn acquisition of two Polish banking entities from Allied Irish Banks. Yorkshire lawyers represent a variety of regional and national clients, while the Manchester and Liverpool offices act for several household names, including Warburtons and Carphone Warehouse. "*Even in Birmingham we handle a lot of deals for large listed companies,*" a Brum source said. "*Around half of the transactions I worked on had an international dimension.*" Because large transactions require significant manpower, trainees "*usually play a supportive role on the team,*" performing due diligence and drafting tasks and occasionally dealing with clients. "*I got to liaise with a client in Chile,*" one interviewee reported. "*It's interesting to see the relationship develop over the course of the seat.*"

"*The atmosphere in real estate is pretty different to a group like litigation,*" found one trainee. "*It's busier and you get quite a lot of responsibility and client contact from the start – on day one you show up and they hand you a file!*" In addition to a core real estate seat, there's also the chance to spend time in property litigation, construction or planning subgroups. London deals with big-ticket commercial transactions for global players like Burberry and Pfizer, and is especially hot when it comes to the hotel sector, acting for chains such as Hyatt, Marriott and Starwood. Leeds is active on the retail front, handling work for several well-known high-street stores, while Sheffield has a specialist plot sales team that handles residential conveyancing and construction work. As a trainee there's "*a lot*" of drafting of leases, reviewing licences to let and post-completion work. Trainees across offices were chuffed at the chance to handle small matters like short-term leases and licences to occupy from start to finish, "*acting as the primary contact. You finish the seat having accomplished a lot.*"

International seats and client secondments are hugely popular. Before each rotation, a list of available postings is sent to each office, to ensure fairness for all applicants. Recent overseas destinations include Dubai, Singapore, Bangkok, Hong Kong and Australia, while for client secondments, "*people have gone to investment banks, hotel chains, hedge funds and retail outlets.*"

Please, sir...

Despite DLA's enormous head count and offices galore, trainees across offices assured us the firm's working environment is anything but aloof. "*People assume that our giant ambitions make us ruthless, but it's the total opposite!*" laughed a source, calling DLA "*the kind of place where you can interact readily with the person next to you, be they a partner or another trainee.*" The following statement was a running theme: "*The firm may be massive, but you're definitely not faceless.*" While graduate recruitment has traditionally shied away from terms like "*mellow*" or "*laid-back*" in favour of the less slacker-attracting word "*open,*" the impression of a rather comfortable atmosphere prevails. "*It's a relaxed place, just not to its detriment,*" explained one trainee. "*You can have a laugh or a jape and get back to your work without anyone telling you off. People are down to earth like that.*" Dress "*isn't quite as insouciant as jeans or anything,*" though trainees had noticed a firm-wide edge towards less traditional vesture. "*It's business casual on Fridays in certain offices.*"

Don't be fooled, though: a DLA training contract is "*not a nine-to-five job, it's an until-the-work-is-done job.*" That said, sources agreed that, generally speaking, "*the hours are never too horrendous.*" Seats like real estate and employment usually see solicitors leave by 6pm, while the volatile nature of transactional work lends itself to a less predictable schedule: "*You just never know when something might get dropped on your desk. Corporate is the absolute worst for all-nighters,*" admitted one trainee, wincing at the memory of a recent early morning departure. "*Sometimes you just have to stick around until the deal closes, which sometimes happens in the early AM. But there's lots of support and you're never alone.*"

Some trainees were rather less chipper when it came to discussing compensation, with several citing the discrepancy between London and regional salaries as a real niggle. "*It's my biggest gripe! The London NQ salary is so much higher that what it is here, and I can guarantee they don't work longer hours than I do,*" a Leeds source said. For reference, London NQs take home £60k compared to the regions' £37k. While some took comfort in the fact that even regional DLA trainee salaries are higher than plenty of other firms' across the UK, others were not so easily persuaded. As one Mancunian pointed out: "*We may be paid highly for our region, but when you consider the level of work we do, and the difference in pay between here and London, it does seem pretty unfair.*"

Party people

An obvious bias existed among our interviewees when it came to describing their office, with more than a few deeming their city's digs the best of the bunch. While we can hardly judge one over the other, there were some standout details such as views of St Paul's in London, high ceilings and glass offices in Leeds and quarterly art exhibitions in Sheffield. All offices are located fairly centrally in their respective cities (an important factor, as anyone who's worked on a business park will tell you) and most have perks like subsidised cafés and Starbucks coffee in the building.

Trainees enjoy a lively social scene outside of the usual Christmas and summer bashes. While there's not much inter-office interaction between trainees – apart from an initial induction week where they all meet "*at a swanky hotel*" – there are plenty of opportunities to mix and mingle at home. Most locations put on a payday drinks do, and there are regular Friday outings to the pub. "*It's not all centred around booze:*" Liverpudlians reported charity-driven events like quizzes and paintball, Londoners enjoy discounted tickets and free popcorn at the Barbican Cinema and Brummies have an informal running club that meets for occasional jogs along the canal. Department-sponsored events include the London's IP group's Friday drinks trolley and the Leeds litigation team is planning a weekend away in Edinburgh. And there's always the odd trainee-organised meal or night out. Whether these are reasonably sedate or absolutely raging affairs remains unclear, though we were left with the following, rather telling hint from an experienced trainee: "*Let's just say people know how to party hard!*" Insert winky-face emoticon here.

And finally...
The qualification process is a "*straightforward*" affair and 75 out of 90 DLA second-years stayed on as NQs in 2012.

DMH Stallard LLP

The facts

Location: Crawley, London, Brighton

Number of UK partners/solicitors: 46/40

Partners who trained at firm: 33%

Total number of trainees: 14

Seats: 4x6 months

Alternative Seats: None

On chambersstudent.co.uk...
• How to get into DMH Stallard
• DMH life in London and Crawley

Headquartered in Crawley with offices in London and Brighton, this Southern stronghold is planning on growing.

Prepare for take-off

DMH Stallard *"wants to be seen as a premier offering in the South East with a strong London presence,"* its trainees said. Training principal Dominic Travers concurs: *"DMH Stallard stands out as the main regional player, with an established London practice."* The firm *"is pretty open about its strategy. There are plenty of networking and marketing initiatives in place and we want to increase our reputation and revenue,"* trainees continued. *"Management has said: 'This has been a tough market, but we're not shying away from growth and we're very openly saying we're prepared to merge with the right people.'"* Dominic Travers again: *"Over the next two years, we will be looking for potential merger partners and new teams joining the firm."*

DMH prefers to call its Crawley HQ the 'Gatwick' office, trading on its proximity to the airport. It provides a full-service offering to an array of local and international clients, while there is still a corporate focus in London. *"Corporate does generate an awful lot of work for the firm and permeates several other practices,"* trainees affirmed. *"On the other hand, practices such as litigation and employment are doing very well, so we have a good balance."*

Brighton – the firm's original and spiritual home – has ceased taking trainees, so new recruits are *"either a London or Gatwick trainee. Although you have an office focus, the official line is that you must expect to do seats in both locations. We have a mobility clause in our contract."* One source said: *"Ultimately, being a 'London trainee' doesn't mean very much. There are more seats in*

Gatwick and it's a bigger part of the firm. DMH is quite clear that's where its headquarters are, and you will go there for AT LEAST one seat." Others did add: *"If you have a good reason to stay in Gatwick, such as a young family, the firm might let you stay based there – it's not a guarantee though."* Bottom line: *"People come here with their eyes open and know moving offices is going to be part of the deal when you get the contract."*

Flight path

The Gatwick office has seats in coco, dispute resolution, private client, personal injury, planning and real estate. The London base only offers corporate, dispute resolution, real estate and employment. *"Beyond dispute resolution, both planning and employment are semi-contentious."* The HR team *"does try and match people with their seat preferences, but are cognisant of business needs."* Trainees advised: *"If you're passionate about a particular department, don't dilly-dally. You need to put a good case forward."* A good tip from one trainee was: *"Rather than focusing on location, choose a seat on the experience that area of the law will give you. It gives more weight to your argument."*

Trainees did complain that *"you don't actually find out about your next allocated seat until a week or two before the change. This can be a potential nightmare if you're having to move city."* One said: *"I know the firm isn't trying to be difficult, but it can be very frustrating."* The firm says: *"We endeavour to let people know as soon as possible about their trainee seats. Sometimes this can be later then the trainees might like; this is because sometimes*

Chambers UK rankings

Banking & Finance	Information Technology
Banking Litigation	Intellectual Property
Construction	Planning
Corporate/M&A	Private Client
Dispute Resolution	
Employment	Real Estate
Environment	Real Estate Litigation

where the trainee seats are may change to reflect changing demand in the business."

Your destinations

The London five-partner corporate team is *"very important to the firm. There are plenty of good mid-market clients, many of whom are the firm's largest."* They include a number of major UK clearing banks and various London Local Authorities. The work for trainees here is *"a real mix. Everyone just mucks in and works with each other."* One said: *"I did everything from commercial contract work and a project finance deal to banking transactions. The range can make the experience quite high-pressured, but the size of the team allows you good exposure and the opportunity to really make your mark."* In Gatwick, *"you can request which corporate team you'd like to join, but although you lean towards that area, you'll end up doing a mix of work."* Furthermore, *"you're never trailing through documents aimlessly. The associates will always keep you up to date with the big picture of a deal."* DMH Stallard advised on the acquisition of the Mid Sussex Golf Club, and represented Pyroban Group on the sale of its entire share capital to the US manufacturing and construction giant Caterpillar.

In Gatwick, the *"really big"* dispute resolution department is broken down into real estate litigation, general commercial litigation and technology, media and telecommunication (TMT). Trainees are allocated to one of these teams and *"stick to that field of work."* Trainees said: *"There is always bundling to do, but you're also given real drafting and writing responsibility."* The TMT team is *"quite small and primarily focused on IP, but has a great range of clients."* Clients *"can range from the lone inventor to the massive brand"* – the team has acted for BSkyB on anti-piracy matters and done trade mark and copyright work for Rock Choir (as seen on ITV). Trainees said they received *"a lot of drafting and client contact."* One mentioned: *"We regularly get technical queries and enquiries coming through, so there's a lot of research for trainees to get stuck into."* The real estate litigation team has a mix of public sector bodies and *"large FTSE 100 companies"* on the books. It has advised Tesco on portions of their rent review and Arora Hotels on the restrictions placed on their car parking facility at Heathrow Airport. Trainees said: *"There's a lot of strategical thinking involved and you can find yourself negotiating with the other side and dealing with the clients directly. It's very autonomous work and a great experience."*

The London dispute resolution team provides *"principally a real estate litigation experience, supported by insolvency work."* Trainees said they were *"always invited to meetings and conferences with counsel."* One added: *"For some of the smaller debt recovery stuff, I was largely left to crack on. It was great."*

Real estate is still *"a big area of law for the firm."* In Gatwick there are several real estate teams, *"mostly defined by their client focus."* The department itself handles planning, commercial property, construction and high-end residential work. *"There is also a lot of focus on regeneration and renewables work, which is very exciting."* DMH is advising the The Brighton West Pier Trust on the development of a proposed 150 metre high tower that will be a tourist attraction in the city. In London, it has completed work for Westminster City Council and Citywest Homes in relation to the installation of solar panels on hundreds of social housing units. One trainee said: *"You get a great overview of projects in this department. I was meeting architects and clients and taking weekly conference call meetings on my own."* Another added: *"There's also a lot of drafting, and in many instances you're the first point of contact for the other side. It's scary, but very satisfying."*

The London employment group's clients are mainly employers, with some high-end employees alongside that. For instance, DMH is advising on the termination of a senior executive for Amazon.co.uk and is acting for the International HIV/AIDS Alliance in their management restructuring. Clients also include Fender Musical Instruments, Canterbury City Council and the Caravan Club. Trainees in both offices said: *"Supervision is taken extremely seriously in the employment department. The quality of training is really good and very focused around research and drafting."*

In-flight entertainment

The Gatwick and London offices are *"really quite different in atmosphere."* London is *"more formal, with a glitzy corporate feel."* Born from 2005 and 2008 mergers with Stallards and then Courts & Co, *"you can still feel the influence of the old firms."* Located on New Fetter Lane, the office is *"on the 11th floor of a sky-rise, overlooking St Paul's. It has big glass windows and is all open-plan."* The provincial lawyers, on the other hand, *"are in Crawley overlooking an ASDA,"* trainees laughed, *"but the office itself is really buzzing and friendly. London is more heads-down, while Gatwick is livelier."* One summed up:

"*The offices are very different, but that doesn't mean that one is better than the other. As a trainee you get to experience both sides of the coin.*"

Trainees are "*extremely supportive of each other.*" One said: "*The other night two stayed to help me when I was swamped!*" It isn't often trainees need to stay extremely late, though. "*If you're in corporate you can find yourself staying regularly until 10 or 11pm, but otherwise there is no shame in leaving at 5.30 or 6pm if you have your work done. There's a 'really focus and work hard during the day' culture, and then you get the rewards in the evening.*"

Trainees felt "*the firm really tries to bridge the gap between the offices. Although Gatwick is definitely the focus, a lot of clients are in London, so people constantly travel between locations.*" Practices such as "*corporate, planning and dispute resolution really communicate,*" while others are "*less connected.*" London is "*definitely more conducive to the social side of things, although the*" Gatwick *office does try.*" The office in the capital enjoys last Thursday of the month drinks, organised trips out and "*weekly informal drinks.*" In Gatwick, "*there's a book club and lots of sport, such as cricket and netball.*" A charity mountain biking event provided "*a hard-core South Downs experience.*"

Unfortunately, NQ retention in 2012 wasn't great, with only four qualifiers out of nine staying on. "*I think the firm do want to keep people,*" one source said, "*but there just doesn't seem to be the capacity. There are currently no London jobs at all and it seems the only positions available are ones where NQs have left. They do try and help us, and it is a difficult market, but the process has been very demoralising.*" Training principal Dominic Travers said: "*Ideally we'd keep all the trainees, but of course it depends on business needs. Our rates are good, but it's not always possible to keep everyone all of the time.*"

And finally...
If you're looking for a broad training in the South East, but fancy a taste of London too, DMH Stallard could be just the ticket.

Dundas & Wilson

The facts

Location: London, Scotland

Number of UK partners/solicitors: 81/249

Total number of trainees: 25 (in England)

Seats: 4x6 months

Alternative seats: None

Extras: Pro bono – Prime Initiative

On chambersstudent.co.uk...
- How to get into D&W
- Interview with training principal Martin Thomas
- Rabbie Burns: a guide for non-Scots

The London office is an important part of Scottish-headquartered Dundas & Wilson, and has strengths in corporate, banking and real estate.

Scot or not?

A Scots firm right the way down to its tartan tootsies, Dundas & Wilson has been around since 1759 and is Chambers-ranked for over 20 different areas of practice north of the border, with an impressive 13 top-tier showings. The firm recently opened a fourth office, in Aberdeen, to add to its existing ones in Edinburgh, Glasgow and London. *"To grow both London and Aberdeen"* will be the focus for the immediate future, said trainees.

"The main preconception" about Dundas & Wilson, said one interviewee, *"is the Scottish thing – that we are big up there and mid-market down here. There is a preconception it's a Scottish firm."* We suppose we're not helping given the tone of our opening paragraphs, but the fact is that the London office has been on the scene for a decade now and has yet to emulate the success of the Scots part of the firm. It does sit at the lower end of the City's mid-market, picking up rankings in corporate, investment funds, real estate and banking. Still, the London office accounts for close to 40% of the firm's overall turnover, so no one can say it's not pulling its weight in that respect. It represents some big names too, including BAE Systems, E.ON, RBS and Lloyds Banking Group.

It must be said that 2011/12 has not been a vintage year for D&W. Revenue fell 12% and profits slumped too. Following the abandonment of merger talks with Bircham Dyson Bell, the managing partner resigned in the middle of his second term. This was followed with a quick-fire round of redundancies, with 28 jobs lost across Scotland and London. Chairman David Hardie also stepped down before his term was due to end, to be replaced by Laurence Ward. In June 2012 elections, the firm's care-taker managers Caryn Penley and Allan Wernham were given a mandate to lead the firm permanently, with *"a growth agenda."* The winds of change have blown a number of other Scottish firms into the arms of English ones – the tie-up with BDB may have fallen through, but we wouldn't bet against other merger talks somewhere down the line. Our trainee sources remained positive about the London office: *"They have a very strong growth plan in place; hopefully we will maintain our footing in the top 50."* If *"six months ago things were less transparent,"* the change at the top has meant trainees now feel a lot more *"in the loop"* about what's going on.

Corporate, banking and corporate recovery services (CRS) are popular seat choices and the firm also *"encourages trainees to do a real estate seat."* Commercial litigation, EU/competition, IP/IT, employment, construction, projects, tax, property litigation and property finance are also on offer. Trainees can also go on a client secondment, to the likes of National Grid and Land Securities.

Hogwarts and all

The real estate department is the *"biggest one by far – there are six or seven seats in it."* Trainees could find themselves working in property finance, planning and environment, utilities, restructuring or general property teams. D&W recently completed an agreement for lease on behalf of Land Securities for Primark to sign a 90,000 sq ft unit at Trinity Leeds, a major new shopping centre due to open in 2013. Juniors are handed individual files which they can manage themselves with some supervision. The restructuring team does *"a lot of work for Scottish & Southern Energy, Scottish Widows, property-holding arms of banks*

Chambers UK rankings

Administrative & Public Law	Intellectual Property
Banking & Finance	Investment Funds
Banking Litigation	Local Government
Charities	Media & Entertainment
Competition/European Law	Outsourcing
Construction	Partnership
Corporate/M&A	Pensions
Dispute Resolution	Planning
Education	Professional Negligence
Employment	Projects
Energy & Natural Resources	Public Procurement
Environment	Real Estate
Financial Services	Real Estate Finance
Franchising	Real Estate Litigation
Healthcare	Restructuring/Insolvency
Immigration	Tax
Information Technology	Transport

experience, responsibility "*builds up to running small files by yourself and attending meetings.*" The CRS department, meanwhile, has been involved in "*high-profile football administrations, especially in relation to Portsmouth FC,*" which recently went into a second round of administration in three seasons.

The firm is "*focusing on building the banking and finance practice,*" and recently acquired a team of five from Stephenson Harwood. These newcomers "*brought some interesting work with them,*" and trainees work on substantive tasks, such as drafting facilities agreements and sending e-mails out to clients in their own name.

D&W is "*really good*" at training – "*that's one of the best things about this firm.*" Trainee-specific sessions are provided "*throughout each seat.*" CRS and banking have "*a two-day introductory course in Scotland to give you an overview.*" The firm also assigns a two-year qualified mentor and an appraiser, usually a "*partner or senior associate*" in every seat. The former is there to answer "*stupid questions,*" while the latter conducts mid and end-of-seat appraisals.

and National Grid." The real estate funds team "*acts for investment funds on their property portfolios*" and again trainees find "*it's a very good seat for independence and responsibility.*" The development and utilities seat "*works with our infrastructure and planning team on projects.*" The matters are more on the infrastructure side, and "*we deal with the real estate aspect of it.*"

The London corporate practice is ranked in the lower mid-market by *Chambers UK* and houses two trainees at a time. "*It's split into general corporate and private equity.*" Dundas represented Endless LLP in its purchase of Cinesite, a digital visual effects company which is working on the latest Bond film as well as having worked on *Harry Potter* and *Pirates of the Caribbean*. The team also acted on one of the largest shopping centre disposals of 2011 – Land Securities' £70m sale of Corby town centre to Helical Bar – and advised the Murray Group on its sale of an 85% stake in football club Rangers to billionaire Craig Whyte. Trainees "*don't get much responsibility,*" in this department as "*there are more levels through which work has to filter down.*" However, they are "*taken to investor meetings and trainees are encouraged to attend drinks with clients.*"

Trainees in commercial litigation "*have every e-mail checked and are reliant on fee earners for what to do next*" in the early stages of the seat, but as they gain more

Will ye go to the Highlands wi' me?

"*When we start, we go to Edinburgh or Glasgow for two days, meet all the Scottish trainees and participate in firm induction.*" It "*does all feel like the same firm,*" – quite apart from "*interoffice bake-offs,*" some practice group are split across London and Scotland. Our sources did find the London office "*a lot more relaxed – in Edinburgh, everyone's always in suits.*" D&W is based in Bush House, "*two minutes from the RCJ and right next to Covent Garden, so it's not suits and glass everywhere.*" The building itself is "*lovely – it's got character.*" Though the lifts are something of a period piece, "*the client meeting rooms are new and quite swanky.*" Elsewhere, everyone sits in pods of four – "*you can be doing your work and turn around for a little break and a random conversation.*" Although this layout "*can be distracting if you're very stressed, at the same time you overhear partners doing their job and pick up on how a particular clients like being dealt with.*" Relationships with partners, by the way, are pretty good: "*One of the senior partners, he's been here for 15 years, is just the most approachable guy – at the risk of sounding lame, everyone's just nice.*" Local haunts such as Sophie's Steakhouse and The Wellington are well frequented on Friday nights. D&W also organises team events such as "*treasure hunts or quizzes*" and puts on "*firm-wide events every quarter that everyone looks forward to.*"

And finally...

Our sources appreciated that the qualification process is "*quick, early and comparatively painless.*" Nine of 12 English qualifiers stayed on 2012.

- 'Commercial awareness' is about more than just following the big commercial stories of the day, but it's a good place to start. 'Like' us on Facebook for frequent updates on the stories that matter: facebook.com/chambersstudentguide

Join us°

Go further

DWF is a business law firm with a distinctive approach, providing a comprehensive range of legal services to corporate bodies, public sector institutions and private individuals. DWF was named "Best National Law Firm" at the 2011 Legal Business Awards.

Looking for the opportunity to take your career further? We are currently looking for a range of lawyers and graduates to join our growing offices across the UK.

Working with us you'll be entitled to a contributory pension scheme, private healthcare, 25 days holiday, life assurance and a discretionary bonus scheme.

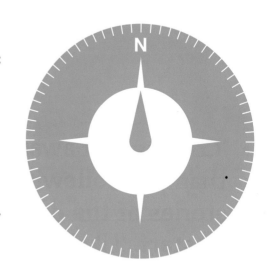

Applications or enquiries can be made to **Alexandra Sutcliffe** at **alex sutcliffe@dwf.co.uk** or call **0161 838 0144**.

All applications are treated in the strictest confidence.

Find out what it's like to work at DWF, meet our people at **www.dwf.co.uk/join-us**

DWF LLP
Voted 'National Law Firm of the Year' in the Legal Business Awards 2011.

www.dwf.co.uk

DWF LLP

The facts

Location: Newcastle, Manchester, Liverpool, London, Preston, Birmingham, Newcastle, Stockton-on-Tees, Scotland

Number of UK partners/solicitors: 166/352

Seats: 6x4 months

Total number of trainees: 44

Alternative seats: Occasional secondments

On chambersstudent.co.uk...

- How to get into DWF
- My, how you've grown: the last five years

Manchester-based DWF has had the explicit aim of becoming a UK top 30 firm for some years now, and 2011–12 saw it finally achieve that goal.

Race to the top

"It is exciting to know you are part of a firm that is so ambitious and has grown rapidly in the past few years," trainees agreed. Just five years ago DWF was a small regional firms with three offices in the North West (Manchester, Liverpool and Preston) and a Leeds outpost. Since then it has opened up shop in Birmingham, London, Newcastle, Stockton-on-Tees and Scotland, and its revenue has doubled. It could have been ever bigger by now: a merger with fellow Nor'wester Cobbetts was discussed in early 2012 and would have propelled the firm into the UK's top 25. In the end nothing came of it, but judging by comments made by managing partner Andrew Leaitherland, a big merger is still very much on the cards.

Mergers are already part of DWF's DNA. A tie-up with Ricksons in 2007 started the firm's current growth spurt. More recently the firm took over Newcastle's Crutes, Birmingham's Buller Jeffries, and Biggart Baillie, one of Scotland's largest firms, adding over 200 fee-earners in all. Revenue topped £100m for the first time in 2011/12. There have also been a ton of lateral hires recently (at least 20 in 2010/11 alone), though we're obliged to point out that the firm has seen partners leave as well as new ones arrive. The firm also currently carries a debt of around 10% of revenue. *"To be successful, a business has to take an entrepreneurial approach,"* training partner Carl Graham told us. *"But we are not a reckless business: we are not unnecessary risk-takers. We always weigh up the pros and cons."*

Insurance work makes up half of DWF's revenue. A big chunk is personal injury (PI) defence, which is DWF's most highly regarded practice – *Chambers UK* regards it as one of the very best in London, the North West, the North East and Yorkshire. There are a variety of insurance seats on offer and trainees can also spend time in real estate, corporate, banking and finance, private client, family, employment, and litigation. The six-seat system means trainees get a varied training contract and *"see a lot of areas of the business."*

Trainees praised graduate programme manager Kate Hasluck for her management of the training contract. *"Her involvement has really helped improve seat allocation and the rotation process."* What seats you can do depends on what office you're in. Manchester and Liverpool offer a broad spread, as does Leeds (although *"it's not as insurance-heavy as Manchester and Liverpool, but more focused on commercial practices"*). London offers seats in employment, family, commercial insurance, catastrophic PI, casualty, regulatory, real estate and corporate. Completing seats in more than one DWF office is not mandatory, but many trainees have done so and found the experience beneficial.

Bumps, bangs and blazes

There's barely any area of insurance that DWF doesn't specialise in. All our interviewees had done at least one seat in this area and they told us *"trainees nearly always end up doing an insurance seat of some sort."* The most common seats in the area are occupational health, catastrophic PI, commercial insurance, fraud, and motor insurance (RTAs). All the work is defendant-side and cases involve simultaneously acting for the insured party

Chambers UK rankings

Administrative & Public Law	Intellectual Property
Banking & Finance	Licensing
Banking Litigation	Local Government
Charities	Parliamentary & Public Affairs
Civil Liberties & Human Rights	Partnership
Competition/European Law	Pensions
Construction	Personal Injury
Consumer Finance	Planning
Corporate/M&A	Police Law
Dispute Resolution	Private Client
Education	Product Liability
Employment	Professional Negligence
Energy & Natural Resources	Projects
Environment	Real Estate
Family/Matrimonial	Real Estate Litigation
Health & Safety	Restructuring/Insolvency
Information Technology	Retail
Insurance	Tax
	Transport

and the insurer. "*For example, if someone has a slip in the workplace and brings a claim against their employer, that employer will look to their insurer, who then might bring us in to make a subrogated claim to recoup expenses from another party.*" Insurers RSA, Aviva, Ageas and MIB are all big clients.

Occupation health trainees deal with workplace disease and accidents at work, including claims over deafness, asbestos-related diseases and syndromes like vibration white finger and RSI. A more unusual case saw DWF defending a £1m claim against the University of Birmingham over exposure to asbestos during an undergraduate course experiment in 1974. "*Many claims have merit and it's a case of getting the best deal for the insurer, who will ultimately have to pay out, but some claims can seem ridiculous,*" one source commented. "*You are expected to do a certain amount of admin, like preparing files and bundles, but it's not a huge amount and you also draft witness statements, make applications to court, go to meetings with counsel and attend hearings.*"

"*I have been surprised how high-value some of the claims are – some are worth millions of pounds,*" a catastrophic PI trainee told us. "*The main ones I have worked on are severe road traffic accidents and brain injury cases.*" The firm has also advised insurers on claims related to the defective French PIP breast implants and recently helped the Brighton & Hove Bus Company bring contempt of court proceedings against three witnesses to an (alleged)

RTA which saw claimants walk away with £1.5m in damages. "*The size and complexity of the claims mean a trainee can't walk straight into a case and deal directly with the other side. You are given tasks on other people's files: contacting medical experts, preparing for settlement meetings and doing case law research.*" Trainees also get to play detective, reviewing surveillance footage to see if what claimants have said about their injuries and disabilities is really true. Trainees also said the work is "*intellectually quite challenging, as there is a lot of medical terminology and complex liability legislation flying around.*"

The commercial insurance team works on business-related insurance squabbles over things like fires in pubs and floods caused by leaky fire hydrants. "*We step into the shoes of the insured and go after who they think is to blame. Then we file a recovery action,*" one trainee explained.

AIM higher

DWF's non-insurance work may seem run-of-the-mill compared to its more highly regarded insurance practice. But the commercial areas of the firm are on the up: DWF's real estate, corporate, banking and restructuring practices all rose in *Chambers UK*'s 2012 North West rankings. Aside from insurance, "*most people also complete a seat in real estate as it's so busy.*" The firm recently advised aeronautics preservation group Avro Heritage on its acquisition of Woodford Aerodrome, near Manchester, from BAE Systems. Other clients include lenders such as the Co-op Bank and Santander, and property owners including Liverpool John Moores University and car park giant Q-Park. House builder Persimmon Homes is another major client. "*I had a few files of my own to run which were residential plot sales in an apartment block in Leeds,*" one trainee told us, "*I took the instruction from the client, completed the transaction and dealt with the moneys; then I was involved with post-completion tasks.*" "*I have been to various meetings with clients and on site visits,*" another source added. "*Day-to-day pieces of work include doing the first drafts of leases, reporting on leases that we have completed, investigating title on pieces of land, preparing Land Registry forms and reviewing leases.*"

In 2011, the corporate department worked on 104 deals with a combined value of over £2.2bn. It counsels a host of AIM-listed companies; for example, helping online conveyancing firm In-Deed with its £10m AIM flotation and Welsh AIM-listed agricultural supplier Wynnstay with its £5m buyout of Shropshire's Wrekin Grain. For trainees, AIM flotations involve "*drafting board meetings and ancillary documents, putting together shareholder resolutions, verification and drafting share purchase agreements.*" Some work can be "*more adminny*" but trainees felt they "*really get involved and are valued as a vital cog in the machine,"* and *"get to meet clients and liaise with them directly."*

The are various litigation seat options include the mysterious-sounding 'insured contracts litigation' which involves work for clients who have taken out legal insurance. So, if they need legal advice they turn to their insurer who turns to DWF. Cases range from debt recovery and breach of contract to IP and property claims. *"All trainees get their own caseload because some of the claims – like debt recovery – are quite straightforward."* Other commercial litigation seats are not terribly common and most trainees fulfil their contentious requirement in an insurance team.

Friday fridge

The larger offices – Liverpool, Leeds and Manchester – *"are all kitted out the same"* with facilities in the same places. And – as one trainee put it rather gushingly – *"the open-plan layout fits with the open spirit and culture that we have."* People *"dress smartly"* but everyone talks to each other informally and on an equal footing. *"One of our core values is 'community'. Our founding partner Jim Davies always stresses his motto: 'Keep the focus on the fun'."* Our interviewees did want us to stress they do work a lot as well. *"In corporate, I got in at 8.30am and on a normal day I would stay until 6.30pm. Sometimes when a deal was completing I would come in at 7am and leave at midnight for three days running,"* said one. Real estate and family are also pretty busy, whereas *"in occupational health it's 8.30am to 6pm and you don't often stay much later than that."* It's a similar story in the other insurance seats, although trainees sometimes stay late if they *"want to finish off little tasks."*

Every office has a monthly 'Friday fridge' – *"free drinks in the canteen after work."* The list of other events is exhaustingly long: networking drinks, days at the races, dinners, shows, bowling, charity events, nights out, meals, team holidays. Liverpool and Manchester lawyers often *"decant"* to the pub after hours: popular watering holes are The Old Grapes and The Alchemist in Manchester and the Cross Keys in Liverpool. Every six months there's a *"quiz with all the current trainees and future joiners so we can to get to know each other."* There are also netball and football teams and rounders and cricket in the summer. *"Socially all the trainees keep in touch. We travel to the other offices for trainee events and we have added each other on Facebook."*

A popular cross-office social is the twice-yearly trainee dinner, held in the Manchester office. *"It's a three-course meal and we are joined by several partners and by Andrew Leaitherland, who will spend three hours giving us a talk on how the firm is doing and answering questions. We can also ask him about problems or areas of improvement. He will then delegate a group of trainees to look into the issues and they report back at the next trainee dinner. The points being raised are often fairly minor, but it is helpful to have that system in place."*

Trainees said they hear a lot from the firm about its plans and goals and enjoy working somewhere which is *"very ambitious where people genuinely want to push the firm forwards."* Perhaps the best thing about DWF's growth is that it has allowed the firm to post stellar retention rates in the past few years. Between 2009 and 2011 just two trainees out of 51 did not remain with the firm on qualification. Sixteen of 20 were kept on in 2012.

And finally...
DWF is one of those firms that likes to ask odd questions at interview. Look up the 'How to get into' bonus feature on our website for more details...

EDWARDS WILDMAN

TRAINEE OPPORTUNITIES IN LONDON

"Being one of a small intake of just eight trainees each year means a high level of exposure, not only to quality work and tailored training but to lawyers from all levels within the firm and the learning experiences that come with that."

JOANNE ELIELI, 2ND YEAR TRAINEE

BOSTON
CHICAGO
FT LAUDERDALE
HARTFORD
LONDON
LOS ANGELES
MADISON NJ
NEW YORK
NEWPORT BEACH
PROVIDENCE
STAMFORD
TOKYO
WASHINGTON DC
WEST PALM BEACH
HONG KONG*
*ASSOCIATED OFFICE

WINNER LC-N
AWARDS 2010
BEST WORK PLACEMENT SCHEME
CITY FIRM

Lex 100 Winner

Apply online for open days, summer placements and training contracts at: trainee.**edwards**wildman.com

Closing date for 2013 summer placement applications: **31 January 2013**
Closing date for 2015 training contract applications: **31 July 2013**

edwardswildman.com

Edwards Wildman Palmer UK LLP

The facts

Location: London

Number of UK partners/solicitors: 30/37

Partners who trained at firm: 16%

Total number of trainees: 15

Seats: 4x6 months

Alternative seats: Secondments

Extras: Pro bono – LawWorks, RCJ CAB, Fair Trials International

On chambersstudent.co.uk...
- How to get into EWP
- Pro bono at the firm

"*Ambition and hunger*" are the watchwords of this London office of a US firm that's seemingly never too far from a merger.

No dodgy ties

It takes concentration to keep up to speed with where this firm is at. Until 1 October 2011, it was Edwards Angell Palmer & Dodge – the result of a 2005 US union between Rhode Island's Edwards Angell and Boston-based Palmer & Dodge. This firm jumped the pond in 2008 following a tie-up with London insurance expert Kendall Freeman, creating its only European base. Bringing us up to date is the 2011 combination with Chicago-born Wildman, Harrold, Allen & Dixon. Why did they settle on the name Edwards Wildman Palmer for the new firm when they had the (we think) more awesome option of something like Angell Wildman & Dodge? No idea.

The new firm has 12 US offices, in addition to a Tokyo outpost and an associated office in Hong Kong. In the USA, Wildman Harrold brought expertise in litigation to complement Edwards Angell's insurance, corporate and IP strengths. The London office, meanwhile, is reaching the culmination of a two-year plan to come into line with the US practice groups. Trainee recruitment manager Sarah Warnes filled us in: "*It made sense to offer the same range of services to clients on both sides of the Atlantic – it's now about building those practices with key expertise.*"

A combination of key partner hires and increased instructions has seen EWP London report a dramatic hike in turnover – from £12.6m in 2009 to £25m in 2011. The focus on insurance work has been diluted – this area is now part of a four-way split with commercial litigation, corporate and IP. Trainees are happy with the progress that has been made. "*Instead of being large and content with broad practices, it has ambitions to specialise – it's an exciting place to be.*"

Despite the changes, EWP is still rooted in contentious work: the "*vast majority*" of trainees still spend six months in both insurance and commercial litigation. First seats are allocated according to stated prior interests and experience; following this, trainees meet with the HR team to discuss each subsequent move. There's always dialogue, but trainees feel allocation "*isn't that transparent. Some people have always got what they wanted, but some have never got their first choice.*" The bottom line is flexibility, Sarah Warnes says. "*We try to take people's desires into consideration, but there's always a bigger picture.*" Officially, seats are offered in insurance, commercial litigation, business law, employment, insolvency/restructuring, IP and competition, in addition to client secondments.

Brand of brothers

Insurance cases are academically complex and can "*rumble on for years.*" Trainees enjoy their time here, although their level of engagement is reliant on "*luck – depending on where the case is at, some people will get good work and the chance to shine; others won't.*" The group continues to work on disputes stemming from Hurricane Katrina, and is representing Munich Re, Centre Re and Swiss Re in their role as reinsurers of T&N's cross-border asbestos liability policy (T&N was a manufacturing company which went bust in 2001 – compensation claims from victims of its asbestos pollution are still being processed). The epic nature of disputes means client contact is unlikely and there's always bundling and admin, though "*this in itself is good experience as you realise someone always has to take responsibility for every part of the case.*" There is more than document management to

Chambers UK rankings

Dispute Resolution	Intellectual Property
Insurance	Public International Law

the seat, with opportunities to write research notes for partners and draft correspondence, and the complexity of claims is always interesting.

The commercial litigation team is *"fast-paced and full of colourful characters"* – great if, like many of our sources, you run on adrenalin and thrive on unpredictability. Trainees often encounter work for industrial and financial clients, and the team is also handling matters for the governments of Nigeria and the Turks and Caicos Islands. Partners with different specialisms *"often seek out the trainee in the department as a resource,"* so work is *"extremely diverse."* Disputes could come from *"anywhere in the world"* – one trainee worked on *"asset recoveries in the Caribbean,"* another on *"a trial to do with money laundering for a Zimbabwean client."* Variety is the order of the day: *"You might come in one morning and find there's been a dawn raid, so we have to go and oversee it to make sure the police are only taking what they're warranted to take from our client."* If hours are unpredictable, be assured that *"a late night means everyone's in the office, so it always feels like we're in it together."* The growing corporate department is another seat where *"trainees are shared by partners,"* and so they gain access to M&A, private equity, banking, capital markets, life sciences and telecommunications work. The level of responsibility *"totally depends on the client you're working for"* – these include Citi, Santander and venture capital firms MVC and Battery Ventures.

The expanding IP group is where a lot of trainees want to be. *"People think of trade mark and patent when they think of IP,"* said one, *"but I get a lot of crossover litigation and commercial licensing too."* The team acts for Warner Bros. and Elizabeth Arden, in addition to many more famous names. *"It helps when it's household names,"* thought one source. *"You're surrounded by these brands all your life then suddenly you're protecting them."* There's the potential for *"smaller discrete tasks to take ownership of,"* in addition to working on EWP's anticounterfeiting programme – where the IP trainee is first point of contact with customs authorities.

The majority of EWP trainees will spend six months with a client. Sources were unanimous that *"all the clichés are true – there's more autonomy and you'll work on high-level matters that your supervisor will just sign off."* Working in-house is necessary development for trainees used to the academic nature of insurance law. *"You realise that you're only one part of what the client's trying to achieve, and most of the time you're just standing in their way."*

The touchy-feely approach

Legacy firm Kendall Freeman had a *"personable, small-firm"* ethos. Has becoming part of a 650-lawyer network changed this? Trainees think *"lines of communication are good"* between offices, though day-to-day there is *"very little interaction with the States."* Overall, EWP seems *"keen to maintain its roots as a UK firm."* Said one source: *"If you walk around the office at 7.30pm it will probably be pretty quiet – we're not doing Debevoise hours yet."* Not overly corporate, an *"old-school"* culture persists. Partners *"aren't touchy-feely,"* and vary in how much they let trainees off the leash. *"It's often better to sit with supervisors who remember what it's like being a trainee,"* thought one. *"Some of the tasks they set take far longer than they remember."* Another hangover from the firm's days as a small insurance practice is the lack of women. Trainee intakes are generally 50% female, dropping to 39% at associate level, but there are no female partners currently in the London office. *"It's not a macho culture, so it's puzzling as to why there aren't more women,"* thought one source, *"but whatever the reason, it doesn't look great from our end."* The firm says it recognises the issue and is working on it.

The firm's social scene remains *"vibrant,"* with a committee that aids the organisation of office-wide events. Between trainees, socialising is *"fantastically impromptu – as simple as an e-mail saying: 'drink tonight?'"* Furthermore, there exists an *"actual ethos of doing pro bono rather than just ticking it off."* Trainees are given the opportunity to work with Fair Trial International and LawWorks on their own projects.

Some partners still have their own offices, but most people share. *"You pick up so much from listening, from their tone on phone calls to their thought process on strategy."* Occupying floors nine to eleven of Dashwood House near Liverpool Street station, there is some competition for views: *"One side gets oddly nice sunsets, the other gets brilliant views of the Gherkin and Heron Tower."*

And finally...
Edwards Wildman Palmer retained five out of eight qualifiers in 2012.

Eversheds LLP

The facts

Location: Birmingham, Cambridge, Cardiff, Leeds, London, Manchester, Newcastle, Nottingham, Ipswich, Scotland

Number of UK partners/solicitors: 296/1129

Total number of trainees: 60

Seats: 4x6 months (occasional split seats)

Alternative seats: Overseas seats, secondments

Extras: Langauge classes

On chambersstudent.co.uk...

- How to get into Eversheds
- Around the offices
- International seats

Eversheds is still a relatively youthful firm, though you'd never guess given its sheer size and global ambitions.

20:20 vision

Eversheds started life only 22 years ago, with a four-way merger between firms in Norwich, Manchester, Sheffield and Birmingham. It grew rapidly and added offices all over the country, including London, and abroad. Between 2008 and 2011, it opened a whopping ten overseas locations. Now the focus is on integration. When we interviewed trainees this year, management was touring the offices giving presentations on its relaunched strategy, entitled 'Eversheds' 2020 Vision'. *"The headline news is one international firm, one brand,"* one trainee summed up. *"We're living in a legal world that's becoming very international, and we're pushing hard on the international pedal."* The firm has over 40 offices around the world and employs well over 1,000 lawyers here in the UK. Check out Eversheds' gazillions of rankings across our global directories to see the huge range of work it does.

This *"big international push"* has clear implications for trainees, around three-quarters of whom are based outside of London. Most obviously, the number of overseas seats on offer is increasing. And, *"I cannot stress enough how important languages are,"* a trainee volunteered. This is a bit of an overstatement as much of the work trainees get involved in is Eversheds' British (and often regional) bread and butter. But the international focus is throwing up opportunities like helping partners with business development in new markets: *"People don't care what level you are if you speak the language – they rope you in."*

Not only have these recent office openings had an impact for those lucky enough to bag one of the international seats on offer, but also trainees around the UK and not just London reported an increase in their international work too. For example, a Nottingham source, like others we spoke to elsewhere, *"went back and forth on the phone between a lot of international offices"* during their corporate seat. Trainees have always told us that they joined Eversheds to do London-quality work *"without having to sniff someone's armpit on the Tube."* This year, they also emphasised international work as a major draw. *"Europe will be stagnant for the next few years,"* one trainee surmised, *"so management wants to find new markets. They're trying to unite all offices as one. It may be of interest to future trainees that the plan is to turn the network of offices into one firm, and encourage cross-pollination between offices. Some future applicants might view this as exciting, others as a hindrance."*

In other words, don't come here if you want to join a sleepy provincial office and work nine to five. Do come here if you want to work hard on big, increasingly cross-border matters. We nearly choked on our morning lattes when one trainee in a regional office suggested doing their interview with us at 7.30am on a Monday morning! Hours vary with department and office, but *"8.30am to 6 or 6.30pm"* is a rule of thumb, *"with peaks and troughs"* in corporate and litigation. Another earlybird who claimed never to be in later than 7.45am said: *"If I didn't have so much work to do, I wouldn't necessarily come in so early."* In commercial, *"you could be regularly working into the early hours,"* whereas real estate *"tends to be far more regular."*

Trainees complete four six-month seats. Until recently, they were allocated their first seat. Now they can indicate preferences, as with all subsequent seats. *"You get sent a list of all vacancies at all offices, plus secondments.*

Chambers UK rankings

Administrative & Public Law	Licensing
Banking & Finance	Local Government
Banking Litigation	Media & Entertainment
Capital Markets	Outsourcing
Competition/European Law	Parliamentary & Public
Construction	Affairs
Consumer Finance	Pensions
Corporate Crime &	Pensions Litigation
Investigations	Planning
Corporate/M&A	Product Liability
Data Protection	Professional Discipline
Dispute Resolution	Professional Negligence
Education	Projects
Employee Share Schemes	Public International Law
& Incentives	Public Procurement
Employment	Real Estate
Energy & Natural Resources	Real Estate Finance
Environment	Real Estate Litigation
Financial Services	Restructuring/Insolvency
Health & Safety	Retail
Healthcare	Shipping
Information Technology	Social Housing
Insurance	Tax
Intellectual Property	Telecommunications
Investment Funds	Transport

You're asked if there's a seat you'd particularly like. The HR team look at it and allocate. There's no guarantee you'll get what you want, though they have been good at saying 'you didn't get it last time, that puts you ahead for next time'." You can apply for a vacancy at any office, and may be offered one in another office if your preference isn't available at your 'home' one. For example, "*the commercial department in London is really popular, but it's unlikely everyone will get a seat here during their training contract.*" Eversheds' core practice areas are company commercial, litigation/dispute resolution, human resources, and real estate. Within these there's a range of seat options. Supervisors are typically associates with over four years' PQE.

Currently, there are four overseas seats in Paris, two in Hong Kong and one in Shanghai. The Hong Kong office only opened in 2009, and we wouldn't be surprised if more overseas options cropped up in the coming years. We also heard of trainees with relevant interest and experience asking to spend time in Sweden, Germany and Abu Dhabi, and being granted permission. See our website for more info.

Olympic feats

One (very) high-profile recent real estate assignment was advising on the construction of The Shard. Other recent work has included acquisitions for an investor buying shopping centres, and advising the Olympic Park Legacy Company throughout West Ham and Tottenham FC's much-publicised tussle for the Olympic stadium. Day to day, sources reported "*drafting, dealing with the client alone on smaller matters*" and being "*in constant touch with surveyors as part of a transaction.*" Unlike some other seats where trainees tend to be more "*reactive*" to specific work requests, "*here I got to see whole files.*" Another said: "*You can ask any questions no matter how silly. My supervisor was great in saying 'I'll talk to so-and-so to see if I can get you this type of work'.*" A trainee in a regional office said: "*Clients were all London-based, or registered in the Channel Islands.*"

Corporate work is more often multi-jurisdictional in nature. A Leeds source said the work is "*predominantly medium-sized acquisitions and disposals. Also public company takeovers. For me it was 50/50 international/UK assignments.*" For example, lawyers across several countries including China, France and the USA acted for Fortune 500 manufacturing firm SPX when it acquired ClydeUnion Pumps. The deal included merger filings in various jurisdictions, including China. On big assignments like this, trainees often "*help project manage the other offices.*" Other tasks include "*basic document drafting and client care stuff, drafting ancillary documents, managing data rooms, doing the board minutes.*" Once a transaction completes the work is far from over: "*Bibles have to be produced, post-completion documents. Original documents have to be sent out. Responsibility is gradually landed on you.*"

The popular commercial seat is "*really general.*" Eversheds also does quite a bit of work for public sector clients. Commercial projects include PFI assignments in the housing, elderly care and education sectors, like Building Schools for the Future (scrapped by the coalition government but still providing lawyers with work). The contracts can run for decades. "*I was involved in a completion: document preparation, liaising with the bank's lawyers.*" Other tasks include "*taking minutes at meetings, reviewing contracts for due diligence reports, drafting contracts, attending seminars and preparing slides.*"

Of commercial dispute resolution (CDR), a London trainee exclaimed: "*God! What didn't I do?*" As a "*paper-heavy department,*" expect plenty of bundling, preparing for trial, but also attending court and helping with seminars. Trainees take on "*all the disclosure, e-disclosure, privilege, and redacting confidential info.*" The team deals with "*huge international clients, especially in arbitration.*" Our sources liked the seat because "*no dispute is like another*" and "*you get to find out a lot about your client's business.*" Clients range from banks to airports to high net worth individuals. The work includes "*simple debt recovery work, and general contractual disputes. I also did some regulatory work for Ofgem and the National Grid.*" Financial services dispute resolution right now involves a lot of "*professional negligence work for high-street banks, still dealing with the fallout from 2008,*" and is one source of opportunities for trainees to visit court.

Employment is another: "*They took me to tribunals and hearings even if I was only the note taker.*" However, a note of caution about this popular seat: "*I enjoyed it so much at law school, but didn't find the practice of it captivated my interest as much as other departments. The employment field is so technical, governed by statute and case law, so the client wants a real specialist who knows the ins and outs.*" Similarly, in restructuring "*sometimes I found myself in court twice a week. The work's really varied – one minute head down in books, the next doing property sales. It's very key you can work quickly and accurately in this seat as things come in quickly. It's great for improving attention to detail.*"

Banking across the board at Eversheds is "*incredibly busy. A lot of my time was something of a project management exercise. As a trainee you get quite involved. There's time pressure, quite a buzz.*" When hours are long, "*there's a team spirit so you're never alone.*" Other smaller seat options include tax, construction litigation, pensions and competition.

Hard-working, not hard-nosed

Eversheds made a lot of redundancies back in the dark days of 2008-10. Combining this background with the "*international push*" of the past few years, we wondered what, if anything, is changing about Eversheds' culture? "*I haven't seen a dramatic amount of cultural change,*" said a final-seater. "*It was a dynamic culture when I joined and still is. The firm moves with the times.*" It has become "*a bit more corporate,*" another thought; one example is the recent reconfiguration of job titles, which included dispensing with the 'solicitor' name, perhaps making them more readily understandable to US and other international clients, some thought. "*The culture is fairly relaxed. There is a business edge. At the end of the day we exist in an incredibly competitive legal world. A lot*

of the time the client will shop for the cheapest quote. We have to be extremely efficient. It does vary by department – in tax there's less focus on that, whereas in banking fees are squeezed a lot.*" Another said: "*I don't think it's hard-nosed. It's generally a friendly place to work. But because it's such a big firm, things are done a certain way across the offices. Everyone's quite ambitious, takes work seriously, but is friendly.*" Some thought that "*centralised functions – like HR, finance – could be more streamlined, more efficient.*"

There's certainly a "*stringent focus on costs,*" and trainees wanting to host even small-scale socials like networking drinks with local young professionals have to "*justify the business case*" of doing so, and apply for money from a relevant budget. Social activities tend to be department-based, like Thursday after-work drinks. The summer and Christmas parties are office-based. Each department has its own firmwide conference, incorporating all the UK offices and overseas if possible. "*We go to lunch together, but not always drinks after work,*" trainees repeatedly told us. See our website for info about Eversheds' main offices in England and Wales, and their favourite nearby watering holes.

Eversheds has a social club which trainees can join for £2 a month – the firm will chip in half the cost of events, which have included Champagne-tasting in Leeds, and a Brum office trip to the darts in Wolverhampton where the inevitable highlight was Phil 'The Power' Taylor. There have also been golf lessons followed by a tournament, and excursions to the theatre, musicals, snooker, and even the British Grand Prix.

Looking ahead to the next few years, anyone with language skills should draw attention to them in their application to Eversheds (a process which interviewees praised for its simplicity and friendliness, incidentally). Many trainees have international experience of some kind, even if it's just travelling. Also, "*I have noticed that we have fewer and fewer trainees coming straight from law school,*" one observed. Another qualified: "*Quite a few have done things before joining, but aren't necessarily much older.*" One who had worked for a while before converting to law said: "*It's difficult to say whether the experience counted. Eversheds recruits according to a competency-based model. It's looking for certain skills. I was able to give concrete examples of them.*"

And finally...
Eversheds' friendly culture, alongside its concerted international push, makes the firm an attractive option for like-minded applicants who want to go that extra mile. It retained 65 of 76 qualifiers in 2012.

Farrer & Co LLP

The facts

Location: London
Number of UK partners/solicitors: 77/136
Partners who trained at firm: 57%
Total number of trainees: 20
Seats: 6x4 months
Alternative seats: None
Extras: Language classes

On chambersstudent.co.uk...
- How to get into Farrer
- A brief history of the firm

A rich history and glamorous client base make training at this 300-year-old institution an "*exciting, challenging and diverse experience.*"

English heritage

Farrer & Co has advised the great and the good since 1701 – highlights include suing playwright Richard Brinsley Sheridan, settling a marital dispute which culminated in pistols at dawn and, in 1856, accepting Charles Dickens as a client. Traditionally, its lawyers were 'men of affairs' – primed to handle all aspects of a client's personal and business life. Today, with a thriving commercial base, the firm's steady growth can be attributed to keeping the link with its past very much alive. *Chambers UK* ranks Farrer as a market leader for private client, family and agriculture, but also recognises it for corporate, sports law, IP and several other areas.

"*The commercial and private client sides work very well together. Often you get 'private client firms' or 'commercial corporate firms', but we're relatively unusual in that we maintain a very good and healthy mix of both,*" trainee recruitment partner Jonathan Eley told us. "*Turnover was £46.6m in 2011 and we're aiming for well over £50m for 2012,*" says Eley. "*The way we achieve this is not by bolt-ons or huge numbers of lateral hires, but through steady growth in good times and bad.*"

Night at the museum

Farrer's wealth of practices means trainees complete six seats, selecting at least one option from each of the firm's four blocks (private client, litigation, property and commercial) then returning to the seat of qualification for their last. "*This system swung it for me,*" said one trainee, "*as I thought it would give me a far better grounding in*

law. Spending eight months in your area of qualification is a real benefit."

Private client work is split into 'onshore' and 'international' seats, while tax and charities are also part of this block. Her Majesty the Queen is the firm's most famous private client, but a mix of landed gentry, politicians, media personalities and international businesspeople instruct the team as well. New starters shouldn't expect to be hobnobbing with Her Maj, or getting much face time with any of the rich and famous for that matter, although they will be trusted with a "*daunting level*" of client contact via e-mail. Explained one: "*Clients expect a lot of you and you constantly have to manage expectations. It's the very top end of Farrer's work, and you just get so much more responsibility and exposure to situations than you would at other firms.*" Tasks are varied – from "*discrete research to doing the probate run and getting copies of wills,*" and trainees might need to rush off to a deceased's house or arrange a funeral. The department recently managed the £15m estate, investments and assets of an elderly lady who had lost her mental capacity.

Trainees are attracted to the charities seat "*for the philanthropic element, but the actual law is incredibly interesting too.*" Top-ranked by *Chambers UK*, the group acts for Age UK, Save the Children, Royal British Legion, many national museums (the V&A, Science Museum, Imperial War Museum), BAFTA, Oxford University, Westminster School and Eton College. It is advising the National Gallery on the digitisation of its collection for the Google Art Project. "*The partners know amazing amounts about how corporate and charity law intersect – they are all at*

Chambers UK rankings

Agriculture & Rural Affairs	Fraud
Charities	Intellectual Property
Corporate/M&A	Media & Entertainment
Defamation/Reputation Management	Partnership
Dispute Resolution	Private Client
Education	Real Estate
Employment	Real Estate Finance
Family/Matrimonial	Sports Law

the top of their game, and the work that comes to trainees is esoteric and interesting – less admin than points of law and notes of advice."

What's black and white and read all over?

Fancy being paid to read *Heat* magazine? Farrer's media defamation practice, which specialises in acting for newspapers and publishers, is second-to-none. Trainees in the media and disputes seat handle a lot of pre-publication work for media groups, "*checking magazines to make sure articles aren't libellous or an invasion of privacy.*" There are "*interesting nuances*" to this type of work. "*Journalists want to be as salacious as possible while holding onto the truth. It's brilliant and interesting, and as a lawyer you have to have faith in the fact that everyone deserves legal defence, and that things are never black and white.*" The firm has carved a reputation in the growing super-injunction business, working on behalf of *The Sun* beating off injunction attempts from John Terry and Gordon Ramsay's father-in-law Chris Hutcheson. Farrer had a long relationship with News Group but this ended in the wake of 2011's hacking revelations. As meddlesome hacks ourselves, we were hoping to hear about trainees' experiences "*at the eye of the News Corp storm*" but they weren't giving much away. Jonathan Eley says: "*We confirm that towards the end of 2011 we decided to cease acting for News Group. We wish the company well in the future. The reasons for the firm deciding to no longer act for News Group are confidential to the company and ourselves.*" The department has "*refocused and realigned itself*" following the exit of the Murdoch empire, with a greater focus on high-end reputation management work and its big remaining clients such as Bauer and Emap expected to fill the gap. The other contentious seat is family. Farrer acted for Katrin Radmacher in *Radmacher v Granatino*, one of the most important divorce cases in recent years, and most matters in this seat will have a lot of money at stake.

Trainees don't typically come to Farrer for its corporate work, but enjoy the mid-market size of the deals and the feel of the department. "*You'll get a whole range of work and you're told to keep an open mind. Partners make an effort to delegate good work down, which is always important as a trainee.*" Trainees get work from different partners, while their supervisor acts as "*work monitor.*" While "*everyone does the big M&A work,*" the department is particularly known for public company offerings and takeovers, private equity and working with entrepreneurs on investments. Clients include private individuals, healthcare services, mining companies and media groups. The group recently acted for Mantle Diamonds in a $25m venture capital fund-raising and a subsequent takeover of the owner of a derelict Botswana diamond mine.

Other commercial seats include employment, IP and banking/financial services. "*I'm a massive geek, and IP didn't disappoint,*" one trainee beamed. "*The precision involved is sort of like being back at university – there's a lot of drafting e-mails of advice on very specific areas of trade mark legislation and copyright.*" Farrer's IP group receives instruction from many of its charities clients, in addition to publishing clients like the *TES*, *The Economist* and medical publishers *BMJ*. The team is counselling The British Library on its digitisation project and the Design and Artists Copyright Society on issues related to the extension of the Artist's Resale Right.

Trainees can choose between a seat in commercial property or estates and private property. Clients of the group include the Duchy of Cornwall, Great Portland Estates, the Joseph Rowntree Housing Trust and London Underground. Trainees enjoy being allowed to manage their own files. "*It's nice to get the end of a matter and feel like you'd done it all. I worked on a conveyance from start to finish, doing all the searches, liaising with clients and looking for restrictions on property.*"

Coal or Tweedy?

"*There are lots of official measures in place to make sure we're okay,*" explained one trainee: "*We each have a supervisor and a recently qualified solicitor as mentors, each intake has a training principal, and there's another principal who's a senior partner. As they're more remote, they're a good sounding board – if something troubles you, they'll take you out for lunch and tell you not to be ridiculous.*" Moreover, sources speak of Farrer's "*collective communal culture. It's genuine – people like spending time with each other, and they're very open about this ethos.*" Farrer, said one source, is "*basically a college, although not in a stuffy, Oxbridge way.*"

And here we come to the nub of the matter, as 'stuffy' and 'Oxbridge' are two words often pinned on this firm. Perhaps it's unavoidable when you act for so many members of the Establishment. Trainees admitted that "*the private client department retains partners who would adhere* to the Farrer stereotypes" but said: "*They are in the minority. Other teams vary due to size, and there are younger associates coming through who are not like that.*" The perceived requirement of "*having to own a horse to get in here is not at all true.*" Farrer recruits from a variety of universities, and rotates through the careers fairs of Manchester, Birmingham, Bristol, Warwick and London universities in addition to Oxbridge. It recently signed up to charity initiative IntoUniversity and offers a week's work experience for young people from disadvantaged backgrounds. If the firm is not stuffy, then "*it's traditional – but I enjoy those traditions,*" said one source. "*We have history and specialist knowledge and a beautiful old building in Lincoln's Inn – these things mean an awful lot to the type of clients we have.*"

Hours are "*less aggressive*" here than in the City, with 9am to 6.30pm being about average for trainees. "*The ethos is to work very hard in the day and then go home.*" Teams "*are very good at taking trainees for lunch,*" and there's a "*real culture of a Friday drink*" at Ye Olde White Horse on St Clement's Lane. Recent networking events have included a talk at the National Gallery and a 'Dickens and Farrer' conference at the firm's offices. "*To an extent we're handing out name tags and taking coats, but after that we're allowed to mingle: the firm trusts trainees to be good ambassadors.*" The social calendar climaxes with the trainee revue at the firm's Christmas party, which this year took the form of a *Grease* medley. "*The senior partner looks through it to make sure there's nothing too defamatory. It's a real mark of the firm – people absolutely love it, so you've got to partake in the madness. Partners really do give you credit if it's good and it raises your profile as a trainee.*"

Jonathan Eley says: "*We look for engaging personalities, people who have other interests and are not one-dimensional, and those who take the same balanced approach to work and life that we do, but who throw themselves into and enjoy work.*" This is a firm where partners and clients often have quite close personal relationships and so good social skills are perhaps even more vital here than elsewhere. Trainees here tend to have "*interesting*" backgrounds – we understand there are a number of second-careerers among the current group of trainees, from professions as diverse as teaching, agenting and physiotherapy. We found it interesting that several of our sources hadn't applied anywhere else, deciding that it was "*Farrer or bust.*" It's that type of firm, with that type of trainee, and that should speak volumes. If you'd be prepared to train anywhere, then look elsewhere.

And finally...

"*The retention rates are testament to the firm's attitude towards trainees – they've invested a lot in us and they want to keep us all on.*" In 2012, all ten second-years were lucky enough to be retained on qualification.

Fisher Meredith LLP

The facts

Location: London

Number of UK partners/solicitors: 14/43

Total number of trainees: 11

Seats: 4x6 months

Alternative seats: None

Extras: Language classes

On chambersstudent.co.uk...
- How to get into Fisher Meredith
- More on the firm's work

Legal aid cuts are forcing Fisher Meredith to reconsider its priorities, but if human rights work is your thing don't leave this fascinating firm off your list.

Taking the bait

Fisher Meredith has a long and proud legacy of legal aid work, having worked on some of the UK's most famous cases in its 37 years. It has represented suspects in the failed July 2005 bombing attempt, one of the youths acquitted of murdering Damilola Taylor, and the Yorkshire Ripper's better half, Mrs Sonia Sutcliffe.

D-day is looming, however, for legal aid. On 1 April 2013, the impact of the coalition government's £350m cuts in the area will become clear. It's not looking good – according to a parliamentary report, the Legal Aid (Sentencing and Punishment of Offenders) Act will lead to 500,000 fewer instances of legal help to individuals, and 45,000 fewer instances of legal representation.

For firms like Fisher Meredith, it's time to face some harsh realities. "*We have to live with the world as it is and not as we'd like it to be,*" sighs managing partner Stephen Hewitt. In the past, up to 60% of the firm's work was legally aided, but with the axing of both its criminal law team in 2008 and its publicly-funded immigration team in 2011, this has dwindled to 40%. "*We anticipate that within 18 months it will be less than that,*" Hewitt adds. Trainees tend to agree with Hewitt that this is a regrettable, but necessary, sacrifice. "*You can't stick your head in the sand,*" one source explained. "*Everyone is open about the fact that, in the current marketplace, if we want to keep doing legal aid work – and doing it well – we need to do private work as well.*"

This being the case, the firm is topping up its best-known practices – family, children, public law and human rights work – with all-private company and commercial, property, private client, immigration, civil and commercial litigation, and crime and regulatory teams. Areas like education, landlord and tenant, community care, and actions against police are also taking on more and more private work. If there's one thing FM is not, it's defeatist. "*We're receiving a number of inquiries about firms interested in us acquiring them or their teams,*" says Hewitt, "*and we hope to grow from a £7m to a £10m turnover firm in a couple of years. We want to be seen as a dynamic, expanding firm.*"

Big kids

The number of seats in each department varies, but in general, opportunities crop up in: police and prison law; housing; children; dispute resolution; immigration; and public services law (PSL). In the latter, trainees can focus on either community care and education issues, or on Court of Protection work. Trainees choose three preferences for each seat, usually returning to their favourite for the final stint, but it's testament to the firm's collaborative streak that, "*once we get the list of available seats, all the trainees sit down together and try to hatch a plan so that we're not in direct competition.*" As a result, "*it usually ends up working out. And everyone gets what they want for their final seats.*"

Children "*is probably the biggest department in the firm,*" and many trainees pass through its doors at some point. "*The bread and butter work is contacts and residence. For example, if a parent fears the other parent might abduct their child from the UK, we arrange orders to prohibit*

Chambers UK rankings

Civil Liberties & Human Rights	Immigration
Court of Protection	Police Law
Family/Matrimonial	Social Housing

that." As in all Fisher Meredith's departments, "there's not very much babysitting that goes on," and trainees should expect to run their own files from day one. "I was seeing clients, taking instructions, briefing barristers, and reading reports as evidence," said one. "Basically everything a solicitor would do." There's plenty of advocacy in the seat, and it's also the department where you're most likely to get to grips with multi-jurisdictional work.

Trainees also regularly pass through PSL. "It's an obscure title," they explain, but "it's kind of an amalgamation of education, community care and Court of Protection work. Different supervisors specialise in different areas." Court of Protection involves "making decisions about what's in people's best interests" when they're unable to judge for themselves. "It can range from young people with severe learning disabilities up to clients in their 90s with severe dementia." Community care work is more about "helping clients get their needs met by social services." This covers a host of issues, like assisting with asylum requirements or helping young people leaving the prison service. "They deal with lots of emergency work in that department," one trainee explained. "You might get a call from someone at 4.45pm on a Friday, and end up making frantic calls to social services trying to help them." There's simply not enough space here to cover all of FM's fascinating seats, but check out our website for more info.

It's worth pointing out that life at FM is no emotional picnic. "You just have to get on with it, because the stakes are so high and they're relying on you. You have to put aside your emotions and be professional. It gives your work a meaning it might not otherwise have." Bear in mind that a healthy dose of maturity will stand you in good stead at FM – not just in terms of the subject matter, but the sheer amount of it. From day one you'll be expected to play a leading role in cases that'll directly impact people's lives. And, while there are regular external training sessions, FM trainees are the sort who are happy to "be thrown in the deep end and work things out for [themselves]."

Fortunately, we received excellent feedback about supervisors. "Everyone's very willing to help. Even more senior solicitors are willing to give time for advice, so you're never afraid to ask questions." Trainees tend to have left the office by 6pm, but are in for the odd later night.

Capital FM

Newbies to Fisher Meredith are genuinely taken aback by the devotion of fee earners to their causes. "In most workplaces, there are a few slackers here and there," they report, "but everyone here is just so committed. They really do care about their clients and go out of their way to get the best for them." Perhaps this is why there's such worry about things changing. "The new people being recruited to do more private work have a slightly different background and a more commercially-minded outlook to some people already here," mused one. While there were a few grumbles that the firm's legacy is being "obscured" by its latest bolt-ons, the general consensus is that it "feels like an addition rather than a replacement. Business and commercial work is necessary to keep afloat, and good management recognises that." Do be advised: "In relation to the commercial-legal aid division, come in with an open mind. If you're looking for either one or the other, this might not be the firm for you. Be very aware of the fact FM's moving towards a more commercial base but not neglecting legal aid entirely."

There's no fancy atrium for FM – it's based "above a Costcutter" in leafy Kennington – but there are plans afoot to move closer to the firm's new private sector clients. "We want to be closer to the hub of the London legal world," Hewitt reveals, "and are looking at potentially moving to a prestigious address that's more central." The firm's private-only Richmond-office is also looking at expanding, Hewitt says. "We're likely to have trainees there before too long."

A straight academic route into FM is "the exception rather than the rule," and current trainees range in age from their mid-20s to late-30s – mostly with some sort of human rights or caseload experience under their belts. "They're some of the smartest, most brilliant people I've ever met," one source buzzed. "Intimidatingly clever and really nice. You get to work with committed, fun, compassionate people." After submitting business plans, five of this 2012's eight qualifiers were kept on at the firm.

And finally...

Fisher Meredith is *"not the type of firm where you come to make a fortune,"* but trainees here were entirely happy with the choice they'd made.

Forbes

The facts

Location: Blackburn, Preston, Chorley, Accrington, Manchester, Leeds

Number of UK partners/solicitors: 36/68

Partners who trained at firm: 44.5%

Total number of trainees: 8

Seats: 4x6 months

Alternative seats: Secondments

Extras: Legal advice clinics in Blackburn, Preston, Chorley and Accrington

On chambersstudent.co.uk...
- How to get into Forbes
- Legal Aid

A chirpy bunch of Lancastrians (or those with an affiliation to the North West region) come to Forbes for both its commercial and criminal practices.

Mancunian candidates

This Blackburn-founded firm has seven offices in its homeland of Lancashire. An hour or so down the A-roads you'll find further Forbes dwellings in Manchester and Leeds. All nine offices are pretty well established, and Forbes has acquired an excellent reputation in the North West. *Chambers UK* ranks the crime department among the top five in the region. It's not all conspiracy, drugs and firearms though, as the firm is also ranked for dispute resolution, personal injury, real estate and social housing work.

As a buffer against cuts to legal aid funding, Forbes has been growing its commercial practice for a number of years. Clients range from national giants, including The Co-operative Bank and ASDA, to locals like the Lake District National Park Authority and Yorkshire Bank. According to trainees, *"football is a big thing at Forbes,"* and it's not just staff debating the merits of Blackburn Rovers over Burnley – the firm has actually represented both football clubs, as well as Liverpool and Manchester United.

Do trainees come to the firm to practise commercial law or have a crack at the renowned criminal practice? *"Trainees seem to be going down the commercial route rather than private client,"* was the general consensus. On the commercial side, the insurance practice was named as *"the big one,"* but *"nearly every year someone will qualify into private client as well."*

Juniors complete four seats of six months each. *"The training partners ask which seats we are interested in doing,"* one interviewee explained. *"They take note of your personality, and where they think we'll fit in. It's well thought through."* *"The advantage of having four trainees each year, and four seats, is that even if there is high demand for a seat, everyone should get a chance to do it."* Some trainees had picked up exactly the seats they asked for, although not all had been quite so lucky.

The available seats are: crime, family, personal injury, insurance, commercial property, employment, business law, commercial litigation, housing litigation, domestic conveyancing, and wills and probate. There are no compulsory destinations. *"It's quite varied: they can put you anywhere."*

Getting down to business

Business law has three core areas: corporate, commercial and IP, the latter of which includes pretty much everything from trade marks to IT-related work. The department recently represented Yorkshire Bank in financing the management buyout of local accountancy firm Douglass Grange. In business law, trainees see *"about five minutes of photocopying in six months. Day to day, it's variable. We might be doing IP, acquisitions, or commercial contracts. You get exposure to an awful lot."*

Insurance and personal injury are thought of as *"two sides of the same fence."* As one trainee explained, personal injury lawyers *"take the first step and file a claim,"* whereas in insurance, *"you defend against that claim."* Both practices are *"hot at the minute."* One interviewee praised the levels of responsibility: *"I had my own client in the first couple of weeks. They really throw you in, and now I have client contact every day."* Forbes acts for both defendants and claimants: the department recently represented Syndicate 2525 (insurer of the Football Association) against claims brought by the former Premier League footballer Dean Ashton, who

Chambers UK rankings

Crime	Social Housing
Dispute Resolution	

suffered a career-ending injury while on England duty. The firm also defended Fylde Borough Council against a claim brought by a gold medal Paralympian who suffered paralysis after falling off the toilet (Forbes unearthed surveillance footage of the claimant pushing his wheelchair through several inches of snow). The insurance team also offers secondments to major supermarkets.

And to the courts

"Those that come to do commercial law couldn't think of anything worse than doing crime," and it's certainly true that a different type of person thrives in these sort of seats – one who can deal with the more rough-and-ready characters who are to be found populating the cells and corridors of police stations. Trainees taking a crime seat spend a lot of time at cop shops and Magistrates' Courts. *"We do a bit of everything, including initial instructions after arrest, drafting defence statements, liaising with the Crown Prosecution Service and research on the nit-picky bits of law. We do everything but represent them at court."* The levels of responsibility are high, which means *"dealing with difficult clients. I'm never overwhelmed by it, though, as and I know I always have someone to back me up,"* one source explained. There is the option to take a seat known as 'crown court', *"which deals with longer and more difficult cases than you'll see in the standard crime seat"* – rapes, murders and the like – and is reserved for those who show a real interest in qualifying there.

Whether or not you complete a seat in crime, there is the opportunity to complete the Police Station Accreditation Course and become a police station representative – someone (not necessarily a qualified solicitor) who advises and assists detainees. *"People who have completed the course continue to use it when they're working in other seats. They spend time at the police station during evenings and weekends."*

Blackburn ravers

Trainees referred to Forbes as a *"family."* With nearly 400 staff in all, that's one long Christmas card list. Yet the kids repeatedly told us: *"Everyone is nice and welcoming. I can go and speak to anybody."* Trainees get a mentor and a seat supervisor. Among the current group there's a lot of banter, and we couldn't stop our sources telling their friends what they'd been saying to us (it's supposed to be confidential). *"We all identified who you'd spoken to last year and made fun of them,"* one declared.

In order for trainees to meet their Forbesian aunties, uncles and second cousins once removed, they are encouraged, although not forced, to take seats in other offices. *"They like you to get a feel for different practices, and to get to know people."* Additionally, not every department has a presence in every office – for example, the crime team is based in Chorley, Preston and Northgate, whereas insurance is in Blackburn, Leeds and Manchester. Although most trainees do move around, *"it's not a prerequisite, and they are very accommodating to your choices."* At the time of our calls, four trainees were beavering away in Blackburn, while the other four were spread across Leeds, Manchester, Preston and Chorley.

"Salaries are a big talking point at Forbes," one of our sources divulged. It's true enough that you might pick up a larger pay packet elsewhere (NQs pick up something in the mid-to-high £20k bracket), but it was generally agreed that *"you don't come to Forbes for the money. We have a great work/life balance."* Hours generally don't stretch too far beyond nine to five.

Our sources advised: *"Forbes emphasises enthusiasm."* At interview, *"you've got to show that this is where you want to be, and where you want to stay."* They might ask what other firms you've applied to: *"Make sure you say other North West firms of a similar size!"*

Social events are *"fun and frequent"* and often involve bowling. *"It's the staple diet of trainee socials,"* we were told. All of our sources mentioned the game: *"It's good because it's competitive – and it's not just bowling, they also give us drinks and nibbles."* There are also regular dinners and quiz nights. Blackburn trainees frequent Molloys, where (according to its website), you can get fish and chips for a fiver, and it's 2-for-1 on all desserts. The more active Forbesians can get involved in another of the firm's *"big things"* – football – while the big event of the year is always the Christmas party at Blackburn Rovers' home ground, Ewood Park. Trainees maintained that what happens at the Christmas party, stays at the Christmas party... but we're not too sure they can remember themselves.

And finally...
Forbes would suit anyone looking for a commercial/high-street mix in the North West. In 2012, the firm retained all four of its qualifying trainees.

Freeth Cartwright LLP

The facts

Location: Nottingham, Leicester, Derby, Birmingham, Manchester, London, Stoke-on-Trent, Milton Keynes, Sheffield

Number of UK partners/solicitors: 97/107

Partners who trained at firm: 35%

Total number of trainees: 18

Seats: 4x6 months

Alternative Seats: None

On chambersstudent.co.uk...

- How to get into Freeth
- Interview with training principal Bob Hughes
- Kimbells & KJD

With several recent mergers and a number of new offices, this Midlands mover is showcasing its national ambitions.

My, how you've grown!

You know when you bump into that kid you played with in the nursery 15 years ago and they've turned into a sexy stunna? Disconcerting, isn't it? It's similar to how we feel about Freeth Cartwright, which we're still prone to thinking of as a nice little East Midlands firm. Even though we've watched it grow steadily over the last half-dozen years, it still comes as something of a shock to realise that it now has nine UK offices. Nine! That's more than DLA Piper! The latest opened in Sheffield in May 2012, which came shortly after the full integration of Stoke-based KJD – previously an associate firm – at the beginning of April. Also within the past two years, it has merged with Milton Keynes' Kimbells in November 2011 and opened a small London office in 2010. Phew! Manage to get all that?

"Our expansion into Sheffield underlines the firm's national growth plans," says Freeth Cartwright chief executive Peter Smith. *"It is becoming increasingly important that we offer enhanced national coverage to our clients while maintaining our commitment to the local market in each of our offices."* Trainees' views? *"It's good to be part of a firm that's growing,"* mused one.

Nottingham remains the firm's largest office and is home to roughly half the trainees, with the others scattered between Leicester, Derby, Manchester, Birmingham, Milton Keynes and Stoke (the trainees currently in the latter two having been hired by pre-merger Kimbells and KJD). Freeth hopes all locations will take trainees by 2014. Applications aren't made to a specific location, but trainees did say that it was generally acceptable to move between offices, either to complete certain seats or for personal reasons.

Corporate and commercial work is a key part of the firm nowadays, while Freeth is also highly ranked in the Midlands by *Chambers UK* for areas including dispute resolution, real estate and banking. It was product liability and clinical negligence that helped form the firm's reputation, and it remains a leader in the Midlands for its clin neg work, recently winning a settlement of more than £5m for a 12-year-old girl who suffered profound brain injuries due to a lack of oxygen at birth.

Faster than the Speedo light

Trainees said: *"You don't get a lot of choice over your first seat,"* but training principal Bob Hughes adds that they *"wouldn't be placed anywhere they definitely didn't want to go."* The process for the remaining seats involves *"an interview with the training principal about a month before rotation, where you give three preferences before they check if the seats are available."* Most of our interviewees had ended up with seats they wanted but did say the process *"can be slightly artificial. If you talk to relevant people in the departments beforehand you can influence the decision."*

The real estate department is top-ranked by *Chambers UK* in the East Midlands and the commercial property subset falls within its remit. *"It's such a big department that it is usually necessary to spend some time here,"* said our sources. The team is generally involved in either *"buying properties for redevelopment or selling big plots*

Chambers UK rankings

Banking & Finance	Licensing
Clinical Negligence	Personal Injury
Construction	Planning
Corporate/M&A	Private Client
Dispute Resolution	Real Estate
Employment	Real Estate Litigation
Energy & Natural Resources	Restructuring/Insolvency
	Social Housing

of land for residential constructions." For example, it acted for Speedo in connection with its new media and hospitality centre for the London 2012 Olympics. The better work on bigger deals often doesn't reach trainees. One source said: "*It involves a lot of complicated intricacies, so it was difficult for the team to give me anything meaty.*" As such, the majority of trainees' work is at "*the banal end of the scale,*" involving "*quite a lot of administrative tasks*" and "*frequent trips to the Land Registry website.*" However, most sources reported that by the end of their seat they had picked up some drafting experience, including work on leases, contracts and title forms.

The clinical negligence department is also top-ranked by *Chambers UK* for the Nottingham area. Trainees were much more positive about time spent here. "*From the outset I was taking new enquiries and discussing them with partners,*" said one happy source. "*It wasn't just paper-pushing.*" There are opportunities to "*see a lot of clients,*" usually by attending witness statement meetings. Our sources also reported "*running small caseloads with supervision.*" The biggest plus for trainees was getting the chance to do their own advocacy. "*It wasn't very long, only a 20-minute slot at an approval hearing, but the department was aware I needed to do it and were very good at accommodating me.*"

Freeth's corporate team represents the likes of Experian and Aldi. Recently, it advised technology company Invotec's shareholders on the company's £12m sale to RG Industries. One source was tasked with the due diligence on a sale worth over £20m; another spent a night in the lap of luxury after being "*put up in a posh hotel*" during a multimillion-pound asset purchase.

Trainees were really impressed with the supervision in this department. While in commercial property our sources had sometimes complained of being "*micro-managed;*" they'd had a polar opposite experience in corporate. "*There was a lot more faith shown in me and they were much happier for me to take the lead on tasks,*" said one source. "*The knock-on effect was that I took a lot more responsibility in checking my own work for silly mistakes.*" Interviewees felt this was an important aid in their development. "*The partners have said they treated me as they would an associate because I demonstrated I was capable,*" reflected one.

Trainees considered their working hours to be more than reasonable, with an average day said to be around 9am to 5.30pm. An extra hour or two can sometimes be the norm in busier groups.

The X-factor

There seems to be no such thing as your typical Freeth-er. As one trainee put it, "*I don't know how HR managed to find people who are so different yet get on so well.*" The current crop of trainees count a former radio DJ and an LPC teacher in their midst. Bob Hughes added: "*All the applicants have the right academics these days, so you have to look at the personality, which often means we do look for some people who are a bit older or have different backgrounds. Ultimately we ask: do they have a bit of spark?*" Furthermore, Hughes says: "*We found that we had quite a few paralegals who couldn't find training contracts elsewhere but were coming up to the standards we looked for in trainees. If you work with them for a few years, you find out more about them than you can during any interview. This has helped us bring in our new secondary system of finding trainees.*" See the extended interview with Bob Hughes on our website for more on this 'secondary system'.

Although the number of offices makes it hard for the trainee group to meet up regularly, we were informed they all tend to meet up for events in Nottingham once every few months. With the firm shelling out for the non-local trainees' travel and accommodation, they are usually well attended. A night out at the races was the next event lined up at the time of our calls. For those located in Nottingham more permanently, there is a good Friday night drinks culture, with the nearby Round House a particularly favourite haunt. For a bit more on the different offices and what they do, check out our website.

And finally...

Quietly moving up the charts, we reckon Freeth is a dark horse. In 2012, six of its seven second-years were retained on qualification.

Freshfields Bruckhaus Deringer LLP

The facts

Location: London

Number of UK partners/solicitors: 170/557

Total number of trainees: 186

Seats: 3 or 6 months long

Alternative seats: Secondments, overseas seats

Extras: Pro bono – Tower Hamlets, Liberty, Oxfam, US/Caribbean death row appeals; language classes

On chambersstudent.co.uk...

- How to get into Freshfields
- A brief history of the firm
- More on overseas seats, secondments and appraisals

"*Prestigious*" peppered our interviewees' descriptions of Freshfields... what else would you expect from one of the oldest firms on the block?

Transaction heroes

London-led Freshfields is known home and away for its 200-year reign as a top corporate City firm. A bevy of international offices – 27 to be exact – ensures a steady influx of some superb global pickings, the results of which have earned the firm more than 100 rankings in *Chambers Global*. Freshfields regularly clocks in as a top earner, and this year's no different – despite a 0.9% dip in revenue, it still pulled in a staggering £1.13bn in 2011/12. The decrease may have caused the firm to swap its second place for fourth in the UK revenue charts, but with numbers this gigantic, who's counting really?

Although Freshfields maintains a historically corporate lilt – which many trainees cited as their main reason for joining – its dispute resolution and finance practices have enjoyed a surge in business lately, causing interviewees to ponder "*whether they might actually catch up to corporate in years to come.*" Training partner Simon Johnson points out that "*around 30 to 40% of work is coming from financial institutions now,*" and "*dispute resolution is tremendously busy at the moment – it's the busiest of any group.*" Still, for the time being, "*corporate is very much the core,*" most sources agreed. "*Let's put it this way: in corporate, you're never working as support for other teams – they all come to you.*"

Tesco, Mars, General Motors, Microsoft and PepsiCo are just a few of the big names instructing this firm. Financial institutions like Goldman Sachs, London Stock Exchange and the Bank of England (on the books for 250+ years) also flock to Freshfields. The following highlights from 2011 are a good illustration of the blink-twice-in-case-you-misread-that-number kind of deals the firm regularly works on: advising CVC Capital Partners on the sale of $1.6bn in Formula One shares, acting for private equity group EQT on its £1.5bn purchase of BSN medical, and leading the way in CGI's £1.7bn takeover of rival IT company Logica. The 2012 calendar year is shaping up to be equally industrious, with the firm acting as the official legal services provider to the London Olympics. The role touches every practice area – the firm's responsible for everything from arranging visa clearance for athletes and sorting out security clearance for staff to negotiating broadcasting rights and advising on sponsorship deals.

Into Deringer fire

The firm is known for its flexible seat system, in which trainees can choose to spend either three or six months in each seat. The system was unanimously applauded among our interviewees. "*You've got the most flexible training contract in the City. I've benefited hugely from dipping my toe into the proverbial pond of legal departments – I've tried out certain areas without having to spend a whole six months in ones I wound up disliking,*" one testified. With nearly 200 trainees, HR is faced with the "*righteous task*" of matching up seat preferences with business need. "*The process is generally okay, although your preferences need to be clear on your application,*" we were told. "*If it seems like you just put something down without much thought, they'll probably give that seat to somebody else.*"

Seats on offer include: corporate; finance; dispute resolution (DR); antitrust, competition and trade; employment, pensions and benefits; IP/IT; real estate; and tax. Within

Chambers UK rankings

Administrative & Public Law	Insurance
Asset Finance	Intellectual Property
Banking & Finance	Investment Funds
Banking Litigation	Outsourcing
Capital Markets	Pensions
Competition/European Law	Private Equity
Construction	Product Liability
Corporate Crime & Investigations	Projects
	Public International Law
Dispute Resolution	Public Procurement
Employee Share Schemes & Incentives	Real Estate
Employment	Real Estate Finance
Energy & Natural Resources	Restructuring/Insolvency
Environment	Retail
Financial Services	Tax
Fraud	Telecommunications
Information Technology	Transport

many are speciality subteams that trainees can visit for three months at a time – for example, the banking faction of the finance department or the EU litigation part of DR. A litigation course can be substituted for those hesitant to chance a whole stint in DR, and there's no requirement to complete any particular seats, though sources admitted "*it would be slightly odd to avoid corporate and finance altogether given our workload – people usually come here to pursue transactional work.*"

The virtual guarantee of an overseas seat has been integral to Freshfields' grad recruitment campaign in years past, but the topic proved a bit of bugbear for our sources. "*They slashed the numbers recently – a few years ago there were slots they couldn't fill, but now it seems like there's room for maybe half of us to go now.*" And yet, "*there's still a culture that everyone goes,*" some thought. "*You come here assuming you can do one because that's the way they advertise it, but it's not like that any more. The firm needs to be careful to no longer mis-sell the notion that you can point at a map and get sent there as a trainee.*" Fortunately, many noticed "*they're starting to tell potential recruits there aren't enough for everybody, which is fair enough.*" Still, an unfortunate consequence of the situation is that "*there's more competition than ever to get a spot.*" Furthermore, "*the application process is a little opaque – it's supposed to operate on the 'best person will go' philosophy, but it occasionally seems like people who fit the bill perfectly are rejected in favour of those who don't have the right experience and no one knows why.*" For the record, Freshfields clarified that there are 20 overseas spots and 20 client secondments every rotation, so the majority can go on secondment, though not

necessarily overseas. Despite their grievances, trainees remained positive about the programme as a whole, and those lucky enough to snag an overseas spot raved about the experience. Read more on our website.

From the menial to the genial

As the firm's largest department, corporate is split into four teams, each of which accepts around ten trainees at a time: All four teams handle a range of corporate work: 'A' focuses on financial institutions; 'B' works for private equity and infrastructure clients; 'C' specialises in the energy and retail sectors; 'D' has clients from the worlds of media, technology and telecommuncations. Last year saw the teams undertake some of the biggest deals around, including the $13.5bn sale of Nycomed to Takeda (Europe's biggest ever private equity trade sale) and Hewlett-Packard's £6.7bn takeover of software giant Autonomy (the European IT sector's largest deal to date).

The trainee experience "*varies wildly*" among teams, "*and most people end up visiting more than one.*" Interviewees who'd sat with Team A spoke of "*working alongside banking on multiple regulatory matters at a time,*" while those on Team C got involved with AIM IPOs and "*oil and gas-related transactions.*" On Team B it's all about the "*mega-mergers,*" while Team D members mentioned "*picking up a lot of securities work and telecommunications matters.*" The unifying characteristic across each team? "*Lots of junior admin work!*" Indeed, proof-reading, annotating, verifying signatures and initialling documents can comprise the bulk of a corporate seat. "*It's not terribly glamorous when you start out. You're like Bambi – you have to find your feet amid what amounts to pretty complicated work.*" "*Menial*" tasks are virtually impossible to avoid at Freshfields, but our interviewees were largely positive when it came to discussing responsibility. "*When you think about it, a training contract closely resembles a traditional apprenticeship, so it makes sense to go through stages of grunt work in order to progress – it's actually a pretty useful way to figure out how documents work,*" said one, while another assured us: "*There are lots of opportunities to step up as soon as you build up a sufficient level of trust.*" Most were happy to trade "*especially meaty work*" for the "*chance to work on market-leading deals with some of the greatest lawyers in the City.*" There's scope to get your hands on tougher stuff "*once you prove yourself*" – we heard from trainees who'd drafted disclosure agreements, performed research tasks, attended client meetings and travelled to clients' offices to get documents signed.

Eurostars

The finance practice handles banking, restructuring and insolvency, structured and asset finance, and energy and infrastructure. In 2011 lawyers handled Europe's largest LBO transaction of the year, private equity firm BC

Partners' $2.6bn acquisition of Swedish broadband giant Com Hem. The firm also advised on the £2.4bn acquisition of Northumbrian Water and Zurich Insurance's new €2.5bn revolving credit facility. "*The transactions are absolutely huge, so in a lot of ways you're back at square one as a trainee. It's process-driven until you prove you're ready for chunkier stuff like drafting and negotiating.*" All the same, we heard positive things from those who'd progressed up the totem pole. "*I worked on an intra-group financing where it was my job to check constitutional documents, take notes on conference calls and draft a share charge and letter to the client... in hindsight, I had quite a lot of client contact.*" Another said: "*I liaised with banks and their lawyers to get certain checks done, and regularly attended meetings with partners and clients.*"

Over in dispute resolution, trainees can choose to sit with the general commercial disputes group (CDG) or in specialist seats like international arbitration or financial institution disputes. Like Freshfields' other core departments, DR work is generally large-scale and multi-jurisdictional – clients include BP, Reed Elsevier and ExxonMobil. Recent highlights include advising an oil consortium in a $3bn dispute with the Kazakhstan government, representing Siemens in a dispute over its €600m contract with Eurostar, and handling a multibillion-dollar claim made by Boris Berezovsky (the total of which is rumoured to be one of the highest in the history of the English courts). A DR seat is "*pretty heavy on the junior work,*" so trainees across different teams can expect "*some stuff on the less glamorous end of the scale – namely doc review and bundling.*" That said, "*each team offers a different experience.*" Sources in CDG reported undertaking "*lots of research,*" while those in EU litigation focused on drafting letters, witness statements and court applications. Court attendance is not uncommon, though client contact is "*pretty limited – reasonable considering the scale of our cases.*"

A stint in one of the firm's specialist departments – "*which corporate probably calls support departments*" – offers "*a pretty different experience – you're a lot more involved, and there's more scope to manage small matters.*" Such seats – which include groups like employment, pensions and benefits (EPB), IP/IT, competition and real estate – are highly coveted, "*mainly because the matters are more accessible.*"

The trainee workload is undeniably intense. "*Your actual schedule varies drastically, but it's safe to say everyone's here late fairly often and occasionally on weekends.*" Be "*prepared to keep your BlackBerry on you at all hours and respond accordingly, even if that means cancelling your plans*" – a pretty frequent occurrence. "*People's experiences across the firm vary,*" but "*pretty strenuous*" hours appear to unite most. Our sources weren't complaining. "*Everyone knows you have to work harder here than at regional firms – nobody comes in expecting anything different.*"

You've got to fight for your right to party

"*The degree to which you have to work on each assignment is the hardest part of this job. The standards are exacting – accuracy and attention to detail are incredibly important.*" Indeed, "*what we're producing has to be top-level, so it's up to you to do it spot-on the first time around.*" Case in point: "*I proof-read a 100-page document and got a bollocking for one misplaced comma in the footnotes! They make it clear how important it is to get things right.*" This culture of perfectionism is accompanied by "*an expectation that you'll be diligent and enthusiastic when approaching your work. If you're tentative, your spirit will be broken in three months here. The genuine willingness of my peers is really impressive – 'Yes, I'd love to work on this spreadsheet until 2am' is something people say in earnest!*" Our sources credit this attitude with sustaining "*a good learning environment – there's a healthy sense of competition with others that raises the stakes and gets you working assiduously.*"

Freshfields may be "*pretty formal*" in its approach to work, but that's not to say the firm isn't welcoming on a personal level. "*People tend to be charming and friendly and down to earth; we're not just a bunch of robots churning out paperwork! There's room for a laugh here and there.*" What about when the pressure's on? "*It never becomes an environment where people are throwing each other under the bus to get ahead – if anything, the sense of camaraderie among trainees heightens right before big closings or hearings – there's a tangible feeling of team spirit in the trenches.*" As one source pointed out, "*being here until 4am obviates a lot of formality among trainees, so we're pretty sociable. There's a tangible work-hard, play-hard attitude.*" Indeed, we heard all about departmental summer parties, a "*fantastic*" black-tie Christmas ball and "*various team bonding activities*" like LaserQuest, treasure hunts, bowling and karaoke. There's also plenty on the sporting side of things, including various firm-funded teams and departmental ski trips.

Trainees across the firm underscored the excellence of the training at Freshfields. "*Even if you plan on departing upon qualification – magic circle firms are built on a model of high turnover, so there are always some who do – you'll leave with an excellent foundation.*"

And finally...
In 2012, the firm kept on 82 out of 94 qualifiers.

Gateley

The facts

Location: Birmingham, Leicester, Nottingham, London, Manchester, Leeds, Scotland

Number of UK partners/solicitors: 151/217

Total number of trainees: 29

Seats: 4x6 months

Alternative seats: None

On chambersstudent.co.uk...
- How to get into Gateley
- A history of mergers

In 2012 this Birmingham-based national firm entered the UK top 50 and opened its eighth British office.

Never say never at Gateley

"*We're now a top-50 law firm,*" training partner Pam Scott tells us. "*We're looking to progress with that. Following the opening of our Manchester office in 2010 we had no firm plans to establish another office but the opportunity was right and we launched in Leeds in the start of 2012.*" That was Gateley's eighth UK office, and followed the successful takeover of collapsed firm Halliwells' Manchester commercial practice in 2010.

Apart from one in London (and a two-lawyer outpost in Dubai, which hardly counts), none of the firm's offices strays further south than the Birmingham HQ. Leicester and Nottingham are the remaining English offices, while the firm trades as HBJ Gateley in Edinburgh and Glasgow. The firm secures plenty of recognition from *Chambers UK* – though you won't often see it gracing the top tier of the rankings, you'll usually find it only a couple of paces behind the big boys in the Midlands and the North West commercial tables. Scott doesn't think that the firm has plans to open elsewhere, "*but we never say never at Gateley.*"

Trainees are required to take one seat in real estate, one in corporate and a contentious option. "*First-years get no choice at all. The party line is that you get a choice in your third seat, but they can't always accommodate everyone.*" For those who could be accommodated, options included tax, banking, construction, corporate recovery (non-contentious) and employment. Take note: not all offices contain every department (for example, family is only available in Manchester and shipping in

London) so if you've got a specific interest, make sure you check before applying.

At the time of our calls in summer 2012, Birmingham had the most trainees, with 12. Manchester had nine, London and Nottingham three apiece, and Leicester two. Although trainees can and have moved between offices over the course of their two years, standard practice is for them to remain in one location. There are client secondment opportunities too.

Ale tales

If you've noticed a monarch in moss-coloured robes showing up on pub signs over the past year or so, you've got Gateley to thank. Brewery Greene King's £93m takeover of The Capital Pub Company was facilitated by the firm's corporate group. That deal was unusually large for the team, which "*generally sees deals around the £50m mark.*" Corporate is a "*dynamic seat. It's less law-based and more practical.*" M&A work is "*the bread-and-butter, but trainees also get to see private equity and other matters. You could be working for anything from a business that makes sick bowls for hospitals to a steel merchant. You really get to know the business.*" Trainees in corporate work on ancillary documents, "*right through from drafting them to agreeing them with the other side.*" They also help out on the bigger documents, organise the completion and, once it's all over, complete a "*bible of documents recording what's happened in the deal.*"

Coming up to completion, we heard trainees could be in the office until 11pm for weeks on end and, on occasion,

Chambers UK rankings

Banking & Finance	Planning
Banking Litigation	Private Client
Construction	Real Estate
Corporate/M&A	Real Estate Litigation
Dispute Resolution	Restructuring/Insolvency
Employment	Shipping
Family/Matrimonial	Social Housing
Intellectual Property	Tax
Pensions	Transport

might still be there when the birds woke up. *"That's the nature of doing deals,"* one trainee said, *"and when we're not busy I've left at 5.30pm."* A more standard departure time is around 7pm.

According to our parent publication *Chambers UK*, Gateley's real estate practice is one of the best in Birmingham. The department has an impressive client roster (including Sainsbury's, NatWest and Carlsberg) and good-sized deals. The residential development team acts for eight of the ten largest house builders in the UK, including Taylor Wimpey, Barratt and Persimmon. Seats can be taken in residential development, straight real estate or property finance. In real estate, trainees *"manage their own files preparing leases for landlords and tenants."* Clients go directly to the juniors with instructions, and trainees see the smaller files through from start to finish. Longer files can be passed through generations of trainees. Residential development sees *"straightforward work, once you've got your head around it. There's a lot of lower-level stuff they can give you without much supervision."* Although *"it's not too heavy on the law, you've got to be super-organised."* Real estate hours are *"good, as all house builders go home at 4.30, so we can be done by 5.30pm."*

Hello nurse!

For the contentious seat the majority of our interviewees had completed commercial dispute resolution, employment or corporate recovery; other options include banking litigation and construction litigation. Corporate recovery was highly recommended by our sources. It features highly in *Chambers UK* regional rankings and has both a contentious and non-contentious side to it. *"It's basically insolvency work,"* one trainee explained. *"We attempt to turn companies around, rescue them out of administration and sell them on or restructure them. It's interesting work and an interesting subject matter. The clients are often interesting characters as well!"* Another source admitted: *"I hadn't expected to enjoy corporate recovery. I'm not a confrontational sort of person but the litigation side is brilliant."* Trainees go along to hearings to represent the

firm. In the office, they *"prepare loads of court work"* such as application forms, witness statements and court bundles, and do quite a bit of research. One trainee described it as a *"deskbound sort of seat where you don't meet so many clients,"* but said *"it's very satisfying to see your documents sent into court."*

Employment is very popular – *"the subject matter is juicy!"* One recent case involved a scandalous tale of a *"sexy nurse"* being fired, as the *Daily Mail* reported. Trainees get to *"go to tribunals and have a hell of a lot of client contact. We also take witness statements and help draft scripts for meetings,"* one told us. And, as with all contentious seats, trainees take on a lot of research.

Gately improved

Gateley's expansion may be great in terms of opportunity, but not for remembering every face in the office – particularly in Birmingham, which is split over six floors. The Brummie and Manchester offices are the largest by some distance, and Birmingham is still very much the centre of operations. Trainees from across the firm get to know each other there during two weeks of training at the start of their contract.

Manchester is a similar size to Birmingham but is rather different in atmosphere. As we've mentioned, this office is still new to the firm and previously belonged to Halliwells, a firm that collapsed in 2010 due to the recession and some poor management decisions. Both this year and last, we spoke to rescued ex-Halliwells trainees, and have been struck by just how different their personalities were from the trainees directly recruited by Gateley. We were interested to hear them say how people remain *"so loyal to Halliwells, even now."* A dissenting opinion came from one trainee who thought: *"It's time people got over Halliwells. Gateley is doing so well and people should be proud to be here."* Despite such differences of opinion, all agreed that Manchester is a *"fun"* office with *"great work"* and that Gateley as a whole has been *"enhanced"* by the Halliwells acquisition. They also agreed that while there was a hands-off approach from Birmingham at first, the Manchester office is slowly becoming Gateleyfied and is increasingly looking South for its direction.

The London, Leicester and Nottingham offices are considerably smaller. The London base is up near the Old Bailey (though a move is planned), while in Leicester and Nottingham Gateley is centrally located, close to De Montfort University and Nottingham Trent's city campus respectively.

Gates mates

"On the whole, Gateley trainees are bold with strong personalities. If you stuck them all in a room with people they

didn't know, within ten minutes they'd all be talking to someone different," one source told us. That's exactly what training partner Pam Scott is looking for: *"Trainees should be confident in themselves and have a sharp mind as well as being able to a hold a good conversation. I want to see someone who is a little bit different, someone who has a spark about them and will fit well with Gateley and our clients."* And the best way to identify those people is through the summer vacation scheme – the majority of trainees are hired through this route. Our sources thought the scheme *"gives an accurate representation of what it's like to work here."*

Charity work is such a big deal here that one of our sources advised candidates to highlight any on their application forms. Trainees organise Gateley's charity events – both firmwide for their chosen national charity and office events for their selected local cause. There are sporting activities such as football matches and *"loads of marathons and half-marathons,"* while the less sporty can enter sweepstakes on horse races, visit care homes at Christmas and mow lawns in schools. And the easiest charitable activity of all – the last Friday of every month is a dress-down day.

Gateley has a reputation: *"If there's an event, we will be there. And be there until the end."* This means that juniors will need to find that balance of *"being good fee earners and entertaining clients,"* and need to find it quickly. Luckily they have a few informal networking lessons before being thrown to the lions at the numerous client events.

On a more fun note, Gateley has a social committee that organises ice skating, bowling, pub quizzes... the usual stuff. The Midlands offices meet up a few times a year to play rounders. Every 18 months the whole firm gets together, including those in Scotland and Dubai. The 2011 event was at Old Trafford to welcome the Manchester office to the firm. We heard it was great and that *"it must have cost them a fortune."*

All our sources were hoping to get an NQ job at the end of their training contract, but at the time of our interviews second-year sources predicted that around only three-quarters would stay on. In the end, five out of 16 were retained in 2012. To be fair to Gateley, that qualifying class was its largest ever. The 2013 intake is smaller, so hopefully retention will be better next year.

And finally...

At interview the firm *"were really interested in what I had to say and my personality. It wasn't a box ticking exercise,"* one trainee told us. So make sure you've been doing something interesting lately... and we recommend charity work.

Gordons LLP

The facts

Location: Leeds, Bradford

Number of UK partners/solicitors: 34/72

Total number of trainees: 11

Seats: 4x6 months

Alternative seats: None

Extras: Pro bono – BeInvolved

On chambersstudent.co.uk...
- How to get into Gordons
- The Yorkshire legal market

Having embarked on a lateral hiring binge, brushed up its brand and invested in a shiny new reception, there's no doubt that "*Gordons is going somewhere.*"

Dukes of Yorkshire

"*Welcome to a different kind of law firm,*" states Gordons' rebranded homepage, beneath its new orange and purple logo, beside an extreme, HD close-up of managing partner Paul Ayre's beaming face. This is a firm that's trying to tell us something. "*We're not the same as other big, faceless, mundane firms,*" explain trainees. "*We want to move away from the stuffy law firm image, and show we have a personality behind us.*" At *Student Guide* HQ we have a list of firms who say they are 'different' ranging from Clifford Chance to The Jeffcoat Firm, South Carolina, so we always take that statement with a pinch of salt, but we can't help but approve of the sentiment behind it.

There are plenty of reasons for managing partner Ayre to look quite so perky. In 2011/12 revenue increased for the 11th year on the trot – up by more than 8% to £25.3m. This means the firm is on track to hit its target of £31m in 2013, the final phase of its ambitious three-year plan. Gordons' desire is to rival the 'Bix Six' firms in Leeds, and it's increasingly nipping at their heels. Having taken on a whopping 50 new fee earners in the past year, overflowed into a new storey of its flagship office and nabbed some impressive new clients, "*there's been a very positive buzz within the place.*"

With offices in Leeds and Bradford (trainees will probably spend time in both), Gordons is a Yorkshire firm and proud. "*They like to stress the roots of the firm,*" said one trainee. Local clients like Morrisons and Yorkshire Bank still bring the bulk of instructions and "*Yorkshire work is still very important, but we're increasingly looking to the rest of the country and international clients.*" The firm has recently added Saudi Arabia Airlines, Chinese retail giant Bosideng and German packaging giant Weidenhammer to its books.

Shopping around

Commercial property, commercial litigation, company/commercial and personal law are likely seat stops. Within these larger departments are smaller subgroups like banking/finance, healthcare, retail, personal injury and employment. In their first year, trainees get allocated two seats at random – "*you can always ask, but second-years get priority.*" We heard no grumbles, largely because "*the firm has few enough trainees that people can speak up if they're unhappy. If there's room for manoeuvre they try to accommodate you.*"

Commercial property is the largest of Gordons' departments. "*There are dedicated Morrisons teams in that department where you can help out on acquisitions of big stores.*" It's not all about the supermarket, however. The group also works with everyone from B&M Home Stores ("*quite prominent in the North,*") down to "*a little café in Wakefield.*" On some of these smaller matters trainees are able to "*run everything from start to finish,*" always with supervision on hand. In general, they're perfectly happy that "*as soon as you demonstrate you can do it, responsibility increases.*"

The commercial litigation department also does the odd bit for Morrisons, but this is topped up with "*work for large retailers and individuals – small-business owners who have issues with suppliers or customers,*" plus a size-

Chambers UK rankings

Banking & Finance	Employment
Construction	Private Client
Corporate/M&A	Real Estate
Dispute Resolution	

able dose of property litigation. "*I basically shadowed my supervisor every day*," said one source. "*I drafted witness statements, pleadings and instructions to counsel, had plenty of client contact, went to hearings and did a lot of my own advocacy.*"

While many other firms' private client teams seem to be shrinking, Gordons' 'personal law' team is expanding. The firm acts for five of the region's 15 wealthiest individuals – many with trusts worth over £50m each. Trainees "*get a few small files to run and on bigger files you can get some really decent tasks.*"

The company commercial team has particular expertise in the retail sector, acting for (again) Morrisons, fashion catalogues Freemans and Grattan, plus Yorkshire-based business The Card Factory. Within the group, insolvency allows trainees to get their hands on contentious and non-contentious matters, working one-on-one with a partner. "*We act for a lot of insolvency practitioners, but on the other side you get companies coming to you who are having problems with suppliers or supply chain issues.*"

Depending on the group, work either trickles down from supervisors, or flies in from different fee earners. Trainees are never left floundering. "*The office is all open-plan, and it's not a big deal to ask questions.*" Supervisors are good at keeping tabs on their trainees. "*I have a weekly meeting where we look at my training records and reflect on the work we've done, ticking off any core skills picked up in the seat,*" said one source. There's also plenty of departmental training on hand – usually seminars or webinars over lunch every few weeks. Trainees report: "*The latest I've ever stayed is probably 7.30 or 8pm. If you do that, people wonder why you're still in the office.*"

So far, so lovely, but the qualification process in 2012 was "*a bit of a sore point*" for our sources. Having reportedly announced there were six available positions, it was finally unveiled that only two of Gordons' seven trainees would be offered NQ jobs in 2012. "*My main grievance is that we only had six weeks to find another job,*" said one. The firm says they weren't let go for performance reasons, but because jobs were not available in their preferred departments.

The Ronseal of law firms?

Gordons' head office is in Leeds, although "*the idea is that trainees do at least one seat in Bradford.*" Once they're past the stigma of the city being "*Leeds' poor relation,*" trainees actually take quite a shine to the place. "*We're in quite an old building, but inside it's nice and modernised. It's a small enough office that you know everyone's names.*" Half an hour's train ride away, the Leeds office is big and getting bigger. "*We used to be across three floors, but now it's four, and we're taking the ground floor for a new reception area.*"

Gordons is so proud of its firm culture that it has opted to design the entire rebrand of the firm around it. So, we asked trainees, what exactly is this culture? "*It's a very Yorkshire attitude really,*" says one. "*It's down to earth, practical and does what it says on the tin.*" These good old-fashioned Yorkshire vibes extend to the atmosphere in the offices, where "*you can have a joke and a laugh with anyone.*" Camaraderie results from Gordons' 'post duty' routine, where bleary-eyed trainees communally rifle through the post at 8am each morning, every alternate week. "*It's a good way to get to know the other trainees and the partner helping out, and learn who's doing what in the firm,*" admitted one trainee. "*Then again, I'd rather have a lie-in!*" There are plenty of non-post-related social occasions, with different events each month, and a strong contingent of Gordonites to be found in their "*dangerously close*" local, Roast, every Friday. There are concerns that with all the changes underway, Gordons may be becoming a bit more "*slick and corporate,*" though trainees say that "*as long as they're careful with who they choose to bring in, which seems to be the case, the firm should be able to keep a hold on its culture.*"

Perhaps unsurprisingly, "*trainees mainly come from the Yorkshire area,*" and there's no denying that a connection to the region will stand you in good stead at Gordons. Paralegalling experience, whether at the firm or elsewhere, will also impress. "*Most of us spent a year or two doing that,*" a trainee stressed. Otherwise, if you show that you're "*very competent and on the ball, but friendly and fun as well,*" you'll fit right in.

And finally...
Every year, we get good vibes from this dynamic regional firm. If you want top responsibility and an excellent training in the Yorkshire region, Gordons should be on your list.

Government Legal Service (GLS)

The facts
Location: London
Number of solicitors: 1,550
Total number of trainees: 50
Seats: 4x6 months
Alternative seats: None

On chambersstudent.co.uk...
- How to get into the GLS
- Much more about the work of the GLS

Choose life. Choose a job. Choose health insurance, gym membership and corporate credit cards. Choose a penthouse flat, designer luggage and wondering who you are at 4am on a Thursday morning. Or... choose the GLS.

Lust for life

Forget the financial press: if you want to work on matters that are seriously in the headlines, then the Government Legal Service may be for you. Its 2,000 lawyers are instructed by the government on advice and litigation for pretty much everything that graces the lips of *Have I Got News For You*'s presenters. Localism Bill? Check. Tuition Fees? Check. Academies? Check. Iraq war? Check. Add to this a manageable workload and the fuzzy feeling you get from knowing that you're not just making the rich guys richer. Our sources summed it up: "*Everything you do has impact on the people you love and care about, as well as yourself. There's an overwhelming idea that you're working together for a greater cause. And most days you come in at 9am and leave at 6pm.*" Add to this the ability to "*see policy you've worked on being debated in Parliament*" and you've got yourself an attractive prospect.

Some of our sources this year had been asked by peers "*if we came to the GLS because we couldn't get in anywhere else,*" but in fact the competition to get in is extreme. The GLS receives nearly 3,000 applications for around 20 places each year: a 2:1 will get you to the online assessments, after which recruiters only see your name and if you did law or not. Interestingly, though, many, though by no means all, of those to whom we spoke had previous – if not necessarily lengthy – careers prior to joining. Here's one's view: "*The questions you'll be asked are designed to show off your skills – so if you've had proper work experience you'll have many more examples. It doesn't have to be volunteering for an NGO, but you have to*

demonstrate a genuine interest in what happens in the world. The interview requires sitting down and thinking about your answers, rather than relying on where you went to university." Visit our website, and theirs, for more details on what the application process involves.

About 35% of trainees are based at the Treasury Solicitor's department (TSol), "*the government's personal litigators.*" Other trainees are employed directly by departments such as the Department for Business, Innovation and Skills (BIS), the Department for Communities and Local Government (DCLG), the Department for Work and Pensions/the Department for Health (DWP/H), Her Majesty's Revenue and Customs (HMRC) and the Ministry of Justice (MoJ). There's a four-seat rotation, with HMRC trainees usually staying in their own department, but trainees based in advisory areas like DCLG or BIS spend six months in a TSol seat to gain contentious experience. TSol trainees have a split contract, usually spending their first year at 'home', taking one public and one private law seat, and their second year in outside departments like the Cabinet Office, the Department for Education, the Ministry of Defence or the Home Office. The GLS also recruits barristers – see page 698 for more.

HMRC vs pasties

TSol bears the most resemblance to a City firm – the GLS's largest department, it acts for the government as both a public and private authority. The department's keenly aware of its "*corporate ID: as when we occasionally have to say 'no' to powerful Whitehall departments, brand* becomes very important." Trainees spend time in teams such as prisons; public law and planning; property; immigration; bona vacantia; and employment. If the nature of work incurs "more typical law-firmy work like filing," be assured that in TSol, "trainees only ever do bundling that's theirs." Initially, private law can be less thrilling than public work, but acting on "unlawful detentions, challenges to customs decisions and personal injury claims" offers "brilliant immediate litigation experience, especially in handling your own small claims." Immigration work "can be emotionally exhausting," and can call into question "the extent to which you view politics dispassionately – the decisions are difficult, but what you're defending is the decision-making capacity, not the decision itself." Working on prisons law is every bit as emotive, and potentially more legally complex. "Prisoners can be very litigious, and a lot of the claims involve their movement around the prison system – you get to see the whole picture, and there's often a human rights element which can be really interesting. As a trainee, it's a great opportunity to draft grounds of defence – these are also the type of claims you see in the papers."

Before George Osborne's 2012 Budget, very few people would have used 'pasty' and 'controversial' in the same breath. But if Pastygate has taught us little else, it's that – very – occasionally, tax can be, well, interesting. HMRC trainees sit in departments ranging from insolvency to 'specialist investigations', "which mainly involves high-profile tax avoidance schemes." Typically these cases analyse the receipts of large companies or individuals (looking at you, Jimmy Carr). There's plenty of opportunity to get on board with smaller bankruptcy petitions, plus the opportunity for advocacy at the employment tribunal. There are also advisory seats in HMRC. "It's harder to pick up and run with matters yourself as the teams run large legislative projects. The role tends to be more supportive, but even if you're taking notes at a meeting, it'll be between two other lawyers, a QC and four clients – still pretty exciting."

The Ministry of Justice involves constitutional work as well as the component parts of the criminal justice system – prisons, probation services and courts. It's "the most interesting place to be – anything of major importance finds its way to the MoJ." Trainees can work on national offender management (or prisons), legal aid and information, data protection and human rights law. The latter "is extremely advisory," and intersects with other departments in a variety of ways. "It's interesting because you get to look at matters from a high level, rather than just seeing each individual case." It's less day-to-day points, as matters are "large and high-profile," but that means "each piece of work on your desk is an interesting point of law." Data protection is a vast area for the MoJ. "Government departments come to us saying they want to share certain data about people – is it possible and what

should they do?" Following new EU regulations protecting people's online identities and the right to control and be forgotten by organisations, there's a lot of work with the European Court of Human Rights. There's always a lot of employment-based work for courts and prisons. "It can be from set-piece advice to prison governors or sentence calculation if a prisoner is saying they should be released, to inquests."

Covering the health, well-being and care of well over 20 million people in the UK, trainees in the Department for Work and Pensions and the Department of Health work on vital matters and are happy to say "trainees elsewhere might draft contracts, but we draft laws." There's a lot of work on the framework for the new public sector pension, after the controversial reforms were put through Parliament to implement a flat-rate scheme. "The policy clients tell us what they want, we then write instructions to parliamentary counsel, then we'll go back to the client to see if it's okay. Our job is to then brief the minister before they debate it in the House of Lords, which is a fascinating way to be introduced to government work."

The bigger picture

The Department for Communities and Local Government encompasses planning and regeneration, housing, environment and fire, although D-Cam's Localism Bill forms the backbone of much work here as employees strive "to build the foundations of the Big Society." Recently, trainees have worked on the Local Government Finance Bill, legislation which aims to drive decentralisation by directly encouraging independent local growth. For more on departments like BIS, the MoD and the Cabinet Office, head to our website where there's a lot more detail on what GLS trainees are getting up to.

"The philosophy's that there isn't specific 'trainee work' – I'm always given interesting things to learn from, and there's the notion of always being given the chance to have a go at meaty tasks." The matters GLS trainees work on should appeal to those keen on "pure law. The work is never just interpreting the law, it's the opportunity to make legislation." Further, supervision is bespoke enough that "if you're doing well, you'd get more to do independently, but if you were tripping up, they might lessen what they gave you." There's a training principal who oversees the entire process, a team leader within each group, and an individual supervisor for each trainee. "In advisory, you work with different lawyers on every piece of work – it doesn't matter who you ask for help, as you always feel well managed."

Black-letter law aside, the primary reason people choose to train with the GLS is public service, be it a rejection of "making money for a corporate boss," or simply having "a significant impact" on communities. "The dynamic between law and politics always fascinated me," said one source. "*Advising ministers and making planning policy law is a huge draw, as you're affecting things that you actually care about.*" Most employees are politically minded, if not with a capital 'P'. "*I'm not a protester,*" said one, "*but I follow the news – it helps to know what's going on, and it's good to know what stories are being reported at what time.*" Though most sources hadn't worked on anything they had personal disagreements with, they were adamant that "*if you had political views that you couldn't reconcile, the GLS wouldn't be for you. You often have to put preconceptions aside and look at what's going on, both for and against.*" Civil servants must learn that "*it doesn't matter what your personal opinion is, or what you really think: if you're professional, then you'll be able to do the work.*" Although "*there are always plenty of people ready to engage in lively debate,*" it's not "*like Yes Minister with people blocking legislation they don't like.*" Keeping on top of the news is all well and good, but "*our client is the government, and the solicitors' code is to give the best service possible.*"

There are further differences between public and private practice – "*there's the chance to specialise, but you are encouraged to move around every few years.*" This is brilliant for those "*who don't want to be pigeon-holed early on,*" although some trainees feel they "*don't have a huge amount of say in where we end up.*" On balance, "*it's probably worth being put where business needs dictate, as there's such job security here.*"

Pub(lic) work

Ah, job security. The last bastion of the public sector – that was, until spending cuts "*decimated*" some departments, notably advisory ones. Current trainees, however, see themselves as being out of the thick of it. "*Lots of people have been visibly reassigned, but we've been protected. The cuts have gone a long way – the previous year was difficult, but we've got through it, and we're getting on with it now.*" Smaller departments offer jobs to selected trainees and "*if they can't accommodate you, they find*

you another spot in the GLS." The job process differs between departments – TSol hopefuls submit a CV and "*a list of our top three preferences.*" There's a general consensus that "*advisory is more popular, so you need to earn your stripes in litigation before you go there. It's possible if there's a position while you're there, but they wouldn't necessarily create a place for you even if you'd impressed.*" The GLS does recruit to retain, and in 2011, as in most years, all qualifiers were kept on. "*It's good to be able to concentrate on working and socialising rather than climbing the greasy pole or getting one up on each other.*"

If you're looking for a hard-drinking culture, the civil service probably isn't for you either. There are sporadic pub visits, and a social committee that has put on quizzes and trips to Somerset House, and official trainee drinks on the first Thursday of every month. There is a Christmas party though, "*which we pay for ourselves at a local, or else the papers would have a field day.*"

"*A lot of people have young families. Especially people who've arrived in the private sector – there's a feeling that they arrive here at a time when work/life balance is necessary.*" Trainees are pleased to report leaving work between 6 and 7pm – and very often at 5.30pm, when the working day officially ends. "*People are supportive of you getting a life, and of taking annual leave – they want you to maintain the right level of knowing what's going on in the world.*" Departments like TSol and HMRC "*can feel more corporate – there's a faster pace, and the day passes quicker.*" Don't read 'corporate' as 'unfriendly', though: there's "*a great sense of camaraderie, and a sense that you're never reinventing the wheel, so there'll always be someone around who's done what you're doing before, so you're able to swap and share stories and advice.*" This "*buzzy*" dynamic runs through to the social scene, which is "*pretty active.*" Advisory departments "*have a more relaxed feel. You have time to think about the nuances that aren't as pressing when you're litigating. People are still phenomenally busy but it's more like a really busy library – there's less chat.*"

And finally...

"*I've never had a bad day here. There's no admin work, and every day we get really difficult points of law to consider. But if you equate money and long hours with success, then don't apply.*"

Harbottle & Lewis LLP

The facts
Location: London
Number of UK partners/solicitors: 37/40
Partners who trained at firm: 10%
Total number of trainees: 10
Seats: 4x6 months
Alternative seats: Secondments

On chambersstudent.co.uk...
- How to get into Harbottle
- Interview with film and TV partner Abby Payne

There's a strong media focus at this West End firm, which has interesting clients and excellent work.

Our lips are sealed

The creation of a pair of drama buffs in the 50s, Harbottle & Lewis initially catered to the upper crust of the film and theatre industry before extending its reach to keep stride with the evolving market. This is now a complete media and entertainment practice taking work from the music, TV, publishing, broadcasting, sport, fashion and advertising sectors. *"We strive constantly to stay ahead of the digital curve, becoming increasingly innovative as the law evolves,"* says film and TV partner Abby Payne, mentioning the firm's ever-growing involvement in the digital industry. Indeed, the prospect of brand damage at the hands of social networking is keeping the reputation management team especially busy, while the digital media group currently has its hands full with web-related data protection and privacy issues.

That's not to say the firm is limited to just a few media-related offerings; it's actually full-service, which helped keep financials up during the recession. In addition to providing general commercial and regulatory advice, lawyers advise on corporate, employment, finance, IP, litigation and tax matters across the aforementioned creative industries, with some niche areas like aviation, charity, family, private client and personal injury too. This broad scope makes for an interesting client list, which includes Penguin, Sega, Gok Wan, Channel 4, Kate Moss, DreamWorks and the England Cricket team to name a few. A couple of recent highlights: acting for the Catholic Church on media issues surrounding the 2010 Papal visit and advising the Royal Family on the broadcast of a certain wedding.

Naked ambition

Trainees choose from six seats – corporate, litigation, employment, property, family and media – with the option of a client secondment at Virgin Atlantic. Trainees list their preferences beforehand and are told their seat schedule upon arrival at the firm. *"You're allowed one preference that they try their best to fulfil, but otherwise you've got to go where the work is,"* one informed us.

Most trainees hit the litigation department at some point in order to fulfil the SRA's contentious requirement. The practice is one of the firm's billing powerhouses and is split into commercial litigation, personal injury and media groups. The last houses the firm's celebrated reputation management team, which regularly acts for some famous – and often confidential – names. *"I was able to attend a hearing for a celebrity, though I can't say who,"* a source revealed. *"It's kind of painful to see recognisable faces in reception and not be able to tell your friends... but it does make for some fun lunchtime gossip!"* Harbottle's litigators also recently defended the founders of Skype against a multibillion-dollar suit brought by eBay, and are currently entangled in a major banking and fraud dispute involving Saudi billionaire Maan Al-Sanea. For trainees, research, drafting, document management and bundling are the norm. They also attend hearings and perform the weekly court run – *"there's a lot of out and about to the seat!"* Endeavouring to collect outstanding client fees is another highlight. *"You get to run the debt collection files yourself, so there are lots of opportunities to take the initiative."*

Chambers UK rankings

Charities	Information Technology
Corporate/M&A	Intellectual Property
Defamation/Reputation Management	Media & Entertainment
Employment	Real Estate
	Sports Law

Corporate is another sizeable practice, handling work for clients including Virgin Holidays, Comic Relief and literary agency United Agents in recent years. Lawyers advise on *"the buying and selling of a lot of TV and film production companies,"* plus private equity financing and venture capital sourcing matters, including the recent joint venture between MAMA Group – a festival and live music venue operator – and HMV. For trainees, this translates into *"a lot of indexing, filing and other due diligence,"* though luckily *"it's not like some firms where you're locked in a data room forever: I got to run a small transaction myself, so there was drafting and such to be done for that,"* one reported. Even the team's more sizeable transactions *"aren't so unmanageably large that you can't get a full view of the deal."*

Harbottle's media seat is without a doubt its most popular. After all, *"it's the whole reason a lot of people apply to the firm."* The seat, which takes on two trainees each rotation, is split into two parts: theatre, film and television work is in one; the other is music, sport, advertising, IP, publishing and interactive entertainment (i.e. video games). While trainees tend to sit with specialists in one grouping or the other, they can request work in all of the areas that interest them, with most undertaking assignments in several different sectors throughout the course of their seat. *"Every bit of work has interesting elements,"* said one, mentioning a recent assignment that entailed making amendments to the nudity clause in a film's cast agreement. *"All the partners are experts, so you're working directly with people who are very well known in their fields."* And pretty well connected, it seems – trainees who sat with the music guys reported tagging along to the odd client's gig after work. For more media highlights and details on secondments, see our website.

007pm and I'm outta here!

Sources reported a good balance of *"young and eager"* and *"more traditional"* people at the firm. *"The trainees bring an enthusiastic energy to the office, but we've also*

got some of the older guys around who're representative of people's impressions of Harbottle in its glory years," one explained. Fortunately, there's little divide between the groups, which trainees put down to the small size of the firm and the relative lack of hierarchy. Case in point: *"A partner in my group offered to get me a choc ice from the corner shop earlier!"* Work/life balance appears equally hunky-dory, with trainees regularly leaving the office before 7pm.

The firm is based in Hanover Square in the heart of the West End. The 'one department per floor' layout of the *"lovely old building"* means trainees remain apart during the day, but the celebrated '007' lunch room – named for the Bond posters adorning the wall, a relic from the firm's early representation of the franchise – provides communal territory and a daily free buffet lunch. In addition to *"quite regular"* after work drinks, there are charity-related activities like fund-raising treasure hunts and firm quizzes. There's also the odd partners/trainees v associates football match, group away days and the British Comedy Awards, to which the firm receives some free tickets. *"It's a big night out, dressing up and walking the red carpet with Mitchell and Webb,"* reported second-years. Sadly, the date of the 2011 awards clashed with Harbottle's Christmas party, but you'll have to excuse our lack of sympathy seeing as the latter was *"a posh do"* at Claridge's in Mayfair.

For all their praise of Harbottle's exciting client list and interesting work, our sources cautioned applicants against *"an assumption that a training contract is really glamorous. Our clients and media focus make the firm seem edgy, but for the most part you'll be doing ordinary trainee tasks, which aren't all that thrilling. You might get a tiny dose of the glamour, but it's naïve to pursue the firm because you want to meet a celebrity – and Harbottle can spot someone like that a mile away."* As one source pointed out, *"the media attraction is a given for most applicants. Make sure you come to an interview prepared to answer what other things you find interesting about the firm."* Despite a raise in trainee salaries in 2011 that now puts first-years on £30,000, compensation remains a gripe among those who are *"sceptical as to why wages are so much lower than firms of equivalent size."* That said, most are content to sacrifice City pay for a decent work/life balance and stimulating workload. *"People come here for the clients and reputation and work more than anything.* The firm retained four of five qualfiers in 2012.

And finally...
While Harbottle doesn't require prior experience in the media sector, it *"definitely helps"* to have something on your CV that shows an interest in the industry.

Henmans LLP

The facts

Location: Oxford

Number of UK partners/solicitors: 22/38

Partners who trained at firm: 16%

Total number of trainees: 5

Seats: 4x6 months

Alternative seats: None

On chambersstudent.co.uk...
- How to get into Henmans
- Interview with training partner Philip Evans

This Oxfordshire firm is nationally recognised for its stellar reputation in private client and commercial work.

Fantastic Mr Ox

Henmans is top-ranked by *Chambers UK* for its agricultural, charities, personal injury and private client departments. Says training partner Philip Evans: "*Although we have a range of services to offer, it is fair to say we're a litigation-dominant firm.*" Litigation-based cases make up 40% of the firm's revenue, while private client services, which include family and charities, make up a steady 30%. "*We're very pleased with how well the firm has done in this economic climate,*" says Evans. "*We're now the largest firm in Oxford and are constantly focusing on how to improve our offering.*"

Trainees say the firm is "*quite traditional and professional, but that's combined with a very warm feeling about the place.*" One added: "*We're an old and established firm, with an excellent reputation, but we're also evolving and adaptable. We're definitely not snotty or stuffy.*"

Trainees "*really are from all over the country,*" although all expressed an interest in private client and related practices, and "*most people are drawn to the firm for its reputation rather than location,*" interviewees reflected. All liked the "*high quality of work*" and the small size of the trainee intake. "*It's great to be in a mid-size firm where you're not just a number.*"

Power to the people

Seats include PI, dispute resolution, property, private client and corporate/commercial. Other than the contentious SRA requirement, "*there aren't any seats you have to do. The second-years definitely get priority though.*" The seat allocation process at Henmans is done "*democratically,*" trainees said. "*There really aren't many of us, so towards the end of the second seat, the future second-years pretty much sort out what they're all going to do between themselves. Of course, the HR team oversees everything, and if there's a particularly sought-after seat, they'll intervene, but ultimately everything is resolved amicably between us.*" One said: "*It's a great system. Everything's out in the open and you have the real potential to get the training contract you want.*" Another added: "*It also means, if it fits with the other trainees, you can do repeat seats, particularly in property.*"

The disputes team is "*joint-largest with private client*" and covers almost every sort of litigation you could think of, from your standard commercial, property and professional negligence disputes, right the way through to contentious probate and even ecclesiastical and equine cases. Trainees have the opportunity of "*experiencing a real range of cases*" and are able "*to get stuck into the work from day one.*" One said: "*As a trainee, you'll always get particularly involved in the contentious probate work. There's a lot to be done and it links us with the other big department.*" Clients include landed gentry – lots of Earls, Lords and Sirs – celebrities, regional start-ups and national household names. "*A lot of our clients are based in London or Oxford, but we also do work with international elements,*" trainees said. "*The range is so interesting.*" Interviewees reported drafting letters, attending meetings, going to court – "*the lot. You're never just stuck doing the really boring tasks.*"

On the OUP

The property department is split into residential, commercial and agricultural teams – the last of which is top-ranked by *Chambers UK*. A trainee said: "*Although you focus on what your supervisor is doing, trainees do work across the board. If you show a particular interest, the team takes that into account and gives you substantial experience.*" As with disputes, commercial clients range from small start-ups to giant plcs, while the residential team caters to the wealthy, nobility and celebrity crowds. Notable clients include Oxford University Press, Sony, Cancer Research and the National Trust. In 2012, the team acted for Clydesdale Bank in its refinancing of Strivesign's property portfolio and sorted out a lease for uranium enrichment plant operator URENCO. Trainees praised the level of responsibility they received in this seat, saying: "*There's plenty of drafting and research. If you're keen, this department loves to get trainees involved.*"

Consistently highly ranked by *Chambers UK* in the Thames Valley, the private client department "*is one of the largest and most prominent in the firm.*" Within the team, "*everyone has their own specialist area. Every partner does general private client work such as wills and probate, but we also have charity, tax and Court of Protection specialists.*" One source added: "*The firm is building up its charity work and that crosses a range of departments.*" Unsurprisingly, clients are of ultra high net worth. Trainees said: "*The team is excellent about giving you responsibility and taking the time to explain the technical details.*" One said: "*I've been doing great work from day one, drafting wills, going to client meetings frequently and assisting on trusts management.*"

The clinical negligence and personal injury departments are "*officially separate, but often work together on matters,*" trainees said. The personal injury team represents "*both claimant and defendants, which is great for getting a full overview of the work.*" The team also undertakes professional negligence work for solicitors and insurers including Hiscox, Travelers and Zurich. Trainees praised "*being thrown right into the deep end of responsibility.*" All had gained experience of drafting, meeting clients and attending hearings.

Olympic spirit

"*Most people at the firm have a friendly and laid-back manner,*" trainees said. "*You're definitely not on your guard all the time!*" This "*openness*" extends right up to partners, who "*definitely know everyone's first name.*" Although certain departments have a more heads-down atmosphere, "*you can chat with everyone. As long as you're getting your work done, people are always up for a natter.*"

"*We actually have loads of organised events at the firm,*" trainees said. "*Because of our location* [Henmans is on one of Oxford's business parks], *informal gatherings and after-work drinks are more difficult; however, there's always something or other going on.*" Trainees were full of funny stories about everything from fashion shows to Halloween parties. "*The Halloween event was an evening quiz, and the partners were definitely the most adventurous with their costumes. One came as Frankenstein and another had this hilarious Harry Potter outfit on.*" As it's an Olympic year, the firm also held a "*sort of sports day, with egg and spoon-type events,*" We hear the personal injury team triumphed on the day, just in case you were wondering. Otherwise there are film nights, punting races and "*we decorated the office for the Jubilee.*" There are also month-end drinks, with "*Wii and table tennis. Ultimately, people don't live that near by, so it normally ends pretty early, but it's always a good opportunity to see everyone.*"

Official working hours at Henmans are 9am to 5pm, and trainees reported: "*By 6pm there really aren't many people left in the office.*" Occasionally, there are "*longer hours when you need to get things done,*" but "*you're certainly never expected to be slogging away until midnight. As long as you stay on top of your work, the firm is extremely reasonable.*"

And finally....
The retention process *"is quite an informal one,"* trainees said, *"but we normally keep most people."* In 2012 the firm retained two out of its three qualifiers.

Herbert Smith Freehills LLP

The facts

Location: London

Number of UK partners/solicitors: 171/337

Partners who trained at firm: 60%

Total number of trainees: 158

Seats: 4x6 months

Alternative Seats: Overseas seats, secondments

Extras: Pro bono: Whitechapel Legal Advice Centre, FRU, RCJ CAB, Asylum Support Appeals Project, death row appeals; language classes

On chambersstudent.co.uk...
- How to get into Herbert Smith
- Herbies' in-house advocacy unit

This accomplished City firm is built on the pillars of corporate and dispute resolution.

Freehills on the horizon

Established in 1882 by Mr Herbert Smith, this firm numbers among the largest in the City. *"We were born out of old English, red-braced litigation, but the firm has proactively evolved into a full-service offering,"* trainees reflected. True enough: while still one of the UK's leading firms for dispute resolution, Herbies now also advises a large proportion of the FTSE 100 on corporate matters from its 19 offices worldwide. Beyond the *"twin engines of disputes and corporate,"* energy and natural resources is a growing field for the firm, while the finance and international arbitration practices are also areas of focus. Revenue in 2011/12 rose by 3% to £480m, although that didn't stop a redundancy round and the loss of over 40 jobs in summer 2012.

"The biggest thing that's happened to us in 2012 is the decision to merge with Freehills," training partner Matthew White said. This tie-up with one of the 'Big Six' – Australia's equivalent of the magic circle – is due to go live on October 1, the day this book goes to press. It will create a new firm that goes by the name of Herbert Smith Freehills and, says White, *"will consolidate our place as the number-one firm in Asia-Pacific. We're also still considering opening offices in South America, Frankfurt, Equatorial Guinea and Seoul. A boutique litigation base in New York opened at the beginning of September. The firm is constantly expanding, which is incredibly exciting for us."*

Trainees themselves stressed how *"international"* Herbies feels: *"Although London is still very much the hub, a global outlook is reflected in the trainees we're hiring and the work we do."* Training partner Matthew White said:

"We only recruit people with a global mindset. We expect people to work abroad at least once and probably twice in their career." A trainee added: *"People that come here are interested in the world. Most have language skills and worldwide experiences. Although it's not fully international yet, you can feel the shift."*

O2 Joy

Trainees can choose from a vast selection of seats. The list includes spots in various types of litigation, corporate, real estate and finance, as well as specialist seats which include: competition; IP; employment, pensions and incentives; advocacy; and tax.

Trainees are strongly encouraged to complete both a litigation and a corporate seat in London, a client or overseas secondment, and no more than one specialist seat. However, all sources agreed that *"there's a lot of flexibility."* One said: *"I think about 90% of us do a London corporate and litigation seat, but there might be the business need for you to head to another department or do the seat in another country for that matter,"* Another added: *"Completing a litigation seat is non-negotiable, but then I don't know of someone coming to Herbies not wanting to do one – it's what we're best at."*

Seat allocation *"isn't sorcery."* Trainees advised: *"When you give in your preferences, make sure you speak with those in charge and have good reasons for your choices. The process is very logical here. Most people get at least two or three of their first choices."*

Chambers UK rankings

Administrative & Public Law	Life Sciences
Banking & Finance	Local Government
Banking Litigation	Media & Entertainment
Capital Markets	Outsourcing
Competition/European Law	Partnership
Construction	Pensions
Corporate Crime & Investigations	Pensions Litigation
	Planning
Corporate/M&A	Private Client
Data Protection	Private Equity
Dispute Resolution	Product Liability
Employee Share Schemes & Incentives	Professional Discipline
	Professional Negligence
Employment	Projects
Energy & Natural Resources	Public International Law
Environment	Public Procurement
Financial Services	Real Estate
Fraud	Real Estate Finance
Health & Safety	Real Estate Litigation
Information Technology	Restructuring/Insolvency
Insurance	Retail
Intellectual Property	Tax
Investment Funds	Telecommunications
	Transport

It would be fair to say that Herbies trainees are blessed with opportunities to go abroad. "*The emphasis on secondments is a big part of pushing that international outlook,*" trainees said. Overseas offerings include Hong Kong, Tokyo and Paris (the three most popular – and most difficult to get), Singapore, Dubai, Abu Dhabi and Moscow. Client secondments are equally numerous and available at several energy companies, banks, plus other organisations including BSkyB, Liberty and O2. Although trainees are now expected to complete some kind of secondment, "*most people want to go on one anyway*" and "*no one's forced to go abroad – that's not in anyone's interest.*" Interviewees did feel, though, that "*if you want to be part of a global, elite firm, you have to be willing to move around. From associate to partner, people are constantly travelling and relocating.*" One added: "*It's also the best way to consolidate your experience in a practice area and truly interact with our international clients in their own cultures. The benefits for your career are numerous.*"

A weekday at Bernie's

The 'disputes' practice encompasses a plethora of specialities and subgroups, including insurance litigation, construction disputes, banking litigation, general commercial (the largest subgroup), shareholder disputes, international arbitration, public law disputes and corporate crime. "*All our clients are massive companies,*" trainees remarked. "*A lot of the stuff we work on is high-profile – it's fascinating.*" Herbies is representing the Queen's bank, Coutts & Co, in four separate High Court claims and is acting for Bernie Ecclestone in a $171m dispute arising from the sale of substantial shareholdings linked with Formula 1. Other clients include BSkyB, Société Générale, the Royal Society of Arts and "*any big bank you can think of really.*"

The general disputes practice is so vast that it's currently split into two massive groups – "*three if you count the energy disputes team as well.*" To define massive, one trainee clarified: "*My group was about 90 fee earners.*" Another admitted: "*It can be difficult to get to know everyone in these large groups, but on the whole everyone is very friendly and keen to help. You do get to work with some of the leading litigators in the world.*" Trainees receive work either from their supervisor or from partners who "*send e-mails round with details of cases that you can volunteer for.*" They can gain experience of tasks such as drafting witness statements but said: "*The responsibility levels are lower in litigation than elsewhere. There's a lot of bundling and copy-checking to be done and you're going to be the one to do it.*"

The hugely popular international arbitration seat acts for "*big multinational companies.*" One trainee said: "*On one case I was dealing with parties from Africa, the Middle East and Russia. It was very exciting.*" Training partner Matthew White says: "*This is an area that's constantly expanding. Our drive to open in New York is a good example of that move forward.*" Trainees feel: "*You get a lot more responsibility in this seat than you do in other litigation teams. It's smaller and there's no outside counsel, so there's a lot more research and drafting to do.*" One added: "*I also attended a number of hearings and the cases are incredibly interesting. The seat allows you to actually use all those years of law school!*"

The "*very popular*" in-house advocacy unit "*is a unique opportunity*" that Herbies can provide. Even though it's within the firm, this QC-led group officially counts as a secondment. Visiting the unit also means trainees can start on the path towards gaining higher rights of audience. Although trainees don't actually get to do much advocacy themselves, "*you watch trials and judgings and learn so much. A lot of your time is also spent doing research and drafting skeleton arguments. It's a small group, so you get extremely interesting things to do.*" The team is also keen for trainees to get involved in pro bono advocacy cases, where they can actually test their skills.

Power up

Energy at Herbies isn't strictly separated into its own department, but the work permeates many of the firm's other groups. "*The firm is really pushing its energy capacity and the energy-related seats are very popular*" with trainees. It's seen as quite glamorous," interviewees agreed. Within corporate, "one group is focused on general energy work, while another does infrastructure work." Clients are big international players; for example, Herbert Smith advised Essar Energy, a London-listed FTSE company, on the £2bn acquisition and capital financing of an oil refinery and other assets owned by Shell. The energy litigation team is headed by top-ranked partner Ted Greeno: "Being able to work with someone like him is phenomenal." Trainees are "present for hearings and arbitrations, and watching the QCs thrash it out is exhilarating." Across the energy departments, trainees said: "There is going to be that due diligence and doc review to do, but the teams get you very involved in the research side of things."

The corporate practice includes general practice work such as "your classic M&A, private equity, capital markets work," as well as sector-specialist work such as the above-mentioned energy, insurance and TMT. Clients include Barclays, Merrill Lynch, UBS, HSBC and Deutsche Bank. Herbert Smith has recently advised The Jones Group on its £215m acquisition of Kurt Geiger, and BSkyB on that ill-fated £7.8bn offer from News Corporation. On the whole, "all the corporate groups are inclusive and as a trainee you get access to a range of work." Although there is plenty of due diligence to do, "the teams really trust you to handle the clients and take responsibility. You definitely get more autonomy here than in most of the litigation seats."

Although finance isn't a practice traditionally associated with Herbies, "the department is actually amazing and you learn so much," trainees said. One elaborated: "I think realistically our teams are only a tenth the size of Clifford Chance's or Allen & Overy's, but we offer a very different model. We'll take on a smaller number of highly complex deals. The idea is when something needs proper attention, clients come to our specialists." Another added: "We're also more borrower-heavy than bank-heavy. There are several non-European clients wanting to invest, and our Asian links give us a big advantage in new markets." Although "there isn't as much finance work around" at the moment, trainees all remarked on the "huge" amounts of responsibility they received. "You have to get trainees involved or you won't meet the tight deadlines. From day one you're expected to be fully functioning." In an interesting development, it's recently been announced that the

real estate practice will be merged with the finance department in a restructure following the Freehills tie-up.

Dancing shoes

The working hours are "as you would expect when you come to a big firm." There are going to be some very late nights here, and some weekend work. One interviewee said: "I think on average it works out at a 9pm finish, with better days and worse." Fortunately, "you're hardly ever sat on your own into the evening. If you're working, it's because your team is working. If you put in the hard effort, people do notice and are appreciative."

Herbies "does still retain that 'formal' reputation, but the negative connotations that accompany that word aren't applicable," trainees thought. One said: "It's formal in the sense that professional integrity and perfectionism are valued extremely highly. People take a lot of pride in what they do and that focus can perhaps be interpreted as formality." There aren't dress-down Fridays "but I certainly don't have to wear a tie every day," an interviewee attested. "The main thing is people have a sense of humour," another added. "Everyone is willing to laugh at themselves. It's extremely refreshing. People are good-natured, but are aware of upholding our reputation." Trainees also felt that, "although it's fair to say that you won't know everyone, people don't get lost within Herbies' size. We're a cohesive firm."

A benefit of Herbies' large size is its thriving social scene. Sports enthusiasts can get involved in the likes of football, sailing, netball, cricket, running and tennis. "We have a really good rugby team and the annual Law Society Sevens is always a good day out." Trainees recently set up a music society. "They've got a choir, band and orchestra going. You can also book yourself individual instrumental lessons." Particular praise was reserved for the annual Burns Night ceilidh. "It's mainly a supper in the canteen, but we have a live band and it's great to see you colleagues doing the dosey-doe!" Every other year the firm throws a trainee ball at Kensington Roof Gardens, while on a Friday night "you'll always find someone out on Exchange Square."

"It's obviously from the legal press that this year's retention rates are going to suffer," trainees admitted. "This year's intake was the last of the really big numbers, and they're not keeping everyone." In fact, 83 out of 100 qualifiers stayed on in 2012, not a bad result, considering.

And finally...
Aspiring litigators in particular should look out for this firm, which can also provide the big corporate experience.

Higgs & Sons

The facts

Location: Brierley Hill

Number of UK partners/solicitors: 29/45

Partners who trained at firm: 55%

Total number of trainees: 10

Seats: 4x4 + 1x8 months

Alternative seats: None

Extras: Pro bono – Birmingham Employment Advice Centre

On chambersstudent.co.uk...

- How to get into Higgs & Sons
- Higgs' new home

Forged in the crucible of the Industrial Revolution, this long-standing Black Country firm can give the bigger Brum outfits a run for their money...

Back to Black

Higgs started out in 1875, at a time when coal coking operations, iron foundries and steel mills made the Black Country one of the most heavily industrialised areas in England. Since then, it has grown to become one of the largest firms in these parts, and life is looking good: revenue for 2011 increased by 12.4% on the previous year, to £12.6m, and the firm's corporate department saw a turnover increase of 23%, signalling positive growth in an area that Higgs isn't traditionally known for. In fact, revenue has increased every year since 2007/08.

Operating out of new headquarters in Brierley Hill, as well as a smaller office in Kingswinford, Higgs appeals to trainees because it's "*going places. We're doing well in comparison to other firms in the area, and I feel confident that I'll have a job in two years' time,*" said one. Geographic expansion isn't likely any time soon, but that doesn't stop Higgs competing strongly against larger firms in Birmingham, securing clients from the West Midlands and beyond such as Computech International, Folkes Group and Claimar Care Group.

Preferential seatment

Seat allocation at Higgs is "*all very fair and balanced, and you can at least have a go at most of the things you'd like to do.*" Trainees rank six preferences before they start, and a seat schedule is drafted based upon this list. This is "*a rough schedule and can be changed. The HR team are accommodating and will make the effort to get you where you want to go.*" Four four-month seats are followed by a final 'double seat', consisting of eight months in the department which the trainee anticipates qualifying into. This structure "*encourages retention, because you have that added level of experience at the end of your training contract – you really are prepared for life as a solicitor.*"

"*There are a good range of departments, so if you're not sure about which direction you're heading in, you have a good opportunity to branch out.*" Both commercial and non-commercial interests are catered for, but it is in the latter area that Higgs is particularly strong. Almost one-quarter of the firm's revenue is derived from its private client practice, while another quarter comes from its personal injury and clinical negligence services.

Chambers UK ranks Higgs' private client practice as one of the best in the entire Midlands. "*Its reputation speaks for itself,*" said one source, while others mentioned that "*it's the main reason why I came here.*" Trainees love the spectrum of potential clients, ranging from "*the standard lady off the street to those who have multimillion-pound estates – it's fantastic in that sense.*" There's a good amount of estate and complex tax planning to be done, as well as dealing with probate matters and "*many house visits – there's usually not a day where you don't meet with a client.*" Trainees also get the chance to draft wills, Lasting Powers of Attorney and deeds of appointment.

Trainees usually split a seat between personal injury and clinical negligence and get a mix of both types of work. On the personal injury side, road traffic accidents can lead to claims worth millions and give trainees exposure

Chambers UK rankings

Corporate/M&A	Family/Matrimonial
Crime	Personal Injury
Dispute Resolution	Private Client
Employment	Real Estate

to round-table conferences, attending trial with counsel, taking witness statements and drafting schedules of special damages. *"It's not just road traffic stuff though,"* and our sources had encountered public and employer liability claims as well. Clinical negligence affords the opportunity to attend inquests and settlement meetings in cases relating to brain and spinal injuries, delayed cancer diagnosis and fatal accidents.

Life in this part of Higgs means that *"you need to be able to adapt your people skills accordingly. Sometimes you have to ask difficult questions, particularly when discerning whether a claim is viable or not."* This sensitive touch must be balanced with a degree of resilience, especially when dealing with clients in harrowing circumstances. *"It's certainly a challenge,"* said one source. *"If you become too involved then you won't think with your legal brain, and you need to be there to explain the legal processes to the client, who may not understand them. You don't want to be a cold-hearted robot, but you can't become too emotionally connected either."*

High up the food chain

Higgs' corporate and commercial practice serves many manufacturing and engineering clients, as well as major banks, a significant fast-food chain and an international IT recruitment consultancy. It provides trainees with a *"stark contrast"* to departments like private client and personal injury. *"The clients are different and expect a different level of service. There are more deadlines, which can be challenging, and you work under more pressure."* While classed as a single department, of the two trainees there are at any given time, one will usually take on insolvency and commercial work while the other will see more corporate law.

Trainees also explained that *"it's not like personal injury where referral companies send you the client – here you have to really build relationships and start networking."* This means being taken along to proposal meetings with clients and *"helping the fee earner bring the work into the*

firm." Research is another *"big part of life"* here, as is drafting stock transfer forms and sales contracts in relation to M&A work. *"You're involved in every point of the deal,"* all the way through to *"the champagne upon completion."*

The commercial property department counts one of the country's largest private landlords, London and Cambridge Properties, among its clients. *"The administration work does fall upon the trainees,"* said one source, *"which is not the most exciting thing, but still important to the client."* There's also *"a lot of working with the Land Registry, and you also get to conduct research relating to specific circumstances, for instance when a site is multi-purpose and contains a mixture of both residential and commercial spaces."* Other seats include dispute resolution, employment, commercial, residential property, family, and motoring and private criminal/regulatory.

Supervisors are good at *"helping you to focus on what you would like to do more of,"* while end-of-seat reviews with the head of department and HR *"give you more of an overview of how you are doing in the firm generally. It's all really constructive, and there's nothing to fear."* Trainees always share an office with a supervisor – in most cases a partner.

Higgs gigs

The *"state of the art"* Brierley Hill office elicited much enthusiastic comment. Located on the Waterfront Business Park, it's a far cry from the firm's former high-street digs. The new building provides trainees with *"a more professional environment with a very modern interior."* The office layout itself helps to promote interaction: there's a *"huge atrium"* where the trainees gather for lunch every day.

All trainees are members of the Birmingham Trainee Solicitors Society and the Wolverhampton Junior Lawyers Division, both of which organise regular events, including tango nights and sporting tournaments. Higgs also hires external venues for Christmas and summer parties, the most recent of which was held *"in a hotel nearby – it was very impressive and lively, with nice food and music and a free bar."* Each year Higgs picks a new charity to support (this year it's the Paul Ackrill Trust) and trainees get involved in the corporate social responsibility committee, which organises related events.

And finally...

"We've so many partners who trained here, so obviously it gives you aspirations." In fact, over half of current partners trained with the firm, and in 2012, both second-years remained with the firm to take the next step on that long career path...

"Graduates should be prepared to be flexible in their careers. The legal profession is in a state of flux: its structure could be very different in five or ten years."

Training Partner

Hill Dickinson LLP

The facts

Location: London, Liverpool, Manchester, Chester, Sheffield

Number of UK partners/solicitors: 200/283

Partners who trained at firm: 15%

Total number of trainees: 39

Seats: 4x6 months

Alternative Seats: Overseas seats, secondments

Extras: Pro bono – Manchester Law Centre; language classes

On chambersstudent.co.uk...
- How to get into Hill Dickinson
- The firm's history
- The story of Halliwells

Hill Dickinson's traditional strengths in areas like marine, insurance and professional negligence have been complemented by an increasingly hefty corporate practice.

North by northwest

If success is determined by revenue, then this has been a very good year for North West firm Hill Dickinson. It posted a turnover of £110.1m in 2011/12, up from £100.1m the previous year. Partner Alastair Gillespie commented: "*We've done extremely well this year in a very difficult economic climate. It's been across the board too: it's not just one area pulling the others through.*" One particular highlight has been the success of HD's corporate practice since it acquired collapsed firm Halliwells' offices in Sheffield and Liverpool in 2010. It now has a "*heavyweight*" corporate presence to complement its renowned marine department, region-leading professional negligence team and money-spinning insurance practice. Managing partner Peter Jackson said: "*The firm continues to buck the trend against a challenging economic backdrop. Our corporate and commercial work has been a key area of success for the firm and is an area we will continue to drive forward.*"

This doesn't mean HD is abandoning its roots. Gillespie adds: "*Our profits have been driven by building on what we already offered. We've stayed loyal to these areas too.*" HD is now recognised for its expertise in seven main practice areas as named on its website: insurance; company and commercial; marine; employment and pensions; healthcare; property and construction; and professional risks.

Shipping news

Hill Dickinson has domestic offices in Liverpool, Manchester, London, Sheffield (acquired from Halliwells) and Chester. The firm has an international presence in Singapore and Piraeus, to which shipping secondments are available. These are open to trainees in all offices, but we were informed that those in London usually had first preference. Alastair Gillespie remained tight-lipped on specific destinations, but did say the firm is looking at other potential international opportunities. Domestic client secondments are also available.

Training contract hopefuls apply to individual offices but those in Liverpool and Manchester will have a wider selection of seat choices and can switch between offices to complete certain seats – this is often actively encouraged to improve internal networking. Trainees who end up in the London office stay there for the duration, barring secondments, and should be prepared to undertake a seat in shipping. Trainees in the City said this wasn't compulsory, but that you can "*expect to do shipping or commodities, as there are not enough seats in other teams. It's definitely more shipping-focused in London.*" Trainees have no choice about which department they visit first but are able to give three preferences before each remaining seat.

The insurance department is responsible for more than one-third of HD's revenue. In 2011/12, it brought in £40m, which was a 12.8% increase on the previous year. The practice group is split into teams dealing with specific areas including fraud, motor claims, regulatory, casual-

Chambers UK rankings

Agriculture & Rural Affairs	Insurance
Banking & Finance	Intellectual Property
Clinical Negligence	Pensions
Commodities	Private Client
Construction	Professional Discipline
Corporate/M&A	Professional Negligence
Court of Protection	Real Estate
Dispute Resolution	Real Estate Litigation
Education	Restructuring/Insolvency
Employment	Shipping
Health & Safety	Social Housing
Healthcare	Transport
	Travel

ty claims and catastrophic injuries. Professional and financial risks is also included under the insurance banner, but many trainees take a whole seat in this specific area. Those who sat in fraud reported *"a team that is happy to delegate responsibility. Not all the cases are high-value, so you get the chance to manage your own caseload. You can see the steps of litigation and the team is prepared to give you your own advocacy."* Trainees in the regulatory team can get involved in a number of specialist areas, including health and safety, sports arbitration, trading standards and sports PI. Sources reported *"a lot of client contact"* and *"plenty of opportunities to get out of the office,"* including numerous trips to court. The professional risks team was succinctly defined by one trainee as *"defending professionals who've messed up or allegedly messed up."* This might include representing surveyors, barristers, doctors, dentists or vets. Unsurprisingly the work was described as *"well varied,"* with day-to-day tasks including drafting court documents and meeting witnesses. Others reported being given their own caseloads but *"only on very small, low-value claims."*

Marine law is where Hill Dickinson made its reputation. Liverpool was the second port of the British Empire when Edward Morrall opened his small practice in the city in 1810, and the firm quickly established itself as a leader in maritime law. It has been involved in many famous cases over the decades – acting for White Star Line, owners of the 'Titanic', after the ship's tragic sinking in 1912, and for the owners of the ocean liner 'Lusitania', after it was sunk by German U-Boats during World War I. But enough of the past, because this area still provides the second-largest revenue stream for the firm. The marine, trade and energy department is split into many subsets. These include: shipping; marine personal injury and regulatory; commodities; and piracy. There's also a specialist yacht team. Unfortunately, much of the work undertaken by the department is confidential, so we can't tell you about the many interesting cases the firm has worked on, but we can tell you that another client is Costa Cruise, and HD is advising on the catastrophic consequences of the 'Costa Concordia' casualty.

"Shipping is a very broad area and there's a lot to learn within it. It's hard to get your head around how big it really is." Contentious shipping is split between 'dry' and 'wet' work (see page 146 for definitions). Sources who'd sat here said they were *"generally assisting with any kind of drafting or research,"* but also went to court and got good client contact via e-mail and phone. The marine personal injury seat involves work for big shipping and cruise authorities. HD often defends them against slip and trip claims, but also in the face of more serious issues, such as people going missing off cruise liners. Sources said this seat *"involves a lot of technical jurisdictional issues,"* but also reported having their *"own caseload, often on very high-value matters."*

Fighting back

"In terms of our size we haven't really punched our weight as a corporate firm," says Alastair Gillespie, *"but we're addressing that now with the takeover of Halliwells."* Trainees agree there's *"certainly more of a corporate commercial feel at the firm now."* The corporate team offers advice to all sorts of clients, from small start-ups and financial institutions to large listed and private companies, both in the UK and abroad. HD's corporate clients include the likes of Everton FC, Chester Zoo and Fayrefields Foods. Recent deals include acting for shareholders in the $20 million sale of Jennic to Dutch company NXP Semiconductors. Sources told us they *"always got quality work"* in this seat, with one trainee being particularly happy to have drafted a share purchase agreement. HD is also a significant force in the health sector, representing more than 100 NHS and private sector clients nationally. It also acts for large private sector regulators, including the Care Quality Commission. The healthcare team in the North West is retained by the NHS Litigation Authority to bail out healthcare professionals or NHS bodies when claims are brought against them for malpractice or other contentious issues. Examples include representing Alder Hey Children's Hospital at the Redfern Inquiry into post mortem organ retention. Trainees who spent time here were extremely positive about the experience. *"There was loads of client contact from the start and I was handling a lot of issues on my own after only a few months. I knew the cases and the clients inside out,"* said one. Our interviewees reported being involved in clinical negligence matters such as a high-value brain injury case, and going to a GMC hearing on a regulatory case. They also frequently *"man the phone line to provide advice to GPs before anything develops into a legal matter."*

"The latest I've stayed is midnight a couple of times," said one source, and we didn't find anyone else who'd stayed beyond that. *"It varies by department. Shipping is about 9.30am to 7pm, property not as long, maybe 9am to 6pm. Employment is as and when you're busy. I've been here until 7pm on a Friday and the partner has told me to go home. There's a 'can it wait?' attitude."*

JLD and Coke

Overall, trainees were very upbeat about their time at Hill Dickinson. Any complaints were almost exclusively made by those in the London office. The quality of work isn't an issue, but we heard consistent grumbles about the *"awful"* offices that are *"really starting to show their age."* Faulty air conditioning and heating systems leave trainees struggling in their own micro-climates. The London contingent also bemoaned the lack of communication, both internally – appraisals were said to be not rigidly adhered to, leaving some feeling *"let down"* by the process – and externally with the northern offices, exacerbating feelings of a north/south divide. *"It does seem like it's the Londoners and the North West from the start,"* said one. Alastair Gillespie said of these complaints: *"We are directly addressing issues with the premises in London and place great importance on ensuring that our London teams are happy."*

Trainees up north had no such complaints and those stationed in the Liverpool HQ gave glowing reports of their stunning offices with spectacular views over the docks. *"It's nice to work in a building that reflects where the firm is at in the market,"* beamed one trainee. Our Liverpool-based interviewees were also keen to note the amazing subsidised café that offers *"a wonderful selection of home-made cakes that are very difficult to resist."*

Trainees' social lives are based around the local Junior Lawyers Division, for which the firm pays membership fees. The JLD runs weekly events like wine tasting and holds formal Christmas and summer balls. Trainees in Liverpool also have close ties with the Merseyside Young Professionals group while those in Manchester are associated with the Manchester Trainee Solicitors Group. These associations showcase the strong emphasis HD puts on its trainees networking. One second-year said: *"You're encouraged to go out and network from about day three. You're never seen as too junior to go out and bring in business."* Networking is also encouraged internally and in the Liverpool office there is a bi-monthly mid-week mingle (complete with sandwiches and drinks) for everyone to participate in. The trainee committee is responsible for the trainee-led social scene and they organise numerous activities such as trips to the races. There is a prevalent Friday night drinks culture up north but in London the social scene seem less well attended: *"If you make the effort there's lots of things to do. Unfortunately lots of trainees don't make the effort."*

Trainees come from a good mix of top universities, many in the North and Midlands. We noticed that when we made our random selection of trainees this year, we hit a lot of pure law graduates rather than those who had completed the GDL. Looking back at the last couple of years, this does seem to be something of a trend and we asked the firm if we were onto something. They said no, and 50% of the 2013 intake are apparently non-law grads. Some of the London trainees, though not all, *"have a Masters in shipping or connections in that industry."* When asked what Hill Dickinson looks for in potential trainees, a larger-than-usual proportion mentioned the dread phrase, *"commercial awareness."* We asked one to be more specific: *"Knowledge of the markets we work in: know our offices' business and their client base. That would stand you in good stead."*

And finally...

"We pride ourselves on recruiting to retain," says partner Alastair Gillespie, and Hill Dickinson does usually retain most of its qualifiers. It kept on 29 of 36 in 2012.

Hogan Lovells

The facts

Location: London

Number of UK partners/solicitors: 155/408

UK partners who trained at firm: 34%

Total number of trainees: 133

Seats: 4x6 months

Alternative seats: Overseas seats, secondments

Extras: Pro bono – Criminal Injuries Compensation Authority, RCJ CAB and others

On chambersstudent.co.uk...
- How to get into Hogan Lovells
- More on the old Hogan & Hartson

Following the transatlantic merger of 2010, Hogan Lovells' London office is seeing more international work, particularly in its main practices: corporate, finance and litigation.

Love in a hot and cold climate

Hogan Lovells is *"now truly international,"* said one trainee. After the merger of City colossus Lovells and US firm Hogan & Hartson, Hogan Lovells now has over 2,300 lawyers in over 40 offices all over the globe. There's no rest for the mighty though: just a few months ago the firm planted a flag in Brazil. *"I'm hoping for a second-ment in Rio,"* joked training partner Ailbhe Edgar. In fact, in our chat with Edgar we touched on the firm's plans for Latin America, Asia (*"a key development area"*), the States and Russia – Hogan Lovells really is keeping lots of balls in the air at the moment. Read more from the interview with Edgar on our website.

In London, Lovells is one of those firms pushing at the magic circle. There's shedloads of international work to be had and deals frequently make headlines in the *Financial Times*. Notably, the Brits have been advising News Corp on its £290m acquisition of the international TV production company Shine Group, working with colleagues in the States, Paris and Berlin. The corporate department was head of the operation but drew upon the expertise of the commercial, tax, employment, share schemes and IP/IT teams (showing that teamwork really does matter). Corporate may be the firm's biggest department, but historically the litigation team has always been the star name. It has recently been working with the Moscow office, acting for BTA Bank on one of the largest alleged fraud cases in the English courts, with well over 100 hearings so far.

The firm's revenue stayed flat between 2010 and 2011 – but we're still talking billions, rather than millions, of dollars. The contribution made by the London office to total revenue rose from 23% to 26% ($433m in total).

Students are drawn to Hogan Lovells for *"the quality of training and the breadth of practices"* and the firm is ranked by *Chambers UK* in over 40 areas. One new starter said: *"It's not just corporate and finance work here, there are strengths in every department."* However, a more seasoned fourth-seater warned: *"People have to be careful if they are coming to the firm for its niche areas. Trainees can't always secure that experience. The seats are primarily in the bigger departments."* A stint in either corporate and finance is compulsory, as is a contentious-based six months.

In fact, the seat allocation system was a major gripe among our sources. Before joining, incomers state preferences for their first seat. However, the remainder of the training contract is determined *"when you've only been in the firm for three months."* Midway through the first seat, trainees get presentations from every subgroup in the firm and then rank six preferences (including an optional secondment). The HR team *"tries to accommodate your choices. After that, there's no flexibility and you get no choice in what order you sit in departments."* This system leaves some *"completely happy,"* and we even heard of trainees securing two niche seats. Others were less satisfied with the process: *"I think the word 'lottery' is too strong a term to describe the system..."* said one, but then used it anyway. The firm says it introduced the current

Chambers UK rankings

Administrative & Public Law	Intellectual Property
Asset Finance	Investment Funds
Banking & Finance	Life Sciences
Banking Litigation	Media & Entertainment
Capital Markets	Outsourcing
Commodities	Parliamentary & Public Affairs
Competition/European Law	Pensions
Construction	Pensions Litigation
Consumer Finance	Planning
Corporate/M&A	Private Equity
Data Protection	Product Liability
Dispute Resolution	Professional Negligence
Employee Share Schemes & Incentives	Projects
	Public International Law
Employment	Public Procurement
Energy & Natural Resources	Real Estate
Environment	Real Estate Finance
Financial Services	Real Estate Litigation
Fraud	Restructuring/Insolvency
Information Technology	Retail
Insurance	Tax
	Transport

system after receiving feedback from former trainees who felt stressed at not having the certainty of fixed seats in place. Maybe there's a happy medium to be found. In consolation, trainees can apply for qualification in any department (regardless of whether they've completed a seat there). Once assigned a seat, our sources recommended approaching the department's training principal to "*find the work you want. You should try to create the training contract that you want it to be.*"

At the time of our calls, the vast majority of Hogan Lovells' fourth-seaters had completed a secondment: "*It's unusual not to,*" they said. Each year, up to 20 trainees jet off to Brussels, Dubai, Hong Kong, Paris and Singapore. In 2012, Hogan Lovells offered a finance seat in New York for the first time – not surprisingly, "*applications for it are through the roof,*" says Edgar. Overseas secondments are "*brilliant, with more responsibility than I could have imagined,*" said one interviewee. If you tick 'yes' to a secondment and the international placements are then filled up, you'll be "*automatically placed on a client secondment, so it's a bit of a risk if you don't want to do one of those.*" Luckily, our sources said client placements are a "*fantastic opportunity – and the work/life balance is great.*" Popular destinations are John Lewis, Save the Children and ITV, while other options include Barclays, ExxonMobil, Prudential and the brewery SABMiller.

Who's Hoganing all the beer?

"*The whole way through, the training has been great and they take it very seriously. There's a nice blend of work experience, seminars and different opportunities. At the start of each seat, you get weeks of training to make sure you're up to date on everything,*" trainees said. "*Real responsibility tends to kick in in the second seat. The more you prove yourself, the better the work.*"

Corporate is the firm's largest department. Its biggest M&A transaction of 2011 was SABMiller's £7.8bn acquisition of Foster's: "*SABMiller is a big client and I occasionally see people wandering around the office with crates of beer,*" said one interviewee. Trainees in the corporate department can enter subgroups such as private equity, corporate finance or regulatory. Daily tasks include "*proof-reading and discrete drafting tasks on documents like share purchase agreements.*" Some trainees felt they had an "*administrative role*" but with frequent client contact "*through e-mail and telephone.*"

If trainees don't complete a stint in corporate, finance is a necessity. The department offers seats in banking; capital markets; project finance; infrastructure and project finance; and restructuring/insolvency. Trainees collate documents, "*which is much harder than it sounds, as you need to know what they are,*" as well as case management and bits and pieces of drafting. There's quite a bit of client contact too and one source had been "*arranging signing meetings, both physically and virtually.*" Infrastructure and project finance is the "*least financey part in the department.*" The seat is "*really enjoyable due to the small, tight-knit team. Trainees manage the conditions precedent for big deals and set up completions. It might not be intellectual work but it's really important. They put loads of trust in you.*"

The real estate department is "*quite big and takes on six to eight trainees per seat.*" It's been busy too, advising Prudential on the £400m sale of its Green Park office near Reading. There are smaller files too which trainees handle: "*You are given a lease to do and you run with that from the start. Most of the work you do will be your own files.*" This means loads of responsibility and more client contact than the other seats. "*As a first-seater it can be quite daunting, but it's a fantastic learning curve.*"

Atticus Finch and chums

The litigation department works on "*big international projects, sometimes with our US colleagues.*" Due to the size of the cases, "*there's more scope for disastrous consequences, so trainees are monitored more heavily than in transactional work,*" sources told us. Trainees described the work as "*research-heavy*" and the department as "*a little more old-fashioned*" than the others. Day-to-day tasks depend on the subgroup trainees are assigned to: one source had been "*preparing bundles with letter-writing restricted to four sentences*," whereas others had enjoyed "*attending meetings with clients and counsel.*" One trainee said they "*enjoyed the creativity in drafting witness statements.*"

All contentious seats come with advocacy training via an in-house Professional Skills Course, which our sources couldn't recommend highly enough. Trainees can put this training into practice working on pro bono projects. These offer trainees high-level work, and luckily "*the firm is excellent at providing pro bono opportunities in any department you work in.*" Trainees had helped start up small charities, advised on life insurance policy and criminal injuries compensation, and represented clients in tribunals. The firm also "*does a lot for the victims of the London bombings as well as smaller-scale work for victims of domestic violence,*" one source added.

But is there time to take on pro bono? Although trainees don't have billable-hour targets, one was miffed that "*pro bono doesn't count as chargeable*" for NQs (though the firm pointed out it does count towards a discretionary bonus). As a trainee "*you have to find time to fit it in around normal work*" and the hours "*totally depend on the department.*" Corporate and finance are notoriously "*up and down,*" with leaving times ranging from 5pm to 5am – more usually somewhere in the middle. Pensions and property "*are well known*" for allowing more regular finishes, perhaps at around 7pm.

Freeedooommmm!

"*Firms often have a stereotype,*" a trainee declared. "*Lovells' is that it's friendly and nice – and that is true, by and large.*" We wouldn't presume to comment on whether it is "*a nice version of Slaughter and May,*" as one source claimed, but it does have a reputation in the City for being quite a pleasant environment to work in. Most interviewees told us: "*As with all big firms, there's no standard culture. It very much depends on what department you are in.*" The general consensus was that "*smaller groups have a sense of community. In bigger departments, that's more difficult.*" And is the old 'lovely Lovells' reputation deserved? "*Friendly isn't the right term. Grounded is,*" argued one source. "*Obviously in a firm of this size not everyone is going to be nice, but on the whole you don't see people walking around thinking they are great because they are a lawyer. They seem more down to*

earth." Our sources felt "*well taken care of on a personal level.*" Said one: "*You feel as if people in this firm are less likely to make you kill yourself because they need something doing. They appreciate I'm a human being who has interests outside of work. I'm not afraid to check BBC Sport on my screen.*"

Since the 2010 merger, the London office hasn't seen much change apart from "*bigger deals and more international contact.*" Trainees reported that the firm is "*very English,*" and has a high proportion of Oxbridge-educated juniors. There are "*a few*" international trainees and the remainder of the class hail from "*universities like Exeter, Nottingham, Warwick and Durham – but you don't need a First from the redbricks to get in.*" The firm says it has increased its number of target universities to 24, and has a strong relationship with Birkbeck. Trainees are generally relatively fresh out of uni, perhaps having completed a Master's degrees or pursued pupillage. Some 57 of 73 second-years stayed with the firm on qualification in 2012.

The office itself is "*one of the best bits of working here. We share a room with our supervisor and we get our name on the door,*" one trainee said. "*The foyer has flower arrangements and Europe's tallest indoor water sculpture.*" Check out the firm's graduate recruitment homepage for a video loop. We heard that lawyers sing carols in the foyer at Christmas.

To work off the cookies dotted liberally around the place, the gym in the basement offers free exercise classes and there are plenty of sports teams to get involved with – "*cricket, football, rugby, ladies' football, hockey, softball...*" For non-sporty types, social activities include charity events such as walks and quizzes. Trainees in the smaller teams sometimes get invited to partners' houses for summer barbecues. Trainees often socialise among themselves: "*The large size of the intake is good from that point of view. There are plenty of lunches arranged and if you go to our nice canteen at 1pm, you'll always know someone. And half the group can be found in the pub on a Friday night.*"

There's a firm-wide summer party which everyone attends, including trainees and support staff. In 2012 it was brought forward to April to coincide with the retirement of Hogan Lovells' co-chair and "*lycra-onesie-wearing*" legal legend John Young. During the summer/retirement party, he zipwired into the venue dressed as Braveheart.

And finally...

"*Consider where Hogan Lovells is going in light of the merger and be aware of its ambitions now it's really international,*" advised trainees. "*We have a unique brand to offer post-merger, and can handle cross-border work more than ever before. We're looking now to leverage that and to compete with very top firms.*"

Holman Fenwick Willan LLP

The facts

Location: London

Number of UK partners/solicitors: 76/114

Total number of trainees: 30

Seats: 4x6 months

Alternative seats: Overseas seats, secondments

Extras: Pro bono – Morden Legal Advice Centre

On chambersstudent.co.uk...

- How to get into HFW
- Piracy: an international problem
- HFW's history

This tip-top shipping firm makes waves in a sea of sectors, so there's superb training to be had across a spate of different areas.

Read all a-boat it

Holman Fenwick Willan is an institution in the maritime world. The firm's origins date back to the late 1800s, when solicitor and seafarer extraordinaire Frank Holman set up shop on London's Lime Street. Riding the wave of his family's historical success in shipping – among their accomplishments were the establishment of two hull insurance organisations and one of the world's first shipping protection clubs – Holman eventually enlisted E.A. Fenwick and W.C. Willan as first mates, and the triumvirate embarked on its maiden voyage as HFW. A century-plus later, it's clear their endeavours have paid off: HFW is celebrated at home and at sea as a leader in shipping law, recognised in *Chambers UK* alongside fellow maritime experts Ince & Co. Thanks to the fairly sturdy nature of the shipping industry and the fact that litigation makes up some 82% of HFW's business, the recession has been relatively smooth sailing. The firm managed to keep revenue afloat throughout the downturn – posting a salubrious 10% rise in 2011 – and even pulled off international office openings in Perth and Sao Paulo in 2011. *"There will always be problems in shipping, so in that respect we're more recession-proof than other firms. We've actually got a lot of work that resulted from the market crash,"* trainees reported. At present, the firm relies on a global network of 14 offices across Europe, Asia and Australia, with flagship London leading the way.

In keeping with management's aim to maintain its status as *"the leading firm in international commerce,"* the last few decades have seen HFW fish for offerings beyond traditional shipping work. Trade and energy, insurance, corporate, finance and aviation all now feature among the sectors covered, tacking the likes of Barclays, BP and Kuwait Oil Company onto the firm's already respectable client list. Transactional work in particular has been lavished with some extra attention lately as the firm endeavours to guarantee its ability to *"actively sell our capabilities across the board,"* in the words of training principal Toby Stephens. That said, we're not talking your run-of-the-mill corporate transactions here; deals tend to retain a heavily industrial flavour. A recent success on the M&A front saw HFW advise on one of the year's largest deals in the mining sector: the sale of a 25% stake in Indonesian coal mining outfit Bumi to Vallar.

Trainees can choose from seats in trade and energy; shipping and transport; insurance/reinsurance; commercial banking and disputes; aerospace; and corporate, projects and finance (CPF for short). No seats are compulsory, though *"pretty much everyone does CPF to satisfy SRA requirements"* as it's the sole transactional seat. Each seat is quite broad, so trainees' exposure to particular matters and sectors can vary wildly depending on the partners they work with and how busy the department is when they visit. *"Sometimes when we compare our workloads, it can seem like we're at different firms!"*

Seats ahoy

Trainees are assigned to their first seat and submit a *"wish list"* for each subsequent one, naming their top three choices to give the HR team an initial idea of where people want to go. *"There's room for specific partner and sub-team requests."* A list is then circulated confirming where spots are available and trainees bid for their prefer-

Chambers UK rankings

Asset Finance	Insurance
Aviation	Shipping
Commodities	Transport
Dispute Resolution	Travel

ence. There are usually a minimum of two spots up for grabs in each seat, so the majority of people end up with their first choice.

While a sizeable chunk of trainees tend to arrive each year with some kind of interest in shipping work, those with alternative interests are well catered for. "*The firm is equipped for a variety of work beyond its traditional reputation for shipping. It's possible to do a training contract without actually touching on shipping law now,*" one pointed out. "*We've just added an aerospace team, and there are new opportunities for trainees all the time. It's an exciting time to be here.*"

The trade and energy department "*is incredibly broad,*" handling everything from contractual disputes and international arbitration matters to insolvency cases and derivatives work. On the commodities front, HFW acts for trading companies like the International Cotton Association and Kuwait Oil Company on quality, pricing and shipping matters. "*Most cases involve contractual disputes between buyers and sellers looking to ship things like wheat, oil, grain and coal,*" trainees informed us. "*That means you occasionally touch on shipping law since clients are often charter parties.*" While some trainees spend their seat working for partners who focus exclusively on one type of work, others "*float around more generally.*" Alongside the occasional research assignments and obligatory bundling comes "*a lot of drafting and client contact – you're involved in case management daily, so you're often meeting with counsel and trade experts. There's not a lot of black-letter law.*"

Commercial banking and disputes "*is a new department – it's sort of a spin-off of trade and energy with some more commercial elements,*" sources explained. As such, "*there's a lot of overlap between the two.*" The group handles disputes across the construction, marine, banking, natural resources and commodities sectors. Thanks to "*drastic changes in the shipbuilding market,*" shipbuilding disputes currently comprise a hefty portion of the work, though the group also contends with fraud, banking and insolvency matters. Clients are "*mostly international*" and range from Abu Dhabi Commercial Bank, which the firm is representing in a litigious matter connected to the infamous Saad/Al Gosaibi fraud case, to WMS Gaming, one of the world's biggest slot machine suppliers. Trainees reported taking a "*very involved*" stance in pro-

ceedings, attending meetings with counsel and interacting "*regularly*" with clients. "*I got to go in front of a couple of masters in the Royal Courts of Justice,*" one said, recalling the experience as "*scary but totally exciting.*"

Maritime = merry times

Shipping and transport is HFW's biggest department, and trainees assured us a seat here is "*great fun.*" The work is broadly split into two factions: wet and dry shipping. The former deals with physical damage to vessels like collisions and salvage, acting for P&I clubs, underwriters, shipowners and salvors (the guys responsible for salvaging ships and their cargo). A recent success saw the team defend a multijurisdictional cargo claim against leading ocean carriage organisation BBC Chartering. The wet team also handles piracy issues, a field in which HFW is a world leader – its lawyers have been involved in more hijacking cases than any other firm globally, contending with the legal issues that arise when pirates seize vessels, rigs and, in some cases, crew. The group's expertise was instrumental in the 2010 release of Paul and Rachel Chandler, the British couple infamously captured and held hostage for more than a year by Somali pirates. On the dry side, there's P&I indemnity claims, charter party disputes and more shipbuilding disputes. "*Unlike commercial, where the litigation is usually court-based, it's more arbitration-based in shipping as we usually deal with insurers rather than owners.*" For trainees, legal research, drafting witness statements and researching various points of shipping law are all part and parcel of the seat. Thanks to "*amazing support staff,*" there's "*less admin and more responsibilities than you'd expect. On a small case I was able to help with the negotiation settlement and draft the settlement agreement,*" one source revealed.

Home and away

The corporate, projects and finance group (aka CPF) is the product of a recent amalgamation between "*what used to be separate corporate finance and ship finance teams.*" Despite the merger, sources still notice a "*firm distinction between deals on the corporate side and the ship finance side.*" While the bulk of corporate work is oil and gas-related projects, the team also advises on multinational regulatory matters and handles M&A in the insurance sector. Trainees identified "*two legs to corporate work: there's an administrative element that means you're often putting together bibles and collating documents for filing; there's also quite a bit of substantive drafting of contracts and shareholder agreements.*" On the finance side "*it's mainly shipping-related deals,*" though the team also handles assets in the superyacht and corporate jet sectors, counting ship finance banks, yacht owners and cruise operators among its clients. HFW's recently been involved with some jumbo ship finance deals, including

Nordea Bank's $750m credit facility for Belgian tanker owner Euronav – the largest financing deal in the tanker market since the onslaught of the recession. *"There's not much research because finance work doesn't really require that,"* trainees told us, describing a stint with the ship finance team as a *"very active"* experience. *"There's a lot of day-to-day case management, which involves drafting mortgages and liaising with various ship registries to make sure certain aspects of the deal can progress."* There's also the odd chance for trainees to run their own matters.

"It's expected that people who come here probably want to go abroad for a seat," said one source, and the vast majority of trainees complete an overseas seat during their training contract. Toby Stephens confirms that demand has risen dramatically in recent years. Each rotation sees seats up for grabs in shipping hubs – which have recently included Paris, Piraeus, Dubai, Hong Kong, Singapore, Geneva, Brussels, Melbourne and Sydney. *"On my first day abroad, I was asked to meet with a client and draft a submission. The degree of responsibility you get is phenomenal,"* one source testified. HFW also sends trainees on secondment to a variety of insurance and banking clients. *"They're department-specific and offered ad hoc."*

Back in the Habit

"If you're not interested in international work, HFW is not the place for you," sources warned. *"There's an international element to almost everything we do."* Indeed, as Stephens points out, *"just short of 50% of our business last year came from outside of London, so giving an international training is something we focus on."* As such, proving you've got not only an interest in but also awareness of international commerce is vital if you want to land a training contract.

Despite the firm's interest in global expansion and an *"increasingly commercial outlook,"* trainees insist HFW's *"miles away from your bog-standard commercial firm –*

the clients aren't just some vague corporate entities." In fact, the firm's maritime roots help the firm retain *"an old-school feel,"* sources thought. *"It's not stuffy or formal, and it's not very hierarchical. But certain practice areas like shipping have an old-fashioned ring to them, so it's rather traditional in that sense."* Moreover, HFW's litigation slant means that corporate cabin fever is rarely an issue. *"Everybody keeps a suit jacket on the back of their chair in case of emergency client meetings or even emergency court hearings. You can never really plan your day – it's quite exciting!"* Of course, *"important deadlines can occasionally keep you working late,"* but late nights aren't the norm. *"The office isn't equipped for late working, which is a good sign – you won't find a late night café or any sleep pods here!"*

Most departments run a weekly drink event, and there's a firmwide buffet lunch every two months or so. *"They lay out a lot of great food. Even before you join, you can attend a Christmas lunch for new joiners as well as a summer one with an outdoor spread – it's buffet central from the off!"* Sources also praise the firm's summer barbecues and sports teams as *"good forums for meeting people from other departments."* Past Christmas dos have included a shindig in the basement and a fancy ball. *"This year there was a live band and Michael McIntyre performed."* A recent summer fête was also a hit, with a fun fair featuring carnival rides and fairground games. *"Throwing wet sponges at the partners was the best,"* one source recalled fondly. Among trainees, ad-lib interaction is pretty frequent, too: most Thursdays and Fridays you can find someone enjoying their Holman's discount at the Habit, a local underground wine bar near the firm's offices behind the Tower of London.

While the firm certainly receives applications from ex-mariners and those with some shipping cred on their CV, landlubbers are welcome all the same. *"An interest in international work is the main thing,"* as is *"the ability to talk about the firm's sectors without bullshitting – they can see right through buzzwords like 'piracy' and 'maritime'."*

And finally...
HFW's a good place to consider if you've a litigious nature and want to be *"more than a slave to the photocopier."* Retention rates aren't too bad either: in 2012, nine of 13 qualifiers stayed on at the firm.

Howes Percival LLP

The facts

Location: Leicester, Northampton, Norwich, London, Milton Keynes, Manchester

Number of UK partners/solicitors: 33/60

Partners who trained at firm: 11% (Midlands), 6% (East Anglia)

Total number of trainees: 15

Seats: 4x6 months

Alternative seats: None

On chambersstudent.co.uk...
- How to get into Howes Percival
- Interview with training partner Chris Houghton

Full-service Howes Percival offers training contracts in the East Midlands and Norwich.

Pour myself a cup of ambition

Trainees and clients alike come to Howes Percival for high-quality work with a regional atmosphere. *"We get the best of both worlds,"* said one trainee. And speaking of two worlds, to trainees, HP is essentially two firms. In the East Midlands, it is made up of the Leicester, Northampton and Milton Keynes offices, while a Norwich base gives it a presence in East Anglia. Two newer offices in Manchester and London are administratively on the 'Norwich' side of the firm. The firm boasts a strong corporate practice in Northampton, Leicester and Norwich, while other important practices include real estate, employment and, in Norwich, private client and agriculture and rural affairs as well.

After a mighty blow to the Milton Keynes office back in 2010, when many of its commercial lawyers defected to what is now SNR Denton, these days HP is *"feeling positive."* Our sources described it as an *"ambitious and forward-thinking firm,"* which provides excellent training, with a good atmosphere, work/life balance and salaries. *"Trainees are valued members of the team – they don't sit there waiting to do the photocopying,"* they said.

And yawnin', stretchin', try to come to life

Trainees are hired either to Norwich or the East Midlands. At the recruitment stage, it's made clear that those recruited to the East Midlands part of the firm can expect to spend time in both Northampton and Leicester during their training contract. Fortunately, the two offices are only about an hour's drive apart.

In the East Midlands, *"the firm's main departments are corporate/commercial, litigation, employment and property."* There's another seat option: private client, but it's not as commonly completed as the others. As per SRA regulations, trainees here must complete a contentious seat and a non-contentious seat. *"For the rest we have free range."* New joiners are *"slotted in anywhere for the first seat,"* and subsequently rank the options in order of preference. First-years, however, are *"at the mercy of second-years' preferences"* and they must pick from the leftovers.

The corporate department has seen *"an increase in corporate deal activity in 2012,"* with corporate partner Robert Colman adding that: *"It is certainly not all doom and gloom. There are cautious, positive movements within the region and in terms of investment coming into the area."* Recently, the team advised BNB Leisure on its acquisition of the share capital of Hoste Arms, a company which owns several leisure and tourism businesses in Burnham Market in Norfolk. HP lawyers also advised the UK subsidiary of Infinitas Learning Group on the purchase of the Norwich based LJ Create Group, a digital education solutions provider. Trainees may complete a seat called company commercial. *"There's the corporate bit, which includes the likes of M&A, share purchase and general transactional work – and then the commercial side which negotiates commercial contracts. You will have heard of most of the main clients we deal with: there are large waste management companies, a bottle manufacturer and a major motorway service operation."* Deals regularly exceed the million-pound mark. However, our sources did *"feel like an integral part of the team"* and had been heavily involved with the partners on larger deals. They were

Chambers UK rankings

Agriculture & Rural Affairs	Planning
Banking & Finance	Private Client
Corporate/M&A	Real Estate
Employment	Restructuring/Insolvency

big fans of the seat, as "*you interact with the entire firm, from employment to commercial property to litigation.*" It's not a nine-to-five job. Trainees had found themselves still in the office at 2am – but this is not a regular occurrence.

Jump in the shower and the blood starts pumpin'

Litigation is another big one. "*Trainees get more responsibility here than in other departments as we can have whole files to ourselves. At the moment, the seat includes litigation work along with some IP,*" we heard. However, the IP team has recently become a department in its own right, so watch out for further developments. Currently trainees in the seat draft witness statements and attend court with counsel, while some had undertaken "*nerve-racking, but fantastic*" advocacy. Additionally, "*the litigation seat should be commended for its client contact,*" one source said. Overall, "*it has a more personal touch than the other seats. Also, it's very varied so it keeps you on your toes. No one case is the same as the next.*"

Employment is the other contentious option in the Midlands offices. Trainees here get exposure to "*juicy*" cases and are heavily involved in drafting and lots of client contact. "*They're certainly not afraid of giving people responsibility but it depends on how much you want. You're always very well supervised and the teaching is excellent,*" our sources told us. The seat has a "*good mix*" of contentious and non-contentious work.

"*I'd say that as well as doing general commercial property, the firm has two big property areas: retail and development. So we get exposure to specialist work as well as general, which is a nice extra element.*" Responsibility in the property department increases with time, but by the end of the seat trainees were speaking to clients or the other side "*pretty much every day.*" There's also loads of drafting and juniors may get assigned their own project. We heard it's great for the more logical and organised personalities as it's "*very procedural.*"

Out on the streets the traffic starts jumpin'

In Norwich, the official seat options include: estates; commercial litigation and asset recovery; commercial property; corporate commercial; planning; and corporate insolvency and recovery. However, as the office only takes on two trainees per year, they are expected to take on work from a variety of senior lawyers and departments at any time... and may also undertake split seats "*which complement each other.*" "*We have other departments like personal injury and employment. They don't have official seats but they use trainees from time to time,*" we heard.

"*Agriculture is a big thing in Norwich, and the estates department focuses on that.*" Estates "*also covers private client and corporate.*" Trainees sitting in the group are "*trusted. I recently did my first completion,*" one said. The department may be viewed as a little more traditional than the others – perhaps due to its head, Jeremy Heal, being "*70 years old. He's very lovely and approachable though,*" an interviewee said. But times are changing. In 2012, the department hired a new partner and a new director, which has "*shaken things up a bit... in a good way.*"

With folks like me...

We think it says a lot about the culture of the firm that trainees told us being at Howes Percival had increased their confidence. It's the level of responsibility they're given that does it: "*Trainees here aren't photocopying robots.*" They are also "*included in the e-mails about the firm's strategy. We know what clients the firm is targeting and it's nice to know that the partners go out there and try and win work. HP is really going somewhere.*" One source even mentioned that although 30 Milton Keynes lawyers defected to Dentons back in 2008, "*some of their clients came back to us.*"

Northampton is the head office but only in that the IT and support systems are based there. The regional managing partner is actually based over in Leicester, and Norwich has a separate one. The East Midlands offices "*have quite a bit of contact and the firm tries to bring us together,*" with regular meetings and a crossover of work. Leicester is a modern-build located out on a business park, whereas Northampton is near the centre in a Victorian building. We get the impression that the buildings reflect the atmospheres in each: Northampton is "*a tiny bit more old-fashioned,*" while Leicester has "*a spring in its step, and maybe a little more corporate.*" The Norwich office is on a pretty street near the city centre, great for easy shopping access in lunch breaks, which at HP are a pleasing 75 minutes long. "*Everyone wants you to have a life outside the office. It's by no means a 9am to 5pm job, but it's not bad. You work to your own workload, and we get paid a lot for the regions.*"

What a way to make a living

When we think of AGMs, the scenario that comes to mind is one of gazing out of the windows at squirrels while the boss drones on about targets. At HP, the AGM involves *"jet skiing, quad bikes, clay pigeon shooting and motorboats."* Once a year, everyone (and by everyone we mean everyone) is bussed out to an activity centre. In 2010 they ended up at Centre Parcs; in 2011 it was Wyboston Lakes. It's one of the few times that staff from Norwich and East Midlands meet each other, and last time round they all had the pleasure of witnessing *"a partner dressing up as Dolly Parton and singing Nine to Five."*

The other big event is the trainee's annual party held in Leicester. The whole of the East Midlands offices and the trainees from Norwich are invited. Generally, Leicester is thought of as a more social than Northampton, with post-work drinks cropping up *"every other Friday or so"* and frequent pub lunches. HP *"doesn't have a culture of drinking every weekend – it's just as and when."* Trainees are involved in a lot of local junior lawyer and marketing events though. *"The firm is very keen on trainees learning to network."* Trainees also get involved in charity work – an East Anglian trainee informed us about an upcoming 'dunk a partner in gunge' event.

The firm recruits heavily in the East Midlands from its vacation scheme – all the current Midlands second-years had completed it. Many of the Norwich trainees, on the other hand, had previously been paralegals at the firm. The 2010/11 trainees came from a *"range of universities,"* including Nottingham, Warwick, UEA, Exeter, Sheffield and Cambridge. *"They look for more than academics though,"* they said. *"Communication and interpersonal skills are a must."* Although the firm likes people to have local connections, that doesn't mean they won't consider those outside the LE, NN or NR postcode areas.

Candidates are advised to do their research and understand *"we are a commercial firm first and foremost, not a private client one."* The most important advice that we were given was that personality is crucial. *"Have something on your CV that is a bit different – something you care about. In my interview, they just talked about my extracurricular,"* multiple sources advised.

And finally...

Our second-year sources were a bit worried about less-than-stellar retention rates from previous years, but in the end six out of eight stayed on – one of three in Norwich and all five in the East Midlands.

Ince & Co

The facts

Location: London

Number of UK partners/solicitors: 57/91

Partners who trained at firm: c.70%

Total number of trainees: 31

Seats: 4x6 months

Alternative seats: Occasional overseas seats

Extras: Language classes

On chambersstudent.co.uk...

- How to get into Ince
- Interview with recruitment partner Kevin Cooper

Small and savvy, Ince & Co provides the perfect setting for those who want to learn the ropes in the worlds of shipping, energy and insurance law.

Making a splash

Shipping law may not inspire quite the same bouncy enthusiasm as, say, helping to put a notorious hoodlum behind bars or hammering home that multimillion-pound corporate deal, but don't rule it out just yet. The lawyers of Ince & Co – heroes of the shipping world – deal with pirated vessels, superyachts and maritime collisions in real time on a daily basis. The law doesn't get much more action-packed than this.

In fact, Ince has racked up an impressive 142 years in the engine room of the maritime industry, and is the only firm to have gained a top *Chambers UK* ranking in shipping every year since 2004. Name a big shipping case in the press in recent years, and chances are that Ince had a hand in it. In January 2012 the firm hit the headlines for its role in the aftermath of the sinking of the 'Costa Concordia', and it continues to advise on high-profile piracy cases in Somalia, the Niger Delta and the Malacca Straits.

While shipping matters account for about half of the work at Ince, energy is on its heels and growing fast. Recruiting partner Kevin Cooper explains: "*The shipping industry as a whole is not in a growth period at the moment, but energy is, so we are matching and manning our skills to that market. It is the fastest-growing area of our practice.*" A trainee confirmed: "*Although historically Ince has been synonymous with shipping, that isn't necessarily still the case.*" Do take into account the firm's litigation focus, though. If you're hoping to become a transactional whizz, perhaps it's best to look elsewhere. "*A lot of people who train here end up doing very little non-contentious work.*"

The global aspect of work at the firm – "*it is all international*" – is another huge draw for trainees. Fittingly based in London's St Katherine Docks, Ince also has offices in Paris, Hamburg, Le Havre, Monaco, Piraeus, Shanghai, Singapore, Hong Kong and Dubai. Its most recent addition – Beijing – sprung up in summer 2012. The sense among trainees is that Ince is blossoming, and Cooper says "*the firm will continue to grow in an organic way over the next few years.*"

Learning the ropes

Ince is set up differently to most law firms in that it has no formal departments, instead favouring a more fluid arrangement involving divisions formerly known as strands but now called groups (because 'strands' was confusing people). "*Partners tend to specialise in one or two groups,*" a trainee explained, "*and as a result, everything is a bit more flexible.*" The firm's work generally falls into the categories of insurance, dry shipping, wet shipping, energy and offshore, commercial disputes, international trade, aviation, and business and finance law.

The 'strand/group' approach has two major consequences for trainees. Firstly, "*we can take work from anywhere,*" and secondly, "*if you start working on a case you are not expected to drop it as soon as you switch strands.*" This means that trainees have heaps of opportunities to dip their toes into all sorts of diverse areas of law, dig out work they're interested in and get really stuck in to every project. "*You physically sit somewhere for six months but that's irrelevant to the type of work you do,*" explained a contented source. "*You can take work from anywhere. I've*

Chambers UK rankings

Asset Finance	Fraud
Aviation	Insurance
Commodities	Professional Negligence
Dispute Resolution	Shipping
Energy & Natural Resources	

worked on a shipbuilding dispute at the same time as insurance, energy and white-collar fraud cases." Ince trainees tend to remain as generalists throughout their training contract, and only narrow their interests down to strands at the end of their first year qualified.

While each six-month period is spent in an office with a partner supervisor, trainees will not necessarily be fed work automatically. Instead, senior lawyers send out 'capacity e-mails' asking who is available and the first trainee to reply jumps aboard the case. "*It's a bit of a free-for-all*" sometimes, as you can imagine. Additionally, a nifty traffic light system allows trainees to update their status on a weekly basis. Red means their plate is full, amber indicates it's limited, and green denotes they're actively seeking work. "*The moment you go onto green you're suddenly bombarded,*" claimed one source, summarising the whole process thus: "*Initially you find work through capacity e-mails, traffic lights and just chatting to people in the lift. It's all about internally marketing yourself.*" Door-knocking is encouraged, and more reserved trainees can find this "*a bit awkward.*" It's best to treat it as part of the learning curve. "*I'd be lying if I said the system of finding work is easy,*" claimed one source, "*but I don't think of it as a negative point – it's just good training.*"

iWreck

On the, quite frankly, off chance that your ship hits an iceberg / is grounded / attacked by pirates, or you're involved in a freak aviation, energy or rail disaster, don't panic – there's an app for that! Ince's international emergency response hotline, contactable 24/7 by phone or iPhone app, deals with such catastrophes in real time. In 2007, for example, a team of tireless Incies helped guide the owners of the 'Hebei Spirit' through a potential PR nightmare as it spilt some 11,000 tonnes of crude oil into the sea off South Korea.

This sort of work is 'wet shipping' at its most exciting. Trainees lap it up, as one explained: "*Wet shipping is all to do with ships crashing and that kind of thing. It can be quite exciting. One of the big differences between wet shipping and most other areas of litigation is that you work on the case as it's unfolding rather than dealing with the legal ramifications in retrospect.*" Essentially, "*it's

much more to do with ships sinking, as opposed to the dry contractual and financial disputes.*" Trainees are able to get stuck in, interviewing all sorts of interesting maritime characters, liaising with experts and occasionally even flying abroad to check out the scene of the incident "*on the ground.*" One trainee soberly reminded us, however: "*There's obviously a lot of interpretation of contracts and practical day-to-day stuff to be done. It's not just paying ransoms, guns, high-speed boats and Somali pirates.*"

The other branch of shipping law may be dry by name, but not by nature – particularly at Ince, with its international outlook. One source explained how this works on a practical level: "*A lot of shipping is dealt with under English law but it's got a worldwide element. On one case I can think of, the ship is in New Zealand, some of the shippers are in China and Taiwan and Brazil, the owners are Greek and the charters are Swiss.*" In the last year the firm has worked on issues including multimillion-pound shipbuilding disputes, drafting contracts for ship purchases and sales, advising clients on international sanctions against Iran and advising on the release of pirated vessels, ransoms and insurance.

The growing energy strand complements the firm's traditional shipping practice, and Ince has long been involved in issues relating to oil rigs and offshore energy. A source explained: "*If you have an oil major who wants to get oil out of the sea bed, he'll hire a contractor to manage the operations, and they'll get a subcontractor to deal with certain parts of the operation or building the platform. In that scenario, there's an enormous amount of money at stake, and things can go wrong.*" On these sorts of big cases trainees report being immersed in a fair amount of doc review, but it's a small price to pay for being in a team that is "*really forward-looking and dynamic. It's a really good place to work at the moment.*"

While big ships and oil rigs may sound like boys' toys, there is a growing female contingent at Ince. "*The subject matter is very male: big ships, drilling machines and pipes. It's very heavy on the engineering and technical sides, and you have to have the right mindset to be interested in that.*" That said, "*while at partner level the firm is very male-dominated, at lower levels there's a higher percentage of females.*"

Ahoy, mateys!

Hours are "*fair and flexible,*" and usually range between 9am and 7pm. There's the odd late night, but "*we're not expected to work late unless we really have to,*" and on Fridays most people have dashed over the road to the pub by 5.30pm – "*an e-mail comes round saying that's where people will be from 5.31pm.*" This is certainly appreciated on pay day, with smug trainees agreeing: "*It's great *that they pay a comparable amount to the top-ten firms, even though we don't work anything like the same hours."*

"It's a lot more relaxed here than I expected for an international law firm," said one source. Several mentioned that *"Ince takes itself a lot less seriously than some of the other places I've worked,"* and its small size works to its advantage: *"People know each individual trainee, what we're good at and what we're interested in. It means there's greater scope for us to follow our interests."* The lack of formal departments encourages people to get to know each other. *"There's no divide between levels – everyone mucks in together and gets on."* One source went so far as to claim that Ince *"feels more like we're part of the shipping and insurance industries, than part of the London legal scene."* As a consequence, the firm is jam-packed with the *"big personalities and colourful characters"* you might associate with these sociable industries, who relish marketing events (often held in-house and catered by the firm's very own former Claridge's chef).

A few sources voiced concerns that as the firm expands, older partners retire and a new generation rises through the ranks, the aura of Ince is becoming *"a bit more corporate."* The consensus is, however, that this is a positive move – *"we need to stay at the cutting edge. There's good leadership at the firm and I feel like it's going in the right direction."* Kevin Cooper agreed: *"Every firm does need to change, but the partnership here feels very strongly about maintaining our firm's ethos as much as possible. It's one of our priorities."*

All above board (well, mostly)

If there's one striking trend when it comes to Ince trainees, it's their international backgrounds. Virtually all of our sources had studied or lived abroad at some stage – *"it's really something you notice throughout the firm. A lot of people have strong foreign links."* It's also clear that the firm values experience in the firm's industry sectors, and not every trainee is a spring chicken: *"A lot are in their 30s or even older."* Age *"doesn't matter – you just need a bit of confidence and maturity,"* explained one source. *"People don't expect you to be a young, naïve 22-year-old. They expect you to be a mature, grown-up 22-year-old."* A hearty dollop of confidence will certainly stand you in good stead. *"You don't need to be overly loud, but if you're not willing to put yourself out there you run the risk of not necessarily having much work to do and missing out."*

Successful candidates should be prepared to *"work hard and play hard."* Monthly 'Ince Drinks' at a local pub are put on the firm's tab, and lawyers of all levels can regularly be spotted in The Living Room bar or The Dickens Inn, both overlooking the docks. The very active sports and social committee arranges the *"brilliant"* May Ball and the Christmas party, as well as ad hoc events like a London Marathon party on the office balcony, carol concerts by the firm's choir, and *"sailing, football, hockey, golf and shooting"* trips. *"You can do as much or as little as you want to."*

Ince has *"a very good track record of keeping trainees on. The policy is that there'll be jobs available for everyone who makes the grade."* In 2012, 12 out of 14 qualifiers took up jobs with the firm.

And finally...
Ince's training contract is not for the faint-hearted, but confident sorts with a proactive approach will reap the rewards at this boisterous firm.

- **You've read the book, now visit the website.** Chambersstudent.co.uk has bonus features for every firm covered in the True Picture, including details of their recruitment process

Irwin Mitchell

The facts

Location: Birmingham, Bristol, Leeds, London, Manchester, Newcastle, Sheffield, Scotland

Number of UK partners/solicitors: 137/355

Partners who trained at firm: 39%

Total number of trainees: 88

Seats: 3x4 + 1x12 months or 4x6 months

Alternative seats: None

Extras: Pro bono – CAB, LawWorks, ProHelp and others

On chambersstudent.co.uk...
- How to get into Irwin Mitchell
- The firm's conversion to an ABS
- Seat and pro bono opportunities listed by location

Best known for its top-notch personal injury and clin neg work, Irwin Mitchell is a legal innovator and has recently become the largest firm to date to convert to an Alternative Business Structure under the Legal Services Act.

ABSolutely fabulous

2012 is Irwin Mitchell's centenary year, but it is the last decade that has really shaped this firm. In that time, it has reorganised practices, expanded across the country and grown to become one of the top 25 law firms in the country. It now has offices in Sheffield, Birmingham, Glasgow, Leeds, London, Manchester, Newcastle and Bristol. All are highly respected for their personal injury (PI) and clinical negligence work. According to *Chambers UK*, no other firm comes close to matching IM for its national standing in these areas. The work is all for claimants rather than defendants, and ranges from *"multimillion-pound"* multi-track claims to smaller five-figure and fast-track ones.

But IM is not all about botched operations and pedestrians tripping over paving stones. In terms of trainee numbers, a quarter of the firm is devoted to 'business legal services' and covers areas such as real estate, corporate, commercial litigation and employment. This side of the firm doesn't quite match the PI and clin neg groups in terms of national standing, and *Chambers UK* primarily recognises it for this type of work in IM's traditional heartland of Yorkshire. Investment in 'business legal services' continues though, with lateral hires from the likes of Lawrence Graham, Nabarro, SJ Berwin and DLA Piper during 2010 and 2011. Trainee numbers are up too, from 21 qualifiers in 2008 to 41 in 2012.

Applicants be warned: trainees here work within either a 'business legal services' (BLS) or 'personal legal services'

(PLS) stream, and only complete seats within the stream they've chosen. So, you can't do a training contract that mixes PI with commercial work. All the offices offer both streams, except for Newcastle and Bristol, which are PLS only. *"It does mean you have to have some idea of what you want to do with your career quite early on,"* trainees pointed out. If that's the case, then the system is *"great."*

The 'stream' system is just one of many changes the firm made in anticipation of its conversion into an Alternative Business Structure. In theory, this move allows for outside investment in the firm, but training partner Lisa Jordan tells us IM's management *"has made no decision whether it will seek outside investment or what form any possible investment may take, but we believe we would be an attractive proposition to investors should we decide to seek investment in our business."* There are already some non-lawyer IM execs who have invested in the firm (this has been allowed since 2009), and Jordan expects this trend will continue. A trainee added: *"The ABS conversion means the firm is having to be more transparent in terms of its costs and overheads. There is also more of a focus on profitability and business development."* Go to our website to read more about ABSs and other changes at the firm.

Up close and Personal

There are a huge range of seats on offer in the PLS stream. The most common are clin neg, serious injury, workplace injury, and industrial/asbestos disease. More

Chambers UK rankings

Administrative & Public Law	Fraud
Banking & Finance	Health & Safety
Charities	Information Technology
Civil Liberties & Human Rights	Personal Injury
	Police Law
Clinical Negligence	Product Liability
Corporate Crime & Investigations	Professional Discipline
Corporate/M&A	Professional Negligence
Court of Protection	Real Estate
Crime	Real Estate Litigation
Dispute Resolution	Restructuring/Insolvency
Environment	Tax
Family/Matrimonial	Travel

obscure personal injury-related seats include travel litigation, neurotrauma, armed forces claims, fast-track claims, public law, public liability, employers' liability and Court of Protection. The PLS stream also offers seats in private client – including family, wills and probate, and pensions. Exactly which seats you can do depends what office you're in. Visit our website for a full breakdown.

Serious injury work covers "*a multiplicity*" of gruesome matters, including brain injuries, orthopaedic injuries and other physical harm resulting from things like RTAs and accidents in the home. As a first-year, "*you assist more senior solicitors with their files, but you get to do everything from taking the initial instruction from the client, through drafting instructions to counsel, to putting into place funding arrangements.*" Trainees get "*good substantive work,*" including taking notes during meetings, drafting court documents, attending case conferences and sitting in on telephone hearings. Second years are even able to run up to 20 or 30 of their own files. Another big area of PI is workplace injury – people getting run over by trucks in warehouses and so on. The team also acts for people with work-related afflictions such as asthma, stress and RSI. A mainstay is acting for claimants who have contracted mesothelioma from exposure to asbestos at work. "*It is a very sad seat,*" one trainee reflected. "*Clients often only have a few months to live, so sometimes you find yourself re-issuing the claim on behalf of the estate after they've died.*" Another added: "*I had to see a lot of clients suffering from mesothelioma – sometimes on my own, sometimes with someone more senior there. They were all really lovely, but it was hard at times.*" For this seat – as well as many of the other PI and clin neg ones – a good bedside manner is required. "*You need to be sympathetic and sensitive, as you are always sitting down with clients and talking about their problems as an individual.*"

Carry on doctor

Unlike PI, the clin neg seat – or to give it its full IM title 'medical law and patient rights' – doesn't trade in subspecialities. There is still "*a wide variety*" of work, however, from complex matters related to the contraction of cerebral palsy at birth to claims over damage sustained during botched hip operations. Common matters include delays in diagnosis (often of cancer), birth defects, mistakes made during operations and negligent care. The firm often acts against the NHS and cases are often highly unusual or complex – take the claim on behalf of a mentally ill patient who nurses failed to try to resuscitate after he attempted to hang himself with a hospital bed sheet. Trainees see cases all the way through: first-years assist solicitors while second-years sometimes get their own caseload. They start by assessing the claim's merits, requesting medical records, contacting experts and analysing the case for the defence, before attending case conferences and going to inquests. Only very rarely do cases go to trial. "*I also took a large number of new client calls,*" a trainee told us. "*Sometimes you have to work with very little information and background knowledge. You have to be on your toes and ready for anything.*" This seat is not for everyone: "*One reason it's different is because we sometimes represent legal aid clients, which means you have to have a different approach to costs and legal action. It is also a very medical-heavy area and you have to understand that side of things.*" Cuts to legal aid funding will doubtless have an effect on this department – once again, head to the bonus features on our website for more detail.

One of IM's most well-known groups is travel litigation. The London-based team deals with slips, trips and illnesses suffered by Brits abroad. This is the reason why IM has two small offices in Spain. Recently, the team was instructed by over 100 victims of the 'Costa Concordia' disaster who are claiming £100,000 each in a class action against the beleaguered Costa cruise company.

Cutting it in business

The BLS side of the firm offers seats in commercial litigation, real estate, corporate, regulatory, employment, insolvency and public sector. Again, the exact selection varies by office.

Corporate works mainly on private company M&A. "*In the North of England we are a big name. We are prominent in the corporate world in Yorkshire,*" one trainee said. "*In London we are not that well known and don't compete with the big names for the big clients. But there is a range of work for smaller and mid-sized companies.*" The team acts for businesses like Evans Cycles, Toni & Guy and the Co-op. It recently helped private equity firm Hardy Mill Holdings with the £10m sale of car servicing business

EMAC. It also does "*a little banking work*" for clients including Yorkshire Bank, Santander and RBS. "*There is the odd bit of mundane work like due diligence and making bibles,*" trainees admitted, "*but you do get to see a lot of clients, go along to meetings, maintain e-mail contact with clients and draft parts of agreements between parties.*"

The level of work in other business teams is similar. In litigation trainees handle "*a bit of research, attend quite a lot of client meetings, prepare instructions for counsel and draft pleadings and letters of advice.*" The London office takes on a lot of work related to FSA investigations. The firm's BLS practice areas are increasingly well regarded by *Chambers UK*: corporate, employment and real estate have all been rising up the rankings, and the latter department is now also recognised for its work in the competitive London market.

Two pints of lager and a packet of bics

Trainees agreed that "*a good work/life balance is still very much part of working here.*" Nevertheless, we have noticed a gradual increase in the hours worked by our interviewees over the past few years. Although "*in some departments it is fairly close to nine-to-five,*" here is a more typical experience: "*I start work at 8am and have usually left by 6.30pm. Sometimes I stay late if I need to.*" PI and clin neg seem to have the best hours, while BLS trainees have more unpredictable workloads and more late nights. Despite this development IM trainees have it pretty good compared to trainees at similar-sized national firms.

While deeming the work/life balance good, trainees had a few grumbles about their salary. "*It is a bit of a bugbear here,*" one said, "*but I expect to be paid less here than at a corporate firm. It would be nice to be paid more, but most people on the PLS side are not fussed about the money: if we were, we'd be working for a firm that acted for defendants.*" Although the business stream trainees naturally didn't exactly make the same comparison, they still reasoned that IM is not a 'long hours, lots of money' firm and the people who come to it aren't looking for that lifestyle.

All IM's offices are open plan and trainees say the "*not too pretentious or formal*" atmosphere within them "*derives from that. There is no lack of interaction between senior and junior people.*" Different departments do have different personalities – "*some are more fun and boisterous, while others are more quiet and industrious.*" The smaller the office, the more personable it tends to be. Newcastle is "*more friendly and everyone knows each other,*" while Sheffield is "*more corporate and professional with a heads-down, work-hard approach.*"

All the offices have a strong social vibe. "*There are monthly bake sales to raise money for charity, and every day someone will bring in biscuits and cakes,*" a Birmingham trainee enthused. "*Lots of people go out for lunch together and sometimes partners will buy everyone coffee. We also have two annual events, a financial-end-of-year party at a local bar and a formal sit-down meal at Christmas.*" All offices have departmental socials, trainee drinks and charity events, and London has an informal "*Friday night pint club.*" There are also "*several plans afoot*" to celebrate IM's centenary, one of which is a firm quiz. "*We always have an annual quiz for charity, but this year we are going to do it in all the offices at the same time and be linked up via video.*"

IM has always had pretty good retention statistics. Trainees said the qualification process is informal, "*fairly relaxed*" and "*open.*" In 2012 most trainees received job offers at the start of May and 31 of 41 qualifiers were kept on.

And finally...
In a rapidly changing legal landscape Irwin Mitchell has been one of the boldest movers. Legal aid cuts will doubtless still have an effect, but the firm looks to have successfully reshaped itself for the new era ahead.

Jones Day

The facts

Location: London

Number of UK partners/solicitors: 53/90 (+12 non-UK-qualified)

UK partners who trained at firm: 45%

Seats: None

Total number of trainees: 28

Alternative seats: Dubai, occasional secondments

Extras: Pro bono – LawWorks, FRU, Waterloo Legal Advice Service, Lawyers Without Borders

On chambersstudent.co.uk...

- How to get into Jones Day
- Headline cases and deals
- More on the non-rotational training

Jones Day's non-rotational training system can be "*daunting*" and "*tricky to manage*" but "*bold and enterprising*" trainees will thrive.

Big deal?

US-founded legal giant Jones Day is one of the ten biggest firms in the world and never seems to stop expanding. In 2011 it opened up shop in São Paulo and established a foothold in Saudi Arabia through an alliance with a local firm. Early 2012 saw an office open up in Düsseldorf, bringing the global total to 34.

JD has been in London for over 25 years but it really started making a noise in 2003 when it took over small, happenin' City firm Gouldens. It's all worked out well and today London is seamlessly integrated into Jones Day World. "*Only this morning I was on the phone to someone in Hong Kong, and in a minute I have to phone someone in our Chicago office,*" a trainee told us. "*A lot of my work relates to the US, and I'm often contacted by our lawyers in the Middle East and Asia to help them understand English law.*"

London is recognised by *Chambers UK* in over a dozen areas. In the City, it sits at the top of the mid-market for M&A and litigation, and its core practices – real estate, banking and restructuring – are ranked at a similar level. Major clients include British Land, the Eurasian Natural Resources Corporation (ENRC) and Procter & Gamble; the latter is, like Jones Day, a native of the state of Ohio.

In slightly perturbing news, the London office literally lost its head in 2011, as office managing partner Russell Carmedy left the firm for Proskauer Rose. A private equity partner followed him there while London's restructuring practice head jumped ship for Weil Gotshal. Jones Day did make at least nine lateral hires of its own in 2011, into practices including energy, construction and financial services regulation.

He got on his bike and looked for work

All this mega-firm business sounds pretty cool, but by now you're probably thinking there are dozens of City firms which offer the same training as Jones Day. Right? Wrong. Unusually among City firms, Jones Day offers a non-rotational training contract. Trainees don't do seats. Instead, they are immediately given their own office and are expected to tout for work from different departments. Scary? You bet. "*It's daunting. On day one you get plonked down in your office, then you have to walk the corridors knocking on doors asking for work and introducing yourself. Luckily, most people keep their doors open. It is scary for the first few weeks, but once you're settled it's fine.*" Trainees also receive initial assignments through contacts made on the vac scheme, during social events or at training sessions. And "*once you've worked with someone, they often come back to you with more work. I can't remember the last time I had to go around knocking on doors,*" a second-year said. None of the trainees we spoke to had had any trouble finding enough work to fill their plates.

The firm's full-service offering gives trainees a range of practices to take work from. London is roughly 25% litigation; 25% corporate; 20% banking and finance; 20% property; and 10% 'other', including energy, construction, competition and IP. Many cases and deals blur the

Chambers UK rankings

Banking & Finance	Environment
Banking Litigation	Fraud
Capital Markets	Pensions
Commodities	Private Equity
Construction	Real Estate
Corporate/M&A	Real Estate Finance
Dispute Resolution	Restructuring/Insolvency
Employment	Tax
	Telecommunications

boundaries between these areas – JD is big in banking litigation, for example.

Provided trainees comply with SRA requirements (making sure they pick up enough contentious work, for example), they can take on work from any department that will have them. "*Some people know instantly what they want to do when they start. I had no idea. I did some competition, some employment, some IP, some finance and some banking litigation. Overall, I have done most of my hours in corporate – maybe 60%.*" Most of our sources tried out a variety of practices in their first six months or year and then focused on one practice group, which they hoped to qualify into. The non-rotational training means there are no 'seats' abroad but recently the firm has sent trainees to Dubai for four to six months, and plans to do so again in future.

...and he kept looking 'til he found it.

Trainees like being able to choose their own areas of work and see matters all the way through. "*I have now done more corporate work than I could ever have done in a seat system,*" one trainee said, claiming: "*I feel more confident about my practice than I would if I had done seats.*" Trainees start their training contract doing some "*admin-type work in the background,*" but as they carve out a niche, their work quickly becomes more substantive, with drafting, legal research and client contact all on the daily roster.

Does the system have any disadvantages? "*There is no one standing over you watching what you are doing,*" one trainee admitted. "*You can't just sit around and expect people to come to you. That is true of mentoring and supervision too. It is incumbent on trainees to seek it out. But once you do that, the support is there.*" Another added: "*It can be tricky to manage your workload. You definitely need to have an ability to work autonomously. You have to make many decisions yourself.*"

The 'free market' system attracts a particular type of person. "*This place is not for shy people who aren't prepared to go out and make themselves known around the office.*" But, more than that, "*many people are quite ambitious. When we hire people, we look for individuals who have shown they really want to achieve something. We want people who are independent-minded, bold and enterprising, without being cocky or arrogant.*"

Doing donuts

Jones Day's corporate team often takes on the financial side of transactions: it advised equity fund WL Ross & Co on its role in the $1bn acquisition of Northern Rock's consumer bank from the government by Virgin Money. It also helped private equity house Alcuin take control of £25m worth of the UK arm of Krispy Kreme. All our interviewees had done at least some corporate work; those who had really got stuck in said they'd "*had exposure to all the various legal stages of a corporate transaction.*" Their work ranged from setting up data rooms and helping with due diligence and verification to drafting diligence reports and other deal documents. "*You get a lot of client contact,*" one trainee said. "*I even gave advice to a client on whether to accept a warrant security.*"

Litigators act on a lot of finance-related breach of contract claims in the country's highest courts. Clients include Bombardier Aerospace and oil giants Total and Chevron. "*When I started I was organising documents and sense-checking submissions,*" a budding litigator told us, "*but when it came to doing the second round of submissions I did the first cut of the draft.*" Another added: "*I produced a memo which was given to the client, and have also done research on points of law and liaised with counsel. I was also reviewing documents for the disclosure and taking notes during witness statements.*" Recently, the firm acted for Standard Bank in £137m High Court proceedings against Saudi businessman Sheikh Mohamed Bin Issa Al Jaber over unrepaid loans. The case involved a worldwide freeze of the Sheikh's assets and was worked on by JD lawyers in Paris, Saudi Arabia, Dallas and London, as well as other co-counsel in Guernsey, Egypt, Portugal and Austria.

The banking and finance team acts for big-name clients such as Goldman Sachs, Bank of America and RBS. One of its main areas of work is dealing with distressed debt sales and acquisitions. For example, the firm advised Bangladesh's GMG Airlines on a $200m white-knight investment, and hotel chain Jarvis on asset sales worth £111m during its pre-pack administration. Lawyers also work on a range of capital markets and financial transactions. "*At the start I did a lot of the diligence and quickly became the go-to guy who knew all about the client's assets. More recently I have been involved with drafting the principal transaction documents,*" a second-year told us.

Real estate lawyers recently advised property developer British Land on the £240m acquisition of Drake Circus Shopping Centre in Plymouth and have also worked for California-based CBRE – the world's largest commercial property firm. "*I have assisted on some straightforward sales and purchases of property,*" a trainee told us, "*but recently I have also worked on some major bank-led property financings.*"

Herding cats

Trainees told us that the non-rotational system means "*everyone – solicitors and trainees – always has to be very approachable and polite.*" The system also means personality clashes are rare. "*There will always be some people who you get on better with than others, but if you don't get on with someone you can just choose to work with someone else in future.*"

Although trainees and solicitors have their own offices, they're up and about all the time. "*You always see people standing in office doorways chatting – it's often about work but there is time for a joke around as well. The non-rotational system means you're always walking around the building.*" We can attest to this: JD trainees' busy schedules and frequent walkabouts made them harder to get in touch with to schedule interviews than at most firms.

Trainees are "*expected to be around between 9.30am and 6pm.*" Most of our interviewees started work around 9am and left between 7 and 8pm on a standard day. "*There are some late nights: how late you stay goes up and down a lot. If you are on a busy deal you can be in until the early hours of the morning. I once stayed until 4am when we had a closing.*" On a brighter note, "*no one expects you to come in on the weekend,*" and "*you are expected to have a life outside work and can take work home in the evenings if you need to.*" Trainees felt well rewarded in terms of pay, career support, office facilities and above all top-down appreciation: "*I worked really late into the night once to finish something. When I came in the next morning, I was given loads of praise, which made me feel really good.*"

When they're not working, Jones Days are "*pretty sociable, actually.*" Alas, we hear the traditional office pantomime is now definitely a thing of the past, but the social offerings include "*a firm event maybe once a month, a Christmas quiz and party, and sports teams.*" The Harrow pub is just across the street and is frequented by trainees, associates and partners. "*It is always the focal point if a partner is organising something. Last Thursday we all got an e-mail from two corporate partners inviting everyone out for a drink, as they'd just finished off a deal. They paid for everything.*" Another trainee gave this advice: "*It pays to go to social events – it is really good to build up contacts that way.*" Happily, "*when you are with someone in the pub, you're equals. There is not much of a feeling of hierarchy. You can have a good laugh with the partners.*"

When we spoke to trainees in spring 2012, the majority were unconcerned about qualification. They were right not to be worried. The firm posted an excellent retention rate in 2012, keeping on 11 of 12 qualifiers. "*They don't make you jump through hoops. The department you are working in will usually give you a good idea of whether there is a job there for you.*"

And finally...
Jones Day's unique training contract is not for the faint-hearted but will suit those who want a really exhilarating challenge.

K&L Gates

The facts

Location: London

Number of UK partners/solicitors: 62/58 (+1 non-UK-qualified)

UK partners who trained at firm: 7.8%

Total number of trainees: 15

Seats: 4x6 months

Alternative seats: Occasional secondments

On chambersstudent.co.uk...

- How to get into K&L Gates
- Words from London administrative partner Tony Griffiths

A mid-sized independent firm called Nicholson Graham & Jones until a 2005 merger, the UK office of this American giant retains a "*softer, laid-back vibe*" and is focused on twin strengths of property and corporate.

Opening up the Gates

"*There are definitely signs that we're looking to progress from being a City mid-sizer to an American full-service heavyweight,*" K&L Gates trainees told us this year. 'How so?' we asked. "*You can feel the ambition in several ways,*" came the response. "*The kind of work that's coming in; the increased worldwide, inter-practice video-conferences; and an increasing amount of lateral hard-hitters being hired.*" The firm's director of HR and development, Tina Two, agreed: "*I've been here ten years and although we still have the legacy NGJ friendliness, the office is unrecognisable in terms of thinking and expansion. This is an optimistic and exciting place to be.*"

Since the 2005 merger, the office's traditional core practices of real estate and corporate haven't really kicked on, remaining solidly in London's mid-market, almost exactly where they were in the days of NGJ. The firm's best rankings come in fairly niche areas – policyholder insurance, electoral law, regulatory travel. So, it's about time there was a concerted push forwards. Administrative partner of the London office Tony Griffiths says: "*One of the major highlights of the last year has been the continued momentum of financial growth for the London office. We managed to increase our turnover by 10% in 2011 and that was in no small part due to our emerging, market-penetrating, practices. Structured finance was probably our fastest growing area, followed by our insurance, and energy and funds practices.*"

No doubt part of the reason for the renewed impetus currently driving K&L is its 2010 move from Cannon Street to the fancy new development at One New Change. "*The space is incredible and has a real American feel. There's a lot of space, and it's full of marble, chrome and frosted glass, with floor-to-ceiling windows. It definitely reflects the image management wants to portray.*"

K&L trainees complete four seats of six months each and "*the assumption is that everyone does a corporate, a real estate and a contentious seat.*" However, "*beyond straight litigation, insurance, employment, IP or the construction secondment fulfil the contentious requirement.*" Banking and competition seats supplement corporate, while "*construction, planning/environment and the secondment can all tick the real estate box.*" Other seats include tax and media/sport. "*The firm still has a big property and corporate reputation but,*" said trainees, "*it is trying to diversify. K&L is definitely trying to bring on its funds, competition and finance departments.*"

Although trainees don't get to choose their first seat, "*the firm really tries to accommodate where you'd like to go*" for the remaining three. "*A perk of there only being 16 trainees is that there is more chance of getting your first or second choice,*" one said. "*As long as you're realistic in your hopes – you can't do four niche seats – then it's a very fair system.*"

Google towers and media powers

The corporate team "*is essentially split between capital markets and M&A work, but as a trainee you really get involved in both. You usually do more of what your supervisor does, but you're encouraged to try all types of corporate issues. You get immersed in everything and are*

Chambers UK rankings

Banking & Finance	Insurance
Capital Markets	Intellectual Property
Competition/European Law	Investment Funds
Construction	Licensing
Corporate/M&A	Parliamentary & Public Affairs
Dispute Resolution	Projects
Employment	Real Estate
Environment	Real Estate Finance
Information Technology	Sports Law
	Travel

very much in attendance for all the deals." The department *"does have a reputation for having the longest hours. The good thing is that those hours are spent doing interesting work."* K&L acted for the mobile marketing and advertising provider Velti on its $150m placing and duel listing on NASDAQ; advised on the acquisition of a UK bank by Habib Allied International Bank; and assisted on the £188m acquisition of a portfolio of buildings in the City of London for Vanquish Properties. Sources reported working on *"standard trainee tasks"* such as drafting ancillary documents and board minutes.

Real estate *"is broken down into subteams, but we all just muck in where needed."* Juniors explained: *"There are some big funds clients, wealthy families or hedge funds with different property portfolios, and then you get the big FTSE 100 transactions and corporate support work. There are also some wonderfully eccentric individual clients who are always interesting to work with."* K&L provided advice to the London Borough of Hounslow on a number of planning matters, including a couple of hotel developments close to Heathrow Airport and wind turbines at BSkyB's Sky Studios in Isleworth. Trainees get *"a whole cupboard full of their own files"* to work on, ranging from rent reviews and licences to residential sales. *"It's a steep learning curve in this department and you end up being very busy."*

Known as *"one of the friendliest in the firm,"* the litigation group handles arbitration, financial litigation, commercial disputes, white-collar crime and ADR. *"It was really good to have the experience of more than one area,"* a trainee said. A long-running dispute the group has been working on is the Farepak litigation – you may remember that the Christmas hamper company went bust in 2006 leaving many customers out of pocket. K&L has been acting for the directors of Farepak's parent company,

European Home Retail. Trainees *"draft witness statements, take on lots of research, and are allowed to run smaller matters. You definitely feel part of the team."*

The ever-popular employment group *"is one of the smaller departments here and has both litigation and corporate support elements to it."* Clients include AOL and Bank of America. The competition team *"works very closely with Brussels,"* predominantly on *"regulatory work and merger and transactional support"* – such as advising horse-racing fixtures company Arena Leisure on issues relating to the 60% shareholder's sale of his interests to the minority shareholder, Northern Racing.

Despite K&L's extensive international network, there are no overseas opportunities open to trainees. *"We are investigating opportunities and discussing secondments with our European and Middle Eastern offices,"* Tony Griffiths told us.

Soberer than thou

"Although London still retains its independence, you're very aware that there's a big international force behind you," said trainees. *"It's not a typical big, scary American firm though. The office has retained that old NGJ friendliness."* One thought: *"Although we are changing, the US isn't belligerent in imposing its style on us. Everyone makes an effort with each other and the general atmosphere is still laid-back."* Trainees sit with partners and all reported good relationships with their seniors. *"There are late hours, but people appreciate how hard you're working. There's no face time issue here."* Outside of the corporate department, trainees tend to be able to get away by 7pm.

"We do socialise," trainees said, *"but it's not a rigid 'thou must go out and get wasted' type of place. People are friends, but have their own hobbies and lives outside work."* Office-wide and departmental Christmas parties keep things convivial over the festive period, and *"we also had Guy Fawkes drinks on a Friday in November. Bonfire Night was actually on the Saturday, so the firm just projected fireworks on one of the back walls."* After a period of scouting to find a regular local near the new office, K&L lawyers appear to have settled on Ping Pong. *"It's two-for-one cocktails before 7pm. You'll always find someone from the firm in there."*

Trainees weren't too clued-up on the qualification process but said that the firm was *"making the right noises"* and it eventually kept six out of eight qualifying trainees in 2012.

And finally...
If K&L London is serious about its expansion plans, then this could be an exciting time to get on board.

Kennedys

The facts

Location: London, Manchester, Birmingham, Cambridge, Chelmsford, Maidstone, Belfast, Taunton, Sheffield

Number of UK partners/solicitors: 114/375

Partners who trained at firm: 18%

Total number of trainees: 32

Seats: 4x6 months

Alternative Seats: Overseas seats, secondments

On chambersstudent.co.uk...
• How to get into Kennedys
• The firm's regional offices

With a heavyweight insurance practice and an expanding global presence, Kennedys is making itself at home in the UK top 50.

International playboy

In 2011/12, litigation-focused Kennedys broke through the £100m revenue mark for the first time. Its pre-audited result of £108m – an 11.6% increase on the previous year – left the firm sitting in 30th place in the UK top 50. Not too shabby for a firm that only entered the chart as recently as 2009. "*You need to grow by at least 10% to do more than stand still in this market,*" said senior partner Nick Thomas. "*Real inflation is always higher than the reported indices suggest and operating a business in London and other capital cities is costly.*"

The firm is headquartered in London and this office is home to most of Kennedys' trainees (21 at the time of our calls). Offices in Birmingham, Manchester, Sheffield, Cambridge and Chelmsford take on a few more each (Manchester had the most with four; Cambridge housed just one), while the UK line-up is completed with offices in Belfast, Maidstone and Taunton. Around £83m of Kennedys' revenue last year was generated in the UK, with the remaining £25m contributed by the firm's international outposts, which are in nine exotic locations including Dubai, Miami and Sydney.

To help cement its international status Kennedys rolled out its first overseas secondment for trainees in June 2011, offering them the chance of a three-month seat in Hong Kong. Graduate recruitment adviser Rowena Bubb said: "*It was very much part of an overall trainee review. As an international law firm we want to offer overseas opportunities to our trainees.*" A trainee went to Singapore in March 2012 and it appears that further opportunities are on the way, as nearly all our interviewees mentioned the current rumour on the grapevine of a new secondment to Dubai.

Toilet humour

Back in Blighty, it is the London office that offers the most seats. These come within the four main departments of insurance, liability, employment and company/commercial – with the latter described as "*quite small and certainly not the main focus.*" Trainees have little say in where they sit first but give three preferences before each remaining changeover. Second-years are given priority but sources did say the system tends to operate on the basis of "*if you get your third choice for one seat then you're likely to get your first choice next time.*" Trainees in regional offices have about half as many seats to choose from.

Kennedys immerses itself in litigation and dispute resolution work for the insurance/reinsurance and liability industries. The insurance litigation practice acts for over 50 top insurers, including Zurich and Chartis, and accounts for roughly 80% of Kennedys' turnover. The firm acted on the fallout from the Potters Bar rail crash, representing a national railway company in the aftermath of the 2002 disaster which killed seven passengers. More recently it represented J D Wetherspoon and its insurers, Zurich, when a man glorying in the name of Ricky Edwards-Tubbs sought damages for an injury received in one of the chain's pubs. Tubbs sought to submit a second expert medical report instead of relying on the first he had received pre-litigation. The final decision swept away the

Chambers UK rankings

Clinical Negligence	Partnership
Construction	Personal Injury
Dispute Resolution	Product Liability
Employment	Professional Negligence
Health & Safety	Real Estate
Insurance	Transport

practice of 'expert shopping' and cherry-picking the most favourable report.

Over half of our random sample of trainees had spent time in an insurance team. Work mainly involves defending claims and assessing liability both in England and internationally. Some London trainees felt the nature of the work left them disconnected. "*The cases were so big that you couldn't get that involved,*" said one. "*I know that a lot of the work they do is very intellectual and includes arguing finite points but I felt like I was only doing research. I only wrote four or five letters in six months.*" Those located in the regional offices gained more hands-on experience. "*I was doing a lot of trial-based work including drafting mediations and court documents,*" one Manchester trainee told us. "*I gained a good knowledge of all the litigation processes.*"

Professional indemnity is one of the major arms of the insurance department and is Kennedys' largest team in terms of fee earners. It represents professionals who've been accused of malpractice or error and their insurers. As such, trainees were involved with "*instructing experts on what the professionals had done and attending mediations or settlement meetings.*" To keep certain matters from going to trial our sources had been tasked with "*drafting first response letters.*" Trainees were really positive about the supervision they received in this seat. "*Even if I was given standard tasks like researching, they would take the time to show me where the work had gone and how it fitted into the whole procedure,*" said one London trainee. Another added: "*If I wanted to get involved in certain work they would take an active role in helping me do that.*"

Construction is another big hitter within the insurance department and carries out both contentious and non-contentious work. The nature of the contentious work gives trainees exposure to some complex international cases. "*It's quite common to get some multi-jurisdictional work. In one multimillion-pound case I was involved with some claims handlers in Romania,*" beamed one interviewee. Indeed, all of the work was said to be on "*massive-value claims –£500,000 minimum.*" As a result, trainees don't handle their own files but there are plenty of drafting opportunities and chances to get out of the office. "*I took the witness statements at a site where there had been a*

flood due to a negligent builder and drafted it into a 40-page document," said one second-year. Non-contentious work involves advising construction consultants, particularly architects, and producing legal documents for the design and supply of certain projects.

Kennedys' liability practice includes the personal injury and medical negligence teams. PI was a seat undertaken by the majority of our interviewees and all were chuffed with the "*huge amount of responsibility*" they were given. "*I was regularly attending meetings with counsel, liaising with them about their availability for trial. I was even pitched against a barrister at a hearing – it was a little bit daunting,*" reflected one. As with insurance, there's plenty of drafting and taking witness statements to contend with, but several of our sources had also been given a couple of smaller-value cases of their own. One chuckling interviewee recalled how they "*always seemed to be given the cases of people who'd been injured in toilets.*"

The healthcare department primarily handles allegations of medical negligence. Its biggest client is the NHS Litigation Authority, but it also represents the Medical Protection Society, the Medical Professional Liability Company and a large number of private hospital groups and clinics. Trainees who'd spent time here reported being given their "*own small caseloads for the NHSLA,*" and felt the overall experience gave them "*a taste of what it was like to be an actual fee earner.*"

Of Kennedys and kings

Non-contentious seats are not prevalent at this litigation-heavy firm, but there are opportunities to sit in commercial property, insolvency, corporate and banking. As this work is "*not the core of what Kennedys does,*" the teams are much smaller. This is not to the detriment of the trainee experience: "*I felt I had more responsibility, as the files were more transferable to trainees,*" said one. A source who'd sat in banking added: "*It was the most hands-on seat I had. I was constantly out and about and worked really closely with the partner.*" The insolvency team was recently involved in the fast-track administration sale of Molinaire, the post-production company behind films such as *Prometheus* and *The King's Speech*. At the time of writing there are no non-contentious seats available in Birmingham, Cambridge or Manchester, but client secondments are available, as is the chance to switch offices to complete certain seats.

The majority of our interviewees were very positive about the supervision they'd received but there were a few grumbles too. Our sources generally reported supervisors being "*very hands-on,*" with many directly involved in helping trainees manage their workloads. However, a few Londoners did moan about their supervision in the insurance department. "*I was generally left to my own devices,* which is fine to an extent, but ultimately I felt isolated," one said. "I felt that if I did have a problem I wasn't able to talk to my supervisor about it." Another added: "When I did get feedback it seemed to be unnecessarily harsh, even if they did have a valid point."

There were almost no complaints about the working hours. An average day starts at about 9am, with the majority of people then out the door by 6.30pm. Those in insurance might expect to do an extra hour or so, while those who are immersed in trials have the occasional late night. "Obviously when there's work to do you might have to hang around, but it's not a 'stay late and pretend to be busy' culture."

London trainees were very happy with their salaries considering the field of work Kennedys specialises in. Those in the regional offices also felt well remunerated for their locations but did think the disparity between their salaries and those the firm offers in the capital did not simply reflect differing living costs. "You would expect a bit of a difference but not as big as it is," commented one. Another point of interest is that unlike many of its top-30 cohorts, Kennedys does not currently pay LPC fees.

Fruits of our labour

The firm's headquarters is right by the Lloyd's building in the heart of the City. Operating in the shadow of the Gherkin, the office is "shiny, new and open-plan." Particular highlights are the top-floor balcony with views over London, which is used for the monthly staff drinks, and the breakout area known as The Writz, which offers free fruit and toast in the mornings. Although we don't have space to talk about all the individual offices (see our website for more), one regional trainee did say: "Kennedys has a general theme that runs throughout all their offices, and that is that they're nice." We also heard of twice-weekly fruit basket deliveries which contain "much more than your bog-standard apples and bananas."

"The social life at Kennedys is great; there's always something going on." Departmental socials are frequent, and a number of sports teams often do battle against nearby clients. Trainee events are often just trips out for drinks (from the sounds of things, you'll never be short of someone to go to the pub with at Kennedys), but have also included activities such as cocktail-making and bowling. The regional offices are perhaps not quite as lively, but all the trainees make the effort to venture out in the capital when training courses or the yearly firm-wide party brings the whole intake together.

Some trainees did think the crossover between offices could be improved. "Kennedys is very London-focused. If you think otherwise you are a bit deluded," one opined. Another, however, did say the firm is "making a concerted effort now to include the regional offices." Symptomatic of this more integrated approach was the involvement of all Kennedys' offices in an Olympic torch bike relay in July – a charity cycle ride between all the firm's UK locations in support of War Child. Every single one of our interviewees raved about it and even chief executive Guy Stobart donned his helmet and lycra to support the cause.

Kennedys' motto is 'legal advice in black and white' and according to trainees "it practises what it preaches. We give good, clear legal advice without the stuffiness and formality." The message resonates through all aspects of the firm, from the no-nonsense website right through to daily office life. "You can go up to a partner and feel free to ask them a question. One of the partners was even talking to me about my holidays in Ibiza. It's just straightforward and normal all around." Likewise, the trainees reflect the firm's tag line. "Everyone is pretty down to earth. No one has a big ego or pretentious attitude."

Kennedys' trainees come from a wide variety of backgrounds and the current intake includes non-redbrick graduates as well as Oxbridge alumni. "There's a real mix," said one second-year. "A couple of trainees have paralegalled, others have taken gap years." One trainee did mention that Kennedys "really values any work or previous experience you may have," and about half of our sample had worked in a relevant field beforehand. Strong academics are important but by no means the be-all and end-all to secure a training contact. In fact, Kennedys is launching an apprenticeship scheme for school leavers in a bid to provide legal career opportunities for students without a degree.

And finally...
Those looking for a life as a litigator could find their match in this contentious-heavy training contract. In 2012, ten of Kennedys' 12 qualifiers stayed on as NQs.

Kingsley Napley LLP

The facts

Location: London

Number of UK partners/solicitors: 44/63

Partners who trained at firm: 18%

Total number of trainees: 10

Seats: 4x6 months

Alternative Seats: None

On chambersstudent.co.uk...
• How to get into Kingsley Napley
• We talk to managing partner Linda Woolley

Kingsley Napley is a London firm with strengths in high-end crime, clinical negligence and professional discipline.

Life of crime

The name Kingsley Napley is practically synonymous with high-profile, top-notch criminal work. Its clients include former UBS trader Kweku Adoboli, charged with £1.5bn's worth of fraud and false accounting; NewsCorp's own Rebekah Brooks regarding the phone hacking investigation; and sports agent/bookie Mazhar Majeed, who was embroiled in the 2010 cricket match-fixing scandal.

"*On a headcount basis, crime and regulatory are definitely our biggest practice areas, but they don't drive the whole firm,*" trainees told us. "*We have a variety of areas on offer, and are ranked highly in a number of practices. Every firm has its strengths, but we offer a service across the board.*" Alongside the crime team, other Kingsley Napley practices include clin neg, real estate, immigration, employment, corporate/commercial, regulatory, public law, private client and family, and there are seats for trainees available in all. "*We're famous for our contentious work, so those areas tend to be the most competitive to get a seat in.*" Trainees issued a further warning: "*You'll probably get a seat in crime if you really want it, but it's the most difficult team to qualify into.*"

Trainees pick all four of their seats at the beginning of their training contract and, in general, "*people get at least two or three of their first choices. Of course, there's no guarantee you'll get every seat you want, but the HR team definitely tries to accommodate you. No one ends up really disappointed.*" Trainees liked being able to choose their seats before starting. One said: "*I don't think there's any benefit in uncertainty. Knowing in advance means you can forge links with your future team.*" Another added: "*Your choices aren't set in stone. There's room for negoti-*ation later. It's not guaranteed that you'll get to change, but it is a possibility*" (the firm says, realistically, it's rare). Trainees also have the option of qualifying into a practice they haven't sat in. "*If there are the places available and you put in a decent application, there is no reason why you wouldn't be considered.*" All five qualifying trainees were kept on as NQs in 2012.

Kings counsel

Top-ranked in London by *Chambers UK*, the clin neg team acts purely for claimants and "*is oriented towards catastrophic injury cases, which are often high-profile,*" trainees said. "*Several partners have specialities such as cerebral palsy claims, spinal injuries or birth defects, and all cases are valued in the millions of pounds bracket. It's not your average PI department.*" The administration that goes with these cases "*is a huge part of the work. There is a lot of scheduling of documents and finance work, which can be a nightmare in terms of organisation.*" The trainee "*is definitely a departmental resource and the team wants to give you a really good mix of work.*" Trainees mentioned meeting with clients, taking on research tasks and drafting letters of claim. "*It's a very good learning experience. Even just taking notes presents a challenge, as the work can be very technical and it's extremely important to record the details.*" The trainees we spoke to very much enjoyed the seat, but did reflect on the emotional nature of the work: "*The reality is that some of these injuries are truly horrendous, and the sufferers will often never recover. This does make you work even harder for them, as what you're doing is so rewarding, but you should be aware of what you're going into.*"

Chambers UK rankings

Administrative & Public Law	Crime
Children: Cross-border Disputes	Employment
	Family/Matrimonial
Clinical Negligence	Financial Services
Competition/European Law	Fraud
Corporate Crime & Investigations	Immigration
	Professional Discipline

The fantastic criminal practice "*is essentially split between general crime and white-collar crime.*" As the biggest part of the firm, it's also KN's best-known. "*You really get a sense of the standard from day one. The partners are really impressive.*" As well as the clients we mentioned earlier, the group is acting for beardy Bristolian Justin Lee Collins in relation to a harassment charge; for Sally Challen, convicted of the murder of her husband; and for Norayr Davtyan, regarding the heavily reported alleged gang-rape on a South-East London college campus. Trainees said: "*To really get the best work, you have to be proactive. If you are, you'll visit police stations and go to court quite a bit and you might even clerk for a trial. There's also lots of drafting and client contact.*"

Although one doesn't immediately associate corporate and commercial work with Kingsley Napley, the firm does have a thriving practice. "*It's based around four partners. One is specifically tech/IP-focused; there's a general corporate partner, with a lean to banking; a public listing partner who does AIM market and general stock exchange work; and then finally a general commercial partner who has a focus on hotels.*" Clients are start-ups and mid-sized companies, and there's "*a really good undercurrent of IP, licensing and gambling work that dips fairly heavily into the FSA and gambling regulations. There's also quite a bit of sports contract work.*" Trainees said: "*To be perfectly honest, you can very much steer what you're doing in coco. The team is open to letting you do work that you're interested in. It's all about putting your hand up and engaging.*

The butler did it

Regulatory work has been so abundant that in May 2011 the team became a practice area in its own right. Clients are regulatory bodies – like the Health Professions Council, Architects Registration Board and the British Society of Plant Breeders – and the work is very litigation-based. "*A lot of it is investigating allegations made against a registrant of a body.*" The firm prosecuted on behalf of the General Teaching Council when teacher Benedict Garrett was suspended in July 2010 after being discovered working as a stripper, naked butler and porn actor going by the stage name of 'Johnny Anglais'. Trainees said: "*From day one you're basically running your own cases. You get into everything: witness handling, case management, you head down to the tribunals and marshal the clients – it's very hands-on.*"

Private client "*is something the firm is really looking to grow.*" Currently split between court of protection and probate teams, there is "*a lot of opportunity to get involved in both contentious and non-contentious work. The matters tend to be small, so you can see everything through.*" As well as expanding this practice, managing partner Linda Woolley says: "*We've also always had a niche property litigation team and are looking to develop it further.*"

Hours do vary between teams, but as a general rule "*people do successfully have families and social lives at Kingsley Napley.*" There will be some longer hours – especially in coco, we're told – "*but in some areas it's basically a ghost town after 6.30pm.*"

The Kings singers

The atmosphere in the office is "*definitely friendly and not particularly quiet. People are genuinely affable.*" One source stressed: "*People who aren't team players are not going to do well here. This isn't a 'clamber to reach the top' place*" Linda Woolley adds: "*Maturity and an enthusiasm for the work we do is also very important. A fixation on money isn't going to keep you going for 40 years.*"

Socially, there's "*absolutely masses going on.*" The Junior Fee Earners group organises a varied social calendar. "*We're heading to Lord's to watch the cricket, there was a bowling night, lots of dinners and we even went to Wimbledon Dogs.*" The newly formed choir received high praise: "*We're definitely improving. I think there's even a video somewhere on YouTube,*" a trainee divulged. We duly found KN's not-bad-at-all a cappella rendition of 'Goodnight Sweetheart'. Finally, one trainee warned: "*Watch those Kingsley Kilos! There is honestly cake everywhere. For birthdays, for half-birthdays – they definitely don't want you to lose any weight...*"

And finally...

"*Ultimately,*" say trainees, "*the firm attracts natural litigators: bright, relatively argumentative and occasionally eccentric. It makes for an interesting and wonderful place to work.*"

Kirkland & Ellis International LLP

The facts

Location: London

Number of UK partners/solicitors: 38/55 (+26 US-qualified)

Total number of trainees: 10

Seats: 4x6 months

Alternative seats: Overseas seats

Extras: Pro bono – LawWorks, A4ID

On chambersstudent.co.uk...

- How to get into K&E
- Interview with training principal Stephen Gillespie

Fifth in the US for gross revenue, Kirkland & Ellis's young training contract is a lure for entrepreneurial sorts, who say "*there's no such thing as trainee work*" here.

Born free (market)

Chicago-born Kirkland established a London presence mid-90s, but only began actively seeking out work in London in 2004. Making numerous magic circle hires, the strategy was to become a leading European private equity player. Since this shift in outlook, Kirkland has "*developed and enlarged corporate M&A and debt finance, made up and brought in a number of tax partners, developed an upstream private funds practice though a team from SJ Berwin, and had notable hires in antitrust,*" training principal Stephen Gillespie told us. London has become Kirkland's largest European office with 120 lawyers. The UK training contract launched in 2009, and the firm expects it to grow rapidly over the next few years.

Hong Kong became the latest centre of accelerated growth in late 2011 when Kirkland made lateral hires to boost its M&A, securities and capital markets practices. The firm's global picture is particularly significant for trainees as there is the opportunity to take seats in the New York and Hong Kong offices – one trainee actually qualifying into HK in 2011. "*As Hong Kong grows, they will probably take as many trainees as we are able to send them,*" Gillespie told us. Regarding further opportunities, he said: "*Kirkland is a pragmatic place – so I wouldn't discount the possibility of other places where trainees might be able to go.*"

Visionaries

Secondments aside, Kirkland trainees choose from the following seats: corporate; competition; banking/finance; restructuring; litigation/arbitration; and funds. Whatever the department, private equity houses make up the bulk of client roster, and in 2012 Kirkland remained the only firm ranked top for investment funds by *Chambers UK*. Trainees' main tip: "*You've got to find the subject matter interesting.*" In a nutshell, the firm assists the client in buying failing companies and improving them, before selling them on at a profit. The luckier trainees in the funds seat get to see the whole lifespan of this process. "*A client will come to you early on wanting to raise a new fund, and we'll put the structure in place, take all agreements from investors and then close it.*" Such diffuse processes means there's a lot of "*liaising with the other side to get signatures,*" but we're assured there are also "*plenty of opportunities for drafting too.*" Furthermore, trainees are "*encouraged to ask questions, sit in on every conference call and get copied in on client e-mails. It's the only way to learn.*" Notable work includes representation of Vision Capital and Deutsche Bank on its sale of a portfolio to a Canadian investor.

Kirkland's banking group only has 17 members, but is ranked alongside Allen & Overy, Skadden and Clifford Chance for sponsor work. This means it advises sponsors on issues such as leveraged finance, distressed investments and acquisition funding. The team recently acted for Bain Capital and Hellman & Friedman on the €1.6bn financing of the purchase of Securitas Direct; Avis

Chambers UK rankings

Banking & Finance	Restructuring/Insolvency
Investment Funds	Tax
Private Equity	

Budget on its $1bn public takeover of Avis UK; and Triton's sale of chemical manufacturer Evonik's Carbon Black business for €900m. Trainees receive "*high-quality, daunting work from day one,*" and often have to juggle multiple matters at once. One assisted clients who were bidding for target companies, "*so my role was to run processes, talk to the other side's lawyers to make sure everything was being done, and negotiate small documents and the small parts of bigger ones.*" Trainees like the support the "*collegial*" department gives them. "*They don't just fling a task at you and let you get on with it – they're very good at explaining the context and showing how it's part of a commercial deal as a whole.*"

Kirkland's corporate group represents private equity investors in large leveraged buyout deals and the corporate aspects of private equity reorganisations. The busy pace means trainees "*can see three different deals in the length of a seat.*" The size of the department (it's Kirkland London's largest) and of transactions means that trainees will pay their due diligence dues at the start – but it's worth it. "*At first I didn't see the point, but the more I did it, the more I got to understand about the company or target,*" one source explained. Juniors may also get discrete tasks sent over from Kirkland US – "*share issuances and allotments, changing a company name or approving board minutes. It's low-level corporate work, but because you're the UK contact, the responsibility is on your head.*" Hours in corporate can and will be tough, but Kirkland trainees have no qualms about that. "*I left at 5am every night for two weeks,*" revealed one. "*When I finally got home one morning, the partner called and told me to come back in. It's a challenge, but the reward of finishing outweighs it.*"

The London office is a hub for Kirkland's international arbitration practice and acts for Samsung, General Motors and technology makers Raytheon. A more moderate pace of work means trainees have time for direct client contact – "*not 24-hour call, but you will respond by BlackBerry. You get to feel a real affinity with the client.*" Trainees may also attend arbitrations: "*There are a lot fewer peo-*

ple there than at trial, so you're right at the front being part of it.*"

Nothing ventured, nothing gained

Kirkland and its private equity clients are an ideal match. "*Their management structure is as pared down as ours: it's exciting because every time you speak to someone, they're a decision maker.*" So too, trainees tell us, is Kirkland's structure. "*It's pretty flat, so you'll chat with a senior in the same way you'd chat with a trainee.*" This system engenders "*entrepreneurialism. Work will always find you, but the way to get really good work is to put yourself out there and chat to people.*" Overall, trainees say, "*it's smaller and more meritocratic. If you demonstrate ability you'll get more work and become a better lawyer, faster.*"

For trainees this translates to accepting long hours, although they still claim these "*aren't as bad as what friends put in at magic circle firms.*" It's intense. "*You have to be hard-working,*" said an interviewee, "*as it's how you learn best here. But even if it is full-on, you're never left to drown.*" The engrained culture of responsibility also means, said one source, "*it would be strange if a deal was closing and I walked out of the door. Part of the responsibility we get means we're not obliged to stay in the office, but we want to be here.*"

Trainees praised the firm's socials, "*which everyone from first-seaters to equity partners attends.*" There's an attorney retreat and a Christmas bash held at the Kensington roof gardens. Generally, "*people socialise out of their own choice rather than being forced to go to events. We might have dinner as a team at the end of a long day, or go for Thursday or Friday drinks.*"

"*It's easy to forget that you work in such an iconic building.*" Kirkland is based in 30 St Mary Axe (better known as the Gherkin), which is good for impressing the parents. Inside, "*it's spacious and modern and we have a chef and get free dinner after 7pm.*" Kirkland lawyers get their own offices after qualification, but "*it's not isolated – people are constantly popping in and chatting.*" The panorama from the offices is "*spectacular,*" but although one second-year did admit to enjoying watching the sun rise, "*we don't have much time to stop and admire the view.*"

And finally...

"*People are happy to be here, and really keen on what they do. People are ludicrously into funds and it shows.*" This year four of six trainees showed their commitment by taking up NQ positions.

LATHAM & WATKINS

MAKE YOUR MOVE

MAKE YOUR MOVE

to a firm where from day one you'll be working on market leading transactions and cases across our global network, dealing directly with clients and rapidly building up your experience.

This is your career at Latham & Watkins.

To find out more about us visit our website LW.com

Abu Dhabi
Barcelona
Beijing
Boston
Brussels
Chicago
Doha
Dubai
Frankfurt
Hamburg
Hong Kong
Houston
London
Los Angeles
Madrid
Milan
Moscow
Munich
New Jersey
New York
Orange County
Paris
Riyadh*
Rome
San Diego
San Francisco
Shanghai
Silicon Valley
Singapore
Tokyo
Washington, D.C.

LW.com

Latham & Watkins LLP

The facts

Location: London

Number of UK partners/solicitors: 44/97

Total number of trainees: 34

Seats: 4x6 months

Alternative seats: Overseas seats, secondments

Extras: Pro bono – LawWorks, ProHelp, Islington Law Centre, ISLP-UK, Human Rights Watch, TrustLaw Connect, Not For Sale and others; language classes

On chamberstudent.co.uk...

- How to get into Latham & Watkins
- Pro bono at Latham

Giant Latham & Watkins attracts high-calibre trainees for its international work and supportive atmosphere.

Califormation

When Dana Latham met Paul Watkins back in 1934, they decided to found a firm based on non-hierarchical management. Over in Blighty, we imagine that bowler-hatted, pinstripe-suited types muttered into their tea and crumpets that the Californian sun had gone to these Americans' heads. But it seems that non-hierarchical management can lead to global domination. Latham is one of the world's largest firms, with 31 offices across the US, Europe, the Middle East and Asia and turnover in excess of $2bn.

Over in the London office (and 2012 is Latham's 23rd year in the UK), the current trainees chime that the firm retains its *"non-hierarchical"* foundations. However, if you simply take this to mean that everyone goes down the pub together, you're not grasping the full implications. Non-hierarchical means that, from NQ to partner level, everyone has the same billing targets and holiday allowance – and are all still working when the birds wake up to welcome the cold dawn. The London office is busy: as a hub for Europe and the States, it's a key player in the firm's strategic plans for global coverage.

Latham's recruits are articulate and intelligent. That's not to say they're all Oxbridge graduates (in fact, at the time of our calls only two of the 12 second-years were) but rather that our sources gave damn good interviews... when they weren't exhausted from a 4am finish the night before. You can be assured that these weren't your stereotypical students who knew more about downing Jägermeister than the content of Monday morning lectures. They're more like grade-eight-on-the-piano, cap-

tain-of-the-rugby-team, multilingual graduates who spent their summer holidays shadowing judges. *"My activities were for enjoyment, not as a CV booster,"* one high-achiever assured us. And that's just the type of people they are... people who enjoy work. *"As a Latham trainee you may be a bit sleep-deprived, but with the adrenaline of working on a big deal, you don't even notice,"* they said.

No virgin to megadeals

Trainees complete one finance seat, one corporate and one litigation. They have a chat with the trainee co-ordinator about preferences as *"the subgroups are flexible."* They can seek work out themselves or *"a partner who needs help may pop their head around the door."* Supervisors are *"helpful at managing workflow. They can shield you from taking on too much and they are always on your side. You can say no to work, but you'll need a good reason,"* one source said.

The M&A team works on billion-dollar deals for clients including Barclays, KKR, Virgin Media and Yahoo!. Like most things at Latham, the work is *"international in its approach,"* and trainees frequently liaise with the firm's European offices. The other seat in the corporate department is capital markets, which has three teams: debt, equity and high-yield products. The latter is the largest and strongest on the market according to *Chambers UK.* Last year alone the team handled over $20.7bn in high-yield offerings. *"I worked on one large deal for my whole seat,"* one corporate trainee explained. *"I was helping to organise the deal, sending updates to clients and proofing and drafting documents. There was lots of client contact*

Chambers UK rankings

Banking & Finance	Information Technology
Banking Litigation	Intellectual Property
Capital Markets	Investment Funds
Competition/European Law	Outsourcing
Corporate/M&A	Private Equity
Dispute Resolution	Projects
Employment	Public International Law
Energy & Natural Resources	Restructuring/Insolvency
	Tax

and e-mails can go out in your name." Another source had spent weeks proof-reading documents which could be anything from five to 500 pages long. "*It can be quite fiddly, so you have to keep really awake as you're doing it,*" they told us, also claiming to "*really enjoy it. It's a great way to learn about corporate and how it all fits together.*"

Deep breath

"*At the start of the banking seat, I was thrown straight into a deal. I barely had time to breathe for six weeks,*" one trainee told us. However, another said: "*I was told in my first meeting that I would start on basic tasks and if I proved myself I'd get more and more responsibility. I was never expected to know anything that I didn't.*" Saying that, they were working on Europe's largest leveraged buyout since 2008 – the €3.6bn sale of Polkomtel, Poland's second largest mobile phone provider network. Once trainees "*show capability and initiative,*" they'll be given drafting experience. Late nights can become the norm – regularly working until 11pm isn't unusual. "*The team are sensitive if you have plans, though. They don't expect you to work weekends, but then it's not good to say no.*"

The litigation department has been busy too: notably changing EU Commission policy while representing ArcelorMittal, the world's largest steel-producing company. After nine years of the high-profile prestressing steel cartel investigation, Latham has argued its case and had the fine against ArcelorMittal reduced from €276m to €45.7m. The case led to two new policy announcements, including lowering fines for future similar cases. For a trainee, however, the public international law seat was described as "*a little dull. The actual cases are fascinating but as a junior I was generally paper-pushing.*" The small department means trainees do a lot of administration on the "*massive trials.*" By contrast, the antitrust competition seat was deemed "*really enjoyable. It's a research-heavy seat with a lot of looking up of EU legislation or case law.*"

Foreign office

Great levels of responsibility come trainees' way in the form of pro bono, which is "*a big deal at Latham.*" Projects include corporate, property and human rights matters and clients include both big international and small local charities and other non-profit organisations. Trainees become heavily involved, especially in quieter periods. "*There's a real mixture, and things you wouldn't be able to do in your normal seats.*" One of Latham's main pro bono objectives is to end human trafficking, and the firm's relationship with Not For Sale (NFS). Trainees have recently been advising NFS on how a UK presence could be incorporated into its global structure.

Have you noticed how everything has an international element yet? It's one of the main draws for trainees. More than half of each intake spend six months in one of Latham's offices abroad. Destinations have included Hong Kong, Singapore, Moscow, Brussels and New York. "*There are more offices wanting trainees than there are trainees, so you will probably get to go, and to the location you want.*" Effort is also put into integration between offices. "*Someone will always know someone else from an international office who can provide advice. They do a great job of keeping everyone interconnected.*" Each department has an annual retreat, to which every department member – from across all the European and Middle Eastern offices – is invited. The corporate department recently met up in Paris, and the tax lawyers in Majorca. Other destinations have included Madrid and Brighton, which probably sounds quite exotic if you're coming from Latham's Qatar office. "*We have meetings throughout the day and events in the evenings.*" For qualified solicitors, there's a firm-wide first-year, third-year and fifth-year 'academy' held in the States. This entails numerous meetings about things relevant to your year group: how to be an associate, business development and, for fifth-years, the partnership track.

Daddy issues?

"*When you tell people you're applying for a US firm, they think you're mad and will have no friends or social life,*" one trainee told us. Well, you can't say you weren't warned. "*But you'd be a fool to apply to a City firm without expecting to work long hours.*" And Latham's trainees are no fools. "*We can still have a joke at 3am. A partner has walked into my office at that time with carrot cake,*" one said. It can't be denied that there are periods of practically living in the office and we all know what a strain bad flatmates can be. Thus, "*at interview, recruiters ask themselves whether they would be happy to be in the office with this person in the early hours of the morning.*"

Many of our sources had completed vac schemes in other firms (and often had more than one training contract offer to choose from). Making comparisons, they agreed that

"*Latham is more collegiate than British firms. There's none of that 'my dad is richer than your dad' culture.*" They regarded UK firms as "*more hierarchical, with an entrenched culture due to their age.*" Equally, however, they denied Latham London's vibe takes its cue from the States: "*We don't have that sickeningly enthusiastic American culture. People are genuine and can laugh at themselves.*" And in true British fashion, one source admitted: "*People cringe when they get delivered the Latham fleece for Associates Academy.*" To balance out the fleece, there's jeans allowed on casual Friday.

The 'non-hierarchical' motto rang true to every interviewee. "*You can talk to anyone*" and "*partners will never wonder why a trainee is asking them a stupid question,*" they said. Juniors share a room with their supervisor. "*When you start you fear that if you look at BBC News they'll think you're not doing any work. But your supervisor has been in your position. Mine has made it my office as well and I can pick up personal calls in there,*" one trainee told us. Supervisors also give trainees two reviews per seat. "*They take it seriously rather than a chore that they have to do.*"

Latham lifers

"*It is achievable to become partner,*" one trainee said – and we heard of some of the class who had already put it on their 'things to do before they're 40' list. It's a tough

ask, but we hear the firm is really good at telling you if you're on track. Those who aren't tend to go in-house or to a smaller firm. "*People don't leave to go to our competitors.*"

Trainees have a billing target of 1,200 hours but such is the workload that trainees tend to pass that mark with ease. The long hours are to be expected but one gripe trainees had was regarding holiday allocation. "*Everyone gets 20 days, from trainees to partners,*" one source mentioned. Barring sick leave and personal days, there is no possibility of getting any more. Of course, an NQ pay cheque of nearly £100,000 is some compensation for the heavy workload. It's almost the highest salary in the market, and stands head and shoulders above those offered by the magic circle.

To bag a training contract, "*do the vacation scheme,*" one source advised. To get on Latham's scheme, there are two interviews: one general one and one on commercial awareness. Then when at the firm, you'll have to produce two pieces of written work and we hear that people who don't take this seriously fail to get through. Also, "*go to social events and meet as many people as possible, as everyone gets asked their opinion on vac schemers.*" Through a diversity charity, Sponsors for Educational Opportunity, the firm "*invites students from non-traditional local universities to the vac scheme.*" Two of these candidates were offered training contracts last time round.

And finally...
In 2012, 12 out of 13 qualifiers stayed with the firm as NQs.

Lawrence Graham LLP

The facts

Location: London

Number of UK partners/solicitors: 69/101

Total number of trainees: 30

Seats: 4x6 months

Alternative Seats: Dubai

Extras: Pro bono – Big Issue

On chambersstudent.co.uk...

- How to get into Lawrence Graham
- The AIM market
- More London

If you're looking for a classic City training contract with a staple diet of corporate, property and litigation, LG can provide the experience you're looking for.

More London

Lawrence Graham is one of London's older firms, dating back to the early 1700s, but its recent history really dates from 2007. That was the year when it spruced itself up, rebranding itself as LG and moving to spiffy new offices in More London, the fancy business development on the South Bank of the Thames next to Tower Bridge. Two assertive moves, and a real statement of intent of the firm's future ambitions.

What success has been achieved since then? It's fair to say the record is mixed. Given the firm's heavy focus on real estate work, you might have been forgiven for fearing the worst, and LG was perhaps unfortunate in that it revved up for a big push forward just before the economy collapsed, which naturally hampered its plans somewhat. Revenue fell and two redundancy rounds dampened the mood in the office. Trainees still hear rumblings of "*cutbacks and making sure you stay within the budget, and everyone is quite aware of that,*" but "*at the same time people are quite optimistic.*"

There have been achievements in this period as well. The firm has opened two new overseas offices to add to an existing one in Monaco serving high net worth individuals. It launched in Dubai in 2007 and Moscow in 2009, while in February 2012 it announced it would be forming an alliance with a local firm in Singapore. Despite not having an extensive international network, LG has worked hard to generate business from abroad, and 40% of its revenue comes from international clients. It still gets big instructions, too, recently being appointed to lead an independent investigation into Libor for the British Banking Association.

What we have, then, is pretty much what we had before the recession – a fairly solid mid-sized, mid-market firm, with core strengths in property and AIM-related capital markets work.

More seats

LG requires trainees to complete a contentious, transactional and property seat. There is little leeway for those wishing to pass over the property seat: "*One person in my intake of 19 skipped it; you'd be very lucky if you could.*" Although three-quarters of the training contract seems predetermined, there are a variety of subsections within the litigation, corporate and real estate department so there is more choice than there first appears to be. But with only one completely 'free' seat, "*you need to really think about what department you want to be in and plan it out in advance – you don't want to get to your fourth seat and realise you didn't get it.*"

Before each seat change, trainees fill out a form, "*setting out your first, second and third choice, which departments and which supervisors you want.*" The HR team also recommends trainees have a chat with their preferred supervisor for "*a bit of background schmoozing;*" however, our sources weren't sure if that carried much weight when factors like department needs and other trainee preferences were taken into account. "*The second-years*

Chambers UK rankings

Banking Litigation	Insurance
Capital Markets	Investment Funds
Construction	Pensions
Corporate Crime & Investigations	Planning
Corporate/M&A	Private Client
Dispute Resolution	Public Procurement
Employment	Real Estate
Fraud	Real Estate Finance
Information Technology	Real Estate Litigation

get preference – the first-years sort of flop around the seats that are left." Most of our interviewees appreciated that seat allocation is a delicate balancing act and that the HR team tries their best to accommodate everyone. "No one has got stuck where they desperately didn't want to go."

Our Graham with a quick recapitalisation

LG has an especially long list of clients listed on the Alternative Investment Market (the sub-market of the London Stock Exchange which allows smaller companies to float shares). In fact, as of May 2012, the firm had more AIM-listed clients than all but three other firms and it regularly acts for Indian plcs that have raised capital on AIM – such as cleantech company Greenko. The firm's M&A practice shouldn't be forgotten: in 2012 it advised Cove Energy, an oil and gas exploration company (and an existing AIM client of LG), on billion-pound takeover bids from Shell and then PTTEP.

Due to the large monetary value of deals in the corporate department, trainees found themselves with relatively low levels of client contact in comparison to other seats. The upside: "I was given lots of responsibility and was very rarely given menial tasks like photocopying," said one source. "On some really big transactions I helped with document reviews and due diligence but on smaller acquisitions I helped an associate run a smaller sub-team."

The corporate tax group is "very good for black-letter law" as trainees spend substantial amounts of time researching "specific laws for specific scenarios." As part of a small group, trainees work for everyone in the team. Corporate recovery is another "technical seat, with a lot of research." The department mostly acts for "the big banks or the accountancy firms that are putting a company into administration."

Graham crackers

Trainees can sample from a smorgasbord of property seats. LG has a place on Sainsbury's legal panel and has been advising the supermarket chain on the purchase and development of numerous stores, including the regeneration project in Bicester town centre. It also acted for the Crown Real Estate Commissioners on the funding and purchase of Stadium MK retail park, a matter worth £60m. Other clients include global insurance conglomerate AXA and Whitbread, owner of the Premier Inn and Costa Coffee chains.

Trainees in the general real estate group enjoyed the responsibility that came with this seat: "You have your own files, like rent reviews, that you are responsible for from the opening to when you close the files. Partners won't chase you up to see if you've done the work." On their own files, trainees had liaised with managing agents or the opposing side. Other tasks include drafting and negotiating aspects of contracts. The department is divided into teams focusing on different clients and each has its own ropes to learn. "I worked for more than one team and no one briefed me on how procedures worked, what the teams did," said one source. As a result, some came away from this seat with mixed reviews – "I felt a bit isolated initially; there wasn't too much of a team or collegiate feeling."

"You might get to run your own matters in other real estate groups, but in construction all the deals are big" and so this is less likely. Trainees receive work from the contentious and non-contentious side of the team, and are able to handle disclosure-related tasks and get involved with drafting. Although it's a busy team, "they have been very good at explaining how things work." The firm has recently launched its first overseas secondment, a construction-heavy seat in Dubai.

The real estate finance team works on financing acquisitions, restructurings and distressed loan sales for "some very big companies," alongside fee earners and associates from the finance department. Clients include RBS, Deutsche Hypo, La Selle Investment Group and Nationwide.

Eastern promise

Those not wanting to go down the corporate or real estate path will find some variety at LG. "We used to be based around old-school clients from England," said a trainee of the top-ranked private client practice, "but now we have partners who specialise in the Middle East and East Asia." Clients could be from "big wealthy Middle Eastern families or international bankers from Hong Kong or Singapore – international wealth is an area we are pushing into." Trainees work on drafting simple documents *"like appointment of trustees or straightforward wills."* Junior associates and trainees are encouraged to get involved in marketing and networking to *"start up their own career – I enjoyed that aspect,"* said one source.

To fulfil the contentious seat requirement, trainees can pick from dispute resolution, employment, real estate litigation or restructuring and insolvency. Dispute resolution trainees see some fascinating work – for instance, LG is acting for the Federal Republic of Brazil and the Municipality of São Paulo in a corruption case that has been brought against the former mayor of São Paulo in the Royal Court of Jersey. It's all to do with kickbacks from a large construction project. *"It's a very big step for democracy,"* one excited source exclaimed, with the significance of the matter more than making up for having to take on bundling and admin tasks. Other seats include banking, insurance and employment/pensions.

Putting in the L(e)G work

"There's no need to work late to impress." Hours tend to be good in most departments, averaging about 9am to 6pm, and some of our sources *"never had to work a weekend."* But it wouldn't be a City firm without someone burning the midnight oil – *"I had a lot of late nights in corporate,"* said one source, *"although none past midnight,"* while another in banking had experienced a stretch of *"non-stop 11pm or midnight finishes and a few all-nighters."*

While most trainees found their supervisors *"love having trainees and love nurturing them,"* we did hear reports, particularly from sources in real estate, of *"supervisors who, for lack of a better word, couldn't give a sh*t,"* or *"have no communication skills whatsoever."* In times of need, trainees find the HR team to be a good first port of call and if they've *"formed good relationships with a past supervisor, could always go back and talk to them."* Of course, the trainees themselves *"get along quite well,"* and form a good informal support network.

"It's hard to sum up LG without regurgitating the spiel that's already out there," one source mused. *"It's a medium-sized firm – that was the attraction for me – and it's got some great clients."* Another source summed up the consensus, saying: *"The partners are nice, like ... normal people. They are not what you would imagine a partner in a large firm would be like, which would be scary and bossy."*

LG trainees have *"solid academics"* but come from a wide range of universities. *"The one thing that I did note about us,"* said one source, *"is that everyone is around my age, in the 26 to 28 bracket. The firm likes people with a little bit of life experience – most of us have travelled or worked before."*

Happy as Larry

There is more of a departmental focus than a firmwide one when it comes to the social calendar. Each department hosts joining and leaving drinks for trainees at the beginning of each seat rotation. Some also host their own summer and Halloween parties and instead of a firmwide Christmas do, each department has its own bash. Tightened purse strings in 2011 saw the end of the trainee Christmas party budget: they were asked to foot their own bill. In the end, not only did the resourceful LG trainees throw their own bash, they even invited the partners. One firmwide event is the annual pub quiz, the proceeds from which go to charity. The firm also looks ahead with *"Next Generation"* drinks sessions, a networking event for everyone from trainees to 2PQE level to bring guests from other businesses. On Friday evenings, trainees send round messages to see who's up for a drink. The Brigade on Tooley Street, a converted fire station, is a popular destination. Trainees are good at heading out spontaneously and often get together on weekends.

What next for Lawrence Graham? *"The firm should be okay as the economy picks up,"* thought one interviewee. *"The only thing I wonder is if the firm might merge, perhaps with a similar mid-sized city firm like Field Fisher or Mishcon or Nabarro."* Clearly that trainee was either particularly insightful or well connected on LG's gossip grapevine, because less than a month after we spoke to them news broke in the legal press that the firm was indeed in talks with Field Fisher Waterhouse about a potential tie-up. Nothing came of the discussions in the end, but of course there are plenty of other potential suitors out there. With a merger or without one, some further international expansion is a probability.

At qualification time, *"you have to go behind the scenes, talk to the partners and find out if there are jobs in the place where you want to qualify."* Due to a cycle of deferrals, the qualifying class of 2012 is one of the larger ones in recent years and second-years feared that as many of half of them might be leaving. In the end, 12 out of 19 stayed on.

And finally...

There's no doubt LG will beef itself up in one way or another over the next few years. For now, its trainees enjoy a proper City experience that's not too hardcore.

Lester Aldridge LLP

The facts

Location: Bournemouth, Southampton, London
Number of UK partners/solicitors: 43/35
Partners who trained at firm: 30%
Total number of trainees: 12
Seats: 4x6 months
Alternative seats: Secondments

On chambersstudent.co.uk...

- How to get into Lester Aldridge
- Interview with managing partner Michael Giddins

Sunny Saturdays on the beach? This Bournemouth-born firm is going to be "*London-facing*" from its South Coast offices.

The Bournemouth identity

Starting life through a merger between two Bournemouth firms in 1988, Lester Aldridge has carved out a place for itself on the South Coast, and now it's focusing on its London office. "*The firm is looking to be London-facing, with London clients, but with out-of-London rates*," managing partner Michael Giddins explains. A third office, in Southampton, also continues to grow.

Despite its small size, this full-service firm scores well in *Chambers UK*. It is ranked in the South for many mainstream areas of practice, such as real estate, litigation, employment, family and private client, while its shipping and healthcare groups gain even wider recognition. "*Dispute resolution is very busy and our fast-track property teams have had some good wins*," Giddins says.

The training contract is offered with Lester Aldridge as a whole, so trainees can expect quite a bit of movement between the three offices. At the time of our calls, there were seven (mostly first-year) trainees in Bournemouth, four in Southampton and one in London. A list of available seats is released three months before rotation and trainees rank their top three preferences. A pleasantly broad spread of options includes property; banking and finance; corporate; marine; Fast Track debt recovery; dispute resolution; care; employment; family; tax, trusts and wills (TTW); and planning and development.

"*I've been lucky in that I've enjoyed all my seats*," one source said, "*but I've never had my first choice*." Another told us: "*The seats we are allocated don't seem very logical, but I can't think of a better way they could operate it.*" This means that "*trainees don't talk among themselves*

about seat allocation. It can be very competitive." Last year, we heard that some had been circumventing the list all together, going straight to partners in the hope that they could pull some strings. This year, "*some trainees have spent twelve or eighteen months in the same seat*," a disgruntled source commented. "*Seats in London are popular*," and although trainees didn't quite say so outright, we got the impression there's some competition for them.

Sea cats and fat cats

Spanning all three offices, the real estate group is one of Hampshire and Dorset's largest. "*In Southampton, we are dealing with businesses which have gone into administration*," whereas trainees in London were seeing "*large commercial sales and acquisitions of sites, a few commercial landlord and tenant matters, and the odd bit of residential work.*" One trainee confessed: "*To be truthful I was surprised by the standard of work. We've been working with large, well-known clients.*" These include Bournemouth-based McCarthy & Stone, which builds retirement homes, and the company behind those storage adverts you see on billboards, Big Yellow. Recently, the team worked on the £4.4m acquisition of Winchester Job Centre. One trainee described the seat as "*fantastic. I was taking matters through to completion by the end.*" Another had "*a lot of client contact. When my supervisor went away I took control and was on the phone to CEOs of massive companies. I went round to an MD's home to interview him by myself. He had a really nice house!*"

Managing partner Michael Giddins leads the dispute resolution team in Bournemouth, as well as sitting as a part-time judge. "*I had decent levels of responsibility*," a

347

Chambers UK rankings

Charities	Partnership
Consumer Finance	Planning
Corporate/M&A	Private Client
Dispute Resolution	Real Estate
Employment	Real Estate Litigation
Family/Matrimonial	Restructuring/Insolvency
Healthcare	Shipping

trainee modestly said, before adding: "*I've had my own cases and I won a trial.*" Another thought: "*It's a great seat. You learn really quickly. You're never left to drown though. There is loads of client contact, and I also drafted court applications and witness statements.*" Clients range from "*individuals wanting to register a trade mark*" right up to nationally recognised names. There's less crossover between offices than in some other seats.

Marine is "*popular because it's so specialist.*" The team covers dry shipping, personal injury claims and marine finance, and is ranked in the top five outside of London by *Chambers UK*. "*There's both contentious and non-contentious work going on, so you could work on the purchase of vessels, breach of contract claims, or a big arbitration case.*" And, "*it's always exciting when we arrest a ship!*"

The employment team acts for both employers, including Condor Ferries and the Bournemouth Symphony Orchestra, and employees. "*Bournemouth has more non-contentious work and Southampton has more contentious.*" Trainees in this seat had split their time between the two offices, drafting contracts for employers, and redrafting company handbooks and contracts. "*I had my own contentious files to manage,*" one added.

The level of responsibility afforded to trainees is "*probably the most gratifying part of the training contract,*" one source said. "*The firm adopts a laissez-faire approach: they really want you to grow as your own solicitor rather than as a clone of a certain partner.*"

"*The firm thinks they get the best out of happy people, so they offer a great work/life balance,*" trainees told us. Across all offices, trainees' working hours were praised and our sources regarded 7pm as a late night. However, one source "*did leave at 10pm a handful of times*" when in London.

The Bournemouth supremacy

Our Southampton and London sources considered the Bournemouth head office to have the most formal atmosphere. However, Bournemouth sources told us of monthly happy hours, dress-down Fridays ("*as long as we don't wear tracksuits*") and a generally "*busy*" social life. "*It's a staple that on Friday lunchtime we go to the pub. When it's sunny we go down to the beach. On Friday nights, there's usually a beer at O'Neills and some of us head in to the town after.*" With "*more clubs and bars per square mile than London,*" it's not a bad place to spend a training contract. The seven-storey office has been recently refurbished. Some of the floors are open-plan, some are broken down into offices, and some are split into 'pods', described by one helpful source as "*like an office but without a door.*" Trainees on the office-based floors "*tend to get their own room, with their supervisor across the corridor.*" Said one such source: "*My name is on the door. It's so cool!*"

Southampton is a "*one-level office with a shared kitchen. Rather than a monthly happy hour we have a breakfast, and the whole office heads down to The Cricketers on Friday lunchtime.*" The London office moved to 70 Chancery Lane in September 2011. Trainees thought the move was a bold statement in the recession. It's largely open-plan but the partners have their own offices. The office is quite partner-heavy and trainees "*don't tend to party with them, but we do go out together for lunches.*" The kitchen area, which is "*big enough to hang out in,*" encourages socialising. "*The old office didn't have anything like that. It encourages people to actually take lunch, rather than eat at our desks.*"

South Coast girls, we're undeniable

Although the trainee salary increased in September 2011, our sources remained unimpressed. "*The firm thinks it pays the highest in Bournemouth; however, for firms of a similar size in Southampton, it's not so good,*" one said. Another complained: "*It's the biggest drawback of the whole training contract. It's a brilliant firm, with brilliant work and brilliant people, but then you see your payslip.*"

"*LA is much more female-heavy than other firms,*" a trainee told us. As of August 2012, some 75% of trainees and a whopping 87% of assistant solicitors were women. One said: "*I was on a completely female team. It's great for the girls to see.*" The fact is, boys, that the ladies come across better at interview, so you really need do your homework on the firm.

And finally...
Retention here is generally pretty good, and Lester Aldridge retained four of six qualifiers in 2012.

Lewis Silkin LLP

The facts

Location: London

Number of UK partners/solicitors: 60/113

Total number of trainees: 13

Seats: 6x4 months

Alternative seats: Occasional secondments

Extras: Pro bono – National Pro Bono Centre, Own-it; language classes

On chambersstudent.co.uk...

- How to get into Lewis Silkin
- The early days of law firm advertising
- Social housing at Lewis Silkin

It's now over a decade since Lewis Silkin moved from SW1 to the City, but with some quirky practice areas, it retains the feel of a West End firm.

The welfare scape

Lewis Silkin reported an epic 27% hike in partner profit between 2010 and 2011, although boasting about the dollar isn't this firm's style. "*There are other measures we believe are indicative of our firm's health besides PEP,*" said training partner Lisa Patmore. "*Financially there is revenue, growth and cash generation, but there are the non-financial factors like client satisfaction and employee engagement.*" There's evidently something a bit different about the ethos at LS, although the difference is tricky to define. Asking trainees why they chose the firm, you're as likely to hear about its "*unstuffy personality and non-aggressive working ethos,*" as you are to hear cool client name-checks, or about the firm's star employment practice.

The original Lewis Silkin rose from legal practice to become minister of town and country planning under Clement Attlee. As well as his name, the firm still bears his legacy in a highly regarded social housing group. The firm's large employment practice is a nationwide leader, and works globally through the Ius Laboris alliance with international firms. "*We have a significant number of clients for whom we co-ordinate support,*" says Lisa Patmore. "*We pick absolute employment law specialists, so when we refer work, we know who we're referring to. For example, we operate a well-established helpdesk for MTV which ensures they are supported in over 30 countries.*" Lewis Silkin's final specialism is in media. There's a specific marketing, brands and technology team, where you'll find household-name clients like E.ON and Bacardi, as well as some of the advertising agencies who helped them become household names.

LS had a strategy to fit these specialisms into three 'scapes' ('landscape, peoplescape and mediascape') but during a recent rebrand the firm has moved to a more conventional focus on client sectors. Little has changed day-to-day: the employment practice still remains the largest by a way, accounting for around 39% of revenue. Property and advertising/media/IP/defamation/IT count for around 17% each, with corporate revenue rising slightly to 14% of business, and litigation making up the remainder.

Smooth as Silkin

Trainees take six four-month seats, "*the extra two making it easier to satisfy people's expectations.*" The idea is that trainees spend time in every department, plus, "*if there's a seat you want to repeat in your second year, you can, or maybe go on a secondment to a client that links to it.*"

Trainees can visit both a straight employment seat and a smaller sports immigration team. Employment is a team that, although huge, embodies the rest of the firm's "*supportive, friendly collective feeling.*" An impressive client list includes many major British law firms, along with Marks & Spencer, Credit Suisse and Nokia. Trainees mainly encounter respondent work, and are able to get stuck in with a wealth of tasks: "*Because it's people-oriented, you don't need to be as versed in technicalities and formalities.*" Even when dealing with vast corporations, the work is pretty personal, and "*it's always interesting to hear about the silly things people do.*" One trainee "*ran a small tribunal case as the first point of contact, from the initial pleading to liaising with counsel to attending the tribunal.*" There's also research on offer, like "*writing a note on the impact of social networking on employment law.*" Meanwhile, the immigration team acts for many Premier League teams and rugby clubs in securing players and staff, and their representation at hearings. The pace is fast, and there's a high turnover of work. The team

Chambers UK rankings

Construction	Intellectual Property
Corporate/M&A	Media & Entertainment
Defamation/Reputation Management	Partnership
	Real Estate
Dispute Resolution	Real Estate Litigation
Education	Retail
Employment	Social Housing
Immigration	Sports Law

allows trainees a lot of client contact "*and the chance to attend meetings and to accompany clients to visa appointments.*" By the end of the seat, sources often have their own files to run.

The litigation seat also has two paths. The first involves working on small debt collection files which trainees can take on themselves: "*It sounds horrible, but is an amazing experience. Lots of people just don't like paying bills, and often relationships have completely broken down – you learn quickly that you can't take it personally.*" The second is mediation-based, where trainees support fee earners on large matters, attending court, researching points and producing attendance notes. Disputes stemming from private equity funds are currently pretty common, and there's plenty of work from tech, energy and sports clients too. The firm represented Fulham FC in a complex issue centring around whether it is possible to stay an Unfair Prejudice Petition in favour of an arbitration. Trainees always "*attend meetings, and are always encouraged to read into case background and discuss the bigger strategy.*"

Freudian slick

The corporate seat offers an atypical City experience, as the firm's staple is lower mid-market work. "*It's not 24-hour days dealing with banks and multimillion-pound transactions.*" There's still a lot of M&A, often with clients from the MCT sector, as well as in the healthcare and energy and natural resources industries. The team acted for Publicis Groupe in the sale of a majority stake of Freud Communications back to PR guru Matthew Freud.

Property takes two trainees a time, one in commercial and one in social housing. Commercial comes down to "*two types of transaction – large-scale development projects that will run and run, and small purchases of newbuilds that trainees can take on themselves.*" Clients include Rio Tinto, PizzaExpress and Electronic Arts – LS advised the

computer games company on the sale of its European headquarters in Chertsey to a pharmaceutical company. For detail on the firm's renowned social housing practice, head to the bonus features on our website.

The firm's media connections are rooted as surely as its social ones. Ex-chairman Roger Alexander (dubbed 'the Don' of advertising law during his 40 years at the top) was famous for thinking as creatively as his clients. Lewis Silkin was even behind the profession's first billboard ad back in the 1980s, when the ban against firms advertising their services was first lifted. Today the firm has trendy agencies like Mother (makers of Coca-Cola's 'Move to the Beat' campaign) and TBWA on the books. LS provided advice to the latter on their 'Wünderful Stuff' ad for Müller – the one featuring the Mr Men, Yogi Bear and Muttley from Wacky Races, intended to blow the 'Yeo Valley' farmers out of the water – on its countless commercial and licensing issues. Trainees in the media, brands and technology (MBT) seat get "*a vast array of work, from litigious IP through to IT advice, to advising on ad clearance.*"

Tutu unique

Trainees receive constant feedback, "*which is very good in terms of reassurance. Appraisals are critical but positive.*" People at LS have a similar outlook – "*they care about who they work with, and aren't stuffy.*" There's certainly something different about Lewis Silkin, and trainees think "*it comes from the clients we work for – we're entrenched in the creative industries so we are creative lawyers.*"

Socialising occurs on an impromptu basis, but on Fridays you can usually "*wander over to Baranis and find a lot of us there.*" Every few months the firm puts on 'Lewis Silkin simply drinks'. "*It's just a tab behind a local bar, but it encourages those who wouldn't normally be out on Fridays to join in.*"

The firm is noticeably "*composed of very unique individuals*" and trainees agreed that character plays a major role in getting in. The assessment process, therefore, "*is designed to bring out people's personalities.*" Partners whittle 600 applications down to interview 30 for the six places on offer. The bottom line? "*They want people who have a bit of a story. We're such a human firm, they just want to know what you're about.*" You'll find an ex-ballet dancer, a professional violinist and maker of video games in the current intake.

And finally...

"*Retention hasn't been amazing in the past, as there is fierce competition for specific departments.*" In 2012, however, five out of the six qualifiers stayed put with the firm.

Linklaters

The facts

Location: London

Number of UK partners/solicitors: 181/670

Seats: 4x6 months

Total number of trainees: 239

Alternative seats: Overseas seats, secondments

Extras: Pro bono – Mary Ward Legal Advice Centre, Disability Law Service, Lawyers Without Borders and others; language classes

On chambersstudent.co.uk...

- How to get into Linklaters
- An interview with training principal Simon Firth
- The Linklaters LPC

'Our aim is to be the leading global law firm,' Linklaters' website says simply – every year this firm competes to be the biggest and best in the world.

You're the strongest Link

Missile-like bands of light emanate from London across the globe on Links' graduate recruitment website. The image leaves little to the imagination: for years now Linklaters has been one of the largest and most global law firms anywhere. It employs over 2,500 lawyers in 27 offices worldwide, and pulled in a revenue of £1.2bn in 2011/12. *"Everyone here is very proud to work at a magic circle firm,"* one trainee said. *"There is no doubt that the prestige is important even if people don't acknowledge it. Once you have that magic circle name on your CV you know it will open a lot of doors in the future."*

Although Linklaters was traditionally known as one of the magic circle's corporate-leaning firms, it would be misstating the case to characterise M&A work as its only trick. *Chambers UK* ranks Links equally highly for its banking and finance, capital markets, competition, energy, regulatory and projects work. But the firm undoubtedly leans towards high-end transactional work. *"I really like finance and corporate work,"* said one trainee. *"As a lawyer your job is to hold everyone's hand and make sure everything moves in the same direction and that everyone is happy."*

Chambers Global awards Links over 100 rankings in 28 jurisdictions. *"I love the fact we have offices all around the world,"* said one trainee. *"Every deal has an international aspect – whether it is a holding company based in the Cayman Islands or a borrower based in Luxembourg. I liaise with lawyers in loads of different countries."* The firm expanded its global web in 2012, entering an exclusive alliance with Australian firm Allens. But Asia is cur-

rently where the big bucks are. *"We have a big presence in the key jurisdictions of Hong Kong and Singapore,"* says training partner Simon Firth, *"and we see a lot of our growth coming from Mainland China."*

It's not all boom for Linklaters at the moment: after a major redundancy round in 2009, which hit associates and partners, *The Lawyer* reported in early 2012 that Links would be laying off a further 70 partners worldwide. Trainees were sanguine about the idea of cuts. *"Obviously it is never nice to hear people are being let go,"* said one. *"But this is a business and unless it works perfectly, management will have to make tough decisions to improve things."*

Spoilt for choice

At the time of our research half of trainees were sitting in the three core transactional departments, divided equally between corporate, banking and capital markets. In addition, there were around 20 trainees in litigation and around a dozen in both projects and real estate. Then there are always a handful in the smaller departments: financial regulation, restructuring, tax, competition, IP, investment management, TMT, pensions, environment and employment/incentives. Any training contract here will be heavily transactional – Links' trainees like things that way. *"It is impossible to focus on seats in smaller departments and avoid transactional work,"* cautioned one. Trainees can also fulfil their contentious requirement on a two-week course at the College of Law.

Chambers UK rankings

Asset Finance	Intellectual Property
Banking & Finance	Investment Funds
Banking Litigation	Life Sciences
Capital Markets	Outsourcing
Commodities	Partnership
Competition/European Law	Pensions
Corporate Crime & Investigations	Pensions Litigation
	Planning
Corporate/M&A	Private Equity
Data Protection	Projects
Dispute Resolution	Public Procurement
Employee Share Schemes & Incentives	Real Estate
	Real Estate Finance
Employment	Real Estate Litigation
Energy & Natural Resources	Restructuring/Insolvency
Environment	Retail
Financial Services	Tax
Fraud	Telecommunications
Information Technology	Transport
Insurance	

Before joining, trainees list four seat preferences, one of which they are assigned as a first seat. A few months into training the three remaining seats are assigned, based on a list of eight trainee preferences (two of which can be in one of the smaller departments). Overseas seats are assigned at a later stage. Seat swaps are possible. Some sources felt that "*there is lobbying to get certain seats which are heavily oversubscribed, like projects, competition, IP and litigation. At the very least you have to stress to HR what you want really hard.*" Others said that to win a stint in a small department it is enough just to list it as your number-one preference. "*There is such a vast number of trainees that it is difficult to accommodate everyone, but they do the best they can.*"

Links has had its Weetabix

Linklaters' huge corporate department does some massive deal making. It advised mining and trading giant Glencore on its $82bn merger with partner firm Xstrata. The size of the deals means for most trainees "*the tasks border on the menial*" – due diligence, data room management, proof-reading and transaction management. Client contact is rare. "*I wouldn't say I'm a small cog in the machine though,*" said one trainee brightly. "*I'm quite a big cog given the number of hours I put in.*" No doubt the hours people work have a bearing on the department's "*intense, adrenaline-driven, work-hard atmosphere*" in which "*people really want to impress the partners.*" But here's the upside: "*All the deals you work on get reported in the FT and sometimes you'll come down to the restau-*

rant for lunch and see the deal announced on BBC News." The work spans the globe and often reflects major trends in global economics: the firm recently advised on the sale of Thames Water's parent company to a Chinese investment firm and helped a Chinese food business buy a controlling stake in Weetabix.

It's not just corporate which demands long hours. "*The toughest part of this job is the hours,*" trainees agreed. "*A good day is when you come in at 9.30am and leave at 7pm – no one usually leaves before then,*" said one. "*On a normal day I work until 9 or 11pm and on a bad day I might work until 2am. During one month I worked up to or past midnight almost every night and worked every weekend.*" This last example may be extreme, but all our interviewees had at some point worked until the small hours. Some trainees relish this more than others. "*Call me mad, but there is something quite fun about being in the office trying to make a deal happen late at night,*" said one. The big plus is that "*they treat you really well if you do stay late – dinners are paid for and you can get a taxi home.*" The Silk Street office boasts many other perks, including a dentist, doctor, gym, beauty salon, prayer room, restaurant and sleep pods. "*It is fantastic, but a bit worrying – because why would I ever need to leave this place?*" said one trainee, only half jokingly.

Comrade, can you spare a dime?

Before we tell you about Links' finance work, here's one trainee's simple explanation of the field: "*Finance is all about loans. If a business wants to borrow money it can do one of two things: take out a private contractual loan, or raise money publicly through bonds or stocks. Banking is the former. Capital markets is the latter.*" Got that? Then keep reading.

The banking department advises both lenders (BNP Paribas, Citi, JPMorgan, Deutsche Bank, UBS...) and borrowers (Rio Tinto, Vodafone, Balfour Beatty, Tate & Lyle) on a whole range of loan and credit agreements. "*While the partners advise on the main loan agreements, as a trainee you make sure all the little documents are ready to go: the board minutes, pieces of legal advice, letters to auditors and the constitutional documents of the companies.*" Trainees recognised their time in capital markets as the "*most technical and challenging seat.*" Terms like 'commercial mortgage-backed securities' and 'special purpose vehicle' are run of the mill. There are three capital markets departments: derivatives and structured products (DSP), equity and debt markets (EDM) and the structured finance group (SFG). Links recently advised the Industrial & Commercial Bank of China on a 1.5bn yuan offshore bond issuance – a so-called 'dim sum bond' – and assisted the Russian government with a 40bn rouble bond issuance. "*There are a lot of smaller deals too. Some of them are really quick – they last maybe four weeks – so you get to see them from start to finish. You have quite an upfront role as a trainee and get a lot of client contact."*

News of the World

Since early 2012 Linklaters has been acting for News International in all its civil phone-hacking cases, making litigators *"ridiculously busy."* More usual fare includes litigating on behalf of finance and corporate clients – RBS, Barclays – in disputes over world-spanning commercial contracts. *"I've done a few long document review tasks,"* said one trainee. *"But if you impress on minor tasks, you get to do more: I wrote up a research memo, which went straight to the client without being touched."* There are a range of other seat options, and we heard positive things about all of them. Projects is particularly popular, partly because *"the results of your work are very real and tangible – it's a bit like real-life Monopoly."* The regulatory department, meanwhile, is *"growing by the minute as things like the Bribery Act and Basel III come into force."*

Overseas seats are immensely popular. There are around 45 spots abroad – see page 532 for a full list – and around two-thirds of trainees spend time overseas. *"It is brilliant,"* enthused one trainee. *"Transport and accommodation are paid for and booked by the firm and my apartment was five minutes from the office."* Another trainee added: *"The amount of responsibility I got was much more than in London and the office was very close-knit and more personable."* The number of overseas seats means *"almost everyone who wants to will go."* At the time of our calls Singapore, Hong Kong and Moscow offered the most seats, while New York and Paris were the most competitive picks. Meanwhile, client secondments to the likes of Barclays, BP and The Prince's Trust offer the chance to *"learn more about a business and what happens before the lawyers get involved."*

Pimm's o'clock

"Each department has its own culture," trainees told us. *"Tax and competition are more techy, other departments are more relaxed, while some – like corporate – are very 'work hard, play hard'. EDM is a sociable department – it has a drinks trolley every Friday and there was a Pimm's party for the Jubilee."* Interviewees praised the firm's bespoke LPC at the College of Law for creating unity in the trainee group. *"My intake has been a real source of support for me,"* one said. *"I make an effort to*

see my closer friends among the trainees outside hours. I usually spend time with my peer group or grab lunch with friends rather than with my department as a whole." Trainees are also encouraged to rub shoulders at the six-monthly seat-swap drinks and the annual summer trainee ball. There are also trainee bowling and karaoke socials as well as departmental retreats to places like Devon, Barcelona and even Monaco.

"Everybody here – well not everybody, but most people – is very ambitious," said one trainee. *"I think some of my colleagues enjoy the long hours in a masochistic way,"* observed one wryly. *"A few trainees already seem to be working towards partnership – they are very conscientious and work extremely hard. Others have realised they don't enjoy it as much and are considering their options. There are lots of people in between. I just work my hardest and make sure I exceed expectations, to improve my chances of being kept on."* All our interviewees possessed a streak of ambition, but they were also a frank and friendly bunch more willing than most to point out the ups and downs of their job.

Linklaters sees the whole planet as its recruiting ground, hiring trainees from around the world. About one-third of trainees are non-white and the firm recruits directly from both India and Australia. *"This is an inclusive firm and it's making an effort to be more diverse,"* observed one trainee. As to universities, one trainee said: *"Many people think the magic circle is all Oxbridge, but my intake included a lot of people from London universities and places like Bristol, Bath and Warwick."* The firm says 31% of the current trainee group are Oxbridge grads.

The six-monthly appraisals and feedback from supervisors didn't provoke any major complaints from trainees. They were also happy with the qualification process. *"Networking is an important part of it,"* sources agreed. *"You are encouraged to keep in touch with people from previous seats. It's good to show you are keen to qualify into a department – perhaps at your appraisal – but sometimes it's best to wait to be asked first."* Trying too hard is definitely frowned upon – we cringed at the story of the trainee who *"sent Christmas cards to everyone in the department he wanted to qualify into, including the partners. That was a bit too blatant."* Ultimately, *"people judge you on the quality of your work. Just being matey with a partner will not get you far."* In 2012, 100 of 122 qualifiers were kept on.

And finally...

A training contract here is best suited to *"people who are quite ambitious, confident and enjoy being pushed,"* but for Linklaters trainees the pain is well worth the gain.

Macfarlanes LLP

The facts

Location: London

Number of UK partners/solicitors: 71/157

Partners who trained at firm: 56%

Total number of trainees: 59

Seats: 4x6 months

Alternative seats: None

Extras: Pro bono – Cambridge House, LawWorks, National Pro Bono Centre, BPP Legal Advice Centre; language classes

On chambersstudent.co.uk...
- How to get into Macfarlanes
- Interview with graduate recruitment partner John Hornby

If it were a person, Macfarlanes would shop in Savile Row, take afternoon tea at Fortnum's and consider behemoth expansionism slightly distasteful. In reality, it's a City firm with a sharp eye for quality.

The few

Born in 1875 and christened 'Macfarlanes' in 1962, what this City firm lacks in size it makes up for in reputation. In fact, such is its corporate expertise, it receives not one but two rankings for M&A in *Chambers UK*. One puts it at the very top of the market when it comes to mid-market transactions; the other recognises that it is also a significant force when it comes to the very biggest deals. Other top Chambers rankings come in the fields of investment funds and – unusually for a City firm of this ilk – private client.

Our initial description of Macfarlanes as a tweedy, English sort of place stem from that strong private client practice acting for "*old-school monied aristocrats,*" as well as the firm's long history and resolute independence (it has never merged). In fact, it's rumoured that until quite recently Macfarlanes didn't even have a formal partnership agreement, with promotion to the top rungs of the firm being solidified though nothing more than a gentlemanly handshake. However, it's only fair to say that trainees described Macfarlanes in different terms, painting a picture of "*a small firm punching above its weight.*" One source even likened it to "*a small, Staffy Bull Terrier that packs a bite.*" Hmm... small, very English, fighting spirit, looks a bit like a dog – perhaps Winston Churchill is the best comparison to this firm.

Macfarlanes "*is a great place to be if you want to get experience in different areas of the law, it has a broad practice for its size.*" The structure of the training contract had a minor revamp after the real estate market took a tumble during the recession. The compulsory real estate seat has been scrapped – instead, trainees must now complete stints in both mainstream corporate M&A and a specialist corporate seat (which could be investment funds; banking and finance; employment, pensions and benefits; commercial; or competition). For the remaining two seats, trainees have a choice between commercial real estate, private client, tax, restructuring and litigation/dispute resolution.

From the first seat onwards, trainees are asked to state their choices, including a "*main preference seat, which is pretty much guaranteed.*" According to trainees, "*partners take the lead in allocation instead of graduate recruitment, and they aren't dogmatic about seat choices: if they can accommodate you, they will.*"

Corporate is king

Trainees find the M&A seat provides opportunities to be involved in headline deals and "*fast-paced, exciting work.*" The firm recently advised Trafigura on the disposal of a 20% stake in Puma Energy. While there isn't much black-letter law to dive into in a seat like this, the practical nature of transactional practice allows trainees to take on project management roles and "*first goes*" at drafting court documents, letters and other documents. On smaller deals, trainees receive more responsibility and more client contact. Depending on their supervisor, some had liaised with chief executives and foreign counsel and had

Chambers UK rankings

Agriculture & Rural Affairs	Information Technology
Banking & Finance	Intellectual Property
Banking Litigation	Investment Funds
Charities	
Competition/European Law	Media & Entertainment
Construction	Pensions
Corporate/M&A	Private Client
Dispute Resolution	Private Equity
Employee Share Schemes & Incentives	Real Estate
Employment	Real Estate Finance
Environment	Real Estate Litigation
Financial Services	
Fraud	Tax

meetings with investment managers and even the chairman of a FTSE 100 company.

The banking practice "*is growing at a huge rate.*" The firm represents the likes of RBS, Goldman Sachs Asset Management and Virgin Group. "*It's a hardcore seat*" as "*trainees are the hub through which all information flows.*" Fortunately, "*it is an incredibly supportive team: they are so careful and helpful with trainees, making sure you are all right with the level of work you are given and the supervision you are getting.*" Banking has a "*monitoring*" session for trainees every Wednesday: "*We have a sandwich and a talk about what we are doing, and if we have little, some or no capacity.*" Trainees get to draft board minutes, conduct completion meetings and email clients directly.

In addition to private equity matters, the investment funds practise has "*quite a lot of private client finance work going on – wealthy people in China and India who have more disposable cash than corporates do, so you get to work on some really interesting deals.*" Macfarlanes recently acted for Montagu Private Equity on the raising of €2.5bn for its fourth fund, which it then used to acquire The College of Law. Trainees we spoke with understood that "*you don't get to run files, as it's a very technical area that you don't study on the LPC.*" Our sources were happy with the tasks meted out to them: researching EU directives, fund reviews, undertaking FSA applications for individuals and firms, drafting compliance procedures of investment banks and looking up provisions to prepare client reports.

The family silver

"*A firm of Macfarlanes' calibre is incredibly popular with the Oscar Wilde kind of fellows, who love the old world of private client,*" a trainee declared. The firm's expertise in offshore tax laws, trust and succession planning and cross-border family wealth management makes it stand out when lined up against other top-end corporate firms, most of which shed their private client departments years ago. In addition to catering to wealthy aristos (whom we don't imagine can really be much like Oscar Wilde), Macfarlanes manages the wealth of "*new entrepreneurs who have set up entities that you've heard of: founders of pub chains, music shops, restaurants.*" Client contact is limited since the "*world-famous figures*" Macfarlanes acts for have "*long-standing personal relationships*" with the team's senior lawyers. However, trainees "*get very interesting work,*" and had spent time "*meeting clients and discussing their wills,*" and bequests where people's "*complicated family arrangements*" (like the existence of step-children) causes trickiness.

There are three property-related seats: private client property, commercial real estate and construction litigation. Private client property involves acting for "*private individuals buying and selling big country estates or houses in Chelsea and Mayfair.*" There are opportunities for trainees to run files as "*some of these clients have smaller property matters – like selling holiday homes and leases on car-parking space.*" Trainees in construction litigation worked on cases valued from "*millions down to the thousands.*" With smaller matters, they can work through an entire case cycle in the course of their seat. One junior had "*gone to do an application myself in court. I was fully briefed and allowed to go and say my piece.*"

In the employment department, "*you're usually the only trainee and get to work on a lot of different matters for everyone in the department.*" Taking on both contentious and non-contentious matters trainees attend meetings with counsel, field calls from clients, draft research notes and explore the employment aspects of corporate deals.

Macfar-flung friends

Macfarlanes doesn't have an international network, but it does have relationships with firms across the world and trainees in seats such as tax and banking will find work involving the Middle East, South East Asia, Luxembourg, the Channel Islands and the Caribbean a recurring theme. Additionally, there is much "*attention to emerging markets,*" such as India and China. The firm is "*really good at encouraging business development at any level and age: if you have a contact that you think could be useful, they will pick up the entertainment bill.*" "*We may not remain a pure one-office firm forever,*" says grad recruitment partner John Hornby, "*but our strategy is to build on our best-friend relationships. We may add a couple of offices in due course as we see client demand, but we have no intention of building a global network.*"

"*Even though with time Macfarlanes has become more flexible with lateral hiring, it tends to promote people who trained here, as if it were breeding a thoroughbred.*" Supervisors are always senior associates or partners – "*never a junior associate, because the firm's obsessed with training.*" Lunch and breakfast seminars, mock trials, departmental updates – trainees find the level of support on offer "*one of the best aspects of the firm.*" In addition, a partner principal is assigned to each trainee for the duration of their training contract. They are involved in appraisals and lobby on trainees' behalf come qualification.

Trainees acknowledged: "*We do have a stuffy reputation but that perception jars with the reality.*" Macfarlanes, they say, is a "*modern firm with values,*" which "*doesn't have the rugby club aggression that you find at other firms – no Jägerbombs, just bottles of red wine.*" The "*Oxbridge reputation*" was "*possibly true in the past, but things have certainly changed – no more than 50% of the current trainee intake come from an Oxbridge background.*" During our research, we came across a fair number of trainees who had attended comprehensive schools, and their university backgrounds certainly went beyond Oxford and Cambridge, although not far past the Russell Group.

Macfarlanes trainees are treated like adults. "*There's no asking for permission to use the toilet like you're in junior school – you learn to deal with your own workload.*" Accordingly, "*if you need to go early, you can leave, but if you have work, you will be expected to stay late and complete it.*" Work hours aren't deemed too terrible. Our sources liked coming in early in order to leave by 7.30 or 8pm.

Gauguin to Gaga

"*You can always pass by and find someone to drink with – by no means just trainees.*" Departments host drinks events to welcome new trainees every six months. "*Banking is known for being very friendly and has a do once every two weeks.*" Most departments also organise a summer party: "*Private client had a barbecue at a partners house where kids and better halves were invited.*" Trainees can be found after work at the Castle, across the road from office.

For those who can tear themselves away from the Castle, Macfarlanes offers art history lectures, normally themed around current exhibitions such as the Da Vinci and Turner shows at the National Gallery. "*An excellent art historian comes in – we did a winter series and now a summer series.*" Throw in a few drinks and canapes and "*it really is a pleasant way to while away an evening.*"

From highbrow pursuits to Camden's cheesiest club: every year the firm (including future trainees) puts on a cabaret at Koko for its charity of the year, and "*everyone from cleaners to senior partners participate in the acting, dancing, make-up and organising.*" For a tenner, guests get to see wonderful sights like grad recruitment partner John Hornby dressed as Cheryl Cole – "*wonderful legs... in a sickening way!*"

Macfarlanes doesn't announce how many NQ jobs are available in each department and this makes some trainees nervous as they are unable to calculate their chances. Still, retention is usually all right, and 25 out of 30 qualifiers stayed on at the firm in 2012. The process is a simple one: "*In April or May we give in our preferences, two weeks after that they interview us and in another two weeks they let us know.*" Trainees talk to partners in departments they are interested in and training principals "*really come into their own, networking on your behalf.*"

And finally...
There will be no dramatic shake-up in this firm's future: that's just not the Macfarlanes style. Choose it for its timeless excellence.

Manches LLP

The facts

Location: London, Oxford, Reading
Number of UK partners/solicitors: 46/65
Partners who trained at firm: 13%
Total number of trainees: 20
Seats: 4x6 months
Alternative Seats: Secondments

On chambersstudent.co.uk...
• How to get into Manches
• Notable divorce cases
• The firm's big-name partners

Manches has a top-notch family team working alongside a host of other practices in London and the Thames Valley.

Manches branches

Founded in 1936 by Sidney and Judith Manches, the first husband and wife partnership to practise in London, the firm has since opened in Oxford and Reading too. Sid and Judith's son Louis Manches is now head of real estate in the London office and their daughter Jane Simpson was chair of the firm until 2011. Although still predominantly known for family law work, the firm "*really is full-service,*" trainees said. Training principal Matthew Martin said: "*We continue to develop our strengths across the board, with a particular focus on the retail and life sciences sectors and growing both our domestic and international private client practice. The London offices will also now be offering a seat for trainees in its private client department from September 2012.*"

A difficult couple of years have seen revenues fall and a CEO brought in to shake things up. She has since departed, having "*refocus[ed] Manches on its core client sectors and revamp[ed] the operational side of the business into a modern corporate structure.*"

Only the London and Oxford offices take trainees: seven to eight are hired into the capital and two to three in Oxford per year. From trainees' perspective, "*the two offices are very separate. If expertise is needed, there is always an exchange of skill, but otherwise they run as separate entities.*" However, the firm says: "*From a commercial and business perspective the offices are very closely associated.*"

Trainees in London have the option of completing their four seats in litigation/TMIP (technology, media and IP),

family, real estate, employment and corporate/commercial. It is "*extremely unusual not to do a family seat – but then, it's also what most people come to Manches for.*" Trainees said: "*The family experience tends to come in the first year,*" and added: "*The litigation department is growing and very busy, so you'll probably do a seat there as well.*" In the first year, "*you don't have much choice in terms of allocation. The HR team are very aware of people coming up to qualification and want to give them priority.*"

Secondments occur on an ad hoc basis: a trainee went to retailer AllSaints for one day a week in 2012. "*This is part of a strategy to grow our expertise in the retail sector,*" Matthew Martin said. Oxford trainees have a choice of family, real estate, litigation, IP/IT, private client, corporate/commercial. "*There aren't any mandatory seats in Oxford,*" trainees said, "*but it's more likely than not you'll do a corporate seat. Family is definitely a much bigger deal in London.*" Family, IP and employment are heavily contentious practices at this firm, so all fulfil the SRA requirement.

The rich and the (not so?) beautiful

The family department is still the firm's most famous. The retirement of Jane Simpson, followed by the shock departure of superstar partner Lady Helen Ward (of Charman v Charman fame) are without question major blows to the team, but it has an established reputation in the marketplace and clients include high-profile names like Paloma Picasso, Lord Lloyd-Webber, Priscilla Waters (in her divorce against Pink Floyd's Roger Waters) and David Seaman.

Chambers UK rankings

Corporate/M&A	Intellectual Property
Dispute Resolution	Private Client
Education	Product Liability
Employment	Real Estate
Environment	Real Estate Litigation
Family/Matrimonial	Retail
Information Technology	Social Housing

"The department is separated into three teams," trainees said. "Each is headed by its own partner and trainees work for a specific team rather than the department as a whole. Two of the teams are more international and ancillary-based, whilst the third focuses more on children." The teams all deal with cases of "über-high net worth – I think the lowest value of case is about £4m and we go all the way up into the billions." Trainees also commented on Manches' "growing international capacity. An element of that has always been there, but now about 80% of the cases are international on some level." The department "brings consistently interesting work, but we do tend to work longer hours. Because of the number and profile of clients, there is a lot to do." On the other hand: "The work is so great you never really notice that you're working that much later." With some of the very high-profile cases, "there's less scope for trainees to get involved, but whenever the opportunity arises, the department will give you really good work." Trainees reported research tasks, attending client meetings, going to court, appearing before masters, and document management.

After family, the litigation/TMIP group is one of the largest in the firm and is always popular with trainees. "Mostly it's commercial litigation, and property litigation also comes under this umbrella." Manches has recently worked on a sex discrimination case against the Department of Health, and for Eurotunnel in a dispute with the union UNITE. Trainees explained: "Week to week you're doing totally different work. The scope is so broad and therefore so interesting. As a trainee you're never stuck at the back – the team wants you involved. There's a fair bit of research and drafting."

The corporate department "handles a wide variety of work, from M&A to restructuring. This is definitely a department the firm is focusing on." Many current clients are "AIM-listed, so perhaps not the biggest companies, but well-known and respected names." In the Oxford office, trainees said: "Clients are a mix of equity funds and fund managers, and public sector clients. The banking practice here is also really developing." The firm advised HSBC on a £15.5m refinancing for a hotel in the Thames Valley and, from the Oxford office, acted for Williams F1 on its €250m listing on the Frankfurt Stock Exchange. A trainee in Oxford said: "Although the work

was interesting, the pace is rather fast and furious and there wasn't much opportunity to get a full overview. I did, however, do some drafting, such as share purchase agreements, stock transfer forms and clauses to amend." By contrast, a London trainee said: "I was given so much more responsibility than I expected. I did a lot of research and then the partners would ask my advice on matters. It was daunting at first, but what you do is respected. You also often attend board and client meetings."

In Oxford the IP/IT department "has a great reputation in the Thames Valley area. We're particularly strong in life sciences, so a lot of our clients are technology and pharmaceutical companies. One partner also does IP work for fashion houses and retailers." The office advised the University of Oxford on the IP aspects of the acquisition of the Institute of Rheumatology from Imperial College, and acted for Fujifilm on the software licensing and development agreement with Boots for digital online photo services.

Let it snow

"Obviously Manches has a history and a heritage that it's proud of, but it's also a young and exciting place to be," trainees said. "The family department is more formal and hierarchical. You're dealing with high-octane lawyers who are public personalities in their own right, so it's almost to be expected. This can translate into a more traditional atmosphere, but still a very friendly one." Departments such as litigation and property "are extremely lively and relaxed. There are no dress-down Fridays or anything like that, but several younger associates and partners continue to shake things up and keep the firm modern." Louis Manches "is great! He speaks to everyone." The same "approachable" atmosphere was stressed in the Oxford office, although "it can be slightly quieter in the day."

"I have said numerous times about how lucky I am with the other trainees," one source said, and this is a close group. Manches sends all future trainees to Kaplan for the LPC, "so we all know each really well before we've even started." Another added: "Because of the size of the intake, and the amount of work there is, people are never competitive or clash. Other trainees will even stay later to help you if you're swamped with work."

"In most departments you'll probably be out about 6.30 to 7pm. However, in family and litigation it's more around the 8pm mark." The Oxford bunch said: "Certainly compared to most London firms, the hours in Oxford are pretty cushty! You start about 9am and really by 6.30pm it's pretty quiet."

Manches' location on Aldwych means its lawyers have "a multitude of options" for after-work pubbing. "The Old

Bank of England or Daly's are always popular, but we often head over to Covent Garden." Unfortunately, in Oxford *"the social stuff is more low-key. We're on a business park that you have to drive to, so it's obviously more difficult to get a drink. We do have the occasional departmental social, but we're not really out every Friday."*

The London office has trainees getting involved in football, netball, cricket and, in the summer, softball. *"The softball is an inter-firm thing. It's hilarious and always followed by the pub after. There's also a partners v trainees football match in the summer."* The firm also organises The Manches Cup, which is an annual sailing competition between law firms. *"You can be on the team even if you haven't sailed, and it's a great way to get to know people in the firm."* Beyond the sporting opportunities Manches *"doesn't really organise that many official events."* There is, however, a Christmas party, *"and this year the theme was 'ski lodge'. It was great: they actually had a fake snow cannon and beautiful decor."* The family department holds drinks on the first Friday of every month and the property team has breakfast together on Wednesdays.

And finally...

"Although Manches does want to retain people, it would be nice if the retention process was a lot more transparent. Telling people in mid-June is late." The firm says it will be addressing trainees' concerns, and retained six of its ten qualifiers in 2012.

Mayer Brown International LLP

The facts

Location: London

Number of UK partners/solicitors: 90/130

Total number of trainees: 52

Seats: 4x6 months

Alternative seats: Overseas seats, secondments

Extras: Pro bono – LawWorks, Islington Law Centre, RCJ CAB and more

On chambersstudent.co.uk...
• How to get into Mayer Brown
• Mayer Brown in Asia

With its global outlook and rip-roaring enthusiasm, this international powerhouse "*ticks all the boxes.*"

State of the union

This year marks the tenth anniversary of Chicago hotshot Mayer Brown's merger with old-school Londoner Rowe & Maw. Since the tie-up, the firm's London office has enjoyed a distinctly transatlantic mix of work, with "*American-driven*" corporate and finance teams working alongside "*traditionally English*" practices like pensions, insurance and employment. A heavy injection of international work permeates the majority of the MB business, particularly on the transactional side: international companies like Morgan Stanley, Thomson Reuters and Unilever have all sought the firm's commercial expertise in recent years.

A spate of mergers and international alliances since the '02 union suggests the firm's thirst for expansion is not totally quenched yet. In 2008, it hooked up with Asian firm Johnson Stokes & Masters, and it combined again with a French litigation boutique in 2009. "*There's a conscious effort to internationalise our work streams as much as possible to make the most of our link-ups,*" trainees told us, explaining that the aforementioned endeavours account for MB's rapid increase in international work over the years.

Despite an epic global network – which includes outposts across the USA, Europe and Asia – and a firmwide turnover that places the firm among the top earners of the profession, the recession has not been kind to the London office: revenue stalled in 2008 and 2009, and deferrals were pressed upon a few of the current intake's trainees. While MB's City digs posted a promising increase in turnover in 2010/11, the state of the office remains rather turbulent: late 2011 saw a series of partner defections, and at the time of publication the office was gearing up for a 20-strong redundancy round and asking some future trainees to voluntarily defer their starts by a year. The moves management has made to get things back on track – which include the recent hire of a high-flying real estate finance partner in London and a new Chicago-based firm chairman – mean "*there's a very cautious optimism that things are getting better,*" trainees thought.

The market may remain uneasy, but MB still attracts a high-value slate of work. This year has seen lawyers act for Genel Energy in a reverse takeover of investment vehicle Vallares that resulted in the creation of an Iraqi oil and gas company valued at $4.2bn. The firm has also continued its work advising the Afghan government on how to expedite international investment in the country's mineral reserves, the potential value of which amounts to a rather stupefying $3 trillion.

Trainees have a relatively structured training contract that entails one contentious seat, one non-contentious seat and one overseas or client secondment. Contentious picks include commercial dispute resolution, insurance, employment or construction, while the non-contentious offerings are finance, corporate or real estate. For the last remaining seat, there's the option to do IP, pensions, EU/competition or tax, though these are considered "*more niche compared to the compulsory ones – they don't take many trainees on at a time, so you might want to look elsewhere if you're desperate to do that kind of work.*" Our sources estimated that "*probably 90%*" of people get their first or second choice each rotation. "*A

Chambers UK rankings

Banking & Finance	Outsourcing
Banking Litigation	Pensions
Capital Markets	Pensions Litigation
Competition/European Law	Professional Discipline
Construction	Professional Negligence
Dispute Resolution	Real Estate
Employment	Real Estate Finance
Energy & Natural Resources	Real Estate Litigation
Environment	Restructuring/Insolvency
Information Technology	Tax
Insurance	Telecommunications
Intellectual Property	

few months into each seat they arrange a meeting to discuss how it's going and where you want to go next – they really look after you in that sense," one testified.

Mayer Brown is unusual in that it has recently made taking an overseas seat or client secondment all but compulsory. *"Around ten or 11"* secondments are up for grabs each rotation, including some finance-based stints in banks, a few corporate-focused ones to multinationals like Unilever and even a couple of IP-related spots at music publisher EMI. Current overseas seats include New York, Hong Kong and Paris. *"The majority of those are finance-based, so you have to spend six months in the finance department beforehand,"* an interviewee clarified. *"I definitely recommend making your desire to go on secondment known in the relevant department because the partners have most weight in that respect,"* one trainee advised.

Part and parcel

MB's corporate team handles capital markets and private equity work as well as *"a good mix of public and private M&A."* The firm advised on JJB Sports' £65m AIM placing and open offer, while lawyers on the M&A front worked on the sale of Bernie Ecclestone and Flavio Briatore's majority stake in QPR football club to Tony Fernandes, founder of the world's first no-frills budget airline. Cross-border work is frequent, and clients include global players like Caterpillar and Dow Chemical. According to our sources, *"the work you do depends on your supervisor – if they specialise in a certain area, you often end up doing a lot of that."* Stock trainee tasks like due diligence, proof-reading and drafting board minutes comprise a hefty portion of the seat, but more meaty work is on the menu for those who step up to the plate: *"They don't push much on you since it's such a big department, but you can definitely get good work. I was working with just two partners on a deal, doing associate-level work*

like attending shareholder meetings and drafting sections of some main transaction documents," one trainee informed us. Others reported undertaking research for large-scale M&A deals and drafting agreements for multi-jurisdictional matters.

Like corporate, finance is *"one of the larger departments"* and has a huge international slant: over 90% of deals have a cross-border element. The team – which handles everything from asset finance and derivatives to securitisation, project finance and restructuring work – regularly serves the crème de la crème of the finance industry (think JPMorgan Chase, Morgan Stanley, HSBC, Deutsche and so on) and has landed some pretty major client wins in the last year, including Credit Suisse and UBS. Long-term advisory stints like MB's four-year rolling instruction on Citi's credit events complement the firm's one-off jobs for financial institutions like Wilmington Trust, which lawyers advised on a $1.8bn telecoms acquisition financing deal. *"Some firms have specific subgroups like capital markets, but we're not structured like that: you're exposed to a variety of work and are encouraged to get experience in multiple areas rather than stick to one type of deal,"* sources said. As far as responsibility goes, *"be ready to dive in the deep end,"* trainees warned, contentedly recalling their time spent drafting facility agreements, liaising with local counsel, amending documents and calling clients. *"I was left to run some of the smaller deals myself,"* one told us, while another reported being *"put in charge of the closing list."* There's also some detail-oriented work like *"doing consistency checks for typos"* and *"other such sweeps – it's a good seat for building your attention to detail."*

The corporate and finance departments have *"reputations for keeping you the longest,"* trainees told us. *"Your hours often coincide with US hours, so it's quite demanding,"* one explained, mentioning that *"people leave between 9 and 10pm quite regularly."* While *"getting used to having dinner at work is part and parcel of a corporate or finance seat,"* trainees assured us their efforts during *"labour-intensive, manic times"* don't go unnoticed. *"I had a few all-nighters coming up to a deal, but once it closed, they made sure everyone working on it got a day off to recover and ordered us to turn off our BlackBerrys. It was arduous, but they recognised that."*

Specialist seats like insurance, IP, and construction are *"pretty oversubscribed,"* seeing as they only take a few trainees at a time. Insurance, a highly ranked practice in *Chambers UK*, is *"pretty fast-paced"* and offers the chance to get involved with disputes *"all over the world since policy holders often reside abroad."* Meanwhile, those in IP are in charge of *"investigating new developments in the law"* and regularly contend with a raft of drafting tasks on documents like contract summaries and trade mark licences. MB's construction team is among the best in the nation, regularly taking instructions from top multinationals, including Alstom, Wates Group and insurance juggernauts QBE and Swiss Re. This focus on international work lends itself to "*a lot of tasks related to arbitration, like mediation and pre and post-hearing duties.*"

Real estate work is "*wide-ranging*" and includes property finance, licensing, commercial property acquisition and leasing work for companies as varied as Selfridges, Wells Fargo and British Land. "*It's quite exciting to manage your own files alongside work on the larger portfolios,*" said trainees, calling the seat "*a nice change from large departments like corporate where all the work is handled in teams.*" Steady client contact is another plus. "*You're dealing with them on a daily basis, and often you're the one they call directly.*"

Like a box of chocolates

"*People often assume we've got a very American culture, but MB seems to have retained its London feel,*" sources said. "*There's still a UK-based working style that feels nurturing as opposed to the cut-throat one people expect from US firms.*" That said, most agreed that "*the Stateside influence is definitely there in corporate and finance,*" where "*the workload can be rough*" and "*profitability is a concept that's constantly pushed.*" Trainees told us that, for the most part, "*the hours are quite humane*" and "*there's no credit for hanging around late just to show your face,*" though a few admitted that "*things might be different if we had more work.*"

While "*the past few years have seen a push towards the Oxbridge end of things,*" sources reported "*a broad spectrum of universities and degrees*" represented throughout the current intake. "*I once heard an associate joke we were like a box of chocolates,*" laughed one. "*People really vary in their backgrounds and paths to the firm – it seems to be something the firm is keen on maintaining.*" Among the trends they could pin down are "*quite a few academically minded people with a Master's or PhD,*" and those with international ties – "*a lot of people have lived abroad or know a foreign language.*" While "*some practices like employment and pensions remain quite national-based,*" there's no denying that international work is manifest across the majority of the firm, particularly in corporate and finance, "*where we mainly do deals with US banks.*" As such, a casual reference to your gap year or foreign language capabilities during interviews would not go amiss, trainees thought. "*Highlight your international interests and experiences because it's something they view very highly.*"

In addition to recently instigated intergroup lunches, each team has a Friday drinks trolley "*now and again,*" and after-work drinks at the White Horse, located ever so conveniently across the road from the office, are "*pretty standard.*" The annual summer party is always a highlight, and we heard things get "*pretty crazy*" around Christmas: "*You do your own thing with your department plus there's a firmwide do... the party ran pretty late into the night last year,*" one source recalled hazily. Other opportunities for mixing and mingling include charity events, sports teams and vac scheme periods. "*That's when there's the most going on. We're invited to the welcome and goodbye drinks, and you can sign up to help look after them, which means you're taken along for the drinks, dinners and bowling stuff.*"

They've still got it...

"*I definitely think communication is something that's improved since I applied a few years ago,*" declared one trainee, echoing a sentiment we heard from many. Indeed, past interviewees have grumbled about "*opaque*" procedures and an unresponsive graduate recruitment team, but things seem to have been set right on that front following a firm-wide survey a while back. "*Now there's a bimonthly newsletter sent around that gives the lowdown on things like who management is looking to hire and where they'd like to improve.*" Moreover, there are regular departmental meetings, which "*make you feel well supported. I've never felt like there wasn't somebody I could turn to if I had a problem.*"

Despite a lagging workflow and the series of redundancies looming at the time of publication, our sources were optimistic when it came to discussing the firm's future. "*The general perception is that we could be busier, but there's hope on the horizon that the market will pick up. Obviously the restructuring affects morale, but it seems if we can keep riding out the recession and making small profits, we'll be okay.*" Indeed, sources reported "*a lot of good applications coming through the door these days,*" so we reckon there's still some decent firepower left in Mayer Brown. "*We've still got the ambition and enthusiasm that drove me to apply years ago – that energy hasn't gone anywhere.*"

And finally...
Retention rates in 2010 and 2011 *"weren't brilliant,"* trainees admitted. In 2012 the firm kept on 16 of its 25 qualifiers.

McDermott Will & Emery LLP

The facts

Location: London

Number of UK partners/solicitors: 20/20 (+8 US-qualified)

UK partners who trained at firm: 5%

Total number of trainees: 10

Seats: 4x6 months

Alternative seats: Overseas seats, secondments

Extras: Pro bono – LawWorks, Own-it, Lawyers Without Borders; language classes

On chambersstudent.co.uk...

- How to get into McDermott
- About the London office's home, Heron Tower

Chicago-born McDermott opened its doors in London in 1998. During the credit crunch, a strategy rethink resulted in a fresh plan for the office in the City.

All change

Partners in structured finance, arbitration and competition have departed, and in came a focus on core practice areas: controversies; transactions; regulatory and government; and tax. The start of 2012 saw the addition of a private equity team from Dewey & LeBoeuf and optimism all round. Said training partner Rashpaul Bahia: "*The private equity addition significantly expanded our corporate capabilities. We will continue to develop the core practice areas that are central to McDermott's strategic growth plans.*"

In 2011, the office relocated to two floors of Heron Tower on Bishopsgate, and recently took out an option on a third. "*It's difficult to predict anything in this market,*" Bahia told us, "*but the firm, and London, is in growth mode: taking on additional space indicates our ambition and plans.*"

"*We have a lot of say in seat allocation, but with so few departments, we were always going to.*" Trainees complete seats from a choice of corporate, employment, IP, energy and tax. Private client is also an option, though we haven't come across anyone who's done it for a couple of years. The private equity group, officially part of corporate, will offer a seat from September 2012.

Now we have Paris

The fast-paced corporate seat deals predominantly in mid-market M&A. Clients are mostly the UK arms of international companies. There's also a focus on energy, healthcare, sports and technology clients. The department is relatively small, and a high proportion of partners have international backgrounds – and indeed, many of the takeovers are multi-jurisdictional. Some examples: MWE advised on the $1.22bn takeover of golf equipment makers Titleist and Footjoy by sports brand Fila. Both Fila and its private equity backer Mirae are Korea-based, while Titleist is a UK company and Footjoy US-run. The firm also advised commodity trader Gunvor Group on its purchase of a share in Signal Peak coal mine for $400m. Gunvor is run from Singapore and Geneva; Signal Peak is a mine in Montana.

For trainees, it's fun "*to not really know what jurisdiction you'll be dealing with,*" while the mid-market size of takeovers means "*there's a broad range of tasks: from average trainee work to some really interesting stuff.*" Trainees get direct contact with the "*fantastic*" partners. "*It's easy to learn through osmosis when you see them work – you see first-hand how much work is coming in and how deep their background understanding is, but equally what a commercially savvy level they're operating on.*"

The wealth of energy clients in the corporate seat is evidence of the project finance group's integration with corporate, finance and regulatory on a global scale. The firm works with Goldman Sachs, JPMorgan and Merrill Lynch as investors into mining, oil and gas and alternative energy projects. The team acted for JPMorgan in its bid to become the biggest player in commodities globally, in its takeover of assets from RBS Sempra in coal, oil, gas and emissions. Trainees find the energy practice "*incredibly broad,*" as they could be working on huge cross-border

Chambers UK rankings

Commodities	Employment
Data Protection	Intellectual Property

transactions, smaller UK-projects or spending time researching and writing contributions to energy journals and the firm's energy blog.

The employment group has a reputation for "*making the trainee feel very at home but also expecting a lot from you.*" The team acts exclusively for employers in disputes involving "*discrimination, unfair dismissal or breach of contract,*" and is lauded by *Chambers UK*, picking up UK-wide rankings alongside the likes of Freshfields, Hogan Lovells and DLA Piper. Trainees see "*predominantly contentious*" work. The team defended brokers BGC in a dispute brought by Tullett Prebon, which claimed the client had unlawfully poached employees. The trial reached the High Court, which ruled in Tullett Prebon's favour: BGC then took it to the Court of Appeal and were rejected. The ruling cast light on issues of forward start contracts and the stress they often put onto relations with an existing employer.

The IP group is also highly ranked, alongside RPC, Linklaters and Mayer Brown in London. There's a focus on disputes in the IT, food, healthcare, media and life sciences sectors and also a growing data protection and privacy practice. Trainees are handed a "*varied*" workload – "*trade mark and copyright, patent and some commercial work*" – and responsibility can be high, sources reporting plenty of drafting. The firm represented online gaming company 32Red in a brand dispute brought against William Hill, whose casino business 32Vegas was said to infringe trade mark. Pharmaceutical conglomerate Novartis is also a client: the team has acted in patent litigations involving vaccines and extended wear contact lenses.

The Paris office, opened last year, now takes London trainees for a full seat. "*We've found that seconding trainees has been an effective way of developing our internal network between Paris and London,*" says Rashpaul Bahia. Our sources were keen to emphasise that although "*work may be in English, you definitely have to speak the language – it's not a holiday.*" A stint in Brussels is also an option.

West Coast and East End

"*Because a lot of clients are West Coast, you might wake up to an e-mail on Saturday morning, which can be nerve-racking.*" This shouldn't, however, be taken as indicative of a heavy hours culture. Trainees are given BlackBerrys, but "*no one's going to chew your head off if you don't get back to someone at the weekend – it's your judgement.*" Early-morning stints in corporate aside, all our interviewees confirmed that "*hours are pretty civilised.*" One added: "*Any time there's been a late night, it's been because of an American client.*"

"*There are so few of us trainees so we're seen as a valuable commodity and are used well,*" thought one. "*We don't just paginate or check documents: we draft, and e-mail clients directly. But by the same token, we're always expected to produce quality work.*" Following mixed feedback on supervision over the last couple of years, a lot of focus has been given to the support trainees receive. There are now "*quarterly meetings with the training partner, and monthly lunches for trainees and associates to give feedback. There's also the option of choosing an associate 'buddy' who you can go to with general queries.*"

Things are pretty British in the office, "*as most partners have come from established London firms. It can be quite formal with partners, and you always know your place – although that's not necessarily a negative thing.*" A US influence comes from the proliferation of committees ("*Americans love having lots of avenues to talk*") and a heavy emphasis on pro bono, with partnerships with LawWorks among other initiatives. When it comes to socialising, there's no set local – instead, employees take advantage of the firm's plum location on the cusp of the old City and trendy Shoreditch and Brick Lane. The firm also puts on "*wind-down drinks*" every other Friday.

The recent move to Heron Tower was extolled by all – and not just because of the 70,000 litre aquarium replete with fish attendants and divers to keep it running. Trainees share an office with "*floor-to-ceiling windows*" with their supervisor.

We couldn't help noticing all MWE's trainees are sometimes a little bit older than the norm. Said one: "*People have worked or done Master's degrees. It could be deliberate on the firm's part, as we are given a decent amount of responsibility and only a certain mindset can cope with that.*"

And finally...
After a lot of changes at MWE London, things are looking rosy: come here for good experience in IP and employment or the growing corporate team. The firm retained four of its five qualifiers in 2012.

Memery Crystal LLP

The facts

Location: London
Number of UK partners/solicitors: 22/36
Partners who trained at firm: 4.5%
Total number of trainees: 8
Seats: 4x6 months
Alternative seats: None

On chambersstudent.co.uk...
- How to get into Memery Crystal
- AIM explained

This pint-sized Chancery Lane firm is best known for top-notch mid-market corporate work.

Memeries are made of this...

Memery Crystal was created 30-odd years ago by the late John Memery and Peter Crystal (who still pops in as a consultant). Alongside a very strong AIM-focused corporate department, it has decent-sized disputes and property teams too. "*You come to Memery Crystal to do corporate law or dispute resolution,*" one trainee declared. "*You don't come here to do family.*"

Well, that's only true up to a point – because in spring 2011, MC hired a crack family team from Howard Kennedy, the first stage of its plan to build a private client practice. Family's now one of the seat options along with corporate, real estate, dispute resolution, tax and employment/IP/commercial contracts. The corporate department took a bit of a beating early in the recession when work dried up, and the firm now has a desire to diversify a little and not rely too much on one area. Everyone does at least one seat in corporate and one in disputes. Trainees may return to a department in their second year if they want to, when their seat preferences get priority. If two trainees want to visit the same department at the same time, they may split the seat with something else.

Going for gold

So, that corporate department first. *Chambers UK* ranks Memery Crystal among the country's very best for capital markets/AIM work. The Alternative Investment Market (AIM) is the one below the main market of the London Stock Exchange and was launched in 1995 to enable smaller companies to raise cash by going public. The team advises a mix of actual companies as well as their brokers and nominated advisers (called Nomads). For example, it recently helped long-standing client Gulf Keystone Petroleum place new shares on AIM, raising $200m to help fund drilling activities in Iraqi Kurdistan. In fact, the natural resources sector (oil and gas, mining) is big business for this team. There's often an international element – the client may be British but "*its activities may be in deepest, darkest Kazakhstan.*" In July, MC launched an 'Africa Desk', and already has lots of clients with interests here, such as jewel miner Petra Diamonds, Chariot Oil & Gas, and New Dawn Mining, a Zimbabwe-focused gold producer. International work is less likely outside the corporate practice.

Corporate as a first seat is "*quite admin-heavy – photocopying, bundling, proofing, quite a lot of company searches, verification.*" Verification is essentially fact-checking a company's prospectus before it lists on the London AIM market. It can involve a trip or two to Companies House but also some old-fashioned Googling. Another source emphasised: "*In your first seat you have to build up trust, get the basics right.*" Trainees sit with a partner or associate, but can also get work from other partners if you express an interest in doing their type of work. "*The supervisor will talk you through what needs to be checked, and how much detail to go into.*" Other tasks include drafting ancillary documents, legal research and "*generally supporting the other solicitors.*"

As a third or fourth-seat trainee, "*there's a lot less admin. You know the systems, the IT, et cetera. You know a lot more, you're almost qualified, and the work they give you reflects this.*" More responsibility includes "*more sophis-*

Chambers UK rankings

Capital Markets	Energy & Natural Resources
Corporate/M&A	Real Estate
Dispute Resolution	Real Estate Litigation
Employment	

ticated drafting, and you're trusted to liaise with clients by yourself." Research tasks might include a visit to the Law Society library, searching Lexis Nexis, Westlaw and other databases, and nipping over to the dispute resolution team to see if anyone there can help answer baffling questions. Memery Crystal also does a fair bit of M&A work, and was actually named 'law firm of the year' at the M&A Awards 2012. One recent highlight was acting for The Garden Centre Group in its £276m acquisition by private equity firm Terra Firma. There were no NQ vacancies in corporate in 2012, although the group did hire a more senior solicitor as a lateral during the course of the year.

On larger cases in dispute resolution, trainees can expect to work in a small team. One mega-case has dominated life here for many months: the *"all-engulfing, huge"* £1bn Gulf Keystone litigation, included in *The Lawyer*'s 'top 20 cases in 2012'. At issue are exploration rights to oilfields in Kurdistan. In another assignment for this key client, MC won a case against a Twitter user who posted 'fantasy' info about the company, causing its share price to tank.

When a new case comes in, the trainee might have the *"lovely task"* of sifting through hundreds – or thousands – of documents. Later, they might draft witness statements and letters of instruction to experts, and build a chronology of events for counsel. *"I worked on a cost schedule, and got to do some disclosure, as part of a team,"* said one. You might also go to court, perhaps for interim hearings. The hours can be *"very long, but they look after you"* – dinner and a cab home are provided – and *"your hard work doesn't go unnoticed."* Smaller cases have included shareholder disputes, when trainees have attended mediations.

Departmental crossover

Real estate clients are mostly commercial. Some are big – like ASDA and Debenhams – and the team's made good inroads into the education sector, advising schools and academies. Small to medium-sized enterprises (SMEs) are more typical clients. *"Right now there's a lot of work on leaseholds rather than outright sales, probably because of the market,"* a trainee reflected. *"If you can run with it there's scope for you to do more. I dealt with clients on a day-to-day basis."* There's some work for

high net worth individuals too, often advising on the personal property of commercial clients.

Sources reported having a fairly *"quiet time"* in the family department so far, probably because the practice is so new. *"I guess it takes time to get established,"* one reflected, though another revealed: *"I got to go to court to observe hearings."* The team does *"a variety of work for high net worth individuals."* The employment/IP/commercial contracts trainee is supervised by head of department and training partner Merrill April: *"She gives lots of responsibility."* Employment is *"a small department but a really good seat."* The team represents *"predominantly employers, but sometimes employees."* AIM-listed clients include Falkland Oil & Gas and wealth management company Ashcourt Rowan, while the group's also advised senior employees leaving such establishments as the BBC, Diageo, Virgin Trains and New Look.

The commercial contracts team is on the same floor as employment as they have a fair bit in common. A trainee would typically spend three months with employment, then toddle down the corridor to sit with commercial contracts for the remaining three months of this seat, or vice versa, thus gaining experience with both sets of partners. Commercial contracts work also often overlaps with corporate. *"If they're working on an acquisition, they may involve you in due diligence. In the commercial contracts team you handle the peripheral documents."* Memery Crystal's IP work is led by a corporate and a commercial contracts partner, so from a trainee's perspective there is still the possibility to do IP-related work during the commercial contacts/employment seat. Finally, tax has been a split seat in the past, but as a rule going forwards there will be no split seats unless circumstances dictate otherwise.

Anchormen

Trainees adopt *"a common-sense approach to hours. If you're busy, you come in earlier. If you're not, you come in at 9.30am and leave at 5pm."* Supervisors won't hold back asking you to put in extra hours when necessary: *"The earliest I've been in is 7am, and the latest I've ever left is 1.30am – though I've been lucky!"*

"All the departments have very nice people. But it feels a bit fragmented, almost as if there are mini-firms within a firm." One source also added: *"Trainees need to go out more!"* MC is making *"a conscious effort"* to remedy this, paying for monthly drinks at local boozers like the Blue Anchor off Chancery Lane, the Old Bank of England on Fleet Street or the Melton Mowbray on High Holborn. There was a nice Christmas bash at the *"swanky"* Mayfair Hotel, and a decent summer party at the Northbank restaurant on the riverbank opposite Tate Modern. The only dampener was the weather...

The qualification process "*is transparent. They say, 'Here are the jobs, go away and think about what you want, then come back.'*" One potential risk at all small firms is that though people may think there will be jobs in your favourite department when you're there, the situation may have changed when qualification comes round. As we've mentioned, there was no vacancy in corporate – the work MC is best known for – in 2012. In the end, three out of five qualifiers stayed on, in the real estate, commercial contracts and dispute resolution departments.

And finally...
This is a pleasant, under-known firm that is worth special consideration if you're looking for a smaller-scale corporate experience.

Michelmores LLP

The facts

Location: Exeter, London, Sidmouth
Number of UK partners/solicitors: 47/71
Total number of trainees: 9
Seats: 4x6 months
Alternative seats: Occasional secondments
Extras: Pro bono – various legal surgeries

On chambersstudent.co.uk...
- How to get into Michelmores
- Interview with HR manager Kim Tomlinson

Michelmores is one of Devon's top firms and offers a three-way mix of business, property and private client work.

Mich-el mucho

When we poor London-bound *Student Guide* researchers think of working in the regions, we imagine the ability to frequent the office local for an after-work pint and still be home in time for *Corrie*. And with fresh air, cheap rents and surfing facilities on the doorstep, there are numerous reasons for City lawyers to relocate to the South West. Michelmores trainees, however, give quite a different answer: "*We come here for the firm's ambition and growth.*" Trainees are "*expected to be driven individuals*" and our sources felt that the rising profile of the firm means "*a wider variety of people*" are applying. "*It used to be all local Devoners*" and though Michelmores still "*likes people who have links to the South West,*" there are one or two from the current intake who don't hail from the region. "*I hope that the firm pushes that more,*" mused one interviewee. "*It's important to express we are not just a Devon firm, we're a national firm, and that we are growing and want to attract the best talent.*"

Is it true to describe Michelmores as a national firm? Headquartered in Exeter, if you look at its Chambers rankings you'll see this full-service firm is an undeniable force in the South West, but outside that region its recognition is limited. A sole UK-wide ranking comes in projects work, thanks in large part to the presence of top partner Carol McCormack OBE. However, it sports an office in London, which moved into new Chancery Lane digs in May 2012, and represents several national and internationally known organisations – like HM Treasury, the Met Office and Power Plate, the company that makes currently fashionable vibrating exercise machines. It also has other big-name clients with links to the South West, such as the airline Flybe and Exeter University. A number of partners here have come from top City firms like Herbert Smith, Freshfields and Clifford Chance. Carol McCormack herself came from Berwin Leighton Paisner back in 2004. So, while Michelmores isn't a national firm in the mould of DLA Piper or Eversheds, it certainly isn't a small-town operation.

"*We want to grow, and grow quickly,*" an interviewee told us. There was a blip during the recession but the firm is "*back on the right path.*" The firm's turnover rose 5% in 2011/12, and to reward all their hard work Michelmores paid all its lawyers and staff a bonus equivalent to 3% of their salary. So it seems this lot aren't running home to catch up on the latest Weatherfield gossip.

A proper chopper deal

Michelmores' practice is split three ways – into business, property and private client – and there are seats available in all those areas. Commercial property and commercial litigation are commonly dished out to the first-years. Other options include clinical negligence, dispute resolution/contentious probate, employment, corporate, government property, insolvency, IP/IT, planning and private client. There's also a popular seat in the London office which is offered to second-years.

Commercial property has been expanding over the past year with hires from Wragge & Co and Nabarro. It's all about "*big commercial property developers,*" and the team's recently been advising Exeter Airport on a £2m helicopter facility for the emergency services. One of our

Chambers UK rankings

Agriculture & Rural Affairs	Information Technology
Banking & Finance	Intellectual Property
Clinical Negligence	Planning
Construction	Private Client
Corporate/M&A	Projects
Dispute Resolution	Real Estate
Employment	Real Estate Litigation
Family/Matrimonial	Restructuring/Insolvency

sources said they'd seen "*five deals of around £2.5m.*" Trainees receive plenty of drafting ("*more than the business seats,*" one compared), conduct client meetings and run smaller files on their own. As a first-year trainee, it can be a little daunting and one commented: "*Sometimes the supervision was lacking.*" There's a related seat in government property which acts for various government departments, NHS trusts, education institutions and police authorities.

Taking silk

In 2012, Andrew Oldland QC joined the firm to head the regulatory team in the elite commercial dispute resolution department (ranked by *Chambers UK* as one of the top two in the region). The department has an impressive client roster including the Met Office, the National Portrait Gallery, Arts Council England and the UK's largest mushroom producer, Monaghan Mushrooms. There's no separate regulatory seat, but in commercial litigation you'll see "*everything from IP disputes to professional negligence.*" Our sources praised the department's excellent fee earners, "*who teach juniors a lot.*" Trainees find themselves running around the country to meet counsel in court and one even had to conduct a mini-hearing with a judge. A bit of administrative work inevitably awaits them back at their desks.

An alternative to commercial litigation is insolvency. "*It's a busy team that deals with international clients,*" including professional services firms like Deloitte. Michelmores acted for Ticketus, advising in relation to the administration of Rangers FC, and also deals with the assets of people who have gone insolvent, "*which sometimes means chucking people out of their homes.*" Our sources advised: "*Take sob stories with a pinch of salt.*" Generally, the tasks are similar to commercial litigation:

"*Claim forms, writing to counsel*" and "*meeting counsel at the Royal Courts of Justice.*" However, "*insolvency law has its own rules which are difficult to get your head around.*" So, if you're a quick-thinking tough cookie, this may be the department for you.

Trainees were quick to tell us that the corporate team's been working on a £610m hotel deal. The client, a founding shareholder of Mint Hotels, is selling to US private equity firm Blackstone. It's been in the press as one of the largest hotel deals in Europe. The other firms involved include Clifford Chance, Freshfields, Allen & Overy, Hogan Lovells and Simpson Thacher & Bartlett. Big deals such as this "*come round every couple of years,*" one source revealed. "*The £20 to £25m range is standard.*" With a team only six partners and six associates big, "*trainees get a lot of hands-on experience. It can be quite full-on. I was trusted to take my own client meetings. There are standard trainee tasks too – due diligence and data room-type stuff,*" said one source. Another had recently drafted a 15-page memo on the Takeover Code. The corporate seat is sometimes offered in the London office, where partner Joe Whitfield specialises in private equity work in Africa.

Office yoga

The firm encourages its trainees to "*pursue interests outside work*" and there's no excuse not to when they can generally leave the office by 6.30pm. In compensation for working the occasional late night, some trainees have been offered a morning off in lieu. There's no official bonus scheme, but "*there is a gesture to trainees and secretaries at Christmas time.*" In 2012, Michelmores announced that if the firm met its April target they'd all get a bonus – and duly kept its promise. "*It was a hard slog to get there,*" one source told us.

The office itself is based on a business park closer to the M5 than to the city centre. Fortunately there is a Michelmores bus link, and the building itself has "*a great café and a gym in the basement.*" A lot of the firm's staff is "*really sporty. A lot of people cycle,*" and the news feed on Michelmores' website is peppered with stories of 5 km runs, swimming to work, bike rides to Nice, office yoga, camping trips and, to top it all off, an Olympic-themed office party. For the less sporty, there are plenty of booze-ups. Michelmores hosts an annual beer festival and a summer party where "*the partners serve champagne as a thank-you.*"

And finally...

Our second-year sources admitted to being "*quite business-oriented*" and were hoping for jobs in those areas. In the end, all seven stayed on after qualification in 2012.

Mills & Reeve LLP

The facts

Location: Cambridge, Norwich, Birmingham, London, Manchester, Leeds

Number of UK partners/solicitors: 98/350

Total number of trainees: 34

Seats: 6x4 months

Alternative seats: Occasional secondments

Extras: Pro bono – LawWorks, Cambridge Citizens Advice Bureau

On chambersstudent.co.uk...

- How to get into Mills & Reeve
- Interview with training partner Brian Marshall

An "*obvious choice*" in East Anglia, and growing across the rest of the UK, this jolly nice firm continues to establish itself as a serious national presence.

A-ha!

The tale of Mills & Reeve is one of local boy done good. For over 100 years, it stayed true to its Norwich roots – refusing to budge from its cosy geographic corner. In 1987, however, it took the tentative step of setting up shop in Cambridge, cementing its reputation as "*the biggest player in East Anglia.*" Since then, it has embarked on a process of expansion that has propelled it into the Birmingham, London, Manchester and Leeds markets. "*I think it really wants to set itself up as a national firm,*" explained one source. "*It's a very realistic aspiration.*"

The firm managed to keep its head above water through the recession and, according to training principal Brian Marshall, "*there's evidence of green shoots*" in the fact that profits rose 3.3% in 2012, to £69.4m. Further expansion seems likely. Marshall says: "*We're always being approached, and you could say there are always discussions going on about possible collaborations or mergers.*" While there's "*nothing concrete at the moment*" to report, our money's on at least one new M&R office popping up in the near future.

M&R works across a wide range of practice areas and sectors, winning top rankings from *Chambers UK* across the board in each of its offices. It is perhaps best known for its private client, corporate and insurance work – the latter of which is "*doing tremendously well*" at the moment and forms the bulk of work in the London office. The firm is also one to watch if you're interested in education or healthcare law – it currently advises more than 70 universities and colleges, and over 100 healthcare trusts and NHS bodies.

Farming talent

The structure of the training contract reflects the firm's national ambitions. Although trainees are only permanently stationed in Norwich, Cambridge and Birmingham – M&R's three full-service offices – they're able to pick and choose seats from any of its six outposts. If they're so inclined, there are plenty of opportunities. Trainees visit six, rather than the traditional four, seats during the two years of their training contract – "*it means you can do seats you don't know anything about but fancy giving a try.*" They're assigned the first of these at random, and second-years get preference over the next two. After this, however, "*HR will do everything they can to accommodate your preferences.*"

Mills & Reeve's family department is one of the finest in the UK and "*one of the biggest family teams in Europe.*" In fact, as proud owner of www.divorce.co.uk, the Divorce UK YouTube channel, and the Divorce UK iPhone app, it almost feels as if the firm has a monopoly on the whole grisly institution. The seat is a favourite among trainees, who are able to get stuck into work for "*high net worth clients, dealing with quite large financial settlements,*" very occasionally seeing their work for celebrities hit the headlines. There's heaps of client contact – "*on average, I had three client meetings a week*" – they're able to run their own small cases, and spend loads of time in court. In recent years, there's even been an increasing international element, acting for cohabitees living abroad – "*it's added a new dimension,*" noted trainees. Also on the private client side lies private tax and estate planning. Involving "*wills and trusts and things,*" the seat deals with a few clients who are "*reasonably well*

Chambers UK rankings

Administrative & Public Law	Information Technology
Agriculture & Rural Affairs	Insurance
Banking & Finance	Intellectual Property
Charities	Licensing
Clinical Negligence	Pensions
Construction	Planning
Corporate/M&A	Private Client
Court of Protection	Private Equity
Data Protection	Professional Discipline
Dispute Resolution	Professional Negligence
Education	Projects
Employment	Public Procurement
Energy & Natural Resources	Real Estate
Environment	Real Estate Litigation
Family/Matrimonial	Restructuring/Insolvency
Healthcare	Tax

off but not super-wealthy, coming back for a new will." On these cases, trainees report *"pretty much taking responsibility for the whole thing, under supervision."*

The agriculture seat may conjure images of a solitary tumbleweed rolling across the Fens, but a bit of due diligence reveals it's *"looking after lots of rich farmers"* in what's basically *"a niche area of real estate."* M&R is well respected for its work in the area, representing clients both in East Anglia and further afield, including the University of Oxford and the Countryside Restoration Trust. *"I learned so much in a couple of weeks,"* claimed one trainee, *"things like EU regulations on farm payments, and tenancies between land owners and tenant farmers."*

Ka-Shing!

Most of M&R's corporate work takes place in the Norwich and Cambridge offices, both of which are ranked among the finest in their cities for this work by *Chambers UK.* The firm has also established an official referral relationship with Freshfields, taking on overflow work from the magic circle firm. One such case is the recent £2.4bn cash sale of Northumbrian Water to the aptly-named Hong Kong billionaire Li Ka-Shing. The firm's own clients range from *"regional stuff"* like Aviva (formerly Norwich Union) and Cambridge Water to *"household names"* such as Ann Summers, Weetabix, the FSA and Macmillan Cancer Support. It's particularly hot in the technology, food, finance and healthcare sectors. Trainees get involved in the lot: *"I saw three significantly sized transactions,"* said one. Responsibility tends to *"start light and increase after that,"* so expect document printing to blossom into running your own matters.

A seat in commercial property is by no means mandatory but trainees say that *"real estate is such a staple part of the firm's work, they'd probably advise you to do it for a rounded training contract."* In East Anglia the group's clients come in all shapes and sizes – investment funds performed particularly well in 2011 – while Birmingham has a high proportion from the healthcare and education sectors. *"I worked on a very high-pressure deal,"* said one source. *"It was largely just me and my supervisor working on it. I had daily client contact, and was more or less told to push forward with things as much as I could."* The real estate disputes seat also offers loads of responsibility. Trainees may not get to run their own files but spend *"on average two or three hours a day talking through problems with partners in a team. I really felt my contribution was useful to them."*

Representing the likes of the Department of Health, a host of brand new clinical commissioning groups and independent clients such as Allied Healthcare, the healthcare department is recognised as being among the strongest in the UK. It recently won in a big judicial review case for North Staffordshire Primary Care Trust, ruling that non-clinical social factors can't be taken into account when deciding which cases qualify for exceptional treatment. A trainee found that *"partners would lead, and I'd support,"* helping out with *"preparing bundles and drafting witness statements and letters of advice."* There are also opportunities to get out and about, visiting clients and going to court.

Insurance is *"one of the firm's busiest and most profitable departments."* The London office is dedicated, almost entirely, to this practice. Very much a love/hate area, those trainees who enjoy insurance and contentious work describe it as *"a great department to sit in."* Responsibility is pitched slightly lower than some other seats. One trainee said: *"I wasn't too involved in drafting technical reports to insurers, but did speak to clients directly and got to go to trial."* There's a real international slant to the work, and a number of current matters are subject to US state law.

"One of the strengths of the firm is the amount of time they spend on growth and training of trainees," chirped one source. M&R has poured resources into ensuring its trainees are supported professionally and personally. This kicks off with a week's training in Cambridge for all newbies, and continues with regular sessions in each department. Reviews take place twice per seat and are usually followed by a chat with trainees' own personal 'principal' – *"a mentor who oversees training – you can speak to them openly about jobs, seats and people."* They're also each allocated a second-year trainee buddy to ensure there's an extra set of eyes looking out for them. We heard that in 2012, *"the firm made a decision to work harder than previous years to keep as many trainees as possible.*

Last year was slightly disappointing in terms of retention [just 36% of 2011's qualifiers were kept on]*, so they moved the timetable forward and brought the jobs list out earlier. It had more jobs than expected and they pushed for more than were on the initial offering. HR tried very hard to make sure that as many people as possible were kept on.*" This paid off in East Anglia. All six trainees were retained in Norwich, and seven out of nine in Cambridge. "*Things are a little trickier in Birmingham,*" however, and the office was unfortunately only able to retain two of its six qualifiers. That adds up to a total of 15 of 21 in 2012.

Chip Thursday, pig Friday

It's a tale of six cities at Mills & Reeve, and each of its outposts has a distinct feel and character. There's no head office, but Cambridge is the biggest of the bunch and houses the most trainees. The current office is "*quite tired – a bit of an 80s supreme,*" but right next door a "*brand new, seven-storey, all-singing, all-dancing Mills & Reeve building*" is shooting up at quite a speed. By early 2013, all 300-odd staff should be moved into this purpose-built, open-plan office, which enjoys "*pretty fantastic, almost panoramic views of the city.*" According to Marshall: "*It's an emblematic building and will be a Cambridge landmark.*" Fortunately, it'll still be a stone's throw from local The Flying Pig. Good job, seeing as "*Friday night is Pig night!*"

A quick hop up the A11 you'll find the "*quite flashy and really nice*" Norwich office. Trainees in other cities joked: "*It's quite an old-fashioned team. They have high tea at four and that kind of thing.*" Norwichians explain this isn't entirely fair: "*There's one department that used to have scones and tea in a teapot, but that's it.*" Well, that's that stereotype quashed then. They continue: "*It's very jolly hockey sticks – and there is a stigma this is country bumpkin-land – but we still do this complex work and have a brilliant rapport with our clients.*" The social life has "*died down a bit*" in recent years, relegated to a "*free bowl of cheesy chips in the pub on Chip Thursdays,*" but trainees tend to hang out informally a few times a month.

The vibe is different again up in Birmingham. Trainees brush over the fact that the building "*could do with an uplift,*" largely because "*it feels like there's a real buzz here.*" This is most likely due to its location in the heart of the city, and its mix of people. Everyone gets together for

"*payday drinks,*" and the social committee tries to arrange something for everyone. "*There's been greyhound racing, a Greek night and there's a quiz in a few weeks' time.*" The London office, located in the City's insurance district, is "*small but growing.*" Manchester and Leeds – the newest additions to the M&R collection – focus largely on family law, private tax and insurance. According to Brian Marshall, it'll be some time until these offices are large enough to take their own trainees, but "*as they grow, more and more will spend time there.*"

Feeling Peaky

Despite all their differences, trainees do "*feel like they're part of one big firm.*" The intranet does a great job of keeping everyone up to date with developments, offices make regular use of each other's expertise, and teams often get together for practice-specific training. The only gripe is: "*We need more coming together of the firm as a whole. At the moment it's just the summer party every two years – otherwise you just have parties within your office or your teams.*" M&R is trying its best to overcome its geographic hurdles, however, taking the rather drastic measure of shipping volunteers up to the Peak District, "*dropping them in random locations, giving them a map and saying 'get back to the hostel'.*" All in the name of charity, of course. There are also plenty of more traditional sporting activities, such as the annual North v South football tournament, to keep trainees on their toes.

Whichever M&R office you end up in, one thing is inevitable: "*There's no elitist feel.*" Every trainee we spoke to commented on the firm's relatively "*flat structure.*" This affects their training – "*I've never asked a partner for help and they've been disinterested*" – and the general atmosphere: "*It doesn't matter who you're speaking to. Everyone will quite happily stop and have a chat and banter with you.*" Brian Marshall says the firm seeks out "*intelligent, articulate people who have done well in all their results,*" and trainees say that an infectious personality and some life experience are just as important. "*We're from a spectrum of academic backgrounds,*" noted one source, "*but we're all quite outgoing, sociable people who want to get involved in the office and the fabric of the firm.*" Whichever office you're interested in joining, a link to the region will stand you in good stead, though it's not essential.

And finally...

Trainees "*don't think it's a big secret the firm recruits quite heavily from the vac scheme if it can,*" and we recommend the programme to get your foot in the door at this close-knit firm.

Mishcon de Reya

The facts

Location: London

Number of UK partners/solicitors: 78/131

Total number of trainees: 18

Seats: 4x6 months

Alternative seats: None

Extras: Pro bono – Queen Mary and Mary Ward Legal Advice Centres, AIRE Centre, Reprieve

On chambersstudent.co.uk...

- How to get into Mishcon
- Interview with training principal Daniel Levy

Despite recording an impressive hike in revenue and feeling the glare of the media spotlight, Mishcon ensures "*you're made to feel part of the team, not just the trainee.*"

The Gaga saga

Even a hermit in the Outer Hebrides would have done well to avoid a Mishcon-related story in 2012. It has represented former MP Chris Huhne against accusations of perverting the course of justice, Gordon Ramsey in his very public family dramas, and Lady Gaga's IP rights owning company, Ate My Heart, against the rise of the nappy-clad animated character Lady Goo Goo. The firm's superstar litigator Charlotte Harris has become a celebrity in her own right, having represented the likes of Ulrika Johnson, Leslie Ash and James Hewitt in the course of the Leveson Inquiry.

It's not all tantrums and tiaras, however. Despite the firm's glamorous sleb clients, about 90% of its revenue comes from the business world. "*Litigation continues to be a powerhouse, and goes from strength to strength,*" says training principal Daniel Levy, but Mishcon Private ("*our offering to private individuals*"), real estate and corporate are also current hotspots.

After a rocky ride through the credit crunch, Mishcon has fought back with all guns blazing, and is currently expanding, launching a brand new office in New York in 2010, and recording a 152% uptick in revenue since 2006/7. The firm is in the final stages of a three-year plan to triple its revenue to an ambitious £80m. "*We are, thank goodness, slightly ahead of target,*" Levy assured us. "*We've grown deliberately. It's in order that we can keep attracting a premium level of work and premium people.*" Will this intergalactic rate of growth continue? Well, "*not at the same pace,*" says Levy. "*We'll probably consolidate a bit more of our growth and concentrate on bedding in the brilliant people we've been trying to attract.*" A new three-year plan is on the way: "*I'm pretty certain we'll remain an independent London-centric firm with a New York litigation office,*" managing partner Kevin Gold told the legal press, but even so, Mishcon is in a period of transformation, moving from its position as a relatively small, relatively niche firm to become more of a mid-size outfit. It has also been a first-mover in the recent shake-up of the profession, applying to become an Alternative Business Structure, which will allow non-lawyers to invest in the firm. It is also thinking about offering non-legal services, like tax advice, to private clients.

Mid-size, huge deals

Many of our interviewees were drawn to Mishcon by its petite size and the "*variety and quality of its work and clients.*" One explained: "*We're a nice, medium-sized firm where you can do private client and family law alongside huge M&A transactions.*" The training contract aims to give trainees exposure to their choice of groups, within the corporate, employment, family, litigation, private client and real estate departments.

Mishcon's prominent litigation department is able to namedrop the likes of Microsoft, Pfizer and BMW as clients. It is involved in all aspects of dispute resolution but the department's fraud litigation team is the cherry on its cake and constitutes the bulk of its work. Fraud cases range from multimillion-pound bribery claims against

Chambers UK rankings

Corporate/M&A	Intellectual Property
Defamation/Reputation Management	Licensing
	Private Client
Dispute Resolution	Real Estate
Employment	Real Estate Litigation
Family/Matrimonial	Sports Law
Fraud	
Immigration	

FTSE 250 companies to one-on-one business disputes. Within these niche areas, trainees find their teams are leanly staffed – "*a partner, an associate and you*" – and "*experience is broad.*" Due to the size of cases in the large mainstream litigation group, "*you get less responsibility and it's up to you to go up to someone and seek out work.*" Trainees should expect to do their fair share of bundling, but are quickly adopted into the "*close-knit team,*" who "*work very hard but also have a lot of fun.*"

"*You hear horror stories about corporate departments,*" mulled one trainee, "*but it's actually really enjoyable.*" This is partly due to the size and nature of Mishcon's corporate work – deals are valued between £1m and £3m, with a focus on opportunist matters such as Google's acquisition of beatthatquote.com and the purchase of WR Technology by Manor Grand Prix Racing (better known as Virgin Racing). "*It's not a case of standing by the photocopier. You have real work, and you're calling clients all the time,*" a source explained. Corporate "*interacts with all the other departments in the firm,*" so as well as working for a range of partners within the department, trainees find it a great way to "*get yourself out there.*"

Mishcon de realty

Real estate is divided into commercial, residential, and litigious work. Deals tend to be large – think Delancey and Qatari Diar's £557m purchase of the Olympic Village, and Capco's multibillion-pound regeneration of Earls Court and Covent Garden. Even the residential team "*don't get out of bed for less than a million.*" Responsibility in the group runs high. "*I had brilliant exposure and ran loads of cases on my own, with supervision,*" enthused one source. "*I'd literally do everything from opening up files to completing transactions.*" Don't worry about being thrown in the deep end – the group is renowned for "*being really reassuring and supportive.*"

Trainees can opt to sit in a private client contentious or non-contentious seat, both of which cover a mosaic of "*little subteams*" ranging from the litigious media, art law and trusts to the more transactional immigration and tax/wealth planning groups. The contentious side is described as "*a riveting department, if you're interested in that sort of thing.*" Trainees are able to get involved in headline-grabbing cases, like former MP Chris Huhne's partner's accusations of harassment by the *Daily Mail*. "*I drafted witness statements, and helped research articles,*" one brimmed. The unusual art law seat covers everything from stolen art to agreements with galleries. "*It's great fun but a lot of responsibility,*" we're informed. The immigration group received rave reviews – trainees agree "*it's an incredible department.*" "*It's pretty high profile, either people with a lot of money or who have a sensitive political background and need assistance. I've been allowed to get involved in anything and everything that comes in.*"

Managing de Responsibility

Trainees think Mishcon has got the balance between responsibility and supervision spot on. Across all seats, "*you're always supervised and if you have any questions, everyone is incredibly responsive.*" Our sources had been asked to get stuck into high-level work early on: "*In my first week I was drafting a witness statement, and went to trial a few weeks later,*" said one. "*Being trusted with so much responsibility in my first seat was an amazing, rewarding experience.*" The firm's training sessions help this process along. A two to three-week induction followed by regular training in every practice group demonstrates that "*they're keen for you to understand what's going on and want you to do real, proper work.*"

Thanks to credit crunch deferrals, Mishcon found itself in somewhat of a quandary in 2012, with an unprecedented 18 second-year trainees vying for coveted NQ positions. At the time of our interviews in late spring, tensions were, unsurprisingly, running high. "*We definitely try to keep on as many qualifiers as we can,*" says Daniel Levy, but on this occasion a large number of qualifiers all wanted to go into one department and it was obvious not everyone was going to be lucky. By early July, however, nine of the 18 qualifiers had smiles on their faces and job offers from Mishcon in their pocket. The firm actively assisted those trainees who weren't staying with application and interview workshops. These efforts didn't go unnoticed by trainees, who were grateful: "*They don't have to help out, but they do.*" "*In coming years it should balance out,*" Levy assures us. "*We'll probably have 12 trainees per intake in the future.*"

Original pranksters

A lot of things have changed about the firm since Mr Mishcon set up his one-man shop in Brixton in 1937, but the culture isn't one of them. "*It sounds terribly clichéd,*" mused one trainee, "*but it really is like one big family.*" In fact, both within and outside the firm, the consensus is that Mishcon is "*a little bit different.*" In a good way. "*There's so much banter it can be quite noisy at times,*" said one interviewee. "*People are always having fun.*" This is largely because "*Mishcon hires a particular type of person – people who are individual, independent and characterful. It makes for an amazing environment to work in."*

The good vibes no doubt trickle down from the firm's spritely partners. *"They all love each other, it's ridiculous,"* laughed one source. *"They enjoy playing pranks on each other!"* It was recounted how *"new partners have to fall in line. One new one arrived and said people mustn't come into his office if he's talking to another partner. Within three minutes all the other partners had charged in and said, 'Er, no, you can't do that'."* There are concerns that this bubbly atmosphere might be a casualty of further growth, but trainees trust that the firm is in good hands: *"If anyone can maintain the culture, they can."*

Perhaps all this talk of pranks and banter is giving you the impression that life at Mishcon is like working in an episode of *30 Rock*, but we must remind you that this is, at the end of the day, a law firm. You'll have to be a pretty high academic achiever just to get though the door, and turning up on your first day with the old fake-arrow-though-the-head gag will probably not endear you in what is first and foremost a highly professional environment. It's also worth saying that hours can get long on occasion, particularly in corporate groups, although the firm's collaborative attitude makes them less painful. *"It's not the kind of office where you'll walk around in the evening and it feels like the middle of the day. If there's nothing to do, your supervisor will tell you to go home. When it's busy, you work late."* Most days trainees manage to leave their desks by 8pm and if they do stay longer, partners have a tendency to hang around for moral support: *"We had a huge demerger and the head of department sat around until 3am even though he had nothing to do."*

Herding into the Cow

Mishcon's recent growth spurt has left its two buildings in Holborn – corporate and real estate bods in one, and everyone else in the other – *"bursting at the seams."* 2012 saw the firm overspill into number three. The offices are perfectly serviceable, but with no canteen or communal area, the feeling among trainees is that an upgrade *"needs to happen."* Daniel Levy kept his cards close to his chest on the topic: *"It'll have to happen eventually."* The word on the street, however, is that *"there are noises we'll look for one building to accommodate everyone, maybe in the next five years or so."*

The lack of communal space clearly doesn't stop Mishconites *"getting a posse together"* on a regular basis. In fact, *"on a Friday pretty much the entire firm bundles into one pub,"* the much-loved Bountiful Cow. Funnily enough, *"once you get in the Cow you forget any hierarchy."* This selective amnesia happens on a regular basis: at trainee drinks; departmental events; and summer and Christmas parties. At the latter, first-year trainees provide the entertainment. *"You can do whatever you want, so long as you embarrass yourself,"* explained one mortified source. *"We did a rendition of Bugsy Malone's 'So you wanna be a boxer?' changed to 'So you wanna be a lawyer?' It was terrible. So terrible. Really, really awful,"* reminisced another, surprisingly fondly. Trainees also receive a generous budget to put on an annual party for employees' lucky kids. Last year the meeting rooms were transformed into a jungle complete with petting zoo.

What characteristics does Mishcon admire in prospective trainees? *"You do have to have some charisma to hold your own in conversations with the big characters who work here – the ones you see on Newsnight and in magazines. We don't want people who will shy away from conversations with people like that."* The current batch of trainees come in all shapes and sizes – some with paralegalling experience or a previous career, others fresh out of law school.

And finally...

A tip from us: *"Getting your face known"* is essential at Mishcon. If you make it onto the *"fantastic"* vac scheme ensure you get involved with all the activities this quirky firm offers and you can't go wrong.

Morgan Cole

The facts

Location: Cardiff, Swansea, Bristol, Oxford, Reading
Number of UK partners/solicitors: 53/127
Partners who trained at firm: 28%
Total number of trainees: 11
Seats: 4x6 months
Alternative seats: Secondments

On chambersstudent.co.uk...
• How to get into Morgan Cole
• Interview with training principal Guy Constant

The Morgan is in Wales; the Cole in the Thames Valley. Put together they make a full-service firm lining the M4.

King Cole

In 1998, Welsh law firm Morgan Bruce merged with the Thames Valley's Cole & Cole. Now known as Morgan Cole, the firm has five offices along the M4 corridor. The insurance and public sector practices loom large, but the firm is ranked by *Chambers UK* in all sorts of areas. Morgan Cole is one of the biggest players in the less crowded Wales market, but even in the more competitive South East region the firm more than holds its own. Furthermore, it is nationally recognised for its education, healthcare and professional discipline work.

Trainees are recruited either to the Thames Valley offices or to Wales and Bristol, and may be expected to take seats anywhere within their region. Cardiff (the largest office) and Reading (where the managing partner is based) could probably be described as the 'main' locations as far as the training contract is concerned. It would certainly be possible (though not necessarily desirable) for a trainee to complete all four seats in Cardiff, whereas that wouldn't be true of Bristol (which only offers one seat), Swansea, Reading or Oxford.

There were 12 trainees at the time of our calls, equally split between the Thames Valley offices and 'Wales and West'. "*We are recruiting more trainees – but gradually,*" training partner Guy Constant told us. "*The number of trainees we have hired for 2014 has slightly increased on 2013. We generally recruit too few so we have NQ jobs when they qualify.*" One trainee said: "*Morgan Cole does retain people. They would rather have you move department than get rid of you. It's really encouraging.*" The firm kept on three out of five qualifiers in 2012.

There are no compulsory seats, but some of the most common are company commercial, property, dispute management and employment. All trainees submit their top three choices and the firm tries to accommodate. "*Welsh trainees have a couple of options those in the Thames Valley don't, such as construction and health, and there are secondment opportunities which vary from year to year.*" Recent secondees have gone to the Welsh government and The Rank Group in Maidenhead.

A safety net

"*One of the strengths of the firm is our slightly different practice base,*" Guy Constant says. "*For example, commercial is one element, but we also have the safety net of a big insurance department which isn't particularly tied to the economy.*" In 2011, insurance accounted for around 40% of the firm's revenue. The department is best known for credit hire litigation and catastrophic injury claims, the latter of which works out of Bristol, an office which has doubled in size since 2010. Clients include big insurers, such as AXA, Aviva, Capita and Cardiff City Council.

Although insurance lawyers can be found all over the firm's network, the seat is only offered in Bristol and Reading. The Wales trainees "*tend to avoid it, possibly because of the commute*" across the Avon, and those in the Thames Valley weren't much more positive: "*Many of us worked in insurance as paralegals and we don't want to do it again.*" All this may sound a bit discouraging but we were assured "*it's a really good seat*" nonetheless and there is the opportunity to go to court for hearings and mediations, although since "*lots of cases have been going on for years*" there are "*hundreds of bundles*" for trainees to negotiate.

Chambers UK rankings

Administrative & Public Law	Intellectual Property
Banking & Finance	Licensing
Construction	Media & Entertainment
Corporate/M&A	Pensions
Dispute Resolution	Personal Injury
Education	Private Client
Employment	Professional Discipline
Family/Matrimonial	Professional Negligence
Health & Safety	Real Estate
Healthcare	Real Estate Litigation
Information Technology	Restructuring/Insolvency
	Social Housing

Health and social care is another large sector at Morgan Cole. "*We do health work for the NHS itself and for private companies that deal with the NHS,*" Guy Constant informs us. Recent client wins include two large NHS Foundation Trusts, three private healthcare companies and the charity MacIntyre.

The commercial property group is working on some "*monumental undertakings with the NHS.*" Other clients include HSBC and Canary Wharf. "*Trainees can get very involved: I felt put to good use. You could always see why you were doing a particular task.*" one told us. Juniors work on multiple smaller matters alongside one or two big ones. "*Some things I was able to do unmanaged, but help was always given to me without question. The whole team are infinitely approachable,*" said a trainee. Another thought: "*It's really good. I managed cases myself and was the first point of contact for clients. I'd say the seat was 70% 'proper' work and 30% assisting solicitors and admin-type tasks.*" The team advised The Vale of Glamorgan Council on a £230m regeneration of former Barry dockland.

Shoes and sunglasses

The employment team "*acts for quite big public sector clients.*" For example, over the past five-and-a-half years it has defended more than 300 equal pay claims on behalf of health boards and NHS trusts. Private sector clients include Avon Cosmetics and Dolce & Gabbana UK. Trainees can expect to correspond with counsel and clients, draft witness statements and instructions to counsel, and attend hearings in England and Wales – as well as taking on a bit of photocopying and scanning duty.

Dispute management is a popular seat. "*We've had some big client wins in South Wales for the National Midwifery Council,*" Constant says. 2011 saw the firm handle some cases worth over £10m, including acting for the former UK sales agents of Crocs. Trainees in this seat felt the level of responsibility they were afforded depended on the case. "*On multi-track cases, trainees don't have the relevant experience, so there's lots of mundane stuff like scanning and photocopying, but I was given a small-track case to run too,*" said one source, whereas another told us: "*I was working on a massive dispute with a massive client with a very senior partner. He gave me loads of drafting experience and I went to several client meetings in my first week.*"

From the university of life

Guy Constant says: "*The job can be stressful so it's important not to be too formal. It would be dull if we weren't allowed to talk to people.*" Trainees agreed: "*It's not stuffy or anything like that.*" The Oxford and Bristol offices are open-plan, trainees in Cardiff sit in an office with their supervisor, while a more unusual arrangement in Reading has teams sharing larger workrooms, with four or five solicitors in each. "*Supervisors are usually partners and they've been brilliant.*"

The hours are not too onerous, although working from 8am to 6pm is perhaps more likely than a nine-to-five shift. "*I've done a couple of nights in the office where I've stayed until 9pm. That's certainly the exception,*" said one source. Corporate tends to demand the longest hours.

"*I think the firm likes people who have some life experience behind them,*" declared one trainee. "*Most of us have done paralegalling work or something similar. We have one ex-nurse. There's not too many of us fresh out of uni.*" Take a look at the trainee pen pictures on the Morgan Cole careers website, which are notable because they give details of successful candidates' past work experience as well as the standard bits about university background (a real mix, by the way) and hobbies.

"*Generally, the firm doesn't place a lot of emphasis on the social life. People do their own thing.*" There are the occasional post-work drinks or Friday lunches, however. All the offices are located fairly centrally in their respective towns and cities with the exception of Oxford, which is out on the ring road, and Swansea, where Morgan Cole shares a very nice building near the port.

And finally...

Whether you go wild for Wales or think the Thames Valley's terrific, Morgan Cole can offer a strong and broad training contract.

Morrison & Foerster MNP

The facts

Location: London

Number of UK partners/solicitors: 12/22

Total number of trainees: 6

Seats: 4x6 months

Alternative Seats: Tokyo, occasional secondments

Extras: Pro bono – Guide to Social Enterprise; language classes

On chambersstudent.co.uk...
- How to get into MoFo
- Interview with director of administration Margaret Mannell

Born in the San Francisco sun in 1883, this US firm, delightfully nicknamed MoFo, prides itself on its individuality.

The MoFo mojo

MoFo worked on the first licence of the Hello Kitty brand, helped create the first ever ATM-friendly bank cards, and was behind the patent of the first heat-tolerant broccoli. Although known in the States for life sciences, IP and IT work, in London the firm offers a balance of corporate, technology and litigation work. "*We offer a range of practices in the UK,*" trainees said. "*It's not a massive office and there are no particularly dominant departments.*" Director of administration Margaret Mannell said: "*We've really weathered the storm in London thanks to the broad nature of our practice. Globally, MoFo's enjoyed its best financial year ever. We're not yet as well known as we'd like to be in London, so we're working hard to build at every level.*"

Although undoubtedly a US firm, MoFo hasn't acquired the fearsome reputation certain other firms enjoy. "*It might be our Californian background,*" interviewees suggested. "*We're not a Wall Street firm. Obviously it's not bean bags everywhere – people do work incredibly hard – but it's in our nature to be gentler and more free-thinking. People are driven and ambitious, but we're not some outfit of fear like other American firms!*"

"*MoFo only really offers corporate, capital markets, litigation and technology as seats*" at the moment, "*so the choice revolves around what order you do them in.*" Despite the limited options, sources say "*there's a lot of flexibility. Departments such as tax, life sciences and financial transactions don't officially have seats, but if you show a real interest, and there's business need, the firm will make it happen.*" There's also a capital markets secondment to Tokyo. "*If capital markets is your thing, lots of people have used the secondment as a way to do a double seat in the area.*"

Cinema and chocolate

Clients in the capital markets department are mostly "*big names, a mixture of UK clients and US-based banks.*" MoFo recently represented Land Bank of Taiwan in litigation against Lehman Brothers, while other clients include Goldman Sachs, RBS, Grupo Santander and the National Bank of Canada. The team is "*a really good bunch*" and "*its size allows the trainee to get a good deal of responsibility,*" drafting ancillary and structured product documents, conducting research and attending client meetings.

"*Every partner in the litigation department has his own speciality,*" be it general commercial litigation, white-collar crime, employment, IP or insolvency. As a trainee "*you can express a focus,*" one source explained, "*but basically you're doing all sorts of work.*" The firm is representing Seiko Epson, which, along with nine other defendants, is being sued by Nokia in the High Court in the largest price-fixing case in Europe. It is acting for Cadbury in a separate price-fixing matter; other clients include Grant Thornton and Landsbanki Islands. "*There aren't loads of trainees, so you will inevitably do some bundling,*" trainees said. "*At the same time, you're constantly in client meetings, drafting letters and sometimes even running your own smaller matters.*"

The corporate department was hit by the departure of several partners in 2011 but, said interviewees, "*we're really*

Chambers UK rankings

Corporate/M&A	Life Sciences
Fraud	Outsourcing
Information Technology	

hiring quite heavily and there's definitely a lot of work coming in. Although we're not at the numbers we were, this is a department the London office is really looking to expand." Margaret Mannell says: "The loss of certain partners and the current rebuilding of the department has meant we've been able to change direction to fit in with where the US and UK markets are going. It's going to be much better in the long run." Clients are predominantly life sciences, energy and technology companies, most of which are AIM-size and American. The team recently advised joint venture company China Africa Resources on the admission of shares on the AIM market. Trainees praised the "commitment" to training in this department. One said: "The team is incredibly responsive to questions and there's a lot of informal seminars. The team is changing and growing, and they are keen for trainees to be a part of that movement forward." Another added: "You're doing everything from company secretarial work to dealing directly with US partners at other firms. The responsibility levels are great. You really learn so much." For now the group is part of London's mid-market, more comparable with the corporate offerings of the likes of small City outfits like Lewis Silkin or Mishcon de Reya than with US corporate powerhouses like Skadden or Cleary but, said trainees, "if you want to be part of an emerging corporate team, this is certainly a firm to keep in mind."

The technologies transactions group (TTG) is one of MoFo's strongest suits. The team covers life sciences, technology, IP and media work. Interviewees pointed out that "although MoFo is really known for its IP work in the States, it's not a heavy focus in this office. The occasional matter comes up, but don't come to the London office expecting to do a lot of IP." Instead, "technology outsourcing is a big part of what we do." The team represented the Odeon & UCI Cinemas Group in the completion of digital film booking and deployment support agreements with a variety of independent film distributors in the UK, and provided English law advice on a gift card programme for Hilton Hotels. Other big-name clients include Universal Pictures, Macmillan Publishing, Sony BMG and EMI Music. "You're the only trainee in the team, so you get involved in everything," one source said. "The department also attends lots of networking and tech events, and trainees are always encouraged to go and engage."

The hours here are "reasonable" – after 7.30pm the office is pretty quiet. "That's the general norm – if you are there past that, people notice and comment, 'Ooh, you're staying late'." Midnight finishes occur on occasion but aren't the norm.

Cakes and sandwiches

"Although the London office is very independent, we're very aware of our big firm backing," trainees said. "Our office feels very connected to the States and the larger MoFo operation. We have people visiting all the time and you're consistently working with the American offices. The chair of MoFo also comes over a couple of times a year." Upon qualification, NQs are sent out to San Francisco for what trainees jokingly referred to as their "MoFo indoctrination." However, sources said: "We're definitely not just a feeder office. The direction this office takes is decided by London management and we have several independent clients. It's good to have the balance between the two."

"The approachability of the office is one of the best things about the firm," one source said. "The vibe is very inclusive. From partners to secretaries, everyone is treated with the same level of respect," trainees said. "A good example," one added, "is that our security guard was leaving, so the firm threw him a party."

The firm holds a cheese and wine night every other Friday, "which is always great to pop into." There's a football team and "throughout the year we have different quizzes and charity events." For the Jubilee, "we held a bake-off and managed to convince the managing partner to walk around the office with a little trolley, selling cake. It was hilarious." The first Monday of every month is "'anything but sandwiches' day. The firm puts on a big lunch for the whole office in one of the meeting rooms." And you'll always find a trainee or four at the Rack and Tenter or the Corney & Barrow near its CityPoint office on Friday evenings.

Special mention needs to go to the office's commitment to pro bono. "Pro bono is a huge part of MoFo," trainees asserted. "Our pro bono hours even count towards our billables, which is definitely rare in London." Trainees are encouraged to take on at least two projects a year, and "you're always supported by the firm. It's viewed as particularly effective training."

And finally...
MoFo retained all three qualifying trainees in 2012.

Muckle LLP

The facts

Location: Newcastle

Number of UK partners/solicitors: 27/41

Total number of trainees: 8

Seats: 4x6 months

Alternative seats: None

On chambersstudent.co.uk...

- How to get into Muckle
- The Newcastle legal market

"*We're North East and proud,*" say trainees at this Geordie firm, which attracts business far beyond the borders of Tyne.

Where there's Muck there's brass

Muckle recorded a double-digit percentage increase in revenue in 2011/12. "*We're not finding it a difficult market,*" said managing partner Steve McNicol, adding that the firm is "*anticipating further growth in this region.*" Muckle is certainly loyal to its North East roots, and it's highly unlikely that the firm will open up shop outside of Newcastle, despite serving many clients with a national focus. "*At this stage we don't see the need to open up offices elsewhere, and in addition we've got room to expand in this office,*" Graduate recruitment executive Kevin Maloney informs us the long-term strategy aims to get the office head count over 200 within five years. One trainee summarised: "*Muckle will continue to be a big regional player. The aim is to keep our reputation constant, despite all the changes in the industry.*"

Roughly one-third of Muckle's revenue is currently generated by its corporate finance, banking and commercial departments; one-third from property, construction and engineering; and one-third from employment, private client and dispute resolution. Muckle receives *Chambers UK* rankings in all of these areas, and has picked up partners from neighbouring firm Watson Burton to strengthen other teams.

It's hard to compare Muckle to nearby firms like Dickinson Dees, Eversheds or DWF: Kevin Maloney says that doing so is "*to a certain extent like comparing apples and oranges as they are national law firms. For instance, Dickinson Dees has over 600 people. It does lots of work in areas in which we have no involvement, but we focus on our core commercial aspects. When you look at the strengths of our teams in these areas, we believe we can compete.*"

Many a mickle...

Trainees don't get a say when it comes to the first seat, but after that they will have a sit down with Maloney to discuss what future options are available: "*They never dictate, but they will make suggestions that they think you might like based on your personality.*" Seats include banking, corporate, commercial, construction/engineering, dispute resolution, employment and property.

Muckle's corporate department is one of the largest in the North East, and has many clients from the motor retail, pharmaceutical and energy sectors. Recently, the department represented RPM International, a manufacturer of sealants and building materials, on its acquisition of Pipeline & Drainage Systems' share capital. Corporate finance has traditionally been a very profitable area for the firm, and a seat here is "*absolutely fantastic.*" Matters can range from working with "*start-ups to dealing with some quite high-end M&A,*" and trainees spend time drafting board minutes and getting to grips with the disclosure process. The banking team has clients including HSBC, Santander and Clydesdale Bank. While there's not as much responsibility for trainees here as there is in other departments, our sources enjoyed witnessing negotiations and "*seeing how stringent the partners have to be when representing the bank – there's often not that much scope for negotiation with the business in question.*"

Seats are available in both property development and corporate real estate. Trainees in development – which encompasses both residential and commercial clients – "*work closely with a few associates,*" helping clients develop plots of land by writing reports and titles. "*It's nice because you're all working towards the same goal, and with a plot of land there may be unforeseen problems,*"

Chambers UK rankings

Banking & Finance	Information Technology
Charities	Intellectual Property
Construction	Real Estate
Corporate/M&A	Real Estate Litigation
Dispute Resolution	Restructuring/Insolvency
Employment	

so it's like putting together a puzzle." Our sources had been given their own files to run and were pleased that *"the team gives us a good amount of responsibility."*

Corporate real estate can be *"quite challenging, as you end up working with everybody."* Trainees enjoyed conducting Land Registry searches, as well as running large parts of some deals. *"It's great responsibility – I ended up leading the client and more or less ran the whole file from start to finish,"* said one source. Another added: *"On day one I had two or three drawers full of my own files, so you have to come up with a strategy and priorities, but the work's really varied and you'll be drafting leases and dealing with a lot of post-completion stuff too."* The team recently supported Muckle's corporate finance group advising on a joint venture between UK Land Estates and Highcross, a major American property fund.

Across the universities

Employment is a *"whirlwind"* of a seat. *"The pace is incredible, as the case law could be different by the next morning, so you have to be on the beat with that constantly."* The team has many clients from the education sector, including London South Bank University and the University of Northumbria. Muckle usually represents the employer in contentious matters, and trainees were mostly exposed to unfair dismissal claims brought against their client. Sources were pleased to be able to squeeze in some attendance at tribunals, and helped to get *"bundles organised – even the trivial things allow you to get to know the case inside out. Discrimination law can be quite complex, but the team eases you in nicely."*

"I'm not going to pretend it's nine to five, as that's unrealistic, but generally the hours are good," said one source. *"There have been one or two occasions where I've worked until 3am, but that's once in a blue moon and gives you an adrenaline rush!"*

Mucking about

"You can do the same type of law here as you can anywhere in the region, so you have to be genuinely motivated to come here: our strength is the culture of our firm, and it's that what we believe makes us different," says Kevin Maloney. Most of our sources knew that they wanted to practise in Newcastle but what appealed to them most was the *"personal and family feel"* that Muckle exuded. *"I wanted a firm where it wasn't just about my grades, or how good I seemed on paper"* said one, applauding the firm for focusing *"on the real person in front of them."* This personable culture is overseen by managing partner Steve McNicol, who is *"the most approachable person – he knows everybody's name."*

"Muckle maintains a focus on the social side, which is nice because working in a law firm can be stressful." The dedicated BEAM team (short for 'Being Engaged at Muckle') is made up of various staff who are responsible for arranging events such as the summer fun-day, the end of financial year bash and the firm-wide Christmas party, which was most recently held at Baltic, the flour mill turned contemporary art gallery on the south bank of the Tyne.

The sister of the BEAM team, is, of course, the Green team, which organises a series of environmentally friendly projects. Grow-your-own veg is one, and over the past couple of years a fierce competition has been waged between each department to grow the largest leeks and marrows on the firm's balcony. *"There's been quite a bit of competition,"* says Maloney, who lamented that *"unfortunately it's been very wet and windy this year, so the leeks have taken quite a bit of damage."* Charity fund-raising and support is a big thing at Muckle, and 1% of the firm's profits is set aside for charitable causes.

Muckle occupies a *"really quite fancy and modern building"* – Time Central on Gallowgate. *"Every boardroom is painted in a different hue"* in accordance with the firm's rainbow-coloured branding, while the open-plan layout means that *"although there is obviously a hierarchy, the office doesn't feel hierarchical."* The canteen, Time Out, is a hit with trainees, who *"muck about"* at lunch among the *"pool tables, plasma TVs and table football."* A little promo video on Muckle's website shows the office in all its glory (although it does also give the impression that the firm is overrun with ghosts).

And finally...

Those with a desire to work in the North East would do well to look up Muckle. In 2012, five out of six qualifiers were retained by the firm.

Nabarro LLP

The facts

Location: London, Sheffield

Number of UK partners/solicitors: 109/263

Partners who trained at firm: 18%

Total number of trainees: 51

Seats: 6x4 months

Alternative Seats: Brussels, secondments

Extras: Pro bono – LawWorks; language classes

On chambersstudent.co.uk...

- How to get into Nabarro
- Interview with partner Justin Cornelius
- Networking 101

Full-service but with strong foundations in property law, Nabarro is your quintessential London mid-market firm.

The house that Nabarro built

A new managing partner and senior partner duo are currently "*resetting the sails*" of Nabarro, says partner Justin Cornelius. Traditionally built on the blocks of property law, this medium-sized City firm also has a highly regarded corporate practice, alongside strong projects, property litigation, capital markets, clinical negligence, funds and pensions teams. "*This year,*" says Cornelius, "*we are focusing on sectors of particular strength – such as financial institutions, real estate, manufacturing, healthcare, infrastructure and renewable energy – and are developing new groups that span across all our practice areas. For example, we have an entrepreneurs group that focuses on small and start-up businesses, which has been very well received by our clients.*" From an internal perspective, "*one of the key themes that we are focusing on is communication and transparency across the firm, from partners to trainees.*"

Headquartered just off Holborn, the firm also has Sheffield, Brussels and Singapore bases. The Brussels office specialises in EU and competition law, while Singapore focuses on construction, engineering and international arbitration. "*In other news, we have just added a new Spanish firm to our European alliance,*" says Cornelius. "*One of our long-term ambitions is to increase our presence in the international markets and expand the Nabarro footprint.*"

In London, trainees take six four-month seats, "*with the idea that you repeat a seat in the department you want to qualify into.*" The party line is trainees must complete a seat in property, corporate and a contentious department.

"*Although that sounds pretty strict, those requirements can be fulfilled in a variety of ways. A number of seats count as 'corporate' – banking and finance, competition, insolvency, funds and indirect real estate, tax and even arguably IP. It's not only pure corporate.*" However, noting that "*it is still 40% of what we do,*" sources agreed that it would be hard to wriggle out of a property seat. Other options include commercial litigation, construction, construction litigation, employment, environment, investments, pensions, planning, projects and property litigation. The HR department "*will generally try and accommodate your preferences, but there is the understandable skew towards second-years getting priority.*" New starters generally get little choice for their first seat, but they then rank four preferences in their first mid-seat review. Trainees agreed: "*You can't always get your first choice, but it's surprising if at least one of your options doesn't come up.*" IP and employment "*are always quite well subscribed,*" while due to the large size of the property department, "*if you ask for a specific seat there, you'll probably get it.*"

The Sheffield office began life as the in-house legal team of British Coal, but over the years has expanded to a range of departments. Seats offered to the handful of trainees hired in the city of steel include construction, corporate, health claims litigation, planning, projects, real estate and environment. "*A number of the practices mirror London ones, so there is cross-communication,*" sources explained. Read more about this office on our website.

Chambers UK rankings

Banking & Finance	Investment Funds
Capital Markets	Local Government
Clinical Negligence	Pensions
Competition/European Law	Pensions Litigation
Construction	Planning
Corporate/M&A	Private Equity
Dispute Resolution	Professional Discipline
Education	Projects
Employment	Public Procurement
Energy & Natural Resources	Real Estate
Environment	Real Estate Finance
Health & Safety	Real Estate Litigation
Healthcare	Restructuring/Insolvency
Information Technology	Retail
Intellectual Property	Tax

They always deliver

The real estate department is split up into five different teams, all with their own mix of clients. The teams are each between 25 and 30 lawyers strong and *"although you'll always get a range of leases and licences to work on, some teams do more commercial/residential work, while others are more focused on the industrial. Some clients are so big they span a couple of teams."* Justin Cornelius says: *"We did well even in the context of an economy that was supposedly not great."* Nabarro has acted for Mitsubishi on its purchase of two adjoining assets in the City of London, and worked on Brockton Capital's acquisition of The Mailbox (Birmingham's distinctive postbox-red former sorting office turned shopping centre). Trainees praised *"the early responsibility"* the seat offers. *"Of course there's supervision, but if you show confidence you can get quite advanced work straight away."* One source said: *"It's such a busy seat. From when you first arrive, you're given ten files to run with – some that are essentially your own. It is, of course, terrifying, but you can really get stuck in."* Another asserted: *"I had client contact every day."* Trainees reported *"drafting all sorts of documents, negotiating and managing schedules."*

"Pure" corporate is a mixture of both private and public work, *"so as a trainee your experience really depends on what the department is doing as a whole – and of course what your capacity is."* The seat covers everything from equity capital markets, public companies and securities work to M&A. *"Of course, partners have areas they prefer to work on, but as a junior you're exposed to all different areas of the law,"* trainees said. *"People e-mail us ad hoc with work all the time, but you're also encouraged to approach partners for work you're interested in taking on."* Recent deals Nabarro has worked on include the

acquisition of $191m worth of Indian-based logistics and hydropower assets on behalf of Infrastructure India; and various acquisitions and disposals for e-gaming operator Sportingbet. Heineken is another big-name client.

A growing department at Nabarro is the funds and indirect real estate team, highly ranked by our parent publication *Chambers UK.* Trainees say: *"The team is very impressive and really looking to continue business development."* The work here *"can be daunting, as it's very specialised and the calibre of partners is so high. If you show enthusiasm and competency however, it's a very inclusive department and you do all sorts."* Although corporate-based, *"there is a lot of interaction with the property and tax departments."*

Breaking camp

Nabarro's contentious teams include commercial, property and construction litigation. The firm has one of the best property litigation teams in the City and recently obtained an injunction for Paternoster Square Management preventing the Occupy London protesters from setting up camp in the square outside St Paul's (they shuffled over a bit instead). Trainees reported *"being anxious about going into the seat. It has a reputation for long hours and being really hard, but the reality is that people love it. There is a lot of pressure, but that's due to getting really involved with the cases. You end up learning so much."* The commercial litigation team does a lot of work for Medical Defence Unit (MDU), basically acting for doctors in disciplinary trouble. *"The MDU work is very specialist and you get really involved with the doctors, which requires a level of empathy,"* trainees explained. Other cases Nabarro has taken on include Ryanair's claim against Her Majesty's Revenue & Customs for recovery of overpayment of Air Passenger Duty, and matters resulting from the Lehman collapse. Trainees *"handle all sorts of work, from drafting to attending hearings."*

Trainees *"love the tax department."* Days are spent *"doing a lot of research, marking up contracts and working heavily alongside other departments. It's very cerebral."* The IP team's partners, meanwhile, *"get the best out of everyone. Trainees get really involved in everything from corporate transactions to trade mark protections."* Among the brands that Nabarro protects are those of Levi Strauss, Twitter and posh-crisp-purveyors Kettle Foods.

Client secondments are regularly available at Mercedes-Benz, Essex County Council and Serco Group. *"There are occasional ad hoc secondments, but they're co-ordinated on a case-by-case basis,"* says Justin Cornelius. A competition-focused overseas seat is also available in the Brussels office and *"the Singapore office is definitely on the radar as an overseas possibility,"* says Cornelius. *"We will be expanding the office this year and I would hope within twelve months we will be sending trainees out there."* Trainees advised: *"Express your interest in sec-ondments as early as possible. It's always a question that comes up in your mid-seat review."*

Let's mingle

Nabarro is serious about networking. Trainees are encouraged not only to get involved in firm networking events, but to run their own: *"It's called Contact Nabarro. Three times a year we set up an event and invite friends, acquaintances and other possible contacts. The idea is that these are clients of the future. We benefit from it by getting excellent networking and communication development practice."* Always on the lookout for a free drink, we attended one of these events – head to the bonus feature on our website to learn the secrets of the 'handicanapé', the correct level of smile to adopt and how to politely escape from a boring conversation.

While noting the *"really relaxed and friendly feel"* at Nabarro, trainees also remarked on the firm's move towards a more *"dynamic energy. Nabarro is switched-on and strives towards innovation. It's really not conservative or stuffy."* Trainees praised newly appointed managing partner Andrew Inkester for his approachability. *"He sits in a totally normal office, as opposed to some special part-ner palace, and he makes an effort to chat with everyone."* Of course *"there are partners who you can't really chat to, but the senior associates are particularly friendly."*

"The beauty of working around Holborn and near to Covent Garden," trainees cooed, *"is you can walk out of the office and find yourself in a good bar or pub."*

Favoured locals include Sfizio, *"which is more like a Nabarro common-room – there doesn't seem to be anyone else in there,"* the Enterprise and the Dolphin. *"People also tend to socialise with their teams a lot,"* juniors explained. *"Partners organise team getaways such as ski trips or countryside fun."* With lashings of ginger beer, we hope. Every couple of months there are firm-wide drinks in the office. *"People genuinely get involved"* in the various firm sports teams (netball, cricket, hockey, football). At Christmas, the firm's choir sings carols in the main atrium. However, the firm organises a 'Trainees in the North' weekend to give Londoners *"a chance to go up to Sheffield and mingle with the trainees up there. The firm puts us up in a hotel and we go out for a meal and drinks."* It's a nice event for the Sheffield trainees, who admitted that at other times, *"socialising has sort of died off here. Not because people don't want to get together, but our location makes it quite difficult. Most people drive."*

Nab a role

"Get on the vac scheme," trainees stressed. This is good advice, since the firm recruits at least 90% of its trainees this way. If you are lucky enough to get a place on it, *"the vac scheme is so good that it normally puts you in good standing for other firms,"* trainees claimed. *"It is intense. It's three weeks of actual trainee experience, alongside socials and extra things to get involved in. It is exhaust-ing, but the best advice is to show enthusiasm and really get involved in everything."* A second piece of recruitment advice comes from Justin Cornelius: *"We are always keen to see a candidate who has taken time to research the firm and is making an informed decision as to why they are sit-ting in front of us in the first place."*

And finally...
Retention rates at Nabarro are generally high, and in 2012 the firm kept on 22 of its 28 qualifiers.

Norton Rose LLP

The facts

Location: London

Number of UK partners/solicitors: 152/360

Seats: 4x6 months

Total number of trainees: 116

Alternative seats: Overseas seats, secondments

Extras: Pro bono – Tooting and Tower Hamlets Law Centres, FRU, CAB; language classes

On chambersstudent.co.uk...

- How to get into Norton Rose
- Going global: Norton Rose's internal network

Snapping at the heels of the magic circle, Norton Rose has experienced explosive global growth in the past few years thanks to four overseas mergers.

Seeking dominion

"Norton Rose used to be happy as a smallish City firm. But we are now making a conscious effort to move away from that. The focus is on being big and global and competing with the best." To achieve this NR has gobbled up four firms in the last three years. After surprising the legal world with an Australian merger in early 2010, it joined with large Canadian and South African practices in June 2011 and then topped off its romp round the Commonwealth with another Canadian merger (this time with Calgary-based Macleod Dixon) in 2012. This last move expanded the size of the firm's energy practice and added offices in oil-rich Venezuela and Kazakhstan.

The Norton Rose Group now employs close to 3,000 lawyers and is structured as a Swiss Verein, split into four regional arms. Its global revenue is more than double what NR's was in 2009. The Norton Rose 'brand' has offices in six continents and clocks up scores of rankings in *Chambers Global*. Africa and the Middle East are particularly key areas of work. NR recently advised South Africa's Standard Bank on a $100m loan for the final stages of the completion of an iron ore mine in Sierra Leone.

"The mergers have gone really well. Legally, the different parts of the firm are separate branches but it doesn't feel like that at all," a trainee opined. *"Every transaction I have worked on has been international and I've also worked with lawyers at our Canadian and Australian counterpart firms."* The US is the one blank spot on NR's global office map and the firm is mighty keen to do something about that. *"The party line is that a US merger is definitely on the cards,"* a trainee told us. Watch this space.

A borrower or a lender be

In London and around the world banking lies at the heart of Norton Rose's work. *"It's important to stress that this is a banking firm rather than a general firm with a strong banking slant,"* trainees agreed. But that doesn't mean the firm just does one thing. The business is focused around six core industry 'headlights': financial institutions; energy; infrastructure, mining and commodities; transport; technology and innovation; and pharmaceuticals and life sciences. In London the firm's M&A, projects, dispute resolution and capital markets work is only one step off the magic circle's pace. NR is also the only firm to sweep top-tier rankings for all areas of asset finance: aviation, shipping and rail.

In autumn 2012, NR replaced its popular six-seat system with a more regular four-times-six-months rotation pattern. The training contract remains heavily banking oriented. Under the 'banking' umbrella, trainees can complete seats in asset finance, project finance or general banking (acquisition finance). Nearly half of all seats are in these three areas. Corporate finance and dispute resolution also encompass a large number of seats, while more niche options include: competition; tax; employment; planning and environment; property; and pensions/incentives.

Under the new system stints in banking, corporate and dispute resolution are all compulsory. An overseas seat no

Chambers UK rankings

Asset Finance	Information Technology
Aviation	Insurance
Banking & Finance	Investment Funds
Banking Litigation	Outsourcing
Capital Markets	Pensions
Commodities	Planning
Competition/European Law	Professional Negligence
Construction	Projects
Corporate Crime & Investigations	Public Procurement
	Real Estate
Corporate/M&A	Real Estate Finance
Dispute Resolution	Real Estate Litigation
Employee Share Schemes & Incentives	Restructuring/Insolvency
	Shipping
Employment	Tax
Energy & Natural Resources	Telecommunications
Environment	Transport
Financial Services	Travel
Fraud	

longer is, and the firm told us trainees will be able to opt to spend their fourth seat option overseas, on client secondment (often to a bank), in one of the niche practice areas or in one of the main banking/corporate transactional teams. Under the old system many sources characterised a typical training contract as follows: "*It's pretty much the case that you do two banking seats, one corporate finance seat, one litigation seat and one overseas seat. That leaves you with one free choice.*" It is unclear what the prevalent model will be under the new system. But as overseas seats remain common, we imagine niche seats will become even rarer in future than they are now.

Most of our interviewees got most of their seat choices, but a few had missed out on favoured choices. Trainees rank their preferences one to four at each move and "*as long as you give a clear reason and justify why you are applying for a certain seat, the HR team will listen.*" One source advised: "*Decide early on if there is one niche seat you really want to do and keep putting it as your number-one choice every rotation.*"

Not such an idiot abroad

The general banking team focuses on acquisition finance: arranging loans for banks – RBS, BNP Paribas, Barclays, Citi – or borrowers to buy or start up new businesses. "*We do a lot of work in Africa,*" one trainee said. "*In some jurisdictions down there it's quite common for governments to renege on agreements, which makes things more interesting...*" NR recently advised UAE-based phone company Etisalat on a $650m loan for its mobile phone business in Nigeria and has helped finance similar enter-

prises in Ghana and Tanzania. Trainees may also get to sample some real estate finance, restructuring or Islamic work and find their day dominated by "*plenty of typical trainee tasks, like proof-reading or preparing corporate authorities, as well as some interesting drafting of loan agreements and ancillary documents.*"

In asset finance, trainees can take seats in shipping, aviation or rail. Clients are often bank lenders, but the firm has also advised train manufacturer Bombardier, ferry operator Stena and easyJet on the financing of trains, ships and planes. While you might occasionally "*go to Hamburg to deliver a plane and be taken to dinner by its new owners,*" trainees admitted that "*the work is quite tedious. You run the conditions precedents list and organise the paperwork and manage documents.*" It doesn't help that that the transactions are all "*commoditised, quick, boilerplated affairs.*" One optimist speculated that "*maybe at a higher level it is more interesting, as you are running the whole deal.*"

A project finance seat focuses on either mining or energy. Both are booming areas – NR advises on world-spanning projects in places as diverse as Rwanda, Bulgaria, Sweden, Nigeria, Abu Dhabi and Saudi Arabia. "*It is great to look at what is being negotiated between the parties and the government of a developing country and see the investment going into that country.*" The team recently worked for Dutch bank ING on $4.1bn worth of funding for a gas-chemical complex in Uzbekistan and advised a European energy trading group on arrangements for a thermal energy plant in Bosnia being built in co-operation with Chinese investors. For trainees, "*the work varies from really simple tasks like making sure document bibles are in order and the right things have been signed, to drafting concession documents, co-ordinating with local counsel and talking directly to clients.*"

Project finance is known as NR's toughest in terms of workload: "*If you do projects you are definitely signing up to do hard hours.*" Across the firm a normal workday lasts from 9am to 7 or 8pm and when deadlines loom the hours can stretch until 10 or 11pm and beyond. Said one source: "*I recognise that the job has its perks and its downsides, and one downside is the demand on your time. A few times a month I stay until 10pm and I have stayed beyond midnight three or four times in the last six months. If I am not busy I make it known and offer my services to anybody in the team who needs them.*"

Toil and trouble

Trainees can complete seats in one of three corporate finance subteams: private equity, capital markets or M&A. The M&A team is split into groups which focus on specific industries – there's a big focus on energy, infrastructure, mining and transport. For example, NR advised the UK arm of Italian oil company Eni on its €590m acquisition of GDF SUEZ's stake in a joint venture with Elf (a subsidiary of Total). Other clients include BMW, AXA and HSBC. Trainees told us corporate work is "*more varied*" and "*more dynamic*" than banking, as there is more of a difference between deals. They also liked the fact you can sometimes mix M&A with capital markets work.

Financial services and regulatory disputes form the backbone of the dispute resolution team. NR has acted for Lloyds in a dispute with the Treasury over tax avoidance and recently worked on three separate FSA enforcement cases defending executives from JPMorgan, Bank of America and Credit Suisse against accusations of insider trading. There is also insurance and arbitration work. One trainee estimated: "*40% of my work was research, 20% was going to client meetings and meetings with chambers, 25% was document management, bundling and bibling and the rest was proof-reading and document review.*"

We mentioned the niche seat options earlier, and corporate support work is a big part in these seats. A trainee explained: "*We work directly with the banking and corporate departments. I get a lot of research queries that have been passed to my supervisor from clients and people in those departments.*" For example, lawyers in the competition and corporate departments recently advised security business G4S on the competition aspects of its £5.2bn acquisition of cleaning and security company ISS.

There are around a dozen overseas seats options (see page 532) for more details). "*They let us know a couple of months beforehand what overseas seats are available. When you rank your seat preferences you can also list where you want to go and what type of work you want to do.*" Where you end up can sometimes be a bit of a lottery – although language skills are taken into account. Singapore and Hong Kong are perennial favourites and in locations like that "*you are usually treated as something between an associate and a trainee. You get greater responsibility than in London.*"

Tudor Rose

NR is a firm with a strong after-hours culture and a bit of "*social flair*" to it. "*There are a few pubs which everyone flocks to on a Friday afternoon – sorry, Friday evening. The Bridge across the road is generally wall-to-wall Norton Rose. There are usually about 20 trainees there each Friday, sometimes more. And there have been times I stayed out drinking there until 3am.*" Some departments organise regular drinks events or outings to the theatre, bowling, quizzes or karaoke. NR is also a sporty firm with lots of teams to join. There is also a trainee social budget which no doubt contributes to the "*good trainee morale.*" We're told "*the trainees all get on very well and there is a real 'band of brothers' mentality.*" The past year's highlight was the Christmas party at the Tower of London – "*it was a good team bonding exercise,*" was all trainees would tell us. Although there is no obligation to attend events, "*it helps to be sociable. If people like you they are more inclined to give you work and help you get on. I think networking is important.*"

All our interviewees spoke positively about their supervisors and a standout feature of NR is its successful partner-mentor programme. "*Your mentor is an independent partner who you don't work with. I have always made the effort to go and chat with mine when I have an appraisal. During my overseas seats we exchanged e-mails about how I was doing. He is curious to know how things are going and is also available to talk if I am having any professional issues.*"

Many of our interviewees had also discussed qualification options with their mentor. The firm has pushed back the timing of the process: September qualifiers now apply in May and hear whether they have an NQ job in July. "*It allows you to take advantage of five or maybe even all six seats as potential areas to qualify into. The reaction has been generally positive, but there have been a few grumbles about the fact that the announcement will come quite late.*" Many of our sources had spoken openly with partners about their interest in qualifying into a particular department – often during appraisals. Because of this trainees "*get a sense of whether and where there will be a job for you before you find out for sure.*" A total of 36 of 46 qualifiers were kept on in 2012.

And finally...
Once again we feel obliged to praise NR for the attention it pays to trainees – especially through its mentoring programme – and we take note of its continuing global expansion. Keep an eye on the press for US merger news.

Olswang

The facts

Location: London, Reading
Number of UK partners/solicitors: 84/154
Partners who trained at firm: 5%
Total number of trainees: 36
Seats: 4x6 months
Alternative seats: Brussels, secondments
Extras: Pro bono – LawWorks, RCJ CAB; language classes

On chambersstudent.co.uk...
• How to get into Olswang
• CSR at the firm

You'll know Olswang for its media work, but don't arrive with stars in your eyes – corporate and litigation are the firm's big earners.

Let's push things forward

No-one would accuse Olswang of not moving with the times. Born media-nosed in Thatcher's golden years, it cemented its rep as legal indie during the swinging 90s. Surviving the dotcom bubble of the early 00s, Olswang has now come of age – but don't make the mistake of equating media with media law. *"The reality is that we advise clients who are in the media sector, which is a subtle difference,"* training principal Stephen Rosen told us. *"Ultimately we are full-service, with a corporate practice which is the largest part of our business. It's not that we're retrenching from media – we're not solely a media law firm, we're a firm with an emphasis on the media sector. We may be helping clients with their corporate matters, their disputes, outsourcings and commercial arrangements."*

The firm announced a 17% hike in revenue in 2011/12, part of which was put down to its flourishing international presence. Madrid, Paris, Munich and Singapore offices have opened in the past three years, adding to established ones in Brussels and Berlin. *"The sectors in which we operate aren't domestic markets, they're global,"* says Rosen. *"Tech, telecoms and media clients like Microsoft, the BBC, Vodafone, ITV and BSkyB by nature offer international exposure."* Trainees have been seconded to Paris and Brussels and there may be opportunities in other offices in the future. *"Not having a second language won't be a bar,"* says Rosen, *"but with increased international work, it'll always be a benefit."* There's also a changing roster of commercial secondments to media outfits.

Moving with the Radio Times

Incoming trainees spend time in corporate (*"a stint in pensions, tax or finance has very occasionally got people out of it"*) and will *"probably"* take a seat in commercial litigation. Other options include real estate, employment, IP, real estate litigation, commercial, construction, competition and MCT (media, communications and technology). Although *"aware there's an element of internal politics,"* our sources concurred that the HR team do a great job when it comes to allocation. Each trainee is allowed one *"hot seat"* as their priority over the two years. *"If there's a seat you're really keen on and you're happy to be put wherever for the other three, you will get it."* There's also an issue with doing two popular litigation seats if you've been placed there to begin with – starting in com lit, for example, may preclude spending subsequent time in employment, IP or real estate. The bottom line: a media seat is by no means guaranteed: accordingly, new intakes are recruited *"with increasingly diverse interests."*

A largely separate, smaller-scale training contract runs in Olswang's Reading office, usually taking around four of its own trainees to swap between real estate, commercial, employment and real estate litigation seats.

Many newbies start in corporate. The team's highly rated by *Chambers UK* for mid-market M&A transactions, like the £293m sale of Shine Group to News Corporation, or the sale of MoneySavingExpert.com to Moneysupermarket.com. The former deal is *"very typical of Olswang's corporate work."* There's a lot of asset transfer and a lot of private equity support across the media, tech and telecoms, retail and leisure sectors. Another

Chambers UK rankings

recent deal was BBC Worldwide's disposal of many of its magazines, including the Radio Times, to a private equity company for £115m. For trainees, there's "*the mundane Companies House admin stuff,*" combined with the ability to "*draft board minutes, research ad hoc points and participate in client meetings.*" Corporate hours are tough, so be prepared to "*come in on Wednesday and not leave the office until Thursday evening.*" There's a lot of camaraderie, though, and "*working with your peers makes it all far better.*" This trench spirit does mean that "*you have to be ready to take on work for other people at any time – for example if you were leaving at 8pm, you'd have to walk around the office and see what's going on first.*" Overall, if there's a natural overflow of grunt work, trainees find joy in "*the hugely interesting context of deals.*"

I'd like to thank the Academy...

Disputes in general commercial litigation will be "*between finance companies, broadcasters and suppliers or banking-related litigations.*" Olswang acted for ITV against STV (broadcaster of much of Channel 3 in Scotland) over disputes related to costs to run Channel 3 and sponsorship rights. Other clients include Microsoft and EMI, and with such high-value disputes, "*there's much bundling and pagination to do.*" It will be rewarding, though: "*It's a menial task, but vital that it's done properly – it's always alarming when you go to court and see the bundles you were in charge of being used by a judge.*" Further, there's "*always a good mixture of court-related work with the due diligence.*" Com lit's got a rep for "*being the most meritocratic department of all – people are extremely bright but super-nice, and partners readily get into debates with trainees.*"

Media litigation can be "*faster-paced, busier and slightly more interesting legally.*" The past twelve months have seen Olswang grace the news more often than Huw Edwards as work has moved from super-injunctions to the phone hacking scandal by way of lots of reputation management. Jeremy Clarkson instructed the team to get an injunction against his ex-wife, who was threatening to break the news that they had had an affair while he was with his current wife. The injunction was eventually dropped and the claims went public, but not before the case raised some serious questions about blackmail and privacy. Exciting stuff, and "*there's a great pleasure to be had in going to the pub and telling your mates that you can't tell them what you've been working on today – because there's an injunction on it.*" Legally, the work is just as fascinating. "*The area of law is still nascent and subject to a lot of development,*" said a source. "*Every week you're there, it's likely that you'll be asking a judge to make a new law.*" Equally, by nature the matters are "*small and self-contained. For the trainee, this means you get cerebral work and they'll push you as far as you can go. I drafted witness statements and court documents, spoke to chambers and lined up counsel.*"

MCT is a "*Rolls-Royce of departments.*" Depending on where they sit, this trainee can work on matters across gaming and gambling, telecoms, technology, outsourcing and digital work, in addition to the staple film and TV matters. The atmosphere tends to be "*more closed-door, in the sense that people just get on with their work.*" There's plenty of it, though, and "*of a brilliant standard.*" Olswang counts Disney, Sony, the BFI and Zodiak Pictures as long-standing clients. Recent flicks the group helped finance include *Hugo*, the new Bond *Skyfall*, and *The King's Speech* – the latter actually being exec-produced by former partner Lisbeth Savill. With clients like YouView, LoveFilm and LG on top of many notable players in the gaming world, it's evident the firm is embracing the digital age. Olswang married its expertise in publishing with the world of e-commerce and new technology when it advised JK Rowling's Pottermore on the imminent arrival of Harry Potter e-books.

Though it's perhaps not best known for real estate, it's worth remembering that this firm began as an offshoot of property-focused Brecher & Co, and acquired property teams from DJ Freeman and Julian Holy mid-noughties. Olswang squares up to Slaughters, A&O and Freshfields on big-ticket real estate work in the capital. And we mean big: the team recently led the sale on behalf of asset managers F&C REIT of St Katherine Docks for £165m. Clients include Legal & General, Royal Mail and Nationwide, and there's a lot of corporate crossover.

Preaching to the choir

In 2000, a two-years-qualified solicitor was made a partner in the tech group. For trainees, the bottom line is *"those who do well are those who do good work,"* and that it doesn't take a certain type of person to succeed here. *"Although people are pretty outgoing and gregarious, there's no particular type they want to keep on – different skills are recognised in different people."* There's an emphasis on being equipped with the tools to succeed, too. The firm *"chooses people who really enjoy the process of teaching – associate supervisors will review work and really aid the process of short-term development. Partners are unbelievably friendly and it's never uncomfortable talking to them."* One trainee's supervisor *"would just sit and ask me random legal questions during the day. They're very keyed in to helping you learn."*

"Friends at other firms can't believe how much social stuff we do." There's a plethora of activities beginning with the letter 'O' (or ending in 'wang') – 'O-Jam', 'The O-Factor', 'Goalswang', and very successfully, 'Ol-sang', a mixed choir, recently made the final of the national Office Choir of the Year contest (Norton Rose won). There's even a book group who meet once a month. *"Traditional sociability"* thrives alongside *"the many organised activities,"* said one trainee. *"I feel that if my day was filled with work it would be really depressing."* On top of monthly in-office drinks, *"it's common to go for a couple of beers with your department."* Rather than a homogeneous culture of after-work boozing, things are *"pretty relaxed. People like doing different things, probably because the firm picks out individuals rather than types."* There's also a strong CSR element to much of Olswang's socialising, plus plenty of opportunities for pro bono, *"especially in your first seat."*

For firms like Olswang that have rapidly developed their image and size, shifts in culture are normal. Although our interviewees all recognised there have been noticeable changes *"within the past year or two years,"* they were uniform in the sentiment that *"these are just necessary steps to survive in this market."* Said one: *"Five years ago, Olswang didn't know what it wanted to be. It was no longer the upstart media boutique of the 90s, and it was unsure if it was going to go down the corporate or the mid-market route, which was unsettling for people."* Now though, sources were clear that *"current focus is to maximise on our traditional reputation while at the same time lining ourselves up to be a broad commercial mid-sizer."*

Trainees see three noticeable products of this strategy. Firstly, *"corporate-style initiatives to increase time efficiency and profitability, like formal billable hours recording."* Secondly, a focus on international expansion, which is *"evidently a priority for the firm."* Thirdly, a change of emphasis in recruitment. Retention in both 2010 and 2011 hovered around the 60% mark – trainees said that those poor results were due to *"heavily media-focused"* intakes not wanting to stay on in other departments. Future intakes are likely to be less set on doing media work. We've noticed that although Olswang has been pushing a 'more than just media' message for a few years, some students have been slow to catch on. So note that there were no NQ jobs in MCT up for grabs in 2011, and only two in 2012. A total of nine of 14 qualifiers were retained in 2012, by the way.

Don't be disheartened if you're media hell-bent: it's still possible to access these departments, but do be aware that *"if you base an application purely on the desire to practise media, you may shoot yourself in the foot."* Equally, as the firm changes, beware of attempting to fit in with *"what people may think is Olswang-y. People think we're trendy and brash. Really, if you manage to click with your interviewers, you'll be fine. Everyone here is pretty laid-back."*

And finally...

Current trainees *"don't have experience of it being an indie upstart, but Olswang's still youthful and light-hearted in its culture, which comes from the top down. No matter what department you're in, this is a place where it's possible to flourish."*

Orrick Herrington & Sutcliffe (Europe) LLP

The facts

Location: London

Number of UK partners/solicitors: 17/34

Total number of trainees: 13

Seats: 4x6 months

Alternative seats: None

Extras: Pro bono – LawWorks, Toynbee Hall Legal

On chambersstudent.co.uk...
- How to get into Orrick
- Interview with training principal Simon Cockshutt

International work and a tiny London office are the defining features of this US operation.

Smoking Herrington

San Fran-founded Orrick has been expanding since the 1980s and now has 24 offices across North America, Asia and Europe. The firm landed in London in 1998 with a focus on structured finance, which, post-credit crunch, gave way to refinancing and litigation work. London's corporate group is now in expansion mode, and trainees see the firm's strategy as pretty forward-thinking. *"The things that you see other firms currently doing – downsizing and refocusing – has already happened. Now, we're seeing new partners coming on board and the firm positioning itself for the markets to pick up."*

Orrick picked up the London office of Coudert in 2005, so there remains a predominantly British vibe around the place. Trainees enjoy, however, that there's *"a US flavour to a lot of the work."* Training principal Simon Cockshutt clarified: *"The greater proportion of work in London is domestically generated, but that doesn't mean they are UK clients. It's often simply English corporate work or an English legal problem."*

Trainees don't choose their first seat, but after that state preferences from the options of corporate, finance, litigation, real estate, employment, IP and tax. A two-partner restructuring team defected to Dewey & LeBoeuf in 2011 (more fool them) to be replaced by a regulatory group which takes one trainee per rotation. *"The firm expects that you do a seat in either finance or corporate,"* explained a source.

Finance, finance and finance

The corporate department encompasses both public and private M&A, equity capital markets, *"which are fairly quiet at the moment,"* and a *"very busy"* venture capital practice, which deals with emerging blue-chip companies and is closely tied to Orrick's home group in Silicon Valley. The team recently advised French TV station Canal+ on its acquisition of a stake in N-Vision BV, owner of a Polish TV station. *"There's a high deal flow,"* explained one source, *"so trainees are expected to step up, get involved and contribute. There's a lot of client contact and a lot of drafting – even at more complex documents you get to take a stab at the first draft."* Trainees underline the point that there's always good work available if they want it: *"If you show initiative and don't make too many mistakes they will give you more responsibility – it's in your interests to perform."*

Finance is another seat split roughly between asset/project finance and capital markets and derivatives. Work is very specific even within these divides – *"it's very easy at law school to think finance is finance, but there's a huge difference even between asset and project."* Trainees on project finance often get to see the full life of a deal: *"The lenders invest money, and at each stage we ensure on their behalf that all the conditions have been filled."* This means a varied array of tasks, from *"research, to drafting agreements, to board minutes."* Securities predominantly involves drafting, although *"once you've done one, they tend to follow a pattern."* Trainees in the new regulatory team have a unique opportunity, both to *"focus on business development"* and to engage in pretty fundamental research. *"The level of work is so good because it often*

Chambers UK rankings

Private Equity	Social Housing

comes down to forming a view on what side of the regulatory fence you're on," explained one. "The answer often isn't that clear to partners either, so your job is to research but then have subsequent dialogue on what the law actually is."

Litigation has gone from two to six partners in the last year, so trainees now have access to specialists in arbitration, and in commercial and property litigation. "You're technically assigned to one partner but seeking work out is encouraged." Work can range from "drafting court orders and corresponding with the other side on minor property disputes, to running through hundreds of e-mails in a data room for multimillion-pound professional negligence claims." Arbitration work is cerebral and varied: "Clients will ask what the chances are of winning in a given scenario, and it's our job to predict." Competition is now part of the litigation group. With clients like Microsoft, Enron Coal and Levi on top of "the work being super-confidential," trainees aren't offered much client contact, but revel in the research-heavy work. "You might look into the Android market one day and the next be researching legal questions." Orrick advised on the competition aspects of Chinese food conglomerate Bright Foods, $2.36bn stake in French Yoplait.

Part of litigation, employment is a seat favoured by trainees for its contentious/non-contentious split and its reputation for "being a department that genuinely cares about its trainees." On the litigious side, work is varied – "liaising with chambers, going along to interview witnesses and being in on conference calls." Handling a different type of client is also a key part of the learning process. "If you're dealing with a banker in the finance department, they'll know an awful lot about their area. But when you're speaking to someone in HR on an employment matter, you'll have far more influence on the way things are going. There's far more problem solving, and with more emotions involved you have to be objective." The employment group acts for SC Johnson, BNP Paribas and Facebook.

Blood on the boardroom table

Orrick London is still partner-heavy. Simon Cockshutt told us: "We work in small, lean-ish teams and there's

scope for significant partner contact. We're not looking at commoditised work: we want to get interesting, innovative matters from high-quality clients. The nature of the work we consequently get is not lots and lots of boring document reviews, so we don't require trainees to sit in data rooms." Sources agree that responsibility is high, but equally that "being proactive helps get better work." For many, this equates to having a "mature" and "realistic" approach – supervision varies between departments, "the perception from some being that there's not enough in corporate." Because of the top-heavy structure and entrepreneurial culture, "the model is different. Trainees don't share offices with supervisors so we're not spoon-fed, and it's more about chatting to different people and seeing how they work."

The "incredibly glassy" London pad is on the top three floors of a building on Cheapside, "just down the road from St Paul's." Fee earners' offices line the outside of the building, "swanky" client suites are decked out with art and flat screen TVs, while trainees share rooms that surround a central atrium. This means "people can see your screen at all times," but also "with glass doors you can see if someone's busy or not if you want to ask them something." Sources think "it's nice to share a room with someone who's going through what you're going through, but there's also no substitute for hearing someone senior on a conference call." The firm has recently moved towards having trainees share with associates.

Pickled Herrington

Popular monthly drinks events take place in the client suites, while end-of-week attendance at local pub the Anthropologist is standard practice for many. There's a women's networking event – "even though there are more women than men here, it's good to have a conversation in a non-legal setting," thought one source. Some social events border on the criminal: "Some trainees organised a murder mystery where one partner had murdered another partner."

"The firm increased the size of its trainee intake with a view to doubling the office size," said one. "That obviously hasn't happened, and there's no attempt by the firm to address or mitigate the situation." Retention was disappointing in 2012: five of 11 took up NQ positions with Orrick – a fact due, says the firm, to the recession having gone on longer than anticipated.

And finally...
"It's a good proposition to be a small, growing office within an international firm – it's a healthy and a motivating environment to work in."

Osborne Clarke

The facts

Location: Bristol, London, Reading
Number of UK partners/solicitors: 96/122
Partners who trained at firm: 7%
Total number of trainees: 32
Seats: 4x6 months
Alternative seats: Secondments

On chambersstudent.co.uk...
- How to get into Osborne Clarke
- Postman's Park
- OC overseas

This once regional firm now has a "*pan-European scope*" and a well thought-out sector focus.

The OC

Osborne Clarke has a long and industrious history in Bristol (dating back to 1748!) and it set up shop in London before any other regional firm in 1987. It took advantage of the 90s dotcom boom by opening in Britain's answer to Silicon Valley – yes, that's the Thames Valley – before opening up in the Californian real McCoy. Since 2012, it has concentrated on four sectors: digital business; energy and utilities; financial services; and real estate and infrastructure. Training principal Nick Johnson asserts: "*The sector approach has really been working well for us. It's something that we have taken much further than other firms. It's about being selective, and saying no to some things – we've chosen our sectors and they are where we focus our energy.*"

Discriminating like this is central to OC's overall aim, which is to develop an in-depth industry knowledge that other firms will find it hard to compete with. Four more sectors will be added in the next few years: life sciences; infrastructure; automotive industries; and retail and recruitment. The firm is big in digital business, and "*we're building up that sector aggressively,*" says Johnson. Elsewhere, financial services work is "*kicking into action in the London market.*"

Broadly speaking, the Bristol office is full-service and is up there with that city's best firms; London has managed to take on a slice of mid-tier M&A and private equity work; while Reading is known for its technology focus. It's a danger to regard OC as simply a worthy Bristol player, but Johnson notes that "*the perception of us as being originally a Bristol-based firm is great in a way, and part of what is special about us. Bristol is very much a key part of our identity, and with Simmons & Simmons arriving in*

the city, I think that we're seeing the market come around to our way of thinking.*"

Osbuongiorno!

OC is also becoming increasingly international. The 'Osborne Clarke Alliance' – a joint venture with a group of foreign firms – is now history, but OC has officially merged with two of the former member firms: Italian outfit SLA Studio Legale Associato and a Spanish firm called, funnily enough, Osborne Clarke Spain. "*It's not a particularly auspicious time to be merging with an Italian or Spanish business,*" says Johnson, "*but these are highly profitable firms and we've known them for quite a while: it will change the outside perception of Osborne Clarke, as we'll go from just having three offices in the UK and two in Germany, to also having four in Italy and two in Spain.*" These latest additions join existing international offices in Silicon Valley and Germany.

Trainees were excited by these latest developments and spoke of potential international secondments and further European growth. "*If you look at Osborne Clarke,*" said one, "*you'll see that we're doing really well for a firm of our size. We're a mid-market firm trying to build up a European profile.*"

The days when it was compulsory to move around the offices are long gone. Trainees can still move between the offices, as long as they "*make out a good business case for doing so, and if there is the business need.*" Trainees are expected to complete one seat in corporate and one in property (or, in Bristol, tax). "*You are bound to get one of your top preferences for the other two seats,*" and "*you can occasionally do banking instead of corporate.*" The

Chambers UK rankings

Banking & Finance	Media & Entertainment
Banking Litigation	Pensions
Capital Markets	Pensions Litigation
Charities	Planning
Competition/European Law	Private Client
Construction	Private Equity
Corporate/M&A	Public Procurement
Data Protection	Real Estate
Dispute Resolution	Real Estate Litigation
Employee Share Schemes & Incentives	Restructuring/Insolvency
Employment	Retail
Environment	Tax
Information Technology	Telecommunications
Intellectual Property	Transport

firm "*certainly doesn't want to pigeon-hole you: it wants you to test the water and try different things.*" Employment, commercial and commercial litigation are especially popular. There is "*some difference in the mix of work the individual offices do, but it's not profound.*" All offices have some of the required seats available, and commercial litigation is present in each location. In Reading there are additional seats in employment or commercial (both with a technology slant). In London there's employment, recruitment and insolvency, while in Bristol trainees enjoy a broader selection including: employment; insolvency; banking; pensions; private client; construction; and incentives.

Digital love

Corporate is a "*key part of the firm.*" OC has been instructed by Carphone Warehouse, Talk Talk and energy services company MITIE. It recently represented Dentsu, a Japanese advertising group, on its acquisition of Steak Group, an international digital marketing business. Trainees get to have a "*first crack at anything that needs drafting,*" such as ancillary documents, and attend completion meetings and liaise with the other side to agree terms and conditions. "*Responsibility grows throughout the seat, the hours are not too bad, and there's a really good team atmosphere.*" The amount of public company work is expanding, and although many of the deals come from across all of OC's sectors, the firm has an especially good track record when it comes to M&A work connected to digital business.

Trainees can take seats in commercial property, residential property or planning. On the commercial side, "*clients tend to be big names and you get less involvement on those bigger deals.*" OC helped Marks & Spencer negotiate the terms of a lease for a new anchor store in Gloucester. On "*smaller, more discrete, matters you get your own files – you're given a long lead, but the lead is still there and you can't really sign anything off.*" Commercial property also comes with "*an awful lot of client contact*" and the chance to attend business development events. Residential property involves working for large house developers, and helping to "*draft transfer documents and the standard forms that go to the Land Registry, as well as going on site to look for potential issues, and completing general conveyancing – it's good fun.*" Planning exposes trainees to some "*really cutting-edge stuff, simply because of the rules by which planning is granted for large infrastructure projects. Not many firms are doing the kind of work we do, and it's very exciting.*" OC works for Associated British Ports in this respect, helping out on planning projects across all 21 of its UK ports, and dishing out advice on a new wind turbine manufacturing facility at the Port of Hull.

Tax is "*technical and challenging,*" but "*a good way to get to know others throughout the firm*" because many of the matters that crop up in tax are connected to the work conducted in other teams. The work is "*heavily research-based.*" Working with the property team to ascertain "*how much stamp duty should be paid*" is common, as is working alongside the incentives team to assist with "*the various incentive options and schemes that employees may have.*"

California scheming

Disputes in commercial litigation are generally complex and intricate. "*It's the nature of commercial litigation to spend most of your time working on a big case,*" said sources, "*but there are a few smaller ones that you can get stuck into and have a first stab at everything.*" Trainees can draft witness statements, claim forms, advice notes and offer letters, and conduct "*lots of research.*" Clients include the Co-operative Bank, Hewlett-Packard and Yahoo!. Significant cases of late include a $300m bondholder dispute related to the financing of a development in Russia. Trainees in London can specialise in IP litigation, which includes "*a lot of trade mark work: one client came in quite late in the day with a bunch of trade marks that hadn't been registered, and a number of issues had arisen out of that.*" Sources had also been involved in producing injunction applications, and liked the "*variety of pace – some matters go on for years and years, while some last for just a week.*"

"*It's a very cool and interesting seat,*" said interviewees of the commercial team. "*We have quite a few American clients, and work with a lot of start-ups.*" On the IP side, trainees help to register trade marks and work on data protection issues for some pretty big clients: Mitsubishi Pharma Europe, Penn Pharmaceuticals and Takeda, a global Japanese pharma company. As you can see from that list, quite a bit of business comes from the life sciences sector, a developing area for the firm. Telecoms lawyers have worked for the likes of Virgin Media and Vodafone, and assisted mobile network operator Everything Everywhere on a partnering agreement with Barclaycard. In IT, OC has represented Dell and Facebook, advising the former on an array of regulatory issues arising out of its Cloud Services offering.

Typical trainee tasks in employment include drafting redundancy letters and *"fairly substantial compromise agreements."* There's also a lot of advisory work to be done, and trainees help counsel clients regularly: *"Often you'll get an employer come to you and they'll ask, 'Does the law permit me to do this?' Then you'll have to analyse the law in connection to the specific situation. It can be quite challenging."* There can be an international edge to work here, and Bristol lawyers advise clients who are looking to set up shop in Europe via OC's office in Silicon Valley.

Secondment opportunities fluctuate, but in the past trainees have spent time at Motorola and News International. Johnson says that OC *"tries to be selective about secondments, as we get asked a lot for secondees. We usually say no to requests unless there will be a clear benefit for the trainee."*

On yer bike, Slick Rick!

"If you are someone who likes to be slick all the time then this isn't the place for you," said one trainee, adding: *"If you can't laugh at yourself then don't even bother applying."* Most of our sources concurred on this point, and enjoyed the open-plan layout of their offices – *"it helps to push away any old-school hierarchy"* – to the point that some sources started to sound rather competitive: *"The Reading office is VERY open-plan. Much more open-plan than it is in Bristol."* Trainees underscored the importance of *"technical excellence"* at the firm, explaining that the sector approach breeds a commitment to *"constantly building up and understanding industry knowledge in a culture dedicated to feedback and teaching."* Trainees are expected to be *"fearsomely bright,"* and attend regular sector meetings to keep their bank of industry expertise updated. A weekly newsletter, 'OC Confidential', also ensures that trainees are on top of the latest firm-wide developments.

The Bristol office, in the Temple Quay part of town, is *"like a vast spaceship, with lots of funky panels of glass everywhere – I remember being quite awestruck when I first saw it, as there's a marble-cast atrium which goes up four storeys."* The atrium is often home to the many social events that take place – *"any old excuse for drinks and nibbles really"* – and recently the Kenyan Olympic team (who just happened to be training in town) popped in for a networking event: *"It was odd because I heard drumming at six o'clock and suddenly I saw Kip Keino in the atrium – he's the coach of the team by the way"* (even more appropriately, the double Olympic gold medallist was made an honorary doctor of law by Bristol Uni in 2007). The atrium has also been utilised as an art gallery. Trainees spend their social budget on events including *"bowling, dinners, go-karting nights and rock climbing."*

Based at One London Wall, with *"DLA Piper above and below,"* perks of the City office include a *"wonderful balcony which overlooks St Paul's,"* and an ideal location between the Barbican and Moorgate. A few mumblings were heard last year about the lack of reputational weight in London, but trainees say that *"the office is expanding, and there has been a real push on the corporate and banking side of things."* Johnson says: *"There's more growth coming out of London than anywhere else. Despite only being in London for 25 years, we'll soon have more partners here than in Bristol, which will be an important moment for the firm."*

The Reading office has *"that intimate and close-knit family feel, but not so much of a strong after-work scene, as most of the staff drive to the office."* It is located at Apex Plaza, which was swanky in the 80s but now is *"not the most glamorous of spots,"* but conveniently placed next to the railway station. Socially, they are *"not divided or segregated: it's a real mix of partners, associates, NQs and trainees."*

The three offices try to operate as a single entity, and *"come together and rent a hotel somewhere along the M4 corridor, usually in Windsor or Wiltshire,"* for the annual summer party. There's always a fancy dress theme which *"people take very seriously,"* as well as a competitive softball match in which each member of the losing team is awarded *"a wooden spoon and a slap around the face. It's a great way to break the ice, but the Bristol lot always win as they're very much into their softball. They don't actually slap us in the face though – I was kidding about that."* This year's party was especially important, as members of the latest OC additions in Italy and Spain were invited over to mingle.

And finally...

Trainees were relieved that *"once the qualification process starts it's over ever so quickly – we all knew within about two weeks."* There were more vacancies than there were candidates in 2012, and ten out of 13 qualifiers stayed with the firm.

Pannone LLP

The facts

Location: Manchester, London

Number of UK partners/solicitors: 71/125

Partners who trained at firm: 27%

Total number of trainees: 28

Seats: 4x6 months

Alternative seats: Secondments

Extras: Pro bono – Manchester University and Manchester Metropolitan University Legal Advice Centres

On chambersstudent.co.uk...

- How to get into Pannone
- Interview with training partner Andrea Cohen
- Clinical negligence and personal injury work

A North West powerhouse with leading personal injury and negligence divisions, Pannone continues to provide an excellent service for trainees and clients alike.

It's pronounced pan-OH-nay

Operating primarily from its Manchester office, Pannone is firmly established as one of the North West's leading firms, providing a full service to corporate, public sector and private clients throughout the UK and internationally. Noteworthy clients include Kellogg, L'Oréal, Manchester City Council, the Isle of Man government and the brilliantly titled Wasabi Frog – more commonly known by its trading name boohoo.com.

Pannone rebranded and refocused in 2011 – that involved a complete internal restructure along with a jazzy new website and corporate logo. The firm is now split into five practice divisions. These are corporate services; dispute resolution and regulatory; 'affinity solutions'; personal injury and medical negligence; and family, personal and financial. *"Our focus in 2012 has been building on the rebrand and continuing to reinforce our message: 'Energy and excellence in all we do',"* training partner Andrea Cohen explained. *"In basic terms this means providing our clients with the best service we can and maintaining our position at the top of the North West region."* Two small satellite offices in Hale and Alderley Edge were closed this year (at the cost of some jobs) as the Manchester HQ covered the work they were doing.

The restructuring has brought with it a slightly more national outlook. The firm is looking more towards London, where an office opened in 2010. Cohen explained that the increased presence in the capital came as a result of the *"high demand for our regulatory prac-*

tice there," and the office now has more practices including clin neg, serious injury and corporate. Will it begin to rival its sole remaining Northern counterpart? *"I can't see that happening,"* said Cohen. *"We're very much a Manchester firm and we want it to stay that way."* The firm's work in ground-breaking clinical negligence and personal injury cases sees it consistently top-ranked in the North West by *Chambers UK*. However, Cohen stressed: *"Pannone has always had a solid PI and clinical negligence base and we continue to have a strong reputation for this type of work. The fact is, though, that our business is more or less equally divided between private client and commercial work."*

If you would like to take your seats

The departments which trainees can choose from are: corporate and commercial; real estate; dispute resolution; employment; regulatory; personal injury; clinical negligence; family law; wills, trusts and probate; court of protection; construction; and corporate recovery. The seat allocation process was described by trainees as being *"as fair as it can be,"* with *"people's wishes catered to as available."* Trainees give their three departmental preferences to the training partner at the start of their contracts and at each mid-seat review – there's no onus on them to prove why they want to be placed somewhere. Split seats are also on offer, which was said to be *"useful if you want to experience another area of law."*

Although by no means compulsory, nearly all trainees do spend some time in either the personal injury or clinical

Chambers UK rankings

Banking & Finance	Fraud
Clinical Negligence	Information Technology
Competition/European Law	Intellectual Property
Construction	Local Government
Corporate Crime & Investigations	Partnership
Corporate/M&A	Personal Injury
Court of Protection	Private Client
Dispute Resolution	Real Estate
Employment	Real Estate Litigation
Environment	Restructuring/Insolvency
Family/Matrimonial	Travel

negligence departments. Specialist areas in PI include catastrophic injury, industrial disease and travel injuries. Trainees spoke of being given "*lots of responsibility*" and "*plenty of client contact*" in this seat. Day to day, there are "*lots of tasks like drafting and obtaining witness statements*" to occupy trainees, but also opportunities to "*undertake case management conferences, attend court hearings and visit clients.*" As their time in the department lengthened, sources reported holding client meetings by themselves on several small-value matters. Advocacy experience is also available here. "*It wasn't rocket science, usually just smaller applications in court,*" said one interviewee, "*but it was good to have the experience.*" With the department being very busy at the moment, trainees are "*expected to get up to speed quickly.*" Sources spoke of "*effectively running caseloads under close supervision. Supervisors will place a lot of trust in you, but also offer as much help as you want or need.*"

The PI team is known for taking on many high-profile and cutting-edge cases – for example, representing the victims of John Worboys, the Black Cab Rapist. The case raised the unprecedented legal question of whether motor insurers are liable not just for injuries caused by road accidents but also for harm resulting from deliberate criminal acts in which a vehicle plays an important part. The department has also acted for the family of Luke Molnar, a gap year student fatally electrocuted in Fiji, as well as recently winning high-value settlements in landmark mesothelioma claims.

Lawyers in the clinical negligence department work closely with their PI counterparts, and trainee experiences were similar in each. They "*assist seniors with all aspects of claims: taking witness statements, attending client meetings, writing up notes, applying for legal aid funding and drafting all court documents as required.*" General client exposure is frequent and the opportunity to man the new-case call line allows trainees to be "*the first point of contact for potential new clients.*" Sources reported being

really involved in a variety of high and low-value cases. "*The work you do feels important,*" said one. "*It's not just doing research for research's sake.*" Supervisors were said to be "*good at judging what you can and can't do, so responsibilities tend to increase as you get more confident.*" Trainees were undoubtedly impressed by their seniors in the department. One second-year said: "*You feel like you're working for the best clinical negligence team in the country.*"

Due the nature of the work the clin neg team often takes on controversial and challenging cases. A notable example is the case of *Rabone v Pennine Care NHS Trust*, where Pannone represented the parents of a girl who argued the trust negligently allowed their daughter to relinquish herself from its care, prompting her subsequent suicide.

Pannone is more than just a PI and clin neg firm, though. Its family department is highly ranked in the North West by *Chambers UK* and trainees say it's the "*perfect learning ground because it's such a well-organised department.*" There is almost constant client contact from the start, with the chance to "*attend client meetings and visit clients in their homes.*" Sources said a lot of drafting is commonplace but so are the opportunities to attend court alone and partake in basic advocacy.

Footballers' dads

Those who'd prefer to steer clear of private client work are well catered for. The corporate department at Pannone is also Chambers-ranked; however, trainees viewed their time as "*certainly less hands-on in terms of client contact. If I was contacting clients it was usually just through e-mail and only to collect contracts,*" said one second-year. On the plus side, trainees were impressed with the variety of matters they could experience. There are opportunities to sample commercial, M&A, banking and IPO work. The department has an international client base, including the American payday loan company Advance America, and the FTSE 100-listed Intertek Group.

Trainees visiting the dispute resolution seat can expect their time to be "*very hands-on.*" However, this can sometimes prove a double-edged sword. "*On the one hand, you get a lot of responsibility. Supervisors are happy to let you run on your own. But I've found the support has not been quite as good,*" said one source. Due to the nature of the work trainees spoke of "*slightly longer hours*" compared to other departments, with specialist areas varying from commercial litigation to IP. Advocacy experience is par for the course, with sources reporting "*going to court for bankruptcy hearings.*" The firm has a reputation for taking on 'big-ticket' litigation and has acted on the fallout of several high-profile disasters, including the Lockerbie bombing and the Bradford City FC fire.

Pannone's regulatory team deals with a range of issues from fraud to general crime. Recently they represented Wayne Rooney's father – Wayne Snr – as he was cleared of alleged involvement in suspected betting irregularities surrounding a Scottish Premier League match.

Trainees were overwhelmingly positive about their time at Pannone but one recurring complaint from second-year sources was the lack of clarity and communication regarding the end of their training contracts. *"There's no jobs list and we're not really made aware of any NQ positions,"* grumbled sources. Many felt they had been left *"in limbo."* Cohen responded: *"If I was a trainee obviously I'd rather know one way or the other. Often we can say: 'Yes you are the right calibre of person we're looking for, but we need to know what the climate is nearer the time.' We always make every effort to keep on all our trainees but we suggest they be prepared and send off applications elsewhere because obviously we can't always keep everyone on."* Retention rates were poor both in 2010 and 2011; despite this, trainees were generally optimistic about their prospects. *"In the past if trainees haven't been kept on then they do tend to get jobs in firms elsewhere in Manchester. Working at Pannone is something you can be proud to have on your CV."* In 2012, nine out of 12 second-years did remain at the firm upon qualification.

Sunday best

Getting a training contract at Pannone does not precede a slip into the social wilderness. *"It sounds a bit of a cliché but they really do value a work/life balance here,"* sources told us. We heard an average working day is 8.30am to 6pm, although this varies slightly between departments. Don't expect to be draining the coffee pot to make it through the night though. Not one of our interviewees had stayed until the early hours and they stressed that *"you're not expected to sit at your desk looking busy if you haven't got any work to do."*

With offices located on bustling Deansgate in the centre of Manchester and just moments from the striking Spinningfields retail and business development, the social life at Pannone is perhaps unavoidably active. Aside from the firm-wide payday drinks sessions, we were told of ski trips to Scotland, outings to Chester Zoo, an array of sports teams and even the chance to take advantage of corporate seats at the MEN Arena. Trainees have Christmas and summer balls, while close ties with the Manchester Trainee Solicitors Group provide plenty more opportunities to don the glad rags. The office building itself was described as *"a bit 80s"*; however, a move to a new city centre location is hoped for in the next few years.

Our sources were keen to emphasise the real family feel at the firm, fostered by little touches such as 4pm birthday finishes and employee of the month awards. *"Everyone looks out for each other. People tend to get on across the board; there's certainly no 'them and us' culture,"* one trainee told us.

We asked our interviewees what sorts of people tend to work at Pannone and the emphatic response was *"Pannone people!"* Yeah, very helpful, thanks guys. What is a Pannone person? *"I think there's a perception that you have to be over-the-top friendly to work here,"* one source mused, perhaps recalling Pannone's long stint as the top law firm on the *Sunday Times'* '100 Best Companies to Work For' charts (it has since stopped entering the annual survey). *"But really, as long as you're down to earth, can hold a conversation and work hard you'll do just fine."* A tangible connection to the North West will also serve you well.

And finally...
Trainees were overwhelmingly positive about their time at Pannone. The firm skilfully combines high-calibre training with its renowned friendliness.

Paul Hastings (Europe) LLP

The facts

Location: London

Number of UK partners/solicitors: 18/30 (+11 US-qualified)

Total number of trainees: 5

Seats: 4x6 months

Alternative seats: Secondments

Extras: Pro bono – LawWorks

On chambersstudent.co.uk...
- How to get into Paul Hastings
- Paul Hastings' global strategy

The London office of this US firm is a small but mighty finance powerhouse.

Long way from LA

From its not-so-humble LA beginnings in 1951, Paul Hastings travelled gradually eastwards, opening offices in the OC, DC, New York and Tokyo before landing in London in the late 90s. PH is one of the top 25 US law firms but is still small in London when compared to other US firms. Its *Chambers UK* rankings come in structured finance, real estate finance and restructuring/insolvency. So, as you can tell, a training contract here will have a strong finance flavour. It's advised on some weighty deals, working for Deutsche Bank on the first commercial mortgage-backed securities (CMBS) issuance in Europe since the financial markets took a plunge in 2007. The firm's London and Hong Kong offices are also advising on SAMSUNG's £198m acquisition of Brit company CSR's smartphone development business.

PH is notably strong in Asia, and plans to open its doors in Seoul when that market opens up to international firms. In a recent article in *The Lawyer*, PH chairman Seth Zachary touched on plans to expand further in London and Germany, renewing the firm's focus on Europe. Trainees predict the City office will flourish: "*I think the London strategy is to consolidate the great team we have at the moment, to hone the expertise we have and upping the ante in that respect.*"

It's a small world after all

"*Paul Hastings takes a very small number of trainees*" so this is a pretty intimate training contract. The seats on offer are capital markets, real estate, general finance, litigation, restructuring, corporate funds, corporate M&A, tax and real estate finance. A few months before each rotation, trainees hand in their top three preferences "*and*

the HR team does try to cater to those. You also have to bear in mind that a specific partner might request you.*" At PH, the "*beauty of the training contract is that you aren't just limited to one seat in any one six-month period. You could be in capital markets, doing some work with the litigation team. So you aren't bogged down by your preferences – you are able to go and get work from elsewhere.*"

"*There is a distinction between capital markets funds and commercial mortgage-backed securities*" in the capital markets department. "*There is also a lot of servicing work, advising servicers of their rights and obligations. It's been quite busy.*" PH advised Deutsche Bank on a £210m CMBS loan backed by the £1bn Westfield Merry Hill Shopping Centre. "*Securitisations are complex and niche – I certainly didn't know much before I started and that inevitably limited my participation, which is fine, I think,*" one source said. The complicated nature of work doesn't allow trainees to be involved in many client meetings or conference calls. Routine tasks include working on "*documents associated with CMBS transactions*" and on doc reviews, drafting letters and notices to the markets, and helping on closings. "*I also worked on a bit of restructuring, with Capita and Hatfield Philips, both major EU servicers. I advised on different types of loans and when loans go into default,*" added one source. There are long nights in the office, "*but if you're there late, the team is also there late, all working and putting hours in together.*"

In the real estate department, "*you'll draft shareholder board agreements, construction advisory agreements and board minutes.*" Trainees will also take on due diligence, man data rooms and respond to buyers' inquiries. The

Chambers UK rankings

Capital Markets

Real Estate Finance

Restructuring/Insolvency

team represented a real estate fund managed by Apollo Global Management in a joint venture to acquire a data-centre on Great Sutton Street (near Old Street) in London.

Working the room

"The corporate department usually does M&A and general corporate advisory work, though recently we've been doing more private equity." PH recently represented Monitise, a mobile banking technology and services provider, on its £109m acquisition of Clairmail. Our sources had encountered *"an acquisition of various EU servicing businesses, split across five different jurisdictions. It was a complete acquisition, and took several months to do."* Trainees had received *"a lot of responsibility, liaising with foreign counsel, reviewing documents"* and *"doing plenty of good drafting."* Happy juniors also reported *"a lot of client contact, even though most of it is over the phone,"* and had been invited to *"business development and networking events."*

Although the London office is small, trainees *"do a lot of financing work with the other US offices"* and *"funds work with a lot of the Asia offices. It's unusual for a transaction to not have an international element."* This lends to the *"one-firm feel, regardless of whether the other person is in Paris or New York."* The culture of *"helping out other offices, even if it's proof-reading memos, makes for a good relationship."*

Trainees spoke of frequent client secondments to Hatfield Philips and Credit Suisse. In the latter, *"at one of our biggest clients,"* the secondee *"works as part of the legal team in the funds-linked products group."* It's a valuable experience, as *"you have to find a balance, working with senior traders and the legal department."* The in-house training Paul Hastings provides used to be *"initially quite US-centric. This was highlighted in a training meeting*

and since then it's improved massively. There is a good training schedule that's just for London now."

Coffee, coffee, COFFEE!

Our sources found it refreshing that *"the firm is a bit more interested in personality than academic credentials."* That said, our sources had come from Russell Group universities. *"People are relaxed but ambitious and very, very bright. You can't take advantage of that friendliness – they are supportive but won't let you slack off."* Though *"hard work doesn't go unnoticed,"* one junior advised: *"I definitely wouldn't apply here if you weren't up for the challenge. You have to be constantly on the go, constantly learning."* Do be warned, *"if you sign up for a training contract at Paul Hastings, you should know you're signing up for some crazy hours. Don't delude yourself."* How crazy is crazy? *"In my current seat probably I work until midnight quite often, I'd say. I've never had the situation where I am free early... when we're quieter and have time I might be catching up with pro bono work, or working on know-how articles to send out to clients."* Fortunately, the financial rewards help make up for the heavy workload. As is typical of US firms, Paul Hastings pays trainees one of the more *"generous"* salaries in the City, starting at £88,000. All four qualifiers were retained by the firm in 2012.

Located just behind Allen & Overy, Paul Hastings' London office sports a *"modern decor but nothing too outrageous."* With Spitalfields *"just below, there are millions of places to eat and drink,"* making up for the lack of a canteen. Trainees keep their motors running on *"endless amounts of coffee – we've got good espresso machines."* On Fridays *"a drinks trolley comes around and there's a ping-pong table set up in the conference room."* We hear partners get *"quite involved"* and there are some *"competitive characters in the office."* Trainees promise they don't just let the partners win (*"he was just better than me!"*). PH has a *"generous"* trainee social budget to enable them *"to get together and catch up. We've done wine tastings, cocktail-making classes or just gone out for dinner."* The firm hosted a Bollywood-themed Christmas party, and at the time of our calls, trainees were looking forward to a partner-led pub quiz.

And finally...

This training contract is one for people looking for the *"hardcore"* experience. But *"despite having the long hours, I've really enjoyed my training contract. It's been stressful sometimes, but those are the moments when you're actually really learning."*

Penningtons Solicitors LLP

The facts

Location: Basingstoke, Cambridge, Godalming, Guildford, London

Number of UK partners/solicitors: 71/87

Partners who trained at firm: 30%

Total number of trainees: 21

Seats: 4x6 months

Alternative seats: Occasional secondments

Extras: Pro bono – LawWorks

On chambersstudent.co.uk...

- How to get into Penningtons
- Interview with chief exec David Raine and business development director Rolland Keane

South-Eastern firm Penningtons' combo of commercial and private client work means there's a variety of seats for trainees to get their hands on.

Home counties ascent

"It's been a year of ongoing integration," Penningtons' chief executive David Raine tells us, reflecting on the consequences of spring 2011 mergers with bite-size City practice Wedlake Saint and struggling Lincoln's Inn firm Dawsons. In addition to padding out Penningtons' London presence and adding some firepower to its private client bill, the mergers also provided a platform for expansion: in March 2012 the firm launched new offices in Guildford and Cambridge. The former complements Penningtons' existing Godalming base – which has *"outgrown its accommodation,"* according to business development director Rolland Keane – while the latter is a move to foster the firm's growing expertise in the technology and education sectors. *"In time we'd like to service other work out of Cambridge as well,"* Raine adds.

The recession was not easy on Penningtons, which suffered trainee deferrals and frozen salaries as a result of the downturn. However, it's safe to say things are looking much brighter for the firm, which not only clung to its spot in the UK top 100 but recorded a whopping 34% rise in revenue in 2011/12 (largely due to those mergers). *"There's a lot of energy at the moment,"* trainees reported, adding that *"any sense of doom and gloom is long gone."* As one elaborated: *"The fact that we're expanding can only be a good thing. There's an encroaching entrepreneurial feel, a sense that we're developing our client base and increasing our expertise. It's quite exciting to witness."*

Penningtons' *"mix of corporate/commercial and people-based work is a real attraction – some days you're work-ing with publicly listed companies, and others for Joe Bloggs around the corner,"* sources said. Like ancient Gaul, the firm is divided into three parts. Unlike ancient Gaul, those parts are business services, commercial real estate and private individual divisions. Divisions aren't restricted to any one office, and particular sectors are cross-divisional, so interoffice interaction is frequent.

Taking care of business

At the time of our interviews, there were 11 trainees beavering away in London, five in Basingstoke and another five in Godalming. Despite the firm's London origins, sources insist that regional offices *"aren't outposts or in any way secondary to the City office."* As Rolland Keane points out, this represents *"a very different dynamic from some firms, where London is clearly the mothership. There's no sense here that a single office dictates terms for the rest of the firm."* Said one trainee: *"It's nice to know that if I stay with the firm, there's the scope to move out of London and still be considered equally important within the firm."*

Trainees typically visit all of Penningtons' three divisions during their training contract, gaining a mix of commercial and private client work. In London, seats in commercial dispute resolution, immigration, employment, private client, commercial real estate, corporate and professional regulation are up for grabs, plus a newly minted clinical negligence seat. In Basingstoke, corporate, private client, clinical negligence, employment and commercial real estate are on the menu, while Godalming offers nearly the same selection, swapping employment for travel – *"effec-*

Chambers UK rankings

Clinical Negligence	Private Client
Corporate/M&A	Professional Discipline
Employment	Real Estate
Family/Matrimonial	Real Estate Litigation
Immigration	Social Housing
Partnership	Tax
Personal Injury	Travel

tively personal injury abroad." Because Godalming's corporate, employment and commercial real estate teams have relocated to the new premises in Guildford – "*just an eight-minute train ride from the office*" – trainees in Surrey can now expect to split their time between the two offices. When it comes to seat allocation, the HR team "*works incredibly hard to keep everybody happy.*" Trainees list their preferences before each seat and "*discuss it among ourselves to see where people are hoping to go.*" The system is flexible, with trainees given the possibility of repeating or splitting a seat, or even swapping with someone in another office.

Penningtons' business services division accounts for a hefty chunk of its revenue. Thanks to the wide spread of services and sectors covered, clients range from individual shareholders to large private companies, and trainees get "*the opportunity to do some commercial and tax work as well as traditional transactional work.*" The corporate team has spent the last year focusing on the education and technology sectors, nabbing some major client wins in each, and has seen an increase in corporate finance work for overseas clients. According to trainees, a seat here is "*academically challenging – there's not a lot of photocopying.*" Sources reported drafting board minutes, preparing documents, assisting with engagement letters and managing their own small transactions by the end. "*There's not much you're not involved in. Every Monday, corporate team members across offices have a live video meeting, so you feel very much part of the team.*" On the commercial side, the firm's IP group handles portfolios for names such as Levi Roots' Reggae Reggae Sauce and the American Institute of Foreign Studies, advising on trade mark issues such as domain name disputes and infringements on eBay. A stint in the commercial dispute resolution team offers "*really good exposure to the whole process – I handled a number of debt claims by myself and was able to meet the clients, attend court and instruct counsel the whole way through,*" one source reported.

London's immigration team is well respected, particularly on the business immigration side. The government's recent changes to the UK points-based immigration system have ushered in a wave of new business. The team has kept busy advising tier 2, 4 and 5 sponsors – which include businesses and universities – on retaining sponsorship licences and acting for foreign investors and entrepreneurs coming to work in the UK. This "*mixture of business and people-based work*" lends itself to an interesting variety of tasks for trainees, who assist on visa and work permit applications and undertake "*a lot of research regarding recent changes to the law.*"

A slice of the PI

Penningtons' private client practice has bulked up considerably since the mergers with Dawsons and Wedlake, both of which had a strong reputation in the field. "*Suddenly, there were twice as many partners and twice as much work. They brought with them some different types of matters, too, like international work for high net worth individuals,*" recalled one source. While pockets of specific work can be found in each office – Basingstoke and Godalming shoulder most of the Court of Protection cases while London tends to focus on international and more complex domestic issues – the department handles a range of issues across its offices, including trusts, estate planning, tax, family, immigration, employment and property matters. As such, trainees are privy to a mixed bag of work. "*Some days you're drafting wills or preparing Lasting Powers of Attorney; others you do research tasks and help with trust management.*" While "*trainees aren't let loose entirely,*" our sources reported a hearty dose of client contact. "*You're usually dealing straight with the individual as opposed to insurers or other people in the middle, so you quickly develop a close working relationship.*"

PI and clin neg is another "*very person-based*" department for which Penningtons has a solid reputation, particularly in the South East. The team, which is based in Godalming but also operates out of other offices, works on complex personal injury claims. "*It could be a misdiagnosis or an accident or a cosmetic surgery gone wrong,*" sources told us. "*You end up doing a lot of research into medical matters, which can get pretty interesting.*" While the majority of cases are kept under wraps, the firm's handled a few that have made it into the papers in recent years, including several claims concerning adverse reactions to swine flu drug Tamiflu. In addition to dealing with legal aid applications, trainees can expect to draft claims forms, witness statements and instructions to counsel. "*Taking enquiries is a big part – we have to interview prospective new clients and consider the legal claims that could be made from their situation.*"

Penningtons' real estate division is broad, and includes banking and finance and construction alongside property litigation, projects and infrastructure, property tax, social housing and (thanks to the Dawsons merger) property investors. The firm recently advised investment company Redicent on the sale of a major government building in Westminster, and acted for Aviva Investors on its £30m supermarket acquisition. Other clients include dairy and livestock supplier National Milk Records, Thames Valley Housing Association and banking giant Santander. Most trainees sit in commercial real estate at some point. Interviewees reported involvement in everything from "*leases for small shops*" to "*sales of multimillion-pound buildings in London – you can experience some very different work across the different subteams.*" More "*routine assignments like completing Land Registry applications and proof-reading large banking documents*" are balanced with "*a fair number of meaty tasks like drafting leases and deeds.*" Those with experience on the residential side mentioned running their own transactions and attending a fair few client meetings – "*it turns out people like to see the lawyers who are selling their houses.*"

Out and about

"*There's something to be said for the work/life balance at Penningtons,*" mused one trainee, praising the firm for its "*practical*" approach to hours. "*You're only expected to hang around when there's work to be done, and the working culture is such that it's rare to be here past 7pm.*" Indeed, an average day sees trainees across offices, including those in London, clock out by 6.30pm, with few ever staying later than 8.30pm. "*Here in Godalming, you have to write your name on a whiteboard if you stay past six so you don't get locked in by the cleaners – that says it all! There's a real ethic of people questioning why you're in the office past seven... that is, if they're in the office themselves.*" Though lawyers' interests outside of work vary, trainees agreed "*there's a sense people work here to earn a living, not to make it their whole life.*"

Thanks to Penningtons' smallish size, the offices retain a palpable "*sense of intimacy,*" according to our sources. "*Even in the London office you know everybody's name.*" Sources credited the firm's open plan set-up with reducing the sense of hierarchy within the office. "*You never feel intimidated by having to knock on a partner's door to ask a question because you're already sitting near them. Being able to hear everyone's phone going lends a real buzz to the atmosphere – you're aware of everything going on around you, so you feel that much more involved.*" While the firm's recent growth is accompanied by a perceptible "*entrepreneurial push*" throughout the firm, trainees are confident the chummy atmosphere will survive any and all changes. "*Penningtons wants to become more dynamic, but not to the jeopardy of its culture or people,*" one said.

Each office has its own sports and social committee in charge of organising get-togethers. Trainees in London reported karaoke outings and pub quizzes, while those in Godalming spoke of curry nights, cinema trips and a particularly memorable "*quiz night at the town hall with a fish and chip supper beforehand.*" Basingstoke is "*perhaps the least social of the offices,*" but trainees assured us they "*still do a lot when possible,*" mentioning a recent trip to the local theatre. Then there's Trainee Thursday, a once-a-month affair in which trainees across offices travel to London or Basingstoke for a training session followed by drinks or seasonal outings such as ice skating at Christmas. Additionally, there are departmental Christmas parties and two firm-wide events each year. The first, an annual sports day, sees everyone gather in Godalming for a barbecue and bean-bag races. The other's an office-wide spring party.

And finally...

With the possibility of further expansion on the horizon, Penningtons is one to watch. Current trainees anticipate "*a lot of good opportunities coming our way,*" including the prospect of higher salaries and a more extensive seat selection. In 2012, seven out of 12 qualifiers were kept on as NQs.

Pinsent Masons

The facts

Location: London, Birmingham, Manchester, Leeds, Bristol, Scotland

Number of UK partners/solicitors: 325/315

Partners who trained at firm: c.28%

Total number of trainees: 185

Seats: 4x6 months

Alternative seats: Overseas seats, secondments

Extras: Pro bono – Goldman Sachs 10,000 Small Businesses, A4ID and others

On chambersstudent.co.uk...
- How to get into Pinsent Masons
- All about McGrigors

Fresh off the back of a merger with McGrigors, Pinsent Masons is looking to boost its prospects in the City and beyond.

Bigger Mac

London-headquartered Pinsent Masons' mid-2012 merger with Scottish outfit McGrigors is big news at the firm. It now has more than 1,500 lawyers spread over 15 offices around the UK, Asia and the Gulf. *"It's been our biggest highlight this year because we've achieved a huge amount in a short period of time – most of our people are in offices together and are now working side by side. We've also worked hard to integrate our NQ recruitment and vacation scheme processes to ensure we get the best of both,"* new head of graduate recruitment Deborah McCormack told us. Legacy trainees from each firm chattered on for yonks about the combination, offering nods to the *"many improvements"* like beefed-up departments and increased opportunities for overseas seats. More on that later; for now, let's talk image – specifically, how the firm is seen at the moment and where it wants to go. *"It's no secret the firm's always wanted to have a strong London office,"* trainees told us, echoing comments we heard last year regarding a *"perceptible focus on upping our status in the City."* Moreover, *"there's a big emphasis"* being placed on increasing PM's international presence. Indeed, *"we've just opened a new office in Munich, with a Paris office scheduled to open in the autumn. Our Doha office consolidates our presence in the Gulf. It's all part of our 2020 vision, which involves a commitment to international growth,"* McCormack revealed.

PM's solid network of UK offices clocks up well over 100 rankings in *Chambers UK*. Trainees in past years have emphasised the firm's weighty construction team – one of the biggest and best in the UK – but the recent merger has boosted PM's profile in other areas, like tax. *"It's one of the few areas for which McGrigors had the bigger team. Our practice has substantially grown in size,"* insiders said. *"We've now become one of the top tax teams in the UK, so if you're trying to capture a snapshot of where the firm's strengths lie, this is an important change to note."* Noted.

Super seven

London welcomed a slew of legacy McGrigors trainees after the merger, boosting its total trainee ranks to 60 at the time of our interviews. Birmingham, meanwhile, had 24, Leeds 23 and Manchester 15. There's also a handful of trainees in Belfast and a considerable number in Scotland, areas which we don't cover here. Trainees tend to stick to their home offices, though cross-office collaboration is becoming more frequent. *"It's not uncommon to get an e-mail from someone in Edinburgh asking if anyone has a spare few hours to help them out on a bit of work,"* testified one Leeds trainee. *"It's all part of everyone trying to get to know each other better and ascertain which teams have strengthened."*

Pinsents now has seven official core practice groups: construction advisory disputes; corporate; financial institutions and human capital; litigation and compliance; projects; property; and strategic business services. Within each are several seat options. Seat allocation is *"fairly transparent,"* with trainees submitting three choices each rotation. *"You get a presentation from each group upon starting so you can make an informed choice."* While most were happy with what they got, trainees on the

Chambers UK rankings

Administrative & Public Law	Licensing
Banking & Finance	Life Sciences
Capital Markets	Local Government
Charities	Media & Entertainment
Competition/European Law	Outsourcing
Construction	Parliamentary & Public Affairs
Corporate Crime & Investigations	Partnership
Corporate/M&A	Pensions
Data Protection	Planning
Dispute Resolution	Private Client
Education	Private Equity
Employee Share Schemes & Incentives	Professional Negligence
Employment	Projects
Energy & Natural Resources	Public Procurement
Environment	Real Estate
Fraud	Real Estate Litigation
Health & Safety	Restructuring/Insolvency
Healthcare	Retail
Information Technology	Shipping
Insurance	Social Housing
Intellectual Property	Tax
	Transport

whole conceded that *"because we're such a big firm, you have to be flexible when it comes to allocation – business needs occasionally take precedence over your choice, and you have to appreciate that."* We did hear a few grumbles about people being *"railroaded into certain areas that didn't have enough trainees"* and grad development proving *"difficult to get hold of if you're in certain offices,"* but most agreed *"any issues here would be present at other firms our size."*

High-powered projects

PM's a big player in the construction arena. The practice – home to a whopping 183 lawyers – handles both advisory and contentious matters, and has worked with high-profile clients including Thames Water, The London School of Economics, and Westfield Shoppingtowns. Lawyers act for contractors on projects in emerging markets like Yemen, Saudi Arabia and Qatar, and for purchasers on big-ticket projects like Wembley Stadium and the new safety confinement at the old Chernobyl nuclear site. Those seeking disputes work head to the construction litigation team, where they get *"involved in every aspect of the cases – drafting witness statements, piecing together documents, attending mediations and hearings."* The only downside to a construction stint is *"there's not too much client contact, because the clients are so massive."*

Corporate is another area to head to *"if you're interested in international work."* Like construction, *"it's very trainee-hungry at the moment."* In London, there's a big focus on corporate finance transactions and commodities work, as well as energy matters like GB Oils' acquisition of Severn Fuels and Production Lubricants. Outside the City it's all about private equity and plc advisory work plus a few commercial deals here and there – the Brum team recently advised on a joint venture between Warwickshire County Cricket Club and Compass Group to establish a vehicle to service match-day food and hospitality needs. *"Corporate's a really good seat for building your organisational skills,"* one trainee informed us, explaining that *"there must be at least 100 ancillary documents per deal that you have to keep track of!"* Across offices sources described drafting board minutes and non-disclosure agreements, proof-reading, managing due diligence, bibling and attending client meetings. In fact, *"they're quite happy to give you a lot of client exposure. I was able to sit down one-on-one with the director of a small company being sold."*

Property's highly ranked in London, where Pinsents is a market leader in the public sector, having acted on significant government projects like Hammersmith & Fulham Council's role in Fulcrum's development of a collaborative care centre. The team also has a good track record in the retail sector – recent matters include acting on House of Fraser's head office move to Baker Street – and on the hotel scene, where lawyers act for clients like Rezidor (European operators of Radisson Hotels and Country Inn & Suites). For trainees, *"there's a huge variety of work – you could be working on ten different matters at once."* As such, *"it's a great seat for learning to manage clients and a big workload. Supervisors check in frequently, but it's up to you to run your own files and pick up the phone to get things done."* In addition to *"bog-standard"* tasks like completing lease registry applications, there's *"quite a bit of research"* and drafting of licences.

Penguin lovers: apply here

PM's tax practice won praise from trainees across the firm. On the advisory side, sources mentioned tackling *"some corporate support work,"* though they insisted the team is not simply a reinforcement for the corporate department: *"We have a lot of standalone clients in our own right."* Such work lends itself to *"a lot of research into technical issues. It's then up to you to persuade the seniors on what you've concluded from your research."* The contentious side of the practice is *"quite McGrigors-heavy"* and is, rather uniquely, home to its very own in-house forensic accounting team. PM's tax litigation lawyers specialise in fraud investigations, both civil and criminal, and advise banks, energy companies and metal traders entangled in MTIC fraud issues. *"You can get involved in some quite exciting disputes,"* one interviewee reported. *"Our job is to review the issues and put ourselves in our clients' shoes, so that involves quite a lot of research and analysis of documents."*

The firm's restructuring practice, part of its financial institutions division, is one of the largest in the UK and has a specialism in construction insolvency. *"It's one of the only seats that's both transactional and contentious, so your work varies day-to-day,"* trainees told us, describing their involvement in drafting sale and purchase agreements, reviewing facility agreements and making court applications.

Trainees typically become eligible for secondments in their second year. There are a few options for regional trainees to take up placements to *"exciting"* clients like Manchester United, though the *"majority"* take place in London – a bugbear for regional interviewees, who said that *"regional trainees aren't really considered for London secondments because of the cost involved. The reasoning makes sense, but it seems unfair to market it to us as an option, even though everyone knows it's not."* There's also the option for one lucky trainee to go overseas to Dubai or even (thanks to the merger) the Falkland Islands. *"With all our recent growth in Europe, we're hoping to see some more options in the future,"* one source said.

Loved-up

While we were keen to find out whether there have been any *West Side Story*-style rumbles between lawyers from the two firms, legacy PM and McGrigors trainees were all quick to assure us *"it's been a brilliant experience all round."* *"The whole motivation behind it was that we were already similar,"* one elaborated, explaining that *"each prided itself on being friendly, laid-back firms that offered bespoke and personal solutions rather than template contracts and all that. Now we each have better resources for operating as such."* When it comes to personalities across the newly enlarged outfit, *"you find mini-cultures in each department, but overall everyone's nice and helpful."* Even in Birmingham, the only non-open-plan office, *"it's easy to ask questions. You generally don't have to tiptoe around anybody."* Thanks to efforts made to assist McGrigors trainees with their transition to the firm, *"it*

hasn't been difficult to start feeling like a part of the team."

In London, trainees were abuzz with praise for their Crown Place office, to which the firm relocated in 2011. *"Luxurious,"* *"shiny"* and *"absolutely lovely"* were just some of the adjectives used to describe the new digs, which include a restaurant, shower rooms with ironing facilities, a *"nice balcony where you can eat your lunch,"* a Costa coffee *"where they know your order"* and an auditorium for client and lawyer events – *"last week they showed The Hunger Games and brought in pizza and beer."* *"You definitely get the sense the momentum is shifting to London,"* trainees thought, sharing stories of *"people moving there if they want to be promoted"* and a few even expressing concern that *"regional offices might start to be seen as satellite outposts within the firm."* For the time being, however, things appear peachy, on the office front at least. Birmingham has recently refurbished its top floor, *"which makes it feel more like a business hub,"* and Leeds has benefited from a new head of office who's *"made it his mission to revamp and reinvigorate us with initiatives like a big office clean-up and a health and well-being week."* In Manchester, the *"scabby"* office of old has been abandoned in favour of *"amazing"* top-floor digs in flash Spinningfields.

"PM trainees are always out on Friday for a drink!" Indeed, the mood in the City may be *"slightly more sombre than five years ago,"* but London trainees still know how to have a good time, mentioning a Jubilee street party, a *"cracking"* Christmas Ball and a *"Welcome to Crown Place"* champagne do. *"The PM trainees have also planned a lot of nights out to help us integrate,"* a McGrigors source revealed. Things are equally jolly outside the City, with Friday drinks trolleys in Manchester, charity quizzes and wine tastings in Leeds and sporting events in Birmingham.

Retention's been *"a little nerve-racking"* this year, not least for the legacy McGrigors bunch, who *"had to apply to a firm they haven't spent that much time at."* In the end, the firm kept on 69 out of 97 trainees. *"There was a panel made up of partners from both firms, so they made the whole process as fair as possible."*

And finally...
Trainees predict nothing but good things to come as a result of the merger. *"It's an interesting turning point for the firm, and the fact that we're bigger can only be a good thing. We've got a lot of opportunities coming our way – watch this space!"*

Reed Smith LLP

The facts

Location: London

Number of UK partners/solicitors: 112/153 (+25 non-UK-qualified)

Total number of trainees: 54

Seats: 4x6 months

Alternative seats: Overseas seats, secondments

Extras: Pro bono – U-Turn, Providence Row, Queen Mary Legal Advice Centre and others

On chambersstudent.co.uk...

- How to get into Reed Smith
- Interview with training principal Peter Hardy
- Changing careeRS

The London office of this US giant is far from being a mere outpost... in fact it is Reed Smith's biggest office globally.

Steel City smithies

The history of Reed Smith is tied to the rise of the steel industry in Pittsburgh in the 1880s – Andrew Carnegie (of Carnegie Hall fame) was one of the firm's earliest clients. Fellow industrialists Messrs Heinz and Mellon followed suit. In testament to *"the amount of effort that goes into building client relationships at Reed Smith,"* The Bank of New York Mellon is still on the client roster today. After a small UK merger in 2001, these Pittsburgh steelers entered into a more substantial tie-up with City firm Richards Butler in 2007. Worldwide, the firm has almost 1,700 lawyers in 23 locations. Training principal Peter Hardy says: *"It's not by accident London is our biggest office – the firm's intention is for London to remain pivotal and we have a fairly aggressive growth strategy to reinforce our strengths."*

"One of the deciding factors when I was weighing up firms was that Reed Smith seemed very focused on where it was going. It's gone and done everything I was told it would do during my interview," a trainee said, and looking at the *Chambers UK* rankings, one can conclude that the merger has met with genuine success. The big ambition was to ramp up the corporate practice in London, and the firm has indeed managed to move up from the 'lower mid-market' category of *Chambers'* M&A rankings into the mid-market. Other practices have progressed too – the dispute resolution, IP and employment teams have all moved up the *Chambers* rankings since 2007, for example, while the banking group made its debut in the charts in 2012. Even the shipping group, where the old Richards Butler was already very strong, has upped its game. It moved into the top tier of the rankings for the first time in *Chambers UK 2013*, joining shipping specialists Ince and Holman Fenwick Willan. *"There is enough diversity in practice areas to ensure the firm will be fine. It is in a strategic global position,"* said a trainee.

So, trainees have plenty of areas to pick from; however, Reed Smith's key market sectors are energy and financial institutions. *"Energy is such a huge focus,"* says Hardy, and in 2011 the firm brought together all of its energy lawyers, previously spread out across many teams, into one dedicated sector group. Financial institutions include the aforementioned Bank of New York Mellon as well as the National Bank of Kuwait, RBS, Lloyds, Santander and HSBC, for which Reed Smith recently won a $90m judgment in a high-profile fraud case.

All at sea

The HR department puts out an extensive seat list with each supervisor identified, as *"if you happen to have an interest in a specific area, this gives the opportunity to drill down further to the supervisor that does that work, instead of putting down a more generic choice."* Trainees mentioned that *"as you progress, you talk to grad recruitment about how your training contract is shaping up and accordingly which seats might be better for you."* Trainees list their top four preferences at each rotation: first choice is guaranteed at least once. Those who don't get any of their top four preferences in any given rotation have first pick of the remaining seats, and first-seaters get what's left over.

Chambers UK rankings

Banking & Finance	Insurance
Banking Litigation	Intellectual Property
Commodities	Life Sciences
Competition/European Law	Media & Entertainment
Construction	Pensions
Corporate/M&A	Product Liability
Data Protection	Professional Negligence
Defamation/Reputation Management	Public International Law
	Real Estate
Dispute Resolution	Real Estate Finance
Employment	Real Estate Litigation
Fraud	Shipping
Information Technology	

International and client secondments are announced on the same seat list, and *"when you state your preferences, secondments are automatically taken to be your first choice."* Trainees then submit a CV and cover letter and interview with the client or international office in question. Current client secondments on offer include stints at BNY Mellon, The Wellcome Trust, Barclays, Bauer Consumer Media and Debenhams, while overseas postings include a corporate seat in Abu Dhabi and shipping in Paris or Piraeus. Hong Kong used to be an option but a recent departure of a team of 15 lawyers and 35 other staff from that office means hosting trainees isn't top priority. *"We have sent one of our most senior shipping partners to Hong Kong to shape up that practice – we aren't pulling back,"* but overseas seats *"have to happen for the right reasons,"* explains Hardy.

Though shipping is divided into wet and dry groups, there's *"definite crossover and overlap between the two."* The majority of trainee work done here is dry shipping –*"mostly contract law in the context of the shipping industry: very case law-heavy."* The floods and fires in Australia have provided work for the group in the form of force majeure disputes – where acts of God have prevented a party from fulfilling the terms of its contract. The fallout from the Japanese earthquake has also been a source of instructions, while other disputes have cropped up about the condition of a vessel's hold for cargo or who is responsible for damages when grain has got damp and sprouted en route from Africa. Trainees spend roughly *"95% of their time on arbitrations,"* researching, writing *"small pieces of day-to-day advice for clients,"* drafting instructions to experts and *"doing some court work"* too. Wet shipping is more about collisions at sea, groundings and jurisdictional disputes. For example, Reed Smith acted for the owners of the 'Jolly Amaranto', a ferry which ran aground in Egypt. A small, technical group, trainees tag along to incident meetings and are the first point of contact when partners go abroad to *"rescue ships."*

According to Peter Hardy, the recent rebrand of 'energy, trade and commodities' to 'energy and natural resources' *"was to reflect an added focus on the energy side of the practice."* Over the last two years, about a dozen new partners have joined this area in London, with some poached from Clifford Chance, SNR Denton and the now defunct Dewey & LeBoeuf. Reed Smith receives top marks from *Chambers UK* for its commodities practice. The firm advises on energy and natural resources projects: the financing, development, management and dispute resolution. It also deals with power generation, oil and gas, renewable energy and energy regulation matters. *"It's probably one of the firm's pre-eminent departments, and you are working with a demanding set of clients. Energy and natural resources is at the centre of where the firm wants to go,"* said one source. The work is *"very similar to shipping, where you are talking about commodities being sold across the world and the disputes that arise in their sale and purchase."* Juniors enthused: *"The department takes training very seriously."*

The vast financial industries group (FIG) covers many areas, including bankruptcy, financial litigation, financial services regulation, investment management and structured finance. The financial services regulatory group *"always acts in an advisory role – we don't work on transactions from start to finish."* Juniors *"research, draft memos, interact with clients"* and deal with Financial Services Authority authorisations. The real estate finance team is small, but for trainees *"it means you can run your own files and attend lots of client events."* The team acts mostly for banks, and trainees receive a good mix of work: drafting, due diligence, ensuring loan conditions are satisfied, dealing with the other side and working on post-completion matters. A secondment to Barclays also counts as a finance seat.

Against the current

Dispute resolution is a Reed Smith staple, especially in bad times. *"You appreciably felt that side of the business was able to step in and pick up the slack as the transactional work fell off in the recession."* Trainees in dispute resolution enjoyed that *"it's a broad department, covering a range of disputes."* They could be working on IP, advertising, financial services, insurance recovery, international arbitration, global regulatory enforcement or professional negligence matters. In this seat, trainees receive capacity requests and if they find themselves available, they are at liberty to *"go and work for people and other areas that they are interested in."* A retail litigation secondment at the Lloyds Banking Group is also on offer. The department *"mainly deals with disputes and complaints from customers or their solicitors."* With more responsibility given to trainees outside the firm, *"you definitely have to hit the ground running. You're the first point of contact and have to think on your feet."* Trainees seconded to the Dubai office came across a fair share of construction arbitration for clients in the region. Some found it *"a novel experience to work with UAE contract law, a foreign jurisdiction compared to what I studied in law school."*

More niche seats include a much-coveted media spot, data privacy and global regulatory enforcement, competition and tax. Starting in September 2012, all future trainees will do a Reed Smith LPC at BPP with business modules leading to a 'bespoke MA'. After they join the firm, there's a *"two-week induction period."* Departmental trainings then take over, varying in scope and routine. There is also *"so much to learn from just listening in when you share a room with a supervisor; most of them are very approachable."*

Tower power

Reed Smith's offices high up Broadgate Tower in Bishopsgate (built a few years ago) boast *"amazing views from every direction."* With trendy *"Shoreditch on the doorstep,"* trainees don't lack for places to eat or stuff to do. But inside these *"beautiful offices"* some grumbled about *"lack of storage space"* and *"having to rely on vending machines for food and coffee after 4pm."* Trainees who have spent time on secondment in Reed Smiths' offices overseas said they're all quite similar decoration-wise, having *"the same theme running through them all."*

Trainees hail from a range of universities, and a variety of international backgrounds and consider themselves to be a *"diverse group."* It's pretty easy to find someone to share a pint or cocktail with on a Friday evening, they said. *"In our intake an e-mail goes around for a Piccolino run. It's the first bar we found, and we never moved."*

"Around Christmas there are several parties: associate, trainee, department and firm-wide. Everyone has a good time," one trainee assured us. However, there was some disappointment among our interviewees that the firm-wide do was held in-house and didn't *"provide an opportunity to actually dress up."* On the 27th floor, FIG holds drinks on Fridays for partners, associates and trainees. Meanwhile, *"shipping is infamously sociable, borderline alcoholic,"* joked a trainee, *"and regularly puts a lot of money behind the bar."* We can almost hear the sea shanties and smell the rum from our office in Holborn...

Reed Smith is an American firm but this office feels very much like a London operation, sources emphasised. *"It's hard to differentiate law firms but Reed Smith stands out as a place where you're not expected to work all night and weekends."* That said, 9am to 8pm days are considered reasonable by trainees. That's still quite a lot of hours. Occasional all-nighters prove that *"we are good, we get the big work and big work requires longer hours."* An annual associates' retreat is held in London where senior management communicates issues of the day and *"always makes a point to encourage trainees to attend. Reed Smith gets top marks in terms of management transparency,"* sources felt. They said they don't feel *"like a weird outgrowth"* as they are usually kept in the *"line of communication."*

And finally...
In 2012, 23 out of 34 qualifiers were kept on as NQs.

1.
RIP UP THE RULE BOOK

If you never go against the grain, always follow the well-trodden path and consistently take the safe option, you could find yourself sleepwalking into a predictable career with a traditional firm. If that's how you see your future, we wish you every success. But please look away now. If you prefer the bold to the boring, however, and find the prospect of joining a different kind of law firm enticing, we'd love to talk to you. We want to break the mould, rewrite the rules and redefine the legal profession. Your mission could be to build the law firm of the future, today. And to define your career at the same time.

Read the full manifesto and find out more at
RPC.CO.UK/MANIFESTO

RPC

THE LAW CAREER FOR PIONEERS

RPC (Reynolds Porter Chamberlain LLP)

The facts

Location: London

Number of UK partners/solicitors: 72/181

Total number of trainees: 31

Partners who trained at firm: 25%

Seats: 4x6 months

Alternative seats: Secondments

Extras: Pro bono – Streets of Growth

On chambersstudent.co.uk...

- How to get into RPC
- Interview with training principal Simon Goldring

A burgeoning corporate division and active engagement with Generation Y has seen RPC go from square to cutting-edge.

RPC gets edgy

Insurance stalwart RPC has got a bit of a buzz about it at the moment. "*We performed well financially in the recession,*" trainees told us. "*We're looking to recruit all the time, our growth plans are ambitious, and it feels like a forward-thinking and innovative environment.*" Gone are the days where the word 'traditional' could be applicable. Today, trainees control the RPC Twitter feed and sit among partners and fee earners in open plan offices, while the CEO and managing partner host lunches to ask: "*How can we make the firm better and your jobs easier?*" The firm's quest for transparency has seen its intranet system, 'Edge', win industry awards. A tax and regulatory blog keeps lawyers up to date with the ever-changing landscape, and a trainee-led business feed is frequently updated.

The process of repositioning started in 2006 when RPC (it now prefers this tag to the cumbersome Reynolds Porter Chamberlain, btw) hopped from Holborn to the Richard Rogers-designed Tower Bridge House. Next came the appointment of managing partner Jonathan Watmough, whose plans to boost RPC's commercial practice have resulted in a move away from reliance on insurance litigation, although this latter area is still an important part of the business. "*The idea is to rapidly increase turnover by growing both divisions in tandem,*" training principal Simon Goldring told us. Growing two fairly diverse practices is not a one-size-fits-all process, as Goldring elaborated: "*We're growing the commercial side by being very selective about what we do. There are certain niche areas where we feel bigger firms aren't interested – like IP. As well as M&A work, we're focusing on commercial litiga-*

tion and competition." The firm's established insurance division requires different tactics. "*It's hard to suddenly double turnover with mature long-term clients,*" Goldring says. "*We've had to be more creative.*"

January 2012 saw the firm poach a 28-strong team from CMS and open an insurance-focused Bristol office. "*We've taken space that can house up to 100,*" Simon Goldring says. RPC also opened the doors of its first international pads, in Hong Kong and the insurance hub of Singapore. "*Our strategy was never to have aggressive international expansion for the sake of it,*" Goldring says, "*but we will continue to look at possibilities. Our size means we are quite opportunistic and fleet of foot – we can move quite quickly.*"

Six weeks before a seat change, trainees give their preferred options, listing "*an insurance, a commercial and a wild card.*" Generally, trainees will get "*one of those three choices.*"

Reading the (1886) Riot Act

Seats available in the commercial division are: corporate; real estate; regulatory; employment; pensions and incentives; and commercial disputes (comprised of tax, general litigation and media defamation). The subsections of the insurance group are: construction; general liability and medical; professional risks; and international risks and reinsurance (IRR). Sought-after secondments are available to household-name construction, media and IP clients. Trainees can put themselves forward, but ulti-

Chambers UK rankings

Banking Litigation	Information Technology
Clinical Negligence	Insurance
Construction	Intellectual Property
Corporate Crime & Investigations	Life Sciences
	Media & Entertainment
Corporate/M&A	Partnership
Defamation/Reputation Management	Product Liability
	Professional Discipline
Dispute Resolution	Professional Negligence
Education	Real Estate
Employment	Retail
Health & Safety	Tax

mately "*a partner has the final say – the firm puts an emphasis on you being the right fit for the client.*"

The professional risks team advises accountants, barristers, surveyors, financial advisers and solicitors on their liability to clients. This area is "*a great place to cut your teeth, as there are a range of small files, but partners allow you to understand the whole litigation process.*" Furthermore, "*the actual law involved is tort, which isn't massively complex, so it's more about the facts of the case, which are often juicy.*" Small claims allow trainees to get a grip on the human side of events. "*In a lot of cases,*" explained one, "*it's very distressing for the people involved as their careers are on the line. Especially when we're acting for solicitors – that's a very interesting area for more reasons than one.*" Trainees working in IRR "*mostly do coverage work – it's very technical.*" The team acts for Munich Re, Allianz, Chartis, Chubb and Swiss Re, among others, and advised 14 major insurers after the August 2011 riots, allowing those affected (and their insurers) to claim compensation from the police authority.

Trainees working in construction may split their time between transactional and litigation work within the department's insurance and non-insurance divisions. A number of our sources had worked on construction disputes. A typical matter might involve "*a dispute between a construction company and a private individual on a building project that had gone wrong.*" Trainees take "*the first stab at letters and witness statements,*" on top of the standard bundling and document management, and often get to go to trial and client meetings.

Deals not to be sneezed at

Regulatory straddles RPC's commercial and insurance divisions and is growing. The group covers a pick-and-mix of matters, from large internal investigations to "*white-collar matters, FSA investigatory work, FSA authorisation, anti-bribery, environmental regulatory and – very occasionally – some actual crime.*" Naturally, case

details in this area are top secret but we can reveal that the team recently worked on a complex anti-bribery case; the investigation of a CEO accused of insider dealing; and the investigation of an insurer accused of fraud. The still-small group means trainees get work from everyone in the team "*and they make it interesting. I had client exposure from day one, and they put a lot of trust in you. There's no associate between you and the partner, so there's less time to faff and less flab on the work that you get.*"

Chambers UK puts RPC's corporate practice at the lower end of the mid-market, alongside the likes of Dundas & Wilson, Farrer and Finers Stephens Innocent, but the firm is aiming to haul itself up the rankings by pushing for deals over the £1bn mark. The group's biggest recent deal was a €1.3bn whopper in the exciting world of hygiene products: the firm acted for SCA (Svenska Cellulosa Aktiebolaget) on its acquisition of Georgia-Pacific's European tissue operations on a deal that spanned 22 jurisdictions. Trainees enjoyed the chance to work on an instruction of this size, as well as on RPC's more usual smaller deals. "*It's mainly proof-reading on the high-value matters, but partners make sure that you're taken along to meetings so you're still learning,*" one said. "*The smaller deals allow you to be autonomous, with more opportunity for drafting.*" Trainees in corporate are exposed to a range of work, as partners from M&A, commercial, insolvency and banking sit together, and "*half the experience in this department is going and getting the work you want to do. Sometimes you'll just get chatting to a partner about a matter and they'll ask you to get involved.*"

Bigmouth strikes again

Part of the firm's commercial disputes division is the star media defamation practice. With an increasing number of news stories being broken and gossiped about online (R**n G***s, anyone?), it's an ever-active area. Trainees reported that matters come in every day, many of which will never make it to court but nevertheless require research. "*It's varied in terms of work,*" sources told us. "*You have to stay on top of things – there's a degree of document management, but you also run smaller claims yourself and basically draft defences for them.*" The team regularly defends Trinity Mirror, *The Daily Telegraph*, *The Financial Times* and *The Spectator*. "*There's always background work to do for newspapers, as you're seeing if the claims made against them can be substantiated.*" This year the team acted for Associated Newspapers, MGN and News Group in major slander claims brought by Joanna Yeates' landlord, Christopher Jefferies. It also defended IPC (owner of music bible *NME*) in a suit brought by Morrissey after he claimed an interview with the magazine implied he was racist. The fast pace of life in the department means, said one source, "*I get as much responsibility as they think they can give me. I'm in the* *loop at all times, I have direct contact with the client on every case, and there are hardly any standard 'trainee' tasks."*

IP is *"growing very fast,"* trainees tell us. *"A few partners have recently been made up – it's quite a young team but one that's pushing to make an impression."* The practice has specialities in media, sports and retail work, and counts Associated Newspapers, HMV, The National Trust, lastminute.com, Sports Direct and Dunlop among its clients. The group also encompasses RPC's competition and outsourcing teams, and trainees' work will cover *"disputes, commercial contracts, data protection, contentious IP and competition work."*

RPC has a reputation for decent hours, and although some sources said *"there's so much work that hours in some departments are getting longer,"* the sensible attitude towards this subject remains. *"There's almost always work, but never the pressure to stay late,"* thought one. *"If you were hanging around at 8pm with nothing to do, people would think you're weird."*

That vision thing

"There's a sort of feeling that we're a little bit different, and we do things our own way," trainees claimed. Certainly in recent years RPC had one of the profession's more unique graduate recruitment campaigns – a bright, pop-arty comic strip featuring puzzled law students facing 'Decision Impossible'. This has now been phased out, but the new graduate website (parts of which remind us of the Sky Movies branding for some reason) still features a bold message. *"We're determined to rewrite the rule book,"* it declares. *"Initiate a sea change in our sector. Challenge ingrained attitudes and question conventional wisdom. Consequently, we've created a radical manifesto for change – and it's not for the faint-hearted."* We'll leave it up to you to decide how much you buy into these words, but we'd advise you to take heed of them and tailor your application accordingly. In our experience, when a firm moves from bland platitudes about itself and starts to use words like *radical manifesto*, it suggests that it actually has that 'vision' thing. If nothing else, you might have a think about the implications of another statement on the website: *"Law firms are changing in response to rapidly changing times. Unfortunately, we're convinced that most of them aren't changing quickly enough."* For his part, Simon Goldring says: *"We're saying to people if you want something a little bit different, and the chance to shine, then come here. We're not looking for people who want something safe. We want people who want to make a difference as lawyers."*

Sources love RPC's open plan office. *"As a trainee, it's invaluable,"* one said. *"People can see when you aren't busy so you get more exposure to work. You also learn more quickly by listening to other people on the phone, and it's always more sociable."* Trainees sometimes head down to the Living Room bar, or often head straight to haunts around Bank, London Bridge or Brick Lane come 6pm.

Despite all the talk of radical manifestos, we were amused to discover a hint of RPC's more traditional side in that its lawyers are divided into houses (imaginatively named 'Reynolds', 'Porter' and 'Chamberlain') and can gain house points during the firm's various quizzes and contests, such as annual talent contest 'The RPC Factor'. If you find yourself in Chamberlain house watch out, because it has produced more dark wizards than any other. Trainees' creativity is brought to the fore during the Christmas party skit, which in 2011 *"was a cover of the Band Aid song 'Do They Know It's Christmas?' – someone completely rewrote the lyrics, someone did a dance routine, someone worked on the editing."* There are both rugby and football teams, and one trainee had the idea of setting up a darts team as a way of connecting with insurance clients.

And finally...
"RPC is becoming a serious corporate competitor, while maintaining the understanding that its lawyers have lives outside work." Retention rates are consistently excellent, and in 2012, 13 out of 15 qualifiers stayed on for the long haul.

SGH Martineau LLP

The facts

Location: Birmingham, London

Number of UK partners/solicitors: 64/82

Partners who trained at firm: 16%

Total number of trainees: 20

Seats: 6x4 months

Alternative seats: London

On chambersstudent.co.uk...
- How to get into SGH Martineau
- Interview with managing partner Bill Barker

A recent merger has given this Birmingham native's London office a boost, which means increased possibilities for trainees in the capital.

Sprecher Sie Brummie?

"*I can remember the feeling of trawling through firms... they all blend into one another after a while. Unfortunately, some are actually really nondescript in real life as well – but we aren't!*" Forceful words from a Martineau second-year, but Chambers will be the judge of how interesting you are. If all you do is give the firm a quick once-over, it doesn't look too promising. This is a medium-sized firm in the competitive Birmingham market. It has plenty of *Chambers UK* rankings to its name, mostly in the second or third tiers of the tables devoted to the Midlands (the much larger Eversheds, Wragge, Pinsent Masons, DLA Piper and Gateley hog the top tiers). An exception is a dedicated group of education specialists regarded as some of the best in the country at acting for universities.

Ironically, given our source's comment about firms blending into one, Martineau has been doing a bit of blending of its own recently. December 2011 saw it merge with a City-based firm with the tongue-twisting name of Sprecher Grier Halberstam (not as German as it sounds). Martineau had long been on the lookout for a match, as managing partner Bill Barker explained: "*We wanted a larger London office, and thought a little merger would be very complementary. We predicted a firm of a quarter to a third of our size would be suitable. SGH was in fact larger than we had in mind.*" With annual turnover of almost half of Martineau's, SGH represents a strong and – dare we say it – interesting fit. "*We realised that we both had slightly different client bases and offerings,*" Barker told us. "*They were very big in insolvency work; we have a strong reputation in banking and lending. We have a*

strong transactional real estate practice; they were strong in contentious real estate. Equally, we have groups like IP, tax and competition, meaning there are opportunities to sell those services to their client base.*" Prior to the merger, Martineau jumped the Channel by opening a Brussels office in collaboration with Becker Buttner Held (exactly as German as it sounds). The office will focus on energy and EU law.

The merged entity has turnover in excess of £30m and a gigantic real estate practice which accounts for just under a third of the firm's practice. Seven industry sectors have been targeted, which are: private wealth; education; leisure; energy; industry and manufacturing; investment funds; and banking and restructuring. The word from trainees: "*Post-merger, it's exciting. The thing that hits home is growth – one of the reasons for merging was to have a stronger presence in London.*" Bill Barker agrees. "*For trainees, the merger is very good news. SGH didn't have any trainees at all, so now we're bigger, it creates opportunities in London that simply weren't there before. We will probably recruit slightly more trainees in future and we might well have trainees permanently in London.*"

The Birmingham Six

Martineau operates a six-seat training system which goes some way towards setting it apart from the other Brummie firms we've mentioned. Trainees liked this way of doing things, as many enter the firm with a spread of interests. "*I wanted exposure to as many areas as possible, and six gives you that opportunity.*" Officially, trainees must tick off a property, a corporate and a contentious seat,

Chambers UK rankings

Agriculture & Rural Affairs	Family/Matrimonial
Banking & Finance	Intellectual Property
Charities	Private Client
Construction	Professional Negligence
Corporate/M&A	Real Estate
Dispute Resolution	Real Estate Litigation
Education	Restructuring/Insolvency
Employment	

although there is room for manoeuvre – some seats fulfil two of these requirements.

First seats are *"sorted before you start and usually based on your background."* Following this, trainees state their preferences, with second-years getting priority. Because the firm *"attracts similar people, most trainees want to do the same things,"* making seat allocation an ongoing issue. The firm recently overhauled the system and put managing partner Bill Barker in charge. *"We're keen to retain trainees, and I'm the best person to see which bits are growing and developing and where is likely to need a September qualifier – it's very important that those bits of the firm get to choose,"* he told us. A sensible strategy, although this naturally narrows choices. Second-years were shocked to be informed that they couldn't take both employment and commercial disputes, *"and then some of us didn't get either choice anyway."* In the firm's defence, *"it starts the NQ process very early on,"* releasing a jobs list in early April. *"It's a fairly open and honest process, so you'll know in early May if you're not successful, which means there's plenty of time to go and find something else."* Eight out of nine qualifiers secured NQ positions in 2012.

University challenges

Property's a department that can hold a lot of trainees at once, and it's where many begin their training contracts. *"It's great as a first seat,"* sources say, as *"the responsibility really sets you up. They give you your own caseload to manage and let you get on with it."* This may include *"reviewing documents and plans, liaising with the Land Registry, drafting leases and being responsible for sales and completions."* The department has many clients in the finance, education, energy and leisure sectors. It recently advised the University of Cumbria on the multimillion-pound restructuring of its higher education programme in relation to the sharing of its campuses. A stint in property 'proper' can be sidestepped by spending time in property litigation, a department that primarily advises pubs, shops and hotels on contentious matters.

Trainees enjoy construction for the *"nice mix of contentious and non-contentious work."* The department has a focus on urban regeneration projects and, like the property group, has lots of energy and education clients. It recently combined both specialities by advising Lancaster University on the planning of a £5m wind turbine. Trainees take on mainly transactional work for individuals, contractors, subcontractors and universities, and enjoy the mixture of tasks offered them. *"You won't just be doing the same thing all the time – you might be looking at building contracts or making professional appointments with architects."*

The commercial disputes team acts for clients including BSkyB on high-value commercial disputes, contentious insolvency cases, professional negligence matters and debt collection. The team acted for npower on a portfolio of claims relating to electricity supply to the value of £350k. Trainees enjoy taking part in the court process: *"I spoke to clients, assisted the partner on files and got to go to the High Court and work one-on-one with the QC."*

Califabrication

Trainees in the IP seat get to grips with problems such as *"the client discovering companies with the same name as them, unfair advertising, defamation and trade mark and patent infringement."* The group takes on licensing and infringement work for universities, and has a line in patent work on behalf of textile clients, recently acting for Lancashire cardigan makers Tulchan Textiles and hip Californian fashion brand Wet Seal. Other seats in the commercial division are employment, education and energy.

Martineau's family team acts for millionaires, entrepreneurs and sports stars on divorce, pre-nup agreements and child custody matters, often with an international aspect. Despite it being very partner-led, trainees emphasised: *"They're very good at giving you hands-on work."* They attend client meetings, and *"you are not just sitting in the corner not saying anything, but are taking notes and being asked your opinion."* Trainees can also take a seat in wills, tax planning and charities.

Corporate choices in Birmingham are M&A, banking and corporate finance, while in London, trainees now have the opportunity to spend time in banking and corporate and a banking/commercial litigation mixed seat. Trainees in the London banking seat reported a lot of Islamic finance work and plenty of partner interaction, while in banking litigation they are the initial point of contact for banks: *"They contact us when the customer defaults on a loan, and the trainee will issue proceedings, draft the particulars of the claim and seek judgment against the debtor. Once we've received judgment, we'll advise the bank on how to enforce it."*

Appraisals come at the end of each four-month seat. *"Supervisors fill in the form, which you get to see before you fill in your half of it,"* one trainee explained. *"You then sit down with the supervisor and* [HR manager] *Jennie Seymour – all three of you know what's coming so it's never a shock."* Some seats offer fortnightly reviews, and trainees are pleased with the feedback they get from their superiors. *"Feedback is always there for you when you want it."*

Grill Bill

Our sources were impressed by how the firm kept them informed during the merger. *"They do communication very well here,"* said one. *"There were lots of talks during the months before, and now one person in each department puts our questions to Bill Barker."* There are frequent opportunities to meet 'n' greet management, *"where you submit questions beforehand and they answer them during a breakfast or over wine and nibbles."* Cultural differences may exist between teams, but overall, trainees feel that *"people are down to earth and have time for you."*

"We're known in Birmingham as one of the more sociable firms," claimed one source. *"We like hanging out with each other."* This *"massively social"* outlook *"reflects the firm's ethos as a whole."* Trainee-organised Friday drinks are well attended, *"and often turn into a big night out for the younger people."* A Christmas party in January was held at the Forest of Arden hotel, *"just off the M42, so it was easy for legacy SGH people to make it from London."* Trainees are also active in the Birmingham Trainee Solicitors Society, putting on sporting and networking events.

The Birmingham HQ opposite Snow Hill station means *"we're connected. Some people commute from Cheltenham, we do business in Manchester and Liverpool, and we're not cut off from City firms because we're not that far away by train."* The office takes up two floors of No 1 Colmore Square, and boasts a freshly rebranded reception in Martineau's corporate colours of orange and grey. Employees sit in pods with partners and associates, and there are quiet rooms and break-out areas with sofas and a small kitchen on each floor. The firm's London base is at One America Square near Tower Bridge, and visiting trainees are put up in a flat nearby.

The vast majority of our interviewees either came from Brum or studied there, and believed that *"local ties are important because the firm wants to know that you're going to stay around."* Some had prior experience in one of the firm's focus sectors, and advised: *"If you have a genuine interest in any of them it's something you should really try and make clear."* Many had applied to other Midlands mid-sizers; some turned down other offers for Martineau. Their reason? *"The people. It's good-quality work but the culture is always friendly. And I would never expect to be here at 8pm. People have outside interests which they encourage because it makes you an interesting person."* However, with a London training contract a probability over the next couple of years, Bill Barker muses: *"We may begin to attract a slightly different breed of individual."*

So, SGH Martineau – bland or grand? Daringly different or dull as ditchwater? As a slightly smaller, independent outfit, it does offer something else for graduates looking to work in Birmingham, a city dominated by Wragge and the large national firms. It scores highly on the trainee satisfaction front, with our interviewees especially praising its openness, sociable nature and broad training contract. And its encroachment into the London market demonstrates a touch of ambition and represents probable opportunities for junior lawyers. None of this is unique to Martineau – but put together it is what makes the firm a very nice place to work, and isn't that the most important thing, anyway?

And finally...

Trainees *"definitely recommend doing the mini-vacation scheme if possible, rather than going straight to the assessment centre. You just get a real feel for whether you'd click or not."*

"A training contract is a two-year interview, so don't relax too much as – you are constantly under scrutiny."

Trainee

SHEARMAN & STERLING LLP

GRADUATE RECRUITMENT

Perform on the big stage

Abu Dhabi

Beijing

Brussels

Dusseldorf

Frankfurt

Hong Kong

London

Milan

Munich

New York

Palo Alto

Paris

Rome

San Francisco

Sao Paulo

Shanghai

Graduates are afforded early responsibility and work at the highest level within the firm. You will play a part in headline-making deals for some of the world's leading organisations, and enjoy many opportunities for international travel.

But don't just take our word for it – go online: ukgraduates.shearman.com

Shearman & Sterling LLP

The facts

Location: London

Number of UK partners/solicitors: 24/53 (+3/19 non-UK qualified)

Partners who trained at firm: 60%

Seats: 4x6 months

Total number of trainees: 25

Alternative seats: Overseas seats

Extras: Pro bono – A4ID, Lawyers Without Borders; language classes

On chambersstudent.co.uk...

- How to get into Shearman
- A history of Shearman

"*Finance-focused*" Shearman & Sterling has one of the longest-established and largest London offices of any US – sorry, "*international*" – firm.

Built like a tank

Shearman & Sterling was founded on Wall Street almost 140 years ago, and early clients included Henry Ford and the Rockefellers, but the Big Apple was not big enough for this mighty beast. Shearman has had an international practice for over a century and has been a global trailblazer: it opened up in Abu Dhabi as far back as 1975 and in Beijing in 1993. The London office celebrated its 40th anniversary in 2012.

"*Finance is what Shearman is all about,*" a trainee told us. The firm's pedigree is best demonstrated by just one of its recent blue-chip deals: the London and Abu Dhabi offices recently advised Dow Chemical on a $20bn joint venture with Saudi Aramco (Saudi Arabia's national oil company and the largest private company in the world) to build an oil refinery in Jubail on the Saudi Gulf coast.

The London office's revenue rose by 5% in 2011 to just under $110m (£70m). That means that if the office were a standalone UK firm, it would be the 40th-largest in the country. The *Chambers UK* rankings show the firm's market standing has remained solid in the past few years. Shearman is particularly rated for its projects, banking and capital markets work.

The firm is powered by its corporate, finance and projects departments. These are the areas where you'll find most trainees: usually four or five in each. Trainees can also complete seats in one or more of the firm's 'advisory' teams: litigation/arbitration, competition, employment, tax, property, and financial services regulation/asset management. Each of these groups takes one trainee at a time.

"*Something you need to realise is that this firm is quite limited in terms of seat options,*" one trainee opined. What they meant is that "*trainees are generally expected to complete seats in two of the three main areas.*" We'll put it as simply as we can: don't apply to Shearman if you aren't very interested in finance and transactional work. Trainees agreed they are "*given free rein to choose the other two seats.*" It's "*not mandatory*" to complete a contentious seat, and trainees can sign up for a two-week course at the College of Law to fulfil the SRA requirement.

Sterling work

Chambers UK reveals that Shearman's finance practice is hot on the heels of the magic circle in terms of its work product. The department is divided into leveraged finance (loan-based buyouts) and structured finance (capital markets) sections. "*Trainees usually normally see either leveraged or structured work, rather than both,*" a source told us. "*The majority of my work comes from my supervisor, although other people in the department sometimes randomly pop up and ask me to help with certain tasks. All my supervisors have encouraged me to seek out work from elsewhere.*" A recent deal trainees might have come across was Brazilian oil giant Petrobras' $7bn bond issue. Shearman acted for the eight underwriting banks which hailed from Brazil, Japan, the US and Europe and included JPMorgan, Morgan Stanley and Santander. The firm also guided Jaguar Land Rover through a £500m high-yield bond offering – its first since being taken over by Tata in 2008 – and acted for Liverpool FC on the refinancing of its debt, having previously worked on the

Chambers UK rankings

Banking & Finance	Energy & Natural Resources
Banking Litigation	Financial Services
Capital Markets	Projects
Competition/European Law	Restructuring/Insolvency
Corporate/M&A	

club's acquisition by New England Sports Ventures in 2010.

"The average burn time for a deal in finance is a month," a trainee told us. *"If you are on the deal from the get-go, your first task is getting all the ducks in a row: arranging the corporate permissions, looking at the lender's assets all over the world, doing board resolutions, getting forms agreed – the organisational side. Then, if your supervisor is happy, you might get to do a first draft of a legal opinion, mandate letter or debenture document. Then you will compile the closing check-list and get the sign-off for each part of the deal. You have long hours while the deal is going on, staying until 7 or 8pm. It was a bit of shock when I started that I was still at work at 9pm sometimes. In the last week you don't get out before 10 or 11pm. Once it's closed there is always stuff to do but you get a fortnight of 'decompression' when you can leave at 6pm or so."* If all our interviewees answered our questions as exhaustively as that one did, our job would be very easy! Trainees also told us they'd been doing definition checks, bibling, document management and proof-reading, and had attended closings.

A lot of projects work is energy-related – that Dow–Aramco deal we've already mentioned, for example. Shearman also recently acted for a Korean, a French and a Japanese bank on a $252m loan to build a sewerage plant in Bahrain and advised Australian mining business Sundance on its role in the $4bn Mbalam iron ore project in Cameroon. *"It's so international,"* one trainee told us of the department. *"We draft documents governed by Islamic finance and I have to call people and chase documents around the world. I have really had to use my brains."* Unlike financings, projects can drag on for years, but the joy of working on them is that *"it is quite nice to see where the money goes that finance lawyers help raise."*

Shearman Steeling

The corporate team has recently worked on Tata Steel's $600m sale of two steel plants on Teesside to Thailand's Sahaviriya Steel Industries, and Citi's $2.2bn sale of EMI to Sony. In fact, over the past year Shearman has worked on a long list of interesting and *"very, very big"* deals. *"There was a massive mining project recently,"* said one source. *"I was given the task of drafting some ancillary*

documents, verification notes and board memoranda. I *also worked on a smaller-value transaction recently, for which they let me draft some of the core deal documents."* You can tell from that example how many overlaps there are between departments: corporate lawyers might be bashing out the terms of a project-based joint venture, while the finance lawyers help claw together the money for it to go ahead.

The advisory teams' bread and butter is *"corporate support work on the big transactions,"* along with some *"standalone matters."* The work is *"more academic"* in tone: less *"document-heavy"* than the transactional seats and involving more research tasks. While still demanding, advisory seats are known for their lighter hours. *"It's more manageable: usually 9.30am to 7pm, although if you are working on a big project you might finish at 8 or 9pm."*

Litigation and arbitration also fall under the 'advisory' umbrella. Litigators work on a lot of finance disputes as well as contract, insurance, IP and fraud cases. Shearman recently won a $2.1bn award for Dow Chemical in a arbitration against a subsidiary of the Kuwait Petroleum Company over its withdrawal from a planned joint venture with Dow.

Anti-American

Now, you may have been seeing plenty of dollar signs reading this True Picture, but trainees insist Shearman is *"not particularly American."* Well, obviously, it is in the sense that that is where it was founded, but *"the firm likes to portray itself as international and we very much have an English culture: the senior management are all English."* One source stated: *"The perception is that at American firms trainees sit in their office getting beasted for weeks on end, but I wouldn't say I work any harder than my peers at magic circle firms."* US firms are also reputed to take a more laissez-faire attitude to training, with more on-the-job learning. Not at Shearman. *"The formal training is very good – if anything there is too much!"* one trainee joked. *"Some of it is compulsory. There is one session for trainees every week and more general training too."* There seems to be a strong teaching ethos too. *"The supervisors are very good at helping you. You are not left to do things on your own. People are very good at explaining the background to a deal and what they want you to do."* First-years get buddied up with a junior associate mentor and trainees praised the quality of their *"thorough"* and *"detailed"* appraisals.

"To me it was important to work somewhere with an international environment," a trainee told us. *"As a trainee you enjoy all the benefits of plugging into intra-firm relationships."* There are overseas seats, in New York, Brussels, Hong Kong, Singapore and Abu Dhabi. The last two are projects-related. *"Getting an overseas seat is just like get-*

ting any other seat," trainees told us. "*You just put it down as one of your preferences. There is no separate interview process. If you want to go abroad you probably will be able to.*" As Abu Dhabi and Singapore are relatively small offices "*the spotlight is on you as the trainee – you get access to interesting work, but you work harder too.*"

Other than loving long hours and international work, there are no clear background traits shared by all Shearman trainees. Our interviewees came from a surprisingly broad range of universities, including Oxbridge, the Russell Group and newer institutions.

In the Light and in the dark

Shearman's London office is just behind Liverpool Street station near Exchange Square. "*It's quite fun being near Shoreditch,*" one trainee enthused. "*It's a good location for going out.*" Trendy hangouts The Light Bar and the Strongroom are popular among trainees, as are The Fox and The Water Poet (over near Spitalfields) for more traditional pub-goers. "*The social calendar is fairly busy,*" one source said. "*Associates and trainees go out for drinks on a Friday when they can. All the trainees know each other very well. If associates or supervisors want to come along they do.*" There are also firm-sponsored "*card

behind the bar*" trainee socials every four months, and touch rugby and five-a-side football teams. We were told one department had recently been go-karting and clay pigeon shooting (not at the same time), and a summer party was held overlooking the Thames in 2012 to celebrate the London office's 40th anniversary.

Shearman trainees spoke positively about the atmosphere inside the office too. "*Because it's such a small office it is quite an informal environment. People wear chinos and smart-casual. There are always people having coffee in the break-out areas. It is a very collegiate atmosphere and people have pally relationships.*" There were no major grumbles about qualification either. Somewhat unusually, the firm does not announce which departments have NQ vacancies. Instead, second-years apply blind to the departments where they want to work. "*The firm wants people to apply where they want to go, not make tactical decisions,*" trainees explained. "*The system encourages informal discussions. Most trainees speak to the partners in the department they have been working in and subtly ask if there is likely to be a job on offer.*" Briefly put: it helps to network. Trainees hear if they have an NQ job in June and in 2012 seven of eight qualifiers stayed on come September.

And finally...

"*Every transaction you will work on will have an international dynamic. It's great that the quality of work we do is similar to the magic circle, but there is a smaller trainee group and you get more one-to-one exposure to partners.*" That, in a nutshell, is why trainees choose Shearman.

Sheridans

The facts

Location: London
Number of UK partners/solicitors: 27/20
Partners who trained at firm: 26%
Total number of trainees: 2
Seats: 4x6 months
Alternative seats: Occasional secondments

On chambersstudent.co.uk...
- How to get into Sheridans
- The amazing life of Bernard Sheridan

There's plenty to get starry-eyed about at this media gem – but beware: with so much changing so fast, it pays to keep abreast of legal and industry developments.

Britpop

Kylie, N-Dubz, Robbie Williams, Leona Lewis. Not, in fact a BRIT Awards retrospective, but a snapshot of Sheridans' frankly illustrious client list. Founded by Bernard Sheridan in 1953, the firm grew its entertainment practice as rapidly as the austere 50s became the swinging 60s. Paul McCartney, Pink Floyd and The Rolling Stones were all clients as Sheridans positioned itself at hip London's creative heart.

Today, the firm advises clients from the worlds of gaming, fashion, telecoms, leisure, advertising and sport as well as from the music, TV, film and theatre industries. Solid company/commercial, employment and property departments traditionally sourced work from creatives, but now "*increasingly generate their own work as well,*" according to partner Claire Lewis. The 'interactive' sector, which encompasses video games, online businesses and other digital media, is a natural area for expansion.

As the humble CD bows to Spotify, the interaction of music and the World Wide Web is something the firm is primed to deal with. Explained Lewis: "*There's a lot of crossover between groups, which we view as one of our big strengths. Within interactive, there will be people who do a lot of music, and if we're working on a large corporate transaction for a music publishing company, obviously music would be working with corporate.*" Trainees take four seats: dispute resolution and employment; TV, film and sport; company and commercial; and music, theatre and media. The interactive team is ever-growing and may become a seat in its own right. Trainees "*sometimes get asked to do work for a department you're not sitting in.*"

And the BAFTA goes to ...

The trainee in TV, film and sport will get to see the life of a movie right from the green light: from receiving financial backing through to being regulated. In film financing, the firm acts for well-established production companies and 'super-indies' like Shine, Avalon and Kudos. Starry Britflicks like *The Sweeney* and *Great Expectations* naturally bring work that is "*high-level. There's no actual involvement in financing for trainees, but there's a lot of post-completion admin, like arranging for multiparty agreements to be counter-signed and bibling all the documents.*" Sheridans worked on script clearance for Thatcher biopic *The Iron Lady* (an arduous process, if reports are to be believed), as well as negotiating terms of Meryl Streep's contract. It's on low-budget films that trainees will see more of a process and get a feel for "*what you'd look for as a client in terms of copyright ownership.*" There's also plenty of research needed, for example "*on compliance with the Ofcom broadcasting code.*" Sports work revolves around the licensing of rights to major events, event organisation and merchandise licensing. Recently the team has worked for FIFA and BSkyB. There are secondment opportunities in this seat – one trainee spent two days a week at production company Big Talk, makers of *Spaced*, *Shaun of the Dead* and *Rev*: "*Fantastic as an experience, and indicative of the flexibility of the training contract here.*" It provided lots of drafting opportunities, in addition to the rather more exciting

Chambers UK rankings

Media & Entertainment	Sports Law

script reads "*and seeing Simon Pegg and Nick Frost around the office*."

"*It's very busy, but never felt too bad*," thought one source of dispute resolution. "*In litigation you have to quickly grasp that there are some deadlines that have to be prioritised.*" The team takes on general commercial disputes, in addition to those from film, music, TV, IP and media clients. Sheridans has been sole adviser to the Press Complaints Committee in relation to the Leveson Inquiry. On smaller matters, trainees "*get the full range of work – from bundling to court applications, to liaising with counsel.*" As the only trainee in the team, it's often necessary to "*go to court yourself and submit an application.*" Smaller tasks can fall solely on the trainee's shoulders. "*Someone might be infringing a client's song by copying it on YouTube. The trainee will review it, put together a letter, and be in constant contact with the client.*" There's also ever-present defamation work in this seat. Sheridans acted for Katie Price when ex-hubby Peter Andre sued her over comments made about his parenting skills. "*The day before the trial, a story came out about it that wasn't particularly accurate. As it's a defamation, it goes before a jury, so the trial had to be postponed and a contempt of court claim brought in. It was fascinating to see how the trial played out in the complete change of circumstances.*"

Clients for the employment and coco teams were traditionally music management and TV and film production houses, but "*increasingly we're seeing online and advertising entrepreneurs coming directly here, giving the ancillary groups their own client base.*" Employment sees "*the full spectrum of clients: from chief execs of record labels or TV companies down to general employees of a model agency or website.*" Corporations advised include Gordon Ramsay Holdings, The Really Useful Group and Channel Four. The team acted for Mark Frith, ex-editor of *Smash Hits* and *Heat*, on his well-publicised exit from *Time Out* and his later appointment as 'super editor' of media conglomerate Bauer. Coco deals range from start-ups to private equity floats via investments and M&A – standalone clients include Octopus Investments and Earlscourt Holdings as well as digital agency Glamoo and mobile app developers Rocket Science. Here, trainees appreciate the range of tasks the deals afford them, which serve as a "*good introduction to how businesses are run and increase their capital.*"

Chances are you'll have heard of everyone the music, theatre and media team acts for. Current trainees have encountered "*a little bit of theatre work – predominantly drafting agreements and clearing the rights for plays.*" The team worked on the Broadway transfer of the successful (if critically sniffed at) *Rock of Ages*. They've also been busy working with the producers of the Jennifer Saunders-penned Spice Girls musical, *Viva Forever!* Music-wise, the work is "*big-ticket.*" Kate Bush's latest album, Dizzee Rascal's new label and Robbie Williams' move to Universal from EMI have all been negotiated by Sheridans. For trainees, "*the negotiation is enjoyable, though working with brand-new artists gives you the responsibility to push for a recording deal and see what it means to them personally.*"

One big Dappy family

Unsurprisingly for a firm that takes on one candidate a year, trainees have a pretty personalised experience. Formal appraisals exist, but "*you can approach someone any time you've done work for them.*" Trainees emphasise that "*when required, you have to put in the hours,*" though only ever because a specific matter means that's necessary. "*Everyone's a real person here, pretty relaxed and informal – it's the way clients like it.*" There are monthly organised drinks, and a large enough contingent of "*young associates*" to always have a drinking buddy should you wish. Formal Christmas and summer parties are staples of the social calendar, most recently taking place at "*a banqueting hall and the rooftop of a Soho hotel*" respectively.

Prospective trainees should heed two pieces of advice. Firstly: "*It's nice to be involved with matters you can tell your friends about, but it's far more important to have an understanding of the legal work that goes into it.*" After all, contracts are contracts whether you're drawing them up for N-Dubz or not. But here's another thought: "*The work is similar to any commercial work at base level, but it's also very niche. The clients dictate you should have a real interest and understanding in what they're doing – you need to be driving things forward rather than just responding.*" Sources encourage wannabes to get "*as much work experience as possible,*" and get up to speed with changes in the firm's key industries, "*the current big thing being the government's crackdown on online piracy.*" Read more on our website.

And finally...
Qualification can be tricky in firms as niche as this, but happily the sole 2012 qualifier stayed on with Sheridans as an NQ.

DON'T MISS
YOUR CHANCE

Join a firm with the scale, stature and clients to provide you with the quality and variety of work and opportunities that you need to grow your career.

Be a part of it.

Apply now at
www.shoosmiths.co.uk

Shoosmiths

The facts

Location: Birmingham, Basingstoke, Milton Keynes, Northampton, Nottingham, Reading, Fareham, London, Manchester, Scotland

Number of UK partners/solicitors: 110/350

Partners who trained at firm: 7.5%

Total number of trainees: 41

Seats: 4x6 months

Alternative seats: Secondments

On chambersstudent.co.uk...
- How to get into Shoosmiths
- Interview with firm chairman Andrew Tubbs

"*Straightforward*" and "*down-to-earth*" are buzzwords at Shoosmiths, which is intent on continuing to grow and upping its profile at the national level.

Skyrockets in flight

The last decade has been one of immense growth for Shoosmiths: the national outfit doubled its turnover between 2002 and 2008. In years past the Northampton-founded firm was known primarily for its active presence in the personal injury and debt recovery sectors, but it now operates a full service, having incorporated practices like litigation, corporate, employment and property into the majority of its ten offices. As *Chambers UK* illustrates, Shoosmiths is strong across the board, with top-tier rankings in practices as varied as banking litigation (Manchester), IP/IT (Milton Keynes), private client (Northampton) and competition (Nottingham).

When the recession came knocking in 2008/09, Shoosmiths took an unfortunate hit in both profit and revenue. Trainee deferrals, voluntary pay cuts and two redundancy rounds contributed to an immediate rebound in profitability – net profit skyrocketed 83% in 2009/10 and another 25% in 2010/11. However, revenue has yet to return to pre-downturn levels, standing at £87m in 2011/12. Moreover, as we went to print the firm announced another round of redundancies, mainly affecting the trainee-free Basingstoke office.

Afternoon delight

Despite this latest bump in the road, trainees across offices insisted: "*There's definitely a good atmosphere at the firm right now – it's all hands on deck and nearly every location is recruiting.*" Shoosmiths' impending merger with Scottish firm Archibald Campbell & Harley – set to go ahead in autumn 2012 – proved a weighty factor in the chirpy attitudes prevalent among our interviewees. "*It's a good example of how we're growing and evolving as a workforce. The firm's ambition is to become the most renowned national law firm, and this is a step towards that.*" Some hefty client wins in the past year – including choccy retailer Thorntons and doughnut king Krispy Kreme – have also cemented a positive impression of the firm's current state and prompted a brand review. "*They're interested in updating our brand to include a new website and logo. Our ethos of offering straightforward delivery of services won't change, but I think the firm as a whole will be perceived as more modern.*"

Crunching the numbers

Training contracts are available in Nottingham, Birmingham, Reading, Fareham, Manchester, Northampton and Milton Keynes (with only half an hour between them, the last two operate as one office as far as trainees are concerned). Of the remaining offices, London operates mainly as a client meeting point while Basingstoke is a hub for the firm's private client arm Access Legal. At the time of our calls, there were ten trainees in Northampton/MK, seven in Birmingham, six each in Reading and Fareham, five in Nottingham and two in Manchester.

Trainees don't get a say in their first seat (unless they're part of the 30 to 40% who are already paralegalling at the firm), but from there on "*graduate recruitment is very flexible and accommodating. You get to discuss your preferences and they make sure you get to sit where you want before qualification.*" Aside from an initial meeting in the

Chambers UK rankings

Banking & Finance	Licensing
Banking Litigation	Pensions
Clinical Negligence	Personal Injury
Competition/European Law	Planning
Corporate/M&A	Private Client
Dispute Resolution	Product Liability
Employment	Real Estate
Environment	Real Estate Litigation
Health & Safety	Restructuring/Insolvency
Information Technology	Retail
Intellectual Property	Tax

Northampton HQ (a business park building called The Lakes), there's not much trainee traffic between offices, though *"you can apply nationwide for client secondments and NQ jobs."* Thanks to small intakes, there's always just one trainee per seat, *"so you're relied on a lot and never have to vie for work."*

The Lakes and MK

The main seats in Northampton revolve around debt recovery services, so financial litigation and recovery work are common. *"Recovery is quite specialist, so it's actually really interesting."* The department is *"responsible for tracking down people who've missed bills like their car payments, so it becomes a bit like detective work. You've got people chasing down third parties and others handling the defence. There are a lot of opportunities to see different sides of cases."* Our interviewees reported handling their own files and attending hearings at the High Court. *"You can seek advice at any time, but they give you work that's similar to the qualified solicitors,"* said one. The office as a whole is Shoosmiths' biggest, and while its interior is admittedly *"dated,"* it benefits from a *"young atmosphere – there are a lot of people under 30, so the dynamic is pretty fun."*

Milton Keynes is *"well positioned as a commercial centre for South Midlands and North London banking work,"* and is regarded firm-wide as *"the place to go for IP."* Indeed, this team has fingers in the education, retail, automotive and technology sectors and a top-drawer client list that includes Red Bull, H&M, McDonald's, Amazon and IKEA. In a recent case of royal proportions (bear with us here), lawyers advised high-street chain LK Bennett on its dispute with New York's The Jones Group over the design rights to a dress worn by the Duchess of Cambridge. MK's also home to the head of the *"very technical"* pensions team and houses a specialist real estate practice that acts for residential developers like Bellway Homes and Barratt Developments. *"It's pretty similar to corporate in that it's all about the deals; you're just selling land*

instead of companies." The office may suffer from a *"commuter culture"* due to its business park location but *"it's not dead by any stretch of the imagination,"* its occupants insisted, filling us in on events like the annual summer ball, regular local junior lawyers dos and five-a-side football matches with local clients.

Berks to Brum

Reading is *"one of the few offices that has a presence in every commercial area."* Seats in corporate, commercial, commercial litigation, IP, banking, employment, real estate and real estate litigation are available. The corporate practice *"has been doing very well lately,"* trainees said, mentioning the team's recent work for sizeable regional clients – such as Ageas, which it advised on a £53m acquisition of Castle Cover share capital – as well as some bigger players, like Krispy Kreme and its £25m management buyout. *"The department's really fast-moving. You're initially handed some admin tasks like filings and filling in forms, but there's a definite progression towards drafting board minutes and sitting in on meetings."* Commercial litigation's been occupied with *"people going to court because of bills they can't pay,"* while employment's *"incredibly busy"* thanks to redundancies connected to the recession. Such contentious seats tend to entail bundling, drafting claims and letters to the other side and occasional court appearances. There's even the chance to *"run some small files – I got to chase some low-value litigation claims all by myself."* Luckily, *"it's not all work, work, work."* There's a big athletic scene – football tournaments, cricket matches and a running club – and low-key affairs like *"drinks at the local pub every first Friday of the month."* Reading, like all the offices, has New Friday, a trainee-instigated informal networking event that occurs every three months or so.

In Nottingham, five seats are on offer: real estate, real estate litigation, corporate, commercial and employment. The commercial team, particularly strong in the white goods and building materials sectors, has clients ranging from health-corp Coloplast to the Open University to tractor manufacturer extraordinaire John Deere. *"There have been lots of changes to commercial law recently, so trainees are encouraged to write articles on these updates,"* one source reported, mentioning that *"a commercial seat also offers the opportunity to get your hands on some competition work too."* As such, the seat's *"a pretty mixed bag – sometimes you get involved in writing first drafts of confidentiality agreements or terms and conditions of sale; other times you're busy with data protection work, which includes reviewing clauses and agreements and preparing presentations."* Like Northampton, the office has a rep as *"one of the younger, cooler and more vibrant"* members of the Shoosmiths clan – *"we've got a lot of keen fancy dressers, and there aren't too many old partners here!"*

Birmingham has one of the widest ranges of seats, with lender services, commercial, commercial litigation, corporate/insolvency, personal injury, employment, construction and real estate/planning all on offer. On the corporate front, clients include local names like Birmingham City Council and Birmingham City FC as well as a few multinationals like publishing corporation Informa, while IT lawyers have recently handled projects for Associated British Foods, Thomas Cook and Experian. The Birmingham office is also home to a specialist construction team, which packs a mighty punch despite its small size – lawyers are currently overseeing English Heritage's construction of a £20m visitor centre at Stonehenge. "*A construction seat's like a cross between commercial and commercial litigation in the building industry, so you get a pretty wide experience.*" Thanks to the office's growth in recent years, its occupants are looking forward to relocating to bigger premises "*in the next year or two.*"

Northern Solent

One of the firm's "*key aims*" is to expand the Manchester base. "*We're all really excited about moving the office forward and developing its client base,*" one source confirmed. "*It's traditionally focused on debt recovery work, but in the last few years they've expanded into more corporate and commercial stuff – the aim is to make it full-service.*" Manchester currently takes on just two trainees a year and offers seats in the real estate, commercial, corporate/banking and finance litigation departments, though interviewees hinted that "*they might be adding more services like IP soon.*"

The Fareham office, referred to as Solent, offers seats in commercial, commercial litigation, corporate, employment and property/planning. Fareham's employment team "*is a good seat for getting a mix of contentious and non-contentious work,*" while its planning practice is highly ranked in *Chambers UK* and handles a substantial amount of public inquiry work as well as projects for local authorities and developers. The office itself may be somewhat isolated in its business park location, but that doesn't stop trainees from "*going for a few drinks after work fairly regularly – we just can't have too many seeing as we have to drive!*"

While interviewees admitted the trainee experience is liable to vary depending on which office you attend, sources firm-wide described a similar policy when it comes to responsibility: "*You get a lot fairly early on, and if you show promise you continue to receive that degree of trust.*" As one elaborated, "*initially you'll be given lower-level stuff that gives you an idea of how admin work fits into the bigger picture, but they're very much willing to give you access to better work as soon as they see you can handle it.*" We did hear about the odd difference in vibe between offices in the South and the North (seeing as some have a "*younger*" feel than others), but for the most part "*Shoosmiths culture shines through*" in all, insiders agreed.

A traditional perk of a Shoosmiths training contract is the virtually guaranteed opportunity to do a client secondment. "*There are easily enough available for everyone.*" Options include some local clients as well as national players like Home Retail (operators of Argos and Homebase). "*I was given a lot of autonomy during mine, like holding my own meetings and assisting with presentations,*" one trainee testified.

Straight shooters

Thanks to open-plan offices, the firm "*isn't an intimidating environment for trainees. You sit among everyone from support staff to senior partners, and there's no air of superiority that might discourage you from approaching someone.*" This "*lack of boundaries*" is "*really great from a development point of view – you witness how the partners negotiate and approach their work, which helps you learn.*" Moreover, "*there's a lot of emphasis on training. Supervisors really invest a lot of time explaining the hows and whys.*"

The few grumbles we heard from trainees mostly revolved around salaries, which start at £24,000 in all offices. "*It would be nice to see it increased as the cost of living rises – I think it would help attract and retain the right people,*" one thought. Still, none could deny the upside to this – namely "*a terrific work/life balance.*" More than one source recounted anecdotes about "*being told to go home at seven*" and "*receiving days off in lieu after you've worked late for a few weeks.*" As one trainee explained, this boils down to "*having a bit of extra time and space you don't get at a high-octane City firm. That's not to say things will never get stressful, but you'll never be so out of your wits that you don't have time to reflect on what it is you're actually learning.*"

And finally...

Our sources encouraged applicants to "*make sure they know the ins and outs of which office you're applying to as they differ in specialisms and head count.*" Following a "*fairly stress-free*" qualification period, all 16 qualifiers were retained in 2012.

Sidley Austin LLP

The facts

Location: London

Number of UK partners/solicitors: 30/63

Partners who qualified at firm: 13%

Total number of trainees: 19

Seats: 4x6 months

Alternative seats: Brussels

Extras: Pro bono – LawWorks

On chambersstudent.co.uk...
• How to get into Sidley
• Capital markets explained

Sidley Austin's finance know-how is undisputed, but with post-recession diversification, there are many more reasons to train here.

Reasons to be cheerful

The Sidley Austin we know today actually comes from the 2001 combination of Chicago native Sidley & Austin and New York's Brown & Wood, a move which created one of the ten largest firms on the planet. In just over a decade, this titan has added offices in Geneva, Brussels, Frankfurt and Sydney to its existing hubs in eight US cities plus Shanghai, Singapore, Hong Kong, Beijing, Tokyo and of course London, which has been around since 1974. London's age and size make it the firm's key European outpost, and its lawyers frequently handle cross-jurisdictional matters.

The focus of London was traditionally quite niche financial work: securitisation and derivatives, financial services regulation and debt capital markets. As the credit crunch hit this kind of work exceptionally hard, Sidley quickly broadened its practice. Using its strengths in the securities arena, it moved into insolvency and restructuring, in addition to other areas that suffer less in recessions, such as insurance, dispute resolution and regulatory. Accordingly, the make-up of the London office has shifted, as HR director Jerry Gallagher told us. "*Global finance is still the largest practice, with 30% of the total in London. This is followed by corporate, then capital markets, dispute resolution, regulatory, insolvency, insurance, tax and funds.*" The diversification of London has borne dividends, with the office reporting a 5% hike in revenue for the 2011 financial year.

The future will see "*continued growth in our European operations,*" says Gallagher. "*We look for opportunities to capitalise on each office's individual strengths and to*

strategically work cohesively as a whole. We recently have seen a senior partner from the States move to the European offices in order to focus on this."

Financial times

New starters can "*mention a preference*" for first seats although the firm "*doesn't make guarantees.*" Subsequent allocation is arranged two months into the training contract, when trainees meet with HR and discuss likes and dislikes. "*No one's ever allocated seats they actively don't want – that's quite a clear policy,*" say trainees. Seats are currently available in the Global Finance Group (GFG), capital markets, funds, tax, insurance, corporate, regulatory, insolvency, dispute resolution, employment and competition. A six-month Brussels secondment is also available.

Diversification has meant that a stint in finance "*is no longer necessary,*" although due to its size, many trainees still spend six months there. The group is split between three teams: derivatives, global finance and real estate. Trainees report a recent uptick in securitisation work, and are thrilled to be at the centre of this process: "*Since 2008, everyone has had a conceptual idea of what it is, but to see it actually operate and comprehend what needs to be done to enact a process is hugely gratifying.*" Briefly, the process involves the pooling of debt such as mortgages, credit card debt and loans and selling this consolidated liability as securities or CMOs to investors. A trainee working on one acted for an originator of mortgages, "*making sure all the documentation was in place, drafting all the purchase documents that investors would need to*

Chambers UK rankings

Capital Markets	Investment Funds
Competition/European Law	Real Estate Finance
Dispute Resolution	Restructuring/Insolvency
Insurance	Tax

subscribe to notes, organising board minutes and dealing with Scottish and Jersey counsel." Despite *"flat-out hours,"* trainees love the seat. *"It's obviously challenging, but everything you do is appreciated, and you're an integrated part of the deal. In finance there's a focus on helping trainees to understand the financial philosophy behind them."* Long hours are also a big part of the expanding capital markets department. Deals often have an international element, like the firm's representation of RBC and Scotia Capital in a $170m sovereign bond offering by the Turks and Caicos Islands. A corporate seat can be split with either tax or employment. Its staple work is cross-border M&A and funds-based transactions, and the team counts eBay, Allied Irish Banks and Western Union among its client base.

(In)sure about it?

Regulatory is an area with *"a lot of changes happening. There's the constant need to review, propose ideas and come up with theses on how they could impact on companies going forward."* The group acts for banks, insurers and fund managers on cross-border compliance issues under UK and EU regulations. One trainee worked *"with fund associations on lobbying new pieces of legislation – making submissions to help the drafting process and ensuring it's coherent. It's interesting because you get to see what debates are going on at EU level."* Another *"liaised with the Financial Services Authority on the progress of applications, prepared lawyer presentations and researched complex FSA rules."* Sidley acts for the Managed Funds Association and the Investment Company Institute, in addition to financial institutions like JPMorgan Chase and MasterCard International. There's also a lot of data protection work in this seat.

Sidley's insurance division covers both contentious and transactional work. The former involves insurance and reinsurance claims for clients such as Pulsar Re, Magnetar Capital and Lonmar. The non-contentious practice uses the firm's depth in structured finance and derivatives to work on de-risking work such as longevity swaps (offsetting the risk of pension scheme members living longer than expected). Trainees enjoy the academic nature of insurance and the depth to which research tasks can lead – one *"looked into how the law defines the word 'price'"* – on top of *"proof-reading, looking at contracts and background reading."* Sidley acts for big hitters such as Prudential and Aviva on transactional matters, recently

advising Aon on restructuring its employee benefits consultancy following a merger with Hewitt.

The dispute resolution team focuses on conflicts from insurance, IP and technology, real estate finance, derivatives, structured finance and product liability. It represented Fondazione Enasarco in derivatives litigation against Lehman Brothers Finance for $100m, and Pulsar Re in relation to the liquidation of Lehman Re. There's plenty of court time and trainees *"will be in on conference calls and in meetings with clients."*

Competition work comprises antitrust, merger control and compliance, and the team works closely with Sidley's Brussels office on EU and regulatory matters. Headline matters include acting for Alberto Culver on merger control issues stemming from its acquisition by Unilever. *"You have to get quite intimately involved in the details of how companies are run. There was a problem with soap sales with that merger – Alberto Culver owns TRESemmé and Simple, and Unilever owns Dove, so we had to make submissions relating to soap, asking if bar soap and liquid soap are different product markets."* Trainees receive *"a broad range of research and writing-based work."*

An education

Sources praised Sidley's emphasis on *"helping trainees to learn the legal principles that are in play. They don't just ask you to go and perform a task, but they take time to explain the client and what they're hoping to achieve. When you have that context, you're never going off and blindly trying to draft something."* There are mid and end-of-seat appraisals which *"the firm takes seriously,"* although the high level of supervisor contact means *"it's more a case of discussing progress informally and then having this reflected at the end."* Trainees share an office with their supervisor. *"It allows for good exposure to a high standard of work,"* thought one. *"If you're working with them then you get to see the overall picture rather than being roped into a tiny aspect of a deal, and you also get to observe how they work and hear them on calls."*

Sidley partners are *"relaxed people, and don't get shirty if you have questions. They know that if you feel confident in approaching them, the work product will end up better – and when partners are like this, juniors adopt a similar approach."* Sources were split when we asked if the office felt American. *"It's a mixture,"* thought one, *"as we market ourselves as having an English ethos and atmosphere to UK clients, although a lot of good work comes from the US."* Fewer than 10% of Sidley's London lawyers are US-qualified. Sources were clear, though, that however British Sidley's accent, there's space for Yank entrepreneurialism. *"You get rewarded for taking on responsibility, so if you're proactive and friendly, it can only go well."*

Trainees here are *"bright, and genuinely interested in complex work."* In the past we've noted the presence of several slightly older trainees and this year was no exception, with plenty of Master's and PhD graduates in the mix. This is not necessarily coincidental. *"Generally speaking, people reconsidering their career don't consider the magic circle, but look for something different. If someone is an ex-banker, for example, they would have already come across us in their career."* NQ positions are released in mid-April and in 2012, seven of the nine qualifiers were kept on to continue their education further.

"The firm's keen to impress that on the day you start, your background and university are irrelevant – there's no reference back, as the day you start it's an opportunity to develop." Accordingly, Sidley's commitment to diversity in recruiting is *"very serious."* The UK office has a number of links with schemes like the Windsor Fellowship and the PRIME initiative: the former a scheme to improve ethnic diversity; the latter a work experience venture for students from disadvantaged backgrounds. The firm recently established a steering group including both lawyers and support staff, who meet quarterly.

The small trainee cohort meet up regularly for lunch and drinks at deli bar The Anthologist and The Old Doctor Butler's Head off Moorgate. Sidley's social committee arranges events like *"cake sales, barbecues, cheese and wine evenings and pub quiz nights,"* as well as frequent interesting client events. *"Tom McNab, who was an Olympic coach and worked on Chariots of Fire, came to speak about his new play, 1936, and how it relates to modern business. There aren't that many internal events, but when the firm puts them on, it pushes the boat out."* The Halloween party sees Sidley HQ transformed into a family-friendly wonderland, this year with a Harry Potter theme.

And finally...

Sidley's ethos is a successful mix of responsibility and development. *"If you want to be one of hundreds and not have client contact, this isn't the place for you – here, responsibility starts on day one."*

Simmons & Simmons LLP

The facts

Location: London, Bristol

Number of UK partners/solicitors: 120/212

Partners who trained at firm: 38.3%

Total number of trainees: 82

Seats: 4x6 months

Alternative seats: Overseas seats, secondments

Extras: Pro bono – LawWorks, A4ID and others

On chambersstudent.co.uk...
- How to get into Simmons
- Simmons' art collection
- More on seats and secondments

Founded by twin brothers in 1896, Simmons & Simmons is one of the most well-known names in the City.

When she was good...

Like the little girl with the curl from the nursery rhyme, when Simmons is good, it's very, very good. For example, the firm is a leader for finance work, and its hedge fund practice is quite simply superb. A client's comment to *Chambers UK* – "*they had the best hedge fund practice 15 years ago and they remain among the best today*" – should give you an idea of the high regard in which this group is held. The other areas in which Simmons is unarguably very, very good are employment, life sciences and IP.

And when she was bad she was horrid? Well, no, not really. Nonetheless, there is something of a perception that Simmons has drifted slightly over the past decade. Peers such as Norton Rose and Lovells have surpassed it in global reach by entering into international mergers, while other firms are pushing up behind. Away from the main pillars of strength we've mentioned, the firm is less of a heavy hitter. For example, it's not that Simmons' corporate group is poor – it is recommended by *Chambers UK* – but it's not in the very highest tiers. Trainees admitted readily enough: "*As soon as you leave the magic circle firms, which are perceived to be good at everything, you have smaller firms that have some practices that rival the magic circle and some that don't.*"

Simmons recently revealed a new three-year strategic plan. In that, it could have attempted to boost its 'some that don't' practices like corporate and real estate but it hasn't done so. Instead, the firm has made a very conscious decision to further enhance what it does best. The key new elements of the strategy, training partner Alex Brown says, are "*more investment into the asset management sector, and to build on our existing funds practice. We have a market-leading hedge funds group, and we want to tack on other funds work – private equity, for example.*" Additionally, says Brown, the recent hire of five partners from BLP has added "*oomph*" to the banking team. All in all, the finance practices appear to be taking centre stage in the firm's future plans, although energy and infrastructure, life sciences, and technology, media and telecoms are also named among Simmons' five key sectors.

The spectre of a potential future merger can't be ignored. Simmons has an international network of 20 offices but if it wants to keep pace with the emerging global elite, a tie-up with a (probably American) firm would look very logical. It has flirted with other firms in the past but never gone all the way. Trainees' opinions on this subject were mixed. From one: "*Do I think it will happen? Absolutely. Who will it be with? I won't speculate.*" From another: "*I don't think it's on the cards now.*" Alex Brown says: "*It isn't in our strategy to merge at all. It would be a flawed strategy only to be out there to get married. Like every other large firm, we would absolutely look at an interesting prospect, but we are not actively out there searching for a bolt-on partner.*" Read an extended interview with him on our website. Anyway, Simmons continues to expand steadily overseas (China, Africa and the Middle East are areas of particular interest at the moment), and also recently opened an office in Bristol focusing on projects, real estate and dispute resolution. That's a sensible move, as it will help keep costs down by doing some work in the West Country.

Chambers UK rankings

Asset Finance	Information Technology
Banking & Finance	Intellectual Property
Banking Litigation	Investment Funds
Capital Markets	Life Sciences
Commodities	Outsourcing
Competition/European Law	Pensions
Construction	Product Liability
Consumer Finance	Professional Negligence
Corporate Crime & Investigations	Projects
Corporate/M&A	Real Estate
Dispute Resolution	Real Estate Finance
Employment	Restructuring/Insolvency
Energy & Natural Resources	Retail
Environment	Tax
Financial Services	Telecommunications
Fraud	Transport
Health & Safety	

Top of its game

Trainees are expected to complete a corporate/commercial seat, a finance-related seat, and one in a contentious area of practice, but there are numerous choices within these three areas. Trainees rank all 14 available seats in order of preference and usually get their first or second choice. A change to the system means new starters now get a say in their first seat, a "*really good*" development. Trainees can also tick a box to go on a client secondment or to an overseas office, and here some grumbling did emerge. "*You can express a preference as to what overseas seat you want, but it's made clear you should basically be willing to go wherever the firm wants.*" That's caused "*a little bit of a kerfuffle,*" as people desperate to go to one location have been shipped off to another.

The financial markets department is central to Simmons and so an interest in this area is vital. In case you're not sold yet, we asked a trainee what's interesting about moving cash from place to place. "*The scale of the transactions makes it exciting, and it's great to see a deal reported in the papers that you have been involved in.*" At Simmons there's also the "*kudos*" of working in a department that's at the top of its game. The renowned hedge funds team is a "*fun, young*" group that can be "*demanding in terms of hours*" but which offers "*brilliant*" work. "*At the beginning of the seat,*" one source told us, "*there are smaller tasks – admin and basic drafting, and you are heavily supervised. But once I'd seen one hedge fund launch, since the documentation stays more or less the same, my supervisor would give me launches to run and let me do initial drafts of documents and contact the client.*" As well as launches, trainees might work on the reorganisation of an existing fund or on negotiations of

agreements with its administrators. The more specialised work is rarer and stays with the partners, but trainees become "*quite practised*" at drafting and dealing with clients and counterparties.

That's my derivative

Life in the derivatives seat received equally good reviews. It can be "*a bit of a headache*" trying to understand the "*very technical*" work but fortunately "*the partners are keen to ensure we feel comfortable asking questions – they realise you haven't a hope in hell of getting your head around derivatives unless you constantly badger your supervisor!*" Other finance-related seats include regulatory, banking and asset finance. Banking is an "*ambitious*" department, recently boosted by those hires from BLP, that wants the same recognition given to other parts of the financial markets group. Asset finance is a smaller group, where "*they are open to it if you want to take on more responsibility*" and which has the "*glamour of being able to travel to aircraft deliveries.*"

Though the corporate group doesn't have the volume of deals that you would find at the magic circle, "*I had heard of most of our clients before I worked here,*" one trainee said. "*I'd say we get the smaller deals of the really big companies, and the big deals of smaller companies.*" For example, Simmons represented HMV in its £53m sale of Waterstones. The work is more "*varied*" than simply M&A: there are also private equity deals and corporate restructuring to contend with, as well as "*public sector work for government bodies.*" The trainee experience in this seat "*can go either way.*" One of our sources had "*got involved in client meetings and negotiations*" and been "*allowed within limits to discuss certain points on agreements. I could see the trainee on the other side of the deal wasn't having that same experience.*" At the same time, "*sometimes on a large deal there is more admin to do,*" and trainees will find themselves with tasks like verification or data

room management.

Simmons has a large dispute resolution department, of which roughly a third is devoted to financial markets litigation, taking on both claimant and defendant instructions from investment and retail banks and other companies in the finance sector. Other areas of work include professional negligence, real estate litigation, contentious construction and general commercial matters. "*In litigation they like to see you get the little things perfect before they trust you with larger matters,*" said one source. "*Saying that, I seemed to do all right: in one particular case I was on the phone to counsel and experts every other day as the main point of contact.*" Some of the work is "*inevitably adminny,*" though: filing, bundling, and "*we have to provide daily updates to the client so there are sta-*

tus tables that I need to update every day." Clients of the IP group include Coca-Cola, BAT and pharma companies Eli Lilly and GlaxoSmithKline. Much of the group's work is 'hard' IP – patent litigation – but "*I did a lot of contentious soft IP work*," said our trainee source, "*writing correspondence, bundling of course, and generally getting really involved.*" In one major matter, Simmons successfully defended Samsung against Apple in a design infringement case (the one where the judge ruled that Samsung's Galaxy tablet was less 'cool' than the iPad). Read about other Simmons seats and secondments on our website.

Come into our world

There is no doubt that Simmons has a reputation for being a slightly more cuddly alternative to the magic circle and, indeed, many of our sources had chosen it for this reason, rather than for the allure of its finance work or the chance of an overseas seat. There are "*no tossers*" here, we were assured. "*We're not a macho firm.*" There may be "*one or two old-school partners who are a bit grumpy sometimes,*" but the quality of supervision and mentoring was roundly praised and "*there is an open-door policy that is actually enforced – I mean, a partner will genuinely go and ask an associate why they have their door closed if they are not on a call.*" Bumping Simmons further up the 'lovely scale', its LGBT efforts have been recognised by Stonewall and sources agreed that this is "*not marketing fluff.*" One trainee affirmed: "*It's not like there's glitter coming from the ceilings and Kylie playing in the lifts but I've never felt anything other than comfortable here.*" Certainly, it's to be commended that Simmons has rolled its LGBT initiatives out across its whole network, including the Middle East – "*a region where it's not purely in its commercial interests to do so.*" Simmons is also strong on pro bono for a UK firm. "*We don't just do the easy stuff like going down to the Citizens Advice centre – though I do that as well – but take on more juicy international human rights cases.*"

Cuddly or not, the workload can still be gruelling – even in litigation, which traditionally has more regular hours, one source had experienced "*quite a bit of weekend and late-night working.*" It would be advisable to apply to Simmons alive to the fact that 'nice' does not equal 'easy'.

The business of law

When the recession required law firms across the City to push back the start dates of their trainees, Simmons came up with the novel idea of giving its own deferred trainees the opportunity to complete an MBA in the time they suddenly had spare. The fourth-seaters at the time of our calls were the first to be offered the MBA. While they agreed that they didn't use the knowledge they'd gained in the day-to-day practice of law, those who had done it had clearly found it useful – several quoted little mantras they had learned on the course. Some also opined that those who had completed the MBA arrived at Simmons "*a lot more confident*" than those who hadn't. While future trainees won't complete a full MBA before starting, they will complete extra business courses during their LPC and training contract, giving them the option to complete an MBA post-qualification.

We've collected comprehensive retention statistics for every firm we cover in the True Picture for some time now. In a normal year, about 80% of trainees will be retained at the firm that trained them. However, since we started keeping records, Simmons never once managed to reach even that average, and has retained just 69% of trainees qualifying between 2002 and 2011. There are some complex reasons for this, which we won't go into here, but we wonder if the firm couldn't help matters by reducing the size of its intakes slightly. The firm kept on 36 of its 46 qualifiers (78%) in 2012: one of its better results.

A lively social scene includes plenty of sports clubs, quizzes and ski trips, a "*soirée*" in Ampersand, the firm's rather good restaurant, every couple of months, and of course spontaneous Friday pubbing in the watering holes around the firm's CityPoint offices. Finally, we can't fail to mention that Simmons has one of the best art collections of any UK firm – see our website for more details.

And finally...
Look to Simmons if you want a full-service training contract with a heavy finance flavour.

SJ Berwin LLP

The facts

Location: London

Number of UK partners/solicitors: 94/170

Partners who trained at firm: 21%

Total number of trainees: 76

Seats: 4x6 months

Alternative seats: Overseas seats, secondments

Extras: Pro bono – Toynbee Hall Law Centre

On chambersstudent.co.uk...
- How to get into SJB
- The world of private equity

"*Young, dynamic and punchy*" sums up this corporate go-getter, which is celebrating its 30th birthday this year.

Founding fathers and pioneer spirits

SJ Berwin represents founder Stanley Berwin's second major stamp on the City's legal scene. After establishing the firm that would later become known as Berwin Leighton Paisner, he departed for an in-house position, returning four years later with a reinvigorated interest in customer service, which he was determined to find room for within the firm's ethos. Opinions on commercial outlooks clashed, however, and so in 1982 Berwin sired a new firm in which clients' commercial interests were prioritised – a radical notion in the staid world of early 80s legal London. And thus SJ Berwin was born, playing the rebellious younger sibling to straight-laced BLP and elbowing its way through the thick of the establishment and right into the UK top 25.

Following Berwin's death in 1988 the firm eventually fell into the custody of David Harrel, whose long stint at the top saw SJB's partnership quadruple in size and its network grow to include multiple European offices. He's also (partly) the man to thank for today's market NQ salaries, having incited an infamous pay war among City firms in the early noughties. The onslaught of the recession marked the start of a rather rocky ride for SJB: the sparkle of its sensational City ascent was slightly dulled by redundancies, lawyer defections and two failed merger negotiations with American firms Orrick and Proskauer Rose.

That said, SJB managed to open offices in Hong Kong, Shanghai and Dubai during the downturn, surpassing the achievements of some peer firms at the time and nabbing a slice of the coveted Asian market. In late 2010, leadership of the firm was passed to Rob Day, who trainees credit with guiding SJB in its "*transition from a European to an international entity.*" Healthy financial results in 2011 and 2012 have no doubt boosted spirits in the office. "*We've certainly turned a corner,*" training principal Nicola Bridge says, emphasising the firm's efforts to "*build up countercyclical practices like litigation so we're balanced for all economic situations.*" According to trainees, "*the message is that they're not looking to close themselves off by limiting the focus to any one area.*" Our sources anticipate an increase in activity for traditional strengths like private equity and fund formation – "*areas SJB's known for*" – and cited certain litigation subgroups, like arbitration and competition, as areas likely to expand over the next few years.

And the prospect of a US merger? Yet more talks, this time with Mayer Brown, reportedly took place in the summer of 2012. Despite SJB's public insistence that it's completely relaxed and in no desperate hurry to push through a merger, it increasingly looks like a question of when, not if. Bridge says: "*It's something we'll continue to consider if we come across an opportunity that enables us to achieve our strategic objectives while protecting our culture and values.*" According to trainees, "*there's a degree of speculation about our macro-planning, but the fact that it's mooted doesn't affect daily life at the firm.*" Indeed, they name the firm's fierce desire to avoid stagnation as "*one of the best things about SJB.*"

Chambers UK rankings

Learning your ABCs

Seat allocation is fairly straightforward: trainees complete a form before each rotation, listing four preferences. Throughout their training contracts, they are meant to complete two corporate seats, one contentious seat and one wild card, which includes areas like real estate, tax and financial markets. According to our sources, there's a *"bit of wiggle room"* with the requirements: for instance, the firm has stretched its definition of corporate to include finance.

SJB's corporate department is split into teams named, quite simply, A, B and C. *"Their main difference is in origin – they were once power circles led by different partners that eventually hardened into groups over time,"* one trainee explained. As such, the teams aren't entirely black and white when it comes to the spread of transactions they handle, and there's crossover between each. As far as we can tell, team B mainly contends with deals, while C manages SJB's famous funds activity and team A *"sweeps up the rest,"* working on a mishmash of transactions *"like IPOs and restructuring deals."*

SJB's breadth of M&A work covers high-end and mid-market deals in both the private and public spheres. The firm has advised on several multibillion-pound deals lately, including Universal's £1.2bn takeover of rival EMI's recorded music division and British Land's £2.1bn stake in Broadgate Estate, an elite East London office district. Lawyers also handle takeovers in speciality sectors like retail, hotels, pharmaceuticals and media. *"It's a pretty lean, mean team,"* trainees said, describing their time in the department as *"one in which you have responsibilities thrust upon you whether you want them or not. You're often the key contact for the client."* On the funds front SJB is among the best, particularly on the private equity side of things, and advises on a host of *"complicated and technical"* structurings including venture capital trusts,

REITs and alternative investment funds for some rather impressive clients – *"the number of prestigious names I worked with was ridiculous,"* recalled one trainee. Another reported *"doing six fund closings in six months,"* mentioning that a stint with the team includes *"quite a bit"* of drafting of agreements and minutes as well as *"some high-pressured moments – one closing saw me thrown into a taxi to deliver the paperwork to the client at the eleventh hour."*

The chance to work on headline transactions is a big draw for trainees, but it comes with a price – *"insane hours – we're talking back-to-back all-nighters."* To put it lightly, after a corporate stint *"you quickly readjust your opinion of what constitutes a late night."* While most celebrate their ordeal as a rite of passage, the pressure to *"get used to sacrificing most of your weekday evenings"* can take its toll on some. *"If there's a deal on, you can forget about girlfriends, mums and birthdays because you probably won't be leaving in the PM,"* we were told. Fortunately, *"everyone's in it together,"* so a lonely experience it ain't. Plus, there's a fair amount of flexibility when it's not busy, and *"for the most part people are pretty good at not dumping things on your desk at 5.30pm and telling you to have fun."*

SJB is a leader for private equity work and most trainees reported working on a deal with a private equity element at some point during their training contract. Accordingly, they advised applicants to *"consider if that's something they're interested in. It's a cliché that you can't get in here without spouting something about private equity in your interview!"* That said, SJB is a full-service firm, as someone took care to point out, so *"there are still really good non-private equity opportunities. Our litigation and property groups make waves too."*

Busy bees

Despite some lawyer departures in 2010, SJB's property department remains a key part of the business. In 2011, it advised on the £480m sale of Chiswick Park, one of the largest transactions for a single property asset that year. Clients include Marks & Spencer, British Land and The Crown Estate, the latter of which it has advised for the last decade on the £1bn regeneration of Regent Street. For trainees, this means involvement with some interesting and often *"highly confidential"* matters, as well as independent files. *"From the get-go, you're running matters yourself, negotiating leases, managing the enquiries list, distributing documents and working on research."*

The litigation department is *"busy, busy, busy"* at the moment. *"We're becoming increasingly recognised as a force in the field, so expansion is on the cards,"* a trainee said. The firm acts on all sorts of litigation and dispute resolution matters – from international arbitration, competition and IP to private equity, employment and tax – and has a stash of clients that includes Morgan Stanley, JPMorgan, Hilton and Qantas, to name a few. *"Because of the size and value and complexity of some of our work, assignments can get fairly bespoke."* There's no shortage of bottom-of-the-totem-pole tasks like bundling and pagination in the department – *"it takes a lot of the moaning-and-groaning sort of work to get things done!"* That said, interviewees reassured us *"there's also really high-quality work to be had,"* like running discrete research assignments, assisting with case analysis and attending summary judgment hearings. *"I had the opportunity to get involved in strategy meetings with both clients and counsel,"* one trainee informed us, while another reported *"working on two high-profile matters that made the front page of the Financial Times. I was leading the conversations with clients by the end of my seat."*

SJB offers regular overseas seats in Madrid, Paris, Dubai, Brussels and Frankfurt as well as occasional seats in other locations, including Hong Kong. The process for landing a seat abroad is broadly similar to a normal seat change: trainees list their desired destination and are given the chance to explain their reasons for wanting to go abroad. They can also expect to be interviewed by lawyers in their office of choice. Work experience and foreign language capabilities can factor in quite heavily, and *"the overseas office usually gets the final say"* in who goes. There's also the option of a client secondment at companies like Universal, Westfield and M&S.

The dog days are over

"SJB still has a quite difficult reputation in the press, but I don't think it's deserved," says Nicola Bridge, referencing the media's long-standing portrayal of the firm as a hard-nosed, rather pugnacious entity. *"We're a very different place than we were many years ago – we still work very hard, but we don't take ourselves too seriously."* Indeed, trainees agree that the firm's *"80s-style aggressively entrepreneurial spirit seems to be fading. The days of the pushy, anti-establishment attitude are over, mostly because the guys who created that dynamic where everyone worked their socks off all the time aren't really around any more."* That said, they insisted that the firm is still a vigorous go-getter, which perhaps accounts for its intense reputation. *"We're massively client-focused, so there's no pushing back deadlines for anything. No one feels sorry for you if you're consistently working late nights because it's expected that we deliver. If there's an impression of pushiness and long hours, that's why."*

Sources *did* concede that *"SJB lawyers are very interested in business – perhaps more interested in business than law sometimes. We tend to enjoy commercial stuff rather than black-letter law."* Indeed, *"the firm encourages us to be forward and use our initiative,"* one trainee said. *"The environment is young, dynamic and punchy, and while we're expected to work hard, we're rewarded for it. The standard is to involve us a lot, particularly in corporate seats – there's lots of ownership of your work there."* While trainees on the whole appreciate the *"exciting, fast-paced"* atmosphere, they warned it's not for everybody: *"You'll be working with clients who are used to having their demands met quickly, so you'd be misguided to think that it's easy. Be prepared to get treated harshly in terms of hours and workload. It's very much a culture of work, work, work, which means you really have to commit."*

Trainees are a tight-knit bunch, thanks in no small part to the firm's free buffet lunches, which are *"a good way to socialise daily"* and, if the following source is anything to go by, *"bloody well cooked, except for the kitchen's love of silver onions – they seem to make their way into every dish!"* When they're not working, you can usually find trainees mingling at the local riverside haunt The Banker or newly opened Oyster Shed, where *"partners tend to lead exoduses on Fridays nights."* Back at the office, the lush roof terrace proves a handy destination for post-deal celebrations and the odd summer barbecue. *"We've got all the hallmarks of a modern firm,"* sources reported rather gleefully, counting a café, restaurant (Stanley's), GP clinic, gym membership, concierge service and, tellingly, sleep pods among the many perks of 10 Queen Street Place (or 10 QSP for those in the know). Our verdict? We tend to agree with the trainee who summarised the office as follows: *"If you've got to be stuck somewhere at midnight, it's not a bad place to be at all."* The firm retained 28 out of 42 qualifiers in 2012.

And finally...

For a closer look at SJ Berwin, check out PLUM, the annual recruitment magazine. Assembled entirely by trainees, it appears to be the product of some pretty playful photoshoots.

Skadden, Arps, Slate, Meagher & Flom (UK) LLP

The facts

Location: London

Number of UK partners/solicitors: 20/130 (+21 US-qualified)

Total number of trainees: 12

Seats: 4x6 months

Alternative seats: Overseas seats

Extras: Pro bono – LawWorks, TrustLaw Connect, Child Rights Information Network; language classes

On chambersstudent.co.uk...

- How to get into Skadden
- Recent cases and deals
- Interview with grad recruitment partner Danny Tricot

"*Entrepreneurial*" Skadden is one of the world's top law firms. The London office is a key hub for its corporate and international arbitration practices.

Who's the Skaddy?

It's a history woven into the fabric of quite a few American law firms: marginalised immigrant Jewish lawyers, politely but firmly turned away at the door by the WASPish legal elite, start their own practice. Skadden became the go-to firm for hostile takeovers in the 1950s when the New York old guard was too genteel to dirty their hands in 'snake pits' – back rooms where shareholder votes were counted over cigars and scotch.

Thanks to this initial entrepreneurship, and a lot of hard work since, Skadden's become one of the most profitable firms in the world, and the founders' legacy of meritocracy and hard graft is expected of all its 1,800 lawyers across the world, including those in London, where it landed in 1988. "*We think of Europe very closely in London, as we head our European operation from this office*," says joint graduate recruitment partner Danny Tricot. To illustrate Skadden's clout on the continent, in the first six months of 2012 it advised on 33 European M&A worth a whopping $71.84bn in total. The firm takes a sans-frontières approach to staffing, mobilising experts from its offices across the world to match its international deals.

Although News Corporation's $11.5bn proposed acquisition of BSkyB fell flat in the face of *News of the World*'s hacking scandal, Skadden has remained on the media conglomerate's retainer. It's now advising on Rupert Murdoch's proposed split of NewsCorp into two divisions: publishing, and film and media. The moguls on Skadden's client list don't end at Murdoch. The firm represented Russian oligarch Roman Abramovich in a multi-billion-pound High Court case brought by Boris Berezovsky involving share sales and breach of contract.

True grit

Trainees say Skadden's "*very international – top of its league*," and matches the magic circle on a global scale. Unlike magic circle firms, however, London trainees are "*one out of five in an intake, not just one of hundreds.*" When asked 'why Skadden?' all answers boiled down to this element of being "*not just a number*" alongside the lure of "*really big deals.*" The firm recently increased the number of people it's taking on its vacation schemes, not with the aim of increasing trainee intake but rather to ensure it's got a larger pool of quality candidates. "*We really try to recruit our trainees from our vacation schemes*," says Tricot. Those who haven't done one are welcome to apply but "*we really prefer those who've done schemes with us.*"

"*In your first year, you will either do litigation, corporate M&A or capital markets.*" Second-years then get to choose from banking, tax, white-collar crime, restructuring and, on occasion, project finance. Given the small size of the intake, the firm is quite flexible in accommodating trainees' wishes, "*if you make a good business case for what you want to do and why.*" This extends as far as secondments to Hong Kong and, more infrequently, Moscow.

Trainees in the corporate seat "*deal with a lot of our private equity clients and their portfolio companies.*" Teams typically consist of one partner, two associates and a trainee, and sometimes they're even smaller: "*When one*

Chambers UK rankings

Banking & Finance	Energy & Natural Resources
Capital Markets	Investment Funds
Corporate Crime & Investigations	Private Equity
	Restructuring/Insolvency
Corporate/M&A	Tax
Dispute Resolution	

of the associates dropped out before a closing, it was just me and one other person preparing documents, I had a lot of exposure to the stages of the transaction from due diligence to closing," one source said. Others reported "a lot of client contact, straight from the first couple of weeks – negotiating non-disclosure agreements and contracts with the other side." Although the immediate teams are small, trainees can be "co-ordinating with local counsel across 16 jurisdictions," or "doing due diligence on a potential M&A transaction within a huge Skadden team led by London." There are a lot of "paper-organising exercises" but on certain matters, said one source, "it felt like I was running the deal myself." Heightened responsibility doesn't come "without a safety net," and supervisors keep an eye on trainee capacity.

"Obviously the markets aren't blooming at the moment," said a trainee of the capital markets seat, "but I had the opportunity to get very involved in several deals." The department has a split between lawyers who do equity and debt, and "as a trainee you mostly do equity." Annotating and drafting prospectuses are routine trainee tasks.

A brave new world

"We don't do lots of little cases, but rather a few big cases," and so most matters in litigation and arbitration are very long-running. Whether a trainee "ends up bundling" or finds themselves doing "mostly substantive work" is dependent on "what case you're on and what stage that case is at." Some of our sources were stuck with "a lot of doc review," but others came away saying "I was so lucky to do such exciting things." For some fortunate sources, being involved with the Abramovich trial was "fantastic – one of those cases that comes your way only once in your career." The "immensely complicated facts dealing with, basically, the foundation of modern capitalism in Russia, and the very colourful characters" certainly made it interesting. These trainees weren't just thumbing through documents to ensure the right order – "my main task was helping develop legal arguments, doing contract analysis, and fiduciary duties," said one.

The banking department's "been extremely busy and I think they are quite understaffed at the moment," which means more work for trainees to get their teeth into. They'd had first goes at drafting things like UK security documents on US deals and worked on "getting financings in place according to German regulations." As this is a second-year seat, trainees are encouraged to have client contact and "are expected to act like associates, juggling multiple tasks, deciding which can be done first and which can be safely put on the back burner."

If trainees aren't busy, "it's looked down upon if people stick around to appear as if they are working long hours." However, the unpredictability of City life means "you might be working 14 or 15 hours for six days straight and then have nothing." One source said: "I think on average I worked four weekends in each seat," and, though "expecting worse," knew about "one trainee who was in seven weekends in a row and didn't have a day off for 50 days." Skadden trainees come in "with their eyes open. We are here to do our job, to do it well, whatever it takes. If it takes staying in late, working elsewhere, flying to clients, that's what people will do." And they are rewarded for their hard work – when the firm did well this year, both first and second-year trainees received a bonus.

Underdog millionaires

"Being a US firm, we are quite modern, rather than traditional, in our approach." Along with Clifford Chance, Skadden is one of the only law firms that has turned its back on the Square Mile in favour of Canary Wharf (the office "has great facilities and the location is very convenient," but after school's out trainees "don't want to stay here beyond a minute"). Nor were the humble origins of the firm lost on our sources. "The legacy of being the scrappy underdog is like a badge of pride." There is real diversity among trainees. Although everyone we spoke to attended a top university, they hailed from all over the world.

"People are dedicated to their work but have their own lives, there is no obligatory socialising. It's just not that sort of a culture." Friday nights are for "doing your own thing," but on Thursdays a few trainees might get together for drinks. Departments hold the occasional drinks events and summer and Christmas parties are open to everyone from the support staff to the partners. Trainees pointed out that the firm is trying to fix the slightly fragmented social scene, hosting monthly drinks in the canteen and a party to celebrate American Independence Day. The firm retained all eight of its qualifiers in 2012.

And finally...

If a more 'traditional' City firm doesn't appeal, then Skadden's tough, go-getting vibe might be more up your street. See our website for more details about the work of the firm.

Slaughter and May

The facts

Location: London

Number of UK partners/solicitors: 110/300

Partners who trained at firm: 81%

Total number of trainees: 178

Seats: 4x6 months (occasional 3-month seats)

Alternative seats: Overseas seats, secondments

Extras: Pro bono – Islington Law Centre, RCJ CAB, LawWorks, A4ID, TrustLaw and others; language classes

On chambersstudent.co.uk...

- How to get into Slaughter and May
- Interview with training partner Graham White

Trainees are expected to bring their A-game at this renowned firm, which puts a premium on excellence in all of its endeavours.

Corporate Kraftsmen

For many of you, Slaughter and May will require little introduction – after all, the firm's had a tight grip on the titles 'most prestigious' and 'most profitable' for some time now. But for those a little less clued-up, here's a quick tutorial. Magic circle member? Check. Global reputation? Check. Multimillion-pound PEP? Top-ranked practice teams? Premier clientele? Check, check, check. Excellent training contract? Well, let's find out...

Slaughters' corporate reputation is second to none. FTSE 100 companies flock in droves to the firm, which counts more than 100 listed companies among its client cache (the only firm ever to smash that benchmark). If there's an exceptionally high-profile transaction on show, such as Kraft's £12bn takeover of Cadbury, Slaughters lawyers are all but guaranteed to be behind the scenes – particularly on the M&A front, where multibillion-pound deals are commonplace. The firm's recent role in Hewlett-Packard's £7bn bid to buy out software giant Autonomy – Europe's largest ever bid in the technology sector – is a pretty good example of the scale we're talking. Recent advisory posts on Thomas Cook's £1.4bn financing package and British Airways' $7bn joint business with American Airlines and Iberia are none too shabby, either.

Other groups – among them finance, litigation, real estate and tax – are equally important ingredients in the Slaughters recipe for success. That said, the training contract is very much oriented towards the firm's traditional strengths: trainees are expected to spend at least two of their seats in the corporate and finance departments, and many even squeeze in three – a recipe known as

"CoCoFin." Beyond corporate and finance are seats in large groups like dispute resolution as well as a handful of three-month stints in specialist ones like tax, employment, pensions and IP. "You can tailor your contract quite well," trainees told us, explaining that while seat patterns are mapped out in advance, "HR is very accommodating if you change your mind about where you want to go next – the whole process is more flexible than people expect."

Slaughters solicitors are trained to be generalists, so there's a real emphasis placed on exposure to a broad scope of work. As executive partner Graham White explains, "it's a huge benefit to the firm to have lawyers with the flexibility to handle a range of different types of work. Quite apart from the fact that it is more stimulating for the lawyers, we think it is better for the clients – there's a risk otherwise that lawyers restricted to a narrow spectrum of transactions will become trapped in following a specific formula and will miss wider points or solutions to problems." As such, each department's lawyers are equipped to handle anything and everything that comes through the door. For trainees, this policy lends itself to "a wide array of work in every seat – you see new stuff every day and rarely do the same thing twice."

The magnificent seven

Slaughters has seven corporate and finance groups, each named for its lead partner's initials. "Each one does all kinds of work, though big-name clients usually remain the property of a single group," one trainee explained, citing one group's proprietary of Arsenal FC as an example. The firm draws some real cream of the crop clients, including

Chambers UK rankings

Administrative & Public Law	Insurance
Banking & Finance	Intellectual Property
Banking Litigation	Investment Funds
Capital Markets	Life Sciences
Competition/European Law	Outsourcing
Construction	Pensions
Corporate Crime & Investigations	Pensions Litigation
	Private Equity
Corporate/M&A	Professional Negligence
Dispute Resolution	Projects
Employee Share Schemes & Incentives	Real Estate
	Restructuring/Insolvency
Employment	Retail
Energy & Natural Resources	Sports Law
Environment	Tax
Financial Services	Telecommunications
Fraud	
Information Technology	

the likes of Westfield, Cadbury, Santander, Unilever, Diageo and Aviva, which lawyers recently advised on its £1bn sale of RAC to jumbo private equity firm The Carlyle Group. Trainees across the various corporate groups reported *"an interesting mix"* of work on IPOs, joint ventures, private share sales, M&A matters and even *"refinancings, which corporate lawyers don't traditionally do – it's all part of the mentality that we become varied practitioners."* Conscious of the stereotypes associated with mega-deals – the notion that trainees are treated to grunt work and little else – our interviewees were quick to enlighten us about their actual experiences: *"It pretty much scales the ladder, from low-level admin stuff like preparing board minutes through to performing discrete research tasks and drafting provisions of agreements,"* one summed up, while others chimed in with tales of liaising with foreign lawyers, *"preparing presentations"* and *"visiting client sites to represent the firm on due diligence exercises."* There's *"a lot of time spent on not-so-exhilarating stuff like check-listing, but you'll also find yourself tested at times and exposed to many different types of deals."*

Much of what's true for corporate is true for finance, largely because of the similarity between the departments' set-ups: *"Again, you're a small part of a very big, general practice where lawyers are working on tons of different matters at any one time."* Indeed, a typical day in finance could involve anything from insolvency, refinancing and restructuring deals to loan agreements, securitisations and capital markets work. In addition to meaty matters for long-standing clients like American Express, HM Treasury and GE, *"there are some smallish one-off deals*

where trainees can end up getting pretty involved." While trainees agreed such projects *"offer the opportunity to learn a lot,"* they noted that the practice area as a whole isn't entirely suited to novices: *"The work requires a lot of knowledge to get to grips with the complicated documents we deal with, so trainees are somewhat on the fringe in that respect."* However, *"there's certainly room to pick up some brilliant experience if you put yourself out there."*

The dispute resolution group's had a smashing year on the media front, acting for Telegraph Media Group in relation to the notorious Leveson Inquiry, and on the arbitration side, advising Alliance Bank of Kazakhstan on two high-value fraud claims. Other notable clients include British Airways, Royal Mail and Nationwide. *"We get a lot of regulatory, insolvency and fraud-related work,"* trainees informed us, warning that those after *"more nuanced cases might want to consider a litigation firm instead."* Much of the work is research-related and requires *"quite a bit of doc review, even at the partner level – there's a lot of admin that goes into these high-profile cases."* That said, a trainee's role goes far beyond bundling and holing up in the corner with a highlighter, our sources assured us: *"I've sat in on witness interviews, met with counsel and private investigators, drafted reports for the fraud office and spent several days in the Court of Appeal – the experience is pretty hands-on."*

The thick of it

"You're expected to be available and knuckle down when the work is in, but the fact that we don't have billing targets is hugely important – it feeds into an ethos where no one expects you to be here if there's no work." On the contrary, one pointed out, *"if you're here later than everybody else, you just look inefficient."* Though *"it's understood that trainees aren't expected to bear the brunt of the hours,"* that can change upon qualification – *"NQ hours are known to be pretty terrible."*

Slaughters keeps a trim international network, preferring a network of 'best friend' firms to launching many outposts of its own. Still, international work is very much part of the firm's fabric. *"It's surprising to get through a whole deal only talking to English lawyers."*

The 'best friends' approach allows for a wide, albeit shifting, variety of international secondment opportunities. *"Every year the list varies slightly."* Upscale firms in New York and Hong Kong prove perennially popular destinations, as does the Slaughters office in Brussels. *"You're really thrust into the thick of it and end up being relied on pretty heavily."* Client secondments *"aren't advertised widely as they're not something trainees usually do,"* though we did hear tell of the occasional ad hoc placement.

The firm takes training very seriously. *"We're trainees in the purest sense as we're trained on absolutely everything. They go over and above what the SRA requires by giving us department-specific instruction, sessions tailored towards the practical side of the trainee role and training delivered by partners and external speakers."*

It's oh so quiet

"When you come here, you realise quite quickly how much everyone cares about the firm's product," said one source, touching on the *"image of excellence"* Slaughters is notorious for. *"People take an earnest approach to their work and do it to an extremely high level. It's crucial to get things right, or at least not wrong twice."* This emphasis on *"quality over quantity"* means *"the environment tends to be pretty serious. It's nothing like Jones Day, where they have mini-golf in their office: you'd never get that kind of jokey attitude here. It's more like working at a library – there's not much messing around."* Still, interviewees insisted: *"It's not as conservative as people think. The firm doesn't over-impose itself, actually – there's a lot of independence when it comes to people's working style. It's kind of like they've put a bunch of geniuses down and let them run free."*

In keeping with the formal atmosphere is a rather conventional approach to etiquette. *"We're encouraged to keep the noise level low, and there are a few antiquated rules like men always letting females in and out of the lift before they enter or leave,"* which *"can lead to some strange dances occurring!"* Moreover, *"there's an expectation to dress smartly,"* and some partners – namely those *"of the old guard"* – take a traditional view of hierarchy wherein *"it wouldn't really do to waltz into their office for a chat."* That said, *"there are also some who would be upset if you didn't swing by and say hello."* While a mildly *"old-fashioned"* ethos definitely prevails, our sources were nothing but content with that. *"I appreciate the firm doesn't pretend to be anything it's not. We're a great law firm, and part of that is making work your first priority. It's not like there isn't room for banter or chit-chat; it's just not that prevalent because people are very respectful of each other's workloads."*

Nobel Prize? Yawn

A consequence of Slaughters' emphasis on hard work is its attraction of *"studious"* and *"bookish"* types. *"It's fair to say the firm's quite academic – Slaughters trainees are always the ones with their hands raised in law school!"* While our interviewees naturally shunned outsiders' accusations of elitism or snobbery, they did say: *"The calibre of people is ridiculously high here... it's almost a bit weird as it gets higher up. You find yourself wondering how people can be that smart."* The down-side? *"You can rarely get away with blagging because everyone's so clever!"* Oxbridge graduates do comprise a hefty portion of trainees, though *"no one is made to feel like anything other than an equal once they've made it to the firm."* Indeed, sources repeatedly insisted: *"The firm operates as a meritocracy – it's all about excellence, no matter where you come from,"* so shining report cards and degrees definitely count in applicants' favour, as do stellar extracurriculars: *"Something you'll notice about people here is that they all have outside interests they've pursued to quite a high standard. You'll find out someone was a fantastic sportsman or a concert pianist, an incredible achievement alongside a university degree."*

The training contract's not all work and no play. Slaughters' trainees kick back on occasion with events like bowling and drinks and regularly gather to hear guest speakers at lunch. A series of sports teams reap the benefits of the social budget – *"the firm sponsors the tours and gives you money to go to the pub afterwards"* – and there's an annual black-tie Christmas ball at the Grosvenor. Most events enjoy *"a pretty good turnout,"* though *"things are very clearly optional – you can either attend things or not and nobody will hold it against you."*

Thanks to Slaughters' ever-high retention rates, our sources had a relaxed approach to the qualification process. *"It's not really on my mind that much because I feel confident that even if I don't get my top choice, they'll find some way of keeping me,"* said one. *"Most people in the past seem to have found a home here except those who didn't want to."* Some 68 out of Slaughters' 77 qualifiers of 2012 (a sound 88%) were retained. On the flip side, *"the attrition after the two-years qualified mark is quite high,"* trainees admitted – after all, *"the work only gets tougher."*

And finally...

Slaughters can look formidable from the outside, but our interviewees urged applicants not to be put off: *"Come look around and do a vac scheme if possible – it'll give you a much better sense of how the majority of people don't actually resemble the snobs you hear about."*

SNR DENTON

RECIPE FOR SUCCESS

Can you take the HEAT?

Do you have the taste for a challenge?
Do you have the taste for law?
Do you have the taste for success?

You knew us as Denton Wilde Sapte. We're now SNR Denton. We'll still demand the best from you, and you can expect even more from us.

You'll develop your career in an open and supportive environment and join a team that achieves success together.

You'll need the skills and ambition to join a top 25 global legal services provider – and the ability to deliver the highest quality services to our clients.

ARE YOU INTERESTED?
Apply now at www.snrdenton.com/graduates

SNR Denton

The facts

Location: London, Milton Keynes

Number of UK partners/solicitors: 115/211

Total number of trainees: 50

Seats: 4x6 months

Alternative seats: Overseas seats, secondments

Extras: Pro bono – PopLaw Clinic; CAB; International HIV/AIDS Alliance, UNICEF

On chambersstudent.co.uk...
- How to get into SNR Denton
- The Milton Keynes office
- Interview with managing partner Brandon Ransley and training partner Jeremy Cape

One of a new brand of international mega-firms and the result of a 2010 US-UK tie-up, SNR Denton is experiencing a "*drive to be more profitable and market the merged firm.*"

Making a Dent(on)

It's now two years since London's banking-focused Denton Wilde Sapte 'combined' (technically, it's not a merger) with Chicago's Sonnenschein Nath & Rosenthal. The aim was to create a leaner, meaner lawyer machine. So how has this new incarnation of Dentons fared? "*There has been a push towards more marketing – we have been liaising a lot with the US side of the firm for client pitches – and there has been a drive to become more strict on financials and billings,*" one trainee observed. "*I haven't noticed a dramatic change in culture, but they are putting a huge effort into making us feel part of one firm.*" There has been the inevitable post-merger turbulence: some partner departures, unexpected "*reshuffling of management positions*" and a decrease in revenues have caused a few market commentators to speculate on the new firm's direction. Revenue for the ex-Dentons part of the firm fell by almost a tenth in 2010/11 and by 5% in 2011/12 (the US side of the business grew, however). As one trainee pointed out: "*Creating a global business is not as easy as sticking a new nameplate on the door.*" The ex-DWS part of the firm had a strategy rethink in early 2011, leading to increased attention on the Middle East and Africa.

Africa and the Middle East have long been a core part of Dentons' identity but, not content, the firm doubled the size of its associate network in Africa in 2011 and now has a presence in 21 countries on the continent. Meanwhile, ten offices in the Middle East make Dentons' presence in that region bigger than that of any other firm.

Add to that the offices in Europe, the rest of Asia, and Sonnenschein's 15 legacy US offices, and you begin to understand what we mean by mega-firm. In London, *Chambers UK* ranks Dentons in almost every area of business law imaginable, placing it at the top end of the City's corporate mid-market. It is perhaps most highly regarded for its banking and energy work. For example, it recently helped Mitsubishi and two other corporations (one from Finland, one from Korea) on a $6bn financing for a 6,000 MW power plant in Jordan.

Desert scenes or Milton Keynes?

The merged firm focuses on eight core sectors: financial institutions and funds; energy, transport and infrastructure; technology, media and telecoms (TMT); real estate, retail and hotels; government; manufacturing; health and life sciences; and insurance. The London office is full service but retains its traditional core strengths of banking, energy and real estate. Banking is the largest department and "*pretty much everyone does a seat there,*" so you'd be mad to join Dentons if you're not interested in this area. There are a few different options within banking, while other seats on offer include energy, project finance, corporate, real estate, dispute resolution, TMT, competition and employment. There are also overseas seats in locations such as Dubai and Abu Dhabi, as well as client secondments to banks and businesses like travel firm TUI.

Mentioning the seat allocation process brings out a few grumbles from trainees. "*We fill in a form listing three*

Chambers UK rankings

Administrative & Public Law	Local Government
Asset Finance	Outsourcing
Banking & Finance	Pensions
Banking Litigation	Planning
Capital Markets	Professional Negligence
Commodities	Projects
Construction	Public Procurement
Corporate/M&A	Real Estate
Data Protection	Real Estate Finance
Dispute Resolution	Real Estate Litigation
Employment	Restructuring/Insolvency
Energy & Natural Resources	Retail
	Sports Law
Environment	Tax
Information Technology	Telecommunications
Intellectual Property	Transport

preferences, but I'm not sure how that gets used. It can be a bit unstructured," one told us. Another added: "If there is a seat you really want to do, you tend to lobby for it, speak to partners, and then you'll get to do it." Trainees also agreed that "sometimes you only get a week's notice of your new seat before a move." Since we spoke to trainees the firm has made changes to make the system more effective.

Dentons also has a 50-lawyer office in Milton Keynes: something you probably didn't expect from a global mega-firm. It has a completely separate training contract and was home to six trainees when we called in early 2012. The seats on offer there are construction, corporate, employment, dispute resolution, property litigation and real estate. It's well-regarded in its region, offers "good training" and (be nice) "doesn't think of itself as being a smaller office." Since our space is limited here, head to the bonus feature on our website, as we have plenty more information about the training on offer in MK.

Cooking on Gazprom

Back in the Big Smoke, the 100-lawyer banking department is divided into general banking, asset finance, trade and regulatory capital markets subgroups. Trainees sit with a partner or associate in one of these teams, but do a mix of work. "We mainly act for lenders and all the top banks," a trainee told us. Lloyds, HSBC, RBS, Citi, Deutsche Bank and BNP Paribas are all clients. Deals range from a few million to hundreds of millions of pounds in value. One of the largest saw the firm advising Bank of Tokyo-Mitsubishi UFJ – Japan's largest bank – and Italy's UniCredit on an $800m loan to Russian energy giant Gazprom. "It is very fast-moving and you have to

keep on top of things," one trainee said. "I was very busy. I got in at 9am and usually finished no earlier than 8pm. Sometimes I was there until 10pm." The work is very international. "I was talking to people in Africa about derivatives surveys and worked on a big Islamic bond issuance in the UAE." The asset finance team has advised on the buying of ships and helicopters but work is usually "90% planes" – the team has advised TAM Airlines, Qatar Airways and the joyfully-named WizzAir on the purchase of new aircraft. As far as trainees are concerned, there is "a lot of handling documents" to contend with. Work ranges from company searches, drafting and proofreading to genuine client contact.

Sainsbury's is one of the real estate department's longest-standing clients, and its lawyers have also acted for John Lewis, the Home Retail group and Westfield. The group helped the latter with scores of leasing agreements for the new Stratford City Westfield. This practice has an international flavour too: "I have been working on a property purchase for a Middle Eastern client," a trainee told us. Trainees work on some "really big deals" as well as "a few smaller ones which you are left to run largely by yourself."

I bless the winds down in Africa

There are several seats in the energy, infrastructure and project finance (EIPF) department, including energy, project finance, rail, environment and construction, but once there, trainees "are not wedded to their group." "It is great to work on projects with tangible results," one trainee remarked. Dentons recently helped Swiss oil trader Addax & Oryx negotiate with the government of Sierra Leone over a £120m loan for the construction of a renewable energy plant in the West African country. Energy is a big area of focus and expertise: from North Sea oil and petrol stations to nuclear power and wind farms. Clients range from Total, EDF Energy and Statoil to the Department for Energy and Climate Change. Trainee tasks include due diligence, preparing conditions precedent and drafting parts of energy supply contracts.

Other sizeable trainee-taking departments are TMT – where work includes "technology and outsourcing agreements as well as general commercial contracts" for media businesses like EMI and Endemol – and corporate. The latter handles IPOs, M&A and "quite a lot of oil and gas work." For example, the team advised Malaysian oil giant Petronas (of Kuala Lumpur twin towers fame) on the £110m sale of a subsidiary to a UK company. Trainee work ranges from verification to "calling the client to check details and attending client meetings." Corporate shares banking's long hours. In the other departments, 7pm finishes, with the occasional late night, are more common.

As you can tell, the training contract is heavily transactional, with most trainees doing three non-contentious seats. They can fulfil their contentious requirement with a stint in dispute resolution, IP litigation (part of TMT) or employment, or by attending a two-week course at the College of Law.

Ménage à trois... quatre... cinq?

"*They have been unrelenting in pumping out marketing about the 'new' SNR Denton,*" trainees agreed. "*You've probably noticed that the grad recruitment advertising has changed from 'friendly' to 'serious' and 'work-hard', which is a more American ethos.*" As we've already mentioned, trainees have noticed an increased emphasis on hours and the firm's finances. "*For us trainees there is a massive focus on billing and time recording,*" one said. So are they made to work harder? "*Some departments have always been busy and worked long hours. That hasn't changed.*"

"*I have seen lots of joint marketing activities, but I haven't worked on a big deal with the US yet,*" one source admitted. Our feeling is that management on both sides of the Atlantic are piling effort into building up the groundwork for cross-office deals with international practice meetings, joint pitches and more, and this effort is now starting to bear fruit. "*US/UK deals are going on,*" one trainee said. "*And I worked on a matter which we only became involved with through introductions from America.*"

The firm is clearly enjoying wedded life – so much so that it appears keen to make it a threesome (we know that metaphor doesn't really work). Rumours in 2012 have suggested merger talks with Salans are underway. "*I think that merger would fit very well,*" one trainee observed.

Barrow boys (and girls)

As in previous years, "*qualification is a bit of a bone of contention.*" We're pleased to report that (after a bit of poking from the *Student Guide* last year) some of the "*frustrating*" hoops that used to be part of the qualification process have been dropped. Notably, a drafting exercise and Watson-Glaser psychometric test have gone, though interviews are still held for NQ jobs. What still irks trainees, however, is the fact that "*the jobs list comes out quite late and you don't get much information up until that point. So, even if you want to stay with the firm, you have to be pre-emptive and apply elsewhere too. That is quite bad for the firm. It wouldn't take much to keep all the trainees in their fourth seat informed, surely? It is something the firm needs to sort out.*" In 2012, trainees found out about NQ jobs in late June, an improvement on previous years. Furthermore, our records show that Dentons' retention rates have been less than impressive for a number of years now, but there has been improvement on this front too, with 29 of 39 qualifiers kept on in 2012.

Whether or not they stayed on as NQs, trainees waxed lyrical about their experience at Dentons, which one described as "*overwhelmingly positive.*" Supervisors came in for unanimous praise. "*Mine have been excellent,*" said one source. "*They have tried to teach me as much as possible. They don't leave you out to dry – there are constant questions about how you are getting on. The other partners have all been very approachable too – no one talks down to you as a trainee.*"

Interviewees agreed there's "*a good mix*" of the opportunity to socialise with colleagues and the ability to get away from the office. "*There are firm socials such as a quiz night and a Halloween party, and sports teams in the summer, but it's not like everyone is best buddies. People have their own lives as well.*" Some departments are more convivial than others. "*Banking is very social. We have a drinks trolley every month on Friday at 5.30pm,*" one source said. "*I tend to go out with associates and trainees maybe once a fortnight, usually to the Corney and Barrow underneath the office.*" Trainees club together by intake or department rather than as one entity, and "*there are a few separate subgroups when it comes to socialising.*" But everyone gets together for the "*big trainee joiners and leavers drinks every six months, which is usually held at*

And finally...

SNR Denton is one to watch. While much of the old Denton Wilde Sapte is still there under the surface, this new firm can no longer pass as a cuddly City mid-sizer.

Do law. Think business.

Graduate careers in law and more

You can build your expertise anywhere. But few firms can give you a commercial perspective to rival ours. We're an ambitious City firm with a fascinating mix of corporate, private client and real estate clients who turn to us for all manner of specialist advice. As a result, we're as much business partners as legal advisers, meaning you will achieve far more out of your career here.

For full details, head to
www.dolawthinkbusiness.co.uk

Speechly Bircham

Speechly Bircham LLP

The facts

Location: London

Number of UK partners/solicitors: 86/103

Total number of trainees: 26

Seats: 4x6 months

Alternative seats: Occasional secondments

Extras: Pro bono – Blackfriars Settlement

On chambersstudent.co.uk...
- How to get into Speechlys
- Some background on Campbell Hooper

This private client ace is intent on boosting its transactional offerings and expanding internationally.

A private affair

Speechly Bircham is still reaping the benefits of its 2009 merger with Campbell Hooper, which served to bolster its real estate and corporate practices and drive up financials in 2010 and 2011. There was a slight dip in this London mid-sizer's revenue this year – which most attribute to the firm's 2011 dismissal from its role as principal property adviser at RBS – but insiders remain upbeat about the state of the firm. *"The loss of that work coupled with the general slowdown did put some pressure on our figures last year, but overall it's busy and improving. Corporate finance in particular has had a very good year, as have private client and tax, and we've hired a significant number of laterals over the past 12 months,"* training principal Chris Putt tells us.

Speechlys may be shifting its focus to the corporate finance group in months to come – *"historically the practice has been too small, and I see it growing quickly relative to the rest of the firm,"* says Putt – but for the time being Speechlys' private client practice continues to trump its transactional offerings in the reputation stakes. The practice is among the biggest in the City and is beloved of the mega-wealthy – most of our interviewees cited the firm's renown in the area as a primary reason for joining. Management capitalised on the weight of this brand in mid-2011 by opening the firm's first overseas offices in Luxembourg and Zürich – the former will focus on funds-related offerings while the latter is *"mainly wealth-related work,"* according to Putt. *"It's an important part of our strategy to pursue this part of the business on an international basis."*

That said, the firm is equally interested in *"making sure all areas complement each other. Private client work constitutes about 25% of the business, but services to the private wealth sector represent more as we service those clients with respect to their transactional corporate and property needs too,"* says Putt. *"With the current economic climate it's important to maintain deep relationships across those sectors and types of clients that play to the firm's strengths."* As such, the firm's private client practice will continue to expand internationally, while property is becoming increasingly specialised by pursuing work with house builders and development funds.

'The Body' of work

"It's almost like being a kid in a candy store here," laughed one trainee in reference to Speechlys' wide variety of seats, which includes *"at least 13 choices."* There are *"no real requirements"* for the training contract (though at least one seat in business services is encouraged), and *"the allocation system is flexible. Before you start, and then at every seat change, you put down the four seats you'd most like to do,"* a source explained. *"Your interests evolve as you get a feel for certain departments, so it's nice to know you're not locked into anything."* Trainees agreed the HR team is *"easily approachable"* and especially praised them for *"having an eye to what's going to happen upon qualification – they're careful to avoid situations where people pursue seats where there won't be many jobs."* In 2012, ten out of 13 second-year trainees landed NQ jobs at the firm, by the way.

Chambers UK rankings

Agriculture & Rural Affairs	Intellectual Property
Charities	Investment Funds
Construction	Pensions
Corporate/M&A	Private Client
Data Protection	Projects
Employment	Real Estate
Family/Matrimonial	Real Estate Litigation
Financial Services	Restructuring/Insolvency
Immigration	

"*Most*" trainees try to land a private client seat, which is a "*brilliant experience*" according to our interviewees. The team has built up an excellent reputation for its tax structuring and wealth protection work, much of which is done for ultra-high-net-worth individuals and families – peppering the almost exclusively confidential client list are flush royals, affluent politicians and loaded entrepreneurs. A name we can, however, mention is that of 'The Body' herself, Elle Macpherson – in 2010 lawyers scored a High Court action on behalf of the supermodel-cum-businesswoman extraordinaire following a dispute with a now-insolvent Icelandic bank. On the contentious trusts side, the firm specialises in acting for offshore trustees entangled in divorce proceedings and regularly defends the legacy funds of charities like Barnardo's and Cancer Research UK. "*The amount of client contact is the single biggest highlight of the seat*," trainees said, explaining that "*you tag along to client meetings frequently, and you're the principal contact for many of the cases you work on*." Day-to-day tasks mainly centre on drafting wills and lasting powers of attorney, though "*if you show interest in a particular side of the business like probates, they'll give that kind of work to you too*." Daily training sessions at the beginning of the seat are a big hit – "*a nice way to get up to speed if you haven't done the LPC elective*."

Corporate finance is "*one of the firm's main engine rooms*." Part of the business services division, the department is solidly mid-market, dealing mainly with M&A, quoted company and private equity/venture capital matters in specialised sectors like financial services, healthcare and hotels and leisure. Recent deals keeping lawyers busy include Ahlstrom's €22.5m acquisition of a Chinese manufacturer and Ecclesiastical Life's disposal of £180m worth of its life assurance business. "*It's one of the seats where you're constantly working on several things at once*," interviewees said, mentioning their involvement in various M&A transactions, schemes of arrangement and corporate governance deals. Fortunately, trainees "*are given proper work*" like drafting agreements, performing due diligence and attending client meetings. "*The group has grown enormously this year, but we work in small*

teams within the larger department, so we get the best of both worlds, really*.*"

Speechlys' real estate group has diversified in recent years and now handles a range of property, construction and engineering work as well as projects and disputes. Transactions for overseas investors and developers are increasingly common undertakings, as are Shari'a finance transactions (the latter are handled in collaboration with the banking group). There's also a regeneration team that works for various non-profit and governmental bodies as well as commercial housing giants like Barratt and Taylor Wimpey – recent matters the team's advised on include the redevelopment of Barnardo's children's charity's headquarters, the refurb of Brighton Marina and Howard de Walden Estates' £34m purchase of several properties on Harley Street from the Crown Estate. To top it off, the firm led the way on Lambeth Myatt's £150m housing regeneration, the largest to be signed in London since the Olympics. "*As a trainee you can put in a preference to be assigned to one of the sub-teams*," we were told. "*You work mainly for your team, but other bits and pieces come in too; it's not rigid.*" Along with contributing to big transactions, trainees are given smaller files to run on their own – "*a really good way to figure out how to manage your workload and deal directly with clients.*"

A balanced diet

A construction seat entails "*quite a lot of research*" and "*is great for honing your knowledge of contract law.*" Along with civil engineering and infrastructure work, the group handles construction and renovation matters, often for overseas clients. As we went to print, the firm was advising on all of the construction elements surrounding the Northacre revival scheme of the former Lancaster Gate Thistle Hotel. "*We do contentious work as well,*" interviewees said, explaining that "*unlike commercial disputes, construction ones can be small – it could be just one person up against a builder.*" As such, there's "*lots of room for trainees to get involved*" – we heard about everything from "*run-of-the-mill work like amending contracts*" to drafting defences and attending adjudications. "*Much of it can be done with minimal supervision.*"

In IPTD (IP, technology and data) "*there's a lot of contract and data protection work on the non-contentious side, which involves tasks like drafting terms and conditions for websites,*" a source explained. "*On the litigation side, it's a lot of research, drafting witness statements and performing the court run for IP disputes.*" There's also "*quite a bit of business development work for trainees – helping out with presentations and so forth.*" A recent triumph saw the team successfully defend World Programming in a copyright software infringement case against SAS (no, not *the* SAS). The team's also made the most of the firm's ties with Elle Macpherson by stepping up to the plate to advise her on various endorsement and appearance agreements (think along the lines of Louis Vuitton and Revlon) as well as the development of her Intimates and 'The Body' brands.

While trainees are assigned a supervisor for each seat, they pointed out that "*supervision isn't just left up to them – people of all levels are keen to help you and go out of their way to make sure you've got the diet of work you want. Everybody's really accommodating in that respect.*" Indeed, "*the firm invests time in you from all angles. Each department has training sessions we're encouraged to attend, and we have two reviews per seat to receive feedback on our progress and raise questions.*"

Dude looks like a lady

Thanks to Speechlys' open-plan office, "*you're never more than a turn of a seat away from someone who can help you out – that dynamic definitely helps break down barriers at the firm.*" Trainees went on to admit that "*it's cliché to say you work at a friendly place, but you do get the feeling that people want to see you do well here.*" Another contributing factor to this collaborative environment is "*the fact that there aren't any weird or aggressive characters here. You get people with niche hobbies or interesting perspectives for sure – there are endless fascinating people to talk to at any gathering – but nobody who walks all over everybody else.*" All in all, the firm is "*pretty down-to-earth,*" trainees agreed, citing recent hullabaloo over the Olympics (an ongoing event at the time of interviews) as an example of the "*nice and normal nature*" of Speechlys lawyers: "*They set up a screen in the café, and people have spent every free moment crowding around it to see the highlights.*"

As for hours, "*it's really reasonable for a City firm,*" sources said, mentioning that "*the office is refreshingly empty*" after the 7pm mark. Of course trainees can expect longer hours here and there, especially in seats like banking or finance, "*but even in those departments it's clear you don't need to be there if the work doesn't require it.*"

Speechlys' "*relatively new*" digs in New Street Square were widely praised by its occupants. "*The office is just around the corner from the courts, so it's handy for passing off documents. Plus the square is awesome – they set up massive screens and deck chairs for events like Wimbledon.*" While there's no doubt the trainees work hard during the day, "*we definitely find time to go out and play.*" A summer bash held in a riverside marquee at Sugar Quay is an annual highlight, as is the Christmas party, which is "*a bit more grand – dinner jackets and dancing and all that. Last year it was held at the Northumberland.*" Those inclined to think formal equals stuffy needn't be too worried – we have it on good authority that "*there's always some senior associate who dresses up as a woman or something!*" There's also a Christmas do exclusively for current and future trainees – "*held at some snazzy venue I'm not cool enough for!*" joked one – plus quarterly firmwide drinks and a sport and social committee "*that organises things like days out at the races or weekend trips to Paris.*"

CSR is a big deal at Speechlys, where trainees regularly get involved with charity walks like the Three Peaks Challenge and London Legal Walk as well as an ongoing project at educational organisation Blackfriars Settlement. "*Once every six months the trainees go down there and put on a presentation about various legal topics for the elderly, who come round the office later in the year for an annual quiz that's always a good laugh.*" Our sources also raved about a reading scheme with a local primary school that, by the sounds of it, is equally fun for students and trainees. "*Once a year we dress up and put on a silly play for them,*" one explained. "*The last one was a mock trial involving Buzz Lightyear and all the other Toy Story characters. I think by the end of it we were actually laughing more than the kids!*"

And finally...
Speechlys' three-week vac scheme is not one to miss – *"it's long enough that you get a decent impression of the firm, and we recruit heavily from it."*

Squire Sanders

The facts

Location: London, Leeds, Birmingham, Manchester

Number of UK partners/solicitors: 130/375 (+30 non-UK-qualified)

Partners who trained at firm: 23%

Total number of trainees: 53

Seats: 6x4 months

Alternative seats: Overseas seats, secondments

Extras: Pro bono – Paddington Law Centre, Birmingham and Hillside Legal Advice Clinics; language classes

On chambersstudent.co.uk...
- How to get into Squire Sanders
- The SSD/Hammonds merger
- An interview with Leeds grad recruitment partner Sally Lodge

Things are "*anything but static*" at this transatlantic firm, which is savouring some serious post-merger perks...

Hello Uncle Squam

In early 2011, the firm formerly known as Hammonds officially linked arms with American Midwesterners Squire, Sanders & Dempsey in a bid to up its stakes in the international market. The combined outfit includes 37 offices in 18 countries. In the year following the merger, Squire Sanders Hammonds was the moniker of choice for the firm's UK branches, but a rebrand in 2012 saw SSH drop the last bit, settling for the smooth-sounding Squire Sanders (and sadly squashing the silly sobriquet "*Squammonds*" it had picked up in the meantime). According to sources, "*things are busier than ever*" on the English side, which can now attract the sort of high-calibre international clients "*Hammonds could have only dreamed of.*"

Hammonds may have disappeared from the letterhead, but the current bunch of trainees – many of whom witnessed the evolution first-hand – assured us that much of the old firm's affable ethos remains. Trainees asserted that "*things have very much stayed the same on a day-to-day basis at all offices*" despite initial concerns that the three UK regional outposts would be neglected in favour of a more London-centric approach.

Indeed, as far as we can tell, the biggest difference to the training contract nowadays is the increased international work on offer: the wide variety of seat choices and down-to-earth approach that traditionally attract applicants have stayed firmly put. "*It's an exciting time to be here,*" trainees agreed, declaring the firm's new global platform a "*positive and welcome*" development. At the time of publication, the firm had just launched a Singapore office and was gearing up for a new outpost in Seoul. Check out our website for more on the ins and outs of the US-UK combination plus a small history lesson on Hammonds' rise to success in the 90s.

Choices and more choices

Thanks to the six-seat system, there's no shortage of opportunity to try out different practice areas. Seats are up for grabs in around 15 different departments, and most are on offer at all four UK offices. As for seat allocation, trainees reported: "*HR is excellent at trying to make business needs and trainee desires match up*" and "*fairly accommodating*" when it comes to personal requests – "*I've heard of them bringing in certain seats that people have asked to do, and they're usually happy to let you repeat one at the end so you can get extra exposure to the area you want to qualify into.*"

At the moment, overseas seats are limited to Brussels and Paris, but trainees anticipate a wider variety of destinations in the future. "*I believe more opportunities will open up over time simply because of need, but there are no plans for additional secondments yet,*" Lodge affirms. In addition to secondments at major clients like Tesco, posts at various banks and companies occasionally arise, some of which are part-time – "*a nice way to gain a better perspective on clients' needs without losing touch with the firm.*"

Going global

The corporate team splits its time between M&A, private equity and capital markets work, regularly handling cross-border deals for investment banks and large corporations.

Chambers UK rankings

Capital Markets	Media & Entertainment
Corporate/M&A	Pensions
Data Protection	Pensions Litigation
Dispute Resolution	Private Equity
Employment	Real Estate
Immigration	Sports Law
Information Technology	

"*You can really see the benefits of the merger in this department,*" one source said. "*Historically we acted for mid-size companies in line with our own size, but our global reach has grown tangibly.*" New clients of note include entertainment promoters Live Nation and Fortune 500 corporation Yum! Brands, the world's largest fast food company. The London office has a strong track record in the sports and media sectors while Leeds is big in renewable energy and Manchester has a growing reputation for technology work. Corporate lawyers recently advised on builders' merchant Travis Perkins' £661m takeover of BSS Group and assisted with North American pharma company Valeant on its multimillion-euro acquisition of a Lithuanian rival's share capital. Trainees mentioned starting off with "*lower-level admin tasks*" before progressing to substantive assignments like negotiating disclosure agreements and drafting ancillary documents; others reported meaty responsibilities from the start: "*I was able to run a small deal on my own, which involved discussing and structuring all the documents myself.*" Sources agreed: "*The firm tries to get you involved with clients from an early stage – we're taken along to all the meetings.*"

Like corporate, a seat in banking offers "*a high degree of exposure to clients early on.*" The team focuses on corporate banking, real estate finance and asset-based lending, mixing national deals with cross-border transactions like Barclays' recent buyout of the Jemella Group, owners of the ghd hair styling company. Squire Sanders lawyers were in charge of the asset-based lending transactions on the £160m deal. "*I was involved in a major refinancing of a multinational corporation, and my role was liaising with overseas counsel and making sure the documents reflected our discussions. I really got to pick it up and roll with it,*" one trainee testified.

The commercial dispute resolution team handles disputes for large corporations like Tesco, Lloyds and Northern Rock. There's also a sizeable chunk of international arbitrations before institutions like the International Chamber of Commerce and International Centre for Settlement of Investment Disputes. "*I was heavily relied upon in the wind-up to trial,*" testified one source, mentioning "*proofing final submissions and preparing trial bundles alongside small-value files I was running by myself for our reg-*

ular clients." Attending court is a "*pretty regular*" feature of a CDR stint: "*I got to go on my own to instruct counsel – the seat is fantastic for building your confidence.*" In finance litigation, asset-based lending and fraud cases constitute the majority of the work – indeed, the firm acts for nearly 90% of asset-based lenders in the UK. While "*there's not too much client contact,*" a finance litigation seat offers a combination of "*small applications you run yourself*" and work on "*bigger disclosures. It's a good team for learning how to deal with tons of documents.*"

Commercial IP offers a mix of contentious and non-contentious work for big-ticket names like Bacardi, who the firm recently advised on advertising and media contracts connected to the booze giant's Bacardi, Martini and Grey Goose brands. In the luxury and fashion circles, it works for high-end retailers like Cath Kidston, Hobbs, Austin Reed and Daks. "*You do a lot of advertising clearances as a trainee: design agencies come to us to ask if they can put a certain feature in an advert and you're responsible for looking at the IP laws.*" There are also some "*rather interesting*" tasks such as "*writing the rules for promotional competitions, like when a high-street store is running a sweepstake.*"

Other seats with contentious aspects include employment, restructuring and insolvency, property litigation and London's ever illustrious sports seat, which represents sports organisations and athletes entangled in disputes and is "*unsurprisingly very popular among male trainees.*" There's "*a lot of anti-doping work, as in acting for sportsmen who test positive for steroids,*" one revealed. The chance to attend tribunals, instruct counsel and perform the court run during a contentious seat proved "*particularly exciting*" for our interviewees.

All in all, our sources were "*quite content*" with the level of responsibility offered at the firm. "*I've probably spent around 3% of my time doing mundane stuff – to be honest, I don't even know how to use the photocopier! Once you show you can do something, they raise the calibre of work they give you.*"

A match made in heaven

How are the old Hammonds crew getting along with their new American comrades? A resounding "*things couldn't be better*" came from all quarters. "*Our cultures have happily coincided,*" one source thought. "*The firm is still full of the same kind of people we all interviewed with years ago – friendly, ordinary, intelligent people you can relate to, people who don't bamboozle you with long words.*" This is all well and good for those whose office set-up was unaffected by the merger, but what did the London trainees – who welcomed 30 UK-based SSD lawyers to their digs in March 2011 – have to say about it all? "*It's gone incredibly smoothly,*" they said, emphasising that "*everyone works together harmoniously. They've integrated so well that an outsider probably couldn't differentiate between Hammonds and SSD lawyers without just singling out the Americans.*"

This isn't to say there's been no US influence on the working environment. "*Certain things have changed to put us more in line with American work standards: for example, the procedure for promotions has become more merit-based rather than the historic UK tenure-type system.*" That said, "*we're not forced to bill 3,000 hours a year or charge US rates all of a sudden. The extent to which we've been Americanised is mainly visible when the firm does stuff like celebrate the Fourth of July with doughnuts.*" Interviewees agreed management is "*really interested in coming across as a global rather than American-led firm. There are a lot of people taking active roles across the world as international partners in charge of international teams.*"

"*People work hard in the daytime but tend to go home between 6 and 7pm most days.*" Seats like corporate and banking require occasional late nights "*since the work comes in peaks and troughs,*" but "*there's a bit of trench spirit going on when you do have to stay, a sense of comradeship that makes it better.*" On the whole, the firm doesn't really go for a "*jackets on the backs of seats*" kind of approach, though trainees did warn that one or two partners "*insist you stay to be seen sometimes.*"

Trainees firm-wide reported a palpable increase in work of late. In Birmingham, "*property work is picking up,*" particularly on the construction side – the office just welcomed an entire team of lawyers from DLA Piper. "*There's no shortage of work*" in London, where a new shipping practice and a number of NQ vacancies "*suggests we've got a steady influx,*" and Leeds trainees reported growth across a number of practice areas. Even in Manchester, which faced some turbulence during the recession and failed to keep on any trainees in 2011, things seem to be back on track: "*Morale is a lot better than this time last year. Some teams are quieter than they should be, but litigation, property and employment have all become noticeably busier.*"

"*Socially, the firm does not disappoint.*" Highlights include end-of-financial-year drinks, pub quizzes, firm-wide and departmental Christmas parties and a summer ball. We also heard about impromptu after-work drinks, the odd curry night and one-off client events like last year's infamous 'White Collar Boxing' – "*think lawyers and accountants whacking each other in the face! What's not to love?*" Trainees across the firm occasionally unite for intra-office activities such as the Three Peaks Challenge, and many get involved with their local trainee solicitor society.

Good vibrations

When we asked our interviewees for final comments regarding their time at Squire Sanders, we continuously heard one version or another of the following statement: "*I think there was a bit of worry for everyone when the merger happened seeing as SSD was not the firm we applied to, but the changes have only been for the better, and the benefits are showing across the board.*" Our sources were unanimously content and couldn't say enough about the many opportunities in store for future trainees. "*They'll be part of an aspirational firm that's constantly growing, so the possibility to move between offices and work with major clients is only going to get greater,*" said one, touching on the "*much anticipated*" prospect of more international secondments for both trainees and fee earners. "*I can honestly say we're progressing into something quite special. Squire Sanders isn't a major global name yet, but it will be over time – the firm's putting a lot of money into making the brand synonymous with success... it's a good time to be applying.*" For those who find all this talk of "*vibrant attitudes*" and "*dynamic teams*" too saccharine for their taste, perhaps the following testimony will prove more palatable: "*I consider myself a normal human being, so I've always thought if I won the lottery I'd quit any job... but this one would honestly make me think twice. It's really great being surrounded by ambitious people, doing different stuff every day. Trust me – this is a commendation from a man who doesn't like working!*" The firm retained 26 of 33 qualifiers in 2012.

And finally...
Those interested in Squire Sanders are well advised to get a place on the vacation scheme as the firm recruits heavily from the pool – one interviewee went as far as to call it *"practically a must."*

"Don't join a firm with your heart set on qualifying into a certain area – you'll almost certainly change your mind after sitting in several different departments."

Trainee

Stephenson Harwood

The facts

Location: London

Number of UK partners/solicitors: 91/136

Partners who trained at firm: 15%

Total number of trainees: 32

Seats: 4x6 months

Alternative seats: Overseas seats, secondments

Extras: Pro bono – Lawyers in Schools; language classes

On chambersstudent.co.uk...

• How to get into Stephenson Harwood

• Interview with training partner Neil Noble

This mid-size international firm has its eye on expansion, especially in the areas of corporate and finance.

Harder, better, faster, stronger

"It's clear that Stephenson Harwood is moving in the direction of becoming a big City firm and is very serious about further international expansion," say its trainees. *"They're hiring new partners every 30 seconds and the new office is a corporate dream."* The firm moved to Finsbury Circus in Moorgate in 2011, and this is still having a positive effect on the general mood of the firm. *"The office has made people prouder,"* trainees said. *"You can really feel the push to drive forward, expand and become a big competitor."* This isn't to say there haven't been one or two blows, like the departure of Sunil Gadhia to Cleary Gottlieb in March 2012. Gadhia served as Stephenson Harwood's CEO between 2003 and 2009, and was widely credited with reviving its fortunes after an early-noughties identity crisis, as well as developing the firm's India practice.

New CEO Sharon White *"addresses the firm every six months, as to how every department is doing and future plans for development. Management are careful in their growth plans, but it's clear that SH is fighting to secure a foothold in emerging and exciting markets."* Having first forged links with East Asia in 1875 and with historical connections to the Hong Kong and Shanghai Banking Corporation (HSBC is still a client today), Stephenson Harwood is already well placed in that region. Over 25% of the firm's lawyers are based in Asia. Two more offices, in Paris and Piraeus, complete the firm's international network – for the moment.

Although known primarily for litigation and shipping work, *"the perception of shipping dominance is just not true,"* trainees said. *"We're definitely not a shipping firm.*

Although the department is revered, it is essentially a small part of what we do. With all the growth in other departments, we're becoming a truly full-service firm." If you were to examine the *Chambers UK* rankings, you would note that alongside the shipping practice, litigation, real estate and asset finance all make strong showings, and the firm gains recognition in many other areas. It certainly has a considerably broader remit than classic shipping firms such as Ince, Thomas Cooper or Holman Fenwick Willan.

Trainees at SH undertake four seats of six months each. There is a varied selection of litigation, corporate and finance teams to choose from. Then the marine and international trade (MIT) seat is *"a mixture of contentious and commercial work to do with ships,"* while employment/pensions and real estate round off the options. *"MIT and commercial litigation fulfil the SRA requirement, so you'll end up doing a seat in at least one of these departments."*

Amazon's warriors

Trainees list three preferences at each seat rotation *"and the HR team really does listen to what you'd like. I think the vast majority end up with their first, or at least second choice,"* trainees said.

The most populous department in the firm, commercial litigation contains insolvency, IP, regulatory (which includes white-collar crime), arbitration, property litigation and general litigation. *"Groups are pretty defensive over their trainees, so you tend to focus on one sub-specialty. If you*

Chambers UK rankings

Asset Finance	Information Technology
Aviation	Investment Funds
Banking & Finance	Outsourcing
Banking Litigation	Pensions
Capital Markets	Pensions Litigation
Commodities	Private Equity
Construction	Professional Negligence
Corporate Crime & Investigations	Projects
Corporate/M&A	Real Estate
Dispute Resolution	Real Estate Finance
Education	Real Estate Litigation
Employment	Shipping
Environment	Social Housing
Financial Services	Tax
Fraud	Transport

have the capacity, however, you're encouraged to pick up work from other teams." As a general rule in com lit, "*there will be some bundling, but the firm gives you plenty of opportunity to get involved and feel creative in argument.*" The insolvency teams "*primarily work for businesses and business creditors rather than banks. We also advise company directors and various individual professionals. We do have some long-standing banking clients, and as our financial practice grows we will be more beholden to those clients. For the moment, however, we're still litigating against a range of opponents.*" For instance SH, is advising the liquidators of MK Airlines on the losses arising from a crash between one of its planes with a South African Airlines aircraft at Johannesburg airport.

The regulatory group work includes advising on FSA investigation, Serious Fraud Office inquiries, insider dealings and market abuse. There are some "*very interesting, high-profile, international clients,*" trainees divulged. This includes advising the Arab Republic of Egypt in connection with the tracing and recovery of between $30bn and $70bn worth of assets misappropriated by former president Hosni Mubarak, his family and his associates. The firm also acted for the former chief executive of UBS's UK wealth management division, John Pottage, in his appeal against a £100,000 FSA fine for compliance failures and misconduct. Furthermore, SH has "*a history of acting for oligarchs, so there is a lot of Russian work.*" Trainees find the work "*really interesting. It's a small team, so there's a lot of first drafts and research to get your teeth into.*" The arbitration team were given particular credit for "*really getting trainees involved.*" One said: "*I went to court about seven times and occasionally it was simply me and the client. It was a daunting, but great learning experience.*"

The corporate department has been hiring of late. In 2011 and 2012, the London office has taken on new partners from firms such as Simmons and Weil Gotshal, while the firm also expanded its corporate expertise in China and Paris and has established a fully separate projects team. "*Projects has emerged as an independent team with real momentum. It serves as an example of the strengthening nature of what we have to offer,*" says training partner Neil Noble. The corporate department covers: corporate finance (which is the general corporate seat incorporating M&A and securities work); projects; tax; funds; and commercial, outsourcing and technology. SH advised LOVE-FILM on the acquisition of all its remaining shares by significant minority shareholder Amazon and acted for the Qatar Investment Fund on its $250m migration from AIM to the main market of the London Stock Exchange. Trainees said: "*There is a lot of crossover between departments, so you can end up doing different types of work.*"

Ship-shape

The finance department is essentially asset finance and includes banking, shipping, aviation, real estate and rail finance. Neil Noble again: "*There's a five-year strategy in place to ensure the growth of this department. There have been several hires in recent years, particularly in the banking team, and we have several other laterals in the pipeline. On the asset finance side of the practice, the rail and aviation teams have picked up several large clients and deals and we have been very lucky with the general growth in every sub-specialty.*" SH advised on a $21.7bn order for 230 Boeing 737 aircraft (including Boeing's new 737 MAX aircraft), and also acted for Santander on its $25m investment-grade facility for InterContinental Hotels. Most of what trainees do is still asset finance-based and "*it's very drummed into you from the beginning that you're there to think and get involved. Of course there's the basic grunt work to do, but if you show an interest, the teams are fantastic in giving you all sorts.*"

The MIT department (aka shipping litigation), deals with "*offshore construction disputes, oil and gas issues, shipbuilding and yard disputes and shipping PI cases. There is also offshore contracts work. A large proportion of clients are Chinese, Korean and Russian.*" As a trainee, "*you're very aware of how knowledgeable the partners are. Clients expect not only legal, but also commercial advice, so it can be quite fast-paced.*" One source said: "*You end up working directly with clients and I even found myself in front of a commercial court master.*"

Sing Kong

Overseas secondments are available in Hong Kong and Singapore, with two trainees going out to each location every rotation. "*The HR team sends an e-mail round and you submit an essay outlining the reasons why you want* to go. *Although secondments are very popular, if you're interested you're highly likely to get the chance to go.*" The Hong Kong office specialises in corporate/finance, litigation and real estate (though trainees tend to focus on just one area when out there) while the Singapore office covers corporate/finance, in particular aviation finance and MIT. Teams in both offices are "*very friendly and you get a lot of good work and exposure. The hours can be long though.*" There are also various client secondments.

"*SH has a very approachable office atmosphere,*" trainees declared. "*The CEO comes to every firm event and knows everyone's name. Even the most senior partners are very personable and genuinely open to helping you. People are interested in your life outside of work as well.*" One source said: "*I'm actually friends with people in my intake and actively socialise with them outside of work, even on the weekends.*"

As the firm grows, is this going to change? "*Management is doing its best to maintain that friendliness, but by virtue of growth, a personality becomes harder to maintain. We seem to be losing our interesting quirks,*" one source mused. Neil Noble said: "*Inevitably as you get larger, it becomes more difficult to uphold that small-firm culture. We are, however, trying to preserve our core values and have found that those that join us buy into that culture and our values.*"

It canapés to work here

Our impression, for what it's worth, is that this was an essentially quite traditional firm (indeed, it only converted to LLP status in May 2012) that suddenly cottoned on to the whole modernisation thing and threw itself forward with gusto – hence the new office, the big corporate and finance push, the talk of expansion, the emphasis on networking events (trainees even hold their own, "*a wine and canapés do where we invite everyone who has the potential of one day becoming a client*"), the LLP conversion, et cetera.

We also think that the experience of future trainees will largely depend on how far the firm continues down this road. While SH's essential decentness is well ingrained, we wouldn't bet on the continued existence of a small-firm environment where everyone knows everyone. Trainees did say: "*The good thing is, we are changing, but nothing seems to be happening very dramatically. SH is careful about the way it's moving.*"

No one can claim there's a shortage of social events. There's an SH choir, football and netball teams, and "*in the summer there's also a lot of cricket. We have client cricket games, interdepartmental cricket games, basic cricket training... people are absolutely obsessed.*" The firm now also hosts Yoga classes. At Christmas, the firm "*always holds a party at a beautiful hotel. Last year it was at the Grosvenor and was casino-themed.*" The trainees organise their own festive bash, too. "*We actually normally go out for a curry around Brick Lane, which is always a lot of fun. The NQs come as well as we're all very close. Certainly on a lower level, everyone is very up for attending social events.*" Trainees also hold their own professional networking event.

Working hours "*differ wildly between departments,*" trainees said. "*In corporate, finance and tax, you can get very close to those magic circle hours. On the other hand there are people who have never had to stay past 8pm through their whole two years.*" One the whole, "*the office does tend to get quieter after about 7pm. If you've finished your work by then, you really are free to go.*" One source added: "*Even if you are there very late, you're never stuck in the office for useless admin stuff. It's always because you have good work to do and your efforts are acknowledged.*"

The firm "*tries to be very open about retention. No one's pulling the wool over your eyes in SH: you know which departments are busy and will need people.*" A total of 12 out of 14 qualifiers stayed on in 2012.

And finally...
Stephenson Harwood would suit anyone searching for a strong, rounded training contract with an international element and probably a shipping twist as well.

Stevens & Bolton LLP

The facts

Location: Guildford

Number of UK partners/solicitors: 36/65

Partners who trained at firm: 14%

Total number of trainees: 8

Seats: 6x4 months

Alternative seats: None

On chambersstudent.co.uk...
- How to get into Stevens & Bolton
- All about Guildford

A slice of London in Guildford? Never! But that is exactly what this conveniently located Surrey firm has to offer...

Wey cool (na na na na...)

It's certainly true that the banks of the River Wey are quieter than those of the Thames, and S&B lawyers get to work inside an office that overlooks these tranquil waters. This is not, however, a sleepy backwater regional firm: the distinct scent of the City is detectable all around S&B's river-perched property. Despite humble beginnings as a small firm drawing in local private client and real estate work, S&B has grown in recent years to become a worthy commercial contender that can give larger outfits a run for their money. S&B is top-ranked in *Chambers UK* for corporate/M&A, employment, IP, dispute resolution and construction work in the South, while the firm's private client and real estate practices still pack a punch. Big-name clients include pizza chain Papa John's, RBS and Lloyds. Trainees proudly declared that "*all areas are strong*" at S&B.

"*I have a lot of trust in the people that run this firm*," said one source, commenting on the management's careful navigation through the country's ongoing economic difficulties. "*You know that they're not going to be sacking people, but you also know that we will be up there, bigger and better – and I say that as a bit of a cynic!*" The gameplan for the future revolves around "*continuing to be a strong force in the South, but also developing links to those bigger City clients who are looking for value for money*." According to managing partner Ken Woffenden, an increasing amount of international work is coming into the firm: "*We feel that's a result of quite a few years spent investing time in building relationships with foreign law firms in Europe and elsewhere.*"

Seat dreams are made of these

Trainees complete six seats of four months during their training contract. Given that there are six seat options, candidates can get the full S&B experience. A stint in coco is compulsory, while others up for grabs are: dispute resolution/IP; real estate; employment, pensions and immigration; family; and tax, trusts and charity. Seat allocation is usually a smooth process, with most getting their first or second choice each time. A small trainee intake means that "*you can discuss your preferences with one another, so that there aren't too many clashes.*"

S&B's coco department is divided into corporate, commercial, franchising, banking and competition. Clients include multinational companies such as distribution and outsourcing company Bunzl and environmental services outfit Veolia. Usually there are two trainees in the department at any given time, with one assigned specifically to corporate, the other to commercial. However, they often get a taste of the rest of the department.

Trainees said of corporate that "*it's here where the firm competes with the City for high-quality work, attracting FTSE 250 companies, while looking after local clients as well.*" The team recently advised international supplier Filtrona on its $110m acquisition of manufacturer Richo. "*A real effort is made to make sure you understand the work and see a deal from start to finish,*" and tasks include "*lots of drafting and marking up disclosure documents. There's a great team spirit and you don't do anything that you feel is beneath you.*" Competition entails "*mainly research tasks*" into issues surrounding EU law, and drafting notes of advice to clients: "*It's interesting work and can be very technical to get your head around.*" Matters can include advising on the competition implications of commercial arrangements, assisting with compli-

Chambers UK rankings

Banking & Finance	Immigration
Competition/European Law	Information Technology
Construction	Intellectual Property
Corporate/M&A	Partnership
Dispute Resolution	Private Client
Employment	Real Estate
Environment	Restructuring/Insolvency
Family/Matrimonial	Tax

ance initiatives in connection with the Office of Fair Trading, and advising on the legality of company rebate schemes.

Dispute resolution is split into general commercial disputes, IP and insolvency teams, which together form one of the largest litigation practices in the region. Clients include Hiscox Insurance and Kia Motors. A big recent case saw the firm represent a Kazakh-registered bank holding company against various allegations – including conspiracy and breach of fiduciary duty – in a matter valued at $1.3bn. Trainees deal with "*all the typical disputes that businesses have, including professional negligence and compliance-based issues.*" Trainees have their own debt collection files to run, while they deal with the disclosure elements of bigger deals.

Real estate is another big area for the firm, and is made up of environment, planning, property litigation, commercial, construction and residential conveyancing teams. There's a mix of "*larger transactions where you'll be assisting associates and partners and smaller matters to cut your teeth on.*" Larger transactions have included acting for property investment company Vfund on a £60m joint venture with Epping Forest District Council to develop a fashion retail park. The smaller matters mean that "*you'll have contact with the client.*" Trainees estimated that around 50% of their time was taken up by commercial work, with the remainder divided up between the other teams.

"*If you have any feeling for numbers and that kind of academic problem solving,*" then the chances are you'll enjoy tax, trusts and charity. The pace of work is "*much slower*" in comparison to other seats, and the "*pressure is different – it's in some ways a more demanding, intellectual pressure.*" Trainees were able to sit with senior partners and "*ran a lot of probate files, drafted powers of attorney and*

conducted quite a bit of historical research into trusts that have been going for over a hundred years.*" On the tax side, they help out with more complicated matters, "*researching tricky aspects of the law and reporting back to the partner.*" Luckily, "*the team is very good at knowing what a trainee can manage,*" and sources enjoyed the esoteric atmosphere and interesting discussions in the department.

Trainees sit in an office with their supervisor, who's often a partner or senior associate. All mid and end-of-seat appraisals are conducted with said supervisor, and are "*useful, even though you get feedback every day.*"

City flitter

"*I love the firm, and I'm not just saying that because I'm being interviewed,*" said one source, echoing the affectionate sentiments expressed by others. Trainees here are clearly very satisfied: "*This is a professional but non-stuffy place, with people at the top of their game, who have been head-hunted to be here. We have City-quality work but we don't charge clients the extortionate amount that City firms often do, meaning that we attract big names.*" The regional location is also conducive to "*having time to have a life,*" while trainees can still "*take advantage of the social scene in London*" – many reverse-commute from Clapham Junction, a 40-minute train journey away. The recent increase in trainee salary to £30,000 has made this even more viable. While reasonable working hours can be expected for the most part, sources did warn that life at S&B is not an easy ride, and that it would be a danger to assume so. There can be periods – especially within corporate and litigation – where trainees work until 11pm or even later.

S&B moved into its office overlooking the River Wey in 2010. It's just opposite the station and within walking distance to the local shops. There is room for expansion, but trainees didn't sound thrilled at the prospect of new lawyers filling the currently empty space: "*Where will we do our pilates?*" At the moment the whole of the third floor is a designated entertainment space, used for not only pilates classes but also Christmas parties and end-of-month drinks.

Trainees meet up for lunch on a weekly basis and sit in the castle grounds, but also organise "*big nights out at least once a month.*" Most recently, they headed to Chelsea for some fancy dining and clubbing. In Guildford, The White House is undoubtedly the watering hole of choice.

And finally...

A firm for those who want the best of both worlds, S&B allows trainees to get to grips with some top-notch work in a peaceful setting. In 2012, three out of four second-years stayed on after qualification.

Taylor Wessing LLP

The facts

Location: London, Cambridge

Number of UK partners/solicitors: 103/169

Partners who trained at firm: 8%

Total number of trainees: 49

Seats: 4x6 months

Alternative seats: Secondments

On chambersstudent.co.uk...
- How to get into Taylor Wessing
- Interview with managing partner Tim Eyles

Over the last decade, TW has blossomed from a newly merged Anglo-German outfit into a profitable mid-tier institution with 22 offices across the globe and a seriously entrepreneurial streak.

Taylor-made

"*Some firms are very set in their ways. I came to Taylor Wessing because I thought it was going places.*" According to its trainees, "*international expansion is something they're really pushing at the moment.*" The first half of 2012 alone saw the firm combine with Singapore buddies RHT Law, and link up with Eurofirm ENWC, bringing its presence into Austria, the Czech Republic, Hungary, Poland, Slovakia and Ukraine. Don't expect it to stop here, though. It looks as if Hong Kong may be next to get the TW treatment, as the firm continues its march into emerging economies. Lateral hires are also high on the agenda: "*We've taken on 19 new partners since the beginning of 2011,*" managing partner Tim Eyles told us. All this effort has helped bump up turnover by 12% in 2011/12, bursting through the £200m barrier for the first time. About half of this was generated outside the UK.

The firm is perhaps best known for its IP work – the bread and butter of the old, pre-merger, Taylor Joynson Garrett – but it ranks just as highly in *Chambers UK* for its mid-market corporate, litigation, real estate and private client teams. It focuses on six major industry sectors, including consumer brands, real estate and life sciences, but its techy expertise remains a big selling point. In October 2011, TW cosied up further to its start-up clients, opening a mini 'Tech City' office near London's so-called 'Silicon Roundabout' at Old Street to "*offer them low-cost advice before they get big.*" Tech clients are also the reason for the existence of TW's small Cambridge office, which doesn't host trainees.

Pick your own

Trainees are free to take their pick of the firm's various seats, so long as one is in a corporate or finance group. The teams falling under this umbrella are: tax and incentives; finance; hotels; corporate; corporate technology; commercial and projects; private equity; and financial institutions and markets (FIM). Naturally, trainees also need to fulfil the SRA's contentious requirement and can choose from seats including: commercial disputes; employment and pensions; trade marks, copyright and media; patents; restructuring and corporate recovery; real estate disputes; and construction. So a pretty varied mix, all in all.

Trainees state a few seat preferences. They're not guaranteed, but most tend to bag one of their top three choices at every stage of their training contract. "*Overall I'm pretty happy with it,*" one source stated, "*although I've had to fight to get what I want sometimes.*" Occasional secondments crop up as well, and in recent years trainees have spent time at the likes of Ricoh.

TW's corporate department is the firm's largest by headcount. Within it, the corporate, commercial and projects subgroup was a particular hit among our sources, mainly due to the diverse nature of its deals. From "*helping mid-size electricity producers set up wind farms,*" to "*reorganising a group of about 30 companies across ten jurisdictions,*" they had been involved in substantial work, "*taking responsibility for certain parts of the deal.*" The corporate technology seat was similarly described as "*a great six months,*" working alongside some of the firm's more techy clients such as medical diagnostics company Oxford Immunotec. Expect a mixture of M&A and

Chambers UK rankings

Agriculture & Rural Affairs	Life Sciences
Banking & Finance	Media & Entertainment
Banking Litigation	Outsourcing
Capital Markets	Pensions
Construction	Pensions Litigation
Corporate/M&A	Private Client
Defamation/Reputation Management	Private Equity
	Product Liability
Dispute Resolution	Professional Discipline
Employee Share Schemes & Incentives	Professional Negligence
	Real Estate
Employment	Real Estate Finance
Financial Services	Real Estate Litigation
Fraud	Restructuring/Insolvency
Information Technology	Telecommunications
Intellectual Property	

restructuring work, as well as "*investment into tech start-ups.*" In private equity, trainees have "*a good mix of drafting and work on wider aspects of the deal.*" This group recently advised on the sale of luxury phone brand Vertu.

There are also a wealth of areas to get stuck into on the finance side. "*It's one big group and I think it's most famous in financial circles for its real estate finance work,*" one source explained. "*I get the impression they're trying to change that, however – they've hired a couple of partners who do more exotic types of finance.*" Trainees receive a mixture of work from across the group, primarily for banks and private equity houses, and often with an international element. "*A lot of transactions are related to the Middle East and Europe, and you spend a lot of time working with the German and French offices.*" Once they've proved their skills, trainee responsibility is pitched high: "*Towards the end of my seat I was given my own £5m deal to run. The department said, 'This is a small one, and we trust you. You can do it.'*" What's more, "*finance departments acting for banks need to build up working relationships with clients, and trainees are very much part of that.*"

A glamour-wess life

Once TW's crowning glory, its IP department may no longer bring in quite as large a cut of the profits, but it remains extremely strong. In fact, 2011 proved to be its busiest ever year, representing industry giants like Teva Pharmaceuticals and KPMG, plus the ever-so-glamorous Vivienne Westwood, Burberry and Christian Dior. It's probably no surprise that "*it's quite a popular seat, and one that draws a lot of trainees to the firm.*" Fortunately, there are plenty of seats to go around and "*if people want to sit there, they will.*" It's unlikely to disappoint – newbies are able to get stuck in to some of the group's biggest cases. For one: "*I was involved in a really exciting defamation case, instructing quite a well-known QC.*"

TW's litigation group has been significantly bolstered of late, taking in a bumper crop of lateral hires. Within its plethora of subgroups, trainees get involved with "*good, interesting tasks,*" such as research, and drafting correspondence and instructions for counsel. Expect the odd bit of bundling, but "*nothing excessive,*" plus some "*exciting international stuff operating in other jurisdictions.*" Taylor Wessing is among the firms working on Bernie Madoff-related litigation, acting for the trustee in bankruptcy and the joint liquidators of the disgraced financier's former companies.

An established private client group is pretty unusual for a City outfit such as this, and as such trainees told us Taylor Wessing's "*is a lot more sophisticated than private client departments at other firms.*" This is largely due to the international scope of the team – spread across the UK, Europe, the Middle East and Asia – and the astronomical wealth of its clients. TW currently represents 20 families whose net worth each exceeds $1bn, so the team's work is where 'private client' meets 'corporate' – many of these families are like mini-conglomerates. For trainees, daily tasks take the form of "*drafting wills and quite simple trusts structures,*" and they're given leeway to run their own cases with supervision. The consensus is that "*the day-to-day management of cases is really useful for training.*"

Employment trainees get involved in both contentious and non-contentious work, "*drafting forms and taking witness statements.*" As well as acting for big names like easyJet and the publishing house Macmillan, the department also helps out some of TW's up-and-coming Silicon Valley clients when their staff relocate overseas. The "*really huge but really friendly*" real estate department tends to work for investors and developers, and allows its trainees to get their hands on their own cases. "*There's quite a lot of research into obscure points of land law,*" one source said. "*I really enjoyed it.*"

Client secondments are still relatively rare, but there may be more in future. "*Last year there were only two people on secondment, but now there's four or five.*" What's more, the firm has responded to trainees' campaigns to instigate some overseas secondments. "*It's something they've started mentioning,*" one trainee revealed. "*They want to have at least 10% of the whole associate group on international secondment at any one time, and to implement something similar for trainees in future.*" Even if they remain in London, trainees can expect plenty of international work. "*More than 60% of our clients in London are headquartered outside the UK,*" Tim Eyles tells us, "*and that number is growing.*"

Across all seats, trainees find they're delegated pretty substantial tasks, both from their supervisor and from others in their department. "*I've had some long hours and some pretty high-level work, but I've appreciated it and enjoyed the responsibility*," mused one. "*In terms of responsibility, I couldn't ask for any more*," said another. The trust imparted to trainees is partially due to TW's rigorous training schedule. It begins with an introduction to the firm, and continues with a "*fairly intense programme*" after each seat move. There are "*maybe three or four sessions a week to get you up to speed*" for the first few months, followed by know-how meetings every two weeks after that. Trainees are always welcome to pop along to any of the firm's other training sessions, and partners tend to be receptive if their trainees are lagging. "*If you say, 'Actually you've given me too much responsibility here,' they sit down and talk it through.*"

Hours are "*not short, but not horrendous*." Trainees manage to leave the office by 7.30pm most evenings, but do work the odd late night or weekend, particularly in the corporate and financial seats. Partners do their best to soften the blow, and "*are genuinely very appreciative*." According to one trainee: "*I stayed until 1am and the head of department came to my office and said he was grateful for my hard work*."

Last year we heard several grumbles about the qualification system, but our sources in this round of research had no such complaints. In general, they agreed that "*it's quite a steady process – we're told the timetable and exactly what's happening from the start*." Trainees can apply for up to two vacancies and are encouraged to take a proactive attitude to the process. "*Most people will speak to partners and ask, 'Will you be recruiting?' and 'Is there likely to be an opportunity for me?' That's the unwritten rule.*" Retention at TW is generally solid, if not spectacular, and 19 of the firm's 22 qualifiers were kept on in 2012.

Head in the clouds

As one of scores of mid-sized London outfits, TW hasn't always stood out from the pack. Therefore, it is continuing a long-term project of "*getting word about the firm out there*." We recall that way back in 2008 the *Student Guide* suggested a radical marketing campaign might be in order for an organisation that was sometimes perceived as a bit

bland, and it seems the firm took our advice, because it invested in a snazzy rebrand the following year. Pouring money into a facelift in the depths of a recession may not seem a great use of resources, but trainees agreed that "*the 2009 rebrand strengthened our identity*." Since then, TW claims to have experienced a '45% increase in media profile,' which we take to mean it's featuring a lot more in the press. The firm's sponsorship of the National Portrait Gallery's high-profile annual photographic portrait prize doubtless plays its part in this increased visibility.

One source remembered: "*On our first day, we had a talk from Tim Eyles, saying you're not just training here – we want you to step up and take responsibility*." Throughout the training contract, it is made quite clear that "*partners don't want us to sit around waiting to be instructed, but to use our initiative*." Basically, Taylor Wessing trainees are treated as adults. "*Without wanting to make you cringe too much, everyone is basically on an even level. We don't put partners on pedestals, and can pretty much walk into anyone's office*." What's more, "*we're encouraged to have good relationships with partners, and have a laugh with them. They're not stand-offish or unapproachable at all*."

In late 2008, TW moved into new purpose-built offices on Fetter Lane, right next to fellow IP supremos Bird & Bird. They're still looking "*very sleek and sophisticated*." Spread across 11 floors, trainees tend to share an office with their supervisor. The jewel in its crown is the "*actually amazing*" Cloud Nine restaurant on the ninth floor. "*It's pretty much the tallest building around*," and trainees can munch on their subsidised lunch while overlooking St Paul's, the London Eye and the Houses of Parliament. The firm takes full advantage of the panorama, holding summer barbecues out on the grassy terrace.

Lawyers also mingle in the Corney & Barrow or The Last on Friday nights, while the most recent summer ball was held at the Royal Courts of Justice, and departments are whisked off for bonding days throughout the year. "*Actually, we're going go-karting tomorrow*," one source told us. Trainees tend to get involved in a healthy dose of community work: painting houses, planting allotments and generally "*getting dirty and moving slabs of concrete around*." There are also plenty of sports teams: a central event in the TW calendar is an inter-office football tournament, in 2012 hosted by the previous year's champions, the Paris office.

And finally...

"*We value creativity. We want people who have done something in their previous private or professional lives that brings a new dimension,*" says Tim Eyles. If this sounds like you, apply for the vac scheme. More than half of TW's trainees come through this route.

Thomas Cooper

The facts

Location: London

Number of UK partners/solicitors: 18/20

Total number of trainees: 8

Seats: 4x6 months

Alternative seats: Overseas seats

On chambersstudent.co.uk...
- How to get into Thomas Cooper
- Interview with managing partner Tim Goode
- P&I clubs

Want to "*put your brains to use in a specialised environment rather than being a corporate cog?*" This international shipping firm may be the place for you.

Learning to sail

Thomas Cooper is a "*specialist shipping firm*" with a "*presence on the world stage.*" The firm debuted in London during the reign of George IV and – despite being sold to a private client, banking and commercial firm in 1870 – plays a leading role in contemporary shipping law. It has international offices in Piraeus, Madrid, Paris and Singapore. "*We're expanding Madrid and Singapore,*" managing partner Tim Goode tells us, and "*South-East Asia is going to be important to us.*"

You should be aware that Thomas Cooper is a pretty niche firm and no one should apply here for anything other than a shipping-heavy experience. "*Trainees complete one seat in finance, one in marine and commercial litigation, and two in shipping,*" sources said. As you'll discover shortly, there are slightly more seat options than that, but while TC does list practices like private client and even sports law on its website, they are areas that trainees will get little or no exposure to.

As long as you know the difference between a ship and a plane, however, the firm doesn't require candidates to have vast experience of its main industry. "*They look for the ability and enthusiasm to learn fast.*"

Getting wet

It's difficult to give an easy overview of what trainees do in the shipping department as "*work is totally dictated by the given supervisor*" and there are "*so many aspects of shipping: wet, dry, insurance, commodities...*" Generally, trainees see a combination of dry (simply meaning con-

tract, cargo claims, commodities disputes and the like) and wet (problems encountered at sea). Check out page 146 for more information. "*I don't think it's possible just to do one or the other,*" one trainee told us; "*you have to be able to handle both.*" The supervisors are the same from year to year and it's possible to "*make a request if you have a particular interest.*" Not to worry though, most new starters don't express a preference, assuring us: "*Until you're doing it, you don't know what it's like.*"

"*The best thing about shipping is when the work relates to the news,*" our sources told us. "*Most shipping cases aren't usually in the public eye,*" one trainee explained, "*but there are some that make front-page news. Then you go in to the office and find that you've been instructed to work on it.*" As you can imagine, it's usually wet shipping in the press – the story often has tragic element. You might remember that back in August 2011 a tug called 'Chiefton' capsized in the Thames causing the closure of the Thames Barrier... sure enough, that case landed on a partner's desk the following morning.

There's a lot of "*good work such as drafting defence submissions and advising to clients on legal merits to claims.*" However, "*big cases are very document-heavy,*" which means trainees see a lot of photocopying and sorting. All of our sources praised the amount of client contact they were given: "*I was expected to communicate on a daily basis with clients, answering their queries and dealing with questions,*" one told us. "*The e-mails go out in our name,*" which means that trainees here must swiftly get up to speed.

Chambers UK rankings

Commodities

Shipping

Riding the waves

If you want to spend time in court, marine and commercial litigation may be your seat. Trainees see *"excellent quality work,"* including *"writing to clients, and attending trials and case management conferences. I was really brought in and did everything with the partner,"* one said. Another forward-thinking interviewee said: *"In case you don't stay at Thomas Cooper, it's a seat that you can take to another firm. Although the majority of clients are shipping companies, the work isn't really shipping-related."* As the only non-contentious seat, trainees must spend at least six months in finance. The tiny size of the team means *"trainees get put where there's a space."* That's not to say it's unimportant: in fact, one interviewee admitted: *"I was surprised our firm was dealing with such huge finance transactions."* Its major clients are overseas banks based in the UK and trainees work on mortgages and ship purchases. As in shipping, both the work and tasks depend on the supervisor. Whereas one trainee told us that due to the *"very high-value transactions,"* there can be *"a lot of hand-holding,"* another said that they had a lot of responsibility for the smaller documents: *"The partner gave them to me first and asked me what I thought about them. Once they trust you, they really use you rather than giving you menial jobs. There is an expectation that you will be self-sufficient after a while."* Such menial jobs include photocopying and bundling and can take up to a third of a trainee's time in the seat... so still plenty of quality work on multimillion-pound transactions.

Third-seat trainees often go to Piraeus. *"There's no application process: you're just told you're going. It's such a great experience,"* trainees told us – and due to the small intake size, almost all spend six months in the sun once they've completed a shipping seat back home. The seat is *"a mix of dry and wet shipping. There's lots of ongoing arbitration and contractual work."* Being the only trainee out there, the work is very hands-on but the hours are good and the support staff are *"amazing."* The firm puts trainees up in a rent-free flat. Athens itself is *"friendly and relaxed"* and *"you are put in touch with trainees from other firms out here..."* so if you meet future Reed Smith, Watson Farley or Norton Rose trainees on the LPC, make sure to get their Facebook details as they may become your best friends. Trainees fluent in Spanish now have the opportunity to complete a seat in Madrid instead.

Land ahoy!

The 40-lawyer London office attracts trainees who *"like the idea of using their brains rather than being a little cog in a big corporate machine."* The office is so small that *"everyone knows each other and what everyone else did on the weekend."* Trainees and partners often go for an after-work pint together and our sources felt the partners had become their friends, but warned that to start with you must *"learn to network quickly. You see the partners as your clients – they give you the work and your feedback."* A small office means that *"your face, your name and your history are known."* Slacking will be noticed, moaning doesn't go down well, and boys: ties should be worn at all times. *"The partners are old-school, they might even tell you off if you're not dressed smartly."*

Although *"shipping is an area of law which is a bit more traditional, don't get the impression that it's all male partners taking long lunches."* The majority of trainees in recent years have been female and these days the firm really scores quite well on the gender diversity front. And it's not all ink pots and quills: *"The IT systems have just been updated."*

Trainees are given BlackBerrys and *"out-of-hours work is required,"* but we heard that if something comes in at 11pm on a Friday and trainees have had one too many at a friend's birthday, saying no is okay. *"Thomas Cooper has a different way of working to corporate firms. We work very, very hard in our working hours, but we don't stay in the office for a crazy amount of time."* Trainees generally leave at around 7pm.

Every three months, trainees meet with the managing partner to chat about seats and the future. *"There's no interview process for qualification. We're just told. It's a more personal approach."* In 2012, three out of four second-years were retained.

And finally...

Tim Goode assured us: *"There are hardly any trainees who have prior shipping experience."* However, one trainee advised: *"Reading TradeWinds and other industry publications may give you the edge at interview."*

"Attention to detail is really important. Every word counts, every attachment you send has to be correct. You don't want clients to think you've rushed your work – they're paying lots of money."

Trainee

TLT LLP

A new kind of law firm

TLT

You want your career to fly.
We'll prepare you for take off.

Training Contracts and Vacation Schemes

We're open here. Open to your ideas. Open to connected working. Open plan and open minded. Here you'll find the future of law – a new way of thinking, and a new way of doing business. Breaking down barriers, encouraging creativity, and caring for the world around us.

As a 'Best Companies' accredited firm, we have accolades from the best in business who agree that our way is the way forward. You need to be part of this. This is where your career really begins.

Whether you join us for your training contract or a one week vacation scheme placement, you'll work on live cases for real clients, get input from a Partner, and develop a broad range of skills across the full legal and business spectrum. Our vacation schemes are held every Easter and summer in Bristol, and every summer in London. Second year law students, final year non-law or law students, graduates and mature candidates can all apply. And, we're recruiting now for trainees to join us in September 2015 and March 2016.

Find out more and apply at www.TLTcareers.com/trainee

TLT LLP

The facts

Location: Bristol, London, Scotland, Northern Ireland
Number of UK partners/solicitors: 75/183
Partners who trained at firm: 18%
Total number of trainees: 23
Seats: 4x6 months
Alternative seats: Secondments

On chambersstudent.co.uk...

- How to get into TLT
- The Anderson Fyfe merger

Year after year, trainees describe TLT as "*ambitious,*" and the firm has made impressive progress up the UK legal charts since its creation.

Are you thinking what we're thinking?

"*TLT is an exciting workplace,*" interviewees chirped. "*It's not stuck in the old ways.*" The firm was created through the merger of two Bristol firms in 2000 and has grown rapidly, doubling its lawyer count since 2005 and tripling turnover since 2002. It expanded into the London market in 2005, and in 2012 TLT announced two more ambitious moves – a merger with Scots firm Anderson Fyfe to give it two offices north of the border, and the opening of a practice in Northern Ireland. There's no getting away from it – TLT can now only be described as a national firm. Trainees love all the energy and ambition. "*There are almost monthly hires in the London office,*" one told us. "*Sometimes they are from magic or silver circle firms. It's great to see, as it tells you they're thinking what you're thinking.*"

Clients include "*big names like EDF Energy, Nationwide, Barclays and WHSmith*" – TLT recently advised the latter on its expansion in the Middle East and Asia. It has adopted a sector-focused strategy, and financial services clients now account for over 40% of the firm's turnover. The other sectors are leisure; retail; technology and media; public sector; housing; and renewables.

There are a potential 20 seats available to trainees in Bristol, although in practice not all of these become available every year. "*A list is sent round with the available seats and we rank our top five preferences.*" There are "*a large number of seats in real estate and in banking and financial services litigation, so trainees tend to work in one or both of these departments in their first year. We might not necessarily choose these seats but they are a*

good introduction to the firm's work." The other choices include: banking and asset finance; commercial dispute resolution; construction; corporate; corporate defence; corporate recovery and insolvency; employment; family; pensions and incentives; professional negligence; regulatory; social housing; and tax and estate planning.

The majority of trainees are based in Bristol but some (seven at the time of our calls) are hired specifically to the London office. This is more heavily geared towards financial services work, but seats in shipping, maritime and international trade, real estate and commercial dispute resolution are also on offer. London trainees chat among themselves about what they want to do and sort things out in a gentlemanly manner. It's unusual for them to take a seat in Bristol, or for Bristolians to spend time in the capital (not counting meetings), but NQ positions are open to all qualifiers regardless of location, and "*quite a few Bristol trainees have qualified in London recently.*"

Coors blimey!

A large chunk of the London-based banking and asset finance team's work is carried out for financial institutions. It has a lot of Indian banking clients: *Chambers Asia* ranks TLT highly for its work for the likes of Bank of Baroda. "*The asset security might be ships or helicopters. The nature of the work means trainees can't get involved in every single aspect of it,*" said one source, "*but I was always going to client meetings. Trainees get given a task that they can take and run with until the end, which is good for building a sense of belonging and purpose.*"

Chambers UK rankings

Banking & Finance	Intellectual Property
Banking Litigation	Licensing
Competition/European Law	Partnership
Construction	Pensions
Corporate/M&A	Planning
Dispute Resolution	Private Client
Employment	Professional Negligence
Energy & Natural Resources	Real Estate
	Real Estate Litigation
Environment	Restructuring/Insolvency
Family/Matrimonial	Retail
Franchising	Shipping
Information Technology	Social Housing

Interviewees said that banking and financial services litigation (BFSL) is "*a good seat to take as the firm has had a lot of success and growth in it. You name a bank, we work for them.*" True enough, this is one of the largest teams of its type outside of London, and clients include Barclays, Bank of Ireland, Nationwide and Bank of India. The work of this department involves chasing down debtors on behalf of banks and recovering money from fraudulent transactions. This makes it a "*very interesting department to work in. They let trainees do advocacy at court on charging order hearings. They really build your confidence.*" Back in the office, "*there is a lot of drafting. I worked on an appeal and wrote general correspondence to clients, the courts and the opposition,*" one source said. Due to the smaller files, "*some trainees don't think it has the prestige of other departments. However smaller files mean more responsibility for us. It definitely has a Marmite element and it depends on personal preference whether they love it or hate it.*" One source declared: "*The work can be a little dry and repetitive.*"

A favourite seat among our sources was commercial dispute resolution, which one source described as "*really hardcore technical stuff.*" The team only takes one trainee in each city at a time, which means "*lots of really meaty stuff and loads of client contact. I worked on a complex international contract case for the majority of my time, where I was exposed to litigation, evidence, investigation and research. There were peripheral matters too, including IP and technical contract cases. My supervisor was more than happy for me to take control, but they looked after me the whole time,*" one trainee enthused. Another claimed: "*It was my favourite seat – very exciting. I had two main roles: acting as trainee support for the team, and taking the first attempt at drafting most documents. You get good practice at cases without dealing with anything too big.*" A "*wide variety*" of clients include WHSmith, Merlin Entertainment and Barclays.

In corporate, trainees "*get less of a shot with clients,*" said one source. "*I got to do the first draft of a few things, like board minutes, but you'd never get to run the case yourself.*" The group advised the shareholders of Cornish brewery Sharp's (makers of Doom Bar, ale fans) on its sale to international giant Molson Coors, and WHSmith on the acquisition of 22 stores from the Sussex chain British Bookshops & Stationers when it entered administration.

The regeneration game

The massive property department is split into several different areas including commercial property, residential property, planning, property litigation and social housing. TLT has recently been advising Swan Housing Association on the Blackwall Reach regeneration project. It's worth around £300m and is going to transform a 1960s housing estate in the East End into 1,600 homes with open spaces and community facilities including a mosque. One trainee described their property seat as "*pretty varied. I did a lot of residential conveyancing and bits and pieces of commercial property. The work goes out in your name and there's lots of client contact.*"

The construction team is "*busy and growing quickly. The work is interesting and complex.*" On the contentious side of the team, said one source, "*I helped with a closure and was involved in an adjudication. On the non-contentious side, I helped prepare building agreements. There are lots of client meetings to attend.*"

Regulatory is all about "*defending the firm's clients against health and safety, trading standards and accusations of environmental violations. The non-contentious side includes advising clients. Trainees deal with a lot of advertising and labelling. A lot of the work was pan-European and it's interesting as a lot of the time we were dealing with new product launches and they want advice on alcohol and food labelling. Those clients tended to be big names such as multinational banks. Health and safety prosecutions are a bit more of a mix, with big and small clients such as household names and some I'd never heard of. It was an interesting and varied seat.*" The outcomes at stake in this seat (in terms of money and prison) mean trainees don't get much client contact.

Trainees in the tax and estate planning seat see "*interesting work, drafting wills, company administration and lots of private client work. I did a preliminary task in a probate process where the client had passed away and we went to their house and checked what was of value. We found £300 cash. I didn't expect that kind of task,*" one said.

Luncheon meet

TLT provides a training programme, Tto2, "*for all trainees and NQs. There are a lot of lunchtime seminars which provide an introduction to different practice areas,*" one trainee explained. Appraisals are "*good,*" another told us. "*We have almost weekly meetings with our supervisor and detailed mid-seat and end-of-seat reviews. My supervisor was hot on the objectives. If I didn't make one, they scrutinised why not.*"

"*Trainees are not treated as babies,*" one interviewee said. "*One of the things I love about TLT is that they really embrace the younger guys. It's not a culture which is reliant on the older generation. We are brought into things and involved in things early. As a trainee, you feel like you and your opinion are worth something.*" Trainees think the firm looks for "*energetic and genuine people.*" The hours, say trainees, are "*excellent,*" and "*the office is pretty empty by 7pm. Working long hours is the exception, not the rule – and when I have worked late, I've got cake,*" a sweet-toothed source chimed.

Skittles and tipples

An active charity committee "*arranges lots of events over the year, such as horse-racing nights, baking sales, fashion shows and balls.*" Otherwise, the social life is "*mainly organised by the trainees.*" In Bristol, "*there's been bowling, pizza nights, karaoke and general drinks. There's a consensus that we should try and do something every couple of weeks, but there's no pressure.*" A few Bristol sources mentioned Toto's wine bar as a venue of choice. The firm organises monthly trainee drinks events "*where they put a tab behind the bar.*" In London, "*the pub is a great way to socialise with people more senior in an informal setting.*" The summer party is the big bash: all lawyers from both offices head to Bristol, where the firm rents out the Ashton Court estate.

Internally, the offices are the spit and image of each other; however, from the street it's a different matter. Londoners are based in a "*nice building*" midway between St Paul's and the Bank of England; Bristolians, on the other hand, walk into a "*bleak*" 1970s tower block every morning, which one trainee referred to as "*the cheese grater.*" We hear the views are great though. There's the occasional chance to get out of the office entirely and go on secondment – recent placements have been at Barclays, Bank of Ireland and Triodos Bank.

The identical offices are open-plan and "*trainees sit with their teams. I sit next to a partner and opposite my supervisor.*" Our interviewees loved this arrangement: "*It breaks down barriers of hierarchy. You hear partners on the phone, dealing with clients, always hearing what's going on. It's great to know what everyone is working on, and it's great for keeping up to date with all the gossip.*"

And finally...

TLT marches boldly onwards and that's just the way trainees here like it. In 2012, 14 out of 17 second-years were retained on qualification.

Travers Smith LLP

The facts

Location: London

Number of UK partners/solicitors: 65/191

Partners who trained at firm: 45%

Total number of trainees: 41

Seats: 4x6 months

Alternative seats: Paris, secondments

Extras: Pro bono – Paddington Law Centre, City Law School Evening Advice Clinic, A4ID; language classes

On chambersstudent.co.uk...
- How to get into Travers
- Travers' commercial department
- Postman's Park

One of the City's most highly regarded mid-size firms, trusty Travers oozes class.

The hare and the tortoise

While so many other firms race towards expansion like their lives depend on it, there's something refreshing about Travers Smith, which jogs along defiantly at its own happy pace. While a number of mid-size firms are urgently seeking to expand overseas or merge in order to consolidate their position in a turbulent market, Travers remains staunchly London-based and independent. Why? Simple. This is a happy band of lawyers with a strong identity, and they don't want to risk losing that. Fortunately, the firm is in a strong enough position to continue to be master of its own fate. That's largely due to its corporate department, which has a reputation for punching far above its weight – *Chambers UK* ranks it alongside giants like Ashurst and Norton Rose. In 2011, corporate activity shot up by 20%, partially due to high-profile deals like NBNK's proposed £1.5bn acquisition of a number of Lloyds businesses. It's also thanks to the firm's artful navigation of the mid-market. "*We have fared reasonably well – on the transactional side, the mid-market where we are most active has suffered less from the downturn than the big-ticket M&A and financing work,*" say newly appointed co-heads of graduate recruitment Anthony Foster and Caroline Edwards.

If the corporate department is Travers Smith's star, it has an able ensemble cast in the form of its other departments. All the usual suspects are there – real estate, litigation, banking, commercial, employment, etc – and most are recognised by *Chambers UK*.

A winning Formula

Seat allocation is a structured affair at Travers. Trainees must choose between a stint in either banking or property, and between litigation or employment. Six months are spent in a corporate seat, while a 'wildcard' option allows them to sample groups like: competition; pensions, funds and tax; or financial services and markets. "*Wherever possible they try to match you up with your choices,*" and all our sources reported spending time in their preferred wildcard seat. Unique to Travers is its quirky room system – three to an office, not two. Trainees usually share with an associate and a partner. "*It works really well,*" they agreed. Not only does it enable trainees to get exposure to work, but "*the guys in your room tend to become your unofficial mentors.*"

Trainees generally sit in one of the corporate department's two primary subteams: corporate finance and private equity. The corporate finance group (CFG) continues to grow. In 2011 alone, its deal activity increased by 20% with the number of associates rocketing by over 50%. Corporate trainees get their hands on heaps of responsibility. Legal research and drafting form the bulk of their work, but "*workload gets adjusted depending on how confident you feel.*" Deals range in value from mid-size to surprisingly large, considering Travers' size. As well as the Lloyds deal, it has also been involved with the Force India Formula 1 team in relation to a $100m investment by Sahara, and Macquarie Bank in its £274m purchase of OnStream, a meter reading and installation business owned by National Grid.

Chambers UK rankings

Banking & Finance	Fraud
Banking Litigation	Information Technology
Capital Markets	Investment Funds
Competition/European Law	Media & Entertainment
Corporate/M&A	Outsourcing
Dispute Resolution	Pensions
Employee Share	Pensions Litigation
Schemes & Incentives	Private Equity
Employment	Real Estate
Environment	Real Estate Finance
Financial Services	Restructuring/Insolvency
Franchising	Retail
	Tax

Litigation *"isn't a department you'd traditionally associate with Travers,"* admitted one source, *"but it's been doing well recently, and bringing in good work."* In fact, it was awarded the title litigation team of the year by *The Lawyer* in 2011 for its work for clients including RBS, Merlin Entertainment and the Argentine Republic. According to Foster and Edwards: *"The volume and status of work has never been higher than last year. It's very high-profile, big-ticket litigation."* Banking disputes take up much of the department's time, but trainees get their hands on some *"very random stuff."* Grunt work is kept to a minimum, and trainees tend to find themselves *"helping with research, drafting witness statements and going to court."* As one put it, *"it seems like I learned really quickly, so by my second month I felt very at home in the department."*

The employment team acts mainly for employers – the likes of financial institutions and hedge funds, as well as listed companies like Groupon, Channel 5 and Virgin Active. Because of its small size, trainees tend to accumulate work from a range of people in the department, rather than purely their supervisor. *"I have a couple of clients that are just my responsibility, overseen by a partner,"* explained one source, *"and generally, I'm the main point of contact."* Trainees often find themselves approached by clients directly for advice on issues like retirement and employee performance. They're also occasionally called in to provide training for clients' HR teams. *"Partners want you to learn as quickly as possible, so they throw as much work at you as they think you can handle."*

"The bread and butter of the banking department is assisting private equity financing." This is mixed in with a dollop of property finance and corporate recovery work. Trainee duties vary depending on deal size. On big ones, such as Bridgepoint's financing for the acquisitions of Pret A Manger and Fat Face, trainees should expect to be *"drafting board minutes and resolutions. On smaller ones you might be able to get involved in drafting the actual substance of the agreement."*

Travers' real estate group is renowned for being a *"great department to work in."* Unlike other groups where *"you might look at two or three matters over a few weeks, your day is very, very busy with a lot of smaller things."* Trainees are encouraged to run their own files, taking them the whole way through to completion.

Where the wildcards are

Of the firm's wildcard seats, commercial is extremely popular. *"I guess because it's nice and generalistic, and there's a lot of different areas you can segue into,"* mused one source. Trainees are involved in everything from *"general contract review to having a first draft yourself."* Those seeking a slower-paced environment should head to the pensions group. *"It's not like anything you'll encounter on the LPC, so training is very rigorous and you get a lot of very good supervision along the way."* The idea is to gear you up to work on *"some absolutely enormous pension schemes."* The more technically-minded will enjoy financial services and markets – *"it's quite a cerebral sort of department."* Their job is to help clients navigate market requirements and regulations and, where necessary, act for those being investigated for breaches. *"I was involved in drafting consultations, but with a lot of support from partners,"* said one contented source. The wildcard option can also be exchanged for a secondment with private equity clients 3i, or with the firm's Parisian corporate team if your French is up to scratch.

Travers might be friendly, but don't expect an easy ride – responsibility is pitched high. Almost all our sources reported feeling out of their depth at some stage, but accepted this is *"not necessarily a bad thing as it pushes you to learn."* Partners welcome questions, *"so long as you've explored every single avenue first,"* and trainees agree that if you're sinking *"there's always someone to throw you an armband or give you an oar."* The firm's thorough and efficient training schedule, tailored to each department, helps.

Bear in mind that, despite its small size, Travers packs a serious punch and trainees' working hours tend to reflect this. Expect peaks and troughs, particularly in corporate and finance departments, with office exit times ranging from 5pm to 3am. Hours might be unpredictable, but trainees find that they manage to balance work and play. As a rule, one trainee told us, *"if I make plans after 7pm I very rarely have to cancel them."* What's more, partners genuinely try to their utmost to encourage a healthy work/life balance. *"They're very much of the school that if there's no pressing work to do, just clock off ASAP,"* and if you have prior plans *"so long as you let people know, they're generally very accommodating."*

Nun for the road

However hard you try to resist, Travers tends to charm your socks off. "*There's just a good spirit here,*" notes one source. "*I always feel I can chat easily with any other trainees, and partners are very sympathetic.*" The firm has managed to create a situation where people feel a genuine sense of loyalty to it. "*There seem to be quite a few people who spend a big chunk of their career here. The continuity helps to create an identity of belonging.*" Retention at Travers is normally good and this trend continued in 2012: the firm kept on 20 of its 22 qualifying trainees although some were on fixed-term contracts. "*We're not just recruiting people for the training contract,*" assure Foster and Edwards. "*We look for people we can really see progressing all the way through the firm.*"

Visiting Travers' recruitment website, you'd almost be forgiven for mistaking the firm's trainee profiles for the cast of a Richard Curtis romcom. Suave-looking Oxbridge graduates abound: "*There are some from other unis, but no one can deny that certain institutions – Oxbridge, London and Durham – are over-represented.*" While in the past this may have played a defining role in the firm's culture, trainees believe that things have changes at Travers. "*When I applied it was renowned for being almost public school-ish, with a lot of laddish banter around the place,*" said one source. However, as one non-Oxbridge trainee confirmed, "*I was slightly worried I'd feel left out, but it was almost conversely the opposite. It doesn't feel cliquey at all.*" Foster and Edwards are currently pushing to diversify incoming trainee groups: "*In the next 2012/13 intake, we have just over 20 trainees arriving representing 12 different universities, so we're currently getting a reasonably broad spread, but continue to try to ensure we attract applications from as many institutions as possible.*"

So, what do recruiters look for in potential recruits? According to trainees, "*they want people who are intelligent with a good academic record, who are good fun, outgoing and affable. Outstanding extra-curriculars are nice to have, but kind of irrelevant.*" Ultimately, "*they look at whether people will want to work with you, and whether you can keep up with the work. That's all.*" Foster and Edwards confirm these sentiments: "*We want people who will not only be strong technically but who will also be comfortable with clients and confident working with, and opposite, other advisers.*"

Travers' City premises are split between two offices, the corporate team in a "*flashy, stainless steel-type building,*" and the rest next door in a "*more traditional, red-brick*" outfit. According to trainees, there's the odd whisper about up-sizing, but "*the consensus is that we're happy where we are.*" We suspect this is due, in part, to the offices' location – just a stone's throw away from local haunt the Bishop's Finger, or "*the BF*" as it's nicknamed. You'll find plenty of Travers faces in there on a Friday night, probably en route to Karaoke Box just around the corner. "*After any kind of drinks things, we always end up in there,*" laughed one trainee. "*Partners put their cards behind the bar and we hire as many boxes as we want.*"

There are plenty of more formal get-togethers, on both a departmental and firm-wide basis. Trainees cite the annual Easter party as a particular highlight. It's a great chance to get to know the incoming batch of trainees, consume "*endless amounts of food and drinks,*" and almost inevitably end up initiating the unsuspecting newbies at the Karaoke Box. The firm is also a haven for sporty types, who can arrange personal training sessions in the firm's tiny basement gym, take their pick from hockey, netball and football teams, and get involved in anything from squash games to ski trips.

And finally...

Travers provides genuinely high-end corporate work in an environment where *"you feel like you're part of a community, rather than just a big empire."*

Trethowans LLP

The facts

Location: Salisbury, Southampton

Number of UK partners/solicitors: 26/27

Partners who trained at firm: 15%

Seats: 4x6 months

Total number of trainees: 7

Alternative seats: Occasional secondments

On chambersstudent.co.uk...

- How to get into Trethowans
- Interview with managing partner Simon Rhodes
- Trethowans' main areas of work

This broad-based South Coast firm has a growing commercial practice and *"there is an openness to new ideas from anyone to improve the firm."*

Rhodes' scholars

With offices in Salisbury and Southampton, Trethowans is one of the Solent region's main commercial firms. Despite its small size it attracts big clients, such as Bacardi, Tate & Lyle, Santander and Ladbrokes. Back in 2009, the firm launched a new business strategy, dubbed 'Destination 2012'. On arrival in the destination year, what has Trethowans achieved? *"We have invested in all aspects of the firm, through wider training, lateral hires, better IT systems and more sponsorships and work in the community,"* managing partner Simon Rhodes told us. *"In 2012, we don't just have quality and breadth of practice but real depth now too."* Trainees like Rhodes' vision and the firm's game-plan. *"Without doubt this is an ambitious firm,"* they agreed. *"Management realise they can't just sit back and watch the world go by. We recently rebranded our website and there are all kinds of initiatives to improve the business."*

Trethowans has around a dozen practice areas and at the time of our research the nine trainees were all located in different departments. Seats on offer include commercial litigation; personal injury; commercial property; corporate; insurance litigation; employment; residential property; private client; and agricultural and rural property. The clinical negligence and PI teams are most highly regarded: both get top-tier mentions for the South in *Chambers UK*. The other main practices – corporate, dispute resolution, property, employment and family – all pick up mid-tier Chambers rankings.

The commercial departments can mostly be found in Southampton, while most of the practices that cater for individuals are in Salisbury. Usually, trainees are based in one office but complete at least one seat in the other. Before starting they hand over a wish-list of their seat preferences to the HR team, who are *"accommodating and listen to our preferences."* Said one trainee: *"We also talk to Nicky* [HR partner Nicola Richards] *about our experiences and where we want to head next. You can go and speak to her at any time and she often ends knowing more about what we want to do than we do ourselves!"*

This cow is small; that cow is far away

The personal injury team acts exclusively for claimants and is especially known for its serious RTA (road traffic accident) and spinal and head injury cases. The firm works closely with the brain injury charity Headway and acts on a large number of six and seven-figure claims. The Southampton-based insurance litigation team, meanwhile, acts for insurers and defendants in PI cases. Recently, one more unusual case saw the firm defend a farmer via his insurer against a £100,000 claim by a man who was trampled by a cow in one of his fields. *"From the start client contact in PI is really good,"* one source informed us. *"I was going to meetings three or four times a week with my supervisor. As time went on I would contribute with questions if we were taking witness statements. I was given meaty tasks like getting my head around five years of litigation and then giving instructions to counsel."* Trainees told us that, right across the firm, they were free to ask to take on tasks they hadn't been able to sample yet. *"In personal injury I didn't run my own caseload, but worked on more complex cases for my supervisor,"* one trainee said. *"I mentioned to my*

Chambers UK rankings

Agriculture & Rural Affairs	Family/Matrimonial
Banking & Finance	Licensing
Clinical Negligence	Personal Injury
Corporate/M&A	Private Client
Dispute Resolution	Real Estate
Employment	

supervisor that I also want to work on some lower-end cases, and I was then able to run a few of those myself."

In property, running your own caseload is par for the course. "*I took over all the files that the previous trainee was working on,*" an interviewee told us. "*One was a low-value lease agreements: I talked the client through the options and the different aspects of the lease. I negotiated some points with the other parties and came back with changes to the lease agreements. Then I completed the documents and sent out copies to everyone. Supervision was excellent: all the official advice I sent out was checked by my supervisor.*" One of the department's core competencies is advising pension funds on their property portfolios. Other clients include builders merchant Jewson and plaster manufacturers British Gypsum.

Commercial litigators handle contractual disputes, as well as professional negligence, IP, property, shareholder and partnership litigation. Clients include Toys R Us and Stannah (of stair-lift fame). The firm recently worked on a $1m dispute over a sponsorship payment to Spanish Formula One team HRT. Advocacy experience is a real possibility here. "*I conducted a few hearings myself and got court experience,*" a trainee told us. "*That was definitely encouraged. I also ran small files on my own and worked on pieces of larger, more complicated files, helping out the partner.*"

The corporate team has recently advised on several multimillion-pound transactions. The size of the deals means there is less individual responsibility for trainees. The firm has advised Ladbrokes on a large number of commercial contracts including HR agreements and IT contracts. "*We have invested heavily in our corporate team,*" Simon Rhodes told us. The firm hired Chambers-ranked corporate partner Paula Eckton at the start of 2012, following on from other hires from Blake Lapthorn and Clarke Wilmott in 2010.

Please sir, may I have some more?

If Mr Rhodes sounds like an interesting chap to you, then you might find employment an interesting seat as "*Simon is usually your supervisor.*" He's a hard worker and "*the workload can be quite heavy and you might have to stay late.*" Along with employment, corporate is the only seat with long-ish hours. "*At the start of my corporate seat, my supervisor sat me down to tell me that the needs of clients and pressure of completions can lead to a few late nights. He said I wasn't obliged to stay, but the department does work as a team and it's good to pull together and get the work done.*" Elsewhere, trainees usually work from around 9am to 6pm.

Trainees told us the Salisbury and Southampton offices are united by the good work they offer trainees, good supervision and an entrepreneurial and open business culture. There are differences though. "*Southampton seems to be more social,*" one source reflected. "*It is near Bedford Place where there are loads of bars and restaurants. We are also in a listed building, so the place has the traditional look you would expect of a law firm.*" Salisbury, by contrast, "*is modern and open-plan. That is a good reflection of the firm's business ethos.*" The business park location means that "*the parking facilities are good, but you can't just pop out for lunch and there is only one pub nearby. We don't do things after work unless they are organised in advance.*" Both offices have been building up their links with the local community. Recent activities include sponsoring a local business award, setting up a free legal advice clinic and organising a local business conference.

We were told "*there are always people travelling between the two offices,*" and the fact that trainees complete seats in both offices creates unity among the group. "*The trainees get given a budget for three events a year. We have been out go-karting and are going to see Oliver! at the Mayflower Theatre. Once you have been recruited here you get invited to attend the trainee socials.*" Trainees also have their own firm-sponsored Twitter account (@TrethTrainees). The year's social highlights are a Christmas and summer party. "*Last year we had a big rounders match and everyone – including the partners – joined in. There was a free bar which was great. And families were invited too: there was a bouncy castle for the kids, though I did have a go on it too.*"

And finally...
Between 2007 and 2011 Trethowans let go of just three of its 19 qualifying trainees. Three of five qualifiers stayed on as NQs in 2012.

trowers & hamlins
training contracts

For further information please contact the graduate recruitment team on
Tel +44(0)207 423 8312 or avithlani@trowers.com

Trowers & Hamlins is an equal opportunities employer

INVESTOR IN PEOPLE

Trowers & Hamlins LLP

The Facts

Location: London, Manchester, Exeter, Birmingham

Number of UK partners/solicitors: 107/147

Partners who trained at firm: 33%

Total number of trainees: 36

Seats: 4x6 months

Alternative Seats: Overseas seats

Extras: Pro bono – PRIME, Kaplan Legal Advice Centre; language classes

On chambersstudent.co.uk...

- How to get into Trowers
- Interview with training principal Tonia Secker
- The Middle East

"*A place with a bit of a social conscience,*" Trowers & Hamlins offers a curious mix of public sector and corporate work in the UK and the Middle East.

Spring and drought

The name above the door might have changed several times, but Trowers & Hamlins has been around in one form or another for the last 230 years. The firm has four offices in the UK – London, Exeter, Birmingham and Manchester – while internationally it has exclusively concentrated on the Middle East, with outposts in Oman, Dubai, Abu Dhabi, Cairo, and Bahrain, as well as another in Malaysia.

This firm is a rather unusual beast in terms of its areas of focus. A trainee described it as "*a three-legged stool*" in that it's supported by "*our Gulf practice, public sector work and everything else.*" The firm has a huge list of public sector clients and supports market-leading local government and social housing practices. By 'everything else', we suppose our source was referring primarily to Trowers' mid-market corporate group, which is well respected in the City.

The Arab Spring is shaking up the Middle East, there are swingeing cuts in the public sector and the larger firms are encroaching on Trowers' mid-market territory in the hunt for corporate work. The question needs to be asked: are any of Trowers' three legs strong enough to hold the weight of the firm?

Our sources were optimistic. As far as the corporate market is concerned, they said: "*Our recent move to Bunhill Row, right next door to Slaughter and May, will emphasise we can do the work bigger players do, and do it very well.*" Trowers' London office was until June 2012 located near the Tower of London, in a district traditionally more associated with shipping and insurance firms – Bunhill Row is certainly a more corporate address. Five of the seven recently promoted partners in London belong to the corporate, IP and banking departments.

In the wake of government spending cuts, the public sector "*is an interesting market. Our view of it is: our clients are not shutting up shop – they are having to be slightly cleverer about what it is that they are trying to achieve,*" says training principal Tonia Secker. And the unrest in the Gulf? We consulted with our colleagues on *Chambers Global*, who gave more detail than we could ever need to know on the region, but pointed out that many businesses moved first their money and then their people out of Manama, Cairo and Tripoli into places like Dubai and Oman, so there is still plenty of work in parts of the Middle East. Among Trowers' deals of note, our colleagues highlighted its involvement in the Naseej project – Bahrain's first social housing project to be implemented on a PPP basis.

Trainees can pick from the following seats: public sector commercial; public sector communities and governance; housing projects; corporate; banking and finance; 'international London'; employment; litigation; commercial property; projects and construction; and tax, trusts and pensions. The graduate manager in London has mid-seat chats with trainees "*about where our career is going and what we're interested in – we give him our first, second and third choice of seats and he collates everyone's preferences. He really listens to you: it's more of a counselling session.*" Trainees are encouraged to complete a 'Trowers seat' – that is, "*a seat particular to the firm's*

Chambers UK rankings

Administrative & Public Law	Healthcare
Banking & Finance	Local Government
Capital Markets	Projects
Charities	Public Procurement
Construction	Real Estate
Corporate/M&A	Real Estate Litigation
Education	Social Housing
Employment	

work – *public sector communities and governance would be one and housing another.*" This isn't seen as a bad thing, and anyway "*it would be logistically difficult for that to not happen.*"

The four trainees in the Manchester office will find "*the office has a large focus on housing association clients, therefore the property department is the busiest and has the most fee earners.*" They will also visit the London office or do an international secondment during their training contract. "*Wearing my hat as a training principal,*" says Tonia Secker about regional trainees visiting London, "*it's important that people come to the mothership, not only to build their own network of peers but also to try to make sure that everyone feels part of the whole UK practice.*"

In addition to London and overseas seats, Exeter trainees can spend time in real estate and construction. The Birmingham office may open its doors to trainees from 2013.

A public display

Public sector communities and governance is "*a bit of a strange seat: it's not clearly explained to trainees what the department does and there are acronyms flying everywhere.*" We'll try and make things clear. The team advises local authorities and public sector entities on PPPs (public-private partnerships), regeneration schemes, finances and outsourcing services. Since the government's spending review, Trowers has been helping the Homes and Communities Agency (HCA) and Registered Providers (RPs) "*generate efficiencies out of the diminished funds that they have, prompting them to look at joint ventures between different local authorities,*" says Tonia Secker. Trowers acted for two RPs and a private developer in a joint venture to establish Triathlon Homes, which will retrofit 1,379 Olympic Village homes to use as affordable housing units after the Games have finished. The department also "*works with a lot of Arms Length Management Organisations for housing associations – ALMOs deal with the responsibilities and duties of local councils and how those are carried out.*"

Much of what goes on in the group is "*like corporate work but in the public sector,*" say trainees, and Tonia Secker agrees. "*A lot of the RPs we act for, were they profit-making corporations, would be listed. If you don't know very much about the local authorities sector, you'd be forgiven for thinking it's in some way cuddly – it isn't.*"

"*You could be selling residential property one day and involved in a multimillion-pound development deal the next*" in the housing projects seat. The department is divided into subgroups such as care (working for care accommodation providers for senior citizens) and development teams. Trainees receive work from their own team as well as others in the department. Routine trainee tasks include applications for the Land Registry, stock rationalisations, title deeds and drafting deed licences. Those parcelling out work are "*keen to give you responsibility. By the end of the seat I was running development deals.*" Others had so many files in their name that "*things were overwhelming, but supervisors sensed that and would talk me through my workload.*" Supervision here is "*much more distant than in seats like corporate, but no one will let you sink.*" Trowers acted for Red Kite Community Housing on the transfer of 6,000 homes from Wycombe District Council, in a deal worth £140m, funded by RBS and Santander. It also advised Aviva Investors in its acquisition of 839 tenanted units from Derwent Housing Association, a matter worth over £42m.

"*The bread and butter of Trowers' corporate work is M&A, AIM, private equity and some public company work.*" It has connections in the leisure industry, and also works on student accommodation matters, which ties up nicely with the housing projects part of the business. Trainees assist on closings and our source had been able to draft "*bespoke articles of association, which were bloody difficult!*" The firm's strategy over the next five years is to "*grow the strong corporate practice further to make sure it gets the prominence and profile it warrants. We're looking to utilise the Middle East as a springboard to expand into emerging markets such as Africa and Malaysia,*" says Secker. Our trainee sources agreed: "*The direction of the firm is changing a bit; we're still strong on social housing but realising we have a strong corporate base.*"

Trainees in the litigation seat mostly come across real estate disputes: landlord and tenant squabbles over rent arrears, leasehold disputes, representing housing associations in repossession cases – that sort of thing. "*You are thrown straight into the deep end, but people are very helpful.*" Work comes through from "*a couple of different sources, and you do bits on bigger cases than running the whole file yourself.*" Some trainees had spoken in court "*a couple of times – you get a bit apprehensive but it boosts your confidence.*"

Trowers of Arabia

Overseas seats are "*very popular,*" but *"you are likely to be able to go if you want."* Trainees are sent to Dubai, Abu Dhabi, Bahrain and Oman, though not the "*much smaller*" Cairo office. The unrest in the region meant some trainees this year were a little delayed in actually getting out on secondment, although we gather once there, they didn't experience any problems. There are plenty of perks of working in the Gulf, although red tape and the slow-moving culture of the region provide a different set of challenges from UK life. "*You have to have a sense of humour about it. The region's exploded so much over the past 20 years – it's a young legal system, not as developed.*" It's certainly "*an education in terms of dealing with people – just as useful as building your knowledge of law.*"

Back in Blighty, the Manchester office is located right across from the town hall and its 280-foot bell tower. We heard them peal loud and clear during our chats with Manc trainees. Trowers' digs are "*easy to get to,*" though "*nothing fancy.*" The Exeter office is also very close to the city centre. Trainees in London are "*very excited*" about their move to a new office. "*We've outgrown this one and are moving somewhere very swish. It was previously used by Linklaters, but we gutted it and did it up.*" For some, knowing "*there are going to be hair-dryers, hair-straighteners and showers*" was enough to keep them revved up; for others the strategy behind the move is the exciting thing. "*The desire is to expand, and the potential is there. We've taken the building knowing the lease for the only two floors we don't have is due to expire in the next few years.*"

Most trainees found themselves working from about 8.30am to 6 or 7pm. "*You'd have a hard time getting hold of a property lawyer any time past 6pm,*" but "*in corporate, towards the end a deal you might be working from 9.30am to midnight.*" Along with a relatively humane work/life balance, our sources across the board had found the firm to be a "*friendly place, as cheesy as it sounds.*" People are generally approachable and "*it's easy to get into a bit of banter with a partner, and just as easy with the staff in the café.*"

"*You get a lot of people here who are very principled, aren't working for material aspirations but truly believe what they are doing will make a difference towards society.*" One trainee declared that Trowers lawyers were mostly "*Guardian-reading, sandal-wearing lefties.*" Certainly, social housing law attracts a certain type of person. Tonia Secker promises us "*there's not a sandal in sight,*" and prefers *The Times*, apparently. But, she says, "*we do look for true independent thinkers*" and in the public sector practices, "*we do have people who are politically quite well informed.*" Once we remove newspaper preferences from the equation, "*Trowers is quite diverse: there are plenty of people of different nationalities and ethnicities.*" A slight point of interest is that at the time of our calls, male trainees outnumbered female ones by 21 to 18 – fairly unusual in an age when two-thirds of law school grads are female. We can't say we've noticed this in past years, however, and we think this is simply a quirk of the current intake.

The down-side to Trowers' good work/life balance is that the social scene is a little thin, as so many people have families and go straight home. Still, trainees "*regularly meet for lunch on Fridays,*" and "*billing-drive drinks is a firm-wide staple – everyone gets the chance to mingle with people from other departments.*" The firm also does hold the standard Christmas parties, a mid-seat meal for trainees in the UK and an event for every new intake, to which future trainees are also invited.

And finally...

Trowers was *"so busy"* in 2012 that departments were crying out for NQs, and 14 jobs were made available for 13 qualifiers. Of those, eight stayed on with the firm.

Veale Wasbrough Vizards

The facts

Location: Bristol, London

Number of UK partners/solicitors: 47/80

Partners who trained at firm: 27%

Total number of trainees: 15

Seats: 4x6 months

Alternative seats: Occasional secondments

Extras: Pro bono – Bristol CAB, BRAVE, Avon & Bristol Law Centre

On chambersstudent.co.uk...
- How to get into VWV
- Trends in the education sector

Veale Wasbrough Vizards continues to work its magic – especially in the education arena.

The best of times...

Veale Wasbrough Vizards is the product of a 2009 merger between Bristol-based Veale Wasbrough and London outfit Vizards Tweedie. The former was particularly known for its education and charities work, while the latter had a 200-year-old history in the capital, with good property, family and private client practices and an impressive literary claim to fame: Charles Dickens found his first job at the firm as a legal clerk back in 1828. With sector similarities making a merger good sense, the pair came together and formed a firm that today employs 300 staff and has a turnover in excess of £20m.

VWV concentrates its efforts on five sectors in particular: education and charities; healthcare; public sector; private wealth; and family businesses. These sectors permeate the work completed throughout the firm's four departments, which are: litigation and employment; charities, corporate and commercial (CCC); private client; and real estate. Education and charities work is arguably VWV's strongest suit – much of the firm's revenue is derived from these areas and both specialities are top-ranked in *Chambers UK*. Education used to be its own department at VWV, but after a bit of a profit-inducing rejig, management *"separated it off into various parts, so that the main bulk or success of the firm could be divided throughout the different departments."*

Trainees are hired to both Bristol and London and mostly come to VWV because they have an active interest in the sectors the firm operates within – *"I saw their specialities and I knew it would suit me,"* said one source. They were optimistic about the future: *"It sounds good from what I hear. I think VWV will continue to be a major player in Bristol but it will also take on a more national guise, or at least be viewed as not just a 'regional firm,"* a trainee declared. Post-merger, *"expansion in London is definitely on the agenda."* In July 2012 news broke that VWV was in merger talks with Hewitsons of Cambridge, Northampton and Milton Keynes. Training partner Tabitha Cave is enthusiastic: *"There has been much excitement about it, and there are synergies in the education, charities and private client work that we do."* If it goes ahead, the merged firm would have a combined turnover of £34m and 480 partners and staff. So keep an eye on that story.

School for scandal

Trainees list three preferences before each seat rotation, and mentioned that *"you're encouraged to speak to the HR team informally as soon as you might have an inkling as to where you would like to go next."* Sources added that if their first preference is not met, then *"you'll always get a worthy substitute."* It's worth mentioning that the London office does not have commercial seats on offer, but has corporate, private client, litigation/employment, real estate and charities groups. Moving between offices for seats is also a possibility, and actively encouraged.

The charities department advises over 1,000 charitable organisations. Clients include educational institutions, national charities like the Community Service Volunteers, and organisations connected to social care and the arts, like the Dunhill Medical Trust and the London Symphony Orchestra. The work is corporate in nature, and trainees

Chambers UK rankings

Banking & Finance	Partnership
Charities	Personal Injury
Construction	Private Client
Corporate/M&A	Real Estate
Dispute Resolution	Real Estate Litigation
Education	Restructuring/Insolvency
Employment	

will "*do a lot with schools that are being converted to academies, and subsequently gain charity status – you'll do quite a bit of drafting, and many articles of association.*" One associate in particular concentrates on academy conversions. Pastoral is another team that comes under the CCC banner: "*It means that we basically represent schools and any issues they may have with relationships between teachers and pupils, or parents and schools. That's the general remit.*" Trainees have drafted circular letters to parents and press releases on behalf of the school if anything "*high-profile*" had happened: "*We drop whatever we've been doing, navigate with the press and provide legal defences where they are needed. It can be fast-paced and dramatic.*" An ongoing strand of work comes from immigration concerns: "*We advise schools about taking on international students and the guidelines that they need to follow, especially because the UK Border Agency are constantly updating their policies. Giving lectures and seminars on this topic at schools is becoming increasingly common.*" On the more 'traditional' or 'pure' charities side – that is, not to do with education – trainees might "*conduct research into how two charities can merge while considering certain aspects of trust law.*"

There are two corporate seats: a general one which incorporates mid-tier M&A and family-run businesses matters, and a second geared specifically towards company secretarial work. It's also possible to split a seat between the two. Trainees on the general path came across deals involving start-up companies, which meant "*drafting lots of shareholder agreements,*" and also got to encounter much of the completion process: "*I co-ordinated the disclosure and really got an idea of what the mechanics of completion involve. There were 20 people in the room, and a lot of responsibility resting on me.*" VWV has increasingly drawn in business from early-stage tech companies in the South West region, like children's luggage manufacturer Trunki. It also worked with health club chain Esporta on its reorganisation before the £77.6m sale of its operating group to Virgin Active, while a specialist team provides advice to family businesses, including Clarks Shoes and Weston's Cider. Trainees did warn, however, that "*big deals are not so commonplace.*" In contrast, commercial has "*had so much work on that there have been more requests for trainees.*" Sources enjoyed

drafting and reviewing contracts, as well as taking on IP trade mark work: the team has been advising The Royal Hospital for Children on its trade mark protection and enforcement strategy, while other commercial clients include coffee business advisers Beyond the Bean, and aircraft manufacturer Airbus.

Headmaster demons

VWV offers "*the whole raft of employment services.*" New clients include the hedge fund QCM, Chartis Insurance and Exotix – a 'niche banking boutique'. There is a mix of contentious and advisory work on offer, and those who had specifically concentrated their seat on the education aspect of the department mentioned "*taking witness statements from teachers, writing out scripts for redundancy, dealing with grievance claims, and there's also a layer of child protection as well – it's everything and anything you can imagine!*" Headmaster changes can prompt strategic reviews of a school's operations, which tackle disciplinary procedures, redundancy programmes and restructuring advice. Some sources found that they were "*more heavily involved on the litigious side,*" and overall the responses we heard were positive: "*It's hard work, but all very worthwhile – employment is quite a fast-moving field, and you'll be taking phone calls from clients who will need immediate legal advice.*"

Other litigation teams at VWV include commercial lit, property lit and personal injury. In commercial litigation, clients include the Yankee Candle Company, EDF Energy and the Bank of Ireland. Matters encompass claimant professional negligence, insolvency-related disputes, debt recovery work and partnership disputes. Property litigation is "*intense, with long hours, good training and a very thorough approach from supervisors.*" The team has worked for the British Railways Board, Esso and Bath Spa University, and represented PricewaterhouseCoopers in a number of estate management disputes. "*I felt like I learnt a lot, repossessing properties on behalf of big clients, handling dilapidation claims and dealing with landlord disagreements,*" said one source. Personal injury can be "*a little bit of a shock to the system,*" but the occasional trainee who'd got a chance to work with VWV's Augustine Injury Law team enjoyed "*really interesting work on high-value claims.*" The team takes on mostly claimant work, and cases can involve fatalities from mesothelioma, accidents in which people have been trampled by cattle and serious bicycle injury claims. Sources explained how the work had affected their outside lives: "*I do find myself worrying about cyclists a lot more, and taking extra care at pedestrian crossings...*"

Real estate is still an important area for VWV. "*We have a lot of commercial clients, but we also work with many schools, charities and hospitals – there's a real mix of work and a lot of crossover with other teams.*" Much of the work with schools revolves around academy conversions, and a few of our sources were able to work closely with the education specialists within the department, "*running a few of my own files for independent schools.*" On top of this, the department gives trainees a chance to sample the many other strands on offer, including acting for local authorities on town centre regeneration schemes, assisting healthcare practices on surgery development initiatives, and representing government departments on property-related matters. Sources described in broad terms that "*much of the commercial property work involves drafting leases, licences and contracts; getting involved with negotiations; and making quite a few Land Registry applications.*" The team itself was praised for being "*very accommodating and happy to take half an hour out to explain anything to you – you're not stuck with mundane tasks.*"

Veale the love

VWV cultivates "*quite a human environment – it's not intimidating at all.*" Sources also appreciated that "*the emphasis is on working effectively during the time that you are in the office. My supervisors have gone out of their way to say that you must have other things in your life.*" Another perceived bonus is "*the fact that despite doing a lot of corporate work, the atmosphere here isn't a corporate one.*"

This is helped by the choice of office location. "*We're smack-bang in the middle of Bristol,*" said one trainee – VWV is positioned just behind the Hippodrome Theatre. "*The building itself is a little dated, and beginning to fall apart a little bit, but that just shows that we're focused on our work! It also makes us stand out, as many Bristol firms have moved into those big corporate glass buildings over at Temple Meads.*" A stone's throw away from Broad Quay, our sources had been taking advantage of a recent heat wave – "*the first day we saw the sun we got together and sat outside down by the waterfront.*"

The London office, formerly Vizards Tweedie, is a little more "*traditional*" in tone, but this was not deemed a negative attribute: "*It's good to learn the traditional side of it as well, to have someone who has worked a certain way for many years to impart their wisdom and teach you. The younger people here do have a different, perhaps more business-oriented perspective, but the old and new do complement each other.*" Again, the location reflects the atmosphere. The Fetter Lane office is "*very near to Fleet Street, which does have a more traditional feel, but we're also within walking distance to Holborn and Covent Garden and all the shops, so the location is like our culture in that way – a mixture of old and new.*" The open-plan layout of both offices was a hit with our sources, who claimed that this fact is "*one of the most valuable resources, as when you're in law school everything is so black and white, but you get to learn the subtleties of that commercial dimension through just listening in to your colleagues.*"

Enter the dragon boat

Trainees say the social life has "*fallen away in conjunction with the recession – there's just less money so there's no trainee budget and we usually only get a small contribution, if anything.*" It would be unfair to say that there's no social life at all: there are social committees in both offices, and recent events have included bowling nights, *Come Dine With Me* cook-offs, departmental Christmas parties and end of financial year celebrations. A major calendar highlight each year is the Dragon Boat Race, in which Bristol law firms compete to raise money for charity: "*It can be quite competitive and last year we dressed up as wizards.*" The London office tends to have "*more lunches than evening events, as a lot of people commute into the City and have families, but the trainees, associates and legal execs go out together.*"

Trainees reflected on the merger positively and said that integration between the two offices "*is definitely improving – they've been really pushing that recently.*" Overall, the process of merging the two firms is coming along, but "*it's still early days, and something we are continuing to work on. There has been more and more synergy, but in terms of socialising not so much.*" Certain teams hold monthly meetings via video conference – "*if we can work the remote control then they usually go well*" – and roughly once every two months trainees across the firm gather in Bristol for a "*knowledge-sharing meeting, and then afterwards we'll go out for dinner or have a drink.*"

And finally...
VWV provided a rounded training contract with a strong education flavour. In 2012, nine out of 12 qualifying trainees were retained by the firm.

Vinson & Elkins RLLP

The facts

Location: London

Number of UK partners/solicitors: 10/27 (+6 US-qualified)

UK partners who trained at the firm: 6.6%

Total number of trainees: 8

Seats: Non-rotational

Alternative seats: Overseas seats

Extras: Pro bono – Anglican Health Network, Toynbee Hall Legal Advice Centre; language classes

On chambersstudent.co.uk...

- How to get into V&E
- A history of the firm
- Energy law

This Texas-founded firm brings a touch of Southern charm to the grey streets of London.

Bags of energy

Vinson & Elkins is a powerhouse for all things energy. In particular, *Chambers Global* ranks its oil and gas practice among the world's top five, while *Chambers UK* recognises the London office's capacity for both projects and energy work.

This was one of the first US firms to open in the UK but as far as size is concerned it has never reached a critical mass – until now. "*The London office has grown substantially over the past 18 months. We've added a tax department and the litigation department doubled in size last year,*" deputy training principal Mark Beeley tells us. Still, compared to the firm's 380-strong Houston HQ, or to most of the other offices featured in this book, V&E London remains a Thumbelina-sized package, with just 44 lawyers as of July 2012.

Still, size is no guarantee of performance, and London lawyers, working from the 32nd and 33rd floors of the CityPoint skyscraper near Moorgate, regularly collaborate with the firm's other offices on deals worth billions of dollars. London acts as an important link between Vinson's ancestral home in the States and its operations across Europe, Asia and the Middle East. "*The London office is seen as a gateway to the rest of the world,*" one trainee stated.

Oil over the world

Trainees technically rotate through four supervisors from four different departments – finance, litigation, ETP (energy, transactions and projects) and M&A – but a "*loose system*" means they don't have to work exclusively within their supervisor's department. In fact, "*it's unusual for a trainee not to take on work from other departments during a seat,*" and once they move on after six months they'll still receive work from their previous team. "*The firm feels it's better for trainees to see transactions through from beginning to end. We're able to have a go at managing projects early on, which we wouldn't be able to do if we'd only seen part of a transaction in one seat,*" one interviewee told us. "*You can ask to work on the areas of law that most interest you and they take that into consideration.*" That's great for trainees who start their training contract knowing what they want to specialise in, although we heard those who don't could potentially find themselves lumbered long-term on a certain deal when they'd rather be sampling other areas.

The finance department is "*involved in sign-of-the-times transactions which are often in the FT,*" one trainee said. Despite this, "*there's not a long client list when it comes to banks.*" Vinson & Elkins has stronger relationships with private equity houses, particularly HgCapital and Texas-based Lone Star Funds. Clients also include energy companies, and the London team has recently been working with their American colleagues to advise oil and gas company Endeavour International on the closing of a £20m secured letter of credit facility with Commonwealth Bank of Australia. In the M&A department, about half of the work comes from Africa-based private equity clients. The firm recently represented TPG Capital in connection with the $500m investment in natural gas company Valerus Compression Services. The department also represents several of the world's largest oil and gas compa-

Chambers UK rankings

Construction	Projects
Energy & Natural Resources	

nies, including Statoil and Sinopec. Those working within the ETP department told us: *"It's a great seat and we get involved in the sector right away."* Mark Beeley says that the team has seen a large number of deals involving Sub-Saharan Africa and Brazil, which *"trainees have been heavily involved in."*

The huge size of the deals means V&E is often *"working alongside magic circle firms."* One interviewee related the story of one such deal, where the magic circle firm *"had an army of trainees,"* while V&E had *"a team of two partners, four associates and me. That meant I was working with associates, rather than trainees, on the other side."* Being in a smaller team, trainees say, means *"access to better and more interesting work. Here, trainees have to be a paralegal, a trainee and a junior associate all rolled into one. We do mundane stuff, but then also help out the partner directly and draft things. We get really involved in every aspect. I get e-mail contact with clients on a daily basis and I am the only trainee cc-ed in to e-mail chains for transactions. More senior lawyers may help you draft the e-mails, but you send them."*

Trainees in the litigation department see *"a lot of drafting and client contact."* One trainee told us *"a lot of the work is in energy,"* and Mark Beeley, a litigator himself, says that the department has also *"recently been working against the government of Ecuador on a matter concerning power generation facilities."* The team also works on non-energy related cases, including advising the Panama Canal Authority on contract disputes relating to its $5.25bn expansion programme.

Trainees have the option to complete a secondment in Hong Kong, Abu Dhabi, Dubai and, from 2012, Beijing and Tokyo. *"They tend to send people out in their second or third seats,"* one trainee told us. *"There's such a small intake of trainees, it's likely that you will get a second-*ment but it's not certain,"* another explained, advising new starters to show their interest early. *"There's no application process. I had a chat with Mark Beeley who noted my interest and said the firm would send me where they need trainees."* Can trainees choose between destinations? *"We take preferences into account but secondments are driven by needs and what is best for our candidates,"* Beeley says. Reflecting on their secondment, one trainee said: *"The work was so varied. I got a whole range of projects, including M&A, litigation and finance. Being the only trainee out there, every department was trying to use me."*

Remember the Alamo!

V&E is *"a very happy place,"* sources said. *"There is a work hard, play hard mentality yet it has a family feel too."* A social committee was recently set up: *"They organise monthly socials, which can take any form. We've just had a bake-off."* There's also a football team, trainee lunches and charity events. *"Going to Wagamama with my group at 11pm on a Friday night to plot our weekend of work has been one of my highlights,"* said one trainee, who paused briefly before adding: *"I guess that should be one of my low points, too."* Yep, that was a weekend OF work, not a weekend OFF work. The flip-side to getting plenty of responsibility is that your hours will reflect that – not that any of our sources were complaining too much.

"There is a nod towards the Texan in the everyday" and every year V&E invites its clients to celebrate Texan Independence Day. *"We play traditional Texan games"* – there's a quick-draw contest and horseshoe-throwing – *"and the cowboy hats come out."* A genuine Texan partner gives a speech explaining the significance of the day. Mark Beeley says: *"The Texan emphasis is very, very important to us. The firm likes to think of itself as having a Deep South charm about it. We try hard to keep that connection."* Of course, the firm's chief practice area is as Texan as it gets, and a genuine interest in energy is helpful to get a foot though the door here. *"A big mistake is confusing energy work and environmental law,"* Beeley warns. V&E wants to know why prospective trainees want to work for an energy firm and where their interest in the field comes from.

And finally...

The precision of Vinson's hiring process is reflected in its retention stats: three of four qualifying trainees were retained in 2012, following on from 100% retention in both 2010 and 2011.

Walker Morris

The facts

Location: Leeds

Number of UK partners/solicitors: 46/120

Partners who trained at firm: 50%

Total number of trainees: 31

Seats: 6x4 months

Alternative seats: Secondments

Extras: Pro bono – Business in the Community, Kidz in Kampz and others

On chambersstudent.co.uk...
- How to get into WM
- Leeds: a UK financial hub
- Football insolvencies

This successful Leeds firm might have *"a Northern feel"* but trainees were *"surprised that a lot of our clients are national and international – I am struggling to think of ones based in Leeds."*

Single-site heavyweight from Yorks

"If it's not broken, why fix it?" says graduate recruitment partner Nick Cannon about the one-office strategy Walker Morris has pursued, well, forever. It operates out of two adjacent buildings in Leeds and successfully competes as an independent firm in a city that's now largely dominated by nationals like Addleshaw Goddard, DLA Piper, Eversheds and Pinsent Masons. *Chambers UK* places WM highly in over a dozen practice areas, with particular recognition coming for dispute resolution, restructuring/insolvency and real estate. *"These have been difficult times over the last few years for all law firms. Having said that, we are increasing our turnover and real estate has been particularly strong. In real estate turnover was up 14% on last year. We are actively looking to recruit in real estate."*

"The big firms can get away with sloppy service more than us. We can't survive and thrive unless we provide excellent service and work," Cannon asserts. Taking a look at the firm's clients, it seems it's doing just that. To name a few, it's been representing Starbucks and Drax Power. Often hailing from the North themselves, trainees are able to appreciate that *"Walker Morris makes a thing about Yorkshire roots, and it has strong links with businesses and companies there."* However, over 70% of WM's work comes from outside the Yorkshire region. Trainees described the firm as *"quite proactive"* when it comes to seeking out business – *"a lot of what I was doing in one of my seats was researching potential new client opportunities for my supervisor."*

Seat options include: corporate; banking and insolvency; banking and real estate litigation; commercial dispute resolution; property litigation; commercial contracts; property; contentious and non-contentious construction; regulatory; planning; public sector and projects; IP; and employment. WM runs a six-seat training contract and is *"quite flexible"* about how trainees chart their own course. In the first year *"we were pretty much allocated what we were going to do, though we were asked what we wanted to do in our second and third seats and HR did try to accommodate us."* In the second year *"you get to choose where you go"* and WM has even created seats when trainees had really wanted experience in a certain practice. Trainees are pretty much free to decide how long they sit in a seat in their final year. There are regular client secondments with clients in the energy and banking sectors.

Waste busters

Those who'd sat in corporate towards the end of 2011 found *"things were a bit quiet,"* but the department was bustling with M&A, public company flotation and private equity work by early 2012. The firm acted on Symington's acquisition of food brands Ragu, Chicken Tonight and La Rochelle. Supervisors play a substantial role in work assignment, though *"you don't just work exclusively for one person."* Depending on how busy the department is, and how many hands are on deck for bigger deals, trainees might get the chance to run smaller transaction on their own, perhaps *"negotiating substantial points in a completion meeting for a private equity investment."* Researching companies, liaising with other depart-

Chambers UK rankings

Administrative & Public Law	Local Government
Banking & Finance	Pensions
Banking Litigation	Planning
Construction	Projects
Corporate/M&A	Real Estate
Dispute Resolution	Real Estate Litigation
Employment	Restructuring/Insolvency
Environment	Retail
Information Technology	Tax
Intellectual Property	

ments, due diligence and drafting ancillary documents are standard tasks. Once in a while *"you do get a stab at drafting share purchase agreements"* and other substantive documents. Among other things, WM is an expert on waste – waste disposal, energy from waste, waste facilities – and corporate trainees come across deals such as a council's disposal of an £8.1m waste collection business (and advising on related pension schemes, neatly tying up with the firm's public sector and employment expertise).

The finance commercial seat consists of banking and insolvency matters – partners tend to specialise in one or the other, with a few who cross over. On the banking side, WM represents big banks. Trainees had the opportunity to be *"involved in a couple of really big transactions, which was great, I was given quite a lot of responsibility."* Bank receiverships make up a significant portion of the insolvency side's work. Trainees tend to be *"quite involved in the process, drafting and sending out letters on behalf of banks."* The firm is also well known for its work on football club insolvencies, including those of Portsmouth, Crystal Palace and Plymouth.

A good hair day for Morris

Work in commercial litigation comes from *"mostly big corporate clients like ghd and Starbucks."* We note that many matters arise from the food, energy, property, retail and public sectors. Trainees appreciated the broad spread of tasks handed to them. They'd dealt with drafting injunctions, witness statements, position statements, correspondence, instructing counsel, researching points of law and getting their hands dirty with tedious disclosure exercises. *"I did everything from running my own cases which were worth £500 to being trainee support on those worth tens of millions of pounds."* There are a lot of bundles to deal with but *"it's almost like a rite of passage for trainees, isn't it?"* mused one of our sources. Making up for that, a lucky few *"ran hearings on behalf of Walker Morris."*

"We used to have banking litigation and property litigation teams, now it's just known as real estate and banking litigation. There is still a divide between the two but there is a substantial crossover with mortgage fraud and banks lending against property,"* one trainee explained. Within this rejigged group, trainees sitting with the property partners mostly work on *"commercial landlord-tenant disputes and the various procedures you need to go through to review, alter or end leases."* There is some contact with clients and opposing counsel, mostly over the phone. There are also seats in construction, offering contentious and non-contentious experiences. This group acts for councils, building and project developers and *"surveyors, especially in relation to negligence claims."* Although there is a *"fair bit of bundling,"* trainees praised the *"exposure to adjudications and injunctions."*

P-P-P-pick up a £550m deal

The public sector and projects team *"is a big one, taking at least two or three trainees at one time."* The group works on large Private Finance Initiatives *"on things like waste and hospital facilities contracts."* There is a focus on education, charities, renewables, waste, and energy from waste. WM represented a Covanta Energy and Kelda Water Services joint venture on the bid and negotiations for a waste treatment project worth £550m. The firm also advised North Lincolnshire Council in procuring a 25-year PPP household waste treatment and disposal contract valued at £300m. Government projects need *"massive contracts that take years to negotiate,"* meaning trainees can't get involved in the day-to-day contract negotiations. Instead they help out with research and keep track of legal updates. They're also responsible for document management and take on discrete bits of drafting, but generally have little contact with *"these very big public sector clients."*

Walker Morris's real estate group acts for student accommodation company UNITE on all sorts of matters, including the acquisition of a development site in Stratford from Westfield. Property is *"a very busy seat that mainly takes on commercial work, but for trainees there are some residential files, since there isn't so much riding on those."* Trainees get to run them from start to finish.

The regulatory department *"does a lot of work for payday lending companies – it's a booming industry at the moment, and it's been on the news a lot, as quite a few of these companies are being investigated."* Clients are mostly the lenders and trainees spend substantive time drafting documents for the lenders to use for their websites and loan agreements. *"We would be given a website to review, making sure it conforms to the requirements of the consumer credit legislative review."*

Trainees might not work in a City firm, but Walker Morris requires long hours and at times, busy weekends.

On average, our sources seemed to leave work no earlier than 8pm, with some recalling *"a couple of 4am finishes."*

Leeds 2012

Located *"right in the centre of Leeds' financial district,"* WM's office is two minutes from the railway station and, for clients driving in, *"it's conveniently located on the ring road."* It's split across two buildings, and all trainees agree: *"The office is getting a bit dated,"* but were quick to defend its honour: *"It's got showers, it's got everything you could need."* As Cannon good-humouredly pointed out: *"It's like being a member of the family... trainees can slag off the building as much as they like but someone on the outside just can't do that!"* He agreed: *"There is a general appetite among people to move, and it would rejuvenate us, give us a real shot in the arm."*

So what is the Walker Morris family like? One trainee described the character of the firm as *"in the same kind of vein as Yorkshire people are."* That translates to *"straight-talking, practical folk,"* who want to get the job done. A little birdie told us: *"Some of the most old-school partners have just retired. We're on to the next generation."* Trainee-partner relations are therefore pretty good.

"Self-reliant, confident, articulate," is what Nick Cannon looks for in trainees. *"Someone who shows they have more strings to their bow, be that sports, travel or voluntary work."* While good grades are a given, WM doesn't blindly sort trainees using only that criteria. *"If someone has gone to a small comprehensive, is one of the only two from the class to make it to university, their two Bs and an A may have been harder to get than the straight As of someone from a public school,"* says Cannon. Trainees find their colleagues *"bright"* but WM *"isn't overly focused on academics; it likes confident people who are comfortable with clients."*

A gregarious bunch, trainees like *"bit of banter,"* and e-mails planning drinks on a Friday evening regularly shoot round. *"Someone recently organised a lads' night out and I know some of the girls have gone on holiday together."* Channelling the spirit of Team GB, Walker Morris Olympics took place in summer 2012 complete with softball and dodgeball. *"I did umpire a Walker Morris softball challenge the other night; I didn't want real estate to win – they were taking it too seriously!"* joked Nick Cannon. Claims won in the end.

Before trainees start their training contract, they are invited to summer events, which most find *"a good way to integrate people into the firm."* Finally, trainees predict WM will remain true to its values as it expands over the next few years, perhaps expanding regulatory and litigation practices. *"I can't imagine it would be a very different place to work at; it knows its personality."* The firm retained 16 of its 19 qualifiers in 2012.

And finally...

Walker Morris remains one of the top independent firms outside London. If you're looking to work in the North, it's a must-view.

Ward Hadaway

The facts

Location: Newcastle, Leeds, Manchester
Number of UK partners/solicitors: 79/102
Partners who trained at firm: 20%
Total number of trainees: 18
Seats: 4x6 months
Alternative seats: Secondments

On chambersstudent.co.uk...
• How to get into Ward Hadaway
• More on seats
• Newcastle's legal market

> *"We are positioned as the second largest firm in Newcastle, but with the Leeds and Manchester offices expanding there is a feeling that we are a firm on the up."*

Ward Hadaway never forgets

In 2013 Ward Hadaway celebrates 25 years on Newcastle's legal scene. For the last decade it has been the second largest firm in the Toon, and *Chambers UK* will tell you it's the second most highly regarded. Most of its 15 ranked practices are one or two steps behind Dickinson Dees, but in the core areas of litigation, employment and property WH stands shoulder-to-shoulder at the top of the market with Newcastle's old-timer.

Revenue has grown slowly but steadily over the past four years and the firm has also been on a few hiring sprees. By our count it took on ten laterals between summer 2010 and summer 2011 from the likes of Watson Burton, Cobbetts and Trowers & Hamlins. The hires have mostly joined the Leeds office, which now has over 70 staff. A full-service Manchester office with nearly a dozen lawyers opened in July 2012.

"One of the main things that made me want to join this firm was its growth, especially in Leeds," trainees said, and this *"is now a full-service office and is doing really well in a difficult market,"* training partner Paula Myers told us. *"In Manchester we are trying to repeat what we did in Leeds. It's not our plan at the moment, but one day we might have half our lawyers outside Newcastle."* On its website the firm styles itself as a Northern rather than North Eastern firm, but its marketing material also contains a photo of an African elephant with the slogan 'We never forget a client'. It may just be a silly joke, but perhaps it also signifies the firm's commitment to never for-get its Geordie roots. Clients include Barratt Homes and Greggs – both Tyneside businesses which have expanded across the country. WH is also one of a small group of firms with a position on the NHS Litigation Authority panel. It does a ton of employment, commercial and clinical negligence work for the National Health.

Leeds-ing the way

Seats are available in corporate, banking, property, coco, commercial litigation, healthcare, employment, matrimonial, private client, IP/IT, insolvency, public sector, and property litigation. *"You have a meeting before every rotation where they ask you where you want to go next,"* a trainee told us. *"On the whole the firm tries to take everyone's preferences into account, but it is difficult. There is an element of luck to it. Some people have got all their first choices; others got none. I got some of mine."*

Trainees either share an office with their supervisor or sit in a 'pod' of four lawyers in an open-plan setting. In the latter instance they get more work from their team rather than just through their supervisor. *"The level of supervision varies from person to person,"* we were told. *"Some will sit you down and explain what they want you to do and the background of the matter. Some just toss a piece of work to you and ask you to do it. But it is very easy to ask people questions – you are not left on your own."*

We should give a bit more airtime to the Leeds office here, as it took on its first batch of trainees in 2011 and currently has five young whipper-snappers on the scene.

Chambers UK rankings

Agriculture & Rural Affairs	Information Technology
Banking & Finance	Intellectual Property
Charities	Licensing
Clinical Negligence	Pensions
Construction	Planning
Corporate/M&A	Private Client
Dispute Resolution	Real Estate
Employment	Real Estate Litigation
Family/Matrimonial	Restructuring/Insolvency
Healthcare	

Employment and property are the biggest departments here, while the other seat options are corporate and commercial. The office is the largest outside Newcastle of any Geordie firm and is home to a quarter of WH's lawyers. Founded as recently as 2008, it is already ranked by *Chambers UK* for its employment work. "*We are still quite small, but we have expanded quite rapidly since I started in September 2011,*" one of the new crop of trainees told us. Though inevitably they had occasionally acted as "*guinea pigs,*" they said that "*training is quickly becoming more structured.*"

That's ASDA price

Back in Newcastle, the corporate department has two teams that deal with M&A and another focused on banking and finance. "*I worked on five transactions of varying scale,*" a trainee told us. "*Some were very large, while some were for owner-managed businesses – for example selling a local car dealership. I saw one or two all the way through to completion.*" In all, "*less than 25% of deals involve two parties in the North East. Often one or both parties are from outside the North East.*" Good examples are Newcastle's Aesica Pharmaceuticals' acquisition of three manufacturing plants in Germany and Italy from Belgian rival UCB, and local energy business Eaga's £300m takeover by multinational construction firm Carillion. On both deals WH advised the North East party. Leeds-based ASDA is also a major client. Regular trainee activities include "*quite a lot of research into company law; drafting supporting documentation like Companies House forms, waiver letters and share certificates; and due diligence: the client prepares their proposed answers to the diligence questionnaire and I look at it to suggest amendments and flag up potential issues, before passing it on to my supervisor.*" Another source added: "*I also went to client meetings and sat in on calls. I was asked to contribute, not just take notes. There are also admin tasks like organisation of disclosure bundles.*"

When it gets busy – especially in the corporate department – "*everyone can be running around like headless chickens,*" but trainees don't feel rushed off their feet most of the time. "*I probably work 8.30am to 6.30pm on average,*" a trainee said. "*Staying until after 7pm is unusual.*" That said, all our interviewees seemed to have experienced one properly late night during their training contract, staying until 10pm or even the early hours of the morning.

A seat in property can be completed in the business, development, residential or public sector sub-teams – the latter primarily acts for NHS trusts and advised Sheffield Primary Care Trust on the £25m development of four new health centres. The commercial team acts for institutional property owners like Santander, Aldi and software firm Sage. Leeds lawyers recently advised the British Waterways Board on the £16m redevelopment of a brownfield site in Cheshire. As well as these high-value matters, "*there are some transactions with a value of a couple of thousand pounds,*" a trainee told us. "*I was given some of those to run myself. I acted for a commercial client who had a portfolio of residential properties.*"

A clean bill

The coco department provides all advice to businesses not related to acquisitions, banking, disputes or employment. So that's "*incorporating companies, doing background research into joint ventures, arranging share transfers, etc.*" Coco also has public sector and IP/IT subteams, which both offer seats. The former handles local government and PFI work, acting mainly for NHS trusts. "*We do public sector work throughout the firm,*" a trainee told us. "*The government cuts haven't seen it decrease, but it has changed in nature. There is less focus on big projects... and the NHS is becoming a more commercial organisation.*"

The litigation department works on shareholder, insurance and contracts disputes, and professional negligence claims. "*We are building up for a trial which starts on Monday at the Royal Courts of Justice,*" one trainee told us. "*They want me to go down to London to attend court.*" Recently the firm acted for Newcastle Airport in a breach of duty claim against Eversheds over changes made to two executive directors' contracts. Litigators were also involved in the judicial review of the scrapping of the Building Schools for the Future programme, acting for Nottingham Borough Council.

The healthcare seat is also contentious in nature and lawyers there do a lot of defendant clin neg work on behalf of the NHSLA. For example, the team defended the North Cumbria University Hospitals NHS Trust against a claim from a woman who suffered obstetrical haemorrhaging during childbirth and required emergency surgery.

Sae leish, sae blithe, sae bonnie

All our interviewees were very talkative and oozed Geordie charm and spirit. That said, they weren't actually all from the North East. Although trainees said "*connections to the region are something they really press you on during the interview,*" it's clear that you can also wangle a training contract by showing a clear commitment to living and working in Newcastle (or Leeds).

Talkative trainees make for a firm with an active social life. "*Pretty much every Friday people are in the Pitcher & Piano opposite the office,*" one trainee told us. Another added: "*It tends to be the younger people who do more socialising, but you do see partners in the pub too. And it's not like trainees stand in one corner and associates in another and partners in a third. Everyone mingles.*" Indeed, social events are a good opportunity for networking. "*You can stroll up to an employment partner and say you are interested in doing a seat in that area.*" WH also encourages trainees to "*get out and about in Newcastle*" at external networking events. Trainees participate in inter-business seminars and conferences as well as sporting events: touch rugby, cricket, five-a-side football and – on one recent occasion – beach volleyball on Newcastle's very own city beach. There are departmental Christmas meals and away-days, as well as an annual "*spring fling*" in March.

Newcastle lawyers are split between two buildings, both on the quayside near Gateshead Millennium Bridge: Sandgate House and Keel Row House (note for non-Geordies: The Keel Row is not a street but a traditional Tyneside folk song). "*Some departments are more studious than others, but most have time for a bit of banter and jokes at the end of the day. Where there are individual offices it's more noisy and bustling, while the open plan floors are usually more quiet and heads-down.*" Another trainee added: "*Everyone is really friendly. We don't just come in, do our work and then go home. Our size is great too: the managing partner knows everyone's name.*"

WH's talkative trainees were frank to us about their one concern. "*The current main bugbear is the issue of retention and where there will be NQ jobs,*" a trainee told us in April 2012. "*I feel we have not had much communication about when we will find out. I heard on the grapevine that it could be May, June or July. Either way, I feel the list comes out quite late. It is something the firm could improve.*" Training partner Paula Myers responded: "*We tell them every year in January what is going to happen. The jobs are advertised in May. We want to promote fairness, which is why we wait until we know where all the jobs are to bring out the list.*" WH's retention since 2009 hasn't been stellar, with the firm keeping on two-thirds of its qualifiers since then. Seven of nine qualifiers stayed on in 2012.

And finally...

Its geographic expansion, Geordie charm, varied practices and interesting clients make Ward Hadaway a great place to train.

"Don't just do it for the money. The law is not an easy place to be if you see it as just a respectable profession. You need to get a kick out of it."

City managing partner

Watson, Farley & Williams

Challenging.

Nick Payne, Trainee

Distinctive.　　Opportunities.　　Integrated.　　Real.

"From my first seat I've enjoyed the challenge of working closely with senior associates, partners and clients on every project."

Vacation Placements
31st January 2013
Training Contracts
31st July 2013 (to start 2015)

www.wfw.com/trainee

Watson, Farley & Williams

The facts

Location: London
Number of UK partners/solicitors: 54/109
Partners who trained at firm: c.15%
Total number of trainees: 28
Seats: 6x4 months
Alternative seats: Overseas seats
Extras: Language classes

On chambersstudent.co.uk...
• How to get into WFW
• We talk to London office chief
  Mike Vernell

Asset finance is a global business. That means plenty of international work and a guaranteed overseas seat at Watson, Farley & Williams.

Fisherman's friend

Thirty years ago, three partners jumped ship from Norton Rose to set up Watson, Farley & Williams. The firm was founded on shipping finance and today *Chambers Global* ranks this practice among the top two in the world (alongside Norton Rose, in fact). The firm has been expanding beyond the relatively narrow area of shipping finance for a while now. "*WFW has a mantra: we are heavily focused on finance and investment in the energy, natural resources, transport, real estate and ICT sectors,*" Mike Vernell, the head of the London office, told us. Has anything changed during the recession? "*The assets we act on are crucial to the well-being of the world: ships, aeroplanes, power plants, mining, property, et cetera. We don't see it dying.*"

WFW is one of the smaller City firms, but has a significant international network. It has offices in nine other countries, often in major shipping hubs. The most recent opening was in Hong Kong in 2012. "*It is likely that trainees will be able to do a seat there. Trainees are a very useful tool and Hong Kong will just be one more opportunity for them,*" Vernell says. It's another addition to what is already a training contract with a distinct international flavour. Time abroad is guaranteed – indeed, required – with corporate, asset finance and litigation-focused seats available in Paris, Piraeus, Singapore and Bangkok.

In addition to that four-month overseas stint, trainees complete five more seats back home in London, and even here "*we work with the other offices on a daily basis.*" Litigation, corporate, asset finance and PCEF (project, commodities and export finance) are compulsory, while the remaining seat options are the more niche areas of employment, tax, property and EU/competition. Trainees advised students to "*apply with your eyes wide open and realise that this is predominantly a finance-oriented firm.*" Qualification opportunities in the smaller teams are limited – WFW retained ten of 12 qualifiers in 2012, with two going into finance and four into corporate.

Watson the menu, Captain?

The asset finance seat was previously named shipping finance and still operates primarily in that area. However, a number of other assets now fall under its remit, such as aircraft, rail stock, real estate and wind farms. This flagship among the firm's departments recently closed several deals worth over $1bn, while the firm's chairman Frank Dunne won Maritime Lawyer of the Year at the *Lloyd's List* Global Awards in 2011. Within the asset finance group is an expanding aviation team, with three corporate jet and helicopter finance lawyers recently joining other new arrivals from Reed Smith and Clifford Chance. It has advised Singapore Airlines on an aircraft sale worth $200m.

"*A few years ago shipping had a negative reputation regarding some of the partners, but they've made a real effort and now it's a friendly place to be,*" a trainee assured us. Trainees handle "*anything from drafting to attending delivery meetings and dealing with shipping registries. Asset finance is really busy and you get a bit of everything,*" one of our sources explained. "*It's great because they really do throw you into it. The training is really good too – we have talks most weeks,*" another

Chambers UK rankings

Asset Finance	Dispute Resolution
Capital Markets	Employment
Commodities	Energy & Natural Resources

commented. One source appreciated how the firm promotes its trainees: "*My name being included in the final press release was one of my high points at the firm.*"

The PCEF seat was a favourite among our sources. "*About two-thirds of my year have taken it,*" a second-year told us. "*It's a really good department with a nice environment. There are quite a few lateral hires coming in, so it's an exciting, changing environment.*" We heard the work is "*very technical, but it's also a nice balance of research, drafting memos and preparing documents. We have a good amount of client contact.*"

"*The overlap between PCEF and corporate is great for experience,*" one trainee told us. The departments are similar in that they have "*interesting work but long hours.*" Corporate is the firm's second largest department and accounts for a third of the firm's global revenue. The work of the department is largely in the sectors of shipping, energy and natural resources. Matters can last anything "*from a few days to two weeks,*" and have included Madagascar Oil and Equatorial Palm Oil's admissions to the AIM. "*Day to day, my work depends on how busy the department is,*" one source informed us. "*Some days I do admin, but other days I'm the only trainee on a transaction, working with one partner and one senior associate.*"

The hours in corporate "*aren't that bad,*" say our sources. "*Trainees tend to leave around 7pm but there are a few late nights and weekend work on occasion.*" Even when the clock strikes midnight and trainees are still in the office, "*we feel part of a team. We are rewarded for our hard work and people will say thank you and appreciate the hours you put in.*"

All trainees must complete the litigation seat. Work here often covers cases relating to the world of (three guesses...) shipping. Recent highlights for the team include acting for Lloyds TSB in a Commercial Court dispute over the termination of a ship finance lease, and for a company against its insurers for the cost of replacing three legs of a drilling rig that were lost while being towed around the Cape of Good Hope. However, the group also covers other areas of litigation and arbitration, recently working on professional negligence and fraud cases. The department has also represented the governments of Pakistan and the Bahamas.

Seats in competition, employment, property and tax are popular among second-years "*looking to broaden their*

expertise." An interviewee who had visited one of these reflected: "*I did enjoy my time there, but those departments tend to be a bit peripheral so, although your work is important, it's not at the core of the firm.*" That said, the property department has grown so much recently that it split away from corporate and became an independent group, while the employment team has a *Chambers UK* ranking.

Sail away, sail away, sail away

Trainees tend to go abroad in their third, fourth or fifth seats. The overseas offices are smaller and more specialised than in London. In Paris and Piraeus, trainees complete an asset finance seat, while Bangkok is litigation-focused. Two trainees at a time go to Singapore, one to do litigation or corporate work and the other to do asset finance. Language tuition is provided, although if you are already fluent you'll find "*they really put your language skills to use.*"

The overseas seat was a big draw for all our sources, and one summed up the experience: "*Overseas, I felt more like an assistant than a trainee. I learned a lot.*" The Paris office is right on the Champs-Élysées, while the Piraeus office is near the port where the Greeks used to keep their warships. "*It's a great office. Piraeus is quite industrial but has a beautiful harbour. They put you up in a flat near the office and there's lots of trainees from other firms around.*" Out in Singapore and Bangkok, "*the opportunities to work on broader transactions are available, and the Asian market is an exciting one to be involved in.*"

A couple of interviewees referred to the "*personality test we completed in our first couple of weeks here,*" which apparently produced "*a mixture of results.*" Perhaps, but we think we spot a WFW type all the same. Generally, trainees here are "*reserved and understated,*" and "*down to earth.*" Our sources repeatedly emphasised that candidates should "*be themselves*" in the recruitment process. "*They like you to have other interests,*" although we don't get the impression that this is one of those firms that scours CVs for wacky hobbies. We hear the current crop of trainees are enthusiastic about the nice, normal pastimes of music, sport, theatre and travelling. All this tallies with our view of WFW as a solid sort of place not given to pretension or flashiness. We do get the impression, though, that an influx of younger associates and lateral hires is giving a slightly more lively feel to a firm that has always been quite traditional in outlook.

Oh loi loi!

As far as backgrounds are concerned, trainees hail from a good mix of universities. Mike Vernell says: "*WFW doesn't just look for academic ability; we look for more rounded candidates with an interest in the commercial world in which they are working. They should be open-minded and willing to see what they get a buzz from working on. Candidates have to be honest with themselves. The law is not an easy place to be if you think it's just a respectable profession to be working in. You need to get a kick out of it."* Having a second language is a *"big thing"* here for obvious reasons, and *"English doesn't necessarily have to be your first,"* one of our sources told us.

"The office stretches over four floors but people generally know who's who. You do feel like there's a sense of community here – if you get involved of course." Social drinks aren't organised by the firm, but one trainee told us: *"I've had a sociable year group and so we arrange it ourselves."* Trainees frequent corporate bar of choice All Bar One or dine at Piccolino nearby. *"If we're feeling adventurous we might go into Spitalfields."* The boys have a football and cricket team, and there's a canteen *"where people sit about and chat."* The last Christmas party was *"really good."* The firm hired out a converted church near Old Street and had a black-tie dinner with 'aerial artists' hanging about on hoops and the like overhead. But the *Student Guide* team were most impressed by tales of WFW's French chef, Philippe, who not only runs the canteen but *"runs wine-tasting events and cookery classes."*

And finally...
There aren't many smallish firms with such a strong finance focus and such a developed international network. If these three factors are on your checklist, WFW is well worth further consideration.

Wedlake Bell LLP

The facts

Location: London

Number of UK partners/solicitors: 54/75

Total number of trainees: 12

Seats: 4x6 months

Alternative seats: Secondments

On chambersstudent.co.uk...
- How to get into Wedlake Bell
- Law on Bedford Row

Nestled among barristers' chambers, Wedlake Bell is outwardly all tradition, but step inside its listed Bedford Row town house and the sleek interior tells a different tale.

Bedford Rose

Wedlake Bell is a firm un-bogged down by a 230-year history, nurturing both private and commercial practices that support each other by cross-referring work. *Chambers UK* picks out the firm's private client, IP and property groups as outstanding.

April 2012 saw a tie-up with 40-lawyer Cumberland Ellis, firmly planting WB in the UK top 100 for revenue. A merger had been on the cards for a while, as training principal Hilary Platt told us: "*We had room for expansion in this building, Cumberland Ellis were about a third of our size and the merger has added depth to our core practice areas.*" CE's lawyers have bolstered property, litigation, family, commercial, corporate and private client groups, while CE's clients now have access to WB's IP, pensions, construction, employment, banking and tax teams. For trainees? "*It's obviously going to benefit them,*" Platt says. "*Bigger teams mean a greater pool of people to provide work, and more variety in their training.*"

Property at WB is "*such a sizeable chunk of business, so a seat there is highly likely.*" This isn't too restrictive, however, as this could be in construction, residential, commercial property or property litigation. The latter is known for being tough, "*but full of influential partners who appreciate that you've survived it.*" Other potential destinations include corporate, pensions, business recoveries, employment, IP/commercial, private client and a brand new and "*extremely popular*" family seat.

Commercial and residential property typify the dual strength of Wedlake Bell's practice. The former deals with all sides of the commercial process (builders, buyers and sellers) and can entail long hours. "*You get a lot of responsibility with your own files,*" said one source. "*People don't micromanage, but it does put pressure on you to manage your own time.*" A typical deal: acting for property fund Greycoat in the £139m sale of a 19-storey block that's currently the HQ of Pinsent Masons. Developers make up some of the residential team's clientele, but there's a lot of crossover with private client, so trainees can expect to work with established landowners and offshore residents. Developer work is "*primarily lease extension, so we'd be renewing leases, or adapting the originals.*" Working with landowners involves delving into history. One client had "*a large Hertfordshire estate, but pockets of land had been disposed of at various points during the past 400 years. Our job was to trawl through old title deeds and work out where the boundaries now lie – it felt very investigative to follow a paper trail.*"

Dream work

The construction team acts for major developer FourFront, and has a number of clients from the healthcare sector, including Bupa and private hospital group Spire. For the child in everyone, a regular client is KIRK-BI – a property investor that's part of the LEGO empire. Recently the team worked on a project involving the demolition, reconstruction and refurbishment of a huge Central London building. We're not sure if it was made of red, blue and yellow bricks, but we like to imagine so. The team is still pretty small, so trainees get drafting experience from the off. Perhaps the seat's key feature is the trade union helpline for contractors, "*which is the construction trainee's telephone number.*" A miscellany of clients, "*from one-man bands to the trade organisations*"

Chambers UK rankings

Construction	Real Estate
Employment	Real Estate Finance
Information Technology	Real Estate Litigation
Intellectual Property	

themselves" call for their entitled free hour of legal advice. Disputes range in value from "*a couple of hundred pounds to a contract worth £5m,*" and the immediacy "*can be scary.*" Thought one source: "*It's helpful for trainees, as when you strip everything back it's just contract law. You learn from just doing it – everything from phone manner to managing their expectations. They're often pretty eager to litigate, and will say things like, 'Let's bring the heavies in,' and you have to convey that it probably won't be cost-effective. It's a snapshot of the entire process.*"

The corporate team advises on many real estate transactions, in addition to M&A work and several AIM listings. Clients "*are from a variety of sectors, but tend to be medium-sized.*" Over in commercial, a dream client base includes Which?, Lacoste, Tesco and, ahem, DreamWorks. Here, trainees get a mix of IP and commercial as "*partners all do a bit of both.*" The firm advised the Spielberg-founded animation studio on the unauthorised use of the *Kung Fu Panda* brand for a martial arts initiative in schools. Commercial work is likely to be contract-based. One trainee "*worked with the procurement team for a major bank on reviewing every single thing they signed, from gym membership to their new software.*" IP work can be more difficult to get. "*That team is partner-heavy – they're fantastically academic, but they can be quite self-contained.*"

Second largest after property, and larger post-merger, the private client team is "*far from the image of old people writing wills and dying,*" sources assured us. It's also far from the landed gentry stereotype: clients range from "*old-school military officers to wealthy engineers to entrepreneurs.*" Work is varied and can be fascinating, even at trainee level: "*There's always something coming in that you couldn't expect, whether it's drafting or research,*" said one. The team acted for the trustees of a Cornish estate in what has become known as 'The Battle of Trevalga'. The estate was left to Marlborough College by a former pupil, with the stipulation that it was preserved in its current state. The college claimed that, due to

a 'defect' in the will, it was theirs to sell. The case is newsworthy for hinging simply on differences of legal opinion. There's also the empathetic human aspect – residents of the estate fear they would quickly be priced out of the market and forced to move away, and the houses sold to property developers.

Led by experienced recent lateral hire Charmaine Hast, the family team concentrates on "*high-profile, big-money divorce – from £3m to £100m.*" The firm has a niche in cross-border cases, which often become "*jurisdictional races, as petitioning in one has benefits over another: in the UK, the wife is favoured, whereas somewhere like Russia the system is set up so that wives don't get anything.*" Dealing with millionaires and billionaires doesn't detract from the principles at the heart of any family-related seat, though. "*It's about relating to everyday problems,*" thought one trainee. "*All humans are affected by marriage or cohabitation, and you feel personally responsible to ensure they get a good result.*"

OMG, this buffet is like so awkward

Post-merger, Wedlake Bell is "*still trying to figure out where it's positioning itself,*" trainees felt. "*Before it was friendly, nice, the hours were not too late.*" That's still the case, but "*now we're top 100: the board are trying to figure out where they want us to go.*" One source said: "*I hope that the culture at the firm doesn't change – one of the reasons I applied was we're mid-size, do good work, but have that balance of work and life.*" Says Hilary Platt: "*It's certainly something that we'll monitor – we pride ourselves on our culture, and we're aware it's one of our greatest strengths.*"

Trainees agree: "*There has been a decline in social events of late,*" although there are plenty of sports activities, including the annual lawyers v clients day at the Oval. Mostly, however, socialising takes place on an informal basis, and, in the words of one source, "*I'd rather pay for my own drinks and still have a job.*"

Trainees here are more rounded than "*OMG, I desperately want to be a lawyer*" types and the partners watch out for this in the application process: "*One of the big tests is whether you'd be comfortable with them in a room on your own.*" Thus, part of the interview "*is an incredibly awkward buffet lunch involving talking to partners while eating sloppy sandwiches.*" If you've got the stomach to survive that, give Wedlake Bell a look.

And finally...

New to the top 100, it remains to be seen just how corporate Wedlake Bell will become. In 2012, five out of six qualifiers were retained as NQs.

Weil, Gotshal & Manges

The facts

Location: London

Number of UK partners/solicitors: 30/89

Total number of trainees: 20

Seats: 4x6 months

Alternative seats: New York, secondments

On chambersstudent.co.uk...

- How to get into Weil
- We talk to grad recruitment partner Jonathan Wood

Interested in transactional law? Ready to push yourself? Extrovert? US firm Weil Gotshal & Manges is a corporate machine and it's looking for you.

Intensely scary?

"*Do something that scares you,*" says Weil's recruitment slogan. "*We're scrapping that,*" one trainee told us: "*It's not scary here. Perhaps intense is a better word.*" Certainly the London office of this New York-headquartered firm has a tough, no-nonsense aura about it. Led by corporate and finance, and still relatively small 16 years since it first opened, *Chambers UK* puts it alongside Clifford Chance as one of the two best firms in the country for private equity buyouts (*Chambers Global* puts it in the top three globally). And it has always had a fairly aggressive lateral hiring policy, stealing prominent partners from competitors – recently including a top funds team from... Clifford Chance.

A recent move to new offices at 110 Fetter Lane has "*given everyone a feeling of pride and encouraged everyone to work harder. It's a brand new office, designed with us in mind.*" We heard there are sleeping pods in the basement, so you see, 'intense' isn't a word that's being bandied around without reason.

Trainees must take seats in corporate and finance (which includes leveraged finance, structured finance, transactional banking and capital markets). Property, employment and pensions, business finance/restructuring, dispute resolution, funds and IP/IT are among the other available seats. Worldwide, Weil is a leader for bankruptcy and insolvency work so trainees may well find themselves involved in work resulting from some of the biggest bankruptcies of the recession, from Lehman Brothers downwards.

The seat allocation process "*has always been a little opaque.*" While there is a formal system, and no one we spoke to was seriously unhappy with the seats they'd ended up with, over the past two or three years we've heard claims that "*when two people want to do a seat, the one who goes to the department, talks to the partner and tells them why they want to be there will get chosen over the person who just went to HR.*" We say this is fair enough, so long as you know them's the rules of the game. Be prepared to network yourself a bit.

Marmighty deals

"*Don't apply here if you're not interested in corporate law,*" one interviewee warned. Not only is corporate a mandatory seat, but office managing partner Mike Francies is one of the City's most prominent corporate lawyers. The department has a strong private equity focus, recently working with the firm's US lawyers advising Mubadala (a public company owned by the government of Abu Dhabi) as part of a consortium (which included Sony and the Estate of Michael Jackson) in an agreement to purchase British music company EMI (advised by – wouldn't you know it – Clifford Chance) for £1.4bn. The complicated deal utilised the expertise of the IP/IT, finance, capital markets, litigation, tax, pensions, employment and real estate departments. Similarly, the M&A team has been involving the IP and employment teams on a £38m sale of a fuel management business for GE European.

Corporate is a "*Marmite seat,*" but sources did agree that the majority of second-years were hoping to qualify into

Chambers UK rankings

Banking & Finance	Investment Funds
Capital Markets	Private Equity
Corporate/M&A	Restructuring/Insolvency
Dispute Resolution	Tax

the department so it seems that more love than hate it at the moment. "*We're in charge of the completion check list, which helps us understand every part of the jigsaw, and I was sent to meet a small client on my own,*" said one trainee. "*There are documents to go through but I was aware of how they fitted into the bigger structure and I helped with the signing and completion.*" The workload is variable. "*During my six months in the seat, I did three months of 150 to 200 hours, two months of over 200 hours and one was quiet.*" To save you reaching for your calculator, 200 hours works out at about ten hours a day, or 6.5 hours if you work on Saturdays and Sundays as well. Of course, manic periods followed by down-time is the lot of every corporate lawyer, and our source said friends at other City firms "*have done much more than me.*"

In 2011, Weil revived its secondment to New York. It's "*always popular,*" as you can imagine. American firms don't have trainees, so those who go to New York are treated as associates and get immediately involved. Secondments have also been offered in Hong Kong and Paris in the past.

In Lehman's terms

The general finance seat is divided into leveraged finance and structured finance. "*Trainees are asked to sit in one or the other and they don't do a mixture of work. However it's not unheard of to work with another team if yours is quiet.*" Leveraged finance is a "*mixture of debt and equity – and we work on big deals. Our clients are private equity firms who make acquisitions and sell them a few years down the line.*" There's no other word for it – the seat is intense, "*but then that's the best way to learn. If you do a seat there, you can do a seat anywhere.*" Structured finance covers "*two main things: securitisation and derivatives work. The securitisation lawyers work a lot for Lloyds, Barclays Capital and RBS. Derivatives sees a lot of Lehman and MF Global work.*" You'll know about the famous Lehman Brothers collapse of 2008, of course, but if you haven't kept an eye on the FT it's possible you might have missed the more recent MF Global story. A major derivatives broker, its demise in 2011 was the eighth largest bankruptcy in US history. "*Being involved in that was brilliant,*" one source said.

As with corporate, the finance seats were likened to Marmite. Though trainees said it is "*a very pleasant team*" that provides access to "*a lot of high-quality work,*"

including plenty of drafting, one source described the down-side in blunt terms: "*The hours are brutal.*"

Away from corporate and finance, the pressure eases a little. The dispute resolution seat is a favourite, due to the "*friendly team, the work and the dramatic court moments.*" Again, much of the work in recent years has been to do with bankruptcy – Lehman-related work is "*still ongoing four years down the line.*" The firm also often handles tax disputes with HMRC, and represented the Barclay Brothers against Irish businessman Paddy McKillen in a dispute regarding the ownership of the Maybourne Hotel Group. "*Litigation certainly doesn't depend on our American offices for work: most of it is generated in London,*" one trainee said. "*The practice is rapidly expanding. It's an exciting time and we're hiring a lot.*" Juniors are exposed to "*typical trainee tasks, but never to the detriment of good work. There are late nights of photocopying, but there is an equal amount of time spent drafting or meeting barristers, and I was in court as much as my supervisor was,*" said one source. The hours are more regular than corporate or finance, but the seat can be just as busy. "*I was working 12-hour days,*" one litigator told us, whereas another said they'd experienced a couple of 2am finishes. Other contentious seats include business finance/restructuring and employment/pensions, or there's the option to take a two-week litigation course instead.

Weiling the hours away

Having read two-thirds of a feature which goes on about brutal hours and intense work, you might be feeling like Weil isn't worth the effort. While we'd would certainly agree that this is not the place for those people seeking a nice easy training contract at a nondescript City firm, it would be wrong to suggest that life at Weil doesn't have its rewards. At other City firms, trainees say they ruled out the magic circle because they didn't fancy the crazy lifestyle. Weil trainees don't mind the crazy lifestyle and continually compare their firm to the magic circle, but ruled out going to the likes of Linklaters or Freshfields because they wanted "*the same level of work but somewhere where trainees are more than just a number.*" The size of the intake means partners can put names to faces and can really "*have opinions on trainees. People talk to each other, and so we have to constantly impress.*" That means hard work is rewarded with recognition: the highlight of one interviewee's training contract came when "*one of the partners I worked with sent me an e-mail congratulating me on my hard work. He copied in Mike Francies and the HR team. It really made all the effort worth it.*" Of course, another great reward is the £95,000 pay cheque for NQs. That's not quite the highest salary in the market, but Weil out-pays the magic circle by a country mile.

Incoming Weil trainees get to know each other on the LPC at College of Law, so "*there's a ready-made bunch of friends before we start.*" About half the current intake are male, "*half went to Oxbridge, and half studied law.*" One trainee declared that the secret of success to getting into the firm is "*about coming across as intelligent rather than getting stellar grades. Trainees should be outgoing and reflect the firm's entrepreneurial attitude.*" Graduate recruitment partner Jonathan Wood had some useful tips on how to answer the 'Why Weil?' question. "*You get all sorts of daft answers to that. Some people say they want to come here as we're an international firm and they want to travel. We want people to be committed to building a career in London, and excited about taking on the challenges of working on a multi-jurisdictional basis from London rather than seeing us as a platform for travel! Another poorly thought out answer is 'for pro bono.' Although we have a strong social conscience and emphasise pro bono work, we are first and foremost an interna-tional corporate law firm – obviously that should be the primary driver for people wanting to join us.*"

Candidates would do better, says Wood, by demonstrating "*understanding the kind of work we do, our practice areas and a genuine enthusiasm about the prospect of working in those practice areas. We look for people who are eager to learn and develop, who are comfortable in smaller teams and are hungry for early responsibility, so being able to demonstrate that those things are important to a candidate – and that they have those qualities – is really important.*"

"*The concern isn't about being kept on, it's about which department you want.*" The majority of our second-year sources this year wanted to join the corporate team. In the final reckoning, nine out of 13 stayed on at Weil, with four striking it lucky and going into corporate.

And finally...

Quite frankly, Weil Gotshal will be a scary proposition for some of you. That's all right – there are 119 more firms in this guide for you to look at. But if you're a fearless character looking for the full-on City experience, Weil can offer you everything you ever dreamed of.

Average trainee starting salary: £26,349

In central London: £34,817

In outer London: £27,387

In the South East: £20,132

In Yorkshire: £19,707

In the Midlands: £19,665

In the North West: £19,476

In the South West: £19,032

In Eastern England: £18,798

In the North East: £18,634

In Wales: £17,790

Source: Law Society Annual Statistical Report 2011

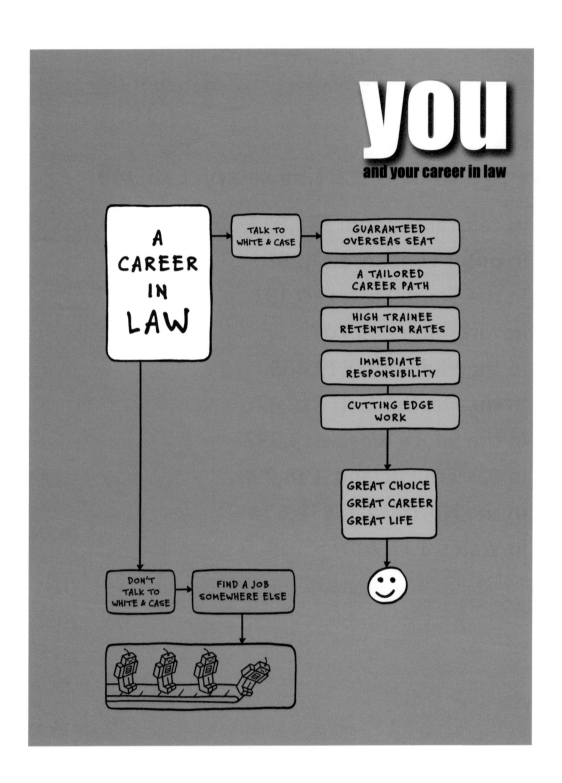

Make the right choice
whitecasetrainee.com

WHITE & CASE

White & Case LLP

The facts

Location: London

Number of UK partners/solicitors: 53/177 (+26 non-UK-qualified)

Total number of trainees: 57

Seats: 4x6 months

Alternative seats: Overseas seats

Extras: Pro Bono – A4ID, LawWorks, Whitechapel Mission Legal Clinic, Innocence Network, RCJ CAB, Lawyers Without Borders; language classes

On chambersstudent.co.uk...
- How to get into White & Case
- A potted history of the firm
- Pro bono at White & Case

American by birth, banking and finance powerhouse White & Case has been an international trailblazer for decades.

The world is not enough

This firm has been around the block: it first established an office outside the US in the 1920s, has been in London since 1971 and has 38 offices in 26 countries. You can get an impression of the firm's international and European standing from the fact that several partners recently advised several of Greece's bank creditors during its £110bn EU bailout. "*This is a genuinely international firm,*" one trainee boasted, "*and that was a major factor in my choice of White & Case.*"

The onset of the global recession put the brakes on global expansion – a bit. Since suffering redundancy rounds and partner defections, the firm has picked itself up, dusted itself off and continued (almost) as if nothing had happened. Revenue grew to $1.33bn in 2011. "*We're currently in more of a maturing phase rather than a growth phase in terms of strategy,*" a senior US source told our sister publication *Chambers Associate*. "*We're trying to make the most out of the network we have.*" And it's quite a network: White & Case has outposts in all the world's major financial centres as well as emerging markets like Mexico and Turkey. The former Soviet Union countries are also a big area of focus.

The UK is a crucial part of the network. "*London and New York are the two drivers of the firm,*" said a trainee. "*This office is of prime importance. Our cross-border deals are often run out of New York, London or Paris.*" A 2008 business review has seen the firm do more to integrate its offices further. "*They are looking to send more London lawyers abroad and move partners around to boost global integration,*" reported one trainee. And it's

not just partners who get a taste of the global jet-set: a big selling point of the training contract is that trainees are guaranteed an overseas seat.

Ever since it was founded in 1901 White & Case has been known for its banking and finance expertise. More recently it has built a stellar reputation for "*ground-breaking*" energy and projects work. For example, the firm advised Qatar Petroleum and ExxonMobil on the $10.3bn Barzan project to build offshore and onshore gas processing plants in Qatar. The firm is top-ranked by *Chambers UK* for projects work, and *Chambers Global* shows that this practice stands out around the world. But *Chambers UK* also ranks the firm in 20 other practices – a big number for a non-native firm – including banking and finance, capital markets, corporate, energy, construction and dispute resolution.

For your eyes only

The finance practice is split into 'banking and capital markets' and 'energy infrastructure, project and asset finance' (EIPAF) departments. There are seats in project finance, asset finance, capital markets (including high-yield debt and structured finance), bank finance and restructuring. Taken together, these finance seats are home to well over half of trainees, with most of those in project finance, bank finance or capital markets. Corporate and litigation/arbitration also take in a sizeable number of recruits, while employment, real estate IP and construction are more rarefied options. "*A lot of people will come in wanting to work in finance, EIPAF or corporate,*" said one trainee. "*More and more people are doing*

Chambers UK rankings

Asset Finance	Dispute Resolution
Banking & Finance	Employee Share Schemes & Incentives
Banking Litigation	
Capital Markets	Energy & Natural Resources
Commodities	Financial Services
Construction	Information Technology
Corporate Crime & Investigations	Private Equity
	Projects
Corporate/M&A	Restructuring/Insolvency
Data Protection	Transport

litigation too, but if you are interested in areas like employment and real estate this is not the best place to go." Trainees are assigned their first seat, and then list three preferences at each rotation: reportedly most get their first choice. Trainees also get to choose their supervisors. Some are more popular than others. "*People choose supervisors based on the word on the street – some are better than others and certain personalities work better together.*"

Trainees usually go overseas in their fourth seat. Singapore and Hong Kong are the most common destinations, while New York is invariably the most popular. Other regular options are Paris, Tokyo, Frankfurt, Beijing, Brussels, Moscow, Johannesburg and Almaty. Overseas seats are assigned a few months into the training contract. Trainees are given a list of all the options and "*then unofficially meet up and put a table together telling HR where we want to go. If two people want to go to the same place, we discuss it amicably and if need be draw names out of a hat.*" Our interviewees had all had good experience abroad. "*Overseas, they don't usually understand what a trainee does so the distinction that normally exists between associate and trainee falls away,*" said one source. "*You get a higher degree of involvement in the work but you need to have a strong personality to adapt to the new role that brings.*"

Whether in London or abroad the firm's office network regularly comes into play. For example, the EIPAF department recently worked with Beijing, Riyadh and New York representing Saudi national oil company Saudi Aramco on a joint venture with Dow Chemical to build a $20bn petrochemical plant in Saudi Arabia. Others projects the firm has worked on include a goldmine in Mongolia, a pipeline under the Baltic Sea, a power station in Turkey and an aluminium smelting plant in the UAE. The department is known for its "*phenomenal work ethic.*" "*I am involved in a variety of transactions and have had clients call me directly with questions,*" a trainee told us. "*Some of the tasks are more tedious – bibling, proof-reading – but they help you gain an understanding of the mechanics*

of the deal. You also know that in a few years' time you will be sent off around the world to negotiate deals.*"

Deutsche Bank is a big client of the bank finance department, which has also acted for Bank of Tokyo-Mitsubishi UFJ, ING, Merrill Lynch, Goldman Sachs and Lloyds TSB. The firm recently advised lenders on three separate $1bn+ loans to businesses in Ukraine, Abu Dhabi and Kazakhstan. "*There is always a big facility agreement at a level that doesn't involve me,*" one trainee said. "*Then there are the additional tasks like organising documents and managing conditions precedent which fall to me. I am usually the first to review the CPs, then I send them to my supervisor. I will then revert to opposing counsel with our combined comments.*" A capital markets seat can be "*intense*" and "*daunting*" as this is a complex area of law. For example, besides working on corporate bonds, White & Case has a line in sovereign bonds too and has advised Namibia and Nigeria on bond issuances. "*There can be a lot of explaining to do,*" said one trainee. "*You learn all about the difficulties of working with developing countries.*" High-yield bonds (or junk bonds) are another area of specialism. The firm recently advised a trio of banks on a £304m debt refinancing bond issuance for Aston Martin Capital.

From Russia with love

Corporate gets good reviews from trainees. "*The work is more varied than in finance,*" said one. "*I got stuck in with client contact, drafted memos, did research into regulatory issues and summarised translations of foreign law.*" Deals are often "*foreign companies buying and selling other foreign companies.*" For example, London, Brussels and Istanbul lawyers advised crisis-hit Belgian bank Dexia on the $3.9bn sale of Turkish-based Denizbank to Russia's Sberbank. Recently, refinancings and restructurings have been a major source of work. The firm advised one of the shareholders in Russia's second largest mobile phone operator MegaFon during its $8.5bn restructuring.

Dispute resolution "*is a popular seat and very competitive to get an NQ job in.*" Trainees attend hearings as well as "*writing letters, pulling bundles together and doing costs schedules.*" It is "*a strong practice area although not one White & Case is known for*" – the arbitration group especially is on the up. It recently acted for Russian investment firm Sistema in a $5bn arbitration with the Indian government after one of its subsidiaries in the subcontinent had its telecoms licence revoked. Litigators, meanwhile, act mainly for banks and other financial institutions in major financial and commercial contract disputes. "*There has been a conscious effort to build the disputes practice and they have increased the number of trainees and qualifiers they want in the group,*" says training principal Philip Stopford. In August 2012 there were seven NQ jobs available in disputes – more than double the number there had been previously.

Like the transactional seats, disputes hands trainees their fair share of dogsbody work. Some trainees put this down to the fact that "*unlike at some firms, there isn't a big army of paralegals to help, so as a trainee you are seen as an all-purpose resource. You do any work from the two or three years PQE level down to paralegal level.*" What's more, the "*paper-heavy*" transactional work means the tasks of junior and mid-level lawyers are primarily organisational. "*At the moment I am a sponge: I will do whatever I am asked and learn from it,*" said one trainee, "*and it always feels as if I am being taught how the documents work rather than just being used to get the deal out of the door.*"

Quantum of solace

Individuality – or independent entrepreneurship – is the key thing White & Case expects from its trainees. "*You are supervised, but you are supposed to take control of your training contract. People coming into the firm should know that: it is quite 'sink or swim' here.*" Undoubtedly this is related to the fact that White & Case operates an 'eat what you kill' partner remuneration system: individuals are paid based on how much work they bring in rather than seniority, making some of them "*hard taskmasters.*" But support is there for those who seek it

out. "*If you need to talk to someone, that is always possible. My appointed supervisors have been great. And ultimately you can always go to HR: Shahnaz in grad recruitment is great.*" Styles of supervision do vary though. "*Depending on your relationship with your supervisor you can get more out if it,*" one source opined. "*Trying to get feedback was tricky in my last seat, but my current supervisor is always on the ball. There are certain difficult personalities, but that is not a reflection of White & Case as a whole.*" The firm is considering implementing upwards reviews of supervisors to help improve quality.

"*7.30pm is a good time to leave and 8pm is pretty standard,*" sources agreed, but most had "*stayed until 11pm or 2am and been called in at the weekend*" at some point. "*But we are given days off in lieu and we are here to work so it doesn't bother me.*" Lawyers do find time to lift their noses from the proverbial grindstone. "*Generally people get on well and we go for drinks after work,*" said one trainee. "*Some departments – like litigation – make an effort to be sociable. The trainees have a social agenda too: when we first started we used to organise drinks once a week, but that has become more difficult now due to people's hours.*" There is also a summer party at the Barbican and an annual winter ball, as well as wine-tasting and sailing events. Every year around 60 London lawyers attend the White & Case World Cup – held in Slovakia in 2012 – with lawyers from around the global network competing.

And finally...

"*White & Case combines the hard-working atmosphere of a New York firm with the we-know-you-have-a-life attitude of English firms. The long hours can be tough, but the high retention rates speak for themselves.*" The firm has done well in this regard over the past few years and in 2012, 25 of 32 qualifiers were kept on.

Wiggin LLP

The facts

Location: Cheltenham, London
Number of UK partners/solicitors: 20/25
Partners who trained at firm: 15%
Total number of trainees: 6
Seats: 4x6 months
Alternative seats: Ad hoc secondments

On chambersstudent.co.uk...
- How to get into Wiggin
- Interview with training principal Simon Baggs

"At the moment I'm sitting in an office with one pink and one green wall. There's film posters in the office, and no one is wearing a suit," mused one source. *"I suppose it's not like a law firm at all."*

What's the buzz?

As one of the UK's leading media firms, Cheltenham-based Wiggin has one foot in the legal profession and the other firmly embedded in stardust. Its client list has more than a touch of glamour: Twentieth Century Fox, HBO and the FA Premier League all feature. This year has seen the firm sprout two offshoots – alternative business models Incopro and Arial Ventures. The former fuses tech and legal expertise to help companies protect their online content; the latter aims to explore new ventures with existing and potential clients. *"It's about using our expertise to develop new ideas,"* says training principal Simon Baggs.

Seat options vary year by year, but usually don't go much beyond litigation, corporate and commercial. Each of these covers media in issues such as broadcast, film, publishing, gaming, tech, music and sport. The majority of trainees also head off on secondment – in the recent past to the BPI, the trade association to the British recorded music industry. One thing, however, is certain. Whichever group you end up in, your clients will be media types – *"99% of the work we do is media-related,"* claimed one source, *"even within corporate."*

Drafting with the stars

The litigation team works for many major newspapers and broadcasters. *"We get incredible work."* Wiggin gets involved in all sorts of disputes, from professional negligence cases and disputed fees to competition law and contentious corporate insolvency. The group recently scored a win for six big-name Hollywood studios against BT, requiring the service provider to take steps to block the pirate download website Newzbin2. In addition, head of the group Caroline Kean has become somewhat of an authority on defamation and the *News of the World* phone hacking scandal. Trainees generally play a role in research and drafting witness statements, as well as attending conferences with clients and counsel. *"I also attended hearings to take notes,"* said one.

The growing film team is currently involved in halting a zombie pandemic, which originated in China but has since caused chaos in the Middle East, the US and Japan, driving Iran and Pakistan to destroy each other in nuclear warfare. Only Brad Pitt can... oh, hang on... phew, that's just the plot of *World War Z*, a blockbuster set to hit the box office in 2013. The team has been involved in the financing of the film, going *"on set, signing production agreements and making sure everything is just so."* Apparently *"some people even got to meet Brad Pitt."* On a daily basis, however, trainees are more likely to find themselves drafting contracts and assisting in the completion of financing these complex deals.

Wiggin's broadcasting team deals with all sorts of techy matters, from gambling regulations to website privacy policies, but according to trainees it's *"mainly about rights"* and who can use them. Trainees love the sheer variety of matters available: *"There are lots of specialisations and I've worked for a lot of people,"* one said. Expect heaps of drafting and research. Firm-wide training sessions are held for a bleary-eyed audience at 8.15am every other Monday.

The corporate department may not be top of Wiggin trainees' wish lists, but most come away from the seat saying: *"I never expected to enjoy it to the extent I did."*

Chambers UK rankings

Defamation/Reputation Management	Media & Entertainment
Intellectual Property	Sports Law
Licensing	

It's "*always really, really busy,*" and recent matters include the high-profile sale of Virgin Media's channel business to BSkyB and the IPO of Perform Group on the London Stock Exchange, as well as work for smaller indie production companies – Endemol's acquisition of Tiger Aspect, for example. "*It is fairly intense but you get a broad range of responsibility and take charge of a lot of your own work.*"

In 2011, Wiggin sent 17 lawyers and trainees on secondment at one time or another. "*There's talk of placements at the Premier League, and a trainee has just gone to Man United,*" while other destinations include Disney and Perform. The firm is also looking to set up secondments with film studios.

Wiggin'a have a ball

So is this trendy boutique based in the hipster-laden media hubs of Shoreditch or Soho? Nope, Wiggin's home is the leafy spa town of Cheltenham. "*It's a breath of fresh air,*" claimed one trainee. "*Cheltenham is a great place to live – I can be at work in ten minutes, or I can get on my old-lady bike and ride out to cute Cotswold villages.*" What's more, the social life is brilliant, because unless they want to become legal hermits (which Wiggsters certainly are not), they have little choice but to get to know each other. "*There's almost an element where you feel like you're back at uni,*" a source explained. "*Most of us have relocated to come here and everyone's in the same boat.*" Every interviewee reported how easy it is to make friends within the Cheltenham bubble. "*There's a contingent of about 15 trainees and NQs who are in each others' pockets. We all live within 15 minutes of each other.*" The firm also puts on frequent events, with more meals and parties than you can shake a stick at.

Naturally, Wiggin's hierarchy inevitably becomes watered down after a few G&Ts or a jog through the hills with the running club, and "*sometimes at socials you'll stop and think: oh hang on, you're my supervisor!*" It also helps foster a "*can-do culture,*" claimed one trainee. "*There's a*

proactive energy that goes all the way from the CEO down to the operations assistant. Everyone is just really on it.*" The firm's relocation to new offices around the corner in July 2012 is intended to push this feeling even further. "*There's curvy walls, loads of glass and a Costa coffee.*" According to Simon Baggs, "*it's going to be quite different to what you'd expect to see in a law firm – there'll be an emphasis on open areas where people can get together throughout the day.*"

Wiggin is always anxious to point out that its clients come from London and the US West Coast, not Cheltenham. Office hours are therefore more reflective of Wiggin's City-style work than its location – when there's work to be done, heads are down until it's finished. The pay, however, matches this: "*It's better than some London firms in terms of trainee salary,*" claimed one source, "*and Cheltenham is so cheap.*" Note also that the firm's small London office has an increasing number of lawyers working there full-time.

A quick scan of current trainees proves that, when it comes to getting hired, age and background are irrelevant. However, "*they did tell us in the recruitment process that they're looking for a certain type,*" a source mused; "*someone who works extremely hard, is ambitious, but at the same time doesn't take themselves too seriously.*" An anecdote from Simon Baggs: "*Last year we had a straight-A candidate whose grades fell down at degree level. He thought he needed to demonstrate staying power, so woke up one day and decided to represent his country in sport – despite not being a sportsman. He went on to represent his country in the Commonwealth Games as a 400 and 800 metre runner. That's what we're looking for: an absolute commitment to success, and no excuses about falling short.*"

Media law has an aura of glitz and glamour, but trainees note: "*Media doesn't mean easier. If anything, it's harder.*" It's crucial that candidates have a thorough grounding in the nuts and bolts of the legal profession. "*Investigate what media law means – look at media investments and different platforms. The last thing Wiggin wants is someone who reads gossip mags and then thinks it's glamorous.*" Simon Baggs confirms: "*Although there's a lot of fun, it's incredibly important we have people who are excellent lawyers. We want to make sure those people who are thinking about the top ten City firms are also thinking about us.*"

And finally...

If Wiggin can keep its trainees on, it will, and in 2012 retained two of its three qualifiers.

Wilsons

The facts

Location: Salisbury, Bristol, London
Number of UK partners/solicitors: 33/31
Seats: 4x6 months
Total number of trainees: 8
Alternative seats: Occasional secondments

On chambersstudent.co.uk...
• How to get into Wilsons
• What's Salisbury like?

Based in the biscuit-tin twee city of Salisbury, Wilsons has "*a great reputation for private client and charities work.*"

Keep the Cathedral Close

A hundred yards from one of the ancient gateways into Salisbury's picturesque Cathedral Close is a large stone-clad building. Formerly the city's Courts of Justice, it's now the home of Wilsons, the largest law firm in Salisbury. It is recognised as one of the South West's top firms for private client, charities and agriculture work, and also picks up *Chambers UK* nods for its dispute resolution, commercial, employment, family and property practices.

Wilsons moved into its new office building in summer 2012, having previously been split between four locations in the city centre. "*People are excited about the move,*" trainees told us, when we spoke to them in the spring. "*It will be nice when we are under one roof. It will give us more of a one-firm feel.*" There have been other changes too. In spring 2012 the firm elected a "*dynamic*" new managing partner, Andrew Roberts. He is ten years younger than the previous firm head and only joined Wilsons in 2007, having previously worked at Boodle Hatfield, DLA Piper, Linklaters and Shell, and as in-house counsel for the Labour Party.

In April 2011 the firm opened a Bristol office, and it has also had a London base since 2009. There are no London trainees at the moment, but at the time of our research there was one based in Bristol.

Wilsons is firmly focused on its private client practice, but is seeking to grow and promote its commercial side too, in areas closely linked to private client. While commercial work ebbs and flows with the tides of the economy, the certainty of death and taxes means private client lawyers have stayed pretty busy. Wilsons doubled its revenue in the mid-2000s, before a slight drop in turnover to £12m in 2009/10. Revenue has been pretty stable since then.

All trainees are expected to complete a property seat, either in the residential, commercial or farms/estates teams. Other common seats are private client; contentious trusts/probate (charities); non-contentious trusts/probate; employment; family; litigation; and company/commercial. "*Seat allocation is an ad hoc process,*" trainees said. "*We are asked before we start what our interests are and a few months before each seat change everyone fires off e-mails to HR to say where they want to go next. They juggle everybody's interests and try to make it work, but nothing is formalised.*"

Private on parade

The private client department is split into offshore/new wealth and landed estates/old money groups, and deals only with those individuals with the highest-value assets. Less wealthy private clients are handled by the non-contentious trusts/probate team. "*We draft and help execute complex wills and trust agreements and all the associated documents,*" a trainee said. "*There is a fair bit of research as well.*" The firm's agricultural expertise shines through here, as lots of the estates have a farmyard-y quality to them. "*I have been to trustee meetings all over the country and worked on agricultural property relief,*" a source informed us. There's also some "*really interesting*" work to be had looking at the world of offshore wealth

Chambers UK rankings

Agriculture & Rural Affairs	Private Client
Charities	Real Estate
Employment	

and tax avoidance. As is often the case in departments like these, rich private clients want face time with the partners, so "*there is not much autonomy for trainees: you don't have your own files and there isn't a huge amount of one-on-one client contact.*" The lower value of work in non-contentious trusts and probate means trainees get more autonomy. "*I was given two or three files which were my responsibility,*" one told us. "*I have drafted codicils, witnessed the signing of wills, and administered estates.*"

In contentious trusts and probate, "*90% of the clients are charities. We act for them in disputes over legacies left to them in wills. If someone contests a will we defend the charity in that dispute. So, you might have to defend the RSPCA if an old granny left them her money, but then a long-lost son shows up and tries to claim it.*" Aside from the RSPCA, other clients include the British Heart Foundation, the Red Cross and the Woodland Trust. There is also "*more basic*" legacy recovery ("*a charity knows it has been left £10,000, but the executors haven't paid out, so we chase after the executors*") and other disputes over wills. "*I ran my own legacy recovery files,*" a trainee told us. "*They are straightforward but still require legal knowledge. I was the main point of contact for clients, set up the file and drafted the initial client letters.*" Another added: "*I was involved with a big Inheritance Act dispute that went to court. I prepared the bundles, drafted witness statements and wrote the instructions to counsel.*" Wilsons also advises charities on constitutional and governance issues, but this is mostly the realm of two London partners and trainees are only occasionally involved.

The commercial and residential property seats offer a chance at "*drafting all the usuals including leases and licences to assign, as well as dealing with Land Registry applications and Stamp Duty Land Tax.*" Clients include the charity Help for Heroes, upmarket estate agent Savills, and Chatsworth, the Duke of Devonshire's country pile. A seat in farms and estates is "*very rewarding,*" a trainee said. "*Halfway through my seat we won a tender to sell off a big rural estate. We set up the sale of the different lots. I collated all of the bundles for the agent to put them on their website. We also spent a day going round looking at all the bits of land.*" While plenty of the work has a local element – like the £14.5m sale of Wiltshire's famous Fonthill Abbey estate – trainees said their work is "*not just Salisbury or South West-based. We have clients from all over the country.*"

Nerds, jocks and preps

At the time of our research, Wilsons' culture was still (in part) defined by its four separate buildings. "*Each department has its own personality. Private client is more nerdy: all the partners have their own office, so it's all a bit old-fashioned and rabbit-warren-like. The commercial and employment building is open-plan and so everyone is always chatting about work.*" Supervision varies too. "*Each supervisor has their own way of doing things. Some want to have regular updates and always explain things to you first; others let you get along with your work and are there for you to ask questions.*" We don't want to over-egg any differences though – especially as everyone will be under one roof by the time you read this. "*It is a unified firm. The dress code and the firm's rules and procedures are the same everywhere.*" Hours are also quite similar across the departments. Trainees usually work from around 9am to 5.30 or 6pm. They sometimes stay late, but this means 7 or 8pm at the very latest.

Trainees see several benefits to the office move. "*In one building I think there will be more potential for cross-referring work, as you'll see more people face to face.*" Trainees also expect a boost to Wilsons' social life. "*At the moment you can't really go over to a different building and ask if people want to go for drinks. The young lawyers, trainees and secretaries pop out on a Friday evening or for lunch. I reckon that will happen more in the new building as you'll bump into people more often.*" The firm doesn't lay on a whole lot of events, but there is a summer party as well as quiz nights and Christmas drinks in the office.

Trainees agreed that "*Wilsons is a lovely organisation to work for,*" but said "*there is one area where the firm falls down a little.*" Communication "*is not brilliant. At the moment, it isn't necessarily clear what our five-year plan is. I would really love to know that. I think the firm needs to sell itself to the trainees a bit more. Our new managing partner wants to be more open.*" Information about qualification filters through slowly, too. When we spoke to trainees in spring 2012 they were unsure when they would find out what NQ jobs were available. Wilsons doesn't have a great recent retention record, with just four of 12 qualifiers staying on between 2009 and 2011. Unfortunately, 2012 wasn't much better, with two of five qualifiers taking jobs at the firm.

And finally...

If you're after a training contract that's heavy on really top-end private client work, Wilsons is one of the best options out there.

Withers LLP

The facts

Location: London

Number of UK partners/solicitors: 59/97

Partners who trained at firm: c.33%

Total number of trainees: 13

Seats: 4x6 months

Alternative seats: Overseas seats

Extras: Language classes

On chambersstudent.co.uk...

- How to get into Withers
- Landmark divorce cases
- Unconventional literary heroines

Withers' illustrious history and global outlook have made it a go-to firm for the wealthy and international.

Welcome to Marlborough country

What links Bernie Ecclestone, the Duke of Marlborough and Princeton University? You've guessed it of course: Withers acts for all of them. The British Horse-racing Authority, CapitalOne Bank, the Tate galleries, and fashion houses Cath Kidson, Lulu Guinness, Max Mara, Valentino and Vera Wang are among the other big names instructing this genteel London firm.

Since a 2002 merger with the US's Bergman Horowitz & Reynolds, Withers has become WithersWorldwide, expanding into New York, Milan, Geneva, Zurich, Hong Kong and the British Virgin Islands. You'll notice they are all major wealth centres, which is a reflection of Withers' most famous area of strength – a *Chambers UK* top-ranked private client group. A new office in Singapore opened in 2012, *"to build on our overall global strategy,"* said training partner Suzanne Todd. *"The hope is that we retain all the traditional Withers strengths, but continue to raise them to an international platform. We embrace our global outlook."* Drawn to the firm for *"its variety of practice areas,"* trainees love *"the prestigious reputation of the firm and the smaller trainee intake." "The family and wealth planning departments still feel very dominant within the firm, but we're highly rated in a variety of areas."* Trainees can choose from a good range of seats. These include commercial litigation, employment, property litigation, contentious trusts on succession, family, wealth planning, reputation management, real estate (which is divided into commercial, residential and landed estates), corporate, banking/finance, IP and charities.

Like clockwork

Consistently highly ranked by *Chambers UK*, the wealth planning department is one of London's finest. It is split

into three groups: the international team (INT), the family (FAB) and business planning team – *"which is more domestic private client work"* – and a funds, investment, trusts and tax team, *"or FITTs, as it's informally known."* Clients are high net worth individuals and well-known corporations, including Barclays Wealth. *"Withers also works with several clients who aren't domiciled in the UK."* Trainees get involved in client meetings *"and take a stab at wills and trusts drafting."* Particular praise went to the FITTs team, who are *"so focused on teaching, and staff you on the full range of work."* The contentious trusts on succession group (CTSG) covers probate and trust disputes and *"90% of the work is people-focused. The client exposure is great and the work is fascinating."* There is also *"a substantial amount of court time and drafting."*

Withers' charity department covers three distinct sectors: medical charities, education charities, and philanthropy in the US and UK. Trainees work across all three. The team has recently reviewed a number of the NSPCC's professional fund-raising agreements and advised University College London Hospitals on charity issues relating to a central London property development. *"You get to work with everyone in the department,"* trainees said. *"It is an extremely busy seat and you're given a huge amount of responsibility. This includes liaising with all sorts of clients and even being involved with your own cases."*

The firm's family department *"is very impressive, and you're a bit in awe of everyone that works here,"* one trainee reflected. *"All the work is done so precisely – it's like being in a clockwork machine."* Clients include wealthy old families, but also *"a number of entrepreneurs."* Although *"the work is top-notch,"* it is *"more difficult to get responsibility"* in this department. *"As the standard is so high, it's hard to make an impact. Senior*

Chambers UK rankings

Administrative & Public Law	Employment
Agriculture & Rural Affairs	Family/Matrimonial
Charities	Private Client
Defamation/Reputation Management	Professional Negligence
	Tax

associates and partners do try though, and you will get some drafting experience." The commercial litigation team "mostly looks after the interests of our entrepreneurial private clients, but we also do insolvency, fraud, professional negligence and arts work. There are also plenty of ADR projects and there's some Italian litigation too." For instance, Withers acted for the Comune di Verona in relation to a claim by Merrill Lynch for declaratory relief in the English courts, represented the Vivienne Westwood label in a £22m dispute over the renewal of a franchise agreement. "No matter how big the claim, you're always included in good work," trainees said. "There is the traditional bundling to do, but you'll be drafting from the beginning, writing letters to clients and going in front of Masters. You can't just sit back in a corner."

Come on, Vogue

The reputation department has clients including gay rights activist Peter Tatchell and pop diva Britney Spears. Most of the individuals the team works for "aren't really tabloid-type celebrities," though. "There is also a lot of work on behalf of charities and smaller companies." From privacy and defamation issues to online protection cases, "the work is very diverse and unpredictable. It's hard, but you get a tremendous amount of responsibility." In the IP department, meanwhile, "we do a lot of work within the fashion world and one of the partners was featured in a Vogue party spread." It's a small team, "so there's a lot for trainees to do."

Finally, a word on the corporate team. "We're working with smaller to mid-size companies, but we do everything you'd expect a corporate department to do." Withers acted for Camilla Fayed on the purchase of luxury fashion business Issa Couture from its administrators. The firm also acted for Bernie Ecclestone in the sale of his stake in Queen's Park Rangers FC to Malaysian businessman Tony Fernandes.

Withers without you, Withers with-ooouuut youuuuu

Although Withers does to a certain extent still have a reputation as an old-school, traditional sort of place, trainees said: "Every department in the firm is so different. The wealth planning and family departments might be more old-school types, but that's more to do with our clients and the nature of the work. The litigation, commercial and corporate departments are dynamic and the attitude of the firm as a whole is very forward-thinking." Trainees stressed: "We have less and less of the landed estate clients and more self-made, international, entrepreneurial individuals. In that market, the firm has to take on a very modern approach."

It was admitted that "on the whole, everyone went to a good university and there are a high percentage who went to public school, but there's none of that stuffy nonsense. Everyone is grounded and friendly." The same goes for those in charge: "There are partners who have been at the firm for a long time, but none are fuddy-duddy cobwebs in the corner. Partners are very approachable and always polite." The atmosphere of the office, although "not boisterous, is smooth and laid-back. People are very close-knit and really support one another." When recruiting, the firm is looking for "mature, bright people, with interests outside the law. They like to hire polite and interesting people, who have had variety in their lives."

Sorting Bovaries from Bennetts

Withers "is not the most sociable firm," but there is "enough" going on in the form of pub quizzes, beer-tasting events, historic walks through London and the like. Informally, "you'll probably always find someone in Jamie's or Corney & Barrow. Both are pretty awful, and yet we're constantly there!"

Working hours "are really quite good." On average, our sources reported leaving between 7 and 7.30pm, depending on how much work they had on. "The very late days are suitably rare," one trainee remarked. "In fact, I can count on both hands the amount of times I've stayed past 11pm."

Withers' initial application form has at least one oddball question on it: 'If you were a fictional character from a novel, who would you be?' A serious tip? "Girls, please don't put Elizabeth Bennett or Hermione Granger. They're such clichés, and you'll probably have your application discarded." To give you a few ideas (but mainly for our own amusement, to be honest), we've come up with some less conventional literary heroines who would make good lawyers – head over to our website to see them.

And finally...

Retention rates are normally okay at Withers. In 2012, nine out of 13 qualifiers stayed on.

Wragge & Co LLP

The facts

Location: Birmingham, London

Number of UK partners/solicitors: 110/288

Total number of trainees: 52

Seats: 4x6 months

Alternative seats: Guangzhou, secondments

Extras: Pro bono – LawWorks, Birmingham Legal Advice Clinic

On chambersstudent.co.uk...

• How to get into Wragge & Co
• Interview with training partner Baljit Chohan

"If you wanted to be at the best firm in Birmingham, you'd be at Wragges."

Birmingham international

London expansion and glamorous new offices in Paris and Abu Dhabi won't dilute Wragge & Co's ID as Birmingham Big Daddy just yet. Around 300 of the firm's 400 fee earners are based at its Midlands HQ, and clients like M&S, Dyson, Birds Eye, Aston Martin and Jockey Club point to a firm with strong ties to UK business.

The 2011/12 year saw Wragges report 5% growth – a shortfall from original targets, but evidence of good things nevertheless, after a couple of weak post-recession years. Growth is, in the words of training partner Baljit Chohan, *"mainly down to the international offices taking off. As time goes on we're becoming increasingly recognised and established as an international law firm which is leading to an increasing number of overseas clients instructing us on inbound UK work."* The firm is consequently seeing a boom in areas like international arbitration and cross-border litigation, international projects and project finance, and corporate. Unusually, property is also an area where Wragges has sought work away from home turf, acting on some megabucks (though top secret) construction projects in Qatar.

For trainees, an international outlook can only be a good thing. *"Technically, it's beneficial as trainees have to translate concepts from UK law into the host jurisdiction,"* explains Chohan. *"Those who want to grab hold of responsibility will feel empowered as they're actually in the position of teaching the client – not just receiving knowledge."*

Wragges' practice is clustered around corporate, litigation and property. Taking a seat in each of these areas is compulsory, with an open option seat for groups like compe- tition, IP and IT. If this *"sounds prescriptive,"* be assured that *"it's not. There's plenty of leeway like employment counting as a litigation or an option seat, and HR is always flexible."* Trainees hired to London have a more reduced range of options than Birmingham, though there are some seats offered in London *"which a Birmingham trainee could request to do."* An overseas stint in Guangzhou, China, is a further possibility.

Best of British

Property encompasses planning and regeneration; retail, energy and leisure; property litigation; residential development; and commercial development and investment. Trainees could work on projects as diverse as developing retail parks, assisting councils with social housing regeneration, dealing with option agreements on a wind farm or helping farmers sell a plot of green field. Depending on the niche, working on large developments can mean *"acting as a general assistant and helping with smaller tasks, rather than being project by project."* Overall though, there's space to get involved, and after a sluggish few years for property, our sources were enjoying the bustle of a busy department. Trainees across all property seats get 30 of their own files on their first day, *"which gives you a complementary balance between small and big project work."* Said one: *"There's scope to move your career on and move fast. On many matters, it's appropriate to have a junior on the file, so we're able to build our own client relationships."* Matters are far from Birmingham-centric. Wragges advised Young's on its massive takeover of 26 pubs for £60m, bringing the brewery's total portfolio to 247 pubs. The team also advised on the pre-let of a new distribution centre for Amazon: as you'd imagine, it's a

Chambers UK rankings

Banking & Finance	Local Government
Banking Litigation	Outsourcing
Competition/European Law	Pensions
Construction	Pensions Litigation
Corporate/M&A	Planning
Dispute Resolution	Projects
Employment	Public Procurement
Energy & Natural Resources	Real Estate
Environment	Real Estate Litigation
Health & Safety	Restructuring/Insolvency
Healthcare	Retail
Information Technology	Social Housing
Intellectual Property	Tax
Life Sciences	

tidy size – 1.1m square feet (about 20 football pitches, we reckon).

A corporate seat could mean six months in areas as diverse as non-contentious construction, projects, tax or finance, but many trainees will spend time in M&A. This might mean an emphasis on publicly registered or traditional private companies – or a mixture of the two, dependent on the supervisor. Deals can be huge, and there's often an international angle, like the £91m takeover of biotech company Astex by SuperGen or the sale of Phones 4U to private equity house BC Partners. Even on deals of this size, trainees don't just do admin tasks – many reported having client contact very early on, and getting experience "*drafting SPAs, shareholder agreements and articles of association for banks.*" The flip side to this is "*the true corporate experience*" that a heavy workload can entail. Hours can be heavy across both offices. Said one corporate trainee: "*Getting away at 10pm would be early – we'd only count it late if we were in past midnight.*"

"*Techy*" construction is "*one of the best seats for atmosphere.*" The team acts for the full spectrum – purchasers, developers, funds, tenants on all manner of different projects. Contentious work tends to come from contractors, and the team is increasingly receiving instructions from insurers. In addition to being "*complex and highly technical by nature,*" disputes are "*extremely high-value,*" meaning at trainee level, "*our input is limited from a legal point of view.*" Example: a delayed construction project which had to come down to minute expert evidence "*to work out the extent of liquidated damages.*" Bundling may form a significant part of work, but trainees will also get to attend adjudications, in addition to being handed their own, smaller files.

Trainees in com lit enjoy the responsibility, insight and variation of clients they gain access to. "*The work puts into context what you read in newspapers,*" thought one. "*We might be advising on deliveries that parties had breached in some way – it's direct evidence of how even really big clients are still suffering from the recession.*" Wragges advised PricewaterhouseCoopers on claims of negligence brought by a publicly listed company's CEO, a claim worth £30m. In London, there's a heavy arbitration bias, but in Birmingham there are multiple subteams to commercial litigation. These include: business, innovation and skills; IT and outsourcing; and health, safety and environment. The latter can naturally take in pretty varied research – "*from personal injury to asbestos claims to researching laser pens or baby monitors.*" There are also seats up for grabs in finance litigation and construction litigation. Many trainees will get a selection of their own debtor files: "*We attempt to claim money back from individuals and get to experience the court system firsthand.*"

Many trainees will take an 'option' seat from the commercial department in IP, IT or competition. The IP team acted for Dyson in a design dispute brought against Vax at the High Court and the Court of Appeal. Wragges also obtained a significant trade mark victory for Play-Doh after another toy manufacturer 123 Nährmittel began using the phrase 'play dough' on its boxes of Yummy Dough. IT clients include BSkyB, Morrisons and Vodafone. There are a lot of commercial secondments open to trainees who want to spend time in-house, including placements at Unilever, Mercedes and E.ON. Learning is rapid, as "*there are fewer people to check if you've done something wrong, and there's no barrier between you and the client – if someone wants an answer, they'll come to you directly.*"

Big ideas, bright sparks

With so much training on offer at Wragges, "*you could easily go to two or three talks a week.*" There's an LPC refresher at the start of every seat, and then department-specific training throughout. Employment has a rep for setting the standard: "*It's junior-run as well as attended, which is often the best way of learning.*" There's also a refreshing lack of social hierarchy: "*Every partner has the same desk and chair as a secretary. People are so outgoing that if you met someone slightly stand-offish it'd be really noticeable.*" Before we go too far though, it's worth noting "*we're still dealing with FTSE 100s in a commercial business – it's not all nicey-nice, making tea for each other and going home at 5pm. But generally, things feel a lot less corporate here than at other firms.*"

Wragges trainees like the fact that they feel accepted on their own terms. This might come out through extra-curriculars being encouraged ("*leaving to play sport is never* an issue") or because of the care taken with training and mentoring. Each new starter gets assigned a personal trainee principal "*who takes you out for lunch, and whom you can ask completely stupid questions.*" They also sit in on three and six-month reviews, ensuring each trainee is fairly judged. Feedback is refreshingly honest, but fair. "*People don't pull any punches, but they truly care about your progression. It's done with a view to making you a better lawyer and staying with Wragges.*" Little things contribute to the feeling of inclusiveness. An initiative called 'Bright Idea' invites practical ways the firm could improve any aspect of the way things are run. "*When it gets implemented you get a personal note from* [senior partner] *Quentin Poole to say thanks.*"

Located in the Colmore Business District, Brum trainees have the pick of bars, a favourite being the Old Joint Stock. There "*are drinks most Friday nights, and because all the law firms are on the same street, you can go into any bar and see someone you know.*" Alcohol aside, there's football and netball, and a plethora of activities organised through the Birmingham Trainee Solicitors' Society. The firm's own trainee social committee pays for a few events a year. There are also classes like yoga and boxercise run by external trainers who come to Wragges HQ. A trainee-run choir is going from strength to strength. "*The repertoire is classical, with some pop – recently we've been learning 'Time to Say Goodbye' and the Westlife classic 'You Raise me Up'.*"

Le Rétropolitain

Brum trainees love their location "*on the Golden Mile,*" but admit the "*outwardly Parisian-looking*" HQ gets "*a bit tired and eighties*" inside. A move to the brand-new Snowhill complex has been on the cards for years, and is now set for January 2014. "*The London office is so nice, so it will be nice to have parity,*" reckon trainees. Situated in Holborn's Woodhouse Square, Wragges London has "*a lot more space, and feels very airy and modern.*" The downside is the atmosphere might "*not be as chatty*" as the Midlands, though.

Talk of a London merger emerged in June 2011, and Baljit Chohan confirmed that "*if we were to merge in the UK, I think realistically it could only be in London. If the right opportunity came along and made sense, we'd take it.*" Don't be mistaken into thinking that London growth might be at the Midlands' expense. Said one trainee: "*A lot of it is about attracting London clients and bringing the work back to Birmingham.*" In many teams, a truly cross-office ethos prevails. "*In commercial litigation, for example, clients and courts are London-centred, but then the cases can be worked on from anywhere, which is a pretty competitive pricing model.*" Chohan gave his perspective: "*Although trainees have training contracts for particular offices, a fee earner wouldn't think in those terms. There's so much crossover right now, that whether we're a national firm, a UK firm or international firm with a Birmingham base doesn't really enter our thinking.*"

Internationally, a similar message prevails. "*Our USP of 'same quality work at Birmingham rates' won't go away,*" think trainees. "*In the future, a lot more work will come from global clients – who bring more fees and a better quality of work. Wragges wants to be viewed as an international firm based in Birmingham rather than a Birmingham firm based everywhere.*"

And finally...

Evidencing the single team ethos, three Birmingham trainees qualified into the London office this year. Elsewhere, retention was rosy, with 27 out of the total 32 who qualified sticking with Wragges.

Refine your search

Refine your search

We know just how disorienting, disheartening and crazily time consuming it can be to get lost in acres and acres of recruitment material from law firms telling you how they're the best thing since sliced bread. We're sure they are, but how can you tell which are most suited to your undoubted talents?

Snap yourself out of that haze and glance at our crystal clear comparison tables. They show you the facts you really want to know, in an instant. Which firms are flashing the cash? Which have moths in their wallets? Which will post you to sunnier climes for a working holiday… ahem, overseas placement? What other carrots are firms prepared to dangle in front of you to secure your signature? Who will pay you to go to law school? And finally, how do you apply?

This section is divided into three easy-to-use reference tables that should help you shorten your long list of target firms. They show at a glance the application and selection procedures of each firm, the number of rival applicants you're likely to compete against for that coveted training contract place, the salaries and benefits on offer, and the locations of overseas seats among those firms that offer them. If you missed it there's a **Vacation Schemes** table on page 29.

Application and selection methods

The table on the following page lets you know how each law firm requires you to apply – whether by a letter crafted in your best joined-up handwriting, via a CV in the post or through an application form online. It shows you what minimum degree is required and how many interviews and/or assessments you face. Finally, and equally crucially, it gives the number of training contracts available alongside how many applications each firm receives.

Salaries and law school sponsorships

Our table of salaries and law school sponsorships on page 521 reveals the current salaries on offer for first and second-year trainees at each firm plus the salary for newly qualified solicitors. It also gives details of sponsorship and awards available to help you pay for law school, along with information about other benefits once you join the firm, like gym membership and health insurance.

Overseas seats

The final table on page 532 lists the firms that ship trainees out to various international locations, so if you've a hankering for Hong Kong, a craving for Chicago or possibly even a fetish for the Falkland Islands, we'll show you where to apply before you can say, 'Money, tickets, passport!'

Applications and Selection

Firm Name	Method of Application	Selection Process	Degree Class	Number of Contracts	Number of Applications
Addleshaw Goddard	Not known	Not known	2:1	35	2,000
Allen & Overy	Online	Interview	2:1	90	2,500
Arnold & Porter	Online	Interview + written assessment	2:1	2	700
Ashfords	Online	Assessment centre + interview	2:1	10-12	400
Ashurst	Online	2 interviews	2:1	45	2,500
Baker & McKenzie	Online	Telephone interview + assessment centre + interview	2:1	34	Not known
Bates Wells & Braithwaite	Online	Interviews	2:1	4	750+
Berwin Leighton Paisner	Online	Phone interview + assessment centre + interview	2:1	40-45	Not known
Bevan Brittan	Online	Not known	Not known	Not known	Not known
Bingham McCutchen	Online	Interviews	High 2:1	Up to 4	Not known
Bircham Dyson Bell	Online	Online test + 2 interviews + assessment centre	2:1 preferred	7	650
Bird & Bird	Online	Not known	2:1	16-17	2,400
Bond Pearce	Online	Assessment days	2:1	10	Not known
Boodle Hatfield	Online	Interviews + test	2:1	6	Not known
B P Collins	CV & handwritten letter	Interview + assessment day	2:1	Not known	Not known
Brabners Chaffe Street	Online	Interview + assessment day	2:1 or post-graduate degree	7	Not known
Bristows	Online	2 interviews	2:1 preferred	Up to 10	2,000
Browne Jacobson	Online	Telephone interview + assessment centre + interview	Not known	8	800
Burges Salmon	Online	Assessment centre + interview	2:1	25	1,700
Capsticks	Application form, CV & letter	Interview	2:1	7	300
Charles Russell	Online	Assessment day + interview	2:1 preferred	18	1,500
Cleary Gottlieb Steen & Hamilton	CV & covering letter	Usually via vac scheme	High 2:1	13-15	Not known
Clifford Chance	Online	Assessment day + interview	2:1	100	Not known
Clyde & Co	Online	Assessment day	2:1	35-40	1,500
Cobbetts	Online	Assessment days	2:1	12	1,100
Collyer Bristow	Online	Test + interview	2:1	Not known	Not known
Covington & Burling	Online	2 interviews	2:1	6	Not known
Cripps Harries Hall	Online	Interview	2:1	8	200
Davenport Lyons	Online	Interviews	2:1	8	400
Davis Polk & Wardell	CV & covering letter	Interview	2:1	4	Not known
Dechert	Online	Assessment day + interviews + tests	2:1	10-12	1,000
Dickinson Dees	Online	Interview + assessments	2:1	Up to 15	800-900
DLA Piper	Online	Interview + assessments	2:1	90	4,050
Dundas & Wilson	Online	Interview + assessment day	2:1 preferred	12 (London)	600
DWF	Online	Interview + assessment centre + selection day	2:1	24	1,300

Applications and Selection

Firm Name	Method of Application	Selection Process	Degree Class	Number of Contracts	Number of Applications
Edwards Wildman Palmer	Online	Assessment morning + interview	2:1	Up to 8	700
Eversheds	Online	Online tests + interview + assessment day	2:1	50-60	4,500
Farrer & Co	Online	Interviews	2:1	10	900
Fladgate	Application form	Assessment day + interview	2:1	4	Not known
Foot Anstey	Online	Assessment day	2:1	4	300
Forbes	Online	Interview	2:1	4	350+
Freeth Cartwright	Online	Interview + selection day	2:1	Not known	Not known
Freshfields Bruckhaus Deringer	Online	2 interviews + tests	Not known	100	2,000
Gateley	Not known	Not known	2:1	Not known	Not known
Gordons	Online	Interview + exercise	2:1	4	400
Government Legal Service	Online	Half-day assessment centre + interviews	2:1	20-25	2,000+
Harbottle & Lewis	Application form	Interview	2:1	5	500
Henmans	Application form	Assessment day + interview + test	2:1	2	250
Herbert Smith Freehills	Online	Assessment centre + tests + interview	2:1	Not known	Not known
Hewitsons	Application form	Interview	2:1	10	850
Higgs & Sons	Online	Interview	2:1 preferred	4-6	350+
Hill Dickinson	Online	Assessment day + tests	Not known	Not known	Not known
Hogan Lovells	Online	Assessment day	2:1	Up to 75	1,500
Holman Fenwick Willan	Online	Assessment centre + interview	2:1	15	Not known
Ince & Co	Online	Interview + tests	2:1	15	1,000
Irwin Mitchell	Online	Assessment centre + interview	None	40	2,000-2,500
Jones Day	Online	2 interviews	2:1	15	2,000
Kennedys	Online	Assessment day	2:1	18	900
Kingsley Napley	Online	Not known	2:1	5	250
Kirkland & Ellis	Online	Interview	2:1	Not known	Not known
K&L Gates	Online	Assessment day + interview	2:1	Not known	1,000
Latham & Watkins	Online	3 interviews	2:1	20	Not known
Lawrence Graham	Online	Interview + tests	2:1	15	800
Lester Aldridge	Application form	Interview + assessment day	2:1	6	133
Lewis Silkin	Online	Interview + assessment day + test	2:1	6	600
Linklaters	Online	2 interviews + tests	2:1	110	4,500
Macfarlanes	Online	Assessment day	2:1	Up to 30	1000
Maclay Murray & Spens	Application form	2 interviews + assessments	2:1	20-25	450
Manches	Online	2 interviews + assessments	2:1	10	850

Applications and Selection

Firm Name	Method of Application	Selection Process	Degree Class	Number of Contracts	Number of Applications
Mayer Brown	Online	Interview + assessments + test	2:1	c. 20	2,000+
Memery Crystal	Online	Interview + assessment centre	2:1	4	300
Michelmores	Online	Assessment days	2:1 preferred	6	200
Mills & Reeve	Online	Assessment centre	2:1	15	c. 850
Mishcon de Reya	Online	Not known	2:1	8-12	1,500+
Morgan Cole	Online	Assessment centre	2:1 preferred	6	Not known
Morgan Lewis & Bockius	Online	Interviews	High 2:1	3	Not known
Muckle	Online	Interviews + assessment day	2:1 preferred	4	230-240
Nabarro	Online	Interview + assessment day	2:1	30	2,000
Norton Rose	Online	Interview + assessments	2:1	55	2,500+
Olswang	Online	Interview + assessments + test	2:1	12	2,000
O'Melveny & Myers	Online	Not known	2:1	Up to 4	Not known
Orrick, Herrington & Sutcliffe	Online	2 interviews	2:1	5	Not known
Pannone	Online	2 interviews	2:1	8	1,200
Paul Hastings	Online	Interview	2:1	3-4	Not known
Penningtons Solicitors	Online	Assessments + interviews	2:1	10-12	1,300
Peters & Peters Solicitors	Application form	Assessment centre + interviews	2:1	2	200
Pinsent Masons	Online	Assessment centre	2:1	80	2,000+
PricewaterhouseCoopers Legal	Online	Not known	2:1	9	Not known
Pritchard Englefield	Application form or online	Interview	2:1 preferred	3	300-400
Reed Smith	Online	Interview + exercise + assessment	2:1	c. 24	1,500
RPC	Online	Interview + assessments	2:1	15	650
SGH Martineau	Online	Mini vac scheme + assessment centre	2:1	10-12	600
Shearman & Sterling	Online	Interviews + assessment centre	2:1	15	900
Sheridans	CV & covering letter	2 interviews	2:1	1	Not known
Shoosmiths	Online	Assessment day	2:1	22	1,600+
Sidley Austin	Online	Interview(s) + test	2:1	10	600
Simmons & Simmons	Online	Online test + assessment day	2:1	c. 40	1,500
SJ Berwin	Online	2 interviews + assessment + test	2:1	40	2,000
Skadden	Online	Interview + exercise	2:1	10-12	1000
Slaughter and May	Online	Interview	2:1	c. 90	c. 2,000
SNR Denton	Online	2 interviews + assessments	2:1	20	1,500

Applications and Selection

Firm Name	Method of Application	Selection Process	Degree Class	Number of Contracts	Number of Applications
Speechly Bircham	Online	Interview + tests	2:1	13	800
Squire Sanders	Online	Interview + assessment	2:1	30	1,500
Stephenson Harwood	Online	Online testing + interview + assessment centre	2:1	16	1,100
Stevens & Bolton	Online	2 interviews + assessments	2:1	4	300
Taylor Wessing	Online	Not known	2:1	c. 22-24	Not known
Thomas Cooper	Online	Interviews + assessments	2:1	4	Not known
TLT	Online	Telephone screening + assessment centre + tests	2:1	Up to 15	c. 700
Travers Smith	Online	2 interviews	2:1	25	2,000
Trethowans	Application form & covering letter	Interview + assessment day	2:1	3-4	100+
Trowers & Hamlins	Online	Interviews + assessment centre + tests	2:1	20	1,500
Veale Wasbrough Vizards	Application form	Interview	2:1 preferred	8-10	Not known
Vinson & Elkins	Online	Interview	2:1	3-4	450
Walker Morris	Online	Interviews + assessment centre	2:1	15	800
Ward Hadaway	Application form	Interview + assessment centre	2:1	10	600+
Watson, Farley & Williams	Online	Interview + assessment centre	2:1	14	700
Wedlake Bell	Application form	2 interviews + open day	2:1	6	Not known
Weil, Gotshal & Manges	Online	Not known	2:1	Up to 14	Not known
White & Case	Online	Interview	2:1	25-30	1,500
Wiggin	Online	Interview + 2 day selection	2:1	3	300
Wilsons Solicitors	Online	Interview + assessment day	2:1	4	Not known
Withers	Online	2 interviews + assessments	2:1	13	700
Wragge & Co	Online	Testing + assessment day	Not known	20	1,000

Salaries and Benefits

Firm Name	1st Year Salary	2nd Year Salary	Sponsorship/ Awards	Other Benefits	Qualification Salary
Addleshaw Goddard	Not known	Not known	GDL & LPC: fees + £7,000 (London) or £4,500 (elsewhere)	Corporate gym m'ship, STL, subsd restaurant, pension, pte healthcare	Not known
Allen & Overy	£38,000	£43,200	GDL: fees + £6,000 (London), £5,000 (elsewhere) LPC: fees + £5,000	Pte healthcare, PMI, in-house medical facilities, STL, gym, music rooms, prayer rooms, subsd restaurant	£61,500
Arnold & Porter	Not known	Not known	GDL + LPC: fees + £8,000	Xmas bonus, child care vouchers, pte healthcare, pte dental, life ass, STL	Not known
Ashfords	£20,000 (regions)	£21,500 (regions)	LPC: £9,000 grant towards LPC	Not known	£31,000 (regions)
Ashurst	£38,000	£43,000	GDL & LPC: fees + £6,500, £500 for first-class degree, language bursaries	Pension, life assurance, STL, subsd gym m'ship, PMI, income protection, in-house medical facilities, restaurant	£61,000
Baker & McKenzie	£38,000 + £3,000 bonus	£43,000	GDL: fees + £6,000 LPC: fees + £8,000	Health ins, life ins, pte medical ins, group pension, subsd gym m'ship, STL, subsd restaurant	£61,500
Bates Wells & Braithwaite	£32,000	£34,000	GDL & LPC: £6,000, interest paid on student loans	STL, subsd gym, subsd restaurant, one month's unpaid leave on qualification, pension	£46,575
Berwin Leighton Paisner	£37,000	£41,000	GDL & LPC: fees + £7,200	Not known	£60,000
Bevan Brittan	Not known	Not known	GDL & LPC: fees + bursary	Not known	Not known
Bingham McCutchen	£40,000	£45,000	GDL & LPC: fees + £8,000	Travel ins, disability ins, STL, life ass, critical illness scheme, subsd gym m'ship, discretionary bonus, PMI	£100,000
Bircham Dyson Bell	£32,000	£33,500	Not known	Bonus scheme, group healthcare, life ass, pension, STL	£52,000
Bird & Bird	£36,000	£38,000	Not known	Not known	£59,000
Bond Pearce	£28,000	£30,000	Not known	Not known	Not known
Boodle Hatfield	£32,750	£34,750	GDL & LPC: fees + maintenance	Pte healthcare, life ass, STL, pension, enhanced maternity pay, childcare vouchers, conveyancing grant, PHI, CTW, EAP	£50,000
B P Collins	£24,000	£25,000	Not known	Not known	Not known

PHI = Permanent Health Insurance; STL = Season Ticket Loan; PMI = Private Medical Insurance; EAP = Employee Assistance Programme; CTW = Cycle to work scheme

Salaries and Benefits

Firm Name	1st Year Salary	2nd Year Salary	Sponsorship/ Awards	Other Benefits	Qualification Salary
Brabners Chaffe Street	No less than £21,000	No less than £21,000	Assistance with LPC funding	Not known	Not known
Bristows	£34,000	£37,000	GDL & LPC: fees + £7,000	Life ass, pension, PMI, PHI, childcare vouchers, EAP, CTW, STL, health assessment	£58,000
Browne Jacobson	£24,500	£25,500	GDL & LPC: fees + £5,000	Life ass, income protection insurance, pension, PMI, corporate discounts	Not known
Burges Salmon	£31,000	£32,000	GDL & LPC: fees + £7,000	Bonus scheme, pension, pte healthcare, life ass, mobile phone, Xmas gift, gym m'ship, sports and social club	£41,000
Capsticks	£29,000	£30,000	GDL & LPC: financial support	Pension, income protection, PMI, life ass, CTW, gym m'ship, childcare vouchers, STL, bonus scheme	£46,000
Charles Russell	£32,500	£33,500	GDL & LPC: fees + £6,000 (London)	Bupa, PHI, life ass, pension, STL	£55,000
Cleary Gottlieb Steen & Hamilton	£40,000	£45,000	GDL & LPC: fees + £8,000	Health club m'ship, pte healthcare (personal & family), life ins, disability ins, EAP, subsd restaurant	£95,000
Clifford Chance	£38,000	£43,000	GDL: fees LPC: fees + maintenance (£4,900 for accelerated LPC)	Subsd restaurant, fitness centre, pension, up to 6 weeks' leave on qual	£61,500
Clyde & Co	£36,000	£38,000	GDL & LPC: fees + £7,000	Pension, life ass, dental ins, PMI, subsd gym m'ship, STL, optional interest free loan, subsd restaurant	£59,000
Cobbetts	£23,695	£25,755	GDL: fees LPC: fees + £5,000	Bupa, gym m'ship, pension, STL, buy-holiday scheme	£31,310
Collyer Bristow	£28,500	£31,500	LPC: fees + £4,000	Not known	Not known
Covington & Burling	£40,000	£44,000	GDL & LPC: fees + £8,000	Pension, PMI, life ass, STL, EAP, PHI	Not known
Cripps Harries Hall	£23,000	£25,000	(Discretionary) LPC fees: 50% interest-free loan, 50% bursary	Not known	£37,500
Davenport Lyons	£33,000 - £33,666	£34,332 - £35,000	No	STL, client intro bonus, subsd gym m'ship, discretionary bonus, life ass, EAP, pension, PHI	Not known

PHI = Permanent Health Insurance; STL = Season Ticket Loan; PMI = Private Medical Insurance; EAP = Employee Assistance Programme; CTW= Cycle to work scheme

Salaries and Benefits

Firm Name	1st Year Salary	2nd Year Salary	Sponsorship/ Awards	Other Benefits	Qualification Salary
Davis Polk & Wardwell	£50,000	£55,000	GDL & LPC: fees + maintenance	PMI, life insurance, pension, STL, subsd gym m'ship, EAP	£100,000
Dechert	£40,000	£45,000	LPC: fees + £10,000	Not known	£61,500
Dickinson Dees	£20,000	£21,000	GDL & LPC: fees + maintenance	Not known	Not known
DLA Piper	£37,000 (London) £22,000 (Regions)	£40,000 (London) £24,000 (Regions)	GDL & LPC: fees + up to £7,000	Not known	£60,000 (London) £37,000 (Regions)
Dundas & Wilson	£30,000 (London)	£33,500 (London)	GDL & LPC: fees + maintenance	Life ass, PHI, pension, STL, holiday purchase scheme	Not known
DWF	£35,000 (London) £25,000 (Regional)	Not known	LPC: fees	Flexible scheme	Not known
Edwards Wildman Palmer	£38,000	£42,000	GDL & LPC: fees + £7,000 (London) or £6,500 (elsewhere)	Bupa, STL, subsd gym, bonus, pension, life ass, subsd cafe, CTW, EAP	£61,000
Eversheds	£36,000 (London) £25,000 (Regions)	£37,000 (London) £26,500 (Regions)	GDL: Fees + £7,000 (London) or £5,000 (Regions) LPC: Fees + £7,000 (London) or £5,000 (Regions)	Not known	NQ Salary £59,000 (London) £36,000 (Regions)
Farrer & Co	£33,000	£36,000	GDL & LPC: fees + £6,000	Flexible scheme	£55,000
Fladgate	£32,000	Not known	Not known	Pension, PHI, life ass, STL, PMI, sports club loan	£52,000
Foot Anstey	£21,500	£23,000	LPC: up to £9,600	Holiday purchase scheme, pension, life ass, CTW, childcare vouchers, free conveyancing	£33,750
Forbes	Not known	£19,500	Not known	Not known	Not known
Freeth Cartwright	£21,500	Not known	Not known	Not known	Not known
Freshfields Bruckhaus Deringer	£39,000	£44,000	GDL & LPC: fees + maintenance	Flexible scheme	£65,000
Gateley	£20,000 - £22,000 (Midlands)	£22,000 - £24,000 (Midlands)	LPC: £5,000	Life ass, STL, library, pvt. health	£32,000 (Midlands)
Gordons	£20,000	£22,000	LPC: £5,000	Pension, life assurance, STL, childcare vouchers, sports club	£34,500

PHI = Permanent Health Insurance; STL = Season Ticket Loan; PMI = Private Medical Insurance; EAP = Employee Assistance Programme; CTW= Cycle to work scheme

Salaries and Benefits

Firm Name	1st Year Salary	2nd Year Salary	Sponsorship/ Awards	Other Benefits	Qualification Salary
Government Legal Service	£23,250 - £25,575	£24,850 - £27,350	LPC and BPTC: fees + £5,000 - £7,000	Pension	£32,000 - £40,000
Harbottle & Lewis	£30,000	£31,000	LPC: fees + interest-free loan	STL, lunch	£50,000
Henmans	£23,000	£25,000	Not known	Pte health care, pension, life ass, EAP, free parking, subsd cafe	Not known
Herbert Smith Freehills	£38,000	£43,000	GDL + LPC: fees + maintenance	Not known	£61,500
Hewitsons	£23,500	£23,500	No	Not known	£35,000
Higgs & Sons	£21,500	£24,000	No	PMI, pension, life ass, BTSS m'ship	£32,000
Hill Dickinson	£32,000 (London) £24,000 (North)	£34,000 (London) £26,000 (North)	LPC: fees + maintenance	Pension, holiday purchase scheme, PHI, life ass, STL, Bupa	Not known
Hogan Lovells	£38,000	£43,000	GDL & LPC: fees + maintenance	PMI, life ass, STL, gym, dentist, GP & physio, subsd restaurant, local retail discounts	£61,000
Holman Fenwick Willan	£36,000	£38,000	Not known	Pension, subsd gym m'ship, STL, life ass, medical ins	£58,000
Ince & Co	£36,000	£39,000	GDL: fees + £6,500 (London & Guildford) or £6,000 (elsewhere) LPC: fees + £7,000 (London & Guildford) or £6,500 (elsewhere)	STL, corporate health cover, pension, subsd gym m'ship, PMI	£58,000
Irwin Mitchell	£22,450	£24,650 (outside London)	GDL & LPC: fees + £4,500	Healthcare, pension, death in service + critical illness cover	Not known
Jones Day	£41,000 increasing to £46,000 after 10 months	£46,000 increasing to £50,000 after 22 months	GDL & LPC: fees + £8,000	Pte healthcare, STL, subsd sports club m'ship, life cover, salary sacrifice scheme, pension	£72,500
Kennedys	£34,000	£37,000	Not known	PHI, pension, PMI, life ins, STL, gym m'ship, CTW, child care assistance, EAP, corporate GP, contribution towards conveyancing fees	£58,000
Kingsley Napley	£28,000	£30,000	Not known	Pte health ins, income protection ins, life ass, pension, corporate cash plan	£49,000

PHI = Permanent Health Insurance; STL = Season Ticket Loan; PMI = Private Medical Insurance; EAP = Employee Assistance Programme; CTW= Cycle to work scheme

Salaries and Benefits

Firm Name	1st Year Salary	2nd Year Salary	Sponsorship/ Awards	Other Benefits	Qualification Salary
Kirkland & Ellis	£41,000	£44,000	GDL & LPC: fees + £7,500	PMI, travel ins, life ins, EAP, gym m'ship	Not known
K&L Gates	£35,000	£38,000	GDL: fees + £5,000 LPC: fees + £7,000	Subsd sports club m'ship, STL, life ass, pension, PHI, GP service	£60,000
Latham & Watkins	£42,000	£45,000	GDL & LCP: fees + £8,000 + £500 for LPC distinction	Healthcare & dental, pension, life ass	£96,970
Lawrence Graham	£35,000	Not known	GDL & LPC: fees + £6,500 (London) £6,000 (elsewhere)	STL, life ass	£57,000
Lewis Silkin	£32,500	£34,500	GDL & LPC: fees + £5,000	Life ass, health ins, STL, pension, subsd gym m'ship, bonus, income protection	Up to £52,000
Linklaters	£39,000	Not known	GDL & LPC: fees + maintenance	Bonus, pensions, PMI, life ass, income protection, STL and others	£61,500 + discretionary bonus
Macfarlanes	£38,000	£43,000	GDL & LPC: fees + £7,000	Life ass, pension, pte healthcare, STL, bonus, childcare vouchers and others	£61,000
Maclay Murray & Spens	£32,000 (London)	Not known	Not known	Pension, death-in-service benefit, income protection, discounted medical/ dental plans and others	Not known
Manches	Not known	Not known	GDL & LPC: fees + £5,000	STL, Bupa, PHI, life ins, pension	Not known
Mayer Brown	£37,500	£42,300	GDL & LPC: fees + £7,000	STL, sports club m'ship, pte health	Not known
Memery Crystal	£30,000	£32,000	GDL & LPC: fees	Bonus, life ass, health cover, travel ins, STL, pension, subsd gym m'ship, CTW	Not known
Michelmores	£20,000	£21,000	LPC: fees up to £8,000	Pension, subsd restaurant, subsd gym with personal trainer, free parking	£33,000
Mills & Reeve	£23,000	£24,000	GDL & LPC: fees + maintenance	Life ass, pension, bonus, sports and social club, STL, subsd restaurant	Not known

PHI = Permanent Health Insurance; STL = Season Ticket Loan; PMI = Private Medical Insurance; EAP = Employee Assistance Programme; CTW= Cycle to work scheme

Salaries and Benefits

Firm Name	1st Year Salary	2nd Year Salary	Sponsorship/ Awards	Other Benefits	Qualification Salary
Mishcon de Reya	£32,000	Not known	GDL & LPC: fees + £5,000	Health screening, life ass, dental ins, PMI, travel ins, critical illness cover, gym m'ship, STL, pension, yoga, childcare, CTW, in-house doctor, bonus and others	Not known
Morgan Cole	Not known	Not known	GDL & LPC: fees	Not known	Not known
Morgan, Lewis & Bockius	£40,000	£43,000	GDL & LPC: fees + £7,500	Life ins, health ins, dental ins, disability ins, STL, travel ins	£75,000
Muckle	£22,000	Not known	LPC: fees subject to eligibility	Pension, PHI, life ass, corporate discounts, salary sacrifice scheme, car parking discount	£33,000
Nabarro	£37,000 (London) £25,000 (Sheffield)	£40,000 (London) £28,000 (Sheffield)	GDL & LPC: fees + (or 50% retrospectively) £6,000 (London GDL) £5,000 (Regions GDL) £7,000 (London LPC) £6,000 (Regions LPC)	PMI, pensions, STL, subsd restaurant, subsd gym m'ship	£59,000 (London) £38,000 (Sheffield)
Norton Rose	£37,000	£41,500	Not known	Life ass, STL, CTW, company car scheme, subsd gym m'ship, EAP, pension, subsd restaurant	Not known
Olswang	£37,000	£41,500	GDL & LPC: fees + £7,000 (London) £6,500 (outside)	Life cover, medical/dental schemes, subsd gym m'ship, subsd restaurant, STL, pension, PHI	£59,000
O'Melveny & Myers	£40,000	£43,000	GDL & LPC: fees + £7,000	Pension, life ass, long term disability ins, travel ins, STL (interest free), corporate rate gym m'ship, pvt health ins	Not known
Orrick, Herrington & Sutcliffe	£38,000	£42,500	GDL & LPC: fees + £7,000	Pension, health ins, subsd gym m'ship, STL, PMI, dental care, childcare voucher scheme	Not known
Pannone	£24,000	£26,000	LPC+: grant for fees	Not known	£35,000
Paul Hastings	£40,000	£45,000	GDL & LPC: fee sponsorship + maintenance	Pte healthcare, life ass, pension, STL, gym subsd	£88,000

PHI = Permanent Health Insurance; STL = Season Ticket Loan; PMI = Private Medical Insurance; EAP = Employee Assistance Programme; CTW= Cycle to work scheme

Salaries and Benefits

Firm Name	1st Year Salary	2nd Year Salary	Sponsorship/ Awards	Other Benefits	Qualification Salary
Penningtons Solicitors	£31,000 (London)	£33,000 (London)	LPC: fees + £5,000	Life ass, critical illness cover, pension, PMI, STL	£47,000 (London)
Peters & Peters	£35,000	£38,000	Not known	Pension, Bupa, STL, subsd gym m'ship, life ass, childcare vouchers, CTW	£50,000
PricewaterhouseCoopers Legal	£30,000	£35,000	GDL & LPC: scholarship for fees + maintenance	Not known	Not known
Pritchard Englefield	Not known	Not known	LPC: fees	PMI, STL, lunch vouchers	Not known
Reed Smith	£37,000	Not known	GDL: fees + £6,000 LPC: fees + £7,000	Pension, life ins, STL, bonus, subsd restaurant, conveyancing allowance, pvt health ins, CTW	£59,000 + bonus
RPC	£37,000	£40,000	GDL & LPC: fees + up to £7,000	Not known	£58,000
SGH Martineau	c. £23,000	c. £25,000	Not known	Not known	£36,000
Shearman & Sterling	£39,000	£40,500	GDL & LPC: fees + £7,000	Life ass, long term disability ins, pension, subsd gym m'ship, PMI, travel ins, dental ins	£78,000
Shoosmiths	£24,000	£25,000	GDL & LPC: assistance + maintenance	Pension, life ass, corporate discounts	£36,500
Sidley Austin	£39,000	£43,000	GDL & LPC: fees + £7,000	Life ass, contribution to gym m'ship, STL, income protection scheme, pension, subsd restaurant, pte health ins	Not known
Simmons & Simmons	£37,500	£41,750	GDL & LPC: fees + £7,500	Not known	£59,000
SJ Berwin	£37,500	£41,500	Not known	Pte healthcare, subsd gym m'ship, life ass, pension, STL, lunch	£59,000
Skadden	£40,000	£43,000	GDL & LPC: fees + £8,000	Life ins, pte health ins, travel ins, subsd gym m'ship, technology budget, EAP, PMI, subsd restaurant	Not known
Slaughter and May	£38,000	£43,000	GDL & LPC: fees + maintenance	PMI, STL, pension, interest-free loan, subsd gym m'ship, accident cover, CTW and others	£61,500

PHI = Permanent Health Insurance; STL = Season Ticket Loan; PMI = Private Medical Insurance; EAP = Employee Assistance Programme; CTW= Cycle to work scheme

Salaries and Benefits

Firm Name	1st Year Salary	2nd Year Salary	Sponsorship/ Awards	Other Benefits	Qualification Salary
SNR Denton	£37,000 (London) £25,500 (Milton Keynes)	£40,000 (London) £27,500 (Milton Keynes)	GDL & LPC: fees + £7,000 (London) £6,000 (Regions)	Sports club m'ship allowance, pte health ins, STL and others	£59,000
Speechly Bircham	£33,000	£35,000	GDL & LPC: fees + maintenance	PMI, life ass, pension, STL, subsd restaurant, corporate discount gym m'ship	£56,000
Squire Sanders	£35,000 (London) £23,500 (Regions)	£37,000 (London) £26,000 (Regions)	GDL & LPC: fees + £6,000 (GDL London) £4,500 (GDL Regions) £7,000 (LPC London) £5,000 (LPC Regions)	Flexible: pension, life ass, subsd gym m'ship, STL	£58,000 (London) £37,000 (Regions)
Stephenson Harwood	£37,000	£40,000	GDL & LPC: fees + maintenance up to £6,000	Subsd gym m'ship, pte health ins, pension, life ass, private GP, critical illness cover, dental ins, STL and others	£60,000
Stevens & Bolton	£30,000	Not known	GDL & LPC: fees (College of Law, Guildford) + £4,000	Pension, private healthcare, life ass, PHI, loan for travel or car parking	Not known
Sullivan & Cromwell	£50,000	£55,000	GDL & LPC: fees + maintenance	Pte health ins, dental ins, life ins, travel ins, pension, subsd gym m'ship and more	£97,500
Taylor Wessing	£37,000	£41,000	GDL & LPC: fees (BPP London) + maintenance	Not known	£60,000
Thomas Cooper	£33,000	£36,500	LPC: fees	PMI, life ass, PHI, pension, loan for dental ins, STL, loan for gym m'ship	Not known
TLT	Not known	Not known	GDL & LPC: fees + maintenance	Flexible scheme	Not known
Travers Smith	£38,000	£43,000	GDL & LPC: fees + £7,000 (London) £6,500 (Regions)	PHI, life ass, subsd bistro, STL, pte health ins, CTW	£61,000
Trethowans	Not known	Not known	LPC: fees	Pension, death in service benefit, PHI, bonus, car parking, new recruit bonus, childcare vouchers, EAP	Not known
Trowers & Hamlins	£35,000	£38,000	GDL & LPC: fees + maintenance	Not known	£55,000
Veale Wasbrough Vizards	£23,000	£25,000	LPC: fees + interest-free loan	Not known	£35,000
Vinson & Elkins	£40,000	£42,000	GDL & LPC: fees + up to £7,500 (LPC)	Private medical and dental, pension, STL, life ass	£80,000
Walker Morris	£24,000	£26,000	GDL & LPC: fees + £5,000	Not known	£36,000

PHI = Permanent Health Insurance; STL = Season Ticket Loan; PMI = Private Medical Insurance; EAP = Employee Assistance Programme; CTW= Cycle to work scheme

Salaries and Benefits

Firm Name	1st Year Salary	2nd Year Salary	Sponsorship/ Awards	Other Benefits	Qualification Salary
Ward Hadaway	£20,000 (Newcastle) £23,000 (Leeds)	£20,500 (Newcastle) £23,500 (Leeds)	GDL & LPC: fees + maintenance	Flexible: death in service ins, pension, travel scheme	£32,000
Watson, Farley & Williams	£35,000	£40,000	GDL & LPC: fees + £6,500/£5,500 (dependent on location)	Income protection scheme, life ass, EAP, pension, STL, subsd healthcare m'ship	£62,000
Wedlake Bell	Not known	Not known	LPC: funding available	Pension, travel loans, gym m'ship, health insurance, life ass	Not known
Weil Gotshal & Manges	£41,000	Not known	Not known	Not known	Not known
White & Case	£41,000 - £42,000	£43,000 - £44,000	GDL & LPC: fees + maintenance + awards for commendation and distinction on LPC	Flexible: PMI, dental ins, life ass, pension, critical illness ins, travel ins, STL and others	£70,000
Wiggin	£32,000	£36,000	GDL & LPC: fees + £6,000	Life ass, pte health cover, pension, PHI, gym m'ship	£55,000
Wilsons	Not known	Not known	Not known	Pension, life ass, PMI, optional benefits	Not known
Withers	£34,000	£36,000	GDL & LPC: fees + £5,000	Not known	£56,000
Wragge & Co	£35,750 (London) £26,250 (Birmingham)	£38,750 (London) £29,250 (Birmingham)	GDL & LPC: fees + maintenance + prizes for first class degree, and distinction GDL/LPC	Pension, life ass, PHI, PMI and others	£58,000 (London) £38,000 (Birmingham)

PHI = Permanent Health Insurance; STL = Season Ticket Loan; PMI = Private Medical Insurance; EAP = Employee Assistance Programme; CTW= Cycle to work scheme

"We're increasingly seeing clients around the world wanting to use English law over US law. That means opportunities for trainees and associates to go abroad will multiply correspondingly."

US firm training partner

Picking a firm for its overseas opportunities

The idea of the international law firm is far from new; UK firms have ventured overseas since the 19th century. What has changed is the number of firms with offices overseas and the increasing desire to plant flags around the globe.

Big firms are canny operators. They understand that thriving in a competitive international legal market requires a network of overseas offices (or relationships with overseas firms) in regions with strong economic growth. China and the Far East are of real interest at present, as are Central and Eastern Europe, the Middle East, Africa and resource-rich parts of Central Asia. Despite its economic draws, India has so far avoided invasions due to its strict Bar Association rules. The downturn in the world economy has, largely, not dampened this thirst for expansion, with firms becoming ever more determined to invest in developing countries where growth has been affected less. The global recession did, however, see some of the magic circle firms retreating in regions such as CEE (which got the former Linklaters offices clubbing together, doing a funky anagram and forming Kinstellar). It's all about following the money and building a presence in the jurisdictions big business clients are hoping to exploit or are already exploiting.

Wherever possible, we've mentioned the main changes from the past year in our True Picture reports. Anglo-American mergers seem to be particularly in vogue – Hammonds, Lovells and Denton Wilde Sapte have all secured transatlantic tie-ups in recent years, while others like Simmons & Simmons and SJ Berwin have openly courted, but so far failed to bag, an American suitor. Several firms – Ashurst, Norton Rose, Clifford Chance, DLA Piper, and most recently Herbert Smith – have made similar gestures towards the Australian market.

There is no question that practising abroad does make your CV shine. So if you're set on squeezing some international work into your training contract, the next step is considering where, and picking a firm where you can be certain of securing an overseas posting. Of course, competition for seats can get tough, and not all firms can guarantee opportunities abroad ahead of time, but the True Picture reports should give you a better idea of where your luck lies. An important thing to bear in mind is language capability – some firms earmark their fluent Russian speakers for Moscow, regardless of whether they'd prefer to head to New York. But let's not get ahead of ourselves here. Language skills in general are undeniably attractive to recruiters. International private client firm Withers, for example, likes to enlist a few fluent Italian speakers in each intake to fill its coveted corporate seat in Milan.

Although time abroad gives you experience of working in another jurisdiction, chances are you won't actually practise foreign law. For UK firms at least, your overseas outpost will be smaller than your home office, so you're likely to receive a greater amount of responsibility. Securing the most popular overseas seats often involves waging a campaign of self-promotion back at home.

Overseas trainees need not worry about feeling isolated in their host country as the local lawyers and staff invariably give a warm welcome to newcomers. In cities with a large influx of UK trainees there's usually a ready-made social scene, so it's likely the first thing to pop up in your inbox will be an invitation to meet other new arrivals. In Singapore, it's not unheard of for trainees to jet off for group weekends on Malaysian or Indonesian islands, while those in Brussels benefit from their proximity to the vast EU machine and all its festive offerings. Another big plus is free accommodation on the firm. Trainees are usually housed in centrally located private apartments. In fact, it may be some time before they can afford such plush digs and domestic perks back home. For more on life as a trainee in an overseas seat, check out our website where we report from the most frequented training locations around the world.

The following table outlines exactly where the overseas seat opportunities are this year. As for international work back in the UK, the nature of a firm's clientèle and worldwide office footprint play a big factor in determining what trainees do day to day. At White & Case there's a considerable amount of project finance work conducted in conjunction with Eastern European offices, while SNR Denton's energy and natural resources work across Africa and the Middle East rakes in heaps of work for London lawyers. Likewise, Trowers & Hamlins' predominance in Islamic finance keeps its City side busy, as do Wiggin's and Lawrence Graham's respective relationships with major film studios in Los Angeles and Indian financial institutions. See our True Picture reports for more details on each.

Overseas seats: Who goes where?

Location	Firm
Abu Dhabi	Allen & Overy, Berwin Leighton Paisner, Clifford Chance, DLA Piper, Herbert Smith Freehills, Linklaters, Norton Rose, Shearman & Sterling, Simmons & Simmons, SNR Denton, Trowers & Hamlins, Vinson & Elkins, White & Case
Almaty	White & Case
Amsterdam	Allen & Overy, Clifford Chance, DLA Piper, Freshfields Bruckhaus Deringer, Linklaters, Norton Rose, Slaughter and May
Athens	Norton Rose
Auckland	Slaughter and May
Bahrain	Charles Russell, Norton Rose, Trowers & Hamlins
Bangkok	Allen & Overy, DLA Piper, Watson Farley & Williams
Barcelona	Slaughter and May
Beijing	Allen & Overy, Clifford Chance, Norton Rose, Vinson & Elkins, White & Case
Berlin	Freshfields Bruckhaus Deringer, Linklaters
Brussels	Allen & Overy, Arnold & Porter, Ashurst, Baker & McKenzie, Berwin Leighton Paisner, Bird & Bird, Clifford Chance, Dechert, Dickinson Dees, Freshfields Bruckhaus Deringer, Herbert Smith Freehills, Hogan Lovells, Holman Fenwick Willan, Linklaters, McDermott Will & Emery, Olswang, Shearman & Sterling, Sidley Austin, SJ Berwin, Slaughter and May, Squire Sanders, White & Case
Bucharest	CMS Cameron McKenna
Budapest	Allen & Overy, CMS Cameron McKenna
Chicago	Baker & McKenzie
Dubai	Allen & Overy, Ashurst, Clifford Chance, DLA Piper, Freshfields Bruckhaus Deringer, Herbert Smith Freehills, Hogan Lovells, Holman Fenwick Willan, Jones Day, Latham & Watkins, Lawrence Graham, Linklaters, Norton Rose, Pinsent Masons, Simmons & Simmons, SNR Denton, SJ Berwin, Trowers & Hamlins, Vinson & Elkins
Dublin	Dechert
Falkland Islands	Pinsent Masons
Frankfurt	Allen & Overy, Ashurst, Clifford Chance, Freshfields Bruckhaus Deringer, Linklaters, SJ Berwin, White & Case
Geneva	Charles Russell, Holman Fenwick Willan, Withers
Guangzhou	Wragge & Co
Helsinki	Bird & Bird, Slaughter and May
Hong Kong	Allen & Overy, Ashurst, Baker & McKenzie, Cleary Gottlieb Steen & Hamilton, Clifford Chance, DLA Piper, Eversheds, Freshfields Bruckhaus Deringer, Herbert Smith Freehills, Hogan Lovells, Holman Fenwick Willan, Latham & Watkins, Kennedys, Kirkland & Ellis, Linklaters, Mayer Brown, Norton Rose, Pinsent Masons, Simmons & Simmons, Shearman & Sterling, SJ Berwin, Skadden, Slaughter and May, Stephenson Harwood, Vinson & Elkins, White & Case, Withers
Istanbul	Allen & Overy, DLA Piper
Johannesburg	White & Case
Kyiv	CMS Cameron McKenna
Madrid	Allen & Overy, Ashurst, Bird & Bird, Clifford Chance, Linklaters, SJ Berwin, Slaughter and May, Thomas Cooper
Melbourne	Holman Fenwick Willan
Milan	Allen & Overy, Ashurst, Bird & Bird, Clifford Chance, Linklaters, Norton Rose, Slaughter and May, Withers
Moscow	Allen & Overy, Baker & McKenzie, Berwin Leighton Paisner, Clifford Chance, CMS Cameron McKenna, DLA Piper, Herbert Smith Freehills, Latham & Watkins, Linklaters, Skadden, White & Case

Overseas seats: Who goes where?

Location	Firm
Munich	Clifford Chance, CMS Cameron McKenna, Norton Rose, Slaughter and May
Muscat	Trowers & Hamlins
New York	Allen & Overy, Cleary Gottlieb Steen & Hamilton, Clifford Chance, Freshfields Bruckhaus Deringer, Hogan Lovells, Kirkland & Ellis, Latham & Watkins, Mayer Brown, Shearman & Sterling, Slaughter and May, Weil Gotshal & Manges, White & Case
Oslo	Slaughter and May
Paris	Allen & Overy, Ashurst, Clifford Chance, Eversheds, Freshfields Bruckhaus Deringer, Herbert Smith Freehills, Hogan Lovells, Holman Fenwick Willan, Ince & Co, Latham & Watkins, Linklaters, Mayer Brown, McDermott Will & Emery, Norton Rose, Simmons & Simmons, SJ Berwin, Slaughter and May, Squire Sanders, Travers Smith, Watson Farley & Williams, White & Case
Perth	Norton Rose
Piraeus	Hill Dickinson, Holman Fenwick Willan, Thomas Cooper, Watson Farley & Williams
Prague	Allen & Overy, Clifford Chance, CMS Cameron McKenna, White & Case
Rio de Janeiro	CMS Cameron McKenna
Rome	Allen & Overy
Sao Paulo	Clifford Chance
Shanghai	Allen & Overy, Clifford Chance, Eversheds, Freshfields Bruckhaus Deringer, Ince & Co, Linklaters, Norton Rose
Singapore	Allen & Overy, Ashurst, Berwin Leighton Paisner, Clifford Chance, DLA Piper, Herbert Smith Freehills, Hill Dickinson, Hogan Lovells, Holman Fenwick Willan, Latham & Watkins, Linklaters, Norton Rose, Shearman & Sterling, Stephenson Harwood, Watson Farley & Williams, White & Case
Sofia	CMS Cameron McKenna
Stockholm	Bird & Bird, Slaughter and May
Sydney	Allen & Overy, Ashurst, Baker & McKenzie, DLA Piper, Holman Fenwick Willan, Norton Rose, Slaughter and May
Tokyo	Allen & Overy, Ashurst, Baker & McKenzie, Clifford Chance, Freshfields Bruckhaus Deringer, Herbert Smith Freehills, Linklaters, Morrison & Foerster, Norton Rose, Simmons & Simmons, Slaughter and May, Vinson & Elkins, White & Case
Toulouse	SNR Denton
Vienna	CMS Cameron McKenna
Warsaw	Bird & Bird, Clifford Chance, CMS Cameron McKenna
Washington, DC	Cleary Gottlieb Steen & Hamilton, Freshfields Bruckhaus Deringer

Note: The availability of overseas secondments is liable to change year by year, so if you have your heart set on a particular destination do check with firms before committing to them.

- **Exclusive to chambersstudent.co.uk: for the first time we bring you law firm diversity surveys.**
Visit the website to find out more.

A-Z of Solicitors

Addleshaw Goddard

Milton Gate, 60 Chiswell St, London EC1Y 4AG
Sovereign House, PO Box 8, Sovereign Street, Leeds LS1 1HQ
100 Barbirolli Square, Manchester M2 3AB
Website: www.addleshawgoddard.com/graduates

Firm profile

As a major force on the legal landscape, Addleshaw Goddard offers extensive and exciting opportunities to all its trainees across the entire spectrum of commercial law, from employment and banking to real estate, corporate finance, intellectual property, employment, PFI and litigation. As a trainee with this firm, you'll be a key member of the team from day one. Wherever you are based, you'll work closely with bluechip clients within a supportive yet challenging environment, and be part of a structured training programme designed to ensure your success – now and in the future.

Main areas of work

The firm has five main business divisions: finance and projects, litigation, commercial services, corporate and real estate. Within these divisions as well as the main practice areas it also has specialist areas such as intellectual property, employment and private client services such as trusts and tax.

Trainee profile

Graduates who are capable of achieving a 2:1 and can demonstrate commercial awareness, teamwork, motivation and drive. Applications from law and non-law graduates are welcomed, as are applications from students who may be considering a change of direction. We also have a Legal access scheme for applicants on GDL or LPC with less conventional academic backgrounds. Further details can be found on our website.

Training environment

During each six-month seat, there will be regular two-way performance reviews with the supervising partner or solicitor. Trainees have the opportunity to spend a seat in one of the firm's other offices and there are a number of secondments to clients available. Seated with a qualified solicitor or partner and working as part of a team enables trainees to develop the professional skills necessary to deal with the demanding and challenging work the firm carries out for its clients. Practical training is complemented by high-quality training courses provided by both the in-house team and external training providers.

Sponsorship & benefits

GDL and LPC fees are paid, plus a maintenance grant of £7,000 (London) or £4,500 (elsewhere in the UK). Benefits include corporate gym membership, season ticket loan, subsidised restaurant, pension and private healthcare.

Vacation placements

Places for 2013 – 80; Duration – 1 or 2 weeks; Location – all offices; Apply by 31 January 2013.

Interviews for our vacation schemes start early January.

Partners 160	
Associates 500+	
Trainees 70	

Contact
grad@addleshawgoddard.com

Closing date for 2015
31 July 2013
Interviews for our training contracts start in early June.

Application
Training contracts p.a. 35
Applications p.a. 2,000
% interviewed 8%
Required degree grade 2:1

Overseas Offices
In 2012 opened up an office in Singapore with an office in Dubai set to open later this year

ADDLESHAW GODDARD

Allen & Overy LLP

One Bishops Square, London E1 6AD
Tel: (020) 3088 0000 Fax: (020) 3088 0088
Email: graduate.recruitment@allenovery.com
Website: www.allenovery.com/careeruk

Firm profile

Allen & Overy LLP is an international legal practice with approximately 5,000 people working across 42 major centres worldwide. The firm's client list includes many of the world's top businesses, financial institutions and governments.

Main areas of work

Banking, corporate, international capital markets, litigation and dispute resolution, tax, employment and benefits and real estate. Allen & Overy partners frequently lead the field in their particular areas of law and the firm can claim both an enviable reputation amongst clients and unrivalled success in major deals.

Training contracts

We recruit 90 trainee solicitors each year across two intakes (March and September).

Final year non-law undergraduates and graduates can apply from 1st November 2012 to 15th January 2013. From 1st June 2013 to 31st July 2013, penultimate year law undergraduates and graduates can apply. We are currently recruiting for our March/September 2015 intakes.

Trainee profile

You will need to demonstrate a genuine enthusiasm for a legal career and Allen & Overy. The firm looks for a strong, consistent academic performance and you should have achieved or be predicted at least a 2:1 degree (or equivalent). At Allen & Overy you will be working in a team where you will use your initiative and manage your own time and workload, so evidence of teamwork, leadership and problem solving skills are also looked for.

Training environment

Allen & Overy offers a training contract characterised by flexibility and choice. The seat structure ensures that you get to see as many parts of the firm as possible and that your learning is hands-on, guided by an experienced associate or partner. Your choice of a priority seat is guaranteed unless exceptional business needs or other extenuating circumstances arise. Given the strength of the firm's international finance practice, trainees are required to spend a minimum of 12 months in at least two of the three core departments of banking, corporate and international capital markets. The firm offers its trainees the option of completing a litigation course. This means that trainees do not need to spend time in the firm's litigation and dispute resolution department to gain their contentious experience if they are sure their interests lie elsewhere. There are also opportunities for trainees to undertake an international or client secondment during their final year of training.

Vacation placements

Allen & Overy offers 60 vacation placements across the year. The winter placement is for finalists and graduates who should apply from 1st October to 31st October 2012. Summer placements are for penultimate year undergraduates who should apply from 1st November 2012 to 15th January 2013.

Benefits

Private healthcare, private medical insurance, in-house medical facilities, interest-free season ticket loan, free in-house gym, subsidised staff restaurants, multi-faith prayer rooms and music rooms.

Sponsorship & awards

GDL and LPC course fees are paid in full along with contributions towards your maintenance costs. For the Allen & Overy LPC, a £5,000 maintenance grant is provided. For the GDL, £6,000 is provided in London and £5,000 elsewhere. Financial incentives are also offered to future trainees achieving a first class undergraduate degree and/or a distinction in the LPC.

Partners 512 worldwide
Associates 1901 worldwide
London Trainees 220

Contact
Graduate Recruitment

Method of application
Online application form

Selection procedure
Interview

Closing date for 2015
Non law candidates
15 January 2013
Law candidates 31 July 2013

Application
Training contracts p.a. 90
Applications p.a. 2,500
% interviewed p.a. 8-10%
Required degree grade 2:1
(or equivalent)

Training
Salary
£38,000 – Year 1
£43,200 – Year 2
£61,500 – NQ
Holiday entitlement 25 days
% of trainees with a
non-law degree p.a. 45%
No. of seats available
in international offices
36 seats twice a year;
9 client secondments

Post-qualification
Salary £61,500 (2012)
% of trainees offered job
on qualification 83%
% of partners who joined as
trainees over 50%

International offices
Abu Dhabi, Amsterdam, Antwerp, Athens, Bangkok, Beijing, Belfast, Bratislava, Brussels, Budapest, Bucharest*, Casablanca, Doha, Dubai, Dusseldorf, Frankfurt, Hamburg, Hanoi, Ho Chi Minh City, Hong Kong, Istanbul, Jakarta*, London, Luxembourg, Madrid, Mannheim, Milan, Moscow, Munich, New York, Paris, Perth, Prague, Riyadh*, Rome, Sao Paulo, Shanghai, Singapore, Sydney, Tokyo, Warsaw, Washington DC.
* associated office

Arnold & Porter (UK) LLP

Tower 42, 25 Old Broad Street, London, EC2N 1HQ
Tel: (020) 7786 6100 Fax: (020) 7786 6299
Email: graduates@aporter.com Website: www.arnoldporter.com

Firm profile
Arnold & Porter is a US-based firm with a deserved reputation for its quality of service and expertise in handling the most complex legal and business problems requiring innovative and practical solutions. The firm's global reach, experience and deep knowledge allows it to work across geographic, cultural, technological and ideological borders, serving clients whose business needs require US, EU or cross-border regulatory, litigation and transactional services.

Main areas of work
The London office is home to the firm's European regulatory, life sciences, IP, competition, corporate, white collar crime, international arbitration, employment and telecoms practices. Chambers UK recently ranked its London office as a top ranked leading firm in EU Competition, Intellectual Property, Media and Entertainment, Corporate: M&A, Life Sciences, Product Liability, Telecommunications and Retail.

Trainee profile
The firm looks for talented law and non-law graduates from all backgrounds who share the firm's commitment to excellence, and want to be part of the continued growth of its London office. Candidates need to demonstrate a consistently high academic background; the firm looks for well-rounded individuals who can demonstrate their participation in a range of extra-curricular activities and achievements.

Training environment
Four six-month seats: pharmaceuticals, IP, corporate and securities, competition, international arbitration or white collar crime. The firm encourages individuals to work across specialisms, and emphasises teamwork, so trainees may find that whilst they are working in one group, they undertake work in a variety of different areas throughout the firm. Trainees will be expected to work on several matters at once, and assume responsibility at an early stage. Trainees may also have an opportunity to work in the firm's Brussels office and where the occasion permits, to work on projects in one of the firm's US offices.

An important aspect of the firm's culture is its commitment to pro bono. Trainees and all lawyers at the firm are encouraged to take part and devote 15% of their time to it, which helps young lawyers develop client management skills from an early stage.

Vacation schemes
The firm takes eight summer vacation students each year. Whether you are a law or non-law student, the firm will introduce you to life in a busy City law firm, spending two weeks working on a variety of projects and workshops with partners and associates throughout the London office. Apply via the firm's website by 1 March 2013.

Benefits
Healthy incentive bonus, Christmas bonus, child care vouchers, private health insurance, private dental insurance, life assurance, season ticket loan.

Sponsorship & awards
GDL/LPC: fees paid; £8,000 per course maintenance.

Partners 20
Assistant Solicitors 22
Total Trainees 2

Contact
Graduate Recruitment

Method of application
Apply via website

Selection procedure
Interview with partners and associates; written assessment

Closing date for 2015
2 August 2013

Application
Training contracts p.a. 2
Applications p.a 700
% interviewed 2%
Required degree grade 2:1

Training salary
1st year US firm market rate
2nd year US firm market rate
Holiday entitlement 25 days

Post-qualification
% of trainees offered job on qualification 100%

Overseas, regional offices
London, Washington DC, New York, Los Angeles, Denver, Northern Virginia, San Francisco, Silicon Valley, Brussels

ARNOLD & PORTER (UK)LLP

Ashfords LLP

Grenadier Road, Exeter EX1 3LH
Tel: (01392) 333634
Email: GraduateRecruitment@ashfords.co.uk
Website: www.ashfords.co.uk

Firm profile

Ashfords is a major regional law firm offering a full service. Our clients range from international companies to start-ups, and from the public sector to private individuals. We are highly regarded for our high profile, 'city' quality work and, combined with our recent expansion into London, we have ambitious plans for the future.

Our core commercial practice areas of Corporate, Property and Commercial Litigation are supplemented by specialists in areas including Employment, Projects, Intellectual Property and Information Technology. Cross firm sector teams include Energy, Marine and Education. Our Private Client services include Family, Trusts and Estates and Equity Release.

Trainee profile

We don't care where you come from, what degree you did or what you look like as long as you are passionate about a career at Ashfords, are confident, a creative thinker with excellent communication skills and a strong academic background.

Training environment

Your training contract will comprise of four six-month seats. Seats are allocated following a face to face trainee meeting with our Trainee Recruitment Manager to ensure that your training contract is structured to suit you. We expect trainees to complete seats in three of our four core areas of Commercial, Property, Litigation and Private Client.

Seats are available in our Bristol, Exeter, London and Taunton offices and as our training contract is not location based your seats may be in any or all of these locations.

We'll give you as much hands-on experience as possible from the start of your training contract as we believe it is a critical part of your training contract. You will have the full support of your supervisor and other lawyers in your team.

We're proud to have been voted a 2012 Guardian UK 300 employer by students and graduates in the UK.

Benefits

Pension scheme (5% employer contribution), life assurance, holiday purchase scheme, childcare voucher scheme, access to corporate rates and discounts, cycle scheme, free legal services.

Sponsorship

£9,000 grant available towards your LPC.

Partners 73
Total Fee Earners 261

Contact
Jess Morris
01392 33 36 34

Method of application
Online application form

Selection procedure
Assessment centre, including group exercises and interviews

Closing date for 2015
Vacation Scheme & Training Contract 31 March 2013
Training Contract only 1 July 2013

Application
No. of training contracts pa 10-12
Applications per annum 400
% interviewed 10%
Required degree grade 2:1

Training
Basic Starting Salary (2012) £20,000 (London uplift will apply)
Holiday Entitlement 30 days

Post Qualification
NQ basic salary (2012) £31,000 (Bristol and London uplift will apply)

Offices
Bristol, Exeter, London, Plymouth, Taunton and Tiverton

Ashfords Solicitors
Incorporating
ROCHMAN LANDAU

Ashurst LLP

Broadwalk House, 5 Appold St, London EC2A 2HA
Tel: (020) 7638 1111 Fax: (020) 7638 1112
Email: gradrec@ashurst.com
Website: www.ashurst.com/trainees
Facebook: www.facebook.com/AshurstTrainees

Firm profile

Ashurst is a leading international law firm advising corporates, financial institutions and governments, with core businesses in corporate, finance, energy, resources and infrastructure. In March 2012, Ashurst and Blake Dawson combined forces to form one global team under the Ashurst brand. We have 24 offices in 14 countries as well as an associated office in Jakarta and a best-friend referral relationship with an Indian law firm.

Main areas of work

Competition and EU law; corporate; employment, incentives and pensions; energy, transport and infrastructure; international finance; dispute resolution; real estate; tax; and technology.

Trainee profile

To become an Ashurst trainee you will need to show common sense and good judgement. The firm needs to know that you can handle responsibility because you will be involved in some of the highest quality international work on offer anywhere. The transactions and cases you will be involved in will be intellectually demanding, so Ashurst looks for high academic achievers who are able to think laterally. But it's not just academic results that matter. Ashurst wants people who have a range of interests outside of their studies. And they want outgoing people with a sense of humour who know how to laugh at themselves.

Training environment

Your training contract will consist of four seats. For each, you will sit with a partner or senior solicitor who will be the main source of your work and your principal supervisor during that seat. Seats are generally for six months. Anything less than that will not give you sufficient depth of experience for the responsibility Ashurst expects you to take on. The firm asks trainees to spend one seat in the corporate department and one seat in the international finance department. Trainees spend their two remaining seats in the firm's other practice areas, on secondment to a client or on secondment to an overseas office.

Benefits

Private medical cover, pension, life assurance, income protection, interest-free season ticket loan, in-house medical facilities, subsidised gym membership and staff restaurant and 25 days holiday per year during training.

Vacation placements

Places for 2013: A spring placement scheme primarily aimed at final-year non-law undergraduates and all graduates. Two summer placement schemes primarily aimed at penultimate-year law undergraduates. Remuneration £275 p.w. Apply from 1st November 2012-15th January 2013.

Sponsorship & awards

GDL and LPC funding plus maintenance allowances of £6,500 per annum. First class degree awards of £500 and language tuition bursaries.

Partners 400
Assistant Solicitors 1700
Total Trainees 100+

Contact
Emma Young, Graduate Recruitment and Development Manager or for general enquiries contact us on gradrec@ashurst.com

Method of application
Online

Selection procedure
Online verbal reasoning test, interview with a member of the Graduate Recruitment and Development Team followed by interview with two Partners

Closing date for 2015
31 July 2013

Application
Training contracts p.a. 45
Applications p.a. 2,500
% interviewed p.a. 10%
Required degree grade 2:1 (or equivalent)

Training
Salary (2012)
First year £38,000
Second year £43,000
Holiday entitlement 25 days
% of trainees with a non-law degree 50%
Number of seats abroad available p.a. 13

Post-qualification
Salary (2012) £61,000
% of trainees offered job on qualification (2011/12) 84%

Overseas offices
24 offices in 14 countries: Australia, Belgium, China, France, Germany, Hong Kong Sar, Indonesia (associated office), Italy, Japan, Papua, New Guinea, Singapore, Spain, Sweden, United Arab Emirates and USA.

Baker & McKenzie LLP

100 New Bridge Street, London EC4V 6JA
Tel: (020) 7919 1000 Fax: (020) 7919 1999
Email: londongraduates@bakermckenzie.com
Website: www.bakermckenzie.com/londongraduates

Firm profile

Baker & McKenzie is a leading global law firm based in 71 locations across 44 countries. With a presence in virtually every important financial and commercial centre in the world, our strategy is to provide the best combination of local legal and commercial knowledge, international expertise and resources. Our trainee solicitors are a vital part of that strategy, exposed to the international scope of the firm from the moment they start. There is also the possibility of an overseas secondment, recent secondees have spent time in Tokyo, Brussels, Moscow, Chicago and Hong Kong.

Main areas of work

London is home to the firm's largest office where Baker & McKenzie has been well established since opening in 1961. With more than 400 legal professionals, we have a substantial presence in the legal and business community.

We deliver high-quality local solutions across a broad range of practices and global advice in conjunction with our 71 international offices. Our client base consists primarily of multinational corporates, based in the UK and elsewhere, and financial institutions. As may be expected of a firm with a very strong international client base, we have considerable expertise in acting on, and co-ordinating, cross-border transactions and disputes.

Our Corporate and Finance teams regularly advise on, and co-ordinate, complex, cross-border transactions for our clients. As a full service office, we cover all the practices expected of a major law firm in the UK, many of which are acclaimed and market-leading.

Trainee profile

The firm strives to enable trainees to be the best they can be. We are looking for trainees who are stimulated by intellectual challenge. Effective communication skills, together with the ability to be creative and practical problem solvers, team players and to have a sense of humour, are qualities which will help them stand out from the crowd.

Training environment

The two-year training contract comprises of four six-month seats which include a corporate and a contentious seat, usually within our highly regarded dispute resolution department, together with the possibility of a secondment abroad or with a client. During each seat you will have formal and informal reviews to discuss your progress and regular meetings to explore subsequent seat preferences. Your training contract commences with a highly interactive and practical induction programme which focuses on key skills including practical problem solving, presenting and the application of information technology. The firm's training programmes include important components on management and other business skills, as well as seminars and workshops on key legal topics for each practice area. There is a Trainee Solicitor Liaison Committee which acts as a forum for any new ideas or concerns which may occur during the training contract.

Benefits

Permanent health insurance, life insurance, private medical insurance, group personal pension, subsidised gym membership, season ticket loan, subsidised staff restaurant.

Sponsorship & awards

CPE/GDL funding: fees paid plus £6,000 maintenance.

LPC funding: fees paid plus £8,000.

Partners 86
Assistant Solicitors 217
Trainees 75

Contact
The Graduate Recruitment
Team 020 7919 1000

Method of application
Online via our website
www.bakermckenzie.com/
londongraduates

Selection procedure
Online application, verbal reasoning test, telephone interview. Successful candidates will then be invited to an assessment centre which consists of Partner interview/case study, Associate interview and group exercise.

Application
No. of training contracts p.a 34
Required degree grade 340
UCAS points and 2:1 degree

Training
Salary for each year of training
1st year £38,000 + £3,000
'joining bonus'
2nd year £43,000

Post-qualification
Salary £61,500

Overseas Offices
71 offices across 44 countries

BAKER & McKENZIE

Bates Wells & Braithwaite London LLP

2-6 Cannon Street, London EC4M 6YH
Tel: (020) 7551 7777 Fax: (020) 7551 7800
Email: training@bwbllp.com
Website: www.bwbllp.com

Firm profile

Bates Wells and Braithwaite is a commercial law firm servicing a wide range of commercial statutory, charity and social enterprises. The firm is expanding, progressive and is doing high quality work for clients and providing high quality training for those who work with the firm.

Whilst the firm is ranked first in three areas of law by the Legal 500 and ranked by them or Chambers in 15 other areas of law, the firm also believes in its staff enjoying a good work/life balance and living a life outside as well as inside the office.

Main areas of work

The firm is well known for its work for a wide range and variety of clients. This includes working with the charities and social enterprise sector, commercial organisations, regulators and individuals. The firm also has particular expertise in the arts and media, sports and immigration arenas together with strong departments dealing with employment, property and dispute resolution.

Trainee profile

The firm is looking for trainees with not only a sound academic background and the ability to communicate clearly and effectively, but most importantly it is looking for trainees who positively want to join a firm such as Bates Wells & Braithwaite. We want the applicant with the character and ability to prosper anywhere, who is positively looking to be in a firm with our work mix and approach.

Training environment

In the first year there are two six month seats, whilst in the second year there are three four month seats which, between them, cover a wide range of the work with which the firm is involved. From time to time the firm arranges secondments to clients on an ad hoc basis.

The firm runs a programme of internal seminars specifically addressed to trainees and operates a mentoring system, all designed to ensure that the trainees enjoy their time with the firm and to maximise the opportunities that are available for them during their training contract and beyond.

Benefits

Interest-free loan for season ticket travel, subsidised use of gym, well being classes and squash court, subsidised restaurant, one month's unpaid leave on qualification and the firm's pension scheme with match funding provided.

Vacation placements

Places for 2013: 24 people for a duration of one week each (£250 paid). Closing date: March 2013. See website for details and to apply.

Sponsorship & awards

We will provide financial support to the value of £6,000 for LPC course fees which commence after the offer has been accepted. Similar support is given for the GDL on a discretionary basis. We also pay interest on student loans on either of these courses from the signing of the training contract to the contract end.

Partners 30
Assistant Solicitors 54
Trainees 8

Graduate recruitment contact
Peter Bennett (020) 7551 7777

Method of application
Online via website

Selection procedure
Interviews

Closing date for 2015
June 2013 - see website

Application
Training contracts per annum 4
Applications p.a. 750+
% interviewed p.a. 5%
Required degree 2:1

Training
Salary
1st year £32,000
2nd year £34,000
Holiday entitlement
5 weeks
Post-qualification
Salary £46,575
% of trainees offered job
on qualification (last 3 years)
92%

Berwin Leighton Paisner

Adelaide House, London Bridge, London EC4R 9HA
Tel: (020) 3400 1000 Fax: (020) 3400 1111
Website: www.blplaw.com/trainee

Partners 226	
Assistant Solicitors 428	
Associate Directors 28	
Total Trainees 84	

Contact
Claire England, Graduate
Recruitment & Trainee
Manager

Method of application
Online application form

Selection procedure
Telephone interview,
assessment centre, partner
interview

Closing date for 2015/2016
31 July 2013

Application
Training contracts p.a. 40-45
Required degree grade 2:1
Required UCAs points 340

Training
Salary
1st year (2011)
£37,000
2nd year (2011)
£41,000
Holiday entitlement 25 days
% of trainees with a
non-law degree p.a. 50%
No. of seats available
abroad p.a. 4

Post-qualification
Salary (2011) £60,000
% of trainees offered job
on qualification (Sept 2011)
95%

Offices
London, Brussels, Paris, Abu
Dhabi, Moscow, Singapore,
Hong Kong, preferred firms
network in 65 countries

Firm profile

Berwin Leighton Paisner is an international, full service law firm with over 850 lawyers, including 226 partners, based across nine global offices. Working in tandem with our international offices, we have flexible and proactively managed relationships with more than 100 leading preferred firms in over 65 countries. Since our 2001 merger, BLP has won over 40 major awards and accolades, including 'UK Law Firm of the Year' five times in a decade - more than any other firm. We have won three FT Innovative Lawyer Awards in the past four years, and at the same awards in 2011 were recognised as the fifth most innovative law firm in Europe.

Main areas of work

We are ranked by leading independent directories in over 70 legal disciplines, we advise a broad range of clients including FTSE 100 companies and financial institutions, major multinationals, the public sector, entrepreneurial private businesses and individuals. We work with 59 Global Fortune 500 companies and eight of the world's top ten banks, and advise the UK's largest retail, water and construction companies. We are market leaders in a number of industry sectors, for example banking and finance, betting and gaming, real estate and hotels. An example of key areas of ranked expertise include: commercial contracts; corporate finance; defence and aerospace; dispute resolution; energy and natural resources; EU and competition; finance; healthcare and education; hotels, leisure and gaming; human resources; insurance; outsourcing; public sector; real estate; retail; regulatory and compliance; restructuring and insolvency; tax; and transport and infrastructure.

LPC+/ GDL+

The firm developed and runs the UK's first tailor-made LPC Course, called the LPC+. Our future trainees study at the College of Law, where tutors are joined by BLP lawyers and trainers who help to deliver some of the sessions, using BLP precedents and documents, and discussing how theory is applied to real cases and transactions. In 2011 we also introduced the GDL+; a programme of BLP led workshops which supplement the content that you study on the GDL course. All BLP future trainees study the GDL at the College of Law (any location).

Trainee profile

In addition to talented individuals with brilliant minds and bright attitudes, we are looking for people who can take complex, often pressurised, commercial situations in their stride. The sort of people our clients want on their side and will ask for by name. People they can trust to help them succeed. In other words, people with BerwinLeightonPaisnericity.

Training environment

Trainees spend six months in four seats and progress is reviewed every three months. The majority of trainees will gain experience within the Real Estate and Corporate Finance departments and undertake a contentious seat during their training contract. Client secondments are a popular choice, and there is the opportunity to undertake an international seat in either our Brussels, Moscow, Singapore or Abu Dhabi office if this is of interest.

Vacation placements

Places for 2013: We run vacation schemes throughout the year, typically during winter, spring and summer. Assessment centres are held from November to March at the firm's London offices.

Sponsorship

CPE/GDL and LPC+ fees paid and £7,200 maintenance p.a.

Bevan Brittan

Kings Orchard, 1 Queen Street, Bristol, BS2 0HQ
Tel: (0870) 194 3050 Fax: (0870) 194 8954
Email: hr.training@bevanbrittan.com
Website: www.bevanbrittan.com

Partners 44	
Total Trainees 15	
Contact HR and Training (0870) 194 3050	
Method of application Online application	
Closing date for 2015 31 July 2013	
Post-qualification % of trainees offered job on qualification (2012) 78%	
Other offices Birmingham, London, Bristol	

Firm profile

Bevan Brittan is a major commercial law firm who provide a comprehensive range of services to clients in the Public, Private and Third Sectors which commission, provide, procure, fund and regulate public services. The firm is the largest specialist provider of commercial legal services to the Public Sector in the UK, with public service clients representing over 90% of their business.

Main areas of work

Our core markets are health, local government, housing, waste, energy and renewables, education, emergency services, public infrastructure, charities and not-for-profit organisations. Our client base reflects this and includes over 30% of all local authorities, 40% of all health trusts and more than 100 private sector organisations - all working together on the delivery of public services. The firm operates in cross-departmental teams across these markets, harnessing the full range of skills and experience needed to provide top-quality legal advice. Teams are established in practice areas such as Employment, Property, Commercial & Infrastructure and Clinical Risk, covering both private and public sectors.

Trainee profile

We recognise that the most important prerequisite of quality service is a team of lawyers dedicated to service excellence. Our success is maintained by attracting and keeping talented legal minds. We are looking for bright, capable and motivated people with sound common sense and plenty of energy, who can think logically and clearly. You need drive, commitment, willingness to take responsibility and the ability to adapt to the ever-changing demands of the legal world.

Trainee environment

We have a widely respected training programme and with our Investors in People accreditation, we are committed to ongoing training and development. Your training will consist of practical work experience in conjunction with an extensive educational programme. The training is aimed at developing attitudes, skills, and legal and commercial knowledge which is essential for your career success. You are encouraged to take on as much work, responsibility and client interface as you are able to handle, which will be reviewed on a regular basis with your supervising partner. We are committed to retaining trainees as qualified solicitors and progression can be rapid, based on individual performance and merit.

Vacation placements

Places available across the three offices for 2013: 18. Closing date: 31st March 2013.

Sponsorship & awards

Bursary and funding for GDL and LPC.

Bevan Brittan

Bingham McCutchen (London) LLP

41 Lothbury, London EC2R 7HF
Tel: (020) 7661 5300 Fax: (020) 7661 5400
Email: graduaterecruitment@bingham.com
Website: www.bingham.com

Firm profile

Bingham London offers you the opportunity to work alongside outstanding individuals in a personal and collegial environment. Our team of over 50 finance, litigation and corporate lawyers is dedicated to providing a seamless and responsive service to the firm's international financial institution clients. Our London office capabilities have been carefully shaped to meet the complex needs of a demanding client base. Through practical experience and in-depth study of the legal and business issues facing these clients, the firm's London lawyers provide counsel in an intelligent and focused way. Widely recognised as one of the world's top-tier financial restructuring firms, Bingham has played a leading role representing creditors in numerous high-profile, precedent-setting workouts and restructurings throughout Europe. Clients include many of the world's largest insurance companies, pension funds, investment banks, hedge funds, distressed debt investors, international agencies, governments and multinational corporate groups. The firm has recently represented the senior noteholders on the restructurings of Technicolor S.A. (formerly Thomson S.A.), the Quinn Group, Connaught Plc, Phoenix Pharmahandel and MJ Maillis; the public noteholders of Wind Hellas, Preem, Petroplus, Sevan Marine, the Icelandic Banks (Kaupthing, Landsbanki and Glitnir), Anglo Irish Bank and Irish Nationwide Building Society; the mezzanine lenders to Gala Goral, Bulgarian Telecommunications/Vivacom, Alinta Energy, Crest Nicholson, European Directories, Alliance Medical, Findus Foods and Dometic; and the bondholders on the majority of restructurings of high yield bonds in Norway including Petrojack and Remedial Offshore. Our Financial Restructuring Practice, which includes recognised leaders in the profession, is ranked in Band 1 by the UK Legal 500 and was awarded a top-tier ranking in the UK by PLC in its Restructuring and Insolvency Handbook 2012-13 for the sixth straight year. We have more than 1,100 lawyers in 14 locations in the US, Europe and Asia.

Main areas of work

Bingham's London office capabilities include financial restructuring, finance, securities and financial institutions litigation, financial regulatory, UK funds, corporate, EU/UK competition and tax.

Trainee profile

We are looking for high-quality candidates who have an exceptional academic record combined with evidence of extracurricular achievement. Prospective trainees will show initiative, be solution-driven and seek to be part of a challenging, yet friendly, environment.

Training environment

We recruit up to four trainee solicitors each year. The training contract currently consists of four six-month seats, rotating between the following practice areas: financial restructuring, finance, corporate, financial regulatory, competition, tax and litigation. The intimate nature of our London office means that you will benefit from a bespoke training programme with a high level of partner involvement. You will assume responsibilities from day one.

Benefits

The firm offers an extensive compensation programme for trainees. As well as a highly competitive salary, the firm offers private health insurance, travel insurance, long-term disability insurance, season ticket loan, life assurance, a critical illness scheme and subsidised gym membership. A discretionary bonus is also payable.

Sponsorship & awards

On acceptance of our offer for a training contract, we will provide LPC and PgDL fees and a maintenance grant of £8,000 per year.

Assistant solicitors 34
Total Trainees 5

Contact
Vicky Widdows, Legal Recruiting/Learning and Development Manager
(020) 7661 5300

Method of application
Online application via firm website at www.bingham.com or via CV Mail

Selection procedure
Currently face to face interviews

Closing date for 2015
31 July 2013

Application
Training contracts p.a. up to 4
Required degree grade
High 2:1 from a leading university and excellent A-levels

Training
Salary
1st year £40,000
2nd year £45,000
Holiday entitlement
25 days

Post-qualification
Salary (2012) £100,000

Overseas offices
Beijing, Boston, Frankfurt, Hartford, Hong Kong, Los Angeles, New York, Orange County, San Francisco, Santa Monica, Silicon Valley, Tokyo, Washington

BINGHAM

Bircham Dyson Bell LLP

50 Broadway, London SW1H 0BL
Tel: (020) 7227 7000 Fax: (020) 7222 3480

Firm profile

Bircham Dyson Bell is a leading London law firm. The firm's approach and track record has enabled it to attract and retain some of the most talented people in the profession. This is achieved through the breadth and variety of work that the firm does. As part of the firm's commitment to providing a high level of service, it has been accredited with the Law Society's Lexcel quality mark and is one of the first law firms to be awarded ISO 14001, the internationally recognised standard for Environmental Management Systems. The firm is a leading member of Lexwork International, a network of 34 mid-sized independent law firms with over 1,700 lawyers in major cities across North America and Europe.

Main areas of work

Bircham Dyson Bell is recognised as having leading practices in the charity, private wealth, parliamentary, planning and public law fields. The firm also has strong corporate, commercial, employment, litigation and real estate teams.

Trainee profile

Applications are welcome from both law and non-law students who can demonstrate a consistently high academic record. The firm is looking for forward thinkers with a practical outlook and lots of initiative to join in the firm's friendly, hard-working environment. If you're focused, positive and a confident leader, get in touch. Many of the firm's current trainees have diverse interests outside law.

Training environment

The firm's training is designed to produce its future partners. To achieve this they aim to provide a balance of both formal and practical training and will give early responsibility to those who show promise. The two-year training contract consists of four six-month seats during which you will work alongside partners and other senior lawyers, some of whom are leaders in their field. As the firm practises in a wide variety of legal disciplines, trainees benefit from a diverse experience. Trainees undergo specific technical training in each seat in addition to the mandatory Professional Skills Course (PSC). Great emphasis is also placed on interpersonal skills training and development so when you qualify you have the breadth of skills required to be an excellent solicitor.

Benefits

Bonus scheme, group health care, life assurance, pension scheme, season ticket loan.

Partners 45
Fee Earners 109
Total Trainees 14

Contact
Graduate Recruitment Team
(020) 7227 7000

Method of application
Please visit the firm's website,
www.bdb-law.co.uk

Selection procedure
Two interviews with members of the Graduate Recruitment Panel, comprising of a number of partners, associates and HR. In addition you will be required to complete an online test and assessment centre exercise

Closing date for 2015
31 July 2013

Application
Training contracts p.a. 7
Applications p.a. 650
% interviewed p.a. 8%
Required degree grade
2:1 or above degree preferred

Training
Salary
1st year £32,000
2nd year £33,500
Holiday entitlement
25 days

Post-qualification
Salary £52,000
% of trainees offered job
on qualification (2011) 57%

BIRCHAM DYSON BELL

Bird & Bird

15 Fetter Lane, London EC4A 1JP
Tel: (020) 7415 6003 Fax: (020) 7415 6111
Website: www.twobirds.com

Firm profile

Bird & Bird is an international law firm with a long-established reputation underpinned by deep client and industry knowledge, for providing cutting-edge legal advice to clients operating at the forefront of their sectors, including: aviation and defence, automotive, communications, electronics, energy and utilities, financial services, food, healthcare, information technology, life sciences, media and sports. We are proud to be working with some of the world's most innovative and technologically advanced companies each of which depend on cutting-edge legal advice to meet their business objectives.

The firm is ambitious and it manages to combine a resilient business approach with a hugely supportive attitude to its employees. With offices in Abu Dhabi, Beijing, Bratislava, Brussels, Budapest, Düsseldorf, Frankfurt, The Hague, Hamburg, Helsinki, Hong Kong, London, Lyon, Madrid, Milan, Munich, Paris, Prague, Rome, Shanghai, Singapore, Stockholm, Warsaw and close ties with firms in other key centres in Europe, Asia and the United States, the firm is well placed to offer its clients local expertise within a global context.

The firm is proud of its friendly, stimulating environment where individuals are able to develop first class legal, business and interpersonal skills. It has an open and collegiate culture reflected in its strong retention rate and assistant involvement. The firm is structured with a very strong international perspective to its culture - integrated teams working for cross-border clients as well as a range of international sport and social activities enables this.

At Bird & Bird, there is a genuine commitment to acting as a responsible employer and also as a proactive member of its local and wider international communities. The firm has a full programme of corporate social responsibility initiatives and policies in place, which fall under three broad areas, people, community and environment.

Main areas of work

Across the sectors listed above, we cover the following practice areas: arbitration, banking and finance, commercial, corporate, corporate restructuring and insolvency, dispute resolution, EU and competition, intellectual property, international HR services, outsourcing, privacy and data protection, public sector, real estate, regulatory and administrative, tax, trade and customs and pro bono.

Trainee profile

The firm recognises that its lawyers are its most important asset and that is why the firm recruits strong graduates capable of developing expert legal skills and commercial acumen. A certain level of intelligence and common sense is a prerequisite (the firm looks for excellent A levels and a strong 2:1), but more importantly it looks for well-rounded individuals who will fit in.

The firm's trainee solicitors are outgoing, articulate team-players, willing to work hard when called upon and genuinely interested in progressing their careers. The firm aims to recruit people who will stay with the firm and therefore seek candidates who have a long-term interest in Bird & Bird and the sectors and areas of legal practice it focuses on.

Training environment

The firm's trainees take on responsibility from day one and enjoy varied and challenging work for industry-shaping clients. If you become a trainee with the firm, you will be given the chance to excel. The firm runs a business skills development programme to provide you with the basic building blocks for your future development within the business of law. Trainees will spend six months in four of the following practice areas: corporate, commercial, employment, banking, tax, intellectual property, dispute resolution and real estate. Trainees are encouraged to join the number of sports teams at the firm and to attend various social events.

Partners Over 230*
Assistant Solicitors Over 580*
Total Trainees 28 in London
*denotes worldwide figures

Contact
Graduate & Trainee
Management Team
london.graduates@twobirds.com

Method of application
Online application form via the firm website

Selection procedure
Insight and selection days in February and March 2013 for summer placements and August 2013 for Training Contracts

Closing date for 2015
31 July 2013 for law and non-law students

Application
Training contracts p.a. 16-17
Applications p.a. 2,400
% interviewed at first stage p.a. 20%
Required degree grade 2:1

Training
Salary
1st year (2012) £36,000
2nd year (2012) £38,000
Holiday entitlement
25 days
% of trainees with a non-law degree p.a. Varies

Post-qualification
Salary (2012) £59,000
% of trainees offered job on qualification (2011) 81%

Overseas offices
Abu Dhabi, Beijing, Bratislava, Brussels, Budapest, Düsseldorf, Frankfurt, The Hague, Hamburg, Helsinki, Hong Kong, Lyon, Madrid, Milan, Munich, Paris, Prague, Rome, Shanghai, Singapore, Stockholm, Warsaw

Bond Pearce LLP

3 Temple Quay, Temple Back East, Bristol BS1 6DZ
Tel: 0845 415 0000 Fax: 0845 415 6900
Email: sam.lee@bondpearce.com
Website: www.bondpearce.com

Vacancies 10
Trainees 28
Partners 76
Total staff 600

Contact
Samantha Lee
Recruitment Manager

Method of application
Online application form

Selection procedure
Assessment days

Closing date
31 July 2013

Application
Training contracts p.a. 10
Minimum qualification 2:1
degree

Training
Salary (2014)
1st year £28,000
2nd year £30,000
Holiday entitlement
25 days

Offices
Bristol, Plymouth,
Southampton, London,
Aberdeen

Firm profile

You'll be surprised what this hidden gem has to offer you! Bond Pearce is a firm that is truly going places. With ambitious growth plans this is an exciting time to be thinking about joining the firm. As our business expands we continue to attract high calibre lawyers as a result of the quality and diversity of the work we undertake both regionally and nationally.

As a trainee you will benefit from excellent supervision from lawyers who are ranked by Chambers as leaders in their fields and who have a breadth and depth of experience that is second to none.

Outstanding client service is something we are passionate about, as it helps to build and reinforce relationships, improve the timeliness of advice and encourage teamwork. The result: commercial legal advice that is proactive rather than simply reactive.

Main areas of work

Our particular strengths lie in our sector expertise and much of our work lies at the cutting edge of developments in key sectors such as energy, retail, financial services, real estate and the public sector. We boast an impressive portfolio of clients which includes, for example: Lloyds TSB, BBC, QBE Group, RWE Npower Plc, Carnival Plc, Associated British Ports, English Heritage, The Crown Estate, Barclays Bank, Royal Mail, Kingfisher, B&Q, Virgin Group, Chemring Group, Carlsberg, Marks & Spencer.

Trainee profile

We are looking for individuals who are capable of combining great legal knowledge with a sound commercial focus; people who are driven, creative and have a genuine enthusiasm for both the law and our business and individuals with a natural ability in dealing with people.

Training environment

You couldn't ask for a better start to your legal career. Our first class training and development programme is recognised amongst the best in the industry and ensures that you qualify with the best possible legal, business and personal skills. We have worked hard to create a culture that encourages, inspires and challenges. Our graduate team, consisting of partners, associates and HR provide all the support and encouragement that you need to see you through your two years with the firm. Structured over four seats we offer a good range of practice areas for you to train and qualify into.

Bond Pearce

Boodle Hatfield LLP

89 New Bond Street, London W1S 1DA
Tel: (020) 7629 7411 Fax: (020) 7629 2621
Email: traineesolicitors@boodlehatfield.com
Website: www.boodlehatfield.com

Partners 30
Other Fee-earners 50
Total Trainees 11

Contact
Alanah Graviles
(020) 7079 8240

Method of application
Online application

Selection procedure
Interviews with the Training
Principal, a Partner and the HR
Director plus an ability test in
verbal reasoning

Closing date for 2015
Graduates and non-law
students 30 June 2013
Law students 31 July 2013

Application
Training contracts p.a. 6
Required degree grade 2:1

Training
Salary
1st year £32,750
2nd year £34,750
Holiday entitlement
25 days

Post-qualification
Salary £50,000

Regional offices
Oxford

Firm profile
Boodle Hatfield is a highly successful law firm which has been providing bespoke legal services for nearly 300 years. They still act for some of their very first clients and are proud to do so. The firm has grown into a substantial practice, serving the full spectrum of commercial and private clients, both domestically and internationally.

Main areas of work
The ethos of facilitating private capital activity and private businesses underpins the work of the whole firm. The interplay of skills between five major areas – private client and tax, property, family, corporate and litigation – makes Boodle Hatfield particularly well placed to serve these individuals and businesses.

Trainee profile
The qualities the firm looks for in its trainees are commitment, flexibility and the ability to work as part of a team. Applicants with a gained/ predicted 2:1 degree in any discipline and a minimum of ABB at A-level should apply.

Training environment
Trainees spend six months in up to four of the firm's main areas: property, corporate, family, private client and tax and litigation. Boodle Hatfield is well known for the high quality of its training. All trainees are involved in client work from the start and are encouraged to handle their own files personally as soon as they are able to do so, (with the appropriate supervision). The firm's trainees therefore have a greater degree of client contact than in many firms with the result that they should be able to take on more responsibility at an early stage. Trainees are given formal appraisals every three months which are designed as a two-way process and give trainees the chance to discuss their progress and to indicate where more can be done to help in their ongoing training and development.

Benefits
Private healthcare, life assurance, season ticket loan, pension scheme, enhanced maternity pay, conveyancing grant, permanent health insurance, employee assistance line, childcare vouchers, cycle to work scheme, give as you earn scheme.

Vacation placements
Two week placement in July, for which 8 to 10 students are accepted each year. Applicants should apply via the application form on the website at www.boodlehatfield.com. The form will be available from 1 November 2012.

Sponsorship & awards
LPC and GDL fees paid in full plus maintenance grant.

B P Collins LLP

Collins House, 32-38 Station Road, Gerrards Cross SL9 8EL
Tel: (01753) 889995 Fax: (01753) 889851
Email: jacqui.symons@bpcollins.co.uk
Website: www.bpcollins.co.uk

Firm profile

B P Collins LLP was established in 1966 and has expanded significantly to become one of Buckinghamshire's largest and best-known practices with an enviable reputation within the Thames Valley. Based to the west of London, our easily accessible offices in Gerrards Cross are close to the M25/M40 interchange and city rail links as well as Heathrow airport. Our location enables us to deliver city quality legal services at highly competitive rates.

The firm's emphasis is on offering the full range of commercial and private client legal services to all our clients from business start-ups to multi-nationals, successful entrepreneurs to retired professionals.

Most of our partners and associates have worked in London but, tired of commuting and long working hours, have opted to work in more congenial surroundings and enjoy a higher quality lifestyle. Gerrards Cross is a very pleasant town surrounded by beautiful countryside but within 30 minutes commuting distance of central London. It is an affluent area conveniently located to serve the extremely active business community which includes West London, Heathrow, Uxbridge, Slough and High Wycombe.

Types of Work
- Corporate and commercial
- Commercial and residential property
- Employment law
- Family law
- Litigation and dispute resolution
- Private client

Training programme

The firm aims to have six to eight trainee solicitors at different stages of their training contracts at all times. Trainees complete five months in four different practice groups of their choice. The final four months is spent in the practice group in which the trainee intends to specialise. The firm has a training partner with overall responsibility for all trainees and each practice group has its own trainee supervisor who is responsible for day to day supervision. Trainees are given early responsibility which includes plenty of client contact and professional work. There are regular meetings between the training supervisor and the trainee to monitor progress and a review meeting with the training partner midway through and at the end of each practice group seat. Trainees are encouraged to participate in social and marketing events. The firm has a very high trainee retention rate.

Trainee profile

Bright, hard working, lateral thinkers who are good communicators with plenty of initiative will thrive in the B P Collins environment. You should be adaptable and self starting in approach and possess a degree of robustness to cope with the changing demands which you will face during the contract.

Partners 16	
Assistant Solicitors 28	
Total Trainees 8	
Contact	
HR Manager Mrs Jacqui Symons	
Method of application	
Handwritten covering letter & CV	
Selection procedure	
Screening interview & assessment day	
Applications for the firm's 2014 intake	
Will be accepted from 1st March to 31 May 2013	
Application	
Required degree grade 2:1, Grades A & B at A level	
Training	
Salary	
1st year £24,000	
2nd year £25,000	

bpcollins
SOLICITORS

Brabners Chaffe Street LLP

Horton House, Exchange Flags, Liverpool L2 3YL
Tel: (0151) 600 3000 Fax: (0151) 227 3185
55 King Street, Manchester M2 4LQ Tel: (0161) 236 5800 Fax: (0161) 228 6862
7-8 Chapel Street, Preston PR1 8AN Tel: (01772) 823921 Fax: (01772) 201918
Email: trainees@brabnerscs.com
Website: www.brabnerschaffestreet.com

Firm profile

One of the top North West commercial firms, Brabners Chaffe Street LLP, in Liverpool, Manchester and Preston, has the experience, talent and prestige of a firm that has a 200-plus-year history. Brabners Chaffe Street LLP is a dynamic, client-led specialist in the provision of excellent legal services to clients ranging from large plcs to private individuals.

Main areas of work

The LLP carries out a wide range of specialist legal services and Brabners Chaffe Street's client base includes plcs, public sector bodies, banks and other commercial, corporate and professional businesses. The LLP's client focused departments include banking, corporate, commercial (including sports law), employment, litigation (including media and sports law), property (including housing association and construction) and private client.

Trainee profile

Graduates and those undertaking CPE or LPC, who can demonstrate intelligence, intuition, humour, approachability and commitment.

Training environment

The LLP is one of the few law firms that holds Investor in People status and has a comprehensive training and development programme. It is listed in the Sunday Times Best 100 Employers to work for in 2006, 2007, 2008, 2009, 2010 and 2011. Trainees are given a high degree of responsibility and are an integral part of the culture of the firm. Each trainee will have partner-level supervision. Personal development appraisals are conducted at three and six-monthly intervals to ensure that trainee progress is valuable and informed. The training programme is overseen by the firm's Director of Training, Dr Tony Harvey, and each centre has a designated Trainee Partner. It is not all hard work and the firm has an excellent social programme.

Sponsorship & awards

Assistance with LPC funding is available.

Partners 77
Associates 51
Assistant Solicitors 46
Fee Earners 50
Total Trainees 14

Contact
Liverpool office
Dr Tony Harvey
Director of Training and Risk
Management

Method of application
Online

Selection procedure
Interview & assessment day

Closing date for 2015
Apply by 30 June 2013 for
training contracts commencing
in September 2015 and for the
summer vacation scheme 2015

Application
Training contracts p.a. 7
Required degree grade
2:1 or post-graduate degree

Training
Salary
Not less than £21,000
Holiday entitlement 25 days

Offices
Liverpool, Manchester, Preston

brabners chaffe street

Bristows

100 Victoria Embankment, London EC4Y 0DH
Tel: (020) 7400 8000 Fax: (020) 7400 8050
Email: trainee.recruitment@bristows.com
Website: www.bristows.com

Firm profile
Bristows is a medium-sized firm that handles the kind of work that might normally be associated with only the very largest firms. Established 175 years ago, the firm has built up a client list that includes leading businesses from a variety of sectors, whether global corporations, growing start-ups, charities or financial institutions. Working with so many ambitious organisations, the firm is often advising on issues that shape entire industries and on which a company's future might depend. For example, advising on whether the business is entitled to launch a new product or assisting a client to buy a rival business.

Main areas of work
Bristows might be known as one of the foremost intellectual property firms in the UK, but this only tells part of the story. The firm's lawyers are also recognised as leading authorities in a wide variety of other legal disciplines and as a firm offer a true breadth of expertise. These are our core practice areas: intellectual property; information technology; corporate; commercial disputes; real estate; regulatory; EU & competition; media & marketing; employment and tax.

Trainee profile
The size of the firm makes this an ideal environment for trainees. As part of a small intake, the trainees work alongside the partners dealing directly with clients right from the start. There's plenty of responsibility but this is matched by an extremely supportive and friendly culture so you're never far from encouragement and advice when you need it. The firm recognises that its reputation as a leading city law firm is entirely down to the individuals who work here, so it places great stock in attracting talented people and doing all it can to make sure they enjoy life at Bristows.

Training environment
Each year the firm asks up to 10 graduates to join its team. The firm is extremely selective because it's looking for the people who will be its future partners. As part of such a select and high calibre intake the firm will give you real responsibility earlier than you might expect. During the two years' training, you'll spend time in each of the firm's main departments, developing your skills and knowledge. You'll also work closely with its partners and senior associates. Part of this training may also involve a secondment to one of a number of leading clients. With the international spread of its clients, the probability of overseas travel is high, especially following qualification.

Benefits
Life assurance; pension scheme; private medical insurance; permanent health insurance; eye care; health assessment; employee assistance programme; cycle to work scheme; childcare voucher scheme; and season ticket loan.

Work experience
For opportunities to spend time with the firm during Winter, Spring and Summer, please see the firm's website for full details.

Sponsorship & awards
GDL and LPC fees paid in full, plus a maintenance grant of £7,000 for each.

Partners 34
Assistant Solicitors 73
Total Trainees 19

Contact
Graduate Recruitment Officer

Method of application
Online

Selection procedure
2 individual interviews

Closing date for 2015
31 January 2013 for February interviews,
31 July 2013 for
August interviews

Application
Training contracts p.a.
Up to 10
Applications p.a. 2,000
% interviewed p.a. 4%
Required degree grade
2:1 (preferred)

Training
Salary
1st year (2012) £34,000
2nd year (2012) £37,000
Holiday entitlement
23 days
% of trainees with
a non-law degree p.a. 90%

Post-qualification
Salary (2012) £58,000
% of trainees offered job
on qualification (2012) 75%
(6 out of 8 trainees)

BRISTOWS

Browne Jacobson LLP

Nottingham, Birmingham, London, Manchester
Tel: (0115) 976 6000 Fax: (0115) 947 5246
Email: traineeapplications@brownejacobson.com
Website: www.brownejacobson.com/trainees.aspx

Partners 78	
Associates 62	
Assistant Solicitors 79	
Total Trainees 16	
Total Staff 605	

Contact
Sophie Potter, HR Manager

Method of application
Apply online at
www.brownejacobson.com/
trainees.aspx

Selection procedure
Telephone interview,
assessment centre and partner
interview

Closing date
31 July 2013 for 2015 training
contracts

Application
Training contracts p.a. 8
Applications p.a. 800
% interviewed p.a. 7%

Training
Salary
1st year (2012) £24,500
2nd year (2012) £25,500
Holiday entitlement 25 days
% of trainees with a
non-law degree p.a. 40%

Post-qualification
Salary Market Rate
Holiday entitlement 25 days
% of trainees offered a job on
qualification (2012) 87.5%

Firm profile

Browne Jacobson a full service national law firm with offices in Nottingham, Birmingham, London and Manchester.

With over 600 people, Browne Jacobson is large enough to attract some of the best talent in the country, but small enough to foster a supportive and flexible working environment. The firm's people are the key to its success and it has a track record of attracting and retaining outstanding people.

Browne Jacobson focuses on long-term relationships that are friendly, flexible and straightforward, with its people, clients and suppliers. The firm's forward thinking environment and its friendly and open culture mean that its people really enjoy working here. This allows good working relationships to develop and provides consistency for clients. It's a simple tactic yet one that works; a large proportion of the firm's client base has been with the firm for a number of years.

Main areas of work

Browne Jacobson offer a comprehensive range of specialist legal services with real strength across the commercial, public, health and insurance sectors.

Trainee profile

Browne Jacobson is looking for talented law and non-law graduates who can bring with them enthusiasm, tenacity, commitment and client focus combined with a flexible and friendly attitude. For more information about life as a trainee visit their blog at www.traineetalk.co.uk or follow them on twitter at www.twitter.com/brownejtrainees.

Training environment

Trainees start with a comprehensive induction programme, a fast track professional skills course and then go on to undertake an extensive internal trainee development programme. They spend four periods of six months in some of the principle areas of the firm, gaining an overview of the practice. Trainees get great training, a friendly and supportive working environment and real career opportunities. They are also given quality work and exposure to clients from early on, but are supported in achieving results and recognised for their contribution.

Sponsorship & awards

LPC/PGDL tuition fees paid, plus maintenance grant for LPC/PGDL of £5,000.

Open days

Browne Jacobson runs an open day in the spring - application deadline for the 2013 open day is 17 March 2013. Apply online at www.brownejacobson.com/trainees.aspx

Benefits

Browne Jacobson offer life assurance, income protection insurance, pension, private medical insurance, dental insurance, travel insurance and corporate discounts.

Burges Salmon

1 Glass Wharf, Bristol BS2 0ZX
Tel: (0117) 307 6982 Fax: (0117) 902 4400
Email: holly.fey@burges-salmon.com
Website: www.burges-salmon.com

Firm profile
Burges Salmon is proof that becoming a top lawyer doesn't have to mean living in London. The firm is consistently ranked among the most profitable UK firms and we continue to win prestigious clients out of the hands of our rivals. Our strategy is client-orientated and we firmly believe it is the way we work that makes us different.

Main areas of work
We provide a full commercial service through five main departments: corporate and financial institutions (CFI); commercial; real estate; private client and wealth structuring; and disputes, environment and planning. Our sector specialisms include energy, infrastructure, financial services, real estate, food, farming and land and transport.

Trainee profile
We recruit future partners, not future trainees and recognise that developing talent is critical to our success. Burges Salmon lawyers are hardworking and motivated with a strong academic background and a genuine enthusiasm for a career in law.

Training environment
Our training contract incorporates six seats as opposed to the usual four which we believe ensures our trainees gain maximum exposure to our varied practice areas. This dedication to trainee development is demonstrated in our consistently high retention rates.

Vacation placements
We run two open days in February and offer 40 two-week vacation placements during the summer. Individuals visit two departments of their choice supervised by a partner or senior solicitor. Current trainees run skills training sessions, sports and social events. Remuneration: £250 per week.

Sponsorship and awards
The firm pays GDL and LPC fees. Maintenance grants of £7,000 are paid to LPC students and £14,000 to students studying for both the GDL and LPC (£7,000 p.a.).

Benefits
Annually reviewed competitive salary, 24 days paid annual leave, bonus scheme, pension scheme, private health care membership, life assurance, mobile phone, Christmas gift, corporate gym membership, sports and social club.

Partners 77
Assistant Solicitors 350
Trainees 46

Contact
Holly Fey, Trainee Solicitor
Resourcing Advisor

Method of application
Application form available via our website

Selection procedure
Assessment centres held in August consist of a verbal reasoning test and a group exercise, followed by an interview conducted by a partner and a member of the HR team

Closing date for 2015
31 July 2013

Application
Training contracts p.a. 25
Applications p.a. 1,700 approx.
% interviewed p.a. 10%
Required degree grade 2:1 in any discipline

Training
Salary
1st year (2012) £31,000
2nd year (2012) £32,000
Holiday entitlement 24 days

Post-qualification
Salary (2012) £41,000
% of trainees offered job on qualification (2012) 100%

BURGES SALMON

Capsticks

1 St George's Road, Wimbledon SW19 4DR
Tel: (020) 8780 2211 Fax: (020) 8780 4811
Email: career@capsticks.com
Website: www.capsticks.com

Firm profile

Capsticks is the leading provider of legal services to the healthcare sector and has over 150 lawyers focusing on healthcare across its offices in London, Leeds and Birmingham. The firm has ambitious plans for further growth, both in its core market and by promoting its broader capability and expanding private sector client base.

Main areas of work

The firm acts for a wide range of healthcare clients, including NHS Trusts and Health Authorities, the NHSLA, regulatory bodies, charities and independent healthcare providers. The firm's main practice areas are clinical law, corporate/commercial, dispute resolution, employment and real estate.

Trainee profile

The firm is committed to recruiting the best people to maintain its market leading position. The firm recruits seven (five in London, one in Birmingham and one in Leeds) trainee solicitors each year and welcomes applications from candidates who are either on course for or have achieved at least a 2:1 (or equivalent) in their undergraduate degree. The firm expects candidates to be committed to a career in healthcare law and to be able to demonstrate they are highly driven, but well rounded, team players, with good problem solving and communication skills.

Training environment

The firm's broad range of practice areas and healthcare clients enables it to give its trainees an opportunity to experience a wide variety of legal work. Trainees are therefore able to acquire an in-depth knowledge of both healthcare law and the healthcare industry, in addition to developing the skills that any good lawyer needs.

The training contract is designed to give trainees maximum exposure to the work of the firm and trainees undertake seats in all of the firm's practice areas, including clinical law, corporate/commercial, dispute resolution, employment and real estate.

Benefits

Bonus scheme, 25 days holiday, pension contribution, income protection, private medical insurance, life assurance benefit, cycle to work scheme, corporate gym 'membership' scheme, childcare voucher scheme and season ticket loan.

Vacation placements

The firm's vacation scheme in London, Birmingham and Leeds runs from the end of June through to the middle of August and placements last for two weeks each. In order to be eligible for the 2013 vacation scheme you should be looking to secure a training contract with the firm in September 2015. The firm welcomes applications for a place on its 2013 vacation scheme between 12 November 2012 and 15 February 2013. Further details are available from the website.

The firm encourages all prospective trainee solicitors to participate in the vacation scheme as this is their primary means for selecting future trainee solicitors.

Sponsorship & awards

The firm offers its future trainees financial support for both the Graduate Diploma in Law and the Legal Practice Course.

Partners 41
Assistant Solicitors 115
Total Trainees 11
Other Fee-earners 21

Contact
HR department,
career@capsticks.com

Method of application
Application form, CV and covering letter

Selection procedure
Interview with Partner and Director of HR

Closing date for 2015
11 August 2013

Application
Training contracts p.a. 7
Applications p.a. 300
% interviewed p.a. 7%
Required degree grade
2:1 or above

Training
Salary
1st year £29,000 p.a. (London)
2nd year £30,000 p.a.(London)
Holiday entitlement
25 days p.a.
% of trainees with a
non-law degree p.a. 40%

Post-qualification
Salary (2011)
£46,000 p.a.
% of trainees offered job
on qualification (2011) 100%

Charles Russell LLP

5 Fleet Place, London EC4M 7RD
Tel: (020) 7203 5000 Fax: (020) 7203 5307
Website: www.charlesrussell.co.uk
Facebook: www.facebook.com/charlesrusselltrainees

Firm profile

Charles Russell is a leading law firm with an impressive reputation and competence in a number of key market sectors. The firm is unusual among top city firms in having a strong private client practice, as well as a commercial focus. It provides a wide range of legal services to companies, institutions and individuals on an international scale.

The practice is well known as a friendly place to work and is committed to fostering a strong team spirit and encouraging personal development, which combined with good quality work and good quality people, makes it a winning combination.

Charles Russell people are actively involved in CSR; helping to promote and organise pro bono, volunteering and fundraising initiatives.

Main areas of work

There are experts in a number of legal service areas, including: corporate and commercial; employment and pensions; litigation and dispute resolution; family; private client; real estate.

These services are focused on the following sector areas: charities and not-for-profit; energy and natural resources; family; healthcare; private wealth; property; retail, design and leisure; sports and media; technology and communications.

Trainee profile

Trainees are expected to get involved with all aspects of the role, so aside from the drafting and research tasks which are a given, trainees can also expect to get more involved directly with clients, run their own files with close support, develop their commercial awareness and participate in business development.

The firm wants to recruit trainees of the highest standard. Trainees will usually have a consistent and strong academic background and will have demonstrated other key attributes outside of academia, such as teamwork, leadership, communication skills and initiative. These attributes can be demonstrated in lots of different ways. The firm is looking for a diverse make up of trainees and welcomes individuals who will bring something different to the role.

Training environment

A small number of trainees are recruited and this allows trainees to undergo the best possible training.

The opportunities to get involved and the experience offered are second to none. Trainees can expect to be challenged and encouraged to go beyond their comfort zone, all with the full guidance, support and encouragement of the team. Trainees are seated with a partner/senior solicitor; there will always be close support at hand. Formal training is in place from day one and the first two weeks are spent completing induction and Professional Skills Course modules. This training provides trainees with the key skills required for their first day in the service area.

Regular feedback is important and mid and end seat appraisals take place to discuss performance and to give guidance on how to develop further. This does not, of course, replace the regular on the job feedback trainees can expect.

Benefits

BUPA; PHI; life assurance; pension; season ticket loan; 25 days holiday; subsidised canteen (London).

Sponsorship & awards

GDL/LPC funding plus £6,000 maintenance grant (London) whilst you are at law school.

Partners 99
Other fee earners 218
Total trainees 38
Total staff 613

Contact
trainee.recruitment@
charlesrussell.co.uk

Method of application
Online application via
www.charlesrussell.co.uk

Selection procedure
Assessment day includes an interview and other exercises designed to assess identified performance criteria

Closing date for 2015
31 July 2013

Application
Training contracts for 2015 18
Applications p.a. Approx 1,500
% interviewed p.a. 7%
Preferred degree grade 2:1

Training
Salary (London)
1st year (2011) £32,500
2nd year (2011) £33,500
Holiday entitlement (2011) 25 days + additional day for house moves

Post-qualification
Salary (2011) £55,000

Regional / Overseas offices
Guildford, Cheltenham, Geneva and Bahrain

CHARLES RUSSELL

Cleary Gottlieb Steen & Hamilton LLP

City Place House, 55 Basinghall Street, London, EC2V 5EH
Tel: (020) 7614 2200 Fax: (020) 7600 1698
Email: longraduaterecruit@cgsh.com
Website: www.cgsh.com/careers/london

Firm profile

Cleary Gottlieb is one of the leading international law firms, with 14 closely integrated offices located in major financial and political centres around the world. For more than 60 years, the firm has been pre-eminent in shaping the internationalisation of the legal profession. Its worldwide practice has a proven track record for innovation and providing advice of the highest quality to meet the domestic and international needs of its clients.

Main areas of work

Core practice groups in London are mergers and acquisitions, financing, capital markets, international litigation and arbitration and competition, plus additional self-standing practices in tax, financial regulation, intellectual property and information technology.

Trainee profile

Cleary looks for candidates who are enthusiastic about the practice of law in a challenging and dynamic international setting. Whilst academic excellence is a pre-requisite, the firm places particular emphasis on recruiting candidates that they and their clients will enjoy working with. A sense of humour is as important as the ability to think critically and creatively about cutting-edge legal issues.

Training environment

By limiting its graduate intake to just 13-15 trainees a year, Cleary is able to offer bespoke training that is individually tailored to the interests, experience and aptitudes of the exceptional individuals that join them. The firm does not believe that the transition from trainee solicitor to associate occurs overnight on qualification, but rather that the transition should be a smooth and gradual one. It therefore encourages its trainee solicitors to accept increased responsibility as soon as they are ready to do so. With appropriate levels of supervision, trainees operate as lawyers of the firm from the day that they join.

Benefits

Health club membership, private healthcare cover (personal and family), life insurance of twice annual salary, long-term disability insurance, employee assistance programme and subsidised staff restaurant.

Vacation schemes

The firm's London office offers 35 vacation places each year (five in winter, ten in spring and ten in each of two summer schemes). The firm actively encourages all candidates that are seriously considering applying for a trainee solicitor position to undertake a vacation placement with the firm. Applications for winter vacation placements should be received by 16 November. The deadline for spring and summer vacation scheme applications is 25 January.

Sponsorship & awards

Cleary funds the LPC for all future trainee solicitors. For non-law graduates, the firm also funds the GDL. A maintenance grant of £8,000 is paid for each year of professional study.

Trainees 22
Partners 196
(17 in London)
Total Staff 2500
(19 in London)

Contact
Graduate Recruitment

Method of application
Cover letter and CV

Selection procedure
Future trainees are primarily selected from among those having completed a vacation scheme with the firm

Closing date for 2015
July 31 2013

Application
Training contracts p.a. 13-15
Required degree grade
High 2:1

Training
Salary
1st year £40,000
2nd year £45,000

Post-qualification
Compensation £95,000

Overseas offices
New York, Washington DC, Paris, Brussels, Moscow, Frankfurt, Cologne, Rome, Milan, Hong Kong, Beijing, Buenos Aires and Sao Paulo

Clifford Chance

10 Upper Bank Street, Canary Wharf, London, E14 5JJ
Tel: (020) 7006 3003
Email: Recruitment.London@CliffordChance.com
Website: www.cliffordchance.com/gradsuk

Firm profile

At Clifford Chance our goal is to be at the forefront of the elite group of international law firms. To join us you will need to share our ambition and our willingness to grasp new opportunities, both in the UK and internationally. You'll need to appreciate the commercial context in which we offer advice and enjoy helping businesses and individuals address the challenges of succeeding in increasingly complex and global markets. And you'll need to enjoy playing an important role – and developing your individual potential – as part of an exceptionally talented legal team.

Main areas of practice

Our business is organised into six global and sector-leading practices – corporate, capital markets, banking and finance – in which you will undertake mandatory rotations as part of your two-year training contract – plus real estate, litigation and dispute resolution, and tax, pensions and employment.

Trainee profile

Clifford Chance is a firm of exceptional lawyers drawn from a wide range of backgrounds – there is no one 'type' here. Instead, we aim to recruit people who can help us to give our clients a competitive edge in challenging situations. We're interested in people who have the potential to become outstanding lawyers – regardless of what you have studied at university. That means you'll need to be able to think on your feet, to offer and embrace new ideas and to play your part in a team that is likely to span practice areas, offices and time zones. We ask a lot of our trainees. Focus and dedication are essential, but you'll also need to be flexible and willing to adapt to new challenges and a lot of responsibility. Counterbalancing this is a level of investment in your career development and a level of international opportunity that is only offered by a handful of professional services firms.

Training environment

Clifford Chance advises multi-national and domestic corporates, financial institutions, regulatory authorities, supranational bodies, governments and government agencies. We work internationally and domestically; under common law and civil law systems; in local and cross-border transactions and disputes; on day-to-day operations and on 'game-changing' transformational deals and issues.

Benefits

As well as a competitive salary, you'll enjoy: a subsidised restaurant; free use of fitness centre, swimming pool, squash courts and wellness centre; the option of up to six weeks' leave on qualification and a pension.

Sponsorship

Fees for GDL and LPC covered.

LPC preferred provider: College of Law Moorgate.

LPC preferred electives: City electives, Private acquisitions, Debt finance, Equity finance.

Maintenance is also provided. £4,900 for the accelerated LPC. Please refer to website for details.

London office
Partners 178
Lawyers 564
Trainees 242

Contact
recruitment.london@clifford
chance.com

Method of application
Applications for the firm's training contract, vacation schemes and insight days should be made via www.cliffordchance.com/gradsuk

Selection procedure
Assessment day: competency interview, case study interview, verbal reasoning test, watson glaser critical reasoning test

Application
Deadlines
Non-law - 31 January 2013
Law - 31 July 2013
Training contract vacancies 100
Minimum requirements
340(28) UCAS points,
Minimum 2:1 degree

Training
Salary
1st year £38,000
2nd year £43,000
Holiday entitlement 25 days
% of trainees with
a non-law degree p.a. 40%

Post-qualification
Salary £61,500
% of trainees offered job on qualification (2011/12) 82%

Overseas offices
Abu Dhabi, Amsterdam, Bangkok, Barcelona, Beijing, Brussels, Bucharest, Casablanca, Doha, Dubai, Düsseldorf, Frankfurt, Hong Kong, Istanbul, Kyiv, London, Luxembourg, Madrid, Milan, Moscow, Munich, New York, Paris, Perth, Prague, Riyadh, Rome, São Paulo, Shanghai, Singapore, Sydney, Tokyo, Warsaw, Washington, DC

Clyde & Co

The St Botolph Building, 138 Houndsditch, London EC3A 7AR
Tel: (020) 7876 5000 Fax: (020) 7876 5111
Email: theanswers@clydeco.com
Website: www.clydeco.com/graduate

Firm profile

Clyde & Co is an international law firm with a pioneering heritage and a resolute focus on its core sectors of aviation, energy, healthcare, infrastructure, industrials, insurance, professional practices, shipping and trade. With over 1,400 lawyers operating from 31 offices and associated offices across six continents, the firm advises corporations, financial institutions, private individuals and governments on a wide range of contentious and transactional matters.

Main areas of work

Core sectors: aviation, energy, healthcare, industrials, infrastructure, insurance, professional practices, shipping, trade and commodities.

Core practice areas: commercial, competition, corporate, dispute resolution, employment, finance, global governance, insolvency and reorganisation, international arbitration, projects and construction, real estate.

Trainee profile

An excellent academic record (including a 2:1 degree) are expected but equally important are your commercial and transferable skills. We look for trainees who take an interest in our clients' business, can apply their knowledge and intellect to practical legal problems, have the confidence to build relationships with clients and colleagues and are committed to a career in commercial law.

Training environment

You will gain early responsibility and be supported through close personal supervision and day-to-day coaching complemented by a wide range of training courses. You will undertake four six-month seats, which will cover both transactional and contentious work. You may also choose to be seconded to one of our overseas offices or have the opportunity for a client secondment.

Benefits

An optional £1,000 interest free loan on joining, pension, life assurance, dental insurance, private medical insurance, subsidised gym membership, interest-free season ticket loan, 25 days holiday per year, we also have a subsidised restaurant.

Vacation placements

The firm runs two-week summer and Easter schemes. Applications are made online at www.clydeco.com/graduate and the closing date is 31 January 2013.

Sponsorship & awards

GDL and LPC fees paid plus a maintenance grant of £7,000.

Partners 295*
Assistant Solicitors 1,034*
Trainees 100*
*denotes worldwide figures

Contact
Caroline Walsh, Head of Legal Trainee Recruitment and Development

Method of application
Online

Selection procedure
Assessment day

Closing date for 2015
31 July 2013

Application
Training contracts p.a. 35-40
Applications p.a. 1500
% interviewed p.a. 10%
Required degree grade 2:1

Training
Salary
1st year £36,000
2nd year £38,000
Holiday entitlement 25 days

Post-qualification
Salary (2012) £59,000
% of trainees offered job on qualification (2012) 96%

Overseas offices
Abu Dhabi, Australia, Belgrade*, Caracas, Dar es Salaam*, Doha, Dubai, Hong Kong, Libya, Montreal, Moscow, Mumbai*, Nantes, New Delhi*, New Jersey, New York, Paris, Perth, Piraeus, Rio de Janeiro*, Riyadh*, São Paulo, San Francisco, Shanghai, Singapore, St Petersburg*, Sydney, Toronto, Tripoli
*associate offices
Alliances: Mongolia - Khan Lex Advocates, Zimbabwe - Scanlen and Holderness

Cobbetts LLP

58 Mosley Street, Manchester M2 3H2
Tel: (0845) 165 5100
Email: gr8training@cobbetts.com
Website: www.cobbettsgraduate.com

Firm profile
Cobbetts LLP is a leading full-service commercial law firm recognised for its client focused relationships and its strong national and international capabilities. Its focus is firmly on delivering innovative solutions in a distinctive and personal way. We require talented individuals with first-class legal expertise and the necessary people skills to deliver outstanding value to both the firm and its clients. Our varied client base gives our trainees the opportunity to get involved in the legal work of major UK and international clients, private individuals, financial institutions, public sector bodies, listed and private companies, emerging enterprises and global multinational corporations. Working in a firm with a reputation for innovative, quality work and surrounded by business focused, forward thinking individuals, our trainees have the perfect opportunity to make their mark in a growing and successful legal business.

Main areas of work
Corporate finance; private equity; taxation; EU competition; state aid; banking and finance; business restructuring and insolvency; asset-backed lending; property finance; commercial; technology, media, trade and infrastructure; ICT and media; IT and IP; low-carbon energy; public sector; education; health; local government; co-operative and mutual services; dispute resolution; banking litigation; debt recovery; employment; pensions; HR advisory service; real estate; construction and engineering; property litigation; planning and environmental; social housing; regulatory; licensing; private client; charities; wills; wealth management and family law; regeneration and renewal; international services.

Trainee profile
We look for high academic achievers who show the potential to offer something above and beyond the undertaking of legal work. Individuals must demonstrate the confidence and commitment to thrive in a strong client centred commercial environment and have a desire for responsibility early in their training.

Training environment
Trainee solicitors are supervised by partners and solicitors who have the expertise to turn our trainees into confident and capable newly qualified solicitors. Trainees are supervised through five seats to gain a broad depth of experience in our core and specialist areas of law including banking and restructuring, commercial and IP, corporate, dispute resolution, employment and real estate. Depending on business needs, opportunities may also arise for a trainee to spend time on secondment at client or partner organisations.

Trainees also have the opportunity to develop their skills through the firm's structured CSR initiatives and various activities with students who will subsequently join as trainees. New trainees are supported before their training contract through the buddy scheme and LPC+ in conjunction with the College of Law, and during their training contract via practice area induction workshops and the PSC.

Benefits
Opportunity to join the BUPA healthcare scheme, gym membership, social club, pension scheme and season ticket travel loan. In addition to annual holiday entitlement, employees are also entitled to a free day's holiday for moving house and wedding day and have an option to buy or sell additional holidays.

Sponsorship & awards
GDL and LPC fees paid. Maintenance grant of £5,000 during the LPC year along with other financial incentives based on performance.

Partners 74
Other fee earners 251
Total Trainees 30

Contact
Katherine Elam
(0845) 165 5053
gr8training@cobbetts.com

Method of application
Online application form

Selection procedure
Assessment days

Closing dates
Training contracts 2015
31 July 2013
Summer vacation scheme
2013 31 January 2013

Application
Training contracts p.a. 12
Applications p.a. 1,100
% interviewed p.a. 5%
Required degree grade
2:1

Training
Salary for each year of training
1st year £23,695
2nd year £25,755
(both reviewed annually)
Holiday entitlement
Starting at 25 days

Post-qualification
Salary NQ £31,310
(reviewed annually)
% of trainees offered job
on qualification 80%

Other offices
Birmingham, Leeds, London

cobbetts

Collyer Bristow LLP

4 Bedford Row, London, WC1R 4DF
Tel: (020) 7242 7363 Fax: (020) 7405 0555
Email: recruitment@collyerbristow.com
Website: www.collyerbristow.com

Partners 29	
Trainees 8	
Total Staff 138	
Contact	
recruitment@collyerbristow.com	
Method of application	
Online application form	
Selection procedure	
Online testing & interview	
Training	
Salary	
1st year (2012) £28,500	
2nd year (2012) £31,500	
(Both reviewed annually)	

Firm profile

This long-established London firm provides a complete legal service to businesses and private individuals. Collyer Bristow is committed to providing a commercial and innovative approach to clients' legal issues, combined with a discrete and personal service, often not available from a large city practice. The firm's client base includes: multinationals, public and private companies, partnerships, entrepreneurs, public sector organisations and high net worth individuals, both in the UK and throughout the world.

The firm's Geneva office provides a base from which to serve clients in Switzerland, Europe and worldwide and, increasingly, to service its expanded private client offering.

The firm is well known for its ground-breaking in-house art gallery and is passionate in its support for the contemporary arts.

Main areas of work

Collyer Bristow has an impressive client base in such diverse sectors as real estate, media and sports, hotels and leisure, financial services and fashion, as well as a substantial private client practice. The firm's main areas of practice include corporate and commercial, real estate, dispute resolution, tax and estate planning, family, defamation and reputation management.

Trainee profile

The firm is looking for individuals who are able to demonstrate a strong academic performance, having gained a 2:1 or at least on track to achieve this. Successful candidates will be motivated individuals who possess strong commercial awareness, common sense and an ability to understand a client's needs.

Training environment

The firm's trainees spend six months in four of the firm's five key practice areas, working with a range of people from senior partners to more recently qualified solicitors. The firm has mentoring, training and appraisal programmes which nurture the development of technical expertise and client advisory skills. Trainees are encouraged at an early stage to take responsibility for their own files and to participate in managing the client's work.

Benefits

25 days holiday and usual benefits.

Sponsorship & awards

Full LPC funding and maintenance grant of £4,000.

Covington & Burling LLP

265 Strand, London WC2R 1BH
Tel: (020) 7067 2000 Fax: (020) 7067 2222
Email: graduate@cov.com
Website: www.cov.com

Partners 241*
Associate Lawyers & Others 601*
Total Trainees London

2010	14
2011	13
2012	13
2013	14

*denotes worldwide figures

Contact

Graduate Recruitment Team
(020) 7067 2000
graduate@cov.com

Method of application

Online application form
See website www.cov.com

Selection procedure

1st & 2nd interview

Closing date for 2015

31 July 2013

Application

Training contracts p.a. 6
Required degree grade 2:1

Training

Salary
1st year £40,000
2nd year £44,000
Holiday entitlement 25 days

Overseas offices

Beijing, Brussels, New York, San Diego, San Francisco, Silicon Valley, Washington

Firm profile

Covington & Burling's LLP London office, situated next to the Royal Courts of Justice, encompasses a broad range of expertise and practice areas. The office, established in 1988, combines deep industry knowledge with lawyers experienced in advising on a wide variety of leading-edge legal issues. The firm has over 800 lawyers globally, in offices in Beijing, Brussels, London, New York, San Francisco, San Diego, Silicon Valley and Washington. We practice as one firm, adhering closely to core values that start with a deep commitment to our clients and the production of top class quality work for them.

The firm has been rated a Top Ranked Leading Law Firm in Chambers UK 2012 and in The Lawyer as a Top 30 International Law firm. The firm is also rated as one of the leading firms by the American Lawyer. Ranked in 'The A-List', Covington & Burling is part of a listing of twenty elite US law firms which are assessed on financial performance, pro bono activity, associate satisfaction and diversity.

At Covington & Burling, you will have an opportunity to work on cutting-edge deals for international and UK corporates, global institutions such as Microsoft, GlaxoSmithKline and Procter & Gamble, Fortune 100 companies and leading technology, life sciences and media companies.

Main areas of work

Corporate advisory (including capital markets, M&A, finance, private equity, venture capital and funds), commercial litigation, data privacy, employment, financial services, insurance coverage disputes, intellectual property, internal investigations and compliance, international arbitration, life sciences, tax, technology and media. In addition, all our lawyers, including trainees, are encouraged to undertake pro bono work.

Trainee profile

We are looking for consistently high academic achievers, (on target for a 2:1 degree or above), commercial orientation, strong interpersonal skills and team players. Whilst some of our trainees read law at university, we welcome graduates from every discipline.

Training environment

You will do four six-month seats, rotating between departments. All trainees will undertake a seat in Corporate and a seat in Dispute Resolution. We can offer optional seats in the following areas: employment, intellectual property, life sciences regulatory, life sciences transactional, tax, technology and media. Client secondments may also be available.

We aim to distinguish our trainee programme by offering a genuine support network which includes assigning associate buddies and undertaking regular performance reviews. We have an excellent record of retaining trainees on qualification and we aim to recruit trainees who are interested in making a long term commitment to the firm.

Benefits

Private medical insurance, life assurance, permanent health insurance, pension, 25 day's holiday, season ticket loan and access to an employee assistance programme. We also have an active social calendar which includes regular firm drinks and sports activities.

Vacation placements

We have 24 places, split over three, week-long programmes. You will be paid £300 per week. Apply by 31 January 2013, online at www.cov.com.

Sponsorship

GDL and LPC course fees and a maintenance grant of £8,000 are paid.

COVINGTON
COVINGTON & BURLING LLP

Cripps Harries Hall LLP

Wallside House, 12 Mount Ephraim Road, Tunbridge Wells TN1 1EG
Tel: (01892) 506006 Fax: (01892) 598206
Email: graduates@crippslaw.com
Website: www.crippslaw.com

Firm profile

A leading regional law firm and one of the largest in the South East, the firm is recognised as being amongst the most progressive and innovative regional practices.

The firm's organisation into client-focused, industry sector groups promotes a strong ethos of client service and ensures the firm's solicitors are not only excellent legal practitioners but also experts in specialist business sectors. The firm is regarded by many businesses, institutions and wealthy individuals as the natural first choice among regional law firms. Although long-established, the firm's profile is young, professional, forward-thinking, friendly and informal. Recognised for the fourth year running as one of the UK's top emloyers having been awarded Best Companies' one star accreditation.

Main areas of work

Commercial 20%, dispute resolution 20%, private client 25%, property 35%.

Trainee profile

Individuals who are confident and capable, with lively but well organised minds and a genuine interest in delivering client solutions through effective and pragmatic use of the law; keen to make a meaningful contribution both during their contract and long term career with the firm.

Training environment

The firm offers a comprehensive induction course, a well structured training programme, frequent one to one reviews, regular in-house courses and seminars, good levels of support and real responsibility.

The training programme is broader than most other firms and typically includes six seats in both commercial and private client areas. Trainees usually share a room with a partner or an associate and gain varied and challenging first hand experience.

Sponsorship awards

Discretionary LPC funding: Fees – 50% interest free loan, 50% bursary.

Partners 38
Assistant Solicitors 62
Total Trainees 15

Contact
Alan Geaney
Director of HR & Development

Method of application
Application form available on website

Selection procedure
One interview with Managing Partner and Director of HR and Development

Closing date for 2015
31 July 2013

Application
Training contracts p.a. 8
Applications p.a. up to 200
% interviewed p.a. 20%
Required degree grade 2:1

Training
Salary
1st year (2012) £23,000
2nd year (2012) £25,000
Holiday entitlement 25 days
% of trainees with a non-law degree p.a. 25%

Post-qualification
Salary (2012) £37,500
% of trainees offered job on qualification (2012) 90%
% of assistants/associates (as at 2012) who joined as trainees 60%
% of partners (as at 1/5/2012) who joined as trainees 22%

Davenport Lyons

30 Old Burlington Street, London W1S 3NL
Tel: (020) 7468 2600 Fax: (020) 7437 8216
Website: www.davenportlyons.com

Firm profile
A leading business law firm offering a partner-led service. The firm provides commercial advice to its clients across a broad range of market sectors. The firm offers a unique combination of very strong corporate, tax, litigation and property capabilities coupled with specialist media and intellectual property expertise. Based in the luxurious surroundings of Mayfair, coupled with the firm's desire to retain its warm and friendly environment, Davenport Lyons is the ideal place to start your career as a successful solicitor.

Main areas of work
The firm provides comprehensive advice from its 17 legal services covering: corporate; intellectual property/rights; dispute resolution; property; commercial; tax; film and TV; employment and immigration; competition; defamation and privacy; information technology; insolvency and corporate reconstruction; licensing; aviation and travel; music; private client and wealth management; and family and children.

Trainee profile
Davenport Lyons is looking for candidates with excellent academic qualifications (2:1 and above, good A level results) and interesting backgrounds, who are practical and can demonstrate good business acumen. Candidates should have a breadth of interests and foreign language skills are an advantage. In short, the firm is looking for well-rounded individuals.

Training environment
The training programme consists of four six-month seats. During each seat trainees receive mid and end of the seat reviews, and each seat has a dedicated trainee supervisor. Davenport Lyons has an on-going in-house training and lecture programme. The firm prides itself on offering interesting, hands-on training with trainees being encouraged to develop their own client relationships and to handle their own files under appropriate supervision, therefore being treated as junior fee earners. The firm aims to make its training contract informative, educational, practical, supportive and, let us not forget, as enjoyable as possible.

Benefits
Season ticket loan; client introduction bonus; contribution to gym membership; discretionary bonus; 23 days holiday; life assurance; Employee Support Programme; pension and private health scheme.

Vacation placements
A limited number of places are available on the summer vacation scheme, which runs during July and August. Remuneration is £250 per week.

Sponsorship & awards
The firm does not offer financial assistance.

Partners 53
Fee Earners 65
Total Staff 193
Trainees 16

Contact
Dawn McEwen
Operations Director
Michael Hatchwell
Training Partner

Method of application
Apply online at
www.davenportlyons.com

Selection procedure
Interviews

Closing date for 2015
30 June 2013

Application
Training contracts p.a. 8
Applications p.a. c. 400
% interviewed p.a. 10%
Required degree grade 2:1, AAB
at A Level (320+ UCAS Points)

Training
Salary
1st Year trainee
£33,000 - £33,666
2nd Year trainee
£34,332 - £35,000
Holiday entitlement 23 days
% of trainees with a
non-law degree p.a. 70%

Post-qualification
% of trainees offered job
on qualification
(2012) 60%

Office
London

Davenport Lyons

Davis Polk & Wardwell London LLP

99 Gresham Street London EC2V 7NG
Tel: (020) 7418 1300 Fax: (020) 7418 1400
Website: www.davispolk.com/careers/londonrecruiting

Firm profile

Davis Polk is a global law firm. For more than 160 years, its lawyers have advised industry-leading companies and major financial institutions on their most challenging legal and business matters. Davis Polk ranks among the world's preeminent law firms across the entire range of its practice. With more than 750 lawyers in New York, Menlo Park, Washington DC, London, Paris, Madrid, Hong Kong, Beijing, Tokyo and Sao Paulo, the firm operates from key business centres around the world to provide clients with seamlessly integrated legal services of the highest calibre.

Main areas of work

We advise European companies, private equity firms, financial institutions and governments on all areas of business and finance, and we are regularly involved in the largest and most important securities offerings and M&A transactions in Europe.

Trainee profile

We seek to hire applicants from a variety of backgrounds with outstanding academic and non-academic achievements, personal skills and creativity, and with a demonstrated willingness to take initiative. We strive to find exceptional lawyers who share our commitment to excellence and who will be collaborative and supportive colleagues.

Training environment

Davis Polk trainees will work closely with and learn from our senior lawyers in London and in our offices around the world as we advise leading British, European and global corporations across the spectrum of their most complex legal matters. Given the quality of instruction, the meaningful legal experience gained on major global transactions and the opportunity to be a part of a dynamic and rapidly expanding practice at one of the world's truly preeminent law firms, there is no better place than Davis Polk for an aspiring solicitor to begin a career. Davis Polk trainees will also have the opportunity to work for a period in our New York office.

Benefits

Private medical insurance, life insurance, pension scheme, season ticket loan, subsidised gym membership, Employee Assistance Programme.

Vacation schemes

Davis Polk plans to offer three- to four-week vacation schemes in the summer for students interested in being considered for training contracts. During each vacation scheme, students will have the opportunity to work on international transactions for a variety of firm clients and attend training programs designed to teach skills required to become an effective solicitor as well as information sessions focused on the work of our UK practice. Students will also have the opportunity to experience Davis Polk's culture through interactions with lawyer mentors and attendance at social events.

We will be accepting applications for 2013 summer vacation schemes (by email to ukrecruitment@davispolk.com) from 1 November 2012 through 31 January 2013. We expect to offer 8-12 places on our vacation schemes in 2013.

Sponsorship & awards

GDL and LPC fees and maintenance grants are paid.

Partners 10
Counsel 2
Associates 30

Contact
ukrecruitment@davispolk.com

Method of application
If interested in applying for a training contract or a place on our vacation scheme, please send a copy of your CV, information on your academic results and a cover letter to ukrecruitment@davispolk.com. In your cover letter, please tell us why you are interested in pursuing a career at Davis Polk.

Selection procedure
Interview

Closing date for 2015
31 July 2013

Application
Training contracts p.a.
Approx. 4
Required degree grade 2:1

Training
Salary
1st year £50,000
2nd year £55,000

Post-qualification
Compensation £100,000

Overseas offices
New York, Menlo Park, Washington DC, Paris, Madrid, Hong Kong, Beijing, Tokyo and Sao Paulo

Dechert LLP

160 Queen Victoria Street, London EC4V 4QQ
Tel: (020) 7184 7000 Fax: (020) 7184 7001
Email: application@dechert.com
Website: www.dechert.com www.careers.dechert.com

Firm profile

Dechert LLP is a dynamic international law firm, with 2,000 professionals across the USA, Europe, Middle East and Asia. London is the third largest office, after Philadelphia and New York.

Main areas of work

The London office has particular strengths in investment funds, corporate and securities including private equity, litigation and finance and real estate; and smaller teams in employment, IP and tax.

Trainee profile

Dechert looks for enthusiasm, intelligence, an ability to find practical solutions and for powers of expression and persuasion. Graduates from any discipline are welcome to apply.

Training environment

The highly personalised six seat rotation system allows trainees to structure their training contract to their interests and aspirations and allows opportunity for secondments to overseas offices as well as to clients. Your seat plan and professional development are guided by both the graduate recruitment manager and by your dedicated trainee partner, who meet with you regularly. Your trainee partner is allocated to you when you start your training contract and acts as a sounding board and a source of support until you qualify.

Vacation placements

Work placement programmes at Easter and in the summer. The firm's work placement programmes are aimed at penultimate year law students. During our placements visitors are supervised by a partner or senior associate and they undertake a variety of tasks such as research projects and attending client meetings. Training sessions are also hosted throughout the scheme, on a range topics, such as presentation and client pitch skills. The closing date for applications is 31 January 2013.

Sponsorship & awards

The firm pays LPC fees plus £10,000 sponsorship.

Partners 41*
Assistant Solicitors 87*
Total Trainees 23*
*denotes London figure

Contact
Robert Girvan
Graduate Recruitment Manager

Method of application
Online

Selection procedure
An assessment morning or afternoon which includes interviews with partners, associates and recruiters and written tests

Closing date for 2015
31 July 2013

Application
Training contracts p.a. 10-12
Applications p.a. 1,000+
% interviewed p.a. Approx 10%
Required degree grade 2:1 (or capability of attaining a 2:1)

Training
Salary
1st year £40,000 +
2nd year £45,000 +
Holiday entitlement 25 days
% of trainees with a non-law degree p.a. Varies
No. of seats available abroad p.a. varies (Brussels, Dublin and others)

Post-qualification
Salary c.£61,500 + (depending on practice area)
% of trainees offered job on qualification 86% (2012)

Overseas offices
Almaty, Austin, Beijing, Boston, Brussels, Charlotte, Chicago, Dubai, Frankfurt, Hartford, Hong Kong, LA, Luxembourg, Moscow, Munich, New York, Orange County, Paris, Philadelphia, Princeton, San Francisco, Silicon Valley, Tblisi, Washington

Dickinson Dees LLP

St. Ann's Wharf, 112 Quayside, Newcastle upon Tyne NE1 3DX
Tel: (0844) 984 1500 Fax: (0844) 984 1501
Email: graduate.recruitment@dickinson-dees.com
Website: www.trainingcontract.com

Firm profile

Dickinson Dees enjoys an excellent reputation as one of the country's leading law firms. Based in Newcastle upon Tyne with additional offices in Tees Valley, Leeds and London, the firm prides itself on the breadth of expertise across its 38 practice areas which enables it to offer services of the highest standards to clients. Whilst many of the firm's clients are based in the North, Dickinson Dees works on a national basis for national and internationally based businesses and organisations.

Main areas of work

The firm has over 600 employees and is organised into four key departments (company and commercial, commercial property, litigation and wealth management) with 38 cross departmental teams advising on specific areas.

Trainee profile

The firm is looking for intellectually able, motivated and enthusiastic graduates from any discipline who have good communication skills. Successful applicants will understand the need to provide practical, commercial advice to clients. They will share the firm's commitment to self development and teamwork and its desire to provide clients with services which match their highest expectations.

Training environment

There are relatively few trainees for the size of the practice which ensures a supportive and friendly environment. You will be fully integrated into the firm and involved in all aspects of the firm's business. The training contract consists of four seats across the different departments. Trainees sit with their supervisors and appraisals are carried out every three months. The firm has its own Training Department as well as a supportive Graduate Recruitment Team. There are induction courses for each seat move with opportunities for trainees to get involved in the firm's training programme. The firm offers a tailored in-house Professional Skills Course.

Work placements

Places for 2013: 40; Duration: 1 week; Remuneration: £200 p.w. The firm's work placement weeks are part of the recruitment process and all applicants should apply online at www.trainingcontract.com. Apply by 31 January 2013 for Easter and summer placements.

Sponsorship & awards

GDL/LPC fees paid and maintenance grant offered.

Partners 59
Total Staff 618
Total Trainees 28

Contact
Joanne Smallwood, Graduate Recruitment Adviser

Method of application
Apply online at www.trainingcontract.com

Selection procedure
Online application, aptitude and ability tests, assessment day, presentation, interview

Closing date for 2015
31 July 2013

Application
Training contracts are based in Newcastle, Tees Valley and Leeds (up to 15 across the three offices)
Applications p.a. 800-900
% interviewed p.a. 10-25%
Required degree grade 2:1 in any subject

Training
Salary
1st year £20,000 (2011)
2nd year £21,000 (2011)
Holiday entitlement 25 days
% of trainees with a non-law degree p.a. 50-60%
No. of seats available abroad TBC

Post-qualification
% of trainees offered job on qualification (2012)
80% (12/15)
% of partners (as at 01/01/2012) who joined as trainees 35%

Other offices
Tees Valley, Leeds, London, Brussels (associated office)

DLA Piper UK LLP

3 Noble Street, London EC2V 7EE
Tel: (0870) 0111 111
Email: recruitment.graduate@dlapiper.com
Website: www.dlapipergraduates.co.uk

Firm profile
DLA Piper is one of the world's largest law firms, supporting clients across the globe with their legal and business needs. They now have 4,200 lawyers working in over 70 offices, across more than 30 countries in the Americas, Asia Pacific, Europe and the Middle East. Their vision is to be the leading global business law firm, delivering quality value-added services to their clients, both internationally and locally. Clients include local and international household name companies, financial institutions, FTSE and Fortune 500 enterprises, public bodies and governments. This means that lawyers at the firm work on a variety of interesting, high-quality deals and matters, that are cutting-edge and newsworthy.

Main areas of work
Corporate; employment, pensions and benefits; finance and projects; intellectual property and technology; litigation and regulatory; real estate; restructuring; and tax.

Trainee profile
DLA Piper feel that their success depends on their people, therefore they place a real emphasis and importance on the trainee recruitment process. The firm has been awarded a commendation for its diversity initiatives and policies, proving a commitment to recruiting and developing people from a wide variety of backgrounds.

DLA Piper welcomes applications from students from all degree disciplines, who have demonstrated consistent academic excellence. In addition they seek enthusiastic and committed individuals, whose good communication and analytical skills enable them to deal with the intellectual challenges of the job.

Training environment
Training at DLA Piper starts from the moment you accept their offer. They want to ensure that you feel part of the firm when you start your training contract. Therefore all future trainees have access to the online portal, 'Inside DLA Piper', where they are kept up to date with news from wherever they are in the world.

Upon starting their training contracts, trainees from across the globe attend a comprehensive residential induction, following which they will undertake four six-month seats in different areas of the firm. Trainees are given an opportunity to express what areas they would like to experience and also have the opportunity to do a seat abroad, or a client secondment.

If you want responsibility, you will be given as much as you can handle and your progress will be monitored via regular performance reviews and informal feedback. Trainees benefit from working closely with people at all levels of the business, as well as having client contact and continuous departmental training. Trainees are also encouraged to take part in business development and corporate responsibility initiatives to develop their professional skills and networks.

All of this combined provides trainees with an excellent grounding on which to build their legal careers.

Vacation placements
DLA Piper runs two week summer placement schemes across all of its UK offices. The scheme aims to give a thorough insight into life at the firm. There will be approximately 150 places available in 2013 and the closing date for applications is 31 January 2013.

Sponsorship & awards
Payment of LPC and GDL fees plus a maintenance grant in both years of up to £7,000.

Partners 300*
Fee-earners 780*
Total Trainees 180*
*denotes UK figures

Contact
Sally Carthy, Head of Graduate Recruitment
recruitment.graduate@dlapiper.com

Method of application
Online

Selection procedure
First interview followed by an assessment day

Closing date for 2015
31 July 2013

Application
Training contracts p.a. 90
Applications p.a. 4,050
% interviewed p.a. 13%
Required degree grade 2:1

Training
Salary 2011
1st year (London) £37,000
2nd year (London) £40,000
1st year (Regions) £22,000
2nd year (Regions) £24,000
Holiday entitlement 25 days

Post-qualification
Salary 2011
£60,000 (London)
£37,000 (English Regional offices)
£34,000 (Scotland)
% of trainees offered a job on qualification 91% (2011)

Regional / Overseas offices
Australia, Austria, Bahrain, Belgium, Birmingham, China, Croatia, Czech Republic, Edinburgh, France, Georgia, Germany, Glasgow, Hong Kong, Hungary, Italy, Japan, Kuwait, Leeds, Liverpool, London, Manchester, Mexico, Netherlands, Norway, Oman, Poland, Qatar, Romania, Russia, Saudi Arabia, Sheffield, Singapore, Slovak Republic, Spain, Thailand, UAE, Ukraine, USA

Dundas & Wilson LLP

Northwest Wing, Bush House, Aldwych, London, WC2B 4EZ
Tel: (020) 7240 2401 Fax: (020) 7240 2448
Email: lorraine.bale@dundas-wilson.com
Website: www.dundas-wilson.com

Firm profile

Dundas & Wilson is a UK commercial law firm, client centric in approach. It is highly rated by clients who value their determined focus and quality of service. Independently recognised for its unquestionable commitment to client service and for building long term sustainable client relationships, Dundas & Wilson is a dynamic and progressive organisation.

Main areas of work

The firm services a wide range of clients including major blue-chip commercial companies and public sector organisations. They are highly regarded for their legal and business expertise in the financial services, energy and infrastructure, real estate and government and public sectors as well as working with a large number of dynamic corporate organisations across a number of industries including food and drink, aerospace and professional services.

Key areas of expertise include construction and engineering, corporate, debt restructuring and recovery, dispute resolution, employment, environment, EU and competition, funds, intellectual property, information technology, outsourcing, pensions, planning, projects, property, property finance, public law, tax and transport.

Trainee profile

Dundas & Wilson are looking for applicants with enthusiasm, commitment, adaptability, strong written and oral communication skills, excellent interpersonal skills, commercial awareness and an aptitude for problem solving and analysis.

Training environment

The two year traineeship is split into four six-month seats. The firm aims to accommodate trainees' preferences when allocating seats as the firm wants to encourage trainees to take an active part in managing their career development.

During the traineeship trainees receive on-the-job training, two day seat training at the beginning of each seat, training in core skills such as drafting and effective legal writing and regular seminars. Trainees receive a formal performance review every three months and are allocated a mentor for each seat.

The firm's open plan environment means that trainees sit amongst assistants, associates, senior associates and Partners – this provides daily opportunities to observe how lawyers communicate both with clients and each other. This type of learning is invaluable and great preparation for life as a fully fledged lawyer.

Benefits

Life assurance, permanent health insurance, group personal pension, season ticket loan, holiday purchase scheme.

Vacation scheme

Dundas & Wilson offers three-week summer placements. To apply, please visit the website and complete the online application form. The closing date is 30 January 2013.

Sponsorship & awards

GDL and LPC fees paid plus maintenance grant.

Partners 83	
Lawyers 323	
Trainees 60	
Contact	
Lorraine Bale	
Method of application	
Online application	
Selection procedure	
Assessment day comprising interview, group exercise	
Closing date for 2015	
31 July 2013	
Application	
Training contracts p.a. 35 (12 in London)	
Applications p.a. 600	
% interviewed p.a. 15%	
Required degree grade 2:1 preferred	
Training	
Salary (2011)	
1st year (Scotland) £19,000 (England) £30,000	
2nd year (Scotland) £22,000 (England) £33,500	
Holiday entitlement 25 days	
Offices	
London, Edinburgh, Glasgow, Aberdeen	

DUNDAS & WILSON

DWF LLP

1 Scott Place, 2 Hardman Street, Manchester M3 3AA
Tel: (0161) 603 5000 Fax: (0161) 603 5050
Email: trainees@dwf.co.uk
Website: www.dwf.co.uk

Firm profile

DWF is a business law firm with a distinctive approach, providing a comprehensive range of legal services to corporate bodies, public sector institutions and private individuals. DWF was named 'Best National Law Firm' at the 2011 Legal Business Awards and ranked third among national firms in the UK for the Legal Week Client Satisfaction Survey 2011.

The firm employs over 1560 people, including 166 partners and 786 fee earners.

Main areas of work

Our legal teams are arranged under seven core practice groups, providing a broad range of expertise which enable us to meet the varied needs of our clients. These practice groups are corporate and commercial, private client and family, banking and finance, insurance, litigation, employment and pensions and real estate.

We align ourselves with our clients through cross-practice group sector groups which reflect the specific service needs of our clients in those sectors. These sector groups include financial services, energy and infrastructure, food, healthcare, outsourcing and technology, public sector, education, retail, transport, insurance and real estate.

Trainee profile

We're looking for people who are committed to a career in law, who enjoy working as part of a busy team and respond positively to a challenge.

Our trainees share ambition and the ability to bring something new and valuable to our team. Commercial accumen, good organisational skills and a fresh way of thinking about client needs are all hallmarks of a DWF team member. We also like to see candidates who have spent some time pursuing interests outside of academia.

We welcome training contract applications from penultimate year law students, final year students and graduates. We only take on a small number of trainee solicitors each year. It's a deliberate policy designed to make sure that each trainee gets plenty of hands-on experience.

Training environment

Our unique training contract is divided into six four-month 'seats'. This allows trainees to get a real taste of the variety of work we offer and make informed decisions about their future career. Trainees have the opportunity to sit in specialist departments within all of our practice groups and return to a preferred department for their final seat; enabling up to eight months pre-qualification experience in their chosen field.

Halfway through each seat, a senior member of our dedicated HR team will meet with each trainee to discuss progress. Trainees are also able to discuss which practice area they would like to target for their next seat rotation. We always do our best to accommodate seat preferences. Having completed four seats our trainees have a detailed discussion with the training principal about their future aspirations.

Vacation placements

Each summer we offer week long vacation scheme placements. During the week you will become fully immersed in one of our many practice groups and also have the opportunity to complete training relating to various legal skills.

Partners 166
Other fee-earners 786
Total Trainees c. 45

Contact
Alexandra Sutcliffe
Graduate Recruitment Officer

Method of application
Apply online via www.dwf.co.uk

Selection procedure
First interview, assessment centre and final selection day

Closing date for 2014/2015
Undergraduates 31 July 2013

Application
Training contracts p.a. 24
Applications p.a. c. 1,300
% interviewed p.a. 10%
Required degree grade 2:1

Training
Salary
1st year (2012)
up to £25,000 (Regional)
£35,000 (London)
Holiday entitlement
25 days p.a.

Post-qualification
% of trainees offered job
on qualification
(2010 and 2011) 100%

Benefits
Flexible benefits scheme including insurance, life assurance, contributory pension and others

Sponsorship & awards
LPC funding for course fees

Offices
Birmingham, Leeds, Liverpool, London, Manchester, Newcastle, Preston, Teeside

Edwards Wildman Palmer UK LLP

Dashwood, 69 Old Broad Street, London EC2M 1QS
Tel: (020) 7583 4055 Fax: (020) 7353 7377
Email: traineerecruitment@edwardswildman.com
Web: www.trainee.edwardswildman.com

Firm profile
Edwards Wildman is an ambitious international commercial law firm growing in strength and capability. Combining the expertise of over 650 lawyers in 30 practice groups across the UK, US and Hong Kong, we offer a full array of legal services to clients worldwide.

Main areas of work
Our key practices are in private equity, venture capital, corporate and finance transactions, complex litigation, insurance and reinsurance and intellectual property. Our work in London also includes: asset recovery; banking and finance, competition; employment; international arbitration; international law; product liability and restructuring and insolvency. Much of the work has an international context.

Trainee profile
Academic excellence is important but we also seek engaging and motivated individuals with the initiative and drive to make their mark. We value good commercial sense, adaptability and those capable of thinking on their feet. Our trainees work hard and have early responsibility and influence over the matters they work on. Therefore, you'll need to understand teamwork, show evidence of taking on responsibilities and communicating well with others. You'll also need great analytical skills and a rigorous approach. We look for people with interesting achievements and those who've made the most of their non-academic opportunities. A range of work/life experiences demonstrating these skills and qualities is key.

Training environment
We believe you learn best by doing, getting involved in real work from the start and because of our size in London, we can offer excellent training with high-quality work in a more personal environment. The firm gives trainees the chance to meet clients and join in marketing and client development activities. Trainees spend six months in four of the firm's major practice areas. Frequent workshops on our tailored training programme help develop the technical skills and knowledge needed in those areas. Secondment opportunities to major clients, or from time-to-time, one of our international offices, gives you the chance to build on and maximise the knowledge and skills gained. Regular structured feedback, reviews and constructive advice enable you to fulfil your true potential. A multi-level support network including buddies, partner mentors and the trainee recruitment team, ensures you have the correct level of guidance and support. Any suggestions or concerns can be voiced via our trainee solicitors' committee.

Benefits
Bupa, STL, subsidised gym membership, bonus scheme, pension scheme, life assurance, subsidised café, cycle to work scheme, confidential employee assistance scheme, free eye tests.

Vacation placements
The firm offers a structured two-week placement for 8-10 students in June/July of each year. We also host open days at Easter, Summer and Christmas – check website for dates and details.

Sponsorship
CPE/GDL and LPC funding, plus a maintenance grant of £7,000 (London) / £6,500 (outside London).

Partners 29
Assistant Solicitors 36
Total Trainees 16

Contact
Sarah Warnes 020 7556 4414

Method of application
Online applications only
www.trainee.edwardswildman.com

Selection procedure
Assessment morning plus one interview with two partners/senior associates

Closing date for 2015
31 July 2013

Application
Training contracts p.a. up to 8
Applications p.a. 700 approx
% interviewed p.a. 10%
Required degree grade 2:1

Training
Salary
1st year £38,000
2nd year £42,000
Holiday entitlement 25 days

Post-qualification
Salary £61,000

Summer placements
No. of places p.a. 8 to 10
Open days 4-5 accomodating up to 100 students in total
Closing date for summer placements 31 January 2013
Closing date for open days check website

Overseas Offices
US - New York, Boston, Chicago, Hartford, Los Angeles, Providence, Stamford, Washington, West Palm Beach, Newport Beach, Madison, Ft Lauderdale
Asia - Hong Kong, Tokyo.

EDWARDS WILDMAN

Eversheds

1 Wood Street, London EC2V 7WS
Tel: (0845) 497 9797 Fax: (0845) 497 4919
Email: gradrec@eversheds.com
Website: www.eversheds.com

Firm profile
Eversheds is one of the world's largest corporate law firms. Committed locally, but connected globally, with over 40 offices based in the world's major economic centres, with a proven track record of delivering consistently high quality legal services across jurisdictions.

Eversheds operates as one team, from 45 offices in 28 countries. Our people share a distinctive culture which has deep client relationships at its core. Whether providing advice which is complex or straightforward, multi-national or local, an attitude of delivering only the very best underscores everything we do.

Main areas of work
Core work: company commercial, litigation and dispute management, real estate, human resources (employment and pensions).

Trainee profile
Our firm attracts great people and we've created an environment where they can achieve great things.

True, you will need a strong academic background and proven ability to apply your intellect to complex problems. But that's just the start. Eversheds trainees need to be multi-faceted people who combine extreme professionalism with outstanding expertise, genuine approachability and real personality.

Training environment
Our training contracts consist of four seats of six months each over two years. At least one seat must be in a contentious area. As part of your training contract, you can also apply to do a secondment at a client office or at another Eversheds office in the UK or internationally. You will also take part in a full programme of personal and commercial development skills training, including finance and business, communication, presenting, business writing, client care, professional standards and advocacy.

Vacation placements
Two week summer placements are available across Eversheds' UK offices. Applications can be made at www.eversheds.com. The application deadline for the 2013 Schemes is 31 January 2013. Please visit the website for the dates of when these will take place.

Sponsorship & awards
GDL fees paid, plus maintenance grant of £7000 (London) or £5000 (other regions).

LPC fees paid, plus maintenance grant of £7000 (London) or £5000 (other regions).

Offices
Amman, Abu Dhabi, Amsterdam, Baghdad, Berne, Birmingham, Bratislava, Brussels, Bucharest, Budapest, Cambridge, Cardiff, Copenhagen, Doha, Dubai, Dublin, Edinburgh, Geneva, Hamburg, Hong Kong, Ipswich, Johannesburg, Leeds, London, Madrid, Manchester, Milan, Munich, Newcastle, Nottingham, Ostrava, Paris, Prague, Riga, Riyadh, Rome, Rotterdam, Shanghai, Singapore, Stockholm, Tallinn, Vienna, Vilnius, Warsaw, Zurich. In addition the firm has close relationships with preferred law firms across Europe, Middle East and America. Further details are available on the firm's website.

Partners 347
Lawyers 1,800
Total Trainees 120

Contact
gradrec@eversheds.com

Method of application
Apply online at
www.eversheds.com

Selection procedure
Application form and online tests, telephone interview, face to face interview, assessment day

Closing date
31st January 2013 for 2013 Summer Vacation Placement
31st July 2013 for 2015 Training Contracts
Applications open for both on 1st October 2012

Application
Training contracts p.a. 50-60
Applications p.a. 4,500
% interviewed p.a. 40%
Required degree grade 2:1 and 300 UCAS points

Training
Salary
1st year (2012)
London £36,000
Other regions £25,000
2nd year (2012)
London £37,000
Other regions £26,500
Holiday entitlement 25 days
% of trainees with a non-law degree p.a. 45%
No. of seats available abroad p.a. 6+

Post-qualification
Salary (2012)
London £59,000
Other regions £36,000
% of trainees offered job on qualification (2012) 85%

 EVERSHEDS

Farrer & Co LLP

66 Lincoln's Inn Fields, London WC2A 3LH
Tel: (020) 3375 7000 Fax: (020) 3375 7001
Email: training@farrer.co.uk
Website: www.farrer.co.uk

Firm profile
Farrer & Co is a mid-sized London law firm. The firm provides specialist advice to a large number of prominent private, institutional and commercial clients. Farrer & Co has built a successful law firm based on the goodwill of close client relationships, outstanding expertise in niche sectors and a careful attention to personal service and quality.

Main areas of work
The firm's breadth of expertise is reflected by the fact that it has an outstanding reputation in fields as diverse as matrimonial law, offshore tax planning, employment, heritage work, charity law, defamation and sports law.

Trainee profile
Trainees are expected to be highly motivated individuals with keen intellects and interesting and engaging personalities. Those applicants who appear to break the mould – as shown by their initiative for organisation, leadership, exploration, or enterprise – are far more likely to get an interview than the erudite, but otherwise unimpressive, student.

Training environment
The training programme involves each trainee in the widest range of cases, clients and issues possible in a single law firm, taking full advantage of the wide range of practice areas at Farrer & Co by offering six seats, rather than the more usual four. This provides a broad foundation of knowledge and experience and the opportunity to make an informed choice about the area of law in which to specialise. A high degree of involvement is encouraged under the direct supervision of solicitors and partners. Trainees attend an induction programme and regular internal lectures. The training partner reviews trainees' progress at the end of each seat and extensive feedback is given. The firm has a very friendly atmosphere and regular sporting and social events.

Benefits
Flexible benefits scheme, sporting teams/clubs, season ticket loan, 25 days' holiday, group income protection, group life assurance, company doctor, subsidised gym membership, subsidised yoga/pilates, pension scheme, private medical insurance after one year, wellwoman/wellman checks.

Vacation placements
Places for 2013: 30; Duration: 2 weeks at Easter, two schemes for 2 weeks in summer; Remuneration: £275 p.w.; Closing date: 31 January 2013.

Sponsorship & awards
CPE Funding: Fees paid plus £6,000 maintenance. LPC Funding: Fees paid plus £6,000 maintenance.

Partners 74
Assistant Solicitors 147
Total Trainees 20

Contact
Trainee Recruitment Manager

Method of application
Online via the firm's website

Selection procedure
Interviews with Trainee Recruitment Partner and partners

Closing date for 2015
31 July 2013

Application
Training contracts p.a.10
Applications p.a. 900
% interviewed p.a. 5%
Required degree grade 2:1

Training
Salary
1st year (Sept 2012) £33,000
2nd year (Sept 2012) £36,000
Holiday entitlement 25 days
% of trainees with non-law degrees p.a. 40-60%

Post-qualification
Salary (2012) £55,000
% of trainees offered job on qualification (2012) 100%
% of partners (as at 2012) who joined as trainees over 60%

FARRER&Co

Fladgate LLP

16 Great Queen Street, London WC2B 5DG
Tel: (020) 3036 7000 Fax: (020) 3036 7600
Email: trainees@fladgate.com Website: www.fladgate.com

Firm profile

Fladgate LLP is an innovative, progressive and thriving law firm which prides itself on its friendly and professional working environment. We are based in modern, attractive offices in London's Covent Garden.

Main areas of work

The firm provides a wide range of legal services to a portfolio of prestigious clients in the UK and overseas, including multinationals, major institutions and listed companies, clearing banks, lenders and entrepreneurs. Fladgate LLP's lawyers have experience in most major areas of practice and the firm combines an accessible and responsive style of service with first-class technical skills and in-depth expertise.

The firm has a strong international dimension based on multi-lingual and multi-qualified lawyers working in London and complemented by access to an extensive network of overseas lawyers. The firm operates specialist teams which serve continental Europe, India, Israel, South Africa, the US and the Middle East.

The firm's principal departments comprise corporate (which includes tax, private capital, restructuring and employment), litigation (which includes media and technology) and real estate (which includes planning, construction and real estate litigation). These are supported by specialist cross-departmental teams that provide co-ordinated advice on a range of issues.

Trainee profile

Fladgate LLP seeks trainees with enthusiasm, leadership potential and excellent interpersonal skills. You must be able to work both independently and in a team, and will be expected to show common sense and initiative. Awareness of the commercial interests of clients is essential. You will have a minimum of a 2:1 degree, although not necessarily in law, together with three excellent A levels or equivalent.

Training environment

Typically, you will complete four six-month seats. Each seat will bring you into contact with new clients and colleagues, and you can expect to gain real hands-on experience of a variety of deals and projects, both large and small. In each seat you will work alongside senior lawyers who will supervise your development and ensure that you are involved in challenging and interesting work. In addition to on-the-job training, each department has a comprehensive training schedule of seminars and workshops covering a range of legal and skills training.

The firm has a modern culture and an open-door policy where trainees are given early responsibility and encouraged to achieve their full potential.

Benefits

Pension, permanent health insurance, life assurance, season ticket loan, sports club loan, private medical.

Partners 50
Assistant Solicitors 37
Total Trainees 8

Contact
Mrs Annabelle Lawrence, Senior Human Resources Manager

Method of application
Please apply using the firm's application form. Further information and an application form are available at the firm's website www.fladgate.com

Selection procedure
Assessment day including interview

Application
For more details please visit www.fladgate.com
Training contracts p.a. 4
Required degree grade 2:1

Training
Starting salary £32,000
Holiday entitlement 25 days

Post-qualification
Salary £52,000

Foot Anstey LLP

Salt Quay House, 4 North East Quay, Sutton Harbour, Plymouth, PL4 0BN
Tel: (01752) 675000 Fax: (01752) 675500
Email: trainingcontracts@footanstey.com Website: www.footanstey.com

Firm profile

Foot Anstey is a premier regional law firm with a reputation for attracting the best talent. Recently awarded the accolade of Regional Law Firm of the Year at the British Legal Awards, the firm provides specialist legal advice to a discerning client base. The firm has a growing reputation for winning prestigious national clients, and for providing commercial advice. The firm continues to invest in people and technology and is committed to improving its significant service offering in order to provide clients with value for money and high quality advice. With strength across the core practice areas of; corporate and commercial, dispute resolution, employment and real estate, the firm has an enviable reputation with several lawyers ranked amongst the best in the UK.

The firm has grown rapidly in recent years and has significantly strengthened the offering with the opening of a Bristol Office. Foot Anstey has a reputation for being easy to do business with and provides a collaborative working environment and an infrastructure to match the leading firms. The firm has successfully attracted top lawyers from London and major regional centres who are able to combine the quality of life offered by the South West with high quality work that emanates from an impressive client portfolio.

Main areas of work

In addition to its core practice areas, Foot Anstey delivers a range of high quality services across key practice areas including media, financial services, education, charities, agriculture, clinical negligence and wealth and succession. Key clients include: Associated Newspapers, Eden Project, Halfords, Hitachi, Kingfisher, Lloyds Banking Group, NFU, Northcliffe Media, Odeon, Santander, Silvergate Media, Screwfix, ShelterBox, UKRD Group and national charities such as Sands.

Trainee profile

The firm welcomes applications from all law and non-law graduates who have a good academic background, exceptional communication skills, excellent commercial awareness and the ability to work as part of a dynamic team. Trainees are welcomed into a friendly and supportive environment where they will find the quality and variety of work both challenging and rewarding.

Training environment

Trainees undertake four seats of six months each. Seats are allocated following a written application process. Individual monthly meetings are held with supervisors and performance reviews take place at the end of each seat. Regular communication between the trainees and supervisors ensures an open and friendly environment. Trainees participate regularly in firm and client events and lunches with the Managing Partner. The Professional Skills Course is sponsored by Foot Anstey and provided by a highly regarded external training provider.

Benefits

Our flexible benefits package includes: 25 days' holiday (plus BH) and the option to buy/sell holiday, contributory pension scheme, life assurance, cyclescheme and childcare vouchers. In addition, non-contractual benefits offered include free conveyancing, discounted shopping and the "Lifestyle Hour" where employees benefit from enjoying one hour off work each week to promote a healthy work/life balance.

Vacation placements

Please see the website for the deadline and application form for the 2013 summer placement scheme.

Sponsorship & awards

Up to £9,600 grant available towards LPC and living expenses.

Partners 56
Assistant Solicitors 93
Trainees 14

Contact
Graduate Recruitment Team
trainingcontracts
@footanstey.com

Method of application
Applications for a training contract should be made using the online application form available at
www.footanstey.com

Selection procedure
Online Training Contract Application Form and Assessment Day

Closing date for 2015
See website

Application
Training Contracts p.a. 4 approx
Applications p.a. 300
% interviewed 10%
Required degree grade Usually 2:1 degree

Training
Salary
1st year (2012) £21,500
2nd year (2012) £23,000
Holiday entitlement 25 days

Post-qualification
Salary (2012) £33,750
% of trainees offered job on qualification (2012) 75%
% of assistant solicitors who joined as trainees 42%
% of partners who joined as trainees 9%

Offices
Bristol, Exeter, Plymouth, Taunton & Truro

Forbes

73 Northgate, Blackburn BB2 1AA
Tel: (01254) 580000 Fax: (01254) 222216
Email: graduate.recruitment@forbessolicitors.co.uk

Firm profile
Forbes is one of the largest practices in the north with 35 partners and over 360 members of staff based in nine offices across the north of England. The firm has a broad based practice dealing with both commercial and private client work and can therefore provide a varied and exciting training contract. The firm is however especially noted for excellence in its business law; civil litigation; insurance; crime; family and employment departments. It has a number of Higher Court Advocates and the firm holds many Legal Service Commission Franchises. Underlying the practice is a strong commitment to quality, training and career development – a commitment underlined by the fact that Forbes was one of the first firms to be recognised as an Investor in People and its ISO 9001 accreditation. For applicants looking for a 'city' practice without the associated hassles of working in a city then Forbes could be it. The firm can offer the best of both worlds – a large firm with extensive resources and support combined with a commitment to quality, people and the personal touch.

Main areas of work
Business law, civil litigation, housing, insurance, crime, family and employment services.

Trainee profile
Forbes looks for high-calibre recruits with strong North West connections and good academic records, who are also keen team players. Candidates should have a total commitment to client service and identify with the firm's philosophy of providing practical straightforward legal advice.

Training environment
A tailored training programme involves six months in four of the following: crime, civil litigation, insurance in Leeds or Blackburn, housing, matrimonial, employment and non-contentious/business law. Trainees may also be given the opportunity to experience secondments at major clients.

Partners 35
Assistant Solicitors 67
Total Trainees 8

Contact
Graduate Recruitment Manager

Method of application
Online application

Selection procedure
Interview with partners

Closing date for 2015
31 July 2013
If no invite to interview is received by 31/08/13 applicants to assume they have been unsuccesful.

Application
Training contracts p.a. 4
Applications p.a. 350 plus
% interviewed p.a. Varies
Required degree grade 2:1

Training
Salary
1st year At least Law Society minimum
2nd year £19,500
Holiday entitlement
20 days p.a.

Post-qualification
Salary
Highly competitive
% of trainees offered job on qualification (2012) 100%

forbessolicitors.

Freeth Cartwright LLP

Cumberland Court, 80 Mount Street, Nottingham NG1 6HH
Tel: (0845) 634 2600 Fax: (0115) 859 9600
Email: carole.wigley@freethcartwright.co.uk
Website: www.freethcartwright.co.uk

Firm profile

Tracing its origins back to 1805, Freeth Cartwright LLP became Nottingham's largest firm in 1994 with successful offices now established in Birmingham, Derby, Leicester, London, Manchester, Milton Keynes, Sheffield and Stoke on Trent. Whilst Freeth Cartwright LLP is a heavyweight commercial firm, serving a wide variety of corporate and institutional clients, there is also a commitment to a range of legal services, which includes a substantial private client element. This enables it to give a breadth of experience in training which is not always available in firms of a similar size.

Freeth Cartwright is extremely pleased to have been awarded The Sunday Times 100 Best Companies to Work for status in 2008, 2009 and 2010. The firm has also won awards for training and recruitment and its IT infrastructure.

Main areas of work

Real estate and construction, commercial services, private client and personal litigation.

Trainee profile

Freeth Cartwright LLP looks for people to bring their own perspective and individuality to the firm. The firm needs people who can cope with the intellectual demands of life as a lawyer and who possess the wider personal skills which are needed in its diverse practice. Successful applicants require a minimum of 320 UCAS points and a 2:1 degree (law or non-law).

Training environment

Freeth Cartwright LLP is committed to providing comprehensive training for all its staff. The firm's training programme is based on in-house training covering technical matters and personal skills, supplemented with external courses where appropriate. The firm endeavours to give the best possible experience during the training period, as it believes that informal training on-the-job is the most effective means of encouraging the skills required in a qualified solicitor. One of the firm's senior partners takes responsibility for all its trainees and their personal development, overseeing their progress through the firm and discussing performance based on feedback. Normally, the training contract will consist of four six month seats in different departments, most of which are available in the firm's Nottingham offices, although it is possible for trainees to spend at least one seat in another location.

Members 97
Assistant Solicitors 107
Total Trainees 18
Contact
Carole Wigley, Principal HR Manager

Method of application
Online application form

Selection procedure
Interview & selection day
Closing date for 2015
14 July 2013

Training
Starting salary (2011) £21,500

Offices
Birmingham, Derby, Leicester, London, Manchester, Milton Keynes, Nottingham, Sheffield and Stoke on Trent

Freeth
Cartwright
LLP

Freshfields Bruckhaus Deringer

65 Fleet Street, London EC4Y 1HS
Tel: (020) 7785 5554 Fax: (020) 7832 7001
Email: uktrainees@freshfields.com
Website: www.freshfields.com/uktrainees

Firm profile
As an international law firm, Freshfields Bruckhaus Deringer advises some of the world's most well known businesses. For graduates keen to pursue a career in commercial law, we offer challenging work that demands a strong intellect and a desire to help ambitious businesses achieve long-term success.

Our lawyers provide clients with a global service from our network of offices across Europe, the Americas and Asia. It is essential that our service is consistent and of the highest quality.

Main areas of work
Our lawyers work in teams, often of no more than three: a partner, an associate and a trainee. Whatever our clients want to achieve, the team's job is to work out how. Is it possible? What will be the most effective way of structuring the deal or tackling the problem? What are the risks? How should it be documented? The team has to provide real commercial solutions, not just what is right or wrong in law.

Organisationally, our lawyers work in one of eight departments: antitrust, competition and trade; corporate; dispute resolution; employment, pensions and benefits; finance; intellectual property/information technology; real estate; and tax.

Trainee profile
Background, university and the degree studied are immaterial. But every successful candidate has three qualities that are non-negotiable: intellectual talent, excellent English (written and verbal), and a generous spirit.

We pursue premium, cross-border work that is nearly always complicated. This means that the learning curve is steep, so the graduates who do best are those who like to be challenged.

Training environment
Graduates who accept a training contract with us have the opportunity to experience up to eight areas of law – twice the number offered by most law firms. The training is largely provided from our London office but many trainees will also spend time on secondment to a client or to one of our US, European or Asian offices.

Benefits
The firm offers a flexible and competitive benefits package.

Vacation placements
We normally take students on our vacation schemes who are in their penultimate year of an undergraduate degree. Again, you will need to submit an online application. The application window for our 2013 schemes is from 1 October 2012 to 13 January 2013. Since we offer places as we go along, the sooner you apply the better.

Sponsorship & awards
Before a training contract starts all graduates complete the Legal Practice Course; and non-law graduates also need to take the Graduate Diploma in Law before the LPC. The firm meets the cost and provides a maintenance grant for both.

Partners 430
Associates 1,634
Total Trainees 187
(London based)

Contact
uktrainees@freshfields.com

Method of application
Online application form

Selection procedure
Online verbal reasoning test, 2 interviews and written test

Closing date for 2015
31 July 2013 (law candidates)
1 May 2013 (non-law candidates)

Application
Training contracts p.a. 100
Applications p.a. c.2,000
% interviewed p.a. c.12%

Training
Salary
1st year £39,000
2nd year £44,000
Holiday entitlement 25 days
% of trainees with a
non-law degree p.a. c. 40%
No. of seats available
abroad p.a. c. 42

Post-qualification
Salary £65,000
% of trainees offered job
on qualification 91% (across
February and August 2012)

Overseas offices
Abu Dhabi, Amsterdam, Bahrain, Barcelona, Beijing, Berlin, Brussels, Cologne, Dubai, Düsseldorf, Frankfurt, Hamburg, Hanoi, Ho Chi Minh City, Hong Kong, Madrid, Milan, Moscow, Munich, New York, Paris, Rome, Shanghai, Tokyo, Vienna, Washington DC

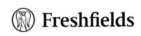 Freshfields

Gateley LLP

One Eleven, Edmund Street, Birmingham B3 2HJ
Tel: (0121) 234 0000 Fax: (0121) 234 0079
Email: graduaterecruitment.england@hbj-gw.com
Website: www.hbjgateleywareing.com

Firm profile

A 100 partner, UK commercial based practice with an excellent reputation for general commercial work and particular expertise in corporate, plc, commercial, employment, property, construction, insolvency, commercial dispute resolution, banking, tax and shipping.

The firm also offers individual clients a complete private client service including FSA-approved financial advice. The firm is expanding (569 employees) and offers a highly practical, commercial and fast-paced environment. HBJ Gateley Wareing has built an outstanding reputation across the UK for its practical approach, sound advice and professional commitment to its clients. The firm is a full range, multi-disciplinary legal business with expertise in many areas.

HBJ Gateley Wareing has an enviable reputation as a friendly and sociable place to work. The firm is committed to equality and diversity across the firm.

Trainee profile

To apply for a placement in England: applications are invited from second year law students and final year non-law students and graduates. Applicants should have (or be heading for) a minimum 2.1 degree, and should have at least three Bs (or equivalent) at A-level. Individuals should be hardworking team players capable of using initiative and demonstrating commercial awareness.

Training environment

Four six-month seats with ongoing supervision and appraisals every three months. PSC taken internally. In-house courses on skills such as time management, negotiation, IT, drafting, business skills, marketing, presenting and writing in plain English.

Benefits

Current trainee offered as a 'buddy' – a point of contact within the firm, library available, private health, life assurance (death in service) and season ticket loan.

Vacation placements

Two-week placement over the summer. Deadline for next year's vacation placement scheme is 11 February 2011 and the closing date for 2013 training contracts is 31 July 2011. Apply online at www.hbjgateleywareing.com. Paper/email applications not accepted.

Sponsorship & awards

LPC maintenance grant of £5,000.

Partners 100 (firmwide)
Vacancies 12 (England)
Total Trainees 16 (England)
Total Staff 569 (firmwide)

Contact
HR Department

Closing date for 2013
Training contracts:
31 July 2011
Vacation placements:
11 February 2011

Training
Salary
1st year £20,000-22,000 (Midlands)
2nd year £22,000-24,000 (Midlands)

Post-qualification
Salary £32,000 (Midlands)

Offices
Birmingham, Dubai, Edinburgh, Glasgow, Leicester, London and Nottingham.

Gordons LLP

Riverside West, Whitehall Road, Leeds, LS1 4AW
Tel: (0113) 227 0100 Fax: (0113) 227 0113
Forward House, 8 Duke Street, Bradford, BD1 3QX
Tel: (01274) 202202 Fax: (01274) 202100
Email: recruitment@gordonsllp.com
Website: www.gordonsllp.com

Firm profile

Gordons is a UK Top 100 law firm and one of the largest law firms based entirely in Yorkshire, with offices in Leeds and Bradford. The firm provides commercial and personal legal services to a wide range of businesses and individuals across the region and beyond, from the individual entrepreneur and small family business to the large PLC, and the firm's private client service is equally as comprehensive. The firm's approach is that of a straight-talking, hard-working, ambitious law firm that puts its clients' success before its own. They aim to be the law firm of choice in their region, providing a genuine alternative to the national firms.

Main areas of work

Commercial property; planning and environmental; construction; corporate; banking; insolvency; commercial litigation; intellectual property; employment; personal injury; contentious and non-contentious personal law; family law and residential property.

Trainee profile

The firm is looking for trainees who are eager to learn, have good interpersonal skills, can relate well to clients and who welcome responsibility at an early stage. Initiative, commercial awareness, IT skills and a friendly and professional manner are all essential qualities along with ambition to succeed. The firm sees its trainees as its partners of tomorrow!

Training environment

The firm's trainees spend a minimum of six months in at least three of the following departments: corporate, commercial property, litigation, private client. During the second year of the training contract trainees may state their preference for a particular department and the firm will try to accommodate the request where possible. The firm's trainees work closely with a partner or senior solicitor in each seat and get 'hands on' training with plenty of client contact. They are actively encouraged to get involved with marketing, networking, training, and other events hosted by the firm and / or clients, and the firm itself has regular social activities on offer, both formal and informal. The environment is supportive and friendly with an open door policy across the firm, and the trainees have regular meetings with their supervisors to ensure their progress. The firm aims to offer its trainees positions within the firm on qualification wherever possible.

Benefits

Group personal pension; life assurance of three x salary death in service benefit; interest-free season ticket loan; childcare vouchers scheme; 24 days holiday per year plus statutory holidays, free fruit; sports and social club.

Sponsorship & awards

The firm contributes £5,000 towards LPC course fees.

Partners 34
Assistant Solicitors 70
Total Trainees 11

Contact
Karen Mills, HR Manager
Philip Paget, Training Partner

Method of application
Online application via website
www.gordonsllp.com

Selection procedure
One stage interview process, including practical exercise and opportunity to meet current trainees

Closing date for 2015
1 July 2013

Application
Training contracts p.a. 4
Applications p.a. 400
% interviewed p.a. 8%
Required degree grade 2:1

Training
Salary
1st year £20,000
2nd year £22,000
(Reviewed annually)
Holiday entitlement 24 days and statutory
% of trainees with a non-law degree p.a. 50%

Post-qualification
NQ Salary £34,500 p.a.
(Reviewed annually)

Government Legal Service

Tel: 0845 3000 793
Email: glstrainees@tmpw.co.uk
Website: www.gls.gov.uk

Firm profile

The Government Legal Service (GLS) is the collective term for the 2000 lawyers working in the legal teams of over 30 of the largest government departments and agencies. These include departments such as the Department for Business, Innovation and Skills, HM Revenue and Customs, Department of Energy and Climate Change, the Ministry of Justice, Home Office and the Treasury Solicitor's Department but there are many more.

Although the legal teams are organisationally separate, together they form the GLS.

Main areas of work

Setting binding agreements to reduce carbon emissions by 2050. Harmonising discrimination legislation to protect individuals from unfair treatment and promote a fair and equal society. Constitutional change in respect of reforming the House of Lords. These are just some examples of the legislation our lawyers have been involved in recently. Providing a wide range of legal services to the Government of the day means that GLS lawyers and trainees operate at the cutting edge of law and politics. Regardless of whether they are advising government ministers on the legality of proposed policy, creating new legislation or representing the Government in high profile litigation cases, it's fair to say that our work is unique, fascinating and challenging in equal measure.

Trainee profile

To join the GLS as a trainee solicitor or pupil barrister, you'll need at least a 2:1 degree (which need not be in law). You must also provide evidence of strong analytical ability, excellent communication and interpersonal skills and motivation for working in public service.

Training environment

The GLS provides a unique and varied training environment for trainees and pupils. Generally, trainee solicitors work in four different areas of practice over a two-year period in the government department to which they are assigned. Pupil barristers divide their year's pupillage between their department and chambers. The GLS prides itself on involving trainees and pupils in the full range of casework conducted by their department. This frequently includes high profile matters and will be under the supervision of senior colleagues.

Benefits

These include professional development opportunities, pension scheme, civilised working hours, generous holiday entitlement and flexible working opportunities.

Vacation placements

A small number of placements may be available. Please check www.gls.gov.uk for further information.

Sponsorship & awards

LPC and BPTC fees as well as other compulsory Professional Skills Course fees. The GLS also provides a grant of around £5,000-7,000 for the vocational year. The GLS is unable to provide funding for the GDL.

Total Trainees around 50 currently working for the Government Legal Service

Contact
glstrainees@tmpw.co.uk or visit www.gls.gov.uk

Method of application
Online application form, situational judgement test and verbal reasoning test

Selection procedure
Half day assessment centre involving a written exercise, a competency based interview and a presentation

Closing date for 2015
31 July 2013

Application
Training contracts p.a. 20-25
Applications p.a. 2000+
% interviewed p.a. 5%
Required degree grade (need not be in law) 2:1

Training
Salary
1st year salary £23,250-£25,575
2nd year salary £24,850-£27,350
Holiday entitlement 25 days on entry

Post-qualification
Salary
£32,000-£40,000
% of trainees accepting job on qualification (2011) 100%

Harbottle & Lewis LLP

Hanover House, 14 Hanover Square, London W1S 1HP
Tel: (020) 7667 5000 Fax: (020) 7667 5100
Email: kathy.beilby@harbottle.com
Website: www.harbottle.com

Firm profile

Harbottle & Lewis provides a wide range of legal services to companies and individuals, primarily within the media and entertainment, technology, advertising, sponsorship, retail, leisure, sport, property, travel and aviation industries. The firm is committed to delivering innovative solutions in the most practical and cost-effective way and has been at the centre of many of these industries' largest and most high profile transactions and cases. Its lawyers are recognised for some of the most pioneering work in the exploitation of digital media and content.

Harbottle & Lewis is large enough to handle virtually any transaction in its specialist industry areas and complementary practices, but it is also of a size that enables it to deliver innovative, focused and commercially relevant advice based on extensive in-depth industry knowledge.

Main areas of work

As a full-service law firm Harbottle & Lewis provides advice on corporate, commercial, employment, financing, intellectual property, IT, litigation, property, tax, regulatory and data protection issues.

The firm offers specialist advice to clients in all areas of the communications and creative industries including advertising, broadcasting, digital media, fashion, film, interactive entertainment, live events, media finance, music, publishing, sponsorship, sport, television and theatre. It also advises on the legal issues faced by organisations and individuals in the media spotlight such as reputation management and private wealth management. The other services provided to individuals include tax, trusts and probate, family, employment, high-value residential property, image rights, asset freezing, mediation and personal injury. It also advises individuals and organisations involved in charities and philanthropy.

Trainee profile

Trainees will have demonstrated the high academic abilities, commercial awareness and initiative necessary to become part of a team advising clients in dynamic and demanding industries.

Training environment

The two year training contract is divided into four six-month seats where trainees will be given experience in a variety of legal skills. Seats include, corporate, employment, family/tax/private client, litigation property, a secondment to a long-standing client as well as seats in the firm's core industries, such as film, interactive entertainment, music, publishing, sport, television and theatre. The firm has a policy of accepting a small number of trainees to ensure they are given relevant and challenging work and are exposed to and have responsibility for a full range of legal tasks. The firm has its own seminar programme in both legal topics and industry know-how. An open door policy and a pragmatic entrepreneurial approach to legal practice provides a stimulating working environment.

Benefits

Lunch provided; season ticket loans.

Sponsorship & awards

LPC fees paid and interest-free loans towards maintenance.

Partners 38
Assistant Solicitors 43
Total Trainees 10

Contact
Kathy Beilby

Method of application
Application form to download from website

Selection procedure
Interview

Closing date for 2015
31 July 2013

Application
Training contracts p.a. 5
Applications p.a. 500
% interviewed p.a. 15%
Required degree grade 2:1

Training
Salary
1st year £30,000 (2012)
2nd year £31,000 (2012)
Holiday entitlement
in the first year 23 days
in the second year 26 days
% of trainees with
a non-law degree p.a. 40%

Post-qualification
Salary (2012) £50k

Harbottle & Lewis

Henmans LLP

5000 Oxford Business Park South, Oxford OX4 2BH
Tel: (01865) 780000 Fax: (01865) 778682
Email: viv.matthews@henmansllp.co.uk
Website: www.henmansllp.co.uk

Firm profile

Henmans LLP is a leading regional law firm and is proud to be the largest in Oxford. The firm has a national reputation in its specialist areas with many of its teams being highly ranked by legal industry commentators. The firm handles business and personal matters for a wide range of clients both nationally and internationally. The firm also acts for a large number of third sector organisations and insurers.

More than half of our partners and senior lawyers are acknowledged as experts within their fields, so clients are confident of receiving the most authoritative advice available. The firm believes that the best advisers are those who thoroughly understand the clients' concerns, so we work hard to ensure that we have a detailed appreciation of our clients' business or personal circumstances and can offer the best possible support and guidance.

Main areas of work

The firm's core service of litigation (including clinical negligence, commercial disputes, personal injury and professional negligence), is nationally recognised for its high quality. We also have an excellent reputation for our corporate, property, private client and charity work. The breakdown of our specialist areas is as follows: dispute resolution: 24%, personal injury and clinical negligence: 16%, property: 19%, corporate/employment: 11%, private client (including family/charities/trusts): 30%.

Trainee profile

Applicants should have sound commercial awareness, solid academic accomplishment including minimum 2:1 degree, intellectual capability, IT literacy, ability to work as part of a team and good communication skills.

Training environment

Trainees are an important part of the firm's future and we are committed to providing a high standard of training throughout the contract. Trainees are introduced to the firm with a detailed induction and overview of its client base. A trainee manual is provided to familiarise the trainee with each department's procedures. Experience is likely to be within the personal injury, property, dispute resolution, commercial (including employment) and private client departments though this can vary from time to time. The firm provides an ongoing programme of in-house education and regular performance reviews within its supportive friendly environment. The firm values commitment and enthusiasm both professionally and socially as an integral part of our culture. Trainees are encouraged to join in social activities and become involved with the life of the firm.

Benefits

Holiday entitlement 23 days + 2 firm days at Christmas, private health care, pension, life assurance, EAP scheme, free car parking and subsidised café.

Partners 21	
Other Solicitors & Fee-earners 33	
Total Trainees 6	
Contact	
Viv J Matthews (Mrs)	
MA CH FCIPD	
Head of HR	
Method of application	
Application form on website	
Selection procedure	
The interview process comprises an assessment day with Head of HR and partners, including an interview, presentation, verbal reasoning test, drafting and team exercise	
Closing date for 2015	
31 July 2013	
Application	
Training contracts p.a. 2	
Applications p.a. 250	
Training	
Salary	
1st year (2011) £23,000	
2nd year (2011) £25,000	
% of trainees with a non-law degree p.a. 40%	
Post-qualification	
Salary market rate	
% of assistants who joined as trainees 16%	
% of partners who joined as trainees 18%	

HENMANS LLP

Herbert Smith LLP

Exchange House, Primrose Street, London EC2A 2HS
Tel: (020) 7374 8000 Fax: (020) 7374 0888
Email: graduate.recruitment@herbertsmith.com
Website: www.herbertsmithgraduates.com

Firm profile

Pre-eminent in dispute resolution and with an outstanding reputation for high value transactional advice, Herbert Smith LLP is a leading international law firm. Its main clients are prominent global and national businesses that it serves from offices in Asia, Europe and the Middle East.

In June 2012, Herbert Smith and Freehills' partnerships announced their decision to merge. At the time of going to print, the firms were targeting 1st October 2012 as the day on which they will combine to form a new firm, Herbert Smith Freehills.

Main areas of work

Alongside Herbert Smith's outstanding reputation in dispute resolution and corporate work, the firm has leading practices in finance, real estate, competition, regulation and trade and employment, pensions and incentives. It is acknowledged as a leader in several industry sectors, including the energy and natural resources and financial institutions sectors.

Trainee profile

As well as a solid academic record, applicants require a strong level of commercial awareness and the common sense to make their own way in a large firm. Combine these qualities with a creative and questioning mind, and Herbert Smith will offer great challenges and rewards.

Training environment

The strength and breadth of the firm's practice areas guarantee excellent training and development opportunities for trainees. Trainees rotate around four six month seats and are encouraged to go on international or client secondment.

Sponsorship & awards

The firm provides funding and a maintenance allowance for GDL and LPC courses.

Vacation placements

Herbert Smith runs four vacation schemes each year, one in winter which is two weeks, and three in the summer, each three weeks long. The firm also runs two day workshops exclusively for first year students around Easter time, designed to give students an early insight into a career at an international law firm.

Partners 268
Fee-earners 1,517
Total Trainees 167

Contact
graduate.recruitment@
herbertsmith.com
020 7374 8000

Method of application
Online at
www.herbertsmithgraduates.com

Selection procedure
Online tests: Verbal reasoning, critical reasoning, situational judgement
Assessment Centre: Group exercise, case study presentation, competency interview.
Minimum 2:1 degree

Closing date for March/September 2015
1 October 2012 – 15 January 2013 for finalists/graduates
1 June – 31 July 2013 for penultimate year students

Training
Salary
1st year £38,000
2nd year £43,000
Holiday entitlement
25 days', rising to 27 on qualification
Approximate percentage law/non-law intake
law   60%
non-law   40%

Post-qualification
Salary (2012) £61,500
% of trainees offered job on qualification (March 2012) 88%

Overseas Offices
Offices throughout Asia, Europe and the Middle East

Herbert Smith

Hewitsons LLP

42 Newmarket Road, Cambridge CB5 8EP
Tel: (01604) 233233 Fax: (01223) 316511
Email: mail@hewitsons.com (for all offices)
Website: www.hewitsons.com (for all offices)

Firm profile
Established in 1865, the firm handles mostly company and commercial work, but has a growing body of public sector clients. The firm has three offices: Cambridge, Northampton and Milton Keynes.

Main areas of work
Three sections: corporate, property and private client.

Trainee profile
The firm is interested in applications from candidates who have achieved a high degree of success in academic studies and who are bright, personable and able to take the initiative.

Training environment
The firm offers four six-month seats.

Benefits
The PSC is provided during the first year of the training contract. This is coupled with an extensive programme of Trainee Solicitor Seminars provided by specialist in-house lawyers.

Vacation placements
Places for 2013: A few placements are available, application is by way of letter and CV to Caroline Lewis; Duration: 1 week.

Sponsorship & awards
Funding for the CPE and/or LPC is not provided.

Partners 41
Assistant Solicitors 33
Total Trainees 12

Contact
Caroline Lewis
7 Spencer Parade Northampton
NN1 5AB

Method of application
Firm's application form

Selection procedure
Interview

Closing date for 2015
31 August 2013

Application
Training contracts p.a. 10
Applications p.a. 850
% interviewed p.a. 10%
Required degree grade
2:1 min

Training
Salary
1st year £23,500
2nd year £23,500
Holiday entitlement 22 days
% of trainees with a
 non-law degree p.a. 50%

Post-qualification
Salary £35,000
% of trainees offered job
on qualification (2012) 83%

Higgs & Sons

3 Waterfront Business Park, Brierley Hill DY5 1LX
Tel: (0845) 111 5050 Fax: (01384) 327291
Email: graduaterecruitment@higgsandsons.co.uk
Website: www.higgsandsons.co.uk

Partners 29	
Fee Earners 86	
Total Trainees 8	

Contact
Helena Flavell

Method of application
Online application form

Selection procedure
Interview with trainee committee

Closing date for 2015
18th August 2013

Application
Training contracts p.a. 4/6
Applications p.a. 350 plus
% interviewed p.a. varies
Required degree grade preferably 2:1

Training
Salary reviewed annually
1st year £21,500
2nd year £24,000
Holiday entitlement
25 days p.a.
Post-qualification
Salary £32,000
% of trainees offered job on qualification 50%

Firm profile

Higgs & Sons is now one of the largest and most respected law firms in the West Midlands, operating out of two offices in Brierley Hill and Kingswinford and employing over 180 staff. During 2010 the firm moved its headquarters to a new purpose-designed facility at the prestigious Waterfront Business Park. The firm is well recognised in the Legal 500 and Chambers Guide to the Legal Profession. In 2011 the firm was awarded Law Firm of the Year (16+ Partners) by the Birmingham Law Society.

Higgs & Sons is different from the typical law firm. The firm successfully combines traditional values with an innovative approach to legal problems which has helped to attract an impressive client base whilst also staying true to the local community. Clients and staff alike are attracted to Higgs' ability to offer an all round service in a number of areas. The firm is proud to provide a supportive and friendly working environment within which both colleagues and clients can thrive. The opportunity for career progression is also clear as more than half of the firm's partners trained with the firm.

Main areas of work

For the business client: corporate and commercial, insolvency, employment law, commercial litigation, commercial property and regulatory.

For the private client: wills, probate, trusts and tax, employment law, personal injury, clinical negligence, conveyancing, dispute resolution, matrimonial/family, motoring and private criminal.

Trainee profile

Applications are welcome from law and non law students who can demonstrate consistently high academic records, a broad range of interpersonal skills and extra curricular activities and interests. The firm would like to hear about what you have done to develop your wider skills and awareness. It is looking for people who want to get involved and participate fully in the business.

Candidates will preferably have a 2:1 class degree.

Training environment

A training contract at Higgs is different from those offered by other firms. There is the unique opportunity to undertake six four-month seats in a variety of departments, including a double seat in the department in to which you wish to qualify as you approach the end of your training contract. Throughout the training contract you will receive a mix of contentious and non-contentious work and an open door policy means that there is always someone on hand to answer questions and supervise your work. Regular appraisals take place at the end of each seat and a designated Partner oversees you throughout the duration of your training contract, acting as a mentor. Participation in BTSS events and an active Higgs social environment ensures the work life balance.

Benefits

Private medical insurance, contributory pension, life assurance, 25 days holiday and BTSS Membership.

Sponsorship

Professional Skills Course.

Hill Dickinson

No. 1 St Paul's Square, Liverpool, L3 9SJ
Tel: (0151) 600 8000
Email: emma.mcavinchey@hilldickinson.com; rebecca.o'regan@hilldickinson.com
Website: www.hilldickinson.com

Firm profile

Hill Dickinson is a large international law firm with big clients, great people, award-winning services and fantastic opportunities. We're based in Liverpool, Manchester, Chester, London, Sheffield, Singapore and Piraeus, and our clients are all over the world.

To give you an idea of the culture here, we'd like to tell you the results of some client research we conducted recently. When we asked our clients to tell us what they think about Hill Dickinson, the three words they used most were 'friendly', 'professional' and 'knowledgeable'. It's true – here you'll find down-to-earth, approachable people who are exceptionally good at what they do.

Main areas of work

We are a full-service firm, so we cover all areas of law and work across a number of sectors, such as: health, insurance, public sector, corporate, banking and finance, property, transport, marine and retail. We pride ourselves on giving our clients a first class experience, so we look after them well and really get to know their objectives.

Trainee profile

For us, brain power is bare minimum. You'll need at least a 2:1, but you'll also need personality, commercial awareness, drive and lots of enthusiasm for your future profession. We'll be looking for people who have done vacation schemes and legal work placements, but we'll also be looking at your previous experiences in business – whether that's three months' work experience in a blue chip company, or eight years working in public services procurement.

Training environment

We're not shy of giving you meaningful responsibilities, and you'll have a chance to make an impact. You'll do four seats, each lasting six months, and will be able to select your preferences from around 18 different areas of law, dependent on your office location. If you train at our London office, you can even do a marine seat abroad.

Our partners will do their best to give you a helping hand and support you in whatever ways they can, and since you'll be sharing an office with them, they will get to know you pretty well!

We'll enrol you on an extensive training programme where we'll teach you about both conventional legal topics and specialised skills and knowledge - contributing to your professional growth and helping to make you the best lawyer you can be. You'll learn how to run a law firm from the top and we'll make sure you have the skills to move up the ranks.

There's also lots of fun to be had: our trainees work really hard, and it's definitely not all fun and games, but they do have a great social scene.

Benefits

As well as a host of fantastic training opportunities, we also provide some pretty good perks: pension, travel insurance, buying and selling holiday entitlement, permanent health insurance and life assurance, bicycle loans, season ticket loans, BUPA cover, and we'll even give you your birthday off (paid).

Sponsorship & awards

We'll pay your LPC fees in full and provide a maintenance grant.

Vacation placements

We offer up to six one-week schemes. There are up to 48 places available for 2013. Apply online by 31 January 2013.

Partners 200
Assistant Solicitors 209
Associates 74
Total Trainees 38

Contact
emma.mcavinchey@
hilldickinson.com;
rebecca.o'regan@hilldickinson.
com

Method of application
Online application form

Selection procedure
Online application, critical thinking test, assessment day

Closing dates for 2015
Vacation schemes 31st January 2013
Training contracts
31st July 2013 Northern Training Contract
30th June 2013 London Training Contract

Training
Salary
1st year (2010) £24,000
2nd year (2010) £26,000
1st year (London) £32,000
2nd year (London) £34,000
Holiday entitlement
25 days & birthday day off

Post-qualification
% of trainees offered job on qualification (2012) 81%

Offices
Liverpool, Manchester, London, Chester, Sheffield, Singapore, Piraeus

HILL DICKINSON

Hogan Lovells

Hogan Lovells, Atlantic House, Holborn Viaduct, London, EC1A 2FG
Tel (020) 7296 2000 Fax (020) 7296 2001
Email : recruit@hoganlovells.com
Website: www.hoganlovells.com/graduates

Firm profile

Hogan Lovells is a top global law firm, with over 2,300 lawyers working in over 40 offices in Asia, Europe, Latin America, the Middle East, and the United States. Our unique balance of ambition and approachability attracts prestigious clients and creates a working culture where the ambition of our trainee solicitors is supported to ensure their success.

Main areas of work

Our global diversity and wide range of practice areas gives us a strong reputation for corporate finance, dispute resolution, government regulatory and intellectual property. Exposure to a variety of legal disciplines provides good training and development opportunities for those joining us.

Trainee profile

We are looking for graduates whose combination of academic excellence and desire for specialist knowledge will contribute to developing business and taking it forward. Although we are one of the largest global legal practices, we work in small, hard-working teams where everybody is committed to our collective success.

The personal qualities our people possess are as important as their qualifications. You need to be happy collaborating with a team yet capable of, and used to, independent action. You will need to demonstrate an ability and desire for lateral thinking, be capable of close attention to detail, and have the energy, resilience and ambition to succeed in a top global law firm.

Training environment

As a trainee solicitor at Hogan Lovells, you will be offered work that sharpens your mind. You will take on as much responsibility as you can handle relating to client work, as well as a comprehensive legal skills training programme, regular reviews and appraisals. After qualification, continuous training and development remain a priority – you will deepen your professional and business expertise throughout your career. Making the best of your expertise enhances the quality of advice we provide to clients, maintains our reputation, and helps you build your career.

We require every prospective trainee solicitor to undertake the accelerated LPC at BPP London. The course will prepare you for practice in the City.

Our two-year training contract is split into four six-month periods of work experience known as 'seats'. As a trainee solicitor, you will move around four different practice areas during this time to gain as much experience as possible – one of your seats will be in either our corporate or finance group, and another in one of our litigation teams. You will also have the option of spending time in the second year of training on secondment to one of our international offices or to the in-house legal team of a major client.

Benefits

PPP medical insurance, life assurance, season ticket loan, in-house gym, access to dentist, doctor and physiotherapist, subsidised staff restaurant, discounts at local retailers.

Sponsorship

GDL and LPC course fees are paid, and maintenance grants are provided for both the GDL and LPC.

Partners 800+
Assistant Solicitors 2,300+
Total Trainees 146

Method of application
Online application form

Selection procedure
Assessment day

Closing date for 2015/2016
Law applications 31 July 2013
Non-Law applications 30 April 2013

Application
Training contracts p.a. up to 75
Applications p.a. 1,500
% interviewed p.a. 25%
Required degree grade 2:1

Training
Salary
1st year (2011) £38,000
2nd year (2011) £43,000
Holiday entitlement 25 days
% of trainees with a
non-law degree p.a. 50%
No. of seats available
abroad p.a. 25

Post-qualification
Salary £61,000

International offices
Abu Dhabi, Alicante, Amsterdam, Baltimore, Beijing, Berlin, Brussels, Budapest, Caracas, Colorado, Denver, Dubai, Dusseldorf, Frankfurt, Hamburg, Hanoi, Ho Chi Minh City, Hong Kong, Houston, Jakarta, Jeddah, London, Los Angeles, Madrid, Miami, Milan, Moscow, Munich, New York, Northern Virginia, Paris, Philadelphia, Prague, Riyadh, Rome, San Francisco, Shanghai, Silicon Valley, Singapore, Tokyo, Ulaanbaatar, Warsaw, Washington DC, Zagreb

Holman Fenwick Willan LLP

Friary Court, 65 Crutched Friars, London EC3N 2AE
Tel: (020) 7264 8000
Email: grad.recruitment@hfw.com
Website: www.hfw.com

Firm profile

We are an international law firm, with over 400 lawyers worldwide. Our culture and our lawyers are innovative and entrepreneurial. We are one of the world's leading specialists in shipping and transport, trade and energy, insurance and reinsurance and commercial law, serving clients globally.

Main areas of work

Admiralty and crisis management; aerospace; arbitration; asset finance; aviation; commercial litigation; competition law - EC and UK; commodities – soft and hard; construction; corporate; corporate finance; dispute resolution and mediation; employment; energy; environmental; fraud; information technology; insurance and reinsurance; intellectual property; logistics; marine litigation and claims; personal injury; port development; professional negligence; real estate; restructuring and insolvency; ship finance; space; world trade.

Trainee profile

We look for trainees with sharp minds, common sense, enthusiasm, ingenuity and a good sense of humour. We look for team players and good communicators who work hard and are client focused. We accept applications from all disciplines and backgrounds; from students and experienced graduates alike.

Training environment

Trainees are involved in a combination of trainee workshops, departmental know-how discussions, mentoring by experienced lawyers and on-the-job training. All our trainees are also encouraged to spend time on our numerous worldwide pro bono and CSR initiatives.

Each year we recruit only a small number of trainees - 15 per year. This enables us to give every trainee our full attention, and means that your individual contribution makes a big difference. Each trainee who joins us is guaranteed an outstanding training contract. You will do interesting, stretching work, very often with an international element. During your training you will have four six-month seats, sitting with a partner or a senior assistant. You may have the opportunity to work in one of our overseas offices (recently trainees have completed seats in Singapore, Hong Kong, Melbourne, Paris, Pireaus and Geneva), or to be seconded to a client.

Benefits

Our salaries are highly competitive. Trainees receive an annual salary of £36,000, increasing to £38,000 after the first year of the training contract. On top of that we offer additional benefits, which include: study assistance and grants; generous contributory pension; subsidised gym membership; season ticket loan; life assurance; medical insurance.

We encourage our trainees to get involved in out of office activities which include: sports teams (football, netball, softball, rugby, golf, cricket and sailing); quiz nights; dragon boat race; and staff parties.

Vacation placements

We run 2 x 2 week vacation schemes in June and July. We have 10 places on each scheme (20 in total). Vacation scheme participants gain practical experience and exposure, as well as attending a final round interview for a training contract during the scheme.

The deadline for 2013 vacation schemes is 14 February 2013.

Partners 142
Assistant Solicitors 240
Total Trainees 30

Contact
Sarah Burson

Method of application
Online application form

Selection procedure
Online application form, assessment centre, vacation scheme (if applied for), final round interview with 2 partners

Closing date for 2015
31 July 2013

Application
Training contracts p.a. 15
Required degree grade 2:1

Training
Salary (2012)
1st year £36,000
2nd year £38,000
Holiday entitlement 25 days
Number of seats available abroad Variable - 8 (2012)

Post-qualification
Salary £58,000 (2012)
% of trainees offered job on qualification
(Sept 2011) 94%

Overseas offices
Rouen, Paris, Brussels, Geneva, Piraeus, Dubai, Shanghai, Hong Kong, Singapore, Perth, Melbourne, Sydney, Sao Paulo

Ince & Co LLP

International House, 1 St Katharine's Way, London E1W 1AY
Email: recruitment@incelaw.com

Firm profile
With over 140 years of experience, Ince & Co LLP is one of the oldest law firms in the City. We've built our success by always taking an innovative approach, looking for new ways to apply legal strategies and create new law. Ince & Co LLP is frequently at the forefront of developments in contract and tort law. With a world leading reputation initially built on shipping and insurance, over the decades we have successfully explored new territory and established our expertise across a number of specific industries.

Main areas of work
We don't have rigid departmental structures here, instead we have five core business groups: aviation, energy and offshore, insurance and reinsurance, international trade and shipping. With clients ranging from insurers, brokers and banks, to oil companies and shipping companies, to airlines, aircraft manufacturers, entrepreneurs and major international trading groups, we can open up a world of opportunity for our trainees.

Trainee profile
Hardworking, competitive individuals with initiative who relish challenge and responsibility within a team environment. Academic achievements, positions of responsibility, sport and travel are all taken into account. We regard our trainees as future solicitors and potential partners, and our training programme is different. Ince trainees get involved in real legal work from day one, and the cases they assist on stay with them throughout their training period and sometimes beyond.

Training environment
Our open, friendly culture allows our trainees to make a real contribution and get involved in all aspects of our practice areas. Trainees will sit with four different partners for six months at a time throughout their training. Under close supervision, trainees are encouraged from an early stage to meet and visit clients, interview witnesses, liaise with counsel, deal with technical experts and handle opposing lawyers. As a result they quickly build up a portfolio of cases from a number of partners involved in a cross-section of the firm's practice.

Benefits
Season ticket loan; corporate health cover; private health insurance; contributory pension scheme; Well Man/Well Woman health checks; subsidised gym membership.

Vacation placements
Places for 2013 > 15; Duration > 2 weeks; Remuneration > £250 p.w.; Closing Date > 31 January 2013.

Sponsorship & awards
LPC fees; £7,000 grant for study in London and Guildford, £6,500 grant for study elsewhere.

GDL fees; £6,500 grant for study in London and Guildford, £6,000 grant for study elsewhere.

Partners 104*
Senior Associates 40*
Solicitors 145*
Total Trainees 35*
* denotes worldwide figures

Contact
Helen Salisbury

Method of application
Online at
http://graduates.incelaw.com

Selection procedure
Interview with HR professional
and a partner from the
Recruitment Committee & 4
tests

Closing date for 2015
31 July 2013

Application
Training contracts p.a. 15
Applications p.a. 1,000
% interviewed p.a. 10%
Required degree grade 2:1

Training
Salary
1st year £36,000
2nd year £39,000
Holiday entitlement 25 days
% of trainees with a
non-law degree p.a. 55%

Post-qualification
Salary £58,000
% of trainees offered job
on qualification (2011)
94% All accepted!
% of partners (as at 2011)
who joined as trainees approx
70%

Overseas offices
Dubai, Hamburg, Hong Kong,
Le Havre, Monaco, Paris,
Piraeus, Shanghai, Singapore

Irwin Mitchell

Riverside East, 2 Millsands, Sheffield S3 8DT
Tel: (0870) 1500 100 Fax: (0870) 197 3549
Email: graduaterecruitment@irwinmitchell.com
Website: www.irwinmitchell.com/graduates

Firm profile

Founded in 1912, the firm has grown from strength to strength and today employ more than 2,100 people. Nationally acclaimed, with strong international capabilities, Irwin Mitchell is one of a few law firms to provide a diverse range of legal services to businesses and private individuals. One of the largest law firms in the UK, Irwin Mitchell provides a wide range of legal services to over 200,000 clients a year, with particular strengths in litigation.

Main areas of work

Personal Legal Services - encompassing all our private client and legal services focussed on individual consumers. Business Legal Services - providing a full range of corporate and commercial legal services to businesses, institutions and organisations.

Trainee profile

The firm is looking for ambitious and well-motivated individuals who have a real commitment to the law and who can demonstrate a positive approach to work-life balance. Irwin Mitchell recruits law and non-law graduates and views social ability as important as academic achievement. Irwin Mitchell believes trainees are an investment for the future and endeavours to retain trainees upon qualification.

Training environment

The firms training contracts are streamed so that as a trainee you would either undertake a training contract based within the Personal Legal Services division, where you can gain experience in areas such as personal injury, clinical negligence, family, or court of protection or you would undertake a training contract based within the Business Legal Services division where you could gain experience in departments such as insolvency, commercial litigation, real estate, corporate or employment. Trainees undertaking a training contract will have three training seats and a qualification seat. This allows trainees to gain practical experience in diverse and innovative areas of law, whilst maximising retention opportunities.

Benefits

Pension scheme, professional subscriptions, Westfield health plan, death in service and critical illness cover.

Work placements

Each summer we run a formal work placement programme. The programme is a great way to get a real insight into what life is like as a trainee solicitor at Irwin Mitchell. An increasing number of our training contracts go to people who have previously undertaken a work placement, so we encourage all those interested in joining us to apply. The closing date for applications is the 1 February 2013.

Sponsorship & awards

GDL and LPC funding, if you have not started or completed your studies when offered a training contract, plus a maintenance grant of £4,500.

Partners 177
Total Trainees 88

Contact
Helen Cannon
Graduate Manager
graduaterecruitment@
irwinmitchell.com

Method of application
Please visit the firm's website
www.irwinmitchell.com/gradua
tes and complete the online
application

Selection procedure
Telephone interview and
assessment centre

Closing date for 2015
31 July 2013

Application
Training contracts p.a. circa 40
Applications p.a. 2,000-2,500
% interviewed p.a. 20%
Required degree grade The firm
does not require a specific
degree grade

Training
Salary
1st year £22,450
2nd year £24,650
(outside London)
reviewed annually in July
Holiday entitlement
24.5 days

Post-qualification
% of trainees offered job on
qualification 77.5%

Overseas / Regional offices
Birmingham, Bristol, Leeds,
London, Manchester,
Newcastle, Sheffield, Glasgow,
Madrid and Malaga

Jones Day

21 Tudor Street, London, EC4Y 0DJ
Tel: (020) 7039 5959 Fax: (020) 7039 5999
Email: recruit.london@jonesday.com
Website: www.jonesdaylondon.com

Firm profile

Jones Day operates as one firm worldwide with 2,500 lawyers in 37 offices. Jones Day in London is a key part of this international partnership and has around 200 lawyers, including around 50 partners and 30 trainees. This means that the firm can offer its lawyers a perfect combination - the intimacy and atmosphere of a medium sized City firm with access to both UK and multinational clients.

Main areas of work

Principal areas of practice at Jones Day include: corporate finance and M&A transactions; investment funds, private equity and corporate tax planning, banking, capital markets and structured finance, business restructuring, litigation, intellectual property, tax and real estate. The London office also has teams of lawyers who are experienced in such areas as competition/antitrust, energy, environmental, employment and pensions law.

Trainee profile

The firm looks for candidates with either a law or non-law degree who have strong intellectual and analytical ability, good communication skills and who can demonstrate resourcefulness, drive, dedication and the ability to engage with clients and colleagues.

Training environment

The firm operates a unique, non-rotational system of training whereby trainees receive work simultaneously from all departments in the firm. The training is designed to provide flexibility and responsibility from the start. Trainees are encouraged to assume their own workload, which allows early responsibility, a faster development of potential and the opportunity to compare and contrast the different disciplines alongside one another. Work will vary from small cases which the trainee may handle alone (under the supervision of a senior lawyer) to larger matters where they will assist a partner or an associate solicitor. The firm runs a structured training programme with a regular schedule of seminars to support the thorough practical training and regular feedback that trainees receive from the associates and partners they work with.

Placement schemes

60 places for 2012/13: Winter 2012 (non-law) - closing date 31 October 2012; Spring 2013 (non-law) - closing date 31 December 2012; Summer 2013 (law) - closing date 31 January 2013. Graduates/postgraduates can apply for any scheme.

Placements last for two weeks with an allowance of £400 per week. Students, graduates and post-graduates can see how the firm's non-rotational training system works in practice by taking on real work from a variety of practice areas. They are also able to meet a range of lawyers at various social events. Those interested in training at Jones Day are encouraged to apply for a placement first as most of the firm's future trainees are recruited from those attending its placement schemes. Applications open early on 1 September 2012 and, because the firm recruits on a rolling basis, it may fill its places ahead of deadlines.

Trainee benefits

Private healthcare, season ticket loan, subsidised sports club membership, group life cover, salary sacrifice schemes and access to stakeholder pension.

Sponsorship & awards

GDL and LPC fees paid and £8,000 maintenance p.a. Fast track LPC for sponsored students from August to February each year, allowing for a 6 month gap before training starts.

Partners approx 50
Assistant Solicitors approx 90
Total Trainees approx 30

Contact
Diana Spoudeas
Manager - Trainee Recruitment and Development

Method of application
Online at
www.jonesdaylondon.com

Selection procedure
Placement schemes
1 interview with partners
Training contracts
2 interviews with partners
Apply for placement first
Placement applications open early on 1 September 2012

Closing date for 2015
Placement schemes
31 January 2013 (unless places fill earlier)
Training contracts
31 July 2013 (unless places fill earlier)

Application
Placements p.a. 60
Training contracts p.a. 15
Applications p.a. 2,000
% interviewed p.a. 20%
Required degree grade 2:1

Training
Salary (2012)
Start £41,000
After 10 months £46,000
After 22 months £50,000
Holiday entitlement
5 weeks

Post-qualification
Salary (2012) £72,500
% of trainees offered job on qualification (2012) 100%

Overseas offices
Continental Europe, Asia, USA, Latin America, Middle East, Asia Pacific

K&L Gates LLP

One New Change, London, EC4M 9AF
Tel: (020) 7648 9000 Fax: (020) 7648 9001
Email: traineerecruitment@klgates.com
Website: www.klgates.com

Firm profile

K&L Gates LLP comprises nearly 2,000 lawyers who practice in more than 40 cities located on four continents. K&L Gates represents leading global corporations, growth and middle-market companies, capital markets participants and entrepreneurs in every major industry group as well as public sector entities, educational institutions, philanthropic organisations and individuals. The firm's practice is a robust full market practice – cutting edge, complex and dynamic, at once regional, national and international in scope. Over the last three years our firm's revenues have exceeded $1 billion and, as stated in the July 2010 issue of the UK publication Legal Business, the firm 'has further cemented its position as the Global 100's fastest growing firm.'

Main areas of work

K&L Gates is active in the areas of corporate/M&A, capital markets, private equity, restructuring and insolvency, finance, funds, antitrust, competition and trade regulation, real estate, planning and environment, intellectual property, digital media and sport, construction, insurance coverage, regulatory work, tax, employment, pensions and incentives, litigation, international arbitration, white collar crime and other forms of dispute resolution.

Trainee profile

The firm welcomes applications from both law and non-law students. Law students should generally be in their penultimate year of study and non-law students should be in their final year of study. The firm also welcomes applications from relevant postgraduates or others who have satisfied the 'academic stage of training' as required by the Solicitors Regulation Authority (SRA). You should be highly motivated, intellectually curious, with an interest in commercial law and be looking for comprehensive training.

Training environment

The firm ensures each trainee is given exceptional opportunities to learn, experience and develop so that they can achieve their maximum potential. Trainees spend six month seats in four of the areas mentioned above. Each trainee sits with a supervisor and is allocated an individual mentor to ensure all round supervision and training. The firm has a thorough induction scheme, and has won awards for its career development programme. High importance is placed on the acquisition of business and professional skills, with considerable emphasis on client contact and early responsibility. The training programme consists of weekly legal education seminars, workshops and a full programme of skills electives. Pro bono and corporate social responsibility activities are also encouraged.

Benefits

25 days holiday per annum, subsidised sports club membership, season ticket loan, permanent health insurance, life assurance, GP service and pension.

Legal work placements

The firm's formal legal work placement scheme is open to penultimate year law students, final year non-law students, other relevant post graduates or others who have satisfied the 'academic stage of training' as required by the SRA.

Sponsorship

GDL funding: fees paid plus £5,000 maintenance grant. LPC funding: fees paid plus £7,000 maintenance grant.

Partners 64
Trainees 16
Total Staff 280

Contact
Hayley Atherton

Method of application
Online at www.klgates.com

Selection procedure
Online testing, full assessment centre and interview

Closing date for 2015
31 July 2013

Application
Training contracts p.a. TBD
Applications p.a. 1,000
% interviewed p.a. 10%
Required degree grade 2:1

Training
Salary
1st year £35,000
2nd year £38,000
% of trainees with a non-law degree p.a. Varies

Post-qualification
Salary £60,000
% of trainees offered job on qualification 80%

Overseas offices
Anchorage, Austin, Beijing, Berlin, Boston, Brussels, Charleston, Charlotte, Chicago, Dallas, Dubai, Doha, Fort Worth, Frankfurt, Harrisburg, Hong Kong, Los Angeles, Miami, Milan, Moscow, Newark, New York, Orange County, Palo Alto, Paris, Pittsburgh, Portland, Raleigh, Research Triangle Park, San Diego, San Francisco, Sao Paulo, Seattle, Shanghai, Singapore, Spokane/Coeur d'Alene, Taipei, Tokyo, Warsaw and Washington.

K&L GATES

Kennedys

25 Fenchurch Avenue, London, EC3M 5AD
Tel: (020) 7667 9667 Fax: (020) 7667 9777
Email: r.bubb@kennedys-law.com
Website: www.kennedys-law.com

Firm profile

Kennedys is a specialist national and international legal firm with unrivalled expertise in litigation and dispute resolution. The firm has over 1000 people globally, across nine UK and nine international locations. Kennedys is a top 30 law firm and the firm's growth and success has been recognised by the 2010 Legal Business Awards, where it was awarded 'Law Firm of the Year' as well as 'Insurance Team of the Year' in the Legal Business Awards. Kennedys is regarded as a leader, not just because it has some of the most respected legal minds in their field - but because they know the importance of being practical, commercial and approachable. Kennedys prides itself on offering its clients clear legal advice.

Main areas of work

Kennedys lawyers provide a range of specialist legal services for many industries including: insurance/reinsurance, healthcare, construction, rail, local government, maritime and international trade – with a particular focus on dispute resolution and litigation.

Trainee profile

The firm is looking for graduates who are articulate, self aware and resourceful. Kennedys' trainees experience early responsibility and client contact, therefore it essential to have a mature and confident approach. Trainees with the firm must have commercial awareness and a strong appreciation of the interests of the client. As Kennedys has a vibrant and supportive working environment it is also looking for sociable, energetic team players.

Training environment

The purpose of the training contract is to give the trainees a mix of experience and skills that will set them up in their legal career as a solicitor with Kennedys. The firm's ability to consistently offer the majority of its trainees positions on qualification is attributable to producing newly qualified lawyers who are competent, confident and commercially driven. A balance of, responsibility, supervision and formal training achieves this. Kennedys ensures that their trainee solicitors are given sound training in the core disciplines. All partners and supervisors are readily accessible and always ready to offer support when needed.

Placement schemes

Kennedys runs summer vacation schemes during June and July. Applications should be made online for the 2013 schemes by 31 January 2013.

Benefits

Permanent health insurance, pension, private medial insurance, life insurance, 25 days holiday increasing to 27 days after five years, interest-free season ticket loan, gym membership, cycle to work scheme, child care assistance scheme, employee assistance scheme, corporate GP, contribution towards conveyancing fees and eye care vouchers.

Partners 154
Solicitors 408
Total Trainees 32

Contact
Rowena Bubb
Graduate Recruitment Advisor
r.bubb@kennedys-law.com

Method of application
Online Application Form

Selection procedure
Assessment Day

Closing date for 2014/2015
31 July 2013
Applications will reopen for 2015 training contacts on 1 October 2013

Application
Training contracts approx 18
Applications 900 (London)
Required degree grade 2:1 and 300 UCAS points or equivalent at A-level

Training
Salary
1st Year £34,000 (London)
2nd Year £37,000 (London)

Post-qualification
Salary £58,000 (London)
% of trainees offered job on qualification 85-90%

Offices
Auckland, Belfast, Birmingham, Cambridge, Chelmsford, Dubai, Dublin, Hong Kong, Lisbon, London, Madrid, Maidstone, Manchester, Miami, Sheffield, Singapore, Sydney, Taunton

Kennedys
Legal advice in black and white

Kingsley Napley LLP

Knights Quarter, 14 St John's Lane, London EC1M 4AJ
Tel: (020) 7814 1200 Fax: (020) 7490 2288 DX 22 Chancery Lane
Website: www.kingsleynapley.co.uk

Firm profile

Kingsley Napley is an internationally recognised law firm based in central London. Our wide range of expertise means that we can provide support for our clients in all areas of their business and private life. Many of our lawyers are leaders in their field and our practice areas are highly ranked by the legal directories.

We are known for combining creative solutions with pragmatism and a friendly, sensitive approach. The relationship between lawyer and client is key. We work hard to match clients with lawyers who have the right mix of skills, experience and approach in order to achieve the best possible outcome.

Main areas of work

Criminal, clinical negligence and PI, immigration, regulatory and professional discipline, dispute resolution, family, employment, real estate, private client, company commercial and public law.

Trainee profile

The firm looks for candidates with a strong academic background. A trainee will also need to demonstrate commercial awareness, motivation and enthusiasm. To be successful you will need excellent communication skills with the ability to be a creative practical problem solver, and to be a team player with a sense of humour.

Training environment

Your training contract will consist of four seats which aim to provide a wide range of practical experience and skills in contentious and non-contentious work. Our training programme is broader than most other firms due to the wide range of law practiced here.

Individual preference for seats is sought and will be balanced with the firm's needs.

Trainees work closely with partners and solicitors in a supportive team structure, and have regular reviews to assist development. The firm maintains a friendly and open environment and it is the firm's policy that each trainee sits with a partner or senior solicitor whilst working for a department as a whole.

The firm gives trainees the chance to meet clients, be responsible for their own work and join in marketing and client development activities.

Benefits

Private health insurance, income protection insurance, life assurance, pension, corporate cash plan and 25 days holiday per year during training. Trainees are also eligible to participate in the firm's flexible benefits scheme.

Partners 45
Assistant Solicitors 70
Total Trainees 10

Contact
Jemimah O'Connor
Tel 020 7369 3733

Method of application
Online only (via the Apply4Law link found on firm website)

Closing date for September 2014
31st May 2013

Closing date for September 2015
31 May 2014

Application
Training contracts p.a. 5
Applications p.a. 250
% interviewed p.a 10%
Required degree grade 2:1

Training
Salary (2012)
First year £28,000
Second year £30,000
Holiday entitlement 25 days
% of trainees with a non-law degree 60%

Post qualification
Salary (2012) £49,000
% of trainees offered job on qualification 80%

Kingsley Napley

Kirkland & Ellis International LLP

30 St Mary Axe, London EC3A 8AF
Tel: (020) 7469 2000 Fax: (020) 7469 2001
Website: www.kirkland.com/ukgraduate

Partners 707
Assistant solicitors 881
Contact Kate Osborne
Method of application Online application form
Selection procedure Interview
Closing date for 2015 31 July 2013
Training Salary 1st year (2011) £41,000 2nd year (2011) £44,000 Holiday entitlement 25 days
Post-qualification (currently no data)
Overseas/ regional offices Chicago, Hong Kong, Los Angeles, Munich, New York, Palo Alto, San Francisco, Shanghai, Washington D.C.

Firm profile
Kirkland & Ellis International LLP is a 1,500-attorney law firm representing global clients in offices around the world.

For over 100 years, major national and international clients have called upon Kirkland & Ellis to provide superior legal advice and client services. The firm's London office has been the hub of European operations since 1994. Here, approximately 120 lawyers offer detailed expertise to a wide range of UK and international clients.

Main areas of work
The firm handles complex corporate, debt finance, restructuring, funds, capital markets, tax, intellectual property, antitrust and competition, litigation and counselling matters. Kirkland & Ellis operates as a strategic network, committing the full resources of an international firm to any matter in any territory as appropriate.

Trainee profile
Your academic record will be excellent, probably culminating in an expected or achieved 2:1. You will have the initiative, the drive and the work ethic to thrive in the firm's meritocratic culture and arrive with an understanding of the work undertaken in the firm's London office.

Training environment
As one of a select number of trainees, you will be given early responsibility to work on complex multi jurisdictional matters.

The principal focus of your training will be on corporate law with a specialism in private equity. You will complete four, six month seats and obtain training in areas such as debt finance, funds, arbitration, IP, antitrust and competition, restructuring and tax. In addition there will be opportunities to undertake an overseas secondment to enable you to experience the international resources and capabilities of Kirkland & Ellis.

Your on the job training will be actively supported by an extensive education programme, carefully tailored to meet your needs.

Benefits
Private medical insurance, travel insurance, life insurance, employee assistance plan, corporate gym membership.

Vacation placements
Places for 2013: up to 20. Duration: 2 weeks. Remuneration: £350 per week. Closing date for applications: 31 January 2013.

Sponsorship & awards
GDL and LPC course fees and a maintenance grant of £7,500 p.a.

KIRKLAND & ELLIS INTERNATIONAL LLP

Latham & Watkins

99 Bishopsgate, London, EC2M 3XF
Tel: (020) 7710 1000 Fax: (020) 7374 4460
Email: london.trainees@lw.com
Website: www.lw.com

Firm profile
Latham & Watkins has more than 2,000 lawyers in 31 offices across Europe, America and Asia and the London office advises on some of the most significant and groundbreaking cross-border transactions in Europe. The firm believes that its non-hierarchical management style and 'one firm' culture makes Latham & Watkins unique.

Main areas of work
Latham & Watkins has strong capabilites in all areas, including banking and finance, corporate, litigation, real estate, employment and tax. Many of the firm's practice groups are award-winning industry leaders, as are many of the firm's partners.

Trainee profile
Candidates should be entrepreneurial and thrive on early responsibility. Those with a strong academic background, excellent communication skills and a consistent record of personal and/or professional achievement will be rewarded with first-class training in a stimulating environment. The firm is dedicated to diversity and equal opportunity and values originality and creative thinking.

Training environment
Latham & Watkins can provide a very different training experience to that offered by the rest of the elite law firms. Each trainee receives bespoke supervision and outstanding support while being encouraged to recognise that they have their own part to play in the growth and success of the firm. Each trainee also has meaningful responsibility from the outset and significant legal experience on qualification. It is also common for trainees to be given the opportunity to spend one of their four six-month seats in one of the firm's overseas offices.

Benefits
Healthcare and dental scheme, pension scheme and life assurance.

Sponsorship & awards
All GDL and LPC costs are paid and trainees receive a maintenance grant of £8,000 per year whilst studying. A bonus of £500 is provided by the firm if a distinction is achieved in the LPC.

Vacation placements
The firm has a two-week Easter vacation scheme for graduates and final year law and non-law students and a two-week summer scheme for penultimate year law students. Students are paid £350 per week. The deadline for Easter scheme applications is 31st December and the deadline for summer scheme applications is 31st January.

Partners 57
Associates 155
Trainees 34

Contact
Lisa Baca

Method of application
Online application form at
www.lw.com

Selection procedure
3 x 30 minute interviews with
a partner and an associate

Closing date for 2015
31 July 2013

Application
Training contracts p.a. 20
Required degree grade 2:1

Training
Salary
1st year (2012) £42,000
2nd year (2012) £45,000

Post-qualification
Salary £96,970

Overseas/regional offices
Abu Dhabi, Barcelona, Beijing, Boston, Brussels, Chicago, Doha, Dubai, Frankfurt, Hamburg, Hong Kong, Houston, London, Los Angeles, Madrid, Milan, Moscow, Munich, New Jersey, New York, Orange County, Paris, Riyadh, Rome, San Diego, San Francisco, Shanghai, Silicon Valley, Singapore, Tokyo, Washington DC

LATHAM&WATKINS

Lawrence Graham LLP

4 More London Riverside, London, SE1 2AU
Tel: (020) 7379 0000 Fax: (020) 7173 8694
Email: graduate@lg-legal.com
Website: http://graduates.lg-legal.com

Firm profile
Lawrence Graham is a distinctive legal practice with a leading reputation in its chosen services and sectors. The firm's approach is relationship-driven and internationally minded, with great people dedicated to their clients.

The firm services its clients from international offices in London, Dubai, Monaco, Russia and Singapore, and also through its close relationships with other advisers in its key jurisdictions. Together, Lawrence Graham advises seamlessly on the most complex cases, cross-border deals and disputes.

Main areas of work
Lawrence Graham offers a full range of legal services with particular focus on commerce and technology, corporate, dispute resolution, employment and pensions, finance, real estate and tax and private capital. It has a specific understanding of the issues facing businesses and individuals operating in its key sectors: energy and natural resources, financial institutions, healthcare, hospitality and leisure, private capital, publishing and media, real estate, support services and technology.

Over 42% of the firm's transactions are now handled for companies outside the UK. The emerging markets of India, South East Asia, the Middle East and South America remain of critical importance to the firm and its clients, while exciting new business opportunities in the more mature markets of Europe and North America keep it firmly centred on those regions.

Lawrence Graham is proud to have a culture that is open and refreshingly straightforward. It employs highly talented individuals, while valuing a strong team ethic - and that is fundamental to the way it works as a business.

Trainee profile
The firm is looking for individuals from a variety of backgrounds with refined communication skills who can demonstrate a commitment to a career in the commercial application of law. A strong academic track record with a minimum of 320 UCAS tariff points and a 2:1 degree is a basic requirement. Also required is a good record of achievement in other areas – indicative of the ability to succeed in a demanding career – and evidence of team working skills and the ability to handle responsibility.

Training environment
Under partner supervision, trainees will be given early responsibility. Training is structured to facilitate the ability to manage one's own files and interact with clients. In addition to the Professional Skills Course, there are departmental training and induction sessions as well as a two year rolling training programme, designed to develop well-rounded lawyers. Training consists of four six-month seats: real estate, transactional and contentious seats are compulsory.

Benefits
Season ticket loan, life assurance.

Vacation placements
Places for 2013: 24; Duration: 3 x 2 weeks between June and July; Remuneration: £350 p.w; Closing date: 31 January 2013.

Sponsorship & awards
GDL Funding: Course fees and maintenance grant. £6k outside London, £6.5k in London.

LPC Funding: Course fees and maintenance grant. £6.5k in London.

Partners 68
Assistant Solicitors 101
Total Trainees 32

Contact
Vicki Thompson
Graduate Recruitment Manager

Method of application
Firm's online application form

Selection procedure
Verbal reasoning test, Partner interview and assessed case study

Closing date for 2015
31 July 2013

Application
Training contracts approx 15
Applications p.a. 800
Required degree grade 2:1

Training
Salary
£35,000
% of trainees with a
non-law degree p.a. 50%

Post-qualification
Salary £57,000
% of trainees offered job
on qualification (2011) 84%

Overseas offices
Dubai, Monaco, Moscow and Singapore

Lester Aldridge LLP

Russell House, Oxford Road, Bournemouth BH8 8EX
Tel: (01202) 786161 Fax: (01202) 786110
Email: humanresources@LA-law.com
Website: www.lesteraldridge.com

Firm profile

Lester Aldridge LLP is an energetic business providing both commercial and private client services on a local, regional, national and international scale. The firm's reputation rests on the expertise of its people who are first-class in every respect, and on the firm's astute approach to its clients. Client satisfaction is always the firm's aim.

History is important in any business – it shows a commitment to its industry and its clients and the firm is proud of its own history. Lester Aldridge's positioning on the south coast offers a positive working environment and a great work life balance; while providing opportunities to work with first class lawyers, impressive clients and opportunity for City experience via LA's London office.

Excellent legal advice is standard. Each client can expect a commitment to excellent service from its staff, a partner led approach, leading legal expertise, comprehensive and cohesive advice, innovative and technological support and value for money.

Main areas of work

LA's work is divided up into 5 groups – Dispute Resolution, Corporate and Commercial, Banking and Finance, Real Estate and Private Client. Within these groups the firm has a number of sectors which offer a cross section of these work types – these include marine, charities, fertility and same sex couples, development, care and medical practices. As a trainee, you will get involved in the broad range giving you choice and experience for your future career in law.

Trainee profile

Candidates should have a consistently strong academic record, be commercially aware and possess a broad range of interpersonal skills. Applicants should be highly motivated and have a desire to succeed working with teams to advise clients in dynamic and demanding industries.

Training environment

When you start at LA you'll be given responsibilities and real jobs to get your teeth into. Direct client involvement is encouraged and you will become an integral part of each team you join.

During the course of your two year contract you will complete four seats of six months duration. This gives you exposure to different areas of the firm and hopefully will help you decide what you would like to specialise in.

Giving constructive feedback is always encouraged at LA, so you can expect to hear the good things about your work from your team (and a few things you need to improve). LA also has an appraisal system where you work with your team leader to set objectives and create an action plan that will measure your progress. In addition each trainee is assigned a mentor to provide guidance and encouragement and regular review meetings are arranged with the Managing Partner where you'll be encouraged to voice your views and opinions.

Vacation placements

The firm offers 2 week work placements in the summer of each year. The application deadline is usually 31 March but please check the firm's website for further details on how to apply.

Sponsorship

LPC loan currently under review.

Vacancies 6
Trainees 12
Total Staff 275
Contact
HR Team
Method of application
Apply to human resources application form
Selection procedure
Interview by a panel of partners as part of assessment and development day
Closing date for 2015
30 June 2013
Application
Training contracts p.a. 6
Applications p.a. 133
% interviewed p.a. 10%
Minimum required degree grade 2:1
Training Salary
Starting salary Competitive market rate for a south coast firm plus additional London allowance where appropriate
Holiday entitlement 22 days
Offices
Bournemouth (2), Southampton & London

 LesterAldridge LLP

Lewis Silkin

5 Chancery Lane, Clifford's Inn, London EC4A 1BL
Tel: (020) 7074 8000 Fax: (020) 7864 1200
Email: train@lewissilkin.com
Website: www.lewissilkin.com

Firm profile
Lewis Silkin is a commercial firm with 60 partners. Due to its expertise and the number of leaders in their respective fields, it has an impressive list of household name clients, ranging from large multinational corporations to brands to government agencies and entrepreneurs, across a wide range of sectors. What distinguishes them is a matter of personality. For lawyers, they are notably informal, unstuffy…well, human really. They are 'people people'; as committed and professional as any good law firm, but perhaps more adept at the inter-personal skills that make relationships work and go on working. They place a high priority on the excellent technical ability and commercial thinking of their lawyers and also on their relationships with clients. Clients find them refreshingly easy to deal with. The firm has a friendly, lively style with a commitment to continuous improvement.

Main areas of work
Lewis Silkin provides services through five departments: Corporate; Employment, Reward and Immigration; Litigation and Dispute Resolution; Real Estate and Development; and Media, Brands and Technology. The major work areas include: commercial litigation and dispute resolution; corporate services, which includes company commercial and corporate finance; intellectual property; media and entertainment; reputation management; employment; marketing services, embracing advertising and marketing law; real estate (including social housing); and technology and communications. They are recognised by commentators as a leading firm in employment and all aspects of brand management.

Trainee profile
They are looking for up to six trainees with keen minds and personalities, who will fit into a professional but informal team.

Training environment
The firm provides a comprehensive induction and training programme, with practical hands-on experience from day one. You will sit with either a partner or senior associate giving you access to day-to-day supervision and guidance. The training contract consists of six four-month seats, working in the firm's five departments and/or client secondments.

Benefits
These include individual and firm bonus schemes, life assurance, group income protection, health insurance, season ticket loan, group pension plan and subsidised gym membership.

Work placements
Please refer to the firm's website for further information.

Sponsorship & awards
Funding for GDL and LPC fees is provided plus a £5,000 maintenance grant for each.

Partners 60
Assistant Solicitors 89
Total Trainees 13

Contact
Human Resources

Method of application
Online application form

Selection procedure
Assessment day, including an interview with 2 partners, a group exercise, analytical and aptitude test

Closing date for 2015 intake
Please refer to website

Application
Training contracts p.a. 6
Applications p.a. 600
Required degree grade 2:1

Training
Salary
1st year £32,500
2nd year £34,500
Holiday entitlement 25 days

Post-qualification
Salary (2012) up to £52,000

lewissilkin

Linklaters LLP

One Silk Street, London EC2Y 8HQ
Tel: (020) 7456 2000 Fax: (020) 7456 2222
Email: graduate.recruitment@linklaters.com
Website: www.linklaters.com/ukgradsCSG

Firm profile

Join Linklaters and you become part of one of the world's most prestigious law firms – a global network of exceptionally talented, highly motivated lawyers working as a team and learning from one another to fulfil its ambition of becoming the leading global law firm.

Main areas of work

While many law firms are strong in particular areas, Linklaters is the only firm to have market-leading global teams across the full range of corporate, finance and commercial practice areas.

This, partnered with its culture of innovation, teamwork and entrepreneurship, means that it has built strong relationships with the world's leading companies, financial institutions and governments and is asked to advise them on their most important and challenging transactions and assignments.

Trainee profile

A truly global firm, Linklaters has 19 practices across 27 cities worldwide, giving you the opportunity to connect with a diverse range of international colleagues and clients on a daily basis.

As part of your training contract you will have the opportunity to be seconded to one of the firm's international offices or to the offices of one of its clients, giving you first hand experience of this global dimension.

Linklaters has high expectations of its trainees and recruits talented and motivated graduates who expect a lot from themselves. In return, the firm offers its trainees global opportunities, entrepreneurial freedom, world-class training and incredible rewards.

Training environment

Linklaters recruits a diverse mix of the most talented graduates from a wide range of universities and backgrounds. Non-law graduates spend a conversion year at law school taking the Graduate Diploma in Law (GDL) and all graduates complete the Legal Practice Course (LPC) before starting their training contracts. The firm meets the cost of the GDL and the LPC and provides a maintenance grant for both. The training contract is structured around four six-month seats, designed to build your knowledge, experience and contacts in a broad range of practice areas and to equip you for your long-term career.

Sponsorship & benefits

GDL and LPC fees are paid in full, plus a maintenance grant. Benefits include eligibility for a personal performance-related bonus, pension, private medical insurance, life assurance, income protection, in-house healthcare services, family friendly benefits, in-house gym, subsidised staff restaurant, interest-free season ticket loan, holiday travel insurance, time bank scheme, cycle2work and give as you earn.

Vacation placements

Linklaters offers vacation schemes for penultimate year students at UK universities (law and non-law), which take place over the summer. The firm also offers first year law undergraduates structured work experience through a two-day insight programme called Pathfinder. All applications begin with an online application form.

Partners 480
Associates 2,200
Trainees 250+*
*(London)

Contact
Graduate Recruitment

Method of application
Online application form

Selection procedure
Critical reasoning test, work simulation exercise and two interviews

Application
Training contracts p.a. 110
Applications p.a. 4,500
Required degree grade 2:1

Training
Salary
1st year (2010) £39,000
Holiday entitlement 25 days
% of trainees with a
non-law degree p.a. 40%

Post-qualification
Salary £61,500 + discretionary performance-related bonus

Offices
Abu Dhabi, Amsterdam, Antwerp, Bangkok, Beijing, Berlin, Brussels, Dubai, Düsseldorf, Frankfurt, Hong Kong, Lisbon, London, Luxembourg, Madrid, Milan, Moscow, Munich, New York, Paris, Rome, São Paulo, Shanghai, Singapore, Stockholm, Tokyo, Warsaw

Linklaters

Macfarlanes LLP

20 Cursitor Street, London, EC4A 1LT
Tel: (020) 7831 9222 Fax: (020) 7831 9607
Email: gradrec@macfarlanes.com
Website: www.macfarlanes.com

Firm profile

Macfarlanes is a leading City law firm. The firm is recognised for the quality of its work, not just in dealing with a full range of corporate and commercial matters, but in advising clients on their private affairs. Clients trust Macfarlanes' judgement and the firm is in a unique position to advise on their most complex matters, whilst at the same time remaining smaller than its competitors.

As advisers to many of the world's leading businesses and business leaders, the firm manages international matters in an effective and seamless manner. It gives clients a single point of contact and co-ordinates advice across all relevant jurisdictions.

Main areas of work

The firm's main areas of practice are in banking and finance; commercial; competition; corporate and M&A; employment, pensions and benefits; financial services regulatory; investment funds; IP and IT; litigation and dispute resolution; private equity; private client; commercial real estate; restructuring and insolvency; and tax and structuring.

Trainee profile

Macfarlanes believes the strongest firm is achieved by choosing a mix of people – reflecting different styles so as to meet the needs that it – and its varied range of clients – will have in the future. The firm looks for a rare combination of intellectual curiosity, character and drive. It is looking for ambitious trainees who will thrive on responsibility and challenge and who are ready to begin their careers on day one.

Training environment

Woven into every aspect of life at the firm is an enduring commitment to the development of trainees. Training begins with tailored electives on the LPC and a week-long induction course at the start of your training contract.

During the two-year training contract you'll be working on real cases, doing real work for real clients from day one. As a trainee you will complete four six-month seats in different areas of practice; typically it is one seat in corporate and M&A, two seats in either private client, litigation, commercial real estate or corporate tax, and then a seat in one of the firm's specialised practice areas within corporate. The precise allocation of seats is flexible so that it can offer you as broad a legal training as possible. Support and guidance are, of course, vital and you will find your supervisor a valuable source of information and inspiration.

Benefits

Life assurance, pension scheme with company contributions, private healthcare, discretionary performance related bonus scheme, season ticket loan, subsidised restaurant, gym membership subsidy, eyecare vouchers and childcare vouchers.

Vacation placements

Places for 2013: 55; Duration 2 weeks; Remuneration: £300 p.w.; Closing date: 31 January 2013.

Sponsorship & awards

CPE/GDL and LPC fees paid in full and a £7,000 maintenance allowance.

Partners 71
Assistant Solicitors 161
Total Trainees 59
Contact
Vicki Wood
Method of application
Online via website
Selection procedure
Assessment day
Closing date for 2015
31 July 2013
Application
Training contracts p.a. up to 30
Applications p.a. 1000
% interviewed p.a. 15%
Required degree grade 2:1
Training
Salary
1st year £38,000
2nd year £43,000
Holiday entitlement 25 days, rising to 26 on qualification
% of trainees with a non-law degree p.a. 60%
Post-qualification
Salary (2012) £61,000
% of trainees offered job on qualification (Sept 2012) 92%
% of partners (as at 1/5/12) who joined as trainees 56%

MACFARLANES

Maclay Murray & Spens LLP

1 George Square, Glasgow, G2 1AL
Website: www.mms.co.uk

Partners 58
Assistant Solicitors 159
Total Trainees 42

Contact
Scott Ross, HR Advisor
scott.ross@mms.co.uk

Method of application
Application forms only,
accessed at
www.mms.co.uk/careers/
traineeship

Selection procedure
Two stage interview process.
During the second stage
candidates will be asked to
complete a role-play and
research exercise.

Closing date for 2014 and 2015
London traineeship July 2013
Scottish traineeship October 2013

Application
Training contracts p.a. 20-25
Applications p.a. 450
Required degree grade 2:1

Training
Salary (2012)
(Scotland) 1st year £18,000
(London) 1st year £32,000
Holiday entitlement 34 days
per year, including public
holidays

Firm profile

Maclay Murray & Spens LLP is a full service, independent, commercial law firm offering legal solutions and advice to clients throughout the UK and beyond. With offices in Aberdeen, Glasgow, Edinburgh and London the firm's objective is to provide a consistently excellent quality of service across the firm's entire service range and from every UK office.

Main areas of work

Banking and finance, capital projects, commercial dispute resolution, construction and engineering, corporate, employment, pensions, EU, competition and regulatory, IP and technology, oil and gas, planning and environmental, private client, property, public sector and tax.

Trainee profile

Applicants should have a strong academic background (minimum 2:1 degree) as well as demonstrate a number of key skills including an inquiring mind and a keenness to learn, commitment, professionalism, determination to see a job through, first class communication skills, the ability to get on with colleagues and clients at all levels, an ability to operate under pressure in a team environment, as well as a sense of humour. The firm welcomes bright non-law graduates.

Training environment

Trainees will have three seats of eight months where you will be provided with a very broad range of practical experience, including legal writing, drafting, research work and an element of client contact. This is one of the firm's strengths as a business and a long standing attraction for candidates.

In addition to on-the-job training, the firm also offers trainees the opportunity of attending in-house seminars and workshops in order to develop their legal and general business skills. By working as a team member on more complex transactions, you are given the opportunity to gain experience over a broad range of work. You will also be encouraged to meet and work alongside clients from different backgrounds and diverse areas of industry and commerce. The firm has an open plan office environment which allows trainees the benefit of working closely alongside solicitors at all levels. This promotes greater communication and team working. Trainees are also able to participate in CSR activities which take place across our offices.

Benefits

At MMS trainees are paid competitive salaries as well as provided with an attractive benefits package. All of the firm's employees receive a combination of fixed and variable holidays totalling 34 days each year. The firm also offers a contributory pension scheme, death in service benefit worth four times your annual salary, support with conveyancing fees, enhanced maternity and paternity pay, income protection insurance, cycle to work scheme, Give As You Earn, season ticket loan for travel, childcare voucher scheme and discounted access to medical and dental plans.

Vacation scheme

MMS offers students the opportunity of a three week summer placement. To apply please visit our website for more details on our application process. The closing date is 31 January 2013.

Sponsorship

Assistance with LPC and GDL funding is available.

 mms | maclay murray & spens LLP

Manches

Aldwych House, 81 Aldwych, London WC2B 4RP
Tel: (020) 7404 4433 Fax: (020) 7430 1133
Email: sheona.boldero@manches.com
Website: www.manches.com

Firm profile

We are a leading law firm based in central London and the Thames Valley (Oxford and Reading) providing legal services to ultra high net worth individuals and growing mid-market companies.

We provide a range of legal services to growing mid-market companies. We focus on a few key sectors, including retail, fashion, technology, life sciences and real estate. We have teams of commercially astute lawyers who are able to help clients find a way through the minefield of complex, confusing and often bureaucratic law that governs the way businesses operate, both in the UK and internationally.

We provide clear and pragmatic advice to high-net worth individuals, successful entrepreneurs, wealthy families, professional trustees and charities in connection with all aspects of wealth management, family law matters and employment law advice.

The firm offers 10 trainee places each September.

Main areas of work

Our main areas of expertise are corporate, dispute resolution, employment law, intellectual property, information technology, property, private client and family law.

The industry sectors in which we have particular expertise are: international wealth; life sciences; real estate; retail/fashion; technology.

Trainee profile

We aim to recruit people who are 'individuals', and who possess a wide cross-section of experience and backgrounds. We look for trainees who can demonstrate that they are intellectually sharp, hard working and ambitious and who show a keen understanding of commercial business issues within both company and private client fields. Excellent academics are required (ie AAB at A level and a strong 2:1 degree or higher). A range of extra curricular interests, team activities and responsibilities are also sought, together with a naturally engaging personality. A sense of humour is an asset!

Training environment

We give high-quality individual training. We initially provide a comprehensive induction week, followed by a highly practical training achieved by trainees being fully involved in supervised client work right from the start. Trainees generally sit in 4 different seats for 6 months at a time under the supervision of either a partner or senior associate. We try where possible to take into account seat preferences. This hands-on approach enables trainees to take on real responsibility from an early stage, ensuring that they become confident and educated solicitors at the point of qualification. Trainees are expected to actively participate in departmental know-how meetings, presentations, client seminars and briefings and they receive regular appraisals on their progress.

Benefits

Season ticket loan, BUPA after six months, permanent health insurance, life insurance, pension after six months.

Vacation placements

Places for 2013: 20 approx; Duration: 1 week; Closing date: 15 February 2013; Remuneration: £225 net of tax.

Sponsorship & awards

GDL and LPC fees are paid in full (for courses yet to be taken) together with an annual maintenance allowance for the academic year (currently £5,000 p.a.).

Partners 59
Assistant Solicitors 65
Total Trainees 20

Contact
Sheona Boldero
sheona.boldero@manches.com

Method of application
Online application form

Selection procedure
1st interview with Graduate Recruitment Manager, 2nd interview (including assessment) with partners

Closing date for 2015
31 July 2013

Application
Training contracts p.a. 10
Applications p.a. 850
% interviewed p.a. 5%
Required degree grade 2:1 min

Training
Salary
1st year (2012)
London under review
2nd year (2012)
London under review
Holiday entitlement 24 days

Post-qualification
Salary
London under review
% of trainees offered job on qualification (2012) 80%

MANCHES

Mayer Brown[1]

201 Bishopsgate, London EC2M 3AF
Email: graduaterecruitment@mayerbrown.com
Website: www.mayerbrown.com/london

Firm profile

Mayer Brown is a leading global law firm with offices in key business centres across the Americas, Europe and Asia. The firm is known for its client-focused approach to providing creative solutions to complex problems on behalf of businesses, governments and individuals. In Asia, the firm operates as Mayer Brown JSM as a result of its 2008 combination with JSM (formerly Johnson Stokes & Master) a leading Asian law firm. In Brazil the firm has an association with Tauil & Chequer Avogados. The firm also has an alliance with Ramon & Cajal in Spain. This presence in the world's leading markets for legal services enables Mayer Brown to offer clients access to local market expertise on a global basis.

Main areas of work

The firm's lawyers practise in a wide range of areas including corporate, finance, litigation and dispute resolution, real estate, insurance and reinsurance, pensions and employment, competition and trade, tax, intellectual property and information technology. The firm advises many of the world's largest companies including a significant proportion of the Fortune 100, FTSE 100 and DAX and Hang Seng Index organisations from the worlds of banking, insurance, communications, industrials, energy, construction, professional services, media, pharmaceuticals, chemicals and mining.

Trainee profile

The firm is looking for candidates who not only have a consistently strong academic record, but also who have a wide range of interests and achievements outside their academic career. Additionally, the firm would like to see innovative candidates who can demonstrate a drive for results, good verbal and written communication skills and an ability to analyse, with good judgement and excellent interpersonal skills.

Training environment

One of the advantages of joining Mayer Brown are the choices available to you. The firm's trainees can tailor their training contract from a range of different seats, including the firm's main practice areas in London and international secondments (Hong Kong and New York). If you don't want to stray too far, a wealth of in-house experience is also available via the firm's client secondments within the UK. For a large international firm, its London office remains a tightly knit team with an open and inclusive culture. You will nevertheless be given significant opportunities to assist on matters which may be multi-disciplinary, cross-border, complex and high-profile in nature.

Benefits

Benefits include 25 days holiday per annum, an interest free season ticket loan, subsidised sports club membership and membership of private health scheme.

Work experience programmes

The firm runs three work experience programmes each year; two three-week schemes in the summer and one two-week programme in the spring. You will gain experience in two key practice areas and be involved in seminars and social events, including a trip to one of our European offices.

Sponsorship & awards

The firm will cover the cost of the GDL and LPC fees and provide a maintenance grant of £7,000.

[1] Mayer Brown International LLP operates in combination with its associated Illinois limited liability partnerships, a SELAS established in France, a Hong Kong partnership, and its associated entities in Asia, and is associated with Tauil & chequer Advogados, a Brazilian law partnership.

Partners 100	
Assistant Solicitors 145	
Total Trainees 52	

Contact
Caroline Sarson,
Graduate Recruitment

Method of application
Online application form

Selection procedure
One stage assessment process including an interview, a written exercise, a group exercise and an online verbal reasoning test

Closing date for September 2015/March 2016
31 July 2013

Application
Training contracts p.a. approx 20
Applications p.a. 2,000+
% interviewed p.a. 8%
Required degree grade 2:1

Training
1st year £37,500
2nd year £42,300
Holiday entitlement 25 days
% of trainees with a non-law degree p.a. 50%

Post-qualification
% of trainees offered job on qualification 80% (March 2012)

Overseas offices
Bangkok, Beijing, Brussels, Charlotte, Chicago, Dusseldorf, Frankfurt, Guangzhou, Hanoi, Ho Chi Minh City, Hong Kong, Houston, London, Los Angeles, New York, Palo Alto, Paris, Shanghai, Singapore and Washington DC

MAYER·BROWN

Memery Crystal LLP

44 Southampton Buildings, London WC2A 1AP
Tel: (020) 7242 5905 Fax: (020) 7242 2058
Email: hseaward@memerycrystal.com Web: www.memerycrystal.com

Firm profile

Memery Crystal LLP has an enviable reputation as a commercial legal practice. We have a strong internal culture, based upon a set of core values, which underpins our individuality, our emphasis on long-term client relationships and our collegiate and entrepreneurial approach. We act for a broad range of clients, from individual entrepreneurs and owner-managed businesses, to City institutions, educational organisations and multi-national corporations.

We offer a partner-led service and pride ourselves on the strength of our client relationships. We set ourselves apart from our competitors through our pragmatism and pro-activity and we have a reputation for punching well above our weight. Unusually for a single-office firm, we have a strong international focus, which we see as vital to our vision of remaining independent in a globalising economy. We have considerable cross-border transactional experience and have built strong relationships with other independent law firms around the world.

Our key strength lies in the quality of our people. We seek to recruit and retain leading individuals, who provide the highest level of service to our clients.

Main areas of work

Our main practice areas include corporate, dispute resolution, employment, family law, real estate and tax. We have particular expertise in a number of industry sectors, including education, digital media, retail and natural resources.

Trainee profile

The firm is looking for candidates who have achieved a high standard of education, show a willingness to take on responsibility, are commercially aware, respond to challenges, have the drive and ambition to succeed, and are seeking fulfilment and recognition in their chosen profession.

Training environment

During your training you will have a balance of formal and practical training. Your development will be closely monitored with appraisals carried out every 3 months. You will sit either with a Partner, associate or senior assistant who will monitor your progress on a regular basis. During the course of your training contract, there will be a regular rotation of seats within the firm.

Benefits

The firm provides a bonus scheme, life assurance, health cover, travel insurance, season ticket loan, group pension plan subsidised gym membership and cycle to work scheme.

Sponsorship & awards

Funding for LPC and GDL fees is provided.

Partners 22
Assistant Solicitors 38
Total Trainees 8

Contact
Helen Seaward

Method of application
Online application form

Selection procedure
First interview followed by assessment centre

Closing date for 2015
31 July 2013 for training contracts

Application
Training contracts p.a. 4
Applications p.a. 300
Required degree grade 2:1

Training
Salary
1st year (2010) £30,000
2nd year (2010) £32,000
Holiday entitlement
25 days p.a.
% of trainees with a non-law degree 40%

Post-qualification
Competitive Salary

Memery Crystal

Michelmores LLP

Woodwater House, Pynes Hill, Exeter EX2 5WR
Tel: (01392) 688 688 Fax: (01392) 360 563
Email: careers@michelmores.com Website: www.michelmores.com
48 Chancery Lane, London, WC2A 1JF
Tel (020) 7659 7660 Fax: (020) 7659 7661

Firm profile

Michelmores LLP, a leading law firm in the South West, is a dynamic, full-service practice with a total complement of over 300 staff. From its Exeter and London offices, the firm provides a first class service to a wide range of local, national and international clients (including several central government departments). The firm has an established track record of attracting quality recruits at every level, enabling its trainees to learn from solicitors who are leaders in their fields. Michelmores has created a great place to work and attracts and retains some of the very best lawyers. The partnership has retained a collegiate style, which has helped to foster a happy law firm renowned for the enthusiasm of its lawyers, from the Managing Partner down to the first year trainees. We have won a number of awards and accolades, culminating in being previously named UK Regional Law Firm of the Year at the British Legal Awards and being listed as 'one to watch' in The Times Best Companies ranking.

Main areas of work

The firm has a good reputation for its work in company commercial law, dispute resolution and commercial property while the firm's Private Client Group (including the firm's Family Team) continues to thrive. The firm also has specialist teams in areas such as projects/PFI, technology, media and communications, construction and medical negligence.

Trainee profile

The firm welcomes applications from both law and non-law graduates. The firm is looking for trainees with a strong academic background who are team players and who genuinely want to share in the firm's success and help it to continue to grow and improve.

Training environment

As a Michelmores trainee you will usually spend six months in each of the firm's main departments (business, property and private client). You will work closely with your supervisor in each department and will be pleasantly surprised at the level of client exposure, responsibility and client involvement. The firm's trainees are given both the opportunity to handle work themselves (while under supervision) and to work as part of a team. The quality of the firm's training is high. You will be expected to attend relevant training sessions on areas such as marketing, IT skills and time management, and will also be encouraged to attend conferences, seminars and marketing events.

Sponsorship & benefits

Optional private medical insurance, pension scheme, payment of LPC fees (up to £8k), subsidised staff restaurant, subsidised gym with personal trainer, free parking.

Vacation placements

The firm runs an annual vacation placement scheme in July in the firm's Exeter office for one week. The online application form is available on the website. Completed forms should arrive by 28 February 2013.

Partners 45
Total Staff (inc. Partners) 320
Assistant solicitors 68

Contact
Claire Kearns
(careers@michelmores.com)

Method of application
Online application form

Selection procedure
Assessment days

Closing date for 2015
1 July 2013

Application
Training contracts p.a. 6
Applications p.a. 200
% interviewed 15%
Required degree grade 2:1
(occasional exceptions)

Training
Salary
1st year (2012) £20,000
2nd year (2013) £21,000
Holiday entitlement
25 days p.a.
% of trainees with a non-law degree 10%
Number of seats available abroad 0 (although occasional foreign secondments available)

Post-qualification
Salary (2012) £33,000
% offered job 100%

Mills & Reeve

112 Hills Road, Cambridge CB2 1PH
Tel: (01223) 222336 Fax: (01223) 355848
Email: graduate.recruitment@mills-reeve.com
Web: www.mills-reeve.com/graduates

Firm profile

Mills & Reeve is a major UK law firm operating from offices in Birmingham, Cambridge, Leeds, London, Manchester and Norwich.

Our business model is straightforward - the highest quality advice, outstanding client service and value for money. We advise more than 70 universities and colleges, over 100 healthcare trusts and NHS bodies, 65 local authorities as well as leading international insurers. Our commercial clients include global and UK-based businesses, FTSE and AIM listed organisations, private companies and startups. We have the largest private tax team outside of London and one of the largest family teams in Europe.

For the ninth year running Mills & Reeve has been listed in The Sunday Times Top 100 Best Companies to Work For, which recognises that we put people at the centre of our business.

Main areas of work

Mills & Reeve's services are delivered through firm-wide core groups: corporate and commercial, disputes, employment, family, health, insurance, private wealth sectors, projects and construction and real estate. Further specialist sector teams focus on agriculture, charities, education, food and farming and real estate investment.

Trainee profile

We welcome applications from penultimate year law students, final year non-law students or graduates. Candidates should already have or expect a 2:1 degree or equivalent.

You'll have a good balance between academic ability, interpersonal skills, drafting skills, common sense, commercial awareness, confidence and a professional attitude.

We look for candidates who have the potential to develop into our solicitors of the future.

Training environment

Trainees complete six four-month seats and are recruited to the Birmingham, Cambridge and Norwich offices. Trainees work alongside a partner or senior solicitor. Regular feedback is given to aid development. Performance is assessed by a formal review at the end of each seat.

Training is supported by a full induction, in-house training programme developed by our team of professional support lawyers and the professional skills course (PSC).

Benefits

Life assurance, a contributory pension scheme, 25 days holiday, bonus scheme, sports and social club, subsidised staff restaurants, season ticket loan. The firm runs a flexible benefits scheme.

Vacation placements

Applications for two week placements during the summer must be received by 31 January 2013.

Sponsorship & awards

The firm pays the full costs of the CPE/GDL and LPC fees and a maintenance grant during the GDL and LPC.

Partners 98
Assistant Solicitors 350
Total Trainees 39

Contact
Fiona Medlock
01223 222336

Method of application
Online

Selection procedure
Normally one day assessment centre

Closing date for 2015
31 July 2013 for training contracts
31st January 2013 for work placements

Application
Training contracts p.a. 15
Applications p.a. Approx 850
% interviewed p.a. 10%
Required degree grade 2:1

Training
Salary
1st year £23,000
2nd year £24,000
Holiday entitlement
25 days p.a.
% of trainees with a non-law degree 40%

Post-qualification
% of trainees offered job on qualification 76%

Offices
Birmingham, Cambridge, Leeds, London, Manchester, Norwich

MILLS & REEVE

Mishcon de Reya

Summit House, 12 Red Lion Square, London WC1R 4QD
Tel: (020) 7440 7000 Fax: (020) 7430 0691
Email: trainee.recruitment@mishcon.com
Website: www.mishcongraduates.com

Partners 78	
Assistant Solicitors 131	
Total Trainees 18	
Contact	
Sisa Sibanda, HR Advisor	
Method of application	
Online application form	
Closing date for 2015	
15 July 2013	
Application	
Training contracts p.a. 8-12	
Applications p.a. 1,500+	
% interviewed p.a. 5%	
Required degree grade 2:1	
Training	
Salary	
1st year £32,000	
Holiday entitlement	
25 days p.a.	
Occasional secondments	
available	

Firm profile

Founded in 1937, Mishcon de Reya is a law firm with offices in London and New York offering a wide range of legal services to companies and individuals.

Our clients are dynamic and sophisticated and we reflect that in our belief in challenging the conventional or accepted ways of working. We like to solve problems quickly. To achieve this consistently, we employ a diverse collection of talented people, from varied backgrounds with differing perspectives, who are capable of addressing issues in a collaborative, non-hierarchical environment.

In every area of the law that we operate, Mishcon de Reya prides itself in providing a best in class service to its clients. Our expertise covers five areas: analysing risk, protection of assets, managing wealth, resolving disputes and building business.

Main areas of work

We are organised internally into six different departments: corporate, employment, dispute resolution, family, Mishcon private and real estate. The firm also has a growing number of specialist groups which include: art; betting and gaming; finance and banking; fraud; immigration; insolvency; and IP.

Trainee profile

Our trainees are typically high-achieving and intelligent individuals with good interpersonal skills and outgoing personalities. Strength of character and ability to think laterally are also important.

Training environment

Trainees have the opportunity to gain experience, skills and knowledge from across the firm in four six-month seats involving contentious and non-contentious work. Because of the relatively few training contracts offered, trainees can be exposed to high-quality work with lots of responsibility early on. Trainees are supported with a wide ranging training and development programme in addition to the Professional Skills Course. Trainee performance is monitored closely and trainees can expect to receive regular feedback in addition to mid-seat and end-of-seat appraisals.

Sponsorship & benefits

The firm provides full LPC and GDL funding, and a maintenance grant of £5,000 payable in the GDL and LPC year. Benefits include 25 days holiday, health screening, life assurance, dental insurance, income replacement insurance, private medical insurance, travel insurance, critical illness cover, gym membership, season ticket loan, stakeholder pension scheme, yoga classes, childcare vouchers, cycle scheme, in-house doctor, bonus scheme and give-as-you-earn schemes.

Vacation placements

Places for summer 2013: 20; duration: 2 weeks; closing date: 31 January 2013.

Our summer vacation schemes have been designed to provide students with an opportunity to gain an insight into the role of a trainee, our culture and our people. We run a fun and informative workshop programme covering all practice areas of the firm, combined with individual and group work sessions.

Mishcon de Reya

Morgan Cole

Bradley Court, Park Place, Cardiff CF10 3DP
Tel: (029) 2038 5385 Fax: (029) 2038 5300
Email: recruitment@morgan-cole.com
Website: www.morgan-cole.com

Firm profile

Morgan Cole is one of the leading regional commercial law practices in the country, providing a comprehensive service both to public and private sector clients as well as individuals. The firm is committed to providing the highest quality legal services and commercially focussed advice from offices in South Wales and southern England.

Main areas of work

The firm's areas of work consist of five practice areas: insurance, corporate commercial, dispute management and regulatory, employment pensions and benefits and commercial property. Within these practice areas the firm's work includes: acquisitions and disposals; technology; insolvency; intellectual property; joint ventures; management buy-outs and buy-ins; construction; professional indemnity; commercial litigation; property and alternative dispute resolution.

Training environment

Trainees spend six months in four different practice areas, and since each practice area handles a wide variety of work within its constituent teams, there is no danger of over specialisation. Training includes client contact and there is always a possibility of a secondment to a major bluechip client! You must show initiative and take responsibility, but the firm will not leave you stranded. You will be assigned a seat supervisor (a partner or senior solicitor) to advise and guide you. You will have a mentor for support to act as a sounding board.

Sponsorship & awards

Payment of fees as per policy.

Partners 50+
Lawyers 230
Total Trainees 8 approx.

Trainee places for 2015
Wales and West 4
Thames Valley 2

Contact
Christine Henderson
Training & Development
Manager

Method of application
Apply online at
www.apply4law.com/morgancole

Selection procedure
Short listing day and
assessment centre

Closing date for 2015
31st May 2013

Application
Training contracts p.a. 6
Required degree grade
Preferably 2:1 and above (law
or non-law)

Training
Salary Competitive and
reviewed annually

Post-qualification
Salary Competitive

Other offices
Cardiff, Bristol, Oxford, Reading,
Swansea

Morgan Cole

Morgan Lewis & Bockius

Condor House, 5-10 St. Paul's Churchyard, London EC4M 8AL
Tel: (020)3 201 5000 Fax: (020)3 201 5001
Email: Londontrainingprogramme@morganlewis.com
Website: www.morganlewis.co.uk

Firm profile

With 24 offices in the United States, Europe and Asia, Morgan Lewis provides comprehensive corporate, transactional, regulatory and litigation services to clients of all sizes and across all major industries. Founded in 1873, Morgan Lewis comprises more than 1,600 legal professionals—including lawyers, patent agents, benefits advisers, regulatory scientists and other specialists. The firm has expanded significantly in London in the past year through the addition of several new teams.

Main areas of work

Debt and equity capital markets; finance and restructuring; labour and employment including employment litigation and immigration advice; private investment fund formation and operation; UK and US tax planning and structuring; international commercial dispute, arbitration, insurance recovery, and white collar matters: life sciences, financial services, energy and technology sector work.

Trainee profile

Morgan Lewis is seeking candidates with a consistently strong academic record, who would respond with confidence to opportunities to work on challenging assignments across a wide variety of areas. Candidates should be able to demonstrate strong interpersonal, communication and client service skills and analytical ability, as well as a proven ability to work effectively both independently and within a team.

Training environment

Our new training programme is led by an experienced training principal. Following a full induction into the firm, including legal research training, the programme will provide trainees with consistently high quality, challenging assignments, working with senior lawyers on complex and frequently cross-border matters. Through this hands-on experience, trainees can expect to gather a thorough understanding of the firm's business and of working with international, high profile clients.

In addition to formal appraisals, the office environment allows regular contact with the training principal, supervisors and other lawyers. Trainees will attend Professional Skills Courses throughout their contract and will have the opportunity to participate in all associate training sessions, pro bono work and business development activities.

Benefits

Life insurance, health and travel insurance, dental insurance, long-term disability insurance and season ticket loan.

Sponsorship & awards

Sponsorship of LPC and GDL. A maintenance grant of £7,500 will be provided.

Partners 19
Assistant Solicitors 22
Total Trainees 7

Contact
Georgia Shearman
0203 201 5620

Method of application
Via our website

Closing date for 2015
31 July 2013

Selection procedure
Interviews

Application
No. of training contracts 3 p.a
Required degree grade
high 2:1

Training
Salary
1st year £40,000
2nd year £43,000
Holiday entitlement
25 days p.a

Post-qualification
Salary £75,000

Overseas offices
Almaty, Beijing, Boston, Brussels, Chicago, Dallas, Frankfurt, Harrisburg, Houston, Irvine, London, Los Angeles, Miami, Moscow, New York, Palo Alto, Paris, Philadelphia, Pittsburgh, Princeton, San Francisco, Tokyo, Washington, Wilmington

Morgan Lewis

Muckle LLP

Time Central, 32 Gallowgate, Newcastle upon Tyne, NE1 4BF
Tel: (0191) 211 7777 Fax: (0191) 211 7788
Email: tmurray@muckle-llp.com Website: www.muckle-llp.com

Firm profile
Muckle LLP is a leading commercial law firm in the North East of England. The firm has an excellent client base of successful private and public companies, property investors and developers, financial institutions and public sector and educational organisations, which recognise that its innovative commercial skills are a major benefit in enhancing its service delivery to them.

Main areas of work
The firm provides the following services – corporate finance, commercial, construction and engineering, property, employment, dispute resolution and private client. The specialist sectors within these services are: banking, special situations, charities, education, energy, manufacturing and sports.

Trainee profile
The firm recruits four trainees a year. The firm is looking to recruit talented individuals who can demonstrate their enthusiasm and desire to become business advisers and a commitment to building their career in the North East. Trainees must have good academic qualifications, interpersonal skills, be a team player and embrace our culture and values.

Training environment
The firm runs an excellent training programme that focuses on the trainees' legal, IT, management and business development skills. During your training contract you may experience training within the following areas: corporate finance, commercial, property, employment, dispute resolution, construction and banking. Training is a combination of on-the-job experience, partner and other lawyer mentoring as well as in-house and external courses. Trainees are encouraged to participate in all aspects of the firm which include engagement, community and 'green' teams.

Benefits
25 days holiday a year and flexible holiday option; pension after six months service; permanent health insurance; life assurance; corporate discounts; salary sacrifice schemes; car parking discounts.

Sponsorship & awards
LPC fees are paid subject to eligibility.

Partners 29
Fee earners 77
Total Trainees 7

Contact
Tracy Murray HR Assistant
0191 211 7843

Method of application
Apply online via our website
www.muckle-llp.com

Selection procedure
Interviews and an assessment day

Closing date for 2013 summer vacation scheme
Friday 25th January 2013

Closing date for 2015 training contracts
Wednesday 31st July 2013

Application
Training contracts p.a. 4
Applications p.a. 230-240
% interviewed p.a. 25%
Required degree grade preferably 2:1

Training
Salary
Starting salary £22,000 (2011) with regular reviews throughout training contract
Holiday entitlement
25 days holiday a year and flexible holiday option

Post-qualification
Salary
Starting salary £33,000 (2012) with regular reviews
Aim to retain 100% of trainees on qualification

Office
Only Newcastle upon Tyne

Muckle LLP

Nabarro LLP

Lacon House, 84 Theobald's Road, London WC1X 8RW
Tel: (020) 7524 6000 Fax: (020) 7524 6524
Email: graduateinfo@nabarro.com
Website: www.nabarro.com

Firm profile

Nabarro is a major UK law firm renowned for its positive, practical approach. The firm operates across a number of industry sectors and legal disciplines and aims to deliver the highest quality legal advice as clearly and concisely as possible.

Main areas of work

Corporate and commercial law; real estate; IP/IT; projects; PPP; PFI; pensions; employment; dispute resolution; construction and engineering; planning; environmental law; banking, finance and restructuring; insolvency and tax.

Trainee profile

The firm is committed to making the most of diverse skills, expertise, experience, attitudes and backgrounds. Accordingly, there is no typical Nabarro trainee. You will need a strong academic record and, in keeping with clients' needs, the firm also wants you to demonstrate a flexibility of thinking and a flair for creative problem solving that will allow you to provide its clients with the best advice and assistance. The firm is also looking for students who demonstrate a proactive approach, strong interpersonal and team working skills as well as commercial acumen.

Training environment

Trainees undertake six four-month seats to ensure maximum exposure to the firm's core practice areas, as well as the opportunity to spend time in more specialist seats or possibly on secondment to a client or Brussels. Your development and future seats are discussed with you mid way through each seat.

Benefits

Private medical insurance, 26 days holidays, pension, season ticket loan, subsidised restaurant, subsidised gym membership. Trainee salaries are reviewed annually.

Vacation placements

Places for 2013: 60

Duration: 3 weeks between mid June and mid August. Closing date: 31 January 2013.

Nabarro's multi award winning three week scheme offers a comprehensive and structured programme of events. You will be based in one department with an allocated supervisor and buddy who will ensure you gain a good mix of work and an excellent insight into life at Nabarro. The firm recruits the majority of its trainees through its vacation scheme.

Sponsorship & awards

Full fees paid for the GDL and LPC plus a maintenance grant: LPC London: £7,000, regions £6,000. GDL London: £6,000, regions £5,000. The firm pays 50% of fees retrospectively if you have completed your GDL/LPC.

Partners 125+
Assistant Solicitors 270+
Total Trainees 50

Contact
Jane Drew

Method of application
Online only

Selection procedure
Assessment Day (including interview)

Closing date for 2015
31 July 2013

Application
Training contracts p.a. 30
Applications p.a. 2,000
Required degree grade 2:1

Training
Salary
1st year (2012)
London £37,000
Sheffield £25,000
2nd year (2012)
London £40,000
Sheffield £28,000
Holiday entitlement 26 days

Post-qualification
Salary (2012)
London £59,000
Sheffield £38,000
(reviewed annually)

Overseas offices
Brussels and Singapore. In Europe the firm has an alliance with GSK Stockmann & Kollegen in Germany, August & Debouzy in France, Nunziante Magrone in Italy and Roca Junyent in Spain.

N A B A R R O

Norton Rose LLP

3 More London Riverside, London, SE1 2AQ
Tel: (020) 7444 2113 Fax: (020) 7283 6500
Email: graduate.recruitment@nortonrose.com
Website: www.nortonrosegraduates.com

Firm profile

Norton Rose LLP is a constituent part of Norton Rose Group, a leading international legal practice. With more than 2,900 lawyers, we offer a full business law service to many of the world's pre-eminent financial institutions and corporations from offices across Europe, Asia, Australia, Canada, Africa, the Middle East, Latin America and Central Asia. Knowing how our clients' businesses work and understanding what drives their industries is fundamental to us. Our lawyers share industry knowledge and sector expertise across borders, enabling us to support our clients anywhere in the world.

Norton Rose Group comprises Norton Rose LLP, Norton Rose Australia, Norton Rose OR LLP, Norton Rose South Africa and their respective affiliates.

Main areas of work

We are strong in financial institutions; energy; infrastructure, mining and commodities; transport; technology and innovation; and pharmaceuticals and life sciences.

Trainee profile

It is important to us that as a trainee you get as much exposure as possible. Therefore, as a trainee in London you will experience our innovative six-seat pattern, which offers one of the most varied among leading City firms. Our flexible seat system allows trainees the widest possible exposure to different practice areas and international offices, in order to enable them to make the best and most informed choice of qualification area.

Throughout the training contract our learning and development programme will ensure trainees continue to develop and succeed at every stage in their career.

At Norton Rose LLP we look for intelligent, ambitious, internationally focused and commercially-minded individuals to drive our business. We will expect you to think creatively and find new ways to solve problems. We expect our trainees to deliver work that meets the highest professional, ethical and business standards for our clients. All applicants must have achieved at least AAB in their A-levels or equivalent and be on course (or already achieved) a 2:1 degree or above.

Applicants should apply before the 31 July 2013 deadline for training contracts commencing in May or September 2015. For non-law students, or those that have already graduated, we recommend you apply before 30th April 2013, as interviews will take place between January and May 2013.

Benefits

Life assurance, private health insurance (optional), season ticket loan, cycle to work scheme, company car scheme, subsidised gym membership, employee assistance programme, subsidised staff restaurant, eligibility to join the firm's group personal pension scheme.

Placement programmes

We offer winter and summer vacation schemes for those considering a career in law. Final-year non-law students and those who have already graduated should apply for the winter vacation scheme. The firm's summer schemes are aimed at penultimate-year students.

Partners 882*
Assistant Solicitors 1724*
Total Trainees 107
*denotes worldwide figures

Contact
Natasha Brady

Method of application
Online only

Selection procedure
Application form and assessment day including written and group exercise plus 1 hour interview.

Closing date for 2015
31 July 2013

Application
Training contracts p.a. 55
Applications p.a. 2,500+
% interviewed p.a. 10%
Required degree grade 2:1

Training
Salary
1st year £37,000
2nd year £41,500
Holiday entitlement 25 days
% of trainees with a non-law degree p.a. 40%
No. of seats available abroad p.a. 22 (per seat move)

Overseas offices
Abu Dhabi, Almaty, Amsterdam, Athens, Bahrain, Bangkok, Bogotá, Beijing, Brisbane, Brussels, Calgary, Canberra, Cape Town, Caracas, Casablanca, Dubai, Durban, Frankfurt, Hamburg, Hong Kong, Johannesburg, Melbourne, Milan, Montréal, Moscow, Munich, Ottawa, Paris, Perth, Piraeus, Prague, Québec, Rome, Shanghai, Singapore, Sydney, Tokyo, Toronto, Warsaw and from associate offices in Dar es Salaam, Ho Chi Minh City and Jakarta.

Olswang LLP

90 High Holborn, London WC1V 6XX
Tel: (020) 7067 3000 Fax: (020) 7067 3999
Email: traineesolicitor@olswang.com
Website: www.olswangtrainees.com

Firm profile

Olswang is a passionate and pioneering firm with a business-minded approach to the law. Our decisive, connected and highly-commercial people are committed to changing the face of business, impacting sectors ranging from real estate to retail and life sciences to leisure. Our progressive culture gives us a definitive edge and has won us an unparalleled reputation in industries such as technology, media and telecoms.

Headquartered in London, our firm comprises over 700 people spanning a network of offices in Belgium, France, Germany, Spain, Singapore and the UK. Our rapidly expanding presence across Europe, combined with our ambitious plans for growth in the territories our clients demand, makes us the firm of choice for true innovation, wherever it may be emerging across the globe.

We represent recognised brands and key industry players such as Guardian Media Group plc, ITV, Legal & General, Lloyds, Microsoft, MTV Networks Europe, Nationwide, UBS and Warner Music International.

Main areas of work

Olswang's practice areas span corporate, commercial, employment, outsourcing, tax, financial services, real estate, regulatory and competition, EU law, litigation, arbitration, intellectual property and data protection, making it a multi-faceted and critical business partner for the clients it attracts.

Trainee profile

Being a trainee at Olswang is both demanding and rewarding. The firm is interested in hearing from individuals who have achieved, or are on course for, a 2:1 degree or above and possess exceptional drive and relevant commercial experience. In addition, it is absolutely critical that trainees fit well into the Olswang environment, which is challenging, busy, individualistic, meritocratic and fun.

Training environment

Olswang wants to help trainees match their expectations and needs with those of the firm. Training consists of four six-month seats in Corporate, Real Estate, Litigation, Finance, Commercial or IP. You will be assigned a mentor, usually a Partner, to assist and advise you throughout your training contract. In-house lectures supplement general training and three-monthly appraisals assess development. Regular social events with the other trainees not only encourage strong relationship building but add to the fun of work as well.

Benefits

Immediately: life cover, medical cover, dental scheme, subsidised gym membership, subsidised staff restaurant, season ticket loan. After six months: pension contributions. After 12 months: PHI.

Vacation placements

Places for 2013: Spring and summer; Remuneration: £275 p.w.; 10 students per scheme; Closing Date: 31 January 2013.

Sponsorship & awards

LPC and GDL fees paid in full. Maintenance grant of £7,000 (inside London), £6,500 (outside).

Partners 111
Fee-earners 313
Total Trainees 36

Contact
Sarmini Ghosh
Graduate Recruiter

Method of application
Online

Selection procedure
Commercial case study, compentency based interviews, psychometric tests and written exercises

Closing date for 2015
31 July 2013

Application
Training contracts p.a. 12
Applications p.a. 2,000
% interviewed p.a. 4%
Required degree grade 2:1

Training
Salary
1st year (2011) £37,000
2nd year (2011) £41,500
Holiday entitlement 25 days
% of trainees with a non-law degree p.a. 50%

Post-qualification
Salary (2011) £59,000

Overseas offices
Brussels, Berlin, Madrid, Paris, Munich, Singapore

OLSWANG

O'Melveny & Myers LLP

Warwick Court, 5 Paternoster Square, London EC4M 7DX
Tel: (020) 7088 0000 Fax: (020) 7088 0001
Email: graduate-recruitment@omm.com
Website: www.omm.com/careers/london

Firm profile

O'Melveny & Myers is a leading global law firm with approximately 800 lawyers practising in 15 offices in the key US, Asian and European economic and political centres. The London office provides transactional and litigation legal services to a diverse group of prominent private equity houses, financial institutions and corporate clients. The team in London comprises mainly English qualified lawyers, as well as some dual qualified (US and UK) lawyers, who advise on cross-border English law matters and work closely with the firm's international network to provide a seamless global service. The London office is known for its entrepreneurial leadership and commitment to excellence, both of which underpin its approach to recruitment. Each year a number of our partners and senior counsel are recognised in the Chambers UK guide as leaders in their practice areas.

Main areas of work

Globally, O'Melveny's capabilities span virtually every area of legal practice. The London office has both a transactions department - which focuses on private equity, corporate finance, M&A and investment funds matters - as well as an international litigation department, with antitrust and competition services support provided through the Brussels office. In September 2012 the firm also extended its top tier entertainment, sports and media practice into London, following the hire of leading entertainment lawyer Lisbeth Savill. London also has the key transactional support functions which are essential to a leading corporate practice; namely tax, regulatory and intellectual property/IT expertise.

Trainee profile

The London office recruits up to four high calibre graduates for training contracts each year. Successful candidates will have proven academic ability, sound commercial awareness, be keen team players and have the ability to carry real responsibility from the outset.

Training environment

Individual preferences can usually be taken into account when tailoring the London training programme, subject to completing the core competencies. Trainees complete seats with partners or senior lawyers usually in each of the corporate, finance, funds and litigation practices. O'Melveny trainees are also regularly seconded overseas to the Hong Kong, Singapore and Brussels offices. They are encouraged to be proactive and take responsibility at an early stage. Trainees work in a very supportive and inclusive environment, with regular formal and informal feedback. Great importance is placed on training for lawyers at all levels, and so trainees participate in both legal and non-legal skills training programmes.

Vacation schemes

Vacation placements are available each summer. All applications for 2013 placements must be submitted online via www.apply4law.com/omm by 31st January 2013.

Benefits

Benefits include: 25 days holiday, pension, life assurance, long term disability insurance, private health insurance, travel insurance, interest-free season ticket loan, corporate rate gym membership.

Sponsorship & awards

O'Melveny & Myers sponsors GDL/LPC fees incurred post-recruitment and awards a maintenance grant (currently £7,000 per annum) during the GDL/LPC course.

Partners 7
Counsel & Associates 16
Trainees 8

Contact
Fiona McEwan
HR Officer

Method of application
Online application
www.apply4law.com/omm

Application
Training contracts p.a. up to 4
Required degree grade 2:1, any discipline

Closing date for 2015
31 July 2013

Training
Salary
1st year (2012) £40,000
2nd year (2012) £43,000

Post-qualification
Market rate

Overseas offices/ regional offices
Beijing, Brussels, Century City, Hong Kong, Jakarta (in association with Tumbuan & Partners) Los Angeles, Newport Beach, New York, San Francisco, Shanghai, Silicon Valley, Singapore, Tokyo and Washington DC

O'MELVENY & MYERS LLP

Orrick, Herrington & Sutcliffe

107 Cheapside, London, EC2V 6DN
Tel: (020) 7862 4600 Fax: (020) 7862 4800
Email: recruitlondon@orrick.com
Website: www.orrick.com/london/gradrecruitment

Firm profile

Orrick is a leading international law firm with more than 1,100 lawyers in 24 offices located throughout North America, Europe and Asia. Orrick has earned a global reputation advising both established and emerging companies, banks and international financial institutions. Much of Orrick's client work involves cross-border transactions which have increased substantially in recent years with the development of the firm's network of global offices.

Main areas of work

Acquisition finance, arbitration and litigation, banking, capital markets, trade and asset finance, competition and European Union law, corporate and corporate finance, employment, energy and project finance, intellectual property, international dispute resolution, real estate, restructuring, structured finance and tax.

Trainee profile

If you set your standards high, have a strong work ethic and are a bright, talented graduate of any discipline looking for a firm offering a broad-based training contract, then Orrick could be for you. Applicants should have at least three A level passes at grades A and B and a 2:1 degree.

Training environment

Orrick is a firm for those looking for a high level of responsibility from day one. The firm values team players and reward collaboration over competition. It aims to give individuals the opportunity to flourish in a lively and supportive work environment and encourage interaction among lawyers across international offices at every level of experience within the firm. It supports learning through a steadfast focus on training and a mentoring programme that will provide you with the right foundation for building your legal career and for working with clients. A genuine open door policy means trainees work closely with partners and of counsel as well as associates to gain practical experience in research, drafting, procedural and client-related skills. There are regular training sessions on legal and soft skills to enhance your development as a lawyer. The two-year training programme is made up of four six-month seats, with regular appraisals throughout. Trainees undertake the Professional Skills Course during their induction programme.

Benefits

Pension, health insurance, subsidised gym membership, season ticket loan, private medical insurance, dental care and childcare voucher scheme.

Sponsorship & awards

GDL and LPC: fees paid plus £7,000 maintenance.

Open days

We hold open days during the year which provide a good opportunity to see the London office of a US law firm in action. Applicants spend the day learning more about the firm and the work on offer in the London office as well as participating in a business game designed to give a flavour of the work of a City lawyer. Applications should be made online via our graduate recruitment website.

Partners 20 (London)
Associates 36 (incl Of Counsel) (London)
Total Trainees 14

Contact
Halina Kasprowiak

Method of application
Online at www.orrick.com/london/gradrecruitment

Selection procedure
2 interviews: 1st round with Recruitment Manager and a senior associate/of counsel; 2nd round with partners

Closing date for 2015
28 June 2013

Application
Training contracts p.a. 5
Required degree grade 2:1

Training
Salary
1st year (2011) £38,000
2nd year (2011) £42,500
Holiday entitlement 25 days
% of trainees retained on qualification (March 2012) 60%

Overseas offices
Beijing, Berlin, Brussels, Dusseldorf, Frankfurt, Hong Kong, Los Angeles, Milan, Moscow, Munich, New York, Orange County, Paris, Portland, Rome, Sacramento, San Francisco, Seattle, Shanghai, Silicon Valley, Taipei, Tokyo and Washington DC.

ORRICK

Pannone LLP

123 Deansgate, Manchester M3 2BU
Tel: (0161) 909 3000 Fax: (0161) 909 4444
Email: graduaterecruitment@pannone.co.uk
Website: www.pannone.com

Firm profile

We are a full-service law firm located in central Manchester, with an office in London. Specialist departments serve a diverse client base which is split almost equally between business and private individuals. We pride ourselves on our ability to work in partnership with our clients and to offer practical and cost-effective solutions, meeting our clients' needs.

Committed to quality and client care, the firm was the first solicitors' practice to be awarded certification to the quality standard ISO 9001 and is a founder member of a European economic interest grouping, Pannone Law Group (although there is no opportunity for trainees to work abroad). The firm has held the Law Society's Lexcel accreditation since 1999 and Investors in People since 2007.

For the seven years that we entered, 2004-2010, Pannone was the highest placed law firm in The Sunday Times 100 Best Companies to Work For.

Main areas of work

Trainees at Pannone benefit from the unusually wide range of law practised within the firm. The departments in which trainees will spend their time include corporate and commercial, real estate, dispute resolution, employment, regulatory, personal injury, clinical negligence, family law, wills, trusts and probate, court of protection, construction and corporate recovery. In many of these fields we are recognised as leading practitioners.

Trainee profile

Selection criteria include a high level of academic achievement, teamwork, organisation and communication skills, a wide range of interests and a connection with the North West.

Training environment

Trainees themselves choose from the above departments to complete four six-month seats. We offer a structured training programme and trainees' progress is closely monitored throughout each of their seats, with an induction programme, lunchtime seminars and departmental training sessions supplementing the main part of the training, which takes place through work in chosen departments. The Professional Skills Course is taken over the two years of the training contract and study leave is given.

Vacation placements

Places for 2013: 60; Duration: 1 week; Remuneration: none; Closing date: 14 April 2013. Recruitment for training contracts is primarily through vacation placements.

Sponsorship & awards

Grant for LPC+ fees at College of Law, Manchester.

Partners 75
Assistant Solicitors 100
Total Trainees 29

Contact
Andrea Cohen

Method of application
Online only

Selection procedure
Individual interview, second interview is informal lunch with partners

Closing date for 2015
31st July 2013

Application
Training contracts p.a. 8
Applications p.a. 1,200
% interviewed p.a. 10%
Required degree grade 2:1

Training
Salary
1st year (2012) £24,000
2nd year (2012) £26,000
Holiday entitlement 23 days
% of trainees with a
non-law degree p.a. 33%

Post-qualification
Salary (2012) £35,000
% of trainees offered job
on qualification (2012) 65%
% of solicitors who joined as
trainees 60%
% of partners who joined as
trainees 25%

PANNONE

Paul Hastings (Europe) LLP

10 Bishops Square, 8th Floor, London, E1 6EG
Tel: (020) 3023 5100 Fax: (020) 3023 5109
Email: yvettecroucher@paulhastings.com
Website: www.paulhastings.com

Firm profile
With lawyers serving clients from 19 worldwide offices, Paul Hastings provides a wide range of services across Europe, America and Asia. Through a collaborative approach, entrepreneurial spirit and firm commitment to client service, the legal professionals of Paul Hastings deliver innovative solutions to many of the world's top financial institutions and Fortune 500 companies.

Main areas of work
Paul Hastings' London office focuses on corporate and real estate finance transactions, M&A, restructuring, capital markets, litigation, employment and tax. The London office has particular experience in multi-jurisdictional European transactions, working together with our offices in Frankfurt, Milan, Paris and Brussels.

Trainee profile
The firm seeks individuals with a wide variety of skills who combine intellectual ability with enthusiasm, creativity and a demonstrable ability to thrive in a challenging environment. The firm expects candidates to have a high level of achievement both at A level (or equivalent) and degree level. This would typically mean an upper second or first class degree. The firm recruits both law and non-law graduates.

Training environment
Paul Hastings will provide you with a first class training and development program, combining on-the-job training and professional courses. The firm will monitor your progress on a formal and informal basis to ensure you receive ongoing training and have the opportunity to give feedback on the program itself and on those areas that are most important to you.

Benefits
Private healthcare, life assurance, pension scheme, season ticket loan and gym subsidy.

Sponsorship & awards
Paul Hastings offers a maintenance grant and also offers sponsorship for the GDL and/or LPC.

Partners 19
Assistant Solicitors 25
Total Trainees 5

Contact
yvettecroucher@paulhastings.com

Method of application
Online application form
available on website

Selection procedure
Interview

Closing date for 2015
31 July 2013

Application
Training contracts p.a. 3-4
Required degree grade 2:1

Training
Salary
1st year (2011) £40,000
2nd year (2011) £45,000
Holiday entitlement
25 days

Post-qualification
Salary (2012) £88,000

Overseas/regional offices
Atlanta, Beijing, Brussels, Chicago, Frankfurt, Hong Kong, Houston, London, Los Angeles, Milan, New York, Orange County, Palo Alto, Paris, San Diego, San Francisco, Shanghai, Tokyo, Washington DC

PAUL
HASTINGS

Penningtons Solicitors LLP

Abacus House, 33 Gutter Lane, London EC2V 8AR
Tel: (020) 7457 3000 Fax: (020) 7457 3240
Email: traineepost@penningtons.co.uk
Website: www.penningtons.co.uk

Firm profile
Penningtons Solicitors LLP is a thriving, modern law firm with a 300-year history and a deep commitment to top quality, partner-led services. Today, the firm is based in London, Cambridge, Hampshire and Surrey and is a member of Multilaw and the European Law Group.

Main areas of work
Penningtons has three main divisions – business services, commercial property and private individuals – which comprise a variety of practice areas. In addition, we have a number of multidisciplinary sector groups that have expertise and experience in particular industries.

Our business services division advises on the full range of corporate and commercial matters including joint ventures, M&A, IT, IP, corporate tax, dispute resolution, business immigration and commercial contracts. We advise on the full range of commercial and residential property matters, including landlord and tenant, conveyancing, planning, construction and property litigation. We help individuals with advice on tax and estate planning, wills, trusts and probate, family law, clinical negligence, personal injury and capacity issues.

Trainee profile
Penningtons seeks high calibre candidates with enthusiasm and resilience. A high standard of academic achievement is expected: three or more good A level passes and preferably a 2:1 or better at degree level, whether you are reading law or another discipline.

Training environment
The firm has five UK offices, giving you the opportunity to work in or outside London. The ability to work outside London, while at the same time being part of a firm with a City presence, appeals to many of the trainees that we recruit. Whichever office you are based in, you will be given a thorough grounding in the law, with four six-month seats across the firm's divisions.

There are occasions when you might be offered a seat in a different office or on secondment with a client. Normally, however, trainees get immersed in the work and culture of their own office, but come together with all the trainees on a monthly basis and with the whole firm at sports and social events.

The firm ensures a varied training programme is given, avoiding too specialised an approach before qualification. Nonetheless, the experience gained in each practice area gives you a solid foundation, equipping you to embark on your chosen specialisation at the end of your training contract with the firm. Penningtons knows its trainee solicitors are happiest and most successful when busy with good quality and challenging work. The value of giving its trainees responsibility and allowing direct contact with clients is recognised. However, experienced solicitors are always ready to give support when needed.

Benefits
Life assurance, critical illness cover, pension, private medical insurance, 23 days holiday, interest free season ticket loan, sports and social events.

Vacation placements
The firm offers both summer vacation placements and information days. Applications are accepted from 1 December 2012 to 31 March 2013.

Sponsorship & awards
Full fees and maintenance for the LPC plus a maintenance grant of £5,000.

Partners 71
Assistant Solicitors 115
Total Trainees 21
* denotes worldwide figures

Contact
Rebecca Philpott
01256 407 195

Method of application
Online form via firm's website, interviews, presentation, written assessment and critical thinking test

Closing date for 2015
31 July 2013

Application
Training contracts p.a. 10-12
Applications p.a. 1,300
% interviewed p.a. 6%
Required degree grade 2:1

Training
Salary
1st year (2012)
£31,000 (London)
2nd year (2012)
£33,000 (London)
Holiday entitlement 23 days

Post-qualification
Salary (2012) £47,000
(London)

Regional Offices
Basingstoke, Cambridge, Godalming, Guildford

PENNINGTONS
S O L I C I T O R S

Peters & Peters Solicitors LLP

15 Fetter Lane, London EC4A 1BW
Tel: (020) 7822 7777 Fax: (020) 7822 7788
Email: jbeckwith@petersandpeters.com
Website: www.petersandpeters.com

Firm profile

This specialist practice is best known as a leading firm in fraud, financial crime, commercial litigation and regulatory work, for which it attracts an impressive client base. It was recognised as 'Niche Firm of The Year' at The Lawyer Awards 2011, and as a 'Stand-Out Firm' for Dispute Resolution at The FT Innovative Lawyers Awards 2011. Peters & Peters was one of the first practices to develop a key multi-disciplinary approach, and the firm has built up a high level of expertise across its practice areas. Much of its work is high-profile and international in scope, and as well as advising corporate and individual clients, it provides advice to foreign regulators, worldwide organisations and governments. In doing so it has forged close working relationships with overseas law firms.

Main areas of work

Business crime, civil fraud and asset tracing, bribery and anti-corruption, commercial litigation, criminal antitrust (cartels), economic sanctions, extradition and international mutual legal assistance. Other areas of expertise: HMRC inquiries and investigations, financial regulation, data protection, freedom of information, professional disciplinary, compliance, regulatory and corporate governance matters, including anti-money laundering compliance, policy-making and risk management.

Trainee profile

We are a friendly firm with a supportive culture. We regard our trainees highly and make every effort to help them become fully integrated into the practice both in our work and socially. We have an excellent retention rate. Four of our seven partners trained with us. We are looking for trainees with strong academic qualifications. We recruit from a wide range of universities, taking both law and non-law graduates who have achieved a degree at 2:1 level or above. Given the nature of our international practice, we are particularly interested in meeting candidates with fluency in foreign languages. You must be committed to hard work and to a steep learning curve. Ideal candidates will have drive, enthusiasm and a sense of humour. Ours is very much a people business so you will also have to demonstrate strong presentation and communication skills.

Training environment

You will sit with a partner who will be the main source of your work and your principal supervisor during that seat, although you will have a lot of contact with the other fee earners in the department.

Your training contract will consist of three seats: Business crime; Commercial litigation/civil fraud; A non-contentious area of law e.g. corporate, dependent upon which exciting secondment you undertake.

Benefits

25 days holiday, pension scheme, BUPA private medical insurance, interest free season ticket loan, subsidised gym membership, interest free cycle purchase loan, free eye tests and contribution towards new glasses, life assurance (3 times annual salary) and a childcare voucher scheme.

Partners (and equivalent level of Special Counsel and Consultant) 11
Associates 19
Total Trainees 4

Contact
Julie Beckwith 020 7822 7721, jbeckwith@petersandpeters.com

Method of application
Application form from Careers section of the Peters & Peters website and send it to Julie Beckwith (see contact details above). Peters & Peters is an equal opportunities employer. If you apply for this job, please also complete the equal opportunities monitoring form.

Selection procedure
First stage, two hour written testing session (admin test and topical essay).
Second stage, interview with a partner and the HR and Training Manager, Sue Bachorski.
Third stage, interview with two senior partners.

Closing date for 2015
Ongoing

Application
Training contracts p.a. 2
Applications p.a. c. 200
% interviewed p.a. 1st stage (testing) 30%, interviewed 5%
Required degree grade 2:1

Training
Salary (2012)
First year £35,000
Second year £38,000
Holiday entitlement 25 days
% of trainees with a non-law degree varies year on year

Post-qualification
Salary (2012) £50,000
% of trainees offered job on qualification (2012) 100%

PETERS & PETERS

Pinsent Masons LLP

30 Crown Place, London EC2A 4ES
Email: graduate@pinsentmasons.com
Website: www.pinsentmasons.com/graduate

Firm profile

Pinsent Masons is a full service international law firm and ranks amongst the top 75 global law firms. We provide legal services to a wide variety of clients across the sectors of energy and natural resources, infrastructure, financial services, advanced manufacturing and technology and core industries and markets. We work with clients including FTSE 100 and AIM listed companies, government departments and public sector institutions. Pinsent Masons is the only firm to operate across all three UK jurisdictions and more recently we have been developing our overseas network of offices in the Asia-Pacific region, continental Europe and the Gulf. Our merger with McGrigors in May 2012 reflects our strategy to become a firm of truly international reach, offering world-class service and excellent value.

Main areas of work

At Pinsent Masons you can expect to get involved in interesting, highly commercial, client-facing work from the earliest stage in your career. Our aim is to develop you as a fully-rounded commercial lawyer and business adviser. To achieve that, we work with you to develop your technical legal expertise, alongside your knowledge of the sectors in which our clients operate.

The firm is organised into seven key practice areas: construction advisory and disputes; corporate; financial institutions and human capital (which includes banking, employment, financial services and pensions); litigation and compliance (including competition and tax); projects; property; and strategic business services (which includes commercial, intellectual property, regulatory and technology, media and telecommunications).

Trainee profile

Pinsent Masons need exceptional individuals with drive, ability and confidence. It is not about the school or university you attended but your unique qualities as an individual and what you can bring to our organisation which will make you successful. Excellent analytical and problem-solving skills are essential, as well as the ability to develop strong working relationships with both clients and colleagues, because fundamentally, the law is about people. How you demonstrate all of this is up to you.

Training environment

A training contract at Pinsent Masons represents the first stage of a focused development programme that will enable you to reach your full potential. Our training programme has been developed in-house, which ensures you receive a balanced and comprehensive introduction to the profession.

Trainees move departments every six months. This gives you the necessary time to develop the legal and commercial depth of understanding required to take on real client-facing responsibility. During the second year of training you may also have the opportunity to undertake a secondment to either a client organisation or one of our international offices.

Vacation placements

We believe that a vacation placement is the best way for you to understand whether a career in commercial law at Pinsent Masons is right for you. We typically recruit 70% of our trainee solicitors through our vacation placement programme and strongly recommend this application route to candidates.

We typically offer c.120 two-week vacation placements and the deadline for applications is 31 January 2013. The dates of our vacation placements can be found on our website.

Partners 350+
Lawyers 1500+
Trainees 180

Contact
The Graduate Team

Method of Application
Online application form

Selection Process
Online ability test and assessment centre

Closing date for 2015
Available online

Application
Training contracts p.a. 80
Applications p.a. 2000+
% interviewed p.a. c.12%
Required degree grade 2:1 (or equivalent)

Training
Salaries Highly competitive (details available on website)
% trainees with a non-law degree p.a. 50%

Regional Offices
London, Birmingham, Leeds, Manchester, Aberdeen, Edinburgh, Glasgow, Belfast and the Falkland Islands

Overseas Offices
Paris, Munich, Dubai, Doha, Beijing, Hong Kong, Shanghai and Singapore

Pinsent Masons

PricewaterhouseCoopers Legal LLP

10-18 Union Street, London, SE1 1SZ
Tel: 0808 100 1500
Website: www.pwclegal.co.uk

Vacancies 9	
Trainees 16	
Partners 22	
Total staff 162	
Work placement Yes	

Method of application
Visit www.pwclegal.co.uk where you'll be directed to our careers site to complete an online application

Closing dates
Training contracts
July 31 2013
Summer vacation scheme 2013
January 31 2013

Application
Required academic grade 2:1 honours degree in any degree discipline plus at least a 320 UCAS tariff or equivalent

Training
Salary London
1st year (2010) £30,000
2nd year (2010) £35,000

Firm profile

PricewaterhouseCoopers Legal LLP (PwC Legal) is an independent member of the PwC international network of firms. We believe we combine the best of both worlds. A firm that's not so large as to be impersonal, yet as part of the PwC network, we can and frequently do call upon professionals in PwC when our clients are looking for rounded solutions incorporating multi-disciplinary advice. Combined with our ambitious growth plans, it's a working model that makes us an exciting place to launch your career.

We offer domestic and international clients both project-based, specialist legal advice and on-going general counsel. Our practice areas include advising on mergers and acquisitions, corporate restructuring, intellectual property, information technology, litigation, immigration, pensions, employment, banking, commercial contracts, real estate, wills and trusts, environment and sustainability.

Our solicitors often work directly alongside PwC tax advisers, human capital consultants, corporate finance experts, actuaries, management consultants and of course, accountants. In terms of global reach, we're unsurpassed, having access to legal expertise in over 70 countries and immigration expertise in over 112 countries. Thanks to resources like this, we believe we can deliver a superior service to clients. One that really addresses their business needs, while offering our lawyers a unique working environment.

Trainee profile

Penultimate-year law students and final-year non-law students with at least a 2:1 honours degree (or equivalent), a 320+ UCAS tariff (or equivalent) and a keen interest in business law.

Training environment

Trainee solicitors have the opportunity to develop their skills in any of our practice groups. At the same time, exposure to the diverse skill sets of professionals in PwC will help you hone strong business advisory skills. You'll also develop lateral thinking skills, gain practical, hands-on experience at a very early stage in your traineeship and be part of teams delivering creative solutions. During your training contract, you'll take the core and elective modules of the Professional Skills Course (PSC) between your second and fourth seats and receive extensive training internally on business development and networking, management and interpersonal skills.

Visit www.pwclegal.co.uk where you'll be directed to the PwC UK careers site to submit your online application form. You need to complete this by 31 July 2013 for training contracts starting in 2015, and by 31 January 2013 for our summer 2013 vacation scheme.

Vacation schemes

Our paid, three-week summer vacation scheme is a great way to find out how we work and why we're unlike any other legal firm. You'll spend time in several of our practice groups, gain invaluable work experience and develop a real flavour for life as a solicitor in PwC Legal. The summer vacation scheme is also the biggest source of candidates for our Trainee Solicitor intake.

Sponsorship & awards

Trainees can apply for a scholarship award to help with the costs of the Graduate Diploma and the Legal Practice Course. If successful, you'll receive the total cost of the tuition and examination fees plus a significant contribution towards living expenses. You can find out more on our website.

Pritchard Englefield

14 New St, London EC2M 4HE
Tel: (020) 7972 9720 Fax: (020) 7972 9722
Email: po@pe-legal.com
Website: www.pe-legal.com

Firm profile
Pritchard Englefield is a full-service English law firm with international scope, experience and expertise. Based in the heart of the City of London, we are ideally placed to meet the modern-day needs of clients on a domestic and cross-border level, while maintaining a friendly yet focused working environment.

Main areas of work
Corporate/commercial (including banking and intellectual property), property, employment, commercial litigation, personal injury and private client (including probate, estate administration and family law).

Trainee profile
The firm is looking for well-rounded, motivated and enthusiastic individuals with a strong academic profile who are fluent in German and/or French. Excellent communication skills and the ability to work as part of a team are essential.

Training environment
Your training will be divided into four six-month seats. Regular two-way appraisals give trainees a forum for direct input into their training. The size of the firm allows trainees to be a valued member of the team with hands on involvement on client files. You will be given responsibility and will frequently have direct client contact. As a trainee, you will be exposed to a diverse range of matters, working with fee-earners at all levels to maximise your breadth of experience and develop your skills. Typical trainee tasks include attending client meetings, researching intricate legal issues and drafting and negotiating a variety of documents. Trainees are also actively involved with practice development and marketing initiatives. Our Corporate Social Responsibility committee organises regular fund-raising and social events that trainees are encouraged to get involved with. The firm also values a genuine worklife balance. The Professional Skills Course is run externally over the two-year training contract.

Benefits
Private medical insurance scheme, 25 days annual leave, interest free loan for annual season ticket and luncheon vouchers.

Sponsorship & awards
Sponsorship for LPC fees.

Partners 17
Other fee-earners (including consultants) 18
Total Trainees 6

Contact
Graduate Recruitment

Method of application
Standard application form available online or contact Graduate Recruitment

Selection procedure
1 interview in September

Closing date for 2015
31 July 2013

Application
Training contracts p.a. 3
Applications p.a. 300–400
% interviewed p.a. 10%
Required degree grade generally 2:1

Training
Salary market rate subject to annual review
Holiday entitlement 25 days
% of trainees with a non-law degree p.a. approx. 50%

Post-qualification
Salary market rate
% of trainees offered job on qualification on average 50%
% of assistants (as at 01/09/11) who joined as trainees approx. 60%
% of partners (as at 01/09/11) who joined as trainees approx. 20%

PRITCHARD ENGLEFIELD
SOLICITORS

Reed Smith

The Broadgate Tower, 20 Primrose Street, London, EC2A 2RS
Tel: (020) 3116 3000 Fax: (020) 3116 3999
Email: graduate.recruitment@reedsmith.com
Website: www.reedsmith.com

Firm profile

Key to Reed Smith's success is its ability to build lasting relationships: with clients and with each other. United through a culture defined by commitment to professional development, team-work, diversity, pro bono and community support, the firm has grown to become one of the largest law firms in the world. Its 23 offices span three continents and London is currently the largest with over 500 people. While the offices benefit from an international framework, each one retains key elements of the local business culture. The team in London is based in The Broadgate Tower, which boasts fantastic views of the city.

Main areas of work

The firm is particularly well known for its work advising leading companies in the areas of financial services, life sciences, shipping, energy and natural resources, advertising, technology and media. It provides a wide range of commercial legal services for all these clients, including a full spectrum of corporate, commercial and financial services, dispute resolution, real estate and employment advice. Much of the work is multi-jurisdictional.

Trainee profile

The firm is looking for individuals with the drive and potential to become world-class business lawyers. They want 'players' rather than 'onlookers' with strong intellect, initiative, the ability to thrive in a challenging profession and the personal qualities to build strong relationships with colleagues and clients.

Training environment

On offer is a four-seat programme with opportunities for secondments to clients and the firm's overseas offices. Trainees also benefit from being able to take a wide range of courses in its award-winning corporate university. There are vacancies for training contracts commencing in August 2015 and February 2016.

Benefits

Pension, life insurance, private health insurance, interest-free season ticket loan, bonus, subsidised staff restaurant, staff conveyancing allowance and cycle to work bicycle purchase scheme.

Vacation placements

The firm offers up to 20 places each year to applicants who will, on arrival, have completed at least two years of undergraduate study.

Sponsorship & awards

GDL Funding: Fees paid plus £6,000 maintenance. LPC Funding: Fees paid plus £7,000 maintenance.

Partners 113*
Fee-earners 302*
Total Trainees 61
* denotes UK figures

Contact
Lucy Crittenden

Method of application
Online application form

Selection procedure
Selection exercise, interview, verbal reasoning assessment

Closing date for 2015/2016
31 July 2013

Application
Training contracts p.a. approximately 24
Applications p.a. 1500
% interviewed p.a. 7%
Required degree grade 2:1

Training
Salary
1st year (2012) £37,000
Holiday entitlement 25 days
% of trainees with a non-law degree p.a. 35%
No. of seats available abroad p.a. 4

Post-qualification
Salary (2012)
£59,000 plus bonus
% of assistants who joined as trainees 43%
% of partners who joined as trainees 45%

Overseas offices
New York, London, Hong Kong, Chicago, Washington DC, Beijing, Paris, Los Angeles, San Francisco, Philadelphia, Pittsburg, Oakland, Munich, Abu Dhabi, Princeton, N Virginia, Wilmington, Dubai, Century City, Piraeus, Richmond, Silicon Valley, Shanghai

ReedSmith

RPC

Tower Bridge House, St Katharine's Way, London E1W 1AA
Tel: (020) 3060 6000
Website: www.rpc.co.uk/manifesto

Firm profile

RPC is a forward thinking commercial law firm with a wide-ranging practice, some of the leading lawyers in their fields and great clients in both the UK and overseas. We offer a depth of knowledge and creativity that few firms can rival and are regularly praised in the leading directories for the quality of our training programmes.

Headquartered in a state of the art site in the City of London, we also have offices in Bristol, Hong Kong and Singapore. We work in an open, collaborative environment designed to bring out the best in our people and to ensure that the service we offer our clients is second to none. We've created a working environment in which knowledge is shared and access to partners is a reality.

Trainee profile

We appoint 20 trainees each year from a law or non-law background. Although proven academic ability is important (we require a 2:1 degree or above) we also value energy, enthusiasm, business sense, commitment and the ability to communicate and relate well to others. Recruitment usually takes place in the September, two years before the training contract begins. Shortlisted candidates will be invited to one of our assessment days during which they will have the opportunity to meet our existing trainees and partners.

Training environment

As a trainee you will receive first rate training in a supportive working environment. You will work closely with a partner and will be given real responsibility as soon as you are ready to handle it. At least six months will be spent in four areas of our practice and we encourage our trainees to express preferences for the areas in which they would like to train. In addition to the Professional Skills Course we provide a complementary programme of in-house training.

Vacation placements

We run summer vacation schemes each year to enable prospective trainees to spend time with us, getting a feel for the work we do and the unique RPC atmosphere. Twelve students at a time spend two weeks with us and are integrated closely with the real working life of RPC, giving you a good idea of whether a career here is right for you.

During the scheme we provide you with real legal work, and expose you to the business side of being a lawyer, including getting an introduction to the importance of business development and marketing and involving you in a 'real-time' business project.

Funding

Bursaries are available for the GDL, if applicable, and the LPC. Bursaries comprise course and examination fees and a maintenance grant of up to £7,000. We request that all our trainees complete their LPC at BPP law school.

Partners 77	
Associates 170	
Total trainees 30	

Method of application
Online or by post

Selection procedure
First interview face-to-face, presentations, aptitude tests, case studies

Closing date for August 2015
Training contract
31 July 2013
Vacation scheme
31 January 2013

Application
Training contracts p.a. 20
Applications received 650
Required degree grade 2:1

Training
Salary
1st year £37,000
2nd year £40,000
% of trainees with a
non-law degree p.a. 50%

Post-qualification
Salary £58,000
% of trainees offered job
on qualification 87%

Overseas offices
Hong Kong and Singapore

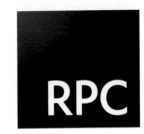

SGH Martineau

No 1 Colmore Square, Birmingham B4 6AA
One America Square, Crosswall, London EC3N 2SG
Tel: 0800 763 2000 Fax: 0800 763 2001
Email: jennifer.seymour@sghmartineau.com
Website: www.sghmartineau.com

Firm profile

We are a commercially orientated law firm that services a diverse range of clients across a number of key sectors. In a changing world, our entrepreneurial spirit and leading-edge expertise in those areas, means that we think, act and do things in a way that delivers the best solution to achieve our clients' business needs.

As a top 70 UK law firm, we provide genuine industry-leading expertise to companies, public sector organisations and private individuals across the globe offering the full spectrum of legal services.

We also have an international reach through Multilaw, LEGUS and AEEC – which means we have on-the-ground representation overseas for our clients with international business operations. Reflecting the importance of UK-US trade links, we are the only firm based outside of North America belonging to State Law Resources.

Main areas of work

Our chosen sectors are energy, education, banking, leisure, private wealth, industry and manufacturing and investment funds. Other sectors in which we have built up strong, cross-disciplinary teams of specialist lawyers include corporate, services to lenders, corporate finance, capital projects, financial services, private capital, commercial disputes, commercial property, mergers and acquisitions, automotive, charities and trusts, construction and engineering, professional negligence, technology, property disputes, real estate and retail.

Trainee profile

We look for our trainees to be enthusiastic, committed, have commercial flair, good business skills and creativity. Trainees also need to have good academic ability.

Vacation placements

We aim to recruit many of our trainees through the mini vacation scheme route. Our mini vacation schemes involve presentations, workshops, networking opportunities and much more.

Training environment

We work in partnership with our trainees and provide mentoring, supervision, support and exposure to the key areas of the firm's practice. Trainees are actively encouraged to be an integral part of our team by delivering legal solutions to our clients while benefiting from quality work.

Trainees benefit from a structured career training programme tailored to their personal development needs. It covers not only legal technical matters but also a business and commercial approach which has never been more central to successful professional careers.

Trainees rotate every four months which results in gaining a broader experience and also the possibility of repeating a seat. Opportunities for seats span across our Birmingham and London offices. The majority of our trainees are based in our Birmingham office however we are looking to recruit trainees into our London office shortly.

Partners 63
Fee earners 108
Total Trainees 19

Contact
Jennifer Seymour

Method of application
Online application form
www.sghmartineau.com

Selection procedure
Mini vacation scheme and
assessment centre

Closing date for 2014 and
2015 training contracts
31 July 2013

Closing date for 2013 mini
vacation schemes
24 February 2013

Application
Training contracts p.a. 10-12
Applications p.a. 600
% interviewed p.a. 10%
Required degree grade 2:1

Training
Salary
1st year (2013) c. £23,000
2nd year (2013) c. £25,000
Holiday entitlement 25 days
% of trainees with a
non-law degree 32%

Post-qualification
Salary (2012) £36,000
% of trainees offered job
on qualification (2012) 100%

Overseas offices
Belgium

Shearman & Sterling LLP

Broadgate West, 9 Appold Street, London EC2A 2AP
Tel: (020) 7655 5000 Fax: (020) 7655 5500
Email: graduates@shearman.com
Website: www.shearman.com

Firm profile

Shearman & Sterling is one of the world's leading premier global law firms and was established over a century ago. The London office opened over 40 years ago and quickly became one of the leading practices, covering all aspects of English, European and US corporate and finance law. Globally there are approximately 900 lawyers, including around 200 partners.

Main areas of work

Our main areas of work include: European corporate (including mergers and acquisitions, equity capital markets and US capital markets), project development and finance, global finance (including capital markets, structured, acquisition and leveraged finance), international arbitration and litigation, antitrust, tax, financial institutions advisory and asset management, real estate and executive compensation and employee benefits.

Trainee profile

There is no 'standard trainee profile' that could describe the trainees that join the firm each year. We look for those who have the potential to become excellent lawyers, developing a range of technical and soft skills throughout their two year training contract and beyond. The role of a trainee solicitor at Shearman & Sterling is as demanding as it is rewarding, with the chance to work on major deals with individuals at all levels, from partners to associates. The diverse range of practices and clients allows for a large variety of work for trainees, who are given real responsibility from day one. Trainees become an integral part of the team working on deals and contributing work that adds significant value to the end result.

Training environment

The two year training contract consists of four seats, each lasting six months. As part of a global firm, trainees may have the opportunity to work in an overseas office for one of their seats, in locations including: New York, Abu Dhabi, Brussels and Singapore. Training at the firm is on the job and formalised. Trainees typically share an office with a partner or senior lawyer, while the structured training programme at the firm ensures trainees get exposure to all the information they need to be a success now and in the future.

Benefits

Life assurance, long term disability insurance, annual eye test, matched pension contributions, subsidised gym membership, private medical insurance, travel insurance and private dental insurance.

Sponsorship & awards

Full sponsorship for the GDL and LPC, and a maintenance grant of £7000 during each year of these courses.

Partners 29
Assistant Solicitors 130
Total Trainees 26

Contact
Charlotte Hannan
Tel: (020) 7655 5000

Method of application
Online at www.shearman.com

Selection procedure
Psychometric test, Interview with HR and a senior lawyer/partner, Assessment centre

Closing date for 2015
31 July 2013

Application
Training contracts p.a. 15
Applications p.a. approx 900
% interviewed p.a. 7%
Required degree grade 2:1 or international equivalent

Training
Salary
1st year (2012) £39,000
2nd year (2012) £40,500
Holiday entitlement
24 days p.a.

Post-qualification
Salary (2012) £78,000
% of trainees offered job on qualification (2011) 84%

Overseas offices
Abu Dhabi, Bejing, Brussels, Düsseldorf, Frankfurt, Hong Kong, Milan, Munich, New York, Palo Alto, Paris, Rome, San Francisco, Sao Paulo, Shanghai, Singapore, Tokyo, Toronto, Washington DC

SHEARMAN & STERLING LLP

Sheridans

Whittington House, Alfred Place, London WC1E 7EA
Tel: (020) 7079 0100 Fax: (020) 7079 0200
Email: enquiries@sheridans.co.uk
Website: www.sheridans.co.uk

Firm profile

Sheridans is a leading leisure, media and entertainment law firm with an established reputation across the creative industries. The firm represents a number of leading organisations, brands and talent across sectors including computer games, entertainment, fashion, film, interactive media, music, sport, television and theatre. Sheridans complements this expertise with a thriving commercial practice offering corporate, dispute resolution, real estate and employment services.

Main areas of work

ENTERTAINMENT & MEDIA: The music department advises recording artists and recording and management companies, on contract negotiation, popular and classical music publishing, merchandising and sponsorship. The film and television departments advise broadcasters, television and feature film production companies, distribution and sales agents, financiers and talent. Other specialist areas include theatre, sport, advertising and branding, fashion and design, trade marks and domain names, technology, computer games and interactive and digital media.

DISPUTE RESOLUTION: The firm provides advice and representation in relation to disputes arising in the media and entertainment industries. The disputes typically range from privacy and defamation claims against the national press to rights disputes.

CORPORATE/COMMERCIAL: The firm advises on commercial contracts, mergers, acquisitions and disposals, management buy-outs and buy-ins, corporate finance, joint ventures, corporate reorganisations, company formations and insolvency.

REAL ESTATE: Services include the sale and purchase of commercial property, involving investment, leasehold and planning matters, secured lending, building and development schemes and property financing, as well as domestic conveyancing for high net worth individuals.

EMPLOYMENT: The employment practice handles contentious and non-contentious matters, representing both employers and senior executives on a wide range of matters from recruitment to severence and change management to TUPE.

Trainee profile

Excellent academic background (2:1 and above, good A levels), commercial awareness, great interpersonal skills and an ability to think strategically. Trainees should have an enthusiasm for, and a demonstrable commitment to, the firm's areas of practice.

Training

The training contract is divided into four six month seats, although trainees are expected to be flexible and assist any department as required. Trainees are given a challenging range of work and exposure to a significant level of responsibility.

Partners 28
Consultants 1
Assistant solicitors 18
Total trainees 2

Contact
Claire Lewis (Training Principal)

Method of application
CV and covering letter, by email to
trainees@sheridans.co.uk

Selection procedure
2 stage interview process

Closing date for 2015
31 July 2013

Application
Training contracts p.a. 1
Required degree grade 2:1

Training
Salary
1st year competitive with similar firms
2nd year competitive with similar firms
Holiday entitlement
20 days

Post-qualification
Salary Competitive with similar firms
% of trainees offered job on qualification (in last two years) 100%

SHERIDANS

Shoosmiths

The Lakes, Northampton NN4 7SH
Tel: (0370) 086 3075 Fax: (0370) 086 3001
Email: join.us@shoosmiths.co.uk
Website: www.shoosmiths.co.uk
Twitter: www.twitter.com/shoosmithsgrads

Firm profile

Shoosmiths is a full service law firm offering you experience in a variety of areas, including commercial, corporate, employment, real estate, intellectual property, banking, planning and dispute resolution. Through our Access Legal consumer brand, we also offer private client, personal injury, medical negligence and conveyancing.

Trainee Profile

You'll be open-minded, forward-thinking, creative and innovative, and be trained in a non-hierarchal, open plan environment.

As a trainee, you will value a social life outside the office. Work-wise, you will care about the quality of service you give to clients, and will want to make a real and direct contribution to the firm's success.

Your experience will be built around a practical workload, complemented by technical and business skills training. We allocate no more than one trainee to each team, which means trainees enjoy high levels of involvement with the team, and are given good quality work and contact with clients.

Over two years, you will complete four, six-month placements, one of which could be an external secondment to a client's in-house legal team, providing an invaluable insight from the client's perspective.

Training environment

There's nothing like diving straight in and having a go and, while we would not ask you to do something you are not comfortable in tackling, we expect you to relish the opportunity to get experience of real cases and deals from the start. In our opinion, it's the best way to learn.

Shoosmiths Trainees take an active part in the CR (Corporate Responsibility) around the firm, and they also create and drive initiatives of their own including "New Friday" a networking event for young professionals.

Your experience will be built around a practical workload, complemented by technical and business skills training. Over the two years, you will complete four six-month placements, one of which possibly being an external secondment to a clients in-house legal team, which provides an invaluable insight into the clients perspective.

Benefits

Regular involvement in sporting and social events, flexible holiday, pension, life assurance, corporate discounts. Please see our website for more benefits.

Vacation placements

Placements provide invaluable experience, allowing you to choose the right firm for you, and can even fast track you to a place on the assessment day for a training contract.

During your time with us, you'll be buddied with a trainee and spend time working with clients, partners and qualified lawyers, making a valuable contribution to the business.

Sponsorship & awards

We are happy to offer you financial assistance in relation to your GDL and/or LPC. We will also provide a living allowance whilst you are studying.

Partners 115
Total Staff 1,300
Total Trainees 41

Contact
Samantha Hope

Method of application
Online application form

Selection procedure
Application & assessment day

Closing date for 2015
31st July 2013

Application
No. of Training Contracts 22
Applications pa 1600+
% Interviewed 10%
Required degree grade 2:1

Training
Salary
£24,000 / £25,000
Holiday entitlement p.a
23 days + flex

Post-qualification
Salary £36,500
% of trainees offered job on
qualification (2012)100%

Offices
Birmingham, Edinburgh,
Manchester, Milton Keynes,
Northampton, Reading, Solent
(please see our website for
locations we are currently
recruiting to)

Sidley Austin LLP

Woolgate Exchange, 25 Basinghall Street, London EC2V 5HA
Tel: (020) 7360 3600
Email: ukrecruitment@sidley.com
Website: www.sidley.com

Firm profile

Sidley Austin LLP is one of the world's largest full-service law firms. With approximately 1,700 lawyers practising on four continents (North America, Europe, Australasia and Asia), the firm provides a broad range of integrated services to meet the needs of its clients across a multitude of industries.

Main areas of work

Corporate, competition, corporate reorganisation and bankruptcy, debt restructuring, debt finance and structured finance, equity capital markets, employment, financial services regulatory, hedge funds, insurance, IP/IT, litigation, real estate and real estate finance, tax.

Trainee profile

Sidley Austin LLP looks for focused, intelligent and enthusiastic individuals with personality and humour who have a real interest in practising law in the commercial world. Trainees should have a consistently strong academic record and a 2:1 degree (not necessarily in law).

Training environment

The firm is not a typical City firm and it is not a 'legal factory' so there is no risk of being just a number. Everyone is encouraged to be proactive and to create their own niche when they are ready to do so. Trainees spend time in the firm's main groups. In each group trainees will sit with a partner or senior associate to ensure individual training based on 'hands on' experience. You will be encouraged to take responsibility where appropriate. Regular meetings with your supervisor ensure both the quality and quantity of your experience. In addition, there is a structured timetable of training on a cross-section of subjects.

Benefits

Private health insurance, life assurance, contribution to gym membership, interest-free season ticket loan, income protection scheme, pension and subsidised restaurant.

Sponsorship & awards

Tuition fees for the GDL/CPE and the LPC. Maintenance grant of £7,000 p.a.

Partners 40
Assistant Solicitors 75
Total Trainees 19

Contact
Kellie Wade
HR Administrator

Method of application
Apply online at
www.sidley.com

Selection procedure
Interview(s) and verbal reasoning test

Closing date for 2015
31 July 2013

Application
Training contracts p.a. 10
Applications p.a. 600
% interviewed p.a. 15
Required degree grade 2:1

Training
Salary
1st year (2010) £39,000
2nd year (2010) £43,000
Holiday entitlement 25 days
% of trainees with a
non-law degree p.a. 50%

Overseas offices
Beijing, Brussels, Chicago, Dallas, Frankfurt, Geneva, Hong Kong, Houston, Los Angeles, New York, Palo Alto, San Francisco, Shanghai, Singapore, Sydney, Tokyo, Washington DC

SIDLEY AUSTIN LLP
SIDLEY

Simmons & Simmons LLP

CityPoint, One Ropemaker Street, London EC2Y 9SS
Tel: (020) 7628 2020 Fax: (020) 7628 2070
Email: recruitment@simmons-simmons.com
Website: www.simmons-simmons.com/graduates

Firm profile
Dynamic and innovative, Simmons & Simmons has a reputation for offering a superior legal service, wherever and whenever it is required. The firm's high quality advice and the positive working atmosphere in its international network of offices has won admiration and praise from both the legal community and business clients.

Main areas of work
We offer our clients a full range of legal services across numerous industry sectors. We have a particular focus on five dynamic sectors, which are: Financial Institutions; Asset Management and Investment Funds; Energy and Infrastructure; Life Sciences; and Technology, Media and Telecommunications (TMT). We provide a wide choice of service areas in which our lawyers can specialise. These include corporate and commercial; information, communications and technology; dispute resolution; employment; EU, regulatory and competition; financial markets; IP; projects; real estate; corporate tax and corporate pensions.

Trainee profile
Simmons & Simmons is interested to find out about your academic successes but will also explore your ability to form excellent interpersonal relations and work within a team environment, as well as your levels of motivation, drive and ambition.

Show us evidence of a rich 'life experience' as well as examples of your intellectual capabilities and we will provide you with everything you need to become a successful member of our firm.

Training environment
The training programme is constantly evolving to build the skills you will need to be successful in the fast moving world of international business. We provide experience in a range of areas of law, and a balanced approach to gaining the knowledge, expertise and abilities you will need to qualify in the practice area of your choice.

Vacation placements
The firm's internship schemes are one of the primary means of selecting candidates for a career at Simmons & Simmons. Your placement will enable you to gain first-hand experience of a busy and dynamic international law firm, as well as exposure to everything from the firm's service areas to the kinds of deals and transactions the firm works on.

The firm's three week summer vacation scheme is open to penultimate year law students, final year non-law students, graduates, mature and international students and those changing career. Applications open 1 November 2012.

The spring vacation scheme is a great opportunity for first year law students and penultimate year non-law students to get an in-depth view of the firm at an early stage of your studies. Applications open 1 November 2012.

Simmons & Simmons also runs winter insight workshops aimed specifically at final year non-law students, graduates of non-law subjects and career changers. Applications open 1 October - 16 November 2012.

Finally, a series of open days, available to all undergraduates, graduates, mature and international students are run throughout the year.

Sponsorship
The firm will cover full tuition fees at law school and offers a maintenance allowance of up to £7,500.

Partners 240+
Fee earners 800+
Total Trainees 85+

Contact
Anna King, Graduate Recruitment and Development Manager

Method of application
Online application, remote online critical reasoning test, assessment day

Selection procedure
Assessment day

Application dates for Training Contracts in 2015/16
Penultimate year law undergraduates
1 June - 31 July 2013
All finalists and graduates
1 November 2012 - 31 March 2013

Application
Training contracts p.a. circa 40
Applications p.a. 1,500
Required degree grade 2:1

Training
Salary
£37,500, 1st and 2nd seat
£41,750, 3rd and 4th seat
Holiday entitlement 25 days
% of trainees with a non-law degree p.a. 50%
No. of seats available abroad p.a. varies

Post-qualification
Salary (2012) £59,000

Overseas offices
Abu Dhabi, Amsterdam, Bristol, Brussels, Doha, Dubai, Düsseldorf, Frankfurt, Funchal*, Hong Kong, Jeddah, Lisbon*, London, Madrid, Milan, Paris, Rome, Shanghai, Tokyo
*Associated office

Simmons & Simmons

SJ Berwin

10 Queen Street Place, London, EC4R 1BE
Tel: (020) 7111 2268 Fax: (020) 7111 2000
Email: graduate.recruitment@sjberwin.com
Website: www.sjberwin.com

Firm profile

SJ Berwin is an international corporate law firm. Clients range from major multinational business corporations and financial institutions to high net-worth individuals. As a result, the firm has established a strong reputation in corporate finance. The firm has 156 partners and over 368 fee-earners.

Main areas of work

SJ Berwin was created and continues to thrive as a leading-edge legal services business, focusing on the European and international marketplace. The firm's clients are sophisticated buyers of legal services, principally entrepreneurial companies and financial institutions, whom the firm advises on a comprehensive range of services including: corporate/M&A, commercial, communications and technology, energy and natural resources, employment and pensions, EU, competition and regulatory, finance, financial markets, intellectual property, investment funds, litigation and dispute resolution, pharmaceuticals and life sciences, private equity, real estate, reconstruction and insolvency, retail and tax.

Trainee profile

The firm wants ambitious, commercially minded individuals who seek a high level of involvement from day one. Candidates must have a strong academic record, be on track for, or have achieved, a 2:1 or equivalent in their undergraduate degree, and have demonstrated strong team and leadership potential.

Training environment

The two-year training contract is divided into four six-month seats. Trainees will spend two seats (which may include a seat abroad) within the following areas: finance, mergers and aquisitions, equity capital markets, private equity, venture capital and investment funds. Trainees are given early responsibility and are supported throughout the training contract.

How to apply

The firm welcomes applications from all disciplines and all universities. Applications must be made using the firm's online form available at www.sjberwin.com. The same form can be used to indicate your interest in an open day, a vacation scheme and/or a training contract.

Benefits

25 days holiday, private healthcare, gym membership/subsidy, life assurance, pension scheme, season ticket loan, free lunch.

Partners 156
Assistant Solicitors 368
Total Trainees 77

Contact
Graduate Recruitment Team

Method of application
Online application form

Selection procedure
2 interviews / case study /
critical reasoning test

Closing date for 2015
31 July 2013
Easter & summer vacation
schemes 31 January 2013

Application
Training contracts p.a. 40
Applications p.a. 2,000
10% interviewed p.a.
Required degree grade 2:1

Training
Salary
£37,500, 1st year
£41,500, 2nd year
Holiday entitlement 25 days
% of trainees with a
non-law degree p.a. 50%

Post-qualification
Salary (2012) £59,000
% of trainees offered job
on qualification (as March
2012) 100%

Overseas offices
Berlin, Brussels, Dubai, Frankfurt,
Hong Kong, Madrid, Milan,
Munich, Paris, Shanghai

Skadden, Arps, Slate, Meagher & Flom (UK) LLP

40 Bank Street, Canary Wharf, London E14 5DS
Tel: (020) 7519 7000 Fax: (020) 7519 7070
Email: graduate.hiring@skadden.com
Website: www.skadden.com/uktraineesolicitors

Firm profile
Skadden is one of the leading law firms in the world with approximately 2,000 lawyers in 24 offices across the globe. Clients include corporate, industrial, financial institutions and government entities. The London office is the gateway to the firm's European practice and has some 250 lawyers dedicated to top-end, cross-border corporate transactions and international arbitration and litigation. The firm has handled matters in nearly every country in the greater European region, and in Africa and the Middle East. The firm is consistently ranked as a leader in all disciplines and amongst a whole host of accolades, the firm has been voted 'Global Corporate Law Firm of the Year' (*Chambers and Partners*), 'Best US Law Firm in London' (Legal Business) 'Best Trainer' and 'Best Recruiter' in the US law firm in London category (Law Careers.Net Training and Recruitment Awards).

Main areas of work
Lawyers across the European network focus primarily on corporate transactions, including domestic and cross-border mergers and acquisitions, private equity, capital markets, leveraged finance and banking, tax, corporate restructuring and energy and projects. The firm also advise in international arbitration, litigation and regulatory matters.

Trainee profile
The firm seeks to recruit a small number of high-calibre graduates from any discipline to join their highly successful London office as trainee solicitors. The firm is looking for candidates who combine intellectual ability with enthusiasm, creativity and a demonstrable ability to rise to a challenge and to work with others towards a common goal.

Training environment
The firm can offer you the chance to develop your career in a uniquely rewarding and professional environment. You will join a close-knit but diverse team in which you will be given ample opportunity to work on complex matters, almost all with an international aspect, whilst benefiting from highly personalised training and supervision in an informal and friendly environment. The first year of your training contract will be divided into two six month seats where you will gain experience in corporate transactions and international litigation and arbitration. In the second year of your training contract, you will have the opportunity to discuss your preferences for your remaining two seats. The firm also offers the opportunity for second year trainees to be seconded to our Hong Kong office for a six month seat.

Benefits
Life insurance, private health insurance, private medical insurance, travel insurance, joining fee paid at Canary Wharf gym, subsidised restaurant, employee assistance programme and technology allowance.

Work placements
Skadden offers the opportunity for penultimate year law and non-law students to experience the culture and working environment of the firm through two week work placements. Placements are paid and take place during Easter and over the course of the summer. The deadline for applications is 12 January 2013 for placements in 2013.

Sponsorship & awards
The firm pays for GDL and LPC course fees and provides a £8,000 grant for each year of these courses.

Partners 31*
Assistant Solicitors 115
Trainees 12*
*London office

Contact
Aidan Connor
Graduate Recruitment
Specialist

Method of application
Online application

Selection procedure
A selection event comprising of an interview and a short exercise

Closing date for 2015
31 July 2013

Application
Training contracts p.a. 10-12
Applications p.a. 1000
% interviewed p.a. 8%
Required degree grade 2:1

Training
Salary
1st year £40,000
2nd year £43,000
Holiday entitlement 25 days
% of trainees with a
non-law degree p.a. 50%

Overseas offices
Beijing, Boston, Brussels, Chicago, Frankfurt, Hong Kong, Houston, Los Angeles, Moscow, Munich, New York, Palo Alto, Paris, San Francisco, São Paulo, Shanghai, Singapore, Sydney, Tokyo, Toronto, Vienna, Washington DC, Wilmington

Skadden, Arps, Slate, Meagher & Flom (UK) LLP

Slaughter and May

One Bunhill Row, London EC1Y 8YY
Tel: (020) 7600 1200 Fax: (020) 7090 5000
Email: trainee.recruit@slaughterandmay.com (enquiries only)
Website: www.slaughterandmay.com

Firm profile

One of the most prestigious law firms in the world, Slaughter and May enjoys a reputation for quality and expertise. The corporate, commercial and financing practice is particularly strong and lawyers are known for their business acumen and technical excellence. As well as its London, Brussels, Beijing and Hong Kong offices, the firm nurtures long-standing relationships with the leading independent law firms in other jurisdictions in order to provide the best advice and service across the world.

Main areas of work

Corporate, commercial and financing; tax; competition; financial regulation; dispute resolution; technology, media and telecommunications; intellectual property; commercial real estate; environment; pensions and employment.

Trainee profile

The work is demanding and the firm looks for intellectual agility and the ability to work with people from different countries and walks of life. Common sense, the ability to communicate clearly and the willingness to accept responsibility are all essential. The firm expects to provide training in everything except the fundamental principles of law, so does not expect applicants to know much of commercial life.

Training environment

Each trainee completes four or five seats of three or six months duration. Two or three seats will be spent in one of the firm's corporate, commercial and financing law groups. The remaining time can be divided between some of the specialist groups and can also include an overseas secondment to one of the firm's offices or to one of its best friend firms. In each seat a partner is responsible for monitoring your progress and reviewing your work. There is an extensive training programme which includes the PSC. There are also discussion groups covering general and specialised legal topics.

Benefits

Private medical insurance, season ticket loan, pension scheme, interest free loan, subsidised membership of health club, 24 hour accident cover, Cycle to Work scheme, childcare vouchers, subsidised restaurant and coffee bar, concierge service and health screenings.

Vacation placements

One or two-week work experience schemes are available at Easter and during the summer period for penultimate year students. We also offer a first year open day at Easter and workshops for non-law finalists and graduates at Christmas. Please visit the website for full details.

Sponsorship & awards

GDL and LPC fees and maintenance grants are paid.

Partners 125
Associates Over 400
Total Trainees 193

Contact
The Trainee Recruitment Team

Method of application
Online (via website)

Selection procedure
Interview

Application
Training contracts p.a. Approx 90
Applications p.a. 2,000 approx
% interviewed p.a. 25% approx
Required degree grade Good 2:1 ability

Training
Salary (May 2012)
1st year £38,000
2nd year £43,000
Holiday entitlement
25 days p.a.
% of trainees with a
non-law degree Approx 50%
No. of seats available
abroad p.a. Approx 30-40

Post-qualification
Salary (May 2012) £61,500
% of trainees offered job
on qualification (March 2012) 93%

Overseas offices
Brussels, Beijing and Hong Kong, plus 'Best Friend' firms in all the major jurisdictions.

SLAUGHTER AND MAY

SNR Denton

One Fleet Place, London EC4M 7WS
Tel: (020) 7246 7000 Fax: (020) 7320 6555
Email: graduaterecruitment@snrdenton.com
Website: www.snrdenton.com/graduates

Firm profile

SNR Denton is an elite client-focused, international legal practice. With over 1,400 high-quality lawyers and professionals in 43 countries, we're one of the world's biggest law firms.

SNR Denton was formed on 30 September 2010 with the combination of Denton Wilde Sapte LLP and Sonnenschein Nath & Rosenthal LLP.

Main areas of work

SNR Denton offers an international legal practice focused on quality in the following industry sectors: energy, transport and infrastructure, financial institutions and funds, government, health and life sciences, insurance, manufacturing, real estate, retail and hotels, technology, media and telecommunications.

Trainee profile

The firm looks for candidates who are talented, and have personality and ambition to join our London, Milton Keynes and Middle East offices. We accept candidates from any degree discipline, but you must have a strong academic and extracurricular record of achievement. SNR Denton lawyers are good team players with excellent interpersonal skills and the flexibility to grow with the firm.

Training environment

As a trainee you will undertake four six-month seats, including a contentious seat or attending an external litigation course. Your transactional experience will include banking (if in London) and corporate, construction or real estate (if in Milton Keynes). Middle East trainees will spend two seats in the UK and two in the Middle East.

Benefits

You'll earn a competitive salary. In London £37,000 in your first year, rising to £40,000 in your second year. In Milton Keynes you'll earn £25,500 in your first year, rising to £27,500 in your second. Other benefits include private health insurance, sports club membership allowance, season ticket loan and many more.

Vacation placements

We offer a one-week summer scheme in Milton Keynes for both law and non-law (July) and in London for law students (July).

In London we also offer open days for non-law students (December).

These placements consist of business games, department visits and social events, giving potential trainees an insight into commercial law and our way of life at SNR Denton.

Sponsorship & awards

We'll pay your GDL / LPC law school fees during actual years of study as well as a study maintenance grant of £6,000 per year of study (£7,000 in London).

Partners 150
Fee-earners 370
Total Trainees 72

Contact
Hemlata Shamji

Method of application
Online application form

Selection procedure
Selection test; occupational personality questionnaire; first interview; second interview and case study

Closing date for 2015
Non-law 29 March 2013
Law 31 July 2013

Application
Training contracts p.a. 20
Applications p.a. 1,500
% interviewed p.a. 10%
Required degree grade 2:1

Training
Salary in London
1st year £37,000
2nd year £40,000
Salary in Milton Keynes
1st year £25,500
2nd year £27,500
Holiday entitlement 24 days
% of trainees with a
non-law degree p.a. 30%
No. of seats available
abroad p.a. Currently 2

Post-qualification
Salary (2011) £59,000
% of trainees offered job
on qualification (2012) 83%

SNR Denton Offices
Abu Dhabi, Almaty, Brussels, Cairo, Chicago, Dallas, Doha, Dubai, Kansas City, Los Angeles, London, Manama, Milton Keynes, Moscow, Muscat, Short Hills, New York, Paris, Phoenix, San Francisco, Silicon Valley, Singapore, St Louis, Tashkent, Washington DC, Zurich
Refer to website for locations of Associate Offices, Facilities and Associate Firms

Speechly Bircham LLP

6 New Street Square, London, EC4A 3LX
Tel: (020) 7427 6400 Fax: (020) 7353 4368
Website: www.speechlys.com

Firm profile

Speechly Bircham is an ambitious, full-service City firm, with over 250 lawyers working with a fascinating mix of clients. We do not see ourselves purely as legal advisers to our clients. Instead, we aim to offer a more rounded, tailored service, where our insight and expertise helps clients achieve their wider aims. We combine expertise, professionalism and hands-on involvement to help our clients both in the UK and internationally with a complete offering across four sectors – financial services, private wealth, technology and real estate and construction.

The firm's international capabilities span three key European centres, with offices in London, Luxembourg and Zurich, making it one of the few UK law firms to offer intergrated corporate, tax, regulatory, funds and private client work to companies, banks, fund managers, wealthy individuals and private offices in Europe.

Main areas of work

Banking and finance, corporate recovery and restructuring, construction and engineering, contentious trusts, corporate finance, corporate tax, employment, family, financial services, IP, technology and data, pensions, private client, real estate, real estate litigation and projects.

Trainee profile

We require candidates to achieve a minimum of a 2:1 in their degree and look for smart, ambitious and intellectually curious individuals. People come to us from all backgrounds and degree disciplines, with a range of views that combine to give us our distinctive perspective on the law.

Training environment

Speechly Bircham divides the training contract into four six-month seats. We only take on 13 trainees per year and emphasis is given to early responsibility and supervised client contact to provide you with a practical learning environment. Trainees are supported by a partner or solicitor and are given in-house legal training complemented by regular performance reviews to promote development. Most of our trainees are selected from our summer schemes however we also accept direct training contract applications and interviews for these take place during August each year.

Vacation scheme

Our scheme is a three-week scheme offering a detailed introduction to the legal world. Each week is spent in a different practice area where you will carry out fee-earning work that could include attending client meetings and going to court. Support is always close at hand, with a current trainee as mentor and an assistant solicitor sponsor for each placement. Our summer scheme also has a programme of sports and social events which help both parties see if we are right for each other personally as well as professionally.

Benefits

Benefits include private medical insurance, life assurance, pension scheme, 25 days holiday, interest-free season ticket loan, subsidised restaurant, 4 weeks unpaid leave on qualification, corporate discount for gym membership.

Sponsorship

GDL and LPC fees paid together with a maintenance grant.

Partners 86
Assistant Solicitors 130
Total Trainees 26

Contact
Katie Summerfield
Human Resources Manager

Method of application
Online application via
www.dolawthinkbusiness.co.uk

Selection procedure
Interview and psychometric
testing

Closing date for 2015
31 July 2013

Application
Training contracts p.a. 13
Applications p.a. 800
% interviewed p.a. 15%
Required degree grade 2:1

Training
Salary
1st year 33,000
2nd year £35,000
Holiday entitlement 25 days

Post-qualification
Salary (2012) £56,000

Speechly Bircham

Squire Sanders

Rutland House, 148 Edmund Street, Birmingham B3 2JR
7 Devonshire Square, Cutlers Gardens, London EC2M 4YH
2 Park Lane, Leeds LS3 1ES
Trinity Court, 16 John Dalton Street, Manchester M6O 8HS
Tel: (0800) 163 498
Email: traineerecruitment@squiresandsers.com
Website: http://trainees.squiresanders.com

Firm profile

We combine sound legal advice with a deep knowledge of our clients' businesses to resolve their legal challenges. We care about the quality of our services, the success of our clients and the relationships that are forged through those successes.

With over 1,400 lawyers in 37 offices located in 18 countries on five continents, our global legal practice is in the markets where our clients do business. We also have strong working relationships with independent firms in Europe and the Middle East, as well as the Squire Sanders Legal Counsel Worldwide Network, which includes independent firms across Latin America.

The client base of our global legal practice spans every type of business, both private and public, worldwide. We advise a diverse mix of clients, from Fortune 100 and FTSE 100 corporations to emerging companies and from individuals to local and national governments.

Main areas of work

Banking and financial services, corporate/corporate finance, environment, safety and health, intellectual property, commercial and IT, international dispute resolution, labour and employment, litigation/disputes, pensions, real estate, regulatory, restructuring and insolvency and tax.

Trainee profile

Squire Sanders seeks applications from law and non-law graduates, and we also welcome applications from individuals seeking a career change. A strong academic background will be key and you will have, or would expect, a 2:1 degree. It is an advantage for applicants to have language skills, but this is not essential. You should also be motivated and ambitious and have a wish to succeed in a client-focused business. Evidence of work experience in the legal sector, excellent communication skills and significant achievement in non-academic pursuits.

Training environment

30 trainee solicitors recruited each year. Trainees undertake six four-month seats during their training contract. Trainees have input in choice of seats and are encouraged to undertake a broad selection of seats to benefit their knowledge on qualification. Trainees benefit from two-tier supervision and challenging work. The firm provides a comprehensive induction programme including on-going departmental training, seminars and workshops throughout the training contract. Trainees undertake formal appraisal meetings with their supervisors during each seat. Trainees also benefit from exposure to clients, cross-border work and opportunity for seats on secondment. Trainees are involved in all aspects of professional life.

Benefits

Pension, life assurance, subsidised gym membership, interest free season ticket loan and a flexible benefits package.

Vacation placements

Places for 2013: 40 summer scheme; Duration: 2 weeks; Remuneration: £230 p.w. (London) £215 p.w. (Birmingham, Leeds, Manchester); Closing date: 31 January 2013.

Sponsorship & awards

PgDL and LPC fees paid and maintenance grant provided. Maintenance grant presently:

GDL: London, £6,000; Regional, £4,500

LPC: London, £7,000; Regional, £5,000

Partners 460
Assistant Solicitors 1000
Total Trainees 60

Contact
Graduate Recruitment Team

Method of application
Online application form

Selection procedure
Assessment and interview

Closing date for 2015
31 July 2013

Application
Training contracts p.a. 30
Applications p.a. 1,500
% interviewed p.a. 10%
Required degree grade 2:1

Training
Salary
1st year (2012)
£23,500 regional
£35,000 London
2nd year (2012)
£26,000 regional
£37,000 London
Holiday entitlement 25 days
% of trainees with a non-law degree p.a. 30%
No. of seats available abroad p.a. 6

Post-qualification
Salary (2012)
London £58,000
Other £37,000
% of trainees accepting job on qualification (2012) 78%

Overseas offices
Squire Sanders Legal Counsel World Wide has offices in the USA, South America, Asia, Europe and the Middle East. For a complete list of our offices, please visit our website.

SQUIRE ◆ SANDERS

Stephenson Harwood

1 Finsbury Circus, London EC2M 7SH
Tel: (020) 7809 2812 Fax: (020) 7003 8346
Email: graduate.recruitment@shlegal.com
Website: www.shlegal.com/graduate

Firm profile

Stephenson Harwood is a thriving, international law firm with over 100 partners and more than 600 staff worldwide. Not only do we act for a wide range of listed and private companies, institutions and successful entrepreneurs. We also offer a full range of services in a wide variety of sectors. What's more, when it comes to delivering sound commercial solutions to complex business challenges, we punch well above our weight.

Main areas of work

Commercial litigation; corporate (including corporate finance, funds, corporate tax, business technology); employment and pensions; finance; marine and international trade; and real estate.

Trainee profile

Firstly we look for a quick intellect. As well as at least a 2:1 in any discipline plus 320 UCAS points or equivalent, you'll need strong analytical skills, sound judgement, imagination and meticulous attention to detail.

Also vital are the communication skills to be persuasive and build rapport, plenty of drive and determination, plus a keen interest in business. Mandarin Chinese language skills are useful.

Training environment

We take just 16 trainees on each year. So you can look forward to a huge amount of individual attention, coaching and mentoring. Your structured programme involves four six-month seats in our contentious and non-contentious practice groups. You can expect on-the-job training complemented by in-house seminars; to share an office with a partner or senior associate; and to benefit from a continuous review of your career development. You could also have the chance to spend one of your six-month seats in Hong Kong or Singapore and to take advantage of client secondment opportunities. We'll give you your own caseload and as much responsibility as you can shoulder – not forgetting free language tuition where appropriate.

Benefits

These include subsidised health club membership, private health insurance and screening, pension, life assurance, private GP services, critical illness cover, dental insurance, retail vouchers, concierge service, subsidised cafe, season ticket loan and 25 days' paid holiday a year.

Vacation placements

Places for 2012/2013: 40

Duration: 1 week winter; 2 weeks spring and summer

Remuneration: £260 p.w.

Closing date: 4 November 2012 for winter; 31 January 2013 for spring and summer.

Open days

16 January 2013, 13 February 2013, 3 April 2013, 24 April 2013

Closing date: 31 January 2013

Sponsorship & awards

Fees paid for GDL and LPC at BPP Law School London and maintenance awards of up to £6,000 (if still studying).

Partners 100+
Associates 200+
Total Trainees 32

Contact
Katy Crosse, Graduate Recruitment Assistant
(graduate.recruitment@shlegal.com)

Method of application
Online application form via www.shlegal.com/graduate

Selection procedure
Application screening, online verbal and numerical testing, face to face interview and assessment centre

Closing date for TC commencing March/Sept 2015
31 July 2013

Application
Applications p.a. circa 1,100
Training contracts p.a. 16
Required degree grade 2:1

Training
Salary
1st year £37,000
2nd year £40,000
Holiday entitlement 25 days
% of trainees with a non-law degree p.a. 50%
No. of seats available abroad p.a. 8 (4 per 6 month rotation)

Post-qualification
Salary £60,000
100% of trainees offered job

Overseas offices
Paris, Piraeus, Hong Kong, Singapore, Shanghai, Guangzhou

Associated offices
Athens, Bucharest, Kuwait, Jakarta

Stevens & Bolton LLP

Wey House, Farnham Road, Guildford GUI 4YD
Tel: (01483) 302264 Fax: (01483) 302254
Email: julie.bounden@stevens-bolton.com
Website: www.stevens-bolton.com

Partners 36	
Associates 65	
Total Trainees 8	
Contact	
Julie Bounden	
(01483) 302264	
Method of application	
Online application form	
available from website	
Selection procedure	
Two interviews and other	
processes	
Closing date for 2015	
31st July 2013	
Application	
Training contracts p.a. 4	
Applications p.a. 300	
% interviewed 10%	
Required degree grade 2:1	
Training	
Salary	
£30,000	
Holiday entitlement 25 days	
Overseas/regional offices	
Guildford only	

Firm profile

Stevens & Bolton LLP is a Guildford-based law firm with a national and international practice. Our vision is to be the South's top independent law firm – and a great place to work. We were named National/Regional Law Firm of the Year at the 2009 Legal Business Awards, UK and Ireland Regional Team of the Year at the 2011/12 STEP Private Client Awards and Corporate Law Firm of the Year at the 2011 Insider Dealmakers South East awards for the fifth year running.

Particular features of our approach to client service include the responsiveness of lawyers and strength in depth in all key areas.

We have a number of active groups in the firm so that everyone is able to contribute ideas in areas such as marketing, profile raising and 'greening the office'. We also have a particularly active corporate and social responsibility committee.

Main areas of work

Corporate and commercial; real estate; dispute resolution and IP; employment, pensions and immigration; tax, trusts and charities; private client and family.

Trainee profile

We welcome applications from candidates with either a law or non-law background who have achieved (or expect to achieve) at least a 2:1 degree. Applicants must also have achieved a minimum of 300 UCAS points in one sitting with at least one grade A. If you are someone with a team spirit, excellent communication skills, notwithstanding initiative and commitment then we'd like to hear from you.

Training environment

The firm provides excellent training to all our trainees and we have won awards for our training and recruitment. From early on our trainees have real client contact and responsibility as we offer equally challenging work to our trainees as we do to our qualified staff. To ensure that you as trainees get as broad a range of experience as possible you will do six four-month seats with the aim of giving you the opportunity (where possible) to spend your final seat in the department you hope to qualify into.

Our trainees attend the Professional Skills Course and we run foundation courses across all the departments which are especially for trainees. All trainees receive regular feedback and career reviews, and sit with either a partner or a senior associate.

There are regular departmental social events and we have drinks for all staff on the last Thursday of every month. We also run other social and client events which include opportunities to get involved in sporting activities. In addition we have trainee dinners for both current and future trainees.

Benefits

25 days holiday, pension, private healthcare, life assurance and an interest free loan for rail travel or car parking.

Sponsorship & awards

The firm will pay the fees at the level set by the College of Law, Guildford for the CPE/GDL and LPC and for a £4,000 maintenance grant for each course of study. Future trainees who have not taken the GDL/LPC are required to attend the College of Law, Guildford.

Vacation placements

We run two programmes each summer of one weeks duration. Please see our website for further information. Applications are accepted between 1 December 2012 and 31 January 2013.

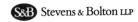 S&B Stevens & Bolton LLP

Sullivan & Cromwell LLP

1 New Fetter Lane, London EC4A 1AN
Tel: (020) 7959 8900 Fax: (020) 7959 8950
Email: traineesolicitors@sullcrom.com
Website: www.sullcrom.com/careers/opps/trainee/

Firm profile

Sullivan & Cromwell provides the highest quality legal advice and representation to clients around the world. The results we achieve have set us apart for nearly 130 years and become a model for the modern practice of law. At S&C, there is no such thing as second best – our culture of meritocracy, responsibility and opportunity ensures the success of each and every new employee. S&C has more than 700 lawyers across an international network of 12 offices on four continents. We maintain a unified firm culture worldwide and provide clients with highly integrated advice on a global basis. The office locations represent our strategy to be present in key financial and business centres where our clients are active. The London office, established in 1972, is S&C's largest office after New York. There are approximately 75 English, US and dual-qualified lawyers working in the office across a number of practice areas.

Main areas of work

S&C London is perhaps unique in the scale, complexity and significance of the work carried out in an office of its size. Our practice areas include: M&A and private equity; capital markets; project finance; leveraged finance and restructuring; real estate; competition law; criminal defence and investigations; and tax.

Trainee profile

We seek trainees who have strong academic credentials (including a projected or achieved First or Upper Second Class honours degree (or equivalent)) as well as an excellent prior academic record. Most important, however, you should also have genuine intellectual curiosity, integrity, common sense, commercial awareness and an ambition to succeed as a lawyer at one of the world's leading law firms. Strong interpersonal skills will also be important: we are looking for genuine team players. If you are interested in working with the worlds leading companies on their most challenging matters, and you feel that you have the qualities we are looking for, we encourage you to apply.

Training environment

We will offer our trainees the opportunity to do superior work, meet exceptional people and grow in a supportive culture. We aim to distinguish our trainee programme by offering genuine mentoring from partners and senior lawyers who will take a keen interest in your career development.

Benefits

Include private health insurance; dental insurance; life insurance; travel insurance; group personal pension scheme with option to contribute via salary sacrifice; subsidised gym membership; concierge service; and 24 days vacation each year.

Vacation placements

Places for 2013: a two-week summer placement scheme primarily aimed at penultimate-year law undergraduates and final-year non-law undergraduates. Remuneration £350 p.w. Apply by CV (including a full classification and percentage breakdown of all academic results) and a covering letter. We will be accepting applications for our 2013 summer vacation scheme from 1 November 2012 through 31 January 2013.

Sponsorship & awards

GDL and LPC funding plus a maintenance grant.

Partners 20
Assistant Solicitors 65
Total Trainees first intake 2013

Contact
Kirsten Davies, Trainee Solicitor Recruitment Manager

Method of application
CV and covering letter

Selection procedure
Interview with Graduate Recruitment and two Partners, meeting with 1-2 associates

Closing date for 2015
31 July 2013

Application
Training contracts p.a. 4-6
Applications p.a. 750
Required degree grade 2:1

Training
Salary (2013)
First year - £50,000
Second year - £55,000
Holiday entitlement – 24 days
Post-qualification
Salary (2012) £97,500

Overseas/regional offices
Beijing, Frankfurt, Hong Kong, London, Los Angeles, Melbourne, New York, Palo Alto, Paris, Sydney, Tokyo, Washington D.C.

SULLIVAN & CROMWELL LLP

Taylor Wessing LLP

5 New Street Square, London EC4A 3TW
Tel: (020) 7300 7000 Fax: (020) 7300 7100
Website: www.taylorwessing.com/graduate
Email: graduate@taylorwessing.com

Firm profile

Taylor Wessing is a leading international law firm where you can move your career forward, faster. We are looking for the trusted advisors of tomorrow who can think creatively, be proactive and stay close to our clients and identify and deliver innovative solutions that help their businesses grow.

Our clients include large and medium size, private and public companies, financial institutions, professional service firms, public sector bodies and wealthy individuals. Our focus is on the sectors that we believe are the industries of tomorrow: Technology, communications and brands; life sciences and healthcare; energy and environment; real estate and infrastructure; financial institutions and services.

We are experts in providing a seamless, high-quality service to global clients across many jurisdictions. Combining a pan-European network with a strong presence in the Middle East, India, China and North America, we are the leading firm for inward investment from North America and experts in IP protection and enforcement rights across the globe. That's why we work for 60% of the world's Top 50 brands.

Main areas of work

We offer industry-focused advice and in-depth sector experience by grouping together lawyers from different legal disciplines including: Banking and finance; capital markets; copyright and media law; corporate; commercial agreements; construction and engineering; employment and pensions; EU competition, IT and telecoms; litigation and dispute resolution; patents; planning and environment; private client; projects; real estate; restructuring and corporate recovery; tax; trade marks and designs.

Trainee profile

We look for people with a minimum of ABB grades at A-level and a 2:1 degree in any discipline. You'll need to be a team player with the communication skills to build vibrant relationships with our clients. You'll have the energy, ambition and creativity to take early responsibility and have a real impact on our business and our clients' business. You'll also be committed to a career in law, with a genuine drive to learn and explore new boundaries.

Training environment

Our training programme combines the in-house Professional Skills Course with six-month seats in four different practice groups, including one contentious seat and one in our corporate or finance areas.

Working closely with partners and associates on high-quality work from the outset, you'll get regular support and feedback every step of the way to align your career to the growth and needs of the firm and our clients. There are also secondment opportunities to our clients and to our international offices.

Vacation schemes

Our vacation schemes are designed for you to experience life as a trainee solicitor in a uniquely innovative City law firm. You'll spend two weeks in two different practice groups gaining first-hand experience under the supervision of associates and partners.

Places: 40+. Duration: 2 weeks. Remuneration: £250 per week. Closing date: 31 January 2013.

Sponsorship

GDL and LPC fees at BPP London sponsored. A maintenance grant is provided.

Partners 354
Trainees 49
Vacancies Circa 22-24

Application
All candidates are required to complete our online application form, which can be found on our website, www.taylorwessing.com/ graduate

Training
Salary
1st year £37,000
2nd year £41,000

Post qualification
Salary £60,000

Offices
Berlin, Bratislava, Brussels, Budapest, Cambridge, Dubai, Dusseldorf, Frankfurt, Hamburg, Kiev, London, Munich, Paris, Prague, Singapore, Vienna and Warsaw
Representative Offices Beijing, Brno, Klagenfurt and Shanghai

TaylorWessing

Thomas Cooper

Ibex House, 42-47 Minories, London EC3N 1HA
Tel: (020) 7481 8851 Fax: (020) 7480 6097
Email: recruitment@thomascooperlaw.com
Website: www.thomascooperlaw.com

Firm profile

Thomas Cooper is an international law firm which was founded in 1825.

Thomas Cooper has experience of dealing with the law in key jurisdictions around the world, with offices in London, Athens, Madrid, Paris and Singapore. The firm takes a pragmatic approach, providing clear advice that helps clients navigate through the complexity of international commerce.

The firm is recommended by and recognised by the major legal directories for its expertise.

The firm's clients operate globally and range from shipowners to charterers and traders, from banks and other financial institutions to underwriters and P&I clubs, from blue chip companies to small businesses and private individuals.

The firm gives insightful and pragmatic advice to clients and allows them to manage their exposure to risk more effectively.

Main areas of work

The firm's core practice areas are maritime, trade, finance, company and commercial, international arbitration, insurance, oil and gas.

Trainee profile

As a trainee with the firm you will be exposed to clients and fee earning work from your first seat. Thomas Cooper works for a wide variety of clients and as such, you can expect to find yourself dealing with finance, personal injury, wet or dry shipping claims.

Thomas Cooper values its trainees because they are vital for the future of the business. If you are bright, confident and a self starter who has a keen interest in maritime then the firm would encourage you to apply to its trainee programme.

Thomas Cooper recruits a maximum of 4 trainees per year.

Training environment

Thomas Cooper has a four-seat trainee programme over two years: two seats in shipping, one in defence and personal injury; and one in finance and international trade. There is also opportunity to do a seat in one of the firm's international offices, this is dependent upon language skills and team workload.

Benefits

Private medical insurance; permanent health insurance; life assurance; 25 days holiday; pension scheme; loan for dental insurance; season ticket loan; loan for gym membership. LPC course fees are paid by the firm.

Partners 29
Assistant solicitors 28
Total trainees 7/8
Contact
Karan Tapley - Human Resources Manager
Tel: (020) 7481 8851
Method of application
Online application form
Selection procedure
Interviews and assessments
Closing date for 2015
31 July 2013
Application
Required degree grade 2:1
Training
Salary
Starting salary for trainees is:
Year 1 £33,000
Year 2 £36,500 (based on 2012 salaries)
25 days holiday
Overseas/ regional offices
Athens, Madrid, Paris and Singapore

TLT LLP

One Redcliff St, Bristol BS1 6TP
Tel: (0117) 917 7586 Fax: (0117) 917 7649
Email: graduate@TLTsolicitors.com
Website: www.TLTcareers.com/trainee

Firm profile
Here, the firm is open. Open to connected working, open plan and open minded. It has reshaped the traditional law firm model into a fresh, bright, inclusive and creative place to work. TLT LLP, TLT Scotland Ltd and TLT NI LLP all operate under the TLT brand and between them have offices in Bristol, London, Glasgow, Edinburgh, Belfast and Piraeus (Greece). Named by the Financial Times as one of Europe's most innovative law firms for four consecutive years and with a 'Best Company' accreditation, TLT is confident its way works. The firm has won awards and gathered accolades, but what matters more is that it has made an impact. TLT continues to win business from FTSE-listed, national and international companies including Punch Taverns, Merlin Entertainments, Dyson, WHSmith, Barclays Bank, Canal & River Trust and EDF Energy, and is forecast to turnover £48million in 2012/2013. So the firm is going places – and quickly. If you want to make your mark in law and work progressively, then this is where your career really begins.

Main areas of work
The firm's full service legal offering spans the financial services, leisure, retail and consumer goods, technology and media, renewables, housing and public sectors, and its core legal specialisms are real estate, banking and finance, commercial, corporate, employment, dispute resolution and litigation, but it believes there's more to legal work than being a lawyer – you need to embrace management, technology and business skills too.

Trainee profile
The firm's trainees are rather special. Genuinely ambitious, talented and technically impressive, you don't just tick all the boxes – you open them up, reshape them and connect them all together.

You'll stand out, stand up for what's right, and stand shoulder to shoulder with your colleagues – you must embrace team working and share a passion for exceptional client service. And while academic achievement is important, your personal qualities also count for a lot here.

Training environment
Whether you join us for your training contract or a one week vacation scheme placement, you'll work on live cases for real clients, get input from a Partner and develop a broad range of skills across the full legal and business spectrum. Our training contracts are designed to have more in them so you get more out of them. So here you'll gain invaluable technical knowledge and professional skills, all backed up by a one-to-one mentor, expert guidance and unlimited support throughout.

Benefits
The firm offers a full and flexible benefits plan, which means you can design your benefits package to meet your lifestyle needs, picking and choosing from a selection of rewards and benefits. As part of the firm's commitment to giving something back, you'll also be encouraged to get involved in community support work, pro bono legal advice, fundraising activities and environmental initiatives.

Vacation placements
Spend a week with TLT and you'll pick up unparalleled experience and a real taste of life at a leading law firm - especially when you consider the amount of Partner contact you'll enjoy, and we've built assessments into the week, which means you won't have to make a separate training contract application or attend an assessment day.

Sponsorship & awards
GDL and LPC fees plus maintenance grant.

Partners 80
Solicitors 223
Total Trainees 23

Contact
Bee Lawson, Graduate
Recruitment Officer
Tel 0117 917 7586

Method of application
Online application form at
www.TLTcareers.com/trainee

Selection procedure
Application form, telephone
screening, verbal reasoning
testing, assessment centre

Closing date
31 July each year

Application
Training contracts up to 15 p.a.
Applications circa 700 p.a.
% interviewed 12% p.a.
Required degree grade
2:1 or above in any discipline at
degree level and a minimum of
300/24 UCAS points at A level

Training
Salary See website for details
Holiday entitlement 25 days

Post-qualification
Salary
See website for details
% trainees offered job on
qualification 80-100%

Offices
Bristol, London, Glasgow,
Edinburgh, Belfast, Piraeus
(Greece)

Travers Smith LLP

10 Snow Hill, London EC1A 2AL
Tel: (020) 7295 3000 Fax: (020) 7295 3500
Email: graduate.recruitment@traverssmith.com
Website: www.traverssmith.com

Firm profile

A leading independent City firm with a major corporate and commercial practice. Although less than a quarter of the size of the largest firms, they handle high profile and top quality work, much of which has an international dimension.

Main areas of work

Corporate (including takeovers and mergers, private equity and funds), commercial, intellectual property and technology law, litigation, banking and corporate recovery, restructuring, financial services and markets, competition, tax, employment, pensions and real estate. The firm also offers a range of pro bono opportunities within individual departments and on a firm-wide basis. For example, it is a legal partner of A4ID (Advocates for International Development) and trainees and associates advise on a voluntary basis at two law centres.

Trainee profile

The firm looks for people who combine academic excellence with common sense; who are determined and articulate, who can think on their feet, and who take their work but not themselves seriously. Applications are welcome from law and non-law undergraduates and graduates.

Training environment

Travers Smith has earned a phenomenal reputation in relation to its size. The work they undertake is exciting, intellectually demanding and top quality, involving blue-chip clients and big numbers. This means that their trainees gain great experience right from the outset.

The firm has a comprehensive training programme which ensures that trainees experience a broad range of work. All trainee solicitors sit in rooms with partners and associates, receive an individual and extensive training from experienced lawyers, enjoying client contact, and the responsibility that goes with it, from day one.

Benefits

Private health insurance, permanent health insurance, life assurance, subsidised bistro, season ticket loan, Cyclescheme.

Vacation placements

Summer 2013: 3 schemes with 15 places on each; Duration: two weeks; Remuneration: £275; Closing Date: 31 January 2013. The firm also offers a two week Christmas scheme for 15 students (places allocated on a rolling basis).

Sponsorship & awards

GDL and LPC paid in full plus maintenance of £7,000 per annum to those in London and £6,500 per annum to those outside of London.

Partners 66
Associates 191
Total Trainees 41

Contact
Germaine VanGeyzel

Method of application
Online

Selection procedure
Interviews (2 stage process)

Closing date for 2015
31 July 2013

Application
Training contracts p.a. 25
Applications p.a. 2,000
% interviewed p.a. 15%
Required degree grade 2:1

Training
Salary
1st year (2012) £38,000
2nd year (2012) £43,000
Holiday entitlement 25 days

Post-qualification
Salary (2012) £61,000
% of trainees offered job
on qualification (2012) 89%

TRAVERS SMITH

Trethowans LLP

London Road, Salisbury, Wiltshire, SP1 3HP
The Director General's House, 15 Rockstone Place, Southampton, SO15 2EP
Tel: 0845 302 4695 Fax: 01722 333 011
Email: recruitment@trethowans.com
Web: www.trethowans.com

Firm profile

Trethowans is a premier law firm based in the South with a team of 135 including 26 partners and 47 lawyers. The firm has a diverse and expanding client base. Our continued success is due to the quality of our people and the growing strength and reputation of our brand. With offices in Salisbury and Southampton our partners and staff enjoy the benefit of living close to the south coast whilst having the quality of work and clients often associated with a city firm. Many of our clients are household name clients. Service excellence is a priority – clients value the firm's ability to deliver top-quality, expert advice, on time, in a very personable manner and at a competitive price.

Main areas of work

On the commercial side, we represent international and national household brand names, owner-managed businesses, entrepreneurs and major regional employers across the UK. When acting for individuals, we represent landowners, entrepreneurs, local families, property developers and trustees amongst others.

Legal advice to businesses include: corporate, commercial, commercial property, commercial litigation, insurance litigation, employment and licensing. Legal advice to individuals include: personal injury, private client (wills, trusts and tax; wealth structuring and inheritance planning), agriculture and rural property, family and residential property.

Many of our teams and individuals are rated in both the Chambers Guide to the Legal Profession and Legal 500, the two independent guides to the legal profession in the UK.

Trainee profile

Trainees should possess sound academic abilities and be able to demonstrate commercial acumen. Flexibility, ambition and enthusiasm are valued. Candidates should be good communicators and adopt a problem solving approach to client work.

Training environment

Trainee solicitors usually undertake four separate specialist seats, each lasting six months. The firm offers a flexible approach in deciding trainees' seats to suit individual needs, while providing a broad training programme in accordance with the Solicitors Regulation Authority guidelines. Trainees work closely with the supervising lawyer/partner to whom they are responsible. They are considered an integral part of each team and become closely involved in the team's work to obtain first-hand legal experience. Each trainee's performance is reviewed regularly by their supervisor and Training Partner and regular feedback is provided. This enables the trainee scheme to be continually evaluated and also ensures that the highest possible standards are maintained. Prospects for trainees are excellent. Most trainees are offered a position as solicitors at the end of their training contract. Trainees are an integral part of the firm from day one. They are responsible for the firm's staff newsletter, participate in business development, and actively communicate via twitter about their work and progress as a trainee (www.twitter.com/trethtrainees).

Benefits

Incremental holiday entitlement up to 28 days, contributory pension scheme, death in service benefit, PHI scheme, performance-related bonus scheme, car parking, new staff recruitment bonus, childcare voucher scheme and employee assistance programme.

Sponsorship & awards

LPC course fees paid provided training contract is secured prior to commencement of LPC.

Partners 26
Solicitors 47
Total Trainees 9

Contact
Kate Ellis
023 8082 0503

Method of application
Applications by online application form and covering letter

Selection procedure
Two stage process; interview and assessment day

Closing date for 2015
26 July 2013

Application
Training contracts p.a. 3-4
Applications p.a. 100+
% interviewed p.a. 25-30%
Required degree grade 2:1

Training
Salary Competitive market rate with regular reviews
Holiday entitlement 23 days

Post-qualification
Salary Competitive market rate with regular reviews
% of trainees offered position on qualification 100% (Nov 2009), 67% (Nov 2010) 75% (Nov 2011)
Holiday entitlement 25 days

Regional offices
Salisbury, Southampton

TRETHOWANS
SOLICITORS

Trowers & Hamlins LLP

3 Bunhill Row, London, EC1Y 8YZ
Tel: (020) 7423 8000 Fax: (020) 7423 8001
Email: avithlani@trowers.com Website: www.trowers.com

Firm profile

Trowers & Hamlins are a medium-sized, full service firm with approximately 650 employees worldwide. The firm has offices in London, Birmingham, Exeter and Manchester, and a long standing presence in the Middle East with offices in Abu Dhabi, Bahrain, Cairo, Dubai and Oman. Although known for its work in the affordable housing and public sector arena, there is far more to the firm, and it is frequently listed as a key player in the corporate, banking and finance, and commercial property sectors.

Main areas of work

Banking and finance, commercial property, corporate, dispute resolution and litigation, employment, housing projects, international, projects and construction, public sector (communities and governance), public sector (commercial) and tax, trusts and pensions.

Trainee profile

The firm recruits around 20 trainees each year, split between September and March intakes. Each year the firm recruits one trainee to join the Exeter office and approximately three to join the Manchester office. The firm is naturally looking for an excellent academic record but, in addition to this, recognises that supplementary skills are important and actively seeks out candidates with good commercial awareness, outstanding communication skills, and a genuine passion for the law and the firm.

Training environment

The training contract is split into four six-month seats. The firm offers secondment opportunities to the Middle East together with seats in a wide range of departments, and it is not surprising that trainees gain a varied and interesting experience. Trainees are paired with either a senior associate or partner as their supervisor to ensure that a suitable level of support is provided. Assessment takes place constantly, with trainees completing both a mid seat and end of seat appraisal. This provides trainees with the opportunity to gain regular feedback and continuously progress.

Responsibility is given from a very early stage with trainees in some departments running files on their own on joining the department. Trainees are encouraged to take as autonomous a role as is possible, safe in the knowledge that there is a structured support system in place to provide assistance should they require it.

Training forms an integral part of the training contract with trainee solicitors receiving regular departmental and firmwide training over the course of their training contract. In addition to this, further professional skills training is provided covering vital skills such as commercial contract drafting and negotiation.

Vacation placements

The firm runs two fortnight long vacation placements which are open to candidates wishing to commence training contracts commencing in September 2015 and March 2016. Online applications should be submitted by 1 March 2013 via the firms website.

Sponsorship & awards

GDL and LPC sponsorship is provided. In addition, those studying for either course will receive a competitive maintenance grant. All London-based future trainees will be required to undertake the LPC at Kaplan Law School.

Partners 132
Assistant Solicitors 195
Total Trainees 39

Contact
Anup Vithlani, Graduate Recruitment and Development Manager

Method of application
Online application form

Selection procedure
Assessment centre, interviews, psychometric tests & practical test

Closing date for 2015
1 August 2013

Application
Training contracts p.a. circa. 20
Applications p.a. 1,500
% interviewed p.a. 4%
Required degree grade 2:1 or higher

Training
London Salary (subject to review)
1st year £35,000
2nd year £38,000
Holiday entitlement 25 days
% of trainees with a non-law degree p.a. 50%
No. of seats available abroad p.a. 14

Post-qualification
Salary (2011) £55,000
% of trainees offered job on qualification (2012) TBC

Offices
London, Birmingham, Exeter, Manchester, Abu Dhabi, Bahrain, Cairo, Dubai and Oman

Veale Wasbrough Vizards

Orchard Court, Orchard Lane, Bristol BS1 5WS
Tel: (0117) 925 2020 Fax: (0117) 925 2025
Barnards Inn, 86 Fetter Lane, London EC4A 1AD
Tel: (020) 7405 1234 Fax: (020) 7405 4171
Email: jobs@vwv.co.uk Website: www.vwv.co.uk Twitter: @vwvlawfirm

Firm profile
Veale Wasbrough Vizards acts nationally for clients in the education and charities, healthcare, private wealth, family owned business and public sectors. The firm also offers a dedicated service to individuals.

Our combination of specialist expertise, genuine teamwork and client commitment sets us apart. That's why we're confident we can deliver the best and most effective legal solutions to help our clients succeed. Our staff of 300 are based at our offices in the heart of two cities; Bristol and London.

As part of our commitment to staff and clients, the firm has three core values which span all work groups and business plans. These are teamwork and collaboration, putting the client at the centre of the firm and commercial approach.

VWV is also a founder member of the Association of European Lawyers and has strong connections with law firms in Southern China.

Main areas of work
The firm is recognised for excellence in specific sectors and for its established commitment to training, teamwork and approachability. Our goal is to help our clients succeed, through high standards, technical expertise, a creative approach and commitment to our people.

As well as offering a wide range of services expected from a commercial law firm, including commercial litigation, construction, family and matrimonial, corporate and real estate, we also deal with residential conveyancing through our dedicated division Convey Direct and personal injury claims through Augustines Injury Law.

Trainee profile
The firm recruits 8-10 trainees annually. It is looking for graduates who will become dynamic lawyers, who will make the most of the training opportunities and positively contribute to the future of the firm. Applicants should have proven academic ability, be good team players, with strong communication skills and commercial awareness.

Training environment
The firm offers its trainees early responsibility. It provides four seats of six months each in a variety of teams, including charities, commercial, commercial litigation, corporate, employment, personal injury, private client and real estate (including construction and property litigation). Trainees also benefit from experience in the five sectors as mentioned above. Many of the firm's partners and senior lawyers trained with the firm and are now widely respected experts in their chosen field.

Sponsorship & awards
Successful candidates may be eligible for sponsorship for the Diploma in Law and/or Legal Practice Course, consisting of a grant for LPC fees and an interest-free loan.

Vacation scheme
The firm's summer vacation scheme offers a week's unpaid work experience, providing an insight into the day to day workings of a large firm of commercial lawyers, as students spend time in different legal teams.

Partners 47
Assistant Solicitors 82
Total Trainees 17

Contact
Ellen Turner, HR Advisor

Method of application
Application form on website

Selection procedure
Interview

Closing date for September 2015
30 June 2013

Application
Training contracts p.a. 8-10
% interviewed (2011) 10%
Required degree grade
Preferably 2:1

Training
1st year £23,000
2nd year £25,000
Holiday entitlement 25 days plus bank holidays

Post-qualification
Salary £35,000
% of trainees offered job on qualification (2011) 80%

Vinson & Elkins

CityPoint, 33rd Floor, One Ropemaker Street, London EC2Y 9UE
Tel: (020) 7065 6000 Fax: (020) 7065 6001

Firm profile

Vinson & Elkins RLLP is one of the largest international law firms and has been repeatedly ranked as the world's leading energy law firm. Founded in Houston in 1917 (and with an office in London for over 40 years), Vinson & Elkins currently has over 700 lawyers with offices in Abu Dhabi, Austin, Beijing, Dallas, Dubai, Hong Kong, Houston, London, Moscow, New York, Palo Alto, Riyadh, San Francisco, Shanghai, Tokyo and Washington, D.C.

Main areas of work

Cross-border M&A, private equity, corporate finance and securities advice (including London Main Market and AIM listings and international equity and debt capital markets), banking and finance, international energy transactions, construction, project development and finance transactions, litigation and arbitration and tax.

Trainee profile

The firm is looking for ambitious individuals with strong academic results, sound commercial awareness and rounded personalities. The ability to think laterally and creatively is essential, as is a need for common-sense and a willingness to take the initiative.

Training environment

The firm currently offers three to four training contracts commencing each September. These are not run on a rigid seat system, but instead a trainee will gain wide experience in many different areas, working with a wide variety of associates and partners from across the firm. V&E is proud of the fact it has twice won LawCareers.Net awards for the quality of its training with a further five nominations.

Whilst the trainees are based in London, the firm is currently regularly seconding its trainees to other offices (particularly its offices in Abu Dhabi, Dubai and Hong Kong).

Benefits

Private medical and dental, pension, season ticket loan, life assurance.

Vacation placements

We view vacation placements as a key part of its recruitment process. For summer 2013 apply by 28 February 2013, by way of online application form.

Sponsorship & awards

The firm pays all GDL and LPC course fees and a discretionary stipend (of up to £7,500) to assist with the LPC year.

Partners 16
Assistant Solicitors 28
Total Trainees 8

Contact
Natalie Perkin (020) 7065 6048

Method of application
Online application form

Selection procedure
Interview

Closing date for 2015
31 August 2013

Application
Training contracts p.a. 3-4
Applications p.a. 450
% interviewed p.a. 10%
Required degree grade 2:1

Training
Salary
1st year £40,000
2nd year £42,000
Holiday entitlement 25 days
% of trainees with a
non-law degree p.a. 40%
No. of seats available
abroad p.a. 4

Post-qualification
Salary £80,000
% of trainees offered job
on qualification 95%

Overseas / Regional offices
Abu Dhabi, Austin, Beijing, Dallas, Dubai, Hong Kong, Houston, London, Moscow, New York, Palo Alto, Riyadh, San Francisco, Shanghai, Tokyo and Washington D.C.

Vinson&Elkins RLLP

Walker Morris

Kings Court, 12 King Street, Leeds LS1 2HL
Tel: (0113) 283 2500 Fax: (0113) 245 9412
Email: hellograduates@walkermorris.co.uk
Website: www.walkermorris.co.uk

Firm profile
Based in Leeds, Walker Morris is one of the largest commercial law firms in the North, with over 450 people, providing a full range of legal services to commercial and private clients both nationally and internationally.

Main areas of work
CDR, commercial, commercial property, construction, corporate, employment, finance, intellectual property, insolvency, PFI/ public sector, planning and environmental, regulatory, sports, tax.

Trainee profile
Bright, articulate, highly motivated individuals who will thrive on early responsibility in a demanding yet friendly environment.

Training environment
Trainees commence with an induction programme, before spending four months in each main department (commercial property, corporate and commercial litigation). Trainees can choose in which departments they wish to spend their second year. Formal training will include lectures, interactive workshops, seminars and e-learning. The PSC covers the compulsory elements and the electives consist of a variety of specially tailored skills programmes. Individual IT training is provided. Opportunities can also arise for secondments to some of the firm's major clients. Emphasis is placed on teamwork, inside and outside the office. The firm's social and sporting activities are an important part of its culture and are organised by a committee drawn from all levels of the firm. A trainee solicitors' committee represents the trainees in the firm but also organises events and liaises with the Leeds Trainee Solicitors Group.

Vacation placements
Places for 2013: 48 over 3 weeks; Duration: 1 week; Remuneration: £175 p.w.; Closing Date: 31 January 2013.

Sponsorship & awards
LPC & PGDL fees plus maintenance of £5,000.

Partners 46
Assistant Solicitors 120
Total Trainees 31

Contact
Nick Cannon

Method of application
Online application form

Selection procedure
Assessment centre & face-to-face interviews

Closing date for 2015
31 July 2013

Application
Training contracts p.a. 15
Applications p.a.
Approx. 800
% interviewed p.a.
Face to face 5%
Required degree grade 2:1

Training
Salary
1st year (2012) £24,000
2nd year (2012) £26,000
Holiday entitlement 24 days
% of trainees with a
non-law degree p.a.
30% on average

Post-qualification
Salary £36,000
% of trainees offered job
on qualification 85%
% of assistants who joined as
trainees 55%
% of partners who joined as
trainees 50%

Ward Hadaway

Sandgate House, 102 Quayside, Newcastle upon Tyne NE1 3DX
Tel: (0191) 204 4000 Fax: (0191) 204 4098
Email: recruitment@wardhadaway.com
Website: www.wardhadaway.com

Firm profile

Ward Hadaway is one of the most progressive law firms in the North of England and is firmly established as one of the region's legal heavyweights. Operating from offices in Newcastle, Leeds and Manchester, the firm attracts some of the most ambitious businesses in the region and has a substantial client base of regional, national and international clients from the private and public sectors.

As a business founded and located in the North, the firm has grown rapidly, investing heavily in developing its existing people and recruiting further outstanding individuals from inside and outside of the region. The firm is listed in the top 100 UK law firms.

Main areas of work

The firm is divided into five main departments; litigation, property, corporate, commercial and private client, with a number of cross departmental teams. The firm is commercially based, satisfying the needs of the business community in both business and private life. Clients vary from international plcs to local, private clients. The firm is on a number of panels including; the Arts Council, NHS (four panels), English Heritage, Department of Education and the General Teaching Council.

Trainee profile

The usual academic and professional qualifications are sought. Sound commercial and business awareness are essential as is the need to demonstrate strong communication skills, enthusiasm and flexibility. Candidates will be able to demonstrate excellent interpersonal and analytical skills.

Training environment

The training contract is structured around four seats, each of six months duration. At regular intervals, and each time you are due to change seat, you will have the opportunity to discuss the experience you would like to gain during your training contract. The firm will give high priority to your preferences. You will work closely with a Partner or associate who will supervise and encourage you as you become involved in more complex work. Your practical experience will also be complemented by an extensive programme of seminars and lectures. All trainees are allocated a 'buddy', usually a second year trainee or newly qualified solicitor, who can provide as much practical advice and guidance as possible during your training. The firm has an active social committee and offers a full range of sporting and social events.

Benefits

25 days holiday (27 after five years service), death in service insurance, contributory pension, flexible benefits package, travel scheme.

Vacation placements

Vacation placements run spring/summer between June and July and are of 1 week's duration. Applications should be received by 28 February 2013.

Sponsorship & awards

CPE/GDL and LPC fees paid and maintenance grants in accordance with the terms of the firm's offer.

Partners 78	
Total Trainees 18	
Contact	
Graduate recruitment team	
Method of application	
Firm's application form	
Selection procedure	
Assessment Centre and interview	
Closing date for 2015	
31 July 2013	
Application	
Training contracts p.a. 10	
Applications p.a. 600+	
% interviewed p.a. 10%	
Required degree grade 2:1	
Training	
Salary 2011	
Newcastle	
1st year £20,000	
2nd year £20,500	
Leeds	
1st year £23,000	
2nd year £23,500	
Holiday entitlement 25 days	
% of trainees with a non-law degree p.a. Varies	
Post-qualification	
Salary (2011)	
£32,000	

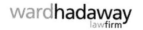

Watson, Farley & Williams LLP

15 Appold Street, London EC2A 2HB
Tel: (020) 7814 8000 Fax: (020) 7814 8017
Email: graduates@wfw.com
Website: www.wfw.com/trainee

Firm Profile

WFW was founded in 1982 in the City of London. It has since grown rapidly to over 120 partners and a total staff of over 600. The firm has offices in London, New York, Paris, Hamburg, Munich, Rome, Milan, Madrid, Athens, Piraeus, Singapore, Bangkok and Hong Kong.

Main areas of work

WFW is a distinctive law firm with a leading market position in international finance and investment, maritime and energy.

In our chosen sectors we compete successfully with some of the best law firms in the world. Building on our origins in ship finance, demand for our maritime work remains as strong as ever. At the same time we have seized opportunities to excel in related areas where our finance expertise has most relevance, such as energy, natural resources, transport, real estate and technology.

Trainee profile

Although there is no typical WFW trainee, there are certain attributes that we look for. You will need a 2:1 or above and at least 320 UCAS points (ABB) – from A-level results, or their equivalent. We also particularly value applicants with initiative, drive and commercial awareness.

Training

At WFW we deal with training and ongoing development in an individual way. During each seat we discuss with you plans for the next one to ensure you gain valuable insight from the six seat programme, including one seat in either Paris, Singapore, Piraeus or Bangkok.

Your training contract will be hands-on, with as much experience of clients and real, high-profile work as possible. You'll also benefit from plenty of exposure to senior lawyers, many acknowledged leaders in their field.

The firm has a reputation for challenging work. Yours will be no exception as we believe that only total immersion can provide you with the experience you require.

Benefits

Various benefits are available to trainees after a qualifying period of service e.g. 25 days holiday, bank holidays, income protection scheme, life assurance, employee assistance scheme, pension scheme, interest-free season ticket loan, £250 contribution towards a sports club and healthcare membership.

Vacation placements

Our vacation scheme is the best way to really familiarise yourself with WFW. The two-week placements are at our London office, either at Easter or during the summer. To appreciate first-hand the kind of work trainees undertake day to day, you will work with solicitors in one of our practice groups for the whole period. To complement this focus on one area, you will also participate in a variety of training and social events designed to give you a general overview of the firm. Places for 2013: 30; duration: 2 weeks, remuneration: £250 p.w.; deadline to apply: 31 January 2013.

Sponsorship & awards

GDL and LPC fees are paid depending on point of offer plus a maintenance grant of £6,500/ £5,500 dependant on location.

Partners 126
Total fee-earners 300+
Total Trainees 26

Contact
Graduate Recruitment Manager

Method of application
Online application

Selection procedure
Assessment centre and interview

Closing date for 2015
31 July 2013

Application
Training contracts p.a. 14
Applications p.a. 700
% interviewed p.a. 20-30%
Required degree grade
Minimum 2:1 and 320 UCAS points (ABB)

Training
Salary
1st year (2012) £35,000
2nd year (2012) £40,000
Holiday entitlement 25 days
% of trainees with a non-law degree p.a. 50%
No. of seats available abroad p.a. 14

Post-qualification
Salary (2012)
£62,000
% of trainees offered job on qualification (2012) 83%
% of assistants (as at 01/09/11) who joined as trainees 30%
% of partners (as at 1/9/11) who joined as trainees 10%

Overseas offices
New York, Paris, Hamburg, Munich, Rome, Milan, Madrid, Athens, Piraeus, Singapore, Bangkok, Hong Kong

Watson, Farley & Williams
www.wfw.com

Wedlake Bell

52 Bedford Row, London, WC1R 4LR
Tel: (020) 7395 3000 Fax: (020) 7395 3100
Email: recruitment@wedlakebell.com
Website: www.wedlakebell.com

Firm profile

Wedlake Bell LLP is a medium-sized law firm providing legal advice to businesses and high net worth individuals from around the world. The firm's services are based on a high degree of partner involvement, extensive business and commercial experience and strong technical expertise. The firm has approximately 120 lawyers in central London and affiliations with law firms throughout Europe and in the United States.

Main areas of work

For the firm's business clients: banking and asset finance; corporate; corporate tax; business recoveries; commercial; intellectual property; information technology; media; commercial property; construction; residential property.

For private individuals: family, tax, trusts and wealth protection; offshore services; residential property.

Trainee profile

In addition to academic excellence, Wedlake Bell LLP looks for commercial aptitude, flexibility, enthusiasm, a personable nature, confidence, mental agility and computer literacy in its candidates. Languages are not crucial.

Training environment

Trainees have four seats of six months across the following areas: business recoveries, commercial property, construction, corporate, employment, family, IP and commercial, private client, pensions, property litigation and residential property. As a trainee, the firm encourages you to have direct contact and involvement with clients from an early stage. Trainees will work within highly specialised teams and have a high degree of responsibility. Trainees will be closely supervised by a partner or senior solicitor and become involved in high quality and varied work. The firm is committed to the training and career development of its lawyers and many of its trainees continue their careers with the firm, often through to partnership. Wedlake Bell LLP has an informal, creative and co-operative culture with a balanced approach to life.

Sponsorship & benefits

LPC funding available subject to the terms and conditions of any offer. During the training contract: pension, travel loans, corporate gym membership, health insurance and life assurance.

Vacation placements

Places for 2013: 8; Duration: 3 weeks in July; Closing date: End of February, 2013.

Partners	60
Assistant Solicitors	75
Total Trainees	12

Contact
The Graduate Recruitment Department

Method of application
Application form

Selection procedure
Two interviews & open day

Closing date for 2015
End of July 2013

Application
Training contracts p.a. 6
Required degree grade 2:1

Training
Holiday entitlement
1st year 23 days
2nd year 24 days
% of trainees with a non-law degree p.a. 50%

Weil, Gotshal & Manges

110 Fetter Lane, London EC4A 1AY
Tel: (020) 7903 1000 Fax: (020) 7903 0990
Email: graduate.recruitment@weil.com
Website: www.weil.com

Firm profile

International law firm Weil, Gotshal & Manges has over 1,200 lawyers, including 300 partners, in 21 cities throughout the US, Europe and Asia.

The London office was established in 1996 and has grown to become the second largest of the firm's worldwide offices, with over 130 lawyers, at least 90% of which are UK-qualified. Approximately 80% of the work completed in London is home grown and many of our European cross-border activities are coordinated from the London office. We pride ourselves on providing our clients with unmatched legal services, which is why the world's most sophisticated clients call upon Weil to provide counsel on their most complex and important issues.

Main areas of work

Private equity is the cornerstone of the London office, with the firm ranked in the top tier of Chambers UK for buyouts with more partners ranked at the top of the individual rankings than any other firm. The establishment of our London funds practice, linking in with our well-established US and Asian teams, provides clients with full coverage for both raising and investing funds.

Our restructuring practice is widely recognised as one of the leading practices in its field, referred to as "the gold standard of bankruptcy bar" (The American Lawyer). The firm has been at the forefront of the credit crisis, advising global financial institutions such as Lehman Brothers, AIG, General Motors and Kaupthing, as well as providing integrated crisis management advice. Our restructuring expertise in the US and Europe has also enabled us to provide corporate and private equity clients with cutting-edge advice on the current markets, how best to weather the current storms and prepare for opportunities in the distressed M&A markets.

We advise on all aspects of domestic and cross-border transactional and general corporate issues, including acquisitions and disposals, corporate governance, demergers and re-organisations, equity capital markets, joint ventures, public and private mergers and strategic alliances.

Full-service transactional support is provided by specialists in the fields of commercial contracts, competition, employment/employee benefits, environment, IP/IT, pensions, real estate and tax.

We have an international finance practice which continues to be among the very best practices in London, and spans asset finance, acquisition finance (including bank / bond financing structures), bank and institutional lending, debt capital markets (including high yield), derivatives, lease financings, refinancings and recapitalisations and structured finance.

Few firms can match the quality and depth of Weil's experience in litigation, arbitration and other forms of dispute resolution. The London dispute resolution team advises upon, manages and conducts all aspects of domestic and international litigation, from strategic advice during the early stages of negotiations to courtroom advocacy.

The London office also works closely with cross-disciplinary teams across the firm on a wide range of industry specialisms, including energy, healthcare, infrastructure and TMT.

Vacation placements

We have up to 30 places for spring and summer. Please refer to the website for further information.

Partners 28
Solicitors 91
Total Trainees 20

Contact
Victoria Wisson

Method of application
Online application form

Closing date for 2015
31 July 2013

Application
Training contracts p.a. up to 14
Required degree grade 2:1

Training
Salary
1st year (2012) £41,000
Holiday entitlement 23 days

Overseas offices
Beijing, Boston, Budapest, Dallas, Dubai, Frankfurt, Hong Kong, Houston, London, Miami, Munich, New York, Paris, Prague, Princeton, Providence, Shanghai, Silicon Valley, Warsaw, Washington DC and Wilmington

Weil

White & Case LLP

5 Old Broad Street, London EC2N 1DW
Tel: (020) 7532 1000 Fax: (020) 7532 1001
Email: trainee@whitecase.com
Website: www.whitecasetrainee.com

Firm profile

White & Case LLP is a global law firm with more than 2,100 lawyers worldwide. The firm has a network of 38 offices, providing the full range of legal services of the highest quality in virtually every major commercial centre and emerging market. They work with international businesses, financial institutions and governments worldwide on corporate and financial transactions and dispute resolution proceedings. Their clients range from some of the world's longest established and most respected names to many start-up visionaries. The firm's lawyers work on a variety of sophisticated, high-value transactions, many of which feature in the legal press worldwide as the firm's clients achieve firsts in privatisation, cross-border business deals, or major development projects.

Main areas of work

Banking and capital markets; construction and engineering; corporate (including M&A and private equity); dispute resolution (including arbitration and mediation); employment and benefits; energy, infrastructure, project and asset finance; IP, PPP/PFI; real estate; tax; and telecommunications.

Trainee profile

Trainees should be ambitious, creative and work well in teams. They should have an understanding of international commercial issues and have a desire to be involved in high profile, cross-border legal matters.

Training environment

Trainees undertake four seats, each of six months in duration. The firm guarantees that one of these seats can be spent overseas. Regardless of where they work, trainees get a high level of partner and senior associate contact from day one, ensuring they receive high quality, stimulating and rewarding work. Trainees are encouraged to take early responsibility and there is a strong emphasis on practical hands-on training, together with plenty of support and feedback. The firm recruits and develops trainee solicitors with the aim of retaining them on qualification.

Benefits

The firm operates a flexible benefits scheme, through which you can select the benefits you wish to receive. Currently, the benefits include private medical insurance, dental insurance, life assurance, pension, critical illness insurance, travel insurance, retail vouchers, gym membership, season ticket loan and green bikes.

Vacation placements

Places for 2013: 12-15 two-week Easter placement and 40-50 two-week summer placements available. Remuneration: £350 per week; Closing Date: 31 January 2013.

Sponsorship & awards

GDL and LPC fees and maintenance paid p.a. Awards for commendation and distinction for LPC.

Partners 71
Assistant Solicitors 209
Total Trainees 57

Contact
Shahnaz Begum

Method of application
Online application via firm website

Selection procedure
Interview
Closing date for August 2015/ February 2016
31 July 2013

Application
Training contracts p.a. 25-30
Applications p.a. 1,500
Required degree grade 2:1

Training
Salary
£41,000, rising by £1,000 every 6 months
Holiday entitlement 25 days
All trainees are guaranteed to spend a seat overseas

Post-qualification
Salary £70,000

Overseas offices
Abu Dhabi, Almaty, Ankara, Beijing, Berlin, Bratislava, Brussels, Bucharest, Budapest, Doha, Düsseldorf, Frankfurt, Geneva, Hamburg, Helsinki, Hong Kong, Istanbul, Johannesburg, London, Los Angeles, Mexico City, Miami, Milan, Monterrey, Moscow, Munich, New York, Paris, Prague, Riyadh, São Paulo, Silicon Valley, Singapore, Shanghai, Stockholm, Tokyo, Warsaw, Washington DC

WHITE & CASE

Wiggin LLP

10th Floor, Met Building, 22 Percy Street, London W1T 2BU
Tel: (020) 7612 9612 Fax (020) 7612 9611
Jessop House, Jessop Avenue, Cheltenham GL50 3WG
Tel: (01242) 224114 Fax: (01242) 224223
Email: law@wiggin.co.uk Website: www.wiggin.co.uk

Firm profile

Wiggin are leading experts in the constantly evolving field of media law. They focus exclusively on media with particular emphasis on film, music, sport, gaming, technology, broadcast and publishing. They are recognised for the uncompromising excellence of their work and an unrelenting determination to deliver the best possible results for their media clients. They have an international reputation for their innovative approach, fresh thinking and cutting edge experience in media law; a sector that is changing with mesmerising speed. The firm offers a highly personalised relationship, working in partnership with its clients to address the complex legal challenges that the fast evolving media industry presents. They have the knowledge and experience, as well as the commitment and confidence, to deliver straightforward and genuine advice motivated only by the need to achieve the best possible outcome for clients. Based primarily out of their Cheltenham office, and also in London, and with blue-chip clients based all over the World the firm goes to where clients need them to be.

Main areas of work

Commercial media 66%, media corporate 18%, media litigation 16%.

Trainee profile

If you want to work on high profile media issues in a forward thinking environment then contact Wiggin. Wiggin are looking for you if you can demonstrate strong academic ability, a commitment to success and a personality that will fit well with the rest of the team. One word of warning though, Wiggin is not for the faint hearted! They need trainees that relish hard work and a challenge.

Training environment

Training is split into four seats and these will be allocated from company/commercial, commercial media (2 seats), media litigation and film. Although based at the Cheltenham office, you will be meeting clients at the firm's London office. The firm often seconds trainees to clients for a period of time if possible.

Trainees are encouraged to take an active role in transactions, assume responsibility and deal directly with clients. In-house seminars are held regularly and training reviews are held every three months. You'll get an experience just like your friends in the City but within the exciting and niche area of media law and within a firm that is able to recognise the importance of a personal approach.

Benefits

Life assurance, private health cover, pension scheme, permanent health insurance, gym membership at corporate rates.

Sponsorship & awards

PgDL and LPC fees and £6,000 maintenance p.a.

Partners 20
Assistant Solicitors 33
Total Trainees 6

Contact
Operations Manager

Method of application
Online application only –
www.wiggin.co.uk

Selection procedure
Interview followed by two-day selection

Closing date for 2015
31 July 2013

Application
Training contracts p.a. 3
Applications p.a. 300
% interviewed p.a. 20%
Required degree grade 2:1

Training
Salary
1st year £32,000
2nd year £36,000
Holiday entitlement 20 days + one day per annum
% of trainees with a non-law degree p.a. 50%

Post-qualification
Salary £55,000
% of trainees offered job on qualification (2011) 100%
% of assistants (as at 2011) who joined as trainees 42%
% of partners (as at 2011) who joined as trainees 12%

WIGGIN

Wilsons Solicitors LLP

Alexandra House, St John Street, Salisbury, Wiltshire SP1 2SB
Tel: (01722) 412 412 Fax: (01722) 427 610
Email: jo.ratcliffe@wilsonslaw.com
Website: www.wilsonslaw.com

Partners 33
Trainees 8
Total Staff 150

Contact
Mrs J Ratcliffe
jo.ratcliffe@wilsonslaw.com

Method of application
Application via website

Selection procedure
Interview and assessment day

Closing dates for training scheme
31 July 2013 for training contract to commence in September 2015

Application
Training contracts p.a. 4

Salary
Above market rate
Holiday entitlement 22 days

Offices
Salisbury, London, Bristol

Firm profile
Ranked as one of the top private client and charity law firms in the country, our 280-year heritage, combined with lawyers who are recognised leaders in their fields, enables Wilsons to provide a unique combination of skills and experience to our clients. Our lawyers are dedicated to ensuring a detailed understanding of their clients' interests and a seamless working relationship across the different specialities of the practice.

Main areas of work
Private Client: We act for clients with business interests, landed and inherited wealth, foreign domiciliaries, UK and offshore trustees and non-resident individuals with links to the UK. Services including tax planning, estate and succession planning, asset structuring, UK and offshore trust formation and advice, wills and trusts and estate administration and probates and intestacies valued at up to £50m.

The family team's expertise ranges from pre-nuptial agreements and civil partnerships to divorce and children's arrangements.

Charity: Wilsons has one of the most highly ranked teams in the UK. We advise on the complete range of legal needs and have a particular specialism in contentious and noncontentious legacy work. The constitutional and governance team has considerable expertise in advising military charities and the charitable care sector.

Agriculture: Wilsons' rural team has developed a practice centred on the needs of rural business and landowners. These include complex sales and purchases, development options for landowners, grants and diversification advice and property litigation, including landlord and tenant, partnership matters, boundary, title and rights of way disputes.

Commercial: The commercial team specialises in employment, commercial property and corporate work. Corporate work focuses on commercial tax and asset planning, transactions and refinancing. The team deals with an unusual breadth of work requiring high-quality, bespoke commercial advice.

Property: Our clients have substantial commercial, agricultural and residential property interests and the firm advises on purchasing, letting and sales, and has a reputation for gaining excellent results in the options over and sales of development land.

Litigation and dispute resolution: Wilsons has one of the largest teams outside London. We advise clients on a wide range of contentious matters to provide an efficient and effective means of dispute resolution. In addition to its expertise in agricultural and probate disputes, the firm has specialists who can advise on all aspects of commercial dispute claims.

Trainee profile
We aim to employ the highest quality people; our reputation relies upon this. We place considerable emphasis on teamwork and look for applicants who are clear team players.

Training environment
The firm has attracted several senior City lawyers and an enviable client base and being based in Salisbury ensures an exceptional quality of work within beautiful surroundings.

Benefits
Pension, life assurance, choice of optional benefits and private medical insurance.

Work experience placements
One week available in July at our head office in Salisbury.

WILSONS

Withers LLP

16 Old Bailey, London EC4M 7EG
Tel: (020) 7597 6000 Fax: (020) 7329 2534
Email: jaya.louvre@withersworldwide.com
Website: www.withersworldwide.com

Firm profile

Withers LLP is a leading international law firm dedicated to the business, personal and philanthropic interests of successful people, their families, their businesses and their advisers.

The firm's mission is to offer a truly integrated legal service to people with sophisticated global wealth, management and business needs.

Withers' reputation in commercial law along with its status as the largest Private Client Team in Europe and leading Family Team sets it apart from other City firms.

Main areas of work

The wealth of today's private client has increased in multiples and many are institutions in their own right. Withers has been able to respond to these changing legal needs and offers integrated solutions to the international legal and tax needs of its clients. The firm has unparalleled expertise in commercial and tax law, trusts, estate planning, litigation, charities, employment, family law and other legal issues facing high net worth individuals.

Work is often international due to the complexity of our client base which includes some of the wealthiest global citizens. Currently we act for around a quarter of the UK Sunday Times 'Rich List' and a significant number from the US 'Forbes' and Asian 'Huran' rich lists. Trainees who speak a relevant language may have the opportunity to complete a seat in one of our offices abroad.

Trainee profile

Each year the firm looks for a diverse mix of trainees who are excited by the prospect of working with leaders in their field. Trainees must have an excellent academic background and great attention to detail. Team players with leadership potential are of interest to the firm, as is an international outlook and foreign language skills.

Training environment

Trainees spend six months in four different departments. Working in a team with a partner and an assistant solicitor provides autonomy, responsibility and fast development. Buddy and mentor systems as well as on the job training ensure trainees are fully supported from the outset.

Application

Apply online by 31 July 2013 to begin training in August 2015. Interviews take place between April and September.

Vacation scheme

The firm runs two-week long placements at Easter and over the summer in London. Apply online by 31 January 2013 for places in 2013. Interviews take place between January and March.

Sponsorship

Fees plus £5,000 maintenance for both the PgDL or CPE and/or LPC are paid.

Partners 108
Total Staff 730
Trainees 39

Contact
Jaya Louvre
Recruitment Manager

Method of application
Application form (available online)

Selection procedure
2 interviews incl. written exercise and presentation

Closing dates for 2015
Training scheme
31 July 2013
2013 vacation placements
31 January 2013

Application
Training contracts p.a. 13
Applications p.a. 700
% interviewed p.a. 20%
Required grades 2:1, AAB at A-Level

Training
Salary
1st year (2012) £34,000
2nd year (2012) £36,000
Holiday entitlement 23 days
% of trainees with a non-law degree p.a. 50%

Post-qualification
Salary (2012) £56,000

Offices
London, Milan, Geneva, Zurich, New York, New Haven, (Connecticut), Greenwich (USA), Hong Kong, Singapore, BVI

Wragge & Co LLP

55 Colmore Row, Birmingham B3 2AS
Tel: 0870 903 1000   Fax: 0870 904 1099
Website: www.wragge.com/graduate
Email: naomi_tuck@wragge.com

Firm profile

Wragge & Co is a UK-headquartered international law firm providing a full service to clients worldwide. The firm has 126 partners, supported by more than 1,000 people in offices in Birmingham, Brussels, Guangzhou, London, Munich, as well as affiliated offices in Abu Dhabi, Dubai and Paris. Committed to delivering first-class legal advice and a partner-led service, Wragge & Co is well known for its technical excellence, creative thinking and single team approach. Its broad client base spans everything from FTSE 100 and 250 companies and multinational corporations to financial institutions and hundreds of public sector organisations.

Main areas of work

We provide a full range of commercial and corporate legal services and have nationally recognised teams in specialist areas including employment, intellectual property, pensions and real estate.

Trainee profile

We're looking for talented people with well-rounded personalities from diverse cultures and different backgrounds. Your age, ethnic origin, gender, sexual orientation, religion or disability are all irrelevant. We recruit only on the basis of ability.

A lot of our people weren't always lawyers, so you may have a variety of career experience and skills, including commercial, technical, social, financial and economic knowledge. Most importantly, it's about who you are.

Training environment

We think that if you're intelligent, talented, willing to learn and work hard, you deserve the chance to prove yourself. This means challenging you with early responsibility and exposure to some of our top clients.

You may find yourself working on high-profile cases in your first few weeks, talking to clients and giving advice. If you can show that you're willing to take on more work and greater responsibility, then we'll trust you with exactly that. And we'll always give you the support you need.

Benefits

We offer all trainees the following: £1,000 interest-free loan, a prize for first class degree, a prize for GDL and LPC distinction, pension scheme (firm makes a contribution after six months), life assurance, permanent health insurance, access to discounted private medical insurance rates, 25 days holiday, optional unpaid leave, social club, access to corporate rates and discounts.

Sponsorship & awards

We cover your Legal Practice Course (LPC) and Graduate Diploma in Law (GDL) fees, as well as providing a maintenance grant for each course.

Partners 126
Assistant Solicitors 103
Total Trainees 54

Contact
Naomi Tuck
Graduate Recruitment Advisor
0121 629 1982

Method of application
Online application, via the
graduate website
www.wragge.com/graduate

Selection procedure
Application form, verbal
reasoning test, situational
judgement test, telephone
interview and assessment day

Closing dates
2013 Vacation scheme
applications 31 January 2013
Training contract applications
for 2015 31 July 2013

Applications
No. of training contracts p.a. 20
Applications p.a. 1,000
% interviewed variable
Required degree grade N/A

Training
Salary for each year of training
1st Year
Birmingham £26,250
London £35,750
2nd Year
Birmingham £29,250
London £38,750
Holiday entitlement 25 days

Post-qualification
Birmingham £38,000
London £58,000
% of trainees offered job on
qualification (September 2012)
74% (March 2012) 100%

Overseas/regional offices
London, Birmingham, Brussels,
Guangzhou, Munich, Abu Dhabi
and Paris

Wragge&Co

The Bar

Barcode

Don't let alien terms used at the Bar confuse or intimidate you!

Baby junior – any barrister who completed pupillage less than two years ago.

Bar Council – the General Council of the Bar, to give it its full title, is the Bar's representative body. It can be found clashing regularly with the Ministry of Justice.

Bar Standards Board – or BSB, the Bar's regulatory body.

Barrister – a member of the Bar of England and Wales.

Bench – the judiciary.

Bencher – a senior member of an Inn of Court. Usually silks and judges, known as Masters of the Bench.

Brief – the documents setting out case instructions.

BPTC – the Bar Professional Training Course. Successful completion entitles you to call yourself a barrister in non-legal circumstances (ie dinner parties), but does not give you rights of audience.

Cab-rank rule – self-employed barristers cannot refuse instructions if they have the time and experience to undertake the case. You cannot refuse to represent someone because you find their opinions or actions objectionable.

Call – the ceremony whereby you become a barrister.

Chambers – a group of barristers in independent practice who have joined together to share the costs of practising. Chambers is also the name used for a judge's private office.

Circuit – the courts of England and Wales are divided into six circuits: North Eastern, Northern, Midland, South Eastern, Western and Wales & Chester.

Clerk – administrator/manager in chambers who organises work for barristers and payment of fees, etc.

Con – short for 'conference', a meeting between a barrister and a solicitor (and their lay client).

Counsel – a barrister.

CPS – the Crown Prosecution Service.

Devilling – (paid) work done by a junior member of chambers for a more senior member.

Direct instruction – since 2004 barristers can be instructed directly by businesses and members of the public without the intervention of a solicitor.

Employed Bar – barristers who are not engaged in private practice at chambers, but are employed full-time by a company or public body.

First and second six – pupillages are divided into two six-month periods. Most chambers now only offer 12-month pupillages.

FRU – the Free Representation Unit. Provides real-life advocacy experience to budding barristers in Employment Tribunals and social security cases.

Independent Bar – the collective name for barristers who practise on a self-employed basis.

Inns of Court – ancient institutions that alone have the power to 'make' barristers. There was a time when there was a proliferation of them but now there are only four: Gray's Inn, Inner Temple, Lincoln's Inn and Middle Temple.

Junior – a barrister not yet appointed silk. Note: older juniors are known as senior juniors.

Junior brief – a case on which a junior is led by a senior. Such cases are too much work for one barrister alone and may involve a lot of research or run for a long time. Ordinarily, junior counsel will not conduct advocacy.

Keeping term – eating the dinners in hall required to be eligible for call to the Bar.

Lay client – barristers' clients are usually solicitors, so the solicitor's client is known as a 'lay client'.

Marshalling – work experience in which you shadow a judge, normally lasting between one and five days.

Mess – the hierarchical groups of four in which students sit during dining sessions. 'Mixed messes' means that barristers and masters sit with students.

Mini-pupillage – work experience at a set of chambers, normally lasting between one and five days.

Moot – a legal debate in which students act as claimants or respondents in an appeal court (ie the Court of Appeal or Supreme Court). Typically, there will be two students on each team, acting as either senior or junior.

Pupillage – the year of training undertaken after Bar school and before tenancy.

Pupillage Portal – the online application system for pupillage.

Pupilmaster – a senior barrister with whom a pupil sits and who teaches the pupil. The Bar Council is encouraging use of the term pupil supervisor.

Queen's Counsel (QC) – a senior barrister, appointed by royal decree to be one of Her Majesty's Counsel. In the reign of a male monarch, the term is King's Counsel (KC).

Set – as in a 'set of chambers'.

Silk – a QC, so named because of their silk robes.

Supervisor – the new name for a pupilmaster.

Tenant/tenancy – permission from chambers to join their set and work with them. A 'squatter' is someone who is permitted to use chambers' premises, but is not actually a member of the set. A 'door tenant' is someone who is affiliated with the set, but does not conduct business from chambers' premises.

Third six – when pupils are not successful in gaining tenancy, they can apply for a third six at another set in the hopes of success there.

A career at the Bar

Being a barrister is, to quote one sage QC, *"quite simply, the best job in the world."* True, the Bar is a highly competitive world in which the hours can be punishing and the work arduous, but the combination of excitement, advocacy, extraordinary experiences, personal fulfilment and kudos it offers is unique.

Essential Bar stats: a harsh reality

It's no secret that becoming a barrister is unfathomably competitive. *"The process is a strenuous and difficult one which is not to be underestimated,"* a current pupil told us. The statistics alone are disheartening: the number of students who successfully completed the BPTC in 2010/11 totalled 1,113. In the same year the number of pupillages on offer was just 446. And don't forget the BPTC grads from all the previous years still hunting for jobs. Hoping to address the problem of over-subscription by raising admission standards for the BPTC, the Bar Standards Board has introduced an aptitude test for BPTC applicants. Called the Bar Course Aptitude Test, it was put in place in autumn 2012 for 2013 starters. It is compulsory for everyone who wants to do the BPTC and is designed to test logic, deduction and interpretation of texts. All this will probably discourage the casual applicant, but the average would-be barrister is made of sterner stuff and usually has a deep-seated commitment to this branch of the profession.

Will you make it?

So, we've established your vocational drive, but what distinguishes you? This is a hard one. Meet enough pupils and barristers and you can see what makes someone successful. The fact that you're gobby/argumentative/confident doesn't mean you'll make it, nor is success guaranteed by superstar academic results and an ability to complete the *Times* crossword in three minutes. Ask a chambers recruiter to define the qualities they look for and they will speak in fairly general terms (academic credentials, people skills, analytical skills, commitment, passion, an ability to express ideas), with the vague caveat that 'you know a good one when you see one'. Perhaps it's best to say that those who thrive at the Bar are people who offer the right traits for their chosen area of practice. Crime is all about guts, personality, advocacy ability and being to-the-point, down-to-earth and capable of assimilating and recalling facts easily. It's not necessary to be a genius.

Commercial practice is a more sophisticated game. Intelligence, an analytical mind, excellence on paper, commercial acumen and an easy manner with business clients are a must. Specialisms like tax and insolvency attract true brainboxes. While advocacy is still important in commercial practice, deriving pleasure from crafting a masterpiece opinion or explaining a phenomenally complex legal argument succinctly is arguably even more so. By reading the **Chambers Reports** and **Practice areas at the Bar** you will understand more about the skills required in the various specialist areas of practices.

Is the cost of training prohibitive?

The GDL conversion course is quite expensive, and the BPTC is painfully steep, so you need to be fairly confident about your prospects of succeeding at the Bar. Many criminal or general common law sets pay their pupils the bare minimum award of £1,000 per month (as prescribed by the Bar Council from 1 September 2011). Some commercial sets make large pupillage awards available in line with the salaries of trainee solicitors at big City firms; they will even advance funds for the BPTC year. Unless you've got a source of cash, getting through law school and pupillage is a pricey business most commonly funded through bank or parental loans. Read our Funding section for more ideas (page 96). Of all the potential sponsors out there, the four Inns of Court have the deepest pockets: they make more than £4.7m available each year to students.

Huge debts aren't so much of a problem if you'll soon be earning a fat income, but the common perception that all barristers are rolling in it isn't quite right. Those determined to serve their community will find the public funding of civil, family and criminal cases in the midst of a rationalisation as legal aid cuts start to bite. Despite this gloomy prognosis, it is worth remembering that privately paying clients still need legal advice and commercial sets continue to thrive. There's no question that tenancy at one of the best commercial sets pays very well indeed: some

Commercial Bar stars earn well over £1m a year, while pupils who make it to tenancy in good-quality sets can outstrip the salaries of their solicitor peers immediately. Do be aware that within each area of practice at the Bar there are a few Premier League sets and many others in lower divisions: the difference in earnings between the top and the bottom is substantial.

Get Bar ready

If you're still at university there's plenty you can do to prepare yourself for a shot at the Bar. If there is anything a little dodgy about your CV – you're mature or you have poor A levels, for instance – getting a First is the best idea. Applicants with 2:1s are two a penny and a 2:2 will scupper your chances unless you can demonstrate some truly remarkable alternative qualities. In general, chambers are more interested in your undergraduate performance than what you can muster up on the BPTC, but frankly you should try to get the best grades at every stage. As for postgraduate degrees – a master's from a very good university, either in the UK or abroad – it must be your choice whether to undertake one or not. Many of the Bar's most successful candidates have such a qualification, but in itself doing a master's degree will not help you win a pupillage.

The best way to demonstrate commitment to the Bar is to undertake mini-pupillages – work experience at a barristers' chambers. Whether assessed or unassessed, minis all involve observing barristers in chambers and probably also in court, although the degree of involvement varies hugely from one set to another. **Read our full feature on mini-pupillages on page 668**.

Not all sets offer mini-pupillages, and some will only take students in the final year of academic legal study (be it degree or GDL), so start off by checking their websites carefully for how and when to apply. In general you should aim for as many as it takes you to decide which areas of practice interest you. Gaining pupillage may be a strictly fair process these days, but personal contacts can still help in obtaining a mini. Apply to an Inn of Court to be assigned a sponsor, or if you've started dining at your Inn then start schmoozing.

Stand out from the crowd

The Bar Standards Board prescribes that BPTC students must undertake a certain amount of pro bono work. To ensure that you do land something that interests you and adds real weight to a pupillage application form, it is a good idea to investigate the options as soon as possible. You should also heed the advice of the QC who said: *"Do everything you can."* Get involved with every debating and mooting opportunity that crops up, enter mock trial competitions at law school and keep an eye out for essay competitions. *"I sacrificed my social life to get the best experience possible,"* a pupil at a top set told us. The scholarships offered by the Inns are not just a way of funding your education: don't underestimate the capacity of a major prize or award to mark you out from other well-qualified candidates.

Competition for pupillage means you increasingly need to do more than just get top grades, win prizes and gain pro bono experience to win a pupillage. Pupils we have spoken to in the past few years have done things like run a charity in South Africa, work for the BBC, intern at the European Commission in Brussels and report on war crimes trials in Tanzania.

Through the Portal

Unless taking time out from academia, most candidates start to make pupillage applications during their final undergraduate year, although in an attempt to snap up the best candidates some of the top commercial sets encourage students to apply in their penultimate year. In general, however, the majority of pupillage offers tend to be made to students following the completion of the BPTC. In 2009, the Bar Council brought in a new pupillage application system called Pupillage Portal, which lets users tailor their applications for each of the sets they apply to. The maximum number of sets users can target through the portal is 12, and the Pupillage Portal operates just once a year. Though participation is voluntary for chambers, if they run their own separate application schemes they must still advertise all vacancies on the Portal website www.pupillages.com and in the Pupillages Handbook, which is published in March each year to coincide with the National Pupillage Fair in London.

The Portal is reasonably easy to use, though drama can be avoided if you fill out all the required details in a word document and then paste it into the required fields. You have to be succinct, using a maximum of around 200 words to answer questions like 'Why do you wish to become a barrister?' and 'What areas of practice are you interested in and why?' You also have 300 words for a 'covering letter' and another 200 to discuss any further experiences you feel are relevant. Additionally, sets are now able to add a unique tailor-made question to the form. 'Identify and summarise a piece of case law and explain why you are interested in it', was one example we heard. Do bear in mind that chambers' recruiters can feel quite worn down by excessively long forms, so try to find the right balance between detailed and snappy answers, and definitely leave out that one time you went to band camp.

Students can be alerted by e-mail, phone call, letter or SMS with the results of their applications. When you do get an offer you have at least two weeks to make a decision. It's important to remember that if you withdraw from the Portal you cannot reapply in the same year, so save yourself the grief and do your research thoroughly before selecting your 12 sets. Be warned: in past years the system operated a 'clearing' round for those unsuccessful in the first round. Due to low uptake the whole clearing round has now been abolished, though, so you have one chance and one chance only to apply to Portal sets.

Beyond the Portal

A good number of sets recruit pupils outside the Portal machinery because they don't like its format or timetable and feel their interests will be better served by other means. The application method at each non-Portal set will be different. Some choose to mirror the Portal timetable in their own application procedures, but many don't and this can bring its own problems: what do you do if a non-Portal set makes you an attractive offer before your 12 Portal applications play out? The decision here must be yours. The good news is that non-Portal sets are generally very good at laying out the specifics of their application processes on their websites.

Interviews: getting them right

So you've got an interview – that's already an achievement. Look the part: dress neatly and discreetly with hair tidy, teeth flossed, tie sober. Most chambers will be grading you on standard criteria that include everything from intellect to personality.

Most sets operate two rounds of interviews/assessments. How sets interview and assess applicants varies quite a bit, but thankfully they are pretty good about detailing their procedures online. The first round is often a sit-down interview. These can be quite brief 10-15 minute affairs. The interview may focus on a topical legal-political question or involve a discussion of the hottest topics in your prospective practice area and some investigation into you and your application form. Remember: you'll face a panel that wants you to stand out. Naturally you should read *The Times'* Law supplement, *Guardian Law* and – an excellent daily blog you can have e-mailed – Current Awareness from the Inner Temple library. Preparation for interviews should consist of more than boning up on the law; now more than ever it's also important to be clued-up on current affairs. You should also think about what is and isn't on your CV and how you can account for disappointing grades or anything that is missing. An increasing number of sets operate a more formalised interviewing system, asking specific set questions to each candidate probing for certain competencies, your analytical ability and advocacy skills. Some sets may also ask you to do a written test or group exercise where you have to argue a point against or alongside others.

If you get through to a second interview round, expect to find yourself in front of a large panel made up of a cross-section of people from chambers. While the format of the interviews may vary between sets, the panel will always want to assess the depth of your legal knowledge, your advocacy potential and your strength of character. This is your moment to show what a brilliant advocate you are. The interview panel will often do its best to catch you out or go against whatever point of view you choose to argue. Don't let them push you around; if you can support your position then stick to it. Resolve is just as necessary for a career at the Bar as receptivity; recruiters want to know that you can fight your corner. As one observed: *"It is amazing how many people can't stand up for themselves, which is all you want to see."*

Criminal and mixed sets will commonly give you an advocacy exercise, such as a bail application or a plea in mitigation (their basic structures will fit on a post-it, so why not note them down and keep them with you at all times). Most sets, if not all, will pose a legal problem, although the amount of preparation time you are given can range from ten minutes to a week. You may be given a piece of statute to interpret or be asked to compare several judgments and give your view on a case study. If you know that this is going to happen then do take an appropriate practitioner's text unless you know that one will be made available to you. That said, chambers generally aren't looking for faultless knowledge of substantive law, but they are trying to get an insight into how your mind works. As one seasoned interviewer explained: *"We are more interested in seeing how a candidate approaches a problem than whether or not they get the right answer."* Of course, other recruiters may not be so forgiving! A second interview is often the time when a professional ethics question may raise its head. You can prepare by reading the Bar's Code of Conduct, which is available on the Bar Standards Board's website.

Try, try and try again?

What if you still don't have pupillage by the time you have finished the BPTC? Rather than seeing an enforced year out as a grim prospect, view it as a time to improve your CV and become more marketable. If you are interested in a specialist area of practice consider a master's degree. If the thought of another year in education brings you out in a cold sweat then seek out some useful practical experience. The most obvious answer is to apply for paralegalling and outdoor clerking jobs at solicitors' firms. Although these positions are hard to come by, the work you do as a paralegal should teach you how cases actually work and how solicitors – your future clients – operate. As a clerk you will be in court all the time, taking notes. This will give you insight into the procedures and politics of trials. The year might also be spent with an organisation that works in an area related to your legal interest. We have interviewed several lawyers who secured pupillages following a period with a company, charity or non-profit organisation.

Pupillage

If you do gain a pupillage, congratulations! Now the hard work really starts. How the pupillage year is divided varies from set to set, but no matter how many pupil supervisors are allotted, the broad division is between the first, non-practising six months and the second, when pupils may be permitted some court action. During the first six, pupils are tethered to their supervisor(s), shadowing them at court, conferences and in chambers. They will also very likely draft pleadings, advices and skeletons or do research for the matters their supervisor is working on. The nature of the second six will depend on the specific area of practice. At a busy criminal set it can mean court every day, and many civil or commercial sets specialising in areas like employment, PI, construction or insurance will send their pupils out up to three times a week. Some big commercial or Chancery sets actively prefer to keep pupils in chambers throughout the year, either for the purposes of assessment or because the nature of the work means pupils are simply too inexperienced to do oral advocacy.

Tenancy

Tenancy is the prize at the end of the year-long interview that is pupillage. Effectively, an offer of tenancy is an invitation from a set to take a space in their chambers as a self-employed practitioner, sharing the services of the clerking and administrative teams. How many tenants a set takes on post-pupillage is usually as dependent on the amount of space and work available in chambers as on the quality of the candidates. If you are curious about a set's growth, check to see how many new tenants have joined in recent years by viewing the list of members on its website, then compare that against the number of pupillages offered in the same period. Usually tenancies are awarded after a vote of all members of chambers, following recommendations from a tenancy committee, clerks and possibly also instructing solicitors. Decisions are commonly made in the July of the pupillage year, allowing unsuccessful pupils time to cast around for other tenancy offers or a 'third six' elsewhere.

There is evidence to suggest that civil and commercial sets have higher pupil-to-tenant conversion rates than criminal sets. Certainly, it is quite usual for a 12-month criminal pupillage to be followed by a third or subsequent six somewhere other than at a pupil's first set. However, plenty of commercial pupils do also find themselves looking for a third six. The general rule is that if a third six is not successful, it is perhaps time to look outside the Bar.

And finally...

One thing is for sure about a career at the Bar: you need to be resolute. Success won't come your way if you doubt your own ambition and ability.

	00-01	01-02	02-03	03-04	04-05	05-06	06-07	07-08	08-09	09-10	10-11
BPTC applicants	2,252	2,119	2,067	2,570	2,883	2,917	2,870	2,864	2,540	2,657	3,100
BPTC enrolments	1,407	1,386	1,332	1,406	1,665	1,745	1,932	1,837	1,749	1,793	1,618
Students passing the BPTC	1,081	1,188	1,121	1,251	1,392	1,480	1,560	1,720	1,330	1,432	1,113
First-six pupils	695	812	586	518	571	515	527	562	464	460	446
Second-six pupils	700	724	702	557	598	567	563	554	515	495	477
Pupils awarded tenancy	535	541	698	601	544	531	499	494	497	467	541

The BPTC replaced the Bar Vocational Course in 2010.

Mini-pupillages

"Honestly, I don't think any Pupillage Portal application should go out without at least one mini-pupillage on it."

At law fairs, one of the most common things students ask about is how they can improve their chances of becoming a barrister. The most obvious answer is: 'Do some mini-pupillages'. Minis are an essential early step because, without at least one under your belt, a pupillage application will look oddly lacking. They are, quite simply, periods of work shadowing and/or assessment within barristers' chambers.

What form do mini-pupillages take?

Unlike the structured vacation schemes you'll encounter at larger solicitors' firms, work experience at barristers' chambers can be more hit-and-miss. Some (especially the most profitable, most prestigious and most forward-thinking) will go about it in a very methodical way. At others it may be a pretty disorganised exercise.

Length: As a rule mini-pupillages last two, three or five days and will be either assessed (ie there will be tests and feedback) or non-assessed. Our sources say: *"You don't need to do a five-day mini unless it's assessed. Three days is more than enough, especially in term-time. It's okay to ask for a three-day mini, even if it specifically says five days on the set's website. Barristers are switching on to the fact that students do have a lot of other stuff to do."*

During a good mini-pupillage you can expect to spend time shadowing a barrister in court, attend conferences with clients and look at paperwork – these are the three fundamentals of the job. *"Students shouldn't expect to be in court the whole time as that's not what the barristers do all day. Chambers will want to see how your brain works."* Besides, depending on what type of chambers you visit, it's always possible that you'll be unlucky and they won't even have anything going on in court while you're there.

On a bad mini-pupillage you might be abandoned in a room with a barrister who doesn't really want you there. *"I got stuck with a costs lawyer. Costs isn't an easily accessible area of law, even for other barristers. He gave me a load of bundles and told me to give them a read. I came back two hours later and asked: 'Where do I start?'"*

An assessed mini is likely to be more structured, with a couple of days out of five dedicated to the assessment process itself. *"It may feel like an academic exercise, but what they want is an 'advice' of sorts, so my efforts also had to be fairly practical. Among other things, the exercise was marked on the quality of the legal analysis, the structure and the language."*

"I was given a factual scenario that filled about one side of A4, and was given a few questions to answer about the scenario. Myself and the other mini-pupil were sent to the nearest Inn library to research and answer the questions using Halsbury's Laws, Westlaw, LexisNexis, etc. I had a day to do this before handing my written answers to a barrister. The following afternoon I had about 30 minutes' worth of feedback with the barrister, who pointed out where I had done well and where I had gone wrong."

It is likely that assessment problems will be on an unfamiliar area of law to give people at different stages of the learning process a fair shot. *"It was suggested that my written answer should be in the form of an opinion, but chambers should understand that if you haven't done the BPTC yet, it's likely you'll produce something more in line with a GDL-style answer. The focus is on content rather than style; they want to know if you can go through the thought processes, aided by the right research tools, to come up with a sensible answer."*

While your written work will be marked, you should also expect to be judged on the quality of your questions, how quickly you pick things up and your general manner. Expect to spend more time on your own than in a non-assessed mini. The advice from those who've been through the process is to try and do some un-assessed minis before an assessed one and not to try one until you've at least started on the GDL. *"They can be very academic and textbooky – a challenge."* In this type of pupillage it is reasonable to ask for feedback on your performance. And as one of our sources pointed out: *"There can be a certain prestige to assessed minis; a lot of the top chambers do them."*

You may be asked to attend an interview for a place on a mini-pupillage, particularly if it is assessed. Be prepared to talk convincingly about why you have chosen to pursue a career as a barrister and perhaps even make a short presentation on a subject selected by the set.

The social scene: A few chambers take as many as five mini-pupils at a time, but usually you'll be alongside just one other. Those sets with more formalised programmes may put on a drinks party but at most others you're unlikely to be invited to any social events.

This is not to say you can't use your visit for some subtle but effective networking. How much you can achieve in this respect will depend on how people in chambers take to you and whether or not your interaction is of the right type. It's about striking a good balance in your interactions with people and being remembered for the right things – enthusiasm, real engagement with the cases you encounter – and not for being a nuisance or a drain on people's time. Pick your moments for questions and conversation carefully.

When should you start applying?

It's never too early. Our sources had each done a couple of minis in their final undergraduate year, a couple while on the GDL course and three while on the BPTC. But if you're sure you want to be a barrister, why wait? There is no rule that says first and second-year undergrads can't do minis. It is true that the less advanced you are in your studies, the less you'll be able to understand, but that doesn't mean it will be a waste of time. You'll learn about your surroundings and how to act around barristers. And of course, it's *"inspirational."* Doing a mini-pupillage, said one of our sources, *"reaffirmed my belief that this was what I wanted to do with my life."*

How do you get a mini?

Two of our sources had used connections within the profession to pick up a couple of minis – you mustn't hesitate to use them if you have them – but for the others they went through the usual application process.

Most sets will give details of mini-pupillages on their website, even if it's just a line saying 'we do them'. If it's not clear whether a set offers minis, *"don't be afraid to ring up the clerks, ask who is dealing with the minis (it's usually a junior barrister) and ask to speak to them."* Then if they're unavailable you will be given the right person's e-mail address to send your application to and know that it's not going to be lost in the ether.

Apply for as many minis as you can because *"it's a numbers game."* That said, never compromise the quality of your applications in your bid to up the quantity. Most sets' procedures will involve a fairly standard CV-based form, or a letter and CV, so it shouldn't require too much brain straining. Make sure your application explains why you are interested in visiting a particular set and shows that you are serious about a career as a barrister. Demonstrating some kind of mooting or public speaking experience will be essential for many sets, given the amount of advocacy involved in the job.

The number of mini-pupillages you are offered should give you an indication of how credible a candidate you are. Likewise, looking at the reputation of the sets that offer you minis will give you *"for lack of a better phrase, an idea of where you stand in the pecking order."* If, for example, you're having no success with leading sets, take the hint and set your sights lower. If you don't hear back from anyone at all, take a long hard look at your CV and ask yourself what you must do to improve it.

Don't expect any feedback after making mini-pupillage applications. Many sets don't even bother to send out rejection letters. If you haven't heard from a set for a couple of months it's likely that you have been unsuccessful. It is possible that the set simply didn't have the space to accommodate you at that point in time, or it may just be a bit disorganised. One of our contacts applied for a mini in March 2008, didn't hear back immediately, and was then surprised when the set contacted her over a year later asking her to come in for the summer 2009 vacation period – *"far too late for a Pupillage Portal application that year!"* Another was rejected for a mini at the set where he eventually gained pupillage.

How many should you do?

We spoke to one barrister this year who told us: *"Mini-pupillages show your commitment to the Bar, but if you do ten that ceases to impress. Three is a decent number."* Having said that, both of our successful sources had completed half a dozen. *"I have been asked why I did so many mini-pupillages. I think there's an idea that doing a lot can project uncertainty as to which area of law you're interested in."* Yes, there is such a thing as overkill, but certainly going past three won't hurt your chances and some sense a change in the way multiple minis are viewed. No one is going to criticise you for sampling different areas of practice.

If you have completed a string of minis, you may wish to consider only putting the more impressive experiences on your CV/application forms. If, for example, you're aiming for a criminal pupillage and have done several crime minis and several civil minis, you could leave some of the civil experiences off your CV. *"It's a case of striking the* right balance between showing your commitment to a practice area and showing that you know what else is out there."

Top tips for making a good impression

- "At the end of every day, mark down every single thing you've done, no matter how small – every little legal point you've looked at, every chat about it you had with a barrister. You will forget it when it comes to subsequent interviews unless you make a note."
- "While you're in court things may go way over your head but stay focused. The barrister who takes you along may ask you how you think the hearing went."
- "Try to be relaxed while you're in chambers. Don't expect too much on a personal or social level. Barristers are different. Some will be very intense. Some will have read your CV and talk to you about your interests. Some won't give a shit and will vaguely resent having to baby-sit you – and you'll know it. Don't take it personally."

- "Later minis are of more use. On my earlier ones I learned that I loved the surroundings of chambers and going to court, but as I did not understand most of the legal principles it was more difficult to engage with the work. By the time I was on later minis, it was much easier to make a good impression."
- "Your knowledge of how to conduct yourself grows and later minis feel less alien and nerve-racking. By the time you're on the BPTC, you're at the stage where you see a set of papers and understand more and get more out of the experience."

And finally...

Applying for pupillage is a tough business and you should be prepared for rejection. Although a mini will get you a certain distance, it will not take you all the way to pupillage. That said, "a mini-pupillage is a real morale boost – it's a reminder that at least somebody thinks you're worth taking a look at."

Does the Bar have an Oxbridge obsession?

"We don't hire people because they went to Oxford or Cambridge. It just so happens those people have all kinds of other interesting things on their CV which make them great candidates."

Pupil recruiter

The Inns of Court

The four Inns of Court appear as oases of calm amid the hustle and bustle of London's legal heartland. Named Lincoln's Inn, Inner Temple, Middle Temple and Gray's Inn, they have many similarities with Oxbridge colleges, not least their libraries, chapels, halls and ancient traditions.

The Inns provide teaching, guidance, scholarships, a social network for members and a calm environment in which to work. Stroll through the Inns and you can practically breathe history. Out in their gardens you can relax with a drink from an on-site bar or play croquet; inside you're surrounded by imposing oil paintings, the austere expressions of past grandees, judges, heads of state and prime ministers gazing out from the wood panelling.

The Inns are the only institutions with the power to 'call' a person to the Bar. Indeed, students must join one of the four Inns before starting their BPTC and, since membership is for life, it's a decision worth mulling over. Although all four provide similar services and facilities, they each have a different flavour and atmosphere, if only due to their differing sizes. Such things are hard to describe, of course, so before picking one take any available opportunity to visit the Inns to see which one most appeals. This is easily done – just call up and ask for a tour. The Inns also produce a wealth of promotional materials/application guides/newsletters all packed with information – soak it up.

At the latest, you'll need to join an Inn before starting the BPTC, but it's a good idea to consider which one much earlier because between them they've got almost £5m to give out in scholarships for GDL and BPTC students as well as pupils. The deadlines for scholarship applications are usually in the calendar year before the course begins, so mark your diary once you have perused the detailed information on the Inns' websites or in their hard-copy brochures.

Getting a scholarship is competitive. Applicants face panels of current members (sometimes including judges) who will examine academic records and set challenges to determine on-the-spot presentation and advocacy skills. Achievements such as 'overcoming hardship' are sometimes also considered, as are extracurricular activities like sporting or musical ability. The top scholarships are the prestigious 'named' scholarships, which can be worth in the region of £15,000. There are also a huge number of smaller awards.

It's advisable to get mini-pupillages and/or other work experience and internships under your belt, especially as there are additional funds to help facilitate these. Check out the Inns' websites or brochures for more information. For students living away from London, there are funds available to help cover transport costs to visit the Inns, and money is available to cover the cost of 'qualifying sessions'. Some of these 'qualifying sessions' are educational, others are purely designed to help students socialise, network and absorb the customs of the Bar. Sessions range from time-honoured dinners in the halls to debates, music evenings, seminars, advocacy weekends or even weekend brunches. During one visit we saw pinball machines being set up by people who would later be dressed as Elvis. Twelve qualifying sessions must be attended before being 'called to the Bar' (the 12th can be the call ceremony itself).

Once a member, a student can be mentored by a practitioner in their chosen field, and there are marshalling schemes whereby students can shadow a judge for a week, observing cases and discussing them at the end of the day. There are educational workshops to polish advocacy skills and seminars discussing areas of law or courtroom technique. Then there are a range of societies for things like drama, music and mooting/debating. All Inns offer mooting at internal, inter-Inn or national level, which we fully recommend you get involved with.

Although this all sounds very exciting, don't get carried away. Ensure that you have this mantra in mind at all times: Securing a Pupillage is Extremely Hard. A BPTC provider is unlikely to turn you away if you've got the cash to spend, but you cannot make your Lord Chief Justice fantasy come true just by completing the course. Even with a much sought-after scholarship, the road to becoming a barrister is neither cheap nor simple. Do remember that the Inns can help you to improve your chances of gaining pupillage, so become adept at networking, study extremely hard and moot, moot, moot.

	Lincoln's Inn	Inner Temple	Middle Temple	Gray's Inn
Contact	Tel: 020 7405 1393 www.lincolnsinn.org.uk	Tel: 020 7797 8250 www.innertemple.org.uk	Tel: 020 7427 4800 www.middletemple.org.uk	Tel: 020 7458 7800 www.graysinn.info
Architecture	The Old Hall was built in 1490 and the larger Great Hall in 1845, the same year as the library. The Stone Buildings are Regency. The largest Inn, it covers 11 acres.	12th-century Temple Church stands opposite the modern Hall built after the original was destroyed in WWII.	Grand. Smoking rooms decked out in oak, Van Dyck paintings and a large private collection of silver. Ornate carvings in the splendid Elizabethan Hall which is tucked down an intricate maze of alleys and narrow streets.	Suffered serious war damage and is largely a 1950s red-brick creation, albeit with its ancient Hall and Chapel intact.
Gardens	Always open, the gardens are especially popular at lunchtimes.	Well kept and stretching down to the Thames. Croquet, chess and giant Connect Four may be played.	Small and award-winning and handy for the bar.	Famous 'Walks' good for nearby City Law School students. Restaurant in gardens during summer.
Style	Friendly, international and large.	Sociable, progressive and switched on.	Musical, arty and very sociable. Christmas revels are notorious.	Traditional and, thanks to its smaller size, offers a personal touch.
Gastronomy	Meals in Hall are subsidised for students.	Lunch served every day. 15% discount for students.	Good-quality lunch served daily.	Lunch served in Hall every day. Subsidised rates for students.
Accommodation	14 flats available for students and 3 are let to pupils. All on-site.	Not for students.	Not for students.	Not for students.
Bar	The stylish Members' Common Room has a restaurant and a terrace bar.	The Pegasus Bar has a terraced open-air area. Good for people watching but not a place to go incognito.	St. Clement's Bar closed recently and is looking for new digs.	The new Bridge Bar, opened in 2011, is above the gateway between South and Gray's Inn Squares.
Old Members	John Donne Lord Hailsham LC Lord Denning MR Muhammad Ali Jinnah H. Rider Haggard Wilkie Collins Some 16 British Prime Ministers	Dr Ivy Williams (first woman called to Bar) Bram Stoker Judge Jeffreys of 'Bloody Assizes' M K Gandhi Lord Falconer of Thoroton	Sir Walter Raleigh William Blackstone Charles Dickens William Makepeace Thackeray	Sir Francis Bacon Thomas Cromwell Dame Rose Heilbron (the first female QC, the first female Old Bailey judge and the first female treasurer at an Inn)
Points of Interest	Together with the Royal Navy, Lincoln's Inn takes the Loyal Toast seated. This commemorates a meal with King Charles II when the entire company got too drunk to stand. Inn offers subsidised trips to The Hague, Luxembourg & Strasbourg.	Temple Church includes part of the Knights Templar's round church, which was modelled on the Church of the Holy Sepulchre in Jerusalem and used as a film set in The Da Vinci Code.	Shakespeare's Twelfth Night first performed here. Hall has a table from the Golden Hind. Every new barrister signs their name in a book on this table.	Shakespeare's Comedy of Errors first performed here. Law teaching on the site of Gray's Inn since the reign of Edward III. The ornate carved screen in the Hall is made from an Armada ship.
Scholarship Interview Process	Panel interview. No set question beforehand. Expect chat about preferred areas of practice and items of legal interest in the news. Scholarship awarded solely on merit then weighted according to financial means.	Panel interview with set question. GDL scholars entitled to automatic funding for BPTC, but can apply for higher award. Merit and academic excellence prioritised, but all awards (save for the top ones) means tested.	Every applicant interviewed. 15 minute panel interview tests a range of skills. Awards based on merit and then weighted according to financial means.	Shortlisted applicants interviewed by a three-person panel looking for an ability to think on one's feet rather than legal knowledge. Extra-curricular achievements taken into consideration - eg music, sport or overcoming adversity.
Scholarship Money	A total of over £1.5m available each year through over 160 scholarships. BPTC: up to 70 scholarships of between £6,000 and £18,000 and up to 40 bursaries of up to £3,000 each.	A total of £1.43m available. GDL: 2 major scholarships and various awards totalling £173,000. BPTC: 7 major grants (of between £17k and £20k), and awards totalling £1m.	A total of around £1m available. A fund of £90,000 for BPTC scholarships and awards. A fund of £90,000 for GDL scholarships and awards. Overseas scholarships totalling at least up to £15,000.	A total of over £850,000 available. GDL: around 18 awards of between c.£3,000 and £9,200. BPTC: around 52 awards of between £6,000 and £17,500 each. Various overseas scholarships and misc awards, eg £10,000 Hebe Plunkett award for disabled.

Practice areas at the Bar

The Chancery Bar

In a nutshell

The Chancery Bar is tricky to define. The High Court has three divisions: Family, Queen's Bench (QBD) and Chancery, with cases allocated to and heard by the most appropriate division based on their subject matter. But what makes a case suitable for the Chancery Division? Historically it has been the venue for cases with an emphasis on legal principles, foremost among them the concept of equity. Put another way, Chancery work is epitomised by legal reasoning. Cases are generally categorised as either 'traditional' Chancery (trusts, probate, real property, charities and mortgages) or 'commercial' Chancery (company law, shareholder cases, partnership, banking, pensions, financial services, insolvency, professional negligence, tax, media and IP). Most Chancery sets undertake both types of work, albeit with varying emphases. The distinction between Chancery practice and the work of the Commercial Bar (historically dealt with in the QBD) is less apparent now. Barristers at commercial sets can frequently be found on Chancery cases and vice versa, though some areas, such as tax and IP, require specialisation.

The realities of the job

- This is an area of law for those who love to grapple with its most complex aspects. It's all about the application of long-standing legal principles to modern-day situations.
- Barristers must be very practical in the legal solutions they offer to clients. Complex and puzzling cases take significant unravelling and the legal arguments/principles must be explained coherently to the solicitor and the lay client. Suave and sophisticated presentation when before a judge is also vital.
- Advocacy is important, but the majority of time is spent in chambers perusing papers, considering arguments, drafting pleadings, skeletons and advices, or conducting settlement negotiations.
- Some instructions fly into chambers, need immediate attention and then disappear just as quickly. Others can rumble on for years.

- Variety is a key attraction. Traditional work can involve human interest, for example wills and inheritance cause all sorts of ructions among families. Commercial Chancery practitioners deal with the blood-on-the-boardroom-table disputes or bust-ups between co-writers of million-selling songs.
- Schedules aren't set by last-minute briefs for next-day court appearances, so barristers need self-discipline and good time management skills.
- The early years of practice feature low-value cases like straightforward possession proceedings in the county court, winding-up applications in the Companies Court and appearances before the bankruptcy registrars. More prominent sets will involve baby barristers as second or third junior on larger, more complex cases.

Current issues

- The Chancery Bar attracts high-value, complex domestic cases and offshore and cross-border instructions. They might involve Russian and Eastern European business affairs or massive offshore trusts in the Cayman Islands, the British Virgin Islands, Bermuda and the Channel Islands.
- The scope of the Chancery Division means that practitioners get involved in some enormous commercial and public law matters.

Some tips

- An excellent academic record is essential. Most pupils in leading sets have a first-class degree. You should enjoy the analytical process involved in constructing arguments and evaluating the answers to problems. If you're not a natural essay writer, you're unlikely to be a natural-born Chancery practitioner.
- Don't wander into this area by accident. Are you actually interested in equity, trusts, company law, insolvency, IP or tax?
- Though not an accurate portrayal of modern practice, Dickens' novel *Bleak House* is the ultimate Chancery saga. Give it a whirl, or buy the DVD.

Read our Chambers Reports on...

Maitland Chambers	South Square
XXIV Old Buildings	Wilberforce Chambers

The Commercial Bar

In a nutshell

The Commercial Bar handles a variety of business disputes. In its purest definition a commercial case is one heard by the Commercial Court or a county court business court. A broader and more realistic definition includes matters dealt with by both the Queen's Bench and Chancery Divisions of the High Court, and the Technology and Construction Court (TCC). The Commercial Bar deals with disputes in all manner of industries from construction, shipping and insurance to banking, entertainment and manufacturing. Almost all disputes are contract and/or tort claims, and the Commercial Bar remains rooted in common law. That said, domestic and European legislation is increasingly important and commercial barristers' incomes now reflect the popularity of the English courts with overseas litigants. Cross-border issues including competition law, international public and trade law and conflicts of law are all growing in prominence. Alternative methods of dispute resolution – usually arbitration or mediation – are also popular because of the increased likelihood of preserving commercial relationships that would otherwise be destroyed by the litigation process.

The realities of the job

- Barristers steer solicitors and lay clients through the litigation process and advise on strategy, such as how clients can position themselves through witness statements, pleadings and pre-trial 'interlocutory' skirmishes.
- Advocacy is key, but as much of it is paper-based, written skills are just as important as oral skills.
- Commercial cases can be very fact-heavy and the evidence for a winning argument can be buried in a room full of papers. Barristers have to work closely with instructing solicitors to manage documentation.
- Not all commercial pupils will take on their own caseload in the second six. At first, new juniors commonly handle small cases including common law matters like personal injury, employment cases, possession proceedings and winding-up or bankruptcy applications.
- New juniors gain exposure to larger cases by assisting senior colleagues. As a 'second junior' they assist the 'first junior' and QC leading the case. They use this as an opportunity to pick up tips on cross-examining witnesses and how best to present arguments.
- In time, a junior's caseload increases in value and complexity. Most commercial barristers specialise by building up expertise on cases within a particular industry sector, eg shipping, insurance or entertainment.
- Developing a practice means working long hours, often under pressure. Your service standards must be impeccable and your style user-friendly, no matter how late or disorganised the solicitor's instruction. In a good set you can make an exceedingly good living.

Current issues

- The Commercial Bar is booming with cases involving ever larger sums of money, ever greater levels of complexity and ever larger teams of lawyers. One recent mega-case has seen Israeli entrepreneur Michael Cherney sue Russian oligarch Oleg Deripaska for £2bn in damages in a spat over the ownership of shares.
- Commercial litigation picked up at the start of the recession, with an especially noticeable increase in the number of disputes related to insurance, professional negligence and financial institutions. The number of cases brought to the High Court increased by a third in 2009. The number fell back to 2008 levels in 2010, but rose marginally in 2011. This trend could be down to a slow market recovery and the double dip recession, as well as the trend for increased mediation and arbitration.
- Many of the big commercial cases of 2012 revolve around energy, technology and especially the financial sector.
- With more claims being settled through mediation, only the big, multi-issue cases tend to reach court, as there are so many other opportunities for dealing with smaller, less complex cases.
- Due to the recession, third-party funding of litigation and costs, risk-sharing arrangements are becoming more prevalent.

Some tips

- Competition for pupillage at the Commercial Bar is fierce. A first-class degree is commonplace and you'll need impressive references.
- Don't underestimate the value of non-legal work experience; commercial exposure of any kind is going to help you understand the client's perspective and motivations.
- Bear a set's specialities in mind when deciding where to accept pupillage – shipping is very different to employment, for example.

Read our Chambers Reports on...

Atkin Chambers	3 New Square
Blackstone Chambers	XXIV Old Buildings
One Essex Court	Pump Court Tax Chambers
39 Essex Street	Quadrant Chambers
Henderson Chambers	South Square
Keating Chambers	3 Verulam Buildings
Maitland Chambers	Wilberforce Chambers

The Common Law Bar

In a nutshell

English common law derives from the precedents set by judicial decisions rather than the contents of statutes. Most common law cases turn on principles of tort and contract and are dealt with in the Queen's Bench Division (QBD) of the High Court and the county courts. At the edges, common law practice blurs into both Chancery and commercial practice, yet the work undertaken in common law sets is broader still, and one of the most appealing things about a career at one of these sets is the variety of instructions available.

Employment and personal injury are the bread and butter at the junior end, and such matters are interspersed with licensing, clinical negligence, landlord and tenant issues, the winding-up of companies and bankruptcy applications, as well as small commercial and contractual disputes. Some sets will even extend their remit to inquests and criminal cases.

The realities of the job

- Barristers tend to engage with a full range of cases throughout their careers, but there is an opportunity to begin to specialise at between five and ten years' call. Although you can express an interest in receiving certain work from the clerks, most sets expect their juniors to be common law generalists.
- Advocacy is plentiful. Juniors can expect to be in court three days per week and second-six pupils often have their own cases. Small beginnings such as 'noting briefs' (where you attend court simply in order to report back on the proceedings) and masters' and district judges' appointments lead to lower-value 'fast-track' personal injury trials then longer, higher-value, 'multi-track' trials and employment tribunals.
- Outside court, the job involves research, an assessment of the merits of a case and meetings with solicitors and lay clients. The barrister will also be asked to draft statements of claim, defences and opinions.
- Dealing with the volume and variety of cases requires a good grasp of the law and the procedural rules of the court, as well as an easy facility for assimilating the facts of each case.
- Interpersonal skills are important. A client who has never been to court before will be very nervous and needs to be put at ease.
- At the junior end, work comes in at short notice, so having to digest a file of documents quickly is commonplace.
- Acting as a junior on more complex cases allows a younger barrister to observe senior lawyers in court.

Current issues

- The trend for mediation and arbitration of disputes, and the trend for solicitors to undertake more advocacy themselves, have reduced work at the junior end to some extent. However, while solicitor advocates frequently take on directions hearings, they are still rarely seen at trial.
- Conditional fee agreements – aka 'no win, no fee'– have definitely affected barristers' remuneration, especially for PI claims. Ongoing changes to the public funding of legal services are also having an impact. On a more positive note, the growth of third-party funding of cases and increased use of risk-sharing arrangements by solicitors is sustaining barristers' volume of work.
- Britons have become increasingly litigious over the past few decades. Personal injury and clinical negligence claims (often against the NHS) are on the rise. Individuals are increasingly aware of the ever-expanding protections afforded by health and safety regulation and professional codes of conduct. The result: more litigation.

Some tips

- Though there are a lot of common law sets, pupillages and tenancies don't grow on trees. You'll have to impress to get a foot in the door and then make your mark to secure your next set of instructions. Personality and oral advocacy skills often matter a lot.
- If you want to specialise, thoroughly research the sets you apply to – many want their juniors to retain a broad practice many years into tenancy, while others do allow some space to carve out a niche.

Read our Chambers Reports on...

Atkin Chambers	Maitland Chambers
1 Bedford Row	Matrix Chambers
Blackstone Chambers	4 New Square
1 Chancery Lane	XXIV Old Buildings
Crown Office Chambers	Old Square Chambers
One Essex Court	South Square
39 Essex Street	2 Temple Gardens
Henderson Chambers	3 Verulam Buildings
11KBW	Wilberforce Chambers
Littleton Chambers	

The Criminal Bar

In a nutshell

Barristers are instructed by solicitors to provide advocacy or advice for individuals being prosecuted in cases brought before the UK's criminal courts. Lesser offences like driving charges, possession of drugs or benefit fraud are listed in the magistrates' courts, where solicitor advocates are increasingly active. More serious charges such as fraud, supplying drugs or murder go to the Crown Courts, which are essentially still the domain of barristers. Complex cases may reach the Court of Appeal or Supreme Court. A criminal set's caseload incorporates everything from theft, fraud, drugs and driving offences to assaults of varying degree of severity and murder.

The realities of the job

- Criminal barristers need a sense of theatre and dramatic timing, but good oratory skills are only half the story. Tactical sense, a level head and great time management skills are important.
- The barrister must be able to inspire confidence in clients from any kind of background.
- Some clients can be tricky, unpleasant or scary. Some will have pretty unfortunate lives, others will be addicted to alcohol or drugs, or have poor housing and little education.
- Barristers often handle several cases a day, frequently at different courts. Some of them will be poorly prepared by instructing solicitors. It is common to take on additional cases at short notice and to have to cope with missing defendants and witnesses. Stamina and adaptability are consequently a must.
- Sustained success rests on effective case preparation and an awareness of evolving law and sentencing policies.
- Pupils cut their teeth on motoring offences, committals and directions hearings in the magistrates' courts. By the end of pupillage they should expect to be instructed in their own right and make it into the Crown Court.
- Juniors quickly see the full gamut of cases. Trials start small – offences such as common assault – and move onto ABH, robbery and possession of drugs with intent to supply.

Current issues

- To save costs, the Crown Prosecution Service is well on the way to its aim of bringing 25% of advocacy in-house. The CPS wants many of its lawyers to develop to become Senior Crown Advocates and handle contested trials in the Crown Court. The move has reduced the work available at the Bar's junior end, and has caused concern about the quality of CPS advocacy.
- Legal aid cuts and reforms are hitting the number of available criminal instructions and remuneration. This is the major issue for all those practising at the Criminal Bar. The Legal Aid, Sentencing and Punishment of Offenders Act 2012 is removing £350m from legal aid's £2.2bn budget. (Read more about legal aid on our website.) A fair chunk of that is due to come from the fees paid to barristers. Criminal barristers have threatened to go on strike in response.
- Partially as a consequence of legal aid cutbacks, many top-end criminal sets are branching out into regulatory, VAT tribunal and professional discipline work.
- Private paying criminal practice is as healthy as ever.
- The Bribery Act 2010, which came into effect in July 2011, has seen UK laws brought in line with the OECD Bribery Convention. It widens the definition of bribery and applies to the activities of UK-based companies anywhere in the world.

Some tips

- Mini-pupillage experience and plenty of mooting and debating is required before you can look like a serious applicant.
- Some top sets will want to see your Pupillage Portal practice area choices restricted to crime and crime/mixed civil.
- The Criminal Bar tends to provide more pupillages than other areas, but these don't necessarily translate into tenancies. Third and fourth sixes are not uncommon.
- There are many ways of getting that all-important exposure to the criminal justice system. See our website for tips on useful voluntary opportunities.

Read our Chambers Reports on...

2 Bedford Row	Matrix Chambers

The Employment Bar

In a nutshell

The Employment Bar deals with any and every sort of claim arising from the relations or breakdown of relations between employees and employers. Disputes relating to individuals and small groups of employees are generally resolved at or before reaching an Employment Tribunal. Such 'statutory' claims may relate to redundancy; unfair dismissal; discrimination on the grounds of gender, sexual orientation, race, religion or age; workplace harassment; breach of contract; and whistle-blowing. In most cases a tribunal will consist of an Employment Judge sitting with two 'wing members', one from a trade union and one from a business background. Appeals are heard by the Employment Appeal Tribunal (EAT).

Accessibility is a key aim of the employment tribunal system, legal representation is not required, and many more cases proceed to a full hearing than in other areas of civil law. Such is the emphasis on user-friendliness that employment claims can even be issued online. Claimants will often represent themselves, meaning a barrister acting for a respondent company faces a lay opponent. In complex, high-value cases both parties usually seek specialist legal representation from solicitors and barristers.

Employees and employers may also bring claims in civil court. High-value claims, applications for injunctions to prevent the breach of restrictive covenants, and disputes over team moves or use of trade secrets are usually dealt with in the county courts or the High Court. These disputes make up a significant proportion of the work undertaken by senior members at sets at the top of the market.

The realities of the job

- For pupils and juniors, most advocacy takes place in employment tribunals or the EAT, where the atmosphere and proceedings are less formal. Hearings are conducted with everyone sitting down and barristers do not wear wigs. The emphasis is on oral advocacy, with witness statements generally read aloud.
- A corporate respondent might pay for a QC, while the applicant's pocket may only stretch to a junior. Solicitor advocates feature prominently in tribunals.
- Tribunals follow the basic pattern of examination in chief, cross-examination and closing submissions; however, barristers have to modify their style, especially when appearing against someone who is unrepresented.

- Large-scale equal pay or City 'team move' cases run much like other high-end litigation in the civil courts.
- Employment specialists need great people skills. Clients frequently become emotional or stressed, and the trend for respondent companies to name an individual (say a manager) as co-respondent means there may be several individuals in the room with complex personal, emotional and professional issues at stake.
- Few juniors act only for applicants or only for respondents. Most also undertake civil or commercial cases, some criminal matters.
- UK employment legislation mirrors EU law and changes with great rapidity. Cases are regularly stayed while others with similar points are heard on appeal.

Current issues

- The tribunals have been overflowing with work during the economic downturn, which has led to long delays in proceedings. The number of claims was up 50% in 2009/10 to 392,800. The figure came down in 2011/12, but is still much higher than before the recession. This means there is ample work for juniors on 'fixed fee' arrangements for insurers or large employers.
- Layoffs, bonus disputes and team moves resulting from the economic downturn are all key sources of claims.
- The Equality Act 2010 was expected to lead to an upturn in discrimination cases. There's been no noticeable increase in this type of litigation, but it's certainly an area to watch.
- Ongoing redundancies in the public and private sector could lead to an increase in strike disputes.

Some tips

- Get involved with the Free Representation Unit. No pupillage application will look complete without some involvement of this kind.
- Practically any kind of job will give you first-hand experience of being an employee – an experience that is not to be underestimated.
- High-profile cases are regularly reported in the press, so there's no excuse for not keeping abreast of the area.

Read our Chambers Reports on...

Blackstone Chambers	Littleton Chambers
11KBW	Old Square Chambers

The Family Bar

In a nutshell

Family law barristers deal with an array of cases arising from marital, civil union or cohabitation breakdown and related issues concerning children. Simple cases are heard in the county courts, while complex or high-value cases are listed in the Family Division of the High Court. Around half of divorcing couples have at least one child aged under 16, and together divorces affect nearly 160,000 children a year. Consequently, a huge amount of court time is allotted to divorce, separation, adoption, child residence and contact orders, financial provision and domestic violence.

The realities of the job

- Financial cases and public and private law children's work each offer their own unique challenges.
- Emotional resilience is required, as is a capacity for empathy, as the work involves asking clients for intimate details of their private life, and breaking devastating news to the emotionally fragile. Private law children's cases can sometimes involve serious allegations between parents and require the input of child psychologists. The public law counterpart (care proceedings between local authorities and parents) invariably includes detailed and potentially distressing medical evidence.
- For many clients, involvement with the courts is out of the ordinary and they will rely heavily on their counsel to guide them through the process. The law can never fix emotional problems relating to marital breakdown or child issues, but it can pacify a situation.
- The job calls for communication, tact and maturity. Cases have a significant impact on the lives they involve, so finding the most appropriate course of action for each client is important. The best advocates are those who can differentiate between a case and client requiring a bullish approach and those crying out for settlement and concessions to be made.
- Where possible, mediation is used to resolve disputes in a more efficient and less unsettling fashion.
- Teamwork is crucial. As the barrister is the link between the client, the judge, solicitors and social workers, it is important to win the trust and confidence of all parties.
- The legislation affecting this area is comprehensive, and there's a large body of case law. Keeping abreast of developments is necessary because the job is more about negotiating general principles than adhering strictly to precedents.
- Finance-oriented barristers need an understanding of pensions and shares and a good grounding in the basics of trusts and property.
- The early years of practice involve a lot of private law children work (disputes between parents), small financial cases and injunctions in situations of domestic violence.

Current issues

- In 2010 the number of divorces rose slightly after having fallen significantly since the early 2000s.
- Despite a push for a greater use of mediation, the volume of litigation over the division of assets after divorce rose in 2010. In a bid to further decrease the number of cases going through the courts, from 2011 onwards all divorcing couples have been obliged to pursue mediation before being allowed to litigate.
- Big divorces are big news. The wealth and assets involved in cases such as that of Boris Berezovsky and his wife Galina far outstrip the reasonable needs of the parties, but precedents for huge payouts have been established and such cases are often accompanied by strategic use of the media.
- Here and there cases involving the division of assets and child law issues following the breakdown of a civil partnership are beginning to appear.
- Prenuptial agreements have become part of the English legal landscape after the landmark *Radmacher v Granatino* case saw the Supreme Court rule for the first time that they should have 'decisive weight' in settlements. Barristers are now often involved with the drafting of such agreements.
- Legal aid cuts are hitting the Family Bar hard.

Some tips

- The Family Bar is quite small and competition for pupillage is intense. Think about how you can evidence your interest in family law. See our **Pro Bono and Volunteering** section.
- Younger pupils might find it daunting to advise on mortgages, marriages and children when they've never experienced any of these things personally. Arguably those embarking on a second career, or who have delayed a year or two and acquired other life experiences, may have an advantage.
- Check the work orientation of a set before applying for pupillage, particularly if you don't want to narrow your options too early. For example, some sets specialise only in the financial aspects of divorce.

Read our Chambers Reports on...

1 Hare Court
Queen Elizabeth Building QEB

Public Law at the Bar

In a nutshell

Centred on the Administrative Court, public law relates to the principles governing the exercise of power by public bodies. Those which most often appear as respondents in the High Court include government departments, local authorities, the prison service and NHS trusts. Often the headline cases are challenges to central government policies, like terror suspect control orders, the extradition of failed asylum seekers and the anonymity of giving evidence. Other big-ticket work comes from public inquires: the Iraq, Baha Mousa and Leveson inquiries are all illustrative examples. However, for all the (in)famous cases reported in the media, there are hundreds of public bodies taking daily decisions that affect just about everybody in the country. It is decisions like these – on immigration, welfare, planning applications or a child's school allocation – which provide most work for private practitioners. The most important process in public practice is judicial review: the administrative court may order that any decision made unlawfully be overturned or reconsidered. Nowadays – much to the dismay of the *Daily Mail* – decisions are often reviewed on the basis of the Human Rights Act 1998 (HRA). Human rights issues continue to be a major source of work for the Public Law Bar. Many barristers also have practices in areas that dovetail with their public law practice. Criminal barristers will, for example, frequently handle issues relating to prisoners or breaches of procedure by police, whereas commercial barristers may handle judicial review of decisions made by the Department of Business, Innovation and Skills.

The realities of the job

- The Administrative Court is extremely busy, so an efficient style of advocacy is vital. Barristers need to cut straight to the chase and succinctly deliver pertinent information, case law or statutory regulations.
- Barristers need a genuine interest in the legislative process and the fundamental laws by which we live.
- A real interest in academic law is a prerequisite. Complex arguments are more common than precise answers.
- While legal intellect is vital, public law's real world issues demand a practical outlook and an ability to stand back from the issue in question.
- Junior barristers often hone their nascent advocacy skills at the permissions stage of judicial review in short 30-minute hearings.

Current issues

- The controversial Health and Social Care Act 2012 is expected to lead to more disputes and more litigation in the health sector.
- The 2012 Legal Aid Act and other reforms to public funding of the Bar are affecting public law cases and the livelihoods of barristers.
- In 2011, the Freedom of Information Act was extended to cover UCAS, the Association of Chief Police Officers and the Financial Ombudsman Service, continuing a trend which is seeing the ever closer scrutiny of public bodies by pressure groups, the media and individuals.
- When it came to power in 2010, the coalition government pledged to scrap the HRA and replace it with a British Bill of Rights, but any such move now looks increasingly unlikely.
- There are an increasing number of coroners' inquests, with prison and military deaths dominating the field.

Some tips

- The competition for public law pupillage is exceptionally fierce.
- Having the highest possible academic credentials is key when applying to a public law set but most successful candidates will also have significant hands-on experience in the public or voluntary sectors.
- Public international law is popular, but it's an incredibly small field with few openings. Moreover, it's dominated by sitting or ex-professors at top universities, alongside Foreign Office veterans and the occasional senior barrister.
- If administrative and constitutional law were not your favourite subjects you should consider your decision before choosing public law.
- As a rewarding alternative, there are opportunities available within the Government Legal Service.
- An interest in current affairs is essential.

Read our Chambers Reports on...

Blackstone Chambers	Henderson Chambers
39 Essex Street	Keating Chambers
Government Legal Service	11KBW
4-5 Gray's Inn Square	Matrix Chambers
1 Hare Court	

Shipping & International Trade at the Bar

In a nutshell

This is such a well-defined specialism at the Commercial Bar it requires its own summary. Shipping and trade work mostly centres upon contract and tort; English case law is awash with examples from the world of shipping. Barristers handle disputes arising from or concerning the carriage of goods or people by sea, air and land, plus all aspects of the financing, construction, use, insurance and decommissioning of the vessels, planes, trains and other vehicles that carry them. There is often a complex international element to such cases, drawing in multiple parties – for example a wrecked vessel might be Greek-owned, Pakistani-crewed, Russian-captained, last serviced in Singapore, carrying forestry products from Indonesia to Denmark, insured in London and chartered by a French company – but English courts are very often the preferred forum for the resolution of such matters, not least because of the worldwide significance of the London insurance market. Trade disputes are often resolved through arbitration conducted in various locations, Paris and London being among the most important.

'Wet' cases deal with problems at sea, while 'dry' cases relate to disputes in port or concerns over the manufacture and financing of vessels. The Bar also has a number of aviation, road haulage and rail specialists, and the sets that dominate these areas also tend to be able to offer commodities trading expertise.

The realities of the job

- Cases are fact-heavy and paper-heavy. To develop the best arguments for a case, barristers need an organised mind and a willingness to immerse themselves in the documentary evidence. This can be time-consuming and exhausting.
- There are opportunities for international travel. Cases can run on for years and involve large teams of lawyers, both solicitors and barristers. Young barristers work their way up from second or third junior to leader over a number of years. New juniors do get to run their own smaller cases, like charter party and bills of lading disputes.
- The world of shipping and trade has its own language and customs.

- Solicitor clients will usually work at one of the established shipping firms, but lay clients will be a mixed bag of financiers, shipowners, operators, traders and charterers, protecting and indemnity associations (P&I clubs), salvors and underwriters.

Current issues

- The last five years have seen a significant increase in shipping litigation, partly fuelled by the economic downturn.
- The recession has had a particular effect on 'dry' shipping. A ship takes a long time to build. Shipyards have churned out scores of vessels ordered in the economic boom times, which no one wants now the recession has hit. The result: disputes.
- P&I clubs (marine insurers) are increasingly watchful of costs. This has sparked an increased interest in mediation and the direct instruction of barristers.
- Recent high-profile maritime disasters like the sinking of the 'Costa Concordia' and the 'MSC Napoli' are just the most well-known examples of the numerous shipping mishaps which happen every year.
- Somali piracy in the Gulf of Aden has been hitting the headlines, but piracy is also affecting waters that have ordinarily been considered safe, like the Baltic Sea. Shipping barristers are increasingly involved in insurance claims related to lost cargoes and ships.
- The Bribery Act 2010 is having a significant effect on international trade activities. The act is especially notable for its extra-territorial reach.

Some tips

- The leading sets are easy to identify. A mini-pupillage with one or more of them will greatly enhance your understanding and chances.
- Despite the prominence of English law, the work calls for an international perspective and an appreciation of international laws. This can be developed during your undergraduate or master's degree and on the BPTC.

Read our Chambers Reports on...

Quadrant Chambers

Chambers Reports: Introduction

Making an informed choice about where to apply for pupillage isn't easy. Having established your desired area of practice, you then need to select a healthy collection of up to 12 Pupillage Portal sets and decide how many sets outside the scheme to apply to. But how do you know where you'll fit in and who will want you?

These days the majority of chambers' websites display all the essential information – not just about their size, nature of work and location, but also about the essence of pupillage and mini-pupillage. Internet surfing can only take you so far though, and there is no substitute for observing the inner workings of a set through mini-pupillage. Because it is impossible to do minis at every set, we've done some of the hard work for you.

Since 2003, we have been calling in on various chambers, taking time to speak with pupils, juniors, pupil supervisors, QCs, clerks and chief execs. The task is not small so we visit each of our chosen sets every other year and refresh the existing Chambers Report in the intervening year. This year's roll call of 26 sets includes 14 new features and 12 refreshed from our 2012 edition. We have tried to visit as many different types of set as possible to paint a picture of the variety of practices available. Our visits took us from the grandeur of the Chancery Bar to the more modest surroundings of sets conducting a significant amount of publicly funded work. There should be something to suit most tastes, be they commercial, common law, criminal, IP, tax, or otherwise. The wild card in our pack is the Government Legal Service, which although not a set operating out of chambers, still offers what we regard as a cracking pupillage.

The sets covered this year are all in London, where the majority of chambers (and pupillages) are based, but in your wider research remember that there are some excellent sets in the regions, mostly in the larger cities of Leeds, Liverpool, Manchester, Birmingham and Bristol. Bear in mind that our selected sets are not the only ones in the Premier League of each practice area. Given the time, we would visit many others. We should also add that the on-the-record nature of our research at the Bar means we can't – and don't pretend to – give the same warts-and-all anonymously-sourced True Picture treatment to sets as

we do to solicitors' firms. You'll have to find out about any warts yourself...

Whichever sets you target, rest assured they are not expecting ready-formed barristers to turn up at their door. If you are committed to the relevant area of practice and can prove it through your extracurricular pursuits – and you've done well academically, of course – they will gladly make allowances for any lack of knowledge or experience on specific legal issues. Much has been said and written about how awful pupillage interviews can be, and how pupillage itself amounts to little more than a year of pain and humiliation. From what we can tell, the former holds true in so far as interviews are a trying and disheartening process that can span anywhere from one to five years. However, in an increasingly modern, business-oriented profession that is taking greater notice of what constitutes good HR practice, sets are more thoughtful towards bar hopefuls. As for pupillage, sets are not trying to push pupils to the edge of sanity – at least not on purpose – rather they try to mentor and challenge pupils so as to gauge compatibility with the set and potential at the Bar. Of course, that still doesn't make it a walk in the park for pupils.

The aim of the Chambers Reports is not merely to get the low-down on pupillage at each set but also to get a feel for each chamber's culture and to pick up tips for applicants. To this end we drank endless cups of tea, selflessly munched our way through kilos of biscuits and took numerous guided tours, checking out artwork and libraries along the way. If we've communicated the qualities that make each set unique then we've done our job and it's over to you to make your choices.

Set	Location	Head of Chambers	QCs/Juniors
Atkin Chambers	London	Nicholas Dennys QC	17/24
2 Bedford Row*	London	William Clegg QC	20/60
Blackstone Chambers	London	Carss-Frisk QC/Peto QC	37/48
1 Chancery Lane	London	John Ross QC	5/39
Crown Office Chambers	London	Richard Lynagh QC	13/73
One Essex Court	London	Lord Grabiner QC	27/49
Thirty Nine Essex Street*	London, Manchester	Jay QC/Tromans QC	31/63
Government Legal Service (GLS)*	London	N/a	450
4-5 Gray's Inn Square*	London	Richard Spearman QC	16/40
1 Hare Court	London	Nicholas Cusworth QC	12/29
Henderson Chambers*	London	Charles Gibson QC	8/39
11KBW	London	James Goudie QC	19/32
Keating Chambers*	London	Paul Darling QC	25/30
Littleton Chambers*	London	Clarke QC/Freedman QC	13/40
Maitland Chambers	London	Christopher Pymont QC	23/44
Matrix Chambers*	London	Tom Linden QC	19/36
Four New Square*	London	Sue Carr QC	22/56
XXIV Old Buildings	London, Geneva	Mann QC/Steinfeld QC	9/29
Old Square Chambers*	London, Bristol	Cooksley QC/McNeill QC	14/57
Pump Court Tax Chambers*	London	Andrew Thornhill QC	10/23
Quadrant Chambers*	London	Persey QC/Rainey QC	15/38
Queen Elizabeth Building (QEB)	London	Lewis Marks QC	6/27
South Square*	London	William Trower QC	19/21
2 Temple Gardens*	London	Benjamin Browne QC	9/44
3 Verulam Buildings	London	Ali Malek QC	22/45
Wilberforce Chambers	London	John Martin QC	23/30

* Sets visited in 2012

Toying with the idea of being a human rights barrister?
Only a handful of the most brilliant people in the
country get to pursue this career.

*"It's ridiculously competitive: there are fewer than
ten human rights pupillages out there. I helped set up
a charity in Africa, had the perfect human rights CV
and still didn't succeed in getting one."*

Pupil

Atkin Chambers

The facts

Location: Gray's Inn, London
Number of QCs/Juniors: 17/24 (10 women)
Applications: 120
Apply through Pupillage Portal
Pupils per year: 2
Seats: 2x3 and 1x6 months
Pupillage award: £50,000 (can advance £10,000 for BPTC)

Construction law can be much more glamorous than a builder's bum might suggest.

Best known as one of London's top two construction sets, Atkin Chambers has "*more to offer than just bricks and mortar.*" Its booming international arbitration work is especially noteworthy.

Sorts of torts and torts of sorts

IT, professional negligence, energy and international arbitration – not areas of law one would immediately associate with construction, but they are all big earners for construction giant Atkin. "*We don't see ourselves as a traditional construction set,*" a baby junior told us. "*What we specialise in is essentially 'the law of obligation'. The industry base for our work has traditionally been construction. But there is no reason we can't apply our expertise to other sectors.*" Another junior added: "*Our work is really just contracts and torts,*" whether they apply to the creation of an IT system, a power plant or a house.

Of course, Atkin doesn't get to be in *Chambers UK*'s top tier for construction without a heap of quality work in this area. Dozens of members have been involved in litigation for the design and construction of the new Wembley in the Technology and Construction Court (TCC). Tenants also represented Linklaters at the TCC in a dispute with engineering firm Sir Robert McAlpine over the corrosion of water pipes at its new Silk Street HQ. Other lay clients include well-known builders like Kier, Carillion, Bovis and Balfour Beatty.

There has been a big increase in the number of international arbitration cases Atkin has undertaken of late – some construction-related, some not. This work now makes up a massive 40% of revenue. "*We still have some major domestic cases,*" senior clerk Simon Slattery tells us. "*But we have really pushed hard with the internation-*al work. It is a significant part of our business at all levels in chambers.*" Members have recently conducted arbitrations in Ireland, Russia, Poland, the Czech Republic, Romania, Dubai, Bahrain, Hong Kong, Singapore and Thailand.

Around the world in 80 hours

Pupils sit with three different supervisors and spend much of their time on shadowing duties at first. "*It's all about learning, because there is an awful lot to learn in this area of law – for example, how to deal with experts.*" A pupil told us: "*Unlike other sets it's not the case that in the second six everything is different*" but "*there is a nice sense of progression throughout the year.*" So, "*in your second seat you get more drafting work of a standard that could be used in small disputes,*" a pupil said. "*My first case was an international arbitration in the telecoms industry over the non-payment of a commission. After that I worked on a fairly simple dispute over the structure of a house.*"

Pupils "*spend a lot of the year drafting pieces of written advice and pleadings,*" although "*there are also a lot of case management conferences to attend.*" Obviously construction barristers aren't the type to be in court every day but one pupil told us: "*Pupils do get quite a lot of chances to attend court – you do spend a week marshalling at the TCC and if another member has something interesting going on in court, they will take you along.*" Sources said: "*There is no real devilling, because the work being done is so difficult and you are still learning.*"

Chambers UK rankings

Construction	Information Technology
Energy & Natural	International Arbitration
Resources	Professional Negligence

Though pupils don't get to spend time on their feet, there are three advocacy exercises during pupillage: two are with either a silk or a High Court judge. Juniors felt pupillage fully prepared them to be an advocate: "*My first day on my feet was a CMC in the County Court. But while shadowing I had picked up so many skills and tactics that I was fully prepared.*" New tenants "*get a mix of their own smaller cases and big cases on which they are led,*" a junior told us. "*There's a mix of the domestic and international too. In one of my current cases we are acting for a Turkish building contractor in an arbitration in Moscow. So I have travelled out to Istanbul and been to Moscow seven or eight times.*" As one pupil rightly said, "*Atkin's international focus is such that members spend a lot of time overseas.*" Construction cases are notoriously lengthy. "*Clients don't really have the time for lengthy cases these days though,*" a junior commented. "*One big case I was on recently was done and dusted in a year, which was impressive. And I never get stuck just doing one case for years. I always punctuate it with my own cases.*" When things get busy tenants work long hours – "*a 12-hour day is what counts as a busy.*"

The Test

Pupils do three "*rigorous*" and "*gruelling*" assessments throughout the year: oral advocacy exercises, 'panel work' and 'the test'. The three oral exercises are spaced throughout the year and build up from "*teaching you your way around a courtroom so you know how to do submissions*" to the final one which is "*a real challenge.*" 'Panel work' puts pupils under "*intense time pressure;*" they are required to do four or five pieces of work for four or five members of chambers in the space of four weeks. All pupils do work for the same members, who provide feedback in writing to the pupillage committee. Finally, 'the test' is a large piece of written work, often an advice on a set of pleadings.

Together these three assessments are the main basis for the tenancy decision, which is made by the pupillage committee; supervisors' reports are also "*important*" although "*doing one bad piece of writing for your supervisor would not be the end of the world.*"

When we visited Atkin in 2011 the set hadn't offered tenancy to any of its pupils since 2008. But it did take on a third-sixer in 2010 who was subsequently offered tenancy. One junior was adamant that potential applicants shouldn't be put off by this: "*People mustn't think it's because we haven't had the work. We want to take on every pupil, but ultimately it depends on whether someone makes the cut in terms of quality.*" Atkin has since taken on one of its two pupils in both 2011 and 2012.

A question of tort

Around 25 applicants are invited to first interview with a panel of six tenants. Applications are judged primarily on academic credentials and personal statements. Candidates are asked two questions, one legal and one ethical. The first might be "*a question related to causation in contract or tort law,*" although "*it can be answered whether or not you have done a law degree,*" the head of the pupillage committee told us. The ethical question might be "*do you think prenuptials should always be binding?*" or "*does it make sense to have intervened in Libya and not in Syria?*" Interviews are as "*fair*" as possible, so there are no questions about your background or experiences. "*We wouldn't talk to someone about their skiing holiday – because that's not relevant to being a good barrister.*"

The set offers several two-day unassessed, unpaid mini-pupillages during July and September. Atkin also sponsors mooting contests at the LSE, Oxford, Cambridge and BPP Law School. The prize for the winners of these contests is a two-day mini and £500.

Atkin is a small set, but the atmosphere is more professional than cosy. That said, "*at the junior end everyone gets on well. There's a lot of popping into each other's offices to say 'hi'.*" The younger members take new pupils out for supper at the start of the year. There's also chambers tea every day at 4pm, but "*it's not like there is a hushed atmosphere where the silks hold forth and we listen,*" said a junior. "*We just have a natter. It's a mix of silks and juniors every day and pupils are encouraged but not required to go.*" A pupil added: "*Depending on who is leading the discussion, it veers from very funny to very informative.*"

And finally...

Whatever you do don't call Atkin 'just a construction set', but its reputation in this field and related areas of contracts and torts is very impressive.

2 Bedford Row

The facts

Location: Bedford Row, London

Number of QCs/Juniors: 20/60 (19 women)

Applications: 457

Apply through Pupillage Portal

Pupils per year: 4

Seats: 2x6 months

Pupillage award: £12,000 grant + £10,000 guaranteed earnings

"We get more exposure to trials in the mags' than anyone else I've heard of."

The crime-heavy pupillage here is *"an amazing thing to be part of,"* providing you are prepared to be on your feet...

Murder and lies

"You often see our QCs on the front of the Metro," one source told us in our visit to chambers this year. The many headline-hitting cases that go through 2 Bedford Row hint at why it has won top-tier rankings for both crime and criminal fraud in *Chambers UK*. The set is home to the mighty William Clegg QC, who made the news this year defending Vincent Tabak in the Joanna Yeates murder trial. The set's line-up of raw talent – and youthful QCs – is a key driver in its success. Outside of the crime and fraud world, 2BR has made a very big footprint thanks to some first-class names: Jim Sturman QC for sports, Ian Stern QC for professional discipline, and Richard Matthews QC for health and safety, to name a few.

In recent years, this defence-focused set has added practices in finance and regulatory work. As such, it has broadened its client base, which now encompasses major City firms and institutions, local councils, high street solicitors, offshore clients, Premier League football teams and public and international bodies. 2BR's latest assignments have seen it working with the European Court of Human Rights, acting for the General Medical Council, and taking cases before the Court of Arbitration for Sport.

Gone in 70 seconds

2 Bedford Row does everything with a no-nonsense attitude, and that includes the hiring process. If all the stuffy tradition and old boys' club stereotypes about the Bar put you off applying, then 2 Bedford Row may be your answer. *"We're not really that bothered if someone's from Oxbridge or not,"* reported a pupil, and head of pupillage

Stephen Vullo echoed this: *"I honestly don't know what uni the current pupils went to. They have to be bright, of course, but what we are really looking for is someone who is a good advocate on their feet."* All interviewees stressed this point, so take note. Two-Bedfordronians spend much more time in court than most, so the interview is built around judging advocacy potential.

Of the 457 applicants, the set aims to interview between 70 and 80. The panel gives the applicant a topic to argue with very brief preparation time. *"We tell candidates to talk for no more than 70 seconds,"* says Vullo. *"We are looking for brevity: half of them talk far too long and that weeds out a lot."* Don't be surprised if the panel gives you a different topic to argue seconds before the interview. That said, our interviewees did claim that the interview process is *"more straightforward than most places I applied to. There was no 'bad cop' on the panel."* In 2012, the set put 22 interviewees through to the second round, and four are usually awarded pupillage. The second round lasts a little longer and applicants are sent the exercise in advance. *They will be expected to give five to ten minutes on their feet. They will respond to our questions on it."*

"If you can't stand up and talk, don't apply," said one interviewee. Vullo elaborated: *"If we feel nervous for the person, they are not right for us. We look for poise and confidence. And we don't cross them off for getting minor legal points wrong."* A pupil also offered: *"Be as succinct as possible. They are looking for spontaneity."* Pupils also strongly recommended equipping yourself with prior experience, which will go some way to boosting your confidence in this advocacy-focused process.

Chambers UK rankings

Crime	Professional Discipline
Fraud	Sports Law
Health & Safety	

Sin City

In one of 2BR's swanky conference rooms, the pupils opened up to us about their lot. During the first six, senior clerk John Grimmer *"has us in court every day from the get-go."* During this time, pupils work for two supervisors simultaneously, but aren't allowed to represent clients themselves. *"During the second six you'll be in court from day one,"* though. *"Most of my work has been in the mags' courts defending cases like theft, assault and harassment,"* remarked one interviewee. The cases tend to be on the lighter end of the criminal scale during pupillage, but one interviewee was starting to get involved in *"cases like violent crime, rape, murder,"* while another mentioned weighty cases like *"child grooming, kidnap and fraud."* One even *"did some research on the Vincent Tabak case."*

"This isn't a glamorous job," thought one pupil, and speaking to those who had done pupillage here it becomes clear a hardy constitution is a must. *"They also need to put in the work,"* Grimmer plainly puts it. Pupils agreed that they often worked *"four out of five evenings a week, sometimes until midnight if you include travel."* One confided: *"When people ask me out for a beer I tell them this is like having two jobs."* The up-side, claimed one source, is that *"we get more exposure to trials in the mags' than anyone else I've heard of."*

This lifestyle evidently suits a certain type of person, and pupils recommended *"doing a mini-pupillage – it's the best way to work out if it's for you."* All agreed that the lifestyle was a price worth paying: *"The pupillage here is an amazing thing to be part of."* Vullo tells us: *"We are conscious not to crush people in pupillage. We always think pupils are worth investing in. Members here are expected to give up time to pupils."* And they really do invest the time; a snapshot of this might include *"Bill Clegg QC giving talks on tactics, Jim Sturman QC on closing speeches and Mark Milliken-Smith QC on cross-examination."* One junior enthused: *"This place is a breeding ground for success. You learn from class acts."*

Call of duty: Blackfriars ops

"Pupillage feels like a year-long interview," admitted a source. Pupils are judged on their performance throughout the year. *"You've got to do well on your feet,"* said one, but added, *"they put more emphasis on the second six."* The year culminates in a mock trial in Blackfriars Crown Court, which 2BR hires out for the purpose. A panel of silks and other members is there to judge the Blackfriars gig, and they give their verdict on tenancy towards the end of September, drawing upon performance throughout the year, too. Aside from the obvious advocacy points, the panel also looks for *"decent written work and recommendations from solicitors."*

So what's the magic formula to gaining tenancy? Awkwardly, the message seems to be: *"Keep a low profile, but impress everyone."* A junior added: *"It's not a popularity contest but you've got to fit with chambers: be respectful, work hard."* John Grimmer shed more light: *"We need to see clearly that in five years' time they will have a practice of their own."*

As we were shown through the doors of the grand Bloomsbury townhouse at no. 2 Bedford Row, it struck us that fitting in here isn't in fact the greatest challenge. Guided though a dark maze of corridors and a cavernous basement, we saw a set comfortable with its own disarray. Down there amid the piles of files we were greeted by a welcoming bunch ready to make friendly chat. Pupils confirmed this: *"The atmosphere is open, collegial and quite different to many sets."* Another chimed: *"There are some sets where pupils are viewed as a subspecies, but not here."* Instead, they are *"always included in things."* This set has no truck with ceremony or needless hierarchy; all interviewees threw around the phrase *"down to earth"* with abandon. The set puts on the usual welcome drinks, Christmas knees-ups and summer parties. Otherwise the hub of chambers' social life is at The Old Nick just round the corner. Friday drinks here are pretty common, unless you're a pupil, it seems, who *"genuinely don't have the time for much socialising."* Stephen Vullo adds: *"Part of the test for pupils is striking the right balance with socialising."* Chambers is also rumoured to take part in white-collar boxing – find out more if you get here...

The recruitment team wanted to stress to ethnic minority applicants that although its current line-up is hardly a beacon of diversity, it is striving to address this with future hiring. This doesn't mean the set is making exceptions. *"It's a level playing field once you're in the interview,"* said a pupil.

And finally...

There is no secret to the rewards of a 2BR pupillage – just make sure you're *"committed to the Criminal Bar and prepared to be in court."*

Blackstone Chambers

The facts

Location: Temple, London

Number of QCs/Juniors: 37/48 (21 women)

Applications: 400+

Apply through Pupillage Portal

Pupils per year: 4-5

Seats: 4x3 months

Pupillage Award: £60,000 (can advance £17,000 for BPTC)

There should be no limit to your ambitions at Blackstone, which is a standout performer in numerous practice areas.

Blackstone has maintained a standard of excellence and integrity in both work and recruitment. A pupillage here is full of promise.

Here comes the sun

Super-slick and smooth as silk – 37 of them to be precise – Blackstone can't help but impress. Sitting on the roof terrace heights and bathed in sunshine it was all too easy to forget the purpose of our visit, while indulging in the generous assortment of chocolate biscuits. But members of this renowned set succeeded in discussing their work as coolly as they did comprehensively. And, as expected, the practice is as varied as the biscuit selection. *Chambers UK* recognises Blackstone's practices in administrative and public law; employment; civil liberties and human rights; financial services; media and entertainment; telecommunications; and sport practices as being at the very top of the profession. Commercial dispute resolution, competition/EU law, immigration and civil fraud practices follow one tier behind in the rankings.

Chambers director Julia Horner broke it down for us. "*45% of chambers' work is under the general commercial umbrella; the rest is split between employment and public law*," she told us. "*Pupils experience all three.*" And it is the pupils who are seriously considered as the future of the set. Those that reach the top of the Blackstone ladder tend to be "*home-grown,*" Horner confirmed. Laterals are only "*specifically targeted to plug levels of seniority.*" Timothy Otty QC – with a glowing human rights, civil liberties, public international practice – is one of five such hires in the last two years. But for most juniors, if they play their cards right, there's no limit to their ascent.

This ascent promises excitement and complexity, as the set's recent work illustrates. Members appeared in the landmark constitutional case *R v Chaytor and Others*, which established that MPs and peers don't enjoy immunity from prosecution for expenses fraud by reason of Parliamentary privilege. It culminated before a nine-judge Supreme Court. In that same court, Blackstone members appeared in a gay asylum seeker's trial in which the Court ruled that refugee status may be granted where asylum seekers can show that revealing their homosexuality would lead to persecution in their home countries. At the other end of the spectrum, a whole host of members represented various parties in judicial review proceedings to determine what should be done with the Olympic Stadium after the 2012 Games. Darling of the Bar (Barling?) Dinah Rose QC and James Segan acted for Tottenham Hotspur FC; Lord Pannick QC, Ben Jaffey and Tom Cleaver for West Ham United FC; Adam Lewis QC, Tom Richards and Tom Mountford for Leyton Orient FC; and John Howell QC, Tom de la Mare and Paul Luckhurst for London Borough of Newham.

The long and winding road

The interview process at Blackstone was never going to be easy. Via Pupillage Portal, chambers receives around 400 applications. Five juniors and one silk – who more often than not is excused from this initial stage – sift through the applications. These are double-marked and if no consensus is reached, triple-marked. The committee looks "*not just at academics, but at FRU or mooting experience and evidence of potential at the Bar.*" References are sought before inviting candidates to first-round interview.

The first interview lasts roughly 15 minutes with about five members on the panel. It entails a general discussion

Chambers UK rankings

Administrative & Public Law	Fraud
Civil Liberties & Human Rights	Immigration
	Insurance
Commercial Dispute Resolution	Media & Entertainment
	Professional Discipline
Competition/European Law	Public International Law
Employment	Public Procurement
Environment	Sports Law
Financial Services	Telecommunications

about the Bar and requires interviewees to select one of six legal discussion points in advance. "*People who do best aren't the ones showcasing their legal knowledge. What they should be doing is exhibiting the relationship they would strike up with a judge,*" pupil supervisor and member of the pupillage committee Ben Jaffey says. One pupil described his 15 minutes as "*challenging, searching, but certainly not hostile.*"

Next comes a three-or-so day mini-pupillage in which at least two days will be spent doing "*actual work,*" with the opportunity to see some court advocacy as well. Those left in the game would do best to demonstrate thoughtfulness and enthusiasm towards the set rather than show off. After all, "*you don't really need to know much law to be a good barrister.*" Those who have already done a mini with Blackstone may skip this stage.

Finally, the second interview rolls around for about 16 "*serious contenders.*" It seems that at this final hurdle (to mix metaphors) the tables turn somewhat. Rather than assessing the remaining candidates, the panel seeks to gauge their keenness: whether they enjoyed the mini, the reasons why, and whether they would accept an offer. Members want to get the right 'fit' among the best of the best, so it's up to applicants to make very clear if Blackstone is indeed the apple of their eye. "*But don't expect a wink and a nudge.*" If you're successful, you won't know until the Pupillage Portal informs you in August…

A day in the life

As far as is possible, pupillage here is "*laid back.*" For starters, there is no limit to the number of tenancies on offer, which means "*pupils don't have to compete. If all four pupils deserve it, they'll all get it.*" Pupils rotate through four supervisors for three months at a time. "*It's incredibly fair. It's the same four supervisors for everyone and nobody is disadvantaged by circumstances.*" In 2011, the supervisors spanned the following specialisms: com-

mercial/financial, public/employment, EU/competition and sports law, exposing pupils to a "*serious breadth*" of work.

Pupils do what their supervisor does. On top of this they see a lot of FRU work. "*It's how we get our sea legs. It's not glamorous but it means that when we appear in court for the first time in a few years, we'll have a head start on our contemporaries in other sets.*" Another added: "*It's a great way to cut your teeth.*" Weirdly, pupils didn't give the impression of working themselves into the ground. "*We are masters of our own fate,*" they said, and any pressure felt is "*self-imposed.*"

But it's not all sunbathing and picnics. Throughout the pupillage year there are two advocacy exercises and six written exercises. A report is written up for each pupil after every seat, which assesses performance and potential. When it comes to tenancy decisions, with the reports and assessments in mind, it's one vote per member. In 2012, two of the five pupils were kept on; the other three were quick to find third sixes.

When I'm sixty-four

So why is it that people come to Blackstone and, more tellingly, stay there? Is it the appeal of wearing a hoodie and trainers to work once you're a tenant (the outfit sported by more than one member on the day of our visit)? Is it the fridge full of beers upstairs (occasionally Champagne, allegedly)? Is it the "*broad church of personalities*" that have congregated to combine and conquer "*equitable values with public law*"? Or perhaps the prominence of advocacy, less emphasised in similar sets? Several of these are bound to appeal.

For one pupil it was "*the feel not of a contrived 'open-door policy' but of doors being open as a natural by-product of the people in this set.*" This ties into the "*flatness*" Julia Horner sought to highlight. "*Everyone is on a first-name basis.*" Pupils enjoy subsidised events, like bowling, and all members join in chambers-wide events like the ever-popular, weather-defying summer garden party. There was even talk of a poetry society for more wistful members.

One thing is for sure, Blackstone won't be tinkering with its winning formula any time soon. And while Horner recognises that "*changes to the Bar mean sets will have to adapt,*" there is certainly no talk of Alternative Business Structures just yet at this one. "*People want to be barristers for the independence it affords them. We have the luxury of working with clients who still want us. We're big enough and good enough to maintain this standard of excellence.*"

And finally…
Keep applications short and sweet. "*And don't think that small things you've done can't be very telling.*"

1 Chancery Lane

The facts

Location: Chancery Lane, London

Number of QCs/Juniors: 5/39 (10 women)

Applications: 250

Outside Pupillage Portal

Pupils: 2 every other year

Seats: 3x4 months

Pupillage award: £40,000+

Known for its PI and clin neg work, 1 Chancery Lane is a mixture of *"the traditional and progressive."*

This go-getting set is a friendly and specialised civil outfit.

Talking happy talk

1 Chancery Lane is renowned for its clinical negligence, professional indemnity, personal injury, property, human rights, police law, education and travel law expertise. Its biggest clients range from local authorities and the NHS to insurers and regulators like the Bar Standards Board. Chambers continues to receive instructions in high-value brain damage and cerebral palsy cases involving substantial claims for future care. In the Admiralty Court, it acted as counsel for the defendant tour operator in a multiparty action arising from a much-publicised incident involving a collapsing iceberg. Public sector clients include Hampshire and Surrey county councils.

Now found at a prime location on Chancery Lane, chambers has come a long way over the last 60 years. *"It was originally a very traditional and varied set. There were about 20 barristers and we did everything from civil to criminal cases,"* explained senior clerk Clark Chessis. *"Chambers then had a vision and decided to develop certain specialisms. In 1991 we moved out of Temple – we were one of the earliest sets to do so – which gave a clear message as to the direction we were moving in. Over the next five to six years, crime left and we became a wholly civil set."* The set moved to its current space in 2006 in *"order to give the best impression to our clients."* It now numbers 44 barristers, *"our largest yet,"* and intends to keep growing.

Chambers takes on two pupils every other year, *"so that we can ensure we're able to give each pupil plenty of individual attention and the best possible chance of obtaining tenancy."* Two candidates have just secured pupillages starting in October. The next intake will be in 2015, with applications welcome from October 2013. The pupillage award, you'll be happy to hear, will be no less than £40,000, and chambers will consider requests to draw down part of the award during the BPTC year.

This chambers operates outside the Pupillage Portal, and has instead fashioned a *"very tailored and structured"* online application form for candidates to fill out. Current pupils explained: *"The application is long and pretty challenging. Beyond the standard high academic credentials, there are a number of 'who are you?' type questions."* For example: 'Please give us an example of a time when you have managed people's expectations or influenced people in some way'; or 'what qualities do you think are required to be a good barrister?' With just 200 words to play with for each answer, *"it's a difficult application to hide in."*

The interview is conducted by a panel of three and there's *"always a junior member of chambers who sits in as an observer."* Current pupils are used to helping candidates around the building and lending an ear to any minor queries. Candidates receive a problem question prior to the panel and are then scored on their reasoning and articulation throughout the interview. The set gets over 200 applications every round, which are *"sifted down to 50 using a selection of members, then to 20 by two different members."*

1 Chancery Lane looks for candidates who are *"hardworking, intelligent, with good communication skills,"* confirmed members Karen Shuman and Geoffrey Weddell. *"Most of our work is actually advocacy, so we need good communicators: those who can make people feel at ease."* Baby juniors added: *"We're a friendly set, so we need someone who is businesslike – but personable. A*

Chambers UK rankings

Clinical Negligence	Professional Negligence
Personal Injury	Travel
Police Law	

lot of the Bar is about networks." Not the 'old boy' type, however – the set is diverse and "*we are not all about certain schools or universities.*" We notice that, as of August 2012, the six most junior tenants are Oxford, Durham, York and Leeds graduates. How to impress? "*People need to have done their homework. You have to know what we do and show you have an interest. Read cases that our senior members do! The information is so accessible.*" Pupils also stressed that current affairs discussions – legal and non-legal – crop up regularly throughout the interview process.

Chances of space

The pupillage is divided into three seats of four months, each with a different supervisor who has completed a specific training course. "*Chambers encourages and leans on people to get the training done. We want to give back to the pupils.*"

During the first six months pupils are exposed to a variety of paperwork, like undertaking written instructions, carrying out legal research and assisting supervisors in the preparation of cases. In the second six, pupils told us, "*you really are in court two or three times a week.*" Pupils receive instructions across a range of County Court matters and interim applications. One explained that they were taking on "*small claims cases, possessions and applications – all representative of junior practice.*"

There are also written assessments to be undertaken throughout pupillage, "*one for each member of ADCO, the admissions committee.*" Interviewees explained that "*generally you won't start your assessed work until the second four.*" As chambers is extremely diligent with feedback, mistakes during the second six and in assessment are frowned upon: "*Really you should have made*

any mistakes during the first half of the pupillage." Tenancy decisions are "*made in June by ADCO.*" As barristers Karen Shuman and Geoffrey Weddell explained, "*at the end of the year, every member of ADCO will meet the supervisors, get feedback from the clerks and assess how pupils have done. Pupil supervisors also supplement the meetings with reports – then a majority vote is taken. It is a long process, but we feel that it's a necessary one.*" Pupils are told mid-July. The set commented: "*Pupils are an investment and we might take them on even if there isn't enough work in that first year. We won't turn people away who we think are good enough for reasons of space.*"

The definition of tea

1 Chancery Lane is a mixture between "*the traditional and progressive. The set is still run by silks, which is obviously more traditional, but our offices are super-modern.*" Though still based in the historic legal hub of London, chambers inhabits a newbuild with hi-tech features. There's plenty of space and light, plus black and white photographs of a capital of yesteryear.

Afternoon tea's still a welcome event. Pupils assured us they're "*always included*" and thought it was "*really nice.*" This inclusiveness was pervasive: "*We all have our own rooms and desks and everyone knows each other. There are lots of different people and we are very collegiate.*" Pupils also thought the pupillage programme encouraged "*support and friendship and at no point do you feel in direct competition with those around you.*"

There are two Christmas parties, the "*themed second one*" coming in February. There are plenty of lunches, "*including taking over Dr Johnson's House one year for a property do,*" and summer parties as well. Pupils also meet regularly for "*informal drinks.*" Hours are, on the whole, not bad for the Bar. "*Pupils are normally kicked out at 6pm and you really don't take anything home.*" Baby juniors feel they are "*here to work, but not for it to take over our lives. You are very much in control of your own diary and it is rare to leave after 8pm.*"

And finally...
Chambers recruits every other year, and both pupils were offered tenancy in 2012.

Crown Office Chambers

The facts

Location: Inner Temple, London
Number of QCs/Juniors: 13/73 (20 women)
Applications: 150-200
Outside Pupillage Portal
Pupils per year: 2-3
Seats: 2x3 and 1x6 months
Pupillage award: £42,500 (can advance £15,000 for BPTC)

COC's diverse areas of practice give it a solid foundation to withstand whatever the economy and changing professional environment might throw at it.

The Bar's biggest common law set boasts a broad practice and is praised by pupils and juniors for its "*focus on early advocacy experience.*"

No objection, your honour

"*This week I started out doing an infant approval hearing. Then yesterday I had a directions hearing in Uxbridge. And tomorrow I'm going to Ilford where I'll be on my feet in a small claims case. My week has been a blur!*" The enthusiastic words of this second-six pupil are a good reflection of the whirlwind pupillage experience at Crown Office Chambers. COC was formed in 2000 as the result of a merger between One Paper Buildings and Two Crown Office Row. Since then it has expanded – though only slightly – from about 75 members to just under 90. Its core practice areas are personal injury, construction, health and safety, insurance, property damage, professional negligence, clinical negligence and product liability work.

On the insurance/property damage side, members have been heavily involved in the Buncefield oil depot explosion as well as in the employers' liability 'trigger' litigation regarding the liability of employers and insurers in asbestos disease claims. COC is recognised as London's premier set for both industrial disease and health and safety work. There are also scores of small cases like the claimant who was attacked by a herd of cows while crossing a field in the Lake District. COC's construction work often relates to engineering, road-building and telecommunications projects, with an increasing number of international and multi-jurisdictional disputes.

In most of these cases COC will be acting for the defendant. "*Traditionally we act for a lot of insurance companies,*" senior managing clerk Andy Flanagan told us. "*And most of our cases will contain insurance issues somewhere along the line.*" Go online to read more about COC's work.

Flanagan tells us COC has been successful in developing the range and amount of work over the past few years. "*The proposed MoJ reforms will no doubt impact slightly on the availability of PI work. However, we are well placed to be able to deal with such challenges and are always looking at new, innovative ways of attracting new work and expanding already established practice areas.*"

Oral specs

COC recruits two to three pupils a year. It's not a member of the Pupillage Portal scheme and you can download the application directly from its website. Mini-pupillages and mooting are pretty much "*prerequisites*" for applicants. What will really make you stand out is good, well-written answers and interesting experiences on your application form. A member of the pupillage committee told us: "*What might be interesting is if someone has a theatrical background and took classes at RADA or put on a play.*"

Of the 150 applicants, 40 to 50 are invited to a first interview with two or three tenants, which lasts 15 minutes. Applicants are asked general CV questions, why the Bar, why COC, and one or two logical reasoning questions. "*I told them my hobbies were yoga and playing the piano, so the logical reasoning question they asked me was to convince them to take up one over the other. Then they asked me to argue the reverse. So you really need to be able to show flexibility of mind.*"

Around ten hopefuls get through to a second-round 30-minute interview with five tenants. Candidates are first asked a problem question for which they get half an hour

Chambers UK rankings

Clinical Negligence	International Arbitration
Construction	Personal Injury
Health & Safety	Product Liability
Insurance	Professional Negligence

to prepare prior to the interview. *"They will often be given a contract to read. Then in the interview they will be given certain facts and asked how the contract would apply. So for example, you have to know if something counts as 'reasonable loss'."* There's also an ethical question like, *"what would you do if you accepted an offer of settlement and then your client revealed there's documentation they have not disclosed?"* In short: good, clear oral skills are the key to gaining pupillage.

Newport state of mind

Pupillage is spent with three supervisors – the same three for each pupil. In the first six pupils shadow their supervisors' work. *"Usually I would be drafting a defence before or just after he is. Then he would show me his and we would look at the work together,"* a pupil told us. *"This is not the sort of set where they are sending out a pupil's drafts from day one."* A baby junior recalled: *"I worked on both live cases and cases which my supervisor had done in the past. It's great because you are doing the work of someone ten to 15 years' call, so it includes some high-profile stuff like the Buncefield Court of Appeals case. I also worked on pleadings, pieces of advice and notes for my supervisor to use."* The set ensures pupils see a mix of work during pupillage. *"One of my supervisors' work was entirely construction and commercial, one's was entirely PI and one's was a mix of PI and insurance,"* said a junior. In their first six, pupils also do four oral advocacy exercises.

Second-six pupils will be on their feet almost immediately. They get small PI cases – often RTAs – or infant approval hearings, and appear in court up to three times a week. (On average pupils make £10,000 in earnings during their second six.) *"The priority in getting you on your feet is to practise putting your case and cross-examination. You get so much responsibility. One of my opponents last week was 25 years' call!"* As if to demonstrate this point, one of the pupils showed us a crammed lever arch file he had just been handed by the clerks. During our visit, another of the pupils was called from the room by the clerks. *"Fast-track PI trial over an RTA with multiple wit-nesses,"* he said, looking excited and just a tad terrified, *"scheduled for tomorrow at 10am at Newport."* Devilling is also expected of pupils in their second six. *"Your supervisor will help you set up work for other members. If they come to you with work they will check with him first."*

COC members are passionate about oral advocacy. *"I wanted to be on my feet day to day, dealing with judges and clients,"* a baby junior told us. For the first two or three years of tenancy PI makes up the *"vast majority"* of cases along with small commercial contract disputes. They are also *"led on one or two big cases a year."* As they become more senior, tenants unofficially specialise in one of three broad areas: PI and clin neg; construction, insurance and prof neg; or health and safety regulatory.

Curry-ing favours

The tenancy decision is based on two written assessments (one six months in and one just before the tenancy meeting), the advocacy exercises in the first six, written feedback from supervisors and written feedback from members of chambers pupils have worked for. Feedback from supervisors is the most important factor in the tenancy decision. The combination of written assessments, individual casework and devilling in the run-up to tenancy can be stressful and hours can shoot up. *"For the first nine months of pupillage you do work 9am to 6pm, but when you start coming up to tenancy the hours are longer and you sometimes end up working till 9 or 10pm."*

COC's size means there is no pervading culture. *"Members have different styles and different approaches, some traditional, some more modern, but the overall result is that we have someone for every client in every core practice area,"* Andy Flanagan told us. *"Chambers is very social at the junior end,"* a junior told us. Juniors frequent Inner Temple's Pegasus Bar and there's a *"juniors' curry night"* at Temple Tandoori. Pupils feel quite *"close"* to this group of juniors and are invited to almost all socials. The relationships between the juniors and clerks is close and friendly. *"I'm on chambers' football and cricket teams with some juniors and some clerks,"* a junior told us.

With time, *"everyone does meet one another"* and *"you come to know everyone well enough to be able to chat with them"* although there are *"different personalities."* Weekly Friday drinks in chambers are patronised by a mix of members and clerks; there's also the annual Christmas *"knees-up,"* held on board 'HMS President' last year.

And finally...

This set has a good track record of keeping on pupils. Between 2007 and 2010 it took on nine pupils out of the 11 who spent time there. In 2011 two of four were taken on. One pupil was offered tenancy in 2012.

One Essex Court

The facts

Location: Temple, London

Number of QCs/Juniors: 27/49 (12 women)

Applications: c.200

Apply through Pupillage Portal

Pupils per year: 4+

Seats: 2x3 and 1x6 months

Pupillage Award: £60,000 + earnings
(can advance £20,000 for BPTC)

"Finding the right set for you is like finding the perfect partner – you have a major part in choosing it, and you shouldn't lose sight of that."

It's *"excellence without arrogance"* at this elite set, which puts a premium on quality work while insisting its tenants remain *"grounded and focused."*

Gold standard for client service

One Essex Court was founded in 1966 as a mixed civil and commercial set. Though a relative newcomer to the market in comparison to some of its old-school neighbours, what OEC lacks in history it makes up for in rapid success: the set quickly overtook its competitors under the direction of former senior clerk Robert Ralphs, who *"recognised the virtues of client service at a time when it was a rarity."* Since reconfiguring its business to serve clients first and foremost, the set has done nothing but flourish.

OEC's strength in commercial law cases has propelled it into the Bar's magic circle, and management claims the set has *"a wider range of work than any other commercial set."* The real engines of OEC are arbitration, banking and finance, civil fraud and energy work, although tenants also take on a sizeable amount of revenue, competition and EU, IP and insolvency work, too. *"The joy of our thriving practice is that every day you're dealing with different problems,"* senior clerk Darren Burrows explains. While tenants dabble in a variety of areas, he says the set *"is hardly rag-tag: our core is commercial, but we're fortunate to have practitioners with niche strengths,"* pointing out that such members are *"credible market specialists, not just barristers who fancy trying out that kind of work."* Indeed, household names such as Google, easyJet, eBay and Yahoo! have all approached the set's renowned IP experts recently to handle complex trade mark and copyright disputes. Because its tenants tackle a wide range of industry sectors, OEC has a broad range of clients – from magic circle City law firms to banks and individuals – and is less susceptible to the market fluctu-

ation experienced by sets that specialise in areas like insolvency. According to Burrows, the set's management has spent the past decade *"focusing hard on attaining new markets and clients with the aim of broadening the practice without losing any of our quality. By working within two or three distinct markets at any one time, we've steadily and healthily climbed to the top."*

Burrows is intent on preserving the high quality of client service ushered in by his predecessors, which entails upholding *"a gold-standard reputation of reliability."* For this reason, the set is one of few that implements a strict no double-booking policy. Chambers is also looking to expand under his leadership, probably into East Asia as *"it's well placed in the market"* and *"there are clear corporate and dispute resolution opportunities out there."*

It's all in the argument

Pupils at OEC are among the highest paid at the Bar, which partially accounts for OEC's substantial volume of applications each year. This translates into a hefty paper sift for the pupillage committee, so current pupils suggest that applicants spend a lot of time on their applications to ensure they aren't discounted at the first stage due to *"silly mistakes like grammatical errors."* It's also important to submit an application that's *"a true representation of yourself."* As one pupil put it: *"Finding the right set for you is like finding the perfect partner – you have a major part in choosing it, and you shouldn't lose sight of that."* Completing a mini-pupillage, while it does *"show a sign of interest,"* isn't required because of limited availability at the set.

Chambers UK rankings

Banking & Finance	Energy & Natural Resources
Commercial Dispute Resolution	Fraud
	Intellectual Property
Competition/European Law	International Arbitration

While successful applicants all have the common quality of academic excellence, members of the pupillage committee say the "*turning point is our assessment of their legal ability: not just how well they do on the day of the interview, but our ability to see them succeeding in the long run.*" For this reason, it's imperative that an applicant be "*a natural advocate – someone who's good at generating confidence in their argument. People who are capable comprise a wide variety of personalities, so we don't pigeon-hole and look for a certain character.*" That said, pupils say that being grounded and focused is important, as is a bit of humility. "*Absolutely no one is arrogant here, even those who have cause to be.*"

The 30-40 applicants who make it through the first stage of the application process face just one interview, which is based on a test of analytical abilities, "*not a chat on whether you can look and act like a barrister.*" One QC explained the process in detail: "*We give them a legal problem and then lock them in the basement with a copy of Chitty on Contracts – and a window if they're lucky! – and let them prep for 90 minutes.*" The problems are "*framed in a manner that doesn't prejudice those without a law degree,*" and pupils claim that "*it doesn't actually matter whether your answer's right – it's all about how you present and support your argument.*"

Over the past decade, OEC's number of pupillage and tenancy offers has been roughly in proportion to the number of applicants with law degrees and those who've completed the graduate diploma in law, so aspiring barristers with "*less traditional*" backgrounds are equally as welcome as the Oxbridge-educated law students who dominate the profession.

Not competitive

Pupils spend time with at least three supervisors during their year at the set, which exposes them to a range of different cases and working styles. "*The aim is to show them variety,*" so they don't always work exclusively for a single supervisor and have the opportunity to follow junior members. According to one, "*it's difficult to generalise*" the kinds of work pupils come into contact with, as it's "*so unbelievably varied: you can be researching code one day and doing admin work like bundling the next.*" Most of this work is live, but luckily "*the support is great*" and there are "*plenty of opportunities to find your feet.*" Court appearances generally occur in the second six, when pupils begin attending "*low-value*" trials such as traffic court cases to gain advocacy experience. Because OEC tends to favour complex, high-value commercial matters that require the expertise of more experienced barristers, it can sometimes be difficult for pupils or even junior members to gain substantive advocacy experience at the beginning of their careers. However, management makes a special effort to offer opportunities to appear in court through an arrangement with a number of provincial firms in which younger juniors work on fixed-fee cases for a lowered rate.

Six months into pupillage, there's a review to evaluate the pupil's progress. According to one QC, "*we never kick anyone out, although sometimes, very rarely, we tell one that they might want to consider other options.*" Each piece of work pupils submit is marked out of ten and collected into a folder, which the pupillage committee examines when making the final tenancy decision in June. Because the set "*aims to keep all pupils on,*" an all-around healthier working environment is fostered. "*We were told on our first day that we're not in competition with each other, which immediately made us all relax. Knowing that has made it so much more enjoyable and has made it possible to have real friendships with each other,*" one told us. "*Being immediately regarded with the potential to become a tenant certainly makes the experience a happier one.*"

The atmosphere of OEC is relatively informal compared to that at some commercial sets, which Burrows attributes to the chambers' "*noticeable evolution over the last 40 years.*" Everyone's on a first-name basis, and barristers maintain relationships in which they get together occasionally, but "*don't live in each other's pockets.*" As one quipped: "*We're a set, not a cult.*" Pupils are invited to all the social events, which are "*not terribly formal*" and include occasional luncheons and Friday night drinks.

And finally...

All four pupils were granted tenancy in 2012, and they called the high retention rate at OEC "*a real selling point. It's a true meritocracy, and you'll get an offer if you're good enough.*"

Thirty Nine Essex Street

The facts

Location: Temple, London; Manchester

Number of QCs/Juniors: 31/63 (29 women)

Applications: 390

Apply through Pupillage Portal

Pupils per year: 3

Seats: 4 (varying duration)

Pupillage award: £47,500 (can advance £8,000 for BPTC)

"I'm so glad I came here, I can't emphasise that enough."

If the quality of the boardroom biscuits is anything to go by, this democratic set means business – albeit with a somewhat cuddly edge.

It's Business Time

"The office has a slicker feel than most chambers," said one interviewee. Our visit to Thirty Nine Essex Street confirmed this. Within this ornate, stone-clad Victorian pile, gone is the barrister's decor of choice: books, wood panels, are eschewed in favour of a frosted-glass-doors look. Glossy brochures and sleek conference rooms were more evocative of a (dare we say it?) law firm than barristers' chambers. To top it off, the set has recently morphed into an LLP in the name of *"business efficiency."* Chief executive – we'd expect nothing less – David Barnes' aim to *"treat the place like a big business"* has evidently paid off, with the set's clients saluting its *"very businesslike"* style. Chambers has extended its brand beyond London, with an office in Manchester and plans to open a Singapore office shortly, with pupillage potential.

The set has beefed up in recent years, with a now 94-strong pack of barristers. This growth has won a broader array of *Chambers UK* rankings – it entered the construction arbitration tables for the first time in 2012. Its core practices continue to wow the market, those being personal injury, environment, Court of Protection, and professional discipline. A big draw for applicants is the set's emphasis on public law, where it wins headline-grabbing cases, such as Robert Jay QC's appointment as lead counsel to the Leveson inquiry. The group also recently acted for Friends of the Earth in a case against the Secretary of State for Energy and Climate Change. The set's immigration and human rights work regularly sees members acting for the Home Office on the international stage. Interviewees agreed that the sheer variety of work on offer is exceptional.

Fou le Fair Fair

Fairness pervades everything during pupillage. Co-head of pupillage Charles Cory-Wright QC has built the hiring process and pupillage around this ethos. The set does *"spread the net wide"* to interview invites, although 2:2 candidates need a stonking CV to be in with a chance. All sources agreed that outside interests are a strong indicator of the well-rounded candidate Thirty Nine Essex Street is looking for. *"You are very much encouraged to be a whole person throughout your time here,"* said a pupil, who received strict orders to *"get the hell down the Barbican!"* for a spot of culture.

Sixty hopefuls made it to interview from the 390 applicants. In the first interview they were faced with a panel of three and given a problem in *"an area of law you know very little about, something high level."* The panel assesses *"rhetorical ability, intellectual agility, and how succinctly you present,"* says Cory-Wright. *"The panel is straightforward. They don't go easy on you, they press you, but it brings the potential out of us,"* a pupil recalled. Eighteen candidates made it through to the second round. For 30 minutes the panel hits candidates with questions covering *"legal problems, politics and morals, and a final question about themselves."* One interviewee admitted: *"The testing is rigorous, as if you were responding to a judge in court. You need to respond quickly and effectively."* The panel wants to see your personality; *"they will test your human side,"* an interviewee remarked. *"If you assess the situation from just the legal perspective, you'll fail."*

From 2012 pupils begin in September, giving the set an extra month to allow for a more thorough, *"fairer assessment."* The pupillage year spans four seats (no, we swear this isn't a law firm), with the first of the four being a

Chambers UK rankings

Administrative & Public Law	International Arbitration
Civil Liberties & Human Rights	Local Government
	Personal Injury
Clinical Negligence	Planning
Construction	Product Liability
Costs Litigation	Professional Discipline
Court of Protection	Professional Negligence
Environment	Tax
Immigration	

law; commercial and construction law; public law, in which pupils raved about doing *"quite advanced opinions early on;"* and environmental and planning law, which for one pupil meant *"lots of wind farm work."* Applicants looking for variety with a public law leaning should consider number 39. David Barnes adds: *"If they have an ambition in a particular area, that's encouraged, but we do also encourage them to embrace chambers' breadth."*

"They are rigorous about pupils working no longer than nine 'til six. They recognise what a difficult year it is," a source told us. Cory-Wright elaborates: *"If you don't enforce that it means the playing field between pupils isn't equal."* There's that fairness thing again. The work during pupillage aims to nurture documenting and advocacy skills above all else. The first six is non-practising, and pupils are assigned a supervisor for each seat, whom they shadow. *"A lot of chambers have pupils doing supervisors' work, but not here. Instead the pupils do the case once the supervisor has done it, so the supervisor can compare and mark it."*

The second six typically sees pupils taking *"two cases a week in court. You're on your own, doing small cases."* That said, one pupil effused: *"My first instruction was for the Supreme Court, it was a big case by an insurance company over fraudulent claims. It was AMAZING! But that's a measure of the generosity of Chambers. They promote us as far as they can."* Another interviewee was let loose on *"a single public enquiry into Iraq, a multimillion-pound gold mine case involving international law, and I worked on the Worboys case"* – that was the cab driver rapist case, for which Edwin Glasgow QC acted for the ten victims. Because pupils often shadow high-level QCs, *"the quality of work is fantastic. The downside is that when you get tenancy, it goes right back down to the lower level."*

Everything I do...

"Everything you do during the first year is assessed for tenancy," said a pupil, *"so you get a pretty good idea of how you're progressing."* Supervisors provide a report during and at the end of each seat, making eight throughout the year, *"so we can see how they have developed."* Supervisors judge the pupils *"on things like rhetorical, intellectual and written ability."* In addition there are two formal assessments, again, dripping with the set's trademark fairness: *"They are assessed by someone who's not your supervisor, and blind-marked."* An interviewee confided: *"This was the worst bit."* They are *"significant pieces of work."* One recent example was in the form of advice in a Court of Protection case. There is also an advocacy exercise in the second six. *"It's a mock courtroom – we don't watch them in court because that would be unfair."* Have we mentioned fairness yet?

One interviewee advised: *"Be aware that everything is assessed and don't pretend you're someone you're not."* And another helping of chambers niceness: *"We don't set up competition between pupils. We don't see any merit in hiring more pupils than you have places for,"* says Cory-Wright. *"You just have to do well rather than better than your team mates."* The other benefit of this is, as one pupil put it: *"The four of us pupils stuck together and learnt from each other."*

Interviewees recounted how the QCs take a personal interest in their success and took one out for *"incredible champagne when I got tenancy."* *"There is a real spirit of giving in these chambers,"* enthused a pupil. Another source said they applied here because *"everyone seemed like brilliant, normal people."* We certainly detected a cuddly, chummy vibe at number 39, and one interviewee told us how *"they value the human side here enormously."*

"Fitting in here is about engaging with people," summed up one source. And there is ample opportunity to do so, whether it's the fortnightly chambers lunches, playing skittles with the clerks at Bloomsbury Bowl, or sharing some refreshment at the Edgar Wallace. The atmosphere is inclusive, *"you never feel watched when socialising here,"* and *"you are not allowed to pay for anything as a pupil."* If freebie nosh is a factor in your applications, then you'll be comforted to know that *"you get fed really well here, there are cakes everywhere... people just give you food."* During our investigation we sampled the boardroom biscuits, and for that moment felt like one pupil reflecting on the year: *"I'm so glad I came here, I can't emphasise that enough."*

And finally...

Over the past five years the set has taken on 12 of the 14 who underwent pupillage, and about half of the members trained at number 39.

Government Legal Service (GLS)

The facts

Location: London

Number of barristers: 450

Applications (solicitor and barrister route): 2,900

Outside Pupillage Portal

Pupils per year: Varies: c.5-15

Seats: 2x6 or 3x4 months

Pupillage award: £23,250-£25,575 + BPTC fees and a maintenance grant of £5,435-£7,625

With a varied pupillage and the chance to work on "*really big cases*," the GLS is an impressive alternative to the independent Bar.

Should you favour stability over independence, generalism over specialism and the chance to draft legislation over the glamour of advocacy, the GLS's unique pupillage could be for you.

Our country's good

Fancy working on issues as varied as prisoners' rights, the Pensions Bill or the cost of drugs to the NHS? More than 30 government departments – from Her Majesty's Revenue & Customs (HMRC) to the Ministry of Justice (MoJ) – employ lawyers. People here tend to be attracted by public service's altruism: "*It all seems a bit more real and everything you work on has a direct effect on someone you know.*"

At the time of our calls there were 16 pupils at the GLS: eight in the Treasury Solicitor's Department (TSol), two in HMRC, and three apiece in Business, Innovation & Skills (BIS) and Work & Pensions/Health (DWP/H). The structure of pupillage differs between 'home' departments. TSol pupils take two six-month seats; those in other departments will more likely spend four months in three different groups. To the envy of their trainee counterparts (see page 295), they qualify after one year and spend two years as 'legal officers' before they notch up the pay scale again to become Grade 7 lawyers. "*As far as the Bar is concerned you're qualified after a year – a good way of looking at it is you spend a year learning to be a barrister and a year learning to be a civil servant. The second year is when you really get to grips with how Whitehall works. The first teaches you about the courts, but you don't understand how policy gets turned into government policy until your second year.*"

Wannabe barristers apply in the same way the GLS's trainee solicitors do, merely specifying their preferred path on the application form. There's not actually that much to distinguish between the two routes after qualification, so why choose the pupillage as opposed to traineeship? "*The skills taught on the BPTC were far more relevant to what we do at the GLS,*" was one person's answer. There's "*still a lot of drafting and opinion-writing,*" though not offering the advocacy opportunities of the private Bar. HMRC still does some of its own though, "*but it's the kind of thing a solicitor advocate would do – people shouldn't come here thinking they'll do vast amounts of advocacy, as it's just not the kind of place where you get to perform in court.*"

Ch-ch-ch-ch-chambers

One seat will be spent away from Whitehall at a leading barristers' chambers. "*Taking a GLS pupil is seen as a sign that you're a top set, as the GLS only sends people places where they also send a lot of work.*" Time spent in chambers has a dual purpose: GLS employees spend a lot of time instructing barristers, so "*it's great to understand how the other side works, get an idea of issues and build contacts.*" Equally, "*there's some training that the GLS just can't give – it's a recognition that should you want to leave the employed Bar, it'd be a bit odd if you'd never had experience in chambers.*"

TSol offers "*legal services to most departments, but mainly litigation.*" The department is divided between public and private work – "*you deal with a lot of different departments and go into a lot of detail on the specifics of other people's working lives.*" Pupils should receive "*work *from one really big case, which should give interesting, headline work.*" There's also the opportunity to deal with smaller files: "*I had a sideline in revoking people's driving licences due to fraud at the testing centre,*" revealed one pupil. There's a lot of breach of contract and inquest work too. In public law and planning "*you can see work that spans trials about tuition fees to arguments about solar panel subsidies.*" The latter involved the government's fight to cut solar panel incentives to 21p per kWh of energy generated from the previous 43p. Proceedings were successfully brought by Friends of the Earth to prevent this. Pupils also help draft new legislation.

The other key strand of work for trainee barristers is policy advice. "*A minister will come up with a great idea, we have to look at it and say they can't do it or they'll get sued – it's all about the ability to communicate.*" In DWP/H there's unsurprisingly a lot of work on the implications of Andrew Lansley's Health and Social Care Act. "*There's a lot of interaction with policy clients, and you then get to see the policy develop as you advise on it.*" There's also work on pharmaceutical pricing: "*It's the question of how much the NHS should pay for its drugs. On one hand they're under patent, but on the other hand, it's such a big purchaser that it could set the price – the work involves analysing how much a drug is actually worth, also against the context of EU legislation on pricing.*"

The Daily Mail test

If you've read our feature on the GLS's training contract on page 295 you won't need telling twice about the benefits of public service. Stability, regular hours and immediate responsibility are only three. If there's a lack of agency in where barristers choose to be, our sources said it was a pay-off worth taking. "*If you're going to have a monthly salary, holidays and a pension, it seems fair that the government is occasionally entitled to have a say in what you do with your life,*" thought one. Remaining generalists and forgoing the sky-high earnings of those at the private Bar – in addition to forgoing advocacy – is a choice, but one it's easier to make when "*you can walk in at 10am and leave at 7pm.*"

But publicly employed barristers didn't get where they are today just because of an aversion to corporate hours. It helps to be extremely into "*the convergence between law and politics. To some extent they're both sides of the same coin, as it's about vital decision-making, albeit in different ways.*" Many see the civil servants' impartiality as an extension of the barristers' cab-rank rule. "*One of the things about government work is you sometimes have to defend things that aren't that nice, but you can't criticise it because you're defending something called a democratically elected parliament. I'm happy defending positions I wouldn't necessarily agree with myself as you're not defending the policy, you're defending the capacity to make it. To work for the GLS, you must ultimately believe that politics works, though.*"

Most departments are "*quite family-oriented,*" though there's "*a good amount of drinking on Fridays.*" TSol's slightly more corporate vibe shouldn't be mistaken for anything hard-nosed. "*Management makes a huge effort to involve staff with the department's plans, and we're encouraged to solve problems collaboratively by e-mailing round.*" If there are grumbles, they come down to the "*irritations*" of a life in the civil service. "*We have to bring in our own tea bags otherwise an MP would end up asking a question in Parliament about staff spending, or if I see a first-class train ticket that's cheaper than second-class I still can't buy it. It's a recognition that politics isn't commercially logical, but part of our training is to understand and manage this.*"

And finally...
Life in the GLS is "*not just about being very smart, it's about communicating effectively with ministers.*"

4-5 Gray's Inn Square

The facts

Location: Gray's Inn, London

Number of QCs/Juniors: 16/40 (12 women)

Applications: 300

Apply through Pupillage Portal

Pupils per year: Up to 3

Seats: 4x3 months

Pupillage award: £40,000 (some can be drawn down for BPTC)

Since 2005 this set has offered tenancy to all 14 of its pupils.

4-5 Gray's Inn Square stands tall for its flair for public law, and offers pupils a solid grounding ion planning cases.

Snug as a bug in a rug

4-5's members excel in a number of areas of public law. Planning is the largest single bread-winner among them, alongside immigration, education, and work for local authorities. The set is active on a ton of judicial reviews and many public inquiries, as well as employment, professional discipline and commercial cases. This range of practices is reflected in the pupillage and junior experience. *"The breadth of practice at the junior end is exceptional,"* one baby barrister told us. *"I do public, planning, environment, commercial and professional discipline work."*

The set has carved out a real name acting for respondents. *"As a whole the set's work is split 75:25 between defendant and claimant,"* a junior estimated. *"People are increasingly doing more claimant work, especially at the junior end. My own work is 50:50 claimant /respondent."* We can't talk about every area of the set's work here, so we'll focus on the set's three main stocks-in-trades: planning, public law and commercial.

Planning work slowed during the recession, but there are a still a high number of ongoing and planned infrastructure projects across the UK. One 4-5 silk recently represented an alliance of 17 local authorities in their opposition to the HS2 high speed line between London and Birmingham. Members have also been involved with inquiries into the Mersey Gateway and Thames Gateway projects. The former is a plan to build the first new bridge over the Mersey in 50 years, while the latter centred around the protection of bug life in Thurrock, Essex. Other barristers have been involved with litigation over various airport and rail projects, including the compulsory purchase of property around Birmingham New Street station for redevelopment.

Recent public law cases which members have been involved with include *R (Adams) v Secretary of State for Justice* concerning the circumstances under which someone can receive compensation for being wrongfully convicted of a criminal offence, and *R (GC) v Commissioner of Police of the Metropolis* – the Supreme Court case which established that the retention of DNA records of non-suspects is unlawful. Members have also worked on judicial reviews on everything from the treatment of a girl who had been trafficked to Britain from Congo as a sex worker, to Westminster City Council's decision to charge motor cyclists a £1 parking fee. Other members recently worked on the inquiry into the death of Baha Mousa in custody in Iraq.

A good chunk of 4-5's commercial work is closely related to public law (with cases heard in the Administrative Court). An example of the former is the case of *British Bankers Association v the Financial Services Authority and the Financial Ombudsman Service* over the mis-selling of Payment Protection Insurance. There is some pure commercial work too and the set expanded this practice in 2011 with the hire of tax and procurement silk Timothy Lyons QC.

Many of the high-profile cases mentioned above are led by silks or senior juniors. Younger barristers often assist on these cases, but we were curious about juniors' own caseload too. *"I led on a number of planning inquiries,"* one told us. *"I like planning because it's quite technical: you get to cross-examine experts about things like the size*

Chambers UK rankings

Administrative & Public Law	Local Government
Education	Planning
Environment	Professional Discipline

of windows or the position of a roof terrace." Another junior told us they did employment, immigration and special educational needs cases and *"drafted grounds for judicial reviews,"* as well as taking on pro bono. Juniors (and occasionally pupils) often go on short secondments to local authorities, Ofgem or the Financial Ombudsman Service.

Careful planning

Public law is a popular area, and 4-5 receives a massive 300 pupillage applications yearly. Those who successfully make it to a first interview are given an advocacy point to argue in favour of or against and a legal problem question. *"The interview includes a few questions on your CV,"* a junior recalled, *"but the main focus is on your advocacy skills and how you tackle the problem question."* In the second round candidates are given a set of papers relating to a case in the morning, asked to draft a skeleton argument during the day and present the oral argument for their case in the evening. *"It is an extremely rigorous process,"* said one member. And with good reason: *"If you get a pupillage with us, the expectation is that you will gain tenancy at the end of the year,"* a source on the pupillage committee said. *"But there are no guarantees: you have to come up to scratch during pupillage."* Impressively, the set has retained every single one of its 14 pupils since 2005, including the single 2012 pupil.

Pupillage is divided into four three-month segments. The first three are spent with different supervisors specialising in public law, planning and commercial work respectively. For the final three months, after the tenancy decision is made, pupils can decide whether they want to switch to a fourth supervisor or stay with their third. *"The first six was really interesting,"* recalled one source. *"It was great to get involved with high-level cases and judicial reviews. I learnt a lot."* In their first few months pupils work primarily for their supervisor. After three months they branch out to work for other members, including silks. *"Your supervisor usually manages what work you do for other members. It's important to make sure other members see your work so they can make an assessment of you."* Pupils work on ongoing cases drafting skeleton arguments and shadowing members in court.

There is a lot of opportunity for advocacy in the second six. *"My first case, a two-day employment tribunal, was on the first day of my first six – but it was adjourned!"* one junior told us. Pupils also do possession hearings in the county court, bail applications, asylum tribunal cases and education cases (*"acting on behalf of parents in school admissions appeals"*). The number of times pupils are on their feet during their second six has increased at this set over the past few years. The 2012 pupil was reportedly active up to five times a week. During their second six pupils also do three *"tough"* assessed advocacy exercises, which *"take the same format as the second-round interview, but are harder."* These exercises *"feed into the tenancy decision,"* but that decision depends mainly on getting the thumbs up from your supervisors.

Sixty shades of Gray

"There isn't a corporate culture here," said one junior. *"We're not always walking around in suits talking about marketing strategies!"* That said, there has been a push to market chambers more in the past year or two, and it now employs a marketing assistant. *"We don't really throw our brand around,"* one member opined, *"but we have been holding an increasing number of academic-tinted seminars and conferences aimed at solicitors and other clients."* Senior clerk Michael Kaplan confirmed this new development and one member added: *"Every set has had to wake up to the idea that this is an increasingly competitive market and that you have to go out there and be more active in winning work."*

Still, we detected a more traditional outlook at 4-5 than at some other sets in the sense chambers is a collection of individuals rather than a monolithic whole with a singular culture. *"All 60 barristers have mutual respect for each other and a lot of us are friends as well as colleagues,"* said one member, *"but there are a variety of personalities here. Our size and diversity of practice and personalities are probably the main things that define us."*

"Everyone speaks to everyone, but the seniors often have family commitments after hours. This is a friendly and open place though, and the junior end gets on particularly well. On an ad hoc basis we go for lunch and coffee." Some members also get together for tennis, and there is an annual sports day at a member's house. A popular place for drinks is the new Bridge Bar – the planning issues for this new hang-out for members of Gray's Inn were handled by one of 4-5's barristers. Well, who better?

And finally...

"I love it here," a baby barrister told us. *"This set offers a real breadth of practice at the junior end."*

1 Hare Court

The facts

Location: Temple, London

Number of QCs/Juniors: 12/29 (17 women)

Applications: 100

Outside Pupillage Portal

Pupils per year: 2

Seats: 3x4 months

Pupillage award: £35,000 (can advance £10,000 for BPTC)

This set is looking for pupils with *"a passion"* for the field of family law.

This top family set encourages pupils *"to spend time with the silks going to court and getting to grips with some high net worth divorces, which throw up really complex issues."*

All that jazz

"Family law melds commercial concerns with the 'people' side of law," enthused pupils at this specialist set. A member added: *"I like it because it blends the social with the practical and the intellectual."* All of 1 Hare Court's barristers are family law specialists, and over half are ranked in *Chambers UK*. The set's work is dominated by ancillary relief (or 'matrimonial finance') – the division of a couple's spoils as part of a divorce. *"Those who instruct us know our specialism is ancillary relief – that is why we have so much of that type of work,"* explains senior clerk Steve McCrone. In all, about 85 to 90% of the set's work falls into this category. The rest includes children's cases and advice on drafting pre-nups.

In the past few years 1HC has been involved in many high-profile family cases. In 2010 silks Richard Todd and Nicholas Mostyn (now a High Court judge) were instructed on both sides of the Supreme Court case which determined that pre-nup agreements are binding under English law. Mostyn also represented Paul McCartney during his divorce proceedings and more recently members acted on the divorce case of Russian oligarch Boris Berezovsky, which saw his ex-wife walk away with a tidy £200m – the largest-ever UK divorce payout. This case was a record-breaker, but several of 1HC's recent instructions have involved eight-figure sums. It's also increasingly common for cases to have an international flavour: quite a few clients hail from overseas or own assets abroad.

"Family law is more rigorous than it used to be," one member told us. *"You need more skills in areas like finance and other disciplines: from forensics to child psychology."* And don't imagine divorce law is about endlessly haranguing opposing counsel either. An increasing number of cases settle out of court. *"The Family Bar is undergoing a big shake up as lots of areas are losing legal aid,"* we were told. *"The government is putting an increasing emphasis on alternative dispute resolution."* 1HC has really been pushing the use of mediation and arbitration and now has three accredited arbitrators and 16 accredited mediators. Emotions do still run high in divorce cases, of course. But: *"We're lawyers, not therapists. We have to be commercial about how we deal with difficult family problems. We have to explain to clients – who might have thought family law was all about sitting on beanbags talking about your problems – what remedies the law offers."*

Follow my lead

Pupils sit with three different supervisors for four months each. They are also encouraged to do work for other members of chambers. *"In my first four months my supervisor would ring around and ask if anyone had suitable work for me. My second supervisor made it clear they wanted me to take the initiative making contact. I often went along to court with other members."* Pupils get stuck in to a range of written work. *"I was asked to do some quite big tasks,"* one told us. *"I have drafted skeleton arguments and one legal opinion as well as doing discrete research tasks. I have also put together schedules of assets and*

Chambers UK rankings

Family/Matrimonial

chronologies of events." One interviewee said they split their time 50:50 between working in chambers and shadowing members in court. Pupils often accompany silks and get a taste of the action in some of 1HC's most high-value cases. These aren't necessarily the most complex or interesting ones though: "*The lower the value of the divorce case, the more intense it often is, as the parties have less to divide up.*"

There are "*not that many differences*" between the first and second six, other than pupils' increasing experience level. Towards the end of the pupillage, they usually get the opportunity to be on their feet two or three times. One we spoke to had done a first appointment in a financial remedies proceeding. "*I was quite pleased to be in a set where I didn't get on my feet too early, as the cases are fairly complex,*" one pupil told us. Pupils do get to practise their advocacy during two non-assessed exercises in the second six.

Keeping it in the family

1HC makes some tough demands of its recruits. Good academics are a given and, as "*nearly all our applicants look really impressive on paper,*" it's vital to show you have a clear interest in family law. "*You have to show a really spirited interest – or, dare I say it, a passion – for family law,*" a member told us. "*When I interview someone, I want to have the impression that they have read the Family Law Journal that week, or know about major issues at the Family Bar.*" The set also likes to see family law mini-pupillages on CVs and it could help if, for example, you did your dissertation on divorce law or shadowed a judge in the Family Division. In addition, the financial nature of ancillary relief means applicants need an interest in, or knowledge, of tax and personal finance. "*I am looking for someone who is either good with numbers or has the capacity to be good with numbers,*" says Ann Hussey, head of the pupillage committee.

1HC operates outside the Pupillage Portal, and applicants first have to impress with a CV and hand-written cover letter. In 2012, 29 candidates were invited to a ten-minute first-round interview. "*It was a CV chat focusing on what I did at university and why I wanted to work here,*" recalled one pupil. As well as questions like 'What makes a good family barrister?' candidates may be asked their views on developments at the Family Bar or, for example, the effects of legal aid cuts. The second-round interview – reached by 11 candidates in 2012 – is more structured. "*I was given three cases plus the judgments and a mock legal question beforehand,*" recalled one pupil. "*In the interview I was asked to analyse the problem, compare the cases and talk about what parts of the judgments were most relevant.*"

1HC has traditionally only taken on one of its three pupils a year and did so again in 2012. It also advertises its tenancy position externally, though the last time it took on a new member this way was in 2005. In future, the set will recruit two pupils with the aim of offering tenancy to one. At the end of pupillage there is an interview for tenancy, consisting of two parts: a general interview and a 15-minute advocacy exercise. "*My impression is that the tenancy decision is predominantly based on that interview,*" a pupil told us. "*But of course our supervisors do give us references which are taken into account by the tenancy committee, along with feedback from other members.*"

The well tempered workplace

"*I think we are a progressive set, but we are still run on a successful traditional basis,*" says senior clerk Steven McCrone. Apparently some of the junior clerks still prefer to call the members Sir and Ma'am, and inside chambers you'll find some traditional fixtures and fittings – we understand the head of chambers even has a harpsichord in his office. That traditional outlook includes a non-expansive approach to the set's membership. "*As we lose people at the top, we recruit new people at the bottom,*" says McCrone. "*We don't usually advertise for new members other than those we take on after pupillage.*"

We don't want to make this set sound like a stuffy place, though. It has "*a strong group of young juniors,*" a youthful head of chambers and a high proportion of female tenants. "*And people often pop into each other's rooms for tea, coffee and a natter.*" The Pegasus Bar in the Inner Temple is popular for a drink and there are also chambers dinners and an annual networking seminar.

And finally...

Take note that a huge chunk of 1HC's work is ancillary relief for divorces, so besides people skills, you'll need a love of numbers, tax and things financial to work here.

Henderson Chambers

The facts

Location: Temple, London
Number of QCs/Juniors: 8/39 (10 women)
Applications: 200+
Apply through Pupillage Portal
Pupils per year: 2
Seats: 4x3 months
Pupillage award: £50,000 (can advance a sum for BPTC)

This top common law set is not afraid to seek out new practices with potential.

From the outside, it has the look and feel of the traditional Bar, but in fact Henderson and its cheery tenants have a thoroughly modern approach to their product liability, consumer and health and safety work.

Crash, bang, wallop

Train crash? Salmonella outbreak? Nasty injury? Defective drugs? Mis-sold PPI? Henderson Chambers is your set. Its expertise lies in health and safety, product liability and consumer credit law, or, as one junior put it, *"things that have broken or gone wrong."* Enthusiastic senior clerk John White gave us a more corporate-style summary: *"We are a recognised leader in a number of specialist fields, like product liability and health and safety. But regulatory and compliance issues have become increasingly important in the past few years."* In addition to these three core areas, Henderson also works on personal injury and disease claims, employment, property, commercial and local government disputes.

Chambers' traditional strength in health and safety has seen its members involved with litigation over the Buncefield oil depot explosion and the Hatfield, Potters Bar, Ladbroke Grove and Grayrigg rail disasters. The Atomic Veterans litigation was another big case – Henderson acted for the MoD in this high-profile injury claim by about 1,000 servicemen involved in atomic tests in the 1950s. On the product liability side, members have acted as counsel for Clover Leaf – the UK distributor of the allegedly defective French PIP breast implants. Members also defended drug maker Sanofi against a group action over the anti-epileptic drug Sabril. Meanwhile, barristers in the *"burgeoning"* consumer finance practice were active on *Sternlight v Barclays Bank* over the interest rates charged on credit cards. Members have also recently been very busy on cases related to the mis-selling of PPI (Payment Protection Insurance).

This broad range of practices certainly appealed to our interviewees when they applied to Henderson. And things could become broader still: the set seems constantly to be seeking out new practice areas with potential. It recently launched a consumer law practice, topping up its consumer finance expertise with the arrival of William Hibbert and Julia Smith from Gough Chambers (Hibbert is a big noise in the world of consumer credit and OFT matters). John White also mentions environmental health and safety actions, insurance, economic torts and technology as growth areas. And speaking of technology: in late 2011 one Henderson barrister was responsible for the first anti-harassment injunction sent to an unknown party via text message.

PI to four significant figures

Pupils spend three months with four different supervisors. Each supervisor usually practises in more than one field, so a seat might combine employment with PI work or property with consumer finance. In their first seat pupils work primarily for their supervisor doing things like preparing skeleton arguments, pleadings, research notes and notes for conference. *"All the work I did was on ongoing cases,"* one pupil told us. *"My very first task was drafting a skeleton argument for a County Court debt action."* One supervisor asks pupils to *"plan and draft an outline – a roadmap – of the cross-examination of the defendant in one of his current cases."* After three months

Chambers UK rankings

Consumer Law	Professional Discipline
Health & Safety	Public Procurement
Information Technology	Real Estate Litigation
Product Liability	

pupils also take on work from other members of chambers. "*There is an informal list of other people you should do work with, including all the members of the recruitment committee and the head of chambers.*" Midway through the year, pupils spend a month seconded to the competition department of US law firm McDermott Will & Emery's Brussels office, picking up commercial experience working with solicitors.

Advocacy comes hard and fast in the second six, when there is "*a big change of pace.*" By the end of this period pupils are on their feet two or three times a week. "*The advocacy is wonderful,*" one pupil cooed. "*I have really had to argue complex points.*" Pupils cut their teeth on RTAs and possession hearings in the Magistrates' and Crown Court, and might eventually even end up in the High Court. Sources we spoke to had gained advocacy experience in a five-day employment tribunal case, a half-hour costs application, and "*possession hearing where the defendant hasn't paid his rent... because he's in prison.*" Pupils also do three or four mock advocacy exercises, the final one in front of a Master at the RCJ.

Easy rider?

In line with Henderson's "*friendly and warm*" ethos, this set isn't intent on beasting its pupils. "*I was told that in the first three months nobody expects you to be marvellously amazing,*" a pupil said, "*but you do push yourself and it's important to show willingness to assist and work with other people.*" A lever-arch file is kept on each pupil containing "*each supervisor's written report and feedback on every piece of written work you have done for other members.*" This file is the main basis for the tenancy decision taken by the recruitment committee. In addition "*the other members are informally canvassed for their opinions,*" and the clerks weigh in too. Chief clerk John White says the first thing he looks for in a pupil is personality – first and foremost as they need to be attractive prospects for solicitor clients. In 2012, Henderson took on both of its pupils as tenants.

One reason personality matters when it comes to tenancy is that the pupillage application process has already weeded out anyone who isn't an excellent barrister. All pupillage applications are marked out of 100, with most weight given to academics followed by non-academic achievements, commitment to the Bar and your interest in Henderson. The highest scorers go through to a first-round interview, based around a "*fairly nebulous*" problem question (back in 2010 applicants were asked about MPs' expenses). There is also a brief CV chat. "*They looked at what I had done and said 'That's interesting!' and we talked a bit about it.*" The second interview is more "*alarming.*" A seven-member panel grills candidates on a more legalistic question, for example about a piece of case law. In addition to its twelve-month pupils, the set takes on a third-six pupil almost every year.

Big bash and the Hendersons

A recent renovation (we could still smell the fresh paint when visiting in summer 2012) has seen Henderson replace its wood panelling and shelves stocked with old law reports with white-painted walls and video-conferencing facilities. But the set retains a cosy – almost homely – feel which fits its location right at the heart of Inner Temple. Sources agreed that this cosy atmosphere is reflected in familial relations among the tenants: "*People are very ready to help you, which means it's easy to keep learning.*" We sense this culture strongly contributes to Henderson's market standing and the quality of the instructions it receives.

We can give you more of a feel of the Henderson 'type' by telling you that one pupil we spoke to used to be a radio DJ for BBC Oxford, while a baby junior previously worked in sales for Channel Four. More senior members don't shy away from non-law activities either: head of chambers Charlie Gibson moonlights as an amateur boxer in the East End (honestly!) and has an electric drum kit in his office. Junior James Purnell is apparently a dab hand at the piano. "*He leads the carol singing at the Christmas party and everyone is 'forced' to join in.*" For more frequent fun there are the "*well-attended*" 5pm Friday drinks: "*What I like about them is that the talk tends not to be about law. At most, people might tell you about funny things that happened in court. It's a nice way to wind down – suddenly all your week's hardships become hilarious anecdotes.*"

And finally...

Stuffed full of bright, charming and diligent barristers and interesting work, Henderson offers pupils great advocacy opportunities and quality feedback on their work – we can't recommend it highly enough.

11KBW

The facts

Location: Inner Temple, London
Number of QCs/Juniors: 19/32 (14 women)
Applications: 210
Outside pupillage portal
Pupils per year: 2-4
Seats: 2x3 and 1x6 months
Pupillage award: £55,000 (can advance £15,000 for BPTC)

"We select people based on hard criteria like their ability to communicate orally and in writing, not based on an impressionistic 'feel' we have about them."

One of London's top public law sets, 11KBW eschews political activism, but does do some of the best education, employment, local government, civil liberties and competition work around.

When Tony met Cherie

11KBW was founded on 7 December 1981 by Alexander 'Derry' Irvine QC. Joining him were nine tenants, including two of Irvine's former pupils: Tony and Cherie Blair. By 1997 the set had grown from ten to 29 members, Blair had become prime minister and he appointed his former pupilmaster Lord Chancellor. Irvine's original senior clerk, Philip Monham, is still with the set today. *"We have expanded a lot over these 30 years,"* he mused, *"but our aim is still to offer top public, employment and commercial practices – tied to that is our education, human rights and information law work."*

Work sees barristers in the thick of major headline-grabbing public law cases. In February 2011 members acted for the Justice Secretary in the High Court in striking down a damages claim brought by 588 prisoners claiming Britain's ban on prisoners' voting rights was a violation of the ECHR. Other clients include HM Treasury, Birmingham Airport and the Secretaries of State for Defence, Justice, Transport and Communities. Members don't just act for the government though – there's an *"exceptionally broad"* client base. One recent case saw members acting for both the Iranian Treasury and state-owned Bank Mellat in a claim relating to economic sanctions against nuclear proliferation.

11KBW is recognised as London's top education and local government set by *Chambers UK*. It has acted for the Department for Education in various challenges to the cancellation of the Building Schools for the Future proj-

ect, and in Sharon Shoesmith's victory against Haringey Council over the Baby P scandal. Other clients include numerous London public and independent schools, as well as the London Boroughs of Brent, Hammersmith & Fulham, Wandsworth and Camden.

Employment and human rights are two commendable pillars of strength, while information law is of growing importance, with an increasing number of Freedom of Information Act cases brought to the fore. Employment lawyers handle a lot of EAT cases, including representation of ASDA in a dispute over terms and conditions of employment. Members also acted for British Airways in a dispute over flight crew holiday payments. Human rights barristers primarily act for respondents. A striking civil liberties case saw the set acting for MI6, the Attorney General, the Foreign Office and the Home Office in civil claims brought by former Guantanamo Bay detainees.

Rigour diggers

Pupillage is divided into two three-month segments and a six-month one. *"In the first three months you work alongside your supervisor, shadowing him on a daily basis and doing the work he does,"* a pupil told us. *"You might do a first draft of documents related to a judicial review, then your supervisor might cannibalise parts of it and ask you to quickly do more research on a more detailed point."* Pupils also observe supervisors in the highest courts in the land. In their second three months, pupils continue to work closely with their supervisors, but will gradually do more devilling for other members. In their second six pupils "*still have a supervisor, but the idea is for you to work with as broad a range of tenants as possible or rather for them to work with you so they can assess your work.*"

Assessment is everything at 11KBW. "*Almost all your work – maybe 90% – is assessed. It is double-marked and then you sit down with two members and they will talk to you for maybe an hour about how to improve. The feedback you get is very detailed. Each piece then goes into your 'pupillage brief' – a thick lever arch file like a coursework folder.*" There are also three assessed advocacy exercises throughout the year in which members play judges and QCs. "*They will be based on real cases but changed to focus more on legal questions.*" There are also several exercises devoted to developing your practice skills – but they are not assessed. Phew.

Assessed pieces of work are the key to tenancy. "*This set is principally concerned with your quality of work, not your personality or being able to network*," a pupil said. "*You don't need to ingratiate yourself with your supervisor or other members*," a baby junior added. "*The onus is on your supervisor to make sure you work with plenty of people.*"

Pupils don't get to spend time on their feet, but baby juniors cut their teeth on employment cases. "*My lay clients are both claimants and respondents, and can range from the retail to financial services sectors.*" Pupils and juniors also assist on major public law cases including judicial reviews, which are "*high-profile, newsworthy and throw up interesting legal issues.*"

Goudie Goudie

11KBW introduced a weekly 'chambers tea' in 2010. "*Chat can range from someone's Supreme Court case to the latest episode of The Apprentice*," a pupil told us. The Witness Box is a favourite Friday evening hangout. "*There are also intermittent drinks and silk parties, a summer garden party and a Christmas party in the club across the road.*" In an attempt to conjure up the set's "*informal*" atmosphere a pupil told us it would be "*hard to spot the difference between one of our QCs and one of our juniors if you just saw them in the hallway.*" Having met both, we can corroborate this. It probably helps that pupils are solely assessed on their work, so "*schmoozing is never of worth at social events.*"

Some public law and employment sets are known for nailing their political colours to the mast. 11KBW does represent respondents more frequently than claimants, but it's not an "*activist*" sort of place. Head of chambers James Goudie may be a former Labour leader for Brent Council, but senior clerk Philip Monham insists that though members "*take an interest in politics*," this is "*not a campaigning set.*" Looking at its work and clients, we're inclined to agree.

With no political stripe in common, members do all share a passion for pro bono. A recent case saw the set act for Camden Community Law Centre in a challenge to Legal Service Commission spending cuts. The set encourages both applicants and pupils to get involved with FRU cases and tenants are encouraged to do at least one pro bono case every year. "*Almost everyone in chambers is involved*," a baby junior told us. "*Quite a lot of cases come through the clerks' room as well as via the Bar Pro Bono Unit. You just put your name forward and get involved.*"

Get your mini into gear

11KBW aims to recruit all its pupils through assessed mini-pupillages. It offers 30 to 40 a year during term time by way of written applications. After the mini, around ten to 12 individuals go through to an interview round. Performing well during your mini is clearly the key to getting a pupillage. So what are recruiters looking for? "*I am always impressed by people with practical insight, people who can get a real sense of a client and the situation in question*," the head of the pupillage committee told us. Beyond this, it's pure skill that matters. "*We select people based on hard criteria like their ability to communicate orally and in writing, not based on an impressionistic 'feel' we have about them.*" He went on: "*The worst thing a mini-pupil can do is to be unwilling or unable to express a view firmly and reach a clear judgement.*"

Advocacy experience or excellent natural advocacy skills are essential. "*I am particularly impressed by people who have taken on real cases through FRU and who have had proper advocacy experience*," the head of the pupillage committee told us. A strong CV helps – whether that includes "*mooting, debating and advocacy experience at university or a ten-year previous career.*" When we visited the set, one pupil had a degree from Harvard, qualified as a solicitor at Linklaters and then worked at the Supreme Court. Though not all recruits have such formidable CVs, if you can match these achievements it certainly won't hurt your chances.

And finally...

This set's commitment to pupils is exemplified by the fact that it took on all three pupils in 2010, its one pupil and third-sixer in 2011, and both pupils in 2012.

Keating Chambers

The facts

Location: Temple, London

Number of QCs/Juniors: 25/30 (15 women)

Applications: 130

Apply through Pupillage Portal

Pupils per year: Up to 3

Seats: 4x3 months

Pupillage award: £50,000 (can advance £15,000 for BPTC)

A background in construction is not a necessity to work at Keating; an interest in commercial law is.

As experts in the field for over three decades, Keating Chambers literally wrote the book on construction law.

The house that Keating built

Indisputably one of London's top two construction sets, Keating has been honing its specialism ever since Donald Keating QC was head of chambers in the 1980s. He first penned the seminal construction tome *Keating on Construction Contracts* in 1955: the ninth edition was published in February 2012, still authored by members of this chambers.

Keating's members have been instructed in disputes over landmark construction projects like Wembley Stadium, the London Eye, the Gherkin, the Millennium Stadium, Portcullis House and the Lowry Centre. The set works on construction cases of all shapes and sizes – its reputation means members are often to be found on both sides of a dispute. For example, members recently advised both Cambridge City Council and engineering firm BAM in a bust-up over the construction of a guided busway.

"Right now we have no real need to go outside our chosen disciplines. We concentrate on those things we are really good at," senior clerk Nick Child tells us. But he doesn't just mean construction contracts disputes. Keating's work extends into squabbles over energy infrastructure projects; professional negligence claims related to engineers, architects and surveyors; and international construction arbitration. Chambers is also expanding its existing presence in technology, procurement and shipbuilding disputes, all areas where the law involved – contract and tort – is closely linked to construction law. On the shipping side members recently acted for Serco in a $30m dispute over the termination of an Abu Dhabi shipbuilding contract. A recent procurement case saw the set represent train manu-facturer Alstom in its appeal against Eurostar's decision to have Siemens build its new Channel Tunnel trains. International disputes – often dealt with through ADR – are a lucrative market at the moment, while the UK construction market remains relatively depressed. So, in the name of marketing Keating overseas, Nick Child has joined the jet-set: Russia, the Middle East and East Asia are all hot sources of work at the moment.

Building your CV

A pupillage at Keating is a hard-won thing. Around 30 applicants are invited to a first-round interview. Candidates have just 15 minutes to impress the four-lawyer interview panel with their legal knowledge, confidence, speaking skills, motivation and interest in construction law. There's room for *"topical"* questions: one example we heard was 'Do you favour compulsory mediation?' while another was 'Should policemen be allowed to serve on juries?' A second-round 30-minute interview includes a presentation, on a (preferably non-legal) topic of the applicant's choice. Past candidates have spoken about the Elgin Marbles and hang-gliding. Applicants are also presented with a legal problem and complete a written test. *"They wanted me to show myself at my best,"* recalled a current pupil. *"I was pushed by the interviewers, who took a purposefully different viewpoint to mine to challenge me."*

"In the interviews we don't usually ask anything about construction," says pupillage committee head Alexander Nissen QC. *"We don't expect any specialist knowledge from applicants: 90% of our barristers do not have any*

Chambers UK rankings

Construction	Professional Negligence
Energy & Natural Resources	Public Procurement
International Arbitration	

technical background at all. *In practice we get assistance from technical experts instructed by the clients and that is sufficient. So, do you need to be an engineer? Definitely not. But do you need an interest in commercial law? Yes absolutely.*" A junior tenant told us: "*I was interested in the language and complexity of contract and tort law. The fact it was complicated is what attracted me.*" If an applicant does have an engineering or construction background this can count as a plus at the initial application stage.

Size matters

Pupils spend time with four supervisors. "*Some individuals focus more on a certain area – like energy or procurement,*" making each 'seat' distinct. Nonetheless, you will need a strong interest in the contractual principles that underlie construction law. You must also have the ability to combine handling stacks of documentation (construction cases are often huge and lengthy) with easy banter among contractor clients. "*Construction is an industry where personality matters a lot. Being a good lawyer isn't enough,*" says a source. "*You have to be able to relate to the man in the street who put his shovel through a cable digging up the road, and to the CEO of the corporation that owned the digger that dug the hole for the cable in the first place.*"

Shadowing is at the core of the first six. "*I did work my supervisor was currently on or had just done, drafting memos, written advice and skeleton arguments. I also attended conferences with clients.*" In contrast to some other commercial sets, pupils have the chance to be on their feet once a week or more in their second six. Not on any construction cases though. The clerks intentionally seek out lower-value work – direction hearings, infant settlements – for pupils to cut their teeth on. "*You get used to the feeling of a courtroom and learn about the type of questions judges ask, which helps when you're preparing briefs.*" Drafting and shadowing continues in this period, and pupils do more live work, such as "*drafting particulars of claim which are sent to the solicitors.*"

Pupils also are put through their paces in three advocacy assessments. "*They are quite tricky and excellent prep for the*

real thing," said one. "*You're given a huge bundle and managing that is a real test.*" Cases are always mocks of recent large matters the set has worked on. Pupils go head to head as opposing counsel and a senior QC sits in judgment.

The tenancy decision is based on a variety of factors including the quality of the pupils' work, their performance in the advocacy exercises and the extent to which the pupils are "*likely to gel well with the clients,*" Alexander Nissen QC says. "*Feedback from supervisors is probably the most reliable source of information upon which to base the decision. The tenancy committee places much store by what they say.*" The decision of the committee is ultimately reviewed by the whole of chambers.

Keating Rocks

Spurning a traditional chambers tea, Keating has a chambers lunch. It's only for members, and pupils are not invited, but rather than a snub we're told this is to "*take the pressure off*" and stop lunch becoming a hob-nobbing affair. Pupils are always invited to other events: the Christmas party, drinks and celebrations. "*There's always a Keating table in halls too which you can join,*" a pupil told us. "*And Daly's Wine Bar is a frequent haunt on Fridays and as a pupil they never let you pay for your own drinks.*"

Pupils usually work 9am to 6pm, but there are exceptions. "*You do put the pressure on yourself sometimes and urgent things can come up. I got a call from the clerks once at 7pm on a Friday, saying some papers had come in, and did I want to take a look at them. It was up to me to say whether I felt I could. In the end I did and worked over the weekend, but I wasn't judged on it. The supervisors are good at applying just the right amount of pressure. You feel busy all the time, but not overburdened.*"

Unusually, Keating is now split fifty-fifty between silks and juniors. Perhaps this contributes to what one source called the "*collegiate*" atmosphere. "*There are plenty of interesting characters, but not a singular chambers personality. Everyone is different, so you do treat everyone differently.*" This doesn't seem to be a set stuffed with eccentrics, although one pupil recalled once hearing the strum of an electric guitar from one silk's office. That would be Marcus Taverner QC. He plays lead guitar in Keating's entry for the Law Rocks 'Battle of the Bands' fund-raiser. The charity – set up by Keating's own senior clerk Nick Child – raised £11,000 at one event in November 2011. Well, rock on, we say.

And finally...
A great set, not just for those interested in construction law, but for anyone who relishes the complexities of contracts law.

Littleton Chambers

The facts

Location: Inner Temple, London
Number of QCs/Juniors: 13/40 (10 women)
Applications: 200
Outside Pupillage Portal
Pupils per year: 2
Seats: 3x4 months
Pupillage award: £45,000 (can advance £10,000 for BPTC)

Since 2006, only one of Littleton's pupils has not been offered tenancy.

"*Proactive in pushing business development,*" Littleton is known for top-drawer employment, commercial litigation and professional negligence work.

Citius, altius, fortius

"*What attracted me to this set is that it is forward-looking, keen at marketing, and progressive,*" a pupil told us. Littleton has indeed 'progressed' of late, increasing in size by a quarter since 2007, from 44 members to 53. It was also one of the first sets to appoint a CEO. That position is now split into administrator and commercial director roles. The latter is currently fulfilled by Nigel McEwen, a solicitor who was previously managing partner of a small City firm. "*It is unusual for a set to hire a solicitor into the role I have,*" he tells us, "*but one of my responsibilities is to go out, meet solicitors and give feedback to members and clerks on what our clients are looking for and what our perceived strengths and weaknesses are.*" A business development manager – also a former solicitor – has been hired to help McEwen in his role. As well as revamping management and marketing, Littleton recently renovated its offices to give them a more modern look and is investing in bringing in more work from overseas, with a particular focus on the CIS region.

Employment law is Littleton's forte and makes up 60% of its work. "*The great thing about this area of law is that it is commercial, but there is a people perspective too,*" a pupil reflected. "*You also get the opportunity for advocacy at an early stage.*" *Chambers UK* ranks Littleton as one of the three best employment sets in London and it has one of the biggest stables of specialist employment barristers anywhere. There are also five Chambers-ranked commercial litigation barristers, and this area makes up around 25% of the set's work, with the remaining 15% being professional negligence and one or two smaller specialisms (sports is one of these, and two Littleton barristers were among the 15 selected to resolve disputes between athletes, coaches and participating nations during the 2012 Olympics).

Employment work breaks down into two broad types (most of Littleton's tenants do both). There's 'statutory' work – unfair dismissal claims, tribunal work and so on. For example, one member defended law firm Clyde & Co in the Employment Appeals Tribunal against a whistleblowing claim by a former partner. Then there are 'civil' or common law employment cases: contractual disputes, bonus claims, breach of fiduciary duty claims, team move cases and the like. These tend to be bigger and hinge around commercial contracts. For instance, Littleton barristers acted on both sides of a High Court case between QBE Insurance and a rival over breach of fiduciary duty and misuse of confidential information by a departing team. The set has also represented Savile Row tailors Ede & Ravenscroft, disgraced police commander Ali Dizaei, Gordon Ramsay's father-in-law and the governor of the Tower of London in employment scraps. Industrial disputes are another breadwinner, and could be on the up given the current state of the economy. Commercial litigation is conducted by a distinct 'practice group' of barristers and Nigel McEwen tells us Littleton aims to expand this practice until it makes up around half of chambers' work.

Pupil people

"*Our barristers deal with people so they have very high levels of interpersonal and emotional skills,*" says Nigel McEwen. But don't think you'll get pupillage at Littleton

Chambers UK rankings

Employment

just by being a people-person. "*There is no substitute for a strong academic background: getting a good degree from a good university,*" says pupillage committee chair Dale Martin. We'd add that a good degree usually means a First, and a good university often means Oxford or Cambridge (although the set's 2011/12 pupil was a King's graduate). The set doesn't expect applicants to have any prior experience of employment law.

Around 20 of the 200 or so applicants make it to a first interview, lasting 30 minutes. Candidates are given documentation about a case study and then asked for their legal opinion on it. Fifteen make it through to the next round: a three-day assessed mini-pupillage. "*It gives us a real chance to observe their interpersonal skills, ability to master information and even things like punctuality; it also allows the applicants to obtain a good feeling for what practising in our chambers is really like,*" says Dale Martin. Mini-pupils are also judged on three pieces of advisory drafting work and an assessed legal exercise. Twelve candidates get through to a final interview, which covers a pre-set legal problem question. "*Our process is fairly intense,*" Martin admits. "*In interviews we look for people able to make points clearly and succinctly and hold out well under fire. Our interviews are culture-free and not based on personality.*"

Employment advocates

Pupillage consists of four three-month seats with four supervisors. Most are employment barristers, although as of 2012 there is also one commercial supervisor and "*you do get to work on purely commercial cases for other members.*" Pupillage starts with a grace period during which "*your supervisor makes sure you don't have too much on your plate and you always finish at 6pm.*" Pupils draft opinions, skeleton arguments, research notes and bits of pleadings. After four months things stop being so "*laid back*" and pupils start to take on work from other members of chambers and shadow them in court. "*Your supervisor is the gatekeeper of that work,*" a pupil tells us. "*If another member wants you to do work for them, they put in a request with your supervisor, who also seeks out interesting pieces of work for you.*"

In addition, second-six pupils have their own caseload and are up on their feet perhaps once a week. "*Oral advocacy is what it is all about. If you don't want to do that don't come here,*" says Dale Martin. "*My first advocacy was on a race discrimination unfair dismissal case,*" recalled one junior tenant. "*I also worked on quite a few multi-day cases and appeared in front of a registrar in Companies Court.*" Pupils also do enforcement applications, case management hearings, pre-hearing reviews and pick up judgments.

As if all this doesn't make pupils busy enough, there are four "*tough*" advocacy assessments and two written assessments to contend with. Furthermore, each supervisor produces a report, while every piece of written work pupils complete for other members of chambers is reviewed and given a mark out of ten. Pupils have full access to these reviews. The tenancy decision is taken "*democratically*" by an all-member meeting. "*There is no official recommendation from the pupillage committee,*" a junior tells us. "*Each supervisor makes a presentation and says whether they are supporting the pupil.*" Our sources agreed that the views of supervisors – and by extension the quality of work – are key to the decision with lesser weight given to feedback on your live advocacy and the assessed exercises. Since 2006 Littleton has offered tenancy to all but one of its pupils.

The ambassador's reception

Some sets leave marketing and business development to the clerks; at Littleton, barristers are closely involved too. "*I am on the business development committee,*" a junior told us. "*We organise a lot of talks and social events, often designed to get young barristers and solicitors together.*" Pupils attend these events and are expected to network their socks off as "*ambassadors for chambers.*"

The slick corporate look of Littleton's offices and its renewed business focus make us suspect that in future the commercial side of chambers will increasingly come to dominate life here. Nevertheless, "*it is a very sociable set – lots of people are friends.*" There's no chambers tea or weekly drinks as apparently "*there is no need to set it up as people naturally get together.*" The set houses "*a variety of personalities and perspectives, from those who want to wear a suit every day to those in tee-shirts and shorts.*" Speaking of shorts... one junior was proud to tell us of a recent "*Caribbean-flavoured leaving do*" which saw shorts-wearing tenants "*limbo dancing surrounded by fake palm trees and flower garlands.*"

And finally...

The quality of training Littleton offers in this interesting area of law means we fully understand why winning a pupillage here is a very competitive business.

Maitland Chambers

The facts

Location: Lincoln's Inn, London

Number of QCs/Juniors: 23/44 (13 women)

Applications: 150-200

Outside Pupillage Portal

Pupils per year: Up to 3

Seats: 1x3 months and 4x2 months

Pupillage award: £60,000 (can advance £20,000 for BPTC)

Maitland's work has an increasingly international flavour, but that won't stop you finding their barristers down the local every Thursday.

Maitland's reputation as one of the biggest and best commercial chancery sets is stronger than ever before.

In the best company

Aside from being the only London set to be top-ranked for commercial chancery work, Maitland receives 11 separate rankings within the top three bands of *Chambers UK*. Work spans company law, partnership disputes, banking and finance, fraud and professional negligence. A prominent traditional chancery practice involving charities, real property and probate work continues to thrive. The set's coverage of commercial law in all its guises is comprehensive to say the least; one pupil succinctly defined Maitland's scope as "*not shipping.*"

Members have worked on high-profile disputes relating to the fallout from the collapse of Lehman and the Madoff fraud, and defended a private equity firm against claims brought by Russian oligarch Boris Berezovsky. They have also advised Asil Nadir over the recent lifting of his bankruptcy discharge suspension. The Turkish Cypriot gained notoriety for absconding UK justice between 1993 and 2010 after being prosecuted for numerous counts of theft and fraud relating to the collapse of Polly Peck, the textile company where he was chief executive. Other lay clients range from banks and football clubs to pop stars and universities: members acted for UCL over campus occupations during the student fees protests.

An increasing amount of the set's work is international – members were recently involved in a $500m fraud claim brought by Russian steel giant Polyus against a Kazakh business family over a gold mine. Internationalisation is one of the strategic goals of pioneering senior clerking duo Lee Cutler and John Wiggs. "*We are encouraging international work by visiting jurisdictions like BVI and Bermuda and by linking members up to specific jurisdictions. We are also promoting chambers as a brand, because that's how our major international and American law firm clients see us. But our real strength – our USP – is that we have strength in so many areas. We can provide one barrister who knows three or four areas of the law.*"

Best Maits

Pupils spend their first three months with one supervisor – after that each seat will last two months. To ensure fairness, pupils sit with the same supervisors. Happily for pupils, the set views the lead up to Christmas as a "*finding-your-feet time when you can ask stupid questions.*" The experience in each seat is contingent on the supervisor's personal style. "*My first supervisor took the view that I should be observing his work,*" one pupil told us, while another added: "*I went straight into doing drafting in my first seat – on my first day in fact.*" One continued: "*Throughout pupillage I did a mix of live and non-live work. If my supervisor didn't think the case he was on would be a useful experience to me, he would set me some drafting or research based on an earlier case of his.*" Pupils sometimes spend time shadowing other members. "*I'm currently observing a trial, so I have been exposed to rules of evidence relating to company cases,*" one told us.

Pupils see all sorts of work during the year. It helps that juniors rarely specialise. One supervisor we heard of worked on commercial, contract, fraud and banking cases. "*My supervisors have all had very broad practices, and yet none of them really overlapped,*" one source told us. After gaining tenancy (fingers crossed), juniors are assigned

Chambers UK rankings

Agriculture & Rural Affairs	Fraud
Chancery	Offshore
Charities	Partnership
Commercial Dispute Resolution	Professional Negligence
	Real Estate Litigation
Company	Restructuring/Insolvency

cases of their own and will be on their feet several times a week. Cases often fall into the traditional chancery ambit – "*personal and company insolvencies, landlord-tenant disputes, spats between companies, contentious probate*." Baby juniors split their time "*fifty-fifty*" between cases like these and being led on commercial chancery cases. "*These are major commercial fraud or finance cases with lots of documents to go through, so they need the manpower. They often have an international flavour and are very high-profile – like our Lehman work*."

Trace the Irascible

Although pupils don't spend any time on their feet during pupillage, there are five assessed advocacy exercises. They increase in complexity and "*in volume in terms of the amount of paper*." The first is usually a simple trial where pupils act opposite each other – and then have to switch sides and argue the opposite position. Ensuing exercises might include applying for injunctions or complex rights of way cases. "*It is a bit scary to a degree*," a baby junior recalled. "*But the exercises really train you up so you are ready to go out there*." In at least one of the exercises, pupillage committee head Anthony Trace QC – noted by our *Chambers UK* colleagues for his "*take-no-prisoners*" approach – will act as judge. His stance can be "*irascible*" (his words not ours) but we can attest to the fact he is one of the set's warmest, most enthusiastic and colourful characters.

"*It is our supervisors' reports which carry the most weight in terms of tenancy*," a pupil informed us. "*The oral advocacy exercises are also taken into account, but they are mostly just a learning experience*." Supervisors inform the tenancy committee of their conclusions by way of a standardised form. "*They mostly assess you on how you develop*." Pupils also receive constant feedback from supervisors throughout the year. No doubt pupils were also comforted by Maitland's impressive track record for taking on its own pupils. One out of the two was offered tenancy in 2012, the first year since 2008 that Maitland hasn't kept on all its pupils.

Pupco to pubco

Maitland is outside the Pupillage Portal scheme – its application form is posted online from mid-January. The application deadline for 2013 is 31 January (a full three months before the Pupillage Portal deadline). So, applicants have only two-and-a-half to three weeks to complete their applications. The application form asks all the standard questions – Why law? Why the Chancery Bar? Why Maitland? There's also a challenging and dangerously open-ended question. It has been known to go a little something like this: 'Choose a proposition and convince us'. One successful applicant wrote on "*why you should go on a National Trust holiday*." The set isn't looking for any specific knowledge, but "*writing skills, your thinking processes and your powers of persuasion*." And a bit of originality certainly wouldn't go amiss.

Around 30 hopefuls are invited to a first-round interview. It starts with "*ice-breakers in relation to your CV*", followed by a reasoning question. A pupillage committee source told us: "*We might give someone a page-long clause from a contract and ask them to discuss how it might operate in certain situations*." A week later ten to 15 people will be invited back for a second interview, which consists solely of a complex legal problem. This involves 40 minutes' preparation where "*the candidate is given a mock instruction setting out the facts of a hypothetical case and will be asked to discuss legal and other issues to which it gives rise*." Although the set assures us the questions can be successfully answered by both law and non-law grads, we note that the questions are quite technical. So, be prepared!

Fitting in to a certain culture or being a specific type of person is not hugely important to Maitland. "*There are different personalities. We have some colourful characters here definitely – Anthony Trace has a piano in his room – but others are quieter*." Although its two newest tenants are both Cambridge law grads, Maitland does not judge candidates based on university background and visits law fairs and universities across the country.

Chambers has a daily 4pm teatime. "*Usually you will go if your supervisor goes, but sometimes if they are busy you will go without them*." Tea is "*a great learning opportunity, especially for juniors. Members have just come back from court and will be talking about their cases*." Outside the chambers' sleek interior and Portland stone façade, 'pubco' organises a weekly Thursday pub outing and there's Friday drinks in the clerks' room. "*The junior end of chambers is very cohesive*" and some members attend tea and drinks "*religiously*."

And finally...
Maitland's strong stable of barristers and its thorough and open approach to pupillage make it very popular with applicants.

Matrix Chambers

The facts

Location: Gray's Inn, London
Number of QCs/Juniors: 19/36 (22 women)
Applications: 250
Outside Pupillage Portal
Pupils per year: 2
Seats: 4x3 months
Pupillage award: £50,000 (can advance £10,000 for BPTC)

"Some sets may put ethics first; some put commerce first: we try to mix the two."

Its pioneering human rights work and a star cast of QCs has made Matrix one of the most famous businesses in the legal profession.

Dodging bullets

"Founded to do things differently to how they are done at the traditional Bar," Matrix caused quite a stir when 22 barristers from seven different sets created it in April 2000. With swish premises and a businesslike brand-focused strategy, not to mention pet fish, it was an outlier in an often staid world. Today, more and more chambers have CEOs, business strategies and contemporary offices, and *"Matrix may be less 'different' to other sets than it used to be."* But its brand and practice have been a roaring success: its casework litters the pages of the mainstream press and revenue is booming, rising from £13.6m in 2008/09 to £18.6m in 2010/11. *"It is important we have a recognisable brand,"* says chief executive Lindsay Scott. That brand includes everything from work quality to job titles: Matrix dubs its clerks 'practice managers' and pupils 'trainees', as *"changing the vocabulary gets rid of the upstairs-downstairs mentality of 'members' and 'clerks'."*

Matrix clocks up ten Chambers rankings and – although best known for its human rights work – trainees said *"there is so much to choose from."* The *"cool"* areas of crime and public law (including human rights, education and immigration) make up about a quarter of the set's work, with the rest split between media, employment, tax/competition, commercial and public international law.

Cool shades

Matrix was founded just after the Human Rights Act came into force, and its barristers have been involved in some of the most famous matters of the past decade. Three silks worked on the landmark 2004 case on the detention without trial of foreign terror suspects. Terrorism-related cases – from the Jean Charles de Menezes shooting to the detention of Iraqi civilians – continue to be a large area of work.

Members also worked on a European Court of Human Rights case on the legality of the police use of 'kettling'.

Immigration barristers were recently active on *HJ (Iran) & Anor v Secretary of State for the Home Department* – concerning an Iranian national using his right to a gay lifestyle as a base for an asylum claim. Other members won the deportation appeal for alleged Russian spy Ekaterina Zatuliveter. And remember those two teenagers who sued the government over the £9,000 recent tuition fee hike? Matrix acted for them too.

"Crime work is quite confronting," a trainee told us. *"In my first week I attended an inquest about a man who had been killed outside a nightclub by a gang of people ten years ago. We actually got an admission during evidence revealing who had done it. It was hugely emotional for the family."* Admittedly crime is overwhelmingly of the privately funded kind, meaning *"there is not so much blood and gore."* Fraud is a mainstay. Barristers recently defended property tycoons Robert and Victor Tchenguiz in a multibillion-pound investigation related to the collapse of Icelandic bank Kaupthing. Trainees get direct access to these high-profile cases. One had *"worked on the Shrien Dewani case, in relation to his extradition to South Africa after allegations he murdered his wife on their honeymoon."*

"Media has been a growth area for us over the past year," says Lindsay Scott: super-injunctions, phone hacking, the Leveson Inquiry, the extradition of Julian Assange – Matrix has been all over it. *"I was thrown straight into the world of phone hacking and super-injunctions,"* one pupil beamed. *"I also worked preparing submissions and closing documents for Module 2 of the Leveson Inquiry."*

Competition and employment are two other major areas of practice we should mention. Rhodri Thompson QC recently

Chambers UK rankings

Administrative & Public Law	Employment
Civil Liberties & Human Rights	Environment
	Fraud
Competition/European Law	Immigration
Crime	POCA Work & Asset Forfeiture
Defamation/Reputation Management	Police Law
Education	Public International Law

acted for MasterCard in a dispute with the European Commission on whether its international credit and debit card fees breached EU competition laws. When it comes to employment, members were active on the much-publicised *Eweida v British Airways* case about the rights of BA staff to wear religious jewellery in the workplace.

Long black coats

Trainees spend time with four different supervisors, often sampling four different areas of Matrix's work. "*I felt like a kid in a candy shop with all the different areas to choose from,*" one told us. One interviewee had completed seats in prison law, education, immigration and competition, while another had done immigration, media, crime and education. Unusually, "*you get genuine input into who you sit with. Half way through my first seat I had coffee with Lindsay Scott and we talked about who I might want to work with next.*"

"*I was never given an old piece of work to practise on,*" one trainee told us. "*Mostly my supervisor would give me their work to do first. For example, I drafted grounds for a judicial review in a prison and police law case. Most of the time he would end up using some of it, but in a significantly amended state.*" All our interviewees had had their own cases as a trainee, most gaining advocacy experience too. Employment Tribunal work is a common first starter, but Magistrates, and Crown Court work are up for grabs too. Through choice, some trainees do more advocacy than others. "*I was on my feet a couple of times during my second six,*" one trainee told us. "*It can be quite a roller coaster. One of my first cases was a bail application hearing. I acted for a man with learning difficulties who had been detained for two years pending deportation.*"

You'll need some pretty impressive credentials to get a look-in here. The four trainees the set took on between 2010 and 2012 had respectively worked: in Afghanistan; for the ECHR in Strasbourg; for the Yugoslavia Tribunal in The Hague; and for the Lord Chief Justice. "*After a Masters degree and two years' work experience I felt more prepared for pupillage,*" one told us. "*We don't penalise people for not having saved the world three times over,*" joked Tom Linden QC, head of Matrix' management committee, "*but having done voluntary or other work which they have really put their heart and soul into is important.*" So perhaps it's not surprising that the young barristers we met were quite down-to-earth and not snooty or aloof as you might expect from people with such stellar CVs.

You can head over to our website for trainee views on the application and two-round interview process and on the tenancy decision. Although neither 2010 trainee was taken on, both were in 2011. At the time we went to press the 2012 tenancy decision had not yet been made.

Taking the red pill

With its record representing individuals against the government in human rights and public law cases, is Matrix on a mission? Well, in part. "*We want to pursue the ethical side of legal practice, as well as being commercial,*" says Tom Linden. "*Some sets may put ethics first; some put commerce first: we try to mix the two. We represent banks and big businesses as well as individuals.*" Matrix is committed to pro bono work, which makes up about 10% of its practice. "*We're pushed to take some on,*" a trainee told us. "*I have a special education needs case coming up soon.*" Members have in the past worked with the charity Reprieve on death row cases and one tenant spent a year in the Gaza Strip working with the Palestinians.

Matrix is one of the few sets that does do corporate culture. "*Our brand and strong identity mean everyone buys into the idea of a sense of community,*" one trainee said. "*We have a weekly Thursday lunch in our 'chill-out area'. Nobody talks about law. We're more likely to talk about the quality of that week's food.*" Maletti's pizzeria apparently provides the best Thursday lunches. It's just across the road, opposite the Yorkshire Grey which is "*Matrix's default pub – we have Matrix drinks there every few weeks. There is always a good mix of barristers and staff, and the Matrix credit card will be put behind the bar.*" We were also told about the "*Matrix*" Christmas and summer parties. And yes, our interviewees did use the word 'Matrix' that often – it seems even going to the pub can't escape the branding exercise.

And finally...

No, it's not named after the 1999 Keanu Reeves movie. According to chief executive Lindsay Scott you want definition #2 from the OED: 'An environment of substance in which a thing is developed'. Aha.

4 New Square

The facts

Location: Lincoln's Inn, London
Number of QCs/Juniors: 22/56
Applications: 160
Outside Pupillage Portal
Pupils per year: 2–3
Seats: 2x3 + 1x6 months
Pupillage award: £60,000 (can advance £15,000 for BPTC)

"If you achieve the appropriate standard, you will be kept on. It's not rocket science at this set."

Located in leafy Lincoln's Inn, this dynamic commercial set has a particular penchant for professional liability work.

Common people

"Our roots are in general common law, but over the years we've developed into a diverse commercial offering," senior clerk Lizzy Stewart told us. Having moved to 4 New Square in 2000, *"we took the opportunity to focus on becoming more modern and businesslike."* Twelve years on, the set is physically expanding, into newly refurbished 2 New Square.

From construction and insurance to public and sports law, this set undertakes a variety of work. *"We are maintaining a focus in professional liability, however,"* Lizzy Stewart maintains. *"The area still generates around 50% of our revenue."* Top-ranked by *Chambers UK* for its professional negligence work, the set was involved in 2012's most complex litigation in the Caribbean, the $2-3bn civil fraud claim arising from the collapse of Trinidad and Tobago's largest insurance company. Members also acted for Barclays Private Lending in a claim for fraud and negligence against a number of property professionals and mortgage introducers, and represented the Bank of Scotland in its £10m claim against firm Dundas & Wilson for failure to detect a potential fraud.

4NS's barristers have also been busy in this Olympic year, among other things representing the Montenegro Olympic Committee in relation to the selection and participation of boxers and working for GB Rhythmic Gymnastics in its Olympic selection dispute against the British Amateur Gymnastics Association. Head of chambers Sue Carr QC has acted as arbitrator in several selection appeals on behalf of British Pentathlon.

Practice, practice, practice

All pupils sit with supervisors who are about nine to 15 years' call. Head of pupillage recruitment Alex Hall Taylor said: *"We feel by that point supervisors will have developed enough of an experienced and varied practice to give pupils a broad seat. We also make a point to regularly mix in new supervisors every year, to ensure variety."* Pupils said: *"All of the supervisors do some sort of professional liability, but make sure you experience different kinds of work."* One added: *"I did the full range, from sports and Chancery to public law."* For the first six, pupils are often doing 'dead' work, but stressed how *"seriously"* feedback is taken throughout. *"Every piece of work is thoroughly discussed and supervisors always sit down and give you a detailed assessment of how you're doing. We also have both mid and end-of seat reviews, so you're very aware of what you need to improve on."*

Make no mistake, feedback is taken so seriously because *"every single piece of work here is assessed."* Obviously, *"for the first couple of weeks, your standard of work is going be lower, but the expectation understandably rises and rises. Everything you do is marked."* Alongside work for supervisors, there are also written and advocacy assessments. A junior explained: *"Throughout pupillage you're assessed on your intellect, advocacy, temperament and motivation, and written work,"* We're told the latter carries the most weight, though *"you really need to meet an excellent standard on each."* Alex Hall Taylor says: *"Pupils also need to display that 'can-do' attitude."*

Gaining tenancy *"is objective here. If you achieve the appropriate standard, you will be kept on. It's not rocket*

Chambers UK rankings

Construction	Professional Discipline
Costs Litigation	Professional Negligence
Insurance	Sports Law
Product Liability	

science at this set," juniors said. Alex Hall Taylor added: "All reports are reviewed and the decision is taken by chambers as a whole. The intention is to create two tenants a year. We have the work, so as long as the standard is reached, we are looking to take the pupils on." Senior clerk Lizzy Stewart said: "We have a very structured program here and it's very strictly regulated. There are no hidden bars to reach."

Toy cars

Advocacy plays a big part of the 4 New Square pupillage. Juniors said: "You're not in court every day, but we're much more involved in advocacy than some other commercial sets." In the second six, pupils are expected to pick up 'real work' and get on their feet. "You're not going to the Court of Appeal, mind you," pupils said. "It's more on the Bow County Court level and you're always supported by your supervisors." Pupils are also supported by a thorough advocacy training programme called 'First Days on Your Feet.' "It's training in all major areas you're likely to be in court for. You'll have one hour on mortgages, one on motor accidents, one for small claims, and so on. It's practical exercises all the way through and is incredibly helpful." One junior added: "As a tradition, whoever gives the road traffic accident session gives a set of toy model cars to the pupil. They're actually a very useful tool in court, but it's also something you can keep and remind you of your learning days." Take in all the training you can, because pupils are required to take part in an assessed moot in their first six. Run by a former member, and now High Court Judge, this experience forms a good part of the tenancy decision.

Strong characters

4 New Square isn't part of the Pupillage Portal. The set has its own application form, which you can download off the website. "In every application we're looking for intellect, motivation, personal qualities, evidence of leadership and potential as advocates," says Alex Hall Taylor. "This assessment process will cut numbers by 70 to 80%." Out of all applicants, about 40 to 50 people are invited for a short CV-focused interview, which reduces the numbers further, to between ten and 20. A second-round, "much

longer and more formal" interview follows. "This is focused on both legal and ethical questions. There's also an advocacy exercise," says Hall Taylor. "Often you're asked to argue a certain point and then argue the complete opposite," junior members disclosed, "to assess how you formulate your arguments." Finally, candidates attend a non-interview based meeting with members of the set, after which offers are made. Increasingly, previous candidates are re-applying and several people have been successful at the second time of asking.

"Realistically, not everyone has a masters from Harvard and a First from Oxford, but those people are out there," says Hall Taylor, so strong academics are a must if you're going to compete. Otherwise, 4 New Square expects a "degree of self-confidence without the arrogance." A junior said: "We are quite an outgoing set and applicants should be excited to be a part of that." As this chambers has a proud advocacy history, "we would also expect our applicants to have a hunger for getting on their feet. That is a vital quality in coming here," says Alex Hall Taylor.

Stars of the Bar in the bar at the Stars

"I wouldn't say this was a fussy, old traditional place by any stretch," pupils reflected. "We're genuinely a lot more informal than other sets and, it sounds like a cliché, but we really are very friendly." Although still residing in beautiful, traditional settings, it's clear there's a bright spark to this set. Our interviewees were dynamic and straightforward, and only one was in a suit – "because I've been in court," we were assured. Clerks and barristers are all on a first-name basis, with juniors adding: "It would be odd any other way, as we all get on so well." Special commendation goes to the female presence in this set. Although there are ultimately fewer women at a senior level, Sue Carr QC is head of chambers, Lizzy Stewart is senior clerk and the set can boast three female QCs. Juniors said: "There are still plenty of chambers where you'll hardly see any women on a senior level, but we have very balanced numbers here. Both Sue and Lizzy are amazing and instil those attitudes of genuine equality."

In keeping with their non-trad vibe, there isn't afternoon tea, "but chambers does regularly get together for breakfasts," juniors said. "Everyone just chats and the QCs are always particularly keen to hear about your early court experiences." There are also drinks "once a fortnight" and all are treated to a summer party. Otherwise "there's a big junior quota and we're all very sociable." On a Friday night, 4 New Squarers can be found at traditional barristers' hangout the Seven Stars.

And finally...
One out of 4 New Square's three pupils was awarded tenancy in 2012.

XXIV Old Buildings

The facts

Location: Lincoln's Inn, London

Number of QCs/Juniors: 9/29 (10 women)

Applications: Not known

Outside Pupillage Portal

Pupils per year: 2

Seats: 4x3 months

Pupillage award: Up to £65,000 pa

Small and unpretentious, but a multidisciplinary and multi-jurisdictional heavy-hitter.

Slick and complex offshore work is the backbone of this increasingly commercial chancery set.

To the Caymans and beyond

Just over 40 years ago, XXIV Old Buildings was born following the merger of an established traditional chancery set with a newer commercial chancery one. Well praised in *Chambers UK* for both traditional and commercial, the set picks up additional rankings in aviation, company, construction, partnership, professional negligence and insolvency and restructuring. Its location in a peaceful corner of ancient Lincoln's Inn belies the set's mightily modern outlook: step inside, and cloisters give way to a glossy and über-modern interior with large, airy boardrooms. It's clear that XXIV Old Buildings is embracing the future.

Around 15 years ago chambers began to *"push itself internationally,"* and now has an annexe in central Geneva, making it unique – maybe even Euro-chic – within the British Bar. Many of the disputes barristers deal with will have a distinctly offshore element: taking in work from Guernsey, the Cayman Islands, the British Virgin Islands, China, Singapore and Africa in a mixture of trust and shareholder disputes and fraud cases. Aside from cross-border expertise, chambers is defined by the multidisciplinary skills of its barristers. Most people have up to five areas of skill, and joint head of chambers Alan Steinfeld QC continues to be Chambers-ranked in an intimidating ten distinct fields, while the entire set's members have 70 individual *Chambers UK* recommendations.

A compact membership of 38 is committed to strengthening core areas in addition to thinking commercially about its *"genuinely broad spectrum of clients."* Indeed, commercial chancery is marked by its breadth of practice –

they can range from Formula 1 bosses to *"the little old lady diddled out of her inheritance,"* via plenty of *"blood on the boardroom table"* type disputes. Centred around trust and estates, the traditional chancery at XXIV Old Buildings will typically be extremely high-value, often with an international flavour. In the last year members have acted on cases involving big names such as Russian oligarch Boris Berezovsky and property developer Robert Tchenguiz.

What unites these seemingly disparate cases? *"The concept of property,"* whether trusts and equity, probate disputes, or conflicts over aircraft or high-value works of art. As for intellectual property, members recently acted on behalf of several car manufacturers who sought to have other F1 competitors disqualified on the grounds that their 'double diffusers' breached FIA regulation. Fundamentally though, *"these are matters of principle,"* a source at the set told us. *"It's good not to be purely fighting cases for big CEOs. We also act for charities."* Elspeth Talbot Rice QC acted for the RSPCA in *Gill v RSPCA*. The well-publicised challenge came from an only child whose parents left their North Yorkshire farm to the charity and made no provision for her: she made a challenge on the grounds of want of knowledge of her mother.

Commercial, with a chancery twist

Pupils, then, must be prepared to deal with cases from the domestic to the multinational. Though it's vital to keep the set's business bent in mind, barristers also delve deeper into technical black letter law than at your average commercial set. To this end, supervisors highlighted the

Chambers UK rankings

Aviation	Offshore
Chancery	Partnership
Company	Professional Negligence
Fraud	Restructuring/Insolvency

"*emphasis on learning*" that will take place at the start of pupillage: "*Very few who come to us will have done insolvency or even contract and tort,*" said pupil supervisor Bajul Shah. "*There's no point in trying to test people before they have grasped the basics.*" Pupils will rotate four times between the same four supervisors. Each has a different emphasis, and they will pick up a mixture of "*insolvency and company; trust and probate; property; aviation; and general contract disputes.*" Having the same supervisors means a level playing field when it comes to the crunch: "*they have all seen your work and can compare opinions.*"

During each seat, pupils will work on "*preparing for applications, drafting pleadings and skeleton arguments,*" as well as attending client conferences. Rather than being used for discrete tasks, "*supervisors use you as a resource.*" One pupil explained: "*It's been great to feel an active contributor to the team. I drafted a letter and my supervisor mentioned my contribution in front of a client.*" If there's no distinct jump in what they are trusted with between the first and second six, pupils mention a change in the second half of the first six. For one, it was being asked for their opinion as part of an appeal. "*To be treated with that level of professional respect instilled a lot of confidence,*" they told us. Day-to-day work is monitored and pupils "*are told to go home at 6.30pm.*"

Pupils assured us that, although "*experience is commensurate to who you're sitting with,*" all supervisors recognise that their primary job is to teach and that assessment comes second. "*Plus,*" added one, "*pupil paranoia goes far beyond anything chambers can do.*" Work is assessed on an ongoing basis, and formal reviews come at the end of each seat. Bajul Shah explains that "*it works both ways. I will give my views on the pupils to the pupillage committee, who also hear feedback from pupils.*" The pupillage committee will see around three lots of feedback before making any decision on tenancy.

At nine months chambers will decide if it will take on junior tenants. By then pupils will have received such extensive feedback that they will know exactly where they stand as the tenancy decision approaches. Feedback then builds up to the point when "*you know how every piece of work has gone.*" In addition to "*looking for the best advocates of their generation,*" supervisors are looking for clear judgement and "*excellent people skills.*" 2012 saw neither pupil granted tenancy. A shift is felt in the final three months of pupillage. Pupils will be "*filling in gaps*" of work and the emphasis shifts towards "*working for other members of chambers.*"

Organic tea

The vibe in chambers is unpretentious. A formal lunch is given for pupils "*hopefully in their first week,*" but it's "*far from the nightmare of crazy etiquette.*" Tea takes place "*organically. There will often be a party heading off to lunch or a group making tea together at the same time in the afternoon.*" If senior members "*single you out as a pupil, it can be scary at first but they just want to get to know you.*" There is "*banter between everyone from juniors to the head of chambers, and interaction will always go beyond just chit-chat,*" pupils happily informed us. The teamwork culture inherent to the set's casework trickles down into regular informal socialising, to the pub or even the occasional theatre trip.

Application for pupillage is made by CV and covering letter before 1 February 2013, and chambers "*tries to see as many applicants as possible*" (36 in the last cycle) for the first-round interview. Initial interviewees are invited to discuss a problem designed to test "*legal analytical skills.*" "*It's a fairly friendly set, so it's a fairly friendly interview,*" a member of the pupillage committee told us. "*The best analogy is the court: we just want to hear what you have to say.*" Current pupils confirm that the panel of "*three to four*" is "*unstuffy*" and crucially "*really takes into account what stage you're at when applying.*" A shortlist of eight to ten will be invited back for a brief advocacy exercise, out of which up to two will gain pupillage.

And finally...

"There's a completely enlightened attitude," pupils told us. "There has never been unfriendliness or boring research work. You are naturally very well treated."

Old Square Chambers

The facts

Location: Bedford Row, London; Bristol

Number of QCs/Juniors: 14/57 (26 women)

Applications: 221 for London and 119 for Bristol

Apply through Pupillage Portal

Pupils per year: 2

Seats: 3x4 months

Pupillage award: £30,000 + £10,000 guaranteed earnings in second six (£8,000 can be drawn down for BPTC)

"You shadow really experienced people, and they try to make sure you see the range of chambers' work."

If employment or PI are your bag, Old Square should be high on your list.

Et in Arcadia ego

Perhaps in a ruse to sift out the weaker candidates, these chambers are housed on Bedford Row, not Old Square. And from the front it looks like every other stately Georgian house on Bedford Row. Step inside, however, and you're confronted with a sweeping hand-carved staircase in an atrium clad with a dizzying display of 18th century murals. The centrepiece is George I astride a steed trotting through some Arcadian playground accompanied by a swarm of cherubs. The rest of this 1717 building received a refurb when the barristers moved in back in 2005.

Chambers itself is one of the hot names in employment, and that, pupils told us, is the big pull: *"It was the quality of the work that attracted me; it's very interesting."* It has an office in Bristol as well as London, which leads the Western circuit in employment and PI. In London the set devotes *"roughly 55% of its time to employment,"* says senior clerk Will Meade, with the remaining key areas being PI, health and safety, and product liability. Pupils will learn from the best, like Mary O'Rourke QC, a trailblazer in professional discipline, and with names like Jennifer Eady QC and John Hendy QC on board, the employment work will have its thrilling moments. This industrial action-heavy practice recently saw Hendy acting for the RMT in challenging UK strike legislation in the European Court of Human Rights, and representing the NUJ in the Leveson Inquiry. On the PI side the set offers a range of expertise, such as Nigel Cooksley QC's specialism in industrial disease cases. Old Square's PI work is more commonly for claimants, an example being acting for the bereaved families in the Camberwell fire inquiry.

Hangin' with Mr. Cooper

With its strong practice-area focus, Old Square will of course be looking for *"candidates who can show an interest in our specialist areas,"* says head of pupillage Ben Cooper. *"This can be demonstrated by work experience in relevant areas, such as with trade unions, mini pupillages, or master's degrees in our areas."* It's clear strong academics are a must, as is being *"a broad, well-rounded applicant,"* a pupil reflected. *"Let your personality come through on the application form."*

The set picks 40 applicants for interview. The first round is 20 minutes long in front of a panel of two or three, which poses a legal problem *"that they are unlikely to have seen before."* A pupil explained: *"It was a discussion of the practical aspects of a legal problem."* The panel feeds candidates a few questions based on their application forms, as well as some *"theoretical or philosophical problems."* One interviewee told us: *"They are looking to determine your advocacy skills. It comes down to persuasiveness, how you present yourself."* As pupils spoke about the interviews like a vague distant memory, it was clear there was no rottweiler on the panel: *"I wasn't being grilled. They gave me the opportunity to talk about myself."*

Old Square asks eight of the 40 for a second interview, which focuses on intellectual agility and flair for advocacy. In this *"we require them to apply their general legal knowledge,"* explains Cooper. *"It takes place in the form of a mock conference, where one person plays the client so we can judge their client-handling skills. It's the problem questions that really sort people out."* One successful candidate boasted that *"it was fairly laid-back,"* although this view is perhaps not one shared by the unlucky major-

Chambers UK rankings

Employment	Personal Injury
Health & Safety	Product Liability

ity. A nugget of wisdom: *"Engage the panel. Allow them to see who you are and what your potential is."*

Strike while it's hot

Pupillage here is *"one of the biggest learning curves I've ever been through,"* according to one source. *"There's a genuine recognition that you're here to learn."* The learning process is shared between four supervisors for three months at a time. The first six sees pupils shadowing supervisors, who arrange the work for them, which ranges from *"doing paperwork"* to *"shadowing them at the Leveson Inquiry."* The true value of the first six is that *"you shadow really experienced people, and they try to make sure you see the range of chambers' work."* For the unions pupils *"went to the tube trains strike injunction and the bus drivers' strike."* On the employers' side pupils witness cases with *"the NHS, Barclays and BP."*

During the second six *"you'll spend a lot of time on your feet."* The clerks arrange the work rather than supervisors *"but they also do work for members."* The principally PI and employment cases the pupils take on are in the form of *"small claims, Mags' Court work, fast-track PI cases."* One pupil gave us a flavour of what to expect: *"I dealt with cases like unlawful deduction of wages, discrimination, road traffic claims and a criminal injuries inquest."* The time spent on their feet gave our interviewees the occasional buzz: *"I won a multi-day discrimination case. I secured a high reward for that."* One also boldly proclaimed: *"I have enjoyed pupillage more than my friends at other places,"* and added: *"It's very different to the Commercial Bar. The emphasis is on court work rather than paperwork. There's an expectation to be on your feet."*

All this action comes at a price. *"The second six is more pressured, but they are good at making sure they're not overloading you and insist on us taking holidays."* Cooper says: *"We impose a limit of three days a week in court in the second six."* Pupils saluted the set's recognition of a work-life balance. During the first six they send them home at 6pm, and although the work increases in the second six, working until 9pm is infrequent: *"We leave at a responsible time."*

"I co-wrote an article," chimed an interviewee in a bid to illustrate how the set offers opportunity early on. Pupils backed Ben Cooper's claim: *"We spend a lot on their training, we treat them like an investment. We pay for them to attend advocacy courses and there's a lot of in-house knowledge-sharing. We do sessions on interesting cases people have had."*

Commoners all

Regarding tenancy, Cooper told us: *"We can't guarantee there'll always be space, but our aim is to take on anyone who meets our criteria."* Thankfully recent tenancy figures indicate that they got the numbers right, with 100% offered rooms in chambers over the past seven years. *"You know whether you've made it at the end of June,"* but before you leap over the finish line there are three assessments to negotiate. The set calls them 'papers' and they tend to be about PI or employment cases. *"They write a skeleton argument, then the panel discusses their opinion, then they present the argument,"* Cooper says. The focus of these tests is on *"advocacy and written skills."* The fun doesn't end there: *"Your supervisors write a detailed report"* and solicitors' opinions also play a role in the tenancy decision. The clerks have a say, too: *"You fit in here if you have the personality to get on with the client. Our philosophy is that we want to be an extension of the solicitors,"* says Will Meade. Pupils do see some benefit of this white-knuckle ride: *"You constantly get feedback, and that's invaluable. The assessment seems more transparent than other chambers."*

Our visit to OSC unearthed a record number of breakout areas, helping to foster that *"friendly atmosphere"* – something of a buzz-phrase throughout our interviews. One source mentioned: *"Junior members have been fantastic to me: after the very first drinks I had all the phone numbers of the baby juniors!"* No doubt this ambience has something to do with the *"pub culture, which is not just on Fridays."* Summer parties, Christmas jollies, and football with the clerks are high points in the social calendar. Our interviewees talked of the *"tolerant and progressive"* feel at OSC: *"We're not a stuck up set, we are all about anti-discrimination."* Nor is hierarchy a big deal: *"John Hendy shares office space with a pupil we took on last year."* Ben Cooper has the final word: *"We are hardworking, but at the same time informal – a lordish attitude would not sit with chambers. We just want people who shine as advocates."*

And finally...

If you're serious about Old Square, make sure your towering intellect and show-stopping advocacy skills come across in interview. The set will be judging *"your ability to analyse information and respond in a short time frame."*

Pump Court Tax Chambers

The facts

Location: Gray's Inn, London
Number of QCs/Juniors: 10/23 (7 women)
Applications: 80
Outside Pupillage Portal
Pupils per year: 2
Seats: 3 core supervisors
Pupillage award: £50,000 (can advance £12,000 for BPTC)

If you're looking for an intellectual challenge, or just get a kick out of taxes, PCTC could be the perfect set.

We don't need to tell you what this chambers specialises in, but we should tell you its reputation in that field is second to none.

Tax doesn't have to be taxing

We'll be honest: tax isn't usually seen as the sexiest area of law. Tax lawyers – deemed to be old fuddy-duddies in cardigans with no social skills – are sometimes held in the same regard as trainspotters or, worse still, accountants. While the bit about the cardigans may be true, we can honestly say that none of the tax lawyers we've ever met are any less socially skilled than most lawyers...

So what's the appeal of this area of law? Well, it's very challenging and academically rigorous – barristers have to get their heads around a heap of complex precedents with names like the 'Ramsay principle', the 'Redrow principle' and 'Francovich damages'. And legislation changes every year with each new Budget. "*It is interesting because it is complicated and very structured,*" says tax silk and Pump Court's pupillage committee secretary, Giles Goodfellow, "*and because taxation affects everybody, the facts of the case and the industries you work with are very diverse.*" If you look at the variety and complexity of the work done by Pump Court Tax Chambers you'll realise there is a lot more to tax law than just sums. In fact sums don't even really come into the equation.

Pump Court Tax Chambers is the only set to be top-ranked in all three categories of tax law by *Chambers UK*. Its revenue comes in equal measure from these three areas. They are: direct tax (income tax, capital gains and so on); indirect tax (including VAT and customs duties) and personal tax or private client (including trusts, inheritance tax and estates). "*It is interesting just how many areas you get involved with as a tax lawyer,*" Giles Goodfellow reflects. "*You might work on anything from a*

dispute over the tax deductibility of travel expenses to a corporate restructuring resulting from a divorce." PCTC's standing is such that in 2011 one silk was even asked by the Treasury to produce an independent study into anti-tax avoidance rules.

Around 20% of PCTC's work is advisory, but the set is increasingly litigation-heavy. Most of that consists of disputes between 'the taxpayer' (corporations, companies and individuals) and HMRC (usually dubbed 'the Revenue'). Most instructions come from the taxpayer, but PCTC is also increasingly a go-to set for HMRC. Its market standing means members frequently appear on both sides of the same dispute – for example, acting for both Marks & Spencer and HMRC in a dispute over EU law and tax relief on losses made by M&S subsidiaries in Belgium and Germany. Chambers also represented the British Film Institute in a case against HMRC, claiming that an EU cultural exemption applied to VAT on cinema tickets. As these two cases indicate, disputes often arise over perceived clashes between EU and UK law. Tax avoidance – now under increasing scrutiny by the government – also brings in a lot of business. For example, chambers acted for Ocean Finance in a dispute over the offshoring of its advertising business to Jersey for tax purposes.

Money matters

Pupils spend their first three months with one supervisor, followed by two months each with two others. "*I drafted opinions for my supervisor, attended meetings and went to court with them and produced notes,*" said one pupil. "*I also did the skeleton argument for a trusts*

Chambers UK rankings

Tax

---

issue." Live work is mixed with some on cases supervisors have already completed. After this first six, pupils spend one or two weeks each with eight to ten other members of chambers. Some are silks, which means "*there is quite a bit of pressure,*" but "*you are usually just given one or two pieces of work and left to get on with it. And the more you draft and research, the more you know what you are doing.*"

"*Different areas of tax require different skills,*" one source told us. For example, issues of VAT and indirect tax often have an EU dimension. They can also be quite political. "*What appeals to me is that public law can play a big part in our cases,*" said one pupil. "*A case may be about a small £100 fine which HMRC imposes on people who pay their taxes late. But if that policy isn't implemented properly it can be a breach of the obligation to treat people fairly, which links to the core of the relationship between the citizen and the state.*" Private client issues can be "*very personal*" and involve "*understanding family dynamics and the fact that some things are more important than money.*" One pupil recalled working on a case regarding taxation on someone's redundancy payments after they lost their job.

The size and nature of PCTC's cases means pupils don't get on their feet in their second six, but they do sharpen their advocacy skills in three assessed moots involving "*a fictional set of facts, but based on a real problem.*" Each moot is more complex than the last, and the final one – which comes just before the tenancy decision – is attended by around 20 members of chambers. The moots are taken into account as part of the tenancy decision, but "*the most important element of that decision is the recommendations from supervisors,*" says Giles Goodfellow. Both pupils gained tenancy in 2012.

The tax haven

Applications to PCTC begin with a CV and covering letter. First-round interviews last 30 minutes, with 20 of those dedicated to a problem question related to interpretation of a statute which candidates are presented with half an hour before the interview. "*The question is self-contained and we make the facts simple to understand. You don't need to be a tax lawyer or even a lawyer to answer them. A few years ago we asked about tax exemptions for principal private residences.*" Up to eight candidates get through to a second round: a piece of written work, which candidates have eight hours to complete and can be up to 2,000 words long. Recently candidates were asked to analyse a Court of Appeals judgment.

A cosy-sized set with just over 30 tenants, PCTC is still managed fairly traditionally as a 'co-operative' of the clerks and members. Change comes at a leisurely pace: membership has increased from 24 to 31 since 2002. "*It is always hard to anticipate what our areas of growth will be as the tax regime changes year by year with new legislation,*" senior clerk Nigel Jones admits, "*and those changes take a while to filter through to tax litigation.*" Chambers' walls are usually decorated with artwork by the rotating artist-in-residence: when we visited we admired some landscapes and still lifes by Emma Elliot.

In the place of the usual chambers tea, members enjoy 11am morning coffee. "*It can be just social chit-chat, but usually people discuss legal issues or the cases they are working on. It can get pretty heavy sometimes, and if the top silks are there the discussion can be pretty entertaining.*" Younger members tend to do more listening then talking. "*As a pupil you don't speak much, but that is because you don't know very much yet, not because they don't want to hear from you. You usually sit back and soak things up.*"

"*This set is small and feels like a bit of a family,*" said one source. Indeed, a few days before we visited, it had organised drinks to celebrate a junior member's engagement. Members enjoy occasional lunches and the odd pint together and there's a "*Christmas jolly*" to which spouses are invited. Mostly, though, members go home at the end of the day as "*everyone has a life outside chambers.*" Asking for examples, we were told that Andrew Thornhill QC collects boats, fellow silk Julian Ghosh QC fences and Chambers-ranked junior Elizabeth Wilson dances the flamenco.

And finally...
PCTC is a real gem and we're surprised more students who love the academic and complex side of law haven't cottoned onto it.

Quadrant Chambers

The facts

Location: Fleet Street, London

Number of QCs/Juniors: 15/38 (9 women)

Applications: 150-200

Outside Pupillage Portal

Pupils per year: 2

Seats: 2x3 months and 1x6 months

Pupillage award: £55,000 (part of which can be drawn during BPTC)

Quadrant operates from swanky modernised historic premises, reflecting its up-to-date and fresh approach to an ancient area of law.

Top of the game in shipping, aviation and general commercial work, Quadrant Chambers continues to be a leader at the modern Bar.

Infinity chambers

"*I think we're a very modern set,*" juniors reflected. "*Quadrant has moved more in the direction of a business, rather than just lots of individuals. We have a CEO and are marketed as a team.*" One added: "*It's all about embracing change and in many ways this is reflected in the building.*" Ah yes, the building. Quadrant definitely has one of the most impressive offices we've ever set foot in. Victorian stucco and grandeur complement open space and light. "*The building is almost like a firm, but its intricacies of rooms are reminiscent of the old Bar. It's a symbol of balance really,*" interviewees thought. Head of pupillage Tom Macey-Dare added: "*We're not a firm – we're still practitioners, but are much more commercial than even five years ago. We do have a corporate ethos, but it only goes so far. We intend to provide the best commercial service, but there is no intention to change business model and we intend to stay an independent chambers.*"

Top-ranked by *Chambers UK* in aviation, shipping/commodities and travel, Quadrant is also looking to increase its offshore energy practice. Members have also developed practices in areas such as insurance and reinsurance, international arbitration, insolvency and banking. Some are currently representing claimants in the alleged $100m fraud by the management of the Latvian state shipping companies. Chambers has also acted for Russian tycoon Boris Berezovsky in his successful appeal for the commission paid on the sale of his $240m super-yacht; represented Coakley (an air speed sensor manufacturer) in its case against Air France in relation to a fatal crash of June 2009; and represented JPMorgan in a $1.3bn dispute regarding oil prospecting licences in Nigeria.

The need for focus

Quadrant runs a pupillage system of two three-month seats followed by a six-month one, with a change of supervisor each time. Supervisors aren't on any kind of rota, but are chosen in regards to the different types of work they have on. Typically, each will do some form of shipping work, but the pupils "*are exposed to a variety of work, in particular the stuff you'll do upon gaining tenancy,*" juniors explained. "*Certainly when you arrive your first three months are a grace period. You take that time to become accustomed to how we do things and mistakes are almost expected. Of course it depends on the size of the mistakes, but really the first three is a learning curve on the way to doing live work.*" From the second three onwards, pupils regularly get involved in real work and become a "*support for their supervisors.*"

As we're talking about the commercial Bar, pupils don't get on their feet until after the tenancy decision. Quadrant "*takes the sensible view that you need to have mastered the theory before being sent to court. By the end of the nine months, you're prepared enough with the knowledge, so can simply concentrate on the traditions of advocacy.*" Once the tenancy decision is made, "*you're in court quite a bit. That's actually only three months later than your peers.*" Juniors focus on a variety of general commercial work in their first couple of years.

Beyond work for their supervisor, pupils undergo written and advocacy assessments. Otherwise pupils are reliant on their supervisors to assess and teach them. "*Your supervisors are protective of you. You don't get ad hoc pieces of work from other members of chambers, so rather*

Chambers UK rankings

Aviation	International Arbitration
Commercial Dispute Resolution	Shipping
	Travel

than allow you to have one bad day and then have a random member holding that piece of work against you, your supervisors fully assess you as a whole."

The process of gaining tenancy is quite straightforward. *"It's definitely not a popularity contest,"* juniors agreed. *"Ultimately it's about your work and competency levels – at every level. Even if it's photocopying or bringing documents to court, your work needs to have been consistent. A lot of pupillage is about being reliable and organised."* The emphasis *"is on learning and enjoying the work itself. If you're meeting a high standard, the expectation is that you will be taken on and they're preparing you for that."* All three pupils stayed on as tenants in 2012.

Thoughts and thinkers

"I think we have one of the most thorough application processes around, actually," says Tom Macey-Dare. Quadrant isn't part of the Pupillage Portal, instead opting for an application form you can download off its website. *"We sift down the numbers to about 50 people. Those are sent out a set of papers, from which they need to write an opinion to be returned to the set."* Don't worry if you haven't written an opinion before. *"I hadn't done anything of the like,"* a junior said. *"Mine wasn't laid out perfectly, but then chambers isn't looking for that. They want to see that you can write well, have analysed the papers and thought of some potential solutions."* The opinion is marked blindly. *"It's one of the best things about the application – because it doesn't matter if you have a starred First from Cambridge: the assessor won't know. Decisions are made totally on the merit of your paper."* The best 16 are called for a panel interview, where they're given two sets of papers to discuss. *"One is a passage from a judgment and the other's an ethical issue."* The interview is a chat about their opinion and the documents, with questions increasing in difficulty. *"It's not about getting the right answer, but about how you develop and present your arguments. At no stage do you require specific legal*

knowledge and all those from halfway through the GDL should be completely comfortable with the level."

Quadrant is looking for people who *"think clearly and rationally and can thoroughly express themselves under pressure,"* says Macey-Dare. Showing interest in the commercial Bar is clearly easier if you've done a law degree, but if you haven't, *"assess which method of learning you enjoy and which GDL subjects you like best. If you enjoy those with more factual detail and intellectual, yet practical issues, then the commercial Bar is suited to you. Applicants need to show that they enjoy the analytical dissecting of problems on a practical scale, rather than an encyclopaedic knowledge of the business world."* Juniors stressed the importance of doing mini-pupillages although it's not a prerequisite to have done one at Quadrant. As for the firm's shipping specialism, *"you definitely don't have to be an avid sailor to want to come here,"* juniors reassured us.

We saw three shipping lawyers...

"We're pretty relaxed within chambers," juniors said. *"Everyone is very close-knit and friendly."* One source had *"even been on holiday with people from Quadrant – that closeness is encouraged here."* Interviewees thought this was partly by virtue of never being directly compared throughout your pupillage. *"I don't think I ever did the same piece of work as my fellow pupils, and ultimately if they want to, Quadrant can take everyone on. It means you can all support each other and actually become friends."* There is a certain amount of hierarchy between juniors and QCs, and pupils are still expected to wear formal dress, but we were assured *"pupils always feel integrated. Part of the suit thing is that you never know when you'll be off to court to help or observe, so it's really more common sense than anything."*

There's no official tea at the set, but *"we have both a summer and Christmas party. The Crimbo do is particularly special."* Well-known (if you listen to Classic FM) choir The Sixteen are partly sponsored by chambers. *"In return they line the balcony of our library for Christmas and sing, while we enjoy mince pies and mulled wine. It's a phenomenal occasion."* Otherwise *"there's always a fairly consistent trickle of people going down to Daly's Wine Bar on a Friday evening."*

And finally...

"You need to be comfortable with the fact that you're going to predominantly be at your desk, undertaking research and analysis. It's less about the theatrics and more about those interested in minute detail." If that's the sort of barrister you'd like to be, look up Quadrant.

Queen Elizabeth Building (QEB)

The facts

Location: Temple, London

Number of QCs/Juniors: 6/27 (15 women)

Applications: 160-180

Apply through Pupillage Portal

Pupils per year: Up to 3

Seats: 3x4 months

Pupillage award: £25,000 pa minimum

You can't choose your family, but you can choose this mightily impressive family law set.

A full array of family services is on offer at QEB and will appeal to candidates looking for a commercial practice that deals with "*real people.*"

Family pride

Eighty years in family law have secured this set a sparkling reputation and a top spot in *Chambers UK*. Queen Elizabeth Building offers an extensive array of family legal services: jurisdictional disputes; cross-border divorces; prenuptial agreements; civil partnerships; financial and domestic injunctions; private children's law; child abduction; Inheritance Act claims; and disputes between former cohabitees. But this understated set is perhaps best known for its international, financial and ancillary work. As senior clerk Ivor Treherne explained: "*We are also moving towards a focus on children's issues throughout matrimonial proceedings.*" There is also a sprinkling of personal injury and professional negligence work going on.

While Legal Aid work accounts for a share of this set's work, QEB is dominated by private clients, from City high-flyers, captains of industry and landed estates, to sport and entertainment stars. In 2010, chambers was instructed to act on both sides of the glossy-mag-selling divorce between Cheryl and dexterous texter Ashley Cole.

The set takes on up to three pupils a year. Tim Amos QC commented that the modest size of the set is "*intentional. There are no plans to expand unless it's done naturally.*"

Anything you can do, I can do...

"*About five years ago*" QEB changed the pupillage rotation system. Now, pupils begin with a four-month seat, followed by a three-and-a-half-month seat, and conclude with a four-and-a-half-month seat to really showcase their skills to their final supervisor before the tenancy decision is made. The idea is "*to give pupils as much exposure as possible to a diversity of work.*" Junior members thought "*the structure means your time in a seat is never too drawn out. You have long enough to learn about the work and your supervisor's ways of doing things.*"

In keeping with the set's specialities, pupils are predominantly exposed to financial and ancillary work, but also witness a variety of family law. "*There is a complete array of clients. We pride ourselves on the complex financial cases, but for juniors, most of the work tends to be more run of the mill.*" Pupils and juniors insisted they "*had never had lots of dogsbody stuff,*" instead the system tends to run under the ethos: "*If your supervisor is drafting, so are you.*" Pupils tackle the same tasks as their supervisors, comparing end results. This allows for regular verbal and written feedback. Otherwise "*there are two informal advocacy projects, followed by a formal assessment; two law notes to write; and two final written assessments. In addition to regular comments, at the end of each seat pupils receive a formal feedback report.*"

At a time when Legal Aid is under threat and family law is being shifted away from the courts to mandatory ADR sessions, is there still the opportunity of actual advocacy experience? According to pupil supervisor Katie Cowton, although Legal Aid issues have had an impact, "*there are plenty of opportunities for pupils to be on their feet. Court time tends to come once or twice a week at QEB, with an increase towards the end of pupillage, and we have a lot of private work that keeps us busy.*" Tim Amos said: "*The Legal Aid cuts are affecting the entirety of the Bar and*

Chambers UK rankings

Family/Matrimonial

although we continue to feel that it is an important part of our practice, it isn't necessarily the whole part. We intend to continue to pay our pupils a minimum of £25,000 pa, excluding earnings."

Sticking around

As member of the pupillage committee Amy Kisser said: *"We only recruit from our own pupils,"* and the entire set comes together to discuss the decision in July. *"The head of chambers takes the final decision, but only in so much as the Queen does! He is always swayed by the majority."* Is the set constricted by space? *"Never: if all three are brilliant, all will be taken on,"* confirmed Tim Amos QC. Pupil supervisor Katie Cowton confirmed: *"The aim is to keep people on, but if we can't we bend over backwards to help them find another set."*

Although the road to tenancy is fraught with competition, junior sources assured us: *"We are all very good friends. We know that not everyone might be kept, but it helps to know we have a respected pupillage programme that never fails to place people. The ethos and culture is friendly and the pupillage experience is never unpleasant. We like each other and chambers encourages that."* As it happened, all three pupils were offered tenancy in 2012.

Cheers

Picture a dinner party among a handful of the intelligentsia: an evening that promises mental acrobatics but also some enjoyment. That's what interviews are like at QEB. *"It isn't about scaring the candidates or being unpleasant: we want to actively engage by giving them a fair and interesting interview,"* Katie Cowton told us. The set had over 170 applications through the Pupillage Portal in 2012, with roughly 20 invited for interviews. Every single application is independently reviewed by three members of chambers.

Tim Amos QC defined the set: *"The common core is our interpersonal skills matched with rigorous academic skill and the ability to deal successfully with people from all walks of life at difficult times in their personal lives. In particular, because of the amount of international and particularly financial/commercial family law we do, QEB represents a real alternative for the clever, aspiring City lawyer who doesn't want to deal with companies and balance sheets, but wants instead to deal with real people."*

Little family

QEB barristers say that chambers has *"changed enormously over the last 25 years. We used to be all horses and divorces, but we've come a long way from that and are looking forward."* With a host of illustrious members (five Family Division judges are former QEB members and one former member, Lord Wilson, sits in the Supreme Court), *"you can see where the 'traditional' tag comes from, but in terms of the people working here, they are very modern in their attitude."* This is evidenced by a distinct lack of hierarchy. As the pupils explained, *"we all know each well and you can talk to everyone in chambers."* Pupil supervisor Katie Cowton commented: *"Our QCs are never separate: they get to know everyone, especially the pupils. It is a very supportive place."* Ivor Treherne added: *"Pupils are the future of our chambers and so are very important. We are too small for there to be politics."* This attitude extends to the clerks and their office. Although *"misters and misses"* are used, juniors thought they *"had a very good relationship with the clerks"* and that they are *"very approachable."*

Tea is very much encouraged at QEB and pupils are encouraged to attend, as it *"gives them the opportunity to interact and get to know what's going on in chambers and work-wise."* There are other chambers gatherings, including Christmas parties, solicitor/client events and junior dinners; however, *"there isn't a big drinks culture. Everyone has their own lives and we don't really head to the pub."*

And finally...

It's said the best things come in small packages and although this set is not the biggest, it's certainly one of the best when it comes to family law.

South Square

The facts

Location: Gray's Inn, London

Number of QCs/Juniors: 19/21 (7 women)

Applications: 150

Outside Pupillage Portal

Pupils per year: 2

Seats: 6x6 weeks

Pupillage award: £60,000 (some can be drawn down for BPTC)

A sleek modern set with a hint of the City about it

South Square does some of the best insolvency and restructuring work in London.

Top billing

Insolvency has always been this set's top focus. *"We have several financial, commercial and business practices here, but insolvency and restructuring is at our core and we intend to stay at the top of our specialism,"* says pupillage director Martin Pascoe QC. Top-ranked by *Chambers UK* for insolvency, South Square is also highly rated for its banking/finance and offshore expertise. About one-quarter of the set's work now involves offshore disputes. *"There's also been an increase in our sport and shipping work this year,"* Pascoe says.

Located in picturesque Gray's Inn, chambers is currently undergoing renovation. *"You have to move with the times,"* says senior practice manager Michael Killick. *"We're expanding into the adjacent building to create a better and more polished space. It's what our client base expects."* Pascoe adds: *"We're actually quite young in comparison to some of our peers, so we aren't 'transitioning' into a modern chambers as such. We started off with a fresh and commercially aware approach."*

"We've basically been involved in every large insolvency that's been," says Michael Killick. Judging from the case list, this is a pretty accurate statement. From Lloyds, Enron, Woolworths, Madoff Securities to Lehman and Swissair, the list of big names brought low is almost endless and in these troubled times, business is good. Interviewees were drawn to the set for its *"excellent reputation"* and market focus, but stressed the set's focus of heads-down research and complex analysis. As one explained, *"insolvency covers a range of legal disciplines, so requires a wealth of legal knowledge. This in turn needs to be intertwined with a full understanding of the business world."*

Southern Exposure

South Square pupils sit with a different supervisor every six weeks (which usually works out at about six to eight supervisors across the course of pupillage). *"It's really one of the best things about doing a pupillage here,"* said one source. *"It not only gives you exposure to the different practices we have, but also allows you to get to know more members of chambers. Six weeks is just the right amount of time to observe and immerse yourself into the work."* Another said: *"It also exposes you to a variety of working styles, helping you develop your own."* Pupillage director Martin Pascoe added: *"From our point of view we think it's better for a greater number of member to assess the pupils on an extended basis. We don't think it's enough, or indeed fair, for them simply to be assessed on the odd piece of work here and there."* Around April, pupils return to their first supervisor, *"so chambers can evaluate your progression,"* Pascoe said. A pupil added: *"It's evidence of how carefully orchestrated the system is, and how seriously training is taken here."*

As with any system, there are downsides. *"It'd be a lie not to say you're thrown into the deep end every six weeks. It isn't a huge length of time, so there is slightly less grace period in which to make mistakes. It also makes it doubly important to make a good personal impression from the offset."* Sources did add: *"Although not always easy, it's very reflective of practice and real life. You're given excellent work from day one, and although nerve-wracking, it's

Chambers UK rankings

Banking & Finance	Offshore
Chancery	Restructuring/Insolvency
Company	

the best way to learn." Each supervisor has an informal review with the pupil at the end of the six weeks, followed by a formalised appraisal after the first six months. "*You know how you're doing throughout.*"

Pupils won't get on their feet until after the tenancy decision. "*The sort of work we do is of labyrinthine complexity, remember,*" sources said. "*There's a huge amount of documentation and research and the emphasis of the pupillage needs to be on how to conduct the appropriate analysis.*" Martin Pascoe added: "*That's the nature of the commercial Bar. Cases are larger and there will inevitably be more paperwork.*" Interviewees agreed they "*would rather be working at a high level of law*" than getting into advocacy earlier. Once they gain tenancy, juniors are in court on average twice a week. New tenants are paired with both a junior of two to three years' call and a senior member of chambers to help them learn the ropes of advocacy.

The tenancy decision is made by the executive committee. "*Ultimately it's working hard and getting on with people,*" one junior said. As obvious as that sounds, "*you have to show that your standard of work has improved throughout and that you have deployed good personal skills. A premium really is placed on your diplomacy and client-facing abilities.*" The set stresses that it never takes on more pupils than it could potentially retain. "*If you're achieving a high enough standard, you will be kept on,*" Pascoe confirmed, and one out of two pupils stayed in 2012.

Analyse this

South Square take on two (sometimes three "*if they're good enough*") pupils a year. The set is not on the Pupillage Portal and applications should be made in writing to the Pupillage Secretary at South Square by post or by e-mail, with a covering letter, CV and two references. "*We review all applications and then take about 30 to 40 candidates on to the next stage,*" says Pascoe. "*The first interview is conducted by two members and aims to test candidates' analytical abilities and ability to identify and discuss important issues.*" Sixteen to 20 applicants are taken on to a second interview with the entire pupillage committee. "*We tend to ask each candidate a set of standardised questions, in order to give each an equal chance. We often ask them to discuss or argue an ethical issue.*" On occasion, candidates are invited for a third interview, "*but normally after two we know enough.*"

Sources advised: "*The most important thing is to do your research on the set. Beyond the internet, we have a chambers magazine with updates of work and cases – so reading that is a good way to get a sense of what's going on.*" Additionally, "*you need to have an interest or be prepared to develop an interest in the financial and business world,*" they continued. "*We're in a service industry and the commercial Bar is all about the needs of clients.*"

The specified academic baseline is a 2:1, but it's important to remember "*of the people applying, the level is very high across the board.*" If you poke around the member bios on South Square's website, you'll find plenty of Oxbridge alumni and those with post-graduate qualifications. "*We are looking for good academics, but a good transcript isn't enough,*" says Pascoe. "*We're looking for those who can flourish in a commercially demanding environment and perform to an excellent standard under pressure.*"

Chambers doesn't do tea and we get the impression there are more sociable sets out there, but the overall atmosphere of the chambers was praised for being "*measured and amiable.*" "*There is a genuine emphasis on personability.*" In our experience, the set is one of calm and sophistication.

And finally...

Pupils are required to wear suits. *"There's some notion of hierarchy I suppose,"* a source said, *"but it's by no means oppressive, everyone is very willing to help you."* By not being in direct competition for places, juniors said, *"the set allows you to foster wonderful and supportive relationships with fellow pupils."*

2 Temple Gardens

The facts

Location: Temple, London

Number of QCs/Juniors: 9/44 (21 women)

Applications: 261

Apply through Pupillage Portal

Pupils per year: 2

Seats: 2x3 and 1x6 months

Pupillage award: £60,000 (can advance up to £22,500 for BPTC)

With an increasingly well-rounded practice 2TG is *"forward thinking,"* but with *"the best elements of the traditional Bar."*

With well-regarded personal injury, clinical negligence, professional negligence and insurance practices, 2 Temple Gardens mixes the old with the new.

A room with a view

2 Temple Gardens' Grade 1-listed building – replete with Edwardian fireplaces and stuccoed ceilings – sits at the southern end of the Temple with panoramic views of Inner Temple Gardens and the River Thames. Some of the antiquity of the building rubs off on its members. *"We retain the best elements of the traditional Bar,"* they say: *"We're not stuffy, but we are quite a mixed bunch and everyone is willing to help each other out."* But this is a *"forward-looking"* set too: its building was recently renovated to give it a contemporary edge and it puts on a large number of seminars for solicitors *"for us as barristers to sell ourselves."*

Chambers' strengths lie in personal injury and clin neg on the civil side, and in professional discipline, professional negligence and insurance disputes on the commercial side. There are also a few smaller areas of practice, such as banking and finance, property, contract disputes and employment. *"In the last two years the commercial side of this set has grown,"* says senior clerk Lee Tyler. *"We rightly have a strong reputation as a defendant insurance claims set, but our commercial practices are rapidly growing."*

Call for Poirot

Personal injury and clin neg make up 30 to 40% of the practice. Most of this is work for defendants, but there is a growing claimant practice too. NHS trusts and strategic health authorities are frequent clients in clin neg cases. Recent cases have centred on the misuse of forceps and the suicide of a mental health patient. On the PI side,

members frequently represent insurers in workplace stress and harassment, asbestos disease and RTA claims. Head of chambers Benjamin Browne QC recently worked on an RTA claim worth £20m and has represented claimants in the atomic test veterans litigation. Other claims have involved a horse startled by pigs, an escaped cow, an arm cut off by a circular saw, a schoolgirl falling out of a window and – we kid you not – an accident on the Orient Express. Appropriately, *"we sometimes have to act like detectives as there are always new factual details which need to be investigated."*

Ranked in *Chambers UK* for both professional negligence and professional discipline work, 2TG is often instructed by professional indemnity insurers and has built a strong reputation for acting on cases against engineers and insurance brokers as well as lawyers and financiers. In one recent case, members defended a refrigeration business against a claim brought by a pharma company over the loss of £1m worth of drugs due to a malfunctioning fridge. The set's barristers have also worked on several insurer-on-insurer disputes recently, including *Municipal Mutual Insurance (MMI) v Zurich* – a £70m spat over the structuring of insurance policies between 1948 and 1992 in relation to the asbestos disease mesothelioma.

Academic results – including A levels – are most important to recruiters, followed by advocacy experience, extracurricular activities (especially leadership and teamwork), any prizes won, and interest in the set's practices. Forty-five applicants are invited to an assessment day, which starts with a group exercise: eight candidates at a time debate a non-legal topic. *"We were told we represent-*

Chambers UK rankings

Clinical Negligence	Personal Injury
Insurance	Professional Negligence

ed small start-up businesses and asked to argue why we should receive funding," one pupil recalled. Following this, applicants are given ten minutes' notice of an "*indefensible*" topic of which they are asked to argue in favour. Chambers also "*sets out its stall*" with presentations on each practice group and a chance to meet some of the maybe 15 tenants present. Fifteen candidates progress to a second interview, which includes a legal problem case study and standardised competency and CV questions.

Bingo!

Pupils sit with three supervisors over the course of the year: usually, each offers experience in a different field. One source had done commercial banking and prof neg work, followed by employment and PI, and then clin neg. "*When you start, you often have a first go at your supervisor's drafting work while they are doing it too. Then they will go through it and explain what you have done right and wrong. It is gratifying if a few of your words are inserted into the final version. As you progress through pupillage more of your work gets used.*" Documents to be drafted include particulars of claim, advice to clients, skeleton arguments and pleadings. "*The drafting work is factually complicated and there are a lot of precedents involved. At the end of the first six you've seen all the major bits of paperwork come by.*" Pupils also receive work from other members of chambers and shadow them in court. "*I did maybe ten or 12 large pieces of work for others during my first six.*"

Oral advocacy dominates the second half of pupillage. "*As soon as the second six starts you are available to be sent off to court.*" Pupils often begin with infant approval hearings, moving on to small claims, fast-track trials and case management on RTA cases. "*Because of the volume and the low value of the cases, the insurers are happy for pupils to take them on. You get experience dealing with everything from shouting judges to missing clients.*" Eventually pupils are on their feet two or three times a week. "*It can be very entertaining: I once had to go to Chelmsford to represent a lorry driver called Johnny*

Bingo. You meet people you would never meet otherwise and for a few hours you get really obsessed by their case.*"

Assessment at 2TG is a "*cumulative process*" – pupils are given appraisals after three months and after six. When it comes to the tenancy decision, "*the supervisors' reports are most important, followed by oral and written feedback from other members.*" Feedback from the clerks and two assessment exercises have weight too, but when it comes to the latter a baby junior says: "*I don't think the exercises impact on the tenancy decision unless you were entirely hapless.*" One of the two pupils gained tenancy in 2012 – a successful continuation of a strong retention rate: 2TG has taken on all but one of its nine pupils since 2008.

Cycling PI

"*This is a sociable set. There is a Christmas do and we also recently had a party with drinks and fish and chips to celebrate part of the building being redecorated.*" Chambers tea is held weekly on Wednesdays. "*There is a rota and a different member hosts and brings a cake each week.*" The chat is "*mostly about law. Members use it as an opportunity to talk about their recent work, but anyone can talk and there is no strict etiquette. And when you've just started your second six, everyone takes an interest and gets all nostalgic about their first time on their feet.*" Weekly Friday drinks also take place and members frequently go for lunch in Middle Temple Hall. "*It is important to meet members during pupillage,*" a junior reflected, "*but it doesn't have to be during tea or the social events.*"

"*You come to know the varying styles and personalities of your supervisors and the other members,*" one pupil said. "*They are all quite different. There is never one chambers view on things.*" For example, *Chambers UK*-ranked silk Martin Porter QC is something of a road safety campaigner. A keen cyclist, he writes a personal blog (thecyclingsilk.blogspot.com) about cycling (obviously) and about the PI cases he's bringing against dangerous drivers.

2TG's marketing strategy revolves around its seminar programme. Held three or four times a month, the seminars are given by members of chambers and are designed to show off practice areas to prospective solicitor clients. Pupils attend too and "*learn new things, pass around drinks and chat to the solicitors.*" The set also recently hosted a "*fabulous*" 'thank you' marketing event for its clients at the top of The Gherkin.

And finally...

Two top tips: first, when applying to this set, showcasing your logical reasoning and advocacy skills matters more than past experiences. Second, doing a mini-pupillage is viewed as a big plus.

3 Verulam Buildings

The facts

Location: Gray's Inn, London

Number of QCs/Juniors: 22/45 (13 women)

Applications: 150-200

Apply through Pupillage Portal

Pupils per year: 3

Seats: 4x3 months

Pupillage award: £60,000 (can advance £20,000 for BPTC)

"From the interview it was clear this was a relaxed group of people who would offer me a great experience."

Pupils at this commercial high-flyer claim: "*It's difficult to imagine anywhere better."*

Wide load

The frequency with which members of 3 Verulam Buildings grace the rankings of *Chambers UK* gives a solid indication of the set's top-tier status in the commercial sector. Indeed, 3VB currently has more juniors in the commercial dispute resolution table than any other set, a clear sign of a strong recruitment force and a definite draw for prospective pupils. "*The pupillage committee has done a great job with recruitment – now our juniors are becoming silks and very strong people are taking their place,*" declared a senior practice manager. "*Pupils know they'll be sitting with the best here.*" As a set that especially favours banking and finance litigation, 3VB may very well be able to attribute its commercial success to changing attitudes towards chambers management: as one QC put it, "*gone are the days of chambers being a collection of independent individuals; barristers now belong to brands and there's a corporate structure and approach to the way they work. We're all engaged in a project here as part of a team.*"

The set has historically leaned towards the banking and finance side of things, but management is keen to emphasise that 3VB is no one-trick pony: while chambers certainly excels in these sectors – barristers do everything from County Court consumer credit cases to interim applications in the High Court – the insurance and media practices are equally praiseworthy, with a number of other commercial services not far behind. "*Our set comprises all the areas of commercial law, including litigation, fraud, insurance, IT and telecoms,*" a practice manager explained. "*Our instructions come from a wide variety of City and national firms as well as banks.*" The last decade

has seen the set gain increasing recognition for these practices: 3VB's international arbitration work in particular has been singled out for its top-tier expertise in commercial disputes. Fortunately, the increase in disputes as a hangover from the recession means 3VB has had an increase in volume of instructions. "*We actually have the question of limitation coming up,*" says the set, implying it now has the luxury of turning work down. It did, however, get embroiled in the aftermath of Rangers FC's recent fall from grace, acting for Collyer Bristow when the firm was sued for at least £25m in damages relating to their role in the club's administration. Rangers' administrators accused Collyer Bristow of professional negligence and breaching their fiduciary duty.

Members give 3VB "*ten out of ten for fantastic accommodations.*" Situated snugly in Gray's Inn, the set supplies a slew of in-house resources, while Gray's Inn Library is a stone's throw away if additional research is needed. Thanks to a large refurbishment several years ago, members enjoy their own rooms, many with views of the garden. As far as internal growth goes, 3VB presently has no plans for expansion beyond its normal annual intake of three pupils, though recruiters aren't opposed to adding people "*ad hoc if they fit the bill.*"

Tabula rasa

Our sources agreed 3VB is the kind of set where "*pupils arrive with the intent of staying here,*" so recruiters are meticulous from the start. Roughly 40 applicants are called to the first round of interviews, where they get a (rather brief) chance to introduce themselves to three

Chambers UK rankings

Banking & Finance	Insurance
Commercial Dispute Resolution	International Arbitration
	Media & Entertainment
Financial Services	Professional Negligence
Fraud	Restructuring/Insolvency
Information Technology	Telecommunications

board members before engaging in a chat on a topic of the board's choosing – usually a current legal issue. The chat *"isn't designed to test knowledge but to explore candidates' ability to speak spontaneously,"* so applicants don't need to memorise anything beforehand but should brush up on their public speaking skills all the same. One successful applicant's advice? *"Read the newspapers so you're clued up on current events – they might ask you anything!"* Around half of candidates go on to the second interview, in which they are asked to address a legal problem in front of a *"much larger"* panel. The problem, given a week in advance, consists of a fake judgment for which applicants must prepare the appeal. All candidates are given the same problem so the panel can *"judge everyone on a level playing field"* and ensure that the interview is fair for GDL, BPTC and post-qualification students alike. A relatively new addition to the second interview is the submission of an accompanying skeleton argument, to check whether candidates' writing skills are up to scratch. *"We were concerned that people's appearances on the CVs and in person were just not enough,"* explained a member of the recruitment committee.

How to impress at interview? *"The best candidates not only produce succinct arguments and convey them persuasively, but show us a new way of looking at the problem,"* recruiters informed us. *"This is how we sort the sheep from the goats."* A mini-pupillage isn't required to get an interview, but the lucky few who make it through successfully will have a few days of work experience arranged for them if they haven't already completed one. While there are certainly a number of conventional Oxbridge law students awarded pupillage, 3VB welcomes applicants with alternative career paths: among the set's current bunch are an ex-solicitor, a former banker and a concert pianist.

Easy does it

Pupils' first and second sixes are split so that they see four different supervisors for three months each. Since most work comes from their supervisors, this system provides pupils with exposure to a wide range of working styles and material. They are encouraged to seek out additional work from shadow supervisors – juniors allocated among pupils to *"consider any extra work that might be useful."* There's a real chance for pupils to get involved in big cases as well as do some advocacy because clients are so varied. *"I've seen such a broad mix of work!"* one informed us, citing exposure to everything from international fraud to construction disputes to IT arbitration cases. *"There's great strength in this variety: our pupils get the chance to spend time in various courts across the country and become very confident advocates in five to six years' time,"* says 3VB. The amount of court time pupils see *"really fluctuates based on your supervisor's cases,"* but all get a chance to observe their superiors in *"high-level court work"* and typically make their own appearances by the second six. Tenancy decisions are made about nine months in, following a formal progress review and a debate among committee members. The set doesn't entertain automatic dismissals for mistakes made during pupillage. As one QC put it, *"life doesn't work like that."* Rather, *"people only fail if they consistently fall below the standards."* Since chambers isn't divided into specific departments, new members can head in any direction they please upon gaining tenancy. *"The borders are porous here."* One of the two pupils up for decision in July 2012 was granted tenancy, while a slightly later starter was still awaiting final confirmation.

"We're a modern place rather than a stuffy or traditional one," a QC told us. *"There's a real informality among everyone here: we don't have a dress code, there's no timid door-knocking and everyone is on a first-name basis. Still, we're professional."* The set's mellow culture is perhaps best encompassed in the informal interaction between members and clerks, whose relationship is far removed from *"master/servant"* or *"us versus them."* *"It's a collegiate culture in which we respect each other mutually,"* believe QCs and clerks. In keeping with informality, you won't find anyone engaging in afternoon tea here, though there are several annual parties and organised drinks to provide social settings for pupils to get to know their superiors. Of course there's always the inevitable feeling of distance as a new starter, but tenants insist: *"People will be amazed at how quickly colleagues become friends."*

And finally...
Recruiters emphasise that *"keenness, drive and a real desire to get stuck in"* are all crucial qualities in would-be pupils.

Wilberforce Chambers

The facts

Location: Lincoln's Inn, London

Number of QCs/Juniors: 23/30 (9 women)

Applications: c.150

Outside Pupillage Portal

Pupils per year: 2

Seats: 6x2 months

Pupillage Award: Up to £65,000
(can advance £20,000 for BTPC)

Wilberforce is *"an actively growing enterprise"* and has offered all its pupils tenancy since 2011.

Confidence, analytical ability and attention to detail are all vital for success at this set.

A Wilberforce to be reckoned with

In the late 1980s, this London set made the decision to adopt the name of Wilberforce, in honour of one esteemed member's great-great-grandfather, William (…Wilberforce). This renaming has fostered an identity that has become widely recognised in the chancery sphere. *Chambers UK* reveals the set's dominance in top-tier traditional chancery work, having triumphed in a number of probate and tax cases. But private clients are hardly the extent of Wilberforce's mighty reach. Its members are involved in pension matters, appearing in several widely reported insolvency cases in the last year and representing seven different parties in 2010's Pilots' National Pensions Fund case, one of the most complex pensions cases to date. The set has also found success on the real estate scene, recently handling several high-value contractual disputes, particularly those concerning development land, and some prolific credit-crunch litigation.

As evidenced by its commercial success, Wilberforce is at the forefront of the chancery sets embracing the ever-diminishing distinction between chancery and commercial work. In addition to private client and professional liability work, the set's chief undertakings are in its business and finance and property groups, which operate both domestically and internationally. The set is also well reputed in the areas of civil fraud, IP and charities. This range of work is a big attraction for pupils, as it surpasses that of purely commercial sets. Recent noteworthy cases include representation of two international banks seeking to recover €40m from confectioner Ferrero in one of the biggest commercial fraud cases tried in the Chancery Division of the High Court; acting for Leeds United FC in its much-publicised proceedings against the Football League after the club was sanctioned with a 15-point deduction; and instructing Nortel and Lehman Brothers administrators during their Supreme Court battle against the Pensions Regulator.

New directions

Wilberforce's 50 or so members currently occupy three buildings on idyllic New Square, though plans to move are in the works: management is *"currently considering the future direction of the set"* and has put in place a long-term development arrangement that includes reorganising chambers' administration and uniting members under one roof. The best way to describe the current premises is swish: a sleek reception and walls dotted with contemporary art suggest that Wilberforce is a modern entity rather than another classic, stodgy set.

The set is *"an actively growing enterprise,"* now more than twice the size it was a decade ago. Steadily amassing pupils is an important part of expansion, so the recruitment committee takes on two a year, with the intention of offering tenancy to both. Around 150 candidates apply for these two coveted spots each year, so having the right credentials is vital: browsing through Wilberforce's website, you will see a tellingly high number of Oxbridge grads, although recruiters stress that they *"make judgements on grades rather than universities."* Successful applicants *"tend to have Firsts"* and, according to current pupils, *"share the unifying characteristic of being irritatingly clever."* Equally important is a clear interest in commercial chancery work and *"some shred of evidence that*

Chambers UK rankings

Chancery	Fraud
Charities	Offshore
Commercial Dispute Resolution	Pensions
Company	Professional Negligence
	Real Estate Litigation

you're a human being." Luckily, the set offers its own bespoke application, so "*you can sell yourself in a tailored way*" that's unavailable on Pupillage Portal.

So what can a hopeful graduate with impressive grades and relevant extracurriculars expect to encounter in the application process? First up is the paper sift, in which two members of the pupillage committee review all the paper applications made that year to weed out the weak from the strong. Proof of your intellectual ability, experience with communication and ability to cope with the kind of work the set handles all weigh heavily, as does demonstration of an interest in the Bar and Wilberforce above all. The committee's advice for getting an interview: "*Sell yourself in the best way possible and take care on paper.*" Around 30 applicants get invited to a 'longlist' interview in which each spends 15 to 20 minutes discussing a topical question raised during the interview, followed by an informal chat to find out interests and ambitions. The subject of debate is usually a "*newsworthy current event with a moral edge,*" such as freedom of the press, and is designed to test analytical abilities, stress tolerance and people skills. Because the committee "*enjoys people who seize the opportunity to fight their corner,*" pupils advise applicants to "*pick a stance and don't give in!*" About half of applicants are given the chop at this point, with the remaining ones returning for shortlist interviews.

The final stage involves a brief chat for the candidates to settle in, followed by a review of a legal problem given half an hour prior to the interview. Current pupils suggest that applicants avoid trying to be "*too clever*" with these problems as "*they're not designed to trip you up.*" Giving a sensible answer and "*talking on a level playing field*" with the panel is much more likely to show that you can fit into the set. Overall, confidence and top-class intellect "*show more than anything that you have the skills for communicating with clients.*"

Moving on

Because the set undertakes such a broad range of work, pupils sit with six different supervisors for two months each. Each seat offers exposure to different tasks, topics and working styles, and a bonus of having only two months with each supervisor means "*you're never stuck for too long with somebody you don't like.*" Day to day, it's largely research and drafting tasks for pupils, along with the occasional visit to court to observe a superior. Pupils don't make many court appearances in their own right, but they get the chance to accompany supervisors "*at every level,*" including the Supreme Court, Court of Appeal, County Court, Chancery Masters and mediation and arbitration sessions. Pupils also participate in mock conferences to practise advising in court. While not all work is live – indeed, pupils often find themselves taking part in a compare/contrast session with a supervisor's old work – pupils agree that "*it's good to do some dead work*" since it's still assessed and the pressure to get it completely right is lower. There's "*little difference*" between the first and second six, although supervisors tend to rely on pupils more during their last few months of pupillage.

Around nine months into pupillage, the committee gathers to make the tenancy decision, a judgement that's made based on confidential reports put together by supervisors. While there's continual assessment throughout pupillage – indeed, pupils stress that "*absolutely everything*" is assessed – "*it's understood that you'll get better as you progress.*" Pupils who have been granted tenancy (and happily, both of those at the set in 2012 were) begin taking on live work exclusively for their remaining three months of pupillage, and they can actually begin practising officially, although a clerk called this time "*a training period and generally just some time to relax before the real work starts.*"

Afternoon tea isn't really Wilberforce's style, but neither does it have a slick suit culture: depending on how senior you are, jeans and jumpers (and the "*occasional tracksuit,*" as one committee member admitted) are acceptable, though pupils and less senior juniors usually stick to formal attire. Occasional banter with the clerks and regular drinks on Friday mean that pupils "*hardly spend every day in sheer terror.*" Basically, Wilberforce is both sociable and professional, which are equally important in securing a place at this prestigious set. As one committee member hinted, "*coming to events like chambers' lunches as a pupil is good for rubber-stamping the tenancy committee's decision.*"

And finally...

According to pupils, the *"mixed bag"* of work at Wilberforce *"shows you pretty much everything chambers does,"* from private client cases and fraud claims to corporate disputes and charity work.

"For many years there had been a culture of preferential treatment being given to students who were known to chambers. I believe that culture has largely disappeared. That said, I have a worry that the increase in university fees and the removal of grant aid to students will make it very difficult for students from less well-off backgrounds to become barristers."

Sir Anthony Hooper, former Lord Justice of the Court of Appeal.

Read the full interview on chambersstudent.co.uk

A-Z of Barristers

Atkin Chambers

1 Atkin Building, Gray's Inn, London, WC1R 5AT
Tel: (020) 7404 0102 Fax: (020) 7405 7456
Email: clerks@atkinchambers.com
Website: www.atkinchambers.com

No of Silks	**17**
No of Juniors	**24**
No of Pupils	**Up to 2**
Contact	
Mr Andrew Burrows	
Email:	
pupillage@atkinchambers.com	
Method of application	
Pupillage: Pupillage Portal	
Mini-pupillage: CV and	
covering letter to contact	
during March 2013	
Pupillages (p.a.)	
Two	
Income	
(2013/14) £50,000	
Tenancies	
Four in the last three years	

Chambers profile

Atkin Chambers was the first set to specialise in the law relating to domestic and international construction and engineering projects. It has a significant and growing international practice at all levels of seniority. Chambers success in this area has been recognised by the grant of the Queen's Award for Enterprise 2005 in the category of International Trade.

Type of work undertaken

Atkin Chambers is a leader in its field: technology and construction law. Members of Chambers have been involved in many of the largest high-profile domestic and international disputes in the fields of construction, technology, power, energy, computers and telecommunications of recent years, both in court and in international and domestic arbitration. Members of Chambers are regular participants as advocates and advisers in all forms of alternative dispute resolution.

Pupil profile

Applicants for pupillage should have a first-class degree or a good 2:1 degree. Postgraduate qualifications are viewed favourably but are not essential. Applications from non-law graduates are welcome. Atkin Chambers is committed to applying equal opportunities good practice.

Pupillage

Atkin Chambers takes recruitment to pupillage and tenancy extremely seriously. The pupillage award (£50,000 for 2013/14 – equivalent to the sums paid by other much larger sets of chambers) reflects this.

The Pupillage year is structured to provide all of the Bar Council's training requirements and the additional training Chambers considers is necessary for successful entry into high-quality commercial work of its practice. Atkin Chambers provides its own advocacy training and assessment in addition to that provided by the Inns.

Full and up-to date details of the structure and goals of Atkin Chambers' pupillage training programme may be reviewed on the website.

Mini-pupillages

Six mini-pupillages are offered each year. Mini-pupillages will be offered to candidates who have achieved or have clear potential to achieve the academic standards required for pupillage. Whilst all applications received will be given consideration, applicants are invited to apply by letter with CV during March 2013.

Sponsorship & awards

Two fully funded pupilages of £50,000 per pupil for 12 months are available. Funding for the BPTC year by way of drawdown is available.

AtkinChambers Barristers

2 Bedford Row (William Clegg QC)

2 Bedford Row, London WC1R 4BU
Tel: (020) 7440 8888 Fax: (020) 7242 1738
Email: clerks@2bedfordrow.co.uk
Website: www.2bedfordrow.co.uk

No of Silks 20	
No of Juniors 61	
No of Pupils 4	
Graduate recruitment contact	
Stephen Vullo	
020 7440 8888	
Method of application	
Pupillage Portal	
Pupillages (p.a.)	
12 months 4	
Tenancies offered according to ability	

Chambers profile

Widely regarded as one of the leading crime sets in the UK, 2 Bedford Row continues to excel in the fields of crime, fraud and regulatory law. Chambers has been described by 'Chambers UK' 2012 as 'one of the strongest sets in fraud', 'packed with extremely talented barristers', and 2011 as 'indubitably one of the best criminal sets in the country'.

Type of work undertaken

Chambers has a broad-based criminal practice and its members have appeared in some of the most high-profile criminal cases of recent years (R v Barry George, R v Levi Bellfield, R v Mark Dixie). In addition, members of chambers have particular experience in the fields of confiscation/restraint, health and safety, financial services law, sports law, professional regulation/discipline and inquests. Members are frequently instructed to appear before regulatory bodies such as the GMC, the FA, the VAT tribunal and the Police Disciplinary Tribunal.

Pupil profile

Chambers recruits candidates from all backgrounds who display the highest intellectual ability, excellent advocacy skills, sound judgement and a real commitment to criminal law and its related fields. Candidates will also be well-rounded individuals who are able to communicate effectively with a wide variety of people.

Pupillage

Chambers offers up to four 12-month pupillages each year. Each pupil will have two pupil supervisors in their first six and a different two in their second six. This ensures that pupils are provided with a thorough grounding in all aspects of chambers' practice. Chambers also provides structured advocacy training throughout the pupillage year and will pay for pupils to attend the 'Advice to Counsel' and 'Forensic Accountancy' courses. Applications for tenancy are usually made after the completion of a 3rd six.

Mini-pupillages

Chambers welcomes applications for mini-pupillage. Please see the website for details.

Funding

Chambers provides a grant of £12,000 to each pupil, paid monthly throughout the year and, in addition, guaranteed earnings of £10,000 in second six.

Blackstone Chambers (Monica Carss-Frisk QC and Anthony Peto QC)

Blackstone House, Temple, London EC4Y 9BW DX: 281 Chancery Lane
Tel: (020) 7583 1770 Fax: (020) 7822 7350
Email: pupillage@blackstonechambers.com
Website: www.blackstonechambers.com

Chambers profile

Blackstone Chambers occupies large and modern premises in the Temple.

Type of work undertaken

Chambers' formidable strengths lie in its principal areas of practice: commercial, employment and EU, public law, human rights and public international law. Commercial law includes financial/business law, international trade, conflicts, sport, media and entertainment, intellectual property and professional negligence. All aspects of employment law, including discrimination, are covered by Chambers' extensive employment law practice. Public law incorporates judicial review, acting both for and against central and local government agencies and other regulatory authorities, all areas affected by the impact of human rights and other aspects of administrative law. EU permeates practices across the board. Chambers recognises the increasingly important role which mediation has to play in dispute resolution. Seven members are CEDR accredited mediators.

Pupil profile

Chambers looks for articulate and intelligent applicants who are able to work well under pressure and demonstrate high intellectual ability. Successful candidates usually have at least a 2:1 honours degree, although not necessarily in law.

Pupillage

Chambers offers four (or exceptionally five) 12-month pupillages to those wishing to practise full-time at the Bar, normally commencing in October each year. Pupillage is normally divided into four sections and every effort is made to ensure that pupils receive a broad training. The environment is a friendly one; pupils attend an induction week introducing them to chambers' working environment. Chambers prefers to recruit new tenants from pupils wherever possible. Chambers subscribes to Pupillage Portal.

Mini-pupillages

Assessed mini-pupillages are an essential part of the pupillage procedure and no pupillage will be offered at Blackstone Chambers unless the applicant has undertaken an assessed mini-pupillage. Applications for mini-pupillages must be made by 26 April 2013; earlier applications are strongly advised and are preferred in the year before pupillage commences.

Funding

Awards of £60,000 per annum are available. The pupillage committee has a discretion to consider applications for up to £17,000 of the pupillage award to be advanced during the BTPC year. Since chambers insists on an assessed mini-pupillage as part of the overall application procedure, financial assistance is offered either in respect of out of pocket travelling or accommodation expenses incurred in attending the mini-pupillage, up to a maximum of £250 per pupil.

No of Silks 37
No of Juniors 50
No of Pupils 5

Contact
Miss Julia Hornor
Chambers Director

Method of application
Pupillage Portal

Pupillages (p.a.)
12 months 4-5
Required degree grade
Minimum 2:1
(law or non-law)

Income
Award £60,000
Tenancies
Junior tenancies offered
in last 3 years
67%
No of tenants of 5 years
call or under
13

1 Chancery Lane (John Ross QC)

1 Chancery Lane, London WC2A 1LF
Tel: 0845 634 6666 Fax: 0845 634 6667
Email: jfensham@1chancerylane.com
Website: www.1chancerylane.com

No of Silks **5**	
No of Juniors **37**	
No of Pupils **2**	
Contact	
Jenny Fensham, Practice Administrator jfensham@1chancerylane.com	
Method of application	
Application form on Chambers website	
Pupillages (p.a.)	
2 every other year (next pupillage intake October 2013)	

Chambers profile

A leading civil common law set, specialising in professional and clinical negligence litigation, personal injury actions, claims for and against public authorities (including the police), disciplinary and regulatory work, property and travel claims.

Reputation: an unstuffy and approachable chambers. Atmosphere: collegiate and supportive. Our pupil and tenant retention rate is very good. We focus on providing a full client service.

Type of work undertaken

We are involved in a wide range of high profile work including education negligence, novel duty of care claims against public authorities, human rights claims, stress related claims, discrimination, social welfare, undue influence claims and judicial review. Members of Chambers have appeared in the Supreme Court in the leading case on duties owed by doctors and social workers investigating child abuse; the leading case on limitation in child abuse claims; and the leading case on police protection and the Human Rights Act. Chambers is listed as a leading set in several practice areas in the Legal 500 and Chambers & Partners and individual members of Chambers are recommended as leading practitioners in additional areas.

Pupil profile

Strong academics are only a small (if essential) part of what we're looking for. Motivation is important; communication skills are absolutely vital; common sense and commerciality are also useful. The desire to excel and a commitment to the profession are important attributes.

Pupillage

Three seats of four months, each with a different pupil supervisor. Pupils are exposed to a variety of paperwork, court work, alternative dispute resolution and conferences and can expect to be in court on average several times each week. There is a mutual feedback and appraisal system in place.

Mini-pupillages

Eight mini-pupillages of a week's duration, four in June and four in July. Please see the recruitment section of our website for further details.

Funding

Pupillages are funded (not less than £40,000 for pupils commencing in 2013).

Cloisters

Cloisters, 1 Pump Court, Temple, London, EC4Y 7AA
Tel: (020) 7827 4000 Fax: (020) 7827 4100
Email: clerks@cloisters.com
Website: www.cloisters.com

No of Silks	9
No of Juniors	42
No of Pupils	2
Contact	pupillage@cloisters.com
Method of application	Pupillage Portal
Pupillages (p.a.)	2 for 12 months

Chambers profile

Cloisters is a leading set advising in employment, discrimination and equality, personal injury, clinical negligence, sports and commercial law with a reputation for delivering exceptional results. It provides responsive first-class client service combined with technical excellence and commercial perspective to resolve the most complex legal problems for individuals and organisations of all sizes.

Type of work undertaken

Employment; discrimination and equality: Cloisters is at the forefront of all aspects of employment law and has unrivalled expertise in discrimination and equality issues. Recent landmark cases include Employees v Birmingham City Council the largest equal pay claim brought against a local authority; Heyday, a case bringing about the end of the default retirement age; Homer v West Yorkshire Police and Seldon v Clarkson Wright & Jakes, two of the first age discrimination cases to go to the Supreme Court and X v Mid-Sussex Citizens Advice Bureau in which the Court of Appeal ruled that volunteers are not covered by the Disability Discrimination Act.

Personal Injury and Clinical Negligence: Cloisters is consistently rated as a top-ranked clinical negligence set in Chambers & Partners and is highly regarded for personal injury. Cloisters continues to be at the forefront of high value litigation involving catastrophic brain and spinal injury, including: Pankhurst v White, Houghton, Mohamed, Iqbal v Whipps Cross University Hospitals, and A v Powys. Chambers also continues to be at the forefront of PI litigation. Recent Court of Appeal case include Crofton v NHSLA (local authority payments and double recovery), Connor v Surrey County Council (psychiatric injury at work/breach of statutory duty), Stanton v Collinson (seatbelts and contributory negligence), Noble v Owens (video surveillance), and Grevil v Redruth Rugby Club (vicarious liability for employed sportsman). Members of chambers have consistently appeared in the leading stress at work cases including: Barber v Somerset County Council, Majrowski v Guys and St Thomas's, and Hartman v South East Essex Mental Health and Community Care NHS Trust. Members of chambers are currently instructed in the Godstone farm ecoli group litigation.

Sport: Cloisters' sport practitioners act for football clubs and players up to Premier League as well as a diverse range of sports bodies and personalities. They handle disciplinary regulations, consultative work, litigation, non-professional sporting activity cases and matters arising from sports and entertainment cases such as employment or contractual issues.

Pupil profile

Chambers welcomes applications from outstanding candidates from all backgrounds and academic disciplines including lawyers coming late to the Bar.

Pupillage

Chambers offers two 12 month pupillages for those wishing to practise full-time at the Bar, normally commencing in October each year. Each pupil is supervised and the supervisor changes every three months to show the pupil different areas of practice. Second six pupils will be allocated work by clerks subject to availability of work and pupil ability.

Mini-Pupillages

Cloisters offers up to ten three day mini-pupillages each year. All applicants must have completed at least their first year at university in any subject. The mini-pupillage is not assessed and is not a requirement for applications for pupillage.

Funding

Cloisters offers two funded pupillages each year. Each pupil will receive an award (currently £40,000 per year). Pupils can also ask for an advance.

Crown Office Chambers

Head of Chambers: Andrew Bartlett QC
2 Crown Office Row, Temple, London, EC4Y 7HJ
Tel: (020) 7797 8100 Fax: (020) 7797 8101
Email: mail@crownofficechambers.com
Website: www.crownofficechambers.com

No of Silks 14
No of Juniors 70
No of Pupils 3

Contact
David Myhill

Method of application
Chambers application form,
downloadable from chambers
website

Pupillages (p.a.)
Up to three per year,
12 months
£42,500 plus earnings

Tenancies
No of tenancies offered in last
3 years 6

Chambers profile

Crown Office Chambers is one of the foremost sets of chambers specialising in civil common law work. The majority of members undertake at least some personal injury work, and some practise solely in that area. Chambers has an established reputation in other areas including construction, professional negligence, commercial contracts, insurance and product liability. It is not a 'pure commercial' set, and pupils will see a range of work during pupillage.

Pupil profile

Members pride themselves on their professionalism, an astute and business-orientated awareness of the practical needs of solicitors and lay clients, combined with an approachable and unstuffy attitude to their work. Chambers looks for the same in its pupils, all of whom are regarded as having strong tenancy potential. Pupils are expected to display the motivation, dedication and intelligence which are the hallmarks of a first-class barrister. Academically, they should have a first or upper second-class honours degree (not necessarily in law), a flair for oral and written advocacy, and a strong and committed work ethic.

Pupillage

Pupils rotate through three pupil supervisors during the course of the year. In their second six, pupils are briefed to attend County Court hearings on their own, probably at least two or three times per week. Generally these will be small personal injury cases. Pupils receive regular feedback on their work from pupil supervisors and other members of chambers. They also undertake a series of advocacy exercises in front of a panel of four members of chambers and receive extensive feedback after each exercise. There are also two assessed written exercises during the course of pupillage. Tenancy decisions are made in early July.

Mini-pupillage

Limited number of mini-pupillages in selected weeks throughout the year. Online application form downloadable from Chambers website.

One Essex Court

Chambers of Lord Grabiner QC, One Essex Court, Temple, London, EC4Y 9AR
Tel: (020) 7583 2000 Fax: (020) 7583 0118
Email: clerks@oeclaw.co.uk Website: www.oeclaw.co.uk

No of Silks 27
No of Juniors 49
No of Pupils 4
Contact
Joanne Huxley, Secretary to the Pupillage Committee
Method of application
Pupillage Portal
Pupillages (p.a.)
4 12-month
Required degree grade
Minimum 2:1
(law or non-law)
Income
Award £60,000

Chambers profile

One Essex Court is a pre-eminent set of barristers' chambers, specialising in commercial litigation. Members provide specialist advice and advocacy services worldwide, which include all areas of dispute resolution, litigation and arbitration.

Type of work undertaken

Chambers' work embraces all aspects of domestic and international trade, commerce and finance. Members of Chambers are recognised specialists in the many diverse fields characterised as commercial disputes, also regularly accepting nominations as arbitrators, mediators and experts. Chambers' work includes, but is not limited to: arbitration, banking and finance, civil fraud, commercial litigation, company and insolvency, competition and EU, energy (oil, gas and utilities), financial services, insurance, IP, professional negligence and revenue law.

Pupil profile

Chambers has for many years maintained a policy of active recruitment and expansion and only offers pupillage to those who are thought capable of becoming tenants. Provided a candidate is proven to have the requisite ability, no distinction is drawn between candidates who do and those who do not have a law degree. Pupils at One Essex Court do not compete against one another for a predetermined maximum intake.

Pupillage

Four guaranteed 12-month pupillages are offered per year, each with substantial funding. From the beginning, pupils assist pupil supervisors with their papers, do legal research, draft opinions, pleadings and skeleton arguments. There are substantial opportunities for advocacy in the second six months of pupillage. Chambers subscribes to Pupillage Portal.

Mini-pupillage

Mini-pupillages last for either one or two days. They are not assessed. A mini-pupillage is not a pre-requisite for pupillage although it is encouraged as it can provide a good opportunity both to see how Chambers works and to meet members of Chambers. Please visit Chambers' website for the application process and deadlines.

Funding

Chambers offers each pupil £60,000, supplemented by earnings in the second six. It is understood that this is amongst the highest, if not the highest, remuneration package available to pupils. An advance of the Award is available, upon request, during a prospective pupil's Bar Professional Training Course ("BPTC") year.

ONE ESSEX COURT

Thirty Nine Essex Street

39 Essex Street, London, WC2R 3AT
Tel: 020 7832 1111 Fax: 020 7353 3978
82 Kings Street, Manchester, M2 4WQ
Tel: 0161 870 0333 Fax: 020 7353 3978
Email: clerks@39essex.com Website: www.39essex.com

No of Silks	30
No of Juniors	64
No of Pupils	up to 3

Contact
Pupillage - Charles Cory-Wright
QC & Marion Smith
anna.markey@39essex.com
020 7832 1111

Method of application
Pupillage Portal

Pupillages (p.a.)
Up to three

Chambers profile

Thirty Nine Essex Street is a long-established civil set. It currently has 94 members, including 30 QCs. Chambers has several members on the Attorney General's Panels for civil litigation. Chambers prides itself on its friendly and professional atmosphere. It was described by *Chambers UK* as 'Home to some "extraordinarily bright people"'. Chambers is fully networked and its clerking and administrative services are of a high standard. Chambers works very hard but it also has extensive social, sporting and professional activities. Thirty Nine Essex Street is an equal opportunities employer.

Type of work undertaken

Commercial law: commercial regulation; construction and engineering; corporate restructuring; costs; employment; insurance and reinsurance; media, entertainment and sports; oil, gas and utilities; project finance; energy.

Common law: clinical negligence; health and safety; insurance; material loss claims; personal injury; product liability; professional negligence; sports injuries; toxic torts.

Environmental and Planning: compulsory purchase; contaminated land; environmental civil liability; environmental regulation; international environmental law; licensing; marine environment; planning; nuisance; rating.

Public law: central and local government (including education, housing, immigration, prisons and VAT); European law; human rights; judicial review; mental health and community care; parliamentary and public affairs.

Regulatory and Disciplinary: medical; legal; social care and education; financial services; broadcasting, communications and media; sport; transport; health and safety; building and housing; local government standards; licensing.

Pupillage

Chambers takes up to three 12-month pupils a year. During the pupillage year, each pupil will be rotated among four pupil supervisors, covering a broad range of Chambers' work. The pupils will also do a number of assessed pieces of written work for other members of Chambers. Pupils work only 9.00 am to 6.00 pm, Monday to Friday.

Chambers is a member of Pupillage Portal. Applicants should consult the Pupillage Portal timetable.

Mini-pupillage

Mini-pupillage is a very useful tool for the assessment by chambers of candidates and vice versa. It is not a prerequisite for potential pupils, but since it is likely to increase the chances of the able candidate in obtaining pupillage, we encourage those intending to seek pupillage to apply for mini-pupillage if they can. There are limited places available. Mini-pupillages are normally for a week. They commence in January and continue until June. Applications should be made between 1 September and 30 November, and (save in exceptional circumstances) while applicants are in their final year before undertaking the BPTC. Selection takes place between 1 December and early January (please check website for details). The deadline for acceptance of offers is mid-January.

Funding

Each 12-month pupillage comes with an award, currently £47,500. Of this, up to £8,000 may be drawn down during the year before pupillage commences. Awards and offers are all conditional upon passing the BPTC.

ThirtyNine
ESSEX STREET

4-5 Gray's Inn Square

Gray's Inn, London, WC1R 5AH
Tel: (020) 7404 5252 Fax: (020) 7242 7803
Email: clerks@4-5.co.uk
Website: www.4-5.co.uk

Pupillages funded **2**	
Tenants **56**	
Tenancies in last 3 years **4**	
Method of application	
Pupillage Portal. Candidates should see chambers' website for full information	
Pupillages (p.a.)	
Up to two 12-month pupillages	
Annexes	
None	

Chambers profile

4-5 Gray's Inn Square is a leading set of chambers specialising in a wide range of work, including in particular public law, judicial review and human rights, planning and environmental law, commercial law and employment. A distinctive feature of chambers is the large number of barristers who practise at the intersection of these various specialisms. Chambers believe its strong reputation owes a lot to this unusual diversity. Chambers is a large set, comprising 56 (16 QCs and 40 junior tenants), and takes a modern and innovative approach to the changing market for legal services. It has well-established links with the academic world and has a number of leading lawyers and academics among its associate tenants. It is fully committed to the Bar's responsibilities as a profession and members of chambers frequently undertake work in a pro bono capacity. Chambers prides itself on being not only a high-quality set, but a friendly one.

Type of work undertaken

General public law (including judicial review applications for and against local government and human rights challenges); planning and environmental law (including inquiries, statutory appeals and judicial review applications) on behalf of developers and planning authorities, and all aspects of domestic and EU environmental law; employment law (including unfair dismissal, discrimination and trade union law); commercial law (including fraud, banking, shipping, regulatory work, insurance and reinsurance); professional negligence (including actions involving property, education and solicitors); education (including human rights and discrimination, special educational needs, admissions, exclusions and transport).

Pupil profile

Chambers has a rigorous selection procedure for pupillage. To obtain a first interview, candidates must show first-class academic ability (though not necessarily a first-class degree) and strong evidence of advocacy potential. Successful interview candidates will be expected to demonstrate exceptional legal problem-solving and advocacy ability.

Pupillage

Pupils will receive a thorough training in the full range of chambers' work during their pupillage. During the pupillage, pupils will generally be assigned to three or four different members of chambers (pupil supervisors) to ensure they see the full range of work in which chambers specialises. Chambers pays for all new tenants to attend the week-long residential Advanced Advocacy Course which is run each year in Oxford by the South Eastern Circuit.

Mini-pupillages

Chambers welcomes applications for mini-pupillages. The deadlines for mini-pupillage applications can be found on our website.

Funding

Chambers normally offers up to two 12-month pupillages, each carrying an award of a minimum of £40,000 (2012 figure) with the possibility to draw down up to £10,000 in the BPTC year at chambers' discretion.

4-5 Gray's Inn Square

1 Hare Court

1 Hare Court, Temple, London, EC4Y 7BE
Tel: (020) 7797 7070 Fax: (020) 797 7435
Email: clerks@1hc.com
Website: www.1hc.com

No of Silks 12
No of Juniors 28
No of Pupils 3 (current)

Contact
Sarah Hardwicke (Chambers Administrator)

Method of Application
Curriculum Vitae with handwritten covering letter

Pupillages (pa)
Two 12 month pupillages

Tenancies offered
7 in the last 5 years

Chambers profile

Chambers is proud to be consistently identified as a market leader in Family and Matrimonial Law, at the forefront of high-end Financial Remedy work.

Type of work undertaken

Chambers work involves the resolution of a broad range of disputes arising out of the breakdown of family relationships, including the dissolution of civil partnerships. Our reputation has been built upon our high net worth financial remedy work, increasingly with an international element. Members of chambers are also regularly instructed in property disputes arising from unmarried parties' cohabitation, Inheritance Act claims, Child Support Act appeals and private law children cases, including child abduction. We have a burgeoning reputation in the area of nuptial agreements.

Our work is undertaken predominantly in and around London, but can be as far a field as Hong Kong and the Cayman Islands. We represent clients at every level of Court and Tribunal, from the Family Proceedings and Magistrates Court to the Supreme Court and Privy Council.

In addition to advocacy and advice, 1 Hare Court provides a comprehensive Dispute Resolution service, including mediation, arbitration and collaborative law.

Pupil profile

Chambers looks to recruit pupils with ability, application and the potential to be first-rate advocates. Candidates should have excellent communication skills, sound judgement, a confident grasp of financial concepts and issues and good academic qualifications (at least a 2:1 honours degree).

Pupillage

Chambers offer two 12 months pupillages, commencing in October each year. Each pupil will have three different supervisors over the year and will be introduced to all aspects of chambers' work. We run in-house advocacy training and pupils will undertake a broad range of written work and research. We have a strong preference for recruiting tenants from our pupils.

Mini Pupillage

Mini-pupillages are available: for further details please consult our website at www.1hc.com/pupillages

Funding

Each pupil will receive an award of £35,000, of which £10,000 may be drawn down in the BTPC year.

Henderson Chambers

2 Harcourt Buildings, Temple, London EC4Y 9DB
Tel: (020) 7583 9020 Fax: (020) 7583 2686
Email: clerks@hendersonchambers.co.uk
Website: www.hendersonchambers.co.uk

No of Silks 8
No of Juniors 37
No of Pupils 2
Contact
Hannah Wilson
pupillages@hendersonchambers.co.uk
Method of application
Pupillage Portal
Pupillages (p.a.)
2 12 month pupillages offered
Remuneration for pupillage £50,000 for 12 months (£42,500 award, £7,500 guaranteed earnings)
Tenancies
5 in the last 3 years

Chambers profile

Henderson Chambers is a leading commercial/common law chambers with acknowledged expertise in all of its principal areas of practice. Members and pupils are frequently involved in high-profile commercial and common law litigation.

Type of work undertaken

Henderson Chambers has unrivalled expertise in product liability (which covers a wide range of commercial work including sale of goods and insurance disputes, multi-party pharmaceutical and medical device claims and regulatory and enforcement proceedings) and is consistently rated as the leading set in this area. Chambers is also widely recognised for the excellence of its health and safety work.

In addition, members are noted for their expertise and experience in areas including: employment law, regulatory and disciplinary proceedings, public law and judicial review, personal injury, property law, and technology and construction.

Pupil profile

Chambers looks for individuals who can demonstrate a first-class intellect whether via the traditional route of an outstanding higher education record or via proof of success in other professions, in business or in employment. It is a friendly and sociable set, and expects candidates to be able to show how they have both worked hard and played hard.

Pupillage

Pupillages are for 12 months, usually with four different pupil supervisors for three months each. Pupils have the opportunity to spend four weeks in Brussels at McDermott Will & Emery in order to experience European practice at first hand. Pupils will attend court regularly during their second six months.

Mini-pupillage

Chambers offers unassessed mini-pupillages. Applications can be made online at www.hendersonchambers.co.uk

Funding

Chambers offers two funded 12-month pupillages with minimum remuneration of £50,000 each. This consists of an award of £42,500 and guaranteed earnings of £7,500 during the second six months.

HENDERSON CHAMBERS

11KBW

11 King's Bench Walk, London EC4Y 7EQ
Tel: 020 7632 8500 Fax: 020 7583 9123
Email: clerksteam@11kbw.com Web: www.11kbw.com

No. of Silks 20
No of Juniors 34
No. of Pupils 2 (current)
Contact
Ms Claire Halas – Chambers Administrator
Method of application
Pupillage Portal
Pupillages (pa)
12 months – 2-3
Required degree: first or upper second class (in any academic field)
Income
£55,000pa
Tenancies
No of tenancies offered in last 3 years: 5

Chambers profile

We are a specialist civil law set providing high quality advice and advocacy to a wide range of private and public sector clients, both claimants and defendants. Current members of chambers include First Treasury Counsel, Chancery.

Types of work undertaken

Pupils can expect to gain a range of experience across the following areas; public law and human rights; employment and discrimination law; business law; European community law; information law and sports law.

Pupillage

The great majority of tenants are recruited from those who have done a 12 month pupillage here. We offer pupillages only to those who we believe have the potential to become tenants and our policy is to offer tenancy to all pupils who meet the required standard during their pupillage. We place a high premium on outstanding intellectual ability, but we are also looking for the strong advocacy skills, determination and practical common sense that will lead to a successful practice.

11KBW is a member of the Pupillage Portal. Applications for pupillage commencing October 2014 should be made in the Pupillage Portal summer round in 2013 (although we accept deferred applications). Interviews will be held in mid-July 2013 and offers of pupillage made in accordance with the Pupillage Portal timetable. We strongly prefer applicants for pupillage to attend an assessed mini pupillage and are only likely to offer an interview to those who have not done an assessed mini pupillage in exceptional cases. When we make pupillage selection decisions we take into account performance in assessed mini pupillages, together with Pupillage Portal application forms and performance at interview. Applicants must have a first or good upper second class degree (in any academic field).

Mini-pupillages

Chambers offers one-week mini pupillages to students who are considering applying to us for a full pupillage. There is considerable demand for the limited number of mini-pupillage places we have available and accordingly they are offered on a selective basis. We strongly recommend an assessed mini pupillage to pupils applying through Pupillage Portal.

We also offer some unassessed mini pupillages for those who are at an earlier stage of their legal studies and who wish to consider practising as a barrister within our areas of expertise.

Awards

We offer a Pupillage Award of £55,000 (Up to £15,000 of the pupillage award may be paid to prospective pupils as an advance in their BPTC year).

Keating Chambers

15 Essex Street, London, WC2R 3AA
Tel: (020) 7544 2600
Fax: (020) 7544 2700

No of Silks 25	
No of Juniors 29	
No of Pupils currently 3	
Contact	
ebrowne@keatingchambers.com	
Method of application	
Pupillage Portal	
Pupillages (p.a.)	
Pupillages (p.a.) 3x12-month pupillages available	
Tenancies	
4 offered in last 3 years	

Chambers profile

Keating Chambers is a leading commercial set specialising in construction, technology and related professional negligence disputes. Disputes often relate to high-profile projects in the UK and overseas and typically involve complex issues in the law of tort, contract and restitution. Chambers is based in modern premises outside the Temple. In their first years of practice, tenants can expect earnings equivalent to those in other top sets of commercial chambers.

Type of work undertaken

Chambers is involved in disputes of all shapes and sizes: from residential building works to multimillion-pound projects for the construction of airports, dams, power stations and bridges. Chambers has been instructed on projects such as Wembley Stadium, the 'Gherkin', the Millennium Bridge, the London Eye and the Channel Tunnel. Much of chambers' work now also includes developing areas such as IT, telecommunications and energy. Chambers acts as advocates in litigation and arbitration throughout the UK and internationally. Some are frequently appointed as mediators, arbitrators and adjudicators.

Chambers' area of practice is dynamic and challenging. As leaders in the field chambers is often in cases that are reported in the law reports. Chambers regularly publishes books, articles and journals.

Pupil profile

No specialist or technical knowledge of construction or engineering is required. A thorough understanding of principles of contract and tort law is essential. Criteria are listed on the website.

Pupillage

Pupils are allocated four supervisors over the course of the year ensuring that each pupil sees a variety of work of differing levels of complexity within chambers. Comprehensive training is provided including a programme of advocacy exercises and provision for attendance at specialist seminars and lectures. For more details, see our website.

Mini-pupillages

Chambers offers a limited number of mini-pupillages each year and undertakes to reimburse reasonable expenses. Applications can be made throughout the year. Please see the website for more details.

Funding

Awards of up to £50,000 are available. Of this, an advance of £15,000 is available during the Bar Professional Training Course.

7 King's Bench Walk

7 King's Bench Walk, Temple, London, EC4Y 7DS
Tel: (020) 7910 8300 Fax: (020) 7910 8400
Website: www.7kbw.co.uk

No of Silks 25
No of Juniors 26
No of Pupils at least 2 and up to 4
Contact
Emma Hilliard (pupillage secretary)
Pupillage@7kbw.co.uk
Method of application
Pupillage Portal
Pupillages (p.a.)
Up to 4 12-month pupillages offered
Required degree grade Minimum 2:1 (law or non-law)
Remuneration for pupillage at least £60,000
Tenancies
Junior tenancies offered in last 3 years 4
No of tenants of 5 years call or under 7

Chambers profile

7 King's Bench Walk is a leading commercial set of chambers, with a reputation for excellence and intellectual rigour. The Legal 500 describes it as "One of the Bar's true elite".

Type of work undertaken

Chambers is at the forefront of commercial litigation, specialising in particular in the fields of insurance and reinsurance, shipping, international trade, professional negligence and private international law. Most of its work has an international dimension. Members regularly appear in the High Court (particularly the Commercial Court), the Court of Appeal and the Supreme Court, as well as in arbitrations in London and overseas.

Pupil profile

Applicants must have at least a good 2:1, coupled with lively intelligence and strong advocacy skills (both oral and in writing). Chambers encourages applications from all outstanding candidates no matter what their background or academic discipline.

Pupillage

Chambers offers up to four (but typically two or three) 12 month pupillages each year (with a review after 6 months). Pupils will sit with four pupillage supervisors prior to the tenancy decision in July. Pupils will assist their pupil supervisors with their work, and accompany them to hearings. Pupils will, particularly after completion of the first three months of pupillage, also do work for other members of chambers.

Mini-pupillage

Mini-pupillages are unassessed, and last three days. They are offered in three separate periods throughout the year: 1 June to 30 September (excluding August), 1 October to 31 January and 1 February to 31 May. Applications for mini-pupillages during these periods must be received by 31 March, 31 July, and 30 November respectively. Application by way of a CV and covering letter should be made to the Secretary to the Mini-Pupillage Committee. Further details of how to apply may be found on chambers' website.

Funding

A pupillage award of at least £60,000 will be available for the 2014/15 and 2015/2016 years, of which up to £10,000 may be drawn down during the BPTC.

Littleton Chambers

3 King's Bench Walk North, Temple, London, EC4Y 7HR
Tel: (020) 7797 8600 Fax: (020) 7797 8699
Email: clerks@littletonchambers.co.uk
Website: www.littletonchambers.co.uk

No of Silks 13	
No of Juniors 42	
No of Pupils currently 1	
Contact	
Felicity Schneider, Administration Director	
Method of application	
Pupillage Portal	
Pupillages (p.a.)	
12 month 2	
Required degree level 2:1 (law or non-law)	
Income	
£45,000 award. Earnings not included.	

Chambers profile

Littleton Chambers is acknowledged as being a top class set in each of its main practice areas. Its success is based upon both the desire to maintain high professional standards and a willingness to embrace change. It prides itself on the skills of its tenants, not only as advocates and advisers on the law, but also for their analytical and practical skills.

Type of work undertaken

Littleton Chambers specialises in commercial litigation, employment law, professional negligence, sports law, mediation and arbitration.

Pupil profile

Chambers takes a considerable amount of care in choosing its pupils and prefers to recruit its tenants from persons who have completed a full 12 months of pupillage with chambers. Chambers endeavours to take on pupils who not only have good academic skills, but who also show flair for advocacy and the ability to understand practical commercial issues.

Pupillage

Chambers generally offers pupillage to two people each year.

During your 12 month pupillage you will have the benefit of three pupil supervisors in succession. Your pupil supervisors will provide support and guidance to you throughout your pupillage, ensuring that you understand not only the nuts and bolts of a barrister's work, but also the ethical constraints which are such a distinctive feature of chambers' professional life.

After six months pupillage, you will be entitled to take on your own work. Typically, pupils in Littleton Chambers have been briefed once or twice a week. Your pupil supervisor will provide assistance in the preparation of these briefs to ensure that your client receives the best possible service from you.

Mini-pupillage

Assessed mini-pupillage forms part of the pupillage application process. Mini-pupillages are not offered outside of this process.

Funding

Each pupillage is funded (currently £45,000 per year) and, if necessary, it is possible to draw down some of this funding during the year of Bar Finals.

LITTLETON

Maitland Chambers

7 Stone Buildings, Lincoln's Inn, London WC2A 3SZ
Tel: (020) 7406 1200 Fax: (020) 7406 1300
Email: clerks@maitlandchambers.com
Website: www.maitlandchambers.com

Chambers profile

Chambers UK has rated Maitland in the top rank of commercial chancery sets every year since 2001.

Type of work undertaken

Maitland is instructed on a wide range of business and property related cases – from major international commercial litigation to disputes over the family home. Its core areas of practice include commercial litigation, banking, financial services and regulation, civil fraud, insolvency and restructuring, media law, pensions, professional negligence, real property, charity law, trusts and tax. Much of the set's work is done in London (as well as in other parts of England and Wales), although instructions often have an international aspect, involving acting for clients and appearing in court abroad. Chambers' work is predominantly concerned with dispute resolution; but it also does non-contentious work in the private client field.

Pupil profile

Academically, Maitland looks for a first or upper second class degree. Pupils must have a sense of commercial practicality, be stimulated by the challenge of written and oral advocacy and have an aptitude for and general enjoyment of complex legal argument.

Pupillage

Maitland offers up to three pupillages, all of which are funded. All pupils in chambers are regarded as potential tenants.

Pupils spend their first three months in Chambers with one pupil supervisor in order that the pupil can find his or her feet and establish a point of contact. For the balance of the pupillage year each pupil will sit with different pupil supervisors, usually for two months at a time. The set believes that it is important for pupils to see all of the different kinds of work done in Chambers.

Chambers believes that oral advocacy remains a core skill of the commercial chancery barrister. The set provides in-house advocacy exercises for pupils during their pupillage. These take the form of mock hearings, prepared in advance from adapted sets of papers, with senior members of Chambers acting as the tribunal. They provide detailed feedback after each exercise. These exercises are part of the assessment process and help develop essential court skills.

Mini-pupillages

Applications are considered three times a year; please see Chambers' website for current deadlines. Applications should be made with a covering letter and CV (listing undergraduate grades) to the Pupillage Secretary.

Funding

Chambers offers up to three 12-month pupillages, all of which are funded (£60,000 for pupils starting in October 2014). Up to £20,000 of the award may be drawn down in advance during the BPTC year or to pay BPTC fees. There is also a cashflow assistance scheme available at the start of practice as a tenant.

No of Silks 23
No of Juniors 43
No of Pupils up to 3

Contact
Valerie Piper
(Pupillage Secretary)
pupillage
@maitlandchambers.com

Method of application
See Chambers' website from January 2013. Application deadline for pupillage in 2014-15 is 5 February 2013

Pupillages (p.a.)
Up to 3 funded

Income
£60,000 p.a.

Tenancies
7 in last 3 years

Matrix Chambers

Griffin Building, Gray's Inn, London WC1R 5LN
Tel: (020) 7404 3447 Fax: (020) 7404 3448
Email: matrix@matrixlaw.co.uk
Website: www.matrixlaw.co.uk
Twitter: @matrixchambers

No of Silks **23**	
No of Juniors **47**	
No of Pupils **2**	
Contact	
Lindsay Clarke	
Tel: (020) 7404 3447	
Method of application	
Our application form can be found on our website. We are not a member of the Pupillage Portal but we follow the same timetable.	
Pupillages (p.a.)	
Up to 2 per year - 12 months	
Tenancies	
4 in the last 3 years	

Chambers profile

Matrix was founded in 2000 with the aim of innovating the way legal services are delivered, and to move beyond traditional divisions at the Bar. "Seen by some as a blueprint for the future of the Bar" (Chambers & Partners), it is primarily our people, approach and attitude that make the atmosphere at Matrix different. Our bright, contemporary offices; our commitment to quality of service; the friendly professionalism of our staff; and the lack of old-fashioned language, hierarchies and attitudes demonstrated by our members – all these core values make Matrix a unique and great place to train.

Type of work undertaken

UK public and private law; the law of the European Union; the European Convention on Human Rights; and public international law.

Pupil profile

Matrix welcomes applications from exceptional candidates from all backgrounds. For further details, please see our traineeship brochure on the 'Opportunities' page of our website.

Pupillage

Matrix offers up to two traineeships, both starting 1 October for 12 months. Traineeships are organised into four periods of three months each. Trainees' preferences are taken into account in assigning them supervisors. In each three month period, trainees will be assigned to a different supervisor with the objective of providing experience of a full range of legal practice. In their second two seats, trainees are encouraged to take on their own cases, in a supervised and well mentored way. Trainees will also be invited to attend internal and external continuing education seminars.

Mini-pupillages

Matrix do not offer mini-pupilages. Instead, we run a Student Open Day in April for those considering applying for traineeship. For more details, please visit our website.

Funding

£50,000 (£10,000 to be drawn down during the BPTC)

4 New Square

4 New Square, Lincoln's Inn, London WC2A 3RJ
Tel: (020) 7822 2000 Fax: (020) 7822 2001
Website: www.4newsquare.com

No of Silks **22**
No of Juniors **53**
No of Pupils **3**

Contact
Georgie Ruane
Tel (020) 7822 2000
Email
pupillage@4newsquare.com

Method of application
Online www.4newsquare.com

Pupillages (p.a.)
Up to 2

Chambers profile

4 New Square is a leading commercial and civil set of barristers comprising 75 members, of whom 22 are Queen's Counsel, with particular expertise and a high reputation in the areas of insurance work and claims against professionals. 4 New Square enjoys a formidable reputation in its principle areas of work: commercial litigation and arbitration, insurance and reinsurance, professional liability and construction and engineering. Its members are also recognised as leading practitioners in the fields of chancery litigation, consumer law, costs litigation, financial services, pensions, product liability, professional discipline, public law and sports law.

Members of 4 New Square appear in a wide range of tribunals (court and arbitral) and are regularly instructed to take landmark cases to the Court of Appeal and the Supreme Court. Recent examples include, the 'Trigger' Litigation (Supreme Court), the Atomic Veterans Litigation (Supreme Court), Jones v Kaney (Supreme Court) and Motto v Trafigura (Court of Appeal). Jackson & Powell on Professional Negligence (the main text in this area) is written and edited by current members of chambers. Chambers attracts a large amount of junior advocacy work which reflects the emphasis on developing pupils and junior tenants into experienced advocates to equip them for a successful career at the Bar.

Type of work undertaken

Professional liability, product liability, chancery, commercial law, construction and engineering, insurance and reinsurance, financial services and banking, human rights, administrative and public law and sports law.

Pupil profile

Chambers does not stream its pupils. Each has an equal prospect of securing a tenancy. Selection criteria: evidence of intellectual ability; potential as an advocate; personal qualities such as self-reliance, integrity, reliability and the ability to work effectively with colleagues and clients; motivation. Equal opportunities: Chambers observes a policy of equal opportunities in accordance with the Bar Code of Conduct. All applicants are required to complete the Bar Council Equality Code questionnaire. This is used for monitoring purposes only.

Pupillage

The first six months: You will go to court and attend conferences with your pupil supervisor. You will also assist your pupil supervisor with their written work: carrying out written advisory and drafting work on their current papers and undertaking detailed research on the law. The second six months: During your second six months, as well as continuing with work for your pupil supervisor, you will take on an increasing amount of your own court work. Chambers places a strong emphasis on advocacy and supports its pupils in gaining valuable practical experience. You can expect to be in court on your own about once a week up to the tenancy decision and potentially on a more regular basis thereafter. You will be expected to complete three assessed pieces of work for members of chambers who are not your pupil supervisors. Advocacy: You will also take part in an assessed moot. Workshop training sessions are run to help you prepare for the moots. Environment: Chambers aims to provide a friendly and sociable atmosphere. Pupils are included in chambers' social events throughout the year.

Mini-pupillages

Mini-pupillages generally last for two days and take place in specific weeks in May, July, November and December of each year. Chambers will pay travelling expenses of £50. Applications must be made on chambers' own mini-pupillage application form, which is available to download from our website.

NEW SQUARE

XXIV Old Buildings

XXIV Old Buildings, 24 Old Buildings, Lincoln's Inn, London, WC2A 3UP
Tel: (020) 7691 2424 Fax: (0870) 460 2178
Website: xxiv.co.uk

No of Silks **9**	
No of Juniors **29**	
No of Pupils **2**	
Contact	
Steven Thompson	
Method of application	
Letter and CV. Please see www.xxiv.co.uk for guidance	
Pupillages (p.a.)	
2	
Tenancies	
Usually 1-2 per year	
Other offices	
Geneva	

Chambers profile

XXIV Old Buildings is a commercial Chancery chambers of 38 barristers based in Lincoln's Inn. Its members provide specialist legal advice and advocacy services in the UK and worldwide on a range of contentious, advisory and transactional matters to the financial, commercial and professional community and to private individuals. Our expertise covers all areas of dispute resolution, litigation and arbitration.

Type of work undertaken

The barristers at XXIV Old Buildings specialise in a variety of commercial Chancery areas with a particular emphasis on trusts and estates and commercial litigation. Areas in which members regularly take instructions include arbitration; aviation; charities; civil fraud, asset tracing and recovery; company; construction and projects; financial services; insolvency; international and offshore; partnership; pensions; professional negligence; real estate litigation and trusts, probate and estates.

XXIV Old Buildings is known for its pre-eminence in international and offshore work, both contentious and advisory. With offices in both London and Geneva, the barristers at XXIV Old Buildings regularly appear in courts and tribunals in offshore centres including the British Virgin Islands, the Cayman Islands, Bermuda, Jersey, the Isle of Man, the DIFC, the Bahamas, Gibraltar, Hong Kong and Malaysia.

Pupillage

The set likes to recruit its junior members from those who have undertaken pupillage with the set. Chambers are therefore careful that its pupils acquire all the skills necessary to make them successful commercial Chancery barristers. During a 12 month pupillage, a pupil will have, on average, four pupil supervisors with whom they will spend the majority of their time. Each year the set is looking for pupils with a first or 2:1 degree, though not necessarily in law, who have an enthusiasm for the type of work the set does, sound judgment and the application required to succeed in a very competitive and intellectually demanding environment. Application is by CV and covering letter.

The closing date for applications for pupillages commencing in October 2014 is 9am on 1 February 2013.

Mini pupillages

Chambers accepts applications for mini-pupillages throughout the year. Application should be made by CV and covering letter. Please see our website www.xxiv.co.uk for details of how to apply.

Funding

Up to £65,000 per pupil.

Old Square Chambers

10-11 Bedford Row, London, WC1R 4BU D: 1046 Chancery Lane
Tel: (020) 7269 0300 Fax: (020) 7405 1384
Email: clerks@oldsquare.co.uk
Website: www.oldsquare.co.uk

No of Silks	13
No of Juniors	58
No of Pupils	2
Contact	
Betsan Criddle	
Gudula Crawford	
Method of application	
Pupillage Portal	
Pupillages (p.a.)	
2 12-month pupillages	
Income	
£40,000 (£30,000 award plus £10,000 guaranteed earnings) Plus additional earnings	
Tenancies	
6 in last 3 years	
Annexes	
Bristol	

Chambers profile

Old Square Chambers is recognised as a premier set in its core specialist areas of employment and discrimination, personal injury and environmental law. Chambers' defining quality is excellence, both in the specialist legal expertise it has to offer and in the customer service which it provides. Members and staff have a reputation for being approachable and unstuffy. Many members hold part-time judicial positions, sit on specialist panels, act as mediators and edit or contribute to leading practitioner texts.

Type of work undertaken

Chambers' strength lies in the depth of experience and expertise in its core practice areas. The Employment and Discrimination Group is widely regarded as one of the foremost in the UK. Work is in all aspects of employment and discrimination law. Clients range from individual employees and directors to major trade unions, private and public sector organisations. Personal injury work covers all aspects of this wide-ranging and complex field, from employers' liability and road traffic claims to high-value head, brain and spinal injury cases, with particular expertise in disaster litigation and multi-party actions. In environmental law, chambers has been at the forefront of developing litigation in the area of toxic torts. Members appear in high-profile multi-party claims arising from pollution of various kinds. Alongside its core areas chambers also has expertise in professional discipline, clinical negligence, product liability, public inquiries, health and safety and ADR.

Pupil profile

Chambers assesses candidates on intellectual ability (usually a first or upper second degree will be required), potential as an advocate, interest in chambers' fields of practice, ability to cope with hard work and pressure and interpersonal skills.

Mini-pupillages

Chambers runs a programme of mini-pupillages during the summer. Applications should be made through chambers' website.

Funding

The current award is £40,000 (£30,000 award plus £10,000 guaranteed earnings). Pupils keep additional earnings from their second six.

OLD SQUARE CHAMBERS

Pump Court Tax Chambers

16 Bedford Row, London WC1R 4EF
Tel: (0207) 414 8080 Fax: (0207) 414 8099
Email: clerks@pumptax.com
Website: www.pumptax.com

No of Silks 10	
No of Juniors 21	
No of Pupils 2 in any given year	
Contact	
Thomas Chacko	
pupils@pumptax.com	
Method of application	
CV and covering letter (non-Pupillage Portal) by 4 February 2013	
Pupillages (p.a.)	
Up to 2 funded	
Tenancies	
3 in the last 3 years	

Chambers profile

Pump Court Tax Chambers is the largest specialist tax set.

Type of work undertaken

All areas of tax work (both contentious and non-contentious) are covered. On the corporate side, clients typically include the 'Big 4' accountants and 'magic circle' solicitors sending a wide variety of work such as M&A, reconstructions and demergers and structured finance. Chambers' private client work comes from a broad range of sources – city solicitors, accountants, regional firms, chartered tax advisers and IFAs, who act for private individuals, trustees and landed estates. Much of chambers' work concerns large scale litigation (especially in the field of VAT) and members of chambers regularly appear in the Tax Tribunals, the High Court, the Court of Appeal, the Supreme Court and the ECJ.

Pupil profile

Chambers looks for applicants who are intelligent, articulate and well-motivated. Successful candidates will have at least a 2:1 honours degree (although not necessarily in law). Prior experience of studying tax law is not required.

Pupillage

Chambers offers up to two 12-month pupillages (terminable after six months by either party) to those wishing to practise full-time at the Bar. Pupillage normally commences in October each year. Pupils will have at least three pupil supervisors and will also sit with other members of chambers so as to receive a broad training in all aspects of the work of chambers.

Mini-pupillages

The programme runs throughout the year. Applications should be made via email to pupils@pumptax.com with accompanying CV and marked for the attention of the Pupillage Secretary.

Funding

Awards of up to £50,000 are available. The pupillage committee has discretion to consider applications for up to £12,000 of the pupillage award to be advanced during the BPTC year.

PUMP COURT
TAX CHAMBERS

Quadrant Chambers (Lionel Persey QC & Simon Rainey QC)

Quadrant House, 10 Fleet Street, London EC4Y 1AU
Tel: (020) 7583 4444 Fax: (020) 7583 4455
Email: pupillage@quadrantchambers.com
Website: www.quadrantchambers.com

Chambers profile

Quadrant Chambers is a leading set of barristers specialising in commercial law. Members of chambers act as advocates in court, arbitrations and inquiries, and advise clients from around the world, in a wide range of industry areas. Many also act as arbitrators and mediators. A number have dual qualifications in other jurisdictions including New York, California, Hong Kong, BVI, Greece, Germany, Australia and South Africa. Former members of Chambers have gone on to chair high profile public enquiries and to sit as judges in the Commercial Court, Admiralty Court, European Court of First Instance (EGC), Court of Appeal, House of Lords, and UK Supreme Court.

Type of work undertaken

Members of Chambers undertake all types of commercial law, including banking and finance, shipping, energy, aviation, insurance and reinsurance, commodities, international trade, sports and media. Over 70% of Chambers' work involves international clients.

Pupil profile

Quadrant Chambers seeks high calibre candidates with good academic qualifications (a first class degree, or at least a high 2:1) who exhibit excellent analytical abilities and outstanding written and oral communication skills.

Pupillage

Quadrant Chambers offer a maximum of three funded pupillages of 12 months duration (reviewable at six months). During their first six months, pupils sit with two pupil supervisors for three months each, and are exposed to a wide range of high quality commercial work. Successful pupils are likely to be offered a tenancy during their second six months. Further information can be found on the website.

Quadrant Chambers will be holding an open day in December 2012 designed for those in the second year of their university degree or above. The open day will provide those interested in pursuing a career at the commercial bar with an opportunity to meet members of Chambers, learn about life as a barrister and see how Chambers works. During the day, members of chambers will give talks about life as a commercial barrister, and a senior Silk will hold an advocacy workshop. Places are limited. Please visit the website for details on how to apply. Quadrant Chambers is not a member of Pupillage Portal. Please consult the Chambers website for application timetable.

Mini pupillages

Mini pupillages are encouraged to enable potential pupils to experience the work of Quadrant Chambers before committing themselves to an application for full pupillage. Please refer to the Chambers website for more details.

Funding

Awards of £60,000 p.a. are available for each pupillage, part of which may be advanced during the BPTC year, at the Pupillage Committee's discretion.

No of Silks **15**	
No of Juniors **37**	
Contact	
Secretary to Pupillage Committee	
Method of application	
Chambers' application form	
Pupillages (p.a.)	
1st 6 months 3	
2nd 6 months 3	
12 months	
(Reviewed at 6 months)	
Required degree	
1st or high 2:1	
Income	
1st 6 months	
£30,000	
2nd 6 months	
£30,000	
Earnings not included	
Tenancies	
Current tenants who served pupillage in chambers 34	
Junior tenancies offered in last 3 years 3	
No of tenants of 5 years call or under 7	

Queen Elizabeth Buildings (QEB)

Chambers of
Lewis Marks QC

Queen Elizabeth Building, Temple, London, EC4Y 9BS
Tel: (020) 7797 7837 Fax: (020) 7353 5422
Email: clerks@qeb.co.uk
Website: www.qeb.co.uk

Number of Silks 6	
Number of Juniors 27	
Number of Pupils up to 3	
Contact	
Miss Amy Kisser, Secretary to the Pupillage Committee	
Method of Application	
Pupilage Portal Summer Season	
Pupillages	
Up to three 12-month pupillages	
Award	
£25,000 minimum pa + earnings in second six and from devilling	
Tenancies	
Five tenancies offered in the last three years	
Annexes	
None	

Chambers profile

QEB is a leading set of family law chambers, particularly well-known for dealing with the financial consequences of divorce, but with immense experience in all aspects of family law including: jurisdictional disputes, foreign divorces, pre-marital agreements, civil partnerships, injunctions both financial and domestic, private law child work, adoption, child abduction, Inheritance Act claims and disputes between former cohabitees. In addition some members practise in general common law, particularly personal injury and professional negligence work.

QEB has been established for well over 100 years and is consistently rated as one of the top-ranking sets for family law. Members of QEB have been involved in many of the most important cases of legal principle, including: White, Sorrell, Miller, Spencer, Marano, Robson, Schofield and Jones.

Many members of chambers have continued into high judicial office. At present, our former members include: Lord Wilson in the Supreme Court and five out of 19 Family Division judges.

Pupil profile

The practice of family law is infinitely varied and clients come from all walks of life. International and conflict of laws issues arise increasingly often. An ability to deal not only with complex financial disputes, often involving commercial issues, but also with child-related or other emotionally fraught and sensitive situations, is essential. We are looking for applicants with a strong academic record (minimum 2:1 law or non-law degree save in exceptional circumstances), good legal and analytical skills, and an ability to communicate sensitively with a wide range of people at a critical time in their lives.

Pupillage

QEB offers up to three pupillages each year. A 12-month pupillage at QEB offers top-quality training and very good financial support in a busy, friendly environment. Pupils have three pupil supervisors, but are also encouraged to work with other tenants at all levels to gain a broad experience of our work. Pupils are automatically considered for tenancy, and our new tenants are only recruited from our pupils. QEB's reputation is such that where a pupil is not taken on, he/she is usually well placed elsewhere. BARMARK has repeatedly singled out the QEB Pupillage arrangements for particular praise.

Chambers is a part of the Pupillage Portal system. Applicants should apply in the summer 2013 season for a pupillage beginning in October 2014. Please consult the latest Pupillage Awards Handbook or website for details of the timetable.

Mini-pupillages

Applications for mini-pupillages are made by CV and covering letter to the Mini-Pupillage Secretary. Please consult our website at www.qeb.co.uk for full details.

Funding

Chambers offers a pupillage award of £25,000 pa minimum, plus earnings in the second six and from devilling. Pupils do not pay Chambers' expenses or clerks' fees. Chambers also funds the compulsory Inn Advocacy and Practice Management Training Courses.

Serle Court

Serle Court, 6 New Square, Lincoln's Inn, London WC2A 3QS
Tel: (020) 7242 6105 Fax: (020) 7405 4004
Email: pupillage@serlecourt.co.uk
Website: www.serlecourt.co.uk

No of Silks **18**
No of Juniors **34**
No of Pupils **2**
Contact
Kathryn Barry
Tel (020) 7242 6105
Method of application
Chambers application form, available from website or Chambers. Not a member of Pupillage Portal.
Pupillages
Two 12-month pupillages
Tenancies
Up to 2 per annum

Chambers profile

"Serle Court is one of the great success stories of the last decade" with "staggeringly fine commercial ability and a marvellous business-like approach". It has an "outstandingly welcoming attitude, charming informality" and "no other set boasts quite so unstuffy an attitude" (*Chambers UK*). Serle Court is one of the leading commercial chancery sets with 52 barristers including 18 silks. Widely recognised as a leading set, Chambers is recommended in 21 different areas of practice by the legal directories. Chambers has a stimulating and inclusive work environment and a forward looking approach.

Type of work undertaken

Litigation, arbitration, mediation and advisory services across the full range of chancery and commercial practice areas including: administrative and public law, banking, civil fraud, commercial litigation, company, financial services, human rights, insolvency, insurance and reinsurance, intellectual property, partnership and LLP, professional negligence, property, sports, entertainment and media and trusts and probate.

Pupil profile

Candidates are well-rounded people, from any background. Chambers looks for highly motivated individuals with outstanding intellectual ability, combined with a practical approach, sound judgement, an ability to develop good client relationships and the potential to become excellent advocates. Serle Court has a reputation for "consistent high quality" and for having "responsive and able team members" and seeks the same qualities in pupils. Chambers generally requires a degree classification of a good 2:1 as a minimum. Serle Court is committed to equality and diversity and encourages and welcomes applications from women, people of minority ethnic origin and people with disabilities, as well as candidates from other groups which are under represented in the legal sector.

Pupillage

Pupils sit with different pupil supervisors in order to experience a broad range of work. Two pupils are recruited each year and Chambers offers: an excellent preparation for successful practice; a genuinely friendly and supportive environment; the opportunity to learn from some of the leading barristers in their field; a good prospect of tenancy.

Mini-pupillages

About 30 available each year. Apply online at www.serlecourt.co.uk.

Funding

Serle Court offers awards of £60,000 for 12 months, of which up to £20,000 can be drawn down during the BPTC year. It also provides an income guarantee worth up to £120,000 over the first two years of practice.

serle court

South Square

3-4 South Square, Gray's Inn, London WC1R 5HP
Tel: (020) 7696 9900 Fax: (020) 7696 9911
Email: pupillage@southsquare.com
Website: www.southsquare.com

No of Silks	19
No of Juniors	21
No of Pupils	2

Contact
Pupillage Secretary
Tel (020) 7696 9900

Method of application
CV with covering letter

Pupillages (p.a.)
Up to two 12-month pupillages offered each year

Chambers profile

Chambers is an established successful commercial set, involved in high-profile international and domestic commercial litigation. Members of chambers have been centrally involved in some of the most important commercial cases of the last decade including Lehman Brothers, Kaupthing, Landsbanki, Woolworths, Madoff Securities and Stanford International.

Type of work undertaken

South Square has a pre-eminent reputation in insolvency and restructuring law and specialist expertise in related areas including banking, financial services, company law, trusts and asset tracing and general commercial litigation. A significant proportion of our work involves international elements: members are called for specific cases in Hong Kong, the Cayman Islands, the British Virgin Islands and Bermuda, and other recent cases have had links to Poland, Russia, Slovakia, Switzerland, Germany, Jersey, Singapore and Dubai.

Pupil profile

Chambers seeks to recruit the highest calibre of candidates who must be prepared to commit themselves to establishing a successful practice and maintaining chambers' position at the forefront of the modern Commercial Bar. The minimum academic qualification is a 2:1 degree. A number of members have degrees in law, and some have BCL or other postgraduate qualifications. Others have non-law degrees and have gone on to take the Graduate Diploma in Law.

Pupillage

Pupils are welcomed into all areas of chambers' life and are provided with an organised programme designed to train and equip them for practice in a dynamic and challenging environment. Pupils sit with a number of pupil supervisors for periods of six to eight weeks and the set looks to recruit at least one tenant every year from its pupils.

Mini-pupillages

Chambers also offers funded and unfunded mini-pupillages – please see the set's website for further details.

Sponsorship & awards

Currently £60,000 per annum (reviewable annually). A proportion of the pupillage award may be paid for living expenses during the BPTC.

SOUTH SQUARE

2 Temple Gardens (Chambers of Benjamin Browne QC)

2 Temple Gardens, London EC4Y 9AY DX: 134 Chancery Lane
Tel: (020) 7822 1200 Fax: (020) 7822 1300
Email: clerks@2tg.co.uk
Website: www.2tg.co.uk

No of Silks 9	
No of Juniors 43	
No of Pupils 2	
Contact	
Leanne McCabe	
Pupillage Administrator	
Method of application	
Pupillage Portal (Summer)	
Pupillages (p.a.)	
Up to three 12-month pupillages	
Award 2013 £60,000	

Chambers profile

2tg is regarded as one of the leading commercial and civil law barristers' chambers. The firm specialises in professional negligence, insurance and personal injury and also has significant practices in banking, employment, technology, construction and clinical negligence, alongside strength in private international law.

Pupil profile

Academically, you will need at least a good 2:1 degree to be considered. Chambers look for applicants who work well in teams and have the ability to get on with solicitors, clients and other members of chambers.

Pupillage

Chambers offers one of the most generously funded, well-structured and enjoyable pupillages at the Bar. It takes pupillage very seriously and aims to recruit the best applicants, and to ensure that its pupils have an excellent foundation from which to start a successful career at the Bar.

Pupils have three different pupil supervisors during pupillage, and will also do work for other members of chambers. The aim is for pupils to experience as much of chambers' work as possible during their pupillage year.

Mini-pupillages

Chambers welcomes 'mini-pupils'. Generally applicants will only be considered after their first year of a law degree or during CPE. Mini-pupillages are a good way to experience life at 2tg first hand. Most mini-pupillages are 2-3 days long. We aim to show you a wide range of barristers' work during your mini-pupillage. It offers an assessment at the completion of your mini-pupillage and encourages you to give feedback too. Chambers also offers help with reasonable expenses (up to £50).

Mini-pupillages are usually unfunded but a few funded mini-pupillages (maximum £250 per person) are also available.

Funding

Chambers offers up to three 12-month pupillages, all of which are funded. Its pupillage award for 2013 was £60,000. Please see our website www.2tg.co.uk for details of the award for 2014.

3 Verulam Buildings (Ali Malek QC)

3 Verulam Buildings, Gray's Inn, London WC1R 5NT DX: LDE 331
Tel: (020) 7831 8441 Fax: (020) 7831 8479
Email: chambers@3vb.com
Website: www.3vb.com

Chambers profile

Sitting comfortably and spaciously in a newly refurbished and expanded row of buildings in Gray's Inn, 3VB is one of the largest and most highly regarded commercial sets, its members being involved in many of the leading cases, recent examples including the test case on overdraft charges, the $700m Springwell professional negligence litigation, the $600m Honeywell dispute, the Rosemary Nelson enquiry, the Lehman Brothers insolvency, and various Russian oligarch disputes.

Type of work undertaken

3VB's 19 silks and 44 juniors lead the field in banking and financial services, and are also among the top practitioners in the fields of professional negligence, civil fraud, insurance, arbitration, and company and insolvency. Chambers also has significant expertise in IT and telecommunications, energy, construction, and media and entertainment.

Pupil profile

Commercial practice is intellectually demanding and 3VB seeks the brightest and the best. The typical successful applicant will have a first or upper second class degree (not necessarily in law) from a good university, with good mooting experience and proven experience of the commercial bar (generally through mini-pupillages with us or elsewhere). Many have a Master's degree or other legal or commercial experience.

Pupillage

Chambers seeks to recruit three 12-month pupils each year through the OLPAS process. Chambers is committed to recruiting new tenants from its pupils whenever it can. Although tenancy is offered to all pupils who make the grade, on average two out of three pupils are successful in any one year.

Mini-pupillages

Two- or three-day mini-pupillages are an important part of Chambers' selection procedure and it is strongly encouraged that prospective applicants for pupillage apply for a mini-pupillage (e-mail Alexia Knight at minipupillage@3vb.com, attaching a detailed CV).

Funding

For the year 2013/2014, the annual award will be at least £60,000, up to £20,000 of which may be drawn during the BPTC year.

No of Silks 20
No of Juniors 44
No of Pupils 3

Contact
Miss Charlotte Eborall
(Pupillage)
Miss Alexia Knight
(Mini-Pupillage)

Method of application
Portal (Pupillage); CV &
covering letter (Mini-pupillage)

Pupillages (p.a.)
12 months 3
Required degree grade
2:1

Income
In excess of £60,000 plus any
earnings

Tenancies
Current tenants who served
pupillage in Chambers Approx
41
Junior tenancies offered
in last 3 years 6
No of tenants of 5 years
call or under 10

Wilberforce Chambers

8 New Square, Lincoln's Inn, London WC2A 3QP
Tel: (020) 7306 0102 Fax: (020) 7306 0095
Email: pupillage@wilberforce.co.uk
Website: www.wilberforce.co.uk

No of Silks	**23**
No of Juniors	**28**
Method of application	**Chambers application form available from website**
Pupillages (p.a.)	**2 x 12 months**
Mini-pupillages	**Total of 28 places**
Award	**£65,000**
Minimum qualification	**2:1 degree**
Tenancies in last 3 years	**5**

Chambers profile

Wilberforce Chambers is a leading commercial chancery set of chambers and is involved in some of the most commercially important and cutting-edge litigation and advisory work undertaken by the Bar today. Members are recognised by the key legal directories as leaders in their fields. Instructions come from top UK and international law firms, providing a complex and rewarding range of work for international companies, financial institutions, well-known names, sports and media organisations, pension funds, commercial landlords and tenants, and private individuals. Clients demand high intellectual performance and client-care standards but in return the reward is a successful and fulfilling career at the Bar. Chambers has grown in size in recent years but retains a united and friendly 'family' atmosphere.

Type of work undertaken

All aspects of traditional and modern chancery work including property, pensions, private client, trust and taxation, professional negligence, general commercial litigation, banking, company, financial services, intellectual property and information technology, sports and media and charities.

Pupil profile

Chambers looks to offer two 12-month pupillages. You should possess high intellectual ability, excellent communication skills and a strong motivation to do commercial chancery work. You need to be mature and confident, have the ability to work with others and analyse legal problems clearly, demonstrating commercial and practical good sense. Chambers looks for people who have real potential to join as tenants at the end of their pupillage. Wilberforce takes great care in its selection process and puts effort into providing an excellent pupillage. There is a minimum requirement of a 2:1 degree in law or another subject, and Wilberforce has a track record of taking on GDL students.

Pupillage

Chambers operates a well-structured pupillage programme aimed at providing you with a broad experience of commercial chancery practice under several pupil supervisors with whom you will be able to develop your skills. Wilberforce aims to reach a decision about tenancy after approximately 9-10 months, but all pupils are entitled to stay for the remainder of their pupillage on a full pupillage award.

Mini-pupillages

Wilberforce encourages potential candidates for pupillage to undertake a mini-pupillage in order to learn how chambers operates, to meet its members and to see the type of work that they do, but a mini-pupillage is not a prerequisite for pupillage. Wilberforce runs four separate mini-pupillage weeks (two in December, one at Easter and one in July). Please visit the website for an application form and for further information.

Funding

Wilberforce offers a generous and competitive pupillage award which is reviewed annually with the intention that it should be in line with the highest awards available. The award for 2014 is £65,000 for 12 months and is paid in monthly instalments. A proportion of the award (up to £20,000) can be drawn down during the BPTC year.

WILBERFORCE CHAMBERS

Contacts

The Law Society
113 Chancery Lane,
London WC2A 1PL
Tel: 020 7242 1222
www.lawsociety.org.uk

Solicitors Regulation Authority
Ipsley Court,
Berrington Close,
Redditch B98 0DT
Tel: 0870 606 2555
E-mail: contactcentre@sra.org.uk
www.sra.org.uk

Junior Lawyers Division
The Law Society,
113 Chancery Lane,
London WC2A 1PL
Helpline: 0800 328 4203
E-mail: juniorlawyers@lawsociety.org.uk
www.juniorlawyers.lawsociety.org.uk

The Bar Council
289-293 High Holborn,
London WC1V 7HZ
Tel: 020 7242 0082
www.barcouncil.org.uk

Bar Standards Board
289-293 High Holborn
London WC1V 7HZ
Tel: 020 7611 1444
www.barstandardsboard.org.uk

Gray's Inn, Education Department
8 South Square, Gray's Inn,
London WC1R 5ET
Tel: 020 7458 7900
E-mail: quinn.clarke@graysinn.org.uk
www.graysinn.info

**Inner Temple, Education &
Training Department**
Treasury Office, Inner Temple,
London EC4Y 7HL
Tel: 020 7797 8208
E-mail: ffulton@innertemple.org.uk
www.innertemple.org.uk

Lincoln's Inn, Students' Department
Treasury Office, Lincoln's Inn,
London WC2A 3TL
Tel: 020 7405 1393
www.lincolnsinn.org.uk

**Middle Temple, Students'
Department**
Treasury Office, Middle Temple Lane,
London EC4Y 9AT
Tel: 020 7427 4800
E-mail: members@middletemple.co.uk
www.middletemple.org.uk

**Institute of Legal Executives
Kempston Manor, Kempston,**
Bedfordshire MK42 7AB
Tel: 01234 841000
E-mail: info@ilex.org.uk
www.ilex.org.uk

**National Association
of Licensed Paralegals**
3.08 Canterbury Court,
Kennington Business Park,
1-3 Brixton Road,
London SW9 6DE
Tel: 020 3176 0900
E-mail: info@nationalparalegals.co.uk
www.nationalparalegals.com

Crown Prosecution Service
Rose Court,
2 Southwark Bridge,
London SE1 9HS
Tel: 020 3357 0000
E-mail: recruitment@cps.gsi.gov.uk
www.cps.gov.uk

Citizens Advice Bureau
Head Office, Myddelton House,
115-123 Pentonville Road,
London N1 9LZ
Tel: 020 7833 2181
Get Advice: 08444 111444
www.citizensadvice.org.uk

Law Centres Federation
22 Tudor Street
London EC4Y 0AY
E-mail: info@lawcentres.org.uk
www.lawcentres.org.uk
Tel: 020 7842 0720

Free Representation Unit
6th Floor, 289-293 High Holborn,
London WC1V 7HZ
Tel: 020 7611 9555
E-mail:
admin@freerepresentationunit.org.uk
www.thefru.org.uk

The Bar Lesbian & Gay Group
E-mail: contactus@blagg.org
www.blagg.org

Lesbian & Gay Lawyers Association
c/o Alternative Family Law,
3 Southwark Street,
London SE1 1RQ
Tel: 020 7407 4007
E-mail: andrea@lagla.org
www.lagla.org.uk

Interlaw Diversity Forum (LGBT)
www.interlawdiversityforum.org

LawWorks
National Pro Bono Centre,
48 Chancery Lane,
London WCA2 1JF
Tel: 020 7092 3940
www.lawworks.org.uk

The Society of Asian Lawyers
c/o Ingram Winter Green Solicitors,
Bedford House, 21A John St,
London WC1N 2BF
E-mail: info@societyofasianlawyers.org
www.societyofasianlawyers.org

Society of Black Lawyers
www.blacklawyer.org

The Association of Muslim Lawyers
E-mail: info@aml.org.uk
www.aml.org.uk

**The Association of Women
Barristers**
E-mail: fj@33cllaw.com
www.womenbarristers.co.uk

**The Group for Solicitors with
Disabilities**
113 Chancery Lane,
London WC2A 1PL
Tel: 020 7320 5793
E-mail:
Judith.McDermott@lawsociety.org.uk
www.gsdnet.org.uk

LPC/CPE Central Applications Board
PO Box 84, Guildford,
Surrey GU3 1YX
Tel: 01483 301282
E-mail: lpc@lawcabs.ac.uk
www.lawcabs.ac.uk/gdl

Pupillage Portal
E-mail: enquiries@Pupillageportal.com
www.pupillages.com
c/o The General Council of the Bar,
289-293 High Holborn,
London WC1V 7HZ
Tel: 020 7242 0082

Career Development Loans
Tel: (freephone) 0800 585505
www.direct.gov.uk

Notes